PRINCIPLES OF FOOD SCIENCE

PART I
FOOD CHEMISTRY

FOOD SCIENCE

A Series of Monographs

Series Editor

OWEN R. FENNEMA

DEPARTMENT OF FOOD SCIENCE
UNIVERSITY OF WISCONSIN-MADISON
COLLEGE OF AGRICULTURE
MADISON, WISCONSIN

PRINCIPLES OF FOOD SCIENCE

Edited by Owen R. Fennema

PART I

FOOD CHEMISTRY

Edited by Owen R. Fennema

Department of Food Science
University of Wisconsin-Madison
Madison, Wisconsin

MARCEL DEKKER, INC.   New York and Basel

MARCEL DEKKER, INC.

270 Madison Avenue, New York, New York 10016

LIBRARY OF CONGRESS CATALOG CARD NUMBER: 75-29694

ISBN: 0-8247-6350-5

Current printing (last digit):
10 9 8 7 6 5

PRINTED IN THE UNITED STATES OF AMERICA

CONTRIBUTORS

A. F. ANGLEMIER, Department of Food Science and Technology, Oregon State University, Corvallis, Oregon

J. ROBERT BRUNNER, Department of Food Science and Human Nutrition, Michigan State University, East Lansing, Michigan

FERGUS M. CLYDESDALE, Department of Food Science and Nutrition, University of Massachusetts, Amherst, Massachusetts

LEROY DUGAN Jr., Department of Food Science and Human Nutrition, Michigan State University, East Lansing, Michigan

OWEN R. FENNEMA, Department of Food Science, University of Wisconsin-Madison, Madison, Wisconsin

F. J. FRANCIS, Department of Food Science and Nutrition, University of Massachusetts, Amherst, Massachusetts

NORMAN F. HAARD, Department of Food Science, Rutgers The State University, New Brunswick, New Jersey

JOHN E. HODGE, Northern Regional Research Laboratory, Agricultural Research Service, U.S. Department of Agriculture, Peoria, Illinois

HERBERT O. HULTIN, Department of Food Science and Nutrition, University of Massachusetts, Amherst, Massachusetts

R. C. LINDSAY, Department of Food Science, University of Wisconsin-Madison, Madison, Wisconsin

MORRIS W. MONTGOMERY, Department of Food Science and Technology, Oregon State University, Corvallis, Oregon

ELIZABETH M. OSMAN, Department of Home Economics, University of Iowa, Iowa City, Iowa

ROSE MARIE PANGBORN, Department of Food Science and Technology, University of California, Davis, California

WILLIAM D. POWRIE, Department of Food Science, University of British Columbia, Vancouver, British Columbia, Canada

T. RICHARDSON, Department of Food Science, University of Wisconsin-Madison, Madison, Wisconsin

GERALD F. RUSSELL, Department of Food Science and Technology, University of California, Davis, California

STEVEN R. TANNENBAUM, Department of Nutrition and Food Science, Massachusetts Institute of Technology, Cambridge, Massachusetts

MARVIN A. TUNG, Department of Food Science, University of British Columbia, Vancouver, British Columbia, Canada

GERALD N. WOGAN, Department of Nutrition and Food Science, Massachusetts Institute of Technology, Cambridge, Massachusetts

PREFACE

For many years, an acute need has existed for a food chemistry textbook that is suitable for food science students with backgrounds in organic chemistry and biochemistry. This book is designed primarily to fill the aforementioned need, and secondarily, to serve as a reference source for persons involved in food research, food product development, quality assurance, food processing, and in other activities related to the food industry.

Careful thought was given to the number of contributors selected for this work, and a decision was made to use different authors for almost every chapter. Although involvement of many authors results in potential hazards with respect to uneven coverage, differing philosophies, unwarranted duplication, and inadvertent omission of important materials, this approach was deemed necessary to enable the many facets of food chemistry to be covered at a depth adequate for the primary audience. Since I am acutely aware of the above pitfalls, care has been taken to minimize them, and I believe the end product, considering it is a first edition, is really quite satisfying - except perhaps for the somewhat generous length. If the readers concur with my judgment, I will be pleased but unsurprised, since a book prepared by such outstanding personnel can hardly fail, unless of course the editor mismanages the talent.

Organization of the book is quite simple and I hope appropriate. Covered in sequence are major constituents of food, minor constituents of food, food dispersions, edible animal tissues, edible fluids of animal origin, edible plant tissues and interactions among food constituents - the intent being to progress from simple to more complex systems. Complete coverage of all aspects of food chemistry, of course, has not been attempted. It is hoped, however, that the topics of greatest importance have been treated adequately. In order to help achieve this objective, emphasis has been given to broadly based principles that apply to many foods.

Figures and tables have been used liberally in the belief that this approach facilitates understanding of the subject matter presented. The number of references cited should be adequate to permit easy access to additional information.

To all readers I extend an invitation to report errors that no doubt have escaped my attention, and to offer suggestions for improvements that can be incorporated in future (hopefully) editions.

Since enjoyment is an unlikely reader response to this book, the best I can hope for is that readers will find it enlightening and well-suited for its intended purpose.

Owen R. Fennema

CONTENTS

PRINCIPLES OF FOOD SCIENCE

PART I
FOOD CHEMISTRY

Chapter 1

INTRODUCTION TO FOOD CHEMISTRY

O. Fennema

Department of Food Science
University of Wisconsin-Madison
Madison, Wisconsin

I. THE NATURE OF FOOD CHEMISTRY

Concern about food exists throughout the world but the aspects of concern differ with location. In underdeveloped regions of the world, the bulk of the population is involved in food production, yet attainment of adequate amounts and kinds of basic nutrients remains an ever-present problem. In developed regions of the world, food production is highly mechanized and efficient, a small portion of the population is involved in food production, food is available in abundance, and much of it is processed or has been altered by addition of chemicals. In these localities, concern is directed mainly to the effects of processing and added chemicals on the wholesomeness, nutritive value, and quality of food. All of these concerns are important and they fall within the realm of food science - the science which deals with the nature of food materials and the principles underlying their spoilage, preservation, and modification.

Food science is an interdisciplinary subject involving primarily bacteriology, chemistry, and engineering. Food chemistry, a major aspect of food science, is the science that deals with the composition, structure, and properties of foods and the chemical changes they undergo. Food chemistry is intimately related to chemistry, biochemistry, physiological chemistry, botany, zoology, and molecular biology. The food chemist relies heavily on his knowledge of the aforementioned sciences to effectively study and control biological substances as sources of human food. Knowledge of the innate properties of biological substances and mastery of the means of studying them are common interests of both food chemists and all other biological scientists. It is important to note, however, that food chemists have specific interests that are distinct from those of other biological scientists. Primary interests of biological scientists include reproduction, growth, and changes that biological substances undergo under environmental conditions that are compatible or almost compatible with life. Food chemists, in contrast, are concerned primarily with biological substances that are dead or dying (postharvest physiology of plants, postmortem physiology of muscle) and are exposed to a wide range of environmental conditions. For example, conditions suitable for sustaining residual life processes are of concern to food chemists during the marketing of fresh fruits and vegetables, whereas conditions incompatible with life processes are of major interest when long-term preservation of food is being attempted, i.e., during thermal processing, freezing, concentration, dehydration, irradiation, and the addition of chemical preservatives. In addition, food chemists are concerned with the chemical properties of disrupted food tissues (flour, fruit and vegetable juices, isolated and modified constituents, manufactured foods), single-cell sources of food (eggs, microorganisms), and one major biological fluid (milk). In summary, food chemists have much in common with other biological scientists, yet they also have interests that are distinctive and of the utmost importance to mankind.

II. HISTORY OF FOOD CHEMISTRY

The origins of food chemistry are obscure and its general history has not yet been properly analyzed and recorded. This is not surprising since food chemistry did not acquire an identity until the twentieth century and its history is deeply entangled with that of agricultural chemistry for which historical documentation is not considered exhaustive [5,15]. Thus the following brief excursion into the history of food chemistry is incomplete and no doubt amateurish since the author claims no expertise as a historian. There is nevertheless much information that even an amateur can gain through moderate study, and some is worth mentioning partly because of simple historical interest but mostly because this information provides needed perspectives as to when, where, and why certain food-related events transpired and as to what long-term changes have taken place in the quality of the food supply.

Although the origins of food chemistry, in a sense, extend to antiquity, the most significant discoveries as we judge them today began in the late 1700's. The best accounts of developments during this period are those of Filby [10] and Browne [5] and the author is indebted to these sources for much of the information presented here. During the period 1780-1850 a number of famous chemists made important discoveries, many of which related directly or indirectly to the chemistry of food. In the writings of Scheele, Lavoisier, de Saussure, Gay-Lussac, Thenard, Davy, Berzelius, Thomson, Beaumont, and Liebig lie the origins of modern food chemistry. Some may question whether these scientists, whose most famous discoveries bear little relationship to food chemistry, have been in fact involved to a significant degree with the origins of food chemistry. Whereas it is admittedly difficult to categorize early scientists as chemists, bacteriologists, food chemists, etc., it is relatively easy to determine whether a given scientist made substantial contributions to a given field of science. From the following brief examples it is clearly evident that many of these scientists have in fact studied foods intensively and have made discoveries of such fundamental importance to food chemistry that their inclusion in any historical account of food chemistry cannot be questioned.

Carl Wilhelm Scheel (1742-1786), a Swedish pharmacist, was one of the greatest chemists of all time. In addition to his more famous discoveries of chlorine, glycerol, and oxygen (3 years before Priestly, but unpublished) he isolated and studied the properties of lactic acid (1780); prepared mucic acid by oxidation of lactic acid (1780); devised a means of preserving vinegar by means of heat (1782 - well in advance of Appert's "discovery"); isolated citric acid from lemon juice (1784) and gooseberries (1785); isolated malic acid from apples (1785); and tested 20 common fruits for citric, malic, and tartaric acids (1785). His isolation of various new chemical compounds from plant and animal substances is considered the beginning of accurate analytical research in agricultural and food chemistry.

The French chemist Antoine Laurent Lavoisier (1743-1794) was instrumental in the final rejection of the phlogiston doctrine and in formulating the principles of modern chemistry. With respect to food chemistry, he established the fundamental principles of combustion organic analysis; he was the first to show that the process of fermentation could be expressed as a balanced equation; he made the first attempt to determine the elemental composition of alcohol (1784); and he presented one of the first papers (1786) on organic acids of various fruits.

(Nicolas) Théodore de Saussure (1767-1845), a French chemist, did much to formalize and clarify the principles of agricultural and food chemistry as provided by Lavoisier. He also (1804) studied CO_2 and O_2 changes during plant respiration, studied the mineral contents of plants by ashing, and made the first accurate elemental analysis of alcohol (1807; by the combustion technique).

Joseph Louis Gay-Lussac (1778-1850) and Louis-Jacques Thenard (1777-1857) devised in 1811 the first method for quantitatively determining the percentages of carbon, hydrogen, and nitrogen in dry vegetable substances. Their oxidative combustion technique, however, did not provide a procedure for estimating the quantity of water formed.

The English chemist Sir Humphry Davy (1778-1829) in the years 1807 and 1808 isolated the elements K, Na, Ba, Sr, Ca, and Mg. His contributions to agricultural and food chemistry came largely through his books on agricultural chemistry, the first edition (1813) being Elements of Agricultural Chemistry, in a Course of Lectures for the Board of Agriculture [7]. His books served to organize and clarify knowledge existing at that time. On page 64 of the first edition he stated: "All the different parts of plants are capable of being decomposed into a few elements. Their uses as food, or for the purpose of the arts, depend upon compound arrangements of those elements, which are capable of being produced either from their organized parts, or from the juices they contain; and the examination of the nature of these substances is an essential part of agricultural chemistry." In the fifth edition ([8], p. 121) he stated that plants are usually composed of only seven or eight elements and that: "...the most essential vegetable substances consist of hydrogen, carbon, and oxygen in different proportion, generally alone, but in some few cases combined with azote [nitrogen]."

The works of the Swedish chemist Jons Jacob Berzelius (1779-1848) and the Scottish chemist Thomas Thomson (1773-1852) resulted in the beginnings of organic formulas, "without which organic analysis would be a trackless desert and food analysis an endless task" [Ref. 10; p. 189]. Berzelius determined by analysis the elemental components of about 2,000 compounds, thereby verifying the law of definite proportions. He also devised a means of accurately determining the water content of organic substances, a deficiency in the method of Gay-Lussac and Thenard. Moreover, Thomson showed that the laws governing composition of inorganic substances applied equally well to organic substances, a point of immense importance.

In a book entitled Considérations générales sur l'analyse organique et ses applications [6] Michel Eugène Chevreul (1786-1889), a French chemist, listed the elements known at that time to exist in organic substances (O, Cl, I, N, S, P, C, Si, H, Al, Mg, Ca, Na, K, Mn, Fe) and cited the processes then available for organic analysis: (1) extraction with a neutral solvent, such as water, alcohol, or aqueous ether; (2) slow distillation, or fractional distillation; (3) steam distillation; (4) passing the substance through a tube heated to incandescence; and (5) analysis with oxygen. Chevreul was a pioneer in the analysis of organic substances, and his classic research on the composition of animal fat led to the discovery and naming of stearic and oleic acids.

Dr. William Beaumont (1785-1853), an American Army surgeon stationed at Fort Mackinac, Michigan, performed classic experiments on gastric digestion that destroyed the concept existing from the time of Hippocrates that food contained a single nitritive component. His experiments were performed during the period 1825-1833 [3] on a Canadian, Alexis St. Martin, whose musket wound afforded direct access to the stomach interior, thereby enabling food to be introduced and subsequently examined for digestive changes.

Among his many notable accomplishments, Jutus von Liebig (1803-1873) studied vinegar fermentation (1837) and showed that acetaldehyde was an intermediate between alcohol and acetic acid. In 1842 he classified foods as either nitrogenous (vegetable fibrin, albumin, casein, animal flesh, and blood) or nonnitrogenous (fats, carbohydrates, and alcoholic beverages). Although this classification was not correct in detail, it served to distinguish differences among various foods. He also perfected methods for quantitative analysis of organic substances, especially by combustion, and he published in 1847 what is apparently the first book on food chemistry, entitled Researches on the Chemistry of Food [16] (edited from the manuscript of the author by William Gregory; Taylor and Walton, London, 1847). Included in this book are accounts of his research on the water-soluble constituents of muscle (creatine, creatinine, sarcosine, inosinic acid, lactic acid, etc.).

It is interesting that the developments just reviewed have paralleled the beginnings of serious and widespread adulturation of food, and it is no exaggeration to state that the need to detect impurities in food has been a major stimulus for the development of analytical chemistry in general and analytical food chemistry in particular. Unfortunately, it was also true that advances in chemistry contributed somewhat to adulteration of food since unscrupulous purveyors of food were able to profit from the availability of chemical literature, including formulas for adultered food, and could replace older and less effective empirical approaches to food adulteration by a more efficient approach based on scientific principles. Thus, the history of food chemistry and the history of food adulteration are closely interwoven by the threads of several causative relationships [Ref. 10; pp. 18-19] and it is therefore appropriate to consider the matter of food adulteration.

The history of food adulteration in the more developed countries of the world falls into at least three distinct phases. From ancient times to about 1820, food adulteration was not a serious problem and there was little need for methods of detection. The most obvious explanation for this situation was that food was procured from small businesses or individuals, and the transactions involved a large measure of personal accountability. The second phase began in the early 1800's, when intentional food adulteration increased greatly both in frequency and seriousness. This development can be attributed primarily to increased centralization of food processing and distribution, with a corresponding decline in personal accountability, and partly to the rise of modern chemistry, to which I have already alluded. Intentional adulteration of food remained a serious problem until about 1920, which marks the end of phase two and the beginning of phase three. At this point regulatory pressures and effective methods of detection reduced the frequency and seriousness of intentional food adulteration to respectable levels and further improvements have been gradually achieved up to the present time.

Some would argue that a fourth phase of food adulteration began about 1950, when foods containing legal chemical additives became increasingly prevalent, when the use of highly processed foods increased to a point where they represented a major part of the American diet, and when contamination of some foods with uncontrolled byproducts of industrialization, such as mercury and pesticides, caused increasing concern with safety of the food supply. The validity of this argument is hotly contested and a consensus is not possible at this time. Nevertheless, the course of action in the next few years seems clear. The rising public concern over the safety of the food supply has already led to some remedial actions, both voluntary and enforced, and more such actions can be anticipated.

The early 1800's also were a period of public concern over the quality of the food supply. Public concern, or more properly public indignation, was aroused in England by Frederick Accum's publication A Treatise on Adulterations of Food [1] and by an anonymous publication entitled Death in the Pot [2]. Accum claimed that: "Indeed, it would be difficult to mention a single article of food which is not to be met with in an adulterated state; and there are some substances which are scarcely ever to be procured genuine" (p. 14). He further remarked: "It is not less lamentable that the extensive application of chemistry to the useful purposes of life, should have been perverted into an auxiliary to this nefarious traffic" (p. 20). Although Filby [10] asserted that Accum's accusations were somewhat overstated, the seriousness of intentional adulteration of food that prevailed in the early 1800's and continued until the early 1900's is clearly exemplified by the following not uncommon adulterants cited by Accum and Filby:

In anatto: Tumeric, rye, barley, wheat flour, calcium sulfate and carbonate, salt, and venetian (ferric oxide; which in turn was sometimes adulterated with red lead and copper!).

In pepper, black: This important product was commonly adulterated with gravel, leaves, twigs, stalks, pepper dust, linseed meal, and ground parts of plants other than pepper (e.g., wheat flour, mustard husks, pea flour, sago, and rice flour).

In pepper, cayenne: Substances such as vermilion (α-mercury sulfide), ochre (native earthy mixtures of metallic oxides and clay), and tumeric were commonly added to overcome bleaching that resulted from exposure to light.

In essential oils: Oil of terpentine, other oils, and alcohol.

In vinegar: Sulfuric acid.

In lemon juice: Sulfuric and other acids.

In <u>coffee</u>: Roasted grains, occasionally roasted carrots or scorched beans and
  peas; also baked horse liver.
In <u>tea</u>: Spent, redried tea leaves, and leaves of many other plants.
In <u>milk</u>: Watering was the main form of adulteration; also common were chalk,
  starch, tumeric (color), gums, and soda. Occasionally encountered were
  gelatin, dextrin, glucose, preservatives [borax, boric acid, salicylic acid,
  sodium salicylate, potassium nitrate, sodium fluoride, or benzoate (formalin)],
  and such colors as anatto, saffron, caramel, and some sulfonated dyes.
In <u>beer:</u> "Black extract," obtained by boiling poisonous berries of <u>Cocculus in-</u>
  <u>dicus</u> in water and concentrating the fluid, was apparently a common additive.
  This extract imparted flavor, narcotic properties, and additional intoxicating
  qualities to the beverage.
In <u>wine</u>: Colorants - alum, husks of elderberries, Brazil wood, burnt sugar,
  etc. Flavors - bitter almonds, tincture of raisin seeds, sweetbrier, oris
  root, and others. Aging agents - bitartrate of potash, "oenathic" ether
  (heptyl ether), lead salts. Preservatives - salicylic acid, benzoic acid,
  fluoborates, lead salts. Antacids - lime, chalk, gypsum, lead salts.
In <u>sugar</u>: Sand, dust, lime, pulp, and coloring matters.
In <u>butter</u>: Excessive salt and water, potato flour, curds.
In <u>chocolate</u>: Starch, ground sea biscuits, tallow, brick dust, ochre, venetian
  red (ferric oxide), and potato flour.
In <u>bread</u>: Alum and flour made from products other than wheat.
In <u>confectionary products</u>: Colorings containing lead and arsenic.

Once the seriousness of food adulteration in the early 1800's was made evident
to the public, remedial forces gradually increased. These took the form of new
legislation to make adulteration unlawful and greatly expanded efforts by chemists
to learn the native properties of foods, the chemicals commonly used as adulterants, and the means of detecting them. Thus during the period 1820-1850 chemistry
and food chemistry began to assume importance in Europe. This was possible
because of the work of the scientists already cited and was stimulated largely by
the establishment of chemical research laboratories for young students in various
universities and by the founding of new journals for chemical research [5]. Since
then, advances in food chemistry have continued at an accelerated pace and some of
the advances and important events that have had a bearing on them are mentioned
below.

Microscopic analysis of food was raised to a position of importance through the
efforts of Arthur Hill Hassall in England during the middle 1800's. He and his associates produced an extensive set of diagrams illustrating the microscopic appearance of pure and adulterated foodstuffs.

In 1860, the first publicly supported agricultural experiment station was established in Weede, Germany, and W. Hanneberg and F. Stohmann were appointed
director and chemist, respectively. Based largely on the work of earlier chemists,
they developed an important procedure for routine determination of major constituents in food. By dividing a given sample into several portions they were able to
determine moisture content, "crude fat," ash, and nitrogen. Then by multiplying
the nitrogen value by 6.25 they arrived at its protein content. Sequential digestion
with dilute acid and dilute alkali yielded a residue termed "crude fiber." The portion remaining after removal of protein, fat, ash, and crude fiber was termed
"nitrogen-free extract" and this was believed to represent utilizable carbohydrate.

Unfortunately, for many years chemists and physiologists wrongfully assumed that like values obtained by this procedure represented like nitritive value, regardless of the kind of food [19].

In 1871 Jean Baptiste Dumas (1800-1884) suggested that a diet supplied only with protein, carbohydrate, and fat was inadequate for support of life.

In 1862 the Congress of the United States passed the Land Grant College Act, authored by Justin Smith Morrill. This act helped establish colleges of argriculture in the United States and provided considerable impetus for the training of agricultural and food chemists. Also in 1862, the United States Department of Agriculture was established and Isaac Newton was appointed the first commissioner.

In 1863 Harvey Washington Wiley became chief chemist of the United States Department of Agriculture, from which office he led the campaign against misbranded and adulterated food, culminating in passage of the first Pure Food and Drug Act in the United States (1906).

In 1887 agriculture experiment stations were established in the United States as a result of enactment of the Hatch Act. Representative William H. Hatch of Missouri, Chairman of the House Committee on Agriculture, was author of the measure. As a result, the world's largest national system of agricultural experiment stations came into existence and this had a great impact on food research in the United States.

During the first half of the twentieth century, most of the essential dietary substances were discovered and characterized. Included in this category are vitamins, minerals, fatty acids, and some amino acids.

The development and extensive use of chemicals to aid in the growth, manufacture, and marketing of foods was an especially noteworthy and contentious event in the middle 1900's, and more is said about this subject in the next section.

This historical review, although brief, makes the current food supply seem almost perfect in comparison to that existing in the 1800's.

III. ROLES OF FOOD CHEMISTS IN SOCIETY

Having defined food chemistry and briefly outlined its history it is appropriate to consider present-day functions of food chemists. These can be conveniently grouped in two categories: scientific endeavors and public service. Analysis of food is an obvious scientific endeavor, the objects being to determine the properties of natural foods, formulated foods, natural foods exposed to processing, and adulterated foods. Analytical information is necessary to assure that commercial foods meet desired standards of wholesomeness, nutritive value, composition, and sensory quality.

A second major scientific endeavor of food chemists is to achieve more effective preservation of foods so that existing food supplies are not wasted and marketed foods are wholesome, nutritious, appetizing, and economical. Food chemists intensively study chemical changes produced in food during handling, processing, and storage, for the purpose of learning the mechanisms of change and the means of controlling these changes. For example, substantial effort is expended to decrease losses of vitamins and minerals during handling, processing, and storage; to control denaturation of proteins and changes in their nutritive value (substantial decreases in the nutritive value of proteins can occur during manufacture of a few foods, such as baked beans and toasted dry cereals, whereas highly beneficial

changes in nutritive value occur during commercial sterilization of many plant
proteins that exist naturally in combination with antinutrititional factors); to control enzyme activity; to lessen oxidation and hydrolysis of lipids; and to minimize
undesirable changes in pigments, flavor, and texture.

Assistance with the development of new or improved foods represents a third
scientific endeavor of food chemists. Existing commercial foods may be improved
with respect to nitritive value (fortification with vitamins, minerals, and amino
acids or modification of handling and processing procedures so as to decrease
losses of nutrients), and sensory quality. Furthermore, entirely new foods may
be developed, such as foods formulated from basic food constituents and food proteins derived from leaves, soybeans, or single-cell microorganisms. In addition,
attention is given to special foods for the young, the old, the obese, and those suf-
fering from food allergies or various illnesses.

The fourth scientific endeavor of food chemists is to design and implement university programs in food chemistry so that the needs of society can be adequately
filled. It is hoped this book can fill a long-standing need in this area.

Food chemists also have an obligation to participate in public service and this
function is often slighted compared to scientific endeavors. One aspect of public
service is participation in the formulation of food regulations, a matter of the utmost importance to consumers and the food industry. A second aspect of public
service is general enlightenment of consumers so that they understand food regulations, food labels, and sound dietary practices and can intelligently assess various
claims involving food and food practices. This line of education is important since,
as Graubard [Ref. 12; p. 19] aptly stated: "...food with man is not just food. It
is the crossroads of emotion, tradition, and habit." It is unquestionably true that
most consumers, even in highly developed regions of the world, are poorly informed
about food and dietary needs. It is highly likely that few could answer questions
such as: "Under what circumstances can thawed foods be refrozen?", "Why is it
claimed by some that red wine is a 'tonic' wine, and that red beets are good for
the blood?" "Why are dogs, cats, insects, snakes, and horses considered unacceptable foods in many developed countries, whereas in other regions they are
consumed without question?" and finally, "What are the relative merits of pesticides, food processing, and chemical additives?" Since the last question is important and controversial, and since it is not dealt with in subsequent chapters, it
is especially appropriate at this point to consider it with the hope of assisting food
chemists in their role of consumer enlightenment.

Should consumers accept the notion that our food supply in the United States is
the best in the world, and that our food industry and the Food and Drug Administration place good nutrition and wholesomeness above economy, efficiency and expe-
dience? Some say yea:

> The U. S. food industry prides itself upon the fact, and I emphasize the
> word fact, that it is now supplying the greatest amount of the most nu-
> tritious, highest quality food at the lowest prices and costs in the history
> of mankind [Ref. 23, p. 30].
>
> The food industry of this country is one of the most enlightened,
> progressive industries in the world. It usually perceived and solved
> potential problems before laws needed to be made, for it learned early
> that sustained profits come only through protection of the consumer
> [Ref. 18, p. 7].

The Federal Food and Drug Administration stands guard over the safest food supply on earth and, in fact, in all history [Ref. 17, p. 81].

The new technology in food processing and preservation has literally transformed our diet. We may bemoan the passing of the cooking that reminded us of Mother, but if we are honest, we would not wish to go back to it - and certainly our wives would not. In variety, wholesomeness, and overall quality our food supply in this country is a model to the world [Ref. 9, p. 302].

A first step toward increased understanding will be, I hope, to bring home to Americans the realization that we have the best, the safest, the most varied food supply in the world. We must point up the obvious fact that today's urbanized living precludes each family from growing its own food; that in a society such as ours we just cannot have the abundance of healthful convenience foods we enjoy without the pesticides, fungicides, antioxidants, mold inhibitors, antibiotics, and other chemicals which can be used - with proper safeguards that eliminate any risk whatsoever to the public health - in the growing, processing, and distribution of food [Ref. 21, p. 65].

And some say nay:

Although scientists had warned of the perils and declining quality of our food at Congressional hearings during the 1950's, they went unheeded. Meanwhile the hazards have escalated. Often with government sanction and encouragement, short-term self-defeating agricultural practices have been recommended, while long-term ecological consequences have been ignored. Results are reflected in problems such as nitrate and mercury poisonings in food chains, water eutrophication, and world-wide pesticidal contamination of all life forms. Also with government sanction, the use of food additives has been allowed to proliferate, despite repeated warnings by scientists that such substances may pose subtle hazards, suspected but at present incompletely understood. In the 1950's, experts were concerned mainly with toxic and carcinogenic properties of food additives as dangers to people eating them; by the 1970's, they are also concerned with possible teratogenic and mutagenic effects on the quality of life for future generations [Ref. 14, p. 11].

Despite all this, any random meal conceivably can contain the seeds of illness ranging from mild nausea to the most agonizing pain and even leading, sometimes, to death. Even more alarmingly, a succession of chemical-laden meals over many years may cause chronic or acute illnesses of varying intensity, all painful and some eventually fatal [Ref. 20, p. 2].

Americans consume more chemicals in their food than any other nation. At the same time American forecasts are the gloomiest in the world about the continued rise of cancer, high blood pressure, heart disease, congenital abnormalities, etc. - in fact all the degenerative diseases. The United States leads the civilized world in chemicalized food and in degenerative diseases. She also leads the world in high living standards and ample food. Both of these should reduce instead

of increasing the degenerative diseases. The only possible explanation
of the United States more than equally sharing with the civilized world
the rise in such diseases is that her food, though the most abundant,
is also the most unwholesome [Ref. 4, p. 7].

Taken together, food industry and FDA distortions make accurate
public information on food safety, quality, and cost a rare commodity.
The keystone myth that ties the FDA and the food industry together is
the FDA assertion that the food industry is primarily concerned with
advancing the interest of the food consumer. This assertion has been
raised to the level of an article of faith as part of the official creed of
the FDA. The agency believes that the overwhelming majority of the
food producers in the country will voluntarily and without regulation
insure that the quality, safety, and cost of the food supply are set at
the level most advantageous to the consumer. It assumes that every-
thing is going pretty well in the food industry. The only problems the
agency feels it has are generated by an insensitive Congress trying to
protect the few small companies that do violate the food law. These
myths, largely composed of disjointed and inaccurate fragments of
scientific research and regulatory history, are cited in office after
office of the FDA as justification for the lack of vigorous protection
of the public interest [Ref. 22, p. 216].

Chemical additives, vitamins, fat labeling, and filth in food all have
important health implications for the American public. All are major
responsibilities of the FDA food protection program, yet none has
received the kind of scientific and regulatory attention that will advance
the quality of American health. In the place of sustained action to
advance health by helping to improve the American diet, the FDA
substitutes a naive faith that the way American food is produced, pre-
served, and distributed is exceptionally fine. It maintains this faith
in the face of increasing scientific evidence that chemical additives
can be extremely dangerous, that the vitamin content of the American
diet is deteriorating, that saturated fat in food may be a contributing
factor to more than 70 per cent of all American deaths, and that American food is getting filthier [Ref. 22, p. 81].

Although heart disease, cancer, stroke, infant mortality, and
hunger are all national health problems related to the fact that large
numbers of Americans do not get enough wholesome food, the FDA
persists in maintaining that there is little wrong with the American
food production and distribution system [Ref. 22, pp. 207-208].

Yet others compound the confusion by presenting substantial inconsistencies within
a single source. "In the field of food additives, the country has legally abolished
the concept of balancing risks against benefits. Food additives must be safe. The
fact that industry officials and regulatory agents still apply the risk/benefit argument to food additives merely widens the gap between them and those who support
the law" [Ref. 22, p. 98]. And in the same document (p. 212), "Even the best
scientific study will not establish perfect safety. Therefore the issue facing the
public and Congress is how much risk the public should be subjected to."

So what is the consumer to believe? A reasonable conclusion to the food-
additives controversy is that proponents of both extreme positions are frequently

guilty of exaggeration, partial truths, and oversimplification. Surely, the strongest advocates of the food industry are likely to admit (at least privately) that the
food industry needs strict regulation, that the wholesomeness and nutritive quality
of the food supply is in need of continual improvement, and that the free-enterprise
system does by its very nature place primary emphasis on product cost and consumer appeal, and secondary emphasis on other aspects.

Similarly, the most ardent and knowledgable critics of the food industry would
surely admit in moments of total honesty that our food supply today is decidedly
superior in quality to that which existed throughout most of history, and that the
vast majority of our food industrialists are honest, conscientious individuals.
Acceptance of these views in no way justifies the status quo. More of our traditional food additives need to be critically evaluated for both safety and necessity.
Since it is impossible to demonstrate with absolute certainty that a given amount of
a given food additive is safe for all humans, the arguments for adding presumably
safe artificial flavors and colors to foods are considerably less convincing than the
arguments for adding presumably safe preservatives that substantially lessen food
spoilage. Furthermore, it is not only food additives that are of concern. Many
foods contain natural toxicants which probably pose greater hazards to human health
than the synthetic, but carefully screened chemicals added by man [11]. Thus the
all too common attitude that what is natural is pure, wholesome and ethical and
what is synthetic is debased, pernicious and wicked is hardly justifiable. Food
chemists have a role in imparting this kind of perspective to the public and it is
hoped this book can be of assistance.

REFERENCES

1. F. Accum, A Treatise on Adulterations of Food, and Culinary Poisons. Ab'm
    Small, Philadelphia, 1820. (A fascimile reprint by Mallinckrodt Chemical
    Works, St. Louis, Missouri, 1966.)
2. Anonymous, Death in the Pot. England, 1831, as cited by Filby, 1934 [10].
3. W. Beaumont, Experiments and Observations of the Gastric Juice and the
    Physiology of Digestion. F. P. Allen, Plattsburgh, New York, 1833.
4. F. Bicknell, Chemicals in Your Food. Emerson Books, New York, 1960.
5. C. A. Browne, A Source Book of Agricultural Chemistry. Chronica Botanica
    Co., Waltham, Mass., 1944.
6. M. E. Chevreul, Considerations Générales sur l'analyse Organique et sur ses
    Applications. 1824, as cited by Filby, 1934 [10].
7. H. Davy, Elements of Agricultural Chemistry, in a Course of Lectures for the
    Board of Agriculture. Longman, Hurst, Rees, Orme, and Brown, London,
    1813, as cited by Browne, 1944 [5].
8. H. Davy, Elements of Agricultural Chemistry. 5th ed., Longman, Rees,
    Orme, Brown, Green and Longman, London, 1836.
9. S. M. Farber, N. L. Wilson, and R. H. L. Wilson, Food and Civilization.
    Charles C. Thomas, Springfield, Ill., 1966, p. 302.
10. F. A. Filby, A History of Food Adulteration and Analysis. George Allen &
    Unwin, Ltd., London, 1934.
11. Food Protection Committee, Toxicants Occurring Naturally in Foods, 2nd ed.,
    Publ. ISBN 0-309-02217-0, National Academy of Sciences, National Research
    Council, Washington, D.C., 1973.

12. M. Graubard, Man's Food, Its Rhyme and Reason. Macmillan, New York, 1943, p. 18.

13. R. L. Hall, Food Prod. Devel., 4(5), 66 (1970).

14. B. T. Hunter, Consumer Beware. Simon and Schuster, New York, 1971.

15. A. J. Ihde, The Development of Modern Chemistry. Harper and Row, New York, 1964.

16. J. von Liebig, Researches on the Chemistry of Food. Edited from the manuscript of the author by William Gregory; London, Taylor and Walton, London, 1847, as cited by Browne, 1944 [5].

17. M. E. Lowenberg, E. N. Todhunter, E. D. Wilson, M. C. Feeney, and J. R. Savage, Food and Man. John Wiley, New York, 1968.

18. T. D. Luckey, in Handbook of Food Additives (T. E. Furia, ed.), Chemical Rubber Co., Cleveland, Ohio, 1968, pp. 1-23.

19. E. V. McCollum, World Rev. Nutr. Diet., 1, 1 (1959).

20. B. Mooney, The Hidden Assassins. Follett Publ. Co., New York, 1966.

21. C. G. Mortimer, in Science and Food: Today and Tomorrow. Food Protection Committee, National Research Council, Washington, D. C., 1961, pp. 63-73.

22. J. S. Turner, The Chemical Feast. Grossman Publ., New York, 1970.

23. B. Wolnak, Food Prod. Devel., 6(5), 28 (1972).

Chapter 2

WATER AND ICE

O. Fennema

Department of Food Science
University of Wisconsin-Madison
Madison, Wisconsin

I. INTRODUCTION

On this planet, water is the only substance that occurs abundantly in all three physical states. It is our only common liquid and is our most widely distributed pure
solid, being ever present somewhere in the atmosphere as suspended ice particles
or on the earth's surface as various types of snow and ice. As is evident from
Table 2-1, water is the major component of most foods, and each has its own characteristic water content. It is essential to life as a carrier of nutrients and waste
products, as a reactant and a reaction medium, as a stabilizer of biopolymer conformation, as a determinant of protein reactivity, and in other ways yet unknown.

TABLE 2-1

Water Contents of Various Foods

Food	Water content (%)
Meat	
Pork, raw, composite of lean cuts	55–60
Beef, raw, retail cuts	50–70
Chicken, all classes, raw meat without skin	74
Fish, muscle proteins	65–81
Fruit	
Berries, cherries, pears	80–85
Apples, peaches, oranges, grapefruit	85–90
Rhubarb, strawberries, tomatoes	90–95
Vegetables	
Avocado, bananas, peas (green)	74–80
Beets, broccoli, carrots, potatoes	80–90
Asparagus, beans (green), cabbage, cauliflower, lettuce	90–95

Its presence in the correct amount, location, and orientation is necessary for viability of biological matter and for acceptable quality of foods. However, the large water content of native foods and biological matter necessitates effective methods of preservation if long-term storage is desired. It is of more than passing interest that removal of water either by conventional dehydration or by separation locally in the form of pure ice crystals (freezing) greatly alters the native properties of foods and biological matter. Worse still, all attempts to return water to its original position (rehydration, thawing) are never more than partially successful. Ample justification exists, therefore, for studying water and ice with considerable care.

II. PHYSICAL CONSTANTS OF WATER AND ICE

As a first step in becoming familiar with water, it is appropriate to consider the physical constants shown in Table 2-2. By comparing water's properties with those of molecules of similar molecular weight and atomic composition (CH_4, NH_3, HF, H_2S, H_2Se, H_2Te) it is possible to determine if water behaves in a normal fashion. When this is done, water is found to have unusually large values for melting point, boiling point, surface tension, dielectric constant, heat capacity, and heats of fusion, vaporization, and sublimation; a moderately low value for density; an unusual density maximum at 3.98°C (not shown in table); an unusual attribute of expanding upon solidification; and a viscosity which in light of the above is strangely normal. In addition, the thermal conductivity of water is large compared to other liquids, and the thermal conductivity of ice is moderately large compared to other nonmetallic solids. Of even greater interest is the fact that the thermal conductivity of ice at 0°C is approximately four times that of water at the same temperature, indicating that ice conducts heat energy at a much faster rate than immobilized water (e.g., in tissue). The thermal diffusivities of water and ice are also of

TABLE 2-2

Physical Constants of Water and Ice[a]

Molecular weight			18.01534	
Phase transition properties				
Melting point at 1 atm (°C)			0.000	
Boiling point at 1 atm (°C)			100.000	
Critical temperature (°C)			374.15	
Critical pressure (atm)			218.6	
Triple point			0.0099°C	
			4.579 mm Hg	
Heat of fusion at 0°C		1.436 kcal/mole;	79.71 cal/g	
Heat of vaporization at 100°C		9.705 kcal/mole;	538.7 cal/g	
Heat of sublimation at 0°C		12.16 kcal/mole;	674.98 cal/g	
Other properties at	20°C	0°C	0°C (ice)	−20°C (ice)
Density (g/cm^3)	0.998203	0.999841	0.9168	0.9193
Viscosity (cp)	1.002	1.787	−	−
Surface tension				
against air (dynes/cm)	72.75	75.6	−	−
Vapor pressure (mm Hg)	17.535	4.579	4.579	0.776
Heat capacity (cal/g °C)	0.99883	1.00738	0.5018	0.4668
			(−2.2°)	(−20.8°)
Thermal conductivity [cal/				
(sec) (cm^2) (°C/cm)]	1.429	1.348	5.35	5.81
Thermal diffusivity (cm^2/sec)	0.0014	0.0013	∼0.011	∼0.011
Dielectric constant				
static[b]	80.36	88.00	91[c]	98[c]
at 3 x 10^9 Hz	76.7	80.5	−	3.2
	(25°)	(1.5°)		(−12°)

[a]From Refs. [7,8,50].

[b]Limiting value at low frequencies.

[c]Parallel to c axis of ice; values about 15% larger if perpendicular to c axis.

interest since these values indicate the rate at which these substances undergo changes in temperature. Ice has a thermal diffusivity approximately nine times greater than that of water, indicating that ice, in a given environment, undergoes a temperature change at a much greater rate than water. These sizeable differences in thermal conductivity and thermal diffusivity values of water and ice provide a sound basis for explaining why tissues freeze more rapidly than they thaw (equal temperature differentials).

III. THE WATER MOLECULE

Water's unusual properties suggest existence of strong attractive forces among water molecules and uncommon structures for water and ice. These features are best explained by first considering the nature of a single water molecule and then of small groups of molecules. To form a molecule of water, two hydrogen atoms approach the two sp^3 bonding orbitals of oxygen (ϕ_3^1, ϕ_4^1) and form two covalent sigma (σ) bonds (40% partial ionic character), each of which has a dissociation energy of 110.2 kcal/mole. The localized molecular orbitals remain symmetrically oriented about the original orbital axes, thus retaining an approximate tetrahedral structure. A schematic orbital model of a water molecule is shown in Figure 2-1a and the appropriate van der Waals radii are shown in Figure 2-1b.

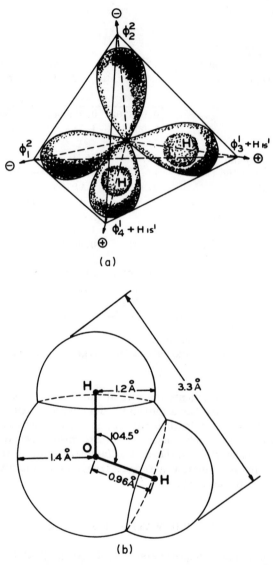

(a)

(b)

FIG. 2-1. Schematic model of a single HOH molecule. (a) sp^3 configuration. (b) Van der Waals radii for a HOH molecule in the vapor state.

The bond angle of the isolated water molecule (vapor state) is 104.5° and this value is near the perfect tetrahedral angle of 109°28'. The O-H internuclear distance is 0.96 Å, and the van der Waals radii for oxygen and hydrogen are, respectively, 1.40 and 1.2 Å.

IV. ASSOCIATION OF WATER MOLECULES

The V-like form of a HOH molecule and the polarized nature of the O-H bond result in an unsymmetrical charge distribution and a vapor-state dipole moment of 1.84D for pure water. Polarity of this magnitude produces intermolecular attractive forces, and water molecules therefore associate with considerable tenacity. Water's unusually large intermolecular attractive force, however, cannot be fully accounted for on the basis of its large dipole moment. This is not surprising, since dipole moments give no indication of the degree to which charges are exposed or of the geometry of the molecule and these aspects, of course, have an important bearing on the intensity of molecular association.

Water's large intermolecular attractive forces can be explained quite adequately by its ability to engage in multiple hydrogen bonding on a three-dimensional basis. Compared to covalent bonds (average bond energy of about 80 kcal/mole), hydrogen bonds are weak (less than 10 kcal/mole) and have greater and more variable lengths. The oxygen-hydrogen hydrogen bond has a dissociation energy of about 3-6 kcal/mole.

Since electrostatic forces make a major contribution to the energy of the hydrogen bond (perhaps the largest contribution), and since an electrostatic model of water is simple and leads to an essentially correct geometric picture of HOH molecules as they are known to exist in ice, further discussion of geometrical patterns formed by association of water molecules emphasizes electrostatic effects. This simplified approach, while entirely satisfactory for the present purpose, must be abandoned if other behavioral characteristics of water are to be explained satisfactorily.

The highly electronegative oxygen of the water molecule can be visualized as partially drawing away the single electrons from the two covalently bonded hydrogen atoms, thereby leaving each hydrogen atom with a partial positive charge and a minimal electron shield; i.e., each hydrogen atom assumes some characteristics of a bare proton. Since the hydrogen-oxygen bonding orbitals are located on two of the axes of an imaginary tetrahedron (Fig. 2-1a), these two axes can be thought of as representing lines of positive force (hydrogen-bond donor sites). Oxygen's two lone-pair orbitals can be pictured as residing along the remaining two axes of the imaginary tetrahedron, and these then represent negative lines of force (hydrogen-bond acceptor sites). By virtue of these four lines of force, each water molecule is able to hydrogen bond with a maximum of four others. The resulting tetrahedral arrangement is depicted in Figure 2-2. Because each water molecule has an equal number of hydrogen-bond donor and receptor sites arranged to permit three-dimensional hydrogen bonding, it is found that the attractive forces among water molecules are unusually large, even when compared to the attractive forces existing among other small molecules which also engage in hydrogen bonding (e.g., NH_3, HF). Ammonia, with its tetrahedral arrangement of three hydrogens and one receptor site, and hydrogen fluoride, with its tetrahedral arrangement of one hydrogen and three receptor sites, do not have equal numbers of donor and receptor

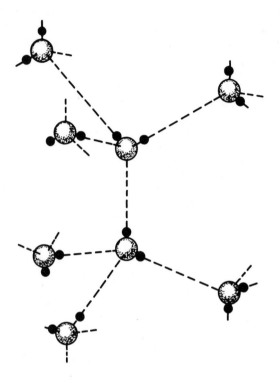

FIG. 2-2. Hydrogen bonding of water molecules in a tetrahedral configuration.
Hydrogen bonds are represented by dashed lines.

sites and therefore can form only two-dimensional hydrogen-bonded networks involving fewer hydrogen bonds per molecule than water.

Water's ability to engage in three-dimensional hydrogen bonding provides a logical explanation for many of its unusual properties. For example, its large values
for heat capacity, melting point, boiling point, surface tension, and heats of fusion,
vaporization, and sublimation are all related to the extra energy needed to break
intermolecular hydrogen bonds.

The dielectric constant of water is also influenced by hydrogen bonding. Although water is a dipole, this fact alone does not explain the magnitude of its dielectric constant. Hydrogen-bonded groups of molecules apparently give rise to multimolecular dipoles which effectively increase the dielectric constant of water.
Water's viscosity is discussed in Sec. VII.

V. STRUCTURE OF PURE ICE

Water, with its tetrahedrally directed forces, crystallizes in an open (low-density)
structure that has been accurately elucidated by studies involving X-ray, neutron,
and electron diffraction and infrared and Raman spectroscopy. As shown in Figure
2-3, the O-O internuclear nearest-neighbor distance is 2.76 Å and the O-O-O bond

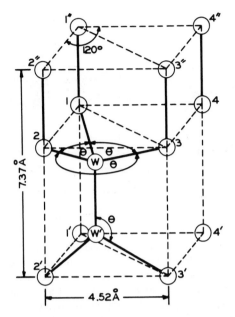

FIG. 2-3. Unit cell of ordinary ice at 0°C. Circles represent oxygen atoms of water molecules. Nearest-neighbor internuclear O-O distance is 2.76 Å ; θ = 109°.

angle is slightly in excess of 109°, or very close to the perfect tetrahedral angle of 109°28'. The manner in which each HOH molecule can associate with four others (coordination number of 4) is easily visualized by considering molecule W and its four nearest neighbors 1, 2, 3, and W'.

When several unit cells are combined and viewed from the top (along the c axis) the hexagonal symmetry of ice becomes apparent. This is shown in Figure 2-4a. The tetrahedral substructure is evident from molecule W and its four nearest neighbors; 1, 2, and 3 being visible, and the fourth lying below the plane of the paper directly under molecule W. When Figure 2-4a is viewed in three dimensions, as in Figure 2-4b, it is evident that two planes of molecules are involved. These two planes are parallel and very close together, and they move as a unit during the "slip" or flow of ice under pressure (in glaciers). Pairs of planes of this type comprise the "basal planes" of ice.

When several basal planes are stacked, an extended structure of ice is obtained. Three basal planes have been combined to form the structure shown in Figure 2-5. Viewed parallel to the c axis, the appearance is exactly the same as shown in Figure 2-4a, indicating that the basal planes are perfectly aligned. Ice is monorefringent in this direction, whereas it is birefringent in all other directions. The c axis is therefore the optical axis of ice.

The location of hydrogen atoms in ice was established during the late 1950's by means of neutron diffraction studies of ice containing deuterium [36]. It is generally agreed that:

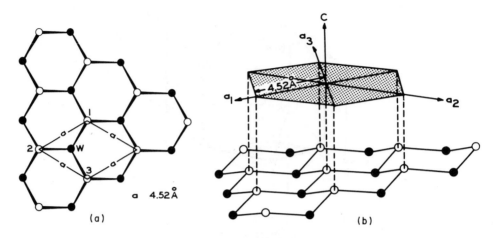

FIG. 2-4. The "basal plane" of ice (combination of two planes of slightly different elevation). Each circle represents the oxygen atom of a water molecule. Open and shaded circles, respectively, represent oxygen atoms in the upper and lower layers. (a) Hexagonal structure viewed parallel to c axis. Numbered molecules relate to the unit cell in Fig. 2-3. (b) Three-dimensional view of the basal plane. The front edge of view (b) corresponds to the bottom edge of view (a). The crystallographic axes have been positioned in accordance with external (point) symmetry.

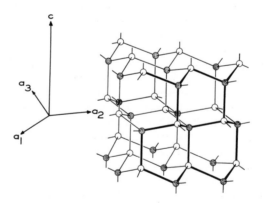

FIG. 2-5. The extended structure of ordinary ice. Only oxygen atoms are shown. Open and shaded circles, respectively, represent oxygen atoms in upper and lower layers of a basal plane.

1. Each line connecting the two nearest-neighbor oxygen atoms is occupied by one hydrogen atom located 1 ± 0.01 Å from the oxygen to which it is covalently bonded, and 1.76 ± 0.01 Å from the oxygen to which it is hydrogen bonded. This configuration is shown in Figure 2-6a.

2. If the locations of the hydrogen atoms are viewed over a period of time, a
   somewhat different picture is obtained. A hydrogen atom on a line connecting two nearest-neighbor oxygen atoms, X and Y, can situate itself in one of
   two possible positions: either 1 Å from X or 1 Å from Y. As predicted by
   Pauling [34] and later confirmed by Peterson and Levy [36], the two positions have an equal probability of being occupied. Expressed in another way,
   each position will, on the average, be occupied one-half of the time. This is
   possible because HOH molecules, except at extremely low temperatures,
   can cooperatively rotate and, additionally, hydrogen atoms can "jump" between adjacent oxygen atoms. The resulting mean structure, known also as
   the half-hydrogen, Pauling, or statistical structure, is shown in Figure 2-6b.

With respect to crystal symmetry, ordinary ice is believed to belong to the di-
hexagonal bipyramidal class of the hexagonal system. In addition, ice can exist
in nine other crystalline polymorphic structures and also in an amorphous or vitreous state of rather uncertain structure. However, of the 11 total structures, only
ordinary hexagonal ice is stable under normal pressure of 0°C.

VI. REAL OR DYNAMIC PICTURE OF ICE

Ice is not a static system consisting solely of HOH molecules precisely arranged
so that one H atom resides on a line between each pair of oxygen atoms. First of
all, pure ice (and water) contains not only ordinary HOH molecules but many other
constituents in trace amounts. In addition to the common isotopes ^{16}O and ^{1}H,
^{17}O, ^{18}O, ^{2}H (deuterium) and ^{3}H (tritium) are also present, giving rise to 18 isotopic variants of molecular HOH. Ice also contains ionic particles, such as hydrogen ions (existing as H_3O^+), hydroxyl ions, and their isotopic variants. Ice
therefore consists of more than 33 chemical derivatives of HOH. Fortunately, the
isotopic variants occur only in small amounts and they can in most instances be
ignored. This leaves for major consideration only HOH, H^+ (H_3O^+), and OH^-.

Second, ice crystals are never perfect and the defects encountered are usually
of the orientational (caused by proton dislocation accompanied by neutralizing orientations) or ionic (caused by proton dislocation with formation of H_3O^+ and OH^-)
types (see Figure 2-7). The presence of these defects provides a means for

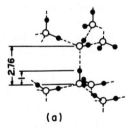

(a)

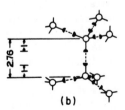

(b)

FIG. 2-6. Location of hydrogen atoms (•) in the structure of ice. (a) Instantaneous structure. (b) Mean structure (known also as the half-hydrogen, (◖)
Pauling, or statistical structure). (o) oxygen.

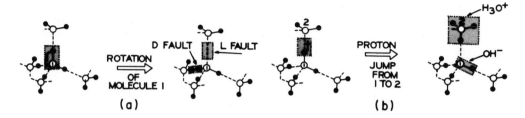

FIG. 2-7. Schematic representation of proton defects in ice. (a) Formation of
orientational defects. (b) Formation of ionic defects. Open and shaded circles
represent oxygen and hydrogen atoms, respectively. Solid and dashed lines, respectively, represent chemical bonds and hydrogen bonds.

explaining the much greater mobility of protons in ice than in water and the small
decrease in dc electrical conductivity that occurs when water is frozen.

In addition to the atomic mobilities involved in crystal defects, there are other
types of activity in ice. Each HOH molecule in ice is believed to vibrate with a root-
mean-square amplitude (assuming each molecule vibrates as a unit) of about 0.4 Å
at -10 °C. Furthermore, HOH molecules, which presumably exist in some of the
interstitial spaces in ice, can apparently diffuse slowly through the lattice.

Ice is therefore far from static or homogeneous, and its characteristics are dependent on temperature. Although the HOH molecules in ice are four-coordinated
at all temperatures, it is necessary to lower the temperature greatly, probably to
-183°C or lower, to "fix" the hydrogen atoms in one of the many possible configurations. Therefore, only at temperatures near -183°C or lower are all hydrogen
bonds intact and as the temperature is raised the mean number of intact (fixed)
hydrogen bonds presumably decreases gradually. It is likely that the amount of
"activity" in ice has some relationship to the rate of deterioration of foods and
biological matter stored at low temperatures.

VII. STRUCTURE OF PURE WATER

Elucidation of the structure of pure water is an extremely complex problem which
in recent years has attracted increasing attention from capable investigators.
Many theories have been set forth but all are no doubt incomplete, overly simple,
and subject to weaknesses which are quickly cited by supporters of rival theories.
This, of course, is a healthy situation which is likely eventually to result in an
accurate structural picture (or pictures) of water. In the meantime, few statements
can be made with any assurance that they are to stand essentially unmodified in
years to come.

To some, it may seem strange to speak of structure in a liquid when fluidity is
the major feature of the liquid state. Yet it is an old and well-accepted idea [40]
that water has structure, not of the long-range rigid type found in ice but of a
short-range order that prevails momentarily over a distance of perhaps several
molecular diameters.

There is considerable evidence supporting the belief that short-range order
exists in water. For example, water is an "open" liquid, being only 60% as dense

as expected on the basis of the close packing that can prevail in nonstructured liquids. Partial retention of the open, hydrogen-bonded, tetrahedral arrangement of ice can easily account for water's density. Furthermore, the heat of fusion of ice, while unusually high, is sufficient to break only about 15% of the hydrogen bonds believed to exist in ice. Although this does not necessarily require that 85% of the total possible hydrogen bonds remain in water (for example, more may be broken, but the change in energy may be masked by a simultaneous increase in van der Waals interactions), it does seem likely that sizeable numbers of hydrogen bonds and extensive association of water molecules do indeed remain. Further evidence of association can be gained from the many additional unusual properties of water, some of which have been discussed earlier, and from direct evidence gained from experiments involving such methods as X-ray, infrared, and Raman spectroscopy.

Theories of water structure are often classified in two major categories: (1) "uniform" theories (also called homogeneous or continuum theories) which embody the idea that intermolecular hydrogen bonds are distributed uniformly throughout water, so that each water molecule has essentially the same environment, and (2) mixture models, wherein intermolecular hydrogen bonds are concentrated, at any given moment, in localized multimolecular clumps or clusters of water molecules. The most widely accepted model appears to be the mixture model, wherein one or more short-lived bulky species (flickering clusters) of yet undetermined structure(s) exist in dynamic equilibrium with at least one species of a more dense nature. This model can be reconciled with many observed properties of water but only a few examples are cited here.

Consideration is first given to the effect of temperature on the coordination number (number of nearest neighbors) and on the distance between nearest neighbors in ice and water. Ice has a coordination number of 4; with nearest neighbors at a distance of 2.76 Å at 0°C. X-Ray diffraction studies by Morgan and Warren [32] and Brady and Romanov [5] indicate that the coordination number of water increases from a value of 4.4 at 1.5°C to 4.9 at 83°C, and the distance between nearest neighbors increases from slightly greater than 2.9 Å at 1.5°C to 3.05 Å at 83°C. (The increase in distance between nearest neighbors represents nothing more than thermal expansion.) It is evident, therefore, that the ice to water transformation is accompanied by an increase in the distance between nearest neighbors (decreases density) and by an increase in the average number of nearest neighbors (increases density), with the latter factor predominating to yield the familiar net increase in density. From a structural viewpoint, melting of ice results in an abrupt loss of long-range order and the presumed beginning of the bulky-dense species equilibrium, with the short-range order of the mixture model.

Further warming above the melting point causes the density value to pass through a maximum of 3.98°C and then to gradually decline. It has already been shown that warming increases the coordination number and the distance between nearest neighbors and that these two factors have opposite effects on density. It is apparent, then, that the effect of an increase in coordination number must predominate at temperatures between 0 and 3.98°C, and that the effect of increasing distance between nearest neighbors (thermal expansion) must predominate above 3.98°C. Based on the mixture model, this simply requires a rather marked reduction in the ratio of the amounts of bulky to dense species (increases the coordination number) as the temperature is raised from 0°C to 3.98°C, and a slower reduction in the ratio above 3.98°C.

The low viscosity of water is readily reconcilable with the concept of short-lived (mean lifetimes of 10^{-10} to 10^{-11} sec) bulky clusters in dynamic equilibrium with dense non-hydrogen-bonded fluid. The rapid formation and collapse of clusters would give a molecule ample opportunity to move about and change neighbors - the essence of flow.

VIII. STRUCTURE OF WATER AND ICE
AS INFLUENCED BY SOLUTES

A. Effect of Small Ions on the Structure of Water

The normal structure of pure water (based on a hydrogen-bonded tetrahedral arrangement) is disrupted by the addition of dissociable solutes. Although exact details of ionic hydration are still a matter of debate, there is abundant evidence indicating that some ions in dilute aqueous solution have a net structure-breaking effect (solution is more fluid than pure water), whereas others have a net structure-forming effect (solution is less fluid than pure water). It should be understood that the term "net structure" refers to all kinds of structures, either normal or new types of hydrogen-bonded structures. However, in the sense of "normal" water structure, all ions are disruptive and all can, for example, pose a hindrance to ice formation.

The ability of a given ion to alter net structure is apparently related closely to its polarizing power (charge divided by radius) or simply the strength of its electric field. Ions which are small and/or multivalent (mostly positive ions), such as Li^+, Na^+, H_3O^+, Ca^{++}, Ba^{++}, Mg^{++}, Al^{3+}, F^-, and OH^-, have strong electric fields and are net structure formers. The structure imposed by these ions more than compensates for any loss in normal water structure, and these ions strongly bind (the bound water is less mobile and more compressed than HOH molecules in pure water) the four to six water molecules that are adjacent to them.

Ions which are large and monovalent (most of the negatively charged ions and large positive ions), such as K^+, Rb^+, Cs^+, NH_4^+, Cl^-, Br^-, I^-, NO_3^-, BrO_3^-, IO_3^-, and ClO_4^-, have rather weak electric fields and are found to be net structure breakers, although the effect is very slight with K^+. These ions disrupt the normal structure of water and fail to impose a compensating amount of new structure.

In concentrated salt solutions the region of normal water structure which is believed to exist far removed from ions in dilute salt solutions is no doubt eliminated and the structure which is common in the near vicinity of ions is likely to predominate. Water near readily hydratable ions apparently assumes a structure similar to that found in crystalline salt hydrates.

Note should be made of a report by Berendsen and Migchelsen [3] indicating that the expected effect of ions on water structure is altered when the water is involved in collagen hydration. This demonstrates that great care is needed when attempting to extrapolate from simple to complex systems.

B. Effect of Hydrogen-Bonding Solutes
on the Structure of Water

Solutes capable of hydrogen bonding might be expected to enhance or at least not disrupt the normal structure of pure water. However, in many instances it is found that the distribution and orientation of the solute's hydrogen-bonding sites are geometrically incompatible with those believed to exist in normal hydrogen-bonded clusters of water. Thus, these solutes frequently have a disruptive influence on the normal structure of water. Urea is a good example of a small hydrogen-bonding solute which for geometric reasons has a marked disruptive effect on the normal structure of water. For similar reasons, most hydrogen-bonding solutes could be expected to hinder freezing.

It should be noted that the total number of hydrogen bonds per mole of solution may not be significantly altered by the addition of a hydrogen-bonding solute that disrupts the normal structure of water. This is possible since disrupted water-water hydrogen bonds are replaced by water-solute hydrogen bonds. From this viewpoint, these solutes frequently have little influence on net structures as defined in the previous section.

These newly formed water-solute bonds may be of particular importance when macromolecules are involved. If hydrogen-bonding sites are properly distributed on the surface of the macromolecule, it is conceivable that a structured zone of water exists at the macromolecule-water interface. A considerable number of polypeptides, proteins, steroid hormones, and carbohydrates appear to have their hydrogen-bonding sites spaced such that the aforementioned interaction with water cannot be discounted.

C. Solutes that Enhance the Structure of Water
(Predominantly Nonpolar Solutes)

Inert solutes, such as hydrocarbons, rare gases, and the nonpolar groups of such compounds as fatty acids, amino acids, and proteins, have a structure-forming action when introduced into water. Solutes of this nature are thought to situate themselves at the boundary of bulky hydrogen-bonded clusters of water molecules and their presence is believed to encourage more extensive water-to-water hydrogen bonding and to thereby cause the solute to become partially surrounded by water with a greater than normal amount of structure. The enhanced structures, in these instances, are thought to be similar to those in pure water. Two types of water-inert solute interactions are of special interest: (1) those bringing about the formation of clathrate hydrates and (2) those involving proteins.

1. CLATHRATE HYDRATES

Clathrate hydrates are icelike inclusion compounds wherein water, the "host" substance, forms hydrogen-bonded, cagelike structures that physically entrap molecules of a second molecular species, known as the "guest" or "hydrate former." Mention is made of them because they may prove of some value for preserving or processing foods and biological matter, because some are stable above 0°C provided the pressure is sufficient and because microstructures of a similar type may occur naturally in biological matter. The guest molecules of clathrate hydrates are low molecular weight compounds with sizes and shapes compatible with the dimensions of host cages comprised of 20-74 water molecules. Typical guests include low molecular weight hydrocarbons and halogenated hydrocarbons, rare gases, carbon dioxide, sulfur dioxide, ethylene oxide, ethyl alcohol; short-chain primary, secondary and tertiary amines; and alkyl ammonium, sulfonium, and phosphonium salts. Interactions between water and guest often involve weak van der Waals forces, but electrostatic interaction occurs in some instances.

Crystals of clathrate hydrates can be formed by mixing water and a suitable guest solute in a closed vessel (to maintain the equilibrium partial pressure of the guest in the vapor space; required pressure ranges from less than atmospheric to 160 atm), cooling to an appropriate temperature (below the decomposition temperature of the hydrate), and initiating crystal formation by any of several conventional means.

Clathrate hydrates are referred to as "icelike" since their structure is based on a hydrogen-bonded tetrahedral arrangement of water molecules, and when developed to visible size they often appear much like ice. However structural differences are evident when molecular tetrahedra are assembled to form macrocrystals. The extended structure of ice has the familiar hexagonal symmetry, whereas tetrahedra of the clathrate hydrates combine to produce groups of polyhedra usually with symmetry other than hexagonal.

Clathrate hydrates can exist in the presence of a broad range of nonguest solutes, such as carbohydrates, proteins, lipids, and intact plant and animal tissues [17,49]. Nonguest solutes depress the decomposition temperatures of hydrates to an extent approximately equal in magnitude to the freezing point depression of water [17].

Although crystalline clathrate hydrates have not as yet been put to any significant practical use, several possible applications have been suggested: demineralizing sea water, concentrating fluid materials in a manner similar to freeze concentration, leavening achieved through decomposition of carbon dioxide hydrate, and inhibiting oxidation by entrapment of oxygen within the hydrate structure [48].

There is evidence that structures similar to crystalline clathrate hydrates may exist naturally in biological matter. If this is so, these structures are likely to be of far greater importance than crystalline hydrates since they are likely to influence the conformation, reactivity, and stability of molecules, such as proteins. It is also possible that clathrate-like structures of water have a role in the anesthetic action of such inert gases as xenon [31,35].

2. INTERACTION OF WATER AND PROTEINS

In most proteins about 40% of the total amino acids have nonpolar side chains, such as the methyl group of alanine, the benzyl group of phenylalanine, the isopropyl group of valine, the mercaptomethyl group of cysteine, and the secondary butyl and isobutyl groups of the leucines. There is good agreement that these nonpolar groups have a structure-forming action on adjacent water and that the interaction between water and the nonpolar groups has an important influence on the reactivity of the protein and on its native tertiary conformation [42]. The mechanisms of interaction between water and nonpolar groups, however, is a subject of disagreement. One point of view, advanced by Kauzmann [18] and by Scheraga and co-workers [33,43], concerns the phenomenon of "hydrophobic association." This involves, after a protein is placed in an aqueous environment, an alteration in tertiary structure so that hydrophobic, nonpolar groups can associate, forming in essence an intramolecular micelle and thereby minimizing contact of these groups with water. Some hydrophobic groups, of course, remain in contact with water and where this occurs water is believed to become more structured than in the absence of these groups. Accordingly, the net effect of the hydrophobic, nonpolar groups is to decrease entropy and increase free energy. Hydrophobic association minimizes these changes but does not eliminate them. A protein with a large number of exposed nonpolar groups would therefore have a substantial structure-forming (entropy-decreasing) effect on water and would have, in spite of hydrophobic association, the greatest likelihood of aggregation and precipitation.

Klotz [19-21] proposed a quite different type of interaction between water and the nonpolar side chains of proteins. He noted that the nonpolar side chains of certain amino acids are analogous to compounds known to form crystalline clathrate hydrates. Since a large number of these groups exist along the protein macromolecule, Klotz has reasoned that they act cooperatively to induce a "stabilized arrangement of water in a microscopically crystalline array," (Ref. 21, p. S-30) with a structure similar to clathrate hydrates. Hydrophobic groups, according to this view, would be abundant on the exterior of the molecule. At this point, neither view can be accepted or dismissed unequivocally.

Enhancement of water structure by nonpolar groups, of course, is not limited to protein side chains. The nonpolar groups of compounds, such as alcohols, fatty acids, and free amino acids, can be expected to have the same effect, but these substances have received less attention than proteins.

D. Effect of Solutes on the Structure of Ice

The amount and kind of solute can influence the quantity, size, structure, location, and orientation of ice crystals. Consideration is here given only to changes in ice structure induced by solutes. Luyet and co-workers [27,28] studied the nature of ice crystals formed in the presence of various solutes, including sucrose, glycerol, gelatin, albumin, myosin, and polyvinylpyrrolidone. They devised a classification based on morphology, elements of symmetry, and the cooling velocity required for development of various types of ice structure. Four major types of structure were observed: hexagonal forms, irregular dendrites, coarse spherulites, and evanescent spherulites. A variety of intermediate types was also observed.

The hexagonal form is the normal and most highly ordered type and it has been found to occur provided the specimen is frozen in a coolant of only moderately low temperature (to avoid extremely rapid freezing) and the solute is of a nature and concentration such that it does not interfere unduly with the mobility of water molecules. Hexagonal crystals were producible in all specimens except those containing large amounts of gelatin. The ice structures observed in gelatin all possessed greater disorder than the hexagonal form.

Frozen gelatin solutions were also studied by Dowell et al. [9], and they found that cubic and vitreous ice became more prevalent with increasing rates of freezing or increasing concentrations of gelatin. Apparently gelatin, a large, complex, hydrophilic molecule, is able to greatly restrict the movement of water molecules and their ability to form highly ordered hexagonal crystals. Although ice crystals other than hexagonal types can be formed in foods and biological matter, they are uncommon.

IX. BOUND WATER AND WATER ACTIVITY

The term "bound water" is frequently used, yet a universally accepted definition does not exist, nor is one likely to in the future. Some authors have followed the inexcusable practice of using the term without defining or describing it, and others have generated such a broad array of definitions that confusion is prevalent. Some have suggested solving the problem by abandoning the term. This is a questionable approach since abondonment of the term does not eliminate the phenomena; it merely necessitates development of a new terminology, and this effort can be best applied to improving our description of "bound water."

Bound water is not a homogeneous, easily identifiable entity and because of this, descriptive terminology is difficult and a concise definition is nearly impossible. If all water is regarded as either "free" or "bound," one can reasonably argue that all water in tissue is bound since it does not freely flow from tissue when a moderate force is applied, and all of it is to some degree under the influence of biological structures or solutes and would therefore behave differently than pure water. Still different approaches to "boundness" arise when one considers water structure (average position of water molecules in relation to each other and in relation to solutes and biological structures), mobility of water molecules (translational and rotational motion), bond-dissociation energies (water-water, water-solute, water-ion), or water activity (defined as p/p_o, where p is the partial pressure of water in a sample and p_o is the vapor pressure of pure water at the same temperature). Although water activity and bond-dissociation energy may, at first, appear to follow a strict inverse relationship, this is not necessarily so since Raoult's law states that solutes decrease the vapor pressure of water and water activity even when the solution behaves ideally (i.e., water-water bond-dissociation energy equals water-solute bond-dissociation energy).

Despite these many complexities, most are likely to agree with the following conclusions concerning "bound water" nomenclature:

1. A classification system of "degrees of water binding" is far superior to a single definition of "bound water."
2. Such a classification should encompass all degrees of water binding that occur in biological systems.
3. Such a classification should include the various attributes of "boundness" that are commonly discussed in the literature.

The classification in Table 2-3 is in accord with these thoughts and it is hoped to assist food scientists in gaining a reasonably accurate mental image of water binding.

Water with full activity (type IV) does not exist except in the pure state. The remaining types of water are present in biological matter and they can be best visualized by considering the changes in water activity that occur during a process of drying or freezing (also a drying process with the removed water deposited internally in the form of pure ice crystals). This approach is greatly facilitated by considering plots of water activity (a_w) vs moisture content. In Figure 2-8 is shown the full range of water contents encountered during removal of water from a typical food. The low moisture (below 25%) end of the curve, where a_w changes greatly with small changes in water content, is shown in greater detail in Figure 2-9. This type of plot is known as a "moisture sorption isotherm." In Figure 2-10 growth rates of microorganisms and rates of various chemical reactions have been superimposed on the isotherm and the isotherm also has been divided into three characteristic zones. These interrelationships are developed further in Table 2-3.

The first water removed (Type III water of Table 2-3, from zone III of Fig. 2-10) has an activity slightly less than that of pure water. This type of water represents the majority of water in plant and animal food tissues, is easily removable, and is readily available for growth of microorganisms and chemical reactions. As it is removed the remaining water gradually assumes a lower activity. When all of the type III water has been removed, the moisture content is about 12-25% and the water activity is about 0.8 (these values depend on the type of product and the temperature).

Type II water is substantially more difficult to remove than type III water, and removal of a given increment of type II water results in a much greater reduction of the remaining water's activity than occurs when a like increment of type III water is removed (note slopes of curves in Fig. 2-10). Partial removal of type II water eliminates the last possibility of microbial growth and greatly reduces most kinds of chemical reactions (Figure 2-10). Complete or near complete removal of type II water (to 3-7% moisture level, depending on the product and temperature) corresponds approximately to optimum stability of dry products that contain significant amounts of oxidizable lipids.

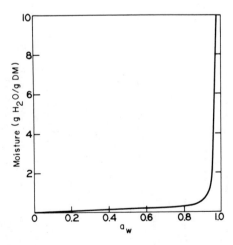

FIG. 2-8. Water activity in food containing a broad range of water contents (20°C).

TABLE 2-3

Degrees of Water Binding in Food and Living Matter[a]

Water type and intensity of binding	Description	Corresponding moisture content of tissue (g H_2O/g DM)[f]	ERH[b] needed to alter quantity of water (%)	Freezing point of tissue	Solvent capacity of water[c]	Translational mobility of water	Relationship to moisture sorption isotherm (see Fig. 2-10): Zone	Relationship to moisture sorption isotherm (see Fig. 2-10): Common deteriorative occurrences
Type IV water Full activity	Pure water	None present	<100	Normal	Normal	Normal	-	-
Type III water Activity reduced slightly	Water physically entrapped in tissue matrix, i.e., by membranes, macrocapillaries (>1 μm diam.), fibers, fibrils, etc.; solution behaves almost ideally	Min ~0.14-0.33 Max 20	80-99	Reduced	Reduced slightly	Reduced very slightly	III	Growth of microorganisms Enzymic activity Hydrolytic and oxidative reactions Nonenzymic browning
Type II water Activity reduced substantially and binding energy increased	Water-solute hydrogen bonds, and water-water hydrogen bonds in multilayers adjacent to solutes; also includes water in microcapillaries (<1 μm diam.); solution properties deviate significantly from ideal behavior	Min ~0.07 to Max 0.14-0.33	25-80	Reduced or unfreezable	Reduced substantially	Reduced slightly	II	Nonenzymic browning Enzymic activity Hydrolytic reactions Oxidative reactions ↑ Decreasing stability

Type I	Water Activity reduced greatly and binding energy increased greatly	Monolayer adsorption of water to solutes; water in chemical hydrates[d], water-ion hydrogen bonding[e], and water-dipole hydrogen bonding of the strongest kind	0-0.07	0-25	Unfreezable	Reduced greatly or totally lost	Reduced greatly	Reduced greatly	I

← Decreasing stability

I Optimum stability

Decreasing stability →

Autooxidation

[a] From Refs. 1a, 1b, 2, 6, 11, 12, 14-16, 22, 23, 26, 29, 38, 39, 44, 45, 47.

[b] ERH is equilibrium relative humidity. ERH/100 = a_W = p/p_o, where a_W is water activity, p is the partial pressure of the sample (vapor pressure of ice if sample is frozen), and p_o is the vapor pressure of pure water at the same temperature (supercooled water if temperature is below the freezing point of the sample).

[c] This category is included because it is frequently mentioned in the literature. It is a poor term since quantitative values vary depending on the solute being tested and the conditions used. Different interpretations also can be applied to the results [2]. In this instance, "solvent capacity" refers to the ability of water in situ to dissolve additional solutes.

[d] Includes water fixed at specific locations within such molecules as DNA.

[e] Binding energies are at least twice that of an average hydrogen bond (4-5 kcal/mole) [41]. Examples include water binding to small ions (Na^+, Ca^{++}, Mg^{++}, OH^-) and to ionic groups on protein ($-COO^-$, $-NH_3^+$).

[f] The notation DM stands for dry matter.

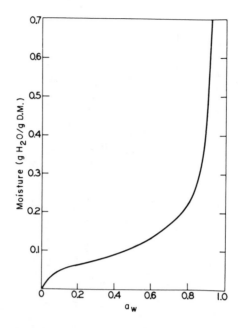

FIG. 2-9. General moisture sorption isotherm for food (20°C).

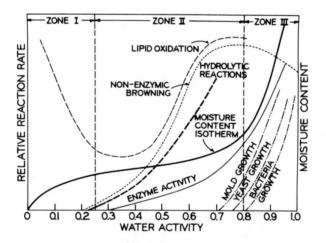

FIG. 2-10. Reaction rates in food as a function of water activity (generalized behavior at 20°C). (Adapted from Labuza [24]; courtesy of the Institute of Food Technologists.)

Partial removal of type I water can be accomplished by conventional dehydration but not by freezing. Type I water is very tightly bound and is what some authors refer to as "true bound water." The degree of binding is such that any reactions depending on solvation are so slow as to be unmeasurable. It is in this region that one sees an acceleration of lipid phase reactions, such as oxidative rancidity (Fig. 2-10). The small amount of water that is needed to inhibit oxidative rancidity apparently functions by [24] (1) facilitating destruction of free radicals, (2) hydrogen bonding to hydroperoxides and slowing the rate of their conversion to other products, and (3) hydrating or reacting with metals and thereby reducing their abilities to catalyze oxidation. As the water content is increased above the optimum level into zone II, lipid oxidation increases, presumably because of increased catalyst mobility and because new catalytic surfaces are exposed as the matrix swells.

A few additional comments about the nature of bound water are in order:

1. The apparent amount of bound water varies depending on the method of measurement.

2. The actual amounts of the various types of bound water vary depending on the product.

3. Although bound water has been grouped in four categories, this is not meant to imply that distinct boundaries exist among these categories. There very likely exists a wide variety of intermediate states of "boundness," not just four, between the extremes of maximum and minimum water binding. This results necessarily from the variety of secondary bonding possibilities available to each water molecule. However, certain bond types may be more prevalent than others, causing discontinuities on some plots.

4. The manner in which a given water molecule is bound to other molecules can change as the total water content of the system is altered. For example, at water levels in excess of the monolayer value (occurs in the high-moisture portion of zone I, Fig. 2-10 and represents the amount of water needed to provide one molecule of water for each binding site), a given water molecule is believed to bond with only one site on a macromolecule, whereas at levels below the monolayer value this same molecule can apparently bond simultaneously with two adjacent sites on a macromolecule [12].

5. Food and living systems contain water molecules bound with a broad range of intensities but it is those molecules that are most mobile and bound least firmly that determine the observed water activity.

6. Water that is bound should not be thought of as totally immobilized. As boundness increases, the rate at which a water molecule changes place with a neighboring water molecule decreases but usually does not decline to zero (an exception occurs in glass structures of samples at low temperatures). The mobility of water is evident even at moisture levels just above the monolayer value, where movement of glucose is facilitated by mobile molecules of water [10].

7. Water that is bound to hydrophilic solutes is more structured than ordinary water but its structure is different from that of ordinary ice.

Up to this point, only isotherms at room temperature have been considered. From Figure 2-11 it is apparent that the moisture content-a_w relationship is temperature dependent and that a reduction in temperature shifts the boundary of zones I and II (inflection point near the low-moisture end of the curve) to points of greater moisture and lower a_w. Values for optimum moisture content also change with temperature but exact predictions are difficult, especially when large changes in temperatures are involved. This is reasonable since determination of optimum

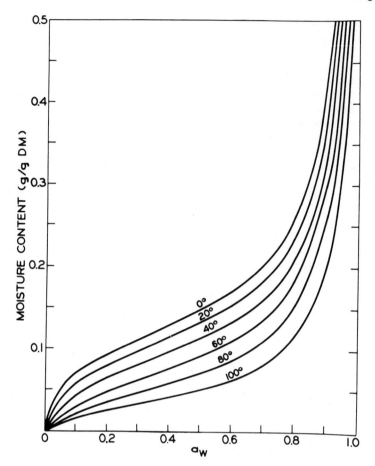

FIG. 2-11. Moisture sorption isotherms of potatoes at various temperatures. (Redrawn from Görling [13]; courtesy of the Society of Chemical Industry.)

stability involves consideration of microbial growth rates and rates of several types of chemical reactions, all of which are influenced to different degrees by changes in temperature.

The moisture content-a_W relationship also is of interest at subfreezing temperatures. When such a plot is prepared, it is advantageous to define a_W exactly as before, the consequence being that supercooled water rather than ordinary water becomes the reference state. Since the partial pressure of water in a frozen food is equal to the vapor pressure of ice at the same temperature [4,46], knowledge of product temperature permits calculation of the associated a_W value. Values of a_W at temperatures between 0°C and -50°C are presented in Table 2-4.

An alternative approach to defining subfreezing a_W values is to compute them using the vapor pressure of ice as the reference state (p_{sample}/p_{ice}). This results in all frozen samples, regardless of temperature, having a_W's of 1.0 (assumes solid-liquid equilibrium). This is not useful since (1) a_W then becomes

TABLE 2-4

Vapor Pressures and Water Activities of Food at
Various Subfreezing Temperatures

Temperature (°C)	Liquid water[a] (mm Hg)	Ice[b] or food containing ice (mm Hg)	a_W (P_{ice}/P_{water})
0	4.579[b]	4.579	1.00[d]
-5	3.163[b]	3.013	0.953
-10	2.149[b]	1.950	0.907
-15	1.436[b]	1.241	0.864
-20	0.941[c]	0.776	0.82
-25	0.605[c]	0.476	0.79
-30	0.382[c]	0.286	0.75
-40	0.142[c]	0.097	0.68
-50	0.048[c]	0.030	0.62

[a]Supercooled at all temperatures except 0°C.
[b]Observed data [50].
[c]Calculated data [30].
[d]Applies only to pure water.

independent of total moisture in the sample and thus can no longer be used to estimate rates of chemical reactions and rates of microbial growth, and (2) isotherms
prepared on this basis cannot be compared to isotherms at temperatures above
0°C. Theoretical reasons also exist for choosing the vapor pressure of supercooled water rather than the vapor pressure of ice as the reference state for com-
puting a_W, and the former method is employed here.

Shown in Figure 2-12 are isotherms for lean beef at various low temperatures,
a freezing point curve for this product, and a curve representing the combined
amount of capillary and other difficult to freeze (DTF) water. The dashed isotherms are hypothetical but realistic. Qualitatively, this graph applies to frozen
foods in general. Freezing involves movement in a horizontal direction from right
to left (constant moisture). The beef sample in Figure 2-12 contained 75% moisture (3 g H_2O/g DM), giving at room temperature the starting conditions depicted
by point T_1. Removal of sensible heat would cause a slight decline in a_W and
freezing would commence at about -2°C (point T_2 and 0.98 a_W). Further cooling
would result in additional ice formation and movement to the left along line T_1-T_3.
During the course of freezing, the freezing point of the unfrozen phase and the
amounts of ice and unfrozen water can be derived from the figure. This is done
by drawing a vertical line from the appropriate point on line T_1-T_3 to the abscissa.
For example, at subfreezing temperature T_3, the freezing point of the unfrozen
phase is -30°C, the amount of ice is represented by the length of line segment T_3-
A and the amount of unfrozen water is represented by segment A-C. The unfrozen

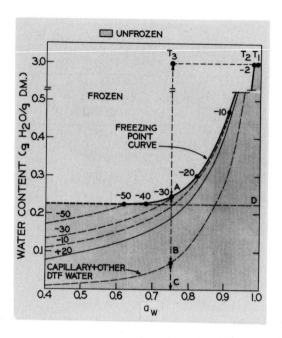

FIG. 2-12. Water activity in lean beef (75% water) at low temperatures. Dashed curves are hypothetical but realistic. DTF is "difficult to freeze." Data from Riedel [38].

water, in turn, consists of firmly bound, unfreezable water (segment A-B) and capillary and other DTF water (BC). As is evident from Figure 2-12, maximum ice formation occurs at about -40°C.

If, prior to cooling, meat is dried to a moisture content of less than 0.225 g H_2O/g DM (point D), then no ice forms regardless of temperature.

Conditions during freeze drying also can be determined from the figure. Consider, for example, that a product of normal water content is placed in a freeze dryer and dried at a constant temperature of -30°C. Conditions then first change from T_1 to T_3 as previously described for freezing (except that a slight amount of moisture is lost during this period causing T_3 to assume a slightly lower position than shown) and then gradually change from T_3 to A as the frozen phase is sublimed. At the conclusion of sublimation, drying would continue (conversion of liquid water and sorbed water to water vapor) and the conditions would move from point A downward and to the left along the dashed -30°C isotherm.

An additional point of interest from Figure 2-12 and Table 2-4 is that frozen foods at a conventional storage temperature of -20°C have an a_w of 0.82. This a_w results in acceptable (not optimum) stability, i.e., rates of chemical reactions are slow and microorganisms cannot grow. At room temperature this a_w would permit growth of some microorganisms as well as undesirably rapid rates of many chemical reactions (see Fig. 2-10). Thus it is clear, as previously noted, that the relationship between a_w and product stability changes with temperature.

A final point of importance with respect to isotherms is that desorption isotherms and resorption isotherms usually do not coincide, i.e., they exhibit hysteresis.

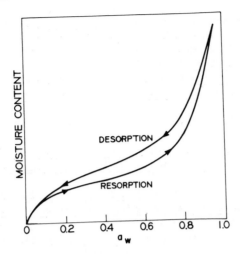

FIG. 2-13. Hysteresis of moisture sorption isotherm.

As is apparent from Figure 2-13, at any given moisture content the a_W during desorption is less than the a_W during resorption, and at any given a_W the moisture content during desorption is greater than that during resorption. The cause is apparently related to (1) interactions of nonaqueous constituents during desorption so that some adsorption sites are irreversibly lost, and (2) differences in water vapor pressure needed to fill and empty capillaries of irregular shape [37]. The lower moisture contents of samples during resorption result in their having greater viscosities than samples of the same a_W during desorption, and one consequence, according to Labuza et al. [25], is that oxidation at a given a_W proceeds more slowly in resorption samples.

Hysteresis with respect to relative amounts of frozen and unfrozen phases has been observed during freezing and thawing of whole blood, collagen, and solutions of polyvinylpyrrolidone (A. P. MacKenzie, personal communication, 1974), but the extent is small compared to that observed during dehydration.

In conclusion, it can be said that water is not only the most abundant constituent in foods but that it also contributes greatly to the desirable native qualities of food; is the cause of food's perishable nature; governs the rates of many chemical reactions; and is instrumental in the undesirable side effects of freezing. It is associated with nonaqueous food constituents in such a complex manner that once these relationships are disturbed by some such means as drying or freezing they can never again be completely reinstated. Finally, water is above all else frustratingly complex, inadequately studied, and poorly understood.

REFERENCES

1a. M. Akiba, Bull. Fac. Fish., Hokkaido Univ., 1(3 & 4), 156 (1950).

1b. P. S. Belton, R. R. Jackson, and K. H. Packer, Biochim. Biophys. Acta, 286, 16 (1972).

2.   H. J. C. Berendsen, Proc. European Biophys. Cong., Baden, Austria, 1, 483 (1971).

3. H. J. C. Berendsen and C. Migchelsen, Fed. Proc., 25, 998 (1966).
4. L. A. Berny, M. S. Thesis, University of Wisconsin, Madison (1973).
5. G. W. Brady and W. J. Romanov, J. Chem. Phys., 32, 306 (1960).
6. J. Brooks, J. Gen. Physiol., 17, 783 (1934).
7. D. A. Copson, Microwave Heating. AVI Publ., Westport, Conn., 1962.
8. N. E. Dorsey, Properties of Ordinary Water-Substance. Reinhold, New York, 1940.
9. L. G. Dowell, S. W. Moline, and A. P. Rinfret, Biochim. Biophys. Acta, 59, 158 (1962).
10. R. B. Duckworth and G. M. Smith, Proc. Nutr. Soc., 22, 182 (1963).
11. E. D. Finch, J. F. Harmon, and B. H. Muller, Arch. Biochem. Biophys., 147, 299 (1971).
12. M. E. Fuller and W. S. Brey, Jr., J. Biol. Chem., 243, 274 (1968).
13. P. Görling, Fundamental Aspects of the Dehydration of Foodstuffs (eds. anonymous), Society of Chemical Industry, London, 1958, pp. 42-53.
14. A. R. Haly and J. W. Snaith, Biopolymers, 10, 1681 (1971).
15. R. Hamm, Advan. Food Res., 10, 356 (1960).
16. C. F. Hazlewood, B. L. Nichols, and N. F. Chamberlain, Nature (London), 222, 747 (1969).
17. C. P. Huang, O. Fennema, and W. D. Powrie, Cryobiology, 2, 109 (1965).
18. W. Kauzmann, Advan. Protein Chem., 14, 1 (1959).
19. I. M. Klotz, Science, 128, 815 (1958).
20. I. M. Klotz, Brookhaven Symp. Biol., 13, 25 (1960).
21. I. M. Klotz, Fed. Proc., 24(2, Suppl. 15), S-24 (1965).
22. I. D. Kuntz, Jr., T. S. Brassfield, G. D. Law, and G. V. Purcell, Science, 163, 1329 (1969).
23. J. Kuprianoff, in Fundamental Aspects of the Dehydration of Foodstuffs. Society of Chem. Industry, London, 1958, pp. 14-23.
24. T. P. Labuza, Proc. 3rd Intl. Cong. Food Sci. Technol., 1970, Washington, D.C., p. 618 (1971).
25. T. P. Labuza, L. McNally, D. Gallagher, J. Hawkes, and F. Hurtado, J. Food Sci., 37, 154 (1972).
26. T. P. Labuza and M. Rutman, Can. J. Chem. Eng., 46, 364 (1968).
27. B. J. Luyet, in Cryobiology (H. T. Meryman, ed.), Academic Press, New York, 1966, pp. 115-138.
28. B. J. Luyet and G. L. Rapatz, Biodynamica, 8, 1 (1958).
29. A. P. MacKenzie and D. H. Rasmussen, in Water Structure at the Water-Polymer Interface (H. H. G. Jellinek, ed.), Plenum Press, New York, 1972, pp. 146-172.
30. B. J. Mason, The Physics of Clouds. Clarendon, Oxford, 1957, p. 445.
31. S. L. Miller, Proc. Natl. Acad. Sci. U. S., 47, 1515 (1961).
32. J. Morgan and B. E. Warren, J. Chem. Phys., 6, 666 (1938).
33. G. Nemethy and H. A. Scheraga, J. Phys. Chem., 66, 1773 (1962).
34. L. Pauling, J. Amer. Chem. Soc., 57, 2680 (1935).
35. L. Pauling, Science, 134(3471), 15 (1961).
36. S. W. Peterson and H. A. Levy, Acta Crystallog., 10, 70 (1957).
37. K. S. Rao, J. Phys. Chem., 45, 522 (1941).
38. L. Riedel, Kältetechnik, 13, 122 (1961).
39. L. B. Rockland, Food Technol., 23, 11 (1968).

40. W. K. Röntgen, Ann. Phys. Chem. (Weid.), 45, 91 (1892).
41. O. Ya. Samoilov, in Water in Biological Systems (L. P. Kayushin, ed.),
    Consultants Bureau, New York, 1969, p. 20.
42. H. K. Schackman, Cold Spring Harbor Symp. Quant. Biol., 28, 409 (1963).
43. H. A. Scheraga, G. Nemethy, and I. Z. Steinberg, J. Biol. Chem., 237,
    2506 (1962).
44. J. L. Shereshefsky and C. P. Carter, J. Amer. Chem. Soc., 72, 3682 (1950).
45. R. O. Slatyer, Plant-Water Relationships. Academic Press, New York, 1967.
46. R. M. Storey and G. Stainsby, J. Food Technol., 5, 157 (1970).
47. M. V. Sussman and L. Chin, Science, 151, 324 (1966).
48. L. U. Thompson and O. Fennema, Agri. Food Chem., 19, 232 (1971).
49. G. Van Hulle and O. Fennema, Cryobiology, 7, 223 (1971).
50. R. C. Weast, ed., Handbook of Chemistry and Physics. 50th ed., Chemical
    Rubber Co., Cleveland, Ohio, 1969.

GENERAL REFERENCES

CLATHRATE HYDRATES

G. A. Jeffrey and R. K. McMullan, in Progress in Inorganic Chemistry (F. A.
    Cotton, ed.), Wiley-Interscience, New York, 1967, pp. 43-107.
I. M. Klotz, in The Frozen Cell (G. E. W. Wolstenholme and M. O'Connor, eds.),
    J & A Churchill, London, 1970, pp. 5-21.

WATER, ICE, WATER ACTIVITY, WATER-SOLUTE INTERACTIONS

D. P. Bone, Food Prod. Devel., 3, 80 (1969).
D. Eisenberg and W. Kauzmann, The Structure and Properties of Water. Claren-
    don, Oxford, 1969.
O. Fennema, W. D. Powrie, and E. H. Marth, Low-Temperature Preservation
    of Foods and Living Matter. Dekker, New York, 1973, Chap. 1.
N. H. Fletcher, The Chemical Physics of Ice, Cambridge University Press,
    London, 1970.
F. Franks, ed., Water, A Comprehensive Treatise. Plenum Press, New York,
    1972.
H. H. G. Jellinek, ed., Water Structure at the Water-Polymer Interface. Plenum
    Press, New York, 1972.
T. P. Labuza, Food Technol., 22, 263 (1968).
S. A. Matz, Water in Foods. AVI Publ., Westport, Conn., 1965.
N. Riehl, B. Bullemer, and H. Engelhardt, eds., Physics of Ice. Plenum Press,
    New York, 1969.

Chapter 3

CARBOHYDRATES

J. E. Hodge

Northern Regional Research Laboratory
Agricultural Research Service
U.S. Department of Agriculture
Peoria, Illinois

and

Elizabeth M. Osman

Department of Home Economics
The University of Iowa
Iowa City, Iowa

Contents

I. INTRODUCTION

The food scientist has a many-sided interest in carbohydrates. He is concerned with their amounts in various foods, availability (nutritional and economic), methods of extraction and analysis, commercial forms and purity, nutritional value, physiological effects, and functional properties in foods. Understanding their functional properties in processed foods requires not only knowledge of the physical and chemical properties of isolated carbohydrates, but also knowledge of the reactions and interactions that occur in situ between carbohydrates and other food constituents and the effects of these changes upon food quality and acceptance. This is a tall order for knowledge. Because processing affects both nutritional and esthetic values of food, knowledge of the changes that carbohydrates undergo during milling, cooking, dehydration, freezing, and storage is especially important.

Students are advised to study the fundamental chemistry underlying useful carbohydrate properties. Of service will be an understanding of the association of polar molecules through hydrogen bonding, ionic effects, substituent effects, chelation with inorganic ions, complexing with lipids and proteins, and decomposition reactions. This background will provide an understanding of properties that affect the texture and acceptance of processed foods (e.g., solubility, hygroscopicity, diffusion, osmosis, viscosity, plasticity, and flavor production and retention), properties that enable the formation of high-quality pastries, gels, coatings, confections, and reconstitutable dehydrated and frozen foods.

Ability to predict what changes in functional properties are likely to ensue from incorporating various types of carbohydrates into processed foods is a practical goal of the food scientist. Such forecasting requires either a wealth of experience with trial-and-error methods or a deep knowledge of carbohydrate properties as related to structure - perhaps both. However, scientific knowledge of cause and effect is highly respected when it shortens industrial development time.

A. Sources, Types, and Terminology

The layman's conception of carbohydrates generally involves only the sugars and starches of foods - those that generate calories and fat. The food chemist knows many other types that are ingested. The types of food carbohydrates, their mono-saccharide composition, and their most common sources are listed in Table 3-1. The monosaccharides are not listed separately because only the sucrose hydrolysis products, D-glucose and D-fructose, are commonly found free in natural foods. These two monosaccharides are frequently added as sweeteners, however, and jointly in the form of invert sugar syrup, isomerized corn syrups, and honey.

Because most people enjoy the sweetness of sugars and the mouthfeel of cooked starches, they become familiar by association with table sugar (sucrose), invert sugar (hydrolyzed sucrose), corn syrup sugars (D-glucose and maltose), milk sugar (lactose), and the more starchy foods. These carbohydrates are nutritionally available; i.e., they are digested (hydrolyzed to component monosaccharides) and utilized by the human body. The carbohydrates of dietary fiber (cellulose, hemi-celluloses, pentosans, and pectic substances), in contrast, tend to be overlooked because they are largely unavailable. They are not hydrolyzed significantly by digestive enzymes; nevertheless, they may be quite important for human health [30,169].

In Table 3-2, the carbohydrates of natural and processed foods are divided into available and unavailable types. The available carbohydrates vary in degrees of absorption and utilization depending upon quantities ingested, accompanying food types, and human differences in complements of digestive enzymes and intestinal transport mechanisms. Malabsorption difficulties and adverse physiological effects are known for all the available carbohydrates but gelatinized starches give little or no trouble [68].

It is important to realize that in ruminants the unavailable and most abundant polysaccharide cellulose is partially hydrolyzed to the same highly available sugar that starch provides upon digestion; i.e., D-glucose. Grazing animals do it through the cellulases generated by the microorganisms of their rumen. Cellulose is, therefore, a contributing source of valuable animal protein. The efficiency and economics of the ruminant's conversion of cellulose to nutrients probably can be improved upon by food chemists. Development of cellulases that are stable outside the cells of microorganisms enables the culturing of fungi and yeasts on cellulose hydrolyzates. Fungi (e.g., mushrooms) can produce protein with the biological value of animal protein [189]. The conversion of cellulosic wastes to animal feed and human food is an intriguing prospect for limiting environmental pollution and for feeding the world's expanding population.

Carbohydrates were first named according to their natural sources; e.g., beet sugar, cane sugar, grape sugar, malt sugar, milk sugar, cornstarch, liver glycogen, and sweet corn glycogen. Trivial names were then formed, often from a prefix related to the source followed by the suffix "-ose" to denote carbohydrate. Names arising in this way, for example, are fructose (fruit sugar), maltose (malt sugar), lactose (milk sugar), xylose (wood sugar), and cellulose (cellular membranes). These short, well-established names are still commonly used. They

TABLE 3-1

Common Food Carbohydrates: Types, Composition, and Sources

Type	Component monosaccharides	Most common food sources
Polysaccharides		
Starch, dextrins	D-Glucose	Cereals, roots, tubers, legumes
Cellulose	D-Glucose	Plant cell walls and fiber
Glycogen	D-Glucose	Liver, animal tissue, sweet corn
Hemicelluloses	L-Arabinose, D-xylose, L-rhamnose, D-galactose, D-mannose, D-glucose, D-glucuronic, and D-galacturonic acids	Plant cell walls and fiber; cereals, legumes, and nuts; flour, bran
Pentosans	L-Arabinose, D-xylose	With hemicelluloses and pectic substances
Pectic substances	D-Galacturonic acid, L-arabinose, D-galactose, L-rhamnose, L-fucose	Fruits, especially citrus and apples; sugar beet, vegetables
Oligosaccharides		
Raffinose, stachyose	D-Galactose, D-glucose, D-fructose	Legume seeds, cereals, tubers
Fructosylsucroses	D-Fructose, D-glucose	Cereals, onion, leek
Maltooligosaccharides	D-Glucose	Starch syrups, malt, amylodextrins
Disaccharides		
Sucrose	D-Glucose, D-fructose	Sugarcane, sugar beets, fruits, and vegetables; sweetened foods
Maltose, isomaltose	D-Glucose	Starch syrups, malt, honey
Lactose	D-Galactose, D-glucose	Milk, cheese, dairy products

TABLE 3-2

Utilization of Dietary Carbohydrates in Human Metabolism[a]

Type of carbohydrate	Available (digested and absorbed)	Unavailable (not digested or poorly absorbed)
Polysaccharides	Starches, gelatinized Amylose Amylopectin Amylodextrins Glycogen	Cellulose Hemicelluloses Pectic substances Pentosans Chitin
Oligosaccharides	Sucrose Malto- and maltose Isomaltose Lactose[b]	Melibiose Raffinose Stachyose Lactulose
Monosaccharides Hexoses	D-Glucose D-Fructose D-Galactose	D-Mannose L-Sorbose
Pentoses	D-Ribose	L-Arabinose D-Xylose[c]
Alditols	Glycerol D-Glucitol (sorbitol) Xylitol	D-Mannitol[c] Galactitol (dulcitol) L-Arabinitol

[a]Compiled from Fordtran and Ingelfinger [55], Gray [68], Southgate and Durnin [187], Touster [198].

[b]Well utilized by most infants and by most adults of North European extraction but poorly utilized by most peoples of the world [68,114].

[c]Moderately absorbed and metabolized.

furnish no information on the chemical structures, however, so a definitive carbohydrate nomenclature has been developed [8,9]. From the definitive names, structural formulas can be written (Section II). Some of the terms involved in the definitive nomenclature are explained in the following paragraphs.

The simple sugars (monosaccharides) are basically aliphatic polyhydroxy aldehydes and ketones: $HOCH_2-(CHOH)_n-CHO$ and $HOCH_2-(CHOH)_{n-1}-C:O-CH_2OH$, called "aldoses" and "ketoses," respectively. However, it must be understood that cyclic hemiacetals of these open-chain forms prevail in solids and at equilibrium in solutions (Section II). In the definitive nomenclature, the suffix "-ose" is appended to prefixes denoting the number of carbon atoms in the monosaccharide; e.g., trioses ($n = 1$), tetroses ($n = 2$), pentoses ($n = 3$), hexoses ($n = 4$). To distinguish aldoses from ketoses, ketoses are designated as "-uloses." Thus, the simplest ketose, $HOCH_2-C:O-CH_2OH$, is a triulose; the most common ketose, D-fructose (levulose), is a hexulose. To designate the configurations of hydroxyl groups on the asymmetric carbon atoms of monosaccharides, the prefixes D and

L are used together with prefixes derived from the trivial sugar names (e.g., D-glycero-, L-arabino-, D-xylo-) followed by pentose, hexose, hexulose, etc. (Section II).

As open-chain hydroxy aldehydes and hydroxy ketones, the monosaccharides are very reactive. They readily enolize in alkaline solutions to reduce ions such as Cu^{2+} and $Fe(CN)_6^{3-}$. Therefore, they are called "reducing sugars." Plants protect the reactive monosaccharides for transport and storage by condensing them, with loss of water, into less reactive oligo- and polysaccharides. For example, the most common reducing sugars, D-glucose and D-fructose, are condensed in such a way that their reactive carbonyl functions are lost to form the disaccharide nonreducing sugar, sucrose. The less reactive sucrose is then transported to all parts of the plant for enzymic syntheses of oligo- and polysaccharides. From thousands or more D-glucose moieties of sucrose, the glucans, starch and cellulose, are built. From the D-fructose moiety of sucrose, fructans, such as inulin and levans are assembled. Other polysaccharides (Table 3-1) are formed from other sugars which arise by enzymic transformations of phosphorylated hexoses and sugar nucleotides [1,78].

The prefix "glyc," is used in a generic sense to designate sugars and their derivatives; e.g., glycoses, glycosides, glycosans, glyconic, glycaric, and glycuronic acids. The generic name for polysaccharides is "glycans." Homoglycans are composed of a single monosaccharide; for example, the D-glucans, cellulose and starch, release only D-glucose by hydrolysis. Other homoglycans (e.g., the hexosans, D-galactan and D-mannan, and the pentosans, L-arabinan and D-xylan) are uncommon in nature. Heteroglycans, composed of two or more different monosaccharides, are more widely distributed than the homoglycans that are not glucans. Galactomannans, glucomannans, arabinogalactans, and arabinoxylans are common diheteroglycans (composed of two sugars). The glycans prevail over free glycoses in natural foods.

The reducing sugars are readily oxidized. Mild oxidation of aldoses yields aldonic acids, $HOCH_2-(CHOH)_n-COOH$; e.g., gluconic acid (n = 4). Oxidation of both ends of the aldose molecule forms aldaric acids, $HOOC-(CHOH)_n-COOH$; e.g., tartaric acid (n = 2). Oxidation of the terminal CH_2OH grouping of hexoses without oxidation of the reducing function (protected) produces hexuronic acids, $HOOC-(CHOH)_4-CHO$. The hexuronic acids are common monosaccharide constituents of many heteroglycans. For example, they are found in acidic hemicelluloses, pectic substances, algin, plant exudate gums, and the mucopolysaccharides of mammalian tissues (Section V). Penturonic acids have not been found in nature.

Reduction of the carbonyl function of aldoses or ketoses yields sugar alcohols, properly called "alditols," $HOCH_2-(CHOH)_n-CH_2OH$. The suffix "-itol" is applied to the trivial prefixes to denote different alditols; e.g., D-glucitol, D-mannitol, xylitol. The triitol, glyceritol (by common usage, glycerol, n = 1), is the alditol moiety of fats. Glycerol and D-glucitol (sorbitol) are acceptable and useful food additives because they are glucogenic and keep foods moist by virtue of their strong affinity for water. Pentitols (n = 3) and hexitols (n = 4) are found in small amounts in many fruits, vegetables, and mushrooms [208]. The heptitol, perseitol (n = 5), and an octitol have been isolated from avocados. Some alditols are nutritionally available; others are not (Table 3-2).

Other types of carbohydrates found in foods are the condensed N-acetylated amino sugars of mucopolysaccharides, glycoproteins, and chitin; the condensed deoxy sugars of gums, mucilages, and nucleotides; glycosides (sugars condensed with nonsugars); glucosinolates (toxic thioglycosides of brassicaceous plants); cyclitols (myoinositol, phytic acid); and the reductone, L-ascorbic acid. These and other types, which are either induced by processing or are added to foods, are presented in later sections.

B. Importance of Dietary Carbohydrates

Carbohydrates provide the main source of calories in the diets of most peoples of the world. However, less than half the caloric intake in the United States is carbohydrate. The affluent and less energetic populace tends to regard carbohydrates as fattening, nonessential, and troublesome; hence, their consumption of high-carbohydrate staples per capita has decreased in favor of high-protein and high-fat meats and oilseeds. With the increased consumption of processed and sweetened foods, dietary sugars are increasing while starches and dietary fiber are decreasing. Reducing diets that severely restrict carbohydrates have caused some concern among nutritionists who believe that appreciable amounts of both available and unavailable carbohydrate are needed for optimum nutrition and health [77,85, 169].

The Food and Nutrition Board of the National Research Council, National Academy of Sciences [11] states:

> Complex carbohydrates, such as cellulose and hemicellulose, are largely indigestible, as are a number of oligosaccharides, certain other carbohydrates, gums, and fibrous matter found in foods of plant origin. These nondigestible substances provide bulk in the diet and aid elimination. Although there is no demonstrated requirement for fiber or bulk, their possible physiological significance has not been adequately explored. A relationship - not yet proven - between lack of dietary "fiber" and certain chronic disorders (noninfectious disease of the bowel, some vascular diseases) has been postulated from epidemiologic evidence [30].
>
> Carbohydrate can be made in the body from some amino acids and the glycerol moiety of fats; there is therefore no specific requirement for this nutrient in the diet. However, it is desirable to include some preformed carbohydrate in the diet to avoid ketosis, excessive breakdown of body protein, loss of cations, especially sodium, and involuntary dehydration. Fifty to 100 g of digestible carbohydrate a day will offset the undesirable metabolic responses associated with high fat diets and fasting [33].

Although protein provides as many calories per gram as carbohydrates, and fat provides more than twice as many, digestible carbohydrate promotes the utilization of fat and reduces the wastage of protein [137]. Essential body-building protein and expensive fats need not be consumed merely to satisfy energy requirements when the more plentiful carbohydrates supply energy efficiently at lower cost.

Apart from their nutritional and economic values, carbohydrates contribute importantly to the appetizing and pleasurable aspects of food. The sweetness of sugars is universally appreciated. Flavors produced in cooked foods by carmelization and sugar-amine browning reactions convert unappealing raw foods into foods with delightful tastes. As the appetite is whetted by volatiles of cooking processes (containing carbohydrate decomposition products), gastric juices flow to improve food digestion.

Carbohydrates are not only fundamental in diets, they provide the main store of utilizable energy from the sun. In the carbon cycle of nature, billions of tons of carbohydrates are produced annually by photosynthesis in oxygen-evolving plants. Directly or indirectly, all animals are energized from this everlasting supply.

C. Origin

1. BIOSYNTHESIS

Carbohydrates are among the first organic compounds to be produced from carbon dioxide and water through the sun's irradiation of the photosynthetic cells of plants. Light energy is thereby converted to chemical energy in substances suitable for food and feed. The routes of carbohydrate synthesis in higher plants show that natural carbohydrates are derived through the carbon reduction cycle of photosynthesis. The carbon reduction cycle itself involves carbohydrate transformations. Details of the chemical reactions, energetics, and enzymology of carbohydrate biosyntheses are available in other texts [1,17,157].

Absorption of light quanta occurs in the chloroplasts of plant leaves, more specifically in layers of the lamellae called "thylakoids." During irradiation, electrons of chlorophyll molecules in the thylakoids are raised to a higher energy level. Some electrons are liberated and are transferred to various acceptor molecules in coupled oxidation-reduction reactions. The result is an oxidation of water to free oxygen, with the formation of reduced coenzymes. Reduction of carbon dioxide occurs in the dark, outside the thylakoids, in the stroma of chloroplasts. Chains of oxygenated carbon atoms are formed. Some of these are converted into carbohydrates and hydroxy acids, others into amino acids and lipids. Small amounts of sucrose and starch are found within the chloroplasts; hence, the enzymes, sugar phosphates, and sugar phosphate nucleotides required for saccharide synthesis and conversions are present. However, the sugars, mainly sucrose, are translocated to cells of plant organs for the synthesis of cellulose, starch, and other polysaccharides.

Cellulose, hemicelluloses, pentosans, and pectic substances provide structural materials (cell walls, fibers, seed coats, peel, and husks) for enclosing the food stores of starch, fructans, sucrose, and their hydrolysis products. Most readily extracted by mechanical operations are the starch granules stored in roots, tubers, fruits, and seeds. The main sources of food carbohydrates for extraction by industrial processes are the cereal grains, manioc (cassava) roots, potato tubers, sugar beets, and sugar cane. Cereal grains provide the most economic sources of food carbohydrates in temperate zones, because they are highest in carbohydrate content, lowest in water content, and easiest to grow, harvest, transport, store, and process.

2. CHEMICAL SYNTHESIS

For more than a century it has been known that a sweet, syrupy mixture of sugars (formose) is spontaneously synthesized merely by storing dilute alkaline solutions of formaldehyde. Condensation of several molecules of formaldehyde produces a racemic (and toxic) (DL) mixture of many aldoses and ketoses, some with branched carbon chains. In a series of brilliant researches conducted in the nineteenth century, E. Fisher and J. Tafel showed that formose contained at least 13% hexoses and that the mixture could be resolved painstakingly into the natural sugars D-glucose, D-fructose, and D-mannose [86]. Much higher percentages of the hexoses have been synthesized since then, but practical procedures for separating the nutritive from nonnutritive sugars are lacking [131].

Present interest in formose stems from considerations that food for astronauts may be synthesized during extended aerospace missions. Catalytic reduction of carbon dioxide to methane followed by oxidation of methane to formaldehyde has been suggested for application of the formose reaction aboard space ships. Through knowledge of the kinetics of the reaction, the triose DL-glyceraldehyde and the triulose dihydroxyacetone have been produced in practical yields and continuous processes have been devised for formose syntheses [131,177]. Reduction of the triose mixture to glycerol is expedient because dihydroxyacetone has proved to be toxic to rats [178]. As a food additive, glycerol is accepted, absorbed, and metabolized; but to replace normal dietary carbohydrate, human feeding experiments under space flight conditions have been required. The results of these and other studies have shown that glycerol, when properly consumed, is well utilized metabolically and in amounts up to 300 g/day. However, the maximum percentage of glycerol compatible with good growth of rats was 40% of the daily diet; whereas 60% of glycerol was fatal within a few weeks [99].

The experimental substitution of glycerol for dietary carbohydrate illustrates an important point for food scientists. Substitution of one carbohydrate for another should not be practiced without specific knowledge of the physiological effects that may be produced, and these should be determined by appropriate feeding tests.

D. Caloric Values and Digestibility

According to the photosynthesis equation, $6 CO_2 + 6 H_2O = C_6H_{12}O_6 + 6 O_2$, 675 kcal of energy are fixed into the chemical bonds of each hexose gram-molecule (mol wt 180). This is known because the reverse reaction, achieved by complete combustion of hexose to carbon dioxide and water in a calorimeter, yields 675/180 = 3.75 kcal/g. When D-glucose is condensed with D-fructose to form sucrose, slightly more energy is stored per gram because 1 mole of water is eliminated between the two hexoses. Combustion of sucrose releases 3.95 kcal/g. Normal humans digest sucrose with 98% efficiency; hence, sucrose calories are calculated at 3.95 x 0.98 = 3.87 kcal/g. When D-glucose is condensed with itself repeatedly, as in the homoglycan starch $(C_6H_{10}O_5)_x$, still more carbon is available per gram. Dry starch provides 4.18 kcal/g upon combustion and cooked starches are digested with 98-99% efficiency. Carbohydrate calories are therefore calculated approximately at 4 kcal/g. This value may be somewhat too high, because the energy released by enzymic hydrolysis of starch in the digestive tract is considered to be unavailable for metabolic processes within the body proper.

The fraction of plant foods called dietary fiber consists of lignin, cellulose, hemicelluloses, pentosans, and pectic substances which have been shown to be practically indigestible in the stomach and small intestine. Southgate and Durnin [187] reported 2% as the maximum contribution of pentosans to metabolic energy and only 0.4% for cellulose, based upon human feeding experiments. Yet, 100% wheat bran was reported to have 56% digestibility and a caloric value of 2.35 kcal/ g [210]. Either the 100% wheat bran contained sugars and starch in excess of the normal 20±% or, more likely, a common source of error in determining the digestibility of unavailable carbohydrates was involved. When digestibility is estimated on a carbohydrate-in, carbohydrate-out (in feces) basis, the values obtained are usually too high. Partially available and unavailable carbohydrates can be fermented in the lower bowel to gases and acids; hence some may never appear in the feces as carbohydrate. Individual variations in intestinal flora and fecal transit time have caused wide variations in digestibility values; hence, "apparent digestibility" is a more suitable term [186].

Another uncertainty involved in the calculation of caloric values arises from the "proximate analysis" used to estimate the carbohydrate composition of foods. "Total carbohydrate," as listed in food composition tables [210], is only a calculated difference between 100% and the sum of the percentages of water, crude fat (by solvent extraction), crude protein (N x factor), and ash. Crude fiber, mainly cellulose and lignin, is often estimated by extracting fat and then determining the residue left after successive hydrolytic extractions with boiling dilute alkali and dilute sulfuric acid. Nitrogen-free extract is the difference between "total carbohydrate" and crude fiber; it represents not only available carbohydrate but also some soluble, unavailable hemicellulose fractions and poorly utilized sugars. Scala [169] has estimated that only 20-50% of the total dietary fiber is represented by the residual crude fiber of proximate analyses. Van Soest and McQueen [204] gave even higher percentages for the extracted hemicelluloses, pentosans, cellulose, and lignin. More exact analytical methods for carbohydrates in foods are needed, particularly to control diets of diabetics and persons with specific carbohydrate malabsorption diseases and to aid investigations of the role of "fiber" in the diet. The instrumental chromatographic methods now available can greatly improve our knowledge of the carbohydrate composition of foods.

Humans vary in their complement of digestive enzymes and especially in the disaccharidases that hydrolyze lactose, sucrose, and isomaltose. Most members of the darker skinned races and many white adults are deficient in lactase. This norm is violated in only a few populations [68,114]. Lactase concentrations in intestinal mucosa decrease at varying rates after age 4 years; therefore no uniformly applicable digestive coefficient can be set for lactose.

Retention of water in the lower bowel by large amounts of undigested hydrophilic carbohydrates or alditols often causes diarrhea. Flatus (fermentation gases) is also discomforting and objectionable. These possible adverse effects must be considered in selecting carbohydrates for addition to processed foods.

E. Carbohydrate Composition of Foods

The dietician's need for more exact information on the carbohydrate composition of foods was discussed in the preceding Section. Food processors also make practical use of carbohydrate composition data. For example, the reducing sugar content of fruits and vegetables that are to be dehydrated or processed with heat is frequently an indicator of the extent of nonenzymic browning that can be expected during processing and storage. The possible hydrolysis of sucrose to reducing sugars during processing also is to be considered. The natural changes in carbohydrate composition that occur during maturation and postharvest ripening of plant foods is therefore of particular interest to food chemists.

Citrus fruits, which normally ripen on the tree and contain no starch, undergo little change in carbohydrate composition following harvest. However, in fruits that are picked before complete ripening (e.g., apples, bananas, pears), much of the stored starch is converted to sugars as ripening proceeds. The reducing sugar content of potatoes also increases during cold storage. According to the activity of endogenous invertase during the sun drying of grapes and dates, sucrose is converted to D-glucose and D-fructose; accordingly, the color of the dried products is deepened by nonenzymic browning reactions.

Green peas, green beans, and sweet corn are picked before maturity to obtain succulent textures and sweetness. Later the sugars would be converted to polysaccharides, water would be lost, and tough textures would develop. In soybeans, which are allowed to mature completely before harvest, the starch reserve is depleted as sucrose and galactosylsucroses (raffinose, stachyose, verbascose, etc.) are formed. In the malting of cereal grains, rapid conversions of reserve carbohydrate to sugars occur as enzymes are strongly activated.

In foods of animal origin, postmortem activity of enzymes must be considered when carbohydrate composition data is obtained. The glycogen of animal tissues, especially liver, is rapidly depolymerized to D-glucose after slaughter, and immediate deep freezing is required to preserve the glycogen. Mammalian internal organs, such as liver, kidney, and brains, also eggs and shellfish, provide small amounts of D-glucose in the diet [210]. Red, fleshy meats contain only traces of available carbohydrate (D-glucose, D-fructose, and D-ribose) and these are extracted into bouillons and broths. Dairy products provide the main source of mammalian carbohydrate. Whole cow's milk contains about 4.9% carbohydrate and dried skim milk contains over 50% lactose [210].

Food composition tables, such as those of Watt and Merrill [210], show "total carbohydrate" that has been calculated by difference in proximate analysis (Section I, D). More recently, foods have been analyzed for specific carbohydrates by chromatographic methods [22,109,117,126,150,209], and by use of glucose oxidase [44]. Table 3-3 shows the approximate carbohydrate composition of some common foods.

Examination of food composition tables shows that, in general, cereals are highest in starch content and lowest in sugars. Fruits are highest in free sugars and lowest in starch. On a dry basis, the edible portions of fruits usually contain 80-90% carbohydrate. Legumes occupy intermediate positions with regard to starch and are high in unavailable carbohydrate.

Glycosides (Section II, D) of many types are widely distributed in plants [129]. Certain biologically active thioglucosides, properly called "glucosinolates," are found in significant amounts in crucifers. Mustard oils, nitriles, and goitrins are released by enzymic hydrolysis. Their suspected goitrogenic properties in humans have been investigated, but the amounts of glucosinolates normally consumed in foods such as fresh cabbage (300-1000 ppm), cauliflower, Brussels sprouts, turnips, rutabagas, and radishes are not now believed to cause adverse physiological effects [203]. Cyanogenetic glycosides, which release hydrogen cyanide by

TABLE 3-3

Approximate Carbohydrate Composition of Selected Food Types[a]

	Cereal grains, whole		Legumes, mature, dry			Fruits, edible portion			Vegetables	
	Corn (%)	Wheat (%)	Navy beans (%)	Soybeans (%)	Peanuts (%)	Apples (%)	Oranges (%)	Prunes (%)	White potatoes (%)	Tomatoes (%)
Monosaccharides										
D-Fructose	0.1-0.4	0.1		Trace		5	1.5	30	0.1	1.6
D-Glucose	0.2-0.5	<0.1		Trace		2	2.5	15	0.1	1.2
Reducing sugars				0-2	0.2	8	5	47	1 (var.)	3.4
Oligosaccharides										
Sucrose	1-2	1	3	5-7	4-5	3	4.6	2	Var.	<1
Raffinose	0.1-0.3	0.3	0.8[b]	1-2						
Stachyose			2.5[b]	3-5						
Other		1-2[c]	3.8[d]	+[d]						
Polysaccharides										
Starch, d.b.[e]	64-78	59-61	35-40	0-2	4	0.6		0.7	75	
Dextrins		6-7	4	1-3	3					
Pectin					+	0.6	1.3	0.9	+	0.3
Pentosans	6	5-6	8	4-5	4		0.3	2.0		
Hemicelluloses	5-6	6	6-7	5-7	4	0.7	0.3	10.7	0.3	0.3
Cellulose	1	2	3	2-3	2-3	0.4	0.3	2.8	0.4	0.2
Water (%)	16	14	11	10	2	84	86	3	80	93

[a]Hardinge et al. [76], Kawamura [104], D'Appolonia et al. [43].
[b]Green mung bean data.
[c]Fructosylsucroses.
[d]Other = verbascose; + = present but not quantitated.
[e]d.b. = dry basis.

enzymic hydrolysis under certain conditions of vegetable maceration, are known to be sources of acute toxicity in certain animal feeds; however, they are not active in the customary foods of developed countries. Certain foreign varieties of lima beans and manioc root (cassava) may yield up to 0.3% hydrogen cyanide by weight, but lima beans distributed in the United States yield less than 0.02% [133]. Saponins, the surface-active glycosides of steroids and triterpenoids, are found in low concentrations in tea leaves, spinach, asparagus, beets, sugar beet (0.3%), yams, soybeans (0.5%), alfalfa (2-3%), and peanuts and other legumes [26]. The toxicity of soybean saponins to tadpoles and guppies and their probable harmlessness in diets of warm-blooded animals have been discussed by Birk [26].

II. STRUCTURE AND NOMENCLATURE

Some primary aspects of carbohydrate structure and nomenclature were presented in Section I, A. In Table 3-2, the differences in absorption of the various sugars are one manifestation of highly specific interactions of sugars with proteinaceous membranes. Some sugars (e.g., D-glucose, D-galactose, and D-fructose) are actively absorbed through the wall of the human small intestine for utilization in metabolic processes, whereas others of the same or smaller molecular size (e.g., 2-deoxy-D-glucose, D-mannose, L-arabinose, and L-sorbose) are absorbed only slightly [16]. Similar specific complexing interactions of sugars are believed to be involved in the sensing of sweet taste [25], in the sequestration of metal ions [7], and in the cell-agglutinating reactions of certain proteins known as lectins [47,179]; for it has been shown that certain configurations and spacings of hydroxyl groups are much more reactive than others in producing the specific responses. Understanding these interactions and defining them requires knowledge of carbohydrate stereochemistry, the important elements of which are D- and L-enantiomorphs, α- and β-anomeric ring forms, configurations about asymmetric carbon atoms, and conformations of the sugar rings. These elements are best understood by reference to stereomodels. Both stick and ball and space-filling models are much more instructive than the conventional formulas that appear in textbooks.

A. Monosaccharides

Carbohydrate structures are customarily represented on paper by one of the three types of formulas shown in Figure 3-1. Only the conformational formula depicts the stereomodel. In the Fischer projection, it is understood that for each tetrahedral carbon atom considered in turn the bonds to the adjacent carbon atoms project backwards below the plane of the sheet upon which the formula is written. Consequently, the other two bonds (to the hydrogen atom and hydroxyl group) project forward above the carbon atom in the plane. In the construction of stereomodels, the lower numbered carbon atom (or ring oxygen) is held upward as the configuration about each carbon atom is determined. When a flexible model of the hydroxylated carbon chain is built for aldehydo D-glucose (Fig. 3-1), it is seen that the oxygen atoms on the fourth and fifth (also the sixth) carbon atoms (counting from the aldehydic carbon as C-1) can be turned to approach within bonding distance of C-1. In Figure 3-1, the oxygen atom on C-5 is shown within bonding distance.

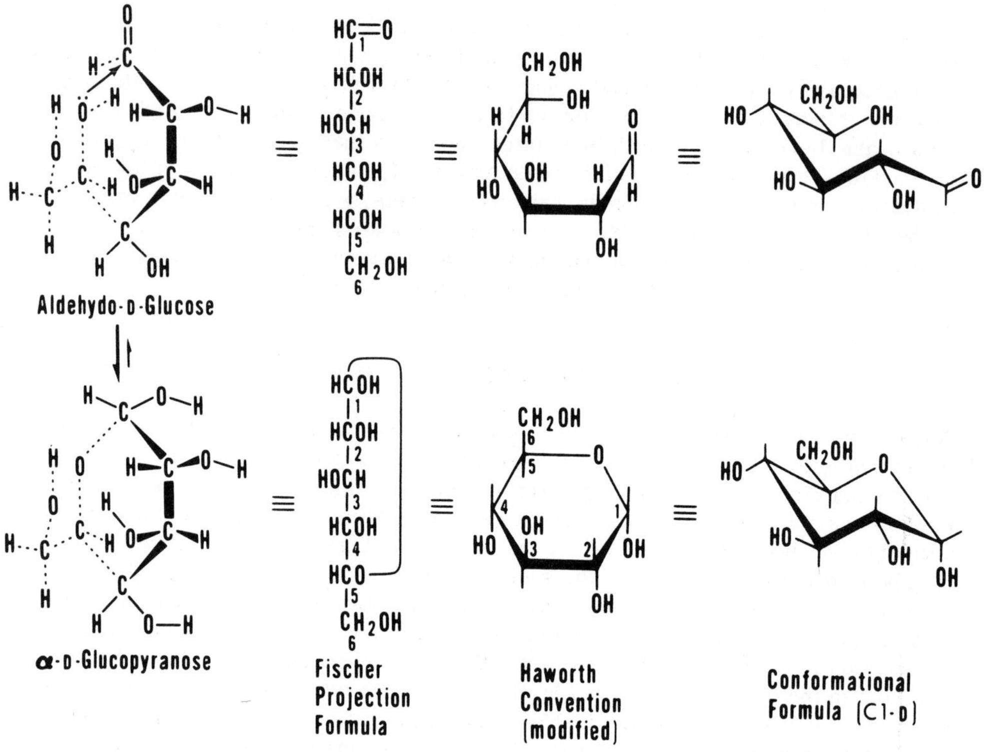

FIG. 3-1. Formulas representing aldehydo-D-glucose and α-D-glucopyranose.

The carbonyl group of an aldehyde readily adds water or simple alcohols to form aldehydrols or hemiacetals in reversible equilibria:

$$\underset{\substack{|\\ -C=O}}{\overset{H}{}} \quad \underset{-ROH}{\overset{+ROH}{\rightleftharpoons}} \quad \underset{\substack{|\\ OR}}{\overset{H}{\underset{}{-C-OH}}} \qquad (R = H \text{ or alkyl})$$

In the same way, the hydroxyl groups on C-4 or C-5 of the sugar molecule will add reversibly to the carbonyl group to form cyclic, internal hemiacetals. If the ring closes by participation of the C-4-OH, a five-membered heterocyclic ring called "furanose" is formed. If the ring closes by participation of the C-5-OH, as shown in Figure 3-1, a six-membered pyranose ring is formed. Seven-membered rings are formed only when the C-4 and C-5 hydroxyl groups are substituted or are not present. Cyclic hemiacetals are formed also with 2-ketoses.

As the hemiacetal rings are formed, the new hydroxyl group on C-1, called the "anomeric hydroxyl group," can project toward either side of the ring. Hence, two different furanoses and two different pyranoses can be formed. When the asymmetric anomeric hydroxyl group is formed on the same side of the ring as the reference hydroxyl group, the furanose and pyranose ring form is arbitrarily called alpha (α-); when it is formed on the opposite side of the ring from the reference hydroxyl group, the anomeric ring form is called beta (β-). The reference hydroxyl group is the one of the highest numbered asymmetric carbon atom, called the "reference carbon atom." This is usually C-5 in hexoses, C-4 in pentoses, and C-3 in tetroses. It is always C-2 in glyceraldehyde, the reference compound upon which the D and L configurational symbols are based. For the D configuration, the reference hydroxyl group is on the right in Fischer projection formulas.

From D- or L-glyceraldehyde all sugars can be synthesized via the cyanohydrin synthesis and other syntheses [86]. By adding hydroxyl groups to the right or to the left of the carbon stem as CHOH groups replace the aldehyde group in each sugar of the ascending series, the configurations of all sugars can be related to the two glyceraldehydes. This operation has been performed in Table 3-4 to show the configurational prefixes that are derived from trivial names of the sugars. Systematic names are formed by adding tetrose, pentose, hexose, etc., to the trivial prefixes with a hyphen; e.g., D-arabinose is D-arabino-pentose. The configurational symbols, D and L usually appear in print as small Roman capitals and the trivial prefixes are italicized, except when they are adjoined to pyranose or furanose without a hyphen.

TABLE 3-4

Configurational Prefixes for Naming Sugars

Trioses	D-glycero	L-glycero		
X = CHO	(D-glyceraldehyde)	(L-glyceraldehyde)		
Y = CH$_2$OH				

$$\begin{array}{ccc}
\text{X} & & \text{X} \\
| & & | \\
\text{HC--OH} & & \text{HO--CH} \\
| & & | \\
\text{Y} & & \text{Y}
\end{array}$$

Tetroses	D-erythro(se)	D-threo(se)	L-erythro(se)	L-threo(se)
X = CHO				
Y = CH$_2$OH				

$$\begin{array}{cccc}
\text{X} & \text{X} & \text{X} & \text{X} \\
| & | & | & | \\
\text{HC--OH} & \text{HO--CH} & \text{HO--CH} & \text{HC--OH} \\
| & | & | & | \\
\text{HC--OH} & \text{HC--OH} & \text{HO--CH} & \text{HO--CH} \\
| & | & | & | \\
\text{Y} & \text{Y} & \text{Y} & \text{Y}
\end{array}$$

Pentoses	D-arabino(se)	D-ribo(se)	D-xylo(se)	D-lyxo(se)
X = CHO				
Y = CH$_2$OH				

$$\begin{array}{cccc}
\text{X} & \text{X} & \text{X} & \text{X} \\
| & | & | & | \\
\text{HO--CH} & \text{HC--OH} & \text{HC--OH} & \text{HO--CH} \\
| & | & | & | \\
\text{HC--OH} & \text{HC--OH} & \text{HO--CH} & \text{HO--CH} \\
| & | & | & | \\
\text{HC--OH} & \text{HC--OH} & \text{HC--OH} & \text{HC--OH} \\
| & | & | & | \\
\text{Y} & \text{Y} & \text{Y} & \text{Y}
\end{array}$$

TABLE 3-4 (Continued)

Hexoses X = CHO Y = CH_2OH				
	X	X	X	X
	$\mid$	$\mid$	$\mid$	$\mid$
	HC–OH	HO–CH	HC–OH	HC–OH
	$\mid$	$\mid$	$\mid$	$\mid$
	HO–CH	HO–CH	HC–OH	HO–CH
	$\mid$	$\mid$	$\mid$	$\mid$
	HC–OH	HC–OH	HO–CH	HO–CH
	$\mid$	$\mid$	$\mid$	$\mid$
	HC–OH	HC–OH	HC–OH	HC–OH
	$\mid$	$\mid$	$\mid$	$\mid$
	Y	Y	Y	Y
	D–gluco(se)	D–manno(se)	D–gulo(se)	D–galacto(se)

To name and formulate the 2-ketoses (glyculoses), consider that X is -C:O- CH_2OH (instead of -CHO) and Y is CH_2OH in Table 3-4. For example, D-fructose is D-arabino-hexulose, L-sorbose is L-xylo-hexulose, and L-xylulose is L-threo-pentulose. Here it is evident that one less asymmetric carbon atom is present in the ketoses than in the corresponding aldoses. Only four of the eight prefixes are given for the hexoses because the other four (D-allo, D-altro, D-ido, and D-talo) are seldom encountered among the names of food sugars. The L series of pentoses and hexoses is formed by transposing each hydroxyl group of the D series to the opposite side of the carbon chain. Complete descriptions of the systematic nomenclature have been published and should be consulted to broaden the simple elements presented here [8,9].

The D or L configuration at the reference carbon atom is readily determined from the Fischer projection formulas but is difficult to assess from Haworth representations of hexopyranoses and hexo- or pentofuranoses. With the ring oxygen in the normal position, as shown for the Haworth convention in Figure 3-1, the highest numbered carbon atom(s) located outside the ring project upward in the D series and downward in the L series. The conformational formula of Figure 3-1 presents a one-sided perspective view of the ball and stick stereomodel. It shows, in sharp contrast to the Haworth convention, that the sugar ring is not planar, that cis hydroxyl groups (at C-1 and C-2) are not eclipsed, that trans vicinal hydroxyl groups (at C-2 and C-3, also at C-3 and C-4) are not necessarily oriented 180° apart, and that the CH_2OH group is normally located in an equatorial, not an axial, position. The conformational formulas should soon displace the conventional formulas because knowledge of the steric relationships in sugar rings has developed rapidly through the use of nuclear magnetic resonance spectroscopy and computer analysis of X-ray diffraction patterns of crystals [6,48,113,192].

The most stable conformations of some sugars of interest to food chemists are shown in Figure 3-2. Chair conformations of the pyranose rings predominate because, in these forms (Cl-D = $^4C_1$), widest separation of the electronegative oxygen atoms is achieved through equatorial orientations of most of the hydroxyl and CH_2OH groups. For α-D-arabinopyranose-1C, the inverted chair conformation shown ($^1C_4$) is the most stable; it allows equatorial orientations for three of the four hydroxyl groups. Furanose rings are also puckered in their most stable forms, so that some of the quasi-axial hydroxyl groups project more toward the

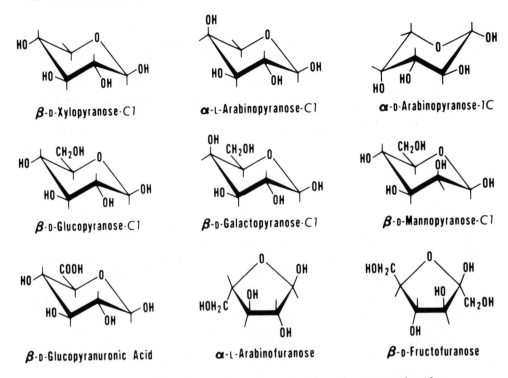

β-D-Xylopyranose-C1   α-L-Arabinopyranose-C1   α-D-Arabinopyranose-1C

β-D-Glucopyranose-C1   β-D-Galactopyranose-C1   β-D-Mannopyranose-C1

β-D-Glucopyranuronic Acid   α-L-Arabinofuranose   β-D-Fructofuranose

FIG. 3-2. Most stable ring conformations of selected monosaccharides.

equator. A uniform nomenclature for the different conformations of five- and six-membered rings in monosaccharides has been proposed [172]. For comprehensive information on sugar conformations, other texts should be consulted [6,48].

Some monosaccharide components of food polysaccharides are deoxy sugars. L-Rhamnose and L-fucose, indicated in Table 3-1, are 6-deoxyhexoses. The prefix "deoxy" indicates removal of the oxygen atom at the carbon position indicated by the preceding numeral with retention of the appended hydrogen atom. From the information that L-rhamnose is 6-deoxy-L-mannopyranose, and that 6-deoxy-L-galactofuranose is one form of L-fucose, definitive formulas for these sugars can be drawn by reference to Table 3-4. Although these sugars contain a terminal methyl group (Y = CH$_3$), they should no longer be called "methylpentoses." The "deoxyribose" of nucleotides (DNA) is 2-deoxy-β-D-erythro-pentose. The common amino sugars, trivially named D-glucosamine, D-galactosamine, and D-mannosamine, are properly named 2-amino-2-deoxy-D-(gluco, galacto, manno) pyranose. The prefix is 2-acetamido-2-deoxy- when the amino group is acetylated. The prefix deoxy-, with the locating numeral, is inserted into the definitive name in alphabetical order, e.g., 6-bromo-6-deoxy-α-D-glucopyranose, but 6-deoxy-6-iodo-β-D-galactofuranose.

To indicate substitution on oxygen atoms (rather than carbon atoms as illustrated above), as in alkyl ethers or acyl esters, the substituent replacing the hydroxyl hydrogen is usually prefixed with an italicized O. For example,

4-O-methyl-β-D-glucopyranuronic acid (see conformational formula in Fig. 3-2) is a natural monosaccharide component of some hemicelluloses. Fully acetylated D-glucose can be named α- or β-D-glucopyranose pentaacetate; however, if the anomeric hydroxyl group is not acetylated, the acetyl positions become specified, as in 2,3,4,6-tetra-O-acetyl-α-D-glucopyranose. Replacement of hydrogen attached to nitrogen or sulfur, as in amino or thio sugars, is indicated in the same way with use of the usually italic capitals N or S. The special case of O substitution at the anomeric hydroxyl group, wherein disaccharides and glycosides are formed, are treated in the following sections.

B. Oligosaccharides

Oligosaccharides are water-soluble polymers of a few condensed monosaccharides. Their degrees of polymerization (DP) range from two to about ten. Those most commonly found in foods are generally homopolymers of D-glucose (e.g., maltose, maltooligosaccharides) or heteropolymers of D-glucose condensed with D-fructose or D-galactose (e.g., sucrose, lactose, raffinose, stachyose). Natural oligosaccharides are synthesized via sugar nucleotides and glycosyl transferases [78, 184]. Some may be present in seeds and tubers as incidental intermediates in the synthesis of reserve polysaccharides; however, others have been shown to be artifacts created by enzymic or acidic hydrolysis during isolation or processing procedures. Some natural and artifactitious oligosaccharides are listed by their trivial names in Table 3-5; their systematic names and most common sources are given in the footnotes.

In the natural polymerization of n molecules of monosaccharides, n - 1 molecules of water are lost between the anomeric hydroxyl group of one monosaccharide unit and one of the several possible hydroxyl positions of the adjacent unit. The sugar radical produced by loss of the anomeric hydroxyl group is called, generically, "glycosyl." The reducing oligosaccharides are therefore named as O-glycosyl-glycoses (Table 3-5, footnotes). When the glycosyl radical is O substituted on any alcoholic or phenolic compound, the resulting compound is called an O-glycoside. The C-O-C bonds between the units of oligo- and polysaccharides are therefore called "glycosidic linkages." The linkage positions are specified in systematic names by -(1→x)-, where 1 and x are the numerals of carbons involved in the C-O-C linkage. When water is eliminated between the anomeric hydroxyl groups of two monosaccharides, nonreducing disaccharides are formed; e.g., trehalose (Table 3-5) and sucrose (Table 3-5, Figure 3-3). These can be named as glycosyl-glycosides. In the formation of the other nonreducing heterooligosaccharides listed in Table 3-5, O-glycosyl substitutions have occurred on sucrose at certain hydroxyl positions. Such additional condensations are regular in their linkage types; thus, homogeneous sections normally are found in the heteropolymers beyond the initial disaccharide to which glycosyl groups have been enzymically transferred.

Many di- and higher oligosaccharides can be formed in small amounts merely by heating glucose or sucrose syrups in the presence of acidic catalysts [194,197]. When starch syrups were manufactured by acid-catalyzed hydrolysis, troublesome amounts of oligosaccharides which were not structural units of starch molecules were formed in the syrups. When these "reversion products" were isolated by

TABLE 3-5

Common Oligosaccharides[a]

Prefix for degree of Polymerization (DP)	Homo		Hetero	
	Reducing	Nonreducing	Reducing	Nonreducing
Di- (2)	Cellobiose[b] Isomaltose[f] Maltose[h] Gentiobiose[j] Laminaribiose[l]	Trehalose[c]	Lactose[d] Lactulose[g] Maltulose[i] Melibiose[k]	Sucrose[e]
Tri- (3)	Maltotriose			Kestoses[m] Melezitose[n] Planteose[o] Raffinose[p]
Tetra- (4)	Maltotetraose			Stachyose[q]
Penta- (5)	Maltopentaose			Verbascose[q]
DP = 6-10	Maltohexa (...deca)ose	Cyclomaltohexa (...deca)ose (Schardinger dextrins)		Ajucose[q] Galactosyl- and Fructosyl- sucroses

[a]From Ref. [14].

[b]4-O-β-D-glucopyranosyl-β-D-glucopyranose (unit of cellulose).

[c]α-D-glucopyranosyl-α-D-glucopyranoside = α,α-trehalose; α,β- and β,β-also known.

[d]4-O-β-D-galactopyranosyl-D-glucopyranose (milk sugar).

[e]β-D-fructofuranosyl-α-D-glucopyranoside (beet or cane sugar).

[f]6-O-α-D-glucopyranosyl-D-glucopyranose (unit of amylopectin, glycogen, dextrans).

[g]4-O-α-D-galactopyranosyl-D-fructofuranose (in heated milks).

[h]4-O-α-D-glucopyranosyl-α-D-glucopyranose (unit of amylose; in starch syrups).

[i]4-O-α-D-glucopyranosyl-D-fructose (in starch hydrolyzates, honey, and brews).

[j]6-O-β-D-glucopyranosyl-D-glucopyranose (unit of natural glycosides).

[k]6-O-α-D-galactopyranosyl-D-glucopyranose (unit of raffinose).

[l]3-O-β-D-glucopyranosyl-D-glucopyranose (unit of laminaran, scleroglucan).

[m]A group of three β-D-fructofuranosylsucroses formed by the transferase action of invertase on sucrose.

[n]O-α-D-glucopyranosyl-(1→3)-O-β-D-fructofuranosyl-(2→1)-α-D-glucopyranoside (commonly abbreviated O-α-D-Glcp-(1→3)-O-β-D-Fruf-(2→1)-α-D-Glcp).

[o]O-α-D-Galp-(1→6)-O-β-D-Fruf-(2→1)-α-D-Glcp (in seeds of many species, cacao beans).

[p]O-α-D-Galp-(1→6)-O-α-D-Glcp-(1→2)-β-D-Fruf (widely distributed in plant tissues and seeds).

[q]Members of the raffinose series with additional α-D-galactosyl groups condensed (1→6) with the preceding galactosyl unit.

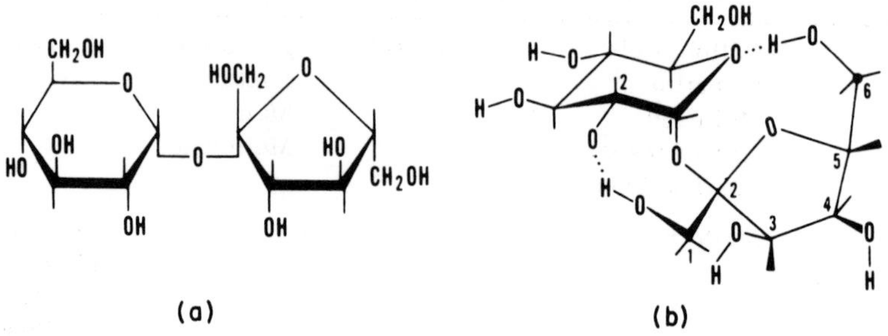

FIG. 3-3.   (a) Haworth and (b) conformational formulas of sucrose.

column chromatography and identified, it was evident that all of the possible α- and β-disaccharides of D-glucose had been formed. However, isomaltose and gentiobiose (which is bitter), containing α- and β-(1→6) linkages, respectively, were formed in largest amounts [197]. Starch syrups are now manufactured mainly by enzymic hydrolysis. When the amylases used are free of transglycosylases, reversion products are not formed and purer syrups are produced. Some maltooligosaccharides remain in these syrups. They inhibit crystallization of D-glucose and provide for suitable textures and humectant properties in the foods to which the syrups are added. The cyclic maltooligosaccharides of DP 6, 7, 8, and higher, known as Schardinger dextrins (Table 3-5), are produced by the trans-glucosylase action of Bacillus macerans enzyme on starch pastes [59,178]. Although they form useful inclusion complexes with many hydrophobic organic compounds, they have not been approved for food use because of unfavorable feeding tests with experimental animals [59].

Oligosaccharides serve as important reference compounds for determining polysaccharide structures via partial hydrolysis. Fragments containing the branching units of a highly branched polysaccharide (e.g., amylopectin fraction of starch, Figure 3-4) can sometimes be isolated after partial hydrolysis with acid or an endo-acting enzyme, such as α-amylase. Such fragments are more easily completely methylated than the original polysaccharide [105]. Complete hydrolysis (methanolysis, acetolysis) of the methylated fragments and identification of the partially methylated monosaccharides defines the positions of interglycosidic linkages. For example, the glucose unit carrying the α-(1→6) linkage at the branch points in amylopectin would yield a 2,3-di-O-methyl-D-glucose, whereas those units between the branch points would yield a 2,3,6-tri-O-methyl-D-glucose, indicating the presence of (1→4) linkages. Exo-acting enzymes, such as β-amylase, can be used to reduce the size of the oligosaccharide and increase the proportion of branching units relative to units of the main chain. The terminal unit at the non-reducing end of the main chain would yield, from amylopectin, a 2,3,4,6-tetra-O-methyl-D-glucose.

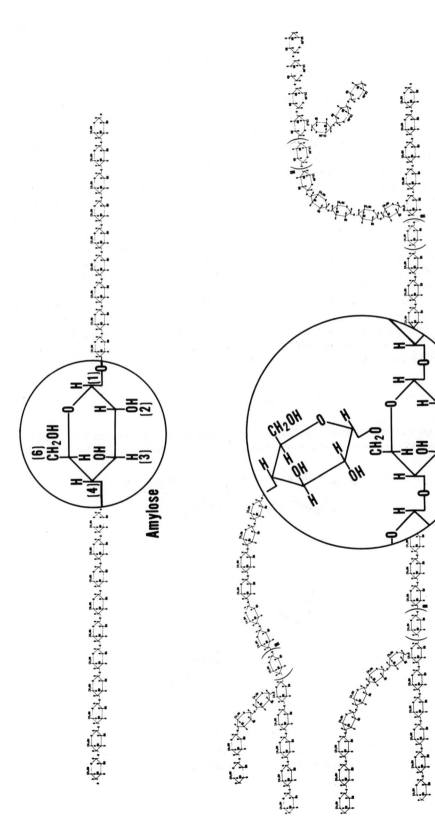

FIG. 3-4. Linear and branched chains of starch fractions.

Methods for preparing, isolating, purifying, identifying, and determining the structure of oligosaccharides are now fully described in the literature [14,40,152, 184], and data for identifying oligosaccharides and their fully acetylated derivatives by melting point and specific optical rotation have been compiled [14,40]. When reference saccharides are available, the oligosaccharides are usually identified by comparative paper chromatography [60]. Solutions of appropriate enzymes are often sprayed onto the developed chromatograms to release the component monosaccharides of nonreducing and higher oligosaccharides for more sensitive detection by spray reagents.

Oligosaccharides may be considered as the repeating units of polysaccharides. The exo-hydrolase β-amylase releases only disaccharide units (maltose) from starch molecules and similar exo-hydrolases release cellobiose units from cellulose. An exo-hydrolase that releases α-maltotriose units from the α-D-glucan, pullulan, has been reported. Figure 3-5 shows the disaccharide repeating units of cellulose and starch in conformational formulas. The hydrogen bonding shown between adjacent D-glucose units is probably the force that directs (or maintains) cellulose molecules into a rigid rodlike shape and amylose molecules into a coil. The hydrogen bonds are deduced from both X-ray diffraction and nuclear magnetic resonance (NMR) data, not only for maltose and cellobiose but also for methyl β-maltoside monohydrate, the cyclic Schardinger dextrins, and amylose [36,40,90, 192]. The same intramolecular hydrogen bond shown for cellobiose is also indicated for lactose by X-ray diffraction data.

C. Polysaccharides

Only a general discussion of polysaccharide structures is presented here. The relationships between structure and functionality in foods are presented in Section

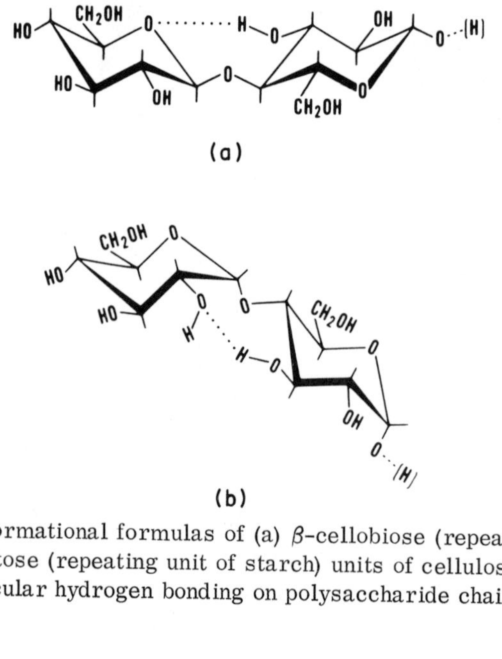

(a)

(b)

FIG. 3-5. Conformational formulas of (a) β-cellobiose (repeating unit of cellulose) and (b) α-maltose (repeating unit of starch) units of cellulose and starch: Effect of intramolecular hydrogen bonding on polysaccharide chain conformation.

3. CARBOHYDRATES

V. Polysaccharides are long chains of glycosidic sugar units synthesized by enzymes from only a few types of hexoses, modified hexoses, and pentoses. The primary chain consists usually of one, but sometimes two, types of monosaccharides. Side chains (branches) may consist of sugars different from those in the main chain with different types of glycosidic linkages. Although the polymerization is seldom absolutely regular, haphazard arrangements and covalently bound network structures have not been found [42].

The glycan nomenclature for polysaccharides was introduced in Section I, A. The names of many well-known polysaccharides end in "-in" (e.g., chitin, dextrin, inulin, pectin) as do the trivial names of natural glycosides. However, the D-glucans, formerly called laminarin and lichenin, are now listed as laminaran and lichenan, and the microbial polysaccharide produced by <u>Xanthomonas</u> <u>campestris</u> has been named xanthan.

As the degree of polymerization (DP) of oligosaccharides increases, it becomes increasingly difficult to isolate one member of a series from its homologs. Even when β-maltose monohydrate is crystallized from starch hydrolyzates, maltotriose and maltotetraose can be detected in the crystals and these higher homologs are not removed by repeated recrystallizations of the maltose from various solvents. Polysaccharides are likewise polydisperse mixtures of homologs which vary widely in DP, even after fractional precipitation procedures have been carefully applied. Because the homologs are so tightly associated, it is difficult to determine the true average molecular weights of discrete undegraded molecules. The methods and problems involved in determining the molecular weights and structures of polysaccharides have been discussed by Danishefsky et al. [42].

Polysaccharides differ from higher oligosaccharides in another important way. As the DP increases during biosynthesis, the opportunity for enzymic synthesis of combinations of chains increases. Branches are formed on the main chains and, sometimes, on branches. The main chain is normally a homoglycan with linkages of the same type, but the branches may be composed of different monosaccharides with different types of linkages. The structural types shown schematically in Figure 3-6 are the most common. The branching probably is not regular with respect to either chain length or spacing. The branched types shown may exist in blocks which are separated by linear portions of the main chain [134]. Long chains tend to adopt folded, helical, and randomly coiled conformations (Section V).

D. Glycosides

Glycosides are condensation products of reducing sugars (glycoses) with nonsugars (aglycons - also spelled "aglycones"). Technically, oligo- and polysaccharides are also glycosides. When a molecule of water is eliminated between the anomeric hydroxyl group of the glycose and the hydroxyl group of an alcohol or phenol, O-glycosides are formed. They are full acetals with different O substituents (mixed acetals). With amino (or imino) and thiol compounds as aglycons, N- and S-glycosides are formed. All three types are minor components of foods and feeds.

Although glycosides abound in all parts of plants, only small amounts normally enter the diet (Section I, E). Nevertheless, the properties of naturally occurring glycosides as related to their structures should be understood because, at very low concentrations, they can affect the acceptability of foods. Certain types (e.g., solanum glyco-alkaloids of potatoes, cardiac glycosides) have potent biological

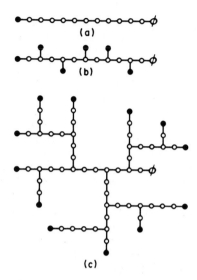

FIG. 3-6. Structural types of polysaccharides. (a) Linear (amylose, cellulose); (b) branched, with single-unit or short side chains (guaran); (c) branch-on-
branch (amylopectin).

activities per se, whereas certain other types are hydrolyzed by natural enzymes
during processing with the release of hydrogen cyanide, mustard oils with pungent
flavors, or polyhydric phenols. Hydroquinones, catechols, and similar phenols
readily undergo enzymic oxidation and reactions with amines or iron(III) to form
dark-colored compounds. The glycose moiety, which may be a simple sugar,
uronic acid, homo- or heterooligosaccharide, generally confers water solubility
upon strongly hydrophobic aglycons, thereby causing them to exhibit strong surface activity. For example, the widespread saponins (steroid or terpenoid O-
glycosides) are added to beverages in minute amounts to create stable foams.
Saponins create foaming problems during the aqueous extraction of sugar beets and
licorice roots. As little as 0.4 ppm in refined sugar causes foaming when the
sugar is dissolved in water. Upon acidification of sugar solutions that contain
soluble carboxylate salts of saponins, precipitates form, as in soft drinks. The
saponins of soybeans and alfalfa form complexes with proteins, and also with the
enzymes α-chymotrypsin and cholinesterase, although the nonspecific and limited
inhibition of these enzyme complexes is counteracted by other proteins in the
legumes [26].

The generally strong bitter tastes of naturally occurring glycosides are often
mentioned. It should also be recognized that the commercial glycyrrhizin of
licorice root (Fig. 3-7), stevioside of the sweet herb of Paraguay (Fig. 3-8), and
osladin of polypody fern rhizomes (Fig. 3-9) are intensely sweet. Although
glycyrrhizin is a monoglycoside and the other two are diglycosides, the similarity
of structures among these and other sweet, and sweetness-inhibiting, glycosides is
interesting and has been discussed [82].

In naming glycosides, the name of the aglycon radical is placed first as a separate word. In place of "glyc-," the trivial sugar prefix is inserted with its configurational symbols and ring form, if known; e.g., methyl α-D-glucopyranoside.

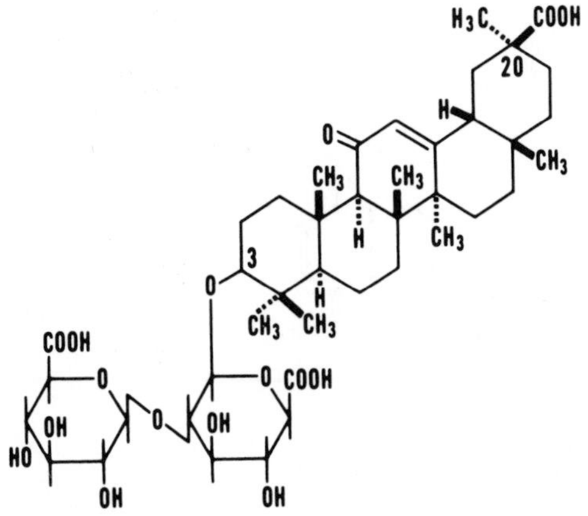

FIG. 3-7. Formula of glycyrrhizic acid (glycyrrhizin), a component of licorice.
Reprinted with permission of Avi Publishing Co. [82].

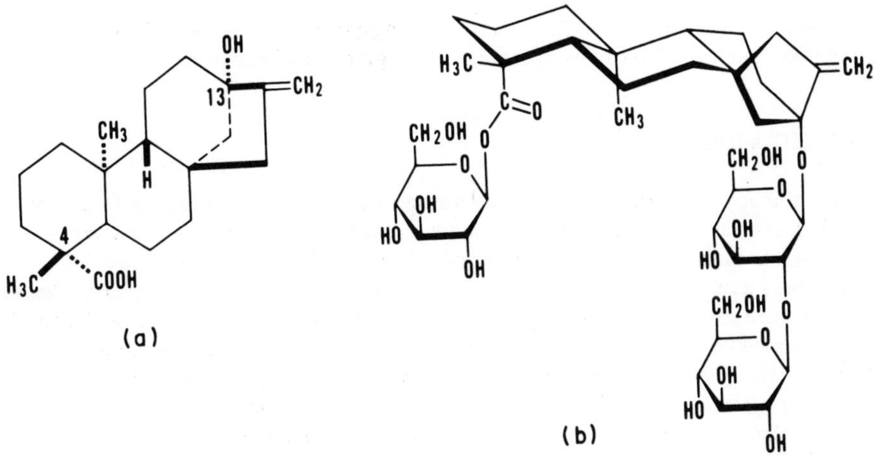

FIG. 3-8. Formulas of (b) stevioside and (a) the aglycon steviol. Reprinted
with permission of Avi Publishing Co. [82].

The suffix "-ide" must appear to denote a glycoside; for example, methyl β-D-
glucopyranuronate is the methyl ester of a uronic acid, whereas, methyl 4-O-
methyl-β-D-glucopyranuronide is the glucoside. To name the methyl ester of this
methyl glucuronide, the form is changed to methyl 4-O-methyl-β-D-glucosiduronic
acid methyl ester. If the aglycon is complex or is not conveniently named as a
radical, the name of the complete aglycon may be used. For example, the cyanogenetic glucoside of manioc root (cassava) is conveniently named acetonecyanohy-
drin β-D-glucopyranoside. Its trivial name, linamarin, gives no clue to its structure. Most of the trivial names of natural glycosides were formed from a prefix
derived from the botanical name of the genus or species from which the glycoside

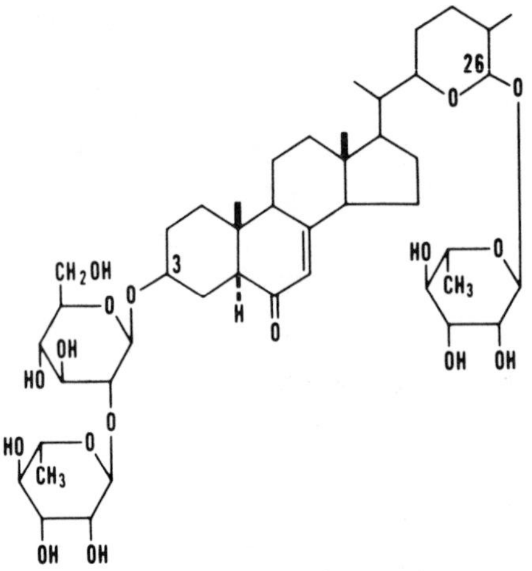

FIG. 3-9. Formula of osladin, a component of polypody fern rhizomes. Reprinted with permission of Avi Publishing Co. [82].

originated, followed by the suffix "-in." The aglycons of complex glycosides are
often called "-genins," as in sapogenins, the aglycons of saponins.

1. O-GLYCOSIDES

The β-D-glucopyranosides predominate among the naturally occurring O-glycosides,
although β-D-glucuronides, β-D-xylosides, α-L-arabinosides, α-L-rhamnosides
(6-deoxy-α-L-mannosides), and the D- and L-fucosides [6-deoxy-D-(or L-)-
galactosides] are fairly common. The common hexoses D-galactose, D-mannose,
and D-fructose are seldom found condensed directly with the aglycon; however, the
glycolipids of wheat flour and many plants contain 1-O-β-D-galactopyranosyl-2,3-
di-O-(palmityl, oleyl, linoleyl, etc.)-D-glycerols. The disaccharide radical O-α-
D-galactopyranosyl-(1→6)-β-D-galactopyranosyl is also found substituted on the
primary hydroxyl group of di-O-acylglycerols [35]. Disaccharides are common in
flavonoid glycosides and more than one may be present.

Many classes of organic compounds form the aglycon of natural O-glycosides.
Most frequently encountered in foods and feeds are the polyhydric phenols, including flavonoids. O-Glycosides of flavonoids are generally nontoxic. Anthocyanidin
glycosides form the red, purple, and blue pigments of many fruits. Other common
aglycones are the steroids and terpenoids of saponins; hydroxy acids and lactones,
including coumarin; cyanohydrins of acetone and benzaldehydes, forming cyanogenetic glycosides; and the hydroxyamino acid units in proteins, forming glycoproteins. The structures of naturally occurring O-glycosides are given in other
texts [39,129] and saponin structures have been discussed separately [26].

O-Glycosidic linkages are stable at the pH of foods; however, they are hydrolyzed in hot acidic solutions or by the action of appropriate enzymes to the component sugar(s) and the aglycon. They are usually stable in alkaline solutions and
are therefore nonreducing. However, when the aglycon is a phenol or enol, or
when the glycosyloxy group stands β to a carbonyl or other electronegative group

in the aglycon, the aglycon is liberated in hot alkaline solutions and reducing substances (sugar decomposition products) can be detected. The elimination of a glycosyloxy group that stands β to a carbonyl function is illustrated in Figure 3-10; i.e., for a serine or threonine residue in one type of glycoprotein. When reduction (hydrogenation) is conducted to immediately follow the elimination reaction, the serine unit is converted to an alanine unit; and the liberated glycose (usually an oligosaccharide) is stabilized by reduction to an alditol. These reactions have been used to determine glycoprotein structures [132]. The anomeric configuration and ring form of O-glycosides can usually be identified by NMR spectroscopy of the acetylated derivatives or by periodate oxidation. Other methods for structure determination and the synthesis and chemical reactions of O-glycosides are discussed by Overend [147].

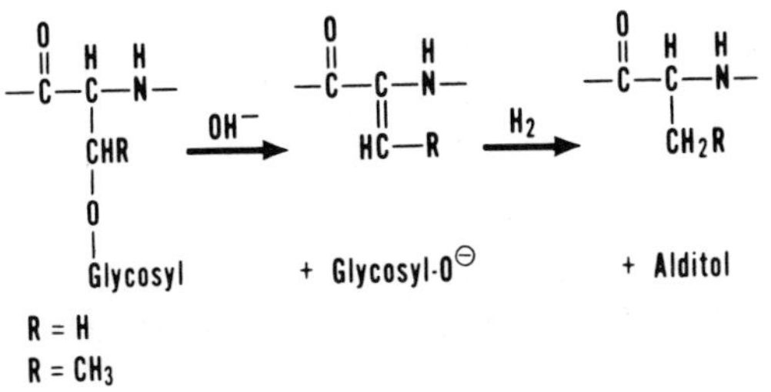

FIG. 3-10. β Elimination of O-glycosyl groups from serine or threonine residues in glycoproteins.

2. N-GLYCOSIDES

In contrast to the O-glycosides, which are stable in the presence of weak acids and bases in the pH range of foods, the N-glycosides of basic amines and their salts readily hydrolyze and decompose in water. Only the N-glycosides of certain resonance-stabilized heterocyclic bases with imide-like imino groups (e.g., imidazoles and hydroxypyrimidines) can match the O-glycosides in stability, and only these are found in natural foods. The N-β-D-ribofuranosyl purines and pyrimidines of nucleosides show amide-like stabilities at the N-glycosyl linkage; hence the furanoside ring does not open to allow enolization and decomposition reactions. The N-glycosyl amides (e.g., N-D-glucosylurea and N-acetyl-D-glucosylamine, also are relatively stable. In contrast, N-glycosyl derivatives of basic amines with no amide-like resonance will slowly decompose with dark color formation merely upon standing at room temperature in moist air. These labile types are called, generically, glycosylamines, and they are named as N-substituted glycosylamines; e.g., N-phenyl-β-D-fructopyranosylamine.

The glycosylamines are not Schiff bases with the azomethine structure $R - C = N - R'$, although this acyclic form is believed to be an intermediate in the interconversion of ring forms, corresponding to the aldehydo and keto open-chain forms of glycoses. The N-substituted D-glucosylamines are hydrolyzed as easily as Schiff bases, but they normally crystallize in the β-D-glucopyranose ring form. The participation of glycosylamines in nonenzymic browning reactions is discussed in Section III.

Certain 5'-nucleotides of 6-hydroxypurine (Figure 3-11; R = H, NH_2, or OH) are used as flavor potentiators. They enhance meaty, brothy, and other food flavors, particularly when they are used in conjunction with monosodium L-glutamate (MSG) and certain other flavor potentiators. Synergistic action between inosine 5'-monophosphate (R = N) or guanosine 5'-monophosphate (R = NH_2) and MSG has been demonstrated [115].

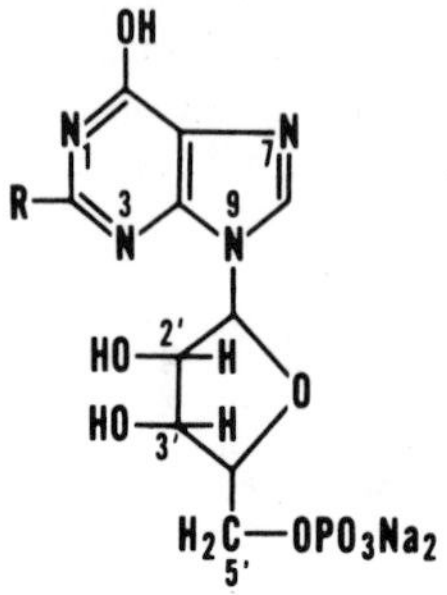

FIG. 3-11. Structure of flavor-potentiating nucleotides: 5'-monophosphates of inosine (R = H), guanosine (R = NH_2), and xanthosine (R = OH).

3. S-GLYCOSIDES

The most important thioglycosides in foods are the glucosinolates (Section I, E). Only D-glucose in the β-anomeric configuration has been found in the glucosinolates of crucifiers. Upon crushing mustard seed or horseradish root, enzymes are activated that catalyze hydrolysis of glucosinolates (Figure 3-12). The steam-volatile, pungent, and lachrymatory mustard oils which arise are the substituted isothiocyanates, where R = allyl, 3-butenyl, 4-pentenyl, benzyl, 2-phenylethyl, or 4-methylthio-3-butenyl. Allyl glucosinolate (sinigrin) is the best-known member of this expanding class of compounds and many other R groups have been defined [203]. Their significance as toxicants in foods and feeds has been discussed [203].

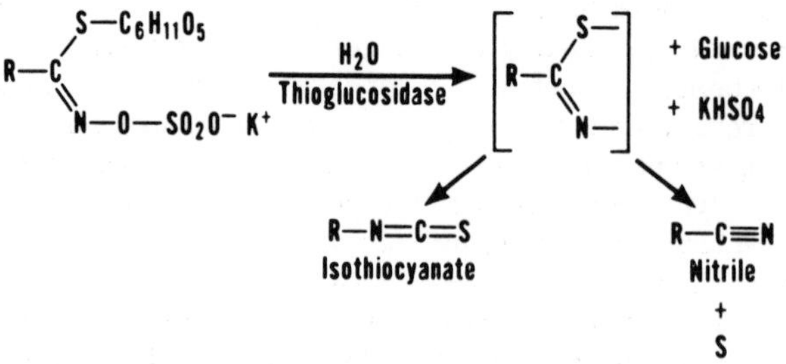

FIG. 3-12. Hydrolysis of glucosinolates.

4. GLYCOSANS

Glycosans are intramolecular glycosides. They are formed by elimination of a molecule of water between the anomeric hydroxyl group and another hydroxyl group within the same glycose. The most common glycosan, levoglucosan, is 1,6-anhydro-β-D-glucopyranose (Figure 3-13). To effect the glycosidic ring closure, the normal Cl-(D) (or $^4C_1$) conformation of the β-D-glycopyranose ring (Fig. 3-2) must be inverted to the 1C-(D) (or $^1C_4$) conformation, wherein all hydroxyl groups and the terminal CH_2OH group are in axial orientations, the most unstable conformation. High temperatures are required to form the somewhat strained, bicyclic structure.

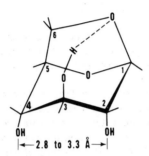

FIG. 3-13. Conformational formula of levoglucosan (1,6-anhydro-β-D-gluco pyranose).

Both levoglucosan and 1,6-anhydro-β-D-glucofuranose are formed together in the pyrolysis (destructive distillation) of D-glucose, starch, or cellulose. They distil from the carbonized residue under vacuum [63,87]. Levoglucosan is prepared also by heating phenyl β-D-glucopyranoside in hot alkali. Probably only trace amounts of levoglucosan would be formed by heating glucose syrups above 100°C under candy-making conditions, but its slightly bitter and astringent taste might be noticed. Levoglucosan yields D-glucose by hydrolysis and D-glucans by thermal polymerization [73,87].

By melting sucrose, or by strongly heating syrups containing D-fructose, small amounts of unfermentable and hydrolysis-resistant di-D-fructose dianhydrides are formed. These are intermolecular glycosidic condensation products that arise by loss of two molecules of water from two molecules of the ketose, as in di-D-fructopyranose 1,2':2,1'-dianhydride. The corresponding di-D-fructofuranose and pyranose-furanose combinations are known. These tricyclic compounds have also been called "diheterolevulosans" [73].

E. Reductones

Reductones are a class of organic compounds in which the distinguishing functional group is derived from conjugated enediol and carbonyl functions. Their outstanding property is exceptionally strong reducing power in cold, acidic solutions. For example, they reduce acidic silver nitrate, gold chloride, and platinum chloride to the free metal, iron(III) to iron(II), copper(II) to copper(I), and free iodine or bromine to their respective ions. Of the many structural types of reductones now classified, those derived by carbohydrate dehydration and fission were the first to be recognized and defined [50].

The reductone functional group, in its simplest form, is represented by the formula $R-C(OH)=C(OH)-C:O-R'$, where R and R' can be alkyl, aryl, or the ends of a cyclizing biradical. Amino analogs ($OH = NH_2$ or $C:O = C:NR$) of reductones are also strongly reducing. As vinylogs of carboxylic acids, most reductones are about as acidic as acetic acid. In water the terminal proton dissociates and the monoanion is stabilized by resonance:

$$^-O-\overset{|}{C}=C(OH)-\overset{|}{C}=O \longleftrightarrow O=\overset{|}{C}-C(OH)=\overset{|}{C}-O^-$$

Resonance of the monoanion tends to protect reductones from air oxidation and catalytic or chemical reduction; however, the dianion which is formed in alkaline solution is not stable. In solutions exposed to oxygen at or above pH 6, free radicals have been detected [19,50].

Both protons of the reductone group are transferred to quinones or quinone-imines as the dehydro reductone, $R-C:O-C:O-C:O-R'$, is formed. When the dehydro form is stable in weakly acidic solution, quantitative titrations of the enediols can be conducted with the oxidation-reduction indicator dye 2,6-dichloroindophenol (Tillmans reagent), or with iodine, in the absence of air. The dehydroreductone can then be reduced back to the enediol form by passing hydrogen sulfide or sulfur dioxide into the solution.

Triose reductone (R = R' = H) is formed in low yields when reducing sugars are heated in strongly alkaline solutions. Monomethyl reductone (R = H, R' = CH$_3$) and diacetylformoin (R = R' = CH$_3$C:O) are formed within the pH range of foods and in sugar-amine browning reactions [80,160].

The alicyclic reductone, reductic acid (RR' = -CH$_2$CH$_2$-), is formed by the decarboxylation and dehydration reactions of uronic acids and pectin in strong acid at temperatures above 100°C [51]. Methylreductic acid [RR' = -CH(CH$_3$)-CH$_2$-] is formed by degradation of the sugar moiety of calotropin, an alkaloid glycoside of North African arrow poisons. Several amino analogs of methylreductic acid have been formed by heating hexoses with secondary amine salts [80]. The cyclic reductones, including the ascorbic acids, are generally more stable than the acyclic reductones in both enediol and dehydro forms. Certain well-browned foods and dark beers resist oxidative deterioration more than the lighter products due to the small amounts of reductones generated in situ by sugar-amine browning reactions. However, the two cyclic reductones shown in Figure 3-14 are much more effective as antioxidants in foods and they are frequently added to foods to inhibit oxidative deteriorations [19] (see Chapter 7).

The confusing nomenclature of the ascorbic acids deserves comment. When the structure of antiscorbutic vitamin C (L-ascorbic acid) was defined, several isomers and homologs were synthesized to determine their antiscorbutic activity [185]. For example, 6-deoxy-L-ascorbic acid was found to be one-third as active as L-ascorbic acid, the D-erythro isomer (Fig. 3-14) one-twentieth as active, and the D-threo isomer (not shown) inactive. Because the isomers were once prepared from the osones of pentoses (now called pentosuloses) by the cyanohydrin synthesis, and seven-carbon homologs were prepared similarly from hexosuloses, the

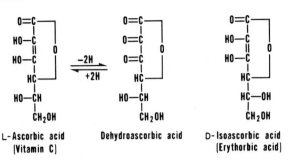

FIG. 3-14. Reductones and dehydroreductones: ascorbic acids.

various ascorbic acids were named from the lower carbon sugars from which they were prepared. Hence, vitamin C is still called L-xyloascorbic acid, and D-isoascorbic acid is called D-araboascorbic acid, although only two asymmetric carbon atoms are present. The trivial name, erythorbic acid, is derived from the D-erythro configuration in D-araboascorbic acid (D-isoascorbic acid) plus "orbic" from ascorbic acid.

III. CHEMICAL REACTIONS

The chemical reactions of carbohydrates that affect food quality and acceptance are discussed in this section. The application of heat in sterilization, cooking, and dehydration processes can cause many complex reactions to occur. The activity of water and protons (or of native glycosyl hydrolases) governs the extent of release of reducing sugars by hydrolysis from their glycosidic conjugates in foods. After release, very few disturbing reactions of sugars occur in watery media at about pH 4. However, should the medium become neutral or weakly alkaline, then the cyclic hemiacetals convert more rapidly to the acyclic carbonyl forms of reducing sugars, i.e., to reactive polyhydroxy aldehydes and ketones, which enolize and begin a series of decomposition reactions.

To the carbonyl groups of acyclic sugars, the basic amino groups of proteins, peptides, and amino acids are readily added and condensed. The deep-seated group of sugar-amine decomposition reactions, known as the Maillard reaction, can then proceed, usually with brown color formation, the starting point being enolization of the glycosylamine.

The decomposition reactions of sugars may occur in a second way, without amine participation, but more heat is required. At pH values less than 4 and at elevated temperatures, the hydroxyaldehydes and hydroxyketones enolize more slowly than in buffered neutral media. However, acid-catalyzed dehydration reactions occur rapidly after the enolization to produce the objectionable furfurals (2-furaldehydes), and dark brown colors are usually formed simultaneously in the foods.

Decomposition reactions may be induced by melting dry sugars and, to a limited extent, by heating their syrups at temperatures above 100°C, as in candy making. Heat hastens the inversion of sucrose to reducing sugars and the opening of their hemiacetal rings. In the hot, highly concentrated syrups, reducing sugars

condense with each other to form di- and higher oligosaccharides and dextrins.
Glycosans of aldoses and cyclic dianhydrides of ketoses (Section II, D,4) also may
be formed. When amino compounds do not participate in the heat-induced decomposition reactions or do so only in trace amounts, the group of complex color-
and flavor-inducing reactions is called "caramelization."

Both the Maillard reaction and caramelization involve a complex group of many
reactions which follow ring opening and enolization of reducing sugars. Both types
taken together are called nonenzymic browning reactions, to distinguish them from
the enzyme-catalyzed oxidative browning reactions of polyhydric phenols and quinones (Chapter 6). The brown to black, amorphous, nondescript polymers formed
in sugar-amine browning reactions are called "melanoidins." The melanoidins
are unsaturated heterogeneous polymers with no regular pattern of repeating units.

A. Hydrolysis

The extent of hydrolysis that saccharides undergo during processing depends primarily on the acidity of the medium, the anomeric form and position of the interglycosidic linkages, the ring form of the sugar units, the extent of hydrogen-
bonded associations between molecules, and the rate of inactivation of native
glycosyl hydrolases. In the home preparation of preserves and jellies, the acidity
of the fruit, the extended boiling times to evaporate water (when commercially
prepared pectin is not added), sucrose hydrolysis, and the hydrolysis of pectin
methoxyl groups can combine to produce gelling failures. Dark colors may develop
in stored preserves due to the release of reducing sugars from nonreducing sucrose
by hydrolysis, followed by nonenzymic browning reactions.

In general, β-D-linked homoglycans and oligosaccharides are less susceptible
to hydrolysis than comparable α-D-linked compounds. Also, α-(1→6)-D-glucosidic
linkages are more stable than α-(1→4, 1→3, or 1→2)-D-glucosidic linkages; the
pyranose ring forms of glycosidic units are more stable than the furanose forms;
and hydrogen-bonded aggregates resist hydrolysis more than amorphous regions in
strongly associated polysaccharides. Mechanisms for hydrolyses of glycosidic
linkages and the influence of structure on rates of hydrolysis have been discussed
by Overend [147] and by Pazur [152].

The furanoside residues of food carbohydrates are very easily hydrolyzed. The
arabinofuranosyl residues which form branches on the main chain of β-D-xylopy-
ranosyl units of pentosans can be selectively hydrolyzed by very dilute acid,
leaving the xylan virtually intact. The β-D-fructofuranosyl linkage in sucrose
makes it labile, even under mildly acidic conditions at low temperatures, and even
when only films of water are present on the surface of, or entrapped in, the
crystals. When sucrose crystals are melted, traces of the constituent monosaccharides can be detected before melting is complete. D-Glucose, D-fructose, and
several condensation, fission, and dehydration products of the sugars are found in
the melt. Thus, sufficient water can be generated by heat-decomposition and condensation reactions of disaccharides to promote their hydrolysis in an apparently
dry state. Acetic, formic, and pyruvic acids, which form by decomposition,
catalyze hydrolysis of sucrose during caramelization [79].

B. Ring-Chain Tautomerism and Mutarotation

The first and simplest structural change in sugars which leads to their decomposition is opening of the hemiacetal ring. The formation of α- and β-pyranose and furanose rings from the acyclic aldehyde or ketone is reversible (Fig. 3-1), and all five isomers (one acyclic, four cyclic) are believed to stand in equilibrium in solutions. The five isomers have been detected by gas-liquid chromatography of evaporated D-fructose solutions [41], and the acyclic keto-D-fructose was estimated at 0.5% of the total mixture [183]. The interconversion of anomers and ring forms through the acyclic form occurs merely upon dissolving crystals of a single anomer in water. Equilibrium may be established in minutes or several hours and is manifest when the optical rotation of the solution is constant.

Among all the ring forms of aldohexoses and aldopentoses, D-glucose and D-xylose have the most stable pyranose conformations (Fig. 3-2). For the β anomers, which predominate among the natural glycosides and polysaccharides, all hydroxyl groups are in equatorial orientations. Because these C1-(D) pyranose conformations are so stable, the furanose and aldehydo forms combined amount to less than 1% of the total in equilibrium mixtures. In aqueous solutions of D-glucose at 25°-30°C only 0.02% of the aldehydo form is present along with about 38% of the α- and 62% of the β-pyranose ring forms. D-Xylose, with the same configuration as D-glucose (Fig. 3-2), shows the same α:β ratio of pyranose anomers but the percentage of acyclic aldehydo form (approximately 0.17%) is increased. Pentoses generally show more of the reducible form than hexoses of corresponding configurations. D-Ribose, with the highest percentage of reducible form in solution, is the least stable toward decomposition reactions [148].

Immediately after crystalline α-D-glucose is dissolved in water, the specific optical rotation begins to decrease from +112° toward +53° where it becomes constant after 4.5 hr at 20°C. Likewise, β-D-glucose shows an increasing optical rotation from +19° to +53°. Such changes are called "mutarotation." They are normally manifestations of the equilibrium that is being established between the anomeric and ring forms of reducing sugars in solution. The mutarotations of other sugars are more complex than those of the α- and β-D-glucopyranoses, particularly when the furanose forms are more involved in the equilibration [5].

Mutarotation occurs only in amphoteric solvents or in mixtures of acidic and basic solvents. A mechanism for simultaneous acid-base catalysis is the most acceptable [188]. However, bases are more effective catalysts than acids. In 0.005N alkali, D-glucose equilibrates immediately; but, in 0.05N alkali, decomposition occurs and mutarotation equilibrium is not established for reasons given in the next section.

C. Enolization and Isomerization

Although a reducing sugar in aqueous solution at pH 3-7 and room temperature equilibrates in several different structural forms, it does not lose its identity. The most stable crystalline form of the sugar usually can be recovered nearly quantitatively from the solution. However, if the solution is strongly heated, or if the pH is shifted to values outside this range, enolization of the acyclic carbonyl form can be expected. Enolization proceeds by acid- and base-catalyzed mechanisms, but bases are much more effective catalysts than acids [92-94,188].

1. ALKALINE MEDIA

Figure 3-15 depicts the instantaneous ring opening of two pyranoses with approximate retention of the initial ring conformation. Rapid abstraction of the weakly acidic α-hydrogen atom at C-2 by a base produces hybrid monoanions of the enediol. If the anomeric oxygen atom remains approximately in its initial orientation (axial for α-D-glucopyranose, equatorial for β-D-mannopyranose), then the cis-enediol would form as shown. The trans-enediol would be formed preferentially from β-D-glucopyranose or α-D-mannopyranose. Some such directive force operates, because the different proportions of D-glucose, D-mannose, and D-fructose (tautomeric forms of the enediol) found in the reaction mixtures, starting with each of the three sugars, indicate that no single acyclic form is the controlling intermediate [93].

By ketonization of the 1,2-enediol shown in Figure 3-15, D-fructose is formed from either D-glucose or D-mannose (only C-1, C-2, and C-3 are shown):

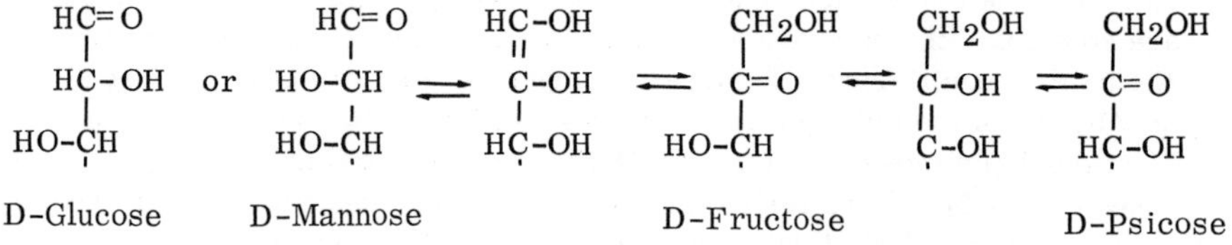

$$
\begin{array}{ccccccc}
\text{HC=O} & & \text{HC=O} & \text{HC-OH} & \text{CH}_2\text{OH} & \text{CH}_2\text{OH} & \text{CH}_2\text{OH} \\
| & & | & || & | & | & | \\
\text{HC-OH} & \text{or} & \text{HO-CH} \rightleftharpoons & \text{C-OH} \rightleftharpoons & \text{C=O} \rightleftharpoons & \text{C-OH} \rightleftharpoons & \text{C=O} \\
| & & | & | & | & || & | \\
\text{HO-CH} & & \text{HO-CH} & \text{HC-OH} & \text{HO-CH} & \text{C-OH} & \text{HC-OH}
\end{array}
$$

D-Glucose   D-Mannose   D-Fructose   D-Psicose

Enolization proceeds in both directions from the carbonyl group of D-fructose, although 1,2 enolization is dominant. Only small amounts of D-psicose (D-ribo-hexulose) are formed by the 2,3 enolization of D-fructose. Although tautomeric equilibria are indicated by the arrows, true equilibrium is not attained, because the open-chain polyhydroxy aldehydes and ketones decompose at the alkalinity (or acidity) required for the enolizations. The interconversions of sugars through their enediols (which have never been isolated) is called the Lobry de Bruyn-Alberda van Ekenstein transformation. The reactions and mechanisms involved have been

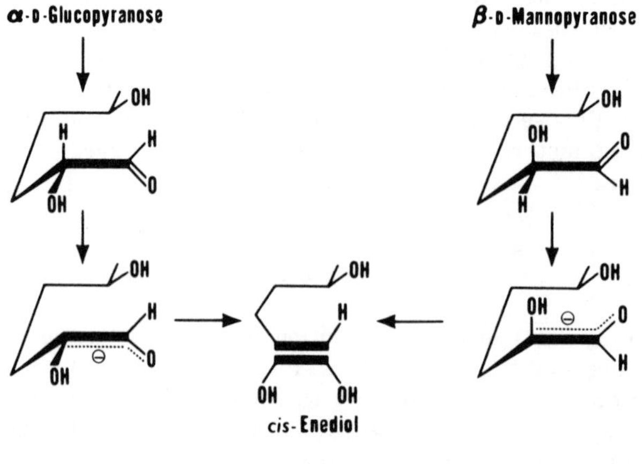

FIG. 3-15. Ring opening of sugars and enolization to the cis-1,2-enediol. Reprinted from Ref. 92.

thoroughly reviewed [188]. In the interconversions shown above, D-mannose and D-glucose have undergone epimerization (inversion of configuration) at C-2. Likewise, D-fructose and D-psicose are epimers resulting from epimerization at C-3.

Formerly calcium hydroxide has been the preferred base for isomerizing aldoses to ketoses; now, sodium aluminate is preferred. Both bases form complexes with D-fructose. Through complexing, decomposition reactions are diminished and yields of ketose are increased. The industrial isomerization of glucose syrup to 40-45% fructose is conducted with glucose isomerase (Chapter 6), but lactulose is produced by the chemical isomerization of lactose with sodium aluminate [202] because 4-O-β-D-galactopyranosyl-D-glucopyranose is not a substrate for glucose isomerase.

Enolization of the sugars in alkali in the presence of oxygen leads to oxidative fission at the double bond. Formic acid and D-arabinonic acid are the main products formed from D-glucose, but other acids are also formed [92].

2. NEUTRAL AND ACIDIC MEDIA

The Lobry de Bruyn-Alberda van Ekenstein transformation has been demonstrated for D-glucose, D-fructose, and D-mannose in the pH range 2.2-2.9 (e.g., at 130°C for 1 hr), with various organic acids as catalysts. The yields of glucose starting with fructose are significant (0.5-7%), whereas only traces of fructose can be detected starting with glucose. In buffered solutions, in the pH range 3.0-6.9, the yields of isomer are increased with increasing pH; still, the yields of glucose (5-20%) from fructose are double the yields of fructose (2-10%) from glucose. Mannose is detected in much lower amounts than glucose, starting with fructose. Below pH 2.2 at 130°C, the dehydration of fructose is strongly catalyzed and the Lobry de Bruyn-Alberda van Ekenstein transformation cannot be demonstrated [154].

These experiments and others show that aldose-ketose isomerizations proceed by acid-base catalysis. The anions of organic acids and hydroxyl ions of water are effective bases in the acidic media at elevated temperatures, even though they are present at low concentrations. Protonation of the carbonyl group and abstraction of the weakly acidic α-hydrogen atom by basic anions act jointly to form the hypothetical enediol intermediate:

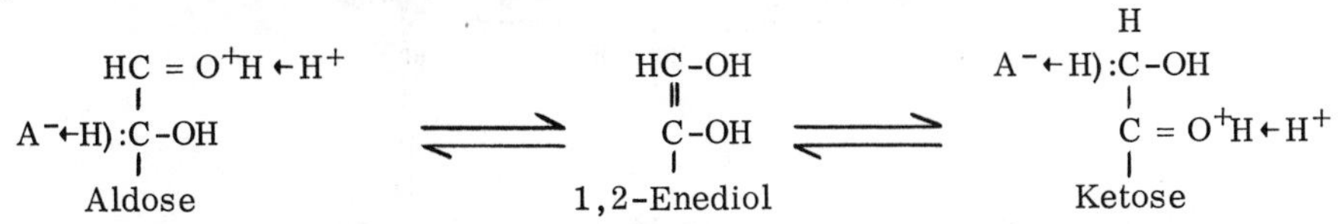

$$
\begin{array}{ccccc}
 & & & & \text{H} \\
\text{HC}=\text{O}^{+}\text{H}\leftarrow\text{H}^{+} & & \text{HC-OH} & & \text{A}^{-}\!\leftarrow\!\text{H}\!):\!\text{C-OH} \\
| & & \| & & | \\
\text{A}^{-}\!\leftarrow\!\text{H}\!):\!\text{C-OH} & \rightleftharpoons & \text{C-OH} & \rightleftharpoons & \text{C}=\text{O}^{+}\text{H}\leftarrow\text{H}^{+} \\
| & & | & & | \\
\text{Aldose} & & 1,2\text{-Enediol} & & \text{Ketose}
\end{array}
$$

The stability of glucose toward enolization, as compared to fructose, can be related to the much lower concentration of the carbonyl form of glucose in solution and to the stability of its β-pyranose ring conformation (Fig. 3-2), which is the most stable of all the sugars.

D. Dehydration Reactions

When sugars are sufficiently heated - as solids, as syrups, or even in dilute acidic solutions - water is eliminated by dehydration reactions. In molten solids and in syrups, water also can be eliminated by condensation reactions (Section II). In contrast to condensation reactions, wherein the sugars remain saturated, dehydration reactions cause sugars to become unsaturated and highly reactive. Dehydration reactions frequently occur during dehydration of food at temperatures well above ambient; however, acid- and base-catalyzed chemical reactions are not inherent in the physical process of drying.

Sugar dehydration reactions begin by elimination of the elements of water that are bound to the α- and β-carbon atoms adjacent to the carbonyl group of the open-chain form. Then, they continue in the same way to extend the conjugated unsaturation of the α,β-unsaturated carbonyl compound. By a series of dehydrations, pentoses and hexoses eliminate three molecules of water in forming 2-furaldehyde and 5-(hydroxymethyl)-2-furaldehyde (HMF).

1. ACIDIC MEDIA

Hexose reducing sugars are partially converted to HMF even by heating in weakly acidic aqueous media, as in the pasteurization of fruit juices. When D-glucose is refluxed in pure water at initial pH 6.5, the unsaturation that develops can be detected by ultraviolet absorption measurements. After the loss of one molecule of water, 3-deoxyglucosone (3-deoxy-D-glucosulose) is formed (Fig. 3-16, R = H). With the loss of a second molecule of water, an absorption band is detected at 228 nm. As refluxing is continued, absorption develops at 284 nm as HMF is formed in increasing amounts. These bands are detected in shorter reaction times as the acidity of the initial solution is increased [218].

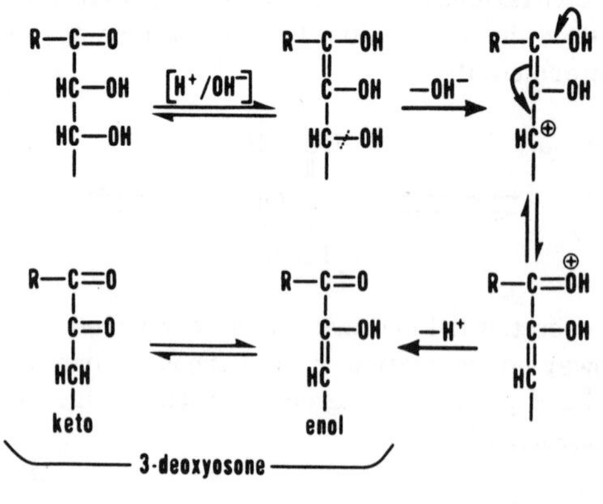

FIG. 3-16. Formation of 3-deoxyosones (R = H) and general β elimination in sugar dehydration reactions.

Sugars are dehydrated mainly by β-elimination reactions. One example of β elimination was illustrated in Figure 3-10. A more general example applicable to sugar hydroxyl groups is given in Figure 3-16. In acidic solutions, wherein the enolization shown would take place slowly, the hydroxyl group standing β to the carbonyl group (i.e., the allylic hydroxyl of the enediol) is quickly eliminated. It is probably protonated and then split out as water. The double bond then shifts as in allylic rearrangements.

With the formation of a new carbonyl group at C-2, or formation of the corresponding enol form (Fig. 3-16), the β- (or allylic) hydroxyl group at C-4 becomes labile. It is eliminated as shown in Figure 3-17 to extend the conjugated unsaturation and resonance along the chain. Whereas complete dehydration of the sugar may occur in this way to form highly unsaturated and polymerizable α-dicarbonyl compounds, an important side reaction is observed. The cis form of the 3-deoxyglucosone-3,4-ene forms a (hemiacetal?) ring between the C-5-OH and the C-2 carbonyl group. Loss of another molecule of water from this heterocycle yields HMF [4]. The trans form can convert to cis and then to HMF; however, the trans form also may be an intermediate in the formation of dark, polymeric humins that accompany the formation of HMF from hexoses or 2-furaldehyde from pentoses.

With unbuffered acids as catalysts, higher yields of HMF are produced from D-fructose than from D-glucose. Also, only the fructose moiety of sucrose is largely converted to HMF under unbuffered conditions that produce the highest yields. In Section III, C experiments were described that showed stronger acid catalysis of the 1,2 enolization of fructose than of glucose; but the enolization of glucose was greatly increased in buffered acidic solutions. It is not surprising, then, that higher yields of HMF are produced from glucose and sucrose when a combination of phosphoric acid and pyridine is used as catalysts than when phosphoric acid is used alone [127]. In fact, the yields of HMF from solutions of glucose, sucrose, and starch (on an equivalent hexose unit basis) are equal during short reaction periods at 200°C or higher. Another factor involved in dehydration reactions leading to HMF is the fragmentation of HMF (or an immediate precursor) to levulinic acid ($CH_3C:OCH_2CH_2COOH$) and formic acid. These two acids are produced in greater abundance when solutions are strongly acidic and this reduces the yield of HMF. Proposed mechanisms for levulinic acid formation have been critically reviewed [51].

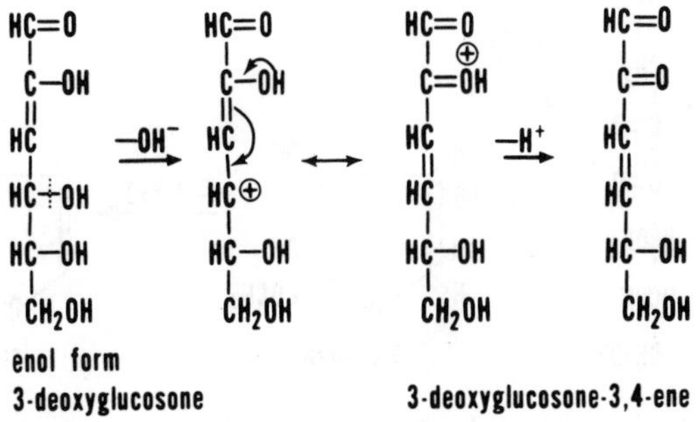

FIG. 3-17. Sugar dehydration leading to 2-furaldehydes.

The 2,3-enediol of a 2-ketose presents two possibilities for allylic hydroxyl eliminations in the same molecule (Figure 3-18). Hydroxyl elimination at C-4 leads to 2-(hydroxyacetyl)furan, which is usually present whenever HMF is present but in much smaller amounts. Hydroxyl elimination at C-1 leads to the methyl α-dicarbonyl intermediate (1-deoxy-D-erythro-2,3-hexodiulose) which, on furanose ring closure, dehydrates to isomaltol (2-acetyl-3-hydroxyfuran). However, the methyl α-dicarbonyl intermediate can also enolize into the reductone structure shown in Figure 3-19, the tautomeric form of which presents a carbonyl group at C-4. The β elimination (shown in allylic form) that follows yields diacetylformoin, another acidic dehydration product of D-fructose [180]. Diacetylformoin has the reducing power of reductones because it can enolize to CH_3-C:O-C(OH)=C(OH)-C:O-CH_3 in aqueous solution. Besides these compounds, 13 others have been identified from dehydrations of D-fructose syrup at 100°C and pH values of 1.0, 2.2, or 3.5 [180]. Similar studies of the thermal degradation products of L-ascorbic acid in model systems have shown that both D-fructose and L-ascorbic acid can be precursors of flavor compounds which are formed during storage of dehydrated orange juice [182].

β-Elimination reactions are invoked also to explain degradation dehydrations of ascorbic acid, uronic acid, and other carbohydrates [51]. The principle of β elimination also applies in general to degradations of polysaccharides containing uronic acid residues [111].

2. ALKALINE MEDIA

Among the common natural foods, only fresh egg white is alkaline. Cereal grains are sometimes treated with alkali for dehulling and for softening of the protein

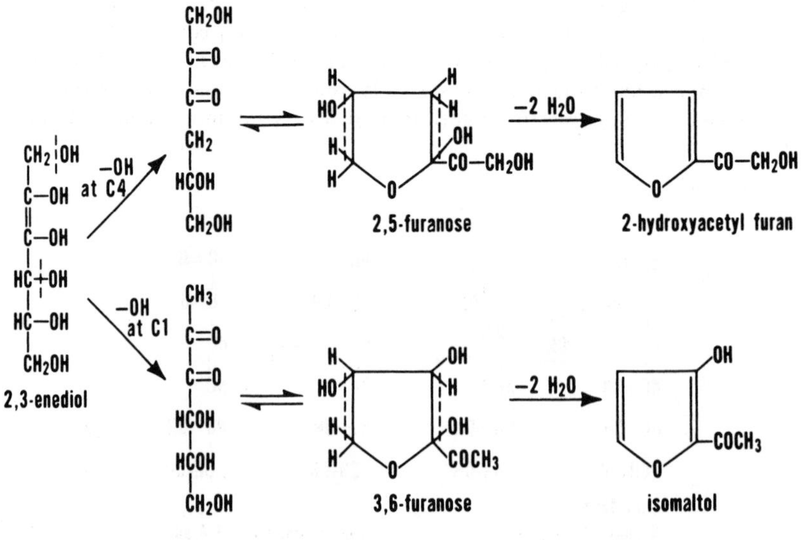

FIG. 3-18. Sugar dehydration leading to 2-(hydroxyacetyl)furan and isomaltol.

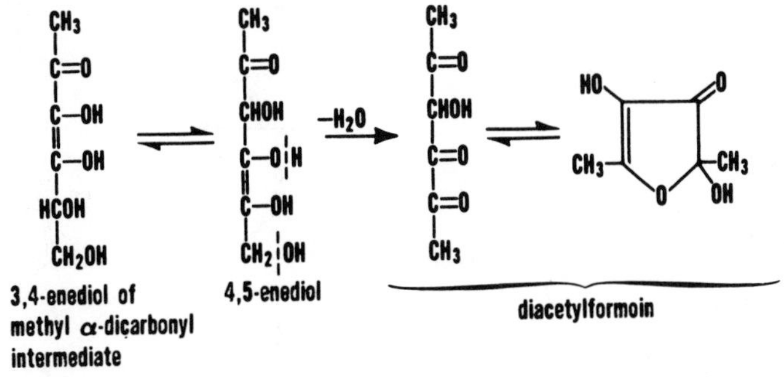

$$\begin{array}{l}
\text{CH}_3 \\
\text{C=O} \\
\text{C—OH} \\
\text{C—OH} \\
\text{HCOH} \\
\text{CH}_2\text{OH}
\end{array}
\rightleftharpoons
\begin{array}{l}
\text{CH}_3 \\
\text{C=O} \\
\text{CHOH} \\
\text{C—O}\,\text{H} \\
\text{C—OH} \\
\text{CH}_2\text{OH}
\end{array}
\xrightarrow{-\text{H}_2\text{O}}
\begin{array}{l}
\text{CH}_3 \\
\text{C=O} \\
\text{CHOH} \\
\text{C—} \\
\text{C=O} \\
\text{CH}_3
\end{array}
\rightleftharpoons
\text{diacetylformoin}$$

3,4-enediol of methyl α-diçarbonyl intermediate   4,5-enediol   diacetylformoin

FIG. 3-19. Sugar dehydration leading to diacetylformoin.

matrix to release starch granules. Finished hominy may be weakly alkaline, and so can alkali-treated pastry, such as pretzels. During open-kettle boiling of maple sap to syrup, the sap (pH 6-7) frequently becomes alkaline (pH 8). Caramelization of the sucrose and invert sugar is then accelerated; however, acidic sugar degradation products soon form to lower the pH to the weakly acidic range. The food chemist should therefore know of the sugar degradation products that are generated in alkaline media. Unfortunately, the reactions in weakly alkaline media are poorly defined.

In acidic media, enolization of sugars is slow, dehydration reactions are rapid and are practically unaffected by air oxidation, and fragmentation products are few. In weakly alkaline media, enolization is rapid, dehydration reactions are slower than enolizations, air oxidation changes the product composition, and reactive fragmentation products abound.

Most of the studies on alkaline sugar reactions have involved strongly alkaline solutions wherein saccharinic acids are the principal products [51]. In weakly alkaline media, the six-carbon saccharinic acids are not detected. The boiling of D-fructose syrup at pH 8-10 for 3 hr produces traces of 2-(hydroxymethyl)furan (furfuryl alcohol) and 2-(hydroxymethyl)-5-methylfuran; however, two-, three-, and four-carbon hydroxycarbonyl compounds, their aldol condensation products (methylcyclopentenolones with caramel aroma), and lower acids comprise the bulk of the ether-soluble products (Figure 3-20). The aldol condensation and cyclization reactions have been formulated [181].

The fragmentation products most commonly detected in alkaline media are acetol ($CH_3C{:}O{-}CH_2OH$), acetoin ($CH_3{-}C{:}O{-}CHOH{-}CH_3$), diacetyl ($CH_3{-}C{:}O{-}C{:}O{-}CH_3$), 1- and 4-hydroxy-2-butanones, γ-butyrolactone, and lactic, pyruvic, propionic, and acetic acids. The prevalence of methyl and acetyl radicals in these products indicates preliminary formation of the methyl α-dicarbonyl intermediate that is derived by 2,3 enolization of D-fructose and β elimination of the C-1-OH group (Figure 3-16, R = CH_2OH, and Figure 3-18). Further dehydration to diacetylformoin (Figure 3-19) would produce alkali-labile reductone structures which would decompose to some of the products mentioned. Cannizzaro and aldol condensation reactions of the first-formed aldehydes and ketones interfere with their detection and with full elucidation of the reaction mechanisms. The proposed sugar fragmentation mechanisms involve dealdolization reactions, and these have been discussed most recently by Feather and Harris [51].

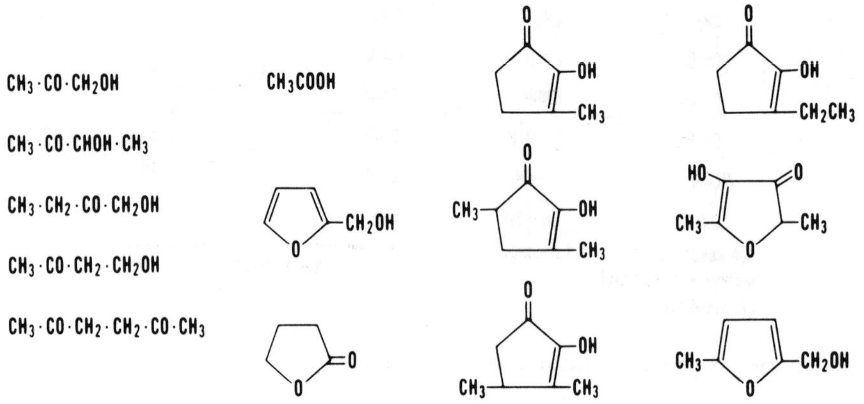

FIG. 3-20. Products of alkaline sugar dehydration and fragmentation reactions.

E. Browning Reactions

Browning reactions are a part of the natural processes of decay; e.g., the drying
and decomposition of vegetation to humus, peat, and coal. When ordered, life-
supporting substances are deprived of the protection of water, they become oxidized
and/or chemically dehydrated to reactive intermediates; these polymerize into
highly disordered, dull-brown humic substances. The dull-brown color itself
indicates a disordered array of red and yellow chromophores and a diffuse light-
absorption spectrum. Browning therefore consists of a series of "downhill,"
exothermic chemical reactions that proceed spontaneously after the "uphill" activation of energy-filled molecules.

The browning reactions of foods should be classified according to the reactions
involved in the initiation steps and not according to the catalysts, as custom now
dictates. The initial reactions are either oxidative or nonoxidative, not enzymic
or nonenzymic, because catalysis by enzymes may or may not be involved in
either type.

1. OXIDATIVE BROWNING

In oxidative browning of the enzymic type, the oxidases (e.g., catechol oxidase,
ascorbate oxidase, lipoxidase) are active only in the first step., i.e., in the conversion of phenol, enediol, or conjugated diene functional groups to reactive carbonyl compounds. The reactions that follow the enzymic oxidations are nonenzymic. Furthermore, the initial oxidations occur, although much more slowly,
in the absence of oxidases. Ascorbic acid can be oxidized enzymically and nonenzymically to dehydroascorbic acid (Figure 3-14), a vicinal tricarbonyl compound
that reacts nonenzymically with amino acids to produce red and brown polymers
[158].

Oxidations and subsequent degradations with browning are induced in carbohydrates by ultraviolet and ionizing radiations. Alditols are oxidized to aldoses, aldoses are oxidized to osones (glycosuloses) and aldonic acids, aldonic acids are

oxidized to 2-keto aldonic acids (which enolize to ascorbic acids), and carbonyl groups are introduced into polysaccharides to initiate their degradation by β-elimination reactions [155,212].

2. NONOXIDATIVE BROWNING

Nonoxidative browning reactions, like the oxidative, may involve enzymes in the first step. In natural products, glycosyl hydrolases initiate the so-called non-enzymic browning reactions by releasing reactive reducing sugars from their con-jugates. This is an important step in color and flavor development in date, honey, maple syrup, chocolate, and vanilla [79]. After the sugars are released, enzy-mically or nonenzymically, they proceed through the sequence of reactions described in Section III,B-D even in the complete absence of oxygen or other oxidants. As a result of reactions involving ring opening, enolization, dehydra-tion, and fragmentation, more reactive hydroxycarbonyl, α-dicarbonyl, and α,β-unsaturated carbonyl compounds are produced. These carbonylic intermediates react to produce brown polymers and flavor compounds, as in caramelization of sugars; however, browning is accelerated tremendously by condensations with amines or amino acids. In the latter instance, nitrogen is found covalently bound in some of the simple end products (e.g., pyrrole aldehydes, alkyl pyrazines, and imidazoles) and also in the brown polymers (melanoidins) of foods and in the humic substances of natural decay.

3. CARAMELIZATION REACTIONS

The fundamental reactions of heat-induced sugar caramelization have been des-cribed in the preceding sections. In review, they are:

1. Inversion of sucrose to D-glucose and D-fructose (Section III,A)
2. Equilibration of anomeric and ring forms (Section III,B)
3. Condensation, intermolecular, i.e., acid-catalyzed reversion of starch sugars to di-, tri-, and higher oligosaccharides (Section II,B)
4. Condensation, intramolecular, i.e., formation of glycosans and difructose dianhydrides (Section II,D,4)
5. Isomerization of aldoses to ketoses (Section III,C)
6. Dehydration reactions (Section III,D,1)
7. Fragmentation reactions (Section III,D,2)
8. Browning (formation of unsaturated polymers)

At the high temperatures of sugar caramelization minimal amounts of acidic and basic catalysts are required, and these are usually present as buffer salts in saps and syrups. Acids generated in molten sugars or added acidic salts catalyze de-hydrations to furans (7, above) and glycosans (5) with little fragmentation (7) [87, 193-195], whereas alkaline salts catalyze fragmentation reactions (8) at the ex-pense of furan and glycosan formation [87,88,167]. Practical caramelization re-actions are conducted with different catalysts to provide either flavoring or coloring caramel for food use.

For flavoring purposes, sucrose is caramelized in concentrated syrups. The sugar fragmentation reactions (7) are promoted by neutralizing and buffering the acids that are formed with basic salts, whereby formation of humic substances is limited to avoid bitter, astringent tastes. The caramel aroma arises mainly from a group of structurally related cyclic alkylenolones, including methylcyclopenteno- lones and methyl "furenolones" (Section IV,C). The methylcyclopentenolones are probably formed by aldol condensations of the hydroxyaldehyde and hydroxyketone fragments (Fig. 3-20). Many other products of sugar caramelization have been identified and their contributions to caramel flavor have been evaluated [53,79, 98,182,193-196,206].

In the manufacture of caramel coloring for use in beverages, glucose syrup is treated with dilute sulfuric acid, partially neutralized with ammonia, then heated in the presence of a sulfite at a pH value of about 4. The sugar is dehydrated and polymerized in unknown ways to form water-soluble polymers of high tinctorial power. Humic substances are filtered off to yield an acidic, very dark, viscous syrup that often polymerizes further in storage as the browning reactions continue. To remain stable in the presence of tannins and in acidic cola drinks, the caramel colloids must be produced to contain strong anionic groups so that they will give an isoelectric pH below that of the beverages to be colored. The apparent role of sulfite is to produce stable sulfonic acid groups in the colloids (the 1,4 addition of sulfite to α,β-unsaturated carbonyl groups has been widely demonstrated [32]). The sugar dehydration intermediate, 3-deoxyglucosone-3,4-ene (Fig. 3-17), con- tains these carbonyl groups and 4-sulfohexosuloses have been isolated after D- glucose has been heated in the presence of sulfites [91,160]. Caramel coloring for confections and baked goods also is produced from glucose syrups (under less drastic reaction conditions) with ammonium salt catalysts, although alkaline salts also have been used, particularly with sucrose and invert sugar. The nitrogen content of caramel coloring should be held at the lowest possible level because some of it participates in the formation of 4(5)-methylimidazole, a toxic compound [216].

4. SUGAR-AMMONIA REACTIONS

The reactions of sugars with aqueous ammonia resemble both alkaline carameliza- tion reactions and the sugar-amine (Maillard) reactions. In a comprehensive re- view [112], sugar-aqueous ammonia reactions were compared with alkaline de- composition reactions. At 25°-38°C, the Lobry de Bruyn-Alberda van Ekenstein transformation (Section III,C) has been demonstrated. Sugar fragmentation occurs, even at 38°C, as is shown by the identification of various substituted imidazoles [e.g., 4(5)methylimidazole is formed from pyruvaldehyde and formaldehyde; 2,2'- bis-4(5)-methylimidazole from pyruvaldehyde and glyoxal]. The reactive alde- hydes and ketones condense with ammonia and cyclize, which aids in their identi- fication. In concentrated solutions of D-glucose and ammonia formation of D- glucosylamine (1-amino-1-deoxy-D-glucose), di-D-glucosylamine, and (by iso- merization) 1-amino-1-deoxy-D-fructose occurs. The ammoniated sugars and sugar fragmentation products, when heated in ammoniacal solutions, form many substituted imidazoles and pyrazines and a few pyridines [112]. Structures of the brown polymers which form have not been determined.

5. SUGAR-AMINE (MAILLARD) REACTIONS

The general properties and identifying signs of the Maillard reaction are given in Table 3-6. The Maillard "reaction" is actually a complex group of many reactions. However, the initial reactions generally follow the same sequence that was outlined for the caramelization reactions. The main difference is that the reacting amino acids, peptides, and proteins condense with the sugar (if the medium is not too dilute or too acidic) and act as their own catalysts for the enolization and dehydration reactions shown in Figure 3-21. Condensations occur as the food is heated and/or dehydrated. Because enolization is so rapid, the glycosylamine usually cannot be found; however, the Amadori compounds (N-substituted 1-amino-1-deoxy-2-ketoses) have been isolated from several different foods [130].

Two of the several branches of the Maillard reaction are shown in Figure 3-21. The major branch leads from the 1,2-eneaminol of the Amadori compound to HMF. The amino acid may be retained in some molecules throughout the dehydration reactions of this pathway. The minor branch (which probably represents less than 5% of the total sugar decomposition) begins with the 2,3-enediol of the Amadori compound; then the amino acid is totally eliminated. More of the methyl α-dicarbonyl intermediate is formed when the more strongly basic secondary amines are

TABLE 3-6

Characteristics of Maillard-type Browning Reactions

Initial Stage (colorless; no absorption in near-ultraviolet)

Reactions: Condensation, enolization, Amadori rearrangement. With proteins, glucose and free amino groups combine in 1:1 ratio

Properties: Reducing power in alkaline solution increases. Storage of colorless 1:1 glucose-protein product produces browning and insolubility

Intermediate Stage (buff yellow; strong absorption in near-ultraviolet range)

Reactions: Sugar dehydration to 3-deoxyglucosone and its -3,4-ene, HMF, and 2-(hydroxyacetyl)furan; sugar fragmentation; formation of α-dicarbonyl compounds, reductones, pigments

Properties: Addition of sulfite decolorizes; reducing power in acidic solution develops; pH decreases; sugars disappear faster than amino acids. With proteins, acid hydrolysis fails to regenerate the sugar (D-glucose). Positive Elson-Morgan test for amino sugars (Amadori compounds)

Final Stages (red-brown and dark brown color)

Reactions: Aldol condensations; polymerization; Strecker degradation of α-amino acids to aldehydes and N-heterocyclics at elevated temperatures. Carbon dioxide evolves

Properties: Acidity; caramel-like and roasted aromas develop; colloidal and insoluble melanoidins form; fluorescence; reductone reducing power in acid solution; addition of sulfite does not decolorize

---

reactants [80]. In addition to the fragmentation products, several important cyclic flavor compounds such as maltol (Figure 3-22), isomaltol (Figure 3-18), and acetylformoin (Figure 3-19), are derived from the 2,3-enediol, as in caramelization reactions. However, maltol and isomaltol are formed in much larger amounts in sugar-amine reactions than in caramelization reactions [80].

Many different types of basic amino compounds can condense with the acyclic carbonyl forms of sugars. α-Amino acids, peptides, and proteins offer basic

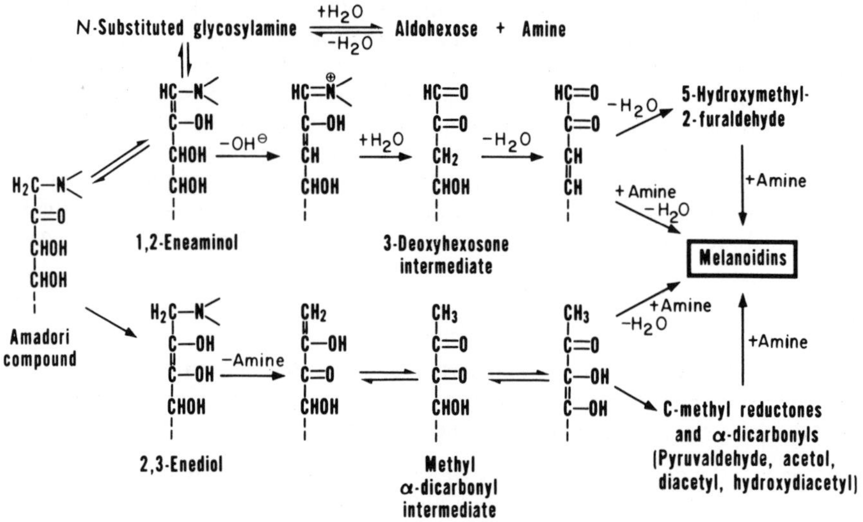

FIG. 3-21. Sugar-amine (Maillard) browning reactions: two pathways to melanoidins and byproducts. Reprinted with permission of Avi Publishing Co. [79].

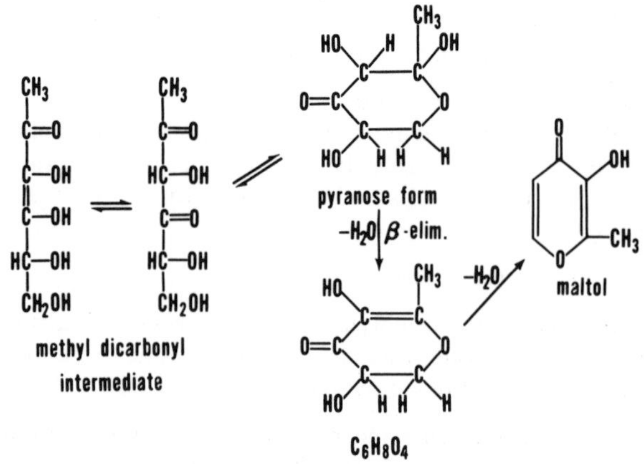

FIG. 3-22. Formation of maltol from the methyl α-dicarbonyl intermediate of Fig. 3-21. Dehydration of the isolated $C_6H_8O_4$ intermediate to form maltol [83].

amino groups when the pH of the adjacent medium rises above the isoelectric point of the amino compound. An exposed ϵ-amino group of lysine residues in proteins reacts like a separate amine, however. Some reactive nonprotein amino compounds (e.g., 4-aminobutyric acid, thiamine, piperidine-2-carboxylic acid) are prevalent in foods and ammonia, methylamines, and histamine can be present if spoilage begins. With ammonia and primary amines or amino acids, a second molecule of aldose can condense with the glycosylamine to form a diglycosylamine. In this event, both condensed glycosyl groups undergo enolization to the keto form; one of the glycosyl radicals readily decomposes to HMF and melanoidins, even in water at pH 5, while the other remains as an Amadori compound [4,160].

The initial rate of browning of a reducing sugar with a given amino compound is directly related to the rate at which the sugar's ring opens to a reducible form [148]. Pentoses and 2-deoxy-D-ribose undergo browning reactions at a faster rate than 2-deoxyhexoses, which in turn brown more rapidly than hexoses. Among the hexoses, D-galactose, D-mannose, and D-glucose show decreasing ring-opening rates and decreasing browning rates in the order listed. D-Fructose forms N-substituted 2-amino-2-deoxy-D-glucose, 2-amino-2-deoxy-D-mannose, and 1-amino-1-deoxy-D-glucose derivatives [116]; therefore, its browning rate differs from that of D-glucose [103]. Although browning in the presence of simple amines (not with proteins) initially occurs more rapidly with D-fructose than with D-glucose, these rates interchange during later stages of browning. In solution, the acyclic form is more prevalent with D-fructose than with D-glucose, and D-fructose also enolizes at a faster rate [92]. However, D-fructose does not form reactive disubstituted amines as does D-glucose. Below pH 3, D-fructose is more reactive than D-glucose because the former is more easily dehydrated to intermediates leading to HMF [103].

A third important branch of the Maillard reaction, not shown in Figure 3-21, involves the Strecker degradation of α-amino acids [79]. At elevated temperatures α-dicarbonyl compounds, such as 3-deoxyglucosone, pyruvaldehyde, glyoxal, or dehydroascorbic acid, will cause the degradation of an α-amino acid to the next lower aldehyde [61,205,207]. This reaction is illustrated in Figure 3-23 for glyoxal and glycine. Not only are carbon dioxide and formaldehyde formed but also pyrazine from the transamination reaction. With pyruvaldehyde as the reactant, 2,5-dimethylpyrazine is formed [205]; with pyruvaldehyde and glyoxal as reactants, pyrazine, methylpyrazine, and 2,5-dimethylpyrazine are formed. With diacetyl, tetramethylpyrazine is formed [161]. The carbon atoms of the pyrazine are therefore derived from a fragment of the reacting sugar. The aldehydes formed from the α-amino acids, the pyrazines, and the sugar fragmentation products combine to produce characteristic aromas of cooked foods. The Strecker degradation has been used commercially to produce the flavors of chocolate, bread, maple syrup, and honey [79].

Many attempts have been made to determine the structure of the melanoidins [37,160]. Some are soluble in water and aqueous alcohol and some are insoluble. Their compositions and molecular weights vary according to the reactants and reacting conditions. Usually they show reductone reducing power, even after dialysis, and antioxidant activity toward linoleic acid and in strongly browned foods and dark beers [102,110].

The chemistry of the Maillard reaction of sugars with proteins is the least understood of all types of browning reactions. Presumably the sugar condenses, enolizes, and is dehydrated but how it forms strong bonds with the protein remains

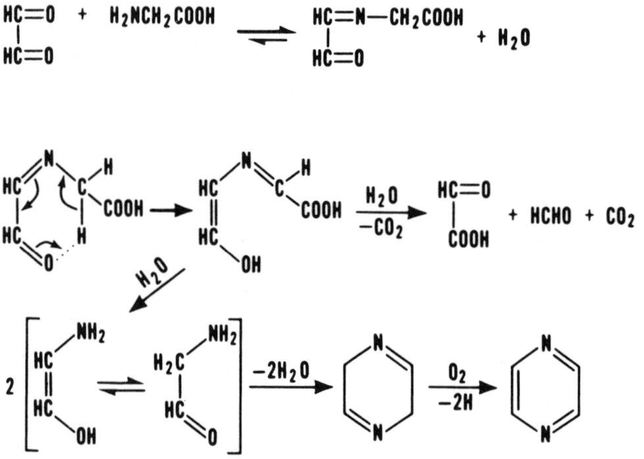

FIG. 3-23. Strecker degradation reactions and products.

to be determined. Furaldehydes and fragmentation aldehydes formed by dehydration and fission of the sugar may condense with the free amino group or the dehydrated sugar may remain combined with the amino groups throughout [37]. Both
types of reaction probably occur in view of the 40 compounds that have been isolated from a lactose-casein model system of browned dried milk [52]. Lysine,
methionine, and the N-terminal amino acids of proteins react most strongly with
pentoses, less strongly with D-galactose and D-mannose, less with D-glucose,
still less with D-fructose and lactose, and least with sucrose. However, sucrose
reacts very strongly with lactalbumin, although not with lactoglobulin [57]. Substantial losses (chemical alteration) of the above amino acids can occur when they
are exposed, in the presence of reducing sugars, to rather drastic heat treatments.
Losses of lysine during heating of crystalline β-lactoglobulin with lactose are
given in Figure 3-24. At 90°C, 40% of the lysine was lost in 2 hr, whereas no
loss was detected for histidine and arginine in the same protein [58]. Similar
studies involving the heating of purified proteins in the presence of reducing sugars
have shown that percent losses of lysine from proteins of egg and milk as well as
from serum albumins and serum globulins are greater than that from gluten proteins (contain much less lysine) [57].

Inhibition of Maillard browning reactions is best accomplished by keeping the pH
below the isoelectric points of the amino acids, peptides, and proteins; by keeping
temperatures as low as possible during processing and storage; and by increasing
the mean distance between reactants (e.g., by using water as a diluent). Use of the
nonreducing sugar sucrose is also preferable to use of reducing sugars when conditions do not favor sucrose hydrolysis (sucrose is hydrolyzed readily in weakly
acidic media, even at low temperatures) [100]. In model systems, browning reactions are prevented by reduction of the reducing sugars to alditols with borohydride.

Sulfurous acid and sulfites are generally effective in extending the storage life
of dehydrated foods, fruit juices, and wines. However, the amount that can be
added is limited by governmental regulations and by taste considerations. The
addition of bisulfite, also carboxymethylcellulose, extends the storage life of

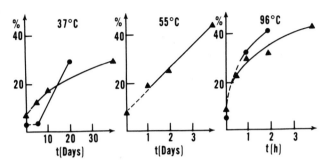

FIG. 3-24. Losses of lysine incurred by heating β-lactoglubulin-lactose mixtures (10% moisture) with one (o–o) and four (Δ–Δ) molecules of lactose per free amino group in the protein. At 0°C, no loss in 35 days, 7% loss after 90 days [58].

dehydrated (instant) orange juice [182]. The complex chemical basis for inhibition of browning reactions by sulfites has been investigated and reviewed [31,91,124, 160].

The losses of lysine and methionine that have been demonstrated in model systems of proteins and sugars were obtained under rather drastic conditions that do not occur during normal processing of high-protein foods. However, losses of these amino acids in roasted and flaked cereals (e.g., breakfast foods) may be significant because they are not abundant at the outset. More important are the off flavors and dark colors that develop from the Maillard reaction in dehydrated products. These sensory defects may cause consumer rejection of otherwise nutritious foods.

IV. FUNCTIONAL PROPERTIES OF SUGARS IN FOODS

Aside from their nutritional values, sugars function as humectants, plasticizers, texturizing agents, flavor-binding agents, flavor-producing agents (via browning reactions), and sweeteners in foods. Some sugars, glycosylamines [211], and amino sugars chelate polyvalent metal ions [7,58], but the usefulness of this property in foods is not as evident with sugars as it is with certain polysaccharides (Section V). The ways in which these functions of sugars are related to their structures are presented in this section.

The outstanding property of carbohydrate molecules is their ability to form hydrogen bonds with water, other polar molecules, and among themselves. They donate the weakly acidic protons of their hydroxyl groups to nucleophiles, and they accept protons at their electronegative oxygen atoms. Even the sweetness of sugars seems to depend on this property.

A. Sugar-Water Relationships

Carbohydrates are hydrophilic to different degrees, depending on their structures. Table 3-7 shows the variations in uptake of moisture from air by different types of carbohydrates. The rate and extent of water absorption by sugars in the dry state

TABLE 3-7

Percentage of Water Absorbed by Carbohydrates from Moist Air[a]

Carbohydrate	Relative humidity (RH) at 20°C		
	60%, 1 hr	60%, 9 days	100%, 25 days
D-Glucose, crystalline	0.07	0.07[b]	14.5[b]
D-Fructose, crystalline	0.28	0.63[b]	73.4[c]
Sucrose, crystalline	0.04	0.03[b]	18.4[c]
Invert sugar, commercial	0.19	5.1	76.6[c]
Invert sugar, pure	0.16	3.0	74.0[c]
Maltose, commercial, anhydrous[d]	0.80	7.0	18.4
β-Maltose hydrate, pure	5.05	5.1	
β-Lactose, anhydrous	0.54	1.2	1.4
α-Lactose hydrate, pure	5.05	5.1	
Raffinose, anhydrous	0.74	12.9	15.9
Cornstarch[e]	1.0	13.0	24.4
Cellulose	0.9	5.4	12.6
D-Mannitol[e]	0.06	0.05	0.42

[a]From Ref. [29].

[b]Water uptake at 29°C increases rapidly above 80% RH for D-glucose, 58% RH for D-fructose, and 83% RH for sucrose. At 90% RH, 25°C, D-glucose equilibrates at 17–18% moisture; D-fructose at 41–43% (syrup); and sucrose at 50–56% moisture [46].

[c]Water uptake still increasing at 25 days.

[d]Commercial crystalline maltose contains oligosaccharides (see text).

[e]For corn syrups, D-glucitol (sorbitol), glycerol, and a review, see Ref. [125a].

depends on their absolute purity, their anomeric purity, whether or not they form stable crystalline hydrates, and the homogeneity of their crystal structures. Water uptake on the surface of crystals causes dissolution; equilibration of anomeric, ring, and acyclic forms; and inversion (hydrolysis) of sucrose, which is promoted in the presence of mild acids or invertase at low temperatures [171]. Hydrolysis of sucrose releases reactive reducing sugars that induce nonenzymic browning reactions [49,100].

Dried solutions of anomeric mixtures, or of two or more different sugars (e.g., invert sugar) generally absorb water at a faster rate than either sugar alone [46], probably because there is less intermolecular hydrogen bonding between unlike sugars. Some sugar anomers, such as α- and β-maltose or α- and β-lactose, form complexes with each other in definite ratios. For example, a crystalline

anhydrous complex of four parts α anomer and one part β anomer of maltose has
been isolated [84]. Even though anhydrous β-maltose is extremely hygroscopic,
its complex with the α anomer does not take up water at 71% relative humidity because of strong intermolecular hydrogen bonding between the two anomers. However, when the α,β complex, or anhydrous, crystalline α(96%)-maltose, is held
at 84% relative humidity, 25°C, for several months (Figure 3-25), both slowly
take up moisture at the crystal surface and convert to the more stable β-maltose
monohydrate without showing any apparent liquid phase or loss of solid form.

The presence of a few percent of maltooligosaccharides in β-maltose monohydrate
crystals (not removed by repeated crystallizations) significantly increases the
hygroscopicity of maltose (Figure 3-26). Pure β-maltose monohydrate does not
take up water at 84% relative humidity, and the pure anomeric forms of lactose (in
this case anhydrous β- and α-monohydrate) are even less hygroscopic (Table 3-7).
The "amorphous commercial anhydrous maltose" in Figure 3-26 was prepared by
spray drying a concentrated solution to a fine beady powder. It contained 8% of
higher oligosaccharides and dextrins, and the α,β anomeric ratio was 1:1 as determined by gas chromatography. It took up 18% water before returning to the
8.5% level, the same level found in vacuum-dried commercial β-maltose which
remained in a solid state. Oligosaccharide-free anhydrous β-maltose (which gave
a different crystalline X-ray pattern from the β-monohydrate) absorbed water up
to 7% by weight, then returned to the 5.0% water content of the crystalline β-
monohydrate. Among the maltooligosaccharides, maltotriose is the most hygroscopic. As the DP increases from three, the water absorption at a fixed relative
humidity decreases [46].

The hygroscopicity of sugars, dextrins, and their mixtures is an important
factor affecting the acceptance of confections, bakery toppings, coffee whiteners,
and instantly reconstitutable powders or granules that must not become sticky.
Maltose and lactose, with their limited uptake of moisture, are particularly useful

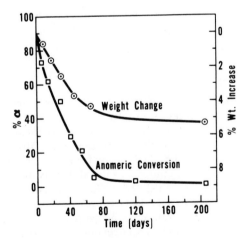

FIG. 3-25. Moisture uptake and conversion of anhydrous α-maltose to β-
maltose hydrate at 84% relative humidity, 25°C. Reprinted with permission of
the American Association of Cereal Chemists [84].

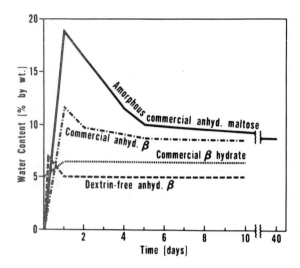

FIG. 3-26. Hygroscopicity of commercial and pure forms of anhydrous β-maltose at 84% relative humidity, 25°C. Reprinted with permission of the American Association of Cereal Chemists [84].

in such products. In contrast, the more hygroscopic liquid sugars (e.g., invert sugar and glucose syrups) help retain moisture in baked goods, plastic candies, and fillings that should not become brittle. If the sugar crystallizes, water is given up and the plasticizing effect is lost. To retain plasticity and inhibit crystallization, the starch hydrolyzates containing noncrystallizing maltooligosaccharides and dextrins, or sorbitol are useful [125a,138].

Fruits are canned in concentrated sugar syrup to give them a firmer texture. In preserves, the activity of water is reduced by hydrogen bonding with sugar, thereby preventing growth of harmful microorganisms. The concentrated syrups withdraw water from the fruit by osmosis, and sugar molecules enter the cells to form complexes with cell-wall polysaccharides [191]. The cell walls are thereby strengthened and the fruit develops a firmer texture.

B. Solute-Binding Properties

The hydroxyl groups of sugars in aqueous solutions are surrounded by hydrogen-bonded water molecules. As water is rapidly removed from concentrated solutions, as in spray drying or freeze drying, the sugar hydroxyls form intermolecular hydrogen bonds which normally lead to crystallization in the absence of a polar solute. However, polar molecules, such as alcohols, esters, and ketones (flavor compounds), become entrapped in the amorphous dried matrix and inhibit crystallization. As much as 1-3% of the freeze-dried residue consists of solutes more volatile than water, unless the amorphous matrix is rehydrated and redried several times. Sucrose, maltose, and lactose entrap more of the polar molecules than do monosaccharides [54]. α,β-Maltose forms amorphous complexes with the lower alcohols, amides, and imidazole in definite ratios, usually two molecules of maltose to one molecule of polar compound. Furthermore, the ratio of α- to β-maltose in carefully formed complexes is 1:1; the complexes are hygroscopic at high atmospheric humidities and the lower alcohols are slowly released. Complexes of maltulose or maltitol with ethanol also have been formed [84].

C. Flavors from Browning Reactions

The flavors derived from nonenzymic browning reactions are essential for recognition and taste acceptance of many processed foods. For example, coffee beans, peanuts, and cashew nuts develop their distinctive flavors only after roasting. Roasted aromas are derived from mixtures of many volatile Maillard reaction products, some of which duplicate those of fats and proteins roasted in the absence of sugars. The sugar-amine condensations and enolizations catalyze decomposition of both sugars and amino acids so that volatile compounds are formed at much lower temperatures than are the pyrolysis products of fats and proteins; hence, Maillard reaction products preponderate in browned foods.

Aromas from coffee, peanuts, popcorn, freshly baked bread, toasted marshmallows, and barbeque can be distinguished by most everyone; yet, they all contain many compounds from browning reactions. Thermal sugar decompositions produce much the same group of certain furans, furanones, pyrones, lactones, aldehydes, ketones, acids, and esters; and also pyrazines, pyrroles, and pyridines when amino acids are involved. The search for so-called "character-impact" compounds among this large group has turned up only a few. The character impact is derived from certain dominant flavor compounds among many other compounds that add identifying flavor notes. Two of the more dominant types from browning reactions are the caramel aroma compounds and the nutty or bready aroma compounds.

Figure 3-27 shows what now appears to be requisite chemical structures for caramel aroma compounds and for popcorny, nutty, or bready aroma compounds. The unbroken bonds and symbols indicate essential parts of the composite molecule. The fragrant caramel aroma compounds are α-enolones which contain carbonyl, enolic hydroxyl, and short alkyl groups (methyl, ethyl, or propyl) on contiguous

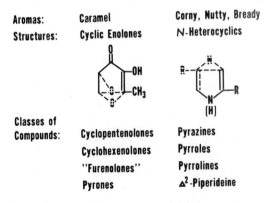

Aromas:	Caramel	Corny, Nutty, Bready
Structures:	Cyclic Enolones	N-Heterocyclics

Classes of Compounds:	Cyclopentenolones	Pyrazines
	Cyclohexenolones	Pyrroles
	"Furenolones"	Pyrrolines
	Pyrones	Δ^2-Piperideine

FIG. 3-27. Composite structures of characteristic aroma compounds derived from nonenzymic browning reactions. Reprinted with permission of the American Association of Cereal Chemists [83].

carbon atoms in five- or six-membered, planar, alicyclic, or O-heterocyclic rings [83,156]. Isomaltol (Figure 3-18), a β-enolone, presents a different arrangement of planar methyl, carbonyl, and conjugated enol groups; yet, it gives an odor somewhat resembling caramel. "Furenolones" in Figure 3-27 refers to methyl-substituted, enolic, dihydrofuranones; viz., 4-hydroxy-2-methyl-3(2H)-furanone and the corresponding 2,5-dimethyl derivative. Both compounds have been found in beef broth, wherein both pentose and hexose precursors are present. The 2,5-dimethyl derivative was first synthesized by the reaction of L-rhamnose with piperidine acetate [80]; later, it was isolated from heat-treated pineapple extract, maple syrup, and other sugar caramelization reactions. It gives an exceptionally powerful fruity-caramel aroma, like that of strawberry and pineapple preserves [80]. Maltol (Figure 3-22) and "ethyl maltol" are said to enhance the sweetness and flavor of soft drinks, fruit juices, baked goods, syrups, and dessert items [141].

The popcorny, nutty, and bready aromas arise mainly from the many different alkyl pyrazines that have been found in foods [125]. N-Acetonylpyrrole, N-acetonylpyrroline, and 2-aceto-1,4,5,6-tetrahydropyridine give bready aromas, and they are probably formed from the Strecker degradation of proline by pyruvaldehyde [83]. Pyrrole-2-carboxaldehydes also form in sugar-amine reactions and they give rise to roasted aromas upon heating [101].

The acyclic aldehydes, such as glyoxal, pyruvaldehyde, and acrolein, give pungent, burnt aromas; whereas Strecker degradation aldehydes, such as iso-butyraldehyde (from valine) and isovaleraldehyde (from leucine), lend flavor notes to malt and bread aromas. Methional, the Strecker degradation aldehyde from methionine, does appear to be a dominant component in cooked cabbage and potato aromas [120].

Some of the flavor compounds generated in Maillard-type browning reactions are deleterious. Odors resembling isonitriles and "scorched turkey skin" have been reported. Caramel flavor is not acceptable in some foods (e.g., orange juice, dehydrated potato, and dried milks) and excessive caramelization in maple syrup is undesirable. The alkyl-substituted pyrazines are fragrant only at the very low concentrations that normally result in food browning reactions. At high concentrations, their odor is best described as stench. Sugar-amine browning reactions must therefore be strictly controlled in food processing to produce fragrant, acceptable products.

D. Sweeteners and Sweetness

Man is accustomed to sweetened foods. Infants, children, adults, many animals, and insects respond favorably to the sweetness of sugars. The major nutritive sweeteners that are added to foods are sucrose, glucose syrups (corn syrups), and dextrose (crystalline D-glucose, monohydrate or anhydrous). Annual consumption of sucrose per capita in the United States is about 100 lb, corn syrups about 16 lb (increasing), and dextrose about 5 lb [149]. Lactose, D-glucitol (sorbitol), D-mannitol, and honey are used in much smaller amounts. Although D-fructose and maltose are not sold as crystalline sugars in significant amounts, they are important constituents of commercial sweeteners. Invert sugar is half D-fructose, and some widely sold corn syrups contain up to 45% D-fructose or maltose. The composition of corn syrup is varied to meet different uses and sweetening requirements. By hydrolysis of cornstarch with different enzymes, syrups are made with high D-glucose, high-maltose, or high-dextrin contents. Some compositions of corn syrups, when mixed with sucrose syrup at high concentrations, give a greater sweetness than predicted from the separate sweetnesses of component sugars [139].

Sweetness is a subjective sensory phenomenon which is influenced by physiological, psychological, and environmental factors [131,151]. Yet, consistent evaluations of the sweetness of sugars relative to the sweetness of sucrose have been obtained by matching equisweet concentrations of their aqueous solutions. Select and trained taste panels working under controlled environmental conditions are required to obtain meaningful results. The abridged results of one exemplary study [220], wherein a panel of 100 was selected from 1000 people based upon their sensitivity of taste, is shown in Table 3-8. With 25 or 50 replications of the matching procedure, relative standard deviations averaged less than 2% of the equisweet concentrations for the sugars listed. The values given in Table 3-8 should be compared with the somewhat differing values reported by Moskowitz [135,136], who found that alditols are generally less sweet than the corresponding aldoses, except for xylitol, and that the pleasantness of sugar and alditol tastes is also a function of concentration. Moskowitz found differences in the relative sweetnesses of D- and L-xylose, α-L- and β-D-fucose, and D- and L-arabinitol, an important consideration for determining the mechanism of sweet taste induction. Food sugars not listed in Table 3-8 are less sweet than D-glucose. Based on sucrose = 1.0, D-galactose is 0.4-0.6, maltose is 0.3-0.5, lactose is 0.2-0.3, and raffinose is 0.15 [135].

TABLE 3-8

Relative Sweetness of Sugars and Alditols (Sucrose = 1.00)[a]

Sucrose concentration (g/100 ml)	Relative sweetness					
	D-Fructose	Xylitol	D-Xylose	D-Glucose	D-Glucitol	D-Mannitol
2.5	1.32	0.96	0.57	0.56	0.55	
5.0	1.33	1.01	0.59	0.56	0.54	0.51
10.0	1.23	1.02	0.65	0.63	0.58	0.56
15.0						0.62
20.0	1.24	1.08	0.78	0.72	0.71	
30.0		1.18		0.77		
40.0				0.83	0.82	

[a]Relative sweetness = (sucrose concentration/sample concentration) for equisweet solutions; calculated from data of Yamaguchi et al. [220].

The older reports on sweetness of sugars should be examined for the method of tasting and purity of the sugars used. Sweetness values determined by the threshold method (minimal concentrations at which sweetness can be detected) have little practical value. For example, erythritol is reported to be more than twice as sweet as sucrose at the threshold level, but it is definitely less sweet at concentrations above 1% by weight. Maltose solutions have been reported to have a malty and disagreeable taste, but this is not true of pure β-maltose monohydrate.

The sweetness of D-fructose solutions relative to sucrose decreases markedly with increasing temperature. At 5°C, D-fructose is about 1.4 times as sweet as sucrose; at 40°C, their aqueous solutions of equal concentration are equally sweet; and at 60°C, the D-fructose solution is only 0.8 as sweet as the sucrose solution. The shift in sweetness was attributed to a change in equilibration of the anomeric forms and ring isomers. Other reducing sugars (D-galactose, D-glucose, L-sorbose) also decreased in sweetness with increasing temperature, but at a slower rate than D-fructose. The sweetness of maltose is essentially independent of temperature [201].

Some sugar solutions differ in sweetness depending on the ratio of α to β anomers. For example, α-D-glucopyranose and β-D-fructopyranose are sweeter than the equilibrium mixtures of their anomers and isomeric ring forms. Furthermore, β-D-mannopyranose is bitter and sweet, whereas the α-D-mannopyranose is only sweet. Solutions of reducing sugars must therefore be allowed to come to equilibrium before sweetness is assessed. The equilibrium composition varies with temperature, concentration, and the presence of solutes, particularly solutes that form complexes with the sugars. At elevated temperatures, the most stable conformations of sugars are subject to change as hydrogen bonding of sugar with solvent, or within and between molecules, is diminished.

Tables of sweetness values can be used only as a rough guide for food formulations. Bitter substances, acids, and salts interfere with sweet taste. Alcohol enhances the sweetness of sucrose; and carboxymethylcellulose, a common food additive, masks it. D-Fructose and sucrose become equally sweet when they are tasted in pear or peach nectars. The medium in which sugars are tasted is therefore highly important and sweetness of the final food products must be evaluated by taste panels [151].

The food sugars differ in pleasantness as well as intensity [135]. High concentrations of most sugars are distasteful; however, concentrated solutions of D-glucose are much less pleasant to taste than equisweet sucrose solutions. Some experimental subjects have rejected a diet in which the carbohydrate is entirely D-glucose, whereas an isocaloric diet with glucose syrup (containing maltose, oligosaccharides, and dextrins) replacing D-glucose has been acceptable [121]. Three isolated sets of experiments have shown that rats prefer maltose solutions to either sucrose or dextrose solutions. Many other factors that affect the evaluation of sweetness should be considered, and these have been reviewed [136,151].

An interesting theory of sweetness, based upon the hydrogen-bonding properties of sweet molecules, has been proposed by Shallenberger and Acree [175]. A sweet compound with electronegative atoms A and B, with a hydrogen atom covalently bonded to A, presumably forms reciprocal hydrogen bonds with a receptor site of similar structure in the taste buds and thereby induces a sweet taste response. AH represents any of the proton-donor groups shown in Figure 3-28, whereas B is a proton-acceptor functional group of the types shown at the bottom

of the figure. The spacing of AH and B should be at least 3 Å, otherwise intramolecular hydrogen bonding between AH and B can occur as shown on the right.
Note that a hydrophobic binding site in the taste bud would be required for such
bonding to be maintained.

This part of the theory has been tested by a taste panel using aqueous solutions
of the simplest cyclic glycols, cis- and trans-cycloalkanediols. Scaled stereomodels were used to determine atomic spacing, and infrared spectra of molecules
in nonpolar solvents were used to determine hydrogen bonding [81]. The cis-1,2-
cyclopentanediol with an interoxygen spacing of less than 3 Å (Figure 3-29) is not
sweet, whereas the trans-diol, with a spacing of 3.5-3.7 Å, is sweet. The cis-
diol shows intramolecular hydrogen bonding and the trans-diol does not.

Taste testing of the cis- and trans-1,2-cyclohexanediols (Figure 3-30) indicated
that the cis form was not sweet, but the trans form exhibited questionable sweetness at the threshold level. The bitterness of both compounds interfered with the
sweetness evaluations. The trans form can adopt the less stable diaxial arrangement of hydroxyl groups (shown in parentheses), whereas the cis form is limited to
an interoxygen spacing of less than 3 Å. Furthermore, the cis- and trans-1,3-
and cis- (but not the trans-) 1,4-cyclohexanediols, with interoxygen spacings much
greater than 3 Å, were evaluated sweet despite accompanying bitterness.

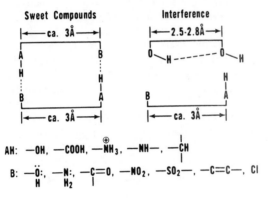

FIG. 3-28. Saporous AH and B functions of sweet compounds and corresponding
functions on taste receptor site as proposed by Shallenberger and Acree [175].

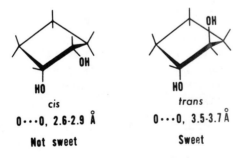

FIG. 3-29. Cyclopentane-cis- and trans-1,2-diols.

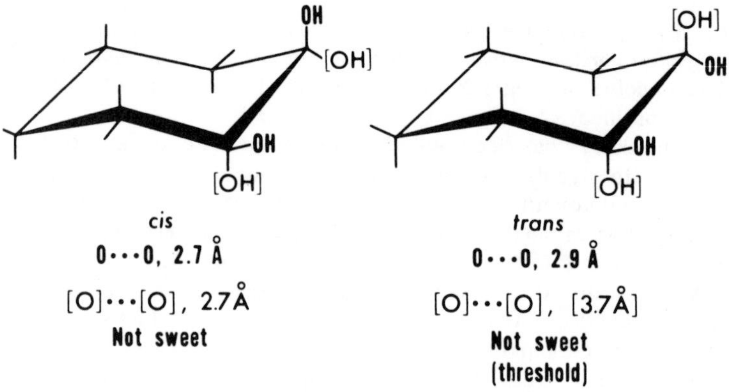

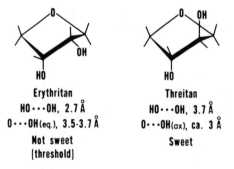

cis

O···O, 2.7 Å

[O]···[O], 2.7Å

Not sweet

trans

O···O, 2.9 Å

[O]···[O], [3.7Å]

Not sweet
(threshold)

FIG. 3-30. Cyclohexane-cis and trans-1,2-diols.

Introduction of an oxygen atom into the ring of the cis- and trans-cyclopentane-diols by synthesis of erythritan and DL-threitan (Figure 3-31) resulted in detection of a threshold level of sweetness for erythritan (possibly due to the spacing of 3.5-3.7 Å between the ring oxygen and one of the hydroxyl groups) and sweetness for DL-threitan. Hence, it appears that hydroxyl groups with interoxygen spacings of 3-5 Å do induce a sweet taste, whereas those outside this range do not.

Levoglucosan, 1,6-anhydro-β-D-glucopyranose (Figure 3-13), said not to be sweet by Shallenberger and Acree, was found to be significantly sweet by a panel trained to taste sweetness in the presence of bitterness [81]. As shown in Figure 3-13, the interoxygen spacing is 3.3 Å for two of the axial hydroxyl groups in the rigid bicyclic structure.

The inhibition of sweet taste by intramolecular hydrogen bonding was further tested with the group of methyl glycosides shown in Figure 3-32. The group with no possible intramolecular hydrogen bonding gave a higher average sweetness than the group in which an axial hydroxyl group was present. Such groups can form an intramolecular hydrogen bond with the ring oxygen. The axial hydroxyl groups of

Erythritan

HO···OH, 2.7 Å

O···OH(eq.), 3.5-3.7 Å

Not sweet
(threshold)

Threitan

HO···OH, 3.7 Å

O···OH(ax), ca. 3 Å

Sweet

FIG. 3-31. 1,4-Anydroerythritol and 1,4-anhydro-DL-threitol.

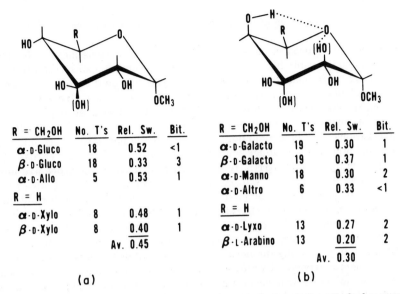

R = CH$_2$OH	No. T's	Rel. Sw.	Bit.
α-D-Gluco	18	0.52	<1
β-D-Gluco	18	0.33	3
α-D-Allo	5	0.53	1
R = H			
α-D-Xylo	8	0.48	1
β-D-Xylo	8	0.40	1
		Av. 0.45	

R = CH$_2$OH	No. T's	Rel. Sw.	Bit.
α-D-Galacto	19	0.30	1
β-D-Galacto	19	0.37	1
α-D-Manno	18	0.30	2
α-D-Altro	6	0.33	<1
R = H			
α-D-Lyxo	13	0.27	2
β-L-Arabino	13	0.20	2
		Av. 0.30	

(a)   (b)

FIG. 3-32. Taste responses with 3% aqueous solutions of methyl glycopyranosides: sweetness relative to sucrose = 1, and bitterness on scale 0-3. (a) No intramolecular H bonding by axial OH; (b) axial OH bonding to ring O.

the second group of methyl glycosides also may have interfered for other steric reasons.

These and other investigations [23-25,107,176] indicate that a stereochemical basis for sweet taste probably does exist among the cyclic glycols, sugars, alditols, and cyclitols, and that further investigations may elucidate mechanistic details of this long-standing mystery.

V. FUNCTIONAL PROPERTIES OF POLYSACCHARIDES

The sources and monosaccharide components of the principal food polysaccharides are given in Table 3-1, and structural types are presented in Section II. To be discussed here are the properties of polysaccharides that relate to their functionality and uses in foods. In both plants and animals, polysaccharides serve in three important ways: They provide structural materials (cellulose, hemicelluloses, and pectic substances in plants; chitin and mucopolysaccharides in animals); they provide food reserves (starch, dextrins, and fructans in plants; glycogen in animals); and perhaps less recognized is the fact that they attract and retain water so that life's enzymic processes are not impeded under dehydrating conditions. Taking a lesson from nature, the food processor sees opportunities to use polysaccharides as structural material and as hydrophilic agents, thus providing control over the form, texture, and shelf life of processed foods.

A. Relation of Structure to Physical Properties

Great differences are found in the solution properties of various polysaccharides. Among those of comparably high molecular weights, some disperse readily in water, some are quite insoluble and others disperse only as discrete, swollen particles or globules. A few form nearly clear solutions of low viscosity at moderate concentrations and others form turbid pastes that show pseudo-plastic rheology at low concentrations. Some form gels at low concentrations, some gel only at high concentrations, and others do not gel at all. Some polysaccharide gels are translucent and others are opaque; some are thermally reversible, whereas others are not. Surprisingly, a few partially substituted polysaccharide types are more soluble in cold water than in hot water. These differences and incongruities are related to the monosaccharide composition of the polymer, to the pattern of chemical linkages among the monosaccharide units, to hydrogen-bonding and ionic interactions within and among polymers, and to gross conformations of the hydrated polymers in solution - subjects that stand in need of further investigation.

The difficulty in predicting the behavior of hydrocolloids in foods can be attributed to the dynamic aspects of water-binding and intermolecular hydrogen-bonding forces in large molecules that contain multiple polar groups. The peripheral polar groups and central hydrophobic stems of polysaccharide molecules give rise to variable interactions with water and electrolytes that are only beginning to be understood [45]. Regulation of the texture of a processed food with polysaccharides is therefore problematical, because the initial state of hydration and interactions between molecules do not remain constant. Nevertheless, selection of certain polysaccharide types over others as food additives can provide for greater stability and more acceptable textures in many different types of foods.

1. POLYSACCHARIDE-WATER INTERACTIONS

Knowledge of interactions between water and polysaccharides is highly important for understanding the functions of carbohydrates in foods. Water forms hydrogen bonds with the hydroxyl groups of polysaccharides in the same way that it does with hydroxyl groups of other molecules. Layers of water molecules adjacent to the hydroxyl groups of polysaccharides are therefore partially ordered and immobilized (Figure 3-33a). Formation of this atmosphere of associated water assists in dissolving or dispersing the large molecules. Application of strong alkali is sometimes necessary to disrupt intermolecular hydrogen bonding among polysaccharide molecules so they can be dispersed. Once the intermolecular associations are broken, layers of partially immobilized water tend to keep the polysaccharide molecules separated in solution.

As the hydrated macromolecules gyrate in solution, the water aggregates shift and can be rearranged or displaced. By folding or coiling, the polysaccharide molecule can associate with itself to form loops (Figure 3-33a) or helices, or possibly even double helices with other coiled macromolecules (Figure 3-33b and c). By stretching out, it can align with sections of other molecules to form crystalloid regions, called "micelles" (Figure 3-33d). The micellar regions become hydrophobic as the bound water is replaced by the intermolecular hydrogen bonds of

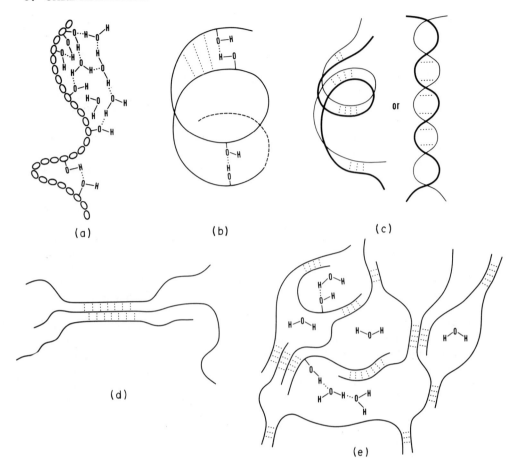

FIG. 3-33. Schemes of intermolecular hydrogen bonding of polysaccharides. See text for description.

carbon-bound hydroxyl groups. If a sufficient number of polysaccharide molecules bind together at separated points, a three-dimensional network arises which entraps substantial amounts of water (Figure 3-33e). Thus, a gel forms from the sol state [159].

When gels form from sols, hydrogen bonding among polysaccharide molecules gradually becomes more extensive, thereby increasing the micellar regions. The growth of micelles results in the gel becoming firmer and, in time, causes a shrinkage that expresses some of the entrapped water - a phenomenon known as "syneresis." In starch gels and dispersions, this process is called "retrogradation." In very dilute solutions of amylose (the linear fraction of starch), the individual molecules are not sufficiently entangled to produce a gel, so the growing micelles eventually cause precipitation.

2. VISCOSITY

Hydrated and extended polysaccharide molecules occupy roughly spherical spaces
as they rotate in solution (Figure 3-34). These moving spheres frequently make
contact with one another, giving even in very dilute solutions a viscosity considerably greater than that of water alone. Incremental increases in concentration of
the polysaccharide result in a very rapid increase in viscosity. For highly branched
polysaccharide molecules, the effective volume (hydrated volume) occupied by the
dissolved polysaccharide is smaller than that resulting from an extended linear
polysaccharide of the same or smaller molecular weight (Figure 3-34a and c).
Highly branched polysaccharides therefore give lower viscosities than linear ones
of the same molecular weight. Linear molecules may coil, however, and occupy
smaller volumes (Figure 3-34a'). If the branches consist of only single monosaccharide units, these stubby projections may inhibit coiling of the molecule and
may extend its effective length (Figure 3-34b). Substitution of a few neutral groups,
such as O-methyl, O-hydroxypropyl, or O-acetyl, on linear polysaccharides also
tends to keep the molecules extended, thereby increasing the viscosity of their
solutions.

Branches on polysaccharides, whether long or short, fend off colliding polysaccharide molecules in solution and inhibit the associative alignment which, with
purely linear polysaccharides, leads to gel formation. The solutions are therefore
more stable. At very high concentrations, the relatively long branches of amylopectin (the branched fraction of starch) may entangle sufficiently to form a gel, but
the bonding among outer branches of these molecules is much less extensive than
those among linear molecules. If solutions of branched polysaccharides are dried,
intermolecular association is not extensive, the films formed by evaporation of
thin layers are brittle, and redissolution can be brought about much more readily
than with linear polysaccharides.

3. MOLECULAR WEIGHTS

Molecular weights of polysaccharides vary greatly, partly because of actual natural
variations and partly because of inaccuracies arising from the techniques used to
separate, purify, and disperse the molecules. In comparing values given for the

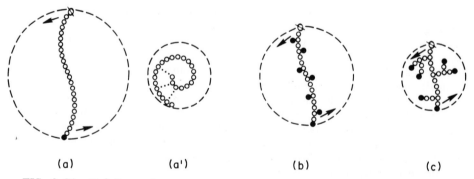

(a)   (a')   (b)   (c)

FIG. 3-34. Relative volumes occupied in sols by polysaccharides of the same
chain length but with different degrees of branching. See text for description.

molecular weights of different polysaccharides, it is important to consider how they have been determined, how the sample has been prepared, and whether or not complete solvation of the molecules has been obtained. Regardless of these experimental difficulties, molecular weight has an important bearing on such properties as viscosity, gel formation, and film formation.

4. ACIDIC POLYSACCHARIDES

The occurrence of acidic groups in a polysaccharide, or their introduction into neutral polysaccharides, leads to different solution properties depending on the acidity of the group. If the groups are weakly acidic carboxyl groups, viscosity is strongly affected by pH. In neutral solutions, the carboxyl groups are anions of salts. Alkali metal salts are largely ionized, and the coulombic repulsion of the negative charges distributed along the molecule tends to keep it in an extended form, producing a highly viscous solution. An additional factor contributing to viscosity is the increased hydration resulting from the carboxylate anions (Figure 3-35a). Furthermore, the ionic repulsion between the carboxylate anions causes the polysaccharide molecules to repel one another and prevent gelation. Polyvalent cations, however, such as calcium, take part in intra- and intermolecular bonding (Figure 3-35b) leading to gel formation or sometimes, if bonding is sufficiently extensive, to precipitation.

When a polysaccharide containing carboxylic acid groups is acidified to about pH 3 or less, the acid groups are only slightly ionized and solution properties more nearly approximate that of a neutral polysaccharide. The acid groups, no longer charged, associate by hydrogen bonding (Figure 3-35c), readily allowing gels or precipitates to form. The need for acid in making fruit jellies is a familiar example of this effect of pH. Such strongly acidic groups as half-ester sulfates, found in some plant gums and seaweed polysaccharides, are much less affected by changes in pH.

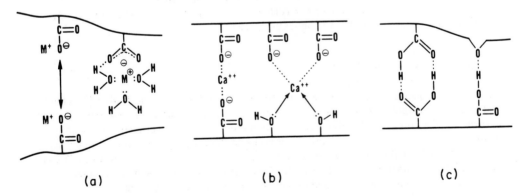

FIG. 3-35. Types of interactions between the anionic groups of acidic polysaccharides in (a) neutral, (b) salted (polyvalent cations), and (c) acidic media (pH < 3).

5. SUMMARY

Polysaccharide structure generally affects sol properties as follows:

1. At the same concentration, solutions of linear polysaccharides have greater viscosities than those of branched polysaccharides of the same molecular weight.
2. Linear polysaccharides can associate through intermolecular hydrogen bonding to form gels or, in more dilute solutions, precipitates. Branching, side chains (substitutions on hydroxyl groups), or negative charges distributed along linear polysaccharide molecules inhibit intermolecular associations.
3. Viscosity is usually more pH dependent in solutions of polysaccharides containing carboxyl groups than in solutions of polysaccharides containing strongly acidic groups.
4. Polysaccharides containing carboxyl groups can form gels at low pH values, because the acidic groups are largely un-ionized. Solutions of polysaccharides containing either weak or strong acidic groups can form gels upon addition of polyvalent cations since these ions readily form intermolecular salt bridges and chelates.

The influence of structure on the properties of polysaccharide solutions has been discussed in greater detail by Whistler [213,214] and Rees [159]. Polysaccharide properties of particular importance in food applications have been reviewed by Glicksman [64].

B. Starch

Starch provides the major source of energy in the diet of man. In nearly all parts of the world, some cereal grain, usually rice, wheat, or corn, constitutes the major source of food, and starch comprises approximately 75% of the grain. Other staple foods, such as taro root, potatoes, and some legumes, are also high in starch content. Much of the starch is consumed without being isolated from the plant material in which it occurs; but refined starch, either natural or modified, plays an important role in food processing [219].

1. MOLECULAR STRUCTURE

Starch is composed of two types of polysaccharide molecules, one linear (amylose) and the other branched (amylopectin). Both are homoglycans of D-glucose. In natural starch, these molecules are closely associated in structured microscopic granules. Granules usually contain both types of starch, with amylose amounting to about 15-30% of the total. Some grains (e.g., corn, sorghum, rice) have "waxy" varieties that contain only amylopectin. Other varieties have been developed in which amylose comprises as much as 85% of the total starch content.

a. Amylose. The condensed D-glucose units occur as α-(1→4)-linked pyranose rings; therefore, the disaccharide repeating unit is maltose (Figure 3-5). The amylose fraction of starch is assumed to be completely linear, although there is some evidence for minor amounts of a very slightly branched glucan that is isolated along with amylose.

The actual molecular weight of amylose varies with its botanical source and the severity of treatment used in its isolation. Apparent molecular weight varies with the method used. Use of improved techniques has led to the realization that these molecules are much larger than once thought. Values of 1.1 million to 1.9 million daltons are now considered valid for amylose [15,70,108]. In general, amyloses from roots and tubers appear to have larger molecular weights than those from cereals.

There is considerable evidence that amylose in solution assumes the form of a long, flexible coil that readily bends in a wormlike fashion [56]. With iodine, amylose molecules readily form a tight helical structure which serves as a host for a core of iodine atoms [165]. This channel-type inclusion compound has a bright blue color, making it useful for the quantitative determination of amylose and as a sensitive indicator of either starch or iodine. Similar but colorless channel-type inclusion compounds are formed by the association of amylose with fatty acids or emulsifiers, such as monoglycerides.

b. Amylopectin. Most of the linkages between the D-glucose units of amylopectin are of the α-(1→4) type, as in amylose. In addition, 4-5% of the glucose units are combined in α-(1→6) linkages (Figure 3-4) giving rise to a branched structure (Figure 3-6). The disaccharide containing the branching linkage is isomaltose.

Foster [56] pointed out that amylopectin isolated by techniques presently available is extremely heterogeneous in molecular weight and probably in the degree of branching. The best estimates of the molecular weight of amylopectin (by light scattering) range from 10 to over 200 million daltons [15].

Chemical determinations have shown one end group for every 20-25 D-glucose units in practically all the amylopectins studied. These figures are often erroneously interpreted as indicating branch lengths of 20-25 units, but this interpretation does not take into account that secondary and higher orders of branching exist and that branch lengths may not be uniform. Lee et al. [118] showed that amylopectin molecules do not have a symmetrically ordered structure. Differences in the fine points of amylopectin structure have been investigated by Gunja-Smith et al. [72] and Robin et al. [162] and may be responsible for differences observed in the properties of starch pastes and white sauces prepared from purified amylopectins from different botanical species [144].

2. GRANULAR STRUCTURE

Starch occurs in plant tissues in the form of discrete granules. These granules remain essentially intact during most types of processing used to prepare starch as a food ingredient, such as milling of meal or flour, separation and purification of starch, or even during most types of chemical modification. In pregelatinized starch, the granular structure of starch is destroyed before it is incorporated in a food product. The structure of the granule and the changes it undergoes during processing of a food product are of major concern to the food scientist. Other food ingredients have important effects on the changes in starch granules which, in turn, affect the texture and stability of the final food product.

The microscopic appearances of starch granules from different botanical species are, in most instances, so unique that identification is possible by this method alone. Unique characteristics are the size, shape, and uniformity of the granules; location (centric or eccentric) of the hilum (a single spot or intersection of two short lines); presence or absence of striations that partly or completely encircle the hilum; and the appearance of the granules under polarized light (birefringence). Some of these features are evident in drawings of common food starches shown in Figure 3-36 (see also Figs. 16-11 and 16-12).

Within the granule, a mixture of linear and branched molecules is arranged radially in concentric shells [13]. When parallel associations exist between adjacent linear molecules or between the outer branches of the branched molecules, they are held together by hydrogen bonds, resulting in crystalline regions or micelles (Figure 3-37a) and causing the granule to be birefringent. A single linear molecule or the outer branches of a branched molecule may be involved in several micelles. More loosely packed, amorphous regions, easily accessible to water, exist between the micelles in each concentric shell and between concentric shells. When granules are crushed, fractures occur along radial lines. Fracturing often reduces the molecular weight of starch, indicating that primary valence bonds are actually broken during this process. Small amounts of noncarbohydrate materials, both organic and inorganic, are naturally present in the granule and some also may be added during processing. Most of the lipid substances can be removed with certain hydrophilic fat solvents (e.g., methanol or dioxane), but this causes some changes in the gelatinization properties of the starch.

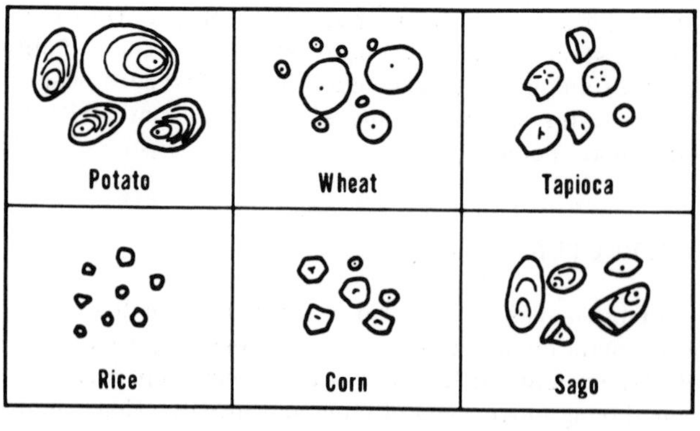

FIG. 3-36. Diagrams of the microscopic appearance of common starch granules. Reprinted from Corn Starch, 1964 edition; courtesy of Corn Refiners Association.

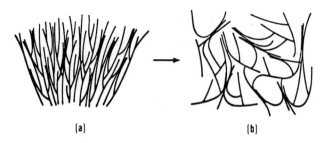

(a)   (b)

FIG. 3-37. Arrangement of molecules in a segment of a common starch granule before and after swelling: (a) nonswollen fragment; (b) swollen fragment. Courtesy of Peter Bernfeld.

3. SWELLING OF THE STARCH GRANULE

a. Gelatinization. The hydrophilic groups in the starch molecule cause it to take up moisture in proportion to the relative humidity of the atmosphere. Under normal conditions, cereal starches, for example, usually have a moisture content of about 12-14%. Cold water can penetrate amorphous regions of the granule without disturbing the micelles, and a maximum water content of about 30% can be obtained by this means. Swelling of the granule is unobservable except under very careful microscopic examination, and the granules settle to the bottom of the mixture unless agitation is applied. Not until the mixture is heated to a temperature sufficiently high to furnish the energy needed to break some of the intermolecular hydrogen bonds in amorphous regions (Figure 3-37b) does the granule begin to swell noticeably. This swelling causes a loss of the radial orientation of the micelles and a loss of birefringence. Further heating causes more loosening of the meshwork, allowing additional water to enter and enlarge the granule. The micelles, however, remain largely intact and hold the granules together in enormously swollen networks unless either the temperature is raised to well above 100°C or agitation is sufficiently violent to tear the swollen granules apart. Agitation of this intensity seldom occurs in food processing. Without such agitation, aqueous suspensions of starch granules being autoclaved at high temperatures may cave in (implode) and gradually fragment. Even when swollen granules are not fragmented by high temperatures or agitation, some of the smaller molecules of amylose become disentangled and are leached into the surrounding water. The resulting starch paste, therefore, can be visualized as consisting of highly swollen but discrete clusters of starch molecules suspended in a starch solution.

The temperature at which starch granules begin to swell rapidly and lose birefringence is called the "gelatinization temperature." More properly it is called the "gelatinization temperature range," because individual granules within any starch sample differ not only in size and shape but also in the energy required to bring about swelling. Because starches from different sources exhibit different gelatinization ranges (Table 3-9), this property is useful for purposes of identification. Gelatinization values do not accurately indicate the temperature at which different starches gelatinize in food systems because of the influence of other ingredients. However, they do provide a relative indication as to how different

TABLE 3-9

Gelatinization Ranges of Various Food Starches[a]

Source	Temperature at loss of birefringence (°C)		
	Initiation	Midpoint	Termination
Corn	62	66	70
Waxy corn	63	68	72
High-amylose corn (55% amylose)	67	80	_[b]
Grain sorghum	68	73.5	78
Waxy sorghum	67.5	70.5	74
Barley	51.5	57	59.5
Rice	68	74.5	78
Rye	57	61	70
Wheat	59.5	62.5	64
Pea (green garden)	57	65	70
Potato	58	62	66
Potato (heat-moisture treated)	65	71	77
Tapioca	52	59	64

[a]From Osman [142]; with permission from Academic Press.
[b]Some granules still birefringent at 100°C.

starches behave. For example, grain sorghum starch, although similar to corn-starch in many ways, gelatinizes at a somewhat higher temperature than cornstarch when compared in food products or in distilled water.

With the initial rapid swelling of starch granules, the clarity of the suspension suddenly increases. Light transmission can be measured to record the progress of gelatinization. Another change that cannot be measured so accurately but that is of significance in some food systems, especially yeast bread, is the increased susceptibility of starch to enzyme attack.

b. Viscosity Changes. As the temperature of the starch suspension is raised above the gelatinization range, the granules continue to swell if sufficient water is present. In some food systems, yeast bread for example, the small amount of water limits further swelling. In more dilute systems, additional swelling may be great but the viscosity increases noticeably only after the granules swell sufficiently so that they collide frequently. In some instances, the friction may be so great that the now fragile granules are torn into fragments, causing a reduction in viscosity. Because viscosity is dependent primarily on the collision and shearing of swollen granules, the temperature at which it shows a noticeable increase, as well as subsequent changes, is highly dependent on the initial concentration of the starch suspension. Also involved in viscosity changes are the size of the granules, the internal forces holding the molecules together within the granule, and the effect of other ingredients in the system.

For accurate comparisons of viscosity changes during cooking of different starches or of the same starch under different conditions, identical conditions of heating and agitation must be used. Several instruments providing such conditions and equipped with devices for continuously measuring and recording viscosity changes are in use. They differ in rate of heating and agitation and in the sensing devices and recording mechanisms employed. To insure homogeneity of the starch mixture and the avoidance of lumps, starch granules must be completely separated and surrounded by water before the temperature of the system is raised to the gelatinization range.

c. Gel Formation. When a starch-thickened mixture is stirred as it cools, its viscosity normally increases. If it is allowed to stand without stirring either before or after cooling, there is a tendency for intermolecular bonds to form (Figure 3-33e). When only amylopectin molecules are present, as in waxy starches, the branches prevent the degree of association required for gel formation, except when extremely high starch concentrations of about 30% or more are present. Root starches gel less readily than those of cereals. The regions of intermolecular bonding in gels grow as the gel stands. The meshwork thus becomes firmer and shrinks to varying degrees depending on the number of micellar regions, their size, and their distribution.

Methods that have been used to evaluate starch gels involve measuring the amount of sag after the gel is removed from the container in which it has been formed, deformation of the gel under a load, elasticity, resistance to cutting, and resistance to breaking under stress. None of these tests relates closely to the sensory properties of the gel. The method that the starch industry has generally found must helpful in predicting the behavior of a starch in practical applications involves use of a disk attached to a rod, the disk being embedded at a prescribed depth under the surface of the sample prior to gelation. Following gelation and a fixed time lapse, the force required to remove the disk is measured. Obviously this test provides only a fraction of the information that is useful when comparing the properties of different gels. Additional information on gels can be found in Chapters 5 and 12.

d. Retrogradation. Retrogradation can be regarded as a normal progression in the firming of a starch gel. The rate and extent of retrogradation are influenced by temperature, size, shape, and concentration of the starch molecules and by other ingredients present. It appears to occur most rapidly at temperatures near 0°C. For this reason, starches are assessed for their tendency to retrograde in frozen foods by examining pastes that have been exposed to several cycles of freezing and thawing. Unmodified waxy starches, which do not form gels except at very high concentration, retrograde under these conditions and also during frozen storage [74,75]. Firming of bread during staling also has been shown to involve retrogradation of the branched fraction of starch [140,170].

Retrogradation of amylopectin can be reversed by heating. The curdled appearance found in thawed sauces and gravies that have been thickened with modified or unmodified waxy starches largely disappears during heating. Bread that has staled with little loss of moisture can be refreshed by heating. Retrograded amylose, in contrast, cannot be reversed by ordinary heating methods. Because the crystalline regions in retrograded starch are not susceptible enzymic hydrolysis, retrogradation somewhat lowers the digestibility of starch.

e. Film Formation. Strong, flexible films can be cast from amylose. These films possess the unusual properties of being water soluble and edible. The presence of amylopectin in large amounts, as in ordinary cornstarch, decreases intermolecular bonding and prevents the formation of self-supporting films. With the advent of commercial procedures for fractionating starch, the development of amylose films for various uses began to receive serious attention. The genetic development of varieties of corn yielding starch in which the level of amylose exceeds 80% provides a natural source of film-forming material that does not require fractionation. Foods can be coated with films of amylose to improve water retention and to decrease surface stickiness in dehydrated fruits.

f. Effects of Other Food Ingredients. Information on the behavior of starch-water systems, although extremely valuable to the food scientist, needs to be augmented by knowledge of the interactions of starch with other components of food systems. Even data obtained by addition of a single ingredient to a starch-water mixture must be applied with caution when attempting to predict the behavior of more complex food products. These effects, as well as information about the role of starch in some specific foods, have been reviewed in somewhat more detail elsewhere [43,142,143].

(1) Sugar. Because of its own hydrophilic character, sugar competes with starch for water present in a mixture, thereby retarding swelling of the starch granules. At low concentrations of sugar, the delay in swelling is not great and the maximum viscosity, in some instances, actually increases slightly (Figure 3-38). The increased viscosity occurs because small amounts of sugar apparently delay fragmentation of the most rapidly swelling granules without preventing swelling of other granules. Higher concentrations of sugar lower both the rate of swelling and the final viscosity obtained. Gel strength, as measured by the embedded disk method, decreases progressively as the amount of sugar added is increased. Sugars other than sucrose show the same qualitative effects but to different degrees (Figure 3-39). Disaccharides exhibit a greater effect than monosaccharides when present at the same concentration by weight [20].

(2) pH. Most foods have pH values in the range of 4-7. Variations within this range produce only minor effects on the rate at which granules swell or on the final viscosity obtained (Figure 3-40). The increased rate of swelling observed in strongly alkaline systems is seldom of any but theoretical interest to food scientists. The effects of acids, however, are of practical importance in numerous food products, including salad dressing, fruit pie fillings, and tomato soup.

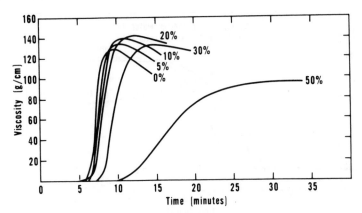

FIG. 3-38. Effect of different concentrations of sucrose on gelatinization of 5% cornstarch in a Corn Industries Viscometer. Reprinted from Bean and Osman [20]; courtesy of the Institute of Food Technologists.

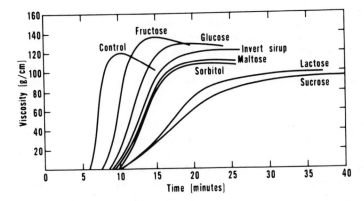

FIG. 3-39. Effect of different sugars on gelatinization of 5% cornstarch in a Corn Industries Viscometer. Reprinted from Bean and Osman [20]; courtesy of the Institute of Food Technologists.

Only a relatively small amount of hydrolytic cleavage of starch hastens the swelling of granules and increases fragmentation so that the maximum viscosity attained is appreciably reduced and rapid thinning of the mixture occurs during storage. In commercial salad dressings, the most effective means of combatting this problem is to use crosslinked starches (Section V,B,4,b). Although these starches may be used in any product of high acidity, they are often not needed in high-acid, high-sugar products since the effect of acid is partially counteracted by the ability of sugar to decrease the swelling of starch (Figure 3-38) [34].

(3) Salts. In the pH range of foods, starch molecules have no ionizable groups; therefore, they are much less sensitive to salt than are proteins. The amylopectin fraction of potato starch has some of its hydroxyl groups esterified with ortho-phosphate groups, making potato starch an exception in this respect. In most

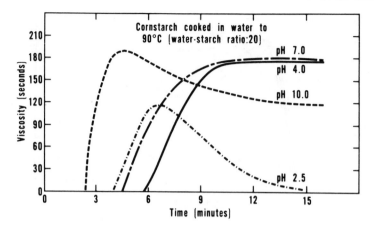

FIG. 3-40. Effect of pH on gelatinization and breakdown of starch. Reprinted from <u>Corn Starch,</u> 1964 edition; courtesy of Corn Refiners Association.

instances, however, the concentrations of salts in foods are so low that their effects on starch are probably much less than those of other ingredients. In proteinaceous foods, the effect of salts on proteins appears to mask the effects, if any, that salts have on starch. Studies of the effects of different ions on starch are abundant and the results often appear contradictory. These studies have been discussed in some detail elsewhere [142]. Suffice it to say that salts can affect starch swelling and this possibility should not be ignored.

(4) Fats and Surfactants. In any discussion of the effects of fats on the swelling of starch and on the resulting viscosity, distinction must be made between fats that contain emulsifying agents and those that do not, because these two groups of substances have opposite effects. Various natural fats composed mainly of triglycerides with aliphatic chains of 16-18 carbon atoms, with no added emulsifiers and with iodine numbers varying from 38 to 132, were found to have identical effects on viscosity curves of starch suspensions obtained with a Brabender amylograph [145]. These fats had no effect on the maximum viscosity reached, but the temperature at which the maximum was reached was progressively lower as more fat was added, up to the point where no more fat could be dispersed in the mixture. The temperature at maximum viscosity for a 6% cornstarch paste fell from 92° to 82°C when 9-12% fat was added.

Monoglycerides and other similar compounds with long hydrocarbon chains attached to hydrophilic groups exert pronounced effects on characteristic starch behavior. The mechanism by which these effects are produced is not clear, although numerous studies have been made of the action of these compounds on granular starch, on amylose, on amylopectin, and on starch-containing foods. Monoglycerides and amylose form colorless channel-type inclusion compounds that are structurally similar to the iodine-amylose complex. However, there is no evidence that monoglycerides form any complex with amylopectin, although formation of such a complex with linear outer branches of amylopectin has been postulated [69]. This complexity would explain the action of surfactants in retarding the staling of bread. In addition to their use in bread, monoglycerides are used in other commercially prepared starch-containing products [28]. They prevent gel formation in a variety of canned sauces, gravies, and soups. Spaghetti and rice to which they have been added are less sticky. Their addition to dehydrated potatoes, either granules or flakes, results in better texture after reconstitution.

The more commonly used surfactants with aliphatic chains of 16-18 carbon atoms cause large increases in the temperature at which starch granules enlarge noticeably and in the temperature at which maximum viscosity occurs. These surfactants also decrease the strength of starch gels. Similar surfactants with chains shorter than 16-18 carbons seem to have an opposite effect.

(5) Proteins. Starch and proteins are closely associated in the endosperm of cereals and legumes. It is evident that starch and protein do not act completely independently of one another in processing seed flours. However, methods for studying their interaction are difficult to devise. Starch-protein interactions in hydrated wheat endosperm, as seen by scanning electron microscopy, are believed to be important for dough structure [21].

(6) Milk. Study of the behavior of starch-milk mixtures is of practical value and the chief interacting components of such systems are undoubtedly starch and milk proteins. However, one cannot ignore the fact that other of the numerous components of milk may influence the results, both by their direct effects on starch (Figure 3-41) [89] and indirectly through their effect on proteins. When 5% cornstarch was added to pasteurized milk from different sources, quite different amylograph viscosity curves were obtained (Figure 3-42). Further study indicated that these differences were caused by the temperature of pasteurization [190]. At the temperature (71.7°C) required for high-temperature, short-time pasteurization, little denaturation of whey proteins occurs, but denaturation begins to occur at slightly higher temperatures and is appreciable at 80°C, a temperature often reached during commercial pasteurization. Raw milk produced a curve of type A, but samples of the same milk heated to 80°C gave a type B curve. Behavior similar to that shown in Figure 3-42 was exhibited by cornstarch pudding (no egg) containing milk that was previously heated to 80°C [67]. In addition, the gel strength (determined by the embedded disk method) of the pudding after cooling was appreciably lower when the milk had been preheated.

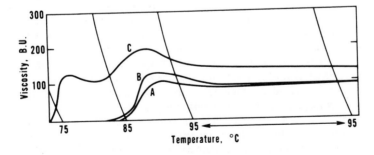

FIG. 3-41. Gelatinization of 5% cornstarch in (A) water, (B) 5% lactose solution, and (C) a natural protein-free milk system. Reprinted from Osman [142]; courtesy of Academic Press.

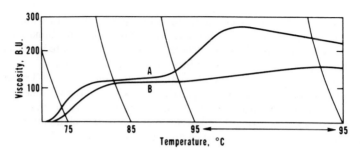

FIG. 3-42. Gelatinization of 5% cornstarch in two samples of pasteurized milk (A and B). Reprinted from Osman [142]; courtesy of Academic Press.

4. TYPES OF FOOD STARCHES

a. Unmodified Starches. That starches from different botanical sources differ in size, shape, general appearance, and gelatinization temperature already has been discussed. Of greater importance to their use in foods are the differences in properties of their pastes and the differences in the characteristics of their gels, if they form gels. For example, in the studies by Osman and Mootse [146], less than one-third as much potato starch as wheat starch was required to give pastes of the same maximum viscosity. However, potato starch failed to form a gel under the conditions used, whereas the wheat starch gel was very strong. Tapioca starch, which, like potato starch, gels under some conditions, also produces no gel at the concentration used in this study. Properties of starches from different plant sources as related to their uses in foods have been discussed by Osman [142].

b. Modified Food Starches. Increasing knowledge of the molecular and granular structure of different starches and their relationship to physical properties has enabled chemists to modify natural starches to meet special needs of the food and other industries. Some modifications are especially useful when applied to waxy starches.

Chemically modified starches must pass rigid tests for toxicity before they are approved for food use in the United States. Available evidence indicates that currently approved chemical modifications pose no danger to health even when the starch is consumed at levels substantially above that expected. The Subcommittee on Safety and Suitability of MSG and Other Substances in Baby Foods of the National Academy of Sciences-National Research Council has stated that "...there appears to be no toxicological basis for excluding the use of modified food starches from the diet of infants, provided the technical limitations on nature and degree of modification, as defined by regulation, are enforced and the amounts used to achieve the benefit do not exceed good manufacturing practice." The digestibility of starches appears to be affected little, if at all, by the chemical modifications used.

Pregelatinized starches are those that have been simply precooked and roll dried to give products that readily disperse in cold water to give moderately stable suspensions. A variety of natural starches are treated in this manner. Drying is accompanied by some breakdown of the swollen granules and some retrogradation. To produce a given viscosity, more pregelatinized than untreated starch is needed. Furthermore, dispersions of pregelatinized starch have a less desirable texture than cooked dispersions prepared from untreated starch. Dispersions of pregelatinized starch, nevertheless, possess some characteristics of the original starches, and the convenience of rapid dispersibility without heating has led to wide use. Their greatest use is in prepared instant puddings and pie fillings, but other food applications are common.

Suspending granular starch in a very dilute acid and holding it at a temperature somewhat below its gelatinization temperature yields an acid-modified or "thin-boiling" starch. This method hydrolyzes enough molecules in the granules so that subsequent heating in water causes ready fragmentation, thus preventing the large viscosity increase that may be obtained with untreated starch. The extent of this hydrolysis can be controlled to give a product with the desired degree of fluidity. Acid-modified starches are used in the manufacture of starch gum candies (e.g., gum drops) because the hot, low-viscosity concentrates can be easily poured into molds, yet they form firm gels upon cooling and aging. The strength of the gel can be at least as great as that resulting from the same starch without acid treatment.

Mild oxidation of starch with alkaline hypochlorite is sometimes carried out on starch slurries by a method similar to that described above for acid modification. This treatment also weakens the granules and produces a thin-boiling starch. However, the resulting gel is less firm.

Because retrogradation of starch is caused by association of hydroxyl groups along the starch molecules, the substitution of acetic ester or hydroxypropyl ether groups for some of the hydroxyl groups greatly increases the stability of starch pastes. This treatment is frequently used in combination with chemical crosslinking.

The extent of swelling and ultimate breakdown of starch granules during cooking can be controlled by introducing variable small amounts of cross-bonding between starch molecules. In general, any bifunctional compound capable of reacting simultaneously with two or more hydroxyl groups can form such crosslinks, but comparatively few reagents are used in preparing crosslinked food starches. These include epichlorohydrin, phosphorus oxychloride, acrolein, sodium trimetaphosphate, succinic anhydride, and adipic anhydride. The greater the amount of crosslinking, the greater the inhibition of swelling. Crosslinking alone does not prevent retrogradation, especially during freezing and thawing; so a few acetyl, hydroxypropyl, or monoesterified orthophosphate groups are often incorporated during the crosslinking process. A wide spectrum of modified properties can thus be realized, depending on the original starch, the reagent used for crosslinking, the extent of crosslinking, and the introduction of various other substituents. Chemical crosslinking, like intermolecular hydrogen bonding, can induce gel formation in the hydrated starch.

Unmodified waxy cereal starches and, to a lesser degree, root starches produce a degree of stringiness that is undesirable in food products. However, the clarity of their pastes and, frequently, their resistance to gel formation are often desirable. When these starches are crosslinked, the desirable characteristics are largely retained, but the degree of swelling that causes long, stringy pastes is prevented.

Introduction of monoesterified phosphate groups as one means of improving freeze-thaw stability has already been mentioned. However, use of such ionic groups requires further mention because their effectiveness results not merely from elimination of some of the hydroxyl groups that may interact to produce retrogradation but also from the repelling action of negative charges. One method of introducing monoesterified phosphate groups into starch results in some degradation of the granules and a cold-water dispersible product. Another method produces both monoesterified phosphate and cross-bonding diesterified phosphate without appreciable breakdown of the starch molecules. This product swells on heating in aqueous media. Both have excellent freeze-thaw stability.

C. Glycogen

Glycogen is a branched polymer of D-glucose similar to amylopectin except that glycogen has a much higher degree of branching than amylopectin. The structure of amylopectin can be compared to a tree, while that of glycogen is more like a bush. The extensive branching gives glycogen excellent freeze-thaw stability [144], and it may be useful as a hydrocolloid in foods if it becomes commercially available. However, its chief interest to food scientists probably lies in its presence in animal muscles at the time of slaughter and the effect it has on postmortem production of lactic acid. Liver glycogen rapidly hydrolyzes to D-glucose after slaughter.

A fraction of the water-soluble polysaccharide of sweet corn is more highly branched than the amylopectin of starch granules; therefore, it is very much like glycogen in structure. The name "phytoglycogen" has been applied to this polysaccharide.

D. Cellulose

1. NATIVE CELLULOSE

Cellulose is the basic structural material of the cell walls of vegetable tissues. In woody tissues, cellulose molecules are associated into partially crystalline microfibrils; however, the cellulose of vegetable pulp cells has little fibrous character. Cellulose is found embedded in an amorphous gel composed largely of hemicelluloses and pectic substances, together with a small amount of protein. Changes in cell-wall constituents surrounding the cellulose, and in the intercellular matrix, are largely responsible for changes in the texture of fruits and vegetables during maturation, storage, and food processing.

Cellulose, like amylose, is a linear polymer of anhydro-D-glucopyranose units united by (1→4)-glucosidic bonds. However, these bonds are in a β configuration rather than the α configuration of amylose. The repeating disaccharide unit is therefore cellobiose rather than maltose (Figure 3-5). As with amylose, the reported molecular weight depends on the source of cellulose, the treatment it has received, and the method used for molecular weight determination. It is conceded to be an extremely large molecule in its native form, whereas the extracted cellulose is generally degraded.

2. MODIFIED CELLULOSES

During controlled hydrolysis of cellulose, the material in amorphous regions is hydrolyzed, leaving the crystalline areas intact in the form of tiny rodlike microcrystals. The dried, white, microcrystalline cellulose sold under the name Avicel is partially soluble in dilute alkali and is insoluble in dilute acid. This substance is sometimes added to foods to contribute bulk without calories; to convert syrups or oil-base foods, such as honey or cheese, into free-flowing granular powders; and to form, with the aid of special dispersion techniques, a gel or creamy colloidal suspension. This product has disadvantages in that it is difficult to hydrate and disperse and that, when used in large amounts, it imparts a dry, chalky mouthfeel.

These drawbacks have been overcome by addition of some carboxymethylcellulose (see below) to the microcrystalline cellulose prior to final drying. This product, known as Avicel-RC, can be much more readily hydrated and dispersed, and the chalky mouthfeel is largely eliminated. When properly dispersed, it forms a weakly bonded gel structure that often prevents coalescence of emulsified oil droplets and settling of suspended solid particles. Avicel-RC imparts heat-resistant properties to emulsions.

The cellulose derivative most widely used in the food industry is the sodium salt of carboxymethylcellulose, also known as CMC or, in its high-purity grades, as cellulose gum. It is produced by first treating purified cellulose with sodium hydroxide, which causes the fibers to swell, and then reacting it with sodium chloroacetate:

$$R\text{-OH} + NaOH \longrightarrow R\text{-ONa} + HOH$$

$$R\text{-ONa} + ClCH_2COONa \longrightarrow ROCH_2COONa + NaCl$$

Theoretically, three carboxymethyl groups can be substituted on each glucose unit, but the maximum average number per glucose unit allowed in food use is 0.9. Solubility of the product and viscosities of solutions depend on molecular weight and on the degree and uniformity of substitution. Obviously, products with a wide variety of solution properties are possible and several grades are marketed.

The viscosity of CMC solutions varies inversely with temperature. Because of the carboxyl groups, CMC solutions may become unstable below pH 5, and precipitation may occur at pH values below 3.

Divalent cations may impart a haze to the solution, and trivalent cations may cause gel formation or precipitation. The properties of some proteins are altered by reaction with CMC. For example, addition of CMC prevents soy proteins and casein from precipitating in their isoelectric ranges and greatly increases the viscosity of gelatin solutions [62].

The major food application of CMC is in manufacture of ice cream. Small percentages of CMC decrease the mobility of water and thereby contribute to good body and smooth texture, retard enlargement of ice crystals during storage, and improve melting characteristics. Applications of CMC in other foods are numerous [18,64].

Methylation of some of the hydroxyls of cellulose separates the cellulose chains so that water can enter and dissolve the product. The method for producing O-methylcellulose is similar to that described for carboxymethylcellulose:

$$R\text{-}OH + NaOH \longrightarrow R\text{-}ONa + HOH$$

$$R\text{-}ONa + CH_3Cl \longrightarrow R\text{-}OCH_3 + NaCl$$

Introduction of groups in addition to methyl can affect solubility and rheological properties of the product. The hydroxypropyl group is most commonly used in products intended for food use, and it is introduced by reaction with propylene oxide:

$$R\text{-}ONa + H_2C\underset{\displaystyle O}{\overset{\displaystyle \diagdown \diagup}{\text{-}CH\text{-}CH_3}} + HOH \longrightarrow R\text{-}OCH_2\underset{\displaystyle OH}{\text{-}CH\text{-}CH_3} + NaOH$$

Hydroxypropylmethylcelluloses differ in molecular weight, total degree and uniformity of substitution, and in the ratio of methoxyl to hydroxypropyl groups present [105]. Since these cellulose derivatives are nonionic, their solubilities and the viscosities of their solutions are little affected by pH or by small to moderate amounts of electrolytes.

The unique property that distinguishes methylcellulose and hydroxypropylmethylcellulose from other commercially available hydrocolloids is their thermogelation. Partially etherified methylcelluloses are soluble in cold water, and the viscosity of their solutions decreases upon heating, as is usual with most gum solutions. This decrease in viscosity continues only to a certain temperature, however, after which the viscosity increases sharply and a gel forms. The gelation temperature and properties of the gel vary with the specific type and degree of substitution and with the amounts and types of other materials in the solution. By way of explanation, it has been suggested that the gelation temperature is the minimum temperature sufficient to dislodge critical amounts of loosely bound water molecules surrounding the polysaccharide chains. When the amount of bound water is sufficiently reduced, the polysaccharide chains are able to interact with one another and produce a gel [168]. Gelation is reversed by cooling and the polysaccharide goes back into solution. The temperature of gelation is depressed by most electrolytes, as well as by sucrose, sorbitol, and glycerol [119]. However, the gelation temperature is raised by ethanol, propylene glycol, and polyethylene glycol 400.

Methylcellulose and hydroxypropylmethylcelluloses are sometimes used in bakery products. Part of their effectiveness stems from their ability to increase the viscosity of the batter or dough and to gel during baking. They have been used successfully with rice, barley, tapioca, soya, potato, and cottonseed flours in the preparation of baked goods for persons allergic to wheat [217]. Numerous other food uses have been described [64, 71].

Two other cellulose ethers that have limited use in foods are hydroxypropylcellulose (Klucel) and methylethylcellulose. Both are soluble in cold water and both precipitate at elevated temperatures, hydroxypropylcellulose at about 40–45°C and methylethylcellulose at about 60°C. In both instances, precipitation is reversed when the mixture cools. Hydroxypropylcellulose is an effective emulsion stabilizer and is used as a stabilizer for whipped toppings. Methylethylcellulose can be whipped to form stiff, stable foams [64].

E. Hemicelluloses and Pentosans

In plant cell walls, cellulose is embedded so intimately in a matrix of noncellulosic substances that some investigators believe chemical linkages are involved. Groups of substances that have been isolated from cell walls, or probably have their origin in cell walls, include cellulose, pectic substances (discussed in Section V, F), hemicelluloses, water-soluble pentosans, and glycoproteins.

The term "hemicellulose" covers a variety of polysaccharides, other than cellulose, starch, and pectic substances, that occur in land plants and are insoluble in water and soluble in aqueous alkali. Some contain only unmodified pentose and/or hexose units; others contain hexuronic acid units; and occasionally the 6-deoxyhexose, L-rhamnose, is found. The morphological distinction between acidic hemicelluloses and pectic substances is not clear in cereals, soybeans, and other vegetables [204]. However, the acidic hemicelluloses have lower percentages of hexuronic acid units and they differ otherwise in chemical structure from the pectic substances.

Some hemicelluloses and water-soluble pentosans, also glycoproteins, have been isolated from wheat flour. In recent years it has become evident that some of these substances influence the baking characteristics of a flour. Most of these hemicelluloses and pentosans consist of single chains of β-(1→4)-linked D-xylopyranose units, sometimes with L-arabinofuranose units attached at C-3, or less frequently, at C-2 positions.

Starch and gluten washed from flour can be recombined to form a dough with baking characteristics somewhat similar to those of doughs from the original flour, but addition of solubles removed in the separation has been found to improve handling properties and loaf volume in most instances. Fractionation of the solubles has indicated that glycoproteins or albumin, rather than a pure pentosan, are probably associated with these improvements. Water-insoluble pentosans were found to have adverse effects on the baking properties of flour. Additional information on pentosans and hemicelluloses is available in a review by D'Appolonia et al. [43].

F. Pectic Substances

Pectic substances occur as constituents of plant cell walls and in the middle lamella. Those present in the middle lamella serve as cementing materials to hold cells together. Because members of this group have varied properties and because they are difficult to isolate in pure condition, much confusion has developed in terminology. To alleviate this confusion, the Division of Agricultural and Food Chemistry of the American Chemical Society appointed nomenclature committees in 1926 and 1941 to make recommendations. The definitions provided by the latter committee [106] in their 1944 report are those used today.

1. Pectic substances: These are complex colloidal carbohydrate derivatives that occur in or are prepared from plants and contain a large proportion of anhydrogalacturonic acid units that are thought to exist in a chainlike combination. The carboxyl groups of polygalacturonic acids may be partly esterified by methyl groups and partly or completely neutralized by one or more bases.

2. Protopectin: This is the water-insoluble parent pectic substance that occurs in plants, and it yields upon restricted hydrolysis, pectin or pectinic acids.

3. Pectinic acids: These are colloidal polygalacturonic acids containing more than a negligible proportion of methyl ester groups. Pectinic acids, under suitable conditions, are capable of forming gels with sugar and acid or, if suitably low in methoxyl content, with certain metallic ions. The salts of pectinic acids are either normal or acid pectinates.

4. Pectin: These are water-soluble pectinic acids with varying methyl ester contents and degrees of neutralization, that are capable of forming gels with sugar and acid under suitable conditions.

5. Pectic acids: These pectic substances are composed mostly of colloidal polygalacturonic acids and are essentially free from methyl ester groups. The salts of pectic acids are either normal or acid pectates.

A linear chain of anhydro-D-galacturonic acid units connected by α-(1→4) linkages is the basic structure of pectic substances (Figure 3-43). Some of the carboxylic acid groups are methylated and others are in the form of salts or free acids. Some pectic substances also contain an appreciable number of acetic ester groups at C-2 and C-3. The difficulty of removing neutral (nonacidic) sugar units from preparations of pectic substances has led to the hypothesis that native pectic substances contain sugar units covalently bonded to the polygalacturonic acid chain and that some of these bonds are broken during purification procedures. Some of these sugar groups are present in purified pectic acid [2]. Furthermore, the association between pectic substances and hemicelluloses in cell walls is such that some investigators believe it likely that they are bonded together to form a continuum of polysaccharides and that covalent bonds are broken during isolation of the various substances from the plant source.

When methyl esters of anhydro-D-galacturonic units are present in pectin, the glycosidic linkage β to the carbonyl of the ester group is readily split (Figure 3-43). The β-elimination mechanism for this reaction is discussed in Section III,D. The nonesterified anhydrogalacturonic acid units are less likely to react in this way. The carboxylic ester group is electron withdrawing (promoting dissociation of the proton on C-5), whereas the carboxylate anion is not. Therefore, if saponification of the ester precedes impending β elimination, the chain remains essentially intact. Both saponification and elimination occur in alkaline solution and also during heating of solutions buffered at pH 7 [3]. An acidic medium is therefore required for extraction and gelling of pectins to minimize degradation of the polysaccharide chains.

Protopectin in fruits decreases during ripening and soluble pectin increases. This change has been found to occur in apples during storage and the change is accompanied by decreased firmness. There follows a period during which the amounts of both types of pectic substances remain essentially constant, and eventually all pectic substances decrease and the texture becomes mealy. Similar changes have been observed in other fruits and vegetables, although formation of stiffening lignin masks this softening in some vegetables. Addition of a calcium salt, such as calcium chloride, often increases the firmness of plant products, such as tomatoes, apples, and green beans, by forming insoluble salts with pectic substances.

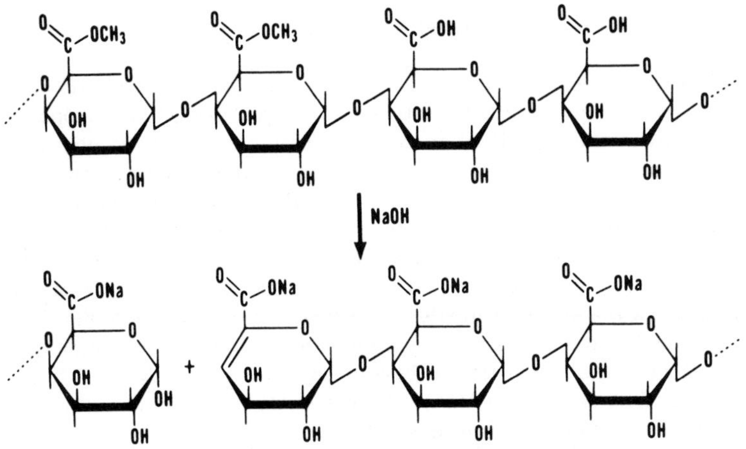

FIG. 3-43. Galacturonic acid and methyl galacturonate units of pectin (above) and alkali-degraded pectin (below).

Most commercial pectin is obtained by extraction of citrus peels with dilute acid, although some is extracted from apple pomace. The major use of pectin is in the manufacture of high-sugar jellies and jams. These products are made from pectins in which at least 50% of the carboxyl groups are methylated [degree of methylation (DM) = 50]. The higher the DM, the higher the temperature at which the gel forms. Rapid-set pectin (about 74 DM) is used in jams and preserves, where rapid setting is important to insure that the fruit is evenly distributed throughout the jelly. For jellies, either rapid-set or slow-set pectin (about 60 DM) can be used.

For gel formation, sugar, acid, water, and pectin must be present. The soluble solids content, mainly sugar, in jelly is generally 65-70%, and the pH is about 2.8-3.2. Protons of the acid shift the equilibrium between ionized and unionized carboxyl groups toward more un-ionized groups, thus decreasing the negative charges, decreasing the attraction between pectin and water molecules, and decreasing the ability of pectin to remain in a dispersed state. Sugar further decreases hydration of the pectin by competing for water. When cooled, the unstable dispersion of less hydrated pectin forms a gel. The gel is reversible and can be liquefied by heating.

Pectins with low methoxyl contents form gels by crosslinkages established between free carboxyl groups and divalent cations, especially calcium (Figure 3-35b). Gel formation does not require the presence of sugar, although a small amount may improve the texture. Gels of this type form over a much wider pH range than gels from high-methoxyl pectins. Low-methoxyl pectins are useful when it is desirable to limit or exclude the use of sugar for flavor or dietary reasons. They are made by controlled hydrolysis of the methyl esters through treatment with acid, alkali, or pectin methyl esterase.

The production, food applications, structure, and properties of pectin have been reviewed most recently by Towle and Christensen [200].

G. Natural Vegetable Gums

The term "gum" has been applied to many substances, both hydrophilic and hydrophobic, that have "gummy" characteristics. In current practice hydrophobic materials of this nature are classified as resins. The term "gum" is confined to hydrophilic substances that give viscous solutions or dispersions when treated with hot or cold water. Included among these hydrophilic gums are some that were formerly classified as mucilages. The term is therefore practically synonymous with "hydrocolloid." Most gums are polysaccharides and some, such as starches, pectic substances, and many derivatives of starch and cellulose, have already been discussed. Most of the other naturally occurring polysaccharide gums that find applications in foods can be classified as seed gums, plant exudate gums, or seaweed gums. Most of these substances have been listed in the Federal Code as "generally recognized as safe" (GRAS). However, limits are set on the amounts that can be added to various food products [10].

Several of the natural gums are so complex that their complete structures have not yet been elucidated. Although present knowledge of the relationships between structure and physical properties of polysaccharides is helpful in predicting the behavior of these materials, it is far from adequate in many food applications. As a result, choice of an appropriate gum remains something of an art. Although a dozen or more different gums may be considered for use in a particular food product, final selection usually devolves upon only one or two - those that interact most favorably with the food constituents at lowest concentrations. Combinations of two or more gums are often advantageous since synergism is sometimes noted. Choice of gums is therefore governed by knowledge of their compatibility with food constituents and with each other.

Many dehydrated, frozen, and "instant" convenience foods would not be acceptable were it not for the small amounts of gums incorporated to improve their textural, water-retention, and rehydration properties. Examples of foods that are much improved by gum additions are ice cream, gelled desserts, salad dressings, baked goods, process cheese, and encased ground meats. Gums may function as thickeners in gravies and sauces, moisture-retaining agents in baked goods, emulsion stabilizers in salad dressings, protective colloids in chocolate milk and syrups, syneresis inhibitors in gels and meringues, foam stabilizers in whipped toppings and beer, clarifying agents for wines and beer, flavor-fixing agents, and lubricants for extruded items [64].

Plant gums that are most frequently added to foods are listed and described in Table 3-10. Among the constituent monosaccharides, D-glucose is conspicuously absent. Although starch is the most common storage carbohydrate found in seeds, certain legumes contain little or no starch at maturity. For example, heteroglycans of D-galactose and D-mannose are found in guar and locust bean endosperm, and these galactomannans provide very useful food-grade gums. Although gums are usually classified according to their sources (Table 3-10), it befits chemists to discuss them in terms of their structures and the effects of their functional groups on useful properties.

TABLE 3-10

Vegetable Gums Widely Used as Food Additives[a]

Type, names, principal source	Relative amounts used[b]	Monosaccharide units of principal glycans	Distinguishing properties
Seed gums (legume endosperms)			
Guar (guaran) <u>Cyamopsis tetragonoloba</u> (India–Pakistan, Texas)	+++	β-D-man, α-D-gal (2:1)	Nonionic, heat stable; hydrates in cold water to very highly viscous, colloidal dispersions
Locust bean (carob) <u>Ceratonia siliqua</u> (Mediterranean)	++	β-D-man, α-D-gal (4:1)	Like guar but heat required for maximum hydration and viscosity
Plant exudate gums			
Arabic (Acacia) <u>Acacia senegal</u> (Rep. of the Sudan)	+++	β-D-gal, L-ara, D-glcA[c], L-rha, 4-O-methyl-D-glcA	Highly soluble, lowest viscosity; Newtonian flow; clear solutions
Karaya (Sterculia) <u>Sterculia urens</u> (India)	+/15	D-galA[c], D-gal, L-rha D-glcA	Insoluble but swells quickly in cold water; O-acetyl groups
Tragacanth <u>Astralagus shrubs</u> (Asia Minor, Turkey)	+/3	D-galA, D-xyl, L-ara, D-gal, L-fuc, L-rha	Soluble and insoluble fractions; forms opaque gels at 2–4% concentration
Seaweed extracts			
Agar <u>Rhodophyceae</u> Red-purple algae	+/15	Agarose: β-D-gal; 3,6-anhydro-α-L-gal (linear) Agaropectin: agarose + sulfate esters, D-glcA	Forms strongest and most stable gels at lowest concentration; gels are transparent and reversible upon heating and cooling

TABLE 3-10 (Continued)

Carrageenans	Rhodophyceae	++	D-gal 2-, 4-, 6-sulfates, 3,6-anhydro-D-gal and its 2-sulfate, D-gal disulfate	Anionic; gel and nongel-forming fractions; forms stable complexes with proteins and other gums
Algin (alginates)	Phaeophyceae Brown algae	++	β-D-manA, α-L-gulA[c] (Na, K, NH$_4$ salts and propylene glycol ester)	Anionic; widely variable sol and viscosity properties in acid and salt forms; forms gels and films

[a]Compiled from Whistler and BeMiller [215].
[b]Each + = approximately 5 million lb for food use in United States.
[c]D-glcA = D-glucuronic acid; D-galA = D-galacturonic acid; L-gulA = L-guluronic acid.

1. SEED GUMS

The galactomannans of guar (guaran) and locust bean gum have relatively simple structures. Guaran consists of long chains of $(1\rightarrow4)$-linked β-D-mannopyranose units; every other mannopyranose unit (on the average) being attached to an α-D-galactopyranose unit through a $(1\rightarrow6)$ linkage. The locust bean galactomannan is structured similarly but with the branched units spaced more widely and irregularly at about every fourth D-mannose unit on the average (Figure 3-44). Because the entire endosperm fraction of the seed is usually powdered to provide either gum, commercial products usually contain protein (5-6%), cellulose (1-3%), pentosans (1%), and ash (1%).

The more highly branched guar is less associated in the solid state and therefore disperses more readily in cold water than the less branched, more hydrogen-bonded locust bean gum. Both have comparably high molecular weights (ca.

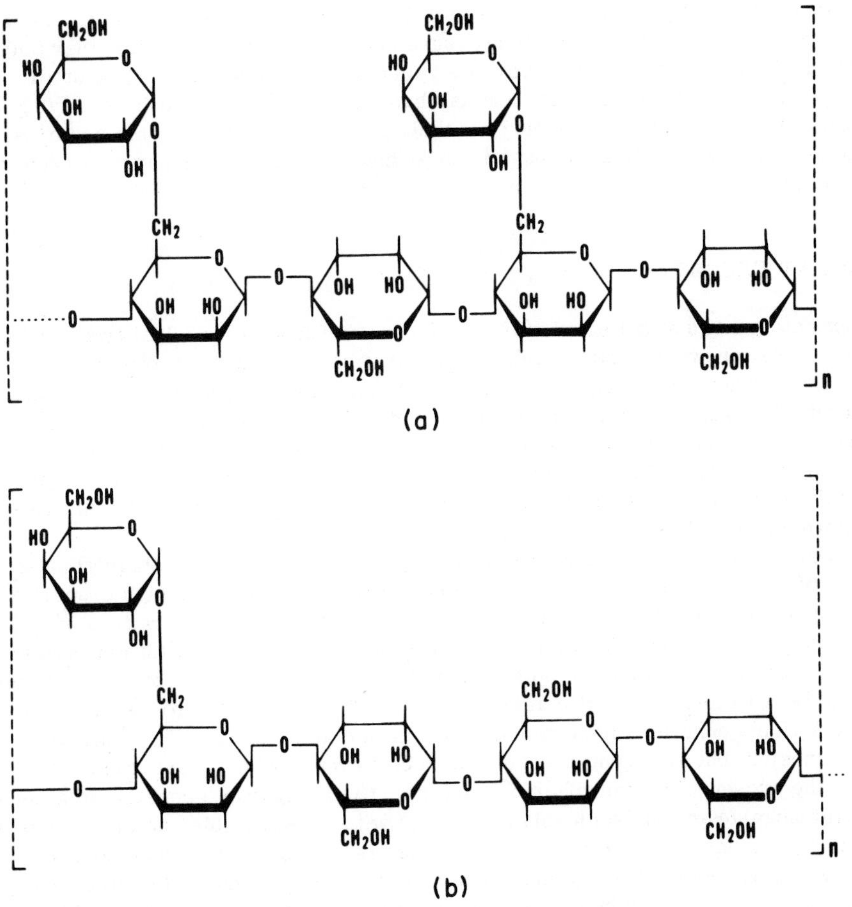

(a)

(b)

FIG. 3-44. Average repeating units in the galactomannans of (a) guar gum and (b) locust bean gum.

300,000 daltons) and can yield colloidal dispersions of comparably high viscosity. However, locust bean gum must be hydrated at elevated temperature to disrupt the micelles in order to produce the fully hydrated, high-viscosity dispersions that can be achieved with guar gum at 25°C. Neither seed gum forms gel per se, but both can be gelled by crosslinking reactions with borate in weakly alkaline media. The hydroxyl groups at C-2 and C-3 of the D-mannopyranose units are oriented cis, which is favorable for borate complexing. Addition of the alditols glycerol or mannitol liquifies the gel because they form stronger complexes with borate than the galactomannans. Decreasing the pH below 7 also liquefies the gel because the borate complexes are not stable in acidic solutions.

    Guar and locust bean gums maintain a nearly constant viscosity over the pH range of foods, unlike most of the anionic gums. Furthermore, their hydrocolloidal stability and rheology are least affected by heat processing, by freezing, and by acids, salts, or proteins in the food product. Sugar decreases the extent of their hydration. They are compatible with starches, cellulose gums, and most of the natural anionic gums. Because the branching units are short and regular, they show some physical properties that are similar to those of linear glycans. They form tough, pliable films and their hydrogen-bonding interactions with other polysaccharides are strong. Locust bean gum forms complexes with certain other gums (e.g., agar, carrageenans, and xanthan gum) that are useful in modifying the texture of their gels and the rheology of their pastes. Esters, ethers, and crosslinked derivatives of both gums have been formed to modify their physical properties [66,164].

2. PLANT EXUDATES

The exudate gums are collected manually from the wounds of tropical trees and shrubs. Best known are gums arabic (Acacia), ghatti, karaya (Sterculia), and tragacanth. They are essentially mixtures of heteroglycans, although common contaminants include proteinaceous and phenolic substances, glycosides, and foreign matter. Because the quality, quantity, and markets of exudate gums are so variable, chemists have sought to replace these natural gums with synthetic derivatives of starch and cellulose and thereby provide more uniform properties and more dependable supplies.

    Exudate gums differ structurally from the neutral seed gums in their greater variety of monosaccharide constituents and inherent acidity. The high proportions of hexuronic acid units in exudate polysaccharides are largely neutralized by calcium, magnesium, and potassium ions. However, when the metallic ions are removed (by precipitation from acid solution, by electrodialysis, or by ion exchange), the acidity of arabic and ghattic acids is comparable to that of lactic acid. Gum karaya not only contains high contents of hexuronic acids (about 37%), calcium, and magnesium but also contains labile O-acetyl groups which yield free acetic acid in the presence of atmospheric moisture. Gum tragacanth consists of a neutral arabinogalactan that is closely associated with more complex heteroglycans containing D-galacturonic acid (43%), D-xylose (40%), L-fucose (10%), and D-galactose (4%). Some of the galacturonic acid units contain O-methyl ether groups. The acidic polymers have been fractionated into water-soluble (tragacanthin) and water-insoluble (bassorin) fractions of similar structure [12].

3. CARBOHYDRATES

Compositional and structural differences among the exudate gums result in wide differences in their solubilities and viscosities. Gum arabic, which is the most highly branched, is by far the most soluble in water despite its high molecular weight (250,000-1,000,000 daltons). Its solutions in water show Newtonian flow up to 40% concentrations, whereas the other natural gums show structural viscosity above 0.5% concentration and are partially insoluble in cold water. Viscosities of gum arabic solutions are also very low in comparison with the other gums. For example, at 5% concentration in water at 25°C, gum arabic gives a relative viscosity of only 3-7 cp, compared with about 100 cp for gum ghatti, 45,000 cp for gum karaya, and over 100,000 cp for gum tragacanth. With increasing concentrations above 40%, structural viscosity and adhesive properties of gum arabic increase rapidly. Aside from the compact, highly branched structure of gum arabic molecules, in contrast to the more extended, rodlike molecular shapes of other gums, the presence of anionic groups at or near the end of the outer branches may account for the paucity of associated molecules in solution [65].

Viscosities of exudate gums vary with the time allowed for hydration and the temperature used to disperse those with insoluble fractions. Autohydrolysis is a factor at elevated temperatures and during long hydration periods. Other factors affecting viscosity are electrolyte type and concentration, rate of shear, and pH. Unlike the other exudate gums, highly heterogeneous gum tragacanth gives a nearly constant viscosity over the acidic pH range and is stable even at pH 2 [128].

Of all the plant exudate gums, gum karaya is the least soluble in water. Its particles swell rapidly in cold water but remain as discrete hydrated entities. Insolubility has been attributed to the 8-13% of O-acetyl groups; however, its high calcium and magnesium contents also may be involved. Addition of sodium or ammonium hydroxide hydrolyzes the acetic ester groups and results in a clearer, more viscous, and ropy dispersion. Autoclaving karaya dispersions improves solubility but lowers viscosity [64].

3. SEAWEED EXTRACTS

Irish moss and giant kelp (red and brown algae) are sources of several types of useful polysaccharides that are not found in land plants. The structural polysaccharides of red-purple seaweeds are mainly β-D- and α-L-galactans which are largely substituted with sulfate half-ester groups in various hydroxyl positions. The acidic sulfate groups are neutralized by the mineral cations of sea water, but these are exchanged for more specific ions during extraction processes with mild aqueous alkali. Some ester hydrolysis may occur during the extractions. Copolymerized with the β-(1→4)-linked sulfated D-galactose units are 3,6-anhydro-α-L-(or β-D-)galactose units linked (1→3). The latter units may or may not be esterified with sulfate at the C-2 hydroxyl group. The many possible combinations of the ester sulfate are evident from the varied types of polysaccharides that are extracted. Fractions with different positions of sulfate half-ester substitution on the different types of galactose residues show different sol and gel properties [153,159].

The sulfated galactans of red algae are represented among the food additives by agar [174], various carrageenan fractions [199], furcellaran [27], and hypnean [166]. The latter two are relatively new food additives. The carrageenans are especially useful in dairy products because they form stabilizing complexes with milk proteins, suspend cocoa powder in milks, and give more acceptable textures to process cheese and ice cream. Both gel- and nongel-forming fractions of carrageenan have been isolated. The structural factors that govern gel formation and strength among the various carrageenans have been discussed by Towle [199] and Pedersen [153].

Agar is essentially the calcium salt of the strongly ionized half-esters of sulfated galactans as described above. However, a neutral fraction, called "agarose" or "agaran," can be separated from agar. Agarose consists of a linear combination of the alternating repeating units given in Table 3-10. As a neutral, linear polymer, agarose resembles amylose in its insolubility in cold water and the need for disruption of solid-state hydrogen bonds before it can be brought into solution. Agarose forms firm gels, but the gels are less flexible and resilient than those formed from the heterogeneous agar. The acidic, sulfated fraction of agar is called "agaropectin." Hexuronic acids and condensed pyruvic acid have been detected in this fraction of some seaweed species. Several uses of agar in stabilizing food products have been described [64,174]. Uses are based on the unique stability of agar during heat processing and its ability to form and reform translucent, resilient gels after heating and cooling cycles.

Cell walls of brown algae contain algin, a linear polysaccharide composed of D-mannuronic and L-guluronic acids in varying ratios. When the miscellaneous natural cations are essentially replaced by a single cation, algins are called (sodium, potassium, ammonium, etc.) "alginates." When the cations are removed, nearly insoluble alginic acid is produced. By interchanging the cations and by converting the carboxyl groups to esters and amides, the rheology of alginates can be varied to fit different uses. Sometimes ion-sequestering agents are used in the formulations. Texture of the clear gels of alginates also can be regulated. Alginates can be gelled by calcium ions, but the complexing of calcium with the α-L-guluronic acid residues differs from that of the low-methoxy pectins [7]. Partial acetylation of the hydroxyl groups inhibits gelation by calcium ions. The role of calcium in forming salt bridges and chelates with vicinal hydroxyl groups in adjacent molecules has been investigated and discussed [7,173]. The food uses of alginates are discussed by Glicksman [64] and McNeely and Pettitt [123].

H. Microbial Gums

Polysaccharides produced by microorganisms only recently have been considered for use in foods. Some of these products appear to have useful properties [95].

1. DEXTRAN

The term "dextran" has been applied for more than a century to carbohydrate slimes originating from microbial action on sucrose syrups and other sugared foods. These slimes are polysaccharides consisting of α-D-glucose units. Dextrans are synthesized by a large number of microorganisms and they exhibit a wide spectrum of properties. Those available today, to which most information on structure and properties relate, are usually synthesized with a strain of Leuconostoc

<u>mesenteroides</u> designated as NRRL B-512 by the Northern Regional Research Laboratory of the United States Department of Agriculture. The reaction may be expressed as:

$$x(Sucrose) \longrightarrow (glucose-H_2O)_x + x(fructose)$$
$$\downarrow$$
$$Dextran$$

In B-512 dextran, some 95% of the D-glucose units are joined by α-(1→6) linkages and the remaining 5% are joined by α-(1→3) linkages to give a branched structure; however, other dextrans are known to contain (1→4) and (1→2) linkages at the branch points. The fermentation can be controlled to give products with molecular weights as low as 50,000 or as high as 100 million daltons. The Food and Drug Administration lists dextran as "generally recognized as safe" provided its average molecular weight is below 100,000 daltons. Dextran is readily soluble in water and has many of the typical characteristics of a hydrocolloid. Properties of dextran of interest to food chemists have been reviewed [96].

2. XANTHAN GUM (POLYSACCHARIDE B-1459)

A gum of very different structure from those previously discussed is obtained from the bacterium <u>Xanthomonas</u> <u>campestris</u> during fermentation in a medium of D-glucose, distillers' solubles, dipotassium hydrogen phosphate, and certain trace elements. This gum has molecular weights on the order of millions and consists of condensed D-glucose, D-mannose, and D-glucuronic acid units in the ratio of 3:3:2. It also contains acetyl and pyruvic acid groups. Xanthan gum has been approved by the United States Food and Drug Administration for use in foods as a stabilizer, emulsifier, thickener, suspending agent, bodying agent, or foam enhancer. It dissolves readily in cold water and its solutions have sufficient structure to prevent fine particles from settling or oil particles from coalescing, yet the solutions pour readily. Temperature has very little effect on viscosity, a property distinguishing xanthan gum from most other hydrocolloids. Also, of all food-grade gums, its viscosity decreases most rapidly with increasing shear rate. Solution viscosity is also essentially independent of pH value and the presence of salts. Xanthan gum forms a gel with locust bean gum but not with guar or other well-known gums [163]. Although xanthan is a new gum, it has already found extensive uses in many food products [122].

Several other microbial polysaccharides are in various stages of development. Microbial fermentation is a promising approach to making many new and potentially useful hydrocolloids for use in foods.

I. Mucopolysaccharides

Plants and animals, also bacteria and fungi, contain protein-carbohydrate complexes that resist physical means of separation into their components. Many of these complexes are known to contain covalent linkages between the carbohydrate and the protein. The covalently linked oligosaccharide-proteins are called "glycoproteins," whereas the chemically linked polysaccharide-proteins are called "proteoglycans." Glycoproteins of cereals, legumes, milk, egg white, blood plasma, enzymes, and other biologically active substances have been studied [97, 132] but their effects on food properties are not yet clear. The polysaccharides that have been isolated from the protein complexes of mammalian mucins are called "mucopolysaccharides." Most of them are acidic glycosaminoglycans; i.e., they are composed of N-acetylamino sugars condensed with uronic acids [97]. Nearly all of the research on these substances has been directed at their role in the living body rather than at their possible effects on the properties of flesh for food use. Mention of some mucopolysaccharides occurring in muscle tissue is made here because they show the water-binding and rheological properties of other polysaccharide gums; hence, they may have some bearing on meat properties.

Connective tissue proteins (e.g., fibrous collagen and elastin) are embedded in an amorphous matrix of extracellular proteoglycans called "ground substance." The ground substance in animals is therefore analogous to the amorphous matrix of hemicellulose, protopectin, and lignin that surrounds cellulose in the structural material of higher plants. Both matrices contain acidic polysaccharides that seem to be covalently bound to the fibrous polymers. Chondroitin sulfates, dermatan sulfate, keratan sulfate, and hyaluronic acid are polysaccharides that have been isolated from mammalian ground substance [97].

1. CHONDROITIN SULFATES

Chondroitin is a polysaccharide consisting of N-acetyl-D-galactosamine and D-glucuronic acid condensed in equimolar ratio. Figure 3-45 shows the assigned repeating unit of chondroitin 4-sulfate (formerly chondroitin sulfate A). Chondroitin 6-sulfate (formerly chondroitin sulfate C), with similar properties, also has been characterized. The polysaccharide formerly designated as chondroitin sulfate B is now known as dermatan sulfate [97]. Chondroitin sulfates are usually the principal components of the ground substance of connective tissue.

2. HYALURONIC ACID

Hyaluronic acid, found in various animal tissues in proportions up to 5% of the dry weight, is a linear polysaccharide of very high molecular weight. Its water solutions show shear-dependent, high viscosities that vary with the pH and ionic strength of the solution. Its structure is closely related to the chondroitin sulfates in that it is composed of an equimolar ratio of N-acetyl-D-glucosamine and D-glucuronic acid connected by the same interglycosidic linkages. Sulfate ester groups, however, are absent in hyaluronic acid (Figure 3-45). Like other polysaccharides that contain uronic acid units, it binds large amounts of water, forms gels, and is susceptible to decomposition by ionizing radiations.

VI. CONCLUSION

The need for acceptable and stable processed foods is increasing as the world population increases. As food supplies and reserves diminish per capita, the

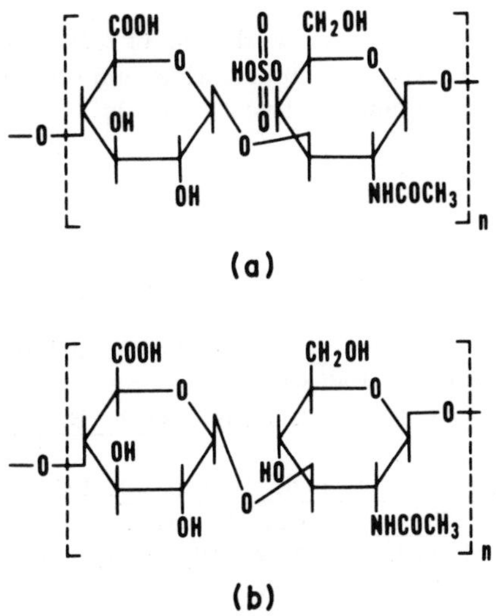

FIG. 3-45. Average repeating units in (a) chondroitin 4-sulfate and (b) hyaluronic acid.

importance of abundant carbohydrates increases. Food scientists should soon find economical ways to convert nonnutritive carbohydrates, particularly cellulose and cellulosic wastes, to nutrients. When this becomes possible, then sugars derived by hydrolysis of nonnutritive polysaccharides can provide suitable substrates for microbial syntheses of nutritive proteins.

Several different types of carbohydrates are now known to be useful in prolonging the storage life of foods and in increasing the acceptability of processed foods. Doubtless more efficient types can be found through study of the interactions of carbohydrates with essential proteins, lipids, and minerals. However, the stability of dehydrated foods is limited by nonenzymic browning reactions of reducing sugars with amino acids and proteins. Development of improved methods for avoiding or inhibiting these chemical reactions in dehydrated and canned foods should permit a significant increase in reserve food supplies.

The complexes that carbohydrates form with proteins are little understood despite their manifest importance in physiological and food chemistry. In foods, as in all living matter, molecular interactions involving noncovalent bonding are as important as reactions involving covalent bonding in determining what is most acceptable and beneficial for human health.

Knowledge of the interactions and reactions of carbohydrates in foods should be accompanied by knowledge of their digestibilities and physiological effects. For certain carbohydrates, the United States Food and Drug Administration stipulates the amounts that can be added to foods. Regulations are based on what is considered to be safe practice by those most knowledgeable in the field. Proposed rules are published first in the Federal Register [cf. 10], and after a specified waiting period for receipt of objections, the proposed or modified rules become a part of the Code of Federal Regulations. Title 21, Part 121 of the Code gives definitions, interpretations, and regulations governing the use of food additives. Both the Register and the Code can serve as an informative guide to chemists who are endeavoring to develop beneficial new additives for foods.

REFERENCES

1. T. Akazawa, in Plant Biochemistry (J. Bonner and J. E. Varner, eds.), Academic Press, New York, 1965, Chapter 12.
2. P. Albersheim, in Plant Biochemistry (J. Bonner and J. E. Varner, eds.), Academic Press, New York, 1965, p. 298.
3. P. Albersheim, H. Neukom, and H. Deuel, Arch. Biochem. Biophys., 90, 46 (1960).
4. E. F. L. J. Anet, Advan. Carbohyd. Chem., 19, 181 (1964).
5. S. J. Angyal, Angew. Chem. Int. Ed., 8, 157–226 (1969).
6. S. J. Angyal, in The Carbohydrates (W. Pigman and D. Horton, eds.), Vol. IA, Academic Press, 1972, Chapter 5.
7. S. J. Angyal, Pure Appl. Chem., 35, 131 (1973).
8. Anonymous, J. Org. Chem., 28, 281 (1963).
9. Anonymous, Biochemistry, 10, 3983 (1971).
10. Anonymous, Fed. Regist., 39(185), 34171, 34181, 34201 (1974).
11. The Food and Nutrition Board, Recommended Dietary Allowances. 8th ed., National Academy of Sciences, Washington, D.C., 1974, p. 34.
12. G. O. Aspinall and J. Baillie, J. Chem. Soc., 1963, 1702, 1714.
13. N. P. Badenhuizen, Chemistry and Biology of the Starch Granule. Springer Verlag, Vienna, 1959.
14. R. W. Bailey, Oligosaccharides. Macmillan, New York, 1965.
15. W. Banks, C. T. Greenwood, and D. D. Muir, in Molecular Structure and Function of Food Carbohydrate (G. G. Birch and L. F. Green, eds.), Wiley, New York, 1973, Chapter 8.
16. J. E. G. Barnett, in Molecular Structure and Function of Food Carbohydrate (G. G. Birch and L. F. Green, eds.), Wiley, New York, 1973, Chapter 14.
17. J. A. Bassham, in Phytochemistry (L. P. Miller, ed.), Vol. I, Van Nostrand-Reinhold, 1973, Chapter 3.
18. J. B. Batdorf and J. M. Rossman, in Industrial Gums (R. L. Whistler and J. N. BeMiller, eds.), 2nd ed., Academic Press, New York, 1973, Chapter 31.
19. J. C. Bauernfeind and D. M. Pinkert, Advan. Food Res., 18, 219 (1970).
20. M. L. Bean and E. M. Osman, Food Res., 24, 665 (1959).
21. J. E. Bernardin and D. D. Kasarda, Cereal Chem., 50, 529 (1973).
22. G. G. Birch, J. Food Technol., 8, 229 (1973).
23. G. G. Birch and C. Y. Lee, J. Food Sci., 39, 947 (1974).
24. G. G. Birch and M. G. Lindley, J. Food Sci., 38, 665, 1179 (1973).
25. G. G. Birch and R. S. Shallenberger, in Molecular Structure and Function of Food Carbohydrate (G. G. Birch and L. F. Green, eds.), Wiley, New York, 1973, Chapter 1.
26. Y. Birk, in Toxic Constituents of Plant Foodstuffs (I. E. Liener, ed.), Academic Press, New York, 1969, p. 169.

27. E. Bjerre-Petersen, J. Christensen, and P. Hemmingsen, in Industrial Gums (R. L. Whistler, ed.), 2nd ed., Academic Press, New York, 1973, Chapter 7.

28. G. Y. Brockaw, Can. Food Ind., 33(4), 36 (1962).

29. C. A. Browne, Ind. Eng. Chem., 14, 712 (1922).

30. D. P. Burkitt, Proc. Nutr. Soc., 32, 145 (1973).

31. H. S. Burton and D. J. McWeeney, Chem. Ind. (London), 462 (1964).

32. H. S. Burton and D. J. McWeeney, and D. O. Biltcliffe, J. Sci. Food Agri., 14, 911 (1963).

33. D. H. Calloway, Environ. Biol. Med., 1, 175 (1971).

34. A. M. Campbell and A. M. Briant, Food Res., 22, 358 (1957).

35. H. E. Carter, R. H. McCluer, and D. Slifer, J. Amer. Chem. Soc., 78, 3735 (1956).

36. B. Casu, M. Reggiani, G. G. Gallo, and A. Vigevani, Tetrahedron, 22, 3061 (1966); 24, 803 (1968); Carbohyd. Res., 12, 157 (1970).

37. A. V. Clark and S. R. Tannenbaum, J. Agri. Food Chem., 18, 891 (1970); 21, 40 (1973); 22, 1089 (1974).

38. E. E. Conn, in Toxicants Naturally Occurring in Foods. 2nd ed., National Research Council, National Academy of Sciences, Washington, D.C., 1973, Chapter 14.

39. J. E. Courtois and F. Percheron, in The Carbohydrates (W. Pigman and D. Horton, eds.), Vol. IIA, Academic Press, New York, 1970, Chapter 32.

40. B. Coxon, Advan. Carbohyd. Chem. Biochem., 27, 7 (1972).

41. H.-Ch. Curtius, M. Mueller, and J. A. Voellmin, J. Chromatogr., 37, 216 (1968).

42. I. Danishefsky, R. L. Whistler, and F. A. Bettelheim, in The Carbohydrates (W. Pigman and D. Horton, eds.), Vol. IIA, Academic Press, New York, 1970, Chapter 35.

43. B. L. D'Appolonia, K. A. Gilles, E. M. Osman, and Y. Pomeranz, in Wheat Chemistry and Technology (Y. Pomeranz, ed.), 2nd ed., American Association of Cereal Chemists, St. Paul, Minnesota, 1971, p. 301.

44. E. S. Della Monica, M. J. Calhoun, and P. E. McDowell, J. Food Sci., 39, 1062 (1974).

45. R. J. Dobbins, in Industrial Gums (R. L. Whistler, ed.), 2nd ed., Academic Press, New York, 1973, Chapter 2.

46. B. J. Donnelly, J. C. Fruin, and B. L. Scallet, Cereal Chem., 50, 512 (1973).

47. R. J. Doyle, S. K. Nicholson, R. D. Gray, and R. H. Glew, Carbohyd. Res., 29, 265 (1973).

48. P. L. Durette and D. Horton, Advan. Carbohyd. Chem. Biochem., 26, 49 (1971).

49. K. Eichner and M. Karel, J. Agri. Food Chem., 20, 218 (1972).

50. H. V. Euler and B. Eistert, Chemie und Biochemie der Reduktone und Reduktonate. Enke, Stuttgart, Germany, 1957.

51. M. S. Feather and J. F. Harris, Advan. Carbohyd. Chem., 28, 161 (1973).

52. A. Ferretti, V. P. Flanagan, and J. M. Ruth, J. Agri. Food Chem., 18, 13 (1970).

53. V. J. Filipic, J. C. Underwood, and C. J. Dooley, J. Food Sci., 34, 105 (1969).

54. J. Flink and M. Karel, J. Agri. Food Chem., 18, 295 (1970).
55. J. S. Fordtran and F. J. Ingelfinger, in Handbook of Physiology, Vol. 3, Alimental Canal (C. F. Code, ed.), American Physiological Society, Washington, D.C., 1968, p. 1475.
56. J. F. Foster, in Starch: Chemistry and Technology (R. L. Whistler and E. F. Paschall, eds.), Vol. 1, Academic Press, New York, 1965, p. 349.
57. R. Fragne and J. Adrian, Ann. Nutr. Aliment., 26, 107 (1971).
58. U. Freimuth and A. Truebsbach, Nahrung, 13, 199 (1969).
59. D. French, Advan. Carbohyd. Chem., 12, 189 (1957).
60. D. French, J. L. Mancusi, M. Abdullah, and G. L. Brammer, J. Chromatog., 19, 445 (1965).
61. M. Fujiimaki, N. Kobayashi, T. Kurata, and S. Kato, Agri. Biol. Chem. (Tokyo), 32, 46 (1968).
62. A. J. Ganz, Food Eng., 46(6), 67 (1974).
63. D. Gardiner, J. Chem. Soc. (C), 1473 (1966).
64. M. Glicksman, Gum Technology in the Food Industry. Academic Press, New York, 1969.
65. M. Glicksman and R. E. Sand, in Industrial Gums (R. L. Whistler, ed.), 2nd ed., Academic Press, New York, 1973, Chapter 10.
66. A. M. Goldstein, E. N. Alter, and J. K. Seaman, in Industrial Gums (R. L. Whistler, ed.), Academic Press, New York, 1973, Chapter 14.
67. V. M. Grant, M. S. Thesis, University of Iowa, 1968.
68. G. M. Gray, Gastroenterology, 58, 96 (1970); Ann. Rev. Med., 222, 391 (1971).
69. V. M. Gray and T. J. Schoch, Staerke, 14, 239 (1962).
70. C. T. Greenwood, Advan. Carbohyd. Chem., 11, 335 (1956).
71. G. K. Greminger, Jr., and A. B. Savage, in Industrial Gums (R. L. Whistler and J. N. BeMiller, eds.), 2nd ed., Academic Press, New York, 1973, Chapter 28.
72. Z. Gunja-Smith, J. J. Marshall, C. Mercier, E. E. Smith, and W. J. Whelan, FEBS Letters, 12, 101 (1970).
73. R. D. Guthrie, in The Carbohydrates (W. Pigman and D. Horton, eds.), Vol. IA, Academic Press, New York, 1972, Chapter 13.
74. H. L. Hanson, A. Campbell, and H. Lineweaver, Food Technol., 5, 432 (1951).
75. H. L. Hanson, K. D. Nishita, and H. Lineweaver, Food Technol., 7, 462 (1953).
76. M. G. Hardinge, J. B. Swarner, and H. Brooks, J. Amer. Diet. Assoc., 46, 197 (1965).
77. A. E. Harper, in Symposium on Foods: Carbohydrates and Their Roles (H. W. Schultz, ed.), AVI Publ., Westport, Conn., 1969, Chapter 15.
78. W. Z. Hassid, in The Carbohydrates (W. Pigman and D. Horton, eds.), 2nd ed., Vol. IIA, 1970, Chapter 34.
79. J. E. Hodge, in Chemistry and Physiology of Flavors (H. W. Schultz, ed.), Avi Publ., Westport, Conn., 1967, Chapter 22.
80. J. E. Hodge, B. E. Fisher, and E. C. Nelson, Amer. Soc. Brew. Chem. Proc., 84 (1963).
81. J. E. Hodge, J. C. Goodwin, E. C. Nelson, and K. A. Warner, Abstracts, 166th Meeting, American Chemical Society, Chicago, Ill., 1973, AGFD-118.

82. J. E. Hodge and G. E. Inglett, in Symposium: Sweeteners (G. E. Inglett, ed.), Avi Publ., Westport, Conn., 1974, Chapter 20.

83. J. E. Hodge, F. D. Mills, and B. E. Fisher, Cereal Sci. Today, 17, 34 (1972).

84. J. E. Hodge, J. A. Rendleman, and E. C. Nelson, Cereal Sci. Today, 17, 180 (1972).

85. R. E. Hodges, Nutr. Rev., 24, 65 (1966).

86. L. Hough and A. C. Richardson, in The Carbohydrates (W. Pigman and D. Horton, eds.), Vol. IA, Academic Press, New York, 1972, Chapter 3.

87. Y. Houminer, in Molecular Structure and Function of Food Carbohydrates (G. G. Birch and L. F. Green, eds.), Wiley, New York, 1973.

88. Y. Houminer and S. Patai, Israel J. Chem., 7, 513, 525 (1969).

89. Q.-S. Hwang, M.S. thesis, University of Illinois, 1963.

90. A. Hybl, R. E. Rundle, and D. E. Williams, J. Amer. Chem. Soc., 87, 2779 (1965).

91. D. L. Ingles, Food Preserv. Quart., 26(2-4), 39 (1966).

92. H. S. Isbell, in Carbohydrates in Solution (R. F. Gould, ed.), Advances in Chemistry Series, No. 117, American Chemical Society, Washington, D.C., 1973, Chapter 5.

93. H. S. Isbell, H. L. Frush, C. W. R. Wade, and C. E. Hunter, Carbohyd. Res., 9, 163 (1969).

94. H. S. Isbell, K. Linek, and K. E. Hepner, Jr., Carbohyd. Res., 19, 319 (1971).

95. A. Jeanes, in Water-Soluble Polymers (N. M. Bikales, ed.), Plenum Press, New York, 1973, p. 227.

96. A. Jeanes, Food Technol., 28(5), 34 (1974).

97. R. W. Jeanloz, in The Carbohydrates (W. Pigman and D. Horton, eds.), Academic Press, New York, Vol. 11B, 1970, Chapter 42.

98. R. R. Johnson, E. D. Alford, and G. W. Kinzer, J. Agri. Food Chem., 17, 22 (1969).

99. V. Johnson, A. J. Carlson, and A. Johnson, Amer. J. Physiol., 103, 517 (1933).

100. M. Karel and T. P. Labuza, J. Agri. Food Chem., 16, 717 (1968).

101. H. Kato and M. Fujiimaki, Agri. Biol. Chem. (Tokyo), 34, 1071 (1970).

102. H. Kato, G. Noguchi, and M. Fujiimaki, Agri. Biol. Chem (Tokyo), 32, 916 (1968).

103. H. Kato, M. Yamamoto, and M. Fujiimaki, Agri. Biol. Chem. (Tokyo), 33, 939 (1969).

104. S. Kawamura, Tech. Bull. Fac. Agri. Kawaga Univ., 18, 171 (1967).

105. J. F. Kennedy, Advan. Carbohyd. Chem. Biochem., 29, 305 (1974).

106. Z. I. Kertesz, G. L. Baker, G. H. Joseph, H. H. Mottern, and A. G. Olsen, Chem. Eng. News, 22, 105 (1944).

107. L. B. Kier, Pharm. Sci., 61, 1394 (1972).

108. P. J. Killion and J. F. Foster, J. Polym. Sci., 46, 65 (1960).

109. M. Kimura, M. Tohma, Y. Okazawa, and N. Murai, J. Chromatog., 41, 110 (1969).

110. N. Kirigaya, H. Kato, and M. Fujiimaki, Agri. Biol. Chem. (Tokyo), 32, 287 (1968).

111. J. Kiss, Advan. Carbohyd. Chem., 29, 229 (1974).

112. M. J. Kort, Advan. Carbohyd. Chem. Biochem., 25, 311 (1970).

113. G. Kotowycz and R. U. Lemieux, Chem. Rev., 73, 669 (1973).

114. N. Kretchmer, Sci. Amer., 227(10), 71 (1972).

115. A. Kuninaka, in Chemistry and Physiology of Flavors (H. W. Schultz, ed.),
     Avi Publ., Westport, Conn., 1967, Chapter 24.

116. C. C. Lee and Y. H. Liau, Cereal Chem., 49, 443 (1972).

117. C. Y. Lee, R. S. Shallenberger, and M. T. Vittum, N. Y. Food Life Sci.
     Bull., No. 1 (1970).

118. E. Y. C. Lee, C. Mercier, and W. J. Whelan, Arch. Biochem. Biophys.,
     125, 1028 (1968).

119. G. Levy and T. W. Schwarz, J. Amer. Pharm. Assoc., 47, 44 (1958).

120. R. C. Lindsay and V. K. Lau, J. Food Sci., 37, 787 (1972).

121. I. Macdonald, in Glucose Syrups and Related Carbohydrates (G. G. Birch,
     L. F. Green, and C. B. Coulson, eds.), American Elsevier, New York,
     1970, p. 86.

122. W. H. McNeely and K. S. Kang, in Industrial Gums (R. L. Whistler, ed.),
     2nd ed., Academic Press, New York, 1973, Chapter 21.

123. W. H. McNeely and D. J. Pettitt, in Industrial Gums (R. L. Whistler, ed.),
     2nd ed., Academic Press, New York, 1973, Chapter 4.

124. D. J. McWeeny, D. O. Biltcliffe, R. C. T. Powell, and A. A. Spark, J.
     Food Sci., 34, 641 (1969).

125. J. A. Maga and C. E. Sizer, J. Agri. Food Chem., 21, 22 (1973).

125a. A. A. Mahdi and W. J. Hoover, Food Technol., 19, 1579 (1965).

126. B. S. Mason and H. T. Slover, J. Agri. Food Chem., 19, 551 (1971).

127. M. L. Mednick, J. Org. Chem., 27, 398 (1962).

128. G. Meer, W. A. Meer, and T. Gerard, in Industrial Gums (R. L. Whistler,
     ed.), 2nd ed., Academic Press, New York, 1973, Chapter 13.

129. L. P. Miller, in Phytochemistry (L. P. Miller, ed.), Vol. 1, Van Nostrand
     Reinhold, New York, 1973, Chapter 11.

130. F. D. Mills, B. G. Baker, and J. E. Hodge, J. Agri. Food Chem., 17, 723
     (1969).

131. T. Mizuno and A. H. Weiss, Advan. Carbohyd. Chem., 29, 173 (1974).

132. R. Montgomery, in The Carbohydrates (W. Pigman and D. Horton, eds.),
     Vol. IIB, Academic Press, New York, 1970, Chapter 43.

133. R. D. Montgomery, in Toxic Constituents of Plant Foodstuffs (I. E. Liener,
     ed.), Academic Press, New York, 1969, Chapter 5.

134. E. R. Morris, in Molecular Structure and Function of Food Carbohydrate
     (G. G. Birch and L. F. Green, eds.), Wiley, New York, 1973, Chapter 8.

135. H. R. Moskowitz, Amer. J. Psychol., 84, 387 (1971).

136. H. R. Moskowitz, in Sugars in Nitrition (H. L. Sipple and K. W. McNutt,
     eds.), Academic Press, New York, 1974, Chapter 4.

137. D. J. Naismith and M. C. Cursiter, Proc. Nutr. Soc., 31, 94A (1972).

138. D. M. Nesetril, Baker's Dig., 28 (June, 1967).

139. C. Nieman, Mfg. Confect., 40(8), 19 (1960).

140. P. P. Noznick, P. P. Merritt, and W. F. Geddes, Cereal Chem., 23, 297
     (1946).

141. R. D. Olsen, Food Process., 25(1), 95 (1964).

142. E. M. Osman, in Starch: Chemistry and Technology (R. L. Whistler and E. F. Paschall, eds.), Vol. 2, Academic Press, New York, 1967, p. 163.

143. E. M. Osman, in Food Theory and Applications (P. C. Paul and H. H. Palmer, eds.), Wiley, New York, 1972, p. 151.

144. E. M. Osman and P. D. Cummisford, Food Res., 24, 595 (1959).

145. E. M. Osman and M. R. Dix, Cereal Chem., 37, 464 (1960).

146. E. M. Osman and G. Mootse, Food Res., 23, 554 (1958).

147. W. G. Overend, in The Carbohydrates (W. Pigman and D. Horton, eds.), Vol. IA, Academic Press, New York, 1972, Chapter 9.

148. W. G. Overend, A. R. Peacocke, and J. B. Smith, J. Chem. Soc. (London), 3487 (1961).

149. L. Page and B. Friend, in Sugars in Nitrition (H. L. Sipple and K. W. McNutt, eds.), Academic Press, New York, 1974, Chapter 7.

150. J. K. Palmer and W. B. Brandes, J. Agri. Food Chem., 22, 709 (1974).

151. R. M. Pangborn, in Symposium: Sweeteners (G. E. Inglett, ed.), AVI Publ., Westport, Conn., 1974, Chapter 3.

152. J. H. Pazur, in The Carbohydrates (W. Pigman and D. Horton, eds.), Vol. IIA, Academic Press, New York, 1970, Chapter 30.

153. J. K. Pedersen, Cereal Sci. Today, 19, 471 (1974).

154. F. Petuely, Monatsh. Chem., 84, 298 (1953).

155. G. O. Phillips, Advan. Carbohyd. Chem., 16, 13 (1961); 18, 9 (1963).

156. A. O. Pittet, P. Rittersbacher, and R. Muralidhara, J. Agri. Food Chem., 18, 929 (1970).

157. E. Rabinowitch and Govindjee, Photosynthesis, Wiley, New York, 1969.

158. S. Ranganna and L. Setty, J. Agri. Food Chem., 22, 719, 1139 (1974).

159. D. A. Rees, Advan. Carbohyd. Chem., 24, 267 (1969).

160. T. M. Reynolds, in Symposium on Foods: Carbohydrates and Their Roles (H. W. Schultz, ed.), AVI Publ., Westport, Conn., 1969, Chapter 12.

161. G. P. Rizzi, J. Org. Chem., 34, 2002 (1969).

162. J. P. Robin, C. Mercier, R. Charbonniere, and A. Guilbot, Cereal Chem., 51, 389 (1974).

163. J. K. Rocks, Food Technol., 25, 476 (1971).

164. F. Rol, in Industrial Gums (R. L. Whistler, ed.), 2nd ed., Academic Press, New York, 1973, Chapter 15.

165. R. E. Rundle, J. F. Foster, and R. R. Baldwin, J. Amer. Chem. Soc., 66, 2116 (1944).

166. R. E. Sand and M. Glicksman, in Industrial Gums (R. L. Whistler, ed.), 2nd ed., Academic Press, New York, 1973, Chapter 9.

167. J. Saunders and F. Jervis, J. Sci. Food Agri., 17, 245 (1966).

168. A. B. Savage, Ind. Eng. Chem., 49, 99 (1957).

169. J. Scala, Food Technol., 28, 34 (1974).

170. T. J. Schoch and D. French, Cereal Chem., 24, 231 (1947).

171. T. Schoebel, S. R. Tannenbaum, and T. P. Labuza, J. Food Sci., 34, 324 (1969).

172. J. C. P. Schwartz, J. Chem. Soc., Chem. Commun., No. 14, 505 (1973).

173. R. G. Schweiger, J. Org. Chem., 27, 1789 (1962).

174. H. H. Selby and W. H. Wynne, in Industrial Gums (R. L. Whistler, ed.), 2nd ed., Academic Press, New York, 1973, Chapter 3.

175. R. S. Shallenberger and T. E. Acree, J. Agri. Food Chem., 17, 701 (1969).
176. R. S. Shallenberger, T. E. Acree, and C. Y. Lee, Nature (London), 221, 555 (1969).
177. J. Shapira, Environ. Biol. Med., 1, 243 (1971).
178. J. Shapira, Proc. West. Pharmacol. Soc., 15, 65 (1972); Chem. Abstr., 78, 155303 (1973).
179. N. Sharon and H. Lis, Science, 177, 949 (1972).
180. P. E. Shaw, J. H. Tatum, and R. E. Berry, Carbohyd. Res., 5, 266 (1967).
181. P. E. Shaw, J. H. Tatum, and R. E. Berry, J. Agri. Food Chem., 16, 979 (1968).
182. P. E. Shaw, J. H. Tatum, T. J. Kew, R. J. Wagner, Jr., and R. E. Berry, J. Agri. Food Chem., 18, 343 (1970).
183. W. R. Sherman and S. L. Goodwin, J. Chromatog. Sci., 7, 167 (1969).
184. I. R. Siddiqui, Advan. Carbohyd. Chem. Biochem., 25, 285 (1970).
185. F. Smith, Advan. Carbohyd. Chem., 2, 79 (1946).
186. D. A. T. Southgate, Proc. Nutr. Soc., 32, 131 (1973).
187. D. A. T. Southgate and J. V. G. A. Durnin, Brit. J. Nutr., 24, 517 (1970).
188. J. C. Speck, Jr., Advan. Carbohyd. Chem., 13, 63 (1958).
189. A. Spicer, Chem. Brit., 9(3), 100 (1973).
190. M. J. Stalder, M.S. thesis, University of Illinois, 1964.
191. C. Sterling and C. O. Chichester, J. Food Sci., 25, 157 (1960).
192. G. Strahs, Advan. Carbohyd. Chem. Biochem., 25, 53 (1970).
193. H. Sugisawa, J. Food Sci., 31, 381 (1966).
194. H. Sugisawa and H. Edo, J. Food Sci., 31, 561 (1966).
195. H. Sugisawa and K. Sudo, Can. Inst. Food Technol. J., 2, 94 (1969).
196. J. H. Tatum, P. E. Shaw, and R. E. Berry, J. Agri. Food Chem., 17, 38 (1969).
197. A. Thompson, K. Anno, M. L. Wolfrom, and M. Inatome, J. Amer. Chem. Soc., 76, 1309 (1954).
198. O. Touster, in Sugars in Nutrition (H. L. Sipple and K. W. McNutt, eds.), Academic Press, New York, 1974, Chapter 15.
199. G. A. Towle, in Industrial Gums (R. L. Whistler, ed.), 2nd ed., Academic Press, New York, 1973, Chapter 5.
200. G. A. Towle and O. Christensen, in Industrial Gums (R. L. Whistler, ed.), 2nd ed., Academic Press, New York, 1973, Chapter 19.
201. T. Tsuzuki and J. Yamazaki, Biochem. Z., 323, 525 (1953).
202. L. Tumerman and J. H. Guth, U. S. Pat. 3,822,249 (1974).
203. C. H. VanEtten and I. A. Wolff, in Toxicants Naturally Occurring in Foods, 2nd ed., National Research Council, National Academy of Sciences, Washington, D.C., 1973, Chapter 10.
204. P. J. Van Soest and R. W. McQueen, Proc. Nutr. Soc., 32, 123 (1973).
205. J. Velisek, J. Davidek, J. Pokorny, K. Grundova, and G. Janicek, Z. Lebensm. Unters. Forsch., 149, 323 (1972).
206. R. H. Walter and I. S. Fagerson, J. Food Sci., 33, 294 (1968).
207. P.-S. Wang, H. Kato, and M. Fujiimaki, Agri. Biol. Chem. (Tokyo), 33, 1775 (1969).
208. J. Washuettl, P. Riederer, and E. Bancher, J. Food Sci., 38, 1262 (1973).
209. J. Washuettl, P. Riederer, E. Bancher, F. Wurst, and K. Steiner, Z. Lebensm. Unters. Forsch., 155, 77 (1974).

210. B. K. Watt and A. L. Merrill, Composition of Foods. Agriculture Handbook No. 8, U.S. Dept. Agriculture, Washington, D.C., 1963, pp. 6, 160, 164.

211. G. Weitzel, H.-U. Geyer, and A.-M. Fretzdorff, Chem. Ber., 90, 1153 (1957).

212. J. H. Wertheim, B. E. Proctor, and S. A. Goldblith, J. Dairy Sci., 39, 1236 (1956).

213. R. L. Whistler, in Encyclopedia of Polymer Science and Technology (N. M. Bikales, ed.), Vol. 11, Interscience, New York, 1969, p. 396.

214. R. L. Whistler, in Industrial Gums (R. L. Whistler and J. N. BeMiller, eds.), 2nd ed., Academic Press, New York, 1973, Chapter 1.

215. R. L. Whistler and J. N. BeMiller, eds., Industrial Gums. 2nd ed., Academic Press, New York, 1973.

216. R. A. Wilks, Jr., A. J. Shingler, L. S. Thurman, and J. S. Warner, J. Chromatog., 87, 411 (1973).

217. F. E. Windover, in Water-Soluble Resins (R. L. Davidson and M. Sittig, eds.), Reinhold, New York, 1962, p. 52.

218. M. L. Wolfrom, R. D. Schuetz, and L. F. Cavalieri, J. Amer. Chem. Soc., 70, 514 (1948).

219. O. B. Wurzburg, in Handbook of Food Additives (T. E. Furia, ed.), CRC Press, Cleveland, Ohio, 1968, Chapter 9.

220. S. Yamaguchi, T. Yoshikawa, S. Ikeda, and T. Ninomiya, Agri. Biol. Chem. (Tokyo), 34, 181, 187 (1970).

GENERAL REFERENCES

R. W. Bailey, Oligosaccharides. Macmillan, New York, 1965.

G. G. Birch and L. F. Green, eds., Molecular Structure and Function of Food Carbohydrate. Wiley, New York, 1973.

J. Bonner and J. E. Varner, eds., Plant Biochemistry. Academic Press, New York, 1966, Chapters 5, 7, 8, 11-13, 22, 30, 34, 35.

T. E. Furia, ed., Handbook of Food Additives, 2nd ed., CRC Press, Cleveland, Ohio, 1973, Chapters 7, 8, 10, 12.

M. Glicksman, Gum Technology in the Food Industry. Academic Press, New York, 1969.

H. S. Isbell, Carbohydrates in Solution (R. F. Gould, ed.), Advances in Chemistry Series No. 117, American Chemical Society, Washington, D.C., 1973.

A. R. Jeanes and J. E. Hodge, Physiological Effects of Food Carbohydrates, ACS Symposium Series No. 15, American Chemical Society, Washington, D.C., 1975.

W. Pigman and D. Horton, eds., The Carbohydrates, Vols. IA, IIA, IIB, Academic Press, New York, 1970, 1972.

H. W. Schultz, R. F. Cain, and R. W. Wrolstad, eds., Symposium on Foods: Carbohydrates and Their Roles. Avi Publ., Westport, Conn., 1969.

H. L. Sipple and K. W. McNutt, eds., Sugars in Nutrition. Academic Press, New York, 1974.

R. S. Tipson and D. Horton, eds., Advances in Carbohydrate Chemistry and Biochemistry. Academic Press, New York, 1969 et seq., annually.

R. L. Whistler and J. N. BeMiller, eds., Industrial Gums. 2nd ed., Academic
Press, New York, 1973.
R. L. Whistler and E. F. Paschall, eds., Starch: Chemistry and Technology,
Vols. I and II. Academic Press, New York, 1967.

Chapter 4

LIPIDS

LeRoy Dugan, Jr.

Department of Food Science and Human Nutrition
Michigan State University
East Lansing, Michigan

Contents

The chemistry of food lipids is complicated because they are diverse types of compounds that undergo many interactions with other components of a food. Many important and well-understood chemical changes that occur in an isolated lipid may be modified by such factors as location of the lipid in a tissue system, the presence or absence of water, and the imposition of such stresses as heat or radiation. Metals, both in the free state as ions and as components of organometallic compounds, affect the chemistry of lipids, especially in oxidation reactions. Nonlipid components of a food may interact with lipids and this can produce changes in food quality.

I.   DEFINITION AND CLASSIFICATION OF LIPIDS

A. Definition

The consumer and the processor of foods utilize substances from the nutrient group known as fats and oils. Fats and oils represent the most prevalent single category of a series of compounds known as lipids. The word "lipide" is defined in Webster's unabridged distionary as "any of a group of substances that in general are soluble in ether, chloroform, or other solvents for fats but are only sparingly soluble in water, that with proteins and carbohydrates constitute the principal structural components of living cells, and related and derived compounds, and sometimes steroids and carotenoids." This definition describes a broad group of substances that have some properties in common and have some compositional similarities.

B. General Classification

A classification of lipids proposed by Bloor [4] contains the following elements which are useful in distinguishing the many lipid substances:

   1. Simple lipids (neutral lipids) - Esters of fatty acids with alcohols.
       a. Fats: esters of fatty acids with glycerol
       b. Waxes: esters of fatty acids with alcohols other than glycerol

2. Compound lipids - Compounds containing other groups in addition to an ester of a fatty acid with an alcohol
   a. Phospholipids (phosphatides): esters containing fatty acids, phosphoric acid, and other groups usually containing nitrogen
   b. Cerebrosides (glycolipids): compounds containing fatty acids, a carbohydrate and a nitrogen moiety, but no phosphoric acid
   c. Other compound lipids: sphingolipids and sulfolipids
3. Derived lipids - Substances derived from neutral lipids or compound lipids and having general properties of lipids
   a. Fatty acids
   b. Alcohols: usually normal chain higher alcohols and sterols
   c. Hydrocarbons

Foods may contain any or all of these substances but those of greatest concern are the fats or glycerides and the phosphatides. The term "fat" is applicable to all triglycerides regardless of whether they are normally nonliquid or liquid at ambient temperatures. Liquid fats are commonly referred to as oils. Such oils as soybean oil, cottonseed oil, and olive oil are of plant origin. Lard and tallow are examples of nonliquid fats from animals, yet fat from the horse is liquid at ambient temperatures and is referred to as horse oil.

C. Fat Group Classification

Fats and oils also can be classed according to "group characteristics." Five well-recognized groups are the milkfat group, the lauric acid group, the oleic-linoleic acid group, the linolenic acid group, and the animal depot-fats group.

The milkfat group pertains essentially to the milk of ruminants and especially to that of the cow, although in certain areas milk of the water buffalo or of sheep and goats may be prominent. Milk fats are characterized by 30-40% oleic, 25-32% palmitic, and 10-15% stearic acids. They generally have substantial amounts of C_4-C_{12} acids and are the only commonly used fats to contain butyric acid, which may be present in amounts from 3% to 15% depending on the source. Milkfat composition is particularly susceptible to variation as a consequence of the animal's diet.

The lauric acid group is characterized by a high proportion (40-50%) of lauric acid (C_{12}) and lesser amounts of C_8, C_{10}, C_{14}, C_{16}, and C_{18} acids. The unsaturated acid content is very low and this contributes to extremely good shelf life. These fats generally melt at low temperatures because of the short carbon chains present. The most widely used fats of this group are from the coconut, seeds of the oil palm, and the babassu or the coquilla nut.

The oleic-linoleic acid group, the largest and most varied group, contain only fats and oils of vegetable origin. These fats usually contain less than 20% saturated fatty acids, with oleic and linoleic acids being dominant. Such fats are commonly derived from seeds of cotton, corn, sesame, peanut, sunflower, and safflower and the seed coat or fruit pulp of the olive and the oil palm.

Fats of the linolenic acid group contain substantial amounts of linolenic acid, although they also may contain high levels of oleic and linoleic acid. The most important food oil of this group is that from the soybean. Others are wheat germ oil, hempseed oil, perilla oil, and linseed oil. The high linolenic acid content contributes to the drying oil characteristic, especially of linseed oil, which contains up to 50% linolenic acid.

The animal fat group consists mainly of lard from the pig and tallows from bovine and ovine sources. These are characterized by 30-40% C_{16} and C_{18} saturated fatty acids and up to 60% oleic and linoleic acids. The melting points of these fats are relatively high, due partly to their contents of saturated fatty acids and to the types of glycerides present. With respect to the latter point, seed fats with as much as 60% saturated fatty acids often contain negligible quantities of trisaturated glycerides, whereas tallow with 55% saturated acids may contain up to 26% trisaturated glycerides. Differences in triglyceride composition affects physical properties, and this in turn greatly influences the use to which a given fat is put.

II. ROLE AND USE OF LIPIDS IN FOODS

A. Role

Fats and oils are the most concentrated source of food energy. They provide 9 kcal of energy per gram which is approximately double the energy provided by proteins or carbohydrates. They are carriers of fat-soluble vitamins, and they contribute to food flavor and palatability as well as to the feeling of satiety after eating.

Lipids in the form of triglycerides, phospholipids, cholesterol, and cholesterol esters are important to the structure, composition, and permeability of membranes and cell walls. They perform a function of energy storage in seeds, fruits of plants, and animals. Lipids are a major component of adipose tissue, which serves as thermal insulation for the body, as protection against shock to internal organs, and as a contributor to body shape.

Fats and oils are used as frying fats or cooling oils where their role is to provide a controlled heat-exchange medium as well as to contribute to color and flavor. As shortenings, they impart a "short" or tender quality to baked goods through a combination of lubrication and an ability to alter interaction among other constituents. As salad oils, they contribute to mouth feel and as a carrier for flavors, and when emulsified with other ingredients they perform the same functions in the form of viscous pourable dressings or semisolid fatty foods known as mayonnaise or salad dressing. Margarines are used both for baking and cooking and as table spreads. Specifically selected or manufactured fats are useful in confections, especially as enrobing or coating agents. These fats must have a short-melting range at body temperature.

Other fatty materials, such as the mono- and diglycerides, and certain phospholipids, such as lecithin, have useful roles as emulsifiers. Mono- and diglycerides contribute to shortening performance and act as staling inhibitors in bakery products. Lecithin is used as a mold-release agent in confections, to control fat bloom in chocolate candies, and as an antispattering agent in cooking margarines.

B. Use of Fats and Oils in Foods

Fats and oils are available in a variety of forms. Butter, cooking oils, margarines, salad oils, and shortenings are essentially all-lipid forms. Salad dressings and mayonnaise are composed of high proportions of fats or oils. Ingested fats and oils include not only those from obvious sources but also those from invisible fat sources, such as cereals, cheeses, eggs, fish, fruits, legumes, meat, milk, nuts, and vegetables. This latter group constitutes approximately 60% of the dietary fat.

Salad and cooking oils are prepared from cottonseed oil, soybean oil, corn oil, peanut oil, safflower oil, olive oil, or sunflower seed oil. These oils are usually refined, bleached, and deodorized. Some oils may be lightly hydrogenated to provide special properties and to enhance flavor stability.

Margarines, used mostly as table spreads and to some extent as cooking fats, are prepared by blending suitably prepared fats and oils with other ingredients, such as milk solids, salt, flavoring materials, and vitamins A and D. The fat content must be at least 80%. Vegetable oils are used predominantly for manufacture of margarine although some animal fats are used. The fats may be single hydrogenated fats, mixtures of hydrogenated fats, or blends of hydrogenated fats and unhydrogenated oil. Special margarines are prepared with increased levels of polyunsaturated fats. These have been prepared in response to medical research which implies a possible superiority for these types of margarines, especially for persons prone to atherosclerotic conditions. The fatty acid compositions of two margarine fats are given in Table 4-1.

Commercial shortenings are semisolid plastic fats made with or without emulsifiers. Plasticity, or ability to be worked, is a major feature distinguishing these from other fats. Original shortenings consisted of lard or tallow, but hydrogenated vegetable oils and various combinations of fats are used to build in specific properties desired for baking. Cottonseed oil, soybean oil, tallow, and lard are the principal fats used in shortenings. However, no natural fat possesses all of the desired characteristics.

TABLE 4-1

General Fatty Acid Composition of Fats in Margarines[a]

	Monoenoic acids (%)	Dienoic acids (%)	Trienoic acids (%)	Saturated acids (%)
Regular vegetable oil margarine	42–63	10–20	0–0.5	16–25
Special vegetable oil margarine	20–57	22–60	0–0.5	13–30

[a]Taken from Food Fats and Oils, Institute of Shortening and Edible Oils (1968).

Butter, obtained by churning cream, is a water-in-oil emulsion containing 80-81% milkfat which is present in a plastic form. Other constituents in small amounts include casein, lactose, phosphatides, cholesterol, calcium salts, and usually 1–3% sodium chloride. Varying but small amounts of vitamins A, E, and D also are present, along with flavor bodies consisting of diacetyl, lactones, and butyric and lactic acids.

Cocoa butter, derived from the cocoa bean, is a fat preferred for confectionary uses. It is usually in insufficient supply and is costly, so that many efforts have been made to substitute for it or to find suitable extenders.

Iodine values and fatty acid compositions of some typical fats and oils are given in Table 4-2.

III. LIPIDS IN FOODS

A. Nomenclature

The nomenclature of lipids includes a broad range of terms because trivial names are used in commerce, because systematic names are useful in scientific literature, and because convenient "shorthand" terms are used to represent substances with involved scientific names.

TABLE 4-2

Composition of Some Typical Fats and Oils

	Iodine value	Percent saturated	Percent oleic	Percent linoleic
Oleo oil	46.8	47.6	50.1	2.3
Butter oil	39.5	57.8	38.3	3.9
Chicken fat	86.5	23.4	52.9	23.7
Cocoa butter	36.6	60.1	37.0	2.9
Corn oil	126.8	8.8	35.5	55.7
Cottonseed oil	105.8	26.7	25.7	47.5
Lard	66.5	37.7	49.4	12.3
Olive oil	89.7	2.9	89.5	7.6
Palm oil	53.6	47.3	42.9	9.8
Peanut oil	93.0	17.7	56.5	25.8
Safflowerseed oil	144.3	5.7	21.7	72.6
Soybean oil	135.8	14.0	22.9	55.2

A nomenclature suitable for describing the stereochemistry of glycerol derivatives has been proposed by the IUPAC-IUB Commission on Biochemical Nomenclature. This system utilizes the Fischer projection of a vertical carbon chain in which the secondary hydroxyl is shown to the left and the top carbon is C-1. The term "sn" (stereospecifically numbered) differentiates this numbering system from conventional systems that convey no steric information. This term is inserted immediately preceding the term signifying glycerol, and is separated from it by a hyphen.

1. TRIGLYCERIDES

Triglycerides are named as derivatives of glycerol and the exact placement of substituents can be indicated in accord with the sn system. Thus a triglyceride containing palmitic (C-1), oleic (C-2), and stearic acids (C-3) is named sn-glyceryl-1-palmitate-2-oleate-3-stearate. Frequently, the glyceryl term is omitted and the same triglyceride is known as palmito-oleo-stearin. A diacid triglyceride containing two molecules of palmitic acid and one of stearic acid could be named dipalmitostearin or stearodipalmitin.

2. PHOSPHOLIPIDS

The phospholipids most important in foods are those containing a molecule of phosphoric acid esterified at one position of the glycerol molecule. The phosphoric acid in turn is esterified to another moiety, such as choline, ethanolamine, or inositol. Nomenclature of the phosphoglycerides is similar to that of triglycerides. Thus, the substance known in commerce as "lecithin" is designated 1,2-diacyl-sn-glycero-3-phosphoryl choline. Lecithin is a choline phosphoglyceride which is also known as phosphatidyl choline or preferably 3-sn-phosphatidyl choline. The term "phosphatidyl" is used for the portion of the molecule exclusive of choline. Similar designations apply to phosphatidylethanolamine, phosphatidylinositol, and others.

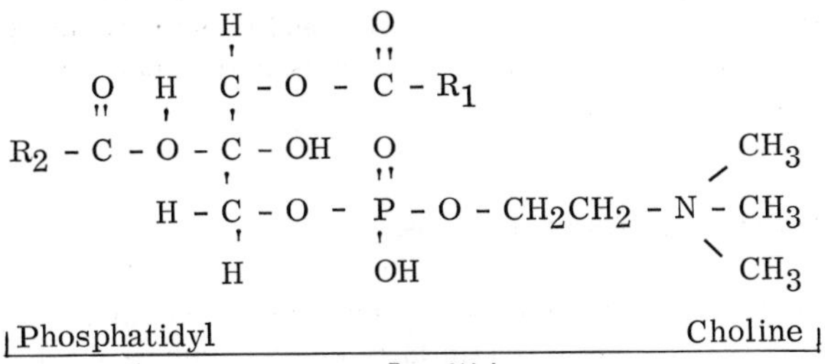

$$
\begin{array}{c}
\overset{\text{H}}{|} \quad\quad \overset{\text{O}}{\overset{||}{}} \\
\overset{\text{O}}{\overset{||}{}}\ \ \overset{\text{H}}{|}\ \ \text{C} - \text{O} - \text{C} - \text{R}_1 \\
\text{R}_2 - \text{C} - \text{O} - \text{C} - \text{OH} \quad \overset{\text{O}}{\overset{||}{}} \quad\quad\quad\quad\quad \text{CH}_3 \\
\overset{|}{\text{H}} - \text{C} - \text{O} - \text{P} - \text{O} - \text{CH}_2\text{CH}_2 - \text{N} - \text{CH}_3 \\
\overset{|}{\text{H}} \quad\quad \text{OH} \quad\quad\quad\quad\quad\quad \text{CH}_3
\end{array}
$$

| Phosphatidyl   Choline |

Lecithin

3. FATTY ACIDS

The fatty acids in lipids are usually aliphatic compounds which may be saturated or unsaturated and, in limited cases, may have branched chains. Nomenclature of the fatty acids requires both a systematic approach and knowledge of trivial names that are frequently encountered.

According to a system adopted at the Geneva Convention, fatty acids are named in accord with the parent hydrocarbon. The final "e" in the name of a hydrocarbon is replaced by "-oic" when referring to the saturated acid. Thus hexadecanoic acid (commonly known as palmitic acid) is related to the 16C hydrocarbon, hexadecane. The suffix "-ene" is used in naming hydrocarbons containing double bonds. Accordingly, the 16-carbon acid with one double bond is hexadecenoic acid and has the trivial name palmitoleic acid. Fatty acids with more than one double bond in the molecule have the suffix "-dienoic," -trienoic," or other suitable designations for the number of double bonds.

Many additional terms are used for purposes of brevity, for designation of double-bond location, or for geometrical configuration. Number designations begin with the carboxyl carbon as number 1. Oleic acid, which is an 18-carbon acid with one double bond in the cis configuration between the 9 and 10 carbons, may be alluded to as oleic acid; octadeca-9-enoic acid; octadeca-cis,9-enoic acid; Δ^9-octadecenoic acid; 18:1 (9c); and $C_{18:1}$. The term $C_{18:1}$ denotes an 18-carbon compound with one double bond and with no specification as to location or geometrical configuration, whereas the term 18:1 (9c) fulfills both requirements. Linoleic acid, an 18-carbon acid with two double bonds located at carbon atoms 9 and 12, has both double bonds in the cis configuration. It may be designated as linoleic acid; octadeca-9,12-dienoic acid; octadeca-cis-9,cis-12-dienoic acid; $\Delta^{9,12}$-octadecadienoic acid; 18:2 (9c, 12c); and $C_{18:2}$. The same limitations apply to these designations as have been discussed for oleic acid.

B. Fatty Acids in Foods

Food lipids, with few exceptions, contain straight-chain compounds with an even number of carbon atoms. Certain fatty acids are found repetitively in almost all fats, oils, or other lipids. These are the three C_{18} acids, oleic, linoleic, and stearic, and the two C_{16} acids, palmitic and palmitoleic.

Unusual fatty acids are found in plants and microorganisms. If unusual fatty acids are found in animals, they usually occur as a consequence of either ingestion or the action of microorganisms, e.g., in the rumen. Examples include most of the branched-chain compounds, hydroxy acids, and those with acetylenic (triple-bond) groups. Through ingestion these fatty acids may appear in depot fats of many animals other than ruminants.

1. STRAIGHT-CHAIN SATURATED ACIDS

Saturated fatty acids with more than 24 carbons seldom occur in food triglycerides but they do occur in waxes. Short-chain fatty acids, such as C_4-C_{10}, are found in milkfats along with longer chain acids. The C_{12}-C_{24} acids usually occur as compounds with an even number of carbon atoms. When fatty acids with odd numbers of carbons occur in animal fats (C_1-C_{23}), fish oils (C_{13}-C_{19}), or in vegetable fats (C_9-C_{23}), they seldom exceed 1-2% of the total fat.

The most commonly encountered saturated acids are lauric, myristic, palmitic, and stearic. Lauric acid is present in amounts of 45-50% in coconut oil or 45-55% in palm kernel oil, and myristic acid in amounts of 15-18% in coconut or palm kernel oil. Palmitic acid is more widely distributed than stearic acid. Palmitic acid is present in cottonseed oil at 22-28%, in palm oil at 35-40%, and at varying levels in other plant fats. It is present at a level of 25-30% in animal fats or milk and at levels up to 15-20% in many fish oils. Stearic acid is found in large amounts in ruminant depot fats (30%), where it probably results from hydrogenation of various unsaturated C_{18} acids in the rumen. It is also present in some plant fats, such as cocoa butter (35%) or Borneo tallow (40%). Some characteristics of saturated fatty acids are listed in Table 4-3.

2. STRAIGHT-CHAIN UNSATURATED ACIDS

The straight-chain unsaturated fatty acids differ with respect to the number of carbon atoms and the double bond characteristics. Double bonds differ in (a) number, (b) location, (c) geometrical configuration, and (d) conjugation. Conjugation is a special case of location in which two double bonds are separated only by a single carbon-carbon bond. Unsaturated acids may have one or as many as six double bonds. Those containing multiple double bonds usually have a methylene

TABLE 4-3

Some Saturated Fatty Acids Found in Food Lipids

Number of carbon atoms	Trivial name	Systematic name	Melting point (°C)	Boiling point (°C)
4	Butyric	Butanoic	− 5.3	164
5	Valeric	Pentanoic	−34.5	186
6	Caproic	Hexanoic	− 3.2	206
7	Enanthic	Heptanoic	− 7.5	223
8	Caprylic	Octanoic	16.5	240
9	Nonanoic	Pelargonic	12.5	256
10	Capric	Decanoic	31.6	271
12	Lauric	Dodecanoic	44.8	130
14	Myristic	Tetradecanoic	54.4	149
16	Palmitic	Hexadecanoic	62.9	167
17	Margaric	Heptadecanoic	61.8	175
18	Stearic	Octadecanoic	70.1	184
20	Arachidic	Eicosanoic	76.1	204
22	Behenic	Docosanoic	80.0	
24	Lignoceric	Tetracosanoic	84.2	

(CH_2) group between the double bond sequence, so the system is not conjugated. Linoleic, linolenic, and arachidonic acids are examples found in food fats. Double bonds occur in many locations but a regularity of position exists in most of those acids commonly found in food fats. Unsaturation at the Δ^9 position with cis orientation is most common. There are several series of unsaturated fatty acids which can be distinguished by the location of the first double bond relative to the omega (ω) or -CH_3 carbon. Thus oleic acid is both a Δ^9 and an ω-9 acid. Linoleic acid is a $\Delta^{9,12}$ acid and an ω-6 acid. Arachidonic acid, which along with linoleic acid is an essential fatty acid, is likewise an ω-6 acid, although it has 20 carbons and four double bonds, all in the cis configuration. Linolenic acid is an ω-3 acid and the hexadecenoic acids are ω-7. The various unsaturated series may be accounted for biochemically by enzymic desaturation of saturated acids beginning at the 9-10 position, and by the addition of two-carbon fragments at the carboxyl end.

Oleic acid is found in almost all fats. It is a dominant component of olive oil in which it is present at levels up to 75%, in cocoa butter at levels up to 40%, and in bovine and ovine fats at levels up to 35-40%. Oleic acid can be transformed into its trans isomer, known as elaidic acid, by nitrogen oxides or selenium and to some extent by the conditions present during catalytic hydrogenation. The latter process is responsible for producing a variety of monoethenoid fatty acids involving changes in both location and geometry of the double bonds.

Petroselenic acid-Δ^6 and vaccenic acid-Δ^{11}t are other octadecenoic acids found in some quantity in food fats. Petroselenic acid is a component of umbelliferous seed oils, and vaccenic acid is found in some animal fats, in several microorganisms, and in some plant sources.

Other monoenes include hexadec-9-enoic or palmitoleic acid found in many fats, especially fish oils and certain seed oils. Erucic acid 22:1, 13c is encountered in mustard seed and rape seed oils at levels of 30-40%. Some typical monoethenoic acids are listed in Table 4-4.

Polyunsaturated acids differ greatly with respect to chain length and double-bond characteristics (number, location, and geometrical configuration). The usual arrangement in food fats is a cis configuration with a methylene group between the double bonds (-CH=CH-CH_2-CH=CH-). Most polyunsaturated fatty acids are in the C_{16}-C_{22} range, although some may have as many as 24 or 26 carbons. The dominant species are diethenoid, although numerous tri- and tetraethenoid acids and some penta- and hexaenoic acids do exist.

Linoleic acid is present at high concentrations in many fats and oils. It is studied widely because it is an essential fatty acid and because it enters into many reactions involving oxidation, polymerization, and lipid-protein interactions. It is a dominant acid in safflowerseed oil (60-80%), cottonseed oil (45-50%), sunflowerseed oil (30-70%), and corn oil (40-60%).

Linolenic acid comprises 50-60% of the fatty acids in linseed oil. It is present in soybean oil at a level of 8-10%, and this poses problems when the oil is used unless it is modified by hydrogenation and other processing.

Arachidonic acid is a C_{20} tetraenoic acid which occurs primarily in animal sources. It is a component of many phospholipids and may be an important element in membranes of organ or neural cell tissues. It is a precursor of one of the prostaglandins.

TABLE 4-4

Some Unsaturated Fatty Acids Found in Food Lipids

Number of carbon atoms	Trivial name	Systematic name	Melting point (°C)	Boiling point (°C)
14	Myristoleic	9-Tetradecenoic		
16	Palmitoleic	9-Hexadecenoic	0	
18	Oleic	9-Octadecenoic	16.3	153 at 0.1 mm Hg
18	Vaccenic	11-Octadecenoic	39.5	
20	Gadoleic	9-Eicosenoic	23.5	
18	Linoleic	9,12-Octadecadienoic	- 5	202 at 1.4 mm Hg
18	Linolenic	9,12,15-Octadeca-trienoic	-11	157 at 0.001 mm Hg
20	Arachidonic	5,8,11,14-Eicosa-tetraenoic	-49.5	

Enzymes capable of promoting hydrolysis of lipids exist in many biological systems. The liberation of free fatty acids and the formation of partial glycerides contribute to flavor, texture, and other properties of foods. Some of these may be desirable while others result in economic loss and rejection of the product for use as food. Lipolytic enzymes are discussed in detail in Chapter 6.

IV. GLYCERIDE COMPOSITION AND STRUCTURE

A. Triglycerides

Properties of triglycerides depend both on the fatty acid composition and on the distribution of fatty acids in the glycerides. Many theories have been advanced to account for the observed distribution of fatty acids.

1. EARLY THEORIES

The "simple glyceride" theory involved the notion that each triglyceride in a fat contained only one fatty acid species. The "even distribution" theory embodied the concept that fatty acids were distributed among glyceride molecules to the greatest possible extent. Thus, each fatty acid would be present in as many glyceride molecules as possible, so that it would not occur twice in a given triglyceride until it exceeded 33% of the fatty acid population. According to the "random distribution" theory, fatty acids combine with glycerol according to the laws of chance.

Thus, representation of a given fatty acid in the total triglycerides of a system is simply proportional to whatever fraction this fatty acid represents of the total fatty acid population.

As accurate methods for determining composition become available, all of these theories were found to be inadequate or wrong.

2. THE 1,3-RANDOM, 2-RANDOM DISTRIBUTION THEORY

According to this concept, the 1 and 3 positions in natural fat molecules are identical and are occupied by identical kinds and proportions of acyloxy groups. The acyloxy groups presumably are distributed in the 1 and in the 3 positions at random. Similarly, those acyloxy groups which occupy the 2 positions of natural fat glycerides presumably are distributed at random among the total glyceride molecules.

By means of gas-liquid chromatography and hydrolysis with pancreatic lipase, the contents and locations of fatty acids in triglycerides can be determined. The fatty acids liberated by pancreatic lipase ($C_{1,3}$) can be separated and identified, and those present at the 2 position (C_2) can then be calculated from the relation $C_2 = 3(C_{1,2,3}) - 2(C_{1,3})$, where $C_{1,2,3}$ represents all fatty acids at all positions. This method does not distinguish between positions C-1 and C-3. Data calculated by this type of procedure are discussed below [11].

Illustrated in Table 4-5 for various natural fats are the triglyceride types in terms of saturated and unsaturated acids and isomeric forms. In the table, GS_3 refers to a fully saturated glyceride and GS_2U refers to a glyceride composed of two saturated acids and one unsaturated acid. Distinguishing between the 1, 3 and 2 positions permits identification of the SUS and SSU isomers of GS_2U and the USU and UUS isomers of GSU_2.

Information of this kind has been valuable in relating the properties of certain natural fats to compositional data. It is especially illuminating to note that pig fat has substantial quantities of GS_2U and GSU_2 but that the dominant isomers are those with saturated fatty acids at the 2 position. However, beef fat also has

TABLE 4-5

Triglyceride Types and Isomeric Forms of Natural Fats[a]

	Types (% wt)				Isomers (% wt)			
	GS_3	GS_2U	GSU_2	GU_3	SUS	SSU	USU	UUS
Pig fat	2.5	22.4	55.7	19.4	1.0	21.4	46.9	8.8
Peanut oil	0.1	9.9	42.5	47.5	9.3	0.6	0.7	41.8
Beef fat	12.6	43.7	35.3	8.4	30.6	13.1	3.4	31.9
Cocoa butter	7.1	67.5	23.3	2.1	65.0	2.5	0.2	23.1
Soybean oil	0	3.7	31.0	65.3	3.7	0	0	31.0

[a]Reprinted from Ref. [36] by courtesy of the American Oil Chemists' Society.

substantial amounts of GS_2U and GSU_2 but the dominant isomers are those with unsaturated acids at the 2 position. This distribution is quite similar to that found in fats or oils of plant origin, as shown in Table 4-5. As noted in Section D.2, pig fat, with its large content of glycerides containing palmitic acid at the 2 position, has properties which without modification give it poor qualities as an all-purpose shortening compared to the properties of beef fat or of plastic fats made by hydrogenating lipids from plant sources.

The kinds and locations of fatty acids in corn oil also have been determined and the results appear in Table 4-6. In Table 4-7 these data have been used to derive the triglyceride types in corn oil.

The 1,3-random, 2-random distribution theory more nearly agrees with the experimentally determined distribution of fatty acids in triglycerides than any other concept.

3. SPECIAL INSTANCES OF 1,3-RANDOM, 2-RANDOM DISTRIBUTION

A. R. S. Kartha [25] proposed that fatty acids were distributed among glycerides in a manner that would permit only that amount of GS_3 (trisaturated glyceride) that is compatible with lipid fluidity in vivo. If this amount of GS_3 is less than that permitted by random distribution, then the fatty acids distribute strictly according to chance among the remaining glyceride types. When the GS_3 content approaches the critical level, esterification of S (saturated fatty acid) at the 2 position is limited such that fluidity of the fat is maintained. The remaining S is then distributed randomly among the 1 and 3 positions.

TABLE 4-6

Total and Positional Analyses of Corn Oil (% Wt)[a]

| Fatty acid | Location in triglycerides | | |
	$C_{1,2,3}$	$C_{1,3}$	C_2[b]
C_{16}	11.8	18.0	-0.6 (0)
$C_{16:1}$	Trace	Trace	0
C_{18}	1.9	3.1	-0.5 (0)
$C_{18:1}$	29.1	28.7	30.0
$C_{18:2}$	56.4	49.3	70.6
$C_{18:3}$	0.8	0.9	0.6
Saturated	13.7	21.1	0.0
Unsaturated	86.3	78.9	100.0

[a]Reprinted from Ref. [37] by courtesy of Academic Press, Inc.

[b]$C_2 = 3(C_{1,2,3}) - 2(C_{1,3})$.

TABLE 4-7

Various Triglycerides in Corn Oil[a]

Triglyceride[b]	% Wt	Derivation
PPP	0	18 x 0 x 18/10,000
OLL	20	28.7 x 70.6 x 49.3 x 2/10,000
LOL	7.3	49.3 x 30 x 49.3/10,000
PLL	12.6	18.0 x 70.6 x 49.3 x 2/10,000
LPL	0	49.3 x 0 x 49.3/10,000
LLL	17.2	49.3 x 70.6 x 49.3/10,000

[a]Derived from data in Table 4-6.
[b]P = Palmitic, O = Oleic, L = Linoleic.

Gunstone proposed three variations of the 1,3-random, 2-random distribution theory [20]   The one that most satisfactorily corresponds with observed distributions involves preferential acylation of C_{18} unsaturated acids at the 2 position. The 1 and 3 positions are acylated subsequently by all remaining acids and by any C_{18} unsaturated acid not required at the 2 position. Within these limits, the distribution of acyl groups at each position is satisfied.

Evidence by other investigators indicates a tendency for specific distribution of palmitic and stearic acids at the 1 and 3 positions along with acids greater than C_{18}. This specificity has the effect of forcing a proportionately higher concentration of unsaturated acids into the 2 position. According to this concept, calculations of glyceride structure in vegetable oils can be based on three rules: (a) fatty acids with chain lengths greater than 18 carbons, as well as palmitic and stearic acid, are randomly distributed between the 1 and 3 positions; (b) oleic and linolenic acids behave similarly and both are distributed randomly and equally in all three positions up to a point beyond which the 2 position become preferentially occupied by these acids; and (c) all remaining glyceride positions are occupied by linoleic acid. Examples of the distributions of oleic, linoleic, and linolenic acid in some vegetable oils are shown in Table 4-8. Oils with a high linoleic content conform well to this concept.

B. Stereospecific Analysis of Fats

For many years, the concept of triglyceride structure was limited to equivalency of fatty acid distribution at the 1 and the 3 positions since it was impossible to differentiate between the two positions. However, the application of recent enzyme technology has provided a means for differentiating between the 1 and the 3 position. This technique is known as "stereospecific analysis" [7]. No investigation of natural fats is complete without the use of stereospecific analysis to identify the fatty acids at the 1, 2, and 3 positions of the various triglycerides.

Such an analysis can be accomplished in the sequence outlined in Figure 4-1.

TABLE 4-8

Unsaturated Glyceride Structure of Vegetable Oils[a]

Oil	Linoleic (%)	Oleic and linolenic (%)	Oleic and linolenic in 2 position (%)	Linoleic to fill 2 position (%)	Percent of linoleic in 2 position	
					Calculated (%)	Found (%)
Soybean	51.0	33.0	11.0	22.3	43.8	45
Linseed	14.5	75.6	25.2	8.1	55.8	47.4
Safflower	78.3	12.0	4.0	29.3	37.4	37.6

[a]Reprinted from Ref. [17] by courtesy of the American Oil Chemists' Society.

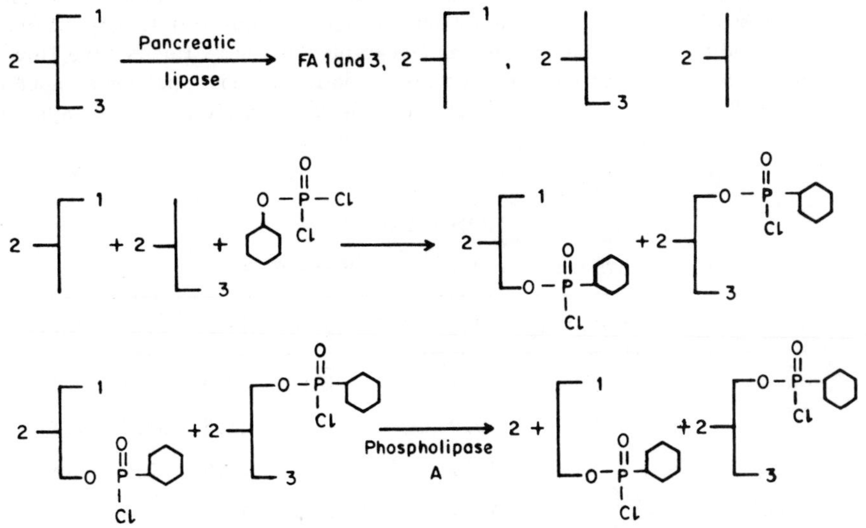

FIG. 4-1. A scheme for stereospecific analysis of triglycerides.

The action of pancreatic lipase on the triglyceride yields fatty acids 1 and 3, the 1,2- and the 2,3-diglycerides, and the 2-monoglyceride. The fatty acids can be isolated readily as a group and so can the diglycerides and the monoglycerides. The fraction containing the diglycerides will react with phenyldichlorophosphate to form two pseudo-phospholipids. The one formed from the 1,2-diglyceride exists in the L form and that from the 2,3-diglyceride exists in the D form. Use of phospholipase A results in hydrolysis of fatty acid 2 from the L form and no alteration of the D form. The lyso compound resulting from liberation of the fatty acid at the 2 position can be separated easily from the unreacted phospholipid and the liberated fatty acid. To complete the procedure an analysis of total fatty acids ($C_{1,2,3}$) is conducted by gas-liquid chromatography. Fatty acids liberated from the 1 and 3 positions can be identified as can fatty acids associated with the 2-monoglycerides. Analysis of the lyso compound provides identification of fatty acids at the 1 position. Fatty acids at the 3 position can be identified by $C_{1,3} - C_1 = C_3$, $C_{1,2,3} - C_{1,2} = C_3$, or $C_{2,3} - C_2 = C_3$. Thus it is possible to account for the quantity and identity of fatty acids located at the 1, 2, and 3 positions in a triglyceride or in triglycerides from natural fats. The results of stereospecific analysis of some fats are presented in Table 4-9.

A number of variations on stereospecific analysis of triglycerides are available for improved specificity, for ease of analysis, or when only limited quantities of material are available for analysis [27].

The distribution of fatty acids in triglycerides obviously is not the same in all fats, since triglycerides from plants and animals differ in this respect. The distribution depends on the various pathways for triglyceride synthesis in a given organism and certain generalizations can be cited. Plants tend to distribute saturated and longer chain acids in the 1,3 positions and dienoic unsaturated acids in the 2 position. Tendencies noted in fatty acid distribution in animal fats are: position 1, saturated; position 2, short chains or unsaturated; and position 3, long-chain fatty acids. Additional variances are that fats of pigs and most fishes have 16:0 in position 2; mammals have essentially none of the longer chain polyenes, such as 20:5, 22:5, or 22:6, in position 2; and fats of birds have nearly random or symmetrical distributions [6].

TABLE 4-9

Stereospecific Analysis of Some Fats

Fat	Position	16:0	16:1	18:0	18:1	18:2	18:3
Soybean	1	13.8		5.9	22.9	49.4	9.1
	2	0.9		0.3	21.5	69.7	7.1
	3	13.1		5.6	28.0	45.2	8.4
Olive	1	13.1	0.9	2.6	71.8	9.8	0.6
	2	1.4	0.7		82.9	14.0	0.8
	3	16.9	0.8	4.2	73.9	5.1	1.3
Corn Oil	1	18.5	0.4	3.5	28.1	48.5	1.0
	2	1.8	0.1	0.2	25.8	71.2	0.9
	3	12.6	0.5	2.2	31.0	52.6	1.1
Rat Liver TG	1	19.0	0.4	2.5	6.2	5.3	
	2	1.2	0.8	0.2	13	18	
	3	6.0	2.8	0.8	14	10	

C. Phospholipids

The phospholipids, or phosphatides, are complex phosphorus-containing lipids which are based on glycerol or on sphingosine. Those based on glycerol are the phosphoglycerides and those on sphingosine are the sphingolipids. The latter have relatively little significance in food systems. Phosphoglycerides can be represented by the general formula:

$$
\begin{array}{c}
\text{H} \quad\;\; \text{O} \\
\quad |\quad\;\; \| \\
\text{O} \;\; \text{H-C-O-C-R}_1 \\
\| \qquad | \\
\text{R}_2\text{-C-O-C-H} \;\; \text{O} \\
\qquad\; | \qquad \| \\
\text{H-C-O-P-O-X} \\
\quad\; | \qquad | \\
\text{H} \qquad \text{OH}
\end{array}
$$

where R_1 and R_2 are the alkyl portions of fatty acids and X is, for example, a base or inositol.

The natural phospholipids are optically active and belong chiefly to one enantiomeric series. They are referred to as L-α or L-3 compounds, although the diglyceride which results from dephosphorylation is the D-1,2-diglyceride.

The fatty acids occupying the sn-1 and sn-2 positions vary in chain length and in unsaturation. Acids at the 2 position are usually highly unsaturated and those at the 1 position can be saturated or monoenoic.

A series of phosphoglycerides commonly found in food materials is illustrated in Table 4-10. The component X specifically defines the compound and no designation is given for the nature of the acyl components.

Phosphoglycerides are important constituents of cell membranes, neural and organ tissues, and blood lipids. Phosphoglycerides are usually complexed as lipoproteins in their natural state so that most techniques for extracting phospholipids require uncoupling of the complex by denaturing the protein.

Oxidation of unsaturated fatty acids in phospholipids occurs readily and in some food systems, particularly meats and fish, the phosphoglycerides oxidize prior to substantial oxidation of the triglycerides. Thus, phospholipids with free amino groups also participate in aldehyde-amine reactions typical of nonenzymic browning. Polymers, Schiff bases, and scission products, some of which fluoresce when excited by ultraviolet radiation, are among the products. The aldehydes for the reactions can be derived from lipid oxidation.

The location of the fatty acids in lecithin can be determined readily by use of appropriate enzymes and application of separation techniques similar to those used with triglycerides. In lecithin from a given source, the fatty acids are distributed among a number of molecular species. This distribution reflects the general tendency for the most highly unsaturated fatty acids to reside at the sn-2 position. The most prevalent molecular species of lecithin in several foods are shown in Table 4-11.

It is seen in Table 4-11 that not all lecithin molecules are alike nor do they all follow the rule of locating saturates at sn-1 and unsaturates at sn-2 [31]. Lecithins from prawn muscles have substantially no stearic acid at sn-2 but 24% of the fatty acids at sn-2 are palmitic.

TABLE 4-10

Phosphoglycerides in Foods

Phosphatidyl Unit	X
Phosphatidic acid	H
Phosphatidylcholine (lecithin)	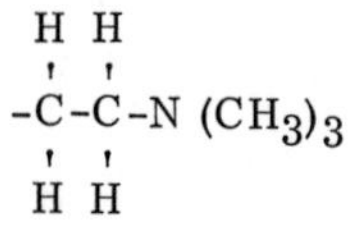 $-CH_2-CH_2-N(CH_3)_3$
Phosphatidylethanolamine (cephalin)	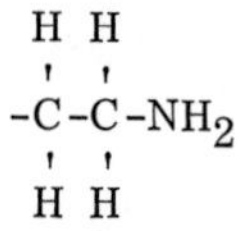 $-CH_2-CH_2-NH_2$
Phosphatidyl serine	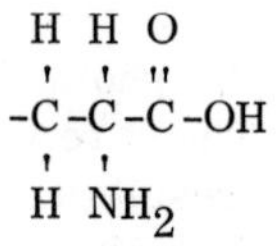 $-CH_2-CH(NH_2)-C(=O)-OH$
Phosphatidylinositol	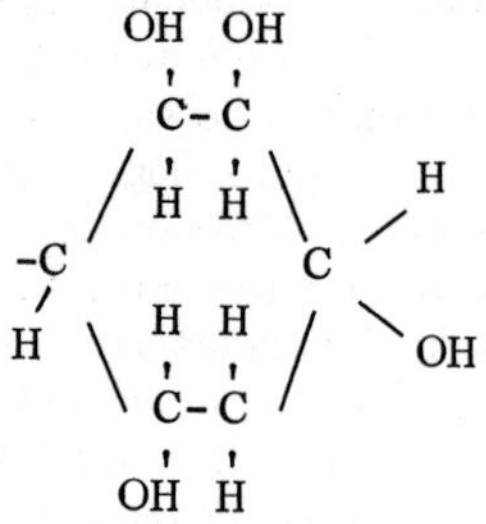 inositol ring (see structure)
Diphosphatidyl glycerol (cardiolipin)	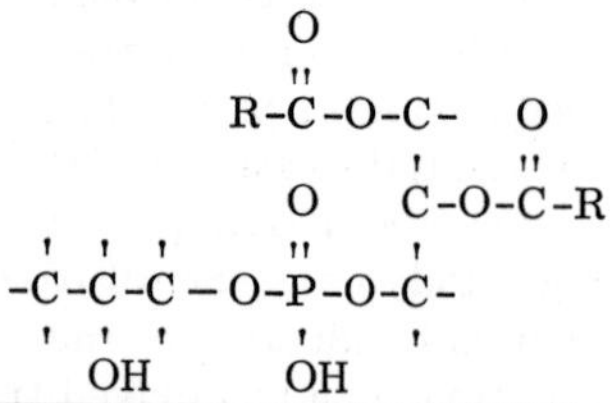 cardiolipin structure

For phosphatidylcholine:

```
      H  H
      |  |
   -C-C-N (CH3)3
      |  |
      H  H
```

For phosphatidylethanolamine:

```
      H  H
      |  |
   -C-C-NH2
      |  |
      H  H
```

For phosphatidyl serine:

```
      H  H  O
      |  |  ||
   -C-C-C-OH
      |  |
      H  NH2
```

For phosphatidylinositol:

```
        OH  OH
        |   |
        C - C
       / H H \      H
     -C         C /
     /  \ H H / \  OH
    H    C - C
         |   |
        OH   H
```

For diphosphatidyl glycerol (cardiolipin):

```
                        O
                        ||
                   R-C-O-C-   O
                        |     ||
                   O    C-O-C-R
                   ||   |
   -C-C-C — O-P-O-C-
    | | |      |
   OH        OH
```

V. PHYSICAL CHARACTERISTICS OF LIPIDS

Physical properties provide useful criteria for evaluating the stage of processing or the utility of a fat for a specific product. Among the physical measurements frequently used are melting point, specific heat, heat of fusion, viscosity, density, and refractive index.

TABLE 4-11

Fatty Acid Type Distribution in Lecithin from Certain Food Lipids

| Lecithin type[a] | | Weight % in lecithin from: | | | | |
sn-1	sn-2	Milk	Soybean	Egg	Wheat germ	Safflower
S	S	10.2				
S	M	28.3		49.3	6.9	4.2
M	S	15.8				
M	M	17.1		3.2	2.5	
S	D	8.2	24.0	31.6	28.4	34.7
M	D	3.9	8.9	3.5	11.8	8.0
D	M	3.7	5.9		4.0	5.0
S	Tr	2.1	3.5		1.7	
D	D	0.5	39.7		36.3	44.8
Tr	D		6.9		3.6	
S	Te	1.6		9.9		

[a]Fatty acids in sn-1 and sn-2 positions where S is saturated, M in monoene, D is diene, Tr is triene, and Te is tetraene. Reprinted from Ref. [30] by courtesy of the American Oil Chemists' Society.

A. Physical Properties

1. MELTING POINT

The melting point or melting range of fats varies from the relatively narrow-range, sharp-melting attribute of fats used for confectionary purposes to the broad-range, gradual-melting range attribute of shortenings. Melting points of pure compounds are sharp, but the variable triglyceride composition of natural and processed fats provides a number of melting points or a melting range within a single sample. Thus the melting point of a fat - the point at which the last trace of solid melts - usually signifies the melting temperature of the highest melting component. Melting point data are useful for animal fats and processed fats but are of little value for vegetable oils since most are liquid at ambient temperatures.

2. SPECIFIC HEAT

Knowledge of specific heats of fats is useful in processing operations. Although the specific heats of most triglycerides in a given physical state are similar, specific heat does increase with increasing unsaturation of fatty acids in both the liquid and solid states of a fat. Of greater importance, liquid fats have specific heat values almost twice those of solid fats, and the solid α form has a greater specific heat than the solid β form. This situation relates directly to the freedom of molecular motion in the various states. Specific heat values of some trisaturated triglycerides are presented in Table 4-12.

3. VISCOSITY

Viscosity is a factor that must be considered when designing systems for handling fats. Viscosity increases with increases in the average chain length of fatty acids in triglycerides and decreases with increasing unsaturation. Viscosity is thus a function of molecular size and molecular packing or orientation. The viscosities of various fats are listed in Table 4-13.

TABLE 4-12

Specific Heats of Some Trisaturated Triglycerides

	Liquid		α Form		β Form	
	Temp (°C)	C_p (cal/g)	Temp (°C)	C_p (cal/g)	Temp (°C)	C_p (cal/g)
Trilaurin	73.6	0.515			-68.6	0.269
Trimyristin	72.1	0.520	-67.5	0.300	-71.8	0.264
Tripalmitin	72.7	0.525	-72.3	0.291	-70.7	0.265
Tristearin	73.3	0.528	-65.5	0.298	-69.5	0.266

TABLE 4-13

Viscosities of Some Fats and Oils

	Viscosity (cp) at			
	38°C	50°C	99°C	100°C
Lard	44	25	9	
Beef tallow		34		10
Cottonseed oil	36		8	
Soybean oil	29		8	
Coconut oil	30		6	
Sunflowerseed oil	33		8	

4. DENSITY

Knowledge of densities of fats is needed for designing equipment but, more important, this property has provided a means for estimating the solid-liquid ratio
(solid fat index, SFI, or solid content index, SCI) of commercial fats. A dilatom-
eter, which measures specific volume (reciprocal of density) is frequently used for
this purpose. The procedure relies on the substantial difference in density between solid and liquid fats. If the specific volume of a fat is known when the fat is
in all-solid and all-liquid states, it is possible to determine the solids content from
specific volume changes, as shown in Figure 4-2. The solid fat expands, with increases in temperature, in accord with the "solids line," and the dotted extension
defines the slope of this line. The "liquid line" indicates the changes in specific
volume of liquid fat with increasing temperature. A fat at point X will consist of
(A/B) x 100% solid fat and (B-A/B) x 100% liquid fat [9].

In practice, the above procedure is simplified by assuming that the solids line
is parallel to the liquid line. This is done since the liquid line is easy to determine
while accurate determination of the solid line is difficult. This greatly simplifies
the procedure, and the resulting errors are not sufficient to make a great difference in assessing the processing performances of fats.

5. TITER

Titer is a measure of fat hardness and it is a criterion for distinguishing, in the
inedible fat market, between tallow and grease. Animal fats of uncertain origin
which have a titer of 40 or greater are designated "tallow," while those with lower
values are designated "grease." Titer is determined by saponifying a fat to obtain
the fatty acids. The melted fatty acids are permitted to cool slowly while the
temperature is observed. At some point, crystallization sets in and the temperature rises slightly. The temperature achieved during this initial crystallization is
the titer.

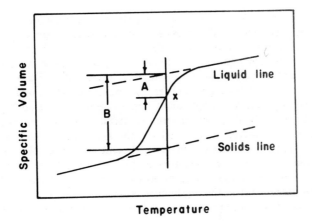

FIG. 4-2. Estimation of solids content of a melting fat.

6. COLD TEST

The cold test is a measure of the time to develop a cloudy appearance in oil held in an ice bath. An acceptable minimum time for salad oil is 5.5 hr. An oil to be used in mayonnaise must pass a cold test so that it cannot crystallize and break the mayonnaise emulsion during storage at refrigerator temperatures.

7. REFRACTIVE INDEX

The refractive index of a fat increases with increasing chain length of fatty acids in the triglycerides or with increasing unsaturation. The iodine value, a measure of the degree of unsaturation in a molecule, correlates with refractive index. Refractive index thus can be utilized as a control procedure during hydrogenation.

B. Other Useful Measurements

1. DIFFERENTIAL THERMAL ANALYSIS

This technique involves the use of a differential thermocouple so that the temperature of a sample being heated or cooled at a constant rate can be measured simultaneously with that of a reference sample. The reference sample is chosen so that it undergoes no change of state over the temperature range investigated. When the sample melts (absorption of heat) or crystallizes (evolution of heat), a temperature difference develops between the sample and reference and the magnitude of the difference is recorded. The resulting plot shows maxima for exothermal effects and minima for endothermal effects and provides a means for ascertaining polymorphic changes in a fat, for determining the temperature at which a fat has been tempered, or for assessing other properties related to changes of state.

2. NUCLEAR MAGNETIC RESONANCE (NMR)

Atoms capable of dipolar orientation under the influence of a magnetic field can assume different energy levels which can be measured spectroscopically. Elements for which mass and charge numbers are both even are incapable of this phenomenon. Thus, ^{12}C and ^{16}O have zero spin and no nuclear magnetic resonance, while ^{1}H has a nonzero spin and is responsive to a magnetic field. Lipids have NMR spectra resulting from responses of hydrogen and from a variety of additional responses provided by the magnetic field of neighboring nuclei. Solids produce line widths that are broad, whereas liquids, with greater molecular motion, average out dipolar broadening and give sharp narrow lines in the spectra. Application of wideline NMR to a lipid system containing liquid lipid enmeshed in a solid fat matrix enables one to determine the solid content of a fat more rapidly than by the dilatometric method. This technique is being developed rapidly but has limited application because the initial cost of the equipment is great.

Additional details of physical properties of fats are discussed by Swern [35].

C. Polymorphism

Certain triglycerides have been found to exist in several different crystal systems, each of which has a characteristic melting point, X-ray diffraction pattern, and infrared spectrum. This phenomenon, known as "polymorphism," arises from different modes of molecular packing in the crystal. Polymorphism is not an uncommon occurrence in nature. For example, ice at elevated pressure can exist in various polymorphic forms and carbon, of course, can exist in the common black form or as diamond. Tristearin can exist in three polymorphic forms with melting points of 53°, 64.2°, and 71.7°C. The lowest melting point form results from rapid solidification of melted tristearin. Slow heating melts this form, which then resolidifies and melts again at 64.2°C. The form derived by crystallization from a solvent melts at 71.7°C.

Crystal forms of monoacid trisaturated glycerides lend themselves best to examination for polymorphism since the various forms are easily achieved and are distinctly different. Analysis of these polymorphic forms by X-ray diffraction provide information as to the "long spacings" and "short spacings" of the crystals. Long spacings are proportional to the number of carbon atoms in acyl groups. Short spacings are measured in a direction approximately perpendicular to the acyl groups. Short spacings correspond to the width or "b" axes of unit cells and are essentially independent of fatty acid chain length. The magnitude of the short spacing varies with the packing density of molecules, and it therefore provides a measure of the degree of randomness of molecular orientation in a given polymorphic form. Presented in Table 4-14 are the short spacings and other polymorphic properties of various monoacid, trisaturated glycerides.

Infrared spectroscopy of the various polymorphic forms shows a single band at 720 cm^{-1} for the α form, a doublet at 719 and 727 cm^{-1} for the β' form, and a single band at 717 cm^{-1} for the β form. These characteristics relate to subcell packing in the crystals, indicating that the α form of monoacid trisaturated glycerides exists in the hexagonal crystal system, the β' form in the orthorhombic system, and the β form in the triclinic system [10].

TABLE 4-14

Polymorphic Properties of Monoacid Trisaturated Glycerides
with even Numbers of Carbons[a]

Melting point	Investigator and short spacing (Å)		
	Density	Malkin	Lutton
Highest	Highest	β 4.6	β 4.6
Lower	Lower	β' 3.4, 4.2	β' 3.4, 4.2
Lower	Lower	α 4.15	–
Lowest	Lowest	Vitreous 4.15 (diffuse)	α 4.15

[a]Reprinted from Ref. [21] by courtesy of the American Oil Chemists' Society.

A form referred to variously as sub-α, vitreous, or γ can be formed at very low temperatures although it is usually short lived. The sub-α form exhibits a doublet at 719 and 727 cm^{-1} indicating a molecular packing essentially similar to that of the β' form of tristearin. At higher temperatures it assumes the α form with greater freedom of molecular motion.

Molecular configurations determined by electron density measurements reveal that β crystals of trisaturated glycerides exist in a "chair" form in which the chains at the 1 and 3 positions of the glyceride point in a direction opposite to that of the chain in the 2 position. The tuning fork model accounts for the β' form (see Fig. 4-3).

Although the lowest melting α form is glassy or vitreous in appearance, dielectric studies and polarized light microscopy indicate the presence of some crystallinity.

Triglycerides containing different fatty acids with varying chain lengths and degrees of unsaturation exhibit exceedingly complex polymorphic behavior. Some crystallize in units consisting essentially of double or triple chain lengths (long spacings). These are given such designations as β-2 or β'-3 to indicate both the packing arrangement and the number of acyl chains associated with it. Triunsaturated triglycerides, such as triolein, form double chain length structures. Mixed oleic-saturated glycerides have a tendency to form triple chain length structures (Fig. 4-4). Triglycerides composed of long and very short carbon chain components have some unusual properties. 1-Stearodiacetin or 1-palmito-diacetin have unusually stable α forms. Films of these substances can be stretched 200-300 times their original lengths. These acetoglycerides can be used as flexible coatings for food products such as cheese. The β form of these substances, which can be obtained by solvent crystallization, cannot be stretched.

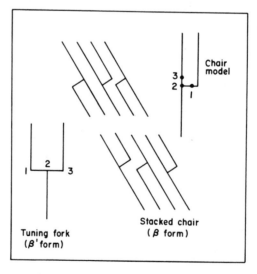

FIG. 4-3.   Models which account for β and β' crystal forms.

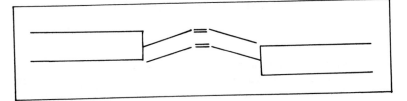

FIG. 4-4. Oleic-disaturated triglyceride in a triple chain length structure.

TABLE 4-15

Characteristics of Fat Crystals

Polymorphic form	Visual appearance	size (μm)
α	Fragile, transparent platelets	5
β'	Tiny delicate needles	1
β	Large coarse crystals with clumping	25–50 (grow to 100)

TABLE 4-16

Crystal Form Tendency of Fats and Oils

β type	β' type
Coconut oil	Cottonseed oil
Corn oil	Herring oil
Olive oil	Menhaden oil
Lard	Milk fat
Palm kernel oil	Palm oil
Peanut oil	Rapeseed oil
Safflowerseed oil	Tallow
Sesame seed oil	Whale oil
Sunflowerseed oil	

Diglycerides exhibit polymorphism and the β' and β forms are most common. The 2-monoglycerides are free of polymorphism, while 1-monoglycerides can exist in three or four forms.

Characteristics of some polymorphic forms are given in Table 4-15. The β' crystals are typical of randomized fats, rearranged lard, tallow, and partially hydrogenated cottonseed oil. In Table 4-16 fats and oils are classified according to the type of polymorphic crystallization that tends to predominate.

D. Implications of Polymorphism in Use of Fats

1. SHORTENING

The quality of shortenings depend on (a) incorporated air, (b) plasticity and consistency, and (c) solid-liquid ratio. These physical characteristics in turn depend on the polymorphic forms of the fats used and the methods of preparation. Plasticity and consistency as well as solid-liquid ratio depend on the melting range. Proper tempering is required to form the mixed crystals required for a broad melting range [5].

Polymorphs differ in their abilities to incorporate air during plasticizing (the whipping of air or nitrogen into a fat during the crystallization stage to give whiter, creamier, smoother, and more uniform shortenings). The β' crystals assist in the incorporation of an abundant quantity of very small air bubbles, while β crystals result in incorporation of a small amount of large bubbles. Forms with double or triple chain length structures, such as β-2 or -3, or β'-2 or -3, have intermediate abilities to incorporate air. The air-incorporating capacity affects the performance of shortenings in applications involving "creaming."

Air incorporation in batters is similar to that during plasticizing. Since the volume, texture, and tenderness of baked products are essentially a function of the size and number of air bubbles in the batter, β' fats are best for use in cakes and also in icings, while β-type fats are usually wholly unsatisfactory.

Good air-incorporation properties can be obtained from random fats, such as cottonseed oil, soybean oil, or tallow. However some modification is necessary since natural vegetable fats at room temperature have crystalline solid contents that are insufficient for good performance and tallow has a solids content that is too great. Lard has too much OPS (oleo-palmito-stearin) to function properly as a plastic fat but this can be corrected by interesterification.

An adequate solids content of vegetable fats is provided by partial hydrogenation in a manner that retains the molecular heterogeneity needed for β' crystals. Tallow can be destearinized and lightly hydrogenated to give improved physical properties and improved flavor stability. Greatly improved bakery qualities for lard can be achieved by destearinization, rearrangement (interesterification), or partial hydrogenation after rearrangement.

Adding flakes of hydrogenated fats aids in creaming performance. Cottonseed oil flakes and tallow flakes perform best in shortenings since they encourage formation of β' crystals. Fats to which flakes have been added exhibit polymorphic forms more nearly like those of the flakes than the original fat. Lard is an exception to this, although the addition of flakes of rearranged lard, tallow, or cottonseed oil tends to slow the transformation of lard to its characteristic β form.

2. MARGARINES

Margarines are produced for table spreads or bakery use from a mixture of fats blended to provide desired properties. A water-in-oil emulsion of the fat is fed into a scraped-surface heat exchanger to rapidly promote partial solidification, then into a crystallizer to complete the crystallization process in a manner yielding the desired plastic properties. Oils that have been hydrogenated to two or three different degrees of hardness are blended to provide SFI values appropriate to the use. Soybean oil, because of its availability and relatively low cost, is frequently used for this purpose. Hydrogenated cottonseed oil, because of its preference for crystallization in the β' form, is often blended with soybean oil. This helps achieve a product which is sufficiently firm to be easily handled and formed and which "sets up" rapidly upon standing. A SFI of 15-20 at 38°C is needed when margarine is used in special applications, such as the manufacture of Danish or puff pastry. In these instances the margarine must not soften unduly when it is rolled into the dough.

3. ENROBING FATS

Cocoa butter has a short melting range at mouth temperature, which makes it a very acceptable confection fat. The composition of the glycerides provides the melting characteristic of the fat; however, for proper results solidification must be carefully controlled to obtain the desired size of crystal and polymorphic form. Cocoa butter has approximately 80% disaturated triglycerides made up of 20% SOS, 55% POS, and 5% POP, where S is stearic, O is oleic, and P is palmitic. The dominant glyceride, POS, exists as the α-2, β'-2, and β-3 polymorphs with the latter melting at 35.5°C. The β-3 form must be achieved by proper tempering because undertempering eventually results in chocolate "bloom" and overtempering results in coarse texture and a dull appearance. Fat bloom is characterized by white spots or a grey surface sheen, and it develops when improperly tempered chocolate is stored at temperatures above normal. Proper tempering requires the formation of stable β-3 crystals produced in small size to provide good structure and gloss to chocolate. Mechanical working of the fat at a temperature just below the β melting point is an effective and rapid tempering technique.

Cocoa butter substitutes or extenders should have glycerides nearly identical to those in cocoa butter and should have no liquid fat, and the polymorphic behavior should resemble that of cocoa butter. Relatively acceptable extenders have been made from cottonseed oil fractions, tallow fractions, fractions derived from inter-esterification of cottonseed oil flakes with olive oils, and hydrogenated coconut or palm kernel oils [8].

4. TEMPERING

Newly processed fats frequently are not in the polymorphic form and physical state in which they are most useful. A process known as "tempering" permits transformation to the proper polymorphic form. During crystallization the heat of transformation must be removed to avoid melting and a later conversion into large

β crystals. Tempering at different temperatures allows the formation of different sets of mixed crystals, giving melting over a wide range of temperature.

The rates at which polymorphic transformations occur depend on the number of polymorphic forms into which the fats can change. Those fats with a relatively limited number of different types of triglyceride molecules exhibit few polymorphic forms and tend to change rapidly into the β form. Fats such as lard flakes, soybean oil flakes, and cocoa butter behave in this manner. Fats with greater randomness of distribution of fatty acids in the triglyceride exhibit more polymorphic forms and transform slowly from one form to another. For example, killing lard, ordinary lard, or hydrogenated lard may pass through the sequence $\alpha \rightarrow \beta'\text{-}2 \rightarrow \beta$, while lard with a high iodine value, rearranged lard flakes, tallow flakes, or cottonseed oil flakes can go through the sequence $\alpha \rightarrow \beta' \rightarrow \beta'\text{-}2 \rightarrow \beta$. The more randomized fats, such as rearranged lard, tallow, partly hydrogenated soybean oil, or partly hydrogenated cottonseed oil, usually go from a $\alpha \rightarrow \beta' \rightarrow \beta'\text{-}2$ but they seldom form β crystals.

Tempering time can be reduced by mixing a fat at a temperature just below the melting point of its most stable form. Initial gross crystallization of the fat mass is followed by agitation and controlled removal of heat to induce rapid formation of additional small crystals and to hasten transformation to the most stable form. The β' form is most stable for hydrogenated vegetable oils, the $\beta'\text{-}2$ form for interesterified lard used in shortening applications, and the $\beta\text{-}3$ form for cocoa butter or its substitutes. Quick tempering permits movement of finished fats from the plant within 24 hr as compared to the 3-10 days needed for conventional tempering procedures.

VI. CHEMICAL PROPERTIES AND REACTIONS

A. Stability and its Characterization

Stability refers to the capability of a fat, oil, or fatty food to maintain a fresh taste and odor during storage and use. It is related to composition of the lipid moiety, the nature and degree of stress on the system, the presence or absence of prooxidants or antioxidants, and the effectiveness of packaging. Fats with substantial unsaturation in the fatty acids are usually unstable or moderately unstable and foods containing them reflect this instability. Vegetable oils usually tend to be more stable than some of the animal fats, such as lard, even though the total unsaturation of the vegetable oils may be greater. This can occur because natural antioxidants are usually present in the vegetable oils.

A challenge has long existed to develop methods which are accelerated in time of execution but which accurately portray the length of time a fat or food remains palatable under conditions encountered during marketing. Most of these methods involve elevation of temperature with or without increased exposure to oxygen, and a suitable objective method of evaluation. Some methods for evaluating the quality of fats are discussed below.

4. LIPIDS

1. ACTIVE OXYGEN METHOD

The active oxygen method (AOM) involves bubbling air at a controlled rate through a tube of fat maintained at 100°C. Rancidity is determined by sniffing the effluent air periodically. Correlations have been made between the development of peroxides and the first presence of odors typifying rancidity. A trained observer can detect rancidity in lard at a peroxide value of about 20; in hydrogenated oils at a value of 70; and in vegetable oils, such as cottonseed and soybean, at a value of 100. Greater objectivity is obtained by determining peroxide values periodically and preparing a plot of time vs peroxide value. The time in hours to obtain the endpoint peroxide value noted above is then interpolated and recorded. This method is widely used to determine the initial stability of a fat or oil with or without the addition of antioxidants. However, attempts to correlate AOM values with the keeping times of fats or foods held under normal storage generally have been unsuccessful.

2. OVEN STABILITY METHOD

The oven stability method, frequently called the Schaal oven test, involves holding the fat or food in a clean glass jar in an oven at 65°C. Samples are sniffed at intervals, usually days, to determine the onset of rancidity. Peroxide values of the fat or oil can be determined if desired but this method usually relies on sensory detection of a rancid odor.

3. OXYGEN BOMB TEST

The oxygen bomb test involves placement of a sample in a bomblike device, the addition of a fixed amount of oxygen, and the monitoring of pressure at constant temperature. The time at which oxygen uptake accelerates, as determined by a decrease in pressure, corresponds to the stability of the sample. This method is useful for measuring the relative effectiveness of antioxidants in prolonging the keeping time of such foods as potato chips.

4. CARBONYL DETERMINATIONS

Extraction of lipids and measurement of carbonyl compounds which have formed provides an indication of the stability of fats in some foods, but the results are undependable in systems containing components which react readily with aldehydes. The method is further complicated by different responses of aldehydes formed from different fats or oils, and by different responses occasioned by the kind of hydroperoxide scission reaction involved. In addition to peroxides, measurements of saturated aldehydes, enals, dienals, and dialdehydes must be made to provide a profile of the oxidative state of the lipid or the food in which it occurs.

Malonaldehyde is measured in some systems since it, or its precursor, develops in meat and fish systems in proportion to the elapsed time for incipient rancidity and to the intensity of rancid odor. This method is also subject to many errors, especially in dry systems, since malonaldehyde reacts readily with free amino groups during nonenzymic browning.

5. OTHER METHODS

Determination of weight gained due to oxygen absorption and reaction has been used to measure stability of some fats or oils. Measurements of oxygen uptake by manometric techniques are useful for some systems, especially for relating the amount of oxygen absorbed to other measurable criteria such as peroxide value, diene conjugation, or the amount of carbonyl compounds. The spectrophotometric analysis of conjugated double bonds reflects early changes during oxidation of dienes, trienes, and other polyunsaturated fatty acids.

B. Lipolysis

The ester linkages of lipids are subject to hydrolysis resulting from enzymes, from thermal stress, or from chemical action. These reactions are collectively known as lipolysis, lipolytic rancidity, or hydrolytic rancidity.

Lipolysis of milkfat has been studied intensively because of the ease with which it occurs in raw milk and its importance to the flavors of various milk products. The common notion that butyric acid is responsible for the flavor of rancid milk has been disproved. All of the even-numbered fatty acids from C_4 to C_{12} contribute to rancid flavor, with no single acid having a dominant influence [23,24].

Lipolysis, regardless of the cause, seriously degrades the quality of cooking and frying fats. As a result of lipolysis, the smoke point [temperature at which vapor (smoke) can be seen in a beam of light over the surface of a heated fat] is severely depressed and fried foods, such as fried cakes and doughnuts, exhibit cracked surfaces, increased tendency to brown, and increased fat absorption. Small amounts of free fatty acids lower the smoke point to objectionable levels (see Table 4-17).

Free fatty acids that develop during storage and processing of oil seeds and animal tissues must be removed by refining processes and deodorization to yield fats and oils of acceptable quality. The resulting yield and cost of processing are of economic importance.

TABLE 4-17

Relation between Smoke Point and
Free Fatty Acid Content of Cottonseed Oil

FFA (%)	Smoke point (°F)
0.01	450
1.0	320
10.0	260
100.0	200

C. Autoxidation

Fats also can become rancid as a consequence of oxidation and this "oxidative rancidity" is a major cause of food deterioration. Lipolytic rancidity usually poses
less of a flavor problem than oxidative rancidity since the former develops off
flavors only in those fats which contain short-chain fatty acids (less than C_{12}).

Energy in the form of heat, light, or ionizing radiation or catalysis by prooxidant metals or enzymes contribute to the oxidation process. Chemical oxidants,
when present, also oxidize lipids.

1. MECHANISMS OF OXIDATION

The reaction of oxygen with unsaturated fatty acids in lipids constitutes the major
means by which lipids or lipid-containing foods deteriorate, Oxidation of fat is
frequently alluded to as autoxidation because the rate of oxidation increases as the
reaction proceeds. Unless mediated by other oxidants or enzyme systems, oxidation proceeds through a free-radical chain reaction mechanism involving three
stages: (1) initiation, formation of free radicals; (2) propagation, free-radical
chain reaction; and (3) termination, formation of nonradical products. Hydroperoxides are the major initial reaction products of fatty acids with oxygen. Subsequent reactions control both the rate of reaction and the nature of products
formed. In the initiation stage an unsaturated hydrocarbon loses a hydrogen to
form a radical, $RH \rightarrow R\cdot + H\cdot$, and oxygen adds at the double bond to form a diradical:

$$
\begin{array}{cc}
\overset{\text{H H}}{\underset{\text{| |}}{R-C=C-R'}} + O_2 \longrightarrow & \overset{\text{H H}}{\underset{\substack{| | \\ \cdot \ | \\ O-O\cdot}}{R-C-C-R'}}
\end{array}
$$

Alternatively, oxygen in the singlet state can apparently interpose between a labile
hydrogen to form a hydroperoxide directly ($RH + O_2 \rightarrow ROOH$). The latter may be
a special case and is referred to here only briefly. Direct formation of hydroperoxides is not necessarily a free-radical chain mechanism, although it can initiate chain processes.

During propagation, the chain reaction is continued by $R\cdot + O_2 \rightarrow ROO\cdot$ and
$ROO\cdot + RH \rightarrow ROOH + R\cdot$ to form peroxy radicals, hydroperoxides, and new hydrocarbon radicals. The new radical formed then contributes to the chain by reacting
with another oxygen molecule.

When two radicals interact, termination occurs:

$R\cdot + R\cdot \rightarrow RR$

$ROO\cdot + ROO\cdot \rightarrow ROOR + O_2$

$RO\cdot + R\cdot \rightarrow ROR$

$ROO\cdot + R\cdot \rightarrow ROOR$

$2 RO\cdot + 2 ROO\cdot \rightarrow 2 ROOR + O_2$

When no radicals are available for further reaction with oxygen, it is necessary for a new initiation reaction to occur if oxidation is to continue.

The initiation reaction is a subject of great interest since it relates both to the site of attack and to the energy requirement. The energy requirement for radical production by rupture of a CH bond is about 80 kcal. Less energy is necessary for addition of oxygen to form a diradical at the double bond, but both requirements appear to be so excessive that numerous energy-reducing postulates exist for involvement of metal activation, enzyme catalysis, or photooxidation.

The hydrogen α to the double bond is most labile because of the electron distribution at the double bond. This hydrogen is therefore readily abstracted by a peroxy radical in the propagation stage. Thus, the primary product of autoxidation is a secondary hydroperoxide located on a carbon α to a double bond.

Initiation by reaction at the double bond to form a diradical may be portrayed as:

1. $-CH_2-CH=CH-CH_2- + O_2 \longrightarrow -CH_2-CH-CH(OO\cdot)-CH_2-$

2. $-CH_2-CH-CH(OO\cdot)-CH_2- \qquad -CH_2-CH-CH(OOH)-CH_2-$
    $\qquad +$ $\longrightarrow$ $\qquad +$
    $-CH_2-CH=CH-CH_2- \qquad\qquad -CH_2-CH=CH-CH-$

3. $-CH_2-CH-CH(OOH)-CH_2 \qquad -CH_2-CH_2-CH(OOH)-CH_2$
    $\qquad + \qquad \longrightarrow \qquad +$
    $-CH_2-CH=CH-CH_2- \qquad\qquad -CH_2-CH=CH-CH-$

Each initiation process thus produces two free radicals, each of which participate in the chain reaction mechanism.

Oxygen normally exists in a triplet state but it has been established that electrophilic singlet oxygen reacts directly with olefinic molecules. Since RH and ROOH are in singlet states, singlet oxygen could react without change of spin and with conservation of energy. Conversion of oxygen to the singlet state can be accomplished by photosensitization in the presence of suitable sensitizers, such as chlorophyll, or possibly by the heme pigments myoglobin or hemoglobin, or by their derivatives. Thus, trace amounts of pigments or other sensitizers may be responsible for the initial formation of hydroperoxides in some systems.

2. HYDROPEROXIDE DECOMPOSITION

Hydroperoxides are readily decomposed by high-energy radiation, thermal energy, metal catalysis, or enzyme activity, with the means depending on the system in which they exist. Hydroperoxides decompose to form additional radicals which add to the chain process. This proliferation of radicals causes acceleration of oxidation without requiring new initiation events.

When the concentration of hydroperoxide is low, decomposition can occur as $ROOH \rightarrow RO\cdot + \cdot OH$, a monomolecular decomposition. When the concentration of hydroperoxide is high, decomposition can occur as $2\ ROOH \rightarrow RO\cdot + ROO\cdot + H_2O$, a bimolecular decomposition. The $RO\cdot$ radicals can participate in the chain propagation stage, although the more energetic $ROO\cdot$ radicals predominate.

Hydroperoxides tend to associate by hydrogen bonding when temperatures are low or when the concentration is high.

$$
\begin{array}{c}
\text{R'} \\
| \\
\text{R--C--O--OH} \\
| \quad \cdot \quad \cdot \\
\text{H} \; : \; : \; \text{H} \\
\cdot \quad \cdot \quad | \\
\text{HO--O--C--R} \\
| \\
\text{R'}
\end{array}
$$

Metallic prooxidants contribute to formation of additional radicals by acting as hydroperoxide decomposers. A metal, capable of existing in two valence states, functions typically as:

$$
\begin{array}{ll}
M^+ + ROOH \longrightarrow RO\cdot + {}^-OH + M^{2+}: & \text{The reduced metal ion is oxidized} \\
M^{2+} + ROOH \longrightarrow ROO\cdot + H^+ + M^+: & \text{The oxidized metal ion is reduced} \\
\hline
2\,ROOH \longrightarrow RO\cdot + ROO\cdot + H_2O: & \text{Net reaction}
\end{array}
$$

In a system containing multivalent metal ions, such as Cu^+ and Cu^{2+} or Fe^{2+} and Fe^{3+}, the hydroperoxides decompose readily with formation of both $RO\cdot$ and $ROO\cdot$ radicals as the metal ions undergo oxidation–reduction.

Heme compounds containing Fe have been implicated as oxidation catalysts either as direct initiators of peroxidation or as peroxide decomposers. A heme concentration exists however at which they actually exert an antioxidant effect, e.g., when heme compounds are present at two to four times the amount most effective for oxidation, no oxidation occurs. In this instance, stable complexes of lipid peroxides and heme compounds apparently form and these presumably inhibit oxidation.

When a hydroperoxide decomposes to form $RO\cdot$ radicals, these in turn are capable of a series of reactions leading to several products which can be isolated from oxidizing lipid systems [3]. The following reactions are apparently involved:

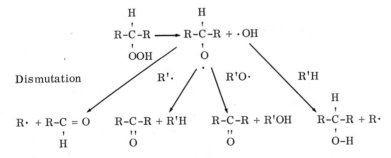

Some of these products are radicals and they are capable of continuing in the chain propagation process. Others, such as the hydroxy acids, keto acids, and aldehydes, are commonly found in oxidizing lipid systems. The aldehydes, many of which are short chain, and the short-chain acids derived by further oxidation of these aldehydes, are largely responsible for the off flavors and odors characteristic of stale or rancid foods.

3. OXIDATION OF MONOENOIC ACIDS

Oxidation of lipids with monoene or polyene structures results in formation of a number of isomeric hydroperoxides. When a monoene is involved, abstraction of hydrogen during the initiation stage occurs from either of the carbons α to the double bond. Thus, two radicals are possible, each of which can assume two forms through resonance. Addition of oxygen at each radical site followed by the addition of a hydrogen free radical results in hydroperoxides at four different positions, two at the carbons involved in the original double bond and two at the α carbons. Formation of the four hydroperoxides in essentially equal amounts has been demonstrated when oleic acid or its esters are oxidized.

Details of the formation of hydroperoxides from oleic acid are illustrated below:

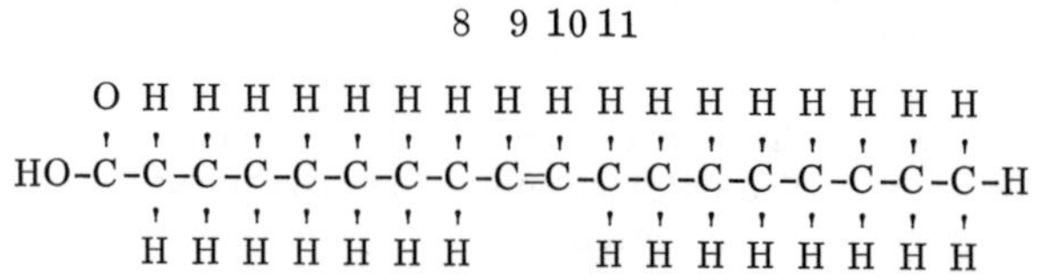

$$
\begin{array}{c}
8\ \ \ 9\ 10\ 11 \\[4pt]
\text{O H H H H H H H H H H H H H H H H H} \\
\text{| | | | | | | | | | | | | | | | | |} \\
\text{HO-C-C-C-C-C-C-C-C-C=C-C-C-C-C-C-C-C-C-H} \\
\text{| | | | | | | | | | | | | | |} \\
\text{H H H H H H H   H H H H H H H H}
\end{array}
$$

If H is abstracted from carbon 8 then two radicals (a) and (b) are possible at C_8 and C_{10}.

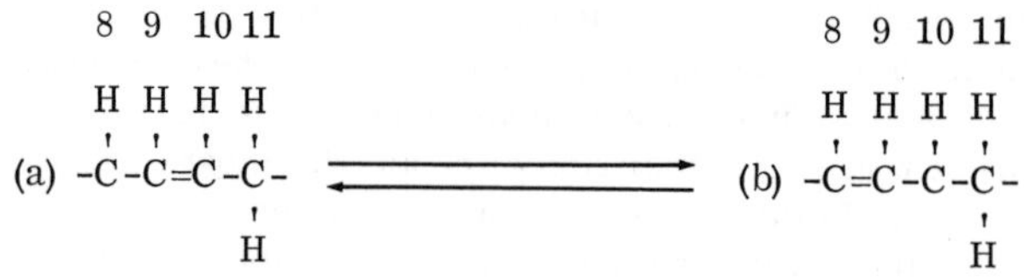

$$
\begin{array}{ccc}
\ \ 8\ \ 9\ \ 10\ 11 & & \ \ 8\ \ 9\ \ 10\ 11 \\[4pt]
\text{H H H H} & & \text{H H H H} \\
\text{| | | |} & & \text{| | | |} \\
\text{(a) -C-C=C-C-} & \longleftrightarrow & \text{(b) -C=C-C-C-} \\
\text{|} & & \text{|} \\
\text{H} & & \text{H}
\end{array}
$$

If H is abstracted from carbon 11 then two radicals (c) and (d) are possible at C_{11} and C_9.

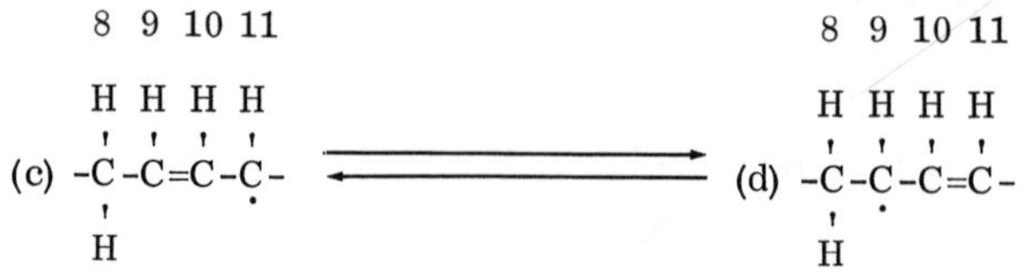

$$
\begin{array}{ccc}
\ \ 8\ \ 9\ \ 10\ 11 & & \ \ 8\ \ 9\ \ 10\ 11 \\[4pt]
\text{H H H H} & & \text{H H H H} \\
\text{| | | |} & & \text{| | | |} \\
\text{(c) -C-C=C-C-} & \longleftrightarrow & \text{(d) -C-C-C=C-} \\
\text{|} \ \ \ \ \ \cdot & & \text{|} \ \ \ \ \ \cdot \\
\text{H} & & \text{H}
\end{array}
$$

Addition of oxygen forms peroxy radicals at C_8, C_{10}, C_{11}, and C_9 to form structures (e), (f), (g), and (h) respectively.

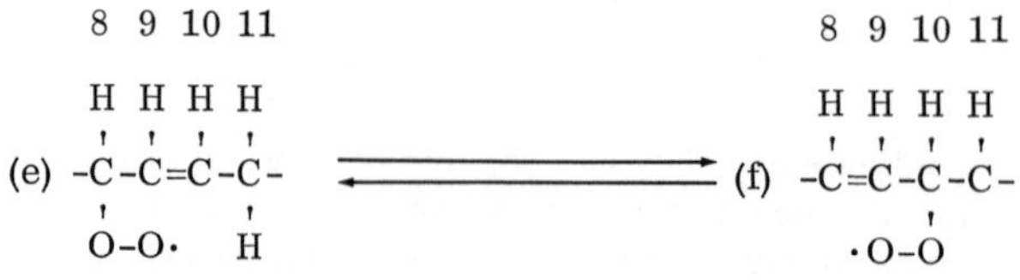

$$
\begin{array}{ccc}
\ \ 8\ \ 9\ \ 10\ 11 & & \ \ 8\ \ 9\ \ 10\ 11 \\[4pt]
\text{H H H H} & & \text{H H H H} \\
\text{| | | |} & & \text{| | | |} \\
\text{(e) -C-C=C-C-} & \longleftrightarrow & \text{(f) -C=C-C-C-} \\
\text{|} \ \ \ \ \ \ \ \ \text{|} & & \ \ \ \ \ \ \ \ \text{|} \\
\text{O-O}\cdot \ \ \ \text{H} & & \cdot\text{O-O}
\end{array}
$$

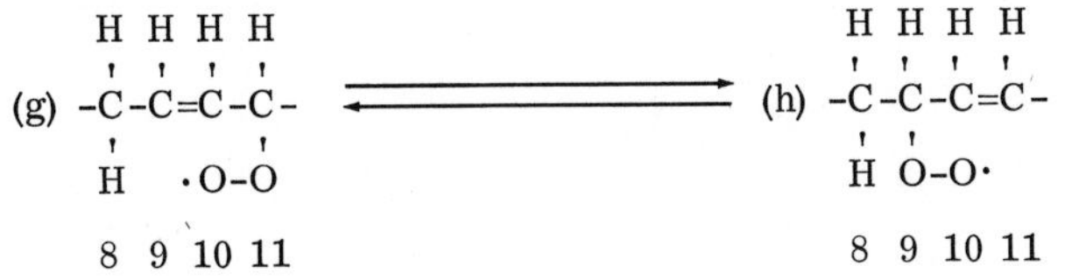

```
          H H H H                                      H H H H
          | | | |                                      | | | |
    (g) -C-C=C-C-     ⇌        (h) -C-C-C=C-
          |   |                                        |   |
          H  ·O-O                                      H  O-O·

     8  9  10 11                                    8  9  10 11
```

Each peroxy radical can abstract H· from an unoxidized molecule to form the four isomeric hydroperoxides (i), (j), (k), and (l).

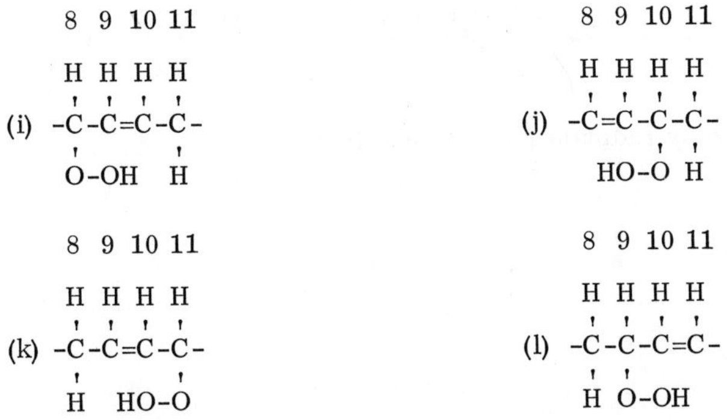

```
    8  9  10 11                                  8  9  10 11

       H H H H                                     H H H H
       | | | |                                     | | | |
 (i) -C-C=C-C-                           (j) -C=C-C-C-
       |       |                                       |   |
       O-OH   H                                      HO-O  H


    8  9  10 11                                  8  9  10 11

       H H H H                                     H H H H
       | | | |                                     | | | |
 (k) -C-C=C-C-                           (l) -C-C-C=C-
       |     |                                       |   |
       H   HO-O                                     H  O-OH
```

The geometry of a double bond is affected by the shift in its location during resonance. In almost all instances, a shift in location of a double bond changes the configuration from cis to trans.

4. OXIDATION OF POLYENOIC ACIDS

Oxidation of polyenes is initiated more readily and proceeds more rapidly than oxidation of monoenes. The greater the number of double bonds, the greater the tendency to oxidize. This is particularly true of most natural lipid molecules since they have 1,4-pentadiene structures: $R-C=C-C-C=C-R$. The methylene group, having contiguous double bonds on both sides, is vulnerable to attack by a peroxy radical. This results in abstraction of hydrogen and creation of a radical at the methylene carbon. The radical thus formed is unstable, and the electrons redistribute to form a conjugated double-bond system. This results in a radical at either the 1 or the 5 carbon of the original pentadiene system.

Details of the formation of hydroperoxides from linoleic acid are illustrated below:

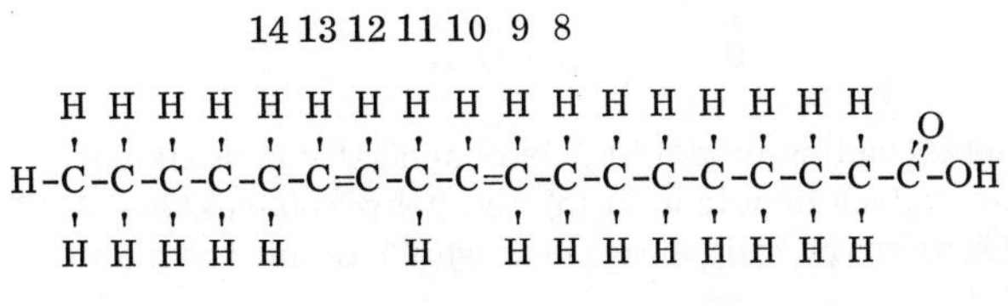

```
               14 13 12 11 10  9  8

    H H H H H H H H H H H H H H H H H    O
    | | | | | | | | | | | | | | | | |   ||
  H-C-C-C-C-C-C=C-C-C=C-C-C-C-C-C-C-C-C-OH
    | | | | |       |   | | | | | | | |
    H H H H H       H   H H H H H H H H
```

Hydrogen is abstracted from C-11 to form three isomeric radicals (a), (b), and (c):

```
    14 13 12 11 9  8

    H H H H H H H
    ' ' ' ' ' ' '
   -C-C=C-C-C=C-C-   (a)
    '         .         '
    H                   H
```

```
       14 13 12 11 10 9  8                      14 13 12 11 10 9  8

       H H H H H H H                            H H H H H H H
       ' ' ' ' ' ' '                            ' ' ' ' ' ' '
  (b) -C-C-C=C-C=C-C-                          -C-C=C-C=C-C-C-   (c)
       '  .        '                            '         .  '
       H           H                            H            H
```

Addition of oxygen forms peroxy radicals (d), (e), and (f):

```
     12 11    9

    H H H H H H H
    ' ' ' ' ' ' '
   -C-C=C-C-C=C-C-   (d)
    '         '    '
    H        O-O·   H
```

```
      13    11   9                         12    10 9

     H H H H H H H                        H H H H H H H
     ' ' ' ' ' ' '                        ' ' ' ' ' ' '
 (e) -C-C-C=C-C=C-C-                      -C-C=C-C=C-C-C-   (f)
     '  '        '                        '         '  '
     H O-O·       H                       H        ·O-O H
```

Each peroxy radical can abstract a H· from an unoxidized molecule to form three isomeric hydroperoxides (g), (h), and (i):

```
     12 11    9

    H H H H H H H
    ' ' ' ' ' ' '
   -C-C=C-C-C=C-C-   (g)
    '         '    '
    H        O-OH   H
```

```
       13    11   9                         12    10 9

      H H H H H H H                        H H H H H H H
      ' ' ' ' ' ' '                        ' ' ' ' ' ' '
  (h) -C-C-C=C-C=C-C-                      -C-C=C-C=C-C-C-   (i)
      '  '        '                        '         '  '
      H O-OH       H                       H        HO-O H
```

The 11-hydroperoxido-9,12-octadecadienoic acid (g) is essentially nonexistent, while 13-hydroperoxido-9,11-octadecadienoic acid (h) and 9-hydroperoxido-10,12-octadecadienoic acid (i) are the primary hydroperoxides which result from auto-oxidation of linoleic acid.

A similar sequence of events occurs during oxidation of linolenic, arachidonic, or other polyenes. When the number of double bonds exceeds two, it is possible to form hydroperoxide systems containing conjugated double bonds, as in the diene system, but isolated from other double bonds. This can occur in linolenic acid.

5. OXIDATION OF SATURATED ACIDS

Saturated fatty acids oxidize only when exposed to conditions of severe stress. When oxidation does occur, the hydroperoxide group generally forms on the carbon β to the carboxyl or ester group. The hydroperoxide then changes to a keto group, giving rise to a β keto acid.

6. OXIDATION OF CONJUGATED DOUBLE-BOND SYSTEMS

Conjugated double-bond systems oxidize with considerable ease by oxidation of the terminal carbons in the conjugated system. Thus a conjugated triene oxidizes 1,6, although it is possible to have 1,4 and 1,2 oxidation in the same system.

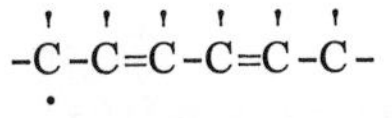

$$-\overset{\cdot}{\underset{\cdot}{C}}-C=C-C=C-C-$$

or

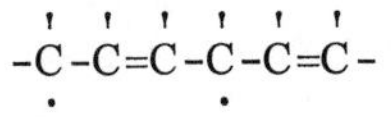

$$-\overset{\cdot}{\underset{\cdot}{C}}-C=C-\overset{\cdot}{\underset{\cdot}{C}}-C=C-$$

or

$$-\overset{\cdot}{\underset{\cdot}{C}}-C-C=C-C=C-$$

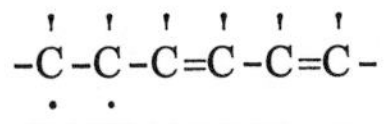

These reactive radical species then form polyperoxides, cyclic peroxides, and peroxide polymers to further complicate the oxidation picture.

7. ALDEHYDES AS SECONDARY OXIDATION PRODUCTS

The scission and dismutation reactions shown earlier yield compounds that are responsible for off flavors and odors. The dominant aldehydes isolated from oxidized fats apparently arise from oleate or linoleate hydroperoxides by these reactions. Typical aldehydes arising from oleate hydroperoxides are listed below:

8-Hydroperoxide

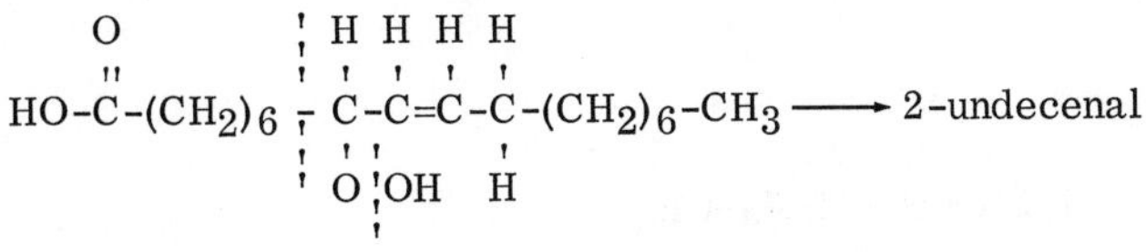

$$
\underset{\text{HO-C-(CH}_2)_6}{\overset{\text{O}}{\overset{\|}{}}} \text{-} \underset{\overset{\|}{\text{O}} \overset{}{\text{OH}}}{\overset{\text{H H H H}}{\text{C-C=C-C-(CH}_2)_6\text{-CH}_3}} \longrightarrow \text{2-undecenal}
$$

9-Hydroperoxide

$$\text{HO-}\overset{\text{O}}{\overset{\|}{\text{C}}}\text{-(CH}_2)_6\text{-}\underset{\underset{\text{H}}{|}}{\overset{\overset{\text{H}}{|}}{\text{C}}}\text{-}\underset{\underset{\text{O}}{|}}{\overset{\overset{\text{H}}{|}}{\text{C}}}\text{-}\underset{\underset{\text{OH}}{|}}{\overset{\overset{\text{H}}{|}}{\text{C}}}\text{=}\overset{\overset{\text{H}}{|}}{\text{C}}\text{-(CH}_2)_6\text{-CH}_3 \longrightarrow \text{2-decenal}$$

10-Hydroperoxide

$$\text{HO-}\overset{\text{O}}{\overset{\|}{\text{C}}}\text{-(CH}_2)_6\text{-}\overset{\overset{\text{H}}{|}}{\text{C}}\text{=}\underset{\underset{\text{HO}}{|}}{\overset{\overset{\text{H}}{|}}{\text{C}}}\text{-}\underset{\underset{\text{O}}{|}}{\overset{\overset{\text{H}}{|}}{\text{C}}}\text{-}\underset{\underset{\text{H}}{|}}{\overset{\overset{\text{H}}{|}}{\text{C}}}\text{-(CH}_2)_6\text{-CH}_3 \longrightarrow \text{nonanal}$$

11-Hydroperoxide

$$\text{HO-}\overset{\text{O}}{\overset{\|}{\text{C}}}\text{-(CH}_2)_6\text{-}\underset{\underset{\text{H}}{|}}{\overset{\overset{\text{H}}{|}}{\text{C}}}\text{-}\overset{\overset{\text{H}}{|}}{\text{C}}\text{=}\underset{\underset{\text{O}}{|}}{\overset{\overset{\text{H}}{|}}{\text{C}}}\text{-}\underset{\underset{\text{OH}}{|}}{\overset{\overset{\text{H}}{|}}{\text{C}}}\text{-(CH}_2)_6\text{-CH}_3 \longrightarrow \text{octanal}$$

Scission of the bond between two carbons, one of which possesses a hydroperoxide group, may result in aldehyde formation at each carbon. The fragment attached to the carboxyl group, as such, or esterified to glycerol is relatively nonvolatile, while the other fragment is more volatile and is readily identifiable since it has only the one functional group.

It is apparent that scission of carbon bonds adjacent to an alkoxy radical may occur at either of two points.

$$\underset{\underset{\text{'H' H \quad H}}{}}{\text{R}\overset{\overset{\cdot}{\text{O}}}{|}\text{C}\text{-}\text{C}\text{=}\text{C-R'}}$$

A B

The two section locations are designated types A and B. In oleate hydroperoxides, type A scission at the 8, 9, 10, or 11 position results in a volatile fraction of C_{10} and C_{11} enals, while type B scission yields C_8 and C_9 alkanals. The B-type scission seems to predominate at moderate temperatures, while higher temperatures or other stresses increase the amount of type A scission. This trend is evident from the data in Table 4-18.

The large C_9 enal fraction can be explained by a B-type scission of the 9-OOH of linoleate as follows:

$$\text{HO-}\overset{\text{O}}{\overset{\|}{\text{C}}}\text{-(CH}_2)_7\text{-}\underset{\underset{\text{OOH}}{|}}{\text{CH}}\text{-CH=CH-CH=CH-(CH}_2)_4\text{-CH}_3$$

TABLE 4-18

Monocarbonyl Aldehydes from Autoxidized Trilinolein Given
Various Treatments[a]

	Fuller's earth (acid washed) 85°C		Cupric stearate 85°C	Heated	
	PV 50	PV 180	PV 50	165°C PV 50	215°C PV 180
Alkanals (%)[b]					
C_5	12	10	5	2	30
C_6	53	64	23	9	19
Enals (%)					
C_6			5	8	4
C_7	1		12	15	16
C_8	1		1		1
C_9	31	23		6	4
Dienals (%)					
C_9					
C_{10}			54	60	43

[a]Reprinted from Ref. [26] by courtesy of the American Oil Chemists' Society.
  PV is peroxide value.
[b]Alkanals from type A scission and enals from type B scission.

$$HO-\overset{O}{\overset{\|}{C}}-(CH_2)_7-\overset{\cdot}{C}H\!\overset{\cdot}{\vert}CH=CH-CH=CH-(CH_2)_4-CH_3$$
$$\overset{\cdot}{O}\ \cdot OH$$

$$HO-\overset{O}{\overset{\|}{C}}-(CH_2)_7-\overset{H}{\underset{\|}{\overset{\vert}{C}}}\ +\ \cdot CH=CH-CH-CH-(CH_2)_4-CH_3$$
$$+ \cdot OH$$
$$HOCH=CH-CH=CH-(CH_2)_4-CH_3$$
$$\overset{H}{\overset{\vert}{}}$$
$$O=\overset{}{C}-CH=CH-CH_2-(CH_2)_4-CH_3$$

8. OTHER SECONDARY OXIDATION PRODUCTS

The number of aldehydes, alcohols, and acids found in an oxidizing system is compounded by secondary and tertiary oxidations in the system. The primary alcohols do not oxidize appreciably at ambient temperatures but substantial conversion to the corresponding acids occurs at temperature above 50°C.

$$R\text{-}CH_2\text{-}OH \xrightarrow{R'OO\cdot} R'OOH + R\text{-}\overset{\cdot}{C}H\text{-}OH \xrightarrow{O_2} \underset{OO\cdot}{R\text{-}CH\text{-}OH}$$

$$R\text{-}\underset{OO\cdot}{CH\text{-}OH} \xrightarrow{R'H} R'\cdot + R\text{-}\underset{OOH}{CH\text{-}OH} \longrightarrow R\text{-}\underset{O}{\overset{\|}{C}}\text{-}OH + H_2O$$

Secondary alcohols convert to the corresponding ketone.

$$H_3C\text{-}(CH_2)_4\text{-}CH(OH)\text{-}CH=CH_2 \longrightarrow H_3C\text{-}(CH_2)_4\text{-}\underset{O}{\overset{\|}{C}}\text{-}CH=CH_2$$

$$\text{1-Octene-3-ol} \qquad\qquad\qquad \text{1-Octene-3-one}$$

Aldehydes presumably are converted to acids by the following mechanism:

$$R\text{-}CHO \xrightarrow{\text{Initiator}} R\text{-}\overset{O}{\overset{\|}{C}}\cdot$$

$$R\text{-}\overset{O}{\overset{\|}{C}}\cdot + O_2 \longrightarrow R\text{-}\overset{O}{\overset{\|}{C}}\text{-}OO\cdot$$

$$R\text{-}\overset{O}{\overset{\|}{C}}\text{-}OO\cdot + R\text{-}CHO \longrightarrow R\text{-}\overset{O}{\overset{\|}{C}}\text{-}OOH + R\text{-}\overset{O}{\overset{\|}{C}}\cdot$$

$$R\text{-}\overset{O}{\overset{\|}{C}}\text{-}OOH + R\text{-}CHO \longrightarrow R\text{-}\overset{O}{\overset{\|}{C}}\text{-}O\text{-}O\text{-}\underset{OH}{CH\text{-}R}$$

$$R\text{-}\overset{O}{\overset{\|}{C}}\text{-}O\text{-}O\text{-}CH(OH)\text{-}R \longrightarrow 2\ R\overset{O}{\overset{\|}{C}}\text{-}OH$$

If the aldehydes are enals or dienals, these may oxidize further to provide yet shorter chain compounds.

9. MALONALDEHYDE

The compound malonaldehyde readily reacts with thiobarbituric acid to form a characteristic pink color. The thiobarbituric acid (TBA) number is related to the development of rancid flavors, particularly in cooked meats, although it is frequently used to estimate the degree of oxidation of other foods. It is not a reliable indicator in dry systems.

Malonaldehyde forms readily when trienoic or tetraenoic acids are present. A proposed mechanism involving one of the β-γ unsaturated peroxido radicals capable of being formed in linolenate or more highly unsaturated acids is [14]:

$$-CH_2-CH=CH-CH_2-CH=CH-CH_2-CH=CH-CH_2-$$

$$-H\cdot \ \Big\downarrow \ + O_2$$

$$-CH_2-CH=CH-CH_2-CH-CH=CH-CH=CH-CH_2-$$
$$\Big\downarrow \ \overset{|}{OO}\cdot$$

$$-CH_2-\overset{\cdot}{CH}-CH-CH_2-CH-CH=CH-CH=CH-CH_2-$$
$$\overset{|}{O}\!\!-\!\!-\!\!-\!\!-\!\!\overset{|}{O}$$

$$\Big\downarrow \ + RH$$

$$-CH_2-CH_2-CH-CH_2-CH-CH=CH-CH=CH-CH_2- \ + R\cdot$$
$$\overset{|}{O}\cdot \qquad \overset{|}{O}\cdot$$

$$\qquad H \ \Big\downarrow \ H$$

$$-CH_2-CH_2\cdot \ + O=\overset{|}{C}-CH_2-\overset{|}{C}=O \ + \cdot CH=CH-CH=CH-CH_2-$$

Malonaldehyde measured in oxidizing systems containing linoleate may be derived from further oxidation of 2-enals or 2,4-dienals.

$$H-C-CH=CH-CH=CH-CH_2-R$$
$$\overset{||}{O}$$

$$\Big\downarrow \ O_2 \text{ and then } R'H$$

$$H-C-CH_2-CH-CH=CH-CH_2-R \ + R\cdot'$$
$$\overset{||}{O} \quad \overset{|}{OOH}$$

$$\Big\downarrow \ \text{Scission and dismutation}$$

$$H-C-CH_2-C-H \ + HO-CH=CH-CH_2-R$$
$$\overset{||}{O} \qquad \overset{||}{O}$$

10. EVALUATION OF THE STATE OF OXIDATION

Measurement of the state of oxidation of a lipid or a lipid-containing food is very complicated and uncertain. Measurement of peroxide value is useful to the stage at which extensive decomposition of hydroperoxides begins. Measurement of carbonyl compounds is useful provided secondary reactions and volatilization have not occurred to a significant extent. The pattern of oxidation may be changed by the reaction of aldehydes with amino groups from proteins, amino acids, and amino lipids, or by the nature of the stress on the system. This, in turn, causes type A or B scission and different carbonyl species to form. Measurement of acid-type carbonyls is not revealing if used alone. A composite of peroxide, TBA, carbonyl type, and acid determinations provides perhaps the best indication of the state of oxidation, yet the data are so variable that no oxidized system has been very well characterized or defined.

D. Lipoxidase–Catalyzed Oxidation

For a full discussion of this subject, see Chapter 6, Section XI,H.

E. Reversion

Some oils develop off flavors and odors even when the peroxide number is as low as a few milliequivalents per kilogram. These flavors, variously characterized as beany, buttery, fishy, grassy, haylike, or painty, are particularly characteristic of soybean oil and hydrogenated soybean oil, and the defect is referred to as "reversion flavor." Flavors and odors of fractions isolated from "reverted" soybean oil have been described as reminiscent of green beans, brown beans, cucumbers, melons, rotten apples, rancid hazelnuts, citrus, licorice, potatoes, fatty aldehydes, or sweet aldehydes [22].

The linolenic acid component of soybean oil has been most frequently implicated in the formation of reversion flavor. Polymers from oxidized soybean or rape seed oils have no flavor characteristic of reversion at ambient temperature, yet when these are heated intense flavor and odor development occurs. These polymers conceivably form by oxidation of the linolenic or linoleic acid components of these oils. Hydrogenation of these polymers does not eliminate the tendency to form flavor compounds, although the nature of the components and the type of flavor does change.

As many as 71 compounds have been identified in the volatile fraction isolated from reverted soybean oil. Each compound apparently makes a contribution to the total flavor, and certain compounds contribute to distinctively different flavors [34]. Examples are given in Table 4-19. Other identified compounds belong to the classes of saturated methyl ketones, esters, saturated aldehydes, 2-enals, 2,4-dienals, saturated acids from C_2 to C_9, 2-cis or 2-trans-enoic acids from C_4 to C_8, hydroxy acids, and keto acids. Benzoic acid also has been isolated.

TABLE 4-19

Flavor Characteristics of Some Compounds Isolated from
Reverted Soybean Oil

Compound	Flavor description
3-cis-Hexenal	Green bean flavor
2-Pentyl furan[a]	Licorice
Diacetyl	Buttery
2,3-Pentanedione	Buttery
2,4-Pentadienal	Potatoey

[a]Imparts beany and grassy odor and flavor at 1-10 ppm, and a licorice odor at high concentrations.

One compound is of special interest because of its acetylenic nature. This is dec-1-yne, which is possibly derived from oleic acid or its esters by the following mechanism:

$$H_3C-(CH_2)_7-\overset{\overset{H}{|}}{C}=\overset{\overset{H}{|}}{C}-CH_2-(CH_2)_6-COOH$$

$\Big\downarrow$ Oxidation

$$H_3C-(CH_2)_7-\overset{\overset{H}{|}}{C}=\overset{\overset{H}{|}}{C}-\underset{\underset{OOH}{|}}{\overset{\overset{H}{|}}{C}}-(CH_2)_6-COOH$$

$\Big\downarrow$ Scission

$$H_3C-(CH_2)_7-\overset{\overset{H}{|}}{C}=\overset{\overset{H}{|}}{C}\cdot$$

$\Big\downarrow$ Disproportionation

$$H_3C-(CH_2)_7-C\equiv C-H + H\cdot$$

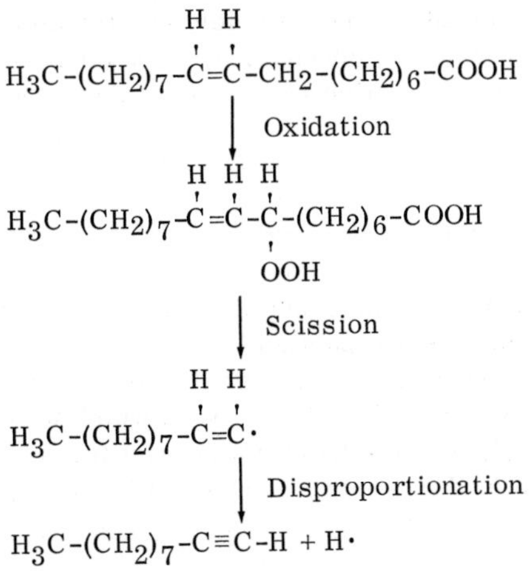

The radical shown here could conceivably combine with a ·OH derived from hydroperoxide scission to give the tautomer of decanal. This compound also has been identified in reverted but not rancid soybean oil.

The compound 2-pentyl furan may be the one substance that is mainly responsible for the characteristic beany or grassy flavor and odor of reverted soybean oil. In concentrated form it has a licorice odor but, when added at 5 ppm to a bland oil, such as freshly deodorized cottonseed oil, it imparts beany and grassy odors reminiscent of reverted soybean oil. It has been proposed that 2-pentyl furan is derived from 4-keto nonanoic acid by the following mechanism:

$$H_3C-(CH_2)_4-\overset{\overset{O}{\|}}{C}-CH_2-CH_2-COOH$$

$\Big\downarrow$

$$H_3C-(CH_2)_4-\overset{\overset{OH}{|}}{C}=\overset{\overset{H}{|}}{C}-\overset{\overset{H}{|}}{C}=\overset{\overset{OH}{|}}{C}-H$$

$\Big\downarrow$ $- H_2O$

$$H_3C-(CH_2)_4-C\overset{O}{\diagup\diagdown}C-H$$
$$\underset{H}{\overset{\|}{C}}—\underset{H}{\overset{\|}{C}}$$

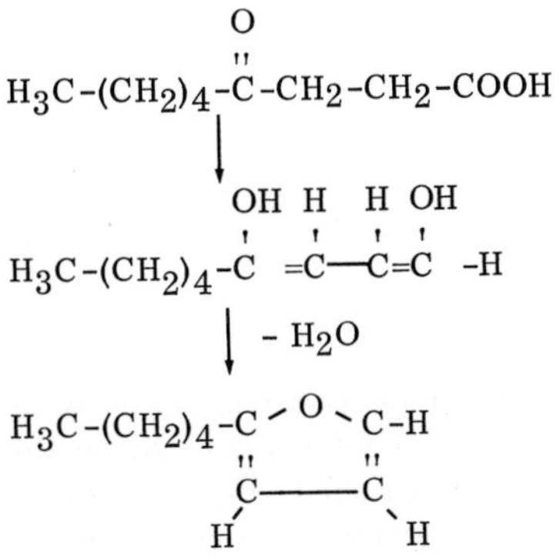

2-Pentyl furan

The 4-keto nonanoic acid presumably could be derived from linoleic acid rather than linolenic acid.

Cottonseed, corn, and several other oils are not subject to reversion flavors even though they contain large amounts of linoleic acid and substantial amounts of oleic acid; these acids are logical precursors of substances which apparently contribute greatly to reversion flavors. A complete explanation of this behavior has not been developed, although it has been suggested that both linoleic and linolenic acid may be essential to the formation of reversion compounds, perhaps because a different pattern of linoleate hydroperoxide decomposition results when the very reactive linolenic acid is present.

F. Antioxidants

An antioxidant is a substance that is added to fats or fat-containing foods to retard oxidation and thereby prolong their wholesomeness and palatability.

Ideally, an antioxidant should: (1) have no harmful physiological effect; (2) not contribute an objectionable flavor, odor, or color to the fat or food in which it is used; (3) be effective in low concentrations; (4) be fat soluble; (5) persist following processing to provide effective protection to food in which it exists; (6) be readily available; and (7) be economical.

1. MECHANISMS OF ANTIOXIDANT ACTION

In food systems, the most effective antioxidants function by interrupting the free-radical chain mechanism, while those used in gasoline, lubricants, rubber, and other applications may function as peroxide decomposers. Antioxidants, such as ascorbic acid, function by being preferentially oxidized and they afford relatively poor protection.

An antioxidant AH apparently reacts with radicals produced during autooxidation according to the scheme:

$$R\cdot + AH \longrightarrow RH + A\cdot$$

$$RO\cdot + AH \longrightarrow ROH + A\cdot$$

$$ROO\cdot + AH \longrightarrow ROOH + A\cdot$$

$$R\cdot + A\cdot \longrightarrow RA$$

$$RO\cdot + A\cdot \longrightarrow ROA$$

This scheme shows that antioxidants interfere with the free-radical, chain oxidation process and that reaction products of antioxidant molecules and oxidized lipid molecules may appear among the final products. Although relatively little evidence exists in support of the latter statement, a tocopherol-linoleic acid compound (Fig. 4-5) has been isolated from an oxidizing linoleate system containing the antioxidant tocopherol [29].

The concentration of an antioxidant in a food fat is important for reasons of cost, safety, sensory properties, and functionality. Functional properties of antioxidants vary. Some antioxidants provide increased protection as the concentration increases, whereas others have optional levels, and higher levels are sometimes

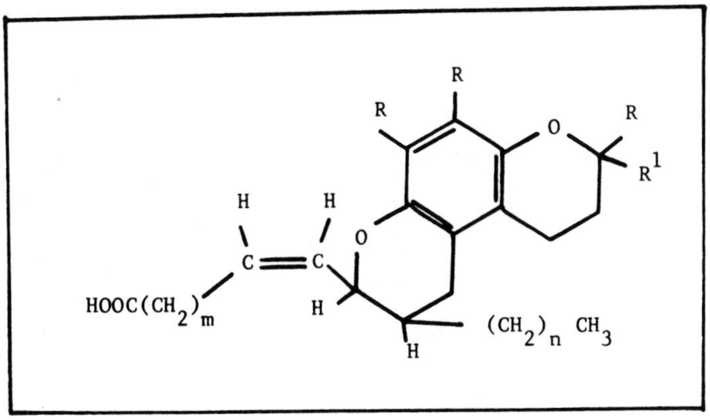

FIG. 4-5. Tocopherol-linoleic acid adduct.

prooxidant. Thus, a proper balance is sought between the quantity which provides maximum stabilization and that which may participate in the chain reaction and thereby intensify oxidation.

Some antioxidants are effective in prolonging the keeping time of both fats and oils and the foods containing them. Such antioxidants are known as "carry through antioxidants" since they "carry through" or survive the thermal stresses, steam distillation, and pH effects of processing to give longer shelf life to the finished food [16].

2. ANTIOXIDANTS USED IN FOODS

Butylated hydroxyanisole (BHA) (a mixture of 2-t-butyl-4-hydroxy anisole and its isomer 3-t-butyl-4-hydroxyanisole), butylated hydroxytoluene (BHT) which is 2,6-di-t-butyl-4-methylphenol, esters of gallic acid, and di-tert-butyl hydroquinone are commonly added to food since they are effective and they comply with safety regulations of the Federal Food and Drug Administration of the United States. These antioxidants are illustrated in Figure 4-6.

Many naturally occurring substances function as antioxidants. Most prominent are the tocopherols (α, β, γ, δ). The tocopherols have vitamin E activity that decreases from α to δ and antioxidant activity that increases from α to δ. The tocopherols act as biological antioxidants in plant and animal tissues, and residual quantities of tocopherols aid in maintaining the keeping quality of refined seed oils. Lecithin or mixtures of phosphatides have some antioxidant activity, as do several flavones, sterols, and sulfhydryl compounds.

When a single antioxidant is added, it may not exceed 0.01% based on the fat content of the food. When more than one antioxidant is added, the combined total may not exceed 0.02%, of which no one antioxidant may exceed 0.01%. When antioxidants and synergists are added, the combined total may not exceed 0.025%, with the same restriction with respect to single additives. These levels have been arrived at from tests of both acute and chronic toxicity in a variety of animals.

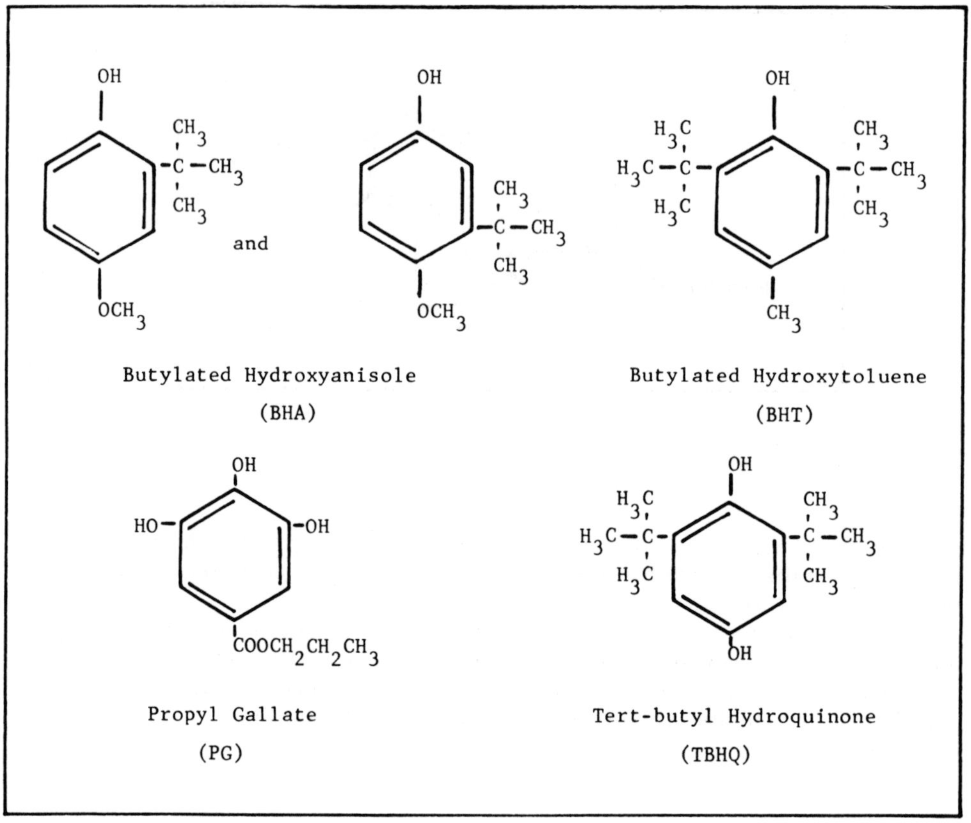

FIG. 4-6. Some antioxidants used in food lipids.

The amount found to cause pathological symptoms or death in test animals is, as a general rule, at least 100 times greater than the amount which is permitted in food fats. Most antioxidants, shortly after ingestion, are excreted as glucuronides and/or ethereal sulfates in the urine, and no serious questions exist relative to the safety of approved antioxidants.

Animal fats, such as lard, have little natural stability and require the use of antioxidants to be effective as commercial fats. The efficacies of BHA and BHT as carry through antioxidants in lard that is subsequently added to different types of food products are illustrated in Table 4-20.

Antioxidants used in combination are sometimes more effective than an equal weight of a single antioxidant. This effect is known as synergism. BHA is synergistic with BHT, with propyl gallate (PG), and with several other antioxidants. Synergism between BHA and BHT is illustrated in Table 4-21.

Although BHA and BHT are synergistic and BHA and propyl gallate are synergistic, the combination of BHT with propyl gallate results in negative synergism, in which the keeping quality of a fat is less than that expected from the sum of the effects of each used alone.

TABLE 4-20

Carry Through Activity of BHA and BHT in Lard

| | Oven stability (days)[a] | | |
	Pastry	Soda crackers	Potato chips
Control lard	7	5	1.5
Lard with 0.01% BHA	44	35	25
Lard with 0.01% BHT	34	34	15

[a]Days to become rancid by odor test at 145°F.

TABLE 4-21

Synergism Between BHA and BHT

	AOM Stability[a] (hr)	Difference	Synergism
Control (lard)	11		
BHT 0.01%	53	42	
BHA 0.01%	46	35	
BHT 0.01% and BHA 0.01%	102	91	$91 - (42 + 35) = 14$

[a]Stability by the active oxygen test.

Addition of certain acidic compounds to fats effectively complexes trace metal prooxidants and frequently provides increased keeping quality. This effect is sometimes confused with synergism. Citric acid is usually used since it is particularly effective in sequestering iron and it generally poses no problem in foods in which the fat is used. Phosphoric and ascorbic acid, their esters, and the esters of citric acid have been used with varying effectiveness.

Commercial effectiveness of antioxidants relies on the varying capabilities of the antioxidants and metal sequestrants as they relate to a particular system. Many combinations of antioxidants and sequestrants are used. Some are used to provide stability to a fat during storage, some to provide processing stability to a fat, and some to provide stability to a product in which the fat is incorporated.

Combinations of BHA with propyl gallate and citric acid, or of BHA with BHT and citric acid, increase the storage life of a fat, provide good processing stability, and help stabilize many processed foods. Propyl gallate loses effectiveness under heat stress and in systems with a high pH. BHA and BHT tend to steam distill or volatilize from a system during frying or baking. This volatility is a useful characteristic in some instances. For example, some cereals and other dry foods are protected against oxidation by incorporating BHT in the liner of the food package. Apparently the antioxidant slowly volatilizes and migrates into the packaged food at a rate sufficient to give some improvement in keeping quality.

Antioxidant discoloration is not a problem except when propyl gallate is used. Propyl gallate forms a blue-black compound with iron and this is occasionally evident as dark specks or streaks in lard or shortening or as a black sludge in tanks used for storing or transporting treated lard.

The use of antioxidants, safely and effectively extends the palatability, acceptability, and nutrient value of many foods and thus eliminates much of the economic waste that derives from discarding foods when they become rancid.

Further information on antioxidants can be found in Chapter 11, Section XII.

G. Polymerization

Conditions leading to polymerization of unsaturated fatty acids in lipids are heat stress, oxidation, and the presence of radical or polar catalysts. Heat stress of fats and oils, such as encountered in severe frying operations, can produce changes in refractive index, molecular weight, color, or viscosity and can cause some conjugation of double bonds and some conversion of cis double bonds to trans double bonds. Not all changes are attributable to polymerization, although the reactions causing the changes may be similar. For example, a crosslinking reaction may occur between two fatty acids in the same triglyceride. This occasions no increase in molecular weight but hydrolysis or saponification of the triglyceride yields a fatty acid "dimer." If crosslinking occurs between fatty acids in two different triglycerides, a triglyceride dimer is formed with a concurrent increase in molecular weight. Saponification yields a fatty acid "dimer" as in intramolecular polymerization. Intramolecular cyclization also can occur.

Some polymers originate by the Diels-Alder reaction between a trans-trans conjugated diene and the olefin group of another molecule. A substituted cyclohexene dimer results.

$$
\begin{array}{c}
\text{H H H H}\\
| \ | \ | \ |\\
R_1\text{-C=C-C=C-}R_2\\
\\
+\\
\\
R_3\text{-C=C-}R_4\\
| \ |\\
\text{H H}
\end{array}
\longrightarrow
\begin{array}{c}
\text{H} \qquad \text{H}\\
\diagdown \qquad \diagup\\
\text{C=C}\\
\diagup \qquad \diagdown\\
R_1\text{-C} \qquad\quad \text{C-}R_2\\
\diagdown \qquad \diagup\\
R_3\text{-C-C-}R_4\\
| \ |\\
\text{H H}
\end{array}
$$

Furthermore, two radicals can unite to form a noncyclic dimer.

$$
R_1\text{-}\overset{\cdot}{\text{C}}\text{H-}R_2 + R_3\text{-}\overset{\cdot}{\text{C}}\text{H-}R_4 \longrightarrow
\begin{array}{c}
R_1\text{-CH-}R_2\\
|\\
R_3\text{-CH-}R_4
\end{array}
$$

Free radicals also can add to a double bond, forming a dimeric radical which may then disproportionate, polymerize further, or abstract hydrogen from another molecule.

$$R_1-CH=CH-R_2 + R_3-CH-R_4$$

$$
\begin{array}{ll}
R_1-CH-CH-R_2 & R_1-CH-CH_2-R_2 \\
\quad | \quad \cdot & \quad | \\
R_3-CH-R_4 \xrightarrow{\;H\cdot\;} & R_3-CH-R_4
\end{array}
$$

Cyclic monomers can result from an internal radical-double bond reaction sequence.

Polymers also form as a consequence of oxidation reactions involving oxy- or peroxy- radicals on "dimer" or greater units which are carbon-carbon linked and/or oxygen linked. Monomeric molecular changes involving cyclization may involve both carbon-carbon bonding and oxygen bonding.

The formation of cyclic monomers, intramolecular crosslinked monomers, and polymers decreases the heat-transfer efficiency of an oil, and also affects the quality of products fried in it. Under extreme circumstances these compounds and others can have an adverse effect on the nutritional quality of the oil and on its wholesomeness.

VII. CHEMISTRY AND TECHNOLOGY OF PROCESSING FATS AND OILS

A. Purification of Fats and Oils

Crude fats and oils contain materials that must be removed to provide satisfactory processing characteristics and to provide desirable color, odor, flavor, and keeping qualities in the finished products. The most frequently used purification processes involve (a) removal of suspended and colloidally dispersed matter by settling, degumming, and acid washing; (b) removal of free fatty acids by refining; (c) decolorization by bleaching; (d) deodorization; and (e) removal of saturated or high-melting glycerides (stearines) by chilling.

1. SETTLING AND DEGUMMING

Settling and degumming are utilized to remove animal or plant proteins, carbohydrate residues, phosphatides, and water. Settling involves storing heated fats quiescently in tanks with conical bottoms. Water and materials associated with water are more dense than melted fat and settle into the cone, where they are drawn off. Some colloidal materials coalesce after direct heating with steam. Another technique involves heating at 200°C in the presence of adsorbents and then filtering.

Purification of soybean oil requires removal of phosphatides. These are usually referred to as "lecithin", which implies that they are phosphatidylcholine although phosphatidylethanolamine may be present in substantial quantity along with lesser amounts of phosphatidylinositol. Degumming is accomplished by mixing the oil with up to 2% water or steam for one-half hour at 54-71°C. The hydrated "lecithin" is separated from the oil by centrifugation or settling.

2. REFINING WITH ALKALI

Refining with alkali removes free fatty acids which can result from lipolysis prior to rendering or extracting the fat or oil. Caustic soda solutions (12–20° Be) are added to the heated fat and stirred vigorously. After a short period, the mixture is allowed to settle. The settlings, called "foots," are collected and sold as "soap stock." In continuous processes appropriate proportions of caustic soda solution and oil are continuously blended at 20–32°C, passed into a heat exchanger which rapidly raises the temperature to 55–70°C to break the emulsion, centrifuged to separate the foots, washed with water, and separated again by centrifugation.

Oils which are removed from seeds or other sources by solvent extraction may be refined while in the presence of the solvent (this solution of oil and various impurities in solvent is known as "miscella") by homogenizing with caustic soda solution (10–14°Be), followed by centrifugal separation and water washing. The solvent ultimately is boiled off.

In addition to removing free fatty acids, refining also removes phosphatides, some solid matter, and some of the colored matter. These substances are removed mainly by occlusion with the soaps.

3. BLEACHING

Bleaching reduces the color of fat or oil and it is achieved by adsorbing the colorants on bleaching earth and/or charcoal or by chemical reactions involving their oxidation or reduction. Chemical methods of bleaching are seldom applied to edible fats. In addition to decolorization, bleaching clay also absorbs suspended matter, soaps, phosphatides, water, and nickel if the treatment occurs after hydrogenation.

Bleaching clay (bentonite) contains not less than 85% of the mineral montmorillonite $Al_4Si_8O_{20}(OH)_4 \cdot nH_2O$. Natural clay is bentonite in which some of the Al has been replaced naturally by H. Activated clay, produced by treating natural clay with mineral acid, has even more Al replaced by H and thus it contains a higher percentage of hydrated silica and an increased adsorptive capacity.

An absence of moisture is necessary in order to achieve maximum adsorption to clay during bleaching. The rate of bleaching increases with temperature; however, if the temperature is too high, darkening may occur by oxidation. An exception is palm oil, which is bleached at 149°C because the color fades during heating.

The clay is added at a temperature lower than optimum so that increased residence time is achieved allowing the water which is slowly released from the clay to form a protective vapor layer over the fat. Bleaching under vacuum is widely used since it diminishes oxidative effects.

Bleaching performance is governed by organic impurities in the oil and the oxidative state of the oil. Bleaching clay more effectively removes green colors (chlorophyll) than red colors (carotenes or xanthophyll). Carotenoid pigments fade due to heat bleaching, but heat may also induce red color formation by oxidation of tocopherol to chroman-5,6-quinones.

Charcoal may be used in conjunction with clay when removal of red color is difficult. It is especially useful in bleaching coconut oil.

4. DEODORIZATION

Natural fats and hydrogenated fats contain substances contributing to undesirable flavor and odor and these substances must be removed. Deodorization is accomplished by placing heated fat in a vacuumized tower and allowing it to cascade over steam moving in a countercurrent direction. This steam-vacuum deodorization process removes volatile odorous substances, such as aldehydes and ketones; destroys peroxides and carotenoid pigments; and strips out residual free fatty acids. Hydrolysis of glycerides is minimal. It is important to preclude oxygen from the system, and citric acid is commonly added to fats being deodorized to counteract the prooxidant effect of trace metals.

5. WINTERIZING

Salad oils are expected to remain clear at low temperatures. If saturated or other high-melting glycerides are present, they crystallize at refrigerator (winter) temperatures and a cloudy appearance results. High-melting glycerides frequently contain substantial quantities of stearic acid and so those glycerides separating on cooling are known as "stearines." Oils are winterized by holding them at 5°C until crystallization is well advanced and then filtering out the solids in a "chill room." Cottonseed oil contains 12-25% of "stearine" and must be winterized when used as salad oil. Corn oil, olive oil, soybean oil, and sunflowerseed oil need not be winterized. Soybean oil which has been partially hydrogenated to alter the linolenic component, however, must be winterized if use at a low temperature is intended.

The processes of refining, bleaching, and deodorizing very effectively remove residual pesticides which may be present; thereby contributing to the overall safety and purity of lipids for food use.

B. Modification of Fats and Oils

1. HYDROGENATION

The physical requirements of many fats used in foods are grossly different from those of natural fats or oils. Hydrogenation, the direct addition of hydrogen to double bonds of fatty acids, is used to modify vast quantities of fats and oils. This process alters molecular configuration and changes the geometry, number, and location of double bonds. These changes, in turn, alter the physical and chemical properties of the fat.

Hydrogenation is used to convert liquid fats to plastic fats, thereby making them suitable for the manufacture of margarine or shortening. Hydrogenated fats also exhibit improved color and stability. Close control of hydrogenation results in highly specific results. For example, salad and cooling oils can be improved by controlled hydrogenation.

During hydrogenation, hydrogen and the fat or oil are mixed at an elevated temperature in the presence of a suitable catalyst. The rate of reaction depends on the nature of the substance to be hydrogenated, the nature and concentration of the catalyst, the concentration of hydrogen, and the temperature, pressure, and degree of agitation. Agitation aids solution of hydrogen in the hot oil, aids movement of unmodified oil to the catalyst surface, and aids movement of converted oil away from the catalyst. Pressure affects the concentration of hydrogen in solution.

a. Catalysis. During catalysis, double-bond sites of triglycerides presumably adsorb, by H bonding or secondary valence forces, at active points on the catalyst surface. The catalyst disassociatively adsorbs hydrogen at these points and when the temperature is sufficient hydrogen adds to the double bonds. The reaction apparently proceeds by the mechanism:

Oil + catalyst $\longrightarrow$ oil-catalyst (complex)

Oil - catalyst + H_2 $\longrightarrow$ hydrogenated oil + catalyst

b. Selectivity. In some instances, hydrogenation is "selective" in that highly unsaturated fatty acids hydrogenate in preference to less highly unsaturated fatty acids. Thus, selective hydrogenation of a fat or oil containing linoleic acid would favor the conversion of linoleic acid to oleic acid or its isomers in preference to the conversion of oleic acid to stearic acid. The ratio of conversion may be 4:1 in nonselective hydrogenation and as great as 50:1 in a very selective hydrogenation.

The term "selective" also applies to the role of catalysts in isomer formation. It is applicable to the formation of "iso" acids or trans-acids during hydrogenation. The term "isooleic acids" defines positional isomers (other than Δ^9) of oleic acid in which the double bond may be in either the cis or the trans configuration. The selectivity refers to production of fewer isooleic acids at a given level of saturated acids or to fewer saturated acids at a given level of isooleic acids.

The complexity of product formation may be illustrated by hydrogenation of linolenic acid.

Reaction rate constants may be determined for each sequence. The K_{Ln} for hydrogenation of linolenate is the resultant of constants for each individual sequence (four) by which linolenate is hydrogenated. Also, K_{Lo} represents the resultant for all reactions by which linoleate is hydrogenated (two). Selectivity then can be expressed as the ratio K_{Ln}/K_{Lo} which denotes the relative rate of hydrogenation of linolenate to that of linoleate [1].

The numerous reactions depicted above, coupled with the numerous triglyceride isomers that exist naturally as a consequence of the many fatty acids present, lead to a very complicated product mix during hydrogenation of a fat or oil. Data in Table 4-22 illustrate the effect of hydrogenation conditions on the types of compounds obtained.

c. Formation of Isomers. Studies of simple systems containing only oleic acid or triolein have established that isomerization occurs during hydrogenation. The double bond migrates, leading to a decrease in 9-octadecenoic acid and an increase in the 8, 10, 7, and 11 isomers. Amounts of the 8 and 10 isomers are essentially equal, as are the amounts of the 7 and 11 isomers. As hydrogenation proceeds,

TABLE 4-22

Hydrogenated Cottonseed Oil

Type of hydrogenation	Iodine value	Trans isomers (%)	Saturated glycerides (%)
Nonselective 0.05% Ni, 140°C, 40 psig	47.5	21.6	45.1
Normal 0.10% Ni, 170°C, 20 psig	47.0	30.9	45.4
Selective 0.20% Ni, 200°C, 5 psig	49.6	37.7	42.3
Original cottonseed oil	109.7	0.0	22.8

the ratio of 9 to 8 positional isomers approaches one and the ratio of trans to cis isomers reaches an equilibrium value of 2:1. The two types of isomerization occur at the same time and with either starting configuration of the double bond.

A concept of partial hydrogenation–dehydrogenation accounts for the shift of double bonds as well as the formation of trans isomers.

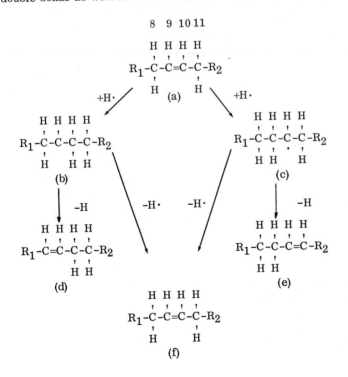

Use of the preceding scheme can be extended to explain formation of 7 and 11 isomers and others shifted further along the chain. The trans-cis ratio reaches an equilibrium which is proportional to the migration of double bonds; however, this ratio cannot be attributed solely to the shift in double bonds, since some geometrical isomerization occurs without positional isomerization when the oil is in contact with the catalyst [2].

Since partial hydrogenation of an oil increases the amounts of fatty acids that are saturated or have trans configurations, the resulting product has an increased solid/liquid ratio and an increased melting point.

Numerous transfer and adsorption steps occur in partial hydrogenation. These require the transfer and/or diffusion of reactants to the surface of the catalyst and in some cases into pores of the catalyst. The saturated and partially hydrogenated isomeric triglycerides then must be transferred back into the main body of the oil. These critical steps must be controlled if selectivity during partial hydrogenation is desired.

d. Catalysts. The catalysts generally used in commercial hydrogenation consist of nickel on various supports. The supports aid in orientation of the catalyst and provide mass, which is important in removing the catalyst from the finished product. The catalysts are activated by various heat and/or acid conditions to provide the irregular surface and active points essential for catalysis. Typical conditions applied to regulate the hydrogenation process are listed in Table 4-22.

e. Other Metal Catalysts. Although nickel is widely used as a hydrogenation catalyst, other metals have the ability to catalyze hydrogenation of fats. These can be used to give a different ratio of trans or positional isomers, to provide other degrees of selectivity, and in some cases to limit the content of saturated fatty acids to that which occurs naturally in the fat. This approach greatly increases the possibility of producing fats tailor made for specific uses. Some of the catalysts available are copper, copper-chromium combinations, and metals of the platinum group.

(1) COPPER-BEARING CATALYSTS.

(a) Copper-Chromium Catalysts. Copper-chromium catalysts have a high selectivity for linolenic acid and almost infinite selectivity for linoleate. Those consisting of approximately CuO 40%, Cr_2O_3 40%, and BaO 10%, and used at 0.1% and 170°C provide the greatest selectivity. Selectivity values expressed as K_{Ln}/K_{Lo} range from 6 to 13. The assignment of infinite selectivity for linoleate over oleate derives when no stearate is produced. Copper-chromium catalysts result in few conjugated dienes, and trans isomer production is less than with nickel.

(b) Copper Dispersed on Solids. Copper dispersed on Cab-O-Sil (a pure form of silica with a large surface area) or on silicic acid provides a selectivity (K_{Ln}/K_{Lo}) of 13-18 and it has greater activity than copper chromite. Hydrogenation can be carried to an oleic content of 72% with no increase in stearic acid and with formation of only 17-32% trans isomers. Some migration of double bonds occurs but monoenes exist primarily as the 9-cis isomer. The trans isomers occur chiefly at the 10 and 11 positions. Refining or treatment with citric or phosphoric acid is necessary to reduce the residual copper content to a level compatible with good stability.

(2) PLATINUM METALS AS SELECTIVE CATALYSTS. The platinum group contains the following metals listed in order of decreasing activity as catalysts for hydrogenation: Pd > Rh > Pt >> Ir > Ru > Os. These catalysts are extremely sensitive to "poisons" at low concentrations. Poisons consist of a variety of substances containing sulfur, arsenic, lead, and other elements capable of reacting with or adsorbing irreversibly with the catalyst so that active areas are covered or eliminated [33].

Catalysts vary in their ability to alter the relative rates of double-bond migration and hydrogenation. Decreasing activity with respect to catalysis of double-bond migration occurs in the order Pd > Ni > Rh > Ru > Os, Ir, Pt, and this order coincides with the abilities of these metals to dissolve hydrogen.

Metal-catalyzed geometric isomerization of olefins occurs more rapidly in the presence of hydrogen than in its absence. Migration of double bonds into conjugation is apparently an essential stage but the catalyst must also be able to hydrogenate these conjugated systems selectively.

Palladium, which is 30-100 times more active than Ni in hydrogenation of oils, normally forms a high proportion of trans isomers but this can be minimized by the choice of process conditions. Soybean oil can be hydrogenated to margarine stock in the presence of only 0.00055% Pd, based on the oil. Efficient recovery of the small amount of catalyst used is difficult and this has prevented wide-scale use of Pd in oil hydrogenation.

f. Homogeneous Catalysis. Hydrogenation accomplished with catalysts that are oil soluble provides greater and more uniform contact between catalyst and the substrate. Furthermore, problems of mass transfer are lessened and new dimensions for control of selectivity and isomerization are introduced.

(1) IRON AND COBALT CARBONYLS. Homogeneous catalytic hydrogenation can be accomplished with soluble ions or organic complexes of certain transition metals. In addition to the advantages cited above, this permits greater selectivity in certain instances.

Iron pentacarbonyl $Fe(CO)_5$ and dicobalt octacarbonyl $CO_2(CO)_8$ catalyze hydrogenation of soybean oil with concurrent migration of double bonds and formation of geometric isomers. The iron compounds form stable π complexes with fatty esters, while the cobalt carbonyls either do not form complexes or form types that decompose during processing. Hydrogenation with these catalysts apparently involves conjugation of a molecule's double-bond system and reduction of one of the double bonds. The linolenate system then can yield a wide range of isomers as illustrated:

```
        9  10 11 12 13 14 15 16
        C=C-C-C=C-C-C=C
         └──A ┴─┘ B ──┘
```

Upon conjugation A yields:

```
        9     11          15
        C-C=C-C=C-C-C-C=C
```

or

```
          10    12       15
        C-C-C=C-C=C-C-C=C
```

B yields:

```
        9      12   14
        C=C-C-C=C-C=C-C
```

or

```
        9           13   15
        C=C-C-C-C=C-C=C
```

Reduction of one double bond in the "A" isomers produces 9,15; 11,15; 10,15; and 12,15 dienes. Reduction of one double bond in the "B" isomers produces the 9,12; 9,14; 9,13; and 9,15 dienes. The large content of trans isomers is attributable to the trans,trans configuration of the conjugated dienes in A and B.

(2) HYDROGENATION WITH CHROMIUM CARBONYLS. Complexes of $Cr(CO)_3$ with methyl benzoate or benzene effect selective hydrogenation of polyunsaturated fatty acids in vegetable oils and have the added advantage of forming products in which double bonds are predominantly in the cis configuration. This is important because liquid salad oils prepared by other hydrogenation methods contain saturated and higher melting trans isomers which must be removed to avoid cloudiness at low temperatures. The all-cis isomers result in retention of the liquid state to quite low temperatures.

By means of hydrogenation catalyzed by chromium carbonyls, simulated olive oil can be prepared from soybean oil (Table 4-23), and simulated cocoa butter can be prepared from certain fractions of cottonseed oil stearines (Table 4-24).

g. Hydrazine Reduction. Unsaturated fatty acids also can be hydrogenated by hydrazine, N_2H_4. In contrast to reduction in the presence of metallic catalysts, there is essentially no formation of trans isomers or migration of double bonds. Reduction of linolenic acid yields three monoenes and three dienes. Monoenes consist of the 9, 12, and 15 isomers. Dienes include the 9,12; 9,15; and the 12,15

TABLE 4-23

Production of Simulated Olive Oil from Soybean Oil[a]

	Hydrogenated soybean oil	Olive oil
Iodine value	95.3	77–94
Palmitate (%)	10.3	7–16
Stearate (%)	4.3	1–3
Other saturates (%)	0.0	0.1–2
Monoene (%)	60.7	65–85
Diene (%)	23.9	4–15
Triene (%)	0.8	
Trans acids (%)	6.8	

[a]Reprinted from Ref. [18] by courtesy of the American Oil Chemists' Society.

TABLE 4-24

Production of Simulated Cocoa Butter from Cottonseed Oil Stearine[a]

	Hydrogenated CSO, stearine fraction	Cocoa butter
Palmitate (%)	58.0	24.4
Stearate (%)	1.0	35.4
Monoene (%)	37.6	38.1
Diene (%)	3.4	2.1
Trans acids (%)	7.2	
Iodine value	38.0	36.7
Melting range (°C)	30–40	24–35

[a]Reprinted from Ref. [18] by courtesy of the American Oil Chemists' Society.

isomers. Any difference in reactivity of the double bonds is small, although some evidence indicates a more rapid reduction of bonds furthest removed from the carboxyl group. This technique, while useful for laboratory reduction, presently holds little promise for commercial use.

h. Triglyceride Composition. Hydrogenation of fatty acids in triglycerides is not
a function of their location. Furthermore, the weight percentage of a given fatty
acid in the 2 position does not change appreciably during hydrogenation, as is evident for soybean oil in Table 4-25. The weight percentage of a given fatty acid in
the 2 position changes little as hydrogenation proceeds over a range sufficient to
eliminate linolenic acid and to reduce linoleic acid to less than 25% of the original
amount.

2. INTERESTERIFICATION

Interesterification, sometimes called "ester interchange" or "transesterification,"
involves an exchange of acyl groups among triglycerides. Since triglycerides have
three ester groups per molecule, many exchange possibilities exist. Acyl groups
may exchange positions within a triglyceride or between triglyceride molecules.

Interesterification can be achieved with the aid of any of several catalytic agents.
These include tin, lead, zinc, cadmium, or their compounds; or compounds of
either alkali metals or alkaline earth metals. The lower alcoholates, amides, and
hydrides are particularly effective at low temperatures. A liquid sodium-potassium
alloy is also effective and it resists fouling, which slows the reaction in some systems.

TABLE 4-25

Weight Percentages of Given Fatty Acids
in the 2 Position of Soybean Oil[a]

	Iodine value	Wt %				
		$C_{16:0}$	$C_{18:0}$	$C_{18:1}$	$C_{18.2}$	$C_{18.3}$
Soybean oil						
Triglyceride	127.6	11.3	4.3	29.1	49.5	5.8
2 Position		1.0	0.7	26.1	66.7	5.5
Proportion		3.0	5.5	30.0	45.0	31.6
Soybean oil (rearranged)						
Triglyceride	127.6	11.1	8.3	38.8	41.4	3.4
2 Position		11.0	4.5	37.5	42.8	3.7
Proportion		33.3	34.8	32.2	34.5	36.0
Soybean oil (hydrogenated)						
Triglyceride	106.2	11.8	4.9	48.4	33.8	1.5
2 Position		11.3	4.7	50.2	31.9	1.5
Proportion		32.0	32.0	34.6	32.4	33.0
Soybean oil (hydrogenated)						
Triglyceride	8.5	12.0	5.8	69.5	11.0	0.0
2 Position		10.6	5.3	69.1	13.8	0.0
Proportion		29.5	30.4	33.1	31.8	0.0

[a]Reprinted from Ref. [28] by courtesy of the American Oil Chemists' Society.

Interesterification can be carried out to an equilibrium condition, at which point the fatty acids assume an almost random distribution among the triglycerides. Directed interesterification is a technique which directs interesterification away from the random condition. This is done at a temperature which permits trisaturated glycerides to crystallize. As these are removed, the equilibrium of the liquid phase is upset and more unsaturated triglycerides are formed in a move toward equilibrium.

A proposed mechanism for both intra- and intermolecular exchange of esters involves the formation of an enolate ion (a) by action of the catalyst.

$$
\begin{array}{ccc}
\text{(a)} & \rightleftharpoons & \text{(b)} \\
& & \\
\text{(d)} & \rightleftharpoons & \text{(c)} \\
& & \\
\text{(e)} & &
\end{array}
$$

A series of reactions lend to formation of a β-ketoester, as in (d), which then yields an intramolecularly rearranged molecule, as in (e) [38]. A similar rearrangement between molecules provides interesterified or rearranged fat in which fatty acids are distributed at random. The following scheme shows a possible rearrangement of fatty acids between two triglycerides.

$$\begin{bmatrix} R_1 \\ -R_2 \\ R_3 \end{bmatrix} + \begin{bmatrix} R_4 \\ -R_5 \\ R_6 \end{bmatrix} \rightleftharpoons \begin{bmatrix} R_5 \\ -R_3 \\ R_1 \end{bmatrix} + \begin{bmatrix} R_6 \\ -R_4 \\ R_2 \end{bmatrix}$$

Interchanges within the same molecule occur more rapidly than those between molecules, and conditions can be chosen to emphasize or deemphasize this type of interchange. By this means, the physical properties of fats can be modified to meet performance requirements in shortenings, margarines, and enrobing fats.

Interesterification can be accomplished in any fat or mixture of fats. However, lard is the fat which is most commonly interesterified commercially. The exact composition of natural lard varies according to the age of pigs from which it is taken, the feed history of the animals, and the carcass location of the fat used. It contains approximately 2% GS_3, 27% GS_2U, 47% GSU_2, and 24% GU_3. The GS_2U fraction is composed of mostly oleopalmitostearin (OPS) which plays a principal role in consistency of lard in the range from 10° to 38°C. As temperature is increased within this range, the solid content index (SCI) decreases from about 26 to about 2. Unmodified lard shortenings tend to become "grainy" due to growth of (1) large crystalline aggregates of OPS which exist in the β' polymorphic state with a triple chain length structure, and (2) large β crystals of trisaturated glycerides. Elimination of graininess is achieved by random interesterification, which reduces the OPS to its "random" proportion and forms a mixture of disaturated glycerides. These crystals have lower melting points and they crystallize in a β'-2 form, which is the type desired in shortenings.

Lard may be given different properties by varying the method of interesterification [39]. One set of conditions favors intramolecular interchange and results in a crystal-modified lard (CML). Conditions favoring random distribution can be controlled to yield a partially modified lard (PML). Conditions favoring directed interesterification can be used to control the GS_3 content of direct interesterified lard (DIL). The effects of these treatments on the baking performance of lard used in pound cake are shown in Table 4-26. All interesterified lards produce pound cake volumes superior to those achieved from ordinary lard. Except for CML lard, tempering and storage of both modified and unmodified lards result in smaller pound cake volumes. However, the relative advantage of all the modified lards as compared to unmodified lard actually increases during storage at elevated temperatures.

VIII. EFFECTS OF PROCESSING ON FUNCTIONAL PROPERTIES AND NUTRITIVE VALUE

Ingestion of fats which have been subjected to thermal stress and oxidation pose questions of nutritive value and safety. A number of fats and oils used in frying

TABLE 4-26

Baking Evaluation of Modified Lards Stored
at Different Temperatures[a]

Storage	Pound cake volume (ml)					
temperature (°C)	24		30		38	
Storage time (wks)	2	16	1	9	1	4
Lard (unmodified)	1475	1435	1400	1190	1400	1100
PML[b]	1500	1445	1470	1335	1400	1295
CML[b]	1525	1565	1535	1550	1510	1555
DIL[b]	1505	1455	1595	1305	1440	1355

[a]Reprinted from Ref. [39] by courtesy of the American Oil Chemists' Society.
[b]PML, CML and DIL are, respectively, partially modified, crystal-modified, and direct interesterified lards.

and other high-temperature applications have been carefully examined to determine the effects and the degree of stress required to create problem situations.

The first concern is related to the presence of hydroperoxides in fats and food which have been stressed and then stored for periods sufficient to develop obvious rancidity. Fats with a peroxide value (PV) of 100 cause no obvious effect when fed to rats, but increasing oxidation up to PV 800 causes loss of appetite and a decreasing ability to gain weight. Fats with a PV of 1200 cause loss of weight, and even death in 3 weeks. Excessive levels of peroxides intensity deficiencies of essential fatty acids and reduce rates of growth and metabolism. Peroxides apparently are not absorbed in the body but lymph lipids have characteristics of peroxide reduction products. Rats and mice tolerate low levels of ingested peroxides with no evidence of harm and they metabolize moderately oxidized fats in a normal manner. If peroxide concentrations are not sufficiently high to cause irritation or intense toxicity, their ingestion apparently has no serious consequence, especially if appropriate quantities of essential lipids and proteins are included in the diet. Peroxide values in excess of 100 are rarely encountered in good commercial practice because secondary product formation then develops sufficiently to make most food fats highly unpalatable.

Heat-induced products of cyclization or polymerization have varying effects when fed to test animals. To detect these products, fats can be saponified and esterified with short-chain alcohols, distilled, then tested for their abilities to complex with appropriate substances such as urea. Urea forms inclusion compounds or adducts with fatty acids or their esters and especially with the more linear saturated acids. Cyclic monomers, dimers, and cyclic dimers formed by thermal or oxidative stress are not adducted by urea after the fats have been saponified. These fractions, designated NUAF (non-urea-adducting fraction), have been found to depress growth in test animals and even to cause death. Cyclic monomers are the most toxic compounds in this category and they appear to form most readily in fats containing linolenic acid [12,13].

Formation of the NUAF correlates well with increasing viscosity in a heated fat and with loss of desirable frying properties. When viscosity increases by 4 centistokes, as much as 11% NUAF may be present. Heat transfer properties decline at least 20% with a viscosity increase of 3 centistokes [32]. This necessitates a longer processing time, which results in fried cakes and potato chips that are misshapen, fat spotted, poorly colored, and lacking in crispness.

Fats that have been severely oxidized by heating yield fractions that are nonadducting and that cause death in weanling rats. If the toxic components are diluted with fresh oil, rats survive but with reduced growth patterns. Additional protein, pyridoxine, or other vitamins in the diet also counters the effects of thermally oxidized oils [31].

The effects of commercial food processing on the wholesomeness and nutritive properties of fats and oils are usually insignificant, although the stresses involved are somewhat similar to those which create the effects noted above. A logical explanation can be offered for the apparent contradiction. In large operations involving deep-fat frying, substantial quantities of food are processed and they usually absorb large quantities of fat. Thus, fresh fat must be added periodically and the mean exposure time of the fat is limited. Furthermore, water evolving from the frying food sweeps oxygen away from the surface of the fat and this tends to retard oxidation. However, less desirable situations also can be encountered. When frying chicken, fatty fish, or pork, the volume of fat can actually increase, so replacement of fat is not required. Furthermore, when the frying operation is done intermittently and on a small scale, such as in restaurants or institutions, oxidation of fat is favored by the large surface to volume ratio of the drying vessel and by the opportunity for fat to absorb oxygen during frequent cooling periods. Fortunately, an automatic safeguard exists since the sensory and functional properties of the fat deteriorate well before the fat becomes unwholesome. Furthermore, any minor amounts of toxic or growth-depressing substances that may enter the final food as a result of fat abuse are believed to be adequately counteracted by proteins and other essential nutrients in the diet [15].

Processes involved in refining and modification of fats have no appreciable deleterious effects on fat, and many of the purifying steps actually enhance its nutrient quality [19]. Trans isomers formed during hydrogenation are utilized as calories without noticeable effect. However trans isomers do not function as essential fatty acids. This poses no particular problem since essential fatty acids are generally abundant in the diet.

Lipid-protein interactions involving nonenzymic browning can substantially decrease the nutritive value of proteins. Aldehydes formed by oxidation of unsaturated lipids react readily with free ϵ-amino groups of proteins to form products which alter the available amino acid pattern of the protein. Products of lipid oxidation can also damage those vitamins that are susceptible to oxidation. Both situations can be controlled easily by the use of antioxidants.

In summary, severe oxidation or thermal abuse of lipids can result in products capable of causing severe physiological damage to or even death of test animals. However, these effects are often negated or diminished by inclusion in the diet of adequate proteins and vitamins, and by the fact that lipids containing substantial concentrations of damaging components are usually so unpalatable that humans do not consume them.

REFERENCES

1. L. F. Albright, J. Amer. Oil Chem. Soc., 47, 490 (1970).
2. R. R. Allen and A. A. Kiess, J. Amer. Oil Chem. Soc., 32, 400 (1955).
3. H. T. Badings, Neth. Milk Dairy J., 14, 215 (1960).
4. W. R. Bloor, Chem. Rev., 2, 243 (1925).
5. W. Q. Braun, J. Amer. Oil Chem. Soc., 37, 598 (1960).
6. H. Brockerhoff, J. R. Hoyle, P. C. Hwang, and C. Litchfield, Lipids, 3, 25 (1968).
7. H. Brockerhoff and M. Yurkowski, J. Lipid Res., 7, 62 (1966).
8. M. H. Chahine, E. R. Cousins, and R. O. Feuge, J. Amer. Oil Chem. Soc., 35, 396 (1958).
9. B. M. Craig, in Progress in the Chemistry of Fats and Other Lipids (R. T. Holman, W. O. Lundberg, and T. Malkin, eds.), Vol. IV, Pergamon Press, London, 1955.
10. D. Chapman, Chem. Rev., 16, 433 (1962).
11. M. H. Coleman and W. C. Fulton, J. Amer. Oil Chem. Soc., 38, 685 (1962).
12. E. W. Crampton, R. H. Common, F. A. Farmer, F. W. Berryhill, and L. Wiseblatt, J. Nutr., 44, 197 (1962).
13. E. W. Crampton, R. H. Common, E. T. Pritchard, and F. A. Farmer, J. Nutr., 60, 13 (1956).
14. K. Dahle, E. G. Hill, and R. T. Holman, Arch. Biochem. Biophys., 98, 253 (1962).
15. L. R. Dugan, Jr., in World Review of Nutrition and Dietetics (G. H. Bourne, ed.), S. Karger, Basel, New York, 1968.
16. L. R. Dugan, Jr., in Encyclopedia of Chemical Technology (R. E. Kirk and D. F. Othmer, eds.), Vol. 2, Interscience Encyclopedia, New York, 1962.
17. C. D. Evans, D. G. McConnell, G. R. List, and C. R. Scholfield, J. Amer. Oil Chem. Soc., 46, 421 (1969).
18. E. N. Frankel, F. L. Thomas, and J. C. Cowan, J. Amer. Oil Chem. Soc., 47, 497 (1970).
19. C. M. Gooding, Chem. Ind., 344 (1966).
20. F. D. Gunstone, Chem. Ind., 64 (1964).
21. C. W. Hoerr and F. R. Paulicka, J. Amer. Oil Chem. Soc., 45, 793 (1968).
22. G. Hoffman, J. Amer. Oil Chem. Soc., 38, 1 (1961).
23. R. G. Jensen, J. Sampugna, R. M. Parry, Jr., K. M. Shahani, and R. C. Chandan, J. Dairy Sci., 45, 1527 (1962).
24. R. G. Jensen, J. Sampugna, and R. L. Pereira, J. Dairy Sci., 47, 727 (1964).
25. A. R. S. Kartha, Studies on the Natural Fats, Vol. 1, published by the author, Ernakulam, India, 1951.
26. W. I. Kimoto and A. M. Gaddis, J. Amer. Oil Chem. Soc., 46, 403 (1969).
27. W. E. M. Lands, R. A. Pieringer, Sister P. M. Slakey, and A. Zschocke, Lipids, 1, 444 (1966).
28. F. H. Mattson and R. A. Volpenhein, J. Amer. Oil Chem. Soc., 39, 3 (1962).
29. W. L. Porter, L. A. Levasseru, and A. S. Henick, Lipids, 6, 1 (1971).
30. O. S. Privett and L. J. Nutter, Lipids, 2, 149 (1967).

31. E. E. Rice, C. E. Poling, P. E. Mone, and W. D. Warner, J. Amer. Oil Chem. Soc., 37, 607 (1960).

32. S. P. Rock and H. Roth, J. Amer. Oil Chem. Soc., 43, 116 (1966).

33. P. N. Rylander, J. Amer. Oil Chem. Soc., 47, 482 (1970).

34. T. H. Smouse and S. S. Chang, J. Amer. Oil Chem. Soc., 44, 509 (1967).

35. D. Swern, ed., Bailey's Industrial Oil and Fat Products, 3rd ed., Interscience, New York, 1964.

36. R. J. VanderWal, J. Amer. Oil Chem. Soc., 37, 18 (1960).

37. R. J. VanderWal, in Advances in Lipid Research, Vol. 2, Academic Press, New York, London, 1964.

38. T. J. Weiss, G. A. Jacobson, and L. H. Wiedermann, J. Amer. Oil Chem. Soc., 38, 396 (1961).

39. L. H. Wiedermann, T. J. Weiss, G. A. Jacobson, and K. F. Mattill, J. Amer. Oil Chem. Soc., 38, 389 (1961).

GENERAL REFERENCES

N. R. Artman, Advan. Lipid Res., 7, 245 (1969).

N. R. Artman and J. C. Alexander, J. Amer. Oil Chem. Soc., 45, 643 (1968).

M. H. Coleman and W. C. Fulton, in 6th Intl. Conf. Biochem., Problems of Lipids (P. Desnuelle, ed.), Pergamon Press, London, 1961.

P. Desnuelle, in Progress in the Chemistry of Fats and Other Lipids (R. T. Holman, W. O. Lundberg, and T. Malkin, eds.), Vol. 1, Pergamon Press, London, 1952.

H. J. Deuel, Jr., The Lipids, Vol. 1, Chemistry. Interscience, New York, 1951.

A. Dolev, W. K. Rohwedder, and H. J. Dutton, Lipids, 2, 28 (1967).

E. W. Eckey, Vegetable Fats and Oils, Rheinhold, New York, 1954.

E. N. Frankel, J. Amer. Oil Chem. Soc., 47, 11 (1970).

A. M. Gaddis, R. Ellis, and G. T. Currie, J. Amer. Oil Chem. Soc., 38, 371 (1961).

H. W. Gardner and D. Weisleder, Lipids, 5, 768 (1970).

W. Grosch and J. M. Schwarz, Lipids, 6, 351 (1971).

F. D. Gunstone, Introduction to the Chemistry and Biochemistry of Fatty Acids and Their Glycerides, 2nd ed., Chapman and Hall, London, 1967.

G. H. deHaas, I. Mulder, and L. L. M. Van Deenen, Biochem. Biophys. Res. Comm., 3, 287 (1960).

D. J. Hanahan, Lipide Chemistry, Wiley, New York and London, 1960.

D. J. Hanahan, H. Brockerhoff, and E. J. Barron, J. Biol. Chem., 235, 1917 (1960).

T. P. Hilditch, The Chemical Composition of Natural Fats, 3rd ed., Rev., Wiley, New York, 1956.

R. T. Holman, in Progress in the Chemistry of Fats and Other Lipids (R. T. Holman, W. O. Lundberg, and T. Malkin, eds.), Vol. 2, Pergamon Press, London, 1954.

A. R. S. Kartha, J. Sci. Ind. Res. (India), 21A, 577 (1962).

J. Kendrick and B. M. Watts, Lipids, 4, 454 (1969).

S. Koritala, J. Amer. Oil Chem. Soc., 45, 197 (1968).

H. R. Kraybill, L. R. Dugan, Jr., B. W. Beadle, F. C. Vibrans, V. Swartz, and H. Rezebek, J. Amer. Oil Chem. Soc., 26, 449 (1949).

D. A. Lillard and E. A. Day, J. Amer. Oil Chem. Soc., 41, 549 (1964).

E. S. Lutton, J. Amer. Oil Chem. Soc., 48, 245 (1971).

E. S. Lutton, M. F. Mallery, and J. Burgers, J. Amer. Oil Chem. Soc., 39, 233 (1962).

T. K. Mag, J. Amer. Oil Chem. Soc., 50, 251 (1973).

T. Malkin, in Progress in the Chemistry of Fats and Other Lipids (R. T. Holman, W. O. Lundberg, and T. Malkin, eds.), Vol. 1, Pergamon Press, London, 1952.

R. F. Matthews, R. A. Scanlan, and L. M. Libbey, J. Amer. Oil Chem. Soc., 48, 745 (1971).

F. H. Mattson and R. A. Volpenhein, J. Lipid Res., 4, 392 (1962).

S. T. Michalski and E. G. Hammond, J. Amer. Oil Chem. Soc., 49, 563 (1972).

J. H. Nelson, J. Amer. Oil Chem. Soc., 49, 559 (1972).

E. S. Pattisen, ed., Fatty Acids and Their Industrial Applications, Marcel Dekker, Inc., New York, 1968.

F. R. Paulicka and C. W. Hoerr, in Encyclopedia of X-rays and Gamma Rays (G. L. Clark, ed.), Reinhold, New York, 1963.

E. G. Perkins, Food Technol., 14, 508 (1960).

O. S. Privett and C. Nickell, Fette, Seifen, Anstrichmittel, 61, 842 (1959).

K. G. Raghuveen and E. G. Hammond, J. Amer. Oil Chem. Soc., 44, 239 (1967).

H. Ralph Rawls and P. J. VanSanten, J. Amer. Oil Chem. Soc., 47, 212 (1970).

R. A. Scanlan, L. A. Sather, and E. A. Day, J. Dairy Sci., 48, 1582 (1965).

C. R. Scholfield, E. P. Jones, J. Nowakowska, E. Selke, and H. J. Dutton, J. Amer. Oil Chem. Soc., 38, 208 (1961).

M. K. Schwitzer, Continuous Processing of Fats, Chemical Publishing, New York, 1959.

R. G. Seals and E. G. Hammond, J. Amer. Oil Chem. Soc., 47, 278 (1970).

K. M. Shahani, J. Dairy Sci., 49, 907 (1966).

D. Swern, ed., Bailey's Industrial Oil and Fat Products, 3rd ed., Interscience, New York, London, Sydney, 1964.

A. E. Waltring and H. Zmachinski, J. Amer. Oil Chem. Soc., 47, 530 (1970).

W. A. Waters, J. Amer. Oil Chem. Soc., 48, 428 (1971).

T. J. Weiss, Food Oils and Their Uses, AVI Publ., Westport, Conn., 1970.

P. B. Wells, Chem. Ind., 1742 (1964).

J. B. Woerfel, R. W. Bates, W. Q. Braun, O. J. Pickens, and H. T. Spannuth, Baker's Dig., 26, 54 (1952).

Chapter 5

AMINO ACIDS, PEPTIDES, AND PROTEINS

A. F. Anglemier and M. W. Montgomery

Department of Food Science and Technology
Oregon State University
Corvallis, Oregon

Contents

I. INTRODUCTION

Proteins are molecules of great size, complexity, and diversity. They are the source of dietary amino acids, both essential and nonessential, that are used for growth, maintenance, and the general wellbeing of man. These macromolecules, characterized by their nitrogen contents, are involved in many vital processes intricately associated with all living matter. In mammals, including man, proteins function as structural components of the body. Muscles and many internal organs are largely composed of proteins. Mineral matter of bone is held together by collagenous protein. Skin, the protective covering of the body, often accounts for about 10% of the total body protein.

Some proteins function as biocatalysts (enzymes and hormones) to regulate chemical reactions within the body. Fundamental life processes, such as growth, digestion and metabolism, excretion, conversion of chemical energy into mechanical work, etc., are controlled by enzymes and hormones. Blood plasma proteins and hemoglobin regulate the osmotic pressure and pH of certain body fluids. Proteins are necessary for immunological reactions. Antibodies, modified plasma globulin proteins, defend against the invasion of foreign substances or microorganisms that can cause various diseases. Food allergies result when certain ingested proteins cause an apparent modification in the defense mechanism. This leads to a variety of painful, and occasionally drastic, conditions in certain individuals.

Food shortages exist in many areas of the world, and they are likely to become more acute and widespread as the world's population increases. Providing adequate supplies of protein poses a much greater problem than providing adequate supplies of either carbohydrate or fat. Proteins not only are more costly to produce than fats or carbohydrates but the daily protein requirement per kilogram of bodyweight remains constant throughout adult life, whereas the requirements for fats and carbohydrates generally decrease with age.

As briefly described above, proteins have diverse biological functions, structures, and properties. Many proteins are susceptible to alteration by a number of rather subtle changes in the immediate environment. Maximum knowledge of the composition, structure, and chemical properties of the raw materials, especially proteins, is required if contemporary and future processing of foods is to best meet the needs of mankind. A considerable amount of information is already available, although much of it has been collected by biochemists using a specific food component as a model system.

In order to meet future requirements for food proteins, several courses of action are necessary. New sources of food proteins are needed, the appropriate technology concerning their utilization must be developed, and more efficient use of conventional proteins must be achieved. Fulfillment of these goals presents a tremendous challenge and opportunity to those involved in food science and related fields.

II. TYPES, STRUCTURES, AND TERMINOLOGY

A. Amino Acids

Amino acids are the "building blocks" of proteins. Therefore, to understand the
properties of proteins, a discussion of the structures and properties of amino acids
is required [65,81]. Amino acids are chemical compounds which contain both
basic amino groups and acidic carboxyl groups. Amino acids found in proteins have
both the amino and carboxyl groups on the α-carbon atom. α-Amino acids have the
following general structure:

$$
\begin{array}{c}
NH_2 \\
| \\
R-C-COOH \\
| \\
H
\end{array}
$$

At neutral pH values in aqueous solutions both the amino and the carboxyl groups
are ionized. The carboxyl group loses a proton and obtains a negative charge,
while the amino group gains a proton and hence acquires a positive charge. As a
consequence, amino acids possess dipolar characteristics. The dipolar, or zwit-
terion, form of amino acids has the following general structure:

$$
\begin{array}{c}
\overset{+}{NH_3} \\
| \\
R-C-COO^- \\
| \\
H
\end{array}
$$

Several properties of amino acids provide evidence for this structure: they are
more soluble in water than in less polar solvents; when present in crystalline form
they melt or decompose at relatively high temperatures (generally above 200 °C);
and they exhibit large dipole moments and large dielectric constants in neutral
aqueous solutions.

The R groups, or side chains, of amino acids exert important influences on
the chemical properties of amino acids and proteins. These side chains may be
classified into four groups as shown in Table 5-1.

Amino acids with polar-uncharged (hydrophilic) R groups can hydrogen bond with
water and are generally soluble in aqueous solutions. The hydroxyls of serine,
threonine, and tyrosine; the sulfhydryl or thiol of cysteine; and the amides of asparagine and glutamine are the functional moieties present in R groups of this class
of amino acids. Two of these, the thiol of cysteine and the hydroxyl of tyrosine,
are slightly ionized at pH 7 and can lose a proton much more readily than others
in this class. The amides of asparagine and glutamine are readily hydrolyzed by
acid or base to aspartic and glutamic acids, respectively.

Amino acids with nonpolar (hydrophobic) R groups are less soluble in aqueous
solvents than amino acids with polar-uncharged R groups. The five with hydrocarbon side chains decrease in polarity as the length of the side chain is increased.
The unique structure of proline (and its hydroxylated derivative, hydroxyproline)
causes this imino acid to play a unique role in protein structure, as is discussed
in Section II.C.

TABLE 5-1

Structures of the Most Abundant Species of L-Amino Acids at pH 6-7

Polar–uncharged R groups		Nonpolar R groups	
Name	Structure	Name	Structure
Glycine	$\overset{+NH_3}{\underset{}{H-CH-COO^-}}$	Alanine	$\overset{+NH_3}{\underset{}{CH_3-CH-COO^-}}$
Serine	$\overset{+NH_3}{\underset{}{HO-CH_2-CH-COO^-}}$	Valine	CH_3 $\overset{+NH_3}{CH-CH-COO^-}$ CH_3
Threonine	$\overset{+NH_3}{\underset{OH}{CH_3-CH-CH-COO^-}}$	Leucine	CH_3 $\overset{+NH_3}{CH-CH_2-CH-COO^-}$ CH_3
Cysteine	$\overset{+NH_3}{\underset{}{HS-CH_2-CH-COO^-}}$	Isoleucine	$\overset{H_3C\ \ +NH_3}{CH_3-CH_2-CH-CH-COO^-}$
Cystine	$\overset{+NH_3}{S-CH_2-CH-COO^-}$ $\overset{+NH_3}{S-CH_2-CH-COO^-}$	Phenyl-alanine	$\overset{+NH_3}{\bigcirc-CH_2-CH-COO^-}$
Tyrosine	$HO-\bigcirc-\overset{+NH_3}{CH_2-CH-COO^-}$	Tryptophan	$\overset{+NH_3}{CH_2-CH-COO^-}$ indole-N-H
Asparagine	$\overset{NH_2\ \ +NH_3}{O=C-CH_2-CH-COO^-}$	Methionine	$\overset{+NH_3}{CH_3-S-CH_2-CH_2-CH-COO^-}$
Glutamine	$\overset{NH_2\ \ \ \ \ +NH_3}{O=C-CH_2-CH_2-CH-COO^-}$		

Negatively charged R groups		Positively charged R groups	
Name	Structure	Name	Structure
Aspartic acid	$\overset{+NH_3}{^-OOC-CH_2-CH-COO^-}$	Lysine	$\overset{+NH_3}{CH_2-CH_2-CH_2-CH_2-}\overset{+NH_3}{CH-COO^-}$

TABLE 5-1 (Continued)

Negatively charged R groups		Positively charged R groups	
Name	Structure	Name	Structure
Glutamic acid	$^+NH_3$ $^-OOC-CH_2-CH_2-\overset{|}{C}H-COO^-$	Arginine	$^+NH_3$ $^+NH_3$ $\overset{||}{C}NHCH_2-CH_2-CH_2-\overset{|}{C}H-COO^-$ NH
		Histidine	$\underset{\underset{H}{|}}{\underset{N}{HN}}\underset{}{\overset{+}{\rlap{—}}}\;CH_2-\overset{+NH_3}{\overset{|}{C}H}-COO^-$

Imino acids			
Proline	$\underset{H_2}{\overset{+}{N}}-COO^-$	Hydroxy-proline	$HO\underset{H_2}{\overset{+}{N}}-COO^-$

The amino acids with positively charged (basic) R groups at pH 6–7 are lysine, arginine, and histidine. The amino group is responsible for the positive charge of lysine, while arginine has a positively charged guanidino group. At pH 7.0, 10% of the imidazole groups of histidine molecules are protonated, but more than 50% carry positive charges at pH 6.0.

The dicarboxylic amino acids, aspartic and glutamic, possess net negative charges in the neutral pH range. An important artificial meat–flavoring food additive is the monosodium salt of glutamic acid.

If we define acids as substances that donate protons and bases as substances that accept protons, amino acids may be visualized as both acids and bases. The carboxyl group acts as an acid and the amino group acts as a base. Dissociation of an acid (the proton donor) may be expressed in the following general manner:

$$AH \rightleftharpoons A^- + H^+ \tag{5-1}$$

If the solution is dilute (so the activity of water can be taken as 1.0), an apparent dissociation constant may be written:

$$K' = \frac{[A^-]\,[H^+]}{AH} \tag{5-2}$$

From this equation it may be seen that if $[A^-]$ is equal to $[AH]$ (at half neutralization), then

$$K' = [H^+] \tag{5-3}$$

Hence, the apparent dissociation constant can be defined as the hydrogen ion concentration (moles per liter) at which the acid is half neutralized. Since it is customary to express the hydrogen ion concentration as a negative logarithm, K' also may be expressed as:

$$pK' = \log \frac{1}{K'} = -\log K' \tag{5-4}$$

Amino acid carboxyl groups have pK' values in the range 2-3, while those for amino groups range from 9 to 10. Hence, if a fully protonated amino acid is titrated with a base, two protons are released. The titration curve for glycine is shown in Figure 5-1. The titration curve is the result of the following two neutralization reactions:

$$\overset{+}{N}H_3CH_2COOH \xrightarrow{OH^-} \overset{+}{N}H_3CH_2COO^- + H_2O \tag{5-5}$$

$$\overset{+}{N}H_3CH_2COO^- \xrightarrow{OH^-} NH_2CH_2COO^- + H_2O \tag{5-6}$$

At half neutralization, pK'_1 in the first reaction, the concentrations of the proton donor and acceptor are equal. The same is true for pK'_2 in the second reaction. At pH 6.06 the net charge of glycine is zero and hence it does not migrate in an electrical field. This pH is called the isoelectric point (pI), and it is the mean of pK'_1 and pK'_2:

$$pI = \frac{pK'_1 + pK'_2}{2} \tag{5-7}$$

The pK''s of the two groups which ionize to change the sign of the net charge on the molecule are used to calculate pI values. Values of pK' for certain amino acids are presented in Table 5-2.

Carboxyl groups of amino acids normally have pK' values that are lower than those of aliphatic acids (acetic acid $pK' = 4.76$). This is presumably due to the location of the positively charged amino group on the same carbon as the carboxyl group. The electron-withdrawing (inductive) effect of NH_3^+ causes the proton to be lost more readily from the carboxyl group resulting in a lower pK'.

Aliphatic R groups have little effect on pK' values of α-carboxyl or amino groups. However, the presence of a carboxyl, amide, sulfhydryl, phenolic, or basic group (as in arginine and lysine) in the R group decreases pK' values of α-carboxyl groups. Ionization of the α-amino group also is influenced by functional groups on the side chain. Particularly noticeable is the higher pK'_2 of cysteine caused by the nearby ionized sulfhydryl group. The strongly basic guanidino group of arginine and the ϵ-amino group of lysine lose protons at a high pH. Histidine is the only amino acid with any appreciable buffering capacity at physiological pH values of 6-8.

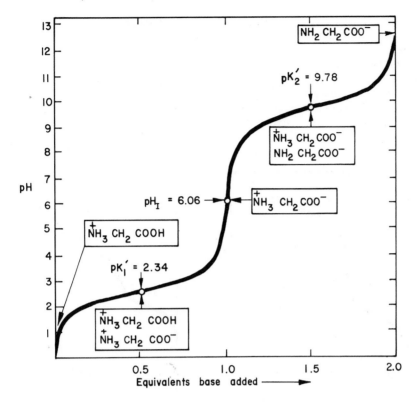

FIG. 5-1. Titration curve for glycine. Modified from Ref. [81].

TABLE 5-2

pK' and pI Values of Certain Amino Acids

	pK'$_1$ α-COO$^-$	pK'$_2$ + α-NH$_3$	pK'$_R$ R group	pI
Glycine	2.34	9.78		6.06
Alanine	2.35	9.69		6.02
Isoleucine	2.36	9.68		6.02
Serine	2.21	9.15		5.68
Aspartic acid	2.09	9.82	3.86	2.97
Asparagine	2.02	8.80		5.41
Glutamic acid	2.19	9.67	4.25	3.22
Glutamine	2.17	9.13		5.65
Histidine	1.82	9.17	6.00	7.58
Cysteine	1.71	10.78	8.33	5.02
Tyrosine	2.20	9.11	10.07	5.65
Arginine	2.17	9.04	12.48	10.76
Lysine	2.18	8.95	10.53	9.74

Titration curves for amino acids with ionizable R groups are complex. The titration curves of aspartic acid, lysine, and histidine are shown as examples in Figure 5-2.

Although the 21 amino acids discussed above make up the majority of the amino acids found in proteins, other naturally occurring amino acids have been observed in minor amounts, and many others have been synthesized chemically. Hydroxylysine has been isolated from collagen hydrolyzates. Both desmosine and isodesmosine have been found in hydrolyzates of elastin, a fibrous protein possessing

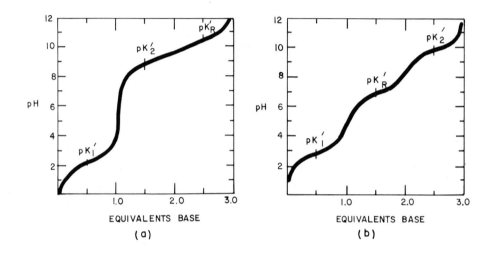

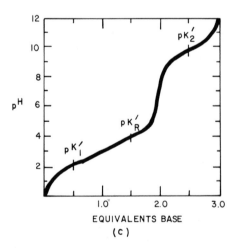

FIG. 5-2. Titration curves for (a) lysine, (b) histidine, and (c) aspartic acid. Modified from Ref. [81].

elastic properties. Several nonprotein amino acids also occur as normal metabolites.

Since all amino acids, with the exception of glycine, contain an asymmetric carbon, both L and D optical isomers are possible. However, only L-amino acids (i.e., those having configuration similar to L-glyceraldehyde) have been found in proteins. This structural similarity of amino acids is an important factor in dictating the structure of proteins. A second center of asymmetry is present in four amino acids: isoleucine, hydroxylysine, threonine and hydroxyproline. The amino acid configurations shown in Table 5-1 are those found in nature.

The aromatic amino acids - tryptophan, tyrosine and phenylalanine - are the only three amino acids that absorb light significantly in the ultraviolet range (Fig. 5-3). Since most proteins contain tyrosine residues, the spectrophotometric measurement of light absorption at 280 nm is a convenient and rapid method for estimating the protein concentration of a solution.

B. Peptides

When the amino group of one amino acid reacts with the carboxyl group of another amino acid, a peptide bond is formed and a molecule of water is released. This C-N bond joins amino acids together to form proteins.

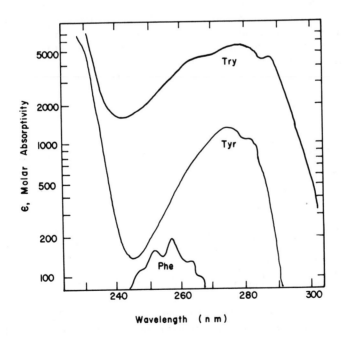

FIG. 5-3. Ultraviolet absorption spectra of phenylalanine (Phe), tyrosine (Tyr), and tryptophan (Try). Modified from Ref. [143].

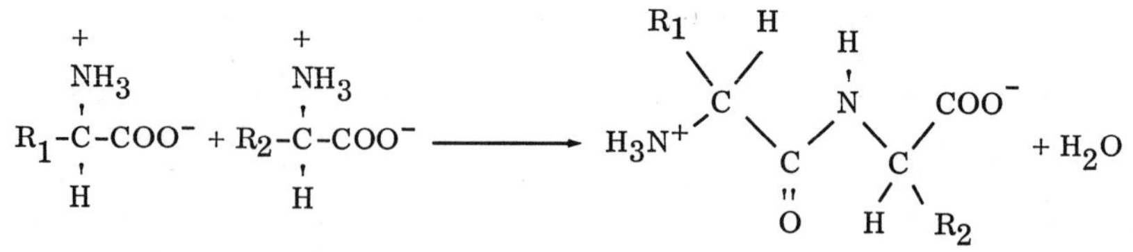

$$\begin{array}{c}\overset{+}{NH_3}\\ |\\ R_1\text{-}\overset{|}{C}\text{-}COO^-\\ |\\ H\end{array} + \begin{array}{c}\overset{+}{NH_3}\\ |\\ R_2\text{-}\overset{|}{C}\text{-}COO^-\\ |\\ H\end{array} \longrightarrow \quad H_3N^+ \quad \begin{array}{c} R_1 \quad H \quad H \\ C \quad N \quad COO^- \\ C \quad C \\ O \quad H \quad R_2 \end{array} + H_2O \qquad (5\text{-}8)$$

The peptide bond is slightly shorter than other single C-N bonds. This indicates that the peptide bond has some characteristics of a double bond, because of resonance stabilization with the carbonyl oxygen. Thus groups adjacent to the peptide bond cannot rotate freely. This rigidity of the peptide bond

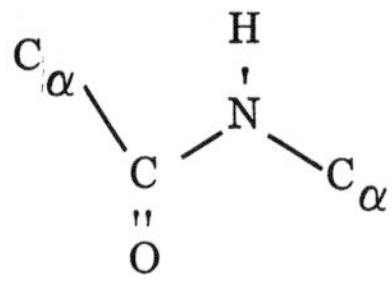

$$\begin{array}{c} C_\alpha \qquad\qquad H \\ \diagdown \quad | \\ C \quad N \\ || \qquad \diagdown C_\alpha \\ O \end{array}$$

holds the six atoms shown above in a single plane [21]. The imino (-NH-) group does not ionize between pH 0 and 14 due to the double-bond properties of the peptide bond [81]. In addition, R groups on amino acid residues, because of steric hindrance, force oxygen and hydrogen of the peptide bond to exist in a trans configuration. Therefore, the backbone of peptides and proteins has free rotation in two of the three bonds between amino acids.

If a few amino acids are joined together by peptide bonds, the compound is called a "peptide." Most natural peptides are formed by the partial hydrolysis of proteins; however, a few peptides are important metabolites. Anserine and carnosine are two derivatives of histidine that are found in muscles of animals. The biochemical function of these peptides is not understood [81].

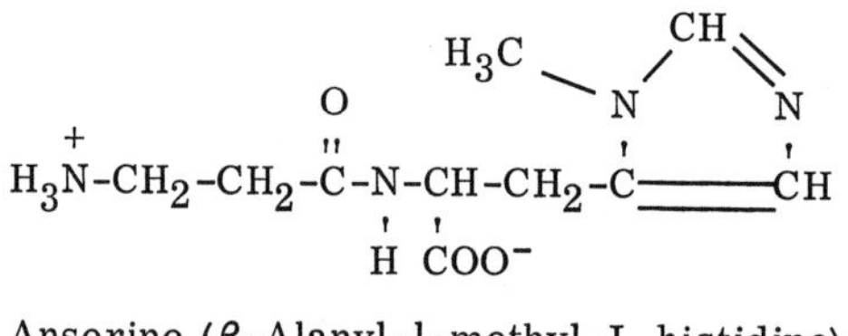

$$H_3\overset{+}{N}\text{-}CH_2\text{-}CH_2\text{-}\overset{\overset{\displaystyle O}{||}}{C}\text{-}N\text{-}CH\text{-}CH_2\text{-}\overset{\overset{\displaystyle H_3C\diagdown_N\diagup^{CH}\diagdown_N}{|}}{\underset{\overset{|}{COO^-}}{C}}\text{====}CH$$

Anserine (β-Alanyl-l-methyl-L-histidine)

$$H_3\overset{+}{N}\text{-}CH_2\text{-}CH_2\text{-}\overset{\overset{\displaystyle O}{||}}{C}\text{-}N\text{-}CH\text{-}CH_2\text{-}\overset{\overset{\displaystyle HN\diagup^{CH}\diagdown_N}{}}{\underset{\overset{|}{COO^-}}{C}}\text{====}CH$$

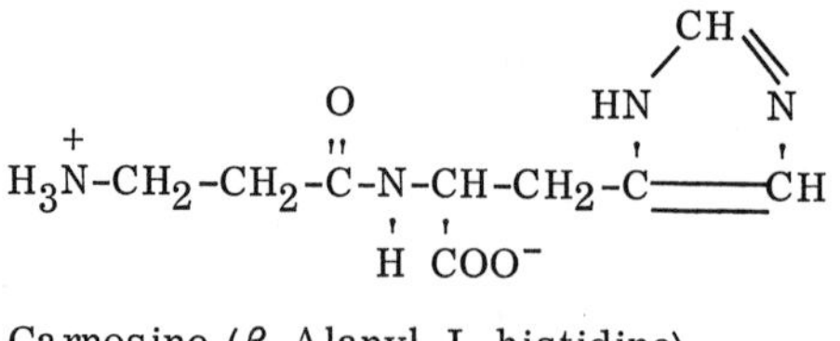

Carnosine (β-Alanyl-L-histidine)

Glutathione occurs in mammalian blood, yeast, and especially in tissues of rapidly dividing cells. It is thought to function in oxidative metabolism and detoxification.

$$\overset{+}{N}H_3 \qquad\qquad O \qquad CH_2SH_H$$
$$^-OOC-CH-CH_2-CH_2-\overset{O}{\overset{\|}{C}}-N-CH-\overset{}{C}-N-CH_2-COO^-$$
$$H \qquad O$$

Reduced glutathione (γ-Glutamylcysteinylglycine)

During oxidation, two molecules of glutathione join via a disulfide bridge (-S-S-) between two cysteine residues. The peptide bond between the γ-carbonyl of glutamic acid and cysteine is not found in proteins.

Other peptides function as antibodies and hormones. Oxytocin and vasopressin are examples of peptide hormones.

The terminal amino and carboxyl groups of peptides are usually free to ionize but as has been mentioned the peptide bond does not form any ionizable groups in the normal pH range of 0-14. Since terminal amino and carboxyl groups of peptides are widely separated, electrostatic interactions are less in peptides than in amino acids. Therefore, the pK' values of the carboxyl groups are increased and those of the amino groups are decreased. For example, the pK'_1 of glycine is increased from 2.34 to 3.06 in glycylglycine, while the pK'_2 is decreased from 9.78 to 8.13 [81]. The pK''s of R groups are approximately the same in short peptides as in the corresponding free amino acids.

C. Protein Structure

Proteins perform a wide variety of biological functions and since they are composed of hundreds of amino acids, their structures are much more complex than those of peptides.

Enzymes are globular proteins produced in living matter for the special purpose of catalyzing vital chemical reactions that otherwise do not occur under physiological conditions [143]. Hemoglobin and myoglobin are heme-containing proteins that transport oxygen and carbon dioxide in the blood and muscles. The major muscle proteins, actin and myosin, convert chemical energy to mechanical work, while proteins in tendons (collagen and elastin) bind muscles to bones. Skin, hair, fingernails, and toenails are proteinaceous protective substances. The food scientist is concerned about proteins in foods since knowledge of protein structure and behavior allows him to more ably manipulate foods for the benefit of mankind.

Nearly an infinite number of proteins could be synthesized from the 21 natural occurring amino acids. However, it has been estimated that only about 2000 different proteins exist in nature. The number is greater than this if one considers the slight variations found in proteins from different species.

1. PRIMARY STRUCTURE

The linear sequence of amino acids in a protein is referred to as "primary structure" (Fig. 5-4). In a few proteins the primary structure has been determined and one protein (ribonuclease) has been synthesized in the laboratory [67]. It is the unique sequence of amino acids that imparts many of the fundamental properties to

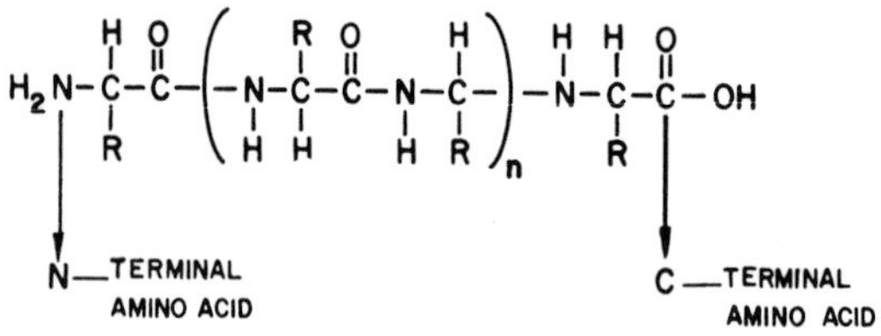

FIG. 5-4. Primary structure of a polypeptide chain showing the N- and C-terminal amino acids.

different proteins and determines in large measure their secondary and tertiary structures [25]. If the protein contains a considerable number of amino acids with hydrophobic groups, its solubility in aqueous solvents is probably less than that of proteins containing amino acids with many hydrophilic groups [21].

2. SECONDARY STRUCTURE

If the primary structure of the protein were not folded, protein molecules would be excessively long and thin. A protein having a molecular weight of 13,000 would be 448 Å long and 3.7 Å thick. This structure allows excessive interaction with other substances, and it is not found in nature. The three-dimensional manner in which relatively close members of the protein chain are arranged is referred to as "secondary structure." Examples of secondary structure are the α-helix of wool, the pleated-sheet configuration of silk, and the collagen helix [40].

The native structure of a protein is that structure which possesses the lowest feasible free energy. Therefore, the structure of a protein is not random but somewhat ordered. When the restrictions of the peptide bond are superimposed on a polyamino acid chain of a globular protein, a right-handed coil, the α-helix, appears to be one of the most ordered and stable structures feasible (Fig. 5-5).

The α-helix contains 3.6 amino acid residues per turn of the protein backbone, with the R groups of the amino acids extending outward from the axis of the helical structure. Hydrogen bonding can occur between the nitrogen of one peptide bond and the oxygen of another peptide bond four residues along the protein chain. The hydrogen bonds are nearly parallel to the axis of the helix, lending strength to the helical structure. Since this arrangement allows each peptide bond to form a hydrogen bond, the stability of the structure is greatly enhanced [39]. The coil of the helix is sufficiently compact and stable that even substances with strong tendencies to participate in hydrogen bonding, such as water, cannot enter the core [99].

Since the α-helix has the lowest feasible free energy, formation of this structure is spontaneous, provided there are no strong interactions of amino acid R groups with the solvent or with each other. Since natural amino acids exist in an L configuration, a right-hand helix is more stable than a left-hand helix. Therefore, if helical structures exist in proteins they are invariably right-handed helices [81]. The helical structure may be interrupted because of interactions between charged R groups or steric hindrance by residues on the larger amino acids. For example, the unique structures of proline and hydroxyproline preclude the formation of hydrogen bonds in the α-helix; thus these imino acids produce bends or kinks in the

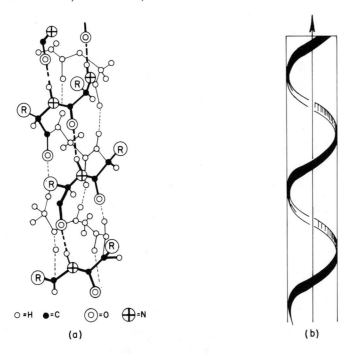

O =H ●=C ◎=O ⊕=N

(a)   (b)

FIG. 5-5. The right-handed α-helix (a) and graphical sketch (b) of the helical structure. Modified from Ref. [75].

protein structure. Examples of protein types in which the α-helix predominates are enzymes and respiratory proteins. These are spheroidal or globular in shape and are concerned mainly with biochemical and physiological metabolism.

A secondary structure found in many fibrous proteins is the β-pleated sheet configuration (Fig. 5-6). In this configuration the peptide backbone forms a zigzag pattern, with the R groups of the amino acids extending above and below the peptide chain. Since all peptide bonds are available for hydrogen bonding, this configuration allows maximum crosslinking between adjacent polypeptide chains and thus good stability. Both parallel pleated sheets, where the polypeptide chains run in the same direction, and antiparallel pleated sheets, where the polypeptide chains run in opposite directions, are possible [40]. Where R groups are bulky or have like charges, the interactions of the R groups do not allow the pleated-sheet configuration to exist. Silk and insect fibers are the best examples of the β sheet, although feathers of birds contain a complicated form of this configuration.

Another type of secondary structure of fibrous proteins is the collagen helix. Collagen is the most abundant protein in higher vertebrates, accounting for one-third of the total body protein. Collagen resists stretching, is the major component of tendons, and contains one-third glycine and one-fourth proline or hydroxyproline. The rigid R groups, and the lack of hydrogen bonding by peptide linkages involving proline and hydroxyproline, prevents formation of an α-helical structure and forces

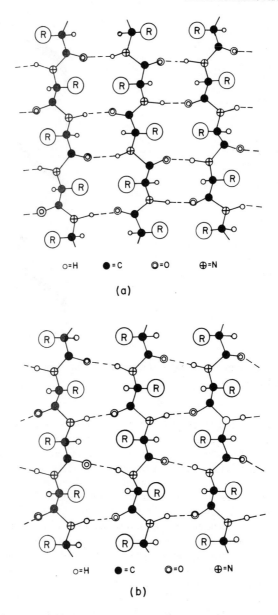

FIG. 5-6. Diagrammatic representation of antiparallel (a) and parallel (b) β-pleated sheets. Modified from Ref. [75].

the collagen polypeptide chain into an odd kinked-type helix. Peptide bonds composed of glycine form interchain hydrogen bonds with two other collagen polypeptide chains, and this results in a stable triple helix. This triple-helical structure is called "tropocollagen" and it has a molecular weight of 300,000 daltons [15].

3. TERTIARY STRUCTURE

The manner in which large portions of the protein chain are arranged is referred to as tertiary structure. This involves folding of regular units of the secondary structure as well as the structuring of areas of the peptide chain that are devoid of secondary structure. For example, some proteins contain areas where α-helical structure exists and other areas where this structure cannot form. Depending on the amino acid sequence, the length of the α-helical portion varies and imparts a unique tertiary structure. These folded portions are held together by hydrogen bonds formed between R groups, by salt linkages, by hydrophobic interactions, and by covalent disulfide (-S-S-) linkages (Fig. 5-7).

Disulfide linkages are the strongest bonds maintaining the tertiary structure of the protein. Hydrophobic interactions occur between nonpolar regions of the protein molecule. Salt linkages are thought to be unimportant in maintaining the tertiary structure of the protein, since ionic groups of proteins have a tendency to react with ions in the surrounding medium and to become highly hydrated.

In proteins for which tertiary structures have been determined, the hydrophobic amino acids tend to be folded to the interior of the protein molecule, while most of the polar or hydrophilic residues are on the surface. The presence of polar R groups on the surface of proteins usually accounts for their solubility in aqueous solutions.

The α-helix content of proteins can vary greatly. Proline, amino acids with like charges, and amino acids that do not readily form α-helical coils (isoleucine and serine) result in bends in the protein structure.

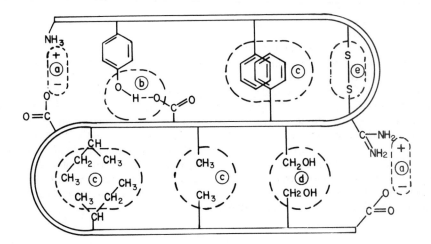

FIG. 5-7. Bonds which stabilize secondary and tertiary structures of proteins: (a) electrostatic interaction, (b) hydrogen bonding, (c) hydrophobic interaction, (d) dipole–dipole interaction, and (e) disulfide linkage. Modified from Ref. [4].

4. QUATERNARY STRUCTURE

The structures discussed so far have involved only a single peptide chain. The structure formed when individual (subunit) polypeptide chains interact to form a native protein molecule is referred to as "quaternary structure" [76]. Combining individual polypeptide chains into quaternary structures, generally in multiples of two, has certain advantages [21,81]. This type of structure minimizes the importance of errors that may take place in the biosynthesis of one of the individual protein chains. Since the polypeptide chains that are combined in these structures may consist of two or more identical proteins there is also an economy of DNA and RNA used in synthesis of the protein. Furthermore, complex structures of several polypeptide chains may be used to regulate the metabolism of individual cells. The combination of different protein subunits into the quaternary structure would also account for isozymes that are found in many enzyme systems [81].

The bonding mechanisms that hold protein chains together are generally the same as those involved in tertiary structure, with the possible exception that disulfide bonds do not assist in maintaining the quaternary structures of proteins.

D. Conjugated Proteins

Many proteins exist in combination with carbohydrates, lipids, nucleic acids, metal ions, or phosphate. These substances are referred to as "prosthetic groups" and they are bound to the protein by linkages other than salt linkages. Proteins that exist in such combinations are called "conjugated proteins." Even though there are major differences that exist among the various conjugated proteins, they share one common characteristic - stabilization of their protein component by combination with a prosthetic group [65].

1. LIPOPROTEINS

Lipoproteins, those proteins that exist in natural complexes with lipids, are found in cells and blood serum. It is believed that these complexes of lipids and proteins serve as transporters of lipids in blood and as components of cellular membranes. Lipoproteins are classified according to their density, and since lipids are less dense than proteins, the greater the amount of lipid, the less dense the lipoprotein. The three classes of proteins are referred to as high density, low density and very low density, and their densities are 1.063-1.21, 1.019-1.063, and 1.0006-1.019 g/ml, respectively [65]. The lipid is firmly bound to the protein and cannot be quantitatively removed by ether extraction. However, high concentrations of acetone or alcohol or very low temperatures (-60°C) will separate the lipid portion from the lipoprotein [135]. Lipids found in lipoproteins are triglycerides, phospholipids, cholesterol, or derivatives of cholesterol [65].

2. GLYCOPROTEINS

Proteins conjugated with heterosaccharides as prosthetic groups are defined as "glycoproteins." The heterosaccharides contain hexosamine, either glycosamine or galactosamine or both, and one or several of the following monosaccharides: galactose, mannose, fucose, and sialic acid. Molecular weight of the branched heterosaccharide varies from 500 to 3500 daltons depending on the glycoprotein. A covalent bond joins the protein to the heterosaccharide by either O-glycosidic bonds to hydroxyamino acids (serine or threonine) or by N-glycosidic bonds to the side chain amide of asparagine residues. A pentose is generally immediately adjacent to the protein in the O-glycoside-type glycoproteins, whereas N-acetylglucosamine is usually the sugar involved in the N-glycoside type [57].

Glycoproteins are found in mucous secretions of mammals where they function as lubricating agents for the surfaces of body tissues. Moreover, many of the blood plasma proteins are glycoproteins. Egg white contains a very viscous glycoprotein, ovomucoid, which cannot be coagulated by heat. Certain fractions of soybean protein contain glycoproteins, such as the hemagglutinin and 7S globulin components [148].

3. METALLOPROTEINS

Another group of conjugated proteins is the metalloproteins - complexes of proteins and heavy metals [134]. In most metalloproteins the metal is very loosely bound and can be easily removed. However, with some proteins the metal is contained in a prosthetic heme group and is firmly bound. Examples of these proteins are hemoglobin and myoglobin, wherein iron is bound to the porphyrin moiety, which in turn is bound to protein. Liver and spleen contain a metalloprotein, ferritin, which consists of about 20% iron. Ferritin appears to be a storage form of iron in animals since the iron is released from the protein when needed. Conalbumin from hen's eggs can form a complex with iron resulting in a salmon pink discoloration. Conalbumin will also combine with copper and zinc [45].

4. NUCLEOPROTEINS

Nucleoproteins are complexes of proteins and nucleic acids. Since nucleic acids are polyionic substances which readily combine with proteins, it is possible that some of the nucleoproteins are artifacts formed during the isolation procedures. However, nucleoproteins are known to be present in viruses and ribosomes (a protein-synthesizing organelle in cells) [81].

5. PHOSPHOPROTEINS

Conjugated proteins containing inorganic phosphates are called "phosphoproteins." The most widely known phosphoproteins are casein and pepsin, the proteolytic enzyme found in the stomach. In these proteins the phosphate is bound through a phosphate ester linkage to the hydroxyl group of serine or threonine [65].

E. Protein Classification

From the previous discussion it is no doubt evident that proteins can be classified in a number of ways. One useful classification is based on protein solubility. Albumins are proteins that are soluble in pure water, while globulins are proteins that are insoluble in pure water but are soluble in salt solutions. Most enzymes and hormone proteins belong in either the albumin or globulin class. Another group of proteins found mainly in plant seeds are the glutelins. These proteins are not soluble in either pure water or dilute salt solutions but are soluble in dilute acids or bases. Yet another class of proteins, the prolamines, are soluble in 70-80% alcohol but are insoluble in water or neutral solvents.

III. PHYSICAL AND CHEMICAL PROPERTIES OF AMINO ACIDS AND PROTEINS

Amino acids and proteins contain amino, carboxyl, sulfhydryl, hydroxyl, indole, and imidazole groups, as well as the imine and carbonyl groups of peptide bonds. These functional groups can react with substances in the environment of the protein and with each other to form either inter- or intramolecular bonds; thus, they determine the physical and chemical properties of the protein.

A. Chemical Reactions of Amino Acids and Proteins

1. REACTIONS OF α-CARBOXYL GROUPS

The α-carboxyl groups of all α-amino acids participate in well-known organic reactions leading to the formation of amides, esters, and acyl halides [50]. Esterification with ethyl alcohol proceeds as follows:

$$R-CHNH_2-COOH + C_2H_5OH \xrightarrow[\substack{\text{in EtOH,} \\ \text{reflux}}]{HCl} R-CHNH_2-COOC_2H_5 + H_2O \qquad (5\text{-}9)$$

The α-carboxyl group can also be reduced to the corresponding alcohol.

$$R-CHNH_2-COOH \xrightarrow[\text{reduction}]{NaBH_4} R-CHNH_2CH_2OH + H_2O \qquad (5\text{-}10)$$

This reaction is often used to identify the terminal carboxyl group of a peptide or protein [81].

Amino acids can be decarboxylated to amines by specific enzymes (see Chapter 6) or by heat, acid, base, or special reagents, such as ninhydrin.

$$R-CHNH_2-COOH \longrightarrow R-CH_2NH_2 + CO_2 \qquad (5\text{-}11)$$

Decarboxylation of histidine to histamine has physiological significance.

$$\text{HN} \diagdown \text{N} \diagup \text{CH}_2\text{-CHNH}_2\text{-COOH} \longrightarrow \text{HN} \diagdown \text{N} \diagup \text{CH}_2\text{CH}_2\text{NH}_2 + \text{CO}_2 \qquad (5\text{-}12)$$

Histamine is one of the major mediators of allergy, shock, and similar states in man [50].

In the presence of strong oxidizing agents, amino acids can be oxidized to alde-hydes.

$$\text{R-CHNH}_2\text{-COOH} + \text{NaOCl} + \text{H}_2\text{O} \longrightarrow \text{R-CHO} + \text{NH}_3 + \text{NaCl} + \text{CO}_2 \qquad (5\text{-}13)$$

2. REACTIONS OF AMINO GROUPS

Acylation of the α-amino group of amino acids by treatment with acid halides or anhydrides leads to the formation of acylamino acids.

$$\text{R-CHNH}_2\text{-COOH} + \text{R'-COCl} \xrightarrow[\substack{\text{room} \\ \text{temp.}}]{\substack{\text{aq.} \\ \text{NaOH}}} \begin{array}{c} \text{R-CH-COOH} \\ | \\ \text{NH-CO-R'} \end{array} \qquad (5\text{-}14)$$

Under mild conditions, the stereochemical integrity of the α-amino group is pre-served. This method is used to protect the amino group during laboratory syn-thesis of a peptide or protein [81].

The ninhydrin reaction is one of the most useful reactions of the α-amino group. An intensely colored product is produced when an α-amino acid is heated with nin-hydrin [50]. This blue colored product can be used to quantify small amounts of amino acids in solutions or on paper strips. Proline and hydroxyproline yield products that have a characteristic yellow color. The reaction proceeds in two steps as follows:

1.

Ninhydrin

$$\text{C=O-H}_2\text{O} + \text{R-CHNH}_2\text{-COOH} \longrightarrow$$

$$\text{HCOH} + \text{R-CHO} + \text{NH}_3 + \text{CO}_2 \qquad (5\text{-}15)$$

2.

$$\text{HCOH} + \qquad \text{C=O} + 2\text{NH}_3 \longrightarrow$$

$$\text{(structure with ONH}_4\text{ and C-N=C ...)} + 2H_2O \qquad (5\text{-}16)$$

The α-amino group can also be arylated by 1-fluoro-2,4-dinitrobenzene. This reaction will quantitatively label the amino groups in amino acids, peptides, and proteins.

$$O_2N\text{-(ring,}NO_2\text{)-F} + R\text{-CHNH}_2\text{-COOH} \longrightarrow O_2N\text{-(ring,}NO_2\text{)-NH-CHR-COOH} + HF \qquad (5\text{-}17)$$

The yellow 2,4-dinitrophenyl derivatives, called DNP-amino acids, are formed with terminal amino groups or with the ϵ-amino group of lysine. These derivatives are easily separated by chromatography and are useful in the identification of N-terminal amino acids in peptides and proteins [81].

At room temperature the α-amino group reacts with nitrous acid to produce 1 mole of nitrogen per mole of amino acid [50].

$$R\text{-CHNH}_2\text{-COOH} + HNO_2 \longrightarrow R\text{-CHOH-COOH} + N_2 + H_2O \qquad (5\text{-}18)$$

This is the Van Slyke reaction and it can be used to follow the release of free amino groups during proteolysis.

The formol reaction also can be used to determine α-amino groups [50].

$$R\text{-CHNH}_2\text{-COOH} + HCHO \longrightarrow R\text{-CH-COOH} \xrightarrow{HCHO} R\text{-CH-COOH} \qquad (5\text{-}19)$$

(with NH-CH₂-OH and NH⁺(H₂COH)(CH₂OH) substructures)

This reaction is the basis of Sorensen's formol titration for determining the amount of amino acids in solutions, such as milk.

A reaction similar to that between amino groups and 1-fluoro-2,4-dinitroben-zene has been developed to label N-terminal amino acids in peptides and proteins. Since the labeling reagent, 1-dimethylaminonaphthalene-5-sulfonyl chloride (dansyl chloride), is highly fluorescent, dansyl derivatives of amino acids can be detected and measured in very low concentrations by fluorimetric methods [81].

$$\text{(dansyl chloride structure)} + R\text{-CHNH}_2\text{-COOH} \longrightarrow \text{(dansyl amino acid structure)} \qquad (5\text{-}20)$$

Dansyl chloride   Dansyl amino acid

The α-amino acids react quantitatively with phenylisothiocyanate to yield phenyl-thiocarbamylamino acid derivatives.

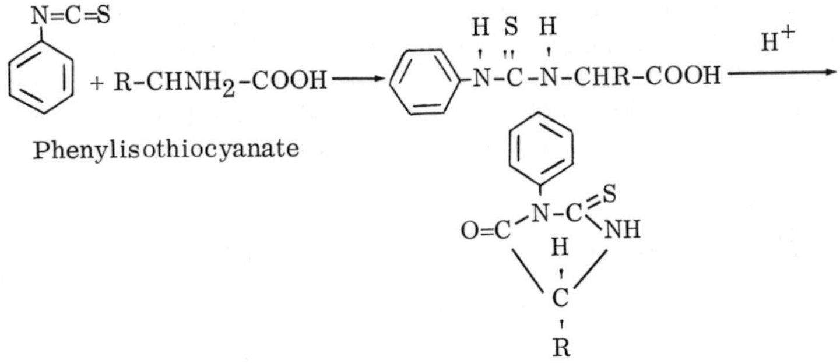

N=C=S

+ R-CHNH$_2$-COOH ⟶

HSH
| || |
-N-C-N-CHR-COOH ⟶ H$^+$

O=C^{-N-C}$\substack{S \\ NH}$
| H
|
C
|
R

(5-21)

Phenylisothiocyanate

Phenylthiohydantoin

Cyclization of the derivatives to phenylthiohydantoin occurs with acid in nitro-methane. This is the Edman reaction, which is widely used to determine the amino acid sequences of both proteins and peptides. The phenylthiohydantoins are colorless, although they are easily separated by chromatographic procedures [81].

Reversible reaction of the α-amino group with aldehydes results in the formation of very labile compounds, called Schiff's bases. These compounds are formed early in nonenzymic browning (Chapter 3).

$$R\text{-}CHNH_2\text{-}COOH + R'\text{-}CHO \rightleftharpoons R\text{-}CH\text{-}COOH + H_2O$$

N
||
HC-R'

(5-22)

Schiff's base

3. REACTIONS OF R GROUPS

The physical and chemical properties of proteins are determined largely by R groups of the component amino acids, since most of the α-amino and α-carboxyl groups are incorporated in peptide linkages. The ϵ-amino group of lysine can of course undergo the reactions of amino groups as presented above.

Hydroxyl groups of serine, threonine, and hydroxyproline can participate in formation of ester linkages and these esters have important influences on the properties of proteins. For example, ester groups can influence the ability of enzymes to bind cofactors, and the phosphate ester shown below imparts special properties to phosphoproteins, such as α-caseins.

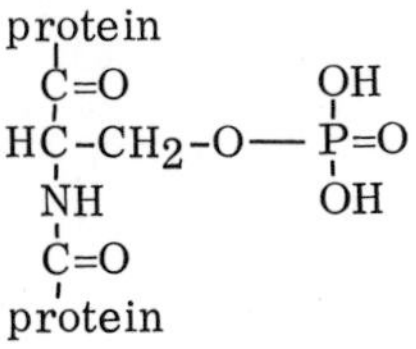

protein
|
C=O   OH
| |
HC-CH$_2$-O — P=O
| |
NH   OH
|
C=O
|
protein

The phenolic hydroxyl of tyrosine contributes to the acidic properties of proteins and this group can be acetylated.

Nonpeptide carboxyl groups of glutamic and aspartic acid residues impart acidic properties to proteins. Many of these carboxyl groups exist in native proteins as the corresponding amines. The aromatic nature of the imidazole structure of histidine allows this amino acid to participate in many of the reactions common to aromatic compounds. The imidazole group of histidine is capable of acting as a general acid or as a general base and it is involved in the active sites of many enzymes [144].

$$H^+ + \quad \mathopen{:}N \underset{\underset{H}{C}}{} N\!-\!H \quad\rightleftharpoons\quad H\!-\!N \underset{\underset{H}{C}}{} N\mathclose{:} \quad + \quad H^+ \tag{5-23}$$

The guanidino group of arginine contributes to the basic properties of proteins. Arginine is found in the muscle of invertebrates in the form of its phosphoric acid derivative, arginine phosphate, and this compound appears to occupy a place in invertebrate muscles analogous to that of creatine phosphate in vertebrate muscles.

$$
\begin{array}{cc}
\mathrm{NH} & \mathrm{OH} \\[-2pt]
\| & | \\[-2pt]
\mathrm{NH\!-\!C\!-\!NH\!-\!P}{=}\mathrm{O} \\[-2pt]
| & | \\[-2pt]
\mathrm{(CH_2)_3} & \mathrm{OH} \\[-2pt]
| \\[-2pt]
\mathrm{NH_2CH\!-\!COOH}
\end{array}
$$

Arginine phosphate

The guanidino group of arginine yields a red color upon treatment with α-naphthol and sodium hypochlorite. This is the basis of the Sakaguchi reaction [65].

The weakly acidic sulfhydryl group of cysteine is extremely reactive and plays a special role as a crosslinking agent in protein structure, since the two half-residues can be reversibly oxidized to yield a covalent disulfide linkage [26].

$$HOOC\!-\!CHNH_2\!-\!CH_2\!-\!SH + HS\!-\!CH_2\!-\!CHNH_2COOH \underset{\text{reduction}}{\overset{\text{oxidation}}{\rightleftharpoons}}$$

$$HOOC\!-\!CHNH_2\!-\!CH_2\!-\!S\!-\!S\!-\!CH_2\!-\!CHNH_2\!-\!COOH + 2H^+ \tag{5-24}$$

Stronger oxidizing agents, such as performic acid, oxidize the disulfide linkage in proteins to cysteic acid. This reaction is used to cleave disulfide linkages prior to determining the amino acid sequence of a protein. The presence of cysteic acid residues in the treated polypeptide chain indicates the positions of former disulfide linkages [138].

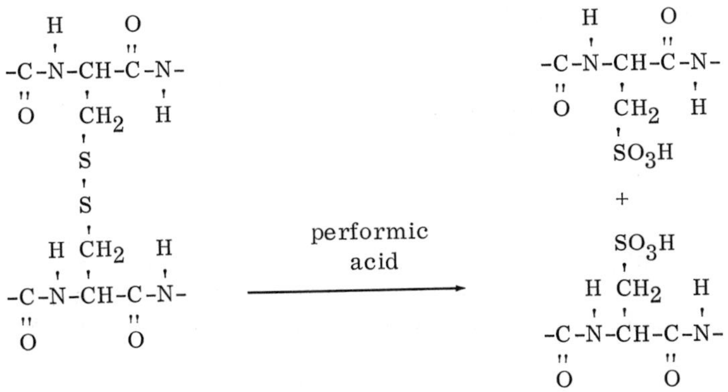

$$
\begin{array}{c}
\underset{\underset{O}{\overset{H}{|}}}{-C}-\underset{}{N}-\underset{\underset{\underset{\underset{S}{|}}{\overset{CH_2}{|}}}{CH}}{-}\underset{\overset{O}{\overset{\|}{}}}{C}-\underset{\overset{H}{|}}{N}- \\
\\
\underset{\underset{O}{\overset{H}{|}}}{-C}-\underset{}{N}-\underset{}{CH}-\underset{\overset{O}{\overset{\|}{}}}{C}-N-
\end{array}
\quad
\xrightarrow[\text{acid}]{\text{performic}}
\quad
\begin{array}{c}
-C-N-CH-C-N- \\
\\
SO_3H \\
+ \\
SO_3H \\
-C-N-CH-C-N-
\end{array}
$$

(5-25)

Disulfide linkage   Cysteic acid residues

Sulfhydryl groups of specific cysteine residues are important components of the active sites of many enzymes. These sulfhydryl groups are capable of reacting with heavy metals or reagents containing heavy metals. The reagent p-chloromercuribenzoate has been used in studying the sulfhydryl groups of enzymes.

$$\text{Protein-SH} + \text{ClHg-}\bigcirc\text{-COONa} \longrightarrow \text{Protein-SHg-}\bigcirc\text{-COOH} + \text{NaCl} \quad (5\text{-}26)$$

Compounds containing sulfhydryl groups, such as cysteine, glutathione, mercaptoethanol, and dithiothreitol, will protect sulfhydryl groups and in many instances will reverse the biological action of heavy metals [138,142].

The irreversible alkylation of protein sulfhydryl groups can be accomplished by many iodo compounds. For example, iodoacetic acid or its amide readily reacts with protein sulfhydryl groups [50].

$$\text{Protein-SH} + \text{ICH}_2\text{-CONH}_2 \longrightarrow \text{Protein-S-CH}_2\text{CONH}_2 + \text{HI} \quad (5\text{-}27)$$

Cyanogen bromide reacts specifically with methionine residues in peptides. This reaction cleaves the peptide bond participated in by methionine. Fragmentation of peptides for analysis of amino acid sequence is accomplished by this reaction [146].

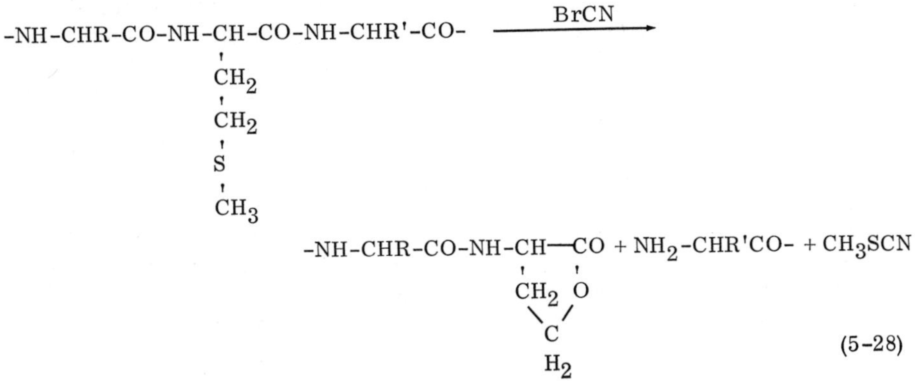

$$
\begin{array}{c}
-NH-CHR-CO-NH-CH-CO-NH-CHR'-CO- \\
\underset{\underset{\underset{\underset{CH_3}{|}}{S}}{\overset{CH_2}{|}}}{CH_2}
\end{array}
\xrightarrow{\text{BrCN}}
$$

$$
-NH-CHR-CO-NH-CH\!-\!\!\!-CO + NH_2-CHR'CO- + CH_3SCN
$$
$$
\underset{\overset{\diagdown}{\underset{H_2}{C}}\diagup}{CH_2 \quad O}
$$

(5-28)

B. Ionic Properties of Proteins

As mentioned previously, hydrophilic R groups generally are located on the exterior of the protein molecule, while hydrophobic or nonpolar R groups generally are located in the interior. The presence of hydrophilic R groups on the surface of proteins causes them to behave somewhat like amino acids. However, the behavior of proteins is much more complex due to the multiplicity of hydrophobic R groups [81].

Since the amino acid composition of individual proteins varies greatly, the net charges on these proteins also vary. As with amino acids, titration curves of proteins indicate the number of nonpeptide carboxyl and amino groups in the protein. In titration experiments it has been shown that nearly all of the potentially ionizable R groups on the protein are capable of ionizing. If a protein contains a rather high content of acidic amino acids (aspartic and glutamic), the protein has a low isoelectric point. Conversely, if the protein contains many basic amino acids (arginine and lysine), the protein has a high isoelectric point. If the protein binds ions of neutral salts, such as magnesium or calcium, a change in both the isoelectric point and the titration curve occurs [65].

This variation in the ionic properties of proteins leads to several methods for fractionating proteins from biological systems. One of these is electrophoresis. Migration of a protein in an electrical field occurs in accord with the relationship

$$\mu = \frac{v}{E} \tag{5-29}$$

where μ is the electrical mobility of the molecule, v is the velocity of migration, and E is the field strength (cm^2/V-sec). Since proteins have a smaller ratio of charge to mass than simple sodium or chloride ions, they migrate more slowly than simple ions in an electric field [81].

There are two types of electrophoresis, free-boundary and zone electrophoresis. Free-boundary electrophoresis is carried out in a solution without any support. It has the disadvantage that large, complex equipment is required to optically observe movement of the proteins and to maintain a constant temperature (to reduce convection in the solution). Furthermore, the method is slow and requires large samples [81].

Zone electrophoresis is carried out on many different types of supports, including paper, cellulose acetate, starch, and polyacrylamide gel [12]. Recent development of polyacrylamide gels has greatly increased the resolving power of zone electrophoresis. In this method, very small quantities of protein (generally unpurified extracts) can be used and electrophoresis is performed in a simple apparatus. Since the porosity of gels can be varied, separation is on the basis of molecular size as well as net charge. Disturbances from convection currents are negligible since zone electrophoresis is carried out in a semisolid medium. Separated proteins are detected in gels by qualitative staining. Shown in Figure 5-8 are results obtained using polyacrylamide gel zone electrophoresis to separate a protein fraction of myofibrillar proteins from bovine muscle.

Ion-exchange column chromatography is another method used to fractionate proteins on the basis of electrical charge. The most successful ion-exchange resins are derivatives of cellulose [100]. Diethylaminoethyl (DEAE) cellulose is an anion exchanger since it contains a positive charge below pH 9. Carboxymethyl

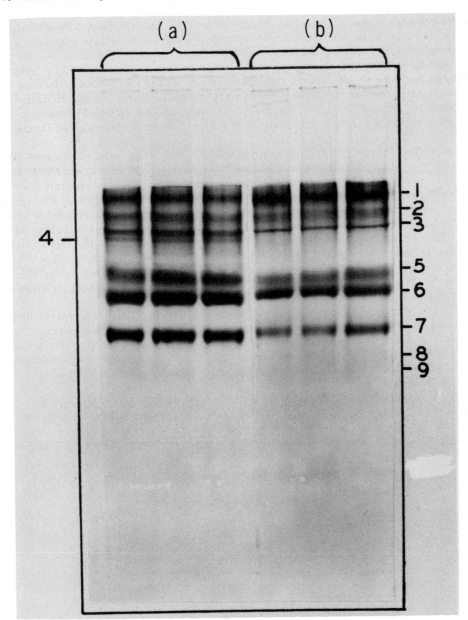

FIG. 5-8. Separation of a protein fraction of bovine myofibrillar proteins by polyacrylamide gel electrophoresis: (a) 0 day postmortem and (b) 12 days postmortem samples [101].

(CM) cellulose contains a negative charge above pH 3, and it is used to fractionate proteins having a net positive charge. Protein is eluted from cellulose ion-exchange resins by increasing the salt concentration (to compete with the protein for the charge), by changing the pH of the buffer (to lessen the protein's charge and thereby decrease its attraction to the resin), or by both of these means. If these changes are slowly accomplished, the mixture of protein can be completely fractionated in one pass through a column. The ability of DEAE cellulose chromatography to separate sarcoplasmic proteins of bovine muscle is illustrated in Figure 5-9.

Electrical charge also influences protein solubility. At pH values other than the isoelectric point, proteins possess like net charges and repel each other. However, as the isoelectric point is approached, the charge difference between protein molecules is lessened. If the charge difference becomes sufficiently small, the proteins touch, aggregate, and sometimes precipitate. Proteins that are water soluble owe their solubilities to water-protein hydrogen bonding and to environmental pH values that do not coincide with their isoelectric points. Establishment of isoelectric conditions is used commercially to precipitate milk casein (pH 4.6). Although proteins possess a number of charged groups at the isoelectric point (net charge is zero), solvation is nevertheless minimal at this pH. This is illustrated for muscle proteins in Figure 5-10.

Ions of neutral salts increase the solubility of proteins. These ions react with charges on proteins, decreasing the electrostatic attraction between opposite charges of neighboring protein molecules. The solvation layer which accompanies ions of neutral salts also tends to increase solvation of the proteins and to enhance their solubilities. Increasing the solubility of proteins by adding neutral salts is called "salting in."

If the concentration of neutral salts is increased to a high level, in many instances the protein precipitates. This phenomenon apparently results because the excess ions (not bound to the protein) compete with proteins for the solvent. The decrease in solvation and neutralization of the repulsive forces allows the proteins

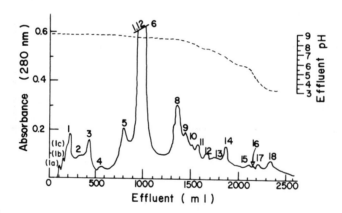

FIG. 5-9. Separation of bovine sarcoplasmic proteins by DEAE-cellulose ion-exchange chromatography. From Ref. [108], courtesy of the Institute of Food Technologists.

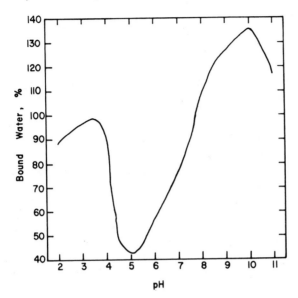

FIG. 5-10. Effect of pH on water-holding capacity of beef muscle. Modified from Ref. [62].

to aggregate and precipitate. This effect is called "salting out." A similar phenomenon occurs when organic solvents, particularly acetone and ethanol, are added to a solution of proteins. These organic solvents compete with the protein for water and thereby decrease the dielectric constant of the solution. A decrease in dielectric constant can decrease the repulsive forces of like charges to the extent that the protein molecules aggregate and precipitate. Since proteins vary in the degree of solvation and surface charge, these methods of precipitation, if performed carefully, can be used to fractionate proteins from biological material [65].

In general, protein solubility increases as the temperature is increased between 0° and 40°C. An exception is β-casein, which is more soluble at 0° than 20°C. Above 40°C proteins tend to denature, which results in a loss of solubility.

C. Denaturation

Proteins undergo profound changes in many specific properties following treatments so mild (no breaking of peptide bonds) that ordinary chemical compounds remain unaltered under the same conditions. These changes in specific properties characterizing the identity of proteins are collectively called "denaturation" [31, 75].

Effects of protein denaturation are: (1) peptide bonds of the protein are more readily available for hydrolysis by proteolytic enzymes; (2) solubility is decreased; (3) enzymic activity, if originally present, is decreased or lost; (4) crystallization of the protein is no longer possible; (5) intrinsic viscosity is increased; and (6) optical rotation of the protein solution is increased. The increase in intrinsic

viscosity would suggest that the protein molecule had unfolded and had become
more asymmetrical. This would expose more hydrophobic residues and would decrease solubility of the protein [21].

The sensitivity of a protein to denaturation is determined by the ease with which
denaturing agents disrupt bonds that are essential to maintenance of three-
dimensional structure. Since proteins differ widely in structure and amino acid
composition, their sensitivities to denaturing agents and the types of alterations
they undergo would be expected to vary. In one protein the tertiary structure may
be most affected, whereas in another protein the secondary structure may be more
susceptible to the denaturing agent.

Since the characteristic properties of different proteins do not exhibit the same
changes during similar denaturing treatments, comparisons of extents of denaturation are difficult. For example, when heat is applied to a solution of casein, the
ultraviolet absorption of α-casein remains unaltered, while that of β-casein increases. When casein solutions are heated, in contrast, solubility and susceptibility to trypsin hydrolysis of the α-casein fraction are modified, whereas these
same properties of β-casein are not altered [129]. The variable responses of proteins to denaturing treatments frequently leads to ambiguities in attempts to precisely define denaturation.

As knowledge of the structure of proteins increases, the concept of denaturation
can be approached in terms of actual structural changes in the protein molecule.
Accordingly, denaturation can be defined as any modification of secondary, tertiary,
or quaternary structure of the protein molecule, excluding breakage of covalent
bonds. Denaturation is therefore a process by which hydrogen bonds, hydrophobic
interactions, and salt linkages are broken and the protein is unfolded [75]. In
some instances the protein completely unfolds and assumes a random coil-type
structure (Fig. 5-11). Proteins in a random coil structure more readily form

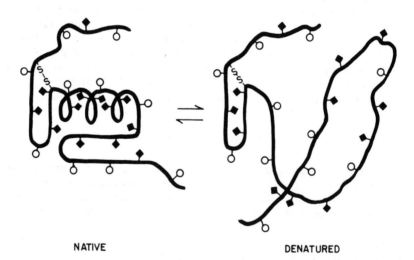

NATIVE   DENATURED

FIG. 5-11. Schematic illustration of the denaturation of a protein molecule.
Polar and ionic side chains are shown by open circles. Filled squares represent
hydrophobic side chains. The latter are mostly located in the interior of the molecule in the native state but are exposed to the solvent upon denaturation. Modified
from Ref. [18].

aggregates. This process may be visualized by the following reactions:

$$N \rightleftharpoons D \longrightarrow aggregation \qquad\qquad (5\text{-}30)$$

where N is native protein and D is denatured protein. Although proteins are difficult to study in their native states, it is generally accepted that native proteins
are those prepared by the mildest extraction methods available.

Denaturation under different conditions does not lead to the same changes in a
given protein molecule. For example, denaturation of a protein by heat does not
result in the same changes produced by dilute acid or alkali. Also, the same kinds
of protein molecules, when exposed to the same denaturation treatment, exhibit a
range of structural differences or microstates (Fig. 5-12). These microstates
represent different degrees of structural order in the polypeptide chain and differences in the structure of water molecules adjacent to the protein. Figure 5-12 also
illustrates that the degree of order in a protein molecule decreases as the severity
of the denaturing treatment increases.

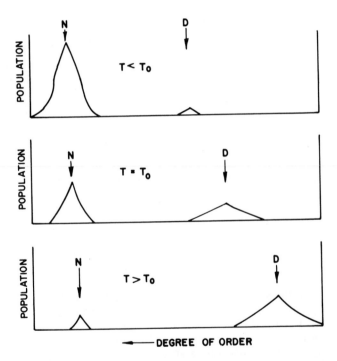

FIG. 5-12. A graphical representation of a two-state protein denaturation. The
relative populations for the numerous microstates of the native (N) and denatured
(D) distributions are indicated by the ordinate. The arrows show the average "degree of order" for the two thermodynamic states and indicate the temperature de-
pendency of this factor as the temperature is increased (top to bottom) through the
transition period. Modified from Ref. [18].

1. ENERGETICS OF DENATURATION

Denaturation is usually an irreversible process if drastic methods of denaturation are used and if the molecular weight of the native protein is very large. However, reversal of denaturation (renaturation, regeneration, reactivation) is observed in some smaller proteins when mild methods of denaturation are used. Under these conditions an equilibrium constant, K, for the reaction $N \rightleftharpoons D$ may be defined as

$$K = \frac{[D]}{[N]} \qquad\qquad (5\text{-}31)$$

The change in free energy, ΔF, can be calculated from the following equation:

$$\Delta F^\circ = -RT \ln K = -2.3\ RT \log K \qquad\qquad (5\text{-}32)$$

where ΔF° is the standard free energy change (i.e., the difference in free energy between a system containing all reactants in equimolar concentration and the same system after it has reached equilibrium), R is the gas content (1.98 cal/mole/deg), and T is the absolute temperature. If the concentrations of N and D are equal, ΔF° is zero, since log 1 is zero. If K is larger than 1.0, log K is positive, ΔF° is negative, and the conversion of N to D brings the system closer to equilibrium. Conversely, if K is smaller than 1.0, log K is negative, ΔF° is positive, and the conversion of N to D is away from the equilibrium state. Without the addition of energy, only reactions with a negative ΔF° can (but may not) proceed spontaneously [65].

Using another thermodynamic relationship,

$$\Delta F = \Delta H - T \Delta S \qquad\qquad (5\text{-}33)$$

it is possible to calculate the change in entropy (ΔS) of the reaction per mole from the change in enthalpy (ΔH) and ΔF. ΔH can be calculated from the Van't Hoff equation:

$$\log \frac{K_2}{K_1} = \frac{\Delta H}{2.3R} \left(\frac{T_2 - T_1}{T_2 T_1} \right) \qquad\qquad (5\text{-}34)$$

where K_1 and K_2 are equilibrium constants at T_1 and T_2, respectively. For reversible denaturation of crystalline trypsin inhibitor, ΔH has been calculated as +57,300 cal/mole and the values of K, ΔF (cal/mole), and ΔS (cal/mole/deg) at various temperatures are listed in Table 5-3. At a temperature between 45 and 47°C, K is equal to 1 and ΔF is zero. At this temperature, native and denatured proteins are present in equal concentrations. The equilibrium is shifted toward the native state below this temperature and toward the denatured state above this temperature. The denaturation process is accompanied by an increase in entropy of 180 cal/mole/deg. This increase in entropy causes ΔF to become negative at higher temperatures, resulting in an increased rate of denaturation [65].

If these results are interpreted in terms of molecular kinetics, the process of denaturation can be compared to the melting of ice. As the temperature is raised, various crosslinking bonds among peptide chains "melt" and the chains acquire a greater mobility [65].

TABLE 5-3

Thermodynamic Data for Reversible Denaturation
of Crystalline Trypsin Inhibitor[a]

Thermodynamic values	Temperature (°C)					
	30	35	40	45	47	50
$K = [D]/[N]$	0.010	0.042	0.220	0.870	2.03	4.35
$\Delta F = -4.58T \log K$	2780	1920	950	87.5	-450	-950
$\Delta S = (\Delta H - \Delta F)/T$	180	180	180	180	180	180

[a]Reprinted from Ref. [65], p. 170, by courtesy of Academic Press.

Before a chemical reaction can proceed, the reacting molecules must become "activated." The energy needed to activate molecules, the activation energy, can be computed from the classical Arrhenius equation:

$$k = Ae^{-E_a/RT} \tag{5-35}$$

where k is the specific reaction rate constant, T is the absolute temperature, R is the gas constant, and E_a and A are empirical constants. E_a is the activation energy and A is called the "frequency factor." When logarithms are taken of both sides of Eq. (5-35), the relationship becomes:

$$\log k = \log A - \frac{E_a}{2.3RT} \tag{5-36}$$

This equation can be integrated between the limits of k_1 and k_2 at T_1 and T_2, respectively, to give

$$\log \frac{k_2}{k_1} = \frac{E_a}{2.3R} \left(\frac{T_2 - T_1}{T_2 T_1} \right) \tag{5-37}$$

The similarity between Eq. (5-37) and the Van't Hoff equation (5-34) should be noted.

The concept of activation energy can be more readily visualized from Figure 5-13. The energy of a native protein, N, must be increased to an activated state, $P^{\ddagger}$, to proceed to a denatured state, D. Activation energy is the energy difference between N and $P^{\ddagger}$ for the forward reaction, and between D and $P^{\ddagger}$ for reversal of denaturation. E_a is determined by plotting log k vs 1/T (Fig. 5-14), the slope of the line being equal to $-0.219E_a$.

E_a values for denaturation of proteins are very high compared to values of other chemical reactions. For example, E_a values for heat denaturation of trypsin, peroxidase, and egg albumen are 40,000, 185,300, and 132,000 cal/mole, respectively, whereas most chemical reactions have much smaller E_a values. Since covalent bonds are not broken during protein denaturation, the large E_a suggests that the number of noncovalent bonds broken must be very large.

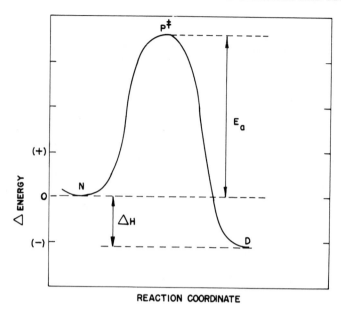

FIG. 5-13. Change in energy during the conversion of native protein (N) to denatured protein (D). The activated molecules ($P^{\ddagger}$) are intermediates in conversion of N to D. Modified from Ref. [144].

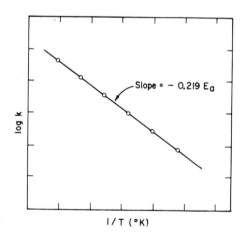

FIG. 5-14. Influence of temperature on the rate constant of a reaction. Modified from Ref. [144].

2. PHYSICAL AGENTS

Denaturing agents may be divided into two classes, physical and chemical. Heat is the most important physical agent. The rate of protein denaturation is highly dependent on temperature. Whereas for most chemical reactions the rate doubles for each 10° rise in temperature, with protein denaturation the rate increases about 600-fold for every 10° rise in temperature. Therefore, by working at low temperatures, the effects of denaturing agents can be greatly reduced. Susceptibility of proteins to heat denaturation depends on a number of factors. Water content of partially dried protein preparations has a large effect on the rate of heat denaturation. For example, wheat gliadin is denatured to the same extent in 1 hr under either of the following conditions (% water, °C): 24% and 60°, or 18% and 70°. Some proteins are stable at temperatures as high as 100°C if the moisture content is very low. Ionic strength, pH, and type of ions present in solution also affect the susceptibility of proteins to heat denaturation [75].

Layering of proteins at an interface or surface can result in denaturation. This apparently results from unfolding of protein molecules along the interface, with hydrophilic residues remaining in the aqueous phase and hydrophobic residues tending to associate with the nonaqueous phase. Thus, it is important, when attempting to preserve the native properties of proteins, to avoid creating interfaces, such as those in foams [65].

Pressures in the range of several thousand kilograms per square centimeter also can cause denaturation of proteins by forcing them into configurations of greater density. Ultraviolet radiation inactivates certain enzymes and decreases the solubility of some proteins. The effects of ionizing radiation on proteins are discussed in Section VI.D.

3. CHEMICAL AGENTS

The pH of the medium has a profound effect on denaturation of proteins. Most proteins are stable within a fairly narrow pH range and exposure to pH values outside this range often causes denaturation. Moving away from the pH of optimum stability increases the proportion of like charges on the R groups and increases repulsive forces within the protein molecule. These changes in ionic forces favor unfolding of the molecular structure. If the resulting structural changes are not too extreme, the protein often can resume its native structure when returned to the stable pH range [21,75].

High concentrations (6-8M) of compounds that tend to break hydrogen bonds, such as urea and guanidine salts, also cause denaturation of proteins. These substances apparently disrupt hydrogen bonds which hold the protein in its unique structure. However, there also is evidence suggesting that urea and guanidine hydrochloride may disrupt hydrophobic interactions by promoting the solubility of hydrophobic residues in aqueous solutions [55].

Synthetic detergents are among the most effective denaturing agents known. These compounds have the ability to form a chemical bridge between hydrophobic and hydrophilic environments, thus disrupting or diminishing the hydrophobic forces needed to maintain native protein structure. Organic solvents, such as acetone and alcohol, also can cause denaturation of proteins although their effects are reduced by low temperatures [65].

D. Gelation

Both carbohydrates and proteins are used to form gels in foods. Attention in this section is given only to gels that are formed with proteins. Additional information on gels can be found in Chapters 3 and 12. Proteins are able to bind by hydration approximately 1 g of water per 5 g of dry protein. However, a few proteins are known to form gels which are capable of "immobilizing" water equal to nearly ten times the combined weight of the hydrated protein. This immobilized water is not tightly bound; rather it is physically entrapped and can be expelled from the gel under conditions much less severe than those needed to remove water of hydration. This kind of immobilized water has the same freezing point, the same dissolving powers, and the same vapor pressure as normal water (see Chapter 2). It is immobilized in the sense that it does not flow freely from the gel (movement of water molecules within the gel can, of course, occur).

Proteins which form gels readily have structures with a high degree of asymmetry. These long proteinaceous fibers form a three-dimensional matrix primarily by establishment of interprotein hydrogen bonds, and this crosslinked structure is sufficiently well developed to hold water in an immobilized (nonflowable) state. Salt bridges probably do not play an important role in the crosslinking process, since they would be highly solvated in aqueous gels. However, ionized functional groups on the protein would aid in immobilizing the water. If the attractive forces of the protein are increased, e.g., by changing the pH to a value closer to the isoelectric point of the protein, the gel would tend to shrink. This shrinkage would expel some of the immobilized water, a process called "syneresis." By decreasing the attractive forces between the protein molecules, however, such as by adjusting the pH away from the isoelectric point of the protein, the gel can be made to immobilize a larger amount of water [62].

Probably the two best-known proteinaceous gels in foods are those of gelatin and the gel formed when casein is coagulated by the action of the proteolytic enzyme, rennin. To better illustrate the properties of gels, the behavior of gelatin will be considered in more detail. Upon heating an aqueous suspension of collagen to a temperature of 62-63°C, it is solubilized (partially hydrolyzed) and converted to gelatin. The temperature at which collagen is solubilized increases as the proline and hydroxyproline content increases. Aqueous solutions of gelatin are viscous and even at concentrations as low as 1% can form gels when cooled to room temperature. As mentioned earlier, collagen contains a high proportion of proline and hydroxyproline, and the peptide bonds from these amino acids are not able to form hydrogen bonds. Therefore, peptide bonds from amino acids other than proline and hydroxyproline are primarily responsible for the interprotein hydrogen bonds that lead to formation of the gel. In addition to these, disulfide linkages, crosslinkages involving bivalent metal ions and two carboxyl groups, as well as crosslinkages involving other substances that are firmly bound to the protein molecule, are important in gel formation. Crosslinking occurs only occasionally along the peptide chain and electrostatic linkages do not appear to be involved, since the masking of polar groups by chemical modification does not greatly influence the mechanical properties of the gel. Nonpolar side chains appear to play no role in the crosslinking of the gelatin molecules. The hydroxy group of hydroxyproline may contribute to gel stability by forming hydrogen bonds with water or other groups on the protein. However, evidence indicates that hydrogen bonding between those peptide bonds capable of doing so is the chief source of bonding among the proteins. This is substantiated by the lack of gel formation when the peptide groups are blocked by the biuret complex with cupric ions. When these ions are removed, gelation can occur again [62].

Gelatin is able to form maximum strength gels in the isoelectric range (pH 5-10) and in solutions of low ionic strength.

E. Hydrolysis of Proteins

Proteins can be hydrolyzed with acid, alkali, or enzymes [66]. Cleavage of proteins by acid hydrolysis is the most widely used method for studying the amino acid composition of proteins. In this method a protein is refluxed in a 20.5% solution of hydrochloric acid for 12-70 hr. The time for hydrolysis can be reduced to 8-10 hr by elevating the temperature to 120°C. Acid hydrolysis avoids racemization of amino acids and a solution of the natural L-amino acids is obtained. However, tryptophan is susceptible to decomposition by mineral acids and is lost during acid hydrolysis of proteins. During acid hydrolysis, asparagine and glutamine are hydrolyzed to aspartic and glutamic acids, and the sulfur and hydroxy amino acids undergo various amounts of oxidation.

Hydrolysis of proteins by alkali results in substantial racemization of the amino acids which causes the preparations to be less useful nutritionally. Generally a solution of 6N sodium hydroxide or barium hydroxide is used for protein hydrolysis. The amino acids arginine and cystine, and a portion of the lysine, are destroyed by this method, although tryptophan is retained [65].

Complete hydrolysis of proteins by the use of proteolytic enzymes is possible [11,109,142]. Unlike acid or alkali hydrolysis, enzymic hydrolysis of proteins does not remove non-amino acid functional groups that are attached to the protein. Details of enzymic hydrolysis of proteins are dealt with in Chapter 6.

IV. DISTRIBUTION, AMOUNTS, AND FUNCTIONS
OF PROTEINS IN VARIOUS FOODS

In this section the major food protein systems are described according to their origin. In discussing food proteins, it is often forgotten that these components, so essential in our diets, are not some kind of delicacy grown strictly for our enjoyment. Both plants and animals require proteins for growth, survival, and propagation of the species. Most proteins must be considered as raw materials requiring some type of processing or modification prior to use by humans.

A. Proteins of Animal Origin

1. MEAT

Generally speaking, meat is the skeletal or striated muscles of animals that are used as food. The flesh of cattle, sheep, and swine provide most of the meat consumed in the United States. Edible muscles from these animals are designated as "red meats," a term descriptive of the color of beef, lamb, and pork as opposed to the light and dark colors of poultry meat. The red color is caused primarily by the respiratory pigment, myoglobin.

A typical adult mammalian muscle stripped of all external fat contains about 18-20% protein on a wet weight basis. Muscle proteins can be categorized on the basis of their origin and solubility as sarcoplasmic, contractile (myofibrillar), or stroma (connective tissue) proteins [15]. Table 5-4 shows the relative distribution of these proteins in muscles from mammals, poultry, and fish. These values must be considered approximate, however, since considerable variability occurs within and among species and in different environments. Detailed information on muscle proteins is given in Chapter 13.

2. MILK

The protein content of fluid milk from cows ranges from 3 to 4%, depending on breed and on a variety of environmental factors. A value of 3.5% protein is often considered average for milk. Milk proteins have been traditionally divided into two classes, casein and whey proteins. The casein fraction contains a heterogeneous group of phosphoproteins that can be precipitated from raw skim milk by acidification to pH 4.6 at 20°C. Proteins remaining in solution after precipitation of casein are collectively known as "whey" or "milk serum" proteins [54,73]. The casein fraction accounts for almost 80% of the total protein content of milk, with whey proteins making up the other 20% (Table 5-5). Detailed information on milk proteins is given in Chapter 14, Section I.

3. EGGS

Chicken eggs consist of about 11% shell, 31% yolk, and 58% white [106,122]. From a food standpoint, the shell and its membranes are nonedible wrappers protecting the major food components contained in the yolk and white. Liquid whole egg con-

TABLE 5-4

Amounts and Kinds of Proteins in Skeletal Muscle from
Different Sources Based on Total Amount of Protein

Fraction	Mammalian (%)	Poultry (%)	Fish (%)
Myofibrillar	49–55	60–65	65–75
Sarcoplasmic	30–34	30–34	20–30
Stroma	10–17	5–10	1–3

TABLE 5-5

Major Protein Components in Cow's Milk[a]

Component	Percent of milk	Percent of total protein
Caseins	2.76	78
β-Lactoglobulin	0.43	12
α-Lactalbumin	0.08	2
Immunoglobulins	0.07	2
Bovine serum albumin	0.03	1
Others	0.18	5

[a]From Refs. [56,112].

sists of about 65% white and 35% yolk. The primary function of egg proteins is to provide food to nourish the young chick. The yolk appears to be the initial source of food, while the egg white seems to act as a protective barrier prior to its eventual use as a source of protein [45]. Because they differ greatly in composition and are distinct parts of the egg, it is convenient to consider white and yolk separately.

a. Yolk. Yolk contains about 50% solids, of which one-third is protein and two-thirds are lipid. Upon centrifugation, yolk can be separated into three fractions, the water-soluble livetins, a granular component composed of phosvitin and lipovitellins, and a low-density fraction containing lipovitellenin [35]. The lipovitellins and lipovitellenin are complex lipoprotein mixtures, the lipids of which can be removed by exhaustive extraction with 80% alcohol, leaving the corresponding phosphoproteins, vitellin and vitellenin [96]. The approximate protein composition of egg yolk and detailed properties of yolk proteins are given in Chapter 15, Section III.

b. White. Egg white is essentially an aqueous solution containing about 12% protein. Four structurally distinct layers can be recognized: an outer fluid (thin) layer, a viscous (thick) layer, an inner fluid (thin) layer, and a small dense layer surrounding the vitelline membrane of the yolk. The last mentioned layer is continuous with the fibrous "chalazae" that maintains the yolk in position. The properties of these layers differ mainly in that the ovomucin content is much greater in the viscous layers than in the fluid layers [96]. The composition of egg white protein and detailed properties of egg white proteins are given in Chapter 15, Section III.

B. Proteins of Marine Origin

1. FISH

The edible portion of fish is the skeletal or flank muscles of the body. Even though the skeletal muscles of different animals are basically similar, fish species used for food are far more numerous and diverse than mammalian species used for food. Since the various species cannot be discussed in detail, the following discussion on fish muscle proteins has been approached on a generalized basis.

Fish usually contain between 40 and 60% edible flesh. The protein content of fresh fish flesh of the more common species ranges from about 10% in mackerel to 21% in Atlantic sardines, although higher values have been reported in isolated catches [51].

In the mid- or lateral line of many fish there exists a layer of heavily pigmented, reddish-brown muscle that may comprise up to 10% of the total body muscle. This muscle layer has a high content of hemoproteins which, following harvest, may catalyze oxidation of lipids and cause pronounced rancidity [33].

Fish muscle proteins, like those of mammalian muscle, are generally classified as sarcoplasmic, myofibrillar, or connective tissue proteins. The relative amounts of these proteins are listed in Table 5-4, and the differences as compared to mammalian muscle and poultry muscle should be noted.

Fish muscle has many similarities to mammalian skeletal muscle with respect to ultrastructure and function. However, fish proteins are not as stable as the proteins of mammalian muscle. They are, for example, easily damaged (degradative changes, denaturation, coagulation) by processing. Although the inherent nature of fish myosin is responsible for much of the instability of fish proteins, not all fish myosins are unstable. Variations in stability appear to be associated with the body temperature of the specimen from which myosin is obtained. Myosins from warm-blooded animals are relatively stable, whereas those from cold-blooded fish residing in temperate or colder waters (cod, haddock) are very unstable. Myosins from tuna, striped bass, and sea mullet, fish living in tropical or warm waters, are considerably more stable than those from cod or haddock [34].

2. SHELLFISH

Information concerning the proteins of crustacean and molluscan shellfish is fragmentary and incomplete.

Shells comprise a large portion of the live weight of shellfish and thus their edible contents are low. The edible portion, expressed as a percentage of the total live weight, ranges from 40 to 47% for various crustaceans, and from 11% (oysters) to about 30% (mussels) for mollusks. The total protein contents of some of the more familiar shellfish are listed in Table 5-6.

The adductor muscle of oysters and clams is a special kind of smooth muscle (catch muscle), which operates to keep the shell closed. This muscle is capable of maintaining an extraordinary tension without using much metabolic energy or exhibiting fatigue. Catch muscles are thought to contain four structural proteins:

TABLE 5-6

Approximate Protein Contents of the Flesh of Certain Shellfish[a]
Based on Fresh Muscle Weight

Species	Percent protein
Crustaceans	
Crab	20.5
Lobster	20.0
Prawn	22.0
Shrimp	22.5
Mollusks	
Oyster	13.0
Mussel	11.0
Scallop	17.5

[a]From Ref. [17].

actin, myosin, paramyosin (tropomyosin A), and tropomyosin. The presence of paramyosin is assumed to account for the unusual properties of the catch muscle [119].

C. Proteins of Plant Origin

For purposes of simplicity and clarity, plant proteins are grouped as vegetable, cereal, or seed proteins in the subsequent discussion.

1. VEGETABLE PROTEINS

Fresh vegetables are not good sources of protein. On a fresh weight basis, the average protein contents of some of the more widely consumed vegetables are: carrots and lettuce, 1%; white potatoes, asparagus, and green beans, 2%; and fresh peas, 6.5%.

Although potatoes contain only 2% crude protein, the protein quality is considered good to excellent because of the relatively high levels of lysine and tryptophan. The outer layers, the so-called "cortex" of potato tubers, contain most of the protein. These layers also have a much higher concentration of essential amino acids than do the inner layers. There are indications that the outer layer portion can be increased by selective plant breeding [116].

2. CEREAL PROTEINS

Cereal grains, properly ripened and dried for optimum storage stability, have protein contents ranging from 6 to 20%. The approximate protein contents of some of the more important cereals are presented in Table 5-7.

TABLE 5-7

Approximate Protein Contents of Cereal Grains[a]
(Moisture Contents Approximately 12%)

Type of grain	Percent protein
Wheat	
Common (hard)	12–13
Club (soft)	7.5–10
Durum (very hard)	13.5–15
Barley	12–13
Rye	11–12
Oats	10–12
Corn (dent)	9–10
Rice	7–9

[a]From Refs. [16;121].

Proteins are found in various morphological tissues of the different grains. In the milling of grain (e.g., wheat), the endosperm is essentially separated from the bran and germ and then pulverized to produce flour for food use [105]. The relative proportions of these fractions in the kernel and their respective protein contents are listed in Table 5-8.

Proteins in the germ (embryo) portion are mainly globulins or albumins, indicating that several enzymes are present which may act as hydrocols in promoting water absorption during germination [137].

The bran or seed coat provides structure and protection to the kernel. Since bran is so poorly digested by man, and the protein difficult to separate, most of this material is used for animal feed.

The endosperm proteins apparently act as structural components and also as a food reserve for the growing seedling. Much of the endosperm storage protein in the kernels of several cereals (barley, corn, rice) is located in subcellular granules or organelles known as "protein bodies" [41]. However, protein bodies have not yet been detected in the endosperm of mature wheat kernels [23].

A major portion of the proteins of corn and wheat are glutelins (soluble in dilute acid or alkali) and prolamines (soluble in aqueous alcohol). Only oats and rice have low levels of prolamines.

a. Wheat Proteins. The starchy endosperm of wheat is the source of flour. Its cells are packed with starch granules which are embedded in a protein matrix. The outer layers of the endosperm (aleurone and subaleurone layers) contain more protein than the inner portion [78]. Roughly 80–85% of the total endosperm protein of wheat is composed of gliadin (a prolamine) and glutenin (a glutelin) in an approximate ratio of 1:1. Glutenin and gliadin are each composed of many different

TABLE 5-8

Approximate Protein Contents of the Major Anatomical Parts
of Wheat and Corn[a] (Expressed on Dry Weight Basis)

Grain	Kernel fractions		
	Germ	Bran	Endosperm
Wheat			
Weight (% of kernel)	3	12	85
Protein (% of kernel fraction)	26	15	13
Corn			
Weight (% of kernel)	12	6	82
Protein (% of kernel fraction)	18	7	10

[a]From Refs. [72,105].

molecular species [13]. These two proteins possess the unusual property of forming an elastic-cohesive mass, gluten, when they are wetted and mixed with water.
Gluten proteins are characterized by high contents of glutamine and proline, which
account for 37 and 14%, respectively, of all the amino acid residues. The polypeptide chains of the gluten proteins are not highly organized into helical arrays.
This is probably due to the high levels of proline residues, which interfere with
helix formation [139].

Glutenin proteins consist of a linear association of polypeptide chains having
molecular weights of 20,000-100,000 daltons. As shown in Figure 5-15, these
subunits are linked together by intermolecular disulfide bonds to form polymers
with molecular weights ranging from 50,000 to several million daltons. These
molecules may also possess some intramolecular disulfide bonds [13,138]. As
mentioned, glutenin forms a very tough, elastic-cohesive mass when hydrated. It
is responsible for most of the cohesion and elasticity of wheat flour doughs. The
nature of the glutenin component of wheat flour largely determines the mixing
properties or requirements of dough [139].

Gliadin proteins are comprised of relatively small, uniform, single-chain subunits maintained in a folded conformation by intramolecular disulfide bonds (Fig.
5-15). Most gliadin proteins have molecular weights in the range of 16,000-50,000
daltons. When hydrated, gliadin yields a viscous fluid mass that is extensible but
has low elasticity. Gliadin proteins govern the loaf volume potential of wheat
flour doughs [71].

The structure of gluten proteins and their elastic and viscous characteristics
depend largely on disulfide bonds [104,138].

Nongluten proteins (albumins and globulins) account for 15-20% of the total
wheat flour proteins. They are not doughforming components but they are soluble,
coagulable, and capable of foaming [105]. Albumins appear to influence the baking
quality of flour, although their mode of action has not been defined.

From a nutritional standpoint, wheat proteins lack adequate amounts of lysine.

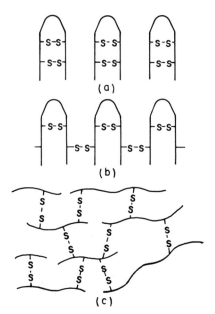

FIG. 5-15. Disulfide bonds in cereal proteins. (a) Intramolecular (wheat gliadin); (b) intramolecular and linear crosslinks (wheat glutenin); (c) three-dimensional crosslinks (corn glutelin). Reprinted from Ref. [138], p. 620, courtesy of the American Chemical Society.

b. Corn Proteins. Two distinct types of proteins are found in the endosperm of normal mature corn; a matrix protein and a granular component (protein bodies) embedded in the matrix. Protein bodies are the main site of zein deposition in corn endosperm [72]. The protein of normal corn consists of about 50% prolamine (zein), this being the largest proportion found in any of the common cereal grains. Zein is practically devoid of two essential amino acids, lysine and tryptophan, and thus is not a high-quality protein.

Corn glutelin is composed of a mixture of proteins of different sizes. These proteins are linked extensively by disulfide bonds (Fig. 5-15) to form a highly complex protein that causes problems during the wet milling of corn [138].

The discovery of a strain of high-lysine corn (Opaque-2) by Mertz et al. [90] has provided a genetic basis for producing corn of higher nutritional quality. A mutant gene in Opaque-2 corn causes a change in the ratio of proteins synthesized. Endosperm protein of normal corn contains 40-50% zein and 20-30% glutelin, whereas the zein and glutelin contents of Opaque-2 are about 20 and 40%, respectively. More importantly, the protein of Opaque-2 corn has almost 70% more lysine and 20% more tryptophan than normal corn. The protein quality of Opaque-2 corn is 90% of that of milk protein when tested in young children [84].

c. Rice Proteins. Protein of rice occurs mainly in protein bodies of the endo-sperm. Whole, milled rice protein has almost the same composition as the protein bodies. About 80% of the protein in milled rice is the alkali-soluble protein, glutelin. Among the cereal grains, rice is unique since it contains high levels of glutelins and low prolamine contents (5%). The lysine content of rice protein is relatively high (3.5–4.0%) due to the low level of prolamine. The latter is a nutritionally poor–quality fraction. As with other cereal proteins, lysine in rice protein is the first limiting amino acid [77].

Since cereal proteins are generally of relatively poor nutritional quality, problems can arise when they constitute the major source of dietary protein. This is true, for example, in developing countries where over 80% of the total available proteins are of plant origin and about 60% of this amount is derived from cereals. In developed countries, plant proteins account for only about 45% of the total proteins consumed.

Another problem with cereal proteins is that they are used inefficiently. Large volumes of corn and wheat are milled and large amounts of germ are produced. Germ comprises about 3% of the weight of wheat and 12% of the weight of corn. Protein contents of the germs of wheat and corn are 26 and 18%, respectively (Table 5-8). More attention should be directed toward greater utilization of these products for human food since the protein quality of the germ of cereal grains approaches that of meat protein [19].

3. SEED PROTEINS

Although a large number of plant species produce seeds having protein contents in excess of 15%, only a few are utilized for food. The protein contents of some high-protein seeds are listed in Table 5-9.

Soybean, cottonseed, peanut, peas, and beans are dicotyledons. Two large leaves or cotyledons are lodged under the seed coat. A distinguishable germ portion lies between the two cotyledons of each peanut kernel. This germ contains

TABLE 5-9

Approximate Protein Contents of Certain Seeds[a]
(Moisture Contents of 5-10%)

Species	Percent protein
Legumes	
Soybean	32–46
Peanut	21–36
Peas, dried	20–25
Bean (Phaseolus spp.)	19–25
Oilseeds	
Sunflower seed	25–27
Sesame seed	24–26
Cottonseed	17–22

[a]From Refs. [1,124].

bitter flavor constituents and compounds that promote rancidity [113]. Proteins of seeds are largely concentrated in protein bodies or aleurone grains which are subcellular granules of the cotyledon cells. These bodies, which are more than 90% protein, account for 70% of the total protein in soybeans [130].

Proteins function in seeds as structural elements of cell walls and various membranes. They are also involved in metabolic mechanisms (various enzymes and cellular components) that keep the cell viable. Proteins comprise a significant portion of the food reserve that is so important during germination [124].

The proteins of most seeds (excluding cereals) are globulins which are soluble in water or dilute salt solutions at pH values above or below their isoelectric points (generally between pH 4 and 5) [147]. Of all the seed proteins, those of the soybean have been investigated the most extensively.

a. Soybean Proteins. Soy proteins consist of a mixture of proteins with molecular weights ranging from 8,000 to 600,000 daltons. The water-extractable proteins can be separated by ultracentrifugation into four major components, designated the 2, 7, 11, and 15S fractions, based on sedimentation rates [147]. The 7S and 11S fractions predominate in the protein bodies and comprise about 70% of the total soybean proteins.

More than one-half of the 7S fraction consists of 7S globulin, and 11S globulin makes up the bulk of the 11S fraction. The 7S and 11S globulins undergo rapid and reversible association-dissociation reactions with changes in ionic environment. The 7S globulin exists as a monomer having a molecular weight of 180,000-210,000 daltons at an ionic strength of 0.5 and pH 7.6, but at 0.1 ionic strength, its molecular weight increases to 370,000 daltons as a result of dimerization. The 11S globulin follows a similar pattern when the ionic strength is lowered from 0.5 to 0.1, although the extent of association is low [148].

Both 7S and 11S globulins contain subunits. The quaternary structure of 11S globulin consists of 12 subunits. A dimer structure consisting of two identical monomers, each containing six subunits, has been proposed for the 11S globulin. The 7S globulin apparently contains nine subunits of single polypeptide chains plus a single polysaccharide unit attached to one of its subunuts [147].

The quaternary structures of the 7S and 11S globulins are disrupted by alkalies, acids, and heat. In the spinning of protein isolates into fibers used for textured food products, the quaternary structures of both globulins are disrupted and subunits are rearranged when the proteins are dissolved in alkali to prepare the spinning solution [148].

b. Cottonseed Proteins. The globulins of cottonseed have been separated by ultracentrifugation into 2S, 7S, and 12S fractions. The 2S fraction (proteins not present in protein bodies) represents about 30% of the total cottonseed protein. This fraction contains several low molecular weight proteins that possess relatively high contents of nutritionally important amino acids, such as lysine and sulfur-containing amino acids [87].

The 7S and 12S fractions (proteins present in protein bodies) together account for nearly 60% of the total proteins in cottonseed. These fractions contain high molecular weight proteins that are characterized by low levels of lysine and sulfur-amino acids. Both the 7S and 12S proteins dissociate in acid solutions to very low molecular weight monomers. These monomers can reassociate and dissolve in alkali, although they may not assume their original configurations. These proteins also undergo association–dissociation phenomena in alkaline solutions with changes in ionic strength [87].

c. Peanut Proteins. About 75% of the total soluble protein of the peanut is located in protein bodies. Two-thirds of this amount is arachin, the major globulin of peanuts. The other major globulin, conarachin, is dispersed in the cytoplasm [37].

Arachin has a molecular weight of 330,000 daltons and possesses the ability to dissociate reversibly to monomers (MW 180,000) with changes in pH, ionic strength, and type of salt. Arachin contains at least four components of which α-arachin is the major fraction. Upon exposure to 8M urea, arachin dissociates into 12 subunits [37,131].

Conarachin contains at least two fractions, α_1- and α_2-conarachins. The major component, α_1-conarachin, associates and dissociates with changes in ionic strength of the medium [3].

Proteins from other seeds (safflower, sesame, sunflower, etc.) have not been studied as extensively as those mentioned above. Some reports, however, are available on these particular proteins [85,91,123].

d. Special Considerations in the Utilization of Seeds. Various processing procedures have been developed that are relatively effective for extracting proteins from seeds. Depending on the type and extent of processing, protein flours, concentrates, and isolates containing approximately 50, 70, and 90% food-grade protein, respectively, can be produced from soybeans, cottonseeds, and peanuts [91,124, 148].

With the application of two additional techniques, the basic protein materials can be modified to yield components possessing ordered fibrous structures. In one procedure, textured protein materials are produced by direct thermoplastic extrusion of protein flours or concentrates under controlled conditions of heat and moisture. With the second procedure, protein isolates are dispersed in alkali and forced through holes of a spinneret (die) into an acid-coagulating bath to form microfilaments (75-μ, diameter), called spun protein fibers. These textured or "shaped" proteins offer considerable technological flexibility in the fabrication of foods [86,145].

Nutritionally, soy proteins contain considerable lysine but they are deficient in the sulfur-containing amino acids, particularly methionine. Cottonseed protein is deficient in lysine, while proteins of the peanut lack lysine, methionine, and threonine.

Antinutritional factors are present in many seeds. Soybeans contain trypsin inhibitors, hemagglutinins, saponins, estrogens, and goitrogens [148]. Gossypol, a very reactive polyphenol that binds lysine and renders it unavailable nutritionally, exists in intercellular pigment glands that are scattered throughout the cotyledons of cottonseed of glanded varieties [136]. Peanuts contain protease inhibitors, goitrogens, and saponins [113]. Allergens have been found in most seeds, leading one to suspect that they may be common components of all seeds.

Proper heat treatments, involving appropriate control of time, temperature, and relative humidity, can be used to destroy or inactivate many of these antinutritional factors and thereby maximize nutritional quality [124]. A specialized nonaqueous processing method, involving centrifugation in the presence of hexane (liquid cyclone procedure), has been perfected for removing or reducing the gossypol content of glanded cottonseed protein to levels acceptable for food use [136]. Through genetic research, glandless cottonseed varieties have been developed that produce high-quality protein seeds free of gossypol [87].

Contamination of certain food-grade seeds and seed meals by mycotoxins, particularly aflatoxins produced by the mold Aspergillus flavus, is a potentially serious problem [91]. Although there is little evidence of aflatoxin in commercial soybeans, there are indications that they may become contaminated when grown under abnormally wet conditions [7]. The problem of aflatoxin contamination is of much greater concern with peanuts and cottonseeds than it is with soybeans [91]. Additional information on plant proteins and mycotoxins can be found in Chapters 15 and 11, respectively.

D. Unconventional Sources of Protein

Problems in achieving adequate protein diets for the world's population have become increasingly apparent since the early 1960's, and these problems are likely to intensify by the end of the current century. People in many areas of the world are already experiencing varying degrees of protein malnutrition, largely because of rapid increase in population. A great need exists to accelerate both the production and yield of edible proteins from conventional sources, as well as to develop procedures for producing proteins from unconventional sources, such as unicellular algae, bacteria, yeasts, and leaves.

1. SINGLE-CELL PROTEIN

Because the words "microbial" and "bacterial" have somewhat undesirable connotations with respect to food, the term "single-cell protein" was proposed to cover the concept of utilizing microorganisms as food [118].

Rapid growth rate, high yields and the high degree of control that can be imposed on growing conditions are attractive advantages when single-cell organisms are considered as a source of food.

a. Yeast. Two species of yeast, Candida utilis and Saccharomyces carlsbergensis, have been used for human food [125]. Candida utilis is also known as torula yeast. It grows well on such substrates as sulfite waste liquor and wood hydrolyzates by utilizing pentoses as a carbon source. Furthermore, C. utilis requires no accessory growth factors and it competes well with bacteria so the possibility of bacterial growth is minimized.

Saccharomyces carlsbergensis, or brewer's yeast, is often recovered after completion of beer fermentation, at which point it can be processed, dried, and used as a nutritional supplement. Candida tropicalis and Candida lipolytica have aroused considerable interest since they are capable of using hydrocarbons as a source of carbon.

The protein content of $\underline{C}$. $\underline{utilis}$ grown on sulfite waste liquor is approximately 53% (dry weight basis). The major deficiency of microbial protein is its low content of sulfur-containing amino acids (methionine, cysteine). Animal feeding trials have been used to evaluate the nutritional attributes of yeast grown on hydrocarbons. Although protein utilization and biological values of only 50-60 were obtained for the original material, the addition of 0.3% methionine consistently increased these values to over 90 [120].

Ingestion of high levels of nucleic acids, particularly those of yeast origin, may cause certain physiological problems in humans. Uric acid, the final metabolic product of the purines contained in nucleic acids, is relatively insoluble in man. Over a period of time, consumption of over 2 g/day of nucleic acids from single-cell proteins in addition to an ordinary mixed diet may lead to the formation of kidney stones in some individuals, or aggravate arthritic or gouty conditions in others [107,140].

b. Bacteria. Bacteria have received much less attention than yeast as a possible source of food protein. However, considerable interest is now being directed toward the use of petroleum hydrocarbons as carbon sources for microbial protein. Accordingly, certain species of $\underline{Nocardia}$, $\underline{Mycobacterium}$, $\underline{Micrococcus}$, $\underline{Bacillus}$, and $\underline{Pseudomonas}$ are being investigated for protein production [125].

c. Algae. During the past two decades considerable interest has been directed to algae as a possible source of food protein. Members of $\underline{Chlorella}$ (green algae) and $\underline{Spirulina}$ (blue-green algae) have been studied rather extensively as producers of edible protein. Under controlled growing conditions, $\underline{Chlorella}$ $\underline{pyrenoidosa}$ and $\underline{Spirulina}$ $\underline{maxima}$ may contain 50 and 60% protein, respectively, on a dry weight basis. Algal protein contains all of the essential amino acids, and it is especially rich in tyrosine and serine. It is, however, low in sulfur-containing amino acids, particularly methionine. Of the algae species examined so far, the blue-green algae have slightly higher levels of the essential amino acids than the green algae [125].

Certain physiological problems are encountered when algal proteins are included in human diets. Diets containing more than 100 g of algal protein per day result in nausea, vomiting, and abdominal pain [53]. The presence of chemically inert cell walls may interfere with the human digestive processes. Poor digestibility (60-70%) is another undesirable characteristic of green algal protein. Removal of the algal pigment component and the use of suitable drying procedures or enzymic treatments result in improved digestibility.

d. Fungi. As a source of human food, mushrooms are the most extensively used filamentous fungi (those developing a true mycelium). They contain no more than 4 or 27% protein on a fresh or dry weight basis, respectively. The protein of the major commercially grown mushroom ($\underline{Agaricus}$ $\underline{bisporus}$) is nutritionally incomplete, being approximately equivalent in quality to wheat gliadin [58].

Mold-type fungi have been used for centuries to prepare certain foods. Penicillium roqueforti and P. camemberti are used to produce Roquefort (blue-veined) and Camembert cheeses that have distinctive flavors and textural qualities. Other mold-type fungi (Aspergillus oryzae, A. soyae, Rhizopus oligosporus, etc.) are employed in Asia to convert soybeans, rice, wheat, peanuts, fish, etc. into a variety of flavorful, nutritious foodstuffs.

It has been proposed that large amounts of food proteins can be produced by culturing fungal mycelia in liquid media containing waste carbohydrates and inorganic nitrogen salts [58]. However, the potential mycotoxin hazards must be assessed fully before any attempt is made to exploit fungi as a food resource.

2. LEAF PROTEIN

A number of studies on extraction of food proteins from various green plant leaves have been completed [103]. The protein content of the final dried product varies from about 50 to 70%, depending on the raw material used. Although leaf protein is very susceptible to heat damage during the drying stage, when prepared under optimum conditions its nutritional value is greater than that of other plant proteins. The lysine content of leaf protein ranges from 5 to 7%.

There is some controversy over the potential value of leaf proteins as a means of alleviating the world shortage of food proteins. Cost, yield, and palatability factors have been cited [19] as major obstacles. However, Pirie [103] has strongly advocated that these problems can be and are being resolved and that the ultimate potential of this source has not yet been approached.

In much of the initial work, proteins from unconventional sources were fed directly or were incorporated in conventional foods without adequate attention to sensory quality. Thus, such foods had a low level of acceptability. However, members of the Chad Republic in Africa have for centuries collected and consumed algae (Spirulina). Furthermore, in Latin America, torula yeast has been successfully added to certain plant protein mixtures (e.g., Incapurina) to adjust for lysine deficiency in the cereal portion.

3. FISH PROTEIN CONCENTRATE (FPC)

Much research effort has been aimed toward greater utilization of fish species (hake, menhaden, etc.) not generally consumed by man directly. For this purpose, raw whole fish is first comminuted and extracted with an organic solvent (isopropyl alcohol only or ethylene dichloride followed by isopropyl alcohol). Lipids and water are removed simultaneously, leaving a protein-rich residue that is steam stripped and dried to remove the residual solvent. This material is ground to the desired particle size to yield a grayish powder or concentrate (FPC) that is virtually odorless and tasteless. FPC prepared in this manner contains over 75% protein, less than 10% moisture, 0.5% lipid, and 10-15% mineral matter [46]. By using eviscerated, deboned fish as the raw material rather than whole fish, a FPC known as EFP-90 can be produced which contains more than 93% protein and about 3% each of moisture and mineral matter.

The amino acid composition of FPC compares favorably with that of whole egg protein and casein. Although methionine is the first limiting amino acid in FPC, lysine constitutes 7.5-10% of the total protein [128].

Even though FPC has high nutritional value, it is practically devoid of the functional properties (solubility, wettability, dispersibility, etc.) required in food fabrication. Until these deficiencies are corrected, utilization of FPC by the food industry is likely to be rather limited. Some of the economic, regulatory and technological problems hindering greater acceptance of FPC have been described in detail [46,68].

V. FUNCTIONS OF PROTEINS IN FOODS

The ability of proteins to form gels, sols, foams, emulsions, etc., provides some indication of their functional roles in foods. In addition, they are important nutrients and they can contribute to color and flavor by participating in Maillard and other browning reactions.

A. Functions of Various Classes of Proteins in Food Systems

The water-holding capacity (WHC) of muscle proteins is an important property influencing taste, tenderness, and color of fresh meat. WHC also affects the quality of meat during most of the subsequent processing operations. When meat emulsions are prepared in large quantities, the ability and capacity of muscle proteins to emulsify fat are extremely important. The water- (sarcoplasmic) and salt-soluble (myofibrillar) proteins have greater emulsifying and stabilizing effects than the stroma proteins [115]. During preparation of meat emulsions, muscle proteins are solubilized with the aid of salt, following which they position themselves at the oil-water interface, thereby stabilizing the emulsion. Poultry and fish muscle proteins also possess WHC and emulsifying properties similar to those of meat proteins.

Coagulation of milk, an essential step in the production of cheese and cultured dairy products, results when large structural aggregates of casein form from the normal dispersion of discrete casein micelles [132]. Coagulation can be accomplished by a variety of agents including acids, heat, enzymes, etc. Aside from being coagulable, milk proteins contribute to flavor and to the formation and stabilization of small air cells in ice cream and whipped cream. In foams, the proteins function at the air-liquid interface.

Various milk powders (fat and water removed) and various milk protein fractions (casein and sodium caseinate, whey proteins, etc.) are used as ingredients in other foods. Nonfat dry milk (NFDM) is used by the baking industry (1) to improve the water-absorption capacity of flour, which in turn increases the viscosity of the dough and the ease with which it can be handled during processing; (2) to improve baking quality of weak flours; (3) to control the rate of gas emission; (4) to strengthen structure and texture; (5) to retard moisture loss; (6) to enhance crust color and flavor development; and (7) to delay the staling process [79]. All dried dairy ingredients used in the baking industry require a proper preheat treatment (e.g., 80-85°C for 30 min) prior to dehydration. This results in desirable changes that have been attributed to denaturation of whey proteins and protein-protein inter-actions. With bread production in particular, the use of milk powders lacking a proper preheat treatment results in doughs of excessive softness, small loaf volumes, and in bread with a coarse texture [79].

Casein promotes low-temperature stability of some frozen foods. Whey proteins (especially lactalbumin) have good whipping characteristics and are used in dessert toppings for stabilization of foam structure. NFDM is added to comminuted meat as a stabilizer for the emulsion and to increase moisture retention. Whey proteins are included in candy and confection formulations (carmels, fudges, taffies, fond-ants, icing formulations) because of their structure-strengthening and moisture-retaining properties. Functions of milk proteins in many food formulations have not yet been determined [79].

The major functional roles of eggs in foods are to facilitate coagulation, gel formation, emulsification, and structure formation [6]. Eggs are used to thicken various heat-treated sauces and custards since egg proteins coagulate between 62 and 70°C. Foam formation with egg proteins results when an aqueous dispersion of appropriate viscosity is whipped. The egg white proteins, ovalbumin and especi-ally the globulins (including lysozyme), are important in foam formation [5]. Ovo-mucin tends to stabilize the foam once it has formed. As proteins form elastic films at the air-water interface, they partially coagulate, thus facilitating retention of air. The entrapped air then provides leavening and volume needed for such items as souffles, angel and sponge cakes, and meringues. During baking, the foam structure of these products is stabilized by further denaturation and coagula-tion of the proteins, especially the globulins and ovalbumin. A layer of denatured protein molecules at the air-liquid boundary retards evaporation, and their charge retards coalescence. An increase in foam stability is noted when conditions favor-ing coagulation are promoted. Elasticity of egg protein films is important in the preparation of some delicate products (cream puffs and popovers). In these in-stances, the protein films stretch when steam is produced during baking, and later coagulate to stabilize the structure of the product.

The emulsifying and stabilizing power of the yolk (mainly lipoproteins) is super-ior to that of whole egg. The lipoproteins of the yolk are hydrophilic colloids that adsorb to the oil-water interface to promote and stabilize the desired oil-in-water emulsion. Egg proteins facilitate dispersion of oil in other ingredients and thus contribute to the consistency of such products as mayonnaise and salad dressings.

Cereal flours, especially wheat flour and to a much lesser degree rye, yield a dough that retains gas and expands under the influence of leavening agents to pro-duce bread, cakes, and biscuits. The unique cohesive-elastic properties of hy-drated gluten (mainly the glutenin fraction) are responsible for this characteristic of wheat flour. Initially, the protein molecules in the flour particles are held in a closely packed, tightly coiled form by hydrogen bonding, salt linkages, and intra-molecular disulfide bonds. The proteins hydrate and swell when flour is mixed with water, and some of the cohesive forces maintaining the contracted conforma-tion begin to weaken. Also, a series of disulfide interchange reactions are initi-ated (Fig. 5-16). As a result, the original protein molecules uncoil and make contact with each other under conditions where linking reactions occur between them [88]. This process is accelerated by mixing, with the eventual result that a three-

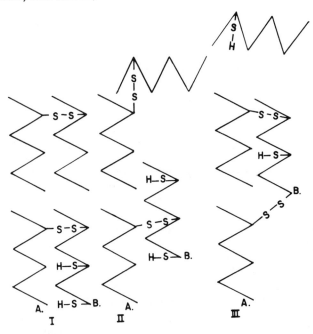

FIG. 5-16. Schematic representation of relief of strain in dough by sulfhydryl-disulfide interchange. Reprinted from Ref. [126], p. 24, courtesy of Baker's Digest.

dimensional mass of protein (gluten) with viscoelastic properties is formed. During fermentation (ripening) further orientation and rearrangement of the protein network continues under the mild influence of growing gas bubbles. The network stresses eventually relax and optimum conditions occur for expansion of gas and retention of structure. During baking, gas expansion causes stretching of the gluten framework to produce an even more porous structure [28]. Gelatinization of starch (65-85°C) and coagulation of egg proteins (80-85°C) contribute to the structure of the baked product. Complete coagulation of gluten does not occur until late in the baking process, when the internal temperature approaches 90°C [97].

Seed proteins, particularly soy proteins, have functional properties that include emulsification, emulsion stabilization, and fat absorption. In meat processing, soy proteins help form a matrix for retaining both moisture and fat and thus help maintain the desired textural stability of the cooked product. Soy proteins promote water absorption in bakery products, thereby minimizing shrinkage and loss of moisture. They are also used in soups and gravies to improve the texture and consistency of these products [30].

Proteins from unconventional sources generally lack many of the functional properties possessed by the more conventional food proteins. They are used mainly for their nutritional value in diets that are low or deficient in protein.

B. Nutritional Attributes of Proteins

The primary function of dietary protein is to supply nitrogen and amino acids for the synthesis of body proteins and other nitrogen-containing substances. The latter category includes such compounds as creatinine, certain hormones (e.g., epinephrine, thyroxine, etc.), and the heme prosthetic group of certain oxidative enzymes and hemoglobin.

Proteins of various body tissues contain 20 or more amino acids. Of this number, nine must be supplied in the human diet since they cannot be synthesized in the body. These amino acids are designated as "essential" and are histidine, isoleucine, leucine, lysine, methionine, phenylalanine, threonine, tryptophan, and valine. The other amino acids are called "nonessential" since they can be synthesized in the body from a utilizable source of dietary nitrogen, usually protein [95]. The diet should provide all the essential amino acids in amounts needed by the body, plus sufficient utilizable nitrogen to allow for biosynthesis of needed nonessential amino acids [94].

In order for biosynthesis of protein to occur in the body, all of the amino acids must be present simultaneously at the sites of protein synthesis. Protein synthesis ceases or is greatly slowed when only one of the amino acids is deficient (mean concentration is too low or intake is too variable). For example, many young children in tropical areas live solely on high-carbohydrate diets derived mainly from cereal grains and cassava. Such diets are inadequate with respect to protein content and protein quality. Children, especially preschool children with high protein requirements, show poor growth characteristics and high susceptibility to infectious diseases when they exist on this kind of diet [19].

The "quality" of "balance" of a food protein depends upon the kinds and amounts of amino acids it contains. A "balanced" or "high-quality" protein contains essential amino acids in ratios commensurate with human needs. Proteins of animal origin generally are of higher quality than those of plant origin. Cereal proteins are often low in lysine and in some instances they lack methionine, tryptophan, and occasionally threonine. Oil seeds and nuts are often deficient in lysine and methionine, whereas legumes often lack sufficient amounts of methionine. Proteins of low nutritional quality usually are deficient in some essential amino acids while containing excesses of others. Those in deficit are designated as "limiting" [93].

If low-quality proteins are fed in amounts sufficient to provide adequate levels of the limiting amino acids, then some amino acids become present in excess of requirements, and these are generally utilized as a source of energy rather than for tissue growth and maintenance. Conversely, when the amount of low-quality proteins just equals the needed amount of an ideal protein, amounts of some essential amino acids become inadequate. This situation, wherein the dietary pattern of amino acids differs greatly from the ideal pattern, is referred to as "amino acid imbalance." Amino acid imbalance can lead to reduced efficiency of amino acid utilization, depressed growth, and permanent impairment of mental capabilities in children. These consequences, with the exception of mental impairment, can be readily corrected by supplementing the diet with the limiting amino acid(s). In individuals consuming the average mixed American diet, it is highly unlikely that deviations in amino acid patterns are sufficient to cause any of the effects described above [94].

"Amino acid antagonism" is a term used to describe a dietary amino acid pattern that causes growth depression of a sort that can be corrected by the addition of an amino acid structurally similar to the antagonist. In contrast to "amino acid imbalance," the supplemented amino acids are not necessarily limiting. For example, an excess of dietary leucine depresses utilization of isoleucine, and this can be alleviated by the addition of small amounts of isoleucine. Both imbalance and antagonism result in increased requirements for an amino acid present in quantities that normally are sufficient [93].

"Amino acid toxicity" is a term used to describe the toxic effects resulting from ingestion of excessive amounts of amino acids. Marked inhibition of growth, reduced food intake, and certain pathological conditions (lesions of the eyes, skin, liver, etc.) are sometimes associated with "amino acid toxicity." Evidence of toxicity has been obtained from animal experiments and is very rarely seen in humans. Furthermore, the amounts of individual amino acids shown to produce toxic effects are much higher than those logically likely to be used as dietary supplements [93]. The toxic effect is likely dependent on the structure and metabolism of the specific amino acid. Methionine, cystine, tyrosine, tryptophan, and histidine appear to be the most toxic amino acids since they enter into many metabolic pathways.

C. Human Requirements

The Food and Nutrition Board of the National Research Council, National Academy of Sciences (United States), has developed nutritional standards entitled Recommended Dietary Allowances [94]. These dietary allowances, often referred to as RDA, are regarded as sufficient to maintain good nutrition in the populace of the United States living under contemporary conditions.

The RDA for protein are listed in Table 5-12 in terms of grams of protein intake per kilogram of body weight. These allowances are based on current knowledge and are revised periodically as new knowledge becomes available.

The recommended intakes are generally higher than average needs and lower than the amounts required in illness or to correct deficiencies. As will be discussed, these allowances are appropriately adjusted for pregnancy and lactation. RDA are primarily intended to serve as guidelines for planning nutritionally adequate diets for various population groups.

In calculating RDA for protein, the efficiency of utilization of dietary protein is considered to be 75% of that of an ideal protein. The latter is defined as a protein that contains adequate and utilizable amounts of all essential amino acids.

1. MAINTENANCE

The RDA for a 70-kg man is 56 g of protein per day or 0.8 g/kg of body weight per day (Table 5-12) based on a total caloric intake of approximately 2,700 kcal. For a 58-kg woman, the daily diet should provide 2,000 kcal and 46 g of protein. These levels of protein intake are considered adequate for maintenance. An expert group from the Food and Agriculture Organization (FAO) and the World Health Organization (WHO), both sponsored by the United Nations, has recommended a

TABLE 5-12

Recommended Daily Allowances for Dietary Proteins[a]

Group	Age	g/kg of body weight
Infants	0 – 6 months	2.2
	6 – 12 months	2.0
Children	1 – 3 years	1.8
	4 – 6 years	1.5
	7 – 10 years	1.2
Adolescents	11 – 14 years	1.0
	15 – 18 years	0.9
Adults	19+ years	0.8

[a]Adapted from Ref. [94].

slightly lower intake of 0.59 g of protein per kilogram of body weight per day for the average individual [20]. The daily requirement for protein remains constant during the lifetime of most adults.

2. GROWTH

Based on the assumption that weight gained by children over 1 year of age is 18% protein, appropriate adjustments for growth must be added to the daily protein allowances for maintenance (Table 5-12). For children (age range 1-10 years) the RDA for protein is highest for the age group of 1-3 years (1.8 g/kg of body weight per day). FAO-WHO suggest a daily intake of 0.88 g protein per kilogram body weight for this age group [20]. Nutritionally, this age span is especially critical because this is when children grow most rapidly and require optimum protein quantity and quality for proper tissue formation. Beyond age 3 years, the RDA for protein decreases gradually until age 18.

3. PREGNANCY AND LACTATION

A pregnant woman must receive adequate nutrients to insure a normal course of pregnancy. About 950 g of protein are required for growth and maintenance of the fetus and growth of maternal tissue. An additional 30 g of protein per day beyond the maintenance requirements will cover these needs [94].

During lactation, an additional intake of 20 g of protein per day is suggested [94] to insure that the lactating mother will receive sufficient dietary protein for the secretion of milk in proper amounts and of adequate quality.

4. ILLNESS AND INJURY

Many diseases and injuries (e.g., infection, trauma, fractures, or immobilization of the body) cause a rapid breakdown of tissue proteins and increased excretion of nitrogen. For example, burns or extensive traumatic damage to the body causes considerable loss of protein externally (because of serum seepage) and increased catabolism of tissue proteins. The more severe the illness or injury, the greater is depletion of protein. Thus, diets must be formulated to compensate for these losses so that recovery can proceed at an optimum rate. It is difficult to specify the particular diet that should be used since each injury or illness must be evaluated on the basis of the individual's physical condition and nutritional status at the time of adversity. However, in most cases it can be assumed that higher levels of protein should be consumed; perhaps 14% or more of the total daily calories should be derived from dietary protein. Furthermore, it is of considerable importance that the dietary protein be of the highest quality available (milk, egg, fish, meat). In this regard the more closely the dietary protein of the absorbed nitrogen conforms to the amino acid pattern utilized for protein biosynthesis, the higher is its biological value (assuming antinutritional factors are absent) [22].

5. PROTEIN REQUIREMENTS EXPRESSED BY AN ALTERNATIVE PROCEDURE

The optimum daily intake of proteins also can be conveniently expressed as a percent of the total caloric intake [2]. Although proteins yield an energy value of 5.65 kcal/g in a laboratory bomb calorimeter, they are inefficiently converted to energy in the body, yielding only 4.1 kcal/g. Thus, on the basis of efficiency of digestion and subsequent utilization by the body, proteins are considered to supply energy at a rate equivalent to that of carbohydrates. An optimum nutritional response seems to result when protein provides 10-14% of the total energy of the diet. This range tends to remain constant irrespective of age, sex, pregnancy, work, or illness. The working capacity of an individual may be affected when the caloric contribution of protein falls below 8% in a mixed diet (i.e., protein from both animal and plant sources). One shortcoming of this procedure is that people eat more as they become more active, and in this situation protein should constitute a smaller percentage of the caloric intake.

In developed countries, such as the United States, the daily per capita protein intake is about 70-90 g, of which 45 to 50 g are of animal origin. It has been suggested that a daily diet containing 30 g of high-quality protein (eggs, milk, meat, fish) will provide nutritional wellbeing irrespective of the quality of the remaining protein [2].

VI. EFFECT OF PROCESSING ON FUNCTIONAL AND
NUTRITIONAL PROPERTIES OF PROTEINS

A. High-Temperature Processing

1. PASTEURIZATION

Heat treatments used for pasteurization of most protein foods must be carefully controlled to minimize damage (loss of functionality) to heat-labile proteins. Thus, temperatures well below 100°C are generally used in various pasteurization processes.

a. Meat. During pasteurization of flesh foods (meat, poultry, and fish), the final internal temperature of the product seldom exceeds a range of about 66-74°C. During the early stages of heat pasteurization (30-50°C), there is an unfolding of peptide chains, formation of relatively unstable crosslinkages, and partial denaturation of the sarcoplasmic proteins. These changes cause a tightening of the myofibrillar structure, resulting in toughness and decreased water-holding capacity. In the latter stages of pasteurization (50-74°C), new stable crosslinkages are formed in conjunction with denaturation and coagulation of both sarcoplasmic and myofibrillar proteins. At appropriate temperatures, collagen shrinks (61-63°C in meat and 45°C in fish) and softens as the ordered helical structure collapses. The overall result is tenderization of connective tissue and toughening of myofibrillar proteins [63].

b. Milk. In current dairy processing operations, milk is generally pasteurized for 15 sec at 72°C. Most of the degradative enzymes are partially or totally inactivated by this treatment. Other changes occurring during pasteurization seem to be quite minor, although a slight denaturation of some whey proteins (β-lactoglobulin and proteins of the fat globule membrane) occurs, and this leads to sulfide formation and a flavor change [79]. In the native state, β-lactoglobulin has a conformation that shields and renders the sulfhydryl groups of cysteine unreactive. As β-lactoglobulin unfolds upon heating, these sulfhydryl groups become more accessible and reactive, yielding H_2S as follows:

$$HOOC-CHNH_2-CH_2SH + H_2O \longrightarrow HOOC-CHNH_2-CH_2O + H_2S \qquad (5\text{-}38)$$

or

$$2\ HOOC-CHNH_2-CH_2SH \longrightarrow (HOOC-CHNH_2-CH_2)_2S + H_2S \qquad (5\text{-}39)$$

Important nutrients in milk are not altered substantially by pasteurization.

c. Eggs. Since raw egg is likely to contain Salmonellae, liquid egg products (whole eggs, yolk products, and egg whites) must be pasteurized prior to being sold for food use. Liquid whole egg must be flash heated to 60°C and held at this temperature for 3.5-4 min [133]. Liquid egg white is more heat sensitive than either whole egg or yolk, and special procedures have been established to carry out pasteurization of egg white without causing a significant reduction in its nutritional and functional properties. These procedures are discussed in Chapter 14, Section II.

2. STERILIZATION

To achieve prolonged storage of foods, heat sterilization is often used to destroy contaminating microorganisms and to inactivate enzymes.

a. Flesh Foods. At temperatures above 80°C, sarcoplasmic and myofibrillar proteins coagulate. Oxidation of the sulfhydryl groups of actomyosin leads to formation of disulfide bonds. Hydrogen sulfide is split from actomyosin at about 90°C. Also, at this temperature Maillard reactions between reducing sugars and amino groups of proteins occur rapidly (see Chapter 3). These reactions decrease the nutritional availability of certain amino acids (e.g., lysine). During sterilization most of the collagen is converted to gelatin. Some essential amino acids are damaged during sterilization of meats, especially cysteine, methionine, and lysine [63]. However, this effect is minor in a well-conducted sterilization process.

b. Milk. Complicated changes occur in milk during heat sterilization. Temperatures exceeding that for pasteurization (72°C) cause instability and coagulation of proteins. Depending on the time-temperature relationships, heat treatments may partially dephosphorylate casein, denature whey proteins, initiate protein-protein and protein-lactose interactions, etc. Several articles [79,111,132] cover these complex changes in detail.

3. SPECIAL PROBLEMS IN HEAT PROCESSING

Of all the major food-processing treatments in current use, heat processing has the most important effect on protein quality. Depending on such factors as time, temperature, moisture content, and the presence or absence of reducing substances, heat treatments may have either a beneficial or detrimental influence.

a. Beneficial Effects. Most proteins of plant origin are nutritionally improved by heating. Trypsin inhibitors and other antinutritional components of several seed proteins are inactivated or destroyed by proper heat treatment. Wheat, rye, and to a lesser extent rice and oats contain a trypsin inhibitor that is destroyed by cooking. Digestibility and availability of the sulfur amino acids also are improved by conventional heat treatments. This is particularly true in soybeans and peanuts. Furthermore, the availabilities of methionine, tryptophan, and threonine are greater in bread than in unground wheat [9]. However, heat treatments must be applied with care so that undesirable effects are minimized.

b. Detrimental Effects. Excessive heating can result in a reduction of palatability and a substantial decrease in nutritive value. Three different types of reactions can result in decreased nutritive value of proteins during improper heat processing: oxidation of amino acids, alteration of some of the linkages between amino acids so that their release during digestion is delayed, and formation of new amino acid linkages that are not subject to hydrolysis by digestive enzymes.

The charring that accompanies gross overheating results in destruction of amino acids and losses of nitrogen, sulfur, and dry weight. Although the effects of pyrolysis complicate the reactions producing these irreversible changes, deamination, decarboxylation, and the oxidation of sulfur are known to occur.

Delayed release of amino acids during digestion may disrupt protein synthesis in body tissues by preventing the simultaneous availability of all essential amino acids. Those that cannot be used in protein synthesis are biologically oxidized [9]. Recent studies have yielded data suggesting that the enzymic release of amino acids can be altered by severely heating proteins [49].

Heat processing can result in the formation of linkages that cannot be hydrolyzed during digestion [9]. Thus, the nutritional availability of some amino acids is markedly reduced even though they sometimes can be recovered by acid hydrolysis. It has been well established that the Maillard or "nonenzymic browning" reaction can account for much of the damaging effect of heat on the protein quality of foods that contain reducing sugars, such as lactose or glucose [83]. Sucrose can also yield reducing sugars if conditions are suitable for its hydrolysis. Lysine readily reacts with lactose to form an amino sugar. The ϵ-amino group of lysine is the preferential site for initiation of the Maillard reaction. The initial Maillard reaction products (prior to the Shiff base) can be cleaved by strong acid but not by enzymic digestion in the gastrointestinal tract [89]. Thus, "bound" lysine has no nutritional value since it cannot be utilized by the body. Arginine, tryptophan, histidine, and threonine also react readily with reducing groups of carbohydrate materials during heating.

The formation of amino sugars may interfere with the specificity requirements for enzyme hydrolysis of proteins in such a manner that amino acids adjacent to the amino sugar site remain unhydrolyzed during digestive processes [43]. Thus, Maillard browning can reduce the availability of many amino acids not directly involved in the reaction.

As the Maillard reaction proceeds, reaction products polymerize (melanoidins), browning intensifies, and significant amounts of amino acids are destroyed (chemically altered irreversibly). In addition to reducing sugars, fats or fatty acids that are undergoing autoxidation may contribute carbonyl groups for a Maillard-type reaction [80].

In the absence of reducing substances, protein-protein interactions (C-N links) can be initiated by exposing proteinaceous tissues to high temperatures ($>110\,^\circ$C) for substantial lengths of time (> 24 hr). New bonds or crosslinkages, such as :CH·N: links, may replace peptide bonds (·CO·NH·). Digestive enzymes are clearly unable to cleave :CH·N: linkages and thus the bound amino acids are not absorbed [43]. According to Bjarnason and Carpenter [14], lysine that becomes unavailable during the heating of carbohydrate-free proteins does so because unnatural amide bonds form between the ϵ-amino group of lysine and the amide groups of asparagine and glutamine (see below). The reacting components may reside either in the same peptide chain or in neighboring molecules.

$$
\begin{array}{ccc}
\begin{array}{l}
\quad\;\; \overset{\displaystyle O}{\overset{\displaystyle \|}{}} \\
-NH-CH-C- \\
\quad | \\
\;\; (CH_2)_n \\
\quad | \\
\;\; C=O \\
\quad | \\
\;\; NH_2 \\
\quad + \\
\;\; NH_2 \\
\quad | \\
\;\; (CH_2)_4 \\
-NH-CH-C- \\
\qquad\;\; \overset{\displaystyle \|}{\underset{\displaystyle O}{}}
\end{array}
&
\xrightarrow{\;\text{Heat}\;}
&
\begin{array}{l}
\quad\;\; \overset{\displaystyle O}{\overset{\displaystyle \|}{}} \\
-NH-CH-C- \\
\quad | \\
\;\; (CH_2)_n \\
\quad | \\
\;\; C=O \\
\quad | \\
\;\; NH \\
\quad | \\
\;\; (CH_2)_4 \\
-NH-CH-C- \\
\qquad\;\; \overset{\displaystyle \|}{\underset{\displaystyle O}{}}
\end{array}
\; + NH_3
\end{array}
\qquad (5\text{-}40)
$$

Such crosslinking reduces the nutritional availability of all essential amino acids.

Cystine is the amino acid most sensitive to heat. During heating of carbohydrate-free proteins at 115 °C for 27 hr (note severity of heating), 50–60% of the cystine is destroyed and H_2S is evolved. The following reactions [14] are at least partly responsible for destruction of cystine during the heating of proteins in the absence of oxygen:

$$R-CH_2-S-S-CH_2-R + H_2O \longrightarrow R-CH_2-SH + R-CH_2-SOH \qquad (5\text{-}41)$$

$$R-CH_2-SOH \longrightarrow R-CHO + H_2S \qquad (5\text{-}42)$$

Cystine loss during heating of proteins becomes of major nutritional significance only if this makes sulfur-bearing amino acids limiting. Generally, the nutritional quality of heated proteins is affected less by loss of cystine than by other changes [14]. Exceptions occur in diets in which sulfur amino acids tend to be limiting. Examples include diets that are heavily dependent on milk, cottonseed protein, or fish meals (limited by methionine plus cystine [9]).

The puffing–exploding type of processing used in the manufacture of certain breakfast cereals causes severe protein damage. Rolled oats boiled in water for 15 min and dried for 15 sec at 130 °C or cooked in steam for 2 min at 100-lb pressure, then exploded and dried for 2 min at 200 °C have protein efficiency ratios (PER) of 1.6. Conversely, when oats are puffed by heating for 5 min at 122 °C and for 2 min at 189 °C, then exploded, the PER decreases to 0.3 [92]. The puffing–exploding heat treatment disrupts many chemical bonds and results in the destruction of substantial amounts of essential amino acids.

Toasting of cereal products also results in considerable damage to the nutritive quality of protein, particularly in the outer layers which are subjected to the greatest heat intensity. Much of this damage is due to the loss and/or unavailability of lysine. The original nutritive value of toasted cereals can be completely restored by the addition of lysine [9].

Although some damage or destruction of protein invariably results from normal commercial heat treatments, such losses are considered as relatively insignificant. In contrast, the more harsh heat treatments such as the puffing–exploding and toasting processes used in the manufacture of certain breakfast cereals are significantly destructive to protein. These foods, however, do not contribute much protein to the American diet since they comprise only a small portion of the daily food intake. Furthermore, most of these products are consumed with milk, which compensates for the lysine lost during these specialized heat-processing treatments [8,9].

c. Alkali Treatment. The use of alkali in food processing, especially when used in conjunction with heat, is cause for some concern because of its damaging effects on protein quality. Alkali treatments are becoming more common in the food industry for preparing protein concentrates and isolates, for modifying proteins to obtain or enhance specific functional properties (foaming, emulsifying, etc.), and for producing protein solutions suitable for spinning fibers. Alkali treatment of proteins may result in formation of new amino acids, such as lysinoalanine, lanthionine, and ornithinoalanine. Cystine, lysine, arginine, and possibly serine are the amino acids involved in these modifications. Since sulfur amino acids and lysine are limiting in a majority of food proteins, reduced nitritive value may result from their exposure to alkali.

Exposure of a high-protein product, soy protein isolate, to aqueous alkali (pH 12.2) for 4 hr at 40°C results in the formation of lysinoalanine (LAL), which is poorly absorbed [38]. The amount of LAL formed increases with rising temperature and with increasing exposure time. The presence of LAL in alkali-treated soy protein isolate is accompanied by a reduction in the cystine and lysine contents. A more severe treatment of the protein with alkali (pH 12.2) at temperatures exceeding 60°C also causes decreases in serine content and in protein digestibility.

The primary change induced in proteins by alkali treatment is apparently a β-elimination reaction [27] leading to formation of dehydroalanine residues from cystine:

$$S-CH_2-CHNH_2-COOH$$
$$|$$
$$S-CH_2-CHNH_2-COOH \xrightarrow{\quad OH^- \quad}$$

$$\overset{-OOC}{\underset{NH_2}{\diagdown}}CH-CH_2-S-S-CH_2-C\overset{COO^-}{\underset{NH_2}{\diagup}} \quad + H_2O \longrightarrow$$

$$\overset{-OOC}{\underset{NH_2}{\diagdown}}CH-CH_2-S-S^- + CH_2=C\overset{COO^-}{\underset{NH_2}{\diagup}}$$

(5-43)

Dehydroalanine

Lysinoalanine is formed by the addition of an ϵ-amino group of a lysyl residue across the double bond of dehydroalanine as indicated below [98]:

$$-NH-CH-CO- + NH-C-CO- \longrightarrow -NH-CH-CO-$$
$$\quad | \qquad\qquad\qquad \| \qquad\qquad\qquad\qquad |$$
$$(CH_2)_4 \qquad\quad CH_2 \qquad\qquad\qquad (CH_2)_4 \qquad \xrightarrow{\quad H_2O \quad}$$
$$\quad | \qquad\qquad\qquad\qquad\qquad\qquad\qquad\quad | \qquad\qquad (HCl)$$
$$NH_2 \qquad\qquad\qquad\qquad\qquad\qquad\quad NH$$
$$\qquad\qquad\qquad\qquad\qquad\qquad\qquad\qquad | $$
$$\qquad\qquad\qquad\qquad\qquad\qquad\qquad CH_2$$
$$\qquad\qquad\qquad\qquad\qquad\qquad\qquad\quad |$$
$$\qquad\qquad\qquad\qquad\qquad\qquad OC-CH-NH-$$

$$NH_2-CH-COOH$$
$$\quad |$$
$$(CH_2)_4$$
$$\quad |$$
$$NH$$
$$\quad |$$
$$CH_2$$
$$\quad |$$
$$NH_2-CH-COOH$$

(5-44)

Lysinoalanine

During alkaline hydrolysis of proteins (boiling wool or lactalbumin for 1 hr in either 0.1N NaOH or 2% Na_2CO_3), Horn et al. [70] noted that cystine residues lost one of the sulfur atoms and were converted into a thiol ether diamino acid, lanthionine:

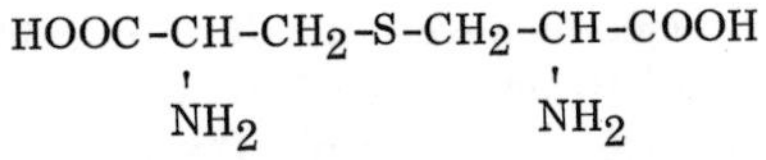

$$HOOC-CH-CH_2-S-CH_2-CH-COOH$$
$$\quad\quad\ \ |\quad\quad\quad\quad\quad\quad\quad |$$
$$\quad\quad NH_2\quad\quad\quad\quad\quad NH_2$$

The heating of egg white (pH 9.0) for 60 min at temperatures exceeding 60°C results in H_2S production and the formation of lanthionine [52]. It was concluded that H_2S was produced from cysteine as a result of nonenzymic reactions while lanthionine was formed by an unknown reaction mechanism. In an earlier study, Chapeville and Fromageot [29] isolated the enzyme cysteine lyase from egg yolk. This enzyme was found to exert a desulfhydration effect and also could lead to the production of ammonia, pyruvic acid, and lanthionine as shown in Figure 5-17. A similar reaction mechanism may function during the heating of egg white [52].

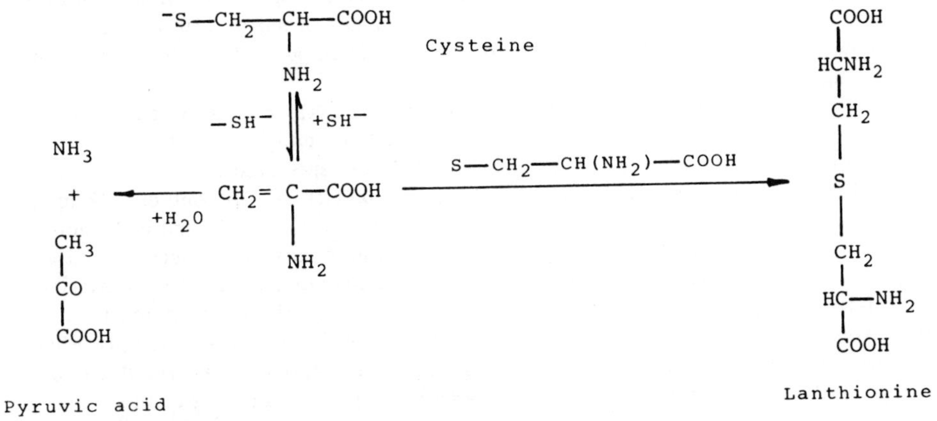

FIG. 5-17. A possible pathway leading to the formation of lanthionine during heating of egg white. Reprinted from Ref. [52], p. 15, courtesy of A. C. Germs.

Free or combined arginine can be degraded by alkali to form ornithine:

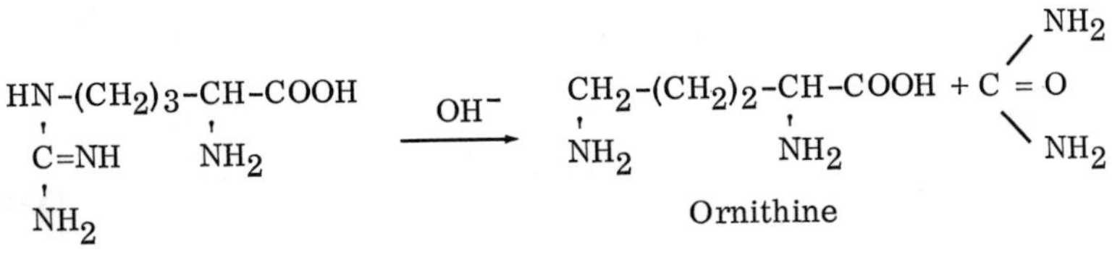

$$HN-(CH_2)_3-CH-COOH \xrightarrow{OH^-} CH_2-(CH_2)_2-CH-COOH + C = O \begin{matrix} \nearrow NH_2 \\ \\ \searrow NH_2 \end{matrix}$$

with $C=NH$, NH_2, NH_2 groups and NH_2, NH_2 on ornithine.

Ornithine   (5-45)

The δ-amino groups of combined ornithine can react with dehydroalanine (produced as decomposition products of cystine and/or serine residues) to yield ornithinoalanine [149]:

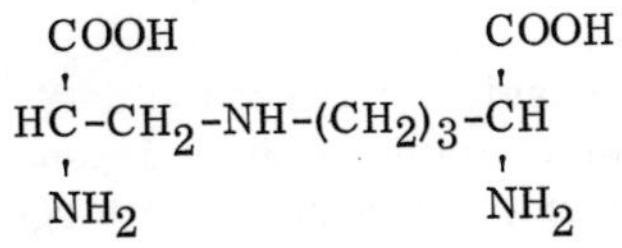

$$\begin{matrix} COOH & & COOH \\ | & & | \\ HC-CH_2-NH-(CH_2)_3-CH \\ | & & | \\ NH_2 & & NH_2 \end{matrix}$$

Although the structures shown above can be obtained by severe alkali processing, they are not commonly encountered during normal alkali processing. How they may affect functional properties of proteins has not been determined. From a nutritional standpoint, they are most likely to be detrimental rather than beneficial.

Hot alkali also causes substantial racemization of arginine, cystine, threonine, serine, and lysine. Amino acids altered by alkaline racemization exhibit decreased nutritive values. Racemization occurs most rapidly when amino acids are involved in peptide linkages.

d. Sulfide Discoloration. Sulfide discoloration has been encountered sporadically in certain canned low-acid, high-protein foods, such as meats and especially seafoods. The discoloration usually consists of black ferrous sulfide precipitated in the head space area of tin-plated steel cans during retorting. The sulfur-containing amino acids, cysteine and methionine, are the sources of sulfur [102]. The ferrous ions originate from the steel base of the can via imperfections in the protective tin coating.

The tin-iron couple which is involved in the electrolytic release of tin or iron ions has unique properties. In the electrochemical series of elements, tin is cathodic to iron (the cathodic half-cell of a battery accepts electrons, while the anodic half-cell releases electrons with resultant oxidation). In contact with many foods, however, the polarity reverses and tin serves as the anode and undergoes slow uniform dissolution. This protects the iron which may be exposed by cracks or pinholes in the coating. In the presence of proteinaceous foods, the polarity of the tin-iron couple remains in accord with the electrochemical series and iron dissolves in preference to tin. This situation apparently arises because proteins bind Sn^{2+} ions very strongly. This binding and reduction of tin ions results in a change in the electromotive force (EMF) because the EMF of a reversible reaction is very concentration dependent. On this basis alone, a ratio of Sn^{2+}/Fe^{2+} of less than 5×10^{-11} would cause iron to be anodic [59].

Because the tin-iron couple is reversible, both green and black discolorations are occasionally observed in a single can of low-acid food. The greenish stain results from the formation of tin sulfide, and the black stain results from the formation of iron sulfide as shown below [102]:

$$
\begin{array}{l}
\text{R-SH + SH-R} \overset{\text{Oxid}}{\underset{\text{Red}}{\rightleftharpoons}} \text{R-S-S-R} \\
\text{S}^{2-}\text{+ R-H} \\
\quad\Updownarrow \text{H}^{+} \\
\text{HS}^{-} \rightleftharpoons \text{H}_2\text{S}
\end{array}
\qquad (5\text{-}46)
$$

$$
Fe^{2+} + S^{2-} \longrightarrow FeS \text{ (black precipitate)} \qquad (5\text{-}47)
$$

$$
Sn^{2+} + S^{2-} \longrightarrow SnS \text{ (green precipitate)} \qquad (5\text{-}48)
$$

The concentration of H_2S in the headspace of cans is closely related to the degree of discoloration. The release of sulfur from the sulfur amino acids is dependent on several factors. The absence of oxygen (high vacuum) contributes to a large concentration of H_2S since the oxidation products of cysteine and methionine (cystine and methionine sulfoxide) do not serve as sources of sulfur [102]. Pyridoxal, in the presence of such ions as Al^{3+}, Fe^{3+}, and Fe^{2+}, exerts a catalytic effect on the rate of desulfhydration of cysteine and methionine [60]. The following reaction may be involved:

$$\underset{\text{cysteine}}{SH-CH_2-\underset{\underset{NH_2}{|}}{CH}-COOH} \xrightarrow[\text{H}_2\text{O, pyridoxal}]{\text{Metallic ions (3}^+\text{)}} \underset{\text{pyruvic}}{CH_3-\overset{\overset{O}{||}}{C}-COOH} + NH_3 + H_2S \qquad (5-49)$$

Several factors are thus involved in sulfide discoloration in canned foods. First, the can itself is important, particularly the integrity of the tin coating and whether or not an organic lining is present. The presence of zinc oxide in an organic lining will effectively prevent sulfide discoloration in low-acid foods by causing the formation of white zinc sulfide instead of undesirable iron or tin sulfides. The composition of the food is also important, especially the amounts of sulfur amino acids, types and concentration of ions, and even the levels of pyridoxal.

B. Low-Temperature Processing

Low-temperature storage delays or inhibits spoilage by retarding microbial growth, enzymic activities, and chemical reactions.

1. CHILLING

Food proteins are relatively stable when held at temperatures just above freezing. However, growth of psychrotrophic microorganisms will eventually become sufficient to cause spoilage as described in Section VII of this chapter.

2. FREEZING

The sensory attributes of food tissues are damaged somewhat by the freezing process (freezing, frozen storage, and thawing), but the nutritive quality of protein is almost unaffected in well-controlled situations.

a. Flesh Foods. Freezing results in some disruption of tissue, including damage to membranes. Upon thawing, enzymes in the damaged tissue are better able to contact substrates, and increased enzyme activity is often observed. This may cause appreciable protein degradation if a long time is involved. Furthermore, irreversible structural changes often result when water-protein associations are disrupted by freezing and replaced by protein-protein interactions or other kinds of interactions. These changes result in damage to textural properties and a loss of water-holding capacity. However, nutritive losses encountered in flesh foods during properly conducted freezing processes are negligible.

Undesirable textural changes often occur in fish during freezing and frozen storage. These changes are largely attributable to the instability of fish proteins, especially myosin. During frozen storage, myosin gradually undergoes denaturation. The denatured myosin appears to interact with native actin, which remains practically undamaged in the muscle. Noncovalent interactions between denatured myosin molecules and between actin and denatured myosin molecules tend to strengthen the muscle structure and decrease WHC. Such changes cause the thawed fish to be dry and tough [34].

In addition, fish lipids may undergo autoxidation during frozen storage, resulting in the formation of free radicals and fairly stable hydroperoxides. These compounds may react with muscle proteins, causing protein polymerization, decreased extractability of myofibrillar proteins, and destruction of amino acids [114]. These undesirable changes can be greatly retarded by storing frozen fish at temperatures of -30°C or lower [34].

b. Eggs. When egg yolk is frozen and stored below -6°C, the thawed material exhibits a gel-like structure and increased viscosity. Yolk lipoproteins are apparently irreversibly damaged by the freeze-induced increase in concentration of yolk salts, and this results in gelation. Gelation can be prevented by adding either 10% sugar or salt prior to freezing [36]. Changes occurring during gelation are discussed in Chapter 14, Section II.

c. Milk. Pasteurized, homogenized, fluid milk can be frozen and held satisfactorily at -24°C for as long as 4 months, but frozen concentrated milk can be satisfactorily stored for only short periods. In both instances, storage stability is limited primarily by the tendency of casein to form a precipitate which fails to disperse upon thawing [42].

C. Dehydration

Removal of water from protein foods by various dehydration methods is an effective means of food preservation. Even though dehydrated foods possess certain advantages (weight reduction, prolonged storage stability without refrigeration, etc.), many undergo undesirable changes in sensory attributes during the dehydration process.

1. CONVENTIONAL DEHYDRATION

The drying of meat, poultry, and fish in moving warm air at atmospheric pressure results in hard, shrunken products that reconstitute very poorly and, when cooked, are very tough and have unnatural flavors [10].

2. VACUUM DRYING

A moderate vacuum of 5-10 mm Hg absolute pressure is used in this procedure. Flesh foods dried by this method are damaged less than by conventional dehydration. The absence of air retards oxidative changes, and the low drying temperatures decrease nonenzymic browning and other chemical changes [110].

3. FREEZE DRYING

In this process, the product is frozen, the pressure is reduced to 1 mm Hg or less, and water is removed by sublimation. The product retains its original size and shape although it shows considerable porosity when dried. This porosity enhances reconstitution [110].

Freeze drying is the best process for dehydrating flesh foods. However, even under optimum operating conditions there are indications that the proteins of freeze dried meat are apparently altered. For example, freeze-dried meat after rehydration and cooking is less tender and juicy than cooked meat that has not been freeze dried. The decreased WHC and toughness may result when actomyosin molecules come closer together, as water is removed during dehydration. Some unfolding of peptide chains may also occur during this period. This is believed to result in aggregation of myofibrillar proteins as new intermolecular salt and/or metal bonds are formed [63,69].

The extent of damage in freeze dried meat or fish is always greater than that resulting merely from a freeze-thaw process. Denaturation of myofibrillar proteins during freeze drying is caused by the removal of "bound" water rather than by the freezing process [34,63].

Dehydration also can result in other deteriorative changes. These involve a loss of nutritive value, especially destruction of lysine by nonenzymic browning, and decreased digestibility which results from interactions of denatured proteins with lipids and carbohydrates. The amount of damage occuring during dehydration of flesh foods increases with the severity of the operating conditions. Elevated temperatures and long exposure to air are particularly harmful. In most instances, however, freeze-dried flesh foods are similar to the fresh products with respect to content of essential amino acids and digestibility.

4. SPRAY DRYING

Spray drying is generally used to produce dehydrated eggs and milk products. In spray drying, the liquid is finely atomized into a stream of rapidly moving hot air. Although heat is the principal agent causing protein alteration during spray drying, surface forces cannot be ignored [32]. In the spray drying of liquid egg white, for example, the shear forces encountered during pumping and atomization operations may have a harmful effect on the protein and on the functional properties of the product. The great surface area generated by atomization also may cause surface denaturation of proteins and a subsequent reduction in whipping and other functional properties. However, the percentage of protein that is usually denatured under standard atomization conditions is relatively small [10].

During spray drying of milk and milk products under properly controlled conditions, changes in milk protein structures and solubilities are relatively minor [61].

5. DRUM DRYING

In drum or "roller" drying, the product is dried in a thin film on a rotating drum that is internally heated with steam. Many operational variables related to time and temperature must be controlled rather rigidly to produce high-quality products [61]. Occasionally, the dry product has a scorched flavor and reduced protein solubility since severe time-temperature conditions are not uncommon.

Two new amino acids, furosine and pyridosine, have been identified in scorched drum-dried milk powders [47,48]. They arise from lysine and their structures are given below:

$$NH_2-CH-(CH_2)_4-NH-CH_2-C-$$
$$\quad\ \ |\qquad\qquad\qquad\qquad\quad\ \|$$
$$\quad\ \ COOH\qquad\qquad\qquad\quad O$$

Furosine

$$NH_2-CH-(CH_2)_4-N$$
$$\quad\ \ |$$
$$\quad\ \ COOH$$

Pyridosine

Furosine and pyridosine are found in relatively large amounts in acid hydrolyzates of drum-dried milk powders, in trace amounts in hydrolyzates of spray-dried milk products, and not at all in freeze-dried milk. Monitoring the formation of furosine might be a useful indicator of heat damage to proteins since it forms well before nutritive damage can be detected. Neither of these new amino acids is readily absorbed in the intestine.

D. Effect of Radiation on Proteins

Although the processing of foods with ionizing radiation has not yet been approved by the Food and Drug Administration of the United States, there is still considerable interest in this prospective means of food preservation. Radiation damage to proteins in aqueous systems, such as foods, is attributable mainly to indirect effects, i.e., irradiation of water produces free radicals ($\cdot$OH, H$\cdot$, etc.) and hydrated free electrons (e_{aq}^-), and these in turn interact with and alter proteins [117]. Since foods contain many components capable of reacting with these water radicals, only a small proportion of these radicals may react with proteins.

Despite considerable research, knowledge of the radiation chemistry of proteins in aqueous solution is still rather limited. More is known about the radiation chemistry of amino acids and simple peptides and it is assumed that the major radiolytic reactions of proteins parallel those of amino acids and peptides [64]. Thus, generalizations drawn from the radiation chemistry of amino acids and peptides appear useful.

Abstraction of a hydrogen atom is the initial reaction most frequently observed during irradiation of amino acids. In the absence of oxygen, this can be initiated by the hydroxyl radical or by e_{aq}^-, whereas in the presence of oxygen the $\cdot$OH radical is responsible. With the α-amino acids, reactions at the α-carbon atom can be divided into three categories [127,141].

1. Reductive deamination: This reaction involves the initial removal of the amino group by e_{aq}^-, resulting in formation of ammonia and a carboxylic acid:

$$R\text{-}CHNH_2\text{-}COOH + e_{aq}^- + H^+ \longrightarrow R\text{-}\overset{\cdot}{C}H\text{-}COOH + NH_3 \qquad (5\text{-}50)$$

$$R\text{-}\overset{\cdot}{C}H\text{-}COOH + R\text{-}CHNH_2\text{-}COOH \longrightarrow R\text{-}CH_2\text{-}COOH + R\text{-}\overset{\cdot}{C}NH_2\text{-}COOH \qquad (5\text{-}51)$$

2. Oxidative deamination: This involves formation of α-carbon free radicals (attack by either e_{aq}^- or $\cdot$OH), which in turn interact to yield an α-carbonyl derivative and ammonia:

$$R\text{-}CHNH_2\text{-}COOH + e_{aq}^- + H^+ \longrightarrow R\text{-}\overset{\cdot}{C}NH_2\text{-}COOH + H_2 \qquad (5\text{-}52)$$

$$R\text{-}CHNH_2\text{-}COOH + \cdot OH \longrightarrow R\text{-}\overset{\cdot}{C}NH_2\text{-}COOH + H_2O \qquad (5\text{-}53)$$

$$2\,R\text{-}\overset{\cdot}{C}NH_2\text{-}COOH \longrightarrow R\text{-}CHNH_2\text{-}COOH + R\text{-}C\text{=}NH\text{-}COOH \qquad (5\text{-}54)$$

$$R\text{-}C\text{=}NH\text{-}COOH + H_2O \longrightarrow R\text{-}CO\text{-}COOH + NH_3 \qquad (5\text{-}55)$$

3. Decarboxylation: This results in carbon dioxide and an amine by an unknown mechanism.

The presence of oxygen affects the reactions at the α-carbon atom. Initially, it suppresses reductive deamination by rapidly removing the reducing species. Second, the mechanism of oxidative deamination is apparently altered even though the products (the carbonyl group and ammonia) are the same:

$$R\text{-}CHNH_2\text{-}COOH + \cdot OH \longrightarrow R\text{-}\overset{\cdot}{C}NH_2\text{-}COOH + H_2O \qquad (5\text{-}56)$$

$$R\text{-}\overset{\cdot}{C}NH_2\text{-}COOH + O_2 \longrightarrow R\text{-}C(\overset{\cdot}{O}_2)NH_2\text{-}COOH \qquad (5\text{-}57)$$

$$R\text{-}C(\overset{\cdot}{O}_2)NH_2\text{-}COOH \longrightarrow R\text{-}C\text{=}NH\text{-}COOH + \cdot HO_2 \qquad (5\text{-}58)$$

$$R\text{-}C\text{=}NH\text{-}COOH + H_2O \longrightarrow R\text{-}CO\text{-}COOH + NH_3 \qquad (5\text{-}59)$$

Radiation-induced modifications in aliphatic side chains are generally initiated by abstraction of hydrogen from a C-H bond. This produces a free radical which can, in the absence of oxygen, combine with similar free radicals to yield dimers, or with CO_2 to form monoaminodicarboxylic acids. In the presence of oxygen, oxidative reactions occur that yield side chain carbonyl, hydroxyl, and carboxyl groups through hydroperoxy intermediates.

The proportion of reactions in the side chain, compared to those at the α-carbon atom, increases with increasing size of the side chain. This proportion is increased further with amino acids having "reactive side chains" (i.e., aromatic and S-containing amino acids).

1. ALIPHATIC AMINO ACIDS

The radiation lability of aliphatic amino acids generally increases with the size of the side chain [127]. Of the amino acids in this category, those containing sulfur are most sensitive to ionizing radiation. The presence of a sulfhydryl or disulfide group in cysteine, cystine, and methionine is responsible for the radiation labilities of these amino acids.

a. Cysteine. Irradiation of cysteine in aqueous solution can result in oxidation to cystine, degradation of the sulfhydryl group with formation of H_2S and alanine, or deamination. The most common chemical reactions of cysteine, especially when oxygen is present, are oxidation to cystine and eventually to SO_4^{2-} [82]. Reactions related to cystine formation are

$$RSH + \cdot OH \longrightarrow RS\cdot + H_2O \tag{5-60}$$

$$RSH + H\cdot \longrightarrow RS\cdot + H_2 \tag{5-61}$$

$$RSH + \cdot OOH \longrightarrow RS\cdot + H_2O_2 \tag{5-62}$$

$$2\ RSH + H_2O_2 \longrightarrow 2\ RS\cdot + 2H_2O \tag{5-63}$$

$$RS\cdot + RS\cdot \longrightarrow RSSR \tag{5-64}$$

Direct decomposition of cysteine during irradiation yields H_2S and alanine:

$$RSH + H\cdot \longrightarrow R\cdot + H_2S \tag{5-65}$$

$$R\cdot + H\cdot \longrightarrow RH \tag{5-66}$$

$$R\cdot + RSH \longrightarrow RH + RS\cdot \tag{5-67}$$

$$RSH + H\cdot \longrightarrow RH + \cdot SH \tag{5-68}$$

$$\cdot SH + H\cdot \longrightarrow H_2S \tag{5-69}$$

During irradiation of cysteine solutions, formation of sulfur may occur as a result of secondary reactions

$$H_2S \longrightarrow H\cdot + HS\cdot \tag{5-70}$$

$$H\cdot + H_2S \longrightarrow H_2 + HS\cdot \tag{5-71}$$

$$HS\cdot + HS\cdot \longrightarrow H_2S + S \tag{5-72}$$

In oxygen-free solutions, irradiation of cysteine is influenced by hydrogen atoms. In acid solutions, cystine is formed

$$H\cdot + RSH \longrightarrow RS\cdot + H_2 \tag{5-73}$$
$$\downarrow$$
$$RSSR$$

whereas in alkaline solutions H_2S is the principal product

$$H\cdot + RS^- \longrightarrow R\cdot + SH^- \qquad\qquad (5\text{-}74)$$
$$\downarrow$$
$$H_2S$$

b. Cystine. During irradiation of cystine solutions, oxidative degradation yields cystine disulfoxide, cysteic acid, cysteine sulfinic acid, and cysteine according to the following reactions:

$$RSSR + \cdot OH \longrightarrow RSOH + RS\cdot \qquad\qquad (5\text{-}75)$$

$$RSOH + RSOH \longrightarrow RSO_2H + RSH \qquad\qquad (5\text{-}76)$$

$$RSO_2\cdot + RS\cdot \longrightarrow RSO_2SR \qquad\qquad (5\text{-}77)$$

$$RSSR + e_{aq}^- + H^+ \longrightarrow RSH + RS\cdot \qquad\qquad (5\text{-}78)$$

$$RSH + RSO_2SR \longrightarrow RSO_2H + RSSR \qquad\qquad (5\text{-}79)$$

$$e_{aq}^- + O_2 \longrightarrow O_2^- \qquad\qquad (5\text{-}80)$$

$$RSOH + O_2^- \longrightarrow RSO_3^- + H\cdot \qquad\qquad (5\text{-}81)$$

$$RSH + RSOH \longrightarrow RSSR + H_2O \qquad\qquad (5\text{-}82)$$

Cysteine produced in the above series can react as shown previously (Eqs. 5-65 through 5-72) to form alanine, hydrogen sulfidem and sulfur. In the presence of oxygen, cystine disulfoxide (5-77), cysteine sulfinic acid (5-79), or sulfenic acid (5-75) can be further oxidized to cysteic acid.

c. Methionine. The characteristic radiation reactions of methionine occur at or near the sulfur atom, with three types of reactions being prevalent: (a) demethylation results in homocysteine, which in turn can be oxidized to homocystic acid; (b) liberation of methylmercaptan results in the formation of aminobutyric acid; and (c) oxidation of sulfur results in methionine sulfoxide and additional decomposition products [82]. These reactions are outlined below:

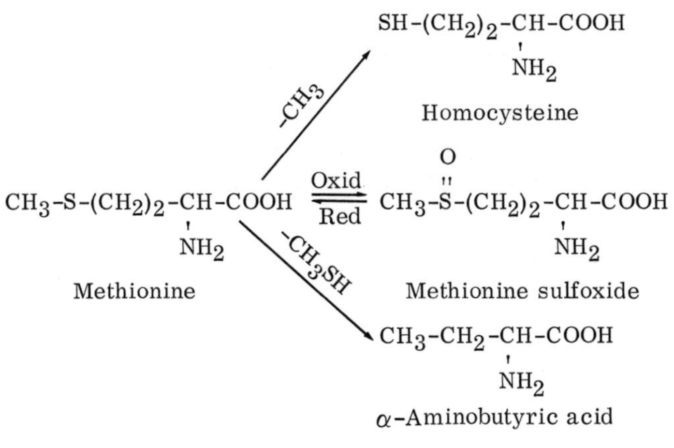

$$SH\text{-}(CH_2)_2\text{-}CH\text{-}COOH \qquad\qquad (5\text{-}83)$$
$$NH_2$$
$$\text{Homocysteine}$$

$$CH_3\text{-}S\text{-}(CH_2)_2\text{-}CH\text{-}COOH \underset{Red}{\overset{Oxid}{\rightleftharpoons}} CH_3\overset{O}{\overset{\|}{-}}S\text{-}(CH_2)_2\text{-}CH\text{-}COOH \qquad (5\text{-}84)$$
$$NH_2 \qquad\qquad\qquad\qquad NH_2$$
$$\text{Methionine} \qquad\qquad \text{Methionine sulfoxide}$$

$$CH_3\text{-}CH_2\text{-}CH\text{-}COOH \qquad\qquad (5\text{-}85)$$
$$NH_2$$
$$\alpha\text{-Aminobutyric acid}$$

2. AROMATIC AND HETEROCYCLIC AMINO ACIDS

Irradiation of these amino acids results in more complex changes than those observed with aliphatic amino acids.

a. Phenylalanine and Tyrosine. Hydroxylation appears to be the main radiolytic
reaction that occurs in solutions of aromatic amino acids [82]. Hydroxylation can
occur in several positions on the aromatic ring. Irradiated phenylalanine solutions
contain o-tyrosine, m-tyrosine, and p-tyrosine and these can be further oxidized
to 2,3-, 2,5- and 3,4-dihydroxyphenylalanine (dopa). The principal hydroxylation
product formed in irradiated tyrosine solutions is 3,4-dopa, which undergoes subsequent oxidation and polymerization to form colored melanine-type pigments.

$$\text{Phenylalanine} \longrightarrow \text{Tyrosine} \longrightarrow \tag{5-86}$$

$$\text{3,4-Dihydroxyphenylalanine} \xrightarrow{\text{Oxid}} \text{melanine-type pigments} \tag{5-87}$$

b. Tryptophan. Reactions analogous to those discussed for phenylalanine and tyrosine are observed with tryptophan. Formylkynurenine is the major degradation
product of irradiated tryptophan in the presence of oxygen [82]. It is assumed to
form from a tryptophan radical, with an organic hydroperoxide radical serving as
an intermediate.

$$\text{Tryptophan} \longrightarrow \text{N-Formylkynurenine} \tag{5-88}$$

c. Histidine. Deamination and decarboxylation are the major types of reactions
occurring during irradiation of histidine solutions, with deamination predominating.

$$
\text{Histidine} \xrightarrow[\text{-CO}_2]{} \text{Histamine (5-89)}
$$

$$
\text{Histidine} \xrightarrow[\text{-NH}_2]{} \text{Imidazolelactic acid (5-90)}
$$

Imidazole ring with $(CH_2)_2\text{-}NH_2$ — Histamine (5-89)

Imidazole ring with $CH_2\text{-}CHOH\text{-}COOH$ — Imidazolelactic acid (5-90)

Histidine: imidazole ring with $CH_2\text{-}CH\text{-}COOH$ and NH_2

Of the aromatic and heterocyclic amino acids, histidine undergoes the greatest decomposition when subjected to ionizing radiation [82].

3. PEPTIDES AND PROTEINS

With aqueous peptide or protein systems, free-radical attack at the peptide bond can result in the formation of a carbonyl and an amide or ammonia [64]. For oxygenated solutions, the proposed overall primary reaction is:

$$
\underset{R}{R\text{-}\overset{O}{\overset{\|}{C}}\text{-}NH\text{-}CH\text{-}R} + H_2O + O_2 \longrightarrow R\overset{O}{\overset{\|}{C}}\text{-}NH_2 + R\overset{O}{\overset{\|}{C}}R + H_2O_2 \qquad (5\text{-}91)
$$

while in oxygen-free solutions a free-radical disproportionation reaction is followed by hydration.

$$
2\,(R\overset{O}{\overset{\|}{C}}\text{-}NH\text{-}\underset{R}{\overset{\cdot}{C}}\text{-}R) \longrightarrow R\overset{O}{\overset{\|}{C}}\text{-}NH\text{-}\underset{R}{\overset{H}{\overset{|}{C}}}\text{-}R + R\overset{O}{\overset{\|}{C}}\text{-}N{=}\underset{R}{C}\text{-}R \xrightarrow{+H_2O} R\overset{O}{\overset{\|}{C}}\text{-}NH_2 + R\overset{O}{\overset{\|}{C}}\text{-}R \qquad (5\text{-}92)
$$

Peptides and proteins containing sulfhydryl or mercaptal side chains are subject to free-radical disproportionation reactions [64]. These reactions result in mercaptans, hydrogen sulfide and disulfides.

$$
\underset{NH_2}{CH_3\text{-}S\text{-}(CH_2)_2\text{-}CH\text{-}COOH} + H\cdot \longrightarrow CH_3S\cdot + \underset{NH_2}{CH_3CH_2\text{-}CH\text{-}COOH} \qquad (5\text{-}93)
$$

The secondary, tertiary, and quaternary structures of various proteins are maintained by disulfide, electrostatic, hydrogen bond, and hydrophobic interactions. Since the energy needed to break noncovalent bonds is considerably less than that required to split covalent bonds, changes in the secondary, tertiary, and quaternary structures may be the earliest critical effects of ionizing radiation on the biological properties of proteins [127]. Breakage of the polypeptide backbone and some alteration of amino acid side chains also can occur if the dose is large enough. Aromatic, heterocyclic, and sulfur-containing amino acids are most sensitive to irradiation.

The extent of radiation damage to proteins is dependent on the properties of the particular protein and the conditions of irradiation. The presence of substances which react with water radicals (scavengers) reduces protein damage by competition, while the presence of oxygen increases protein damage. The pH of the system has some effect on the production of water radicals, but it may have greater effect on the interaction of radicals with buffers or other compounds. As the temperature is increased, irradiation damage to proteins increases. Furthermore, irradiated proteins are more susceptible to denaturation by heat than native proteins. The irradiation dose also affects the extent of radiation damage.

The effects of 2-50 Mrad doses of high-energy electron or γ radiation on the amino acids of ground beef were studied by Johnson and Moser [74]. Regardless of the source of radiation, cystine was the amino acid most sensitive to irradiation, followed by tryptophan and histidine. About 50% of cystine and 10% of tryptophan were destroyed under the most damaging conditions used (24 mev, 200 μamps electron beam, 50 Mrad total dose). The authors concluded that, in general, little damage to amino acids and to the nutritive value of beef was produced by irradiation.

The application of rather high levels (4.8 Mrad) of ionizing radiation are required for complete sterilization of meats. In most instances, this treatment leads to adverse changes in color, flavor, and texture and to only partial inactivation of enzymes [24,64]. The biological value of meat exposed to sterilizing doses of ionizing radiation is reduced about 8-10% compared to the original material. This is comparable to that normally encountered in thermal processing. A major problem still under study is whether any of the radiation-induced reactions lead to the formation of toxic compounds.

VII. PUTREFACTION OF PROTEINACEOUS FOODS

Microorganisms are capable of causing deterioration of protein foods, such as meat, eggs, milk and fish. Whenever inadequate processing and/or unsatisfactory conditions allow for the presence and growth of spoilage microorganisms in proteinaceous foods, undesirable changes occur in flavor and texture. Changes in flavor are attributable to the production of protein metabolic products, such as skatole, indole, and cadaverine, and to the spoilage organisms themselves. Hydrolysis of proteins by microbial proteases can cause texture changes in proteinaceous foods [44].

Growth of spoilage organisms occurs when suitable conditions exist with respect to (1) available nutrients, (2) temperature, (3) pH, (4) water activity, (5) osmotic pressure, and (6) oxidation-reduction potential. In proteinaceous foods, adequate nutrition in the form of amino acids, carbohydrates, lactic acid, and vitamins is generally available. These nutrients are rapidly utilized by the microorganisms, and the metabolites of these amino acids and peptides are responsible for the production of offensive odors and flavors (putrefaction). Eventually, the spoilage microorganisms cease growing because of the accumulation of toxic metabolites.

Listed in Table 5-13 are the metabolites responsible for putrefaction in protein foods, their precursors, and the reactions involved in their formation. Decarboxylation of amino acids is catalyzed by a series of amino acid decarboxylases found in many microorganisms. Deamination is accomplished by amino acid dehydrogenases. NAD serves as the hydrogen acceptor for deamination of alanine and glutamate, while FAD functions similarly for deamination of isoleucine and tryptophan. Aspartate is deaminated by the enzyme aspartase. Serine dehydratase and threonine dehydratase are specific enzymes for deamination of serine and threonine. Pyridoxal phosphate serves as a hydrogen acceptor in these reactions. Hydrogen sulfide results from the action of cysteine desulfhydrase on cysteine. Pyridoxal also is the hydrogen acceptor in this reaction.

TABLE 5-13

Metabolites of Amino Acids

Precursor	Name	Structure
Formed by decarboxylation		
Lysine	Cadaverine	$^+NH_3(CH_2)_4CH_2-\overset{+}{N}H_3$
Ornithine	Putrescine	$^+NH_3(CH_2)_3CH_2-\overset{+}{N}H_3$
Glutamate	Aminobutyric	$^+NH_3(CH_2)_2CH_2COO^-$
Valine	Isobutylamine	$(CH_3)_2CHCH_2NH_3{}^+$
Tyrosine	Tyramine	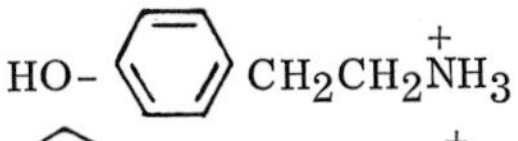 HO-⟨ ⟩ $CH_2CH_2\overset{+}{N}H_3$
Tryptophan	Tryptamine	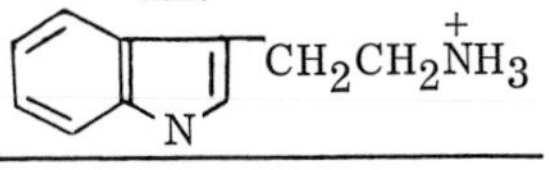 $CH_2CH_2\overset{+}{N}H_3$ (indole ring)
Formed by deamination		
Alanine	Pyruvate	$CH_3CO-COO^-$
Isoleucine	β-Methyl α-ketovalerate	$CH_3CH_2CH-CO-COO^-$ $\quad\quad\quad\quad CH_3$
Tryptophan	Indole	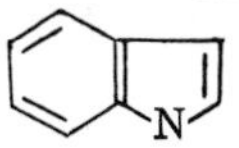 (indole ring)
Glutamate	α-Ketoglutarate	$^-OOC(CH_2)_2CO-COO^-$
Aspartate	Fumarate	$^-OOC-CH=CH-COO^-$
Serine	Pyruvate	$CH_3CO-COO^-$
Threonine	α-Ketobutyrate	$CH_3CH_2CO-COO^-$
Cysteine	Pyruvate Hydrogen sulfide	$CH_3CO-COO^-$ H_2S

TABLE 5-13 (Continued)

Precursor	Name	Structure
Formed by Strickland reaction		
Alanine	Acetate	CH_3COO^-
Valine	Isobutyrate	$(CH_3)_2CH\text{-}COO^-$
Leucine	Isovalerate	$(CH_3)_2CH\text{-}CH_2COO^-$
Isoleucine	α-Methyl butyrate	$CH_3CH_2CH\text{-}COO^-$ $\overset{\mid}{CH_3}$
Proline	γ-Amino valerate	$^+NH_3(CH_2)_4COO^-$
Hydroxyproline	γ-Amino-α-hydroxyvaleric	$^+NH_3(CH_2)_2CH\text{-}CH_2COO^-$ $\overset{\mid}{OH}$

The Strickland reaction involves oxidative deamination of alanine and reductive deamination of another amino acid. The general reaction is:

$$\overset{+NH_3}{\underset{\mid}{CH_3CHCOO^-}} + 2\ \overset{+NH_3}{\underset{\mid}{R\text{-}CHCOO^-}} + 2\ H_2O \longrightarrow \longrightarrow$$

Alanine Amino acid

$$CH_3COO^- + 2\ R\text{-}CH_2COO^- + 3\ NH_4^+ + CO_2 \qquad (5\text{-}94)$$

Acetate Fatty acid

Ferredoxin, NAD, and FAD are involved as coenzymes in the multistep reaction. Glycine, proline, and hydroxyproline are reductively deaminated, while the hydrogen donors are alanine, valine, leucine, and isoleucine.

In fish and fish products, the putrefactive amines trimethylamine and dimethyl-amine are produced by spoilage microorganisms. The amounts of these amines and volatile acids are used as a measure of spoilage of fish and meat products.

REFERENCES

1. A. M. Altschul, in Symposium on Foods: Proteins and Their Reactions (H. W. Schultz and A. F. Anglemier, eds.), AVI Publ., Westport, Conn., 1964, p. 295.
2. A. M. Altschul, Proteins: Their Chemistry and Politics. Basic Books, New York, 1965.
3. A. M. Altschul, L. Y. Yatsu, R. L. Ory, and E. M. Engleman, Ann. Rev. Plant Physiol., 17, 113 (1966).

4. C. B. Anfinsen, The Molecular Basis of Evolution, Wiley, New York, 1959.

5. C. M. Baker, in Egg Quality (T. C. Carter, ed.), Oliver and Boyd, Edin-
    burgh, Scotland, 1968, p. 67.

6. R. E. Baldwin, in Egg Science and Technology (W. J. Stadelman and O. J.
    Cotterill, eds.), AVI Publ., Westport, Conn., 1973, p. 241.

7. G. A. Bean, J. A. Schillinger, and W. L. Klarman. Appl. Microbiol., 24,
    437 (1972).

8. A. E. Bender, J. Food Technol., 1, 261 (1966).

9. A. E. Bender, J. Food Technol., 7, 239 (1972).

10. D. H. Bergquist, in Egg Science and Technology (W. J. Stadelman and O. J.
    Cotterill, eds.), AVI Publ., Westport, Conn., 1973, p. 190.

11. S. A. Bernhard, The Structure and Function of Enzymes, W. A. Benjamin,
    New York, 1968.

12. M. Bier, ed., Electrophoresis. 2nd ed., Academic Press, New York, 1968.

13. J. A. Bietz and J. S. Wall, Cereal Chem., 49, 416 (1972).

14. J. Bjarnason and K. J. Carpenter, Brit. J. Nutr., 24, 313 (1970).

15. C. E. Bodwell and P. E. McClain, in The Science of Meat and Meat Products
    (J. F. Price and B. S. Schweigert, eds.), Freeman, San Francisco, 1971,
    p. 78.

16. A. Bondi, in Processed Plant Protein Foodstuffs (A. M. Altschul, ed.),
    Academic Press, New York, 1958, p. 43.

17. G. Borgstrom, in Fish as Food (G. Borgstrom, ed.), Vol. 2, Academic
    Press, New York, 1962, p. 115.

18. J. F. Brandts, in Thermobiology (A. H. Rose, ed.), Academic Press, New
    York, 1967, p. 25.

19. R. Bressani and L. G. Elias, Advan. Food Res., 16, 1 (1968).

20. W. D. Brown, in Present Knowledge in Nutrition. 3rd ed., The Nutrition
    Foundation, New York, 1967, p. 6.

21. L. Bulter, J. Amer. Oil Chem. Soc., 48, 101 (1971).

22. B. T. Burton, ed., The Heinz Handbook of Nutrition. 2nd ed., McGraw-Hill,
    New York, 1965.

23. W. Bushuk, in Symposium: Seed Proteins (G. E. Inglett, ed.), AVI Publ.,
    Westport, Conn., 1972, p. 193.

24. R. F. Cain and A. F. Anglemier, in Enzymological Aspects of Food Irradia-
    tion (A. Ericson, ed.), International Atomic Energy Agency, Vienna, 1969, p. 91.

25. R. E. Canfield and C. B. Anfinsen, in The Proteins (H. Neurath, ed.),
    Vol. 1, Academic Press, New York, 1963, p. 311.

26. R. Cecil, in The Proteins (H. Neurath, ed.), Vol. 1, Academic Press, New
    York, 1963, p. 379.

27. R. Cecil and J. R. McPhee, Advan. Protein Chem., 14, 272 (1959).

28. N. Chamberlain, in Proteins as Human Food (R. A. Lawrie, ed.), AVI
    Publ., Westport, Conn., 1970, p. 300.

29. F. Chapeville and P. Fromageot, Biochim. Biophys. Acta, 49, 328 (1961).

30. S. J. Circle and A. K. Smith, in Symposium: Seed Proteins (G. E. Inglett,
    ed.), AVI Publ., Westport, Conn., 1972, p. 242.

31. J. R. Colvin, in Symposium on Foods: Proteins and Their Reactions (H. W.
    Schultz and A. F. Anglemier, eds.), AVI Publ., Westport, Conn., 1964,
    p. 69.

32. J. J. Connell, in Fundamental Aspects of the Dehydration of Foodstuffs.
     Macmillan, New York, 1958, p. 167.
33. J. J. Connell, in Symposium on Foods: Proteins and Their Reactions (H. W.
     Schultz and A. F. Anglemier, eds.), AVI Publ., Westport, Conn., 1964,
     p. 255.
34. J. J. Connell, in Proteins as Human Food (R. A. Lawrie, ed.), AVI Publ.,
     Westport, Conn., 1970, p. 200.
35. W. H. Cook, in Egg Quality (T. C. Carter, ed.), Oliver and Boyd, Edinburgh,
     Scotland, 1968, p. 109.
36. O. J. Cotterill, in Egg Science and Technology (W. J. Stadelman and O. J.
     Cotterill, eds.), AVI Publ., Westport, Conn., 1973, p. 143.
37. J. Daussant, N. J. Neucere, and L. Y. Yatsu, Plant Physiol., 44, 471 (1969).
38. A. P. DeGroot and P. Slump, J. Nutr., 98, 45 (1969).
39. R. E. Dickerson, in The Proteins (H. Neurath, ed.), Vol. 2, Academic
     Press, New York, 1964, p. 603.
40. R. E. Dickerson and I. Geis, The Structure and Action of Proteins. Harper
     and Row, New York, 1969.
41. J. W. Dieckert and M. C. Dieckert, in Symposium: Seed Proteins (G. E.
     Inglett, ed.), AVI Publ., Westport, Conn., 1972, p. 52.
42. F. J. Doan and P. G. Keeney, in Fundamentals of Dairy Chemistry (B. H.
     Webb and A. H. Johnson, eds.), AVI Publ., Westport, Conn., 1965, p. 711.
43. G. O. Donoso, A. M. Lewis, D. S. Miller, and P. R. Payne, J. Sci. Food
     Agri., 13, 192 (1962).
44. N. A. M. Eskin, H. M. Henderson, and R. J. Townsend, Biochemistry of
     Foods. Academic Press, New York, 1971.
45. R. E. Feeney, in Symposium on Foods: Proteins and Their Reactions (H. W.
     Schultz and A. F. Anglemier, eds.), AVI Publ., Westport, Conn., 1964,
     p. 209.
46. R. Finch, CRC Crit. Rev. Food Technol., 1, 519 (1970).
47. P. A. Finot, R. Viani, J. Bricout, and J. Mauron, Experientia, 24, 1097
     (1968).
48. P. A. Finot, R. Viani, J. Bricout, and J. Mauron, Experientia, 25, 134
     (1969).
49. J. E. Ford and C. Shorrock, Brit. J. Nutr., 26, 311 (1971).
50. S. W. Fox and J. F. Foster, Protein Chemistry. Wiley, New York, 1957.
51. E. Geiger and G. Borgstrom, in Fish as Food (G. Borgstrom, ed.), Vol. 2,
     Academic Press, New York, 1962, p. 29.
52. A. C. Germs, J. Sci. Food Agri., 24, 7 (1973).
53. J. F. Gordon, in Proteins as Human Food (R. A. Lawrie, ed.), AVI Publ.,
     Westport, Conn., 1970, p. 328.
54. W. G. Gordon, in Milk Proteins (H. A. McKenzie, ed.), Vol. 2, Academic
     Press, New York, 1971, p. 331.
55. J. A. Gordon and J. R. Warren, J. Biol. Chem., 243, 5663 (1968).
56. W. G. Gordon and E. O. Whittier, in Fundamentals of Dairy Chemistry
     (B. H. Webb and A. H. Johnson, eds.), AVI Publ., Westport, Conn., 1965,
     p. 54.
57. A. Gottschalk and E. R. B. Graham, in The Proteins (H. Neurath, ed.),
     Vol. 4, Academic Press, New York, 1966, p. 96.
58. W. D. Gray, CRC Crit. Rev. Food Technol., 1, 225 (1970).

59. D. W. Gruenwedel and H. C. Hoa, J. Agri. Food Chem., 21, 246 (1973).
60. D. W. Gruenwedel and R. K. Patnaik, J. Agri. Food Chem., 19, 775 (1971).
61. C. W. Hall and T. I. Hedrick, Drying of Milk and Milk Products. 2nd ed., AVI Publ., Westport, Conn., 1971.
62. R. Hamm, in Recent Advances in Food Science (J. M. Leitch and D. N. Rhodes, eds.), Butterworths, London, 1963, p. 218.
63. R. Hamm, in Proteins as Human Food (R. A. Lawrie, ed.), AVI Publ., Westport, Conn., 1970, p. 167.
64. J. W. Harlan, F. L. Kauffman, and F. Heiligman, in Radiation Preservation of Foods (F. S. Josephson and J. H. Frankfert, eds.), American Chemical Society, Washington, D. C., 1967, pp. 35-57.
65. F. Haurowitz, The Chemistry and Function of Proteins. 2nd ed., Academic Press, New York, 1963.
66. R. L. Hill, Advan. Protein Chem., 20, 37 (1965).
67. R. Hirschmann, R. F. Nutt, D. F. Veber, R. A. Vitali, S. L. Varga, T. A. Jacob, F. W. Holly, and R. G. Denkewalter, J. Amer. Chem. Soc., 91, 507 (1969).
68. C. Holden, Science, 173, 410 (1971).
69. S. D. Holdsworth, J. Food Technol., 6, 331 (1971).
70. M. J. Horn, D. B. Jones, and S. J. Ringel, J. Biol. Chem., 138, 141 (1941).
71. R. C. Hoseney, K. F. Finney, and Y. Pomeranz, Cereal Chem., 47, 135 (1970).
72. G. E. Inglett, in Corn: Culture, Processing, Products (G. E. Inglett, ed.), AVI Publ., Westport, Conn., 1970, p. 123.
73. R. Jenness, in Milk Proteins (H. A. McKenzie, ed.), Vol. 1, Academic Press, New York, 1970, p. 17.
74. B. C. Johnson and K. Moser, in Radiation Preservation of Foods (E. S. Josephson and J. H. Frantfort, eds.), American Chemical Society, Washington, D. C., 1967, pp. 171-179.
75. M. Joly, A Physico-chemical Approach to the Denaturation of Proteins. Academic Press, New York, 1965.
76. R. T. Jones, in Symposium on Foods: Proteins and Their Reactions (H. W. Schultz and A. F. Anglemier, eds.), AVI Publ., Westport, Conn., 1964, p. 33.
77. B. O. Juliano, in Symposium: Seed Proteins (G. E. Inglett, ed.), AVI Publ., Westport, Conn., 1972, p. 114.
78. N. L. Kent, in Proteins as Human Food (R. A. Lawrie, ed.), AVI Publ., Westport, Conn., 1970, p. 280.
79. J. E. Kinsella, Advan. Food Res., 19, 147 (1971).
80. C. H. Lea, in Fundamental Aspects of the Dehydration of Foodstuffs, Macmillan, New York, 1958, p. 178.
81. A. L. Lehninger, Biochemistry, Worth Publishers, New York, 1970.
82. J. Liebster and J. Kopoldova, Advan. Radiat. Biol., 1, 157 (1964).
83. I. E. Liener, in Nutritional Evaluation of Food Processing (R. S. Harris and H. Von Loesecke, eds.), AVI Publ., Westport, Conn., 1960, p. 231.
84. G. H. Luna-Jaspe, J. O. Mora Parra, C. Rozo Bernal, and S. Perez de Serrano, Dairy Sci. Abstr., 34, 549 (1972).
85. C. K. Lyon, J. Amer. Oil Chem. Soc., 49, 245 (1972).

86. R. E. Martin and D. V. LeClair, Food Eng., 39(4), 66 (1967).
87. W. H. Martinez, L. C. Berardi, and L. A. Goldblatt, J. Agri. Food Chem., 18, 961 (1970).
88. D. K. Mecham, Cereal Chem., 36, 134 (1959).
89. E. Menden and H. Cremer, in Newer Methods of Nutritional Biochemistry (A. A. Albanese, ed.), Vol. 4, Academic Press, New York, 1970, p. 123.
90. E. T. Mertz, L. S. Bates, and O. E. Nelson, Science, 145, 279 (1964).
91. E. W. Meyer, J. Amer. Oil Chem. Soc., 48, 484 (1971).
92. A. F. Morgan, J. Biol. Chem., 90, 771 (1931).
93. National Academy of Sciences-National Research Council, Evaluation of Protein Quality, Publ. No. 1100, Washington, D. C., 1963.
94. National Academy of Sciences-National Research Council, Recommended Dietary Allowances, 8th ed., Publ. No. 0-309-02216-9, Washington, D.C., 1974.
95. National Dairy Council, Dairy Council Dig., 43(6), 31 (1972).
96. T. L. Parkinson, J. Sci. Food Agri., 17, 101 (1966).
97. D. A. Parry, in Proteins as Human Food (R. A. Lawrie, ed.), AVI Publ., Westport, Conn., 1970, p. 365.
98. A. Patchornik and M. Sokolovsky, J. Amer. Chem. Soc., 86, 1860 (1964).
99. M. F. Perutz, Eu. J. Biochem., 8, 455 (1969).
100. E. A. Peterson and H. A. Sober, in Methods in Enzymology (S. P. Colowick and N. O. Kaplan, eds.), Vol. 5, Academic Press, New York, 1962, p. 3.
101. H. J. Petropakis and A. F. Anglemier, unpublished data, 1972.
102. G. M. Piggott and A. M. Dollar, Food Technol., 17, 481 (1963).
103. N. W. Pirie, in Proteins as Human Food (R. A. Lawrie, ed.), AVI Publ., Westport, Conn., 1970, p. 46.
104. Y. Pomeranz, Advan. Food Res., 16, 335 (1968).
105. Y. Pomeranz and J. A. Shellenberger, Bread Science and Technology. AVI Publ., Westport, Conn., 1971.
106. W. D. Powrie, in Egg Science and Technology (W. J. Stadelman and O. J. Cotterill, eds.), AVI Publ., Westport, Conn., 1973, p. 61.
107. Protein Advisory Group of the United Nations System, PAG Bulletin, 2(1), 2 (1972).
108. J. H. Rampton, A. F. Anglemier, and M. W. Montgomery, J. Food Sci., 30, 636 (1965).
109. G. Reed, Enzymes in Food Processing. Academic Press, New York, 1966, p. 123.
110. E. Rolfe, in Proteins as Human Food (R. A. Lawrie, ed.), AVI Publ., Westport, Conn., 1970, p. 107.
111. D. Rose, J. Dairy Sci., 48, 139 (1965).
112. D. Rose, J. R. Brunner, E. B. Kalan, B. L. Larson, P. Melnychyn, H. E. Swaisgood, and D. F. Waugh, J. Dairy Sci., 53, 1 (1970).
113. G. D. Rosen, in Processed Plant Protein Foodstuffs (A. M. Altschul, ed.), Academic Press, New York, 1958, p. 419.
114. W. T. Roubal, J. Amer. Oil Chem. Soc., 47, 141 (1970).
115. R. L. Saffle, Advan. Food Res., 16, 105 (1968).
116. W. Schuphan, in Proteins as Human Food (R. A. Lawrie, ed.), AVI Publ., Westport, Conn., 1970, p. 245.

117. H. A. Schwarz, Advan. Radiat. Biol., 1, 1 (1964).

118. N. Scrimshaw, in Single-Cell Protein (R. I. Mateles and S. R. Tannenbaum, eds.), MIT Press, Cambridge, Mass., 1968, p. 3.

119. S. Seifter and P. M. Gallop, in The Proteins (H. Neurath, ed.), Vol. 4, Academic Press, New York, 1966, p. 153.

120. C. A. Shacklady, in Proteins as Human Food (R. A. Lawrie, ed.), AVI Publ., Westport, Conn., 1970, p. 317.

121. J. A. Shellenberger, in Wheat Chemistry and Technology (I. Hlynka, ed.), American Association of Cereal Chemists, St. Paul, Minn., 1964, p. 1.

122. F. S. Shenstone, in Egg Quality (T. C. Carter, ed.), Oliver and Boyd, Edinburgh, Scotland, 1968, p. 26.

123. A. K. Smith, J. Amer. Oil Chem. Soc., 48, 38 (1971).

124. K. J. Smith, J. Amer. Oil Chem. Soc., 48, 625 (1971).

125. H. E. Snyder, Advan. Food Res., 18, 85 (1970).

126. H. A. Sokol and D. K. Mecham, Baker's Dig., 34(6), 24 (1960).

127. E. M. Southern and D. N. Rhodes, in Radiation Preservation of Foods (E. S. Josephson and J. H. Frankfort, eds.), American Chemical Society, Washington, D. C., 1967, pp. 58-77.

128. B. R. Stillings, O. Hammerle, and D. G. Snyder, J. Nutr., 97, 70 (1969).

129. M. M. Swirski, R. Allouf, and H. Cheftel, Bull. Soc. Chim. Biol., 43, 909 (1961).

130. M. P. Tombs, Plant Physiol., 42, 797 (1967).

131. M. P. Tombs and M. Lowe, Biochem. J., 105, 181 (1967).

132. L. Tumerman and B. H. Webb, in Fundamentals of Dairy Chemistry (B. H. Webb and A. H. Johnson, eds.), AVI Publ., Westport, Conn., 1965, p. 506.

133. United States Department of Agriculture, Egg Pasteurization Manual, ARS 74-48, (1969).

134. B. L. Vallee and W. E. C. Wacker, in The Proteins (H. Neurath, ed.), Vol. 5, Academic Press, New York, 1970, p. 25.

135. F. A. Vandenheuvel, J. Amer. Oil Chem. Soc., 43, 258 (1966).

136. H. L. E. Vix, H. K. Gardner, Jr., M. G. Lambou, and M. L. Rollins, in Symposium: Seed Proteins (G. E. Inglett, ed.), AVI Publ., Westport, Conn., 1972, p. 212.

137. J. S. Wall, in Symposium on Foods: Proteins and Their Reactions (H. W. Schultz and A. F. Anglemier, eds.), AVI Publ., Westport, Conn., 1964, p. 315.

138. J. S. Wall, J. Agri. Food Chem., 19, 619 (1971).

139. J. S. Wall and A. C. Beckwith, Cereal Sci. Today, 14, 16 (1969).

140. C. I. Waslien, D. H. Calloway, S. Margen, and F. Costa, J. Food Sci., 35, 294 (1970).

141. B. M. Weeks, S. A. Cole, and W. M. Garrison, J. Phys. Chem., 69, 4131 (1965).

142. H. H. Weetall, Food Prod. Devel., 7(3), 46, and 7(4), 94 (1973).

143. D. B. Wetlaufer, Advan. Protein Chem., 17, 303 (1962).

144. J. R. Whitaker, Principles of Enzymology for the Food Sciences. Marcel Dekker, New York, 1972.

145. M. D. Wilding, J. Amer. Oil Chem. Soc., 48, 489 (1971).

146. B. Witkop, Science, 162, 318 (1968).

147. W. J. Wolf, J. Agri. Food Chem., 18, 969 (1970).
148. W. J. Wolf and J. C. Cowan, CRC Crit. Rev. Food Technol., 2, 81 (1971).
149. K. Ziegler, I. Melchert, and C. Lurken, Nature (London), 214, 404 (1967).

Chapter 6

ENZYMES

T. Richardson

Department of Food Science
University of Wisconsin
Madison, Wisconsin

Contents

I. INTRODUCTION

Enzymes are complex globular protein catalysts that accelerate chemical reaction rates by factors of 10^{12}-10^{20} over that of uncatalyzed reactions at temperatures around 37°C [85]. By contrast, industrial catalysts (inorganic substances) are orders of magnitude less effective than enzymes under comparable conditions. For example, the reduction of hydrogen peroxide catalyzed by catalase occurs 10 million times faster than it does when catalyzed by colloidal platinum at 37°C [117].

The catalytic efficiency of enzymes is very high, whereby one molecule of enzyme can transform as many as 10,000-1,000,000 molecules of substrate per minute [117]. It is this catalytic efficiency of enzymes at low temperature which makes them important to the food scientist. This means that foods can be processed or modified by enzymes at moderate temperature, say 25-50°C, where food products would not otherwise undergo changes at a significant rate. It also means, however, that endogenous enzymes are active under these conditions as well, and this can be beneficial or deleterious.

Furthermore, enzymes because of their tremendous catalytic power and low activation energies are active at subfreezing temperatures and therefore can be important stimulants of degradative reactions in refrigerated or frozen foods [102].

Of course, one basis for heat processing is to denature and inactivate enzymes so that the food is not subjected to continuing enzymic activity. The food scientist must have an understanding of the denaturation phenomenon in order to properly process foods.

Another important aspect of enzymic activity in addition to catalytic power is the specificity of enzymic reactions. Industrial catalysts lack this specificity of reaction, and so cannot be used for modifying specific components of a food system. The specificity of hydrogen ion catalysts, for example, is very broad, whereas many enzymes perform only a single function, such as hydrolysis of a single bond or bond type. It is this enzymic specificity which allows the food scientist to selectively modify individual food components and not affect others.

The sensitivity and specificity of enzymes also make them important to the food scientist as analytical tools. Analysis for food constituents in many instances can be simplified using enzymic techniques which are detailed by Bergmeyer [8] and Guilbault [41].

Thus, enzymes are of great significance to the food scientist, and the many facets of food enzymology are explored in the following sections.

II. ENZYME NOMENCLATURE

Over the years, the number of enzymes isolated and characterized has continued to increase at an enormous rate. Previously it was the custom for the individual who isolated and characterized the enzyme to also name it. However, in many instances the same enzyme was given different names or two different enzymes were given the same name. Consequently, the nomenclature for enzymes became so chaotic that the International Union of Biochemistry instituted a Commission on Nomenclature and Classification of Enzymes to prepare a system of nomenclature that has become standard and should be used in enzyme work [52]. Each enzyme is assigned a code number of four numerals, each separated by periods and arranged according to the following principles. The first numeral is the main division to which the enzyme belongs, i.e. (1) oxidoreductases, (2) transferases, (3) hydrolases, (4) lyases, (5) isomerases, and (6) ligases; the second is the subclass which identifies the enzyme in more specific terms; the third precisely defines the type of enzymic activity; and the fourth numeral is the serial number of the enzyme in its sub-subclass. Thus the first three numerals clearly designate the nature of the enzyme. For example, 1.2.3.4 denotes an oxidoreductase with an aldehyde as a donor and O_2 as an acceptor, and it is the fourth numbered enzyme in a particular series. In addition to the code number, each enzyme is assigned a systematic name which in many instances is too cumbersome to be used in the literature on a routine basis. Consequently, a trivial name has been recommended for common usage. The trivial name is sufficiently short for general use but is not necessarily very exact or systematic; in a great many instances it is the name already in current use. The 1972 recommendations of the International Union of Biochemistry on Nomenclature and Classification of Enzymes [52] catalogued over 1700 enzymes of which the oxidoreductases, transferases, and hydrolases included over 400 enzymes each.

Aside from enzymes involved in postmortem and postharvest physiology, few of the catalogued enzymes are of direct interest to the food scientist. By far the largest group of enzymes used in food processing is the hydrolases. A few oxidoreductases and isomerases are used, but hardly any transferases, lyases, or ligases.

III. DEFINITIONS

The following terms are often encountered in the enzymology literature.

1. Holoenzyme: The protein portion of the enzyme and the coenzyme, if needed for catalytic activity.
2. Apoenzyme: The thermolabile protein component of the enzyme that determines specificity.
3. Coenzyme, cofactor, prosthetic group: These terms are often used interchangeably to describe cocatalysts which act in conjunction with the apoenzyme to catalyze a reaction. However, Bernhard [9] draws a distinction between cofactors and coenzymes. Prosthetic groups are usually those cocatalysts that are very tightly bound to the protein.
4. Isoenzymes or isozymes [53]: Multiple forms of an enzyme occurring in the same species. They catalyze the same reaction and arise from genetically determined differences in primary structure. The term "multiple forms of the enzyme" should be used as a broad term covering all proteins possessing the same enzymic activity and occurring naturally in a single species.

IV. COMPARTMENTALIZATION OF ENZYMES IN CELLULAR SYSTEMS

Over the years it has become evident that enzymes and enzyme systems are compartmentalized both at the subcellular level and the tissue level. This distribution of enzymes among subcellular particles and tissues of plants and animals is of profound significance to the food scientist.

In general, there are several ways in which the maintenance or destruction of the integrity of enzyme localization is important in food systems. The maturation and ripening of plant foods is an integrated and dynamic sequence of biochemical events [33,86]. Consequently, the integrity of the plant tissue must be maintained to insure proper ripening. Since most fruits and some vegetables are harvested when mature but still unripe, a wide variety of enzymically induced changes must still occur to obtain acceptable quality [33,86]. For example, the loss of some pigments and gains in others, the accumulation of sugars, softening, and biosynthesis of flavor components must occur in a manner which requires the biochemical integrity of the food [9,10].

In some instances the food scientist has learned to control these integrated biochemical changes to produce better and more abundant food. Controlled atmosphere storage of fruits and vegetables, for example, regulates the rate of metabolism of some fruits (notably apples and pears) and lengthens the time these products can be stored [33]. Another example of enzymic control by the food scientist is accelerated aging of meat (increased hydrolase activity) at higher than normal temperatures under ultraviolet light (Tenderay process) [59].

Disruption of the cellular and enzymic integrity of foods is often used by the food scientist in processing operations. Indeed, Schwimmer [91] put forth the thesis that "food processing and technology may be considered as the art and science of the promotion, control and/or the prevention of cellular disruption and its

metabolic consequences at the right time and at the right place in the food processing chain." Of course, cellular disruption is accompanied by the release of enzymes which can be beneficial or deleterious. For example, the interaction of
released enzymes with substrates not formerly available is important in developing
flavor in dehydrated onions [92]. In contrast, disruption of cells and the release
of polyphenoloxidase to combine with oxygen and phenols results in the well-known
enzymic browning reaction, which can be desirable in tea fermentation or undesirable in fruits and vegetables [33]. One objective of the food scientist is to control enzymic reactions of this kind.

Alterations that have occurred in the normal distribution of enzymes in cellular
systems often can be used by the food scientist to determine the history of a food
product. For example, freezing and thawing of tissues is known to disrupt biological membranes. A consequence of this is the release of enzymes from formerly intact organelles. Thus the dislocation of enzymes characteristic of cellular
organelles may mean that such tissues as seafood or meats have been frozen and
thawed [38,44]. This information is valuable to regulatory agencies to detect
fraud.

Furthermore, the products of enzymic reactions often can be used as indicators
of freshness of fish [98]. As autolysis proceeds with time and enzymes are released from their binding sites, the increase in products of autolysis often can be
used as objective measures of freshness.

These few examples give some indications of why knowledge of enzyme localization is important to food scientists. Consideration of the distribution of various
enzymic systems in tissues and subcellular particles is now appropriate.

A. Distribution of Enzymes at the Subcellular Level [15, 88]

Of the many enzymes in a typical cell, very few are in true solution [15]. Most of
them exist bound to membranes of the subcellular elements. Furthermore, those
enzymes in true solution (in the cytosol) are probably subjected to different conditions than encountered in a typical in vitro reaction mixture. A thesis of increasing
importance has been developed which implicates a reversible association of enzymes with membranes as a metabolic control mechanism in postharvest and postmortem physiology [51].

As we shall see, some enzymes are characteristic of a particular subcellular
organelle; however, others are ubiquitous in nature. Although these latter enzymes
may catalyze the same reaction at different subcellular or tissue locations, they
may differ with respect to primary, secondary, tertiary, or quaternary structure.
These isozymes thus may yield different kinetics or respond differently to allosteric
effectors. The significance of isozymes and isozyme distributions in food tissues
is being learned very slowly.

Now, let us look at the enzymic patterns in specific subcellular organelles.
Listed in Table 6-1 are the locations and activities of various enzyme systems associated with subcellular organelles of animal and plant cells. Individual subcellular particles are considered in slightly more detail below.

TABLE 6-1

Enzyme Activities in Various Organelles

Location	Activities in which enzymes are involved
Nucleus	Rich in nucleic acids which control the genetics of protein and enzymic syntheses in the cell. Some essential enzymic cofactors are synthesized in the nucleus
Mitochondria	Produces adenosine triphosphate, from oxidation of metabolites in tricarboxylic acid cycle, to drive anabolic processes. Acetyl coenzyme A is oxidized with formation of NADH. Formation of acetyl coenzyme A from fatty acids and pyruvate. Glutamic acid oxidized to α-ketoglutarate
Chloroplasts	Site of pigment production. Light and dark photosynthetic reactions occur here (production of NADPH and reduction of CO_2 to carbohydrate)
Ribosomes	Contain nucleic acids and enzymes that control protein synthesis
Endoplasmic reticulum (ER)	Ribosomes associated with rough endoplasmic reticulum govern protein synthesis. Smooth ER, ribosome free, is involved in the biosynthesis of lipids, such as cholesterol and long-chain fatty acids
Plasma membrane	Concerned with maintaining water balance of cells. Certain enzymes are involved in the uptake and elimination of ions
Cytosol	Carbohydrates are broken down to pyruvate via glycolysis. Fats are hydrolyzed to glycerol and fatty acids. Site of the pentose phosphate pathway, which produces NADPH for anabolic processes
Lysosomes	Contain an array of hydrolases with acidic pH optima that can hydrolyze most tissue constituents
Peroxisomes (microbodies)	Contain catalase, urate oxidase, D-amino acid oxidase, and L-α-hydroxy acid oxidase
Glyoxysomes	Plant microbodies containing enzymes of the glyoxylate cycle
Amyloplasts	Starch granules that synthesize starch from sugars
Protein bodies of seeds	Aleurone grains in seeds are analogous to lysosomal particles

1. ENDOPLASMIC RETICULUM-RIBOSOMES.

Over 100 enzymes in the endoplasmic reticulum are responsible for a wide variety
of biosynthetic reactions. In postharvest tissues, enzymes involved in the ripening process are synthesized by an intact endoplasmic reticulum. Also, cytochromes in close association with lipoproteins of this organelle can catalyze oxidation of lipids resulting in off flavors [101].

2. PLASMA MEMBRANE

Enzymes associated with the plasma membrane include: Mg^{2+}- (or Ca^{2+}-) dependent ATPase; $Na^+ + K^+ + Mg^{2+}$ ATPase; K^+-p-nitrophenyl phosphatase; K^+ acetyl-
phosphatase; 5'-mononucleotidase; NAD pyrophosphatase; alkaline glycerolphos-
phatase; and phosphodiesterase, cytidinetriphosphatase, inosine diphosphatase,
adenosine diphosphatase, and leucine aminopeptidase. The cell wall and membrane
delimit the contents of the cell, and such treatments as freezing and thawing or
osmotic shock, which disrupt membranes, cause release of cellular contents including enzymes.

3. GOLGI APPARATUS (DICTYOSOMES)

Enzymes existing in the Golgi apparatus include nucleoside diphosphatase, thiamine
pyrophosphatase, acid and alkaline phosphatases, esterase and β-glucuronidase.

4. MITOCHONDRIA

The mitochondrion is of central importance to the food scientist involved in postharvest and postmortem physiology. During the ripening of postharvest fruits,
continued oxidative phosphorylation is essential to supply energy for synthetic reactions [86]. Furthermore, the utilization of tissue oxygen by mitochondrial oxidation reactions is a factor which hinders aerobic glycolysis in postslaughter
meats. Since mitochondria are ubiquitous and occur in cells in substantial numbers, their cytochromes (heme pigments) may be an important factor in lipid
peroxidation of lipoprotein membranes [101]. Hydrolases released from damaged
mitochondria may also be important in the degradation of tissue components during
postharvest or postmortem handling. Coenzymes, such as flavin adenine dinucleotide (FAD), which contain riboflavin may also be important in deteriorative reactions that are photocatalyzed.

5. NUCLEI

Since the nucleus is deeply involved in the genetic apparatus of the cell, it is hardly
surprising to find enzymes associated with synthesis and degradation of nucleic
acids and nucleotides. Also found in the nucleus are enzymes involved in glycolysis,
in the hexose monophosphate shunt and possibly in the citric acid cycle, and in
electron transport.

6. CHLOROPLASTS

A wide variety of reactions are carried out by the chloroplast, including conservation of light energy through photophosphorylation and the fixation of carbon dioxide, which is linked to synthesis of carbohydrates, lipids, and proteins. The chloroplast also synthesizes chlorophyll and carotenoids (source of vitamin A) which are important colorants in foods. Chlorophyll pigments can discolor during processing and they can catalyze photooxidation of lipids, leading to peroxides and resultant off flavors. The chloroplast is also a site of polyphenoloxidase [104] and chlorophyllase activities.

7. PEROXISOMES (MICROBODIES)

This recently discovered subcellular particle is found in both plants and animals. Enzymes which are characteristic of peroxisomes include catalase, urate oxidase, D-amino acid oxidase, and L-α-hydroxy acid oxidase. It is interesting that catalase destroys hydrogen peroxide, whereas the other three enzymes generate hydrogen peroxide as a product. Since catalase is ultimately destroyed by hydrogen peroxide [74], it is possible that an abundance of hydrogen peroxide resulting from oxidases in the peroxisome causes oxidative deterioration of food tissues.

8. GLYOXYSOMES (MICROBODIES)

Glyoxysomes contain enzymes of the glyoxylate pathway, which is instrumental in converting storage lipid to carbohydrate during early postgerminative growth of plants. Glyoxysomal enzyme activity declines in plant tissue after the early stages of plant growth.

9. LYSOSOMES [103]

Of all the subcellular particles, lysosomes may be the most important to food scientists. At least 37 hydrolytic enzymes have been detected in lysosomes. These hydrolytic enzymes all have acidic pH optima and are referred to as "acid hydrolases." Enzymes of lysosomes are capable of hydrolyzing nucleic acids, lipids, proteins, polysaccharides, phosphates, glycoproteins, and glycolipids. Lysosomal enzymes can completely hydrolyze proteins to amino acids. Hydrolytic reactions of lysosomal enzymes, particularly the cathepsins, have been implicated in the aging of meat and in autolysis of animal tissues. It is interesting that lysosomal enzymes are apparently quite resistant to lysosomal proteases.

   Enzymes are released from lysosomes by processes which are detrimental to membrane structure, such as freezing and thawing or osmotic shock. Although the vast bulk of research on lysosomes has been performed on animal tissues, these particles have been found in a variety of plant tissues, including tomato fruit [47].

   As in other subcellular particles there is a subparticulate distribution of enzymes. Some enzymes, such as α-N-acetylglucosaminidase, are constituents of

the organelle membrane. Other enzymes, such as aryl sulfatase, are bound to the
organelle membrane to varying degrees.

10. CYTOSOL

Enzymic activities of the soluble phase of the cytoplasm are many and varied.
Major enzyme systems in the cytosol include those for synthesis of proteins, nucleic acids, and fatty acids; glycolysis; the pentose phosphate oxidative cycle; and
glycogen metabolism. Probably of most interest to the food scientist is the glycolytic enzyme system since postmortem metabolism in meats is anaerobic [33].

11. AMYLOPLASTS

Starch granules not only serve as storage organs for starch but also possess a significant degree of metabolic activity. Enzymes in starch include sucrose-UDP
glucosyltransferase, sucrose phosphate-UDP glucosyltransferase, UDPG pyrophosphorylase, ADPG pyrophosphorylase, and nucleoside-diphosphate kinase [112].
Starch is synthesized in the granules from endogenous substrates, a process
accompanied by a decrease in sucrose content.

B. Distribution of Enzymes in Selected Food Materials

In addition to their subcellular and subparticulate distribution, the kind and concentration of enzymes differs among food systems and tissues. Often the significance
of enzyme compartmentalization at the tissue level is obscure; however, at times
it may affect the processing procedures or the type of product that is produced.
For example, in the preparation of Blue cheese, milk is separated into lipase-rich
skim milk and cream. Subsequently the cream is bleached and homogenized and
then recombined with the skim milk so that the natural lipases can aid in developing
the typical Blue cheese flavor.
The enzyme distribution in milk, eggs, grains, and meats illustrates enzyme
compartmentalization in food materials. At least 20 enzymes native to milk are
distributed among the soluble phase, the micellar phase, and the fat globules [94].
Approximately 19 other enzymes have been detected in milk, but these actually may
be constituents of leukocytes and microorganisms in milk.
Eggs are not a rich source of enzymes, although lysozyme constitutes 3.5% of
the egg white solids. About 12 enzymes have been measured in egg white and seven
enzymes in the yolk [95].
Approximately 55 enzymes have been measured in the wheat kernel [84]; however, a limited number of these enzymes have been studied with respect to distribution. In general, the outer layers of the kernel have very low enzymic activities
(see Chapter 16 for structure of the wheat kernel). The aleurone layer, however,
contains substantial amounts of various enzymes. Although the endosperm usually
contains low concentrations of enzymes, the absolute quantities of enzymes are
relatively high because the endosperm comprises about 82% of the kernel. The
germ is a rich source of various enzymes. This might be expected since germination and growth of the seed involves the enzymic machinery of the germ.

Centrifugal fractionation of disrupted muscle tissue leads largely to the subcellular particles of animal origin (listed in Table 6-1) with their attendant enzymic activities. In broad terms, white muscle, capable of rapid but brief contractions, largely utilizes glycolysis for energy production, whereas red muscle, which can contract for long periods of time, primarily utilizes an oxidative form of metabolism [6].

V. ENZYME SPECIFICITY

The specificity of enzymes distinguish them from nonbiological catalysts. Enzymes show varying degrees of specificity as follows [33]:

1. Stereochemical specificity: Many enzymes show a preference for a particular optical or geometrical isomer.
2. Low specificity: The enzyme is not discriminating as to substrate and exhibits only specificity toward the bond being split.
3. Group specificity: The enzyme is specific for a particular chemical bond that is adjacent to a specific group. For example, trypsin is specific for peptide bonds on the carboxyl side of arginine and lysine.
4. Absolute specificity: The enzyme will attack only one substrate and catalyze only a single reaction. Most enzymes fall into this category.

The specificity of enzymes is very important in food processing, where it is often desirable to modify only a single component in the process. In food analysis, the accuracy of enzymic methods depends on specificity.

VI. ENZYME ACTIVITY AS INFLUENCED
BY ENVIRONMENTAL CONDITIONS

The importance of enzymes to the food scientist is often determined by the environment within the food. Control of the environment is necessary to control enzymic activity during food preservation and processing. In this section, the major factors affecting enzymic activity are discussed. These factors include pH, temperature, moisture, ionic strength, ionizing radiation, shearing, pressure, and interfacial effects.

A. pH Effects [33,83]

Extremes in pH will generally inactivate enzymes. Enzymes usually exhibit maximal activity at a particular pH value, termed the pH optimum. The relationship between pH and activity is illustrated in Figure 6-1. Most enzymes show maximum activities in the pH range of 4.5-8.0, and maximum activity is usually, but not always, confined to a rather narrow pH range. There are, however, enzymes with extreme pH optima, such as pepsin, which has a pH optimum of 1.8, and arginase, which has a pH optimum of 10.0. Depending on the enzyme, the activity can correspond to either a sigmoidal or a bell-shaped curve. At extremes in pH, enzyme

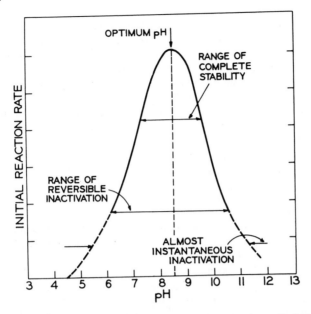

FIG. 6-1. Effect of pH on enzyme activity. Redrawn from Ref. [115], p. 75.

activity usually decreases irreversibly because of protein denaturation. However, as shown in Figure 6-1 there is a pH range of reversible inactivation. This apparently involves the reversible ionization of functional groups in the active site or in areas which control conformation of the enzyme.

Control of pH as it relates to enzymic activity is important to the food scientist. In an industrial process, where enzymic activity is desirable, the pH should be controlled to maximize that activity. However, the food scientist may wish to prevent or inhibit an enzymic reaction. For example, unwanted phenolase activity can be avoided by reducing the pH of the system well below (< 3.0) the optimum pH of 6.5. This is frequently accomplished in fruits by adding natural acidulants, such as citric, malic, or phosphoric acids.

The pH optimum of an enzyme may occur as a result of (1) a true reversible effect of pH on the maximum velocity of the reaction, (2) an effect of pH on the affinity of substrate for the enzyme, and (3) an effect of pH on the stability of the enzyme.

B. High-Temperature Effects [33,83,116]

The effects of temperature are very complex and may result from the summation of a variety of causes. For example, high temperatures may affect the velocity of breakdown of the enzyme-substrate complex; the pH values of functional groups involved in the enzymic reaction; the affinity of the enzyme for activators or inhibitors; and ancillary matters, such as solubility of oxygen, which may be a substrate in the reaction. In addition, heat inactivation of the enzyme can occur, and this is one of the reasons for heat processing foods. Basically, the food scientist must consider two major opposing factors as the temperature is increased: the increasing rate of enzymic reactions and the increasing rate of enzymic destruction (above certain critical temperatures). As the temperature is increased, the rate of destruction increases faster than the rate of catalysis. These effects of temperature on one enzyme are shown in Figure 6-2.

In general, enzymes function very slowly at subfreezing temperatures, and their activities increase as the temperature is increased up to about 45°C. A term which is often used to express the effect of temperature on rates of enzymic reactions is the temperature coefficient, Q_{10}, where

$$Q_{10} = \frac{\text{reaction velocity at temperature } (t + 10°C)}{\text{reaction velocity at temperature } t}$$

For enzymic reactions, a Q_{10} of approximately two is often encountered which indicates that the reaction rate approximately doubles for each 10° increase in temperature until denaturation occurs.

Most enzymes show "optimal activity" in the 30–40°C range and begin to denature above 45°C. However, there are thermostable enzymes available commercially that resist inactivation at temperatures mugh higher than 45°C.

The Arrhenius equation, $k = Ae^{-E/RT}$, indicates the exponential relationship between the rate constant, k, of the reaction and absolute temperature T. The logarithmic form of the equation,

$$\text{Log } k = \frac{E}{2.303R} \cdot \frac{1}{T} + \log A$$

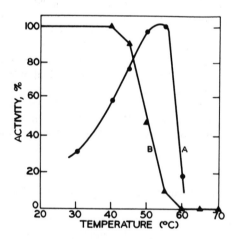

FIG. 6-2. Temperature–activity curve (a) and heat–stability curve (b) for endo-polygalacturonase III at pH 4.4. Curve A: 10-min reaction at each temperature shown. Curve B: exposure of enzyme for 10 min at indicated temperature followed by activity determination. Reprinted from Ref. [30], p. 555, by courtesy of Agrigculture Chemists' Society Japan.

indicates that the log of the rate constant k is inversely proportional to absolute temperature, T. This equation conforms to the equation of a straight line, so that when log k is plotted against $1/T$, the term $(-E/2.303R)$ is the slope of the line. With the slope known, the energy of activation, E, can be easily obtained. Activation energies for enzymic catalysis usually vary from 6,000 to 15,000 cal/mole, whereas those for enzymic denaturation fall within the range of 50,000-150,000 cal/mole. The fact that activation energies for enzyme inactivation exceed those for catalysis means that as the temperature increases above a certain critical zone for the enzyme in question, catalytic activity increases more slowly than the rate of inactivation. Furthermore, at temperatures well below the critical zone, the enzyme will be relatively stable and will have good catalytic activity.

Food scientists probably are more interested in time-temperature relationships for total inactivation of enzymes than in Arrhenius plots for denaturation rates. In these instances, the log of time for inactivation is plotted against temperature, as shown in Figure 6-3.

Inactivation of enzymes sometimes serves as a convenient indicator for the effectiveness of heat treatments for foods. For example, pasteurization of milk at 63°C for 30 min destroys Coxiella burnetti and also inactivates milk alkaline

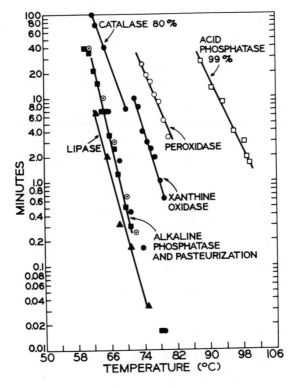

FIG. 6-3. Time-temperature relationships for inactivation of milk enzymes. Reprinted from Ref. [56], p. 201, by courtesy of John Wiley and Sons.

phosphatase. As shown in Figure 6-3, the time-temperature relationships for inactivation of alkaline phosphatase are considered adequate for milk pasteurization.
Notice that after adequate pasteurization some milk enzymes other than alkaline
phosphatase remain active. Similarly, fruits and vegetables are sometimes
blanched in hot water or steam partly for the purpose of inactivating enzymes, such
as lipase, phenolase, lipoxygenase, chlorophylase, catalase, peroxidase, and ascorbic acid oxidase. This process is regarded as effective when the heat-resistant
enzyme, peroxidase, is no longer active.

If the heat treatment given to an enzyme system is marginal and the bulk of the
inactive enzyme exists in a reversibly inactive form (see Chapter 5), enzyme reactivation or regeneration occurs upon storage at a lower temperature. This can
be an extremely important matter in some heat-processed foods. As shown in
Figure 6-4, reactivation of peroxidase following various processes of equal thermal severity is proportional to the rate of heating. Consequently, in high-temperature, short-time (HTST) processes, the enzyme may not be irreversibly destroyed
but only reversibly inactivated. This creates a dilemma for the processor and
regulatory agencies when, for example, milk properly pasteurized by a HTST
method exhibits a positive phosphatase test (indicative of improper pasteurization)
because of regeneration. Regeneration of such enzymes as peroxidase and lipoxygenase can have a detrimental effect on the sensory quality and nutritional value
of foods.

C. Low-Temperature Effects [35,46,102]

Although some enzymes are denatured at subfreezing temperatures, most remain
quite active after freezing and thawing. In addition, many enzymes exhibit significant activity in partially frozen systems. As the temperature of an enzyme solution is decreased from 0° to about 10° below its freezing point, enzymic activity

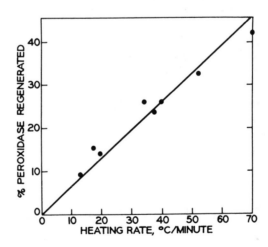

FIG. 6-4. Regeneration of turnip peroxidase as a function of heating rate. Reprinted from Ref. [91], p. 531, by courtesy of the Institute of Food Technologists.

can either increase or decrease, depending upon the enzyme and the system. A
further decline in temperature almost always results in decreased activity. The
following factors appear to be involved in this inconsistent behavior of enzymes in
partially frozen systems.

1. Composition of the medium
2. Rate and extent of freezing
3. Concentration effect of freezing
4. Viscosity
5. Complexity of the sample (intact tissue versus simple systems)

Enzymes in simple systems are especially susceptible to permanent damage
after freezing and thawing if they are highly purified and in an initially dilute solution. Simple systems thus may behave differently than intact tissues [35].

As intimated above, deviations from the Arrhenius relationship do occur with
enzyme-catalyzed reactions. Data for the oxidation of guaiacol by purified peroxidase and for hemin in 40% methanol from +25°C to -30°C are plotted according to
the Arrhenius relationship in Figure 6-5. A similar nonlinear behavior in the
Arrhenius relationship has been observed with invertase [16,17]. The unexplained
decrement in activity between observed rates and the linear extrapolation of the
Arrhenius plot may be due to the following factors: increased intraenzymic hydrogen bonding, yielding inactive enzyme conformers; increased hydrogen bonding between water and either the substrate or the enzyme active site, resulting in decreased specific activity; formation of enzyme polymers, resulting in decreased
specific activity; decreased ionization of enzyme, substrate, and buffers as the
temperature is decreased; and increased viscosity of the system.

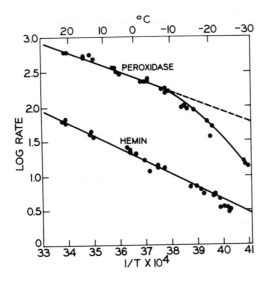

FIG. 6-5. Arrhenius plots of peroxidase- and hemin-catalyzed oxidation of
guaiacol. Reprinted from Ref. [102], p. 166, by courtesy of Academic Press.

During freezing, solutes concentrate in the unfrozen pools of water. The increased concentration of electrolytes and the change in pH that often occurs simultaneously is a major cause of biochemical damage and no doubt affects enzymic activities in frozen systems. Whether the effect is activation, stabilization, or inhibition depends on the enzyme, the nature and concentration of the salts, the pH, the temperature, and the types of other substances present. Increases in the concentrations of solutes can result in inhibition of some enzymes and activation of others.

The rate of freezing can also influence enzymic activity in partially frozen systems. Rate of freezing influences the size of and concentration of solutes in unfrozen pools and this, in turn, presumably influences enzymic activity. In frozen systems high viscosity results in decreased rates of diffusion of enzyme and substrates and thereby tends to limit the rate and extent of enzymic activity. Slow freezing and slow thawing generally result in more loss of enzymic activity than fast freezing and thawing.

The freezing and/or thawing of tissues results in damage to the membranes of subcellular organelles, such as mitochondria and lysosomes, and delocalization of enzymes. Enzymes that are released by freezing and thawing or other disruptive manipulations are known as "latent enzymes." Lysosomes are easily disrupted by osmotic and salt effects that accompany freezing and thawing. Since lysosomes contain a wide array of hydrolytic enzymes, tissue damage can be extensive. To minimize tissue destruction, attention should be paid to minimizing damage to the lysosomes.

Some enzymes can be damaged by exposure to low, nonfreezing (chilling) temperatures, a phenomenon known as "cold denaturation." This occurrence, which is the exception rather than the rule, has been observed with purified enzymes, such as catalase, lactate dehydrogenase, glutamate dehydrogenase, and glyceraldehyde phosphate dehydrogenase. Apparently, some enzymes are thermodynamically unstable at low, nonfreezing temperatures.

D. Water Activity and Enzymic Activity [1,42]

Although it is difficult to believe that enzymes can act at very low water levels, it is well known that dried vegetables soon acquire a haylike aroma if they are not blanched prior to drying. Furthermore, dried oat products become bitter upon storage unless the enzymes are first inactivated by heat. Thus it is common knowledge that foods protected against microbial spoilage by low water content are still susceptible to enzymic spoilage. For example, as shown in Figure 6-6, lipolysis in wheat flour can occur at very low moisture levels. As the moisture level increases so does lipolysis, until at 14% moisture lipolysis is very rapid.

Because enzymes are compartmentalized so they are effectively separated from their substrates, dried grains and seeds can be stored for long periods of time without evident enzymic deterioration. Cereal grains, for example, can be stored for months or years at a water content of 13% without evident deterioration; however, grain that has been mechanically damaged rapidly deteriorates at the same water content.

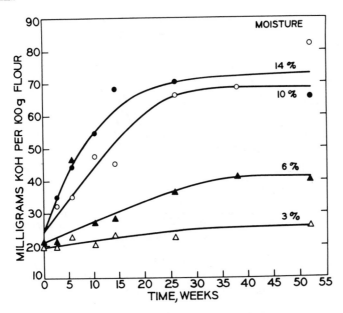

FIG. 6-6. Effect of moisture content and time of storage in sealed containers at 37.8°C on the fat acidity of unbleached patent flour. Reprinted from Ref. [25], p. 380, by courtesy of the American Association of Cereal Chemists.

In addition to endogenous enzymes, concern also should be given to adventitious enzymes derived from microorganisms. These enzymes can be important in cereals, as well as in egg products where bacteria have proliferated before drying.

The absolute water content of a food is not necessarily a decisive factor, but the "boundness" of the water is important (see Chapter 2). Consequently, water activity (a_W) or relative humidity are more suitable parameters than water content when considering enzymic activity in dried foods. Much information on enzymic reactions at low water activities has been obtained from model systems in which an inert material, such as cellulose, is impregnated with enzyme and then freeze dried. Subsequently, this material can be mixed with substrate and studied at various water activities.

Based on data from model systems, as illustrated in Figure 6-7, the following generalizations can be made: (1) at a sufficiently high water activity, enzymic activity may be measurable in a matter of hours; (2) at a sufficiently low water activity, enzymic reactions do not proceed (this is true even though enough water may be present to theoretically cause a hydrolytic reaction to go to completion); and (3) reactions at different water activities tend toward different final values of product accumulation. In this latter instance, the enzyme could be inactivated; however, this clearly was not so in the study shown in Figure 6-7. After 48 days of storage at the original a_W, the a_W of the system was increased, with a resultant increase in enzymic activity to a level characteristic of the new a_W. This apparently occurred because only part of the substrate was dissolved and available at a relatively low water activity. Once the dissolved substrate was used up and the

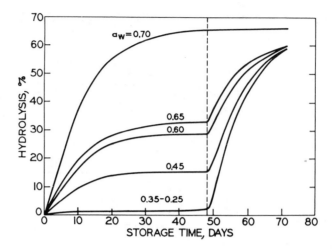

FIG. 6-7. Rates of enzymic hydrolysis of lecithin in a mixture of ground barley malt and 2% lecithin stored at different water activities at 30°C. Reprinted from Ref. [2], p. 351, by courtesy of J. F. Bergmann-Verlag.

reaction products had accumulated, the reaction stopped. An increase in relative humidity would then increase the amount of free water, which would dissolve additional substrate and would dilute the reaction products, thereby allowing the reaction to resume.

Enzymic activity, in general, parallels the sorption isotherm (see Chapter 2), with significant enzymic activity evident only above the region of monomolecular adsorption. Increasing amounts of free water then become available to serve as a vehicle for enzymic processes. However, certain enzymic reactions can occur even below an a_W corresponding to monolayer adsorption of water. This is possible if the substrate is sufficiently mobile and fluid to associate with the enzyme. An example involves the lipolysis of oily, unsaturated triglycerides. At very low a_W's, oily triglycerides, because of their mobilities, are more available and are hydrolyzed much more rapidly than solid triglycerides. In this regard, the temperature at which a dried food is stored would also have a bearing on the mobility and rate of degradation of triglycerides.

Although substrate mobility is important, solid substrates can be attacked at low a_W's, particularly if they are in intimate contact with the enzyme.

Thus, the rate of enzymic reactions in dried foods is limited by the rate at which the substrate diffuses to the enzyme. This may explain why high molecular weight substrates in dried foods are not attacked very rapidly. For example, wheat gluten in flour containing proteinases does not hydrolyze appreciably even at 65% relative humidity. Diffusion effects involving macromolecular substrates may also result in qualitative changes in the enzymic reaction. In an aqueous medium, amylase attacks soluble starch to form oligosaccharides. However, in the dried state, glucose and maltose appear first and only at higher water activities are oligosaccharides formed.

The activities of nonhydrolytic enzymes are also influenced by water activity. This behavior has been observed in model systems containing glucose oxidase and polyphenol oxidase [1] and in wheat protein concentrate containing lipoxygenase [114]. Water serves as a medium for the reaction and as a vehicle for the substrate, but where water is tightly bound, enzymic oxidation is either not possible or is slow.

Enzymes are known to be more heat stable in the dry state. As the moisture content increases, the susceptibility of the enzyme to heat inactivation increases. This can be of practical significance during dehydration of cereals, malt, etc., and in some baked goods where not all enzymes are inactivated in baking.

E. Effect of Electrolytes and Ionic Strength on Enzymes [28]

1. ACTIVATION AND INHIBITION

Some enzymes require certain ions for activity, whereas other enzymes are not particularly affected by ions. Heavy metal ions, such as Hg^{2+}, Pb^{2+}, or Ag^{+}, usually poison enzymes. Ionic effects vary from one enzyme to another; e.g., an ion may be toxic for one enzyme and activate another. Furthermore, a given ion may act as an inhibitor of an enzyme at one level but may activate the same enzyme at another level. Although ions have nonspecific effects on the enzyme as a protein, they also may be required as components of the active site.

Anions tend to be fairly nonspecific in their action on enzymes, whereas the cation requirement of an enzyme is sometimes specific. Some enzymes are activated by more than one cation and other enzymes are activated only by one ion. Cations known to activate enzymes incude Na^{+}, K^{+}, Rb^{+}, Cs^{+}, Mg^{2+}, Ca^{2+}, Zn^{2+}, Cd^{2+}, Cr^{3+}, Cu^{2+}, Mn^{2+}, Fe^{2+}, Co^{2+}, Ni^{2+}, Al^{3+}, and NH_4^{+}. The ionic radii of these ions fall within a fairly narrow zone in the middle range of observed atomic radii; however, the ions are not always interchangeable.

There are also instances of competitive antagonisms between ions. For example, Ca^{2+}-activated myosin ATPase is inhibited by Mg^{2+}.

Ions may activate enzymes by a variety of mechanisms, including (1) becoming an integral part of the active site, (2) forming a binding link between enzyme and substrate, (3) changing the equilibrium constant of the enzyme reaction, (4) changing the surface charge on the enzyme protein, (5) removing an inhibitor of the reaction, (6) displacing an ineffective metal ion from the active site or from the substrate, and (7) shifting the equilibrium of a less active conformer to a more active conformer.

2. SALTING IN AND SALTING OUT

Large quantities of electrolytes have an effect on the solubility of proteins in general. Salts are often necessary to solubilize, or "salt in" a protein in an aqueous system. However, salts can be used to insolubilize, or "salt out," an enzyme, a phenomenon used to isolate enzymes. Ammonium sulfate is often used to fractionate enzymes because it is highly soluble in water and is not harmful to most enzymes.

The solubility of enzymes varies inversely with the concentration of added ammonium sulfate according to the well-known linear relationship, $\log S = -K_2 (\lambda/2) + B'$. The solubility of the enzyme in grams per liter is S, the "y" value when plotted. The ionic strength in moles per liter of solution is $\lambda/2$, the "x" value. The intercept of the "y" axis is B' and the slope of the straight line is $-K_s$. Both of the last two terms are characteristic of the enzyme. As the concentration of ammonium sulfate is increased, enzyme solubility decreases to a point where precipitation eventually occurs. In the case of ammonium sulfate, the actual position of the precipitation range is determined by pH, temperature, and concentration of enzyme.

3. STABILITY OF ENZYMES [12]

In such food processes as brining, enzymes may be inactivated because of the high concentration of electrolytes. In some instances, small concentrations of particular cations and anions can alter the stability of enzymes. The effects are specific and differ from one enzyme to another. These specific effects of electrolytes apparently result from strong preferential binding to the enzyme in either its native or its denatured state.

However, at greater concentrations all electrolytes alter enzyme stability, presumably by nonspecific effects since all enzymes are affected similarly.

F. Inactivation of Enzymes by Shearing

Figure 6-8 illustrates the inactivation of rennet by shearing at 40°C [19]. When the shear rate (sec^{-1}) times the exposure time (sec) is greater than 10^4, inactivation becomes detectable. At shear values on the order of 10^7 about 50% inactivation has been observed for solutions of catalase, rennet, and carboxypeptidase [42]. Moreover, rennet undergoes reactivation after shear inactivation, reminiscent of reactivation after reversible thermal inactivation.

G. Effect of Pressure on Enzymes [83]

Very high pressures usually inactivate enzymes; however, the necessary pressures are much higher than normally encountered in food processing. Consequently, pressure effects on enzymes are of little concern to food scientists.

H. Effect of Ionizing Radiation on Enzymic Activity [61,83,96,109]

Ionizing radiation, such as γ rays, has been proposed as a means for pasteurization or sterilization of foods. Although enzymes are inactivated by ionizing radiation, the dosage required for complete inactivation in situ is about an order of magnitude greater than that necessary to destroy the microorganisms of concern. Although food can be made microbiologically stable by ionizing radiation, residual enzymic activity in a food can harm its desirable sensory properties and nutritive value.

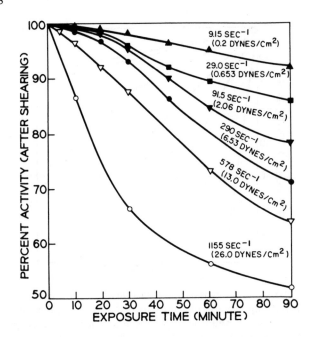

FIG. 6-8. Inactivation of rennet by shearing at 4°C. Reprinted from Ref. [19], p. 505, by courtesy of Academic Press.

In general, the destruction of enzymic activity by ionizing radiation is affected by the particular enzyme being tested, water activity, enzyme concentration, enzyme purity, in vitro vs in situ effects, oxygen concentration, pH, and temperature. As shown in Figure 6-9, an enzyme, such as trypsin, is most resistant to radiation damage in the dry state, presumably because only the direct effects of irradiation are operative. In the presence of water, inactivation is greater presumably because "indirect effects" become important. This involves the radiolysis of water and the damaging effects of resultant free radicals (see Chapter 5). In foods, such as fillet of sole, water contents in the range of 20-30% result in optimum enzymic destruction during irradiation. At lower water levels, the inefficient direct effect mechanism predominates, whereas at higher water levels rapid recombination of resulting free radicals apparently reduces their effectiveness.

Individual enzymes vary greatly in radioresistance. Catalase is about 60 times more resistant to irradiation inactivation than carboxypeptidase.

In general, within certain limits, the more dilute the enzyme solution, the smaller the dose needed to destroy the same percentage of initial enzyme activity. This phenomenon is called the "dilution effect." More impure enzymic preparations are usually more resistant to irradiation damage. The presence of oxygen in the system often sensitizes the enzyme to radio destruction. The effect of pH on enzymic inactivation can be considerable but is not easily predictable (see Fig. 6-9). Thus the effect of radiation on enzymes in meats will be influenced by postmortem pH.

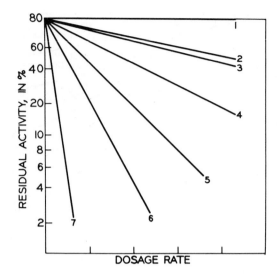

FIG. 6-9. Inactivation of trypsin upon irradiation under various conditions.
(1) dry trypsin, (2) 10 mg trypsin per milliliter solution at pH 8 and -78°C, (3)
80 mg trypsin per milliliter solution at pH 8 and ambient temperature, (4) 10 mg
trypsin per milliliter at pH 2.6 and -78°C, (5) 80 mg trypsin per milliliter at pH
2.7 and ambient temperature, (6) 10 mg trypsin per milliliter at pH 2.6 and ambient
temperature, (7) 1 mg trypsin per milliliter at pH 2.6 and ambient temperature.
Redrawn from Ref. [61], p. 88.

In general, inactivation of enzymes by irradiation is more easily accomplished
as the temperature is raised. In frozen systems little damage to enzymes is evident, presumably because free radicals are immobilized.

Many of the above effects undoubtedly combine to yield differing results in situ
(food systems) compared to in vitro (purified enzymes). In tissues, enzyme compartmentalization is a factor of importance, as are such factors as water activity,
the protective effects of other cellular constituents, and the effect that time elapsed
postharvest or postmortem has on pH.

Combination treatments have been suggested in some instances. For example,
a mild heat treatment to inactivate enzymes coupled with radiation to destroy
microorganisms has been proposed. Alternatively, irradiation followed by refrigeration may be employed for such foods as fresh fish, strawberries, tomatoes, and
mushrooms.

Further details of changes occurring during irradiation of proteins are given in
Chapter 5.

I. Interfacial Inactivation of Enzymes [16, 55, 66]

Proteins in general tend to adsorb at interfaces and this often results in denaturation. The high interfacial tension at the air-water or oil-water interface is apparently responsible. As a result, the secondary and tertiary structure of the enzyme

unfolds rapidly and the molecule spreads over the interface. In an air-water system, hydrophobic amino acid residues orient toward the air and hydrophilic residues toward the water. In an oil-water emulsion, the hydrophobic residues associate with the oil and hydrophilic side chains extend into the water. Simple foaming of enzyme solutions can produce air-water interfaces for surface denaturation. The resulting loss in enzymic activity is not regained readily upon compression or by retrieval of the films in a variety of forms.

Some effects of adsorption at an oil-water interface are similar to adsorption at an air-water interface. However, when enzymes adsorb at an interface already occupied by a close-packed film of another protein or "protective" molecule, unfolding and loss of activity does not appear to occur. The recoverability of enzyme activity from oil-in-water emulsions depends on the charge on the oil droplets, the stability of the emulsion, and the concentrations of protein at the interface and in the bulk solution. Even lipase, which is thought to be especially adapted for activity at oil-water interfaces, can be denatured by adsorption at a triglyceride-water interface [13]. Lipase also can be inactivated at an air-water interface.

VII. KINETICS OF ENZYME ACTIVITY [22,26,70,71,93]

Enzyme kinetics has developed into a discipline in its own right; however, much of the work is related to mechanisms of enzymic activity. Unless the food scientist is involved in basic research on the biochemistry of postharvest plant and postmortem animal tissues, or on the chemistry of enzymes, detailed knowledge of sophisticated enzyme kinetics is usually not essential. For the most part, the food scientist will require sufficient knowledge of enzyme kinetics to prepare an assay for enzymic activity or substrate concentration. Consequently, an understanding of elementary Michaelis-Menten kinetics is usually adequate.

A. Initial Velocity

In enzymic reactions the conversion of substrate S into product P (S→P) is characterized by a progress curve which depicts the rate of utilization of substrate or the rate of formation of product as shown in Figure 6-10. As the reaction proceeds, the rate decreases with time. Causes for this decreased rate include (1) in a reversible reaction, the back reaction (P→S) becomes significant as P increases; (2) the rate decreases if the initial substrate concentration is not $\geq 20\ K_m$ (enzyme is essentially saturated; K_m is equal to the substrate concentration at which the reaction proceeds at half its maximum initial rate; Fig. 6-11); (3) the activity of an unstable enzyme decreases rapidly; and (4) the product of the reaction may inhibit the enzyme.

To minimize the above factors, the initial rate of an enzyme reaction should be measured. It is best to use a continuous measuring device, such as a recording spectrophotometer, to observe initial reaction rates.

Alternatively, aliquots can be taken during the initial phases of the reaction for measurement and manual plotting. Despite the importance of measuring initial rates in enzymic assays, there exist numerous assays whereby a single reading is

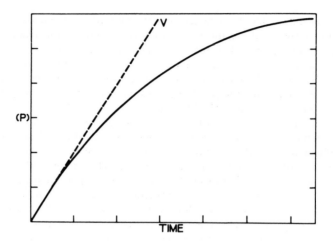

FIG. 6-10. Progress curve of an enzyme-catalyzed reaction. The rate (v) of the reaction (tangent to the curve at the moment of interest) decreases as the reaction proceeds. Reprinted from Ref. [116], p. 171.

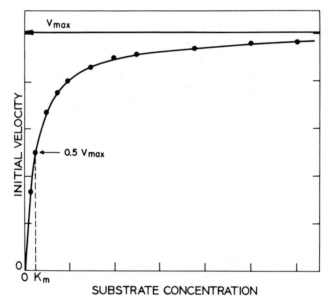

FIG. 6-11. Plot of initial velocity, v, versus concentration of substrate, (S), for a typical enzyme-catalyzed reaction. Reprinted from Ref. [116], p. 176.

taken after a given reaction time. Assays of this type should be suspect until it is established that the single reading falls on a linear portion of the reaction curve.

As shown in Figure 6-11, initial velocity increases with increases in substrate concentration up to a certain point, beyond which initial velocity becomes independent of substrate concentration. Thus, at low substrate concentrations ($\leq 0.1\,K_m$) the enzyme reaction is approximately first order with respect to substrate. This region is important when enzymes are used to analyze for substrate concentration. At high substrate concentrations ($\geq 20\,K_m$) the reaction is essentially zero order with respect to substrate, and the rate of reaction is proportional to enzyme concentration. It is in this region that enzyme concentration can best be determined.

B. Michaelis–Menten Equation

If we assume that an enzymic reaction involves the reversible formation of an enzyme-substrate (ES) complex with the reversible breakdown of the ES complex to enzyme and product, the following situation exists:

$$E + S \underset{k_2}{\overset{k_1}{\rightleftharpoons}} ES \underset{k_4}{\overset{k_3}{\rightleftharpoons}} E + P \tag{6-1}$$

Furthermore, if we assume that after the first few milliseconds of the reaction the rate of formation of ES is equal to its rate of decomposition, the concentration of ES reaches a steady state. From the law of mass action for this steady state, we have:

$$k_1\,[E]\,[S] + k_4\,[E]\,[P] = k_2[ES] + k_3[ES] \tag{6-2}$$

If we consider only the initial stages of the reaction, where [S] is essentially constant and [P] is close to zero, the term $k_4[E][P]$ can be neglected, giving

$$k_1\,[E]\,[S] = [ES](k_2 + k_3) \tag{6-3}$$

This can be rearranged to yield

$$\frac{[E]}{[ES]} = \frac{k_2 + k_3}{k_1\,[S]} \tag{6-4}$$

where the rate constants can be combined into a single constant called the Michaelis–Menten constant, K_m. Therefore

$$\frac{[E]}{[ES]} = \frac{K_m}{[S]} \tag{6-5}$$

Note that K_m is not simply the dissociation constant for the ES complex since it contains the k_3 term. The true dissociation constant of [ES] would be k_2/k_1. Consequently, if k_3 is very small compared to k_2, then K_m is more identifiable as the dissociation constant (stability constant) of the ES complex. However, for enzymes with high molecular activities, such as catalase, k_3 is much greater than k_2, and K_m is better considered as a kinetic constant.

The total amount of enzyme in the reaction, E_T, is equal to the free enzyme in addition to that involved in the enzyme-substrate complex.

$$E_T = E + ES \tag{6-6a}$$

or

$$E = E_T - ES \tag{6-6b}$$

Substituting these values into Eq. (6-3) yields

$$k_1 \left([E_T] - [ES] \right) [S] = k_2 [ES] + k_3 [ES] \tag{6-7}$$

In order to solve for [ES] it is necessary to expand the left side of Eq. (6-7) to give

$$k_1 [E_T] [S] - k_1 [ES] [S] = k_2 [ES] + k_3 [ES] \tag{6-8}$$

Rearranging and combining terms, we get

$$k_1 [E_T] [S] = (k_1 [S] + k_2 + k_3) [ES] \tag{6-9}$$

thus

$$(ES) = \frac{k_1 [E_T] [S]}{k_1 [S] + k_2 + k_3} \tag{6-10}$$

Dividing the numerator and denominator by k_1 yields:

$$[ES] = \frac{[E_T] [S]}{[S] + \dfrac{k_2 + k_3}{k_1}} \tag{6-11}$$

Since the rate of formation of P from ES is proportional to [ES]

$$v = k_3 [ES] \tag{6-12}$$

or

$$[ES] = \frac{v}{k_3} \tag{6-13}$$

Substituting v/k_3 for [ES] and rearranging gives

$$v = \frac{k_3 [E_T] [S]}{[S] + \dfrac{k_2 + k_3}{k_1}}$$

or

$$v = \frac{k_3 [E_T] [S]}{[S] + K_m} \tag{6-14}$$

If [S] is very large (>20K_m) so that K_m is negligible, K_m can be neglected. From Figure 6-11, V_{max} is obtained at these high substrate concentrations, therefore, ignoring K_m and cancelling [S]

$$V_{max} = k_3[E_T]$$

If this is substituted into Eq. (6-14), we get the Michaelis-Menten equation

$$v = \frac{V_{max}[S]}{[S] + K_m}$$

which describes the rectangular hyperbola in Figure 6-11 that is characteristic of many enzyme reactions.

C. Properties of the Michaelis-Menten Constant, K_m [71]

1. K_m has units of concentration (moles/liter).
2. K_m is equal to the substrate concentration at which the reaction proceeds at half its maximum initial rate. This can be shown by substituting 1/2 V_{max} for v in the Michaelis-Menten equation.
3. Most enzymic reactions involving single substrates have K_m values between 10^{-5}M and 10^{-2}M.
4. For practical purposes, we may assume that $v = V_{max}$ (i.e., "zero-order" kinetics are observed) when $[S] \geq 20K_m$, or that $v = k[S]$ (i.e., "first-order" kinetics are observed) when $[S] \leq 0.1K_m$. These values are significant when analyses for substrate or enzyme concentrations are developed.

D. Experimental Determination of Values of K_m and V_{max}

It is very difficult to determine K_m and V_{max} from the plot shown in Figure 6-11 because if the experimental points are scattered, it is difficult to draw an accurate hyperbola. Furthermore, it may not be possible to supply sufficient substrate to achieve V_{max} or to measure the low initial velocities obtained with small concentrations of substrate. However, if the Michaelis-Menten equation is rearranged to yield a straight-line plot, these difficulties are overcome. The Lineweaver-Burk method of plotting the data makes use of the fact that the reciprocal of the equation of a rectangular hyperbola is the equation of a straight line. Thus, the reciprocal of the Michaelis-Menten equation is

$$\frac{1}{v} = \frac{[S]}{V_{max}[S]} + \frac{K_m}{V_{max}[S]}$$

which upon rearrangement becomes the Lineweaver-Burk equation

$$\frac{1}{v} = \frac{K_m}{V_{max}} \cdot \frac{1}{[S]} + \frac{1}{V_{max}}$$

Therefore, if $1/v$ is plotted against $1/[S]$, a straight line is obtained the slope of which is K_m/V_{max} and the $1/v$ intercept is $1/V_{max}$. Extrapolation of the straight line to the negative "x" axis yields $-1/K_m$, which can be used to calculate K_m.

Figure 6-12 depicts a typical Lineweaver-Burk plot and illustrates the determination of V_{max} and K_m from the graph. The experimental values are given above the figure. The extrapolated portion of the line intercepts the negative portion of the "x" axis at -2.5. Therefore, $1/K_m$ is 2.5×10^4 and K_m is 4×10^{-5}M. Also, $1/V_{max}$ is 1.25×10^{-2} and V_{max} is 80 μmoles/liter min.

E. Enzyme Inhibition

The kinetics of enzyme action also can be used to study the effects of inhibitors on enzymic activity. There are essentially two groups of enzyme inhibitors, reversible and irreversible. With reversible inhibition, the enzyme activity is restored when the inhibitor is removed. However, irreversible inhibition is progressive and becomes complete when all the enzyme is combined with the inhibitor. Removal of the excess inhibitor does not lead to reactivation of the enzyme. Heavy metals, such as mercury, are good examples of irreversible inhibitors.

There are three groups of reversible inhibitors, competitive, noncompetitive, and uncompetitive. Competitive inhibition affects the apparent K_m; noncompetitive inhibition largely affects V_{max}; whereas uncompetitive inhibition affects both the apparent K_m and V_{max}. Competitive inhibitors have a close structural resemblance to the natural substrate and can compete with the substrate for the active site of the enzyme. In competitive inhibition the degree of inhibition by an inhibitor is inversely related to substrate concentration. In noncompetitive inhibition, the degree of inhibition is affected only by inhibitor concentration and not by substrate concentration. Uncompetitive inhibition is not relieved by increasing the concentration of substrate.

The differences among competitive, noncompetitive, and uncompetitive inhibitors can be determined experimentally, and for mathematical derivations and plots dealing with inhibition, specialized references should be consulted [22,26,70,71, 93].

F. Measurement of Enzyme Activity [71]

The following rules should be observed when determining the catalytic activity of an enzyme:

1. It is preferable to measure initial rates with a continuous monitoring technique.
2. Reactants including substrate and cofactors must be in sufficient excess over enzyme in order to achieve the maximum catalytic rate. If the Michaelis-Menten constants are known for the various reactants, a substrate concentration ≥ 20 times K_m assures maximum velocity of the reaction.
3. The optimal reaction conditions for the enzyme reaction should be maintained and reported.

$[S]$ M	v μMOLES/ LITER-MIN	$\dfrac{1}{[S]}$	$\dfrac{1}{v}$
8.35×10^{-6}	13.8	12×10^4	7.24×10^{-2}
1.00×10^{-5}	16.0	10×10^4	6.25×10^{-2}
1.25×10^{-5}	19.1	8×10^4	5.23×10^{-2}
1.67×10^{-5}	23.8	6×10^4	4.20×10^{-2}
2.0×10^{-5}	26.7	5×10^4	3.75×10^{-2}
2.5×10^{-5}	30.8	4×10^4	3.25×10^{-2}
3.3×10^{-5}	36.2	3×10^4	2.76×10^{-2}
5.0×10^{-5}	44.5	2×10^4	2.25×10^{-2}
1.0×10^{-4}	57.2	1×10^4	1.75×10^{-2}
2.0×10^{-4}	66.7	0.5×10^4	1.50×10^{-2}

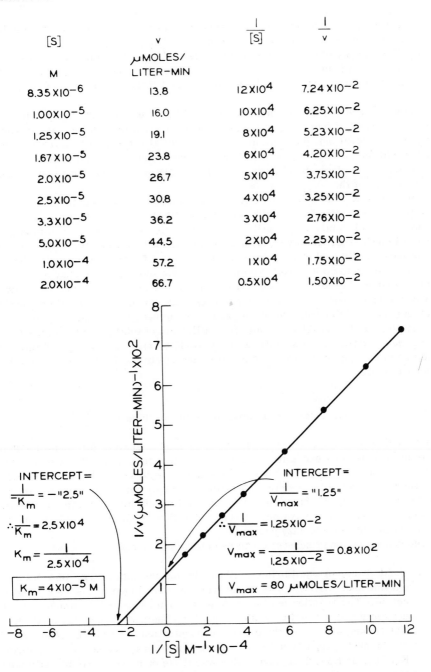

INTERCEPT=

$\dfrac{1}{=K_m} = -\text{"2.5"}$

$\therefore \dfrac{1}{K_m} = 2.5 \times 10^4$

$K_m = \dfrac{1}{2.5 \times 10^4}$

$\boxed{K_m = 4 \times 10^{-5} \text{ M}}$

INTERCEPT=

$\dfrac{1}{V_{max}} = \text{"1.25"}$

$\therefore \dfrac{1}{V_{max}} = 1.25 \times 10^{-2}$

$V_{max} = \dfrac{1}{1.25 \times 10^{-2}} = 0.8 \times 10^2$

$\boxed{V_{max} = 80 \ \mu\text{MOLES/LITER-MIN}}$

FIG. 6-12. Double-reciprocal (Lineweaver–Burk) plot of $1/v$ versus $1/[S]$ for an enzyme reaction. Reprinted from Ref. [93], pp. 220-221, by courtesy of John Wiley and Sons.

4. The rate of the nonenzymic reaction should be determined using a sample heated so as to inactivate the enzyme.
5. The quantity of enzyme should be measured so that specific activities can be calculated (usually a total protein estimation is made, although the enzyme may constitute only a small part of the total if the preparation is crude).

The validity of the assay can be determined by (a) establishing that the initial rates are directly proportional to enzyme concentration (plot initial rates against enzyme concentration); (b) confirming that the initial rates do not increase upon further addition of reactants (substrates, cofactors, etc.); and (c) establishing for discontinuous or single-point assays that the measurements are made on a meaningful portion of the reaction curve.

Once the maximum catalytic activity of the enzyme has been determined, it can be reported as "units of enzyme." The usual unit of enzyme activity is that amount of enzyme which catalyzes the utilization of 1 μmole of substrate per minute under standard conditions. However, with commercial food enzymes the units of activity do not necessarily conform to the above definition. Most enzymes used in food systems are crude so it is not possible to measure the amount of enzymically active protein responsible for substrate transformation. Consequently, the concentration of enzyme in a crude preparation is given as units per milliliter solution, or if the protein content of the preparation has been determined, the specific activity of the preparation can be reported as units per milligram of total protein. In the latter case, the standard unit of specific activity would be micromoles of substrate utilized per minute per milligram protein at stated conditions of temperature, pH, and other variables.

G. Analysis of Substrate with Enzymes [8,41]

Due to their specificity, enzymes often can be used to analyze for specific components in foods without extensive purification procedures. In addition, many enzyme reactions are very sensitive, estimating as little as 10^{-10} g of material.

Precise control of the reaction conditions is important when enzymes are used for substrate analysis. Since the analyses are for substrates, these must be the limiting component in the system. Thus, activators, cofactors, etc., should be sufficient to saturate the enzyme.

The concentration of substrate can be determined in one of two ways.

1. Total change or equilibrium method: In this instance, large amounts of enzyme and small amounts of substrate are employed to ensure a rapid reaction. The reaction is allowed to go to completion and the amount of product formed is estimated by some specific chemical or physical method.
2. Kinetic method: When the enzyme concentration is fixed, the reaction rate can be made proportional to substrate, inhibitors, activators, etc. (provided K_m, K_i, or $K_A \leq 0.1$), and in this way these compounds can be estimated from the initial reaction rate of the enzyme.

In determining substrate concentration, it is obvious from the Michaelis-Menten relationships that [S] must be less than K_m in order for the reaction to be approximately first order with respect to substrate. Analyses can be performed when [S] $\leq 0.2 K_m$ [41].

VIII. ENZYMES IN FOOD PROCESSING [43,83,106,107,111,118]

The food industry is one of the largest users of industrial enzymes. In 1969, the United States fermentation industry produced 64 million dollars worth of enzymes of which the food industry used 30%. In general, enzymes are used in the food industry for upgrading quality and byproduct utilization, for preparing synthetic foods, for achieving higher rates and levels of extractions, for improving flavor, and for stabilizing food quality.

Enzymes that are produced for the food industry are rather crude by biochemical standards. Most enzyme preparations contain a predominating enzyme as well as other enzymes.

The advantages of using enzymes for food processing include: (1) they are natural, nontoxic substances; (2) they catalyze a given reaction without causing unwanted side reactions; (3) they are active under very mild conditions of temperature and pH; (4) they are active at low concentrations; (5) the rate of reaction can be controlled by adjusting temperature, pH, and the amount of enzyme employed; and (6) they can be inactivated after the reaction has proceeded to the desired extent.

Table 6-2 lists most of the common enzymes either currently employed or of potential value in food systems. Inspection of the list indicates that the total number of enzymes of value to the food industry is rather limited, considering the thousands of enzymes that have been studied. The overwhelming majority of enzymes employed by the food industry are hydrolases, consisting chiefly of carbohydrases followed by proteases, lipases, and esterases. A few oxidoreductases are of value to food processing, but only one isomerase and one transferase are of potential value to the industry. Also, it is evident that only a few animal and plant enzymes are in use, whereas the majority of enzymes are of microbial origin.

In using enzymes for food modification, one should know the type of substrate one wants to modify and should be aware that extraneous enzymes in the preparation may result in deleterious effects. The concentration of enzyme needed depends on the time available, pH, the operating temperature, and the degree of conversion desired. In most instances the substrate is present in excess so that the enzyme becomes the rate-limiting factor. Because of the enzyme-time relationship, the time required to complete a process is then inversely proportional to the amount of enzyme used. Thus, if twice as much enzyme is used, the processing time should be halved. Usually, the amount of enzyme preparation used will be in the range of 0.01-0.2% based on the substrate.

The two major environmental factors that must be considered are pH and temperature. The activity of the enzyme at the pH of the food must be considered, and the possibility of inactivation of enzymes at extremes in pH must be kept in mind. The best temperature for an enzyme reaction depends on the time available for the reaction, the amount of enzyme that can be afforded, and the temperature sensitivity of the enzyme and the food. Usually, the process is run at the highest temperature consistent with good final quality. The reaction rate approximately doubles for every 10° rise in temperature until a maximum, termed the "temperature optimum," is reached.

Enzymes require moisture for activity, and enzymic reactions are usually carried out at moisture levels ranging from 50 to 95%. More dilute solutions make the reaction inefficient and expensive. However, in some cases, such as chillproofing beer, one must work with dilute solutions of substrate.

TABLE 6-2

Enzymes of Significance in Food Processing

Enzyme	Reaction	Use or potential use
Isomerase		
Glucose isomerase	D-Glucose $\rightleftharpoons$ D-fructose	For production of fructose-containing syrups
Transferase		
O-Methyl transferase	O-Dihydroxy phenols $\longrightarrow$ O-methoxyl phenol	Block oxidation of O-phenols by phenolase to inhibit browning
Oxidoreductases		
Lipoxygenase	cis,cis-1,4-pentadiene unsaturated fatty acids $+ O_2 \longrightarrow$ Fatty acid hydroperoxide	Improve dough and flavor of bread; bleach bread to produce white crumb
Diacetyl reductase	Diacetyl + NADH $\longrightarrow$ acetoin	Reduce concentrations of diacetyl in beer
Glucose oxidase	β-D-Glucose + $O_2 \longrightarrow$ D-glucono-δ-lactone + H_2O_2	Remove glucose and oxygen from foods
Catalase	$H_2O_2 + H_2O_2 \longrightarrow O_2 + 2 H_2O$	Destroy hydrogen peroxide used for food sterilization. Used to remove H_2O_2 from glucose oxidase reaction
Hydrolases		
1. α-Amylase	1. Internal random hydrolysis	1. Starch liquefaction
2. β-Amylase	2. Successive maltose units removed	2. Produce maltose in bread fermentations and in high-maltose syrups
3. Glucoamylase	3. Successive glucose units removed	3. Produce glucose from starch

Hydrolyze α-1,4-glucan links in starch

Enzyme	Reaction	Use
Invertase	Sucrose + H$_2$O ⟶ α-D-glucose + β-D-fructose	Produce invert sugar for candies, confections, etc.
Lactase	Lactose + H$_2$O ⟶ α-D-glucose + β-D-galactose	Hydrolyze lactose in dairy products
Cellulase complex	Hydrolyze β-1,4-glucan links in cellulose	Convert cellulose to glucose
Pectic enzyme complex	Hydrolyze pectin to pectic acid, intermediate uronides, galacturonic acid, and 4-deoxy-5-ketogalacturonic acid	Clarify fruit juices and wines; degrade fruit pulp and increase extractability of juices
Pullulanase	α-D-1,6 linkages ⟶ α-D-1,4-oligosaccharides susceptible to amylase of starch	Used with α- and β-amylases to effect high-maltose conversion of starch; increase fermentable sugars in brewing
Pentosanases	Pentosans ⟶ D-xylose + L-arabinose	Decrease bread staling
Hemicellulases	D-Xylans ⟶ Xylooligosaccharides + D-xylose + L-arabinose	Reduce viscosity of coffee concentrates
β-Glucanases	β-Glucans ⟶ β-D-glucose	Facilitate filtration of barley wort in brewing with barley
Naringinase	Naringin ⟶ naringenin + rhamnose + glucose	Debitter citrus fruit products
Stachyase	Stachyose ⟶ monosaccharides Rafinnose	Reduce flatulence due to starchyose and rafinnose in leguminous products

TABLE 6-2 (Continued)

1. Papain 2. Ficin 3. Bromelain 4. Fungal proteases 5. Bacterial proteases 6. Pepsin 7. Rennin (chymosin) 8. Microbial rennets 9. Chymotrypsin 10. Trypsin 11. Collagenase 12. Elastase	Proteolytic enzymes that hydrolyze a variety of peptide bonds	Proteases 1, 2, 3, 4, and 5 used to tenderize meat; 1, 2, 3, 4, 5, and 6 can chill-proof beer; 6, 7, and 8 coagulate milk for cheese manufacture; 4 used to modify flour for baking; 10 retards oxidized flavor in milk; 1, 11, and 12 soften and tenderize connective tissues of meats; selected proteases produce protein hydrolyseates used for condiments; 6 and 9 used to prepare "plasteins" (resynthesized protein hydrolyzates)
Pregastric esterases	Milk fat + $H_2O \longrightarrow$ fatty acids + glycerol + partial glycerides	Develop flavor in Italian cheese and flavor concentrates for candy and baking industries
Lipases	Triglycerides + $H_2O \longrightarrow$ fatty acids + partial glycerides + glycerol	Retard staling of bread; enhance whipping properties of egg whites; develop cheese flavor
Ribonucleases	Ribonucleic acids $\longrightarrow$ nucleotides	$5'$-Nucleotides are flavor enhancers

It is important to remember that such factors as time, substrate and enzyme concentrations, pH, and temperature are interrelated. Thus, the variation of a parameter often affects the enzymic response to the other factors.

Microbial enzymes for food applications are actually derived from few sources. Table 6-3 lists the microorganisms generally recognized as safe (GRAS) by the FDA, and the major enzymes associated with them. In addition to the enzymes produced by GRAS microorganisms, enzymes from other microorganisms are sometimes permitted if a special request is made to the FDA.

There are numerous advantages to obtaining enzymes from microorganisms: (1) microorganisms are very versatile, and it is theoretically possible to find a microorganism to produce any enzyme; (2) microorganisms can be altered by mutations or genetic engineering to produce a greater quantity of enzyme or different enzymes; (3) recovery of enzymes is often easy since many microbial enzymes are extracellular; (4) readily available raw materials are used to produce microbial enzymes; and (5) microorganisms have a very high rate of growth and enzyme production.

TABLE 6-3

Enzymes Prepared from GRAS Organisms[a]

Organism	Resulting Enzyme
Bacillus subtilis	Amylase (high temperature)
	Protease, neutral
	Protease, alkaline
Aspergillus oryzae, Aspergillus niger	Amylase
	Glucamylase
	Protease
	Acid protease
	Catalase
	Glucose oxidase
	Lipase
	Anthocyanase
	Naringinase
	Cellulase
	Hemicellulase
	Pentosanase
	Pectinase
Saccharomyces cerevisiae	Invertase
Saccharomyces fragilis	Lactase

[a]Reprinted from Ref. [43], p. 122, by courtesy of Arlington Publ. Co.

IX. IMMOBILIZED ENZYMES [121]

Ordinarily, after a food process is completed, the added soluble enzymes are inactivated with heat or allowed to continue their activity to develop desirable flavor and texture. Also, in analytical applications, the enzyme is used once for a single analysis. Recent developments in enzyme technology have led to the preparation of immobilized enzymes which in principle can be used repeatedly in batch operations or on a continuous basis.

An immobilized enzyme is chemically or physically restricted in movement so that it can be physically reclaimed from the reaction medium. The major reasons that a food scientist may be interested in immobilizing enzymes include such operational advantages as reuseability, possibility of improved batch or continuous operational modes, rapid termination of reactions, controlled product formation, greater variety of engineering designs for continuous processes, and possible greater efficiency in consecutive multistep reactions. Furthermore, it may be possible to selectively modify the properties of the enzyme by immobilization.

There are two broad classes of immobilization, physical and chemical. Chemical methods of immobilization include any that involve the formation of at least one covalent bond between residues of an enzyme and the functionalized, water-insoluble polymer or between two or more enzyme molecules. Chemical methods are essentially irreversible in that the original enzyme cannot be regenerated or recovered. Physical methods include means for immobilizing enzymes that do not involve the formation of covalent bonds. For example, enzymes can be adsorbed on insoluble matrices, entrapped in gels or microcapsules, and contained within special semipermeable membranes. In principle, the physical immobilization of enzymes is completely reversible.

Many methods of enzyme immobilization require the use of noxious chemicals. Furthermore, use of immobilized enzymes in continuous processing of foods which support microbial growth may present public health problems. Consequently, the food scientist must be aware of possible restrictions on the use of some of these systems for food processing by the Federal Food and Drug Administration.

The user of immobilized enzymes should also be aware that immobilization of an enzyme often affects such properties of an enzyme as activity, stability, specificity, pH optimum, and Michaelis-Menten constant.

A. Immobilized Enzymes in Food Processing

Table 6-4 lists enzymes which have been immobilized and are of potential value in food processing.

B. Immobilized Enzymes in Food Analysis

Enzyme immobilization, whereby the enzyme can be used repeatedly or continuously, can allow for the automation of analytical procedures. For example, enzymes have been immobilized on the inner surface of nylon tubing to develop a flow system for analyses. In addition, enzymes can be immobilized on the tip of conventional ion-selective electrodes or oxygen-sensing electrodes to measure product

TABLE 6-4

Immobilized Enzymes of Potential Value in Food Processing

Enzyme	Process	Method of immobilization[a]
Glucose oxidase	a. Deoxygenate foods b. Desugar eggs	co; cr; ad; le
Catalase	Cold sterilization of milk	co; cr; ad; le; mi
Lipase	Develop flavors with milkfat	co; ad; mi
α-Amylase	Starch liquefaction	co; cr; ad; le; ul
β-Amylase	High-maltose syrups	co; ad; le; ul
Glucoamylase	Production of glucose from starch	co; ad; ul
Pullulanase	Starch debranching in conversion of starch	ul
β-Galactosidase	Hydrolyze lactose in dairy products	co; cr; ad
Invertase	Hydrolyze sucrose for invert sugar and confections	co; ad
Naringinase	Debitter citrus juices	co
Proteases	Coagulation of milk, chillproof beer, prepare protein hydrolyzates	co; cr; ad; le; ul
Aminoacylase	Resolution of D- and L-amino acids	co; ad
Glucose isomerase	Production of fructose from glucose	co; ad

[a]co, covalent; cr, crosslinked; ad, adsorbed; le, lattice entrapped; ul, ultra-filtration membranes; mi, microencapsulated.

or the utilization of oxygen due to enzymic activity. The principal of these "enzyme electrodes" has been applied to analyses of a variety of substrates, including glucose, urea, L- and D-amino acids, glutamine, and asparagine.

X. ENZYME INHIBITORS [3,24,34,60,63,81,83,99,113]

A variety of naturally occurring enzyme inhibitors are found in plant and animal tissues. The food scientist is interested in the relationship of enzyme inhibitors to postharvest physiology of plants. He is also concerned about the nutritional implications of inhibitors.

Enzyme inhibitors can be grouped into two main categories, plant and animal.

A. Enzyme Inhibitors in Plant Tissues

Plant enzyme inhibitors can be conveniently divided into those that inhibit mammalian enzymes and those that act on plant enzymes. The former category is of nutritional significance, whereas the latter group has implications in the postharvest
physiology of plants.

1. INHIBITORS OF MAMMALIAM ENZYMES

The principal enzyme inhibitors from plants are those which inhibit mannalian proteolytic enzymes. Of all the inhibitors, soybean trypsin inhibitors have been
studied the most.

Most proteolytic enzyme inhibitors are active against trypsin, although they
also tend to inhibit related enzymes, such as chymotrypsin. Proteinase inhibitors
are found in virtually all the Leguminosae; in grains, such as wheat, rice, and
corn; and in potatoes and beet roots. Because of the importance of legumes, cereals, and potatoes in world nutrition, much research has developed regarding the
nutritional significance of proteinase inhibitors.

The first known enzyme inhibitor from plants was a protein discovered in soybeans in 1944. Since then, approximately eight proteinaceous protease inhibitors
have been observed in soybeans. However, the inhibitors that have received the
greatest attention are the Kunitz inhibitor and the Bowman-Birk inhibitor. The
purified Kunitz inhibitor retains its activity from pH 1 to 12 below 30°C. It is reversibly denatured by short heating to 80°C and irreversibly denatured by heating
to 90°C. Trypsins of various species, including humans are inhibited by the Kunitz
inhibitor. The Bowman-Birk inhibitor appears to be more stable to denaturation
than the Kunitz inhibitor. There is no loss of activity when it is heated in the dry
state at 105°C or in 0.02% aqueous solution for 10 min at 100°C. Autoclaving for
20 min at 15-lb pressure destroys its activity. The inhibitor is stable to acid (pH
1.5, 2 hr, 37°C) and to peptic and pronase digestion. It inhibits the proteolytic
and esterolytic activities of trypsin and chymotrypsin.

2. DISTRIBUTION OF INHIBITORS IN PLANT TISSUES

Most of the protease inhibitors have been found in the seeds of various plants; however, they are not restricted to this part of the plant. For example, in sweet potato, a trypsin inhibitor is found in the tuber as well as in the leaves.

In the white potato, the tuber and the young leaves are rich in a chymotrypsin
inhibitor. However, in the double bean and field bean, trypsin inhibitors are distributed throughout all parts of the germinating seed and growing plant, but the
levels depend on the stage of growth. Apparently, trypsin inhibitors are absent
from leaves, stems, and pods of soybean. This appears to be true as well for the
navy bean. Within the cotyledons of soybean, chick pea, and kidney bean the
trypsin inhibitors seem to be concentrated in the outer part of the cotyledon mass.
In wheat, a trypsin inhibitor is found in the cotyledon as well as in the germ. In
addition, a papain inhibitor is evident in the germ of soybean, haricot, broad bean,
and garden pea.

3. NUTRITIONAL SIGNIFICANCE OF PROTEINASE INHIBITORS

As early as 1917, Osborne and Mendel observed that unless soybeans were cooked for several hours, they would not support the growth of rats, an observation since extended to a variety of experimental animals.

Supplementation of unheated soybean meal with methionine or cystine improves protein utilization to essentially the same extent as proper heating. However, heated soybean meal plus methionine has even greater nutritive value. Methionine is the most limiting amino acid for soybeans, and it has been observed that feeding proteins containing lysine, arginine, isoleucine, or tryptophan at limiting levels in the presence of raw soybean meal results in deficiencies of these amino acids. Thus, it appears there is general interference with protein digestion by the inhibitors.

However, there is compelling evidence to indicate that the growth-retarding effect of trypsin inhibitor may have little to do with inhibition of protein digestion in the intestines, at least in rodents. Active antitryptic preparations have been shown to inhibit the growth of rodents when incorporated into diets containing predigested proteins or free amino acids. In contrast to their affect in chicks, raw soybeans or trypsin inhibitor do not depress proteolytic activity in the intestinal tract of rats and mice. How, then, does trypsin inhibitor retard the growth of rats without affecting intestinal proteolysis and also increase the requirement for methionine?

The feeding of raw soybeans to chicks and rats also results in pancreatic hypertrophy. Thus the growth depression resulting from trypsin inhibitor may be due to endogenous loss of essential amino acids via secretions of a hyperactive pancreas responding to the trypsin inhibitor. It has also been postulated that soybean trypsin inhibitors are somehow directly involved in the metabolism of methionine and thus may be responsible for the apparent methionine deficiency.

Other growth inhibitors may also be present in raw soybeans. For example, it has been estimated that only 30 and 60% of the decrease in the growth rate and protein efficiency, respectively, of raw soybeans fed to rats can be accounted for by the trypsin inhibitor.

4. EFFECT OF HEAT ON TRYPSIN INHIBITOR

Most of the plant proteinase inhibitors are destroyed by heat, with a concomitant increase in the nutritive value of the protein. Simple cooking is often sufficient to inactivate trypsin inhibitors.

The destruction of trypsin inhibitors is a function of temperature, duration of heating, particle size, and moisture conditions; with high temperatures, long heating, reduced particle size, and increased moisture levels leading to greater destruction of trypsin inhibitors. However, excessive heating has a detrimental effect on the nutritional quality of the protein, so a balance must be struck to optimize the heat treatment.

B. Enzyme Inhibitors in Animal Tissues

Proteolytic enzyme inhibitors have been reported in a variety of body secretions, beef pancreas, blood, and egg whites from various avian species.

There are two principal inhibitors of proteinase activity in egg whites, ovomucoid and ovoinhibitor. Purified chicken ovomucoid possesses unusual stability to heat. For example, between pH 3 and 7 after 30 min at 80°C, more than 90% of the activity remains. Ovomucoid complexes porcine, ovine, and bovine trypsins in a 1:1 ratio; however, it has no inhibitory activity on human trypsin. Purified chicken ovoinhibitor reacts with trypsins and chymotrypsins of bovine and avian origin. Ovoinhibitor is quite stable in acid solution, with 93-95% retention of activity after 15 min at 90°C and pH 3 or 5. However, at pH 7 its activity is lost in 15 min at 90°C.

Apparently the proteinase inhibitors of egg whites are of limited nutritional significance. Ordinary cooking does not destroy the antitryptic activity of raw egg white. Yet the feeding of commercial egg white, raw or heated, in the presence of added ovomucoid of known antitrypsin activity has no effect on nitrogen retention by humans. Furthermore, in young rats, the feeding of purified trypsin inhibitor from egg white at a level of 2.5% in a casein diet has no effect on growth or protein efficiency. The dog, however, appears to be sensitive to the antitryptic factors in egg whites.

C. Physiological Significance of Enzyme Inhibitors

1. OVOMUCOID AND OVOINHIBITOR

None of the inhibitors in egg white have been shown to inhibit naturally occurring proteolytic enzymes in egg white. Possibly, they serve some function during embryological development, or they serve an antimicrobial or antiviral function.

2. PLANT ENZYME INHIBITORS

The inhibition of enzymes by endogenous proteins may represent a regulatory mechanism in plants. For example, potato invertase inhibitor was one of the first inhibitors discovered to act on endogenous enzymes and one of the most extensively studied. The invertase system is also of economic importance in the relationship between sugar accumulation in stored tubers and processing quality. The concentration of the invertase inhibitor increases during tuber growth and is in excess over invertase so that enzymic activity is undetectable. Thus, mature tubers are known to contain a low level of invertase relative to a large excess of invertase inhibitor. During curing and storage at warm temperature, the total invertase increases but the excess inhibitor persists. However, when the potatoes are placed in cold storage, invertase activity increases dramatically until it exceeds the inhibitor. The invertase converts sucrose to reducing sugars, which rapidly accumulate until a maximum is reached after several weeks. Subsequently, invertase activity decreases and an excess of invertase inhibitor develops. The changes in invertase, invertase inhibitor, and reducing sugars involve a reversible system which shifts when the tubers are subjected to alternate cold and warm storage.

3. RIPENING OF FRUITS

Polygalacturonase, which is involved in the degradation of pectin in ripening fruits, is inhibited by a polygalacturonase inhibitor. Thus, the degradation of the polygalacturonase inhibitor may trigger polygalacturonase activity in fruits, such as avacados, during ripening.

Selection of plant varieties based on amount of enzyme inhibitors elaborated may lead to improved storage properties and allow control of ripening. A potential application in food processing may be the addition of isolated inhibitors to fresh products to control degradative reactions.

XI. MODIFICATION OF FOOD BY ENDOGENOUS ENZYMES

Since foods are complex biological materials, they are subject to a wide variety of modifying agents. Among these are microorganisms that cause undesirable spoilage or beneficial fermentations; endogenous chemicals that undergo changes, such as autoxidation; and endogenous enzymes that cause numerous desirable and undesirable changes. Enzymic alterations can encompass entire areas of food science, as the postharvest physiology of plants and the postmortem physiology of animal tissues. For example, the ripening of fruits or the conversion of muscle to meat are the results of complex biochemical changes mediated by enzymes. The biochemical reactions involved in these processes are discussed in Chapters 13 and 15 and in specialized texts [33,50,82], so it is not appropriate to deal with them here. Considerations here are limited to those endogenous enzymes which are of predominant interest to the food scientist in terms of changes in color, texture, flavor, and nutritive value of foods. Thus the discussion is limited largely to the activities of hydrolases and oxidoreductases, and only the more important ones are considered in detail.

A. Enzymic Browning [33,62,78,80,83]

Basically, there are four types of browning reactions in foods: Maillard, caramelization, ascorbic acid oxidation, and phenolase browning. The former three are nonenzymic in nature (oxidation of ascorbic acid is sometimes catalyzed by enzymes) and are not considered further here. Phenolase or enzymic browning (enzyme-catalyzed oxidative browning) is of commercial significance, particularly in plant tissues, and it is dealt with in detail.

Normally, the natural phenolic substrates are separated from phenolase in intact tissue and browning does not occur. Enzymic browning can be observed on the cut surfaces of light colored fruits and vegetables, such as apples, bananas, and potatoes. Exposure of the cut surface to air results in rapid browning due to the enzymic oxidation of phenols to orthoquinones, which in turn rapidly polymerize to form brown pigments or melanins. The enzyme which catalyzes this oxidation is commonly known as phenolase, polyphenol oxidase, tyrosinase, or catecholase. The Enzyme Commission designates the enzyme as o-diphenol: oxygen oxidoreductase, E.C.1.10.3.1. Thus, the enzyme is an oxidoreductase in which the phenol is oxidized and oxygen serves as a hydrogen acceptor.

Phenolase enzymes contain copper as a prosthetic group. Consequently, enzymic activity is evident when oxygen and copper are present. Thus, if damage to plant tissue is sufficient and oxygen is present, browning occurs. Such operations as cutting, peeling, and bruising are sufficient to cause enzymic browning.

Phenolase catalyzes two types of reactions, as illustrated in Figure 6-13: hydroxylation (A) (referred to as phenol hydroxylase or cresolase activity), and oxidation (B) (referred to as polyphenol oxidase or catecholase activity). The first reaction results in ortho hydroxylation of a phenol and the second in oxidation of the diphenol to an orthoquinone. If tyrosine is the substrate (Fig. 6-13), phenolase catalyzes its hydroxylation to dopa; and subsequently catalyzes oxidation of dopa to dopa quinone.

The remaining portions of the reaction sequence involve nonenzymic oxidations and ultimate polymerization of indole-5,6-quinone to brown melanin pigments. Moreover, the melanins can interact with proteins to form complexes. Hydroxylation of monophenols is the slow or rate-determining step. Consequently, monophenols undergo the slower hydroxylation reaction before oxidation to orthoquinone. Furthermore, there are some phenolase enzymes, such as those in tea, tobacco, and sweet potatoes, that do not hydroxylate monophenols. However, those from mushroom and potato perform both functions.

Although tyrosine is a major substrate for certain phenolases, other phenolic compounds of fruit, such as caffeic acid, protocatechuic acid, and chlorogenic acid, also serve as substrates. As shown in Figure 6-14, these latter compounds are o-diphenols that are readily attacked by the catecholase component of phenolase. However, as is illustrated in Table 6-5, phenolase does not necessarily attack these substrates at the same rate. Chlorogenic acid is oxidized at 67% the rate of catechol, caffeic acid at only 41% the rate of catechol, and protocatechuic acid is not oxidized at all.

In general, phenolase is active between pH 5 and 7 and does not have a very sharp pH optimum. At lower pH values of approximately 3 the enzyme is irreversibly inactivated. Furthermore, reagents which complex or remove the copper from the enzyme also inactivate it.

1. CONTROL OF ENZYMIC BROWNING

For the most part, phenolase activity in fruits and vegetables is undesirable because of the browning reaction during processing. Consequently, a variety of methods have been developed to inhibit enzymic browning. The methods are predicated on eliminating from the reaction one or more of its essential components, that is, oxygen, enzyme, copper, or substrate.

Heat treatments, or the application of sulfur dioxide or sulfites, are commonly used methods of inactivating phenolase. Phenolase activity can be inhibited by the addition of sufficient amounts of acidulants, such as citric, malic, or phosphoric acids to yield a pH of 3 or lower. Oxygen can be excluded from the reaction site by such methods as vacuumization or immersing the plant tissues in a brine or syrup. Phenolic substrates can be protected from oxidation by reaction with borate salts, but these are not approved for food use. Another promising way to inactivate the substrate involves antiphenolase enzymes. Figure 6-15 describes two enzyme systems that modify the orthophenolic substrates so that they are no longer

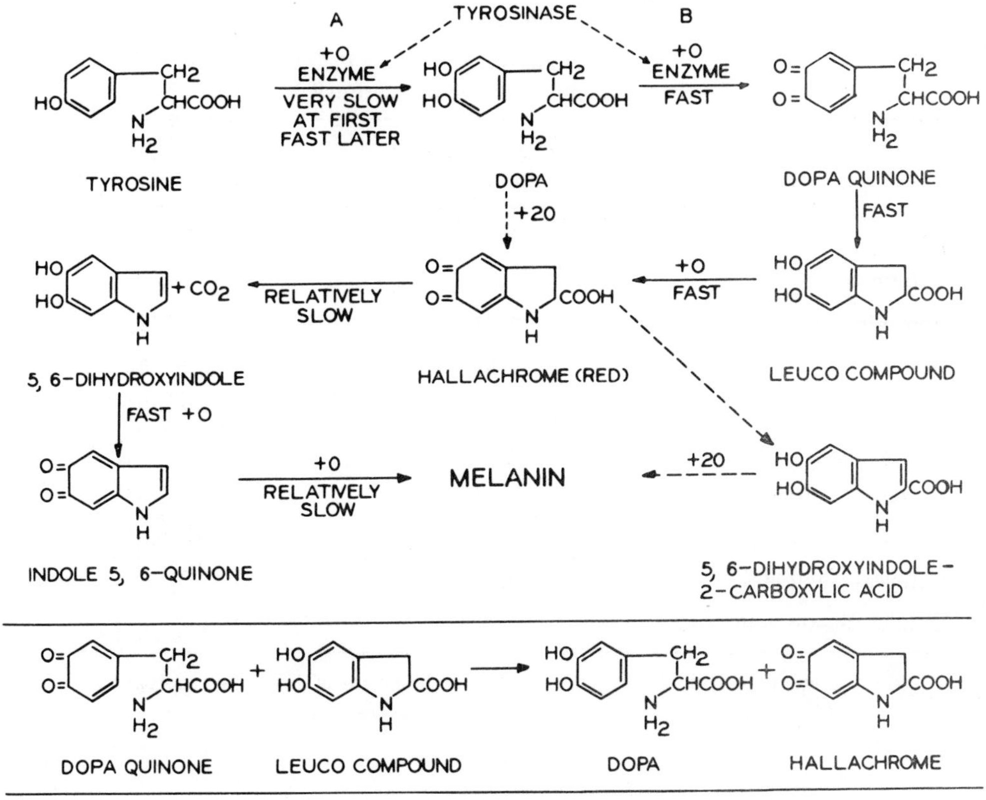

FIG. 6-13. The formation of melanin pigments resulting from the oxidation of tyrosine by phenolase. Reprinted from Ref. [62], p. 95, by courtesy of the American Physiological Society.

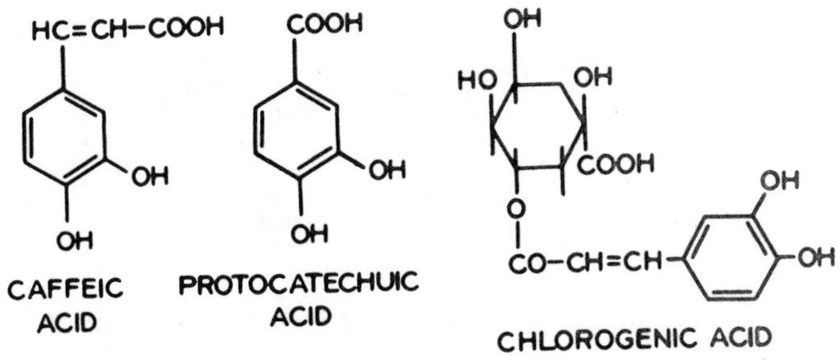

FIG. 6-14. Some o-diphenols that serve as substrates for phenolase.

TABLE 6-5

Action of Phenolase from Cling Peaches
on Various Phenolic Substrates[a]

Substrate	Concentration at pH 6.2 (M)	Relative activity (%)
Catechol	0.01	100
Caffeic acid	0.01	41
Dopamine	0.01	34
Quinic acid	0.01	5
Shikimic acid	0.01	2
Ferulic acid	0.01	0
Protocatechuic acid	0.01	0
D-Catechin	0.003	250
Chlorogenic acid	0.003	67
Isochlorogenic acid	0.003	0

[a]Reprinted from Ref. [65], by courtesy of Institute of Food Technologists.

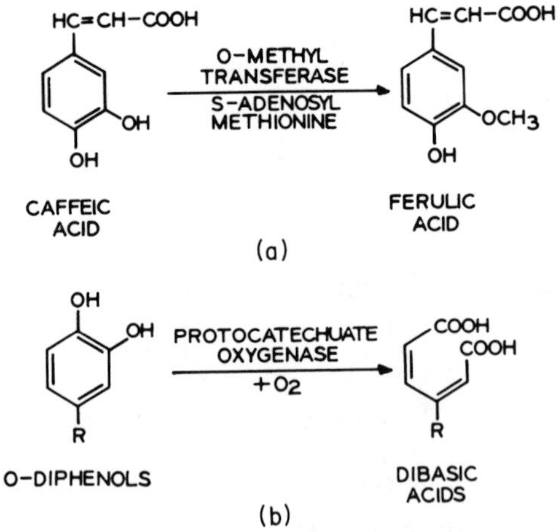

FIG. 6-15. Two enzyme systems that modify phenolic substrates to inhibit phenolase activity.

subject to oxidation and subsequent polymerization. An o-methyl transferase in the presence of a methyl donor methylates the orthophenols, as illustrated for caffeic acid (Fig. 6-15a). In this case, ferulic acid is not oxidized by the polyphenol oxidase.

A second enzyme system which can modify the substrate is protocatechuate oxygenase, which modifies o-diphenols to yield a dibasic acid which is no longer susceptible to oxidation and polymerization (Fig. 6-15b). The disadvantage of both enzymes is that they require alkaline conditions for activity and this limits their use in fruit processing. However, it may be possible to obtain similar enzymes with a lower optimum pH.

B. Pectic Enzymes [27,50,79,83,87]

Pectin is a complex carbohydrate polymer which serves a structural role in plants. The major building blocks of pectin are units of galacturonic acid linked by α-1,4-glycosidic bonds. Approximately two-thirds of the carboxylic acid groups are esterified with methanol.

Listed in Table 6-6 are a variety of enzymes that attack the pectin molecule. A number of microorganisms elaborate these enzymes and serve as a source of commercial enzymes used for clarifying fruit juices. In addition, microbial plant pathogens generally produce pectic enzymes which facilitate invasion of the plant tissue. Undoubtedly, microbial spoilage of fruits and vegetables involves the activity of pectic enzymes. Plant tissues, of course, contain endogenous pectic enzymes that are important in ripening and in subsequent processing.

Figure 6-16 gives an indication of the specificities of the various pectic enzymes. Pectinmethylesterase (PE) cleaves the methyl ester, whereas polygalacturonase

TABLE 6-6

Designations of Pectic Enzymes[a]

Enzymes acting on pectin
  Pectin methyl esterase (PE)
  Polymethylgalacturonases (PMG)
    Endo-PMG (acid and alkaline)
    Exo-PMG
  Pectin transeliminase (PTE)
    Endo-PTE
    Exo-PTE

Enzymes acting on pectic acid

Polygalacturonase (PG)
  Endo-PG
  Exo-PG
  Pectic acid transeliminase (PATE)
    Endo-PATE
    Exo-PATE

---

[a]Reprinted from Ref. [83], p. 75, by courtesy of Academic Press.

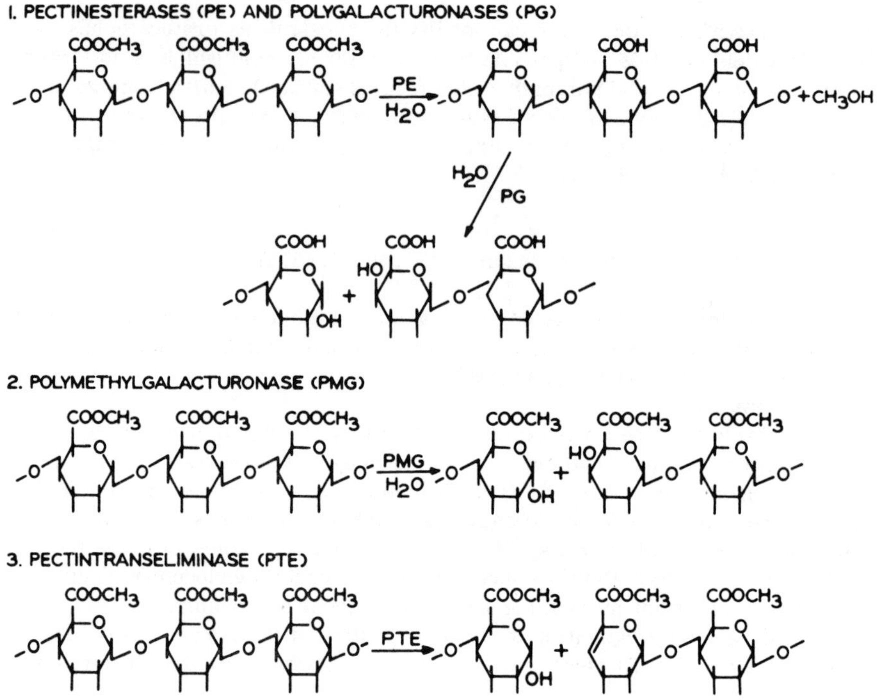

I. PECTINESTERASES (PE) AND POLYGALACTURONASES (PG)

2. POLYMETHYLGALACTURONASE (PMG)

3. PECTINTRANSELIMINASE (PTE)

FIG. 6-16. Enzymic degradation of pectin. Reprinted from Ref. [54], p. 788, by courtesy of the American Chemical Society.

(PG) acts on the resultant pectic acid. There also exist (Table 6-6) an endo-PG, which attacks the interior of pectic acid, and an exo-PG, which cleaves a galacturonic acid residue from the nonreducing terminus of pectic acid. In addition, there are endo- and exo- polymethylgalacturonases which hydrolyze pectin without prior demethylation. Recent additions to the pectic enzyme family are the trans-eliminases. The action of these enzymes either on pectic acid (PATE) or pectin (PTE) results in the formation of unsaturated derivatives of galacturonic acid.

Pectic enzymes are of interest to the food scientist for a variety of reasons, including their roles in ripening of fruit, in maintenance of viscosity in processing fruit products, and in textural changes [4,64,108].

C. Amylases [27,83,100]

The enzymes that hydrolyze starch are termed "amylases." Two amylases have been studied in greatest detail, α- and β-amylase. α-Amylase, an endo-enzyme, hydrolyzes α-1,4-glucan linkages in an apparently random manner. The random attack of α-amylase on amylose in solution results in a rapid decrease of viscosity, the loss of ability to stain with iodine, and an increase in reducing power due to generation of reducing groups. The decrease in viscosity is proportionately greater than the increase in reducing groups since α-amylase attacks interior bonds. α-Amylase attacks amylopectin in a similar fashion; however, the α-1,6 branch points are not hydrolyzed, and a small amount of panose, the trisaccharide containing these α-1,6 linkages, is formed. α-Amylase is often referred to as the "liquefying" enzyme because of its rapid action in reducing the viscosity of starch solutions. Treatment of amylose or amylo pectin with α-amylase results in a mixture of maltose, glucose, and also some panose if the reaction continues for a long period.

β-Amylase is an exo-enzyme; i.e., it attacks only the end units of starch chains. More specifically, β-amylase removes maltose units from the nonreducing end of the starch chain by hydrolyzing alternate glycosidic linkages. Since maltose increases the sweetness of the starch solution, β-amylase is referred to as a "saccharifying" enzyme. The β in β-amylase refers to the fact that there is an inversion of the α-1,4 linkage in starch to the β configuration. The occasional 1,3 linkages in amylose and the 1,6 bonds in amylopectin are not attacked by β-amylase, resulting in incomplete degradation of the starch. If a debranching enzyme is present to cleave these bonds, β-amylase activity continues. With amylopectin, β-amylase activity stops two to three glucose units from the branch point, and the residual molecules are referred to as "limit dextrins." β-Amylases are known to occur only in vegetable tissues.

Amylases are important in fruit ripening, potato processing, production of corn syrup and corn sugar, and bread making.

D. Cathepsins [72,119]

Cathepsins are proteinases that exist intracellularly in animal tissue and are active at acidic pH values. These enzymes are located in the lysosomal fraction of the cell and are thus distinguished from proteolytic enzymes, such as trypsin and chymotrypsin, which are secreted by cells.

Five cathepsins have been observed, and these are designated by the letters A, B, C, D, and E. In addition, a catheptic carboxypeptidase has been isolated.

Cathepsins may be involved in changes observed during the aging of meats [36]; however extensive proteolysis in the aging of meats has not been observed [77,119].

E. Myosin ATPase [68,73]

This enzyme apparently plays a key role in cold shortening and thaw rigor of muscle, and these occurrences affect the tenderness and water-holding capacity of the resulting meat. Apparently the postmortem shortening of muscle proceeds by a mechanism similar to normal muscle contraction. Both cold and thaw shortening appear to be attributable to the inability of the sarcoplasmic reticulum (a very fine network of tubules throughout the muscle) to retain calcium ions. The freed calcium ions diffuse to the contractile proteins, where they release adenosine triphosphate (ATP) from its inert complex with magnesium and also stimulate myosin ATPase. The resultant hydrolysis of ATP furnishes the energy necessary for muscle contraction.

F. Flavor Enzymes [45,48,58,83,89,92,105]

The development of flavor compounds, particularly in fruits and vegetables, has
been linked to enzymic conversion of flavor precursors. Given in Table 6-7 are
the classes of flavor-forming mechanisms in food systems. The first three mechanisms require the direct or indirect activity of enzymes. Examples of each of
these mechanisms are given in the following discussion.

1. BIOSYNTHETIC

The typical flavor of such fruits as bananas, apples, and pears does not arise during growth and normally is not present at the time of harvest. Flavors in these
fruits are developed during a short ripening period related to the climacteric rise
in respiration. During the preclimacteric period small amounts of ethylene, the
"ripening hormone," are released to stimulate the biosynthetic development of
flavor.

   The development of flavor in bananas is a typical biosynthetic process and it
has been studied in some detail. The principal flavor precursors in bananas are
certain of the nonpolar amino acids and fatty acids. Postclimacteric banana tissue
converts L-leucine into 3-methyl-1-butanol, 3-methylbutyl esters, 3-methyl buty-
rates, and 2-ketoisocaproate. In an analogous fashion, L-valine is converted into

TABLE 6-7

Classes of Flavor-Forming Mechanisms in Food Systems[a]

Class	Description	Examples
I. Biosynthetic	Flavor constituents formed directly by bio-synthetic processes	Flavors based on terpen-oid and ester compounds, such as mint, citrus, muskmelon, pepper, banana
II. Direct enzymic	Flavor constituents formed by enzymes act-ing on specific flavor precursors	Formation of onion flavor by action of allinase on sulfoxides
III. Oxidative (indirect enzymic)	Flavor constituents formed by oxidation of flavor precursors by enzymically formed oxi-dizing agents	Flavors characterized by presence of carbonyl and acid compounds, such as tea (see text for addi-tional details)
IV. Pyrolytic	Flavor constituents formed from precursors by a heating or baking treatment	Flavors characterized by presence of pyrazines (coffee, chocolate, etc.) furans (bread), etc.

[a]Reprinted from Ref. [89], p. 583, by courtesy of American Chemical Society.

2-methyl-1-propanol, 2-methyl propyl acetate, 2-methyl propionic acid, and 2-ketoisovaleric acid. In addition, L-phenylalanine apparently serves as a precursor for β-phenylethanol and phenolic ethers, such as eugenol and eugenol methyl ether. In this latter case, enzymes which are thought to be involved in the transformations include phenylalanine ammonia lyase, cinnamic acid-4-hydroxylase, phenolase, and methyltransferase.

Most unripe fruits produce a variety of fatty acids from C_1 to C_{20}. During ripening, short-chain fatty acids, such as acetic, butyric, hexanoic, and decanoic, are converted to a wide variety of flavorful, aromatic esters, alcohols, and acids. Shown in Figure 6-17 is a reaction scheme for the conversion of octanoic acid into esters.

2. DIRECT ENZYMIC

This flavor-forming mechanism involves the direct action of a single enzyme on a precursor to directly generate a flavor. As indicated in Table 6-7 this mechanism is amply demonstrated by the formation of onion and cabbage flavors.

a. Cabbage Family. Cabbage, mustard, horseradish, and watercress are members of the Crucifera, the flavor of which depends largely upon the generation of mustard oils (isothiocyanates). As shown below, mustard oils are produced by the action of enzymes, thioglycosidases, on thioglycosides, such as sinigrin or sinalbin.

$$R\text{-}C\begin{matrix} \diagup S\text{-}C_6H_{11}O_5 \\ \diagdown\!\!\diagdown N\text{-}O\text{-}SO_2O^-K^+ \end{matrix} + H_2O \xrightarrow{\text{Thioglycosidase}} \underset{\text{isothiocyanate}}{R\text{-}N\text{=}C\text{=}S} + C_6H_{12}O_6 + KHSO_4$$

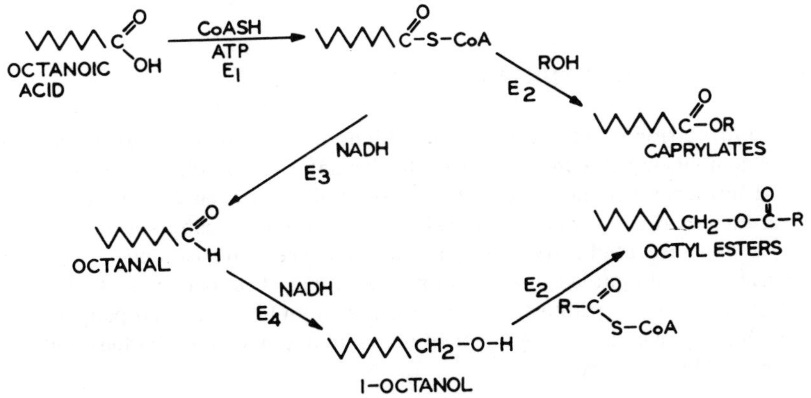

FIG. 6-17. Reaction scheme for conversion of octanoic acid into esters. E_1, Acyl-thiokinase; E_2, acyl-CoA-alcohol-transacylase; E_3, acyl-CoA-reductase; E_4, alcohol-NAD-oxidoreductase. Reprinted from Ref. [105], p. 564, by courtesy of the American Chemical Society.

Thus the products of the reaction are glucose, bisulfate, and an isothiocyanate where the R group can be an alkyl or alkenyl radical. A major component of the flavor appears to be allylthiocyanate. Dimethyl sulfide and related sulfides formed from S-methyl cysteine sulfoxide also play a part in the formation of typical cabbage flavor.

b. Onions. The flavor of onions is attributable to the action of endogenous S-alkyl-L-cysteine sulfoxide lyase on S-substituted L-cysteine sulfoxides as follows:

$$
2 \ \underset{\underset{NH_2}{|}}{R-\overset{\overset{O}{\uparrow}}{S}-CH_2-CH-COOH} + H_2O \xrightarrow[\text{sulfoxide lyase}]{\text{S-alkyl-L-cysteine}} R-\overset{\overset{O}{\uparrow}}{S}-S-R + 2 \ NH_3 + 2 \ CH_3-CO-COOH
$$

The resulting volatile sulfur products are responsible for the characteristic pungent aroma and taste of onions. The naturally occurring substrate for onion cysteine sulfoxide lyase is trans-(+)-S-propenyl-L-cysteine sulfoxide, which is the most efficient substrate yet found. In addition, small but significant quantities of (+)-S-methyl and (+)-S-propyl derivatives are also found in onion. Cysteine, cystine, and S-substituted derivatives of L-cysteine do not serve as substrates. As the onion tissue is damaged, the substrates and enzyme are mixed, thus generating the volatile sulfur compounds.

Part of the flavor precursors in onion are present as γ-L-glutamyl peptides, which are not susceptible to the action of endogenous cysteine sulfoxide lyase. Furthermore, unsprouted onions do not contain the necessary enzymes to release the flavor precursors from the γ-L-glutamyl peptides, thus preventing the onion from reaching its full flavor potential. This has prompted the suggestion that addition of exogenous γ-L-glutamyl transpeptidases from kidney to onions may release the flavor precursor. Subsequent action of exogenous L-cysteine sulfoxide lyase from Albizzia lophanta seeds would yield the volatile sulfur products. This coupled enzyme reaction would thus release the full flavor potential of onions.

3. OXIDATIVE (INDIRECT ENZYMIC)

The enzymic formation of oxidizing agents which, in turn, oxidize precursors to yield flavor components is exemplified in the formation of black tea aroma. In the formation of black tea aroma, catechol oxidase oxidizes flavonols, and the oxidized flavonols in turn oxidize susceptible constituents of the tea such as amino acids, carotenes, and unsaturated fatty acids, to yield flavorful constituents.

Lipoxygenase, a ubiquitous enzyme in plants, forms hydroperoxides which are capable of oxidizing susceptible food constituents to yield flavor components. In addition the hydroperoxides are subject to enzymic and nonenzymic degradation to form flavorful aldehydes and ketones.

4. FLAVORASE CONCEPT

For several years food scientists have been studying the use of enzymes to regenerate flavor in processed foods. This is often referred to as the "flavorase" concept. This concept is predicated on the observation that much of the volatile food flavors is lost during processing, but the flavor precursors are sufficiently nonvolatile to be retained in the food. Although the original flavorase enzymes that generate flavor are destroyed during processing, the addition of exogenous enzymes from a homologous source can act on the excess precursor to regenerate the flavor. This concept has been verified by a number of research workers and is illustrated in Figure 6-18.

Processed foods or food components in which flavor has been partially or fully regenerated by this means include cabbage, potato, tomato, broccoli, peas, carrots, raspberries, bananas, grapefruit juice, orange juice, watercress, mustard, horseradish, and onions. These studies clearly indicate that the generation of flavor in certain plant products is an enzymic process involving endogenous enzymes.

With some vegetables the natures of the flavor precursor, the volatile flavor, and the enzymes have been fairly well established. However, in most instances water extracts of fresh foods have been used to restore the flavor of processed foods. The enzymic nature of flavor regeneration by these extracts has been established by their heat lability.

The flavorase systems that have been studied in greatest detail relate to the cabbage family and the onion, and both involve direct enzymic conversions.

G. Lipolytic Enzymes

1. LIPASES [57,83]

Lipases can be defined as enzymes that hydrolyze ester linkages of emulsified glycerides at an oil-water interface. Lipolytic enzymes are widely distributed,

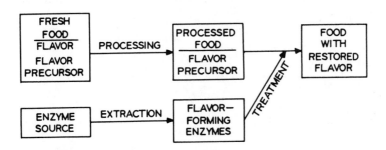

FIG. 6-18. Scheme of flavor formation by enzymes [32]. Reprinted from Ref. [48], p. 488, by courtesy of Institute of Food Technologists.

occurring in plants, animals, and microorganisms. Lipases are found in many biological fluids, cells, seeds, organs, and various other tissues.

In general, lipases hydrolyze triglycerides in a stepwise fashion as follows:

$$\text{Triglyceride} \begin{matrix} \nearrow \text{1,2-diglyceride} \searrow \\ \searrow \text{2,3-diglyceride} \nearrow \end{matrix} \text{2-monoglyceride}$$

However, there are exceptions depending on both positional and fatty acid specificities of the enzyme. The above reaction sequence is for lipases with primary ester specificity, which seem to be the predominant type.

There are four types of specificities associated with lipases. These are: glyceride, positional, fatty acid, and stereospecificities. Glyceride specificity is characterized by a preferential hydrolysis of low molecular weight triglycerides over high molecular weight substrates. The best-known example of positional specificity is that of pancreatic lipase, which hydrolyzes only the primary esters of triglycerides. Lipase preparations which hydrolyze fatty acids from the primary and secondary positions of a triglyceride probably contain more than one enzyme, possibly a triglyceride lipase and a monoglyceride lipase. A lipase which hydrolyzes only the secondary ester from a triglyceride molecule has not been reported to date. Fatty acid specificity occurs when one type of fatty acid is more rapidly hydrolyzed than another type, both being attached to the same positions of like triglyceride molecules. Although it may be difficult to spearate glyceride and fatty acid specificities, one principal example of fatty acid specificity exists. This is the specificity of a lipase from the microorganism Geotrichum candidum for oleic acid. Oleic acid preferentially is hydrolyzed regardless of the position in the triglyceride molecule. However, minor amounts of other fatty acids are also released.

Endogenous lipases are important to the food scientist since fatty acids produced from their hydrolytic action on triglycerides can lead to off flavors.

2. PHOSPHOLIPASES (This section is by L. R. Dugan)

A number of phospholipases react with phosphoglycerides. The acyl group esterified at the sn-1 and sn-2 positions are hydrolyzed according to the nature of the substrate. Most work has been done with lecithin but other phosphoglycerides respond in similar fashion if conditions for hydrolysis are adjusted to the needs of the system.

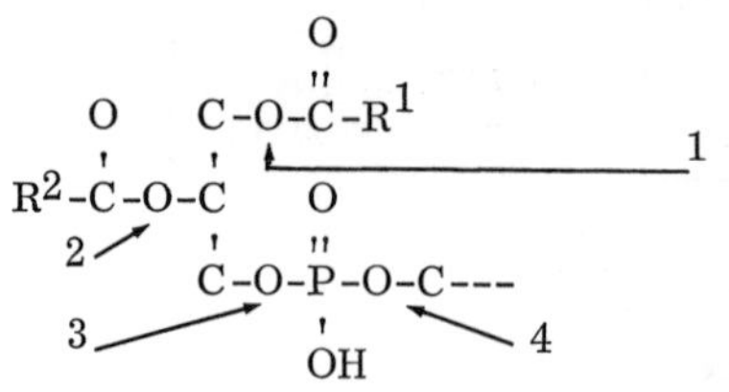

As shown in the above diagram, there are four ester functions which can be hydrolyzed. The enzymes responsible for hydrolysis of these ester linkages are referred to as "phospholipases," although other terms are encountered in the literature. Phospholipase A, also designated lecithinase A (present in snake and bee venoms), hydrolyzes the ester group at the 2 position when lecithin is in the L form. (This designation was the result of early misinterpretation, when it was thought that hydrolysis was achieved at the 1 position of lecithin.) The resulting compound with a hydroxyl at the sn-2 position is known as "lysolecithin." Lecithinase B hydrolyzes a molecule of fatty acid from lysolecithin, leaving glycerylphosphorylcholine. Other phospholipase A enzymes have been isolated. One catalyzes hydrolysis at position 1, and it is designated phospholipase A. The other catalyzes hydrolysis at position 2, and is designated phospholipase A_2. Pancreatic lipase, capable of catalyzing hydrolysis at the 1,3 positions in a triglyceride, catalyzes hydrolysis at the 1 position in lecithin when suitable conditions exist. Pancreatic lipase preparations frequently contain phospholipase A_2 as a contaminant, and both acyl groups may be split off unless the phospholipase is suppressed. Phospholipase C, high in molds and bacteria, catalyzes hydrolysis at position 3, giving a diglyceride and phosphoryl choline. Phospholipase D, found usually in plants (red cabbage is a good source) is a choline-hydrolyzing enzyme (position 4).

H. Lipoxygenase [83,101]

Lipoxygenase, also known as "lipoxidase," catalyzes the stereospecific oxygenation of polyunsaturated fatty acids, their esters, and glycerides containing the cis,cis-1,4-pentadiene double-bond system to yield an optically active hydroperoxide containing a conjugated cis,trans double-bond system. Naturally occurring substrates include such polyunsaturated fatty acids as linoleic, linolenic, arachidonic, and marine oil fatty acids [5]. With linoleic acid, the principal oxygenation products are the conjugated, isomerized 9- and 13-hydroperoxides (see diagram below).

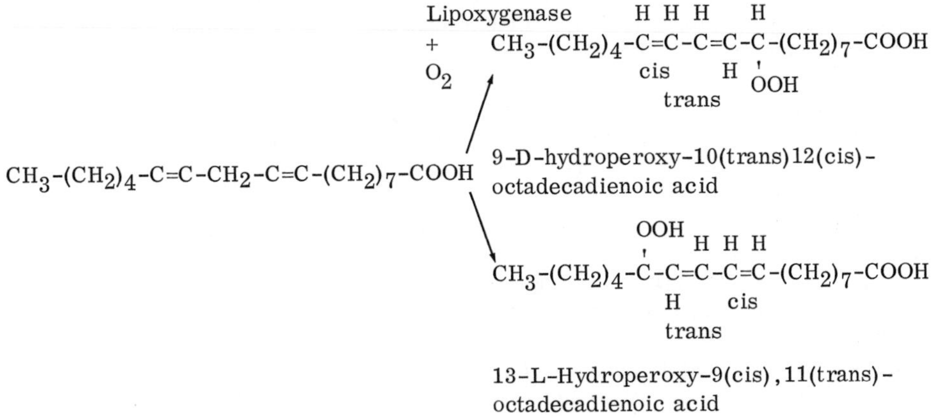

Lipoxygenase + O_2

$$CH_3-(CH_2)_4-C=C-C=C-C-(CH_2)_7-COOH$$

9-D-hydroperoxy-10(trans)12(cis)-octadecadienoic acid

$$CH_3-(CH_2)_4-C=C-CH_2-C=C-(CH_2)_7-COOH$$

$$CH_3-(CH_2)_4-C-C=C-C=C-(CH_2)_7-COOH$$

13-L-Hydroperoxy-9(cis),11(trans)-octadecadienoic acid

Lipoxygenase is principally a plant enzyme and is distributed mainly in legumes, such as soybeans, mung beans, navy beans, green beans, and in cereals, such as wheat, oats, barley, and corn. It has also been definitely identified in potato tubers [36], cauliflower [75], alfalfa [18], apples [120], and a wide variety of plant leaves [49]. Lipoxygenases are a heterogeneous and diverse group of enzymes.

This is also evident from their substrate specificities. For example, one isozyme of soybean is more specific for ester substrates than for the free acid, whereas the others are specific for the free acid [23]. Furthermore, the ester enzyme catalyzes oxygenation of linoleic acid at neutral pH but is practically inactive at pH 9, where the acid enzyme possesses maximal activity [110].

The principal products of the oxygenation of linoleic acid are the 9- and 13-hydroperoxide isomers. The enzyme apparently abstracts a hydrogen atom stereospecifically from position 11 of the linoleic acid molecule. The enzyme then stereospecifically adds oxygen at either end (9 or 13) of the resonating free radical to yield an optically active hydroperoxide [29]; thus, corn germ lipoxygenase yields a 9-D-hydroperoxy-trans-10,cis-12-octadecadienoic acid [37] and a soybean lipoxygenase forms a 13-L-hydroperoxy-cis-9,trans-11-octadecadienoic acid [29]. The mechanism of lipoxygenase activity is obscure; however, the enzyme is thought to activate oxygen in some way, possibly by the formation of singlet oxygen [17].

Lipoxygenase is of practical importance to the food scientist for a number of reasons, some of which are discussed below. Most vegetables contain linoleic and linolenic acids, which are subject to peroxidation by lipoxygenase. For example, the accumulation of carbonyl compounds in unblanched frozen peas is due to lipoxygenase, and failure to blanch plant tissue containing this enzyme may lead to rapid development of off flavors. Consequently, in order to minimize the activity of enzymes, such as lipoxygenase in stored vegetables, blanching is necessary before the vegetables are frozen or dried. However, it is important to remember that the distribution of the enzyme in the food material may affect its heat response. For example, in peas, lipoxygenase activity is highest in the center of the pea but lowest in the skin [32]. However, peroxidase activity is higher in the skin than in the center of the pea [31].

Lipoxygenase can have an undesirable bleaching effect on pigments during spaghetti processing. In addition, lipoxygenase will cooxidize pigments, such as β-carotene and xanthophylls [69]. Lipoxygenase also has been found to have a bleaching effect on chlorophyll [76]. These destructive effects of lipoxygenase are hardly surprising in view of free radicals generated during peroxidation and peroxide decomposition. Thus, it is very likely that other food constituents, such as vitamins, are also destroyed. In fact, the reaction catalyzed by lipoxygenase is so destructive that lipoxygenase inactivates itself by a process first order with respect to enzyme [97].

The lipoxygenase of wheat is thought to have an important effect on the rheology of flour doughs. In addition, wheat flours are often supplemented with soy flours to get the bleaching and improving effect of the soy lipoxygenases. Absorption of occluded atmospheric oxygen during dough mixing improves the rheological properties of the dough. Absorption of oxygen involves the flour lipids and is largely an enzymic process characteristic of lipoxygenase activity. Lipoxygenase is thought to mediate its dough-improving effect by the oxidation of thiol groups on proteins, resulting in crosslinking through disulfide bridges [39].

I. Peroxidases [67,83,90]

Peroxidase is a ubiquitous enzyme occurring in all higher plants that have been investigated and in leukocytes. In addition, a peroxidase is present in milk which is one of the best-known sources of this enzyme [56]. Of the plant peroxidases horseradish peroxidase has been studied in greatest detail.

Peroxidases from various sources all contain a heme (ferriprotoporphyrin IX) prosthetic group.

Peroxidases catalyze the following reaction:

$$ROOH + AH_2 \longrightarrow H_2O + ROH + A$$

The catalytic process of peroxidase appears to result in the transient oxidation of ferric iron to higher valance (ferryl) states. The peroxide (ROOH) may be hydrogen peroxide or an organic peroxide, such as methyl or ethyl hydrogen peroxide. In the above reaction the peroxide is reduced while an electron donor (AH_2) is oxidized. The electron donor may be ascorbate, phenols, amines, or other organic compounds. In many instances the oxidation product is highly colored, and this serves as a basis for the colorimetric estimation of peroxidase activity. For example, the oxidation of aromatic amines, such as diamino benzidine and o-dianisidine, have been used in peroxidase analyses. However, it should be pointed out that aromatic amines of this type can be carcinogenic and should be handled with care. These peroxidatic color reactions are also of value to the food scientist in enzymic analyses of foods. For example, in enzymic reactions where hydrogen peroxide is a product this can be coupled to a peroxidase reaction to develop an analytical procedure. This can be illustrated in the analysis of glucose using glucose oxidase, which generates hydrogen peroxide as follows:

$$\text{Glucose} + O_2 \xrightarrow[\text{oxidase}]{\text{Glucose}} \text{gluconic acid} + H_2O_2$$

The H_2O_2 can be estimated with the peroxidatic reaction above, and from the stoichiometry of the glucose oxidase reaction the concentration of glucose can be estimated [5].

Since peroxidase is very resistant to heat inactivation and is widely distributed in plant tissues, and because very sensitive and simple colorimetric tests are available to measure its activity, it has been used as an indicator for the effectiveness of substerilizing heat treatments. If peroxidase is destroyed so are other enzymes of concern.

Peroxidases also appear to be important from the standpoint of nutrition, color, and flavor. For example, peroxidase activity can lead to the oxidative destruction of vitamin C [10]. Also, peroxidase has been shown to catalyze the bleaching of carotenoids in the absence of unsaturated fatty acids [7] and the decoloration of anthocyanins [40]. Peroxidase, like most heme pigments, catalyzes the peroxidative degradation of unsaturated fatty acids, yielding volatile and flavorful carbonyl compounds which contribute to oxidized flavor. Apparently, heme pigments, such as peroxidase, catalyze the decomposition of hydroperoxides as shown in Figure 6-19 [101] with the generation of free radicals. These free radicals could cause the destruction of a wide variety of food components.

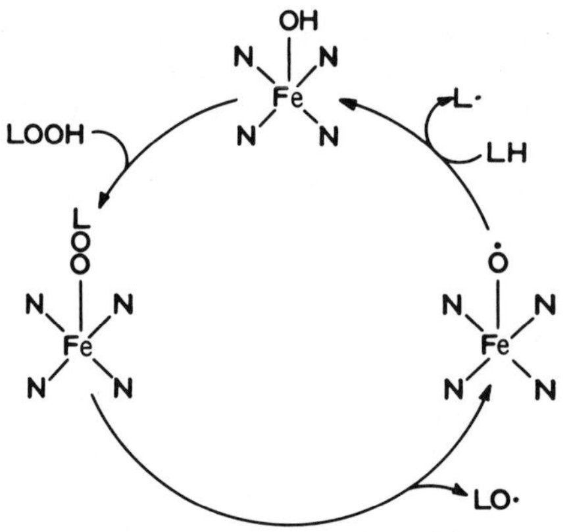

FIG. 6-19. Mechanism of hematin-catalyzed peroxidation of unsaturated lipids. Reprinted from Ref. [101], p. 130, by courtesy of AVI Publishing Co.

J. Thiaminases [11,14]

In certain foods, enzymes exist that hydrolyze thiamine to 2-methyl-6-amino-5-hydroxymethyl pyrimidine and 4-methyl-5-hydroxymethyl thiazole, thus destroying this vitamin. Thiaminase enzymes are found commonly in most fresh water fish and in many marine fish. The enzymes are either an intrinsic part of the flesh or occur adventitiously from microorganisms. Boiling or cooking the fish in most cases inactivates the enzyme. Some fish possessing antithiamine activity are listed below:

Marine species	Freshwater species
Capelin	Carp
Herring	Chub
Menhaden	Smelts
Garfish	Minnow
Whiting	

Many shellfish also exhibit thiaminase activity.

The consumption of raw fish or unheated fermented fish products as practiced in Asia could contribute to thiamine deficiency diseases, such as beriberi. Consumption of raw fish or shellfish and of salted or cured herring may raise the vitamin requirements for thiamine. Salted herring has been shown to destroy 50-60% of added thiamine within 6 hr.

In addition to fish, certain plant materials contain thiaminase. Bracken fern and horsetail plants are especially high in thiaminase activity. This enzyme has also been observed in rice polishing, beans, and mustard seed. Where people consume an exclusive rice diet, especially of unpolished rice, the thiamine requirements may not be met.

Certain microorganisms that can inhabit the buccal cavity or the intestinal tract produce substantial quantities of antithiamine agents. The persistence of beriberi as an endemic condition in certain regions of the world, despite the administration of thiamine, may result from bacterial thiaminase disease.

K. Ascorbic Acid Oxidase [10,33]

Ascorbic acid oxidase is a copper-containing enzyme which catalyzes oxidation of vitamin C (ascorbic acid) as follows:

$$\text{L-Ascorbic acid} + 1/2\ O_2 \longrightarrow \text{dehydroascorbic acid} + H_2O$$

Contrary to a number of oxidase enzymes, one product of the reaction is water instead of hydrogen peroxide. However, in the presence of atmospheric oxygen and no enzyme, ascorbic acid is oxidized to yield dehydroascorbic acid and hydrogen peroxide. This reaction is catalyzed by copper ions, and the resultant hydrogen peroxide leads to further destruction of ascorbic acid.

The enzymic oxidation of ascorbic acid is important in the citrus industry. Ascorbic acid oxidase is present in oranges and other citrus fruits. In the intact fruits the oxidases are presumably balanced by the reductases and the interaction of these two systems determines the final level of ascorbic acid. However, during extraction of juices, the reductases suffer the greatest damage, leaving the oxidases to destroy the ascorbic acid. Thus, it becomes important to inhibit the ascorbic acid oxidase by holding juices for only short times and at low temperatures during the blending stage, by deaerating the juice to remove oxygen, and finally by pasteurizing the juice to inactivate the oxidizing enzymes.

Enzymic oxidation also has been proposed as a mechanism for the destruction of ascorbic acid in orange peels during the preparation of marmalade. Boiling the grated peel in water substantially reduces the loss of ascorbic acid.

Other oxidases, such as cytochrome oxidase, peroxidase, and phenolase, also catalyze destruction of ascorbic acid.

L. Pigment Degrading Enzymes

Chlorophyllases and anthocyanases both exist in plants and can catalyze destruction of chlorphyll and anthocyanins, respectively, if they are not inactivated [20,21].

REFERENCES

1. L. W. Acker, Food Technol., 23, 1257 (1969).
2. L. Acker and H. Kaiser, Z. Lebensm. Untersuch. u Forsch., 110, 349 (1959).
3. A. M. Ambrose, in Toxicants Occurring Naturally in Foods, National Academy of Sciences–National Research Council, Publication 1354, Washington, D. C., 1966, p. 105.
4. L. G. Bartolome and J. E. Hoff, J. Agri. Food Chem., 20, 266 (1972).
5. J. L. Beare-Rogers and R. G. Ackman, Lipids, 4, 441 (1969).

6. C. H. Beatty and R. M. Bocek, in The Physiology and Biochemistry of Muscle as a Food (E. J. Briskey, R. G. Cassens, and B. B. Marsh, eds.), Vol. 2, University of Wisconsin Press, Madison, 1970, p. 155.

7. A. Ben Aziz, S. Grossman, I. Ascarelli, and P. Budowski, Phytochemistry, 10, 1445 (1971).

8. H. U. Bergmeyer, Methods of Enzymatic Analysis. Academic Press, New York, 1965.

9. S. Bernhard, The Structure and Function of Enzymes. W. A. Benjamin, New York, 1968, p. 206.

10. H. A. W. Blundstone, J. S. Woodman, and J. B. Adams, in The Biochemistry of Fruits and their Products (A. C. Hulme, ed.), Vol. 2, Academic Press, New York, 1971, p. 561.

11. G. Borgstrom, Principles of Food Science, Vol. 2, Macmillan, New York, 1968, p. 51.

12. J. F. Brandts, in Structure and Stability of Biological Macromolecules (S. N. Timasheff and G. D. Fasman, eds.), Vol. 2, Marcel Dekker, Inc., New York, 1969, p. 213.

13. H. Brockerhoff, J. Biol. Chem., 246, 5828 (1971).

14. H. P. Broquist and T. H. Jukes, in Modern Nutrition in Health and Disease (M. G. Wohl and R. S. Goodhart, eds.), Lea and Febeger, Philadelphia, 1968, p. 452.

15. H. D. Brown and S. K. Chattopadhyay, in Chemistry of the Cell Interface (H. D. Brown, ed.), Part A, Academic Press, New York, 1971, p. 73.

16. H. B. Bull, Advan. Protein Chem., 3, 95 (1947).

17. H. W. S. Chan, J. Amer. Chem. Soc., 93, 2357 (1971).

18. C. C. Chang, W. J. Esselman, and C. O. Clagett, Lipids, 6, 100 (1971).

19. S. E. Charm and C. C. Matteo, in Methods in Enzymology (W. B. Jakoby, ed.), Vol. 22, Academic Press, New York, 1971, p. 476.

20. C. O. Chichester and R. McFeeters, in Biochemistry of Fruits and their Products (A. C. Hulme, ed.), Vol. 2, Academic Press, New York, 1971, p. 717.

21. C. O. Chichester and T. O. M. Nakayama, in Chemistry and Biochemistry of Plant Pigments (T. W. Goodwin, ed.), Academic Press, New York, 1965, p. 439.

22. H. N. Christensen and G. A. Palmer, Enzyme Kinetics. W. B. Saunders, Philadelphia, 1967.

23. J. Christopher, E. Pistorius, and B. Axelrod, Biochim. Biophys. Acta, 198, 12 (1970).

24. J. R. Couch and F. G. Hooper, in Newer Methods of Nutritional Biochemistry (A. A. Albanese, ed.), Academic Press, New York, 1972, p. 183.

25. L. S. Cuendet, E. Larson, C. G. Norris, and W. F. Geddes, Cereal, Chem., 31, 362 (1954).

26. E. A. Davies, Quantitative Problems in Biochemistry. E and S. Livingstone, London, 1967.

27. D. R. Dilley, in The Biochemistry of Fruits and Their Products (A. C. Hulme, ed.), Vol. 1, Academic Press, New York, 1970, p. 174.

28. M. Dixon and E. C. Webb, Enzymes. 2nd ed., Academic Press, New York, 1964.

29. M. R. Egmond, J. F. G. Vliegenthart, and J. Bolingh, Biochem. Biophys. Res. Comm., 48, 1055 (1972).

30. A. Endo, Agri. Biol. Chem., 28, 551 (1964).
31. C. E. Ericksson, J. Food Sci., 32, 438 (1967).
32. C. E. Ericksson and S. G. Suensson, Biochim. Biophys. Acta, 198, 449 (1970).
33. N. A. M. Eskin, H. M. Henderson, and R. J. Townsend, Biochemistry of Foods. Academic Press, New York, 1971.
34. R. E. Feeney and R. G. Allison, Evolutionary Biochemistry of Proteins. Wiley-Interscience, New York, 1969.
35. O. R. Fennema, W. D. Powrie, and E. H. Marth, Low-Temperature Preservation of Foods and Living Matter. Marcel Dekker, New York, 1973, p. 217.
36. T. Galliard and D. R. Phillips, Biochem. J., 124, 431 (1971).
37. H. W. Gardner and D. Weisleder, Lipids, 5, 678 (1970).
38. Edith Gould and M. J. Medler, J. Assoc. Off. Anal. Chem., 53, 1237 (1970).
39. A. Graveland, J. Amer. Oil Chem. Soc., 47, 352 (1970).
40. R. Grommeck and P. Markakis, J. Food Sci., 29, 53 (1964).
41. G. G. Guilbault, Enzymatic Methods of Analysis. Pergamon Press, New York, 1970.
42. A. Guilbot, J. L. Multon, and R. Drapron, Dechema Monograph, 70, 279 (1972).
43. G. J. Haas, Food Prod. Devel., 5(6), 120 (1971).
44. R. Hamm, D. Masic, and L. Tetzlaff, Z. Lebensm. Unters. Forsch., 147, 71 (1971).
45. D. A. Heatherbell and R. E. Wrolstad, J. Agri. Food Chem., 19, 281 (1971).
46. U. Heber, Cryobiology, 5, 188 (1968).
47. E. Heftman, Cytobios, 3, 129 (1971).
48. E. J. Hewit, D. Mackay, K. S. Konigsbacher, and T. Hasselstrom, Food Technol., 10, 487 (1956).
49. M. Holden, Phytochemistry, 9, 507 (1970).
50. A. C. Hulme, ed., The Biochemistry of Fruits and Their Products. Vol. 2, Academic Press, New York, 1971.
51. H. O. Hultin, J. Food Sci., 37, 524 (1972).
52. International Union of Biochemistry, Standing Committee on Enzymes, Enzyme Nomenclature Recommendations, 1972, Elsevier, Amsterdam, 1973.
53. International Union of Biochemistry, Biochemistry, 10, 4825 (1971).
54. S. Ishii and T. Yokotsuka, J. Agri. Food Chem., 20, 787 (1972).
55. L. K. James and L. G. Augenstein, Advan. Enzymol., 28, 1 (1966).
56. R. Jenness and S. Patton, Principles of Dairy Chemistry. Wiley, New York, 1959, p. 201.
57. R. G. Jensen, in Progress in the Chemistry of Fats and Other Lipids (R. T. Holman, ed.), Vol. 11, Pt. 3, Pergamon Press, New York, 1971, p. 349.
58. E. B. Johns, H. E. Pattee, and J. A. Singleton, J. Agri. Food Chem., 21, 570 (1973).
59. R. L. Joseph, Proc. Biochem., 5(11), 55 (1970).
60. B. Kassell, in Methods in Enzymology (G. E. Perlmann and L. Lorand, eds.), Vol. 14, Academic Press, New York, 1970, p. 839.
61. A. M. Kuzin, Radiation Biochemistry. D. Davey, New York, 1964.
62. A. B. Lerner and T. B. Fitzpatrick, Physiol. Rev., 30, 91 (1950).
63. I. E. Liener and M. L. Kakade, in Toxic Constituents of Plant Foodstuffs (I. E. Liener, ed.), Academic Press, New York, 1969, p. 8.

64. B. S. Luh and H. N. Daoud, J. Food Sci., 36, 1039 (1971).
65. B. S. Luh and B. Phithakpol, J. Food Sci., 37, 264 (1972).
66. A. D. McLaren and L. Packer, Advan. Enzymol., 33, 245 (1970).
67. H. R. Mahler and E. H. Cordes, Biological Chemistry. 2nd ed., Harper and Row, New York, 1971.
68. B. B. Marsh, in Proceedings of the Meat Industry Conference. American Meat Institute Foundation, Chicago, 1972, p. 109.
69. R. R. Matsuo, J. W. Bradley, and G. N. Irvine, Cereal Chem., 47, 1 (1970).
70. R. Montgomery and C. A. Swenson, Quantitative Problems in the Biochemical Sciences. W. H. Freeman, San Francisco, 1969.
71. J. G. Morris, A Biologist's Physical Chemistry. Addison-Wesley, Reading, Mass., 1968.
72. Mary J. Mycek, in Methods of Enzymology (Gertrude Perlmann and L. Lorand, eds.), Vol. 19, Academic Press, New York, 1970, p. 285.
73. R. P. Newbold and P. V. Harris, J. Food Sci., 37, 337 (1972).
74. S. P. O'Neill, Biotechnol. Bioeng., 14, 201 (1972).
75. S. O'Reilly, J. Prebble, and S. West. Phytochemistry, 8, 1675 (1969).
76. F. T. Orthoefer, Diss. Abstr. Int., B30, 2531 (1969).
77. I. F. Penny, J. Sci. Food Agri., 21, 303 (1970).
78. W. Pilnik and F. M. Rombouts, Dechema Monograph, 70, 187 (1972).
79. W. Pilnik and G. J. Voragen, in The Biochemistry of Fruits and Their Products (A. C. Hulme, ed.), Vol. 1, Academic Press, New York, 1970, 1970.
80. J. D. Ponting, in Food Enzymes (H. W. Schultz, ed.), AVI Publ., Westport, Conn., 1960, p. 105.
81. R. Pressey, J. Food Sci., 37, 521 (1972).
82. J. F. Price and B. S. Schweigert, eds., The Science of Meat and Meat Products. W. H. Freeman, San Francisco, 1971.
83. G. Reed, Enzymes in Food Processing. Academic Press, New York, 1966.
84. G. Reed and J. A. Thorn, in Wheat: Chemistry and Technology, (Y. Pomeranz, ed.), American Association of Cereal Chem., St. Paul, Minn., 1971, p. 453.
85. J. Reuben, Proc. Natl. Acad. Sci. U.S., 68, 563 (1971).
86. R. J. Romani, J. Food Sci., 37, 513 (1972).
87. F. M. Rombouts and W. Pilnik, Crit. Rev. Food Technol., 3, 1 (1972).
88. D. B. Roodyn, Enzyme Cytology. Academic Press, New York, 1967.
89. G. W. Sanderson and H. N. Graham, J. Agri. Food Chem., 21, 576 (1973).
90. B. C. Saunders, A. C. Holmes-Seidle, and B. P. Stark, Peroxidase. Butterworth, Washington, D.C., 1964.
91. S. Schwimmer, J. Food Sci., 37, 530 (1972).
92. S. Schwimmer and M. Friedman, Flavour Ind., 3, 137 (1972).
93. I. H. Segel, Biochemical Calculations. Wiley, New York, 1968.
94. K. M. Shahani, W. J. Harper, R. G. Jensen, R. M. Parry, and C. A. Zittle, J. Dairy Sci., 56, 531 (1973).
95. F. S. Shenstone, in Egg Quality - A Study of the Hen's Egg (T. C. Carter, ed.), Oliver and Boyd, Edinburgh, 1968, p. 26.
96. R. G. H. Sin, in Radiation Preservation of Food. U. S. Army Quartermaster Corps, Washington, D. C., 1957, p. 169.
97. W. L. Smith and W. E. M. Lands, Biochem. Biophys. Res. Comm., 41, 846 (1970).
98. J. Spinelli, Proc. Biochem., 6(5), 36 (1971).

99. R. F. Steiner and V. Frattali, J. Agri. Food Chem., 17, 513 (1969).
100. W. F. Talburt and O. Smith, Potato Processing. AVI Publ., Westport, Conn., 1967, p. 180.
101. A. L. Tappel, in Lipids and Their Oxidation (H. W. Schultz, E. A. Day, and R. Sinnhuber, eds.), AVI Publ., Westport, Conn., 1962, p. 122.
102. A. L. Tappel, in Cryobiology (H. T. Merryman, ed.), Academic Press, New York, 1966, pp. 163-177.
103. A. L. Tappel, in Lysosomes Biology Pathology (J. T. Dingle, ed.), Vol. 2, North Holland Pub. Co., Amsterdam, 163 (1969).
104. N. E. Tolbert, Plant Physiol., 51, 234 (1973).
105. R. Tressel and F. Drawert, J. Agri. Food Chem., 21, 560 (1973).
106. G. Uhlig, Naturewissenschaft, 57, 261 (1970).
107. L. A. Underkofler, in Handbook of Food Additives (T. E. Furia, ed.), Chemical Rubber Co., Cleveland, 1968, p. 51.
108. J. P. van Buren, J. C. Moyer, and W. B. Robinson, J. Food Sci., 27, 291 (1962).
109. K. Vas, in Food Irradiation, Proc. Symp. 6-10 June 1966, Karlsruhe. I.A.E.E., Wien, p. 253.
110. W. M. Verhue and A. Francke, Biochim. Biophys. Acta, 285, 43 (1972).
111. K. J. S. Villadsen, Dechema Monograph, 70, 135 (1972).
112. P. N. Viswanathan, Ind. J. Biochem., 6, 124 (1969).
113. R. Vogel, I. Trautschold and E. Werle, Natural Proteinase Inhibitors. Academic Press, New York, 1968.
114. J. M. Wallace and E. L. Wheeler, Cereal Chem., 49, 92 (1972).
115. F. C. Webb, Biochemical Engineering. Van Nostrand, New York, 1964.
116. J. R. Whitaker, Principles of Enzymology for the Food Sciences. Marcel Dekker, New York, 1972.
117. A. White, P. Handler, E. L. Smith and D. Stetten, Principles of Biochemistry. 1st ed., McGraw-Hill, New York, 1954, pp. 221-255.
118. H. Wieland, Enzymes in Food Processing and Products. Noyes Data Corporation, Park Ridge, N.J., 1972.
119. J. Wismer-Pederson, Dechema Monograph, 70, 215 (1972).
120. L. S. C. Wooltorton, J. D. Jones, and A. C. Hulme, Nature (London), 207, 999 (1965).
121. O. Zaborsky, Immobilized Enzymes. Chemical Rubber Co., Cleveland, 1973.

Chapter 7

VITAMINS AND MINERALS

Steven R. Tannenbaum

Department of Nutrition and Food Science
Massachusetts Institute of Technology
Cambridge, Massachusetts

Contents

I. INTRODUCTION

One of the major quality aspects of our food supply is its content of vitamins and minerals. From a biological point of view, we eat to survive, and the pattern of our nutrient requirements has developed during a long evolutionary process in which man has adapted to his environment. Although certain food processes, such as cooking, are indeed very old, it is only within the last 150 years that we have begun to consume a significant part of our food in a factory-processed form.

Our modern processed food supply has contributed enormously to the public health status of the population. Certain nutritional diseases, which were common in parts of the United States 50 years ago, such as pellagra, have all but disappeared. A recent ten-state nutritional survey [89] demonstrated that while nutritional deficiencies did exist, they were minimal compared to what existed prior to the modern era of nutrition and food technology. Consider that it is now possible to eat a diet balanced in all types of foods at any time of year and in any geographical location.

At the same time, modern process technology has also introduced its share of problems. Sometimes this has been a result of inadequate knowledge, but tragic cases of illness and even death have occurred where essential nutrient value has been lost because of ignorance, carelessness, and lack of adherence to "good manufacturing practice." In the past, new food processes have seldom been assessed for their contribution to nutrient loss or retention. Multiple processes, such as freezing of reconstituted dehydrated foods, may lead to benefits in process scheduling, but they may also lead to higher than normal losses of vitamins. New forms of food products, such as intermediate moisture foods, may lead to accentuated problems of vitamin stability. A food product, to have acceptable nutritional quality, should generally be capable of providing those nutrients normally characteristic of its food group.

It is the purpose of this chapter to summarize the available information on the chemistry of vitamin and mineral losses in processed and stored foods. This is a subject which has been treated in many review articles, some of which are listed in the references [5,17,19,42]. Special mention must be made of Nutritional Evaluation of Food Processing [46], which contains a large amount of detailed information on various foods both in the raw and finished state. Rather than recapitulate and summarize the many studies carried out on individual foods and processes, the approach in this chapter is to review analytically the chemistry of the individual vitamins and the general factors leading to nutrient losses.

It is apparent from the literature that information on the fate of vitamins in processed foods is reasonably adequate for only a few vitamins. Considerable information is available on ascorbic acid, provitamins A, and thiamine; less on riboflavin and vitamin B_6; and very little on folic acid and vitamin B_{12}. This is due partially to the relative importance past investigators have attached to these nutrients and also to analytical problems. The amount of space devoted to an individual nutrient in this chapter is influenced both by the complexity of its chemistry and the amount of available information. At some future time, it is hoped that sufficient additional information will accumulate to fill in some of the more obvious gaps.

II. VITAMIN AND MINERAL REQUIREMENTS AND ALLOWANCES

In order to understand whether a specific treatment of a specific food leads to acceptable nutrient quality, it is necessary to have an understanding of both human requirements and the amount of a specific nutrient present in the food after normal preparatory procedures.

The concentrations of many of the key nutrients are given for fresh and cooked foods in USDA Handbook No. 8 [95]. Although data in this compilation are occasionally inaccurate, they afford the only major source of information apart from direct analysis of the product in question. In many instances, inaccuracies are caused by analytical procedures of insufficient specificity, and users of these data should be especially cognizant of the appropriateness of the methodology. Special problems in vitamin analysis are briefly noted in this chapter under the particular vitamin in question.

The presently accepted status of human dietary requirements is well summarized in the recommended dietary allowances (RDA) of the Food and Nutrition Board, National Academy of Sciences-National Research Council: "The allowances are designed to afford a margin of sufficiency above average physiological requirements to cover variations among essentially all individuals in the general population. They produce a buffer against increased needs during common stresses and permit full realization of growth and productive potential; but they are not to be considered adequate to meet additional requirements of persons depleted by disease or traumatic stresses."

Since both males and females of different age classes have been assigned different RDA's, it is simpler to consider a mean value for each nutrient. Mean values for men and women ages 23-50 years are summarized in Table 7-1. It is appropriate to deal with nutrients that have neither established nor approximated RDA's in a quantitative fashion. However, one should remain aware of the fact that they are essential.

III. ENRICHMENT, RESTORATION, AND FORTIFICATION

The addition of nutrients to foods may be undertaken for a variety of purposes [9]. Definitions of the various terms associated with addition of nutrients are:

1. Restoration: Addition to restore the original nutrient content.
2. Fortification: Addition of nutrients in amounts significant enough to render the food a good to superior source of the added nutrients. This may include addition of nutrients not normally associated with the food or addition to levels above that in the unprocessed food.
3. Enrichment: Addition of specific amounts of selected nutrients in accordance with a standard of identity as defined by the United States Food and Drug Administration.

The Joint Policy Statement by the Council on Foods and Nutrition of the American Medical Association and the Food and Nutrition Board of the National Academy of Sciences-National Research Council, published in August 1968, endorses continuation of nutrient addition programs. The specific endorsement states:

> The enrichment of flour, bread, degerminated corn meal, corn grits, whole grain corn meal, and white rice (with thiamine, riboflavin, niacin, and iron); the retention or restoration of thiamine, riboflavin, niacin, and iron in processed food cereals; the addition of vitamin D to milk, fluid skimmed milk, and nonfat dry milk; the addition of

TABLE 7-1

Essential Nutrients Classified by the Food and Nutrition Board[a]

Nutrient	Unit	Mean dietary allowance for normal, healthy men and women age 23–50 years
Nutrients with recommended dietary allowances		
Calories	kcal	2350
Protein	g	51
Vitamin A	IU	4500
Vitamin E	IU	14
Ascorbic acid (vitamin C)	mg	45
Folacin	μg	400
Niacin	mg equiv	16
Riboflavin (vitamin B_2)	mg	1.4
Thiamine (vitamin B_1)	mg	1.2
Vitamin B_6	mg	2.0
Vitamin B_{12}	μg	3.0
Calcium	mg	800
Phosphorus	mg	800
Iodine	μg	115
Iron	mg	14
Magnesium	mg	325
Zinc	mg	15
Nutrients with approximated dietary allowances		
Copper	mg	2
Potassium	mg	2.5
Pantothenic acid	mg	5–10

Nutrients for which dietary allowances are neither recommended nor approximated
Choline,[b] biotin,[b] vitamin D,[b] vitamin K,[b] chloride, chromium, cobalt, fluorine, manganese, molybdenum, nickel, selenium, silicon, sodium, tin, vanadium

[a]Publication ISBN 0-309-02216-9, National Academy of Sciences, National Research Council, Washington, D.C., 1974.
[b]Requirement for normal, healthy men and women age 23–50 is usually satisfied by dietary and nondietary sources.

vitamin A to margarine, fluid skimmed milk, and nonfat dry milk; and the addition of iodine to table salt; the protective action of fluoride against dental caries is recognized, and the standardized addition of fluoride is endorsed in areas in which the water supply has a low fluoride content.

In addition, the Council on Foods and Nutrition and the Food and Nutrition Board in the same policy statement continue to endorse the addition of nutrients to foods under all of the following circumstances:

1. When the intake of the nutrient is below the desirable level in the diets of a significant number of people
2. When the food used to supply the nutrient is likely to be consumed in quantities that make a significant contribution to the diet of the population in need
3. When the addition of the nutrient is not likely to create an imbalance of essential nutrients
4. When the nutrient added is stable under proper conditions of storage and use
5. When the nutrient is physiologically available to the consumer
6. When there is reasonable assurance against excessive intake to a level of toxicity

IV. GENERAL CAUSES FOR LOSS OF VITAMINS AND MINERALS

All foods which undergo processing are subject to some degree of loss of their vitamin and mineral content, the only exceptions being those instances in which the availability of the nutrient is increased or in which some antinutritional factor is inactivated. In general, we attempt to carry out a process in a manner which minimizes nutrient losses and maximizes safety of the product. In addition to losses from processing, there are significant preprocess factors which influence nutrient content. These include genetic variation, degree of maturity, conditions of soil, use and type of fertilizer, climate, availability of water, light (length of day and intensity), and postharvest or postmortem handling.

A. Genetics and Maturity

Numerous examples of genetic variation are given by Harris and Von Loesecke [89]. Data on the effect of maturity are more difficult to find, but an excellent example is tomatoes (Table 7-2). Not only does the ascorbic acid content vary over the period of maturity, but maximum vitamin content occurs when the tomato is in an immature state.

TABLE 7-2

Influence of Degree of Maturity on Ascorbic Acid Content of
New Yorker Variety Tomatoes[a]

Weeks from anthesis	Average wt (g)	Color	Ascorbic acid (mg %)
2	33.4	Green	10.7
3	57.2	Green	7.6
4	102.5	Gr.-Yel.	10.9
5	145.7	Yel.-red	20.7
6	159.9	Red	14.6
7	167.6	Red	10.1

[a]Ref. [68].

B. Other Preprocessing Variables

Most of the other agricultural variables listed above are known to influence content of some vitamin or mineral, but results are poorly documented or come from poorly designed experiments. The last category, which involves the history of the food from time of harvest or slaughter to time of processing, causes considerable variation in nutritional value. Other chapters in this volume deal with various biochemical processes in plant and animal tissues. Since many of the vitamins are also cofactors for enzymes or may be subject to degradation by endogenous enzymes, particularly those released after death of the plant or animal, it is fairly obvious that postharvest or postmortem practices can cause substantial fluctuations in nutrient content.

C. Trimming

Plant tissues in particular are subject to trimming and subdividing practices which lead to losses in nutrient content of the edible portion compared to the whole plant. The skins and peels of fruits and vegetables are usually removed. It has been reported that the level of ascorbic acid is higher in the apple peel than in the flesh, and the waste core of the pineapple is also higher in vitamin C than the edible portion. Similarly, niacin is reported to be richer in the epidermal layers of the carrot root than in the root which remains after processing [17]. It is likely that similar concentration differences can be found in such foods as potatoes, onions, and beets. When peeling is accomplished by such chemically drastic procedures as lye treatment, significant losses of nutrients also occur in the outer fleshy layer. Trimming of such vegetables as spinach, broccoli, green beans, and asparagus involves discarding bits of stems or tougher portions of the plant and undoubtedly causes losses of some nutrients.

D. Milling

A special category of trimming involves the milling of cereals. All cereals which are milled undergo a significant loss of nutrients, the extent of the loss being governed by the efficiency with which the endosperm of the seed is separated from the outer seed coat (bran) and germ. Ths loss of each nutrient follows its own characteristic pattern, as shown for wheat in Figure 7-1.

The loss of certain vitamins and minerals from milled cereals was deemed so relevant to health in the United States populace that the concept of adding nutrients in the final stages of processing was proposed in the 1940's. After a long series of hearings the Food and Drug Administration issued regulations for a standard of identity for enriched bread. These standards required that four nutrients, thiamine, niacin, riboflavin, and iron, be added to flour, along with the option of including calcium and vitamin D. Currently, if bread is to be labeled "enriched" it must meet these standards, but mandatory enrichment is required only by certain state laws.

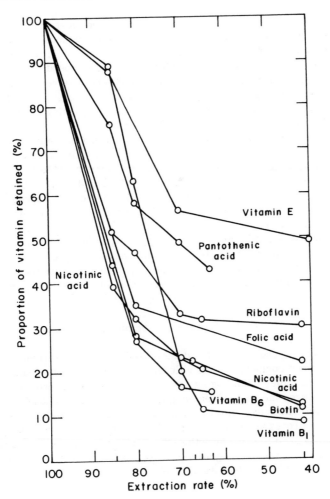

FIG. 7-1. Relation between extraction rate and proportion of total vitamins of the grain retained in flour (from Ref. [2], courtesy of the F.A.O. of the U.N.).

E. Leaching and Blanching

One of the most significant routes for the loss of water-soluble nutrients is via extraction from cut or sensitive surfaces. Food-processing operations which lead to losses of this type include washing, flume conveying, blanching, cooling, and cooking. The nature and extent of the loss of course depend on pH, temperature, ratio of water to food, surface to volume ratio, maturity, etc.

Operations of this type may also lead to secondary influences on nutrient content, such as contamination with trace metals and additional exposure to oxygen. In some foods an improvement in mineral content can occur, e.g., increased calcium from exposure to hard water.

Of the operations listed above, blanching leads to the most important nutrient losses. A discussion of blanching, including blanching methods and the influence of blanching time and temperature, was published by Lee [62]. Blanching is normally accomplished with steam or hot water, the choice depending on the type of food and the subsequent process. Steam blanching generally results in smaller losses of nutrients since leaching is minimized in this process. Leaching during blanching or cooking can be almost entirely eliminated by using microwave cookers [77], since the need for a heating medium is eliminated.

An example of typical vitamin losses from cooked broccoli and the distribution of vitamins between the solid and liquid portions is shown in Table 7-3. If both liquid and solid portions are considered, there is no measurable loss of B vitamins and a 10-15% loss of vitamin C. If the liquid is discarded, as is the usual practice, substantial losses can be found for both boiling and microwave cooking. Losses during microwave cooking are atypically high and can possibly be minimized by using less cooking water.

Under conditions of good manufacturing practice, leaching, blanching, and cooking losses in the food plant should be no greater and possibly even smaller than those found for average practice in the home. A voluminous quantity of data on the vitamin content of canned foods provides verification for this statement [18,23].

F. Processing Chemicals

A number of different chemicals are added to foods as preservatives or processing aids. Some of these compounds have a detrimental effect on the content of certain vitamins. For example, oxidizing agents are generally destructive to vitamins A, C and E. Therefore, the use of bleaching or improving agents for flour may lead to a loss of vitamin activity. However, the older process of aging flour through natural oxidative processes would undoubtedly lead to similar losses.

Sulfite (SO_2) is used to prevent both enzymic and nonenzymic browning of fruits and vegetables. As a reducing agent it protects ascorbic acid, but as a nucleophile it is detrimental to thiamine (see Section VI, A, 2).

TABLE 7-3

Vitamin Content and Distribution in Cooked Broccoli[a]

| Cooking method | Vitamin content (%)[b] | | | | | |
| | Solid portion | | | Liquid portion | | |
	C	B_1	B_2	C	B_1	B_2
Microwave	64	76	71	23	31	31
Pressure (steam)	72	90	94	6	8	8
Boiling	60	75	69	25	33	33

[a]Expressed as a percent of broccoli's original vitamin content.
[b]Ref. [91].

Nitrite is used to preserve meats and may either be added as such or formed by microbial reduction of nitrate. Certain vegetables which contain high concentrations of nitrate, such as spinach and beets, may also contain nitrites because of microbial activity. Nitrite reacts rapidly with ascorbic acid [26] and can also lead to the destruction of carotenoid provitamins, thiamine, and possible folic acid. Nitrite can act either as an oxidizing agent,

$$NO + H_2O = H^+ + HNO_2 + e^- \qquad E_O = -0.99 \text{ V}$$

or by nucleophilic substitution on N or S, or by addition to double bonds. These reactions are pH sensitive since the reacting species is N_2O_3 (formed as follows):

$$H^+ + NO_2^- \rightleftharpoons HNO_2 \qquad pK_a = 3.4$$

$$H^+ + NO_2^- + HNO_2 \rightleftharpoons N_2O_3 + H_2O$$

Thus, the reaction with ascorbic acid is pH sensitive, occurring at a negligible rate above pH 6 and proceeding very rapidly at pH's close to or below 3.4.

Ethylene and propylene oxides are used as sterilizing agents. They are biologically active because of their abilities to alkylate proteins and nucleic acids, and they can react with vitamins, such as thiamine, via a similar mechanism. Their primary use in the food industry is for sterilizing spices.

Alkaline conditions are often employed to extract proteins. Conditions of high pH are also encountered where alkaline baking powders are used. Special instances are found where cooked foods, such as eggs, have a pH in the vicinity of 9 due to loss of CO_2. The destruction of some vitamins (see sections on individual vitamins), including thiamine, ascorbic acid, and pantothenic acid, is greatly increased under alkaline conditions. Strong acid conditions are only rarely encountered in foods and few vitamins are sensitive to this condition.

G. Deteriorative Reactions

There are a number of general reactions which impair sensory properties of processed and stored foods and which also cause loss of nutrients. Enzymic reactions have already been mentioned, but enzymic contamination by added ingredients should also receive consideration. Examples include ascorbic acid oxidase from plant materials or thiaminase from fishery products, when foods containing these enzymes are added to foods which normally do not contain these enzymes.

Lipid oxidation (see Chapter 4) causes formation of hydroperoxides, peroxides, and epoxides which, in turn, oxidize or otherwise react with carotenoids, tocopherols, ascorbic acid, etc. The fate of other readily oxidizable vitamins, such as folic acid, B_{12}, biotin, and D has not been adequately investigated, but serious losses are not unexpected. The decomposition of hydroperoxides to reactive carbonyl compounds could lead to further losses, particularly for thiamine, some forms of B_6, pantothenic acid, etc.

Nonenzymic browning reactions of carbohydrates also lead to highly reactive carbonyl compounds (Chapter 3) which may react with certain vitamins in a fashion similar to that proposed for carbonyls derived from lipid oxidation.

V. OPTIMIZATION OF NUTRIENT RETENTION

In the course of processing and storing foods there is an inevitable decline in nutrient value. It is the responsibility of the food manufacturer to insure that these losses be minimal. The correct approach to optimization of nutrient content will of course vary depending on the type of food or process. A few illustrations follow.

A. High-Temperature, Short-Time Processing (HTST)

One of the most significant of recent food processing developments is HTST processing combined with aseptic canning. The aim and purpose of most heat processes (pasteurization or sterilization) is to reduce the microbial population of the product to a point providing safety and a reasonable shelf life.

It can be demonstrated mathematically that for a commercial sterilization process of any type, a HTST process is preferable because the Arrhenius activation energy of spore inactivation is high compared to that of vitamin destruction.

Consider two simultaneous reactions:

1. Spore inactivation, $N/N_0 = e^{-k_1 t}$

where N_0 is the initial spore count, N is the count after any heating time t, and k is the first-order rate constant for spore inactivation.

2. Vitamin destruction, $V/V_0 = e^{-k_2 t}$

where V_0 and V are the respective vitamin concentrations at times o and t, and k_2 is the rate constant (assumed first order) for vitamin destruction.

The time for completion of any commercial sterilization process will be determined by the level of safety chosen for the product. In low acid, commercially canned foods the safety level is conventionally taken as a reduction to approximately 10^{-12} the original population of spores of <u>Clostridium</u> <u>botulinum.</u> More generally, any indicator organism and any probability level may be chosen. Thus the time for completion of a process, neglecting heating time and cooling time will be given by:

a. Choosing N/N_0 for the particular organism.
b. Finding k_1 and k_2 as a function of temperature (T). The latter condition is usually met by determining the activation energy for the specific reaction using Arrhenius equations:

$$k_1 = A_1 \, e^{-Ea_1/RT}$$
$$k_2 = A_2 \, e^{-Ea_2/RT}$$

where A_1 and A_2 are collision frequency constants, E_{a1} and E_{a2} are the activation energies in kcal/mole, R is the gas content, and T is the absolute temperature. Experimentally, these values are usually determined by studying the reaction kinetics over a suitable temperature range and plotting ln k vs 1/T, the slope being equal to -Ea/R.

c. Solving the two rate equations simultaneously. Thus, if the time for completion of the process is t_c, then

$$t_c = (\ln \frac{N_0}{N}) k_1^{-1}$$

$$= (\ln \frac{N_0}{N})(A_1^{-1})(e^{E_{a1}}/RT)$$

and

$$\ln (V/V_0) = k_2 k_1^{-1}(\ln \frac{N}{N_0}), \text{ etc.}$$

Therefore, the vitamin retention, V/V_0, can be determined for any process as a function of T if the appropriate constants are known. Since the activation energy for spore inactivation is usually greater than the activation energy for vitamin destruction, the rate constant for spore inactivation increases faster as temperature is raised than does the rate constant for vitamin destruction. As a consequence, a temperature can be found where the overall rate of spore inactivation is high compared to the rate of vitamin destruction, and the process can be completed with minimal loss of the vitamin.

As a specific example, consider inactivation of thiamine and spores of Bacillus stearothermophilus, a common thermophilic contaminant of foods. The appropriate constants are as follows.

For thiamine, $k_2 = 0.014$/min at 102°C, $E_{a2} = 22$ kcal/mole; for B. stearothermophilus $k_1 = 0.07$/min at 125°C, and $E_{a1} = 69$ kcal/mole. The results of solving the appropriate equations for a variety of processing temperatures, and for two levels of commercial sterility are shown in Table 7-4. It is evident that much less destruction of thiamine occurs when commercial sterilization is conducted under HTST conditions.

B. Prediction of Vitamin Losses in Storage

Another approach to optimization of nutrient content requires knowledge of the nutrient content of a processed food at various times during distribution. With this knowledge, the manufacturer can specify the minimum nutrient content of the product at time of sale, which is essential if nutrient claims are to be made on the label or in advertising associated with the product.

Suppose one wished to predict the nutrient content of a food product at some point in time. The minimal required information would be (a) initial nutrient composition, (b) time-temperature history of the product in all distribution channels (e.g., this would differ for products sold in New Orleans and in New England), (c) package performance (permeability to oxygen, water vapor, light), and (d) influence of other time-dependent environmental factors, e.g., light, relative humidity, and oxygen.

For products which have a relatively simple composition it is feasible to guarantee nutrient content under known circumstances. An actual case history of a commercial juice product fortified with vitamin C is shown in Figure 7-2. The goal of

TABLE 7-4

Sterility level $N/N_0 = 10^{-10}$

Temperature (°C)	Time for sterility (min)	Percent thiamine loss
100	527	99.99
110	47	75
120	4.7	6
130	0.52	2
140	0.067	1
150	0.009	Approx. 0

Sterility level $N/N_0 = 10^{-16}$

Temperature (°C)	Time for sterility (min)	Percent thiamine loss
100	843	99.99
110	75	89
120	7.6	27
130	0.85	10
140	0.11	3
150	0.015	1

the manufacturer was to maintain at least as much ascorbic acid as specified on the label. If the warehouse temperature had been above 100°F this would not have been possible with an initial vitamin excess of 33%. Furthermore, in this particular instance ascorbic acid is lost through two different reactions (see Section VI, A,1 for details). One reaction is fairly rapid and involves ascorbic acid oxidation by oxygen present in the bottle. The other is a slower reaction in which oxygen is not a reactant.

Figure 7-2 indicates that the second, slower reaction has a high activation energy; i.e., there is little additional loss at ambient temperatures following the initial consumption of residual oxygen, whereas the reaction continues at a significant rate at 100°F. To predict the ascorbic acid content in this product would require knowledge of the initial oxygen content and of the rates and activation energies of the two reactions. One can then set up equations for the simultaneous reactions in a manner similar to that shown earlier for HTST processing.

$$\text{Ascorbic acid} + O_2 \longrightarrow \text{products} \qquad \overline{\text{Find}} \atop E_{a1}, k_1$$

$$\text{Ascorbic acid} \longrightarrow \text{products} \qquad E_{a2}, k_2$$

The actual solution of this problem is left as an exercise for the reader (hint: the amount of O_2 in the headspace is usually much less than the amount of ascorbic acid in the product). Numerical solutions for a number of variables would clearly require the services of a computer.

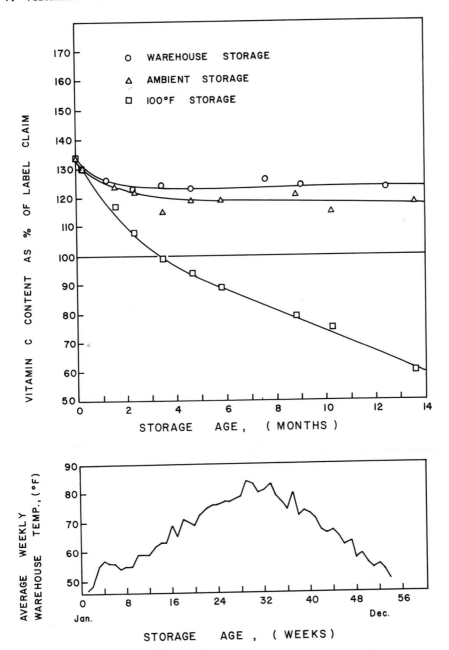

FIG. 7-2. Effect of storage time and storage temperature on the stability of vitamin C in cranberry cocktail (courtesy of Ocean Spray, Inc.).

For more complex products which have nonuniform structures, and for vitamins which exist in multiple forms, the prediction process is very complex. For this reason it seems illogical to promulgate federal or state regulations which apply across the board to all vitamins and all products. On the basis of the previous discussion it appears more reasonable to specify quality characteristics for individual vitamins in certain classes of foods.

VI. CHEMICAL PROPERTIES OF VITAMINS AND MINERALS

A. Water-Soluble Vitamins

1. ASCORBIC ACID (VITAMIN C)

Ascorbic acid is a highly soluble compound that has both acidic and strong reducing properties. These qualities are attributable to its enediol structure which is conjugated with the carbonyl group in a lactone ring.

L-ascorbic acid   L-dehydroascorbic acid

In solution, the hydroxyl on C-3 readily ionizes ($pK_1 = 4.04$ at 25°C) and a solution of the free acid gives a pH of 2.5. The second hydroxyl is much more resistant to ionization ($pK_2 = 11.4$). The compound also absorbs moderately in the UV range and absorption is dependent on pH as shown in Table 7-5.

There are a variety of analytical procedures for detecting ascorbic acid, but none is entirely satisfactory because of lack of specificity and because most foodstuffs contain numerous interfering substances. Analysis usually involves oxidation by a redox dye, such as 2,6-dichlorophenolindophenol. This procedure does not take into account dehydroascorbic acid, a compound which can be readily reduced to ascorbic acid and thus has essentially the same activity as ascorbic acid. Redox procedures are therefore often employed in conjunction with or after treatment of the sample extract with reductants, such as H_2S [E_o' (pH 7) $H_2A \rightarrow A = -0.08$ V]. An alternative approach utilizes the carbonyl properties of A to form the bisphenyl-

TABLE 7-5

UV Absorption Characteristics of Ascorbic Acid[a]

pH	λ_{max} (nm)
2	244
6-10	266
>10	294

[a]$E_{1cm}^{1\%} = 500$.

hydrazone from phenylhydrazine. This procedure is obviously susceptible to errors introduced by the presence of similarly reactive carbonyls, which have no vitamin activity.

Since ascorbic acid is soluble in water, it is readily lost via leaching from cut or bruised surfaces of foods. However, in processed foods, the most significant losses after processing result from chemical degradation. In foods which are particularly high in ascorbic acid, such as fruit products, loss is usually associated with nonenzymic browning. Composition tables may be unreliable for estimating expected concentrations of ascorbic acid since significant amounts of ascorbic acid are used in many types of foods as a processing aid [3].

The exact route of ascorbic acid degradation is highly variable and dependent upon the particular system. Factors which can influence the nature of the degradative mechanism include temperature, salt and sugar concentration, pH, oxygen, enzymes, metal catalysts, amino acids, oxidants or reductants, initial concentration of ascorbic acid, and the ratio of ascorbic acid to dehydroascorbic acid [21, 22,38,49,50,55-58,85].

Since so many factors can influence the nature of ascorbic acid degradation it is not feasible to construct clearly defined precursor-product relationships for any but the earliest products in the reaction pathway. Reaction mechanisms and pathways have been based upon both kinetic and physicochemical measurements, as well as on structure determination of isolated products. Many of these studies have been conducted in model systems at pH's less than 2 or in high concentrations of organic acids and therefore may not duplicate the exact pattern in a particular ascorbic acid-containing food product.

The scheme shown in Figure 7-3 demonstrates the influence of oxygen and heavy metals on the route and products of the reaction [49,53-57,65].

When oxygen is present in the system, ascorbic acid is degraded primarily via its monoanion (HA^-) to dehydroascorbic acid (A), the exact pathway and overall rate being a function of the concentration of metal catalysts (M^{n+}) in the system. The rate of formation of A is approximately first order with respect to $[HA^-]$, $[O_2]$, and $[M^{n+}]$. When the metal catalysts are Cu^{2+} and Fe^{3+} the specific rate constants are several orders of magnitude larger than for spontaneous oxidation, and therefore even a few parts per million of these metals may cause serious losses in food products. The uncatalyzed reaction is not proportional to O_2 concentration at low partial pressures of O_2, as shown in Table 7-6. Below a partial pressure of 0.40 atm O_2 the rate seems to level off, indicating a different oxidative path. One possibility is direct oxidation by hydroperoxyl radicals ($HO_2 \cdot$) or hydrogen peroxide. In contrast, the rate in the catalyzed pathway is proportional to O_2 concentration for partial pressures down to 0.19 atm. The postulated pathway involves formation of a metal-anion complex, $MHA^{(n-1)+}$ which combines with oxygen to give a metal-oxygen-ligand complex, $MHAO_2^{(n-1)+}$. This latter complex has a resonance form of a diradical, which rapidly decomposes to give the ascorbate radical anion $A^{\bar{\cdot}}$, then rapidly reacts with O_2 to give dehydroascorbic acid, A. The O_2 dependence of the catalyzed and uncatalyzed reactions is a key to establishing this mechanism, in which O_2 takes place in the rate-determining step of $MHAO_2^{(n-1)+}$ formation. This O_2 dependence is of considerable importance in explaining the influence of sugars and other solutes on ascorbic acid stability, where at high solute concentrations there is a salting-out effect on dissolved O_2.

In the uncatalyzed oxidative pathway the ascorbate anion (HA^-) is subject to direct attack by molecular O_2 in a rate-limiting step to give first the radical anion

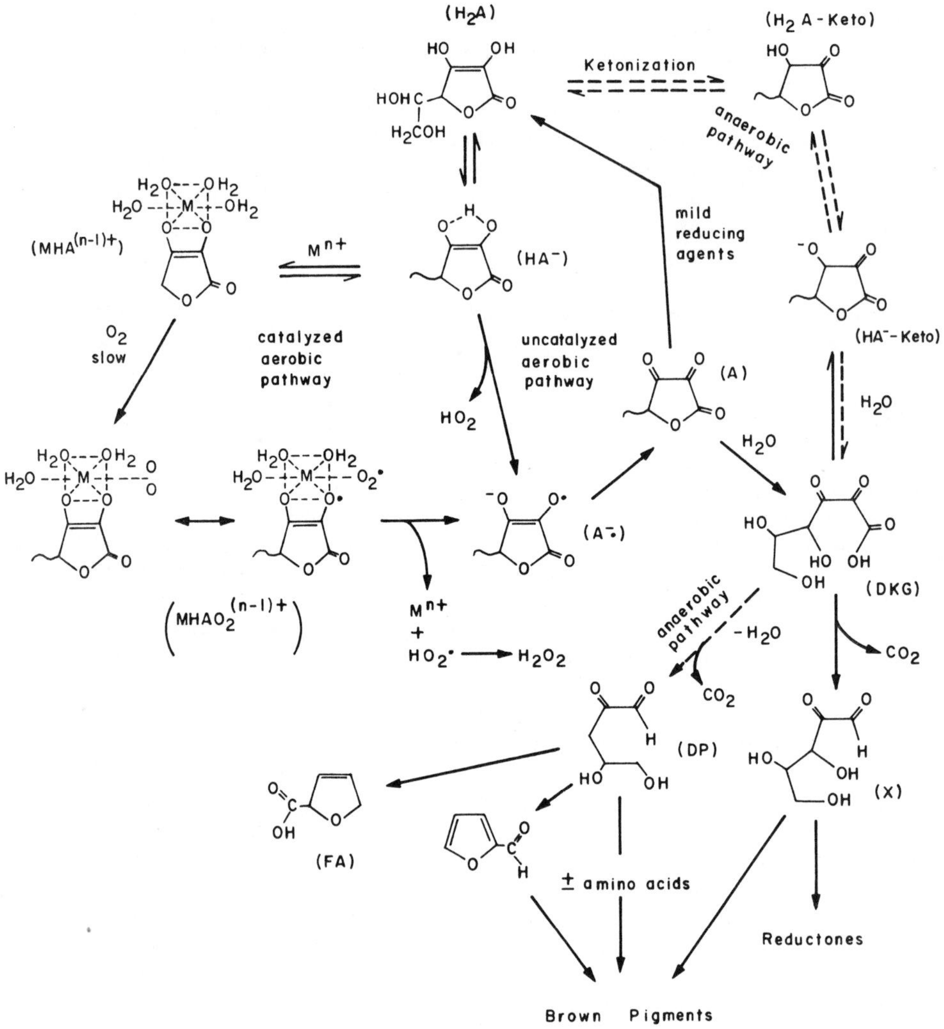

FIG. 7-3. Degradation of ascorbic acid.

A·⁻ and HO₂·, followed rapidly by formation of A and H_2O_2. Thus, the catalyzed and uncatalyzed pathways have common intermediates and are indistinguishable by product analysis. Since dehydroascorbic acid is readily reconverted to ascorbate by mild reduction, loss of vitamin activity comes only after hydrolysis of the lactone to form 2,3-diketogulonic acid (DKG).

The pH-rate profile for uncatalyzed oxidative degradation is an S-shaped curve which increases continuously through the pH corresponding to pK_1 of ascorbic acid and then tends to flatten out above pH 6. This is taken as evidence that it is primarily the monoanion that participates in oxidation. In catalyzed oxidation the rate is inversely proportional to [H⁺], indicating that H_2A and HA⁻ compete for O_2. However, the specific rate constant for HA⁻ is 1.5-3 orders of magnitude greater than for H_2A [53]. Under anaerobic conditions the rate reaches a maximum at pH

TABLE 7-6

Variation of Rate Constants (sec^{-1}) of Uncatalyzed Ascorbic
Acid Oxidation with Oxygen Partial Pressure[a]

Partial pressure of O_2 (atm)	Specific rate constant for ascorbate anion x 10^4
1.00	5.87
0.81	4.68
0.62	3.53
0.40	2.75
0.19	2.01
0.10	1.93
0.05	1.91

[a]Ref. [53].

4, declines to a minimum at pH 2, and then increases again with increasing acidity [49]. The characteristics of the reaction below pH 2 are of little significance in foods, but the maximum at pH 4 is of considerable practical significance and remains the object of much experimentation and speculation. The scheme for anaerobic degradation shown in Figure 7-3 is speculative. Following the suggestion of Kurata and Sakurai [55-57] ascorbic acid is shown to react via its keto tautomer, H_2A-keto. The tautomer is in equilibrium with its anion, HA$^-$-keto, which undergoes delactonization to DKG.

Although the anaerobic pathway can also contribute to ascorbic acid degradation in the presence of O_2, even the uncatalyzed oxidative rate is very much greater than the anaerobic rate at ambient temperatures. Therefore, both pathways may be operative in the presence of O_2, with the oxidative pathways being dominant. In the absence of O_2 there is no added influence of metal catalysts. However, certain chelates of Cu^{2+} and Fe^{3+} are catalytic in a manner independent of O_2 concentration, with catalytic effectiveness being a function of metal chelate stability [54].

In Figure 7-3 further degradation is shown beyond DKG. Although these reactions are not of nutritional importance (nutritional value is already lost at this point), the decomposition of ascorbic acid is closely tied to nonenzymic browning in some food products. Evidence accumulated so far tends to indicate a major divergence of products formed, depending on whether or not decomposition has been oxidative. Since the divergence appears to occur following DKG formation it is somewhat paradoxical that the reactions themselves do not require molecular O_2. However, in oxidative degradation a relatively large proportion of ascorbate is rapidly converted to A, which in turn influences the reaction chemistry via interactions not explicitly shown in the scheme. Xylosone (X) may be formed by simple decarboxylation of DKG, whereas 3-deoxypentosone (DP) is formed by β elimination at C-4 of DKG followed by decarboxylation. It may be the rate of accumulation of DKG which influences its mode of decomposition, or it may be a more specific interaction with A. In either case, the reaction begins to assume the characteristics of typical nonenzymic browning reactions at this stage (see Chapter 3). Xylosone is further degraded to reductones and ethylglyoxal, while DP is degraded to furfural (F) and 2,5-dihydrofuroic acid (E). Any or all of these compounds may combine with amino acids to contribute to the browning of foods [50].

The most critical study of factors influencing ascorbic acid degradation is that of Spanyar and Kevei [85], who have examined the copper-catalyzed reaction with respect to O_2 concentration; Fe^{3+} catalysis; pH, temperature; ascorbate, dehydroascorbate, and isoascorbate concentrations; cysteine and glutathione; and polyphenols. The most interesting findings of this study were the interactions of cysteine, Cu^{2+}, and pH. If sufficiently high concentrations of cysteine are present, ascorbate is completely protected, even when ascorbate is still in molar excess. This protection might be related to interaction of cysteine with copper, since the pH-rate profile of ascorbate degradation was no longer related to the reciprocal of $[H^+]$ but showed a minimum in the vicinity of pH 4. Although I am unaware of any foodstuffs that behave in this manner, an insufficient number of cases has been examined, and the cysteine effect may prove of significance.

In such foods as canned juices, the loss of ascorbic acid tends to follow consecutive first-order reactions; a rapid initial reaction which is oxygen dependent and which proceeds until residual dissolved or headspace oxygen is completely exhausted, followed by anaerobic degradation. In dehydrated citrus juices, degradation of ascorbic acid appears to be only a function of temperature and moisture content [51]. The influence of moisture on stability of ascorbic acid in a variety of foods is shown in Figure 7-4 [60]. Although ascorbic acid appears to be degraded even at very low moisture contents, the rate becomes slow enough that long storage can be used without excessive ascorbate loss.

Although the stability of ascorbic acid generally increases as the temperature of the food is lowered, certain investigations have indicated that there may be an accelerated loss on freezing or frozen storage. This has been shown to be unlikely for most practical food situations [92]; however, storage temperatures above -18°C can ultimately lead to significant losses [48]. In general, the largest losses for noncitrus foods will occur during heating. This is illustrated in Figure 7-5 for peas processed by a variety of techniques. It is apparent that the leaching loss during heating far exceeds losses during other process steps. This observation applies to most water-soluble nutrients.

2. THIAMINE

Thiamine, or vitamin B_1, consists of a substituted pyrimidine linked to a substituted thiazole by a methylene group. It is widely distributed throughout the plant and animal kingdom; it plays a key role as a coenzyme in the intermediary metabolism of α-keto acids and carbohydrates. As a result of this coenzymic role, thiamine can exist in foods in a number of forms, including free thiamine, the pyrophosphoric acid ester (cocarboxylase), and bound to the respective apoenzyme. The details of these various structures are shown in Figure 7-6.

Since thiamine contains a quaternary nitrogen function, it is a strong base and is completely ionized over the entire range of pH normally encountered in foods.

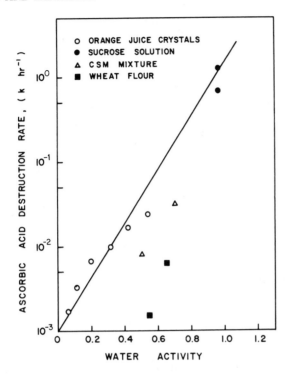

FIG. 7-4. Relation between water activity and rate of destruction of ascorbic acid.

In addition, the amino group on the pyrimidine ring will be ionized, the extent dependent on pH ($pK_a = 4.8$). The coenzyme role of thiamine is elaborated through position 2 of the thiazole ring, which in its ionized form is a strong nucleophile. Studies on deuterium exchange at this position have shown a half-life at room temperature of 2 min at pH 5. At pH 7 the exchange reaction is too fast to follow by ordinary techniques [12].

Thiamine is also characterized by strong UV absorption bands with pH-dependent absorption maxima (Table 7-7). These spectral characteristics are useful for analysis under only the most limited circumstances, since many thiamine degradation products are also UV absorbing. The method of choice for analysis is usually the thiochrome procedure, which involves treatment of thiamine with a strong oxidizing agent (e.g., ferricyanide, hydrogen peroxide) to effect conversion to strongly fluorescent thiochrome (Figure 7-6). Adaptation of this procedure to foods requires enzymic hydrolysis of combined forms of the vitamin to free thiamine, and a chromatographic cleanup prior to conversion to thiochrome.

Thiamine is one of the least stable vitamins. Extensive losses occur in cereals as a result of cooking or baking; in meats, vegetables, and fruits as a result of various processing operations; and during storage. The literature up through 1953 has been analyzed and summarized by Farrer [36], and only typical examples are used here for didactic purposes. The stability of thiamine is so strongly influenced

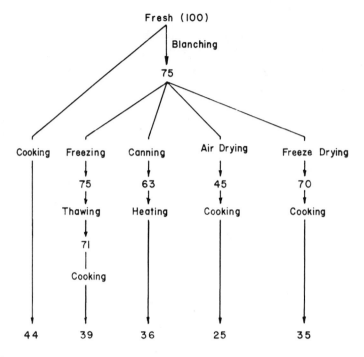

FIG. 7-5. Retention of ascorbic acid in processed peas. (After Bender [5] and Mapson [69].)

TABLE 7-7

Molar Absorptivities of Thiamine Solutions

System	λ_{max} (nm)	ϵ
0.005N HCl	247	14,500
pH 7.0	231	12,000
	267	8,600

by the nature and state of the system that it is difficult to extrapolate between systems, and numerous unexplainable differences between similar investigations exist in the scientific literature (see Farrer for examples).

Since thiamine can exist in multiple forms, the overall stability of vitamin activity depends on the relative concentrations of the various forms. Within given animal species the ratios also depend on the nutritional status prior to death, vary from one type of muscle to another, and for both plants and animals depend on postharvest or postmortem physiological stresses. In the relatively few studies that have been conducted, the enzyme-bound forms (e.g., cocarboxylase) have been

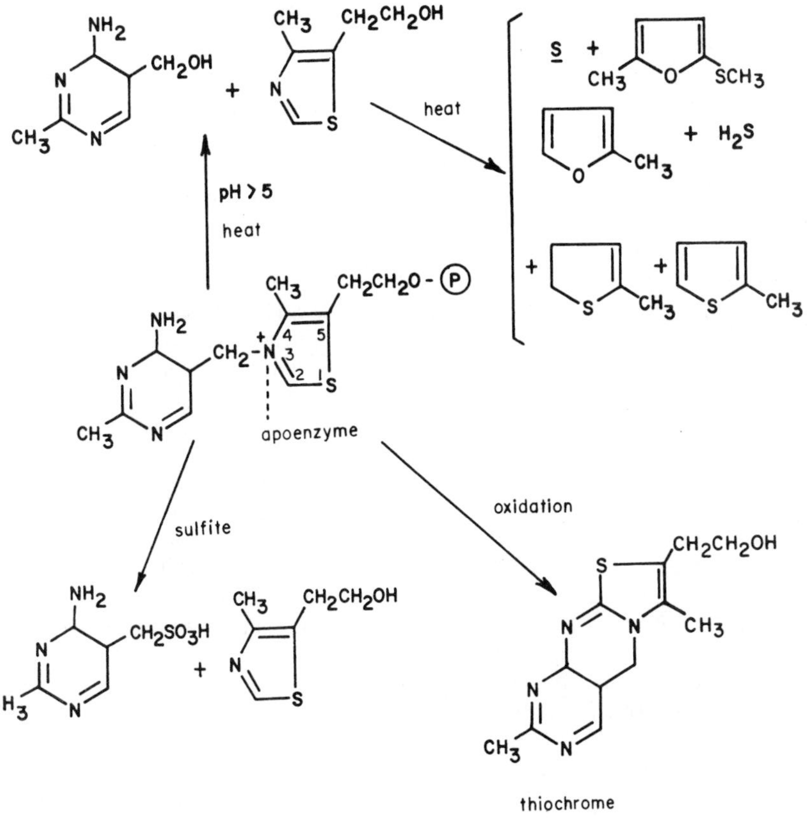

FIG. 7-6. Degradation of thiamine. The circled P is pyrophosphate.

found to be less stable than the free vitamin. Farrer [36] has suggested that the relative concentrations of the various forms of the vitamin may account for some discrepancies in the literature.

The stability of thiamine is also determined by pH, temperature, ionic strength, buffer type, and other reacting species [4,70]. The typical degradative reaction appears to involve a nucleophilic displacement at the methylene carbon joining the two ring systems. Therefore, strong nucleophiles, such as HSO_3^- (sulfite), readily cause destruction of the vitamin. The similarity of the chemistry of degradation either by sulfite or at alkaline pH is shown in Figure 7-6. Both processes yield 5-β-hydroxyethyl-4-methylthiazole and a corresponding substituted pyrimidine. In the case of sulfite, this is a 2-methyl-5(methylsulfonic acid) pyrimidine, while in the case of alkali it is the corresponding hydroxymethylpyrimidine. The chemistry of sulfite cleavage has been extensively analyzed [63] and this reaction is of particular significance in dehydrated vegetables and fruits treated with sulfite to inhibit browning (see Chapter 6).

Thiamine is also inactivated by nitrite, possibly via reaction with the amino group on the pyrimidine ring. It was noticed very early [4] that this reaction was mitigated in meat products compared to buffer solutions, implying a protective effect of protein. Casein and soluble starch also exhibit protective effects against destruction of thiamine by sulfite [64]. In the latter case the protective effect was shown to be unrelated to binding of reactants, oxidation of reactive sulfhydryl groups, or competitive oxidation of sulfite by protein. Although the mechanism of the protective effect is still unclear, it is probable that the effect itself extends to other degradative mechanisms and may be another important source of discrepancies in the literature.

Temperature is an important factor in thiamine stability. Table 7-8 shows differences in thiamine retention among various foods held at two storage temperatures. Rate constants for thiamine degradation in various foods, including peas, carrots, cabbage, potatoes, and pork, range from 0.0020 to 0.0027 per minute at 100°C, but these values cannot be extrapolated to other temperatures unless the Arrhenius activation energy is known for the particular system. Activation energies summarized by Farrar [36] vary by a factor of more than two depending on the system and the reaction conditions. In phosphate buffer at pH 6.8, Goldblith et al. [43] found the activation energy to be 22 kcal/mole for both conventional and microwave heating, similar to the value in pureed meats and vegetables found by Feliciotti and Esselen [37]. Leichter and Joslyn [63] found that sulfite lowered the activation energy to 13.6 kcal/mole. Since it is also possible that catalytic concentrations [8] of such metals as copper can accelerate the rate of degradation at a given pH, differences in activation energies are conceivably ascribable to small compositional differences of the system. However, Feliciotti and Esselen [37] found similar values for activation energies in a wide variety of meats and vegetables, irrespective of sample pH.

Thermal destruction of thiamine leads to formation of a characteristic odor which is involved in the development of "meaty" flavors in cooked foods. Some of the probable reactions [1,32-35,71] are summarized in Figure 7-6. The reaction leading to formation of pyrimidine and thiazole rings has already been described. Significant secondary products are then thought to arise from the thiazole ring,

TABLE 7-8

Thiamine Retention in Stored Foods[a]

System	Retention after 12 months storage	
	38°C	1.5°C
Apricots	35	72
Green beans	8	76
Lima beans	48	92
Tomato juice	60	100
Peas	68	100
Orange juice	78	100

[a]Ref. [41].

and these include elemental sulfur, hydrogen sulfide, a furan, a thiophene, and a dihydrothiophene. Reactions leading to these products are unclear, but extensive degradation and rearrangement of the thiazole ring must be involved.

As previously indicated, the rate of thiamine degradation is extremely sensitive to pH. The pH–rate profiles for heated thiamine and cocarboxylase are shown in Figure 7-7. It is apparent that either the starch and/or the protein components of cereal products exert a protective effect over the range of pH examined. Cocarboxylase is more sensitive than thiamine, but the difference in sensitivity is a function of pH, disappearing completely at pH values greater than 7.5. Since both the amino group on the pyrimidine ring and the 2 position on the thiazole ring are strongly influenced by pH in the region of interest for thiamine stability, either function may be implicated in the degradative reactions. However, based upon the nature of the secondary products it appears that the thiazole ring is the most likely site for the reaction.

In addition to thermal destruction, loss of thiamine can occur in raw fishery products because of thiaminase activity. This does not seem to be a significant human problem but has proved fatal to unwary animal breeders who have included raw fish waste in their rations.

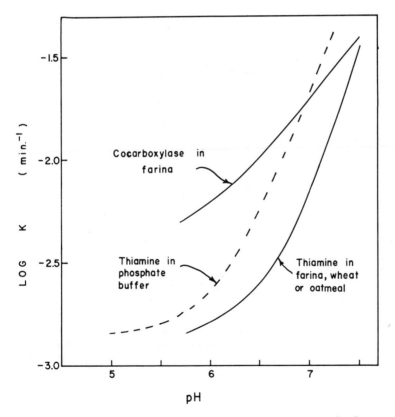

FIG. 7-7. pH stability of thiamine and cocarboxylase. (Ref. [36], courtesy of Academic Press.)

As is true of other water-soluble vitamins, thiamine is extensively lost by leaching during cooking operations (Table 7-3) and during milling of cereals (Fig. 7-1). Little information is available on thiamine stability in dehydrated foods. Studies in dehydrated corn-soy-milk (CSM) indicate that degradation is influenced strongly by moisture content [7]. For example, storage at 100°F for 182 days caused no loss when the system is maintained below 10% moisture content, but extensive loss occurs at 13% moisture. Because of multiple possibilities of physical separation and chemical degradation, substantial losses of thiamine can occur in many foods unless great care is taken during all handling, storage, and processing operations.

3. VITAMIN B$_6$

There are three chemical compounds found in foods which have vitamin B$_6$ activity: pyridoxal (I), pyridoxine or pyridoxol (II), and pyridoxamine (III). This vitamin is widely distributed throughout the plant and animal kingdom, since pyridoxal phosphate is a key coenzyme for almost every type of biochemical transformation of the amino acids (e.g., racemization, transamination, decarboxylation, dehydration).

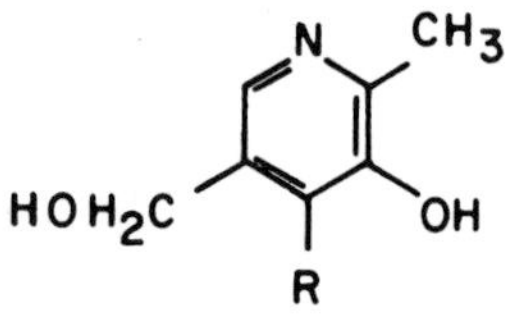

$$\underline{R}$$

I $-CHO$

II $-CH_2OH$

III $-CH_2NH_2$

Information on the distribution of vitamin B$_6$ in its various forms in foods has become available only recently [75,76]. Although many foods have not been systematically studied for vitamin B$_6$ destruction during processing, it is nevertheless apparent that both the quantity and the form of the vitamin are influenced by the processes of heating, concentration, and dehydration. Analysis of the three forms of B$_6$ requires chromatographic separation followed by bioassay, and the entire procedure should be carried out with minimum exposure to light.

The pyridoxol form of the vitamin is extremely stable and is the form used for fortification. Pyridoxal exerts its coenzyme action via a carbonyl-amine condensation, with the amino acid yielding a Schiff base which is stabilized by chelation to a metal ion (IV).

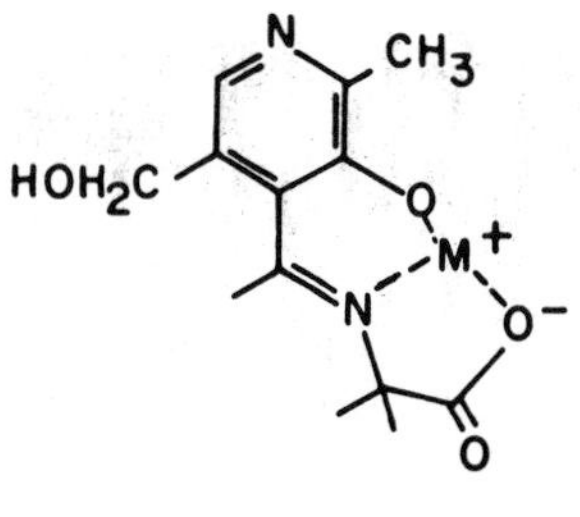

IV

If a solution of pyridoxal is heated with glutamic acid, a mixture including pyridoxamine and α-ketoglutaric acid results. In fact, heating a mixture of amino acids, pyridoxal, and polyvalent metal cations at 100°C at any of a wide range of pH values leads to the same products that normally result from the conversion involving the holoenzyme [84].

In view of the above, it is not surprising to find an entirely different distribution of vitamin B_6 forms in fresh and processed foods. When some of the data of Polansky and Toepfer [76] are recalculated, it is evident that pyridoxal increases and pyridoxamine decreases going from fresh to dried eggs. In fresh milk the main form is pyridoxal; in dried milk pyridoxal is still dominant but there is more pyridoxamine than in fresh, fluid milk; while in evaporated milk pyridoxamine is the main form. In raw pork loin the dominant form is pyridoxal, while in fully cooked ham it is pyridoxamine.

A great deal of attention has been paid to the stability of vitamin B_6 in heat-processed milk. When pyridoxol is added to milk it is stable during sterilization. However, the dominant natural form of vitamin B_6 in milk is pyridoxal. Studies have shown that sterilized liquid milks and formula milks contain less than half their original vitamin B_6 activity, the decrease continuing 7–10 days after processing [47,93]. In addition, feeding tests with rats indicated that the decrease was even more substantial than that found using the test organism S. carlsbergensis. Vitamin B_6 is believed to react with substances released from milk proteins upon heating. A leading candidate for this reaction appears to be cysteine, which reacts with pyridoxal phosphate to form a thiazolidine (V) [6,13].

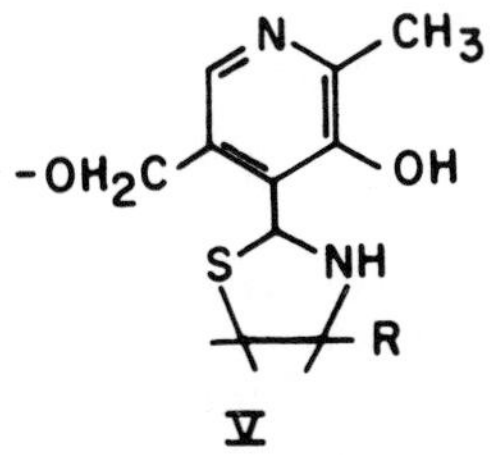

V

When cysteine and pyridoxal are allowed to react under conditions similar to those encountered in the sterilization process, the reaction products have no vitamin B_6 activity for rats and approximately 20% activity for S. carlsbergensis. A resulting product of this reaction appears to be bis–4–pyridoxyldisulfide [97] possibly arising via (V). A similar reaction sequence is possible by direct reaction of

pyridoxal with sulfhydryl groups of milk serum proteins [86]. Since the main result of the interaction of vitamin B_6 with amino groups appears to be the interconversion between pyridoxal and pyridoxamine, both with full vitamin B_6 activity, the
cysteine reaction may be the cause of instability of this vitamin in heat-processed
foods.

Another reaction of vitamin B_6 is its photoconversion to biologically inactive
products. A key reaction product is 4-pyridoxic acid [80] and the reaction is dependent on the presence of oxygen. This reaction is probably of little importance
in food systems.

The sensitivity of vitamin B_6 to conditions of processing led to a situation in
1952 which exemplified the need for food processors to have concern about the nutrient content of processed foods [73]. An infant food, available in liquid and dry
form, was identified as the cause of at least 50-60 cases of convulsive seizures.
The seizures occurred after consumption of the liquid form of the food and were
attributed to instability of pyridoxal in the presence of milk proteins. The situation
was solved by fortifying the product with the more stable pyridoxol.

4. FOLIC ACID

This vitamin is a precursor of coenzymes involved in the biological transfer of one-
carbon units (formyl, formaldehyde, hydroxymethyl). Its chemistry, function, and
biosynthesis have been recently summarized [87] and only a brief consideration of
its properties are possible within the scope of this chapter.

The structure of folic acid is shown below. It consists of a pteridine ring linked
to p-aminobenzoic acid, which in turn is coupled by an amide linkage to glutamic
acid. In many food systems folate contains more than one glutamate moiety, with
the glutamates linked through peptide bonds involving the γ-carboxyl group. In
addition, the 5, 6, 7, and 8 positions of the pteridine ring may be reduced in various forms to yield a variety of di- or tetrahydrofolates (i.e., 5,6,7,8-tetrahydro-
folate; 5,6-, 5,8-, or 7,8-dihydrofolate).

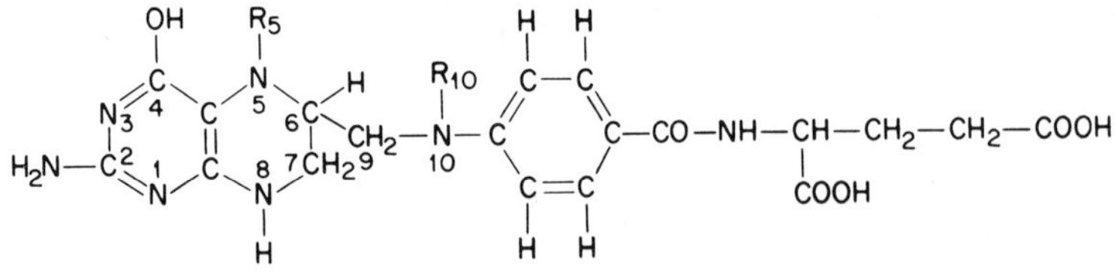

In foods, folic acid content must be assayed (by microbiological methods or by
chromatographic separation) after the various glutamate conjugates are enzymically cleaved to give free folic acid. The natural free folic acid content varies for
individual foods [81]. In typical American diets the total folate content has been
found to be about 180 μg/day [16]. These values are significantly lower than the
RDA (Table 7-1) and folate deficiency is thought by some to be a significant public
health problem [89].

The extent and mechanism of loss of folic acid in processed foods is not clear.
However, studies of processed and stored milks indicate that the primary inactivation process is oxidative [14,15,39,40]. The destruction of folate parallels that of

ascorbate, and added ascorbate can stabilize folate. Both vitamins in milk are greatly stabilized by deoxygenation, but both also inevitably decline during 14 days of storage at room temperature (15°-19°C).

5. RIBOFLAVIN

Vitamin B_2 (riboflavin) is also an important enzyme cofactor and exists in tissues primarily as the coenzyme flavin adenine dinucleotide (FAD). The enzymes associated with this vitamin are called "flavoproteins" and they typically catalyze oxidations or dehydrations of such compounds as amino acids, aldehydes or pyridine nucleotides.

Riboflavin is quite stable in food under ordinary conditions. However, it is lost in trimming, milling, and leaching operations to an extent similar to that of other water-soluble vitamins. Riboflavin is more stable under acid than under alkaline conditions. It is most readily lost if exposed to light, which causes the interesting photochemical cleavage of ribitol shown below, yielding lumiflavin.

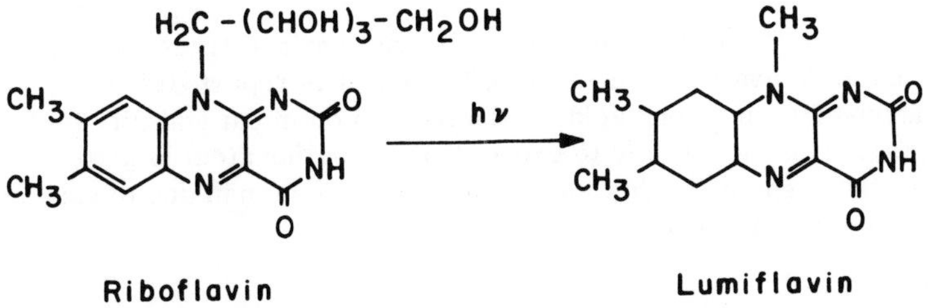

Riboflavin   Lumiflavin

Lumiflavin is apparently a stronger oxidizing agent than riboflavin and can catalyze destruction of a number of other vitamins, particularly ascorbic acid. Some years ago when milk was sold in transparent bottles the reaction sequence described above was a significant problem, leading not only to a loss of nutritional value but also to an acceptability problem known as "sunlight off flavor." With the advent of the paper or plastic milk container the problem disappeared.

6. NIACIN

This is one of the most stable vitamins, being relatively resistent to heat, acid, or alkali. It exists in foods either as nicotinic acid, as nicotinamide, or as one of the nicotinamide coenzymes (NAD, NADP). Its losses from foods occur via trimming, leaching, etc., and parallel losses of other water-soluble vitamins.

Nicotinic Acid

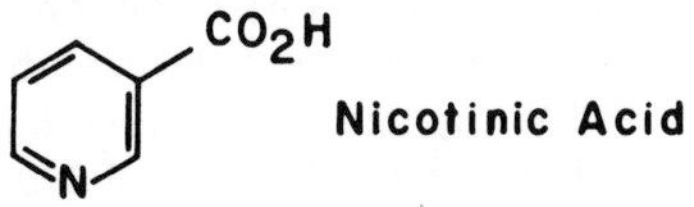

7. PANTOTHENIC ACID

This water-soluble member of the vitamin B group is most stable in the pH range 4-7. It occurs in foods primarily as a moiety of coenzyme A. Outside the stable pH region the amide group is susceptible to hydrolysis, yielding β-alanine and pantoic acid. Based on limited data [75], losses in excess of 50% are not uncommon in thermally processed foods.

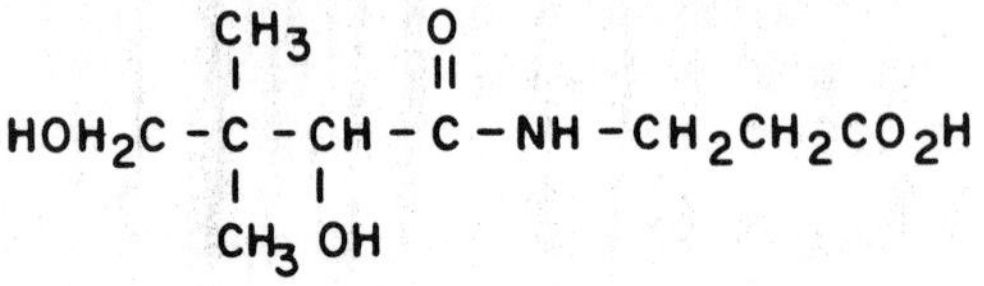

$$HOH_2C - \underset{\underset{CH_3}{|}}{\overset{\overset{CH_3}{|}}{C}} - \underset{\underset{OH}{|}}{CH} - \overset{\overset{O}{\parallel}}{C} - NH - CH_2CH_2CO_2H$$

Pantothenic Acid

8. BIOTIN

Biotin, shown below, is a coenzyme for carboxylations and transcarboxylations. Little information is available on its stability, but it is reportedly stable to heat and light and unstable in strong acid or alkali, with optimum stability in the pH range 5-8 [10]. It is reasonable to expect that the sulfur atom is also susceptible to oxidation. Deficiencies of this vitamin are unlikely in man due to extensive synthesis in the intestinal tract.

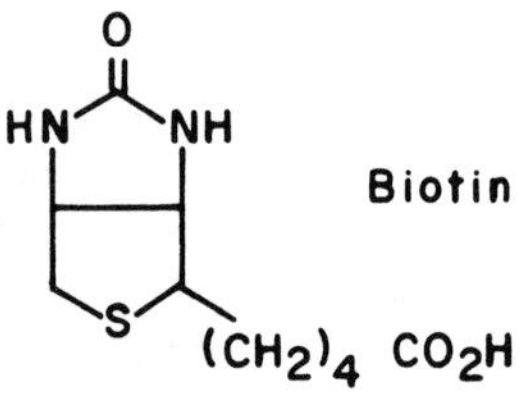

$$HN \underset{}{\overset{\overset{O}{\parallel}}{\diagup}} NH$$

Biotin

$$S \quad (CH_2)_4 \quad CO_2H$$

9. VITAMIN B$_{12}$

This red substance is by far the most complex of the vitamins and has been the last to have its structure elucidated. Vitamin B$_{12}$ is also known by the name "cyanocobalamin" since it is most commonly found as a coordination complex with cobalt. Its structure is shown in Figure 7-8. Because of its complex structure and the possibility of existing in multiple forms, analysis of vitamin B$_{12}$ must be carried out biologically. A compilation of its distribution in foods is given by Orr [75]. It is found only in animal tissues and fermented vegetable products. It is generally found in concentrations of 10-100 μg/kg of fresh food and the human nutritional requirement is correspondingly very small (RDA of 5 μg/day).

Little information is available about the stability of vitamin B$_{12}$ in foods. The region of optimal pH stability is pH 4-6 and in this region only small losses are

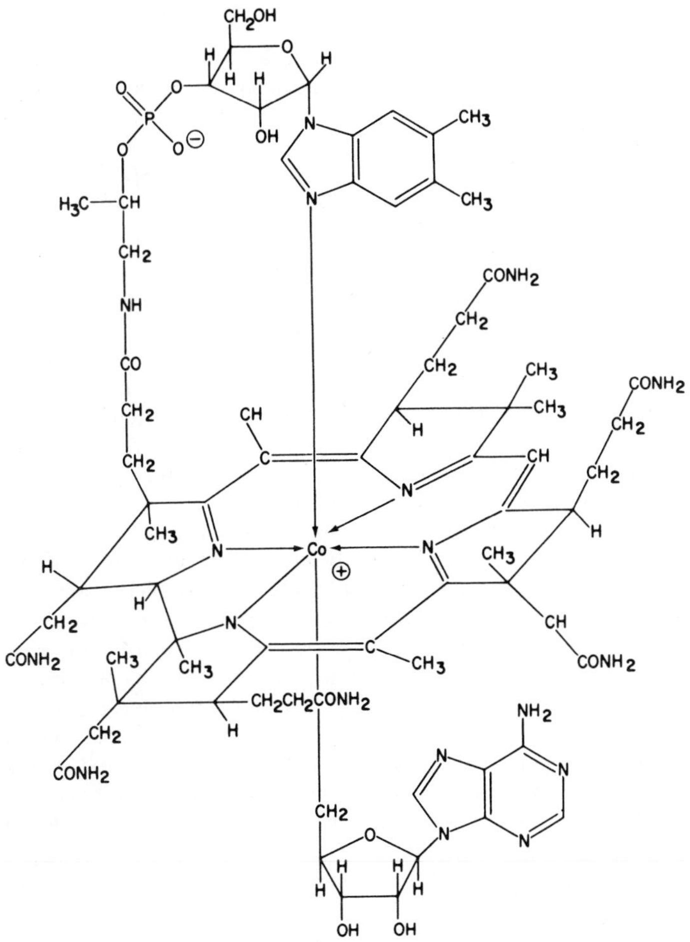

FIG. 7-8. Structure of vitamin B$_{12}$ (from Whitaker [98]).

found, even after autoclaving [10]. At higher pH's or in the presence of reducing agents, such as ascorbic acid or sulfite, losses may be severe. A great deal of work has been done on the stability of this vitamin in pharmaceutical preparations but much of this work is inapplicable to foods.

B. Fat-Soluble Vitamins

1. VITAMIN A

Vitamin A activity is contained in a series of C-20 and C-40 unsaturated hydrocarbons which are widely distributed in the plant and animal kingdom. The structure of the vitamin is shown below, and it may occur as the free alcohol, esterified to fatty acids, or as the aldehyde or acid. In animals the vitamin is found in highest concentration in the liver, where it is stored, existing generally as the free alcohol or in esterified form.

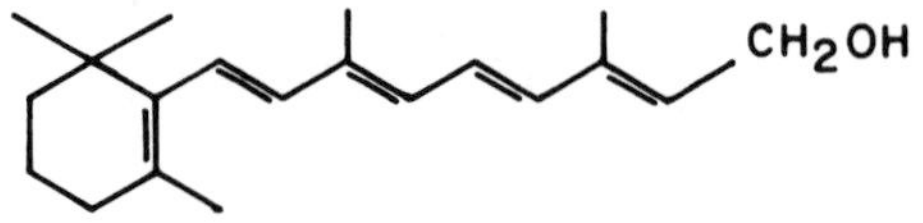

Vitamin A Alcohol

In plants and fungi, vitamin A activity is contained in a number of carotenoids which are metabolically converted to vitamin A after absorption by the ingesting animal. The structures and provitamin A activities of a number of commonly occurring carotenoids are given in Table 7-9, the most potent provitamin being β-carotene, which yields two equivalents of vitamin A.

Since the carotenoids are predominantly hydrocarbon in nature, they are fat soluble and water insoluble and are naturally associated with lipidlike structures. Carotene-protein complexes also occur [74] and they may be associated with an aqueous phase. The highly unsaturated carotenoid systems give rise to a series of complex UV and visible spectra (300-500 nm) which account for their strong orange-yellow pigmentation. Extensive listings of carotenoids, their spectra, and their provitamin A activities are given in Deuel [31] and Zeichmeister [99]. A review of the chemistry of carotenoids in foods is given in Borenstein and Bunnell [11].

It is now generally accepted that the vitamin A activity of a food is best determined by chromatographic separation of the carotenoids, followed by summation of the activities in the various geometric and stereoisomers. The early analytical procedures, including the Carr-Price reaction with antimony trichloride, gave erroneously high values and especially neglected the possibility of cis-trans isomerization following food processing.

The destruction of provitamins A in processed and stored foods can follow a variety of pathways depending on reaction conditions, and these are summarized in Figure 7-9. In the absence of oxygen there are a number of possible thermal transformations, particularly cis-trans isomerization. This has been shown to occur in both cooked and canned vegetables [88,96]. Overall losses may vary from 5 to 40% depending on temperature, time, and nature of the carotenoids. At higher temperatures, β-carotene can fragment to yield a series of aromatic hydrocarbons, the most prominent being ionene [29,67].

If oxygen is present, extensive losses of carotenoids occur, stimulated by light, by enzymes, and by cooxidation with lipid hydroperoxides. Chemical oxidation of β-carotene appears to yield primarily the 5,6-epoxide, which may later isomerize to mutachrome - the 5,8-epoxide. Light-catalyzed oxidation yields primarily mutachrome [83]. Isomerization of the 5,6-epoxide to mutachrome has been studied in orange juice [25]. Further fragmentation of the primary oxidation products yields a complex of compounds [94] similar to those found following oxidation of fatty acids. Oxidation of vitamin A results in complete loss of vitamin activity.

TABLE 7-9

Carotenoids: Structure and Provitamin A Activity

	Relative activity
β-Carotene (widely distributed)	++++
β-apo-8'-carotenal	+++
Cryptoxanthin (orange)	++
α-Carotene (widely distributed)	++
Echinenone (sea urchin)	++
Astacene (crustacea)	0
Lycopene (tomato)	0

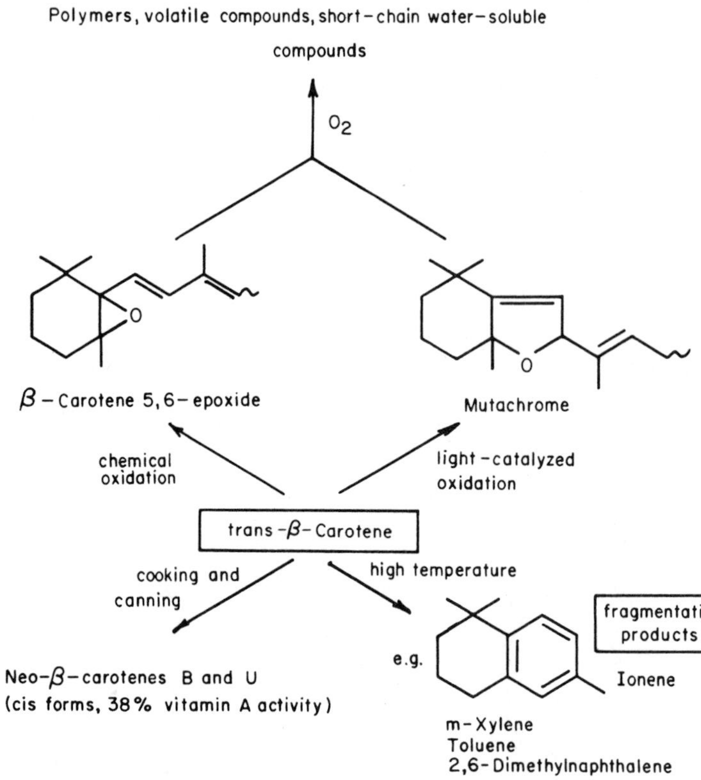

Polymers, volatile compounds, short−chain water−soluble
compounds

FIG. 7-9. Degradation of β-carotene.

Dehydrated foods are most susceptible to loss of vitamin A and provitamin A activity on storage [66] because of their propensity to undergo oxidation [61]. Overall losses of vitamin A resulting from a number of types of dehydration processes are shown in Table 7-10.

As is the case for lipids, the rate of oxidation is a function of enzymes, water activity, storage atmosphere, and temperature [20,79]. Therefore, the expected loss will depend on the severity of drying conditions (Table 7-10) and the degree of protection during storage. The influences of water and O_2 concentrations are shown in Table 7-11. There is a measurable rate of loss even at very low O_2 partial pressures. Although the rate of loss in shrimp decreases with increasing moisture, other foods (corn) show more complex behavior [78]. In general, the stability of carotenoids can be expected to parallel that of unsaturated fatty acids in a given food, and the complex interactions of carotenoid stability with water activity and other constituents of food are beyond the scope of this chapter (see Chapter 4 and Ref. [59]).

TABLE 7-10

Concentration of β-Carotene in Cooked Dehydrated Carrots[a]

Sample	Range of concentration (ppm solids)
Fresh	980–1860
Explosive puff dried	805–1060
Vacuum freeze dried	870–1125
Conventional air dried	636–987

[a]Ref. [30].

TABLE 7-11

Carotenoid Destruction Rates[a]

Product	Percent H_2O	Gas	k (hr^{-1})
Carrot flakes, 20°C	5	Air	6.1×10^{-4}
		2% O_2	1.0×10^{-3}
Shrimp, 37°C	<0.5	Air	1.1×10^{-3}
	3	Air	0.9×10^{-3}
	5	Air	0.6×10^{-3}
	8	Air	0.1×10^{-3}

$E_a = 19 \; K_{cal}/mole$

[a]Ref. [60].

2. VITAMIN K

Vitamin K activity is found in a number of fat-soluble naphthaquinone derivatives and occurs primarily in green plants. The structure of vitamin K is shown in Fig. 7-10a. Aside from the fact that these compounds are photoreactive, little is known of their chemical behavior in foods.

3. VITAMIN D

Vitamin D activity is found in certain sterol derivatives, the structure of one member of this group being shown in Figure 7-10b. These compounds are fat soluble and are sensitive to oxygen and light. A significant fraction of milk sold in the United States is fortified with vitamin D and stability in foods does not appear to be a significant problem.

4. VITAMIN E

There are a variety of tocopherol compounds which have vitamin E activity, the most potent being α-tocopherol, shown in Figure 7-10c. The tocopherols also have antioxidant activity; however the most potent antioxidant is not the most potent vitamin. There is relatively little information available on distribution of vitamin E in foods, particularly in complex diets [27,28]. Vegetable oils, whole wheat, and other whole grains appear to be excellent dietary sources. The influence of storage and processing on retention of vitamin E in foods has been reviewed by Harris [45]. In the course of processing vegetable oils to margarines and short-enings, vitamin E activity is lost. It is also extensively decreased if autooxidation

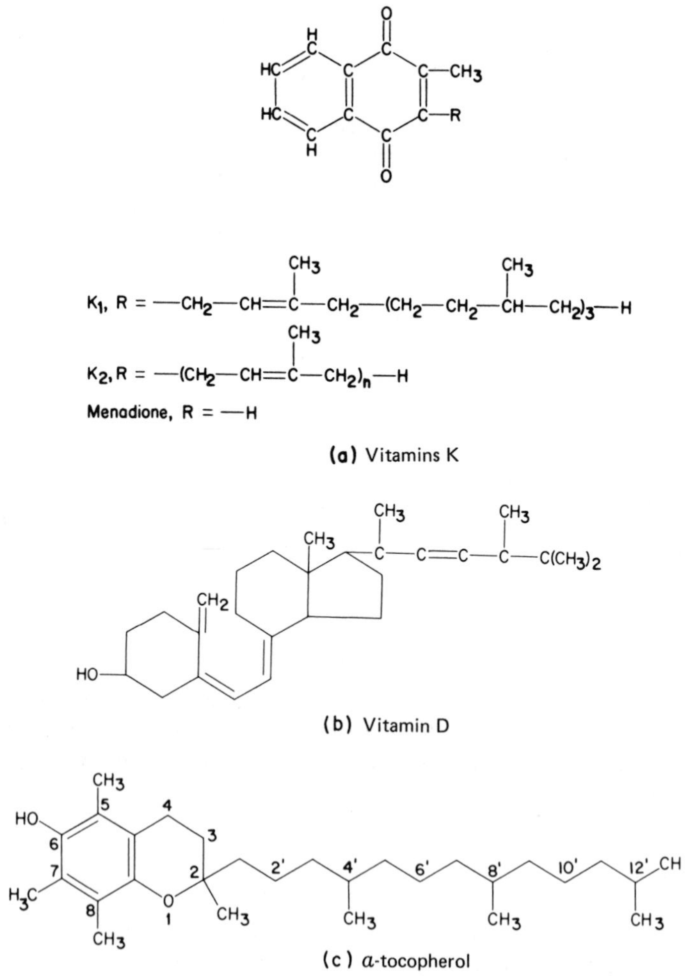

(a) Vitamins K

(b) Vitamin D

(c) α-tocopherol

FIG. 7-10. Structures of some fat-soluble vitamins. (From Whitaker [98].)

of lipids in foods is severe. Dehydrated foods are particularly susceptible for the reasons discussed under vitamin A. The decomposition products of oxidized tocopherols include dimers, trimers, dihydroxy compounds, and quinones [24]. A mechanism for forming some of these compounds has been suggested [44], and the effects of pH, water content, and temperature have been investigated for the case of tocopherol oxidation with methyl linoleate hydroperoxides.

C. Minerals

Table 7-1 contains eight mineral substances with established or approximated RDA's and several others which are required by man but have not had RDAs established. In contrast to the vitamins, the mineral content of foods can vary greatly, depending on such environmental factors as soil composition or nature of the animal feed. Losses occur not so much through destruction by chemical reaction as through physical removal or combination in forms which are not biologically available. Current knowledge on distribution of these food components has been reviewed [52], and an attempt to summarize processing losses is also available [82].

The primary mechanism of loss of mineral substances is through leaching of water-soluble materials and trimming of unwanted plant parts, as discussed earlier in this chapter. Major losses of all minerals occur in the milling of cereals.

Equal in importance is the interaction of mineral substances with other constituents of the food. These interactions can be of a positive or a negative nature. Polyvalent anions, such as oxalate and phytate, can form salts with divalent metal cations and these are extremely insoluble and pass through the digestive tract unabsorbed. The availability of iron depends not only on the nature of the salt or ligand but also on oxidation state. The iron in egg yolk presents a particularly complex case in point [72]. The relative biological value (RBV, ferrous sulfate = 100) of raw yolk was 29 compared to 32 for cooked and 20 for spray-dried yolk. These low availabilities are apparently due to binding of iron to yolk proteins and can be increased to RBV's of 100 by treatment with reducing agents, such as ascorbic acid or cysteine. In similar fashion, it has been shown unwise to judge iron availability except after normal processing of the food since unavailable forms can be altered to increase their biological value [90].

REFERENCES

1. R. G. Arnold, J. Agri. Food Chem., 17, 390 (1969).
2. W. R. Aykroyd and J. Doughty, Wheat in Human Nutrition. Food and Agriculture Organization of the U.N., Rome, 1970.
3. J. C. Bauernfeind and D. M. Pinkert, Advan. Food Res., 18, 219 (1970).
4. B. W. Beadle, D. A. Greenwood, and H. R. Kraybill, J. Biol. Chem., 149, 339 (1943).
5. A. W. Bender, J. Food Technol., 1, 261 (1966).
6. F. Bergel and D. R. Harrap, J. Chem. Soc., 4051 (1961).
7. G. N. Bookwalter, H. A. Moser, V. F. Pfeifer, and E. L. Griffin, Jr., Food Technol., 22, 1581 (1968).
8. R. G. Booth, Biochem. J., 37, 518 (1943).

9. B. Borenstein, Crit. Rev. Food Technol., 2, 171 (1971).
10. B. Borenstein, Vitamins and Amino Acids; in Handbook of Food Additives (T. E. Furia, ed.), 1968, pp. 107-137.
11. B. Borenstein and R. H. Bunnell, Advan. Food Res., 15, 195 (1966).
12. R. Breslow, J. Amer. Chem. Soc., 80, 3719 (1958).
13. V. Buell and R. E. Hansen, J. Amer. Chem. Soc., 82, 6042 (1960).
14. H. Burton, J. E. Ford, J. G. Franklin, and J. W. G. Porter, J. Dairy Res., 34, 193 (1967).
15. H. Burton, J. E. Ford, A. G. Perkin, J. W. G. Porter, K. J. Scott, S. Y. Thompson, J. Toothill, and J. D. Edwards-Webb, J. Dairy Res., 37, 529 (1970).
16. C. E. Butterworth, Jr., R. Santini, and W. B. Frommeyer, J. Clin. Invest., 42, 1929 (1963).
17. R. F. Cain, Food Technol., 21, 998 (1967).
18. E. J. Cameron, L. E. Clifcorn, J. R. Esty, J. F. Feaster, F. C. Lamb, K. H. Monroe, and R. Royce, Retention of Nutrients During Canning, Research Labs., National Canners Assoc., 1955.
19. C. O. Chichester, World Rev. Nutr. Diet, 16, 104 (1973).
20. Hung-En Chou and W. M. Breene, J. Food Sci., 36, 66 (1972).
21. K. M. Clegg and A. D. Morton, J. Sci. Food Agri., 16, 191 (1965).
22. K. M. Clegg, J. Sci. Food Agri., 17, 546 (1966).
23. L. E. Clifcorn, Advan. Food Res., 1, 39 (1948).
24. A. Csallany, Mei Chiu, and H. H. Draper, Lipids, 5, 1 (1970).
25. A. L. Curl and G. F. Bailey, J. Agri. Food Chem., 4, 159 (1956).
26. H. Dahn, L. Loewe, and C. A. Bunton, Helv. Chim. Acta, 43, 320 (1960).
27. C. Davis, Amer. J. Clin. Nutr., 25, 933 (1972).
28. K. C. Davis, J. Food Sci., 38, 442 (1973).
29. W. C. Day and J. G. Erdman, Science, 141, 808 (1963).
30. E. S. Dellamonica and P. E. McDowell, Food Technol., 19, 1597 (1965).
31. H. J. Deuel, Chapters 6 and 7, in The Lipids, Interscience, New York, 1951, pp.
32. K. Dwivedi and R. G. Arnold, J. Agri. Food Chem., 19, 923 (1971).
33. K. Dwivedi and R. G. Arnold, J. Food Sci., 37, 886 (1972).
34. K. Dwivedi and R. G. Arnold, J. Agri. Food Chem., 21, 54 (1973).
35. K. Dwivedi, R. G. Arnold, and L. M. Libbey, J. Food Sci., 37, 689 (1972).
36. K. T. H. Farrer, Advan. Food Res., 6, 247 (1955).
37. E. Feliciotti and W. B. Esselen, Food Technol., 11, 77 (1957).
38. P. Finholt, R. B. Paulssen, and T. Higuchi, J. Pharm. Sci., 52, 948 (1963).
39. B. A. Rolls and J. W. G. Porter, Proc. Nutr. Soc., 32, 9 (1973).
40. J. E. Ford, J. W. G. Porter, S. Y. Thompson, J. Toothill, and J. Edwards-Webb, J. Dairy Res., 36, 447 (1969).
41. M. Freed, S. Brenner, and V. O. Wodicka, Food Technol., 3, 148 (1949).
42. S. A. Goldblith and S. R. Tannenbaum, Proc. 7th Intl. Cong. Nutr., 1966.
43. S. A. Goldblith, S. R. Tannenbaum, and D. I. C. Wang, Food Technol., 22, 1266 (1968).
44. E. H. Gruger, Jr., and A. L. Tappel, Lipids, 5, 326 (1970).
45. R. S. Harris, Vit. Horm., 20, 603 (1962).

46. R. S. Harris and H. Von Loescke, Nutritional Evaluation of Food Processing, Wiley, New York, 1960.

47. J. B. Hassinen, G. T. Durbin, and F. W. Bernhart, J. Nutr., 53, 249 (1954).

48. J. L. Heid, Effects of Freezing on Food Nutrients, in Nutritional Evaluation of Food Processing (R. S. Harris and H. Von Loesecke, eds.), Wiley, New York, 1960, p. 146.

49. F. E. Huelin, I. M. Coggiola, G. S. Sidhu, and B. H. Kennett, J. Sci. Food Agri., 22, 540 (1971).

50. M. A. Joslyn, Food Res., 22, 1 (1957).

51. M. Karel and J. T. R. Nickerson, Food Technol., 18, 104 (1964).

52. H. D. Kay, J. Food Technol., 2, 99 (1967).

53. M. M. T. Khan and A. E. Martell, J. Amer. Chem. Soc., 89, 7104 (1967).

54. M. M. T. Khan and A. E. Martell, J. Amer. Chem. Soc., 89, 4176 (1967).

55. T. Kurata and Y. Sakurai, Agri. Biol. Chem., 31, 177 (1967).

56. T. Kurata and Y. Sakurai, Agri. Biol. Chem., 31, 170 (1967).

57. T. Kurata, H. Wakabayashi, and Y. Sakurai, Agri. Biol. Chem., 31, 101 (1967).

58. V. Kyzlink and D. Curada, Z. Lebens.-Unter. Forsch., 143, 263 (1970).

59. T. P. Labuza, Crit. Rev. Food Technol., 2, 355 (1971).

60. T. P. Labuza, Crit. Rev. Food Technol., 3, 217 (1972).

61. T. P. Labuza, S. R. Tannenbaum, and M. Karel, Food Technol., 24, 543 (1970).

62. F. A. Lee, Advan. Food Res., 8, 63 (1958).

63. J. Leichter and M. A. Joslyn, Biochem. J., 113, 611 (1969).

64. J. Leichter and M. A. Joslyn, Agri. Food Chem.,

65. G. Levandoski, E. M. Baker, and J. E. Canham, Biochemistry, 3, 1465 (1964).

66. G. Mackinney, A. Lukton, and L. Greenbaum, Food Technol., 12, 163 (1958).

67. I. Mader, Science, 144, 533 (1963).

68. W. Malewski and P. Markakis, J. Food Sci., 36, 537 (1971).

69. L. W. Mapson, Brit. Med. Bull., 12, 73 (1956).

70. F. C. McIntire and V. Frost, J. Amer. Chem. Soc., 66, 1317 (1944).

71. T. D. Morfee and B. J. Liska, J. Dairy Sci., 54, 1082 (1971).

72. E. R. Morris and F. E. Greene, J. Nutr., 102, 901 (1972).

73. E. M. Nelson, Publ. Health Repts., 71, 445 (1956).

74. M. Nishimura and K. Takamatsu, Nature (London), 180, 699 (1957).

75. M. L. Orr, Pantothenic Acid, Vitamin B6 and Vitamin B12 in Foods. Home Economics Research Report No. 36, U.S. Department of Agriculture, Washington, D.C., 1969.

76. M. Polansky and W. Toepfer, J. Agri. Food Chem., 17, 1394 (1969).

77. B. E. Proctor and S. A. Goldblith, Food Technol., 2, 95 (1948).

78. F. W. Quackenbush, Cereal Chem., 40, 266 (1963).

79. D. G. Quast and M. Karel, J. Food Sci., 37, 584 (1972).

80. H. Reiber, Biochem. Biophys. Acta, 279, 310 (1972).

81. R. Santini, C. Brewster, and C. Butterworth, Jr., Amer. J. Clin. Nutr., 14, 205 (1964).

82. A. Schroeder, Amer. J. Clin. Nutr., 24, 562 (1971).

83. G. R. Seely and T. H. Meyer, Photochem. Photobiol., 13, 27 (1971).

84. E. E. Snell, Vit. Horm., 16, 77 (1958).

85. P. Spanyar and E. Kevei, Z. Lebens.-Unter. Forsch., 120, 1 (1963).

86. V. Srncova and J. Davidek, J. Food Sci., 37, 310 (1972).

87. E. L. R. Stokstad and J. Koch, Physiol. Rev., 47, 83 (1967).

88. J. P. Sweeney and A. C. Marsh, J. Amer. Diet. Assoc., 59, 238 (1971).

89. Ten-State Nutrition Survey 1968-1970, DHEW Publication No. (HSM) 72-8134.

90. C. Theuer, K. S. Kemmerer, W. H. Martin, B. L. Zoumas, and H. P. Sarett, J. Agri. Food Chem., 19, 555 (1971).

91. M. H. Thomas and G. H. Berryman, J. Amer. Diet. Assoc., 23(11), 941 (1949).

92. L. U. Thompson and O. Fennema, J. Agri. Food Chem., 19, 232 (1971).

93. R. M. Tomarelli, E. R. Spence, and F. W. Bernhart, J. Agri. Food Chem., 3, 338 (1955).

94. M. Walter, Jr., E. Purcell, and Y. Cobb, Agri. Food Chem., 18, 881 (1970).

95. B. K. Watt and A. L. Merrill, Agriculture Handbook No. 8, U.S. Department of Agriculture, Washington, D.C., 1963.

96. K. G. Weckel, B. Santos, E. Hernan, L. Laferriere, and W. H. Gabelman, Food Technol., 16, 91 (1962).

97. G. Wendt and F. W. Bernhart, Arch. Biochem. Biophys., 88, 270 (1960).

98. J. R. Whitaker, Principles of Enzymology for the Food Sciences, Marcel Dekker, Inc., New York, 1972.

99. L. Zechmeister, Cis-Trans Isomeric Carotenoids, Vitamin A and Aryloply-enes. Academic Press, New York, 1962.

Chapter 8

PIGMENTS

Fergus M. Clydesdale and F. J. Francis

Department of Food Science and Nutrition
University of Massachusetts
Amherst, Massachusetts

Contents

The quality of food, aside from the microbiological aspects, is generally based on color, flavor, texture, and nutritive value. Depending on the particular food, these factors may be weighted differently or equally in assessing overall quality. However, one of the most important sensory quality attributes of a food is color. This is based on the fact that no matter how nutritious, flavorful, or well textured a food is, it is never eaten unless it is the right color.

Acceptability of color in a given food is influenced by many diverse factors, including cultural, geographical, and sociological aspects of the population. Indeed, color as well as other eating habits may be viewed as a type of culinary anthropology indigenous to a specific region. However, no matter what the biases or habits of a given area, certain food groups are acceptable only if they fall within a certain color gamut. Moreover, acceptability is reinforced by economic worth since in many cases raw food materials are judged as to value by their color.

It is obvious that the color of a food is due to natural pigments present, except in cases where colorants have been added. Therefore, in order to achieve the desirable color and acceptability, an understanding of such pigment systems is essential.

I. CHLOROPHYLLS

A. Structure

The name "chlorophyll" was originally intended to describe those green pigments involved in the photosynthesis of higher plants. However, it has been extended to all classes of photosynthetic porphyrin pigments. Functionally this appears to be proper except in certain very specific, isolated cases [2].

In any discussion of the chlorophylls, there is a necessary prerequisite of defining structures and chemical terminology. Through the years, terminology has been used, deleted, and revised so that a rather special language has arisen which has become generally acceptable. The following simplified classification of terminology should be an aid in understanding this chemistry [2,6]:

1. Pyrrole: one of four cyclic components of the porphyrin nucleus.
2. Porphine: the completely conjugated tetrapyrrole skeleton, consisting of four pyrrole rings connected by four methyne bridges.
3. Porphyrin: in chlorophyll chemistry it is assumed that the term "porphyrins" includes the entire class of closed, completely conjugated tetrapyrroles. The parent compound of this class is porphine, which may be substituted by various groups, such as methyl, ethyl, or vinyl. All other subclasses of porphyrins are referred to the state of oxidation of this compound. Thus, di-, tetra-, or hexahyhdroporphines may be formed when reduction occurs only on the periphery of the pyrrolic rings. When reduction occurs at the methyne carbons, a class of compounds known as porphyrinogens results.
4. Chlorins: dihydroporphines.
5. Phorbin: a porphyrin with the addition of a C_9–C_{10} ring.
6. Phorbide: all naturally occurring porphyrins have a propionic acid residue at position 7. In the chlorophylls, this position is esterified with a long-chain alcohol (phytol or farnesol). The corresponding structure with a free acid is known as a phorbide if it does not contain magnesium.
7. Phytol: a 20-carbon alcohol with an isoprenoid structure, as shown in Figure 8-1.
8. Chlorophyll a: the structure of chlorophyll a is shown in Figure 8-1. It is a magnesium-chelated tetrapyrrole structure with methyl substitutions at the 1, 3, 5, and 8 positions; vinyl at the 2; ethyl at the 4; propionate esterified with phytyl alcohol at the 7; keto at the 9; and carbomethoxy at the 10. The empirical formula is $C_{55}H_{72}O_5N_4Mg$.

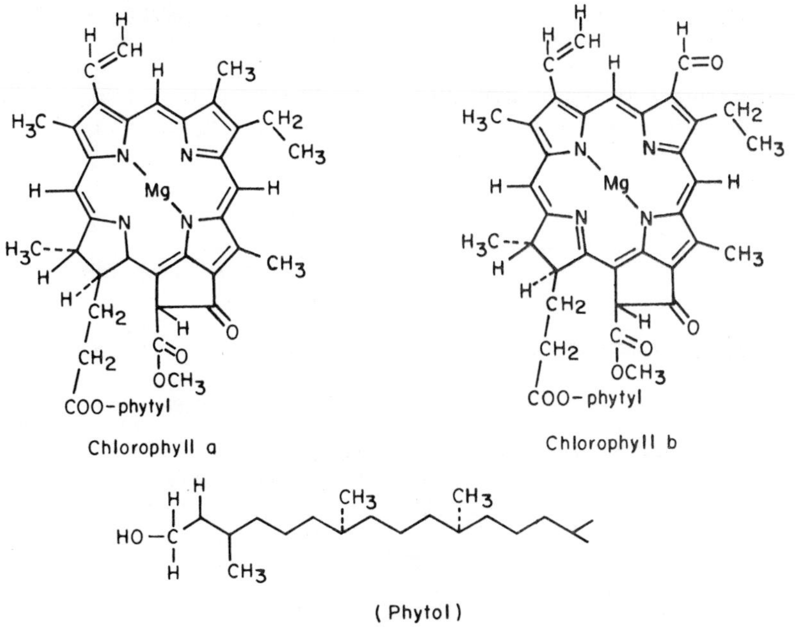

Chlorophyll a   Chlorophyll b

(Phytol)

FIG. 8-1. Structural formulas of chlorophylls a and b and the phytol moiety. (From Aronoff [2], courtesy of Academic Press.)

9. Chlorophyll b: as may be seen in Figure 8-1, chlorophyll b has the same configuration as chlorophyll a except that in the 3 position there is a formyl group rather than a methyl group (circled in Fig. 8-1). The empirical formula is $C_{55}H_{70}O_6N_4Mg$.
10. Pheophytin a: chlorophyll a minus magnesium.
11. Pheophytin b: chlorophyll b minus magnesium.
12. Chlorophyllide a: chlorophyll a minus phytol.
13. Chlorophyllide b: chlorophyll b minus phytol.
14. Pheophorbide a: chlorophyllide a minus magnesium.
15. Pheophorbide b: chlorophyllide b minus magnesium.

This is not intended to be a complete discussion of the chemistry of the chlorophylls but merely an overview of the terminology associated with the chlorophylls normally found in higher plants which are utilized for food.

A diagrammatic summary of the chlorophylls and some of their conversion products, which may or may not be found to occur during food processing, are shown in Figure 8-2.

B. Location in Plants

There have been a variety of chlorophylls described, such as chlorophylls a, b, c, and d; bacteriochlorophylls a and b; and chlorobium chlorophylls.

In foods we are mainly concerned with chlorophylls a and b which occur in the approximate ratio of 3:1 in higher plants. In leaves, these chlorophylls are located within plastid bodies, called chloroplasts. The chloroplasts have an ordered fine structure and appear in the light microscope as green saucer-shaped bodies about 5-10 μm long and 1-2 μm thick. Within the chloroplasts are smaller particles, called grana, which are 0.2-2 μm in diameter and are composed of lamellae which range in size from 0.01 to 0.02 μm. Between the grana are the stroma. Chlorophyll molecules are imbedded in the lamellae and are closely associated with lipids,

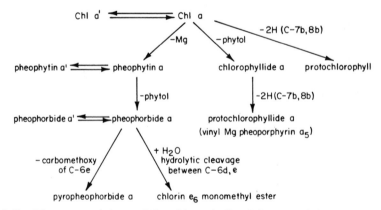

FIG. 8-2. The nomenclature of the chlorophylls and some of their breakdown products. (From Aronoff [2]; courtesy of Academic Press.)

proteins, and lipoproteins. They are held together in a monolayer both by mutual attraction and by the affinity of each molecule's phytol "tail" for lipids and the affinity for each molecule's hydrophobic planar porphyrin ring for proteins. Therefore, within the chloroplast, the chlorophylls may be visualized as being imbedded between a layer of protein and lipid with a carotenoid positioned alongside the phytol chain of the chlorophyll.

C. Physical Properties

Chlorophyll a and pheophytin a are soluble in alcohols, ether, benzene, and acetone. When they are pure, they are only slightly soluble in petroleum ether. They are insoluble in water. Chlorophyll b and pheophytin b are soluble in alcohols, ether, acetone, and benzene. When pure, they are almost insoluble in petroleum ether and insoluble in water.

The chlorophyllides and pheophorbides, which are counterparts to the chlorophylls and pheophytins, respectively, lack only the phytol side chain and are generally oil insoluble and water soluble.

D. Spectral Absorption Properties

A great many workers have established absorption curves for the chlorophylls and their derivatives. The absorption spectra of all pigments derived from the basic porphine or porphyrin structure are characterized by a number of relatively sharp bands in the yellow, red, or near-infrared region, and in the violet or near-violet region. These latter bands are the so-called "Soret bands" and their presence indicates that breakdown of the basic porphyrin structure has not occurred.

The absorption maxima and millimolar absorption coefficients and their derivatives are shown in Table 8-1. Although these values are extremely important in the analysis of the pigments, it should be noted that small differences exist both in the wavelength positions of the maxima and in the absorption coefficients obtained by different workers using the same solvents. This emphasizes the need for determining spectroscopic constants in the laboratory where determinations are to be carried out.

Fluorescence spectral data are also available for the chlorophylls and are a useful tool in quantitative analysis.

TABLE 8-1

Absorption Maxima and Millimolar Absorption Coefficients of
the Chlorophylls and Their Derivatives[a]

Chlorophyll or derivative	Solvent	Wavelength (mμ) maximum	Millimolar absorption coefficient
Chlorophyll a	Diethyl ether	662	90.2
Chlorophyll a	Diethyl ether	661	91.1
Chlorophyll a	Diethyl ether	660	91.1

TABLE 8-1 (Continued)

Chlorophyll or derivative	Solvent	Wavelength (mμ) maximum	Millimolar absorption coefficient
Ethylchlorophyllide a	Diethyl ether	660	89.3
Methylchlorophillide a	Dioxane	660	100.0
Pheophytin a	Diethyl ether	667	55.5
Pheophytin a	Diethyl ether	667	56.6
Pheophytin a	Diethyl ether	666.5	52.4
Ethylpheophorbide a	Diethyl ether	666.7	51.4
Pheophorbide a	1% Pyridine in diethyl ether	662.5	48.9
Methylpheophorbide a	Dioxane	666.0	52.8
Chlorophyll b	Diethyl ether	644	56.3
Chlorophyll b	Diethyl ether	642.5	58.5
Chlorophyll b	Diethyl ether	642.5	52.2
Ethylchlorophyllide b	Diethyl ether	640.5	53.3
Pheophytin b	Diethyl ether	655	37.3
Pheophytin b	Diethyl ether	655	37.0
Pheophytin b	Diethyl ether	653	33.2
Ethylpheophorbide b	Diethyl ether	653	33.2
Pheophorbide b	5% Pyridine in diethyl ether	650.9	31.8
Methylpheophorbide b	Dioxane	652.5	30.6

[a]From Jones et al. [23], courtesy of the Institute of Food Technologists.

E. Chemical Properties

Chemically, the chlorophylls may be altered in many ways but in food processing the most common alteration is pheophytinization, which is the replacement of the central magnesium by hydrogen and the consequent formation of the dull olive-brown pheophytins. It is difficult to explain the drastic color shift of green chlorophylls to the dull olive-brown pheophytins by simply visualizing the replacement of magnesium by hydrogen. The accepted structural formula of pheophytin is normally shown this way, but it is likely that some shift in the porphyrin resonance structure is also involved.

Chlorophyllides may be formed by the removal of the phytol chain. These compounds are green and have essentially the same spectral properties as the chlorophylls; however, they are more water soluble than the chlorophylls. If the magnesium in the chlorophyllides is removed, the corresponding pheophorbides are formed which have the same color and spectral properties as the pheophytins.

These relationships may be illustrated diagrammatically as follows:

Chlorophyll   — Phytol   →   Chlorophyllide

−Mg ↓   −Mg ↓

Pheophytin   — Phytol   →   Pheophorbide

There are many other reactions which may occur due to the functional side groups of the chlorophylls, the isocylic ring which may be oxidized to form allomerized chlorophyll, and the rupture of the tetrapyrrole ring to form colorless end products. During food processing, it is likely that such reactions do proceed to some extent, but this is limited compared to pheophytinization.

F. Effects of Food Handling, Processing, and Storage

Almost any type of food processing alone or combined with storage will cause some deterioration of the chlorophyll pigments. It has been shown that dehydrated products packed in clear containers undergo photooxidation and loss of desirable color. It has also been observed that the conversion of chlorophyll to pheophytin occurs in dehydrated foods and that this conversion is directly related to the degree of blanching which the foods have undergone before dehydration. It has been shown [27], using freeze-dried, blanched spinach puree and model systems at 37°C and with water activities (a_W) higher than 0.32, that the most important mechanism of chlorophyll a transformation is 2.5 times faster than that for chlorophyll b. It has been found that the relationship between a_W and log time for 20% chlorophyll degradation is linear and therefore the chlorophyll/pheophytin ratio may be predictable as a function of a_W. At a_W levels lower than 0.32, chlorophyll was not converted to pheophytin to such a large degree but other chemical components were formed.

Chlorophyll-containing vegetables also show some color changes upon freezing and subsequent storage. These color changes have been found to be influenced by the time and temperature of blanching prior to freezing.

As well as a conversion of chlorophyll to pheophytin, there is destruction of the porphyrin ring system so the chlorophyll-like spectra are lost. Both Wagenknecht et al. [43] and Walker [44] observed degradation in peas and beans to nonchlorophyll compounds and attributed this to the action of lipoxygenase, producing free radicals which in turn degraded chlorophylls. Holden [21] created a system which contained legume seed extracts and long-chain fatty acids and which degraded chlorophylls to non-chlorophyll-like products.

Gamma irradiation and subsequent storage produces a conversion of chlorophyll to pheophytin, as well as degradation of both chlorophylls and pheophytins.

Fermentation can also cause color changes. Jones et al. [23] noted that pheophytins as well as chlorophyllides and pheophoribides were formed during blanching. They also found that upon development of acetic brines, pheophorbides produced off colors within the cucumbers.

Due to the tremendous volume of heat-processed vegetables produced and also to the startling effects which heat processing have on the degradation of chlorophyll, such processes must be considered as the most important in terms of food materials.

The color of processed green vegetables rapidly turns from a bright green to a dull olive brown upon heat processing and subsequent storage. The cause of this color degradation has been found to be conversion of chlorophyll to pheophytin. The formation of pheophytin from chlorophyll is related to the amount of acids produced within the system during heating and storage. One of the major postulates for the production of acids has been that such acids are released from plant tissue during heating and storage. However, Lin et al. [30] and Clydesdale et al. [10] have shown that acids are not released from the plant tissue but are actually formed during heat processing and storage. Although in green spinach ten different acids have been found and a like number exist in processed green beans and peas, it has been found in all cases that certain major acids are responsible for the increased acidity during processing and storage which in turn degrades the chlorophyll to pheophytin. These acids are acetic and pyrrolidone-carboxylic acid (PCA).

The reaction rate of the conversion of chlorophyll to pheophytin has been studied by Joslin and McKinney [24]. Gupte et al. [18] found the reaction to be first order in vivo, as Schanderl et al. [36] did in vitro. Several workers have also found that chlorophyll a is converted to pheophytin a 5-10 times faster than chlorophyll b is converted to pheophytin b.

G. Preservation of the Green Color

There has been a tremendous amount of work aimed at preserving the green color of heat-processed green vegetables. Unfortunately, none of the proposed methods has been really successful. One of the earlier suggestions, based on the assumption that chlorophyllides are more stable than chlorophylls, was to convert chlorophylls to chlorophyllides by means of the naturally occurring esterase, chlorophyllase. This enzyme in vivo has some rather unusual characteristics. Unlike most other enzymes, it functions at room temperature only in the presence of high concentrations of organic solvents; and when in an aqueous media, it functions only at temperatures in the range of 65°-75°C. This may be due in part to its physical orientation since it has been postulated that chlorophyllase is tightly bound to lipoproteins of the lamellae.

Boroden in 1882, although he did not recognize the conversion of chlorophylls to chlorophyllides, postulated that under certain conditions the chlorophylls were "fixed" and were thus more stable. These conditions were promoted by the action of chlorophyllase and his "fixed chlorophylls" were obviously chlorophyllides. Later Thomas, in 1928, and Lesley and Shumate, in 1937, received patents for processes based on a blanch of 67°C for 30 min prior to heat processing. However, their experimental evidence for the greater stability for chlorophyllides was not conclusive.

Schanderl et al. [36] showed that chlorophyllides were slightly less resistant to acid hydrolysis than chlorophylls when HCl and acetone extracts were used. However, these results were found using model systems and pure pigments which do not simulate the conditions which the pigments in plant tissues are subjected to under heat processing. In Europe some workers produced evidence that chlorophyllides might be more stable than chlorophylls in plant tissues, and in this country Clydesdale and Francis [9] also showed this possibility with processed spinach puree. Unfortunately, in these studies it was not possible to produce enough chlorophyllide within the tissue to conclusively prove a gain in stability.

Another method which has been attempted is the use of alkalizing agents to produce a higher pH in the system and thus minimize pheophytin formation. Blair [3,4] received two patents for the use of calcium or magnesium hydroxides or their respective oxides. This was known as the "Blair process" and it produced an attractive product immediately after processing but not upon storage. Several other patents have been issued which make use of alkalizing agents, but none has completely solved the problem.

There has been some concern voiced about the effect of alkalizing agents on Vitamin C present in green vegetables. This concern, however, is unfounded. Green vegetables are a low-acid product and as such must be given a reasonably severe thermal process. Under such conditions, the effect of increasing the pH slightly does not significantly worsen the already poor environment for Vitamin C. However, increased pH does have a significantly undesirable effect on texture.

Attempts have been made to use alkalizing agents in conjunction with an enzyme conversion system of chlorophylls to chlorophyllides. In most studies some gains were noted, but results were not conclusive enough to suggest a new process.

High-temperature, short-time (HTST) processing, because of its obvious advantages on other areas, has also been used in an attempt to stabilize the chlorophyll molecules during heat processing. This method produces a very attractive product immediately after processing but the beneficial effects are quickly lost upon storage. Several combinations also have been attempted with HTST processing. One such combination is the use of alkalizing agents along with HTST processing; another is the use of alkalizing agents, enzyme conversion of chlorophylls to chlorophyllides, and HTST processing. Again, in all instances, some gains were noted immediately after processing but were quickly lost upon storage. Clydesdale et al. [10] have shown that during storage after HTST processing, many acids are formed, and these are the same as those formed during conventional heat processing, i.e., acetic and PCA. This would seem to indicate that the same acids which cause the replacement of magnesium in chlorophyll by hydrogen to form pheophytin during heat processing also cause the conversion during storage.

Workers have tested various buffering agents, such as phosphate, but again have been largely unsuccessful in their attempts to stabilize the chlorophyll molecule.

Undoubtedly some process which would stabilize the chlorophyll molecule and produce an attractive bright green color in thermally processed green vegetables would be invaluable. Investigations so far have met with little success. Perhaps utilizing the features of the processes described, along with appropriate handling, might be the answer. For instance, it has been shown [45] that under controlled-atmosphere (CA) storage of asparagus that chlorophyll retention was increased, particularly as the concentration of CO_2 in the atmosphere was increased.

At the present time, the best way to maintain chlorophyll stability in various products is to use high-quality raw materials, handle the products with the utmost care, employ optimum storage conditions, and use a quality-maximized process to create the final product.

II. MYOGLOBIN AND HEMOGLOBIN

According to the Animal Health Institute, in 1970, 203 million Americans consumed a total of 48 billion lb of meat and poultry. The average American consumed 236 lb of meat and poultry - close to 5 lb/week for each of us. In 1960, the average American ate 190 lb of meat. By 1980, with a population of 230 million, the average consumption is predicted to zoom nearly 40% to an estimated 264 lb per person. This tremendous consumption in 1970 and the even higher consumption predicted for 1980 is likely to be influenced tremendously by color.

The chemistry of the color of meat is the chemistry of heme pigments. More specifically, it is primarily the chemistry of one pigment, myoglobin. In the live animal, myoglobin accounts for only 10% of the total iron, but during slaughter, the bleeding process removes most of the iron as hemoglobin, and in a well-bled piece of beef skeletal muscle as much as 95% or more of the remaining iron is accounted for as myoglobin. Myoglobin, and its various chemical forms, is not the only pigment in muscle, nor is it the most important biologically; but it is generally the only pigment present in large enough quantities to color meat. Muscle pigments which are of considerable importance to the living tissue but which contribute little or nothing to the total color include cytochromes; red heme pigments, which contain iron in a similar porphyrin-protein complex structure; vitamin B_{12}, a much more complex structure than myoglobin and one that contains the same porphyrin ring as the hemes and the cytochromes but that contains a cobalt atom instead of iron; and the flavins, yellow coenzymes involved with the cytochromes in electron transport in the cell.

Myoglobin is a complex muscle protein, similar in function to the blood pigment, hemoglobin, in that both serve to complex with the oxygen required for metabolic activity of the animal. The hemoglobin in red corpuscles contains four polypeptide chains and four so-called heme groups, which are planar collections of atoms with an iron atom at the center. The function of the heme group is to combine reversibly with a molecule of oxygen, which is then carried by the blood from the lungs to the tissues. Myoglobin is a junior relative to hemoglobin, being a quarter its size and consisting of a single polypeptide chain of about 150 amino acid units attached to a single heme group. It is contained within the cells of the tissues and it acts as a temporary storehouse for the oxygen brought by the hemoglobin in blood.

A. Structure

John C. Kendrew, the pioneer who was able to deduce the actual arrangement in space of nearly all of the 2,600 atoms in myoglobin, compared his first view of the three-dimensional structure of a myoglobin molecule to that of the early explorers of America when they made their first landfall and had the unforgettable experience of glimpsing a new world that no European had seen before. This, indeed, was a pioneering experience for all of protein chemistry and it does underline specifically the complexity of the myoglobin structure. Both hemoglobin and myoglobin are complex proteins, which means that in addition to the protein portion of the molecule there is another moiety, nonpeptide in nature, complexed to the peptide chain. The protein moiety is known specifically as globin and the non-peptide portion is called heme. Heme is composed of two parts; an iron atom and a large planar ring, porphyrin. Porphyrin is made up of four subunits, the heterocyclic compound pyrrole, linked together by methyne bridges.

Hemoglobin may be considered as the linking together of four myoglobins; therefore, discussion of the chemistry of these pigments can be limited to myoglobin. Figure 8-3 shows the isolated heme group, which, when attached to the protein globin, forms myoglobin. Figure 8-4 shows a vastly simplified diagrammatic structure of myoglobin. In reality a very complex situation exists which only recently has been defined thanks chiefly to the protein structure studies Kendrew,

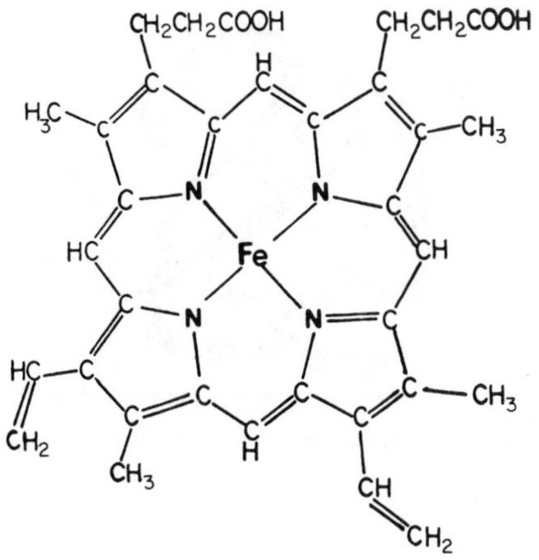

FIG. 8-3. The isolated heme group.

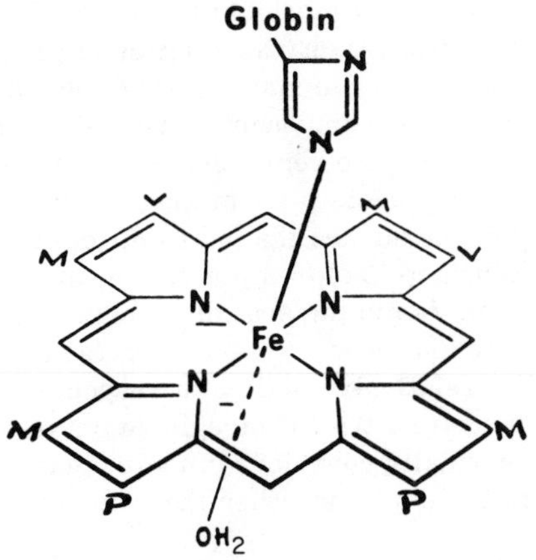

FIG. 8-4. A simplified diagrammatic structure of myoglobin. (From Price
and Schweigert [35], courtesy of W. H. Freeman and Co.)

Perutz, and Edmundson. In simplified terms one may view the protein portion
folded around the iron of the heme group in eight α-helical segments, forming the
total complex molecule. A three-dimensional representation of this myoglobin
molecule peptide chain is shown in Figure 8-5. The heme iron is represented by
the circle in the upper central portion of the figure and the helical peptide segments
are labeled A-H beginning at the amino end and ending at the carboxyl end of the
molecule. Obviously, a complete description of this complex structure requires
much more space than is available here.

FIG. 8-5. A three-dimensional representation of the myoglobin molecule peptide chain.

B. Physical Properties

Myoglobin is part of the sarcoplasmic protein of muscle. It is soluble in water and
in dilute salt solutions.

Any attempt to explain the color of myoglobin in a muscle tissue matrix must
take into account not only the spectral characteristics of the pigment but also the
scattering characteristics of the muscle matrix. The total reflectance characteristics of meat are due to two major components. One of these components, absorption of the meat pigments, may be represented by the symbol K; the other,
the scattering coefficient of the muscle fiber matrix, may be represented by the
symbol S. The ratio K/S then describes the total impact of both absorption and
scattering on the eye. In a brightly colored piece of meat, K, the absorption coefficient, would be high in relation to the scattering coefficient S. As K decreases
with respect to S the characteristic peaks on the spectral curve of myoglobin tend
to decrease until K becomes relatively small with respect to S and the spectral
curve bears little resemblance to a typical myoglobin curve. These are physical
parameters which are not normally considered in a discussion of myoglobin pigments but which are extremely important when the color of meat is considered as
a major quality factor.

C. Chemical Properties

In considering meat pigments in relation to quality one must be concerned mainly
with the various complexes of heme, globin, and ligands which surround iron in an
oxidized (Fe^{3+}) or a reduced (Fe^{2+}) state. The reaction defining the covalent complex formed between myoglobin and molecular oxygen to form oxymyoglobin is
known as oxygenation and is distinct from the oxidation of myoglobin to form metmyoglobin. Furthermore, such complexes may be grouped into ionic and covalent
bond types, with the covalent bond types producing the bright red pigments desired
in meat. Oxymyoglobin, nitrosomyoglobin, and carboxymyoglobin are examples
of the ferrous covalent complexes of myoglobin with molecular oxygen, nitric oxide,
and carbon monoxide, respectively. Spectrally, these complexes are characterized

by relatively sharp absorption maxima at 535–545 nm and 575–588 nm, such as metmyoglobin and myoglobin, respectively.

Cyanmetmyoglobin and metmyoglobin hydroxide are examples of ferric iron covalent complexes which have the characteristic red color. In the case of such ferric covalent complexes, the negative charge of the ion may be thought of for conceptual purposes as having neutralized the third positive charge of the ferric ion. In general, it may be said that an electron-pair forms a stable red covalent complex with myoglobin (ferrous) if it is neutral, or with metmyoglobin (ferric) if it is negatively charged.

In the absence of strong covalent complexers, myoglobin and metmyoglobin form ionic complexes with water. In these complexes, the oxygen of water binds to iron by a dipole–ion interaction since the oxygen atom is not as strong as electron-pair donor as the oxygen molecule.

Myoglobin is characterized by an absorption band with a maximum at 555 nm in the green portion of the spectrum and is purple in color. In metmyoglobin, the major peak is shifted to 505 nm in the blue end of the spectrum and a smaller peak exists at 627 nm in the red, with the net visual appearance being brown. The spectral curves of myoglobin, oxymyoglobin, and metmyoglobin are shown in Figure 8-6.

The color cycle in fresh meats is reversible and dynamic, with the three pigments, oxymyoglobin, myoglobin, and metmyoglobin being constantly interconverted. Remember that brown metmyoglobin, the oxidized or ferric form of the pigment, cannot bind oxygen even though it is oxidized by the same oxygen which converts myoglobin to the red oxymyoglobin (oxygenation). Therefore, in the presence of oxygen, the purple myoglobin may be oxygenated to the bright red oxygenated pigment oxymyoglobin, producing the familiar "bloom" of fresh meats, or it may be oxidized to metmyoglobin, producing the undesirable brown of less acceptable meats. Figure 8-7 shows the heme pigment reactions of both fresh and cured meat and meat products. At high oxygen pressures the reaction of myoglobin (Mb) to oxymyoglobin (O_2Mb) shown in Figure 8-7 is shifted to the left. The red O_2Mb, once formed, is stabilized by the formation of a highly resonant structure, and as long as the heme remains oxygenated no further color changes take place. However, the oxygen is continually associating and dissociating from the heme complex, a process which is accelerated by a number of conditions, among them low oxygen pressures. When this happens, the reduced pigment (Mb) is oxidized to metmyoglobin (MMb). It is not known whether the oxidation takes place during association or dissociation, as indicated by the dashed arrow in Figure 8-7. However, it is known that there is a slow and continuous oxidation to MMb. In fresh meat, the production of indigenous reducing substances constantly reduces MMb to Mb and the cycle continues if oxygen is present.

A summary of the pigments, their mode of formation, and their properties is shown in Table 8-2.

D. Effects of Food Handling, Processing, and Storage

1. CURED MEAT PIGMENTS

Certainly, a very important aspect of the chemistry of meat pigments had to do with the curing process. This process is extremely important because of the large

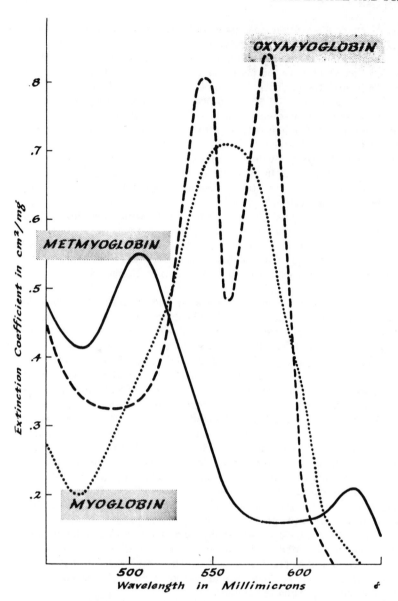

FIG. 8-6. Spectral curves of myoglobin, oxymyoglobin, and metmyoglobin. (From Price and Schweigert [35], courtesy of W. H. Freeman and Co.)

volume of meat products which are cured. Figure 8-7 shows the pathways which form the cured meat pigment nitrosylhemochrome in the presence of nitrate, nitric oxide, and reductants. All of these reactions have been observed in vitro but most of them take place only under fairly strong reducing conditions, since many of the intermediates are unstable in air. If the system in which the cured meat pigment

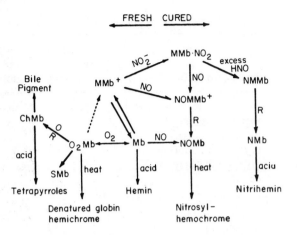

FIG. 8-7. Heme pigment reactions for both fresh and cured meats. (From Fox [11], courtesy of the American Chemical Society.)

TABLE 8-2

Pigments Found in Fresh, Cured, and Cooked Meat[a]

Pigment	Mode of formation	State of iron	State of haematin nucleus	State of globin	Color
Myoglobin	Reduction of met-myoglobin; deoxygenation of oxymyoglobin	Fe^{2+}	Intact	Native	Purplish red
Oxymyoglobin	Oxygenation of myoglobin	Fe^{2+}	Intact	Native	Bright red
Metmyoglobin	Oxidation of myoglobin, oxymyoglobin	Fe^{3+}	Intact	Native	Brown
Nitric oxide myoglobin	Combination of myoglobin with nitric oxide	Fe^{2+}	Intact	Native	Bright red (pink)
Metmyoglobin nitrite	Combination of metmyoglobin with excess nitrite	Fe^{3+}	Intact	Native	Red
Globin hemochromogen	Effect of heat, denaturing agents on myoglobin, oxymyoglobin; irradiation of globin hemichromogen	Fe^{2+}	Intact	Denatured	Dull red

TABLE 8-2 (Continued)

Pigment	Mode of formation	State of iron	State of haematin nucleus	State of globin	Color
Globin hemichromogen	Effect of heat, denaturing agents on myoglobin, oxymyoglobin, metmyoglobin, hemochromogen	Fe^{3+}	Intact	Denatured	Brown
Nitric oxide hemochromogen	Effect of heat, salts on nitric oxide myoglobin	Fe^{2+}	Intact	Denatured	Bright red (pink)
Sulfmyoglobin	Effect of H_2S and oxygen on myoglobin	Fe^{3+}	Intact but reduced	Denatured	Green
Choleglobin	Effect of hydrogen peroxide on myoglobin or oxymyoglobin; effect of ascorbic or other reducing agent on oxymyoglobin	Fe^{2+} or Fe^{3+}	Intact but reduced	Denatured	Green
Verdohaem	Effect of reagents as in sulfmyoglobin in excess	Fe^{3+}	Porphyrin ring opened	Denatured	Green
Bile pigments	Effect of reagents as in sulfmyoglobin in large excess	Fe absent	Porphyrin ring destroyed; chain of porphyrins	Absent	Yellow or colorless

[a]From Lawrie [28], courtesy of Pergamon Press.

is formed contains nitrite, the heme pigments are in the oxidized state initially, nitrite being a strong heme pigment oxidant. In general, the formation of the cured meat chromophore or pigment is generally viewed as two processes: (1) biochemical reactions which reduce nitrite to nitric oxide and reduce the iron in heme to the ferrous state and (2) thermal denaturation of globin. The latter occurs only when the cured meat product is heated to 150°F or higher and may involve the co-precipitation of the heme pigment with other proteins in meat. Although the mechenisms involved in the complete reaction have not been determined in meat or meat products, it has been established that the end product is either nitrosylmyoglobin if uncooked or the denatured globin nitrosylhemochrome if cooked [11].

Several other factors in addition to those previously mentioned are important in cured meat color. Fox et al. [13], working with frankfurters, found that a lag period in color production, attributed to the presence of oxygen, was reduced by chopping under nitrogen, by vacuum mixing, or by adding ascorbate or cysteine. It was also found that the temperature of cooking was critical to the rate of color formation, to the percentage of cured meat pigment formed, and to the level of color maintained during storage.

Board and Ihsan-Ul-Haque [5], using canned, cured ox tongues, investigated the effect of copper contamination, which causes a black discoloration in cured meats. They found that traces of copper dissolved in curing brines become concentrated about 10-fold in the skin of the blade of ox tongues. Brines containing as little as 0.5 ppm copper produced a noticeable discoloration of canned tongues, whereas 5 ppm gave an intense black discoloration. These investigators have recommended use of an acid treatment prior to scalding and canning, which prevents discoloration but does not impair organoleptic quality.

There are many other aspects of cured meat pigment chemistry which are lengthy and involved. For an excellent review of this area, the reader is referred to Fox [11], and for a more detailed report of the role of reductants in the formation of nitric oxide myoglobin the work by Fox and Ackerman [12] is recommended.

2. PACKAGING

Packaging is an extremely important consideration when speaking of meat pigments whether fresh or cured. In the case of fresh meats this may be easily understood because of the reactions which the pigments undergo with oxygen to produce either an acceptable oxygenated product or an unacceptable oxidized product. Meat is packaged for five primary reasons: (1) to protect the product from contamination with bacteria and filth, (2) to retard or prevent loss of moisture from the product, (3) to shield the product from oxygen and light, (4) to facilitate handling, and (5) to aid in maintaining attractiveness.

The accelerated rate of oxidation of the heme pigment at low partial pressures of oxygen is of particular importance when considering packaging films for fresh meats. If oxygen permeability of the film is low but significant, oxygen utilization by the tissue can exceed oxygen penetration of the film and a low partial pressure of oxygen can develop which favors oxidation of O_2Mb to brown MMb. If the packaging material is completely impermeable to oxygen, the heme pigments convert to fully reduced purple Mb and then "bloom" to red O_2Mb when the package is opened and exposed to oxygen.

There has been an increase in shelf life of fresh meats due in part to constantly improving sanitation techniques, automated methods of meat handling, and pasteurization and sterilization techniques. However, as Fox [11] points out, "To keep pace, information is needed on the factors which govern color stability. The area of greatest concern and interest is that of mechanisms whereby the oxidized pigments are reduced, both by endogenous and exogenous reductants and/or reducing systems."

3. MISCELLANEOUS

Aside from the factors which have been considered so far, there are a few others which should be considered relative to the stability of meat pigments. For instance, carbon monoxide has been used with air to flush packaged beef prior to sealing. This treatment was found very effective for preserving and stabilizing the color of fresh beef for about 15 days. Several packaging films were also tested and saran-mylar-polyethylene pouches seemed to be the best. However, when carbon monoxide is used, toxicity must be considered.

Light used in display environments of food is also an important factor in fresh meat color. Color changes have been noted in packaged fresh meat exposed to 215 ft-c of fluorescent light and to heat generated by incandescent light.

Other factors, such as the presence of certain metallic ions, also affect oxidation of O_2Mb and thus the color of fresh meat. It has been shown that copper is extremely active in promoting autoxidation of O_2Mb to MMb, while other metals, such as Fe, Zn, and Al, are less active.

Meat pigments and the changes which they undergo comprise a very complex and important area of food quality. As of yet there is no way to package fresh meat and obtain long storage life. However, with current basic research it is hoped that enough of the metabolic changes that meat pigments undergo can be learned so that new viable approaches to this problem soon can be undertaken.

III. ANTHOCYANINS

Anthocyanins are a group of reddish water-soluble pigments which are very wide-spread in the plant kingdom. Many fruits, vegetables, and flowers owe their attractive coloration to this group of water-soluble compounds, which exist in the cell sap. The very obvious red color has led to an interest in their chemical structure which dates back to the classic work of Paul Karrer. The structures of the anthocyanin group are fairly well known today but the physical chemistry of the pigment complexes and the degradation reactions are less well known.

A. Structure

All anthocyanins are derivations of the basic flavylium cation structure (1). Twenty anthocyanidins are known but only six, pelargonidin (2), cyanidin (3), delphinidin (4), peonidin (5), petunidin (6), and malvidin (7), are important in foods. The others are comparatively rare and are found in some flowers and leaves. Table 8-3 shows the structure of the above six anthocyanins.

Flavylium cation (I)

TABLE 8-3

Substitution on the Flavylium Cation Structure to
Produce the Major Anthocyanidins

	Substituent on carbon number[a]		
	3'	4'	5'
Pelargonidin (2)	H	OH	H
Cyanidin (3)	OH	OH	H
Delphinidin (4)	OH	OH	OH
Peonidin (5)	OMe	OH	H
Petunidin (6)	OMe	OH	OH
Malvidin (7)	OMe	OH	OMe

[a]Compounds (2)-(7) have OH groups on carbons 3, 5, and 7 and hydrogens on all other carbon atoms.

An anthocyanin pigment is composed of an aglycone (an anthocyanidin) esterified to one or more sugars. Free aglycones rarely occur in foods except possibly as trace components of degradation reactions. Only five sugars have been found as portions of anthocyanin molecules. They are in order of relative abundance glucose, rhamnose, galactose, xylose, and arabinose. Anthocyanins may also be "acylated," which adds a third component to the molecule. One or more molecules of p-coumaric, ferulic, caffeic, or acetic acids may be esterified to the sugar molecule.

The anthocyanins can be divided into a number of classes depending on the number of sugar molecules. The monosides have only one sugar residue, usually in the 3 position, rarely in the 5 or 7 position, and never elsewhere. The biosides contain two sugars, with either both on the 3 position, or one each on the 3 and 5 position or, rarely, in the 3 and 7 positions. The triosides contain three sugars, usually two on the 3 position with one on the 5 position, often three in a branched structure or a linear structure on the 3 position, or rarely with two on the 3 position and one on the 7 position. No anthocyanins with four sugar residues have been reported but there is some evidence that they exist. Approximately 120 anthocyanins have been reported in the literature.

B. Separation

The importance of the anthocyanins in plant taxonomy has led to development of a number of separation and identification methods. Usually, these are based on paper chromatography, but lately thin-layer methods have received more attention probably because they take less time.

The usual extraction methods involve maceration with 1% hydrochloric acid in methanol, filtration, and concentration of the filtrates. The crude extract is chromatographed on paper or thin-layer systems and the separated bands are cut out. Usually aqueous and oily solvent systems are alternated and three to five chromatographings are usually adequate to prepare a pure pigment. A number of solvent systems are available [38].

C. Identification

Methods for identifying individual anthocyanins are well established [19]. Usually the required criteria for proof of identity are as follows: (1) Rf data with four or more solvent systems, (2) absorption peaks in the uv and visible range, (3) a ratio of absorption at 440 nm to that of the visible maxima, (4) identification by chromatography of the sugars and aglycones after acid hydrolysis, (5) identification of sugars after peroxide oxidation, and (6) identification of intermediate pigments upon controlled hydrolysis. With the above information, the structure of any known anthocyanin can be determined. If one has access to authentic anthocyanins or wishes to isolate them from known sources, then the identification procedure is much simpler. Identical Rf values of an unknown pigment with a known anthocyanin in five different solvent systems is accepted as proof that they are identical. Details of these analyses may be found in a book by Harborne [19] and in numerous papers on pigment identification [38].

D. Quantitative Analysis

Many methods have been reported for the quantitative estimation of anthocyanins in foods [14]. The analysis of total anthocyanins in fresh material is relatively simple. One need only macerate the sample in acidic methanol and measure the absorption of an aliquot of the solution at the visible absorption maxima. The concentration of the pigment can be determined from the E values reported in the literature [14]. The E value is usually defined in two ways. The molar extinction coefficient, also called the molar absorption coefficient, is the absorption in a 1-cm cell at a specified wavelength of one molecular weight of a compound in 1 liter of solution. E values are also expressed as $E_{1cm}^{1\%}$ which means the absorption in a 1-cm cell, at a specified wavelength, of 1 g of a compound in 100 ml of solvent. An example for cyanidin 3-galactoside, in 85 parts of 95% ethanol and 15 parts 0.1N HCl at 535 nm, is $E_{1cm}^{1\%} 535 = 920$. If a reliable E value is not available, the data should be reported in terms of a known pigment (e.g., cyanidin glucoside or galactoside). When accurate E values become known, the data can be easily recalculated. One should not attempt to calibrate an absorptimeter directly with an anthocyanin since pure pigments can seldom be purchased and are very difficult to prepare.

Accurate estimations of anthocyanin content in samples which have undergone some degradation require methods which measure only anthocyanins and not the colored degradation products. These usually depend on the difference in absorption at two pH values since anthocyanins change color with pH [14]. The change in optical density with pH can be related to pigment content in the same manner as the E value.

Approximate indications (±5%) of the content of individual anthocyanins in a product can be obtained by chromatographing an extract and using a densitometer to measure reflectance or transmittance of the separated bands. If the percentage of each band, as compared with the total for all bands, is calculated against an estimate of total pigment obtained by the pH differential method, a reasonable estimate of each pigment can be obtained [14]. This assumes that each pigment can be separated on paper or thin layer with one run. This is true only for fairly simple mixtures of pigments. If several runs are required to separate the pigments, thus requiring several elutions with attendant losses, the error in estimation rises very rapidly.

E. Stability in Fruit Products

The flavylium nucleus of the anthocyanin pigments is electron deficient and therefore highly reactive. The reactions usually involve decolorization of the pigments and are usually undesirable in fruit and vegetable technology. The rate of anthocyanin destruction is pH dependent, being greater at higher pH values. The rate of reaction is dependent on the amount of pigment in the colorless carbinol base form (10), as described later, and is temperature dependent. Meschter calculated the half-life of the pigment in strawberry preserves to be 1,300 hr at 20°C and 240 hr at 38°C [33]. The reactivity of the anthocyanin molecule with air and many components normally present in fruits and vegetables has led to numerous studies on anthocyanin stability [8].

Cyanidin-3-
rhamnoglucoside (VIII)

F. Effect of pH

Anthocyanins show a very marked change in color with pH changes. Figure 8-8 shows the absorption spectra of cyanidin 3-rhamnoglucoside (8) with changes in pH.

Quinoidal or
anhydrobase (IX)

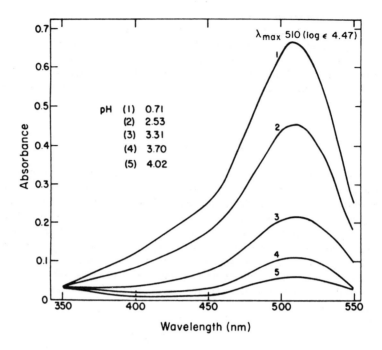

FIG. 8-8. Absorption spectra of cyanidin 3-rhamnoglucoside in buffer solutions at pH values of 0.71-4.02. The concentration of pigment is 1.6×10^{-2} g/liter. (From Chichester [8], courtesy of Academic Press.)

At pH 0.71 the color is an intense red and the pigment is primarily in form (8). As the pH value rises, the pigment changes to the quinoidal or anhydro base (9) and then to the carbinol base (10). Compound (10) is a colorless chromenol, which is fairly stable but does decompose slowly on long standing. The pigment (8) is instantly regenerated upon acidification. No evidence is available for ring fission to produce a chalcone form. In contrast to the anthocyanins, anthocyanidins (with an OH at position 3) produce unstable chromenols which degrade to produce α-diketones.

Carbinol base (X)

Figure 8-9 illustrates the changes that pelargonidin undergoes with changes in pH [20]. The often observed instability of the anthocyanidins, produced by removing the sugar portion of the anthocyanins, is probably due to instability of the chromenols. The latter decompose to produce phenolic benzoic acids. Anthocyanidins

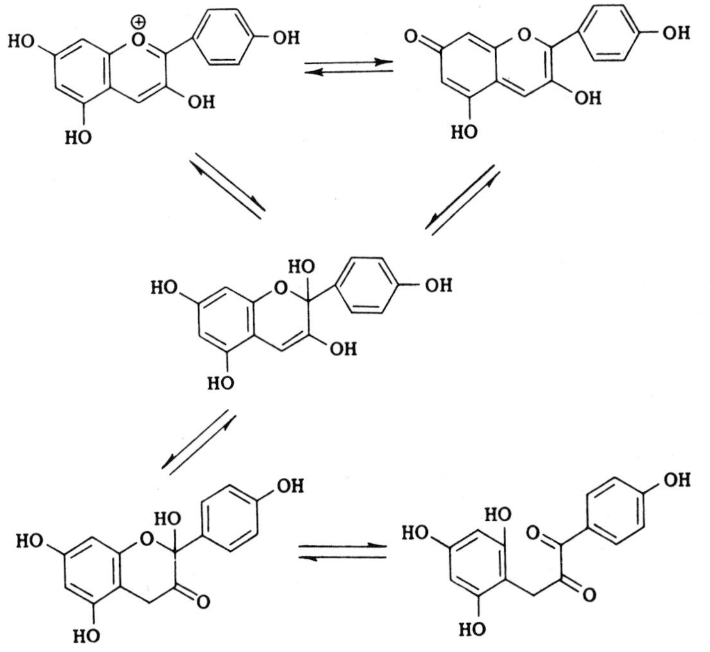

FIG. 8-9. Effect of pH on the structure of pelargonidin. At pH 1, the pigment exists primarily in the form shown in the upper left. At pH 3, the pigment is primarily in the quinoidal form (upper right). At pH 4, the carbinol base (middle) predominates. The structures at the bottom exist primarily at pH values above 4.

are seldom found in stored products in more than trace amounts. They are also relatively unstable on chromatograms during purification and identification.

G. Chemical Reactions

Sulfiting of fruits is an important commercial process for bulk storage of fruit prior to making jams, preserves, or marchino cherries. In recent years, the process has become less important for jams because of the increased use of frozen fruit, which makes a better quality product. Addition of sulfite, or sulfur dioxide, results in rapid bleaching of the anthocyanins, in turn resulting in yellowish colors attributable to other pigments in the fruit. The process is a simple sulfite addition reaction at positions 2 or 4, producing compounds which are colorless but quite stable [26]. Removal of the sulfite by boiling and acidification in jam manufacture results in regeneration of the anthocyanins.

The reaction of anthocyanins with ascorbic acid has been documented by many workers. An interaction occurs which results in degradation of both compounds. For example, cranberry juice cocktail with approximately 9 mg per 100 g of anthocyanins and 18 mg per 100 ml ascorbic acid may lose approximately 80% of the anthocyanin in 6 months at room temperature [39]. The juice will still be brownish red due in part to the color of degradation products. The actual mechanism of this reaction is not completely clear but it may involve an intermediate, peroxide, produced by degradation of ascorbic acid. The reaction of peroxide with anthocyanin has been known for a long time and forms the basis of a method to identify the sugar compound on position 3 of the flavylium compound. Peroxide oxidation of flavylium salts, depending on the conditions, produces a series of different compounds [8]. Oxidation of ascorbic acid is catalyzed by copper and iron compounds and this results in a greater rate of destruction of anthocyanins. Even at low pH values (pH = 2.0) where anthocyanins are more stable, destruction caused by interaction with ascorbic acid is considerable [39]. The presence of metal ions may exert a slight protective effect at low pH values but this is insignificant compared to the amount of degradation caused by ascorbic acid [40].

Accelerated decoloration of anthocyanins in the presence of ascorbic acid, amino acids, phenols, sugar derivatives, etc., may be caused by actual condensation reactions with these compounds. The polymers and degradation compounds produced in these reactions are probably quite complex [8]. Some of the reaction products form compounds called "phlobaphens," which are brownish red in color. For example, strawberry jam after 2 years of storage at room temperature has no detectable anthocyanins left but is still reddish brown in color. Compounds of this type are believed to contribute to the color of aged red wines.

H. Enzymic Reactions

Enzyme systems which decolorize anthocyanins have been reported by a number of workers [8]. They may be glycosidases, which hydrolyze the protective 3-glycosidic linkage to yield unstable aglycones, or phenolases, which require the interaction of o-dihydroxy phenols. Peng and Markakis [34] suggested the scheme shown in Figure 8-10. Catechol is enzymically oxidized to an o-quinone, which then oxidizes the anthocyanin nonenzymically to colorless breakdown products.

I. Anthocyanin Complexes

The observation that red anthocyanin pigments can be isolated from blue flowers (e.g., cornflowers) has stimulated considerable research on possible structures

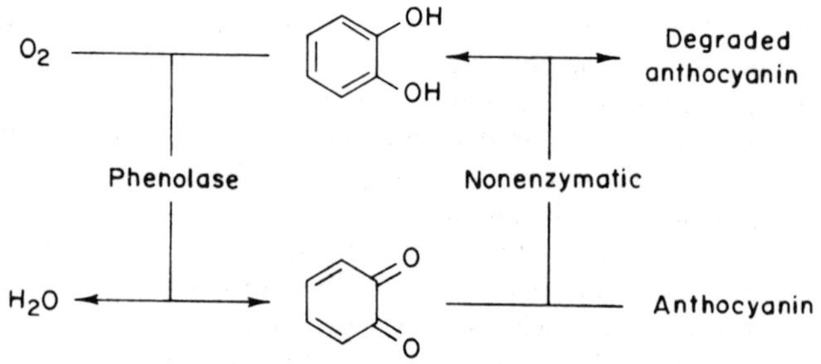

FIG. 8-10. The interaction of anthocyanins with polyphenols and oxygen. (From Peng and Markakis [34], courtesy of MacMillan, Ltd.)

which can produce the blue color. The colors have been ascribed to "copigmentation" of anthocyanins with yellow flavonoids and other polyphenols and to complex formation with a number of components. A number of such complexes have been isolated and they are reported to contain cations, such as Al, K, Fe, Cu, Ca, and Sn; amino acids; proteins; pectin, carbohydrates; or polyphenols. All the previous complexes were reported from flowers, but Van Teeling et al. [42] reported a very high molecular weight (77,000,000) complex isolated from canned blueberries.

J. Anthocyanidin Derivatives

Restrictions on the use of red food colors have led to interest in the potential of anthocyanin-type compounds as food colorants. Jurd [25] described a whole series of compounds differing in the substituents at the 3 position. These have been patented in the public domain (United States Patents 3,266,903 and 3,314,975) but unfortunately they are subject to reactions with sulfur dioxide, ascorbic acid, pH, etc. Timberlake and Bridle [41] recently reported that anthocyanidins with a methyl or a phenyl group at position 4 were very stable in the presence of the above compounds, even more so than some of the permitted red colors. However, this class of 4-substituted flavylium compounds would be considered as new compounds and would have to undergo full toxicity clearance procedures.

IV. FLAVONOIDS

The yellow flavonoids comprise a diverse, almost ubiquitous class of pigments, with chemical structures similar to the anthocyanins. Approximately 400 flavonoids are known and the number is increasing rapidly.

One major group is the flavonols, such as kaempferol (11), quercetin (12), and myricetin (13). Another group, less common than the flavonols is the flavones, such as apigenin (14), luteolin (15), and tricetin (16). Note the similarity in structure to pelargonidin, cyanidin, and delphinidin. Sixty other aglycones, based on hydroxy and methoxy derivatives of the flavonol and flavone structures, are known.

Five other minor groups are known: the chalcones (17), the aurones (18), the flavanones and isoflavanones (19), and the biflavonyls (20).

The above aglycones usually exist in the glycoside form with glucose, rhamnose, galactose, arabinose, xylose, apiose, or glucuronic acid. The sites of substitution are varied, but the 7; 5; 4'; 7,4'; and 3' positions are common. In contrast to the anthocyanins, the 7 position is the most frequent site of substitution because it is usually the most acidic of the hydroxyl groups. The flavonoid compounds also may occur with acyl substituents in a manner similar to the anthocyanins. Compounds have also been isolated in which glucose is attached by a carbon-carbon bond in either the 6 or the 8 position. Such compounds are completely resistant to acid hydrolysis and although not strictly glycosides, they have closely related properties. The two most common members are vitexin and isovitexin.

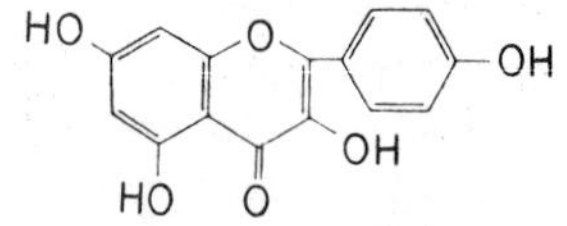

Kaempferol (XI)

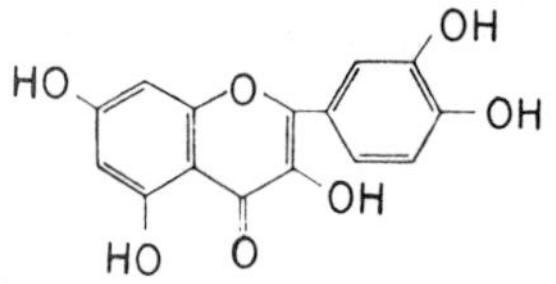

Chalcone (XVII)

Quercetin (XII)

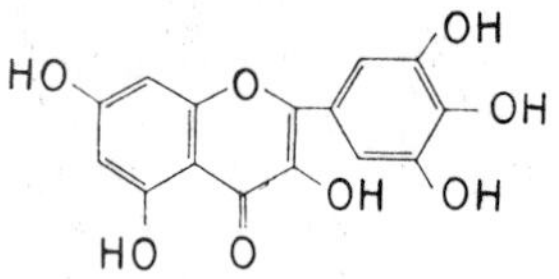

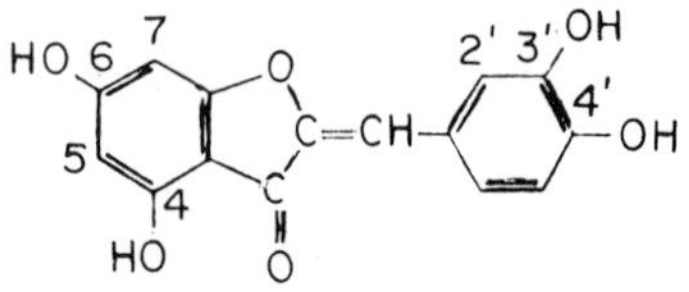

Aurone (XVIII)
(Aureusidin)

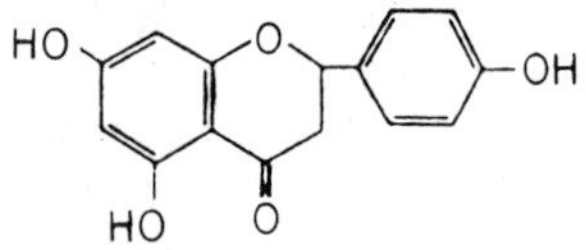

Myricetin (XIII)

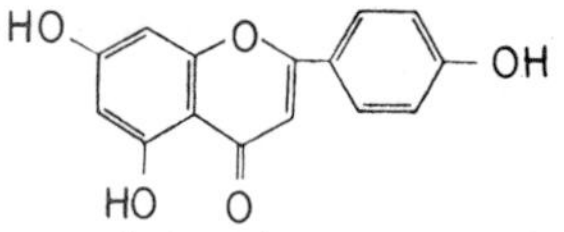

Flavanone (XIX)
(Naringin)

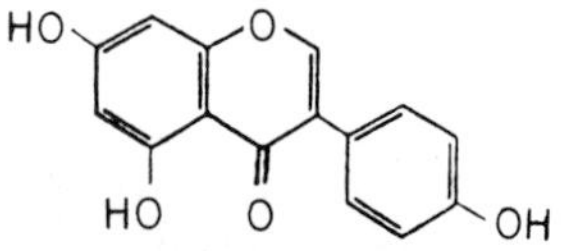

Apigenin (XIV)

Isoflavanone
(Genistein)

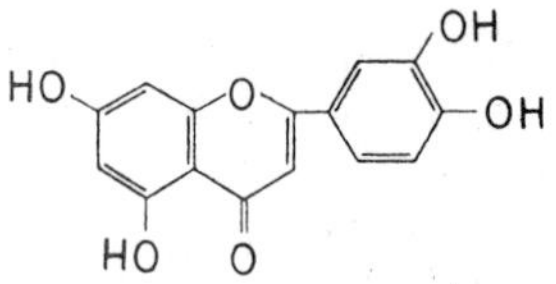

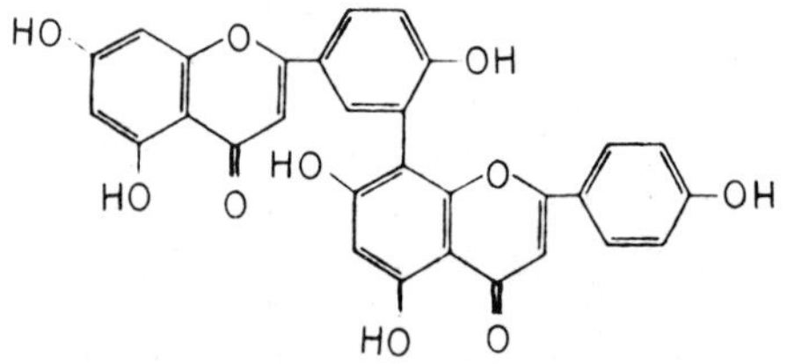

Luteolin (XV)

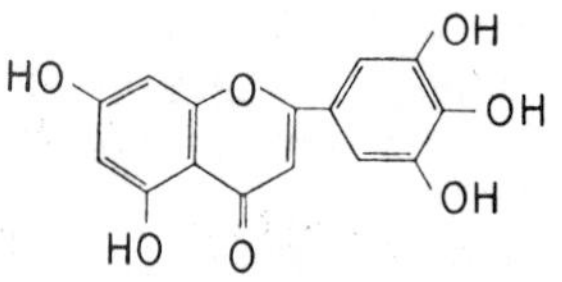

Tricetin (XVI)

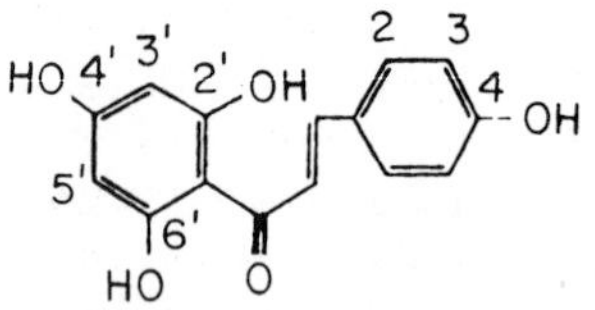

Biflavonyl (XX)
(Amentoflavone)

A. Isolation and Identification

The flavonoid compounds are usually more stable to heat and oxidation than the
anthocyanins and can be isolated from plant tissue in essentially the same manner
as described for the anthocyanins. Most will stand higher temperatures than anthocyanins, so the plant tissue is often placed in boiling ethanol to inactivate
enzyme systems which may degrade the pigments. The identification procedures
for the aglycone, sugars, and possible acyl components involve hydrolysis and

chromatography. Controlled hydrolysis is very useful but is not as reliable as with anthocyanins, since occasionally some theoretical intermediates do not occur. Pigment identifications are usually based on Rf values in five or six solvents, hydrolysis products, spectral changes with several reagents, methylation with identification of hydrolysis products, and, of course, identification of degradation products. Many of the groups have characteristic colors under UV light with and without ammonia fumes. In view of the large number of possible compounds, identification procedures are beyond the scope of this chapter. Interested readers should consult suitable references [15,19,32].

B. Importance in Foods

The flavonols quercetin and kaempferol glycosides are almost ubiquitous in the plant kingdom, having been found in over 50% of all plants tested. Glycosides of myricetin have been found in over 10% of all plants tested. Many plants contain flavonoid pigments. There is a large number of research papers on them primarily because these compounds are useful in plant taxonomy and this has stimulated a great deal of excellent biochemical research.

With a number of notable exceptions, flavonoids in foods have not been extensively investigated. Possibly, the lack of good quantitative analytical methods has contributed to this, but methods are becoming available. Individual methods based on absorptivity in the 300-400 nm range [29] or fluorescence with aluminum chloride are examples.

The three flavonol aglycones, quercetin, kaempferol, and myricetin, are found in considerable amounts in "instant" tea powders where they contribute to astringency. In green tea, the three compounds and their glycosides may comprise as much as 30% of the dry weight. One flavonoid, rutin (quercetin 3-rhamnoglucoside), was studied years ago when it became apparent that the compound complexed with iron to form an unsightly dark discoloration in canned asparagus. The tin complex, in contrast, produces a desirable yellow color.

The flavanones, a minor group of flavonoids found mainly in citrus plants, are much in the news currently because of their potential as synthetic sweeteners. Naringin, a flavanone with neohesperidose in the 7 position, is an intensely bitter substance, whereas an isomer of the above compound with rutinose in the 7 position is tasteless. Neohesperidose has rhamnose and glucose in an α-1$\rightarrow$2 linkage, whereas rutinose has an α-1$\rightarrow$6 linkage. This difference is accentuated when the ring structure is opened to produce chalcone structures with the neohesperidose sugar. One derivative, neohesperidin dihydrochalcone, synthesized from naringin, has a sweetness nearly 2,000 times that of sucrose. One thousand pounds of this compound were synthesized in 1970 for toxicity studies, and preliminary reports look promising. Because of the current problems with the cyclamates, amino acid derivatives, and saccharin, a new artificial sweetener would be very welcome.

The citrus flavonoids were in the news many years ago for their alleged "bioflavonoid" (vitamin P) synergistic activity with ascorbic acid in promoting better "capillary fragility." There may well be a small effect of bioflavonoids in maintenance of stronger capillary walls but the physiological effects have been very largely discounted in normal individuals. The latest promotional effort for citrus flavonoids involves deodorization and disinfection of rooms. It remains to be seen whether this application is successful.

The isoflavones have also received attention lately for their weak estrogenic activity. Three isoflavones have been implicated in the lowered fertility of sheep pastured on clover containing these compounds. There are possible benefits also, because the flush of milk in cows on spring pasture may be due to estrogenic iso-flavones. Other isoflavones are also noteworthy, such as the well-known fish toxicant rotenone and the glycosuria-producing phloridzin.

The polyphenolic character of the flavonoids and their ability to sequester metals has aroused interest as to their possible value as antioxidants for fats and oils. However, their limited solubility in oil has restricted their use and several deriva-tives with increased lipid solubility have been suggested.

The flavonoids are relatively stable toward heat processing in aqueous canned foods but little research has been done on this aspect.

The bioflavonyls are an interesting group but their significance in foods is largely unknown. They are dimers, usually of apigenin (14), with three parent groups made up of the 8-8, 8-3', and 8-4' linkages. Two compounds of this class were isolated from the ginkgo tree, the "living fossil" which has been is existance for over 250,000,000 years.

V. LEUCOANTHOCYANINS

Although leucoanthocyanins are colorless, they are considered here because they have structural similarity to anthocyanins and because under conditions of food handling and processing, they can be converted to colored products. The term "leucoanthocyanin" is somewhat misleading and alternate names, such as proan-thocyanidins, anthoxanthins, anthocyanogens, flavolans, flavylans, and flavylo-gens, have been suggested, although none has gained acceptance.

The basic building block of leucoanthocyanins is usually flavan-3,4-diol (21), forming a dimer through a 4-8 or a 4-6 linkage, but trimers and higher polymers are common. All produce an anthocyanidin, such as pelargonidin, cyanidin, pe-tunidin, or delphinidin, when heated in the presence of a mineral acid. The main leucoanthocyanin in apples is a dimer of two 1-epicatechin units linked through a C_4-C_8 bond (22). This compound gives cyanidin and (-)epicatechin on hydrolysis. It has been found in many varieties of apples, pears, cola nuts, cocoa beans, hawthorn berries, etc.

Flavan-3,4-diol (XXI)
(catechin and epicatechin
are the trans and cis forms
of carbons 2 and 3)

Leucoanthocyanin (XXII)

The leucoanthocyanin compounds are interesting in foods because they contribute to the astringency or "puckeriness" of foods. In apple cider they contribute significantly to the characteristic taste and they are important in the flavor of many other fruits and beverages, such as persimmons, cranberries, olives, bananas, chocolate, tea, and wine. They also contribute to enzymic browning reactions in fruits and vegetables, through their orthohydroxy groups, and to haze formation in beer and wine.

In order to be astringent, they must have the ability to react with protein, and this restricts the size of the leucoanthocyanin polymer. Monomers are apparently too soluble so the effective molecular size is usually within the range of two to eight repeating units. However, the actual structure may be more complex than merely a repeating unit of flavan-3,4-diol. The inability to react with protein in a manner analogous to the reaction of tannic acid in the tanning of skin to form leather has led to the term "condensed tannins." This is an unfortunate term but one that is apparently well entrenched.

VI. TANNINS

The term "tannin," also tannic acid, gallotannic acid, and incorrectly digallic acid, is defined in the Merck Index as a complex mixture found in the bark of oak, sumac, and myrobalen. Its appearance ranges from colorless to yellow or brown. Turkish and Chinese nutgalls contain 50 and 70%, respectively, of tannin. Tannic acid, as purchased from a chemical supply house (e.g., Fisher) has a formula $C^{76}H^{52}O^{46}$ and molecular weight of 1,701 and probably consists of nine molecules of gallic acid and one of glucose.

The term "tannin" as used in foods includes two types of compounds. The first type is the "condensed tannins" which may be 4,8 or 2,8 C-C dimers as described previously, or 3,3-ether-linked dimers of catechin and related compounds. Other linkages, such as 2C,7O or 4C,7O compounds have been reported. The second type is the "hydrolyzable tannins" including the gallotannins and the ellagitannins. These compounds are best noted for their ability to tan hides for leather manufacture. The latter are polymers of gallic acid (23) and ellagic acid (24). A typical ellagitannin containing gallic acid, ellagic acid, and one molecule of glucose is shown in structure (25). Compounds have been reported which are combinations of the two types of tannins, e.g., theaflavin gallate, a possible intermediate found in tea fermentation.

Tannins contribute to the astringency of foods and also to enzymic browning reactions, but their mechanisms of action are not well understood.

VII. BETALAINS

The betalains are a group of compounds resembling the anthocyanins and flavonoids in visual appearance. They were called, incorrectly, in the older literature "nitrogen-containing" anthocyanins. They are found only in ten families of Centrospermae, of which the best known is the red beet. They are also found as water-soluble compounds in the cell sap in chard, cactus fruits, pokeberries, and a number of flowers, such as bougainvillia and amaranthus [31].

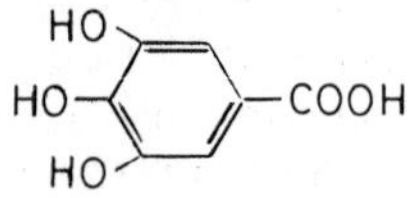

Gallic acid (XXIII)

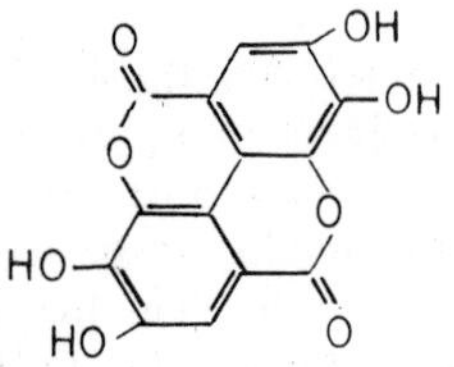

Ellagic acid (XXIV)

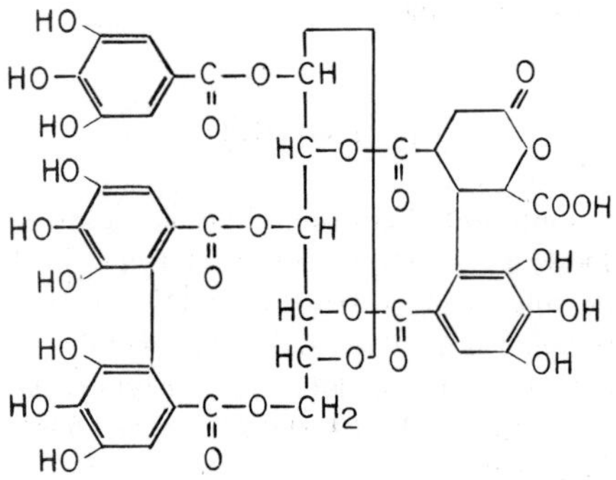

Chebulagic acid (XXV)

About 70 betalains are known and they all have the same basic structure (26), in which R and R' may be hydrogen or an aromatic substituent. Their color is attributable to the resonating structures (29) and (30) as shown in Figure 8-11. If R or R' does not extend the resonance, the compound is yellow and is called a betazanthin. If R or R' does extend the resonance, the compound is red and called a

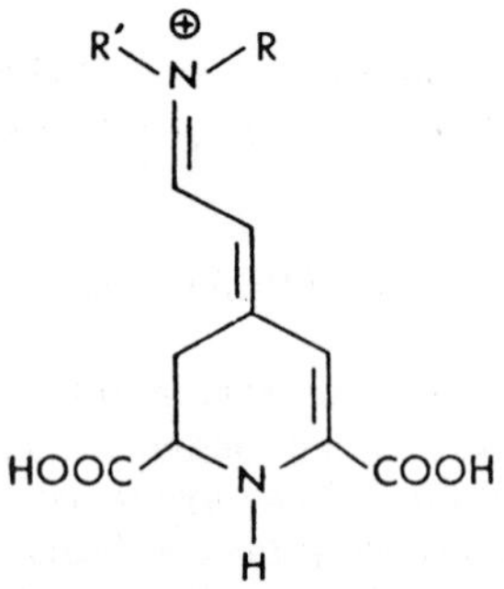

1, 7-Diazoheptamethin
(XXVI)

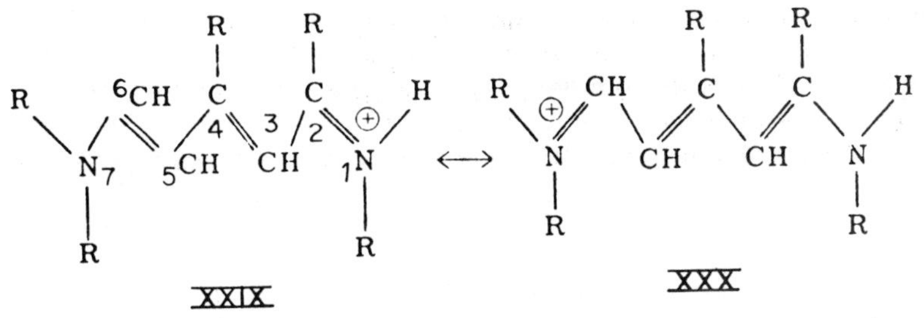

FIG. 8-11. Betacyanin resonating structures (29) and (30). (From Mabry and Dreiding [31], courtesy of Appleton-Century-Crofts.)

betacyanin. For example, the aglycone of the betacyanin in red beets is called betanidin (27). With glucose, it is called betanin (28). The only compounds forming glycosides are glucose and glucuronic acid. The betalains may also occur naturally in the acyl form in a manner similar to the anthocyanins and flavonoids, but the pattern is more complicated. Malonic, ferulic, p-coumaric, sinapic, caffeic, and 3 hydroxy-3-methyl glutaric acids have been found attached to the sugar portion of the betalains.

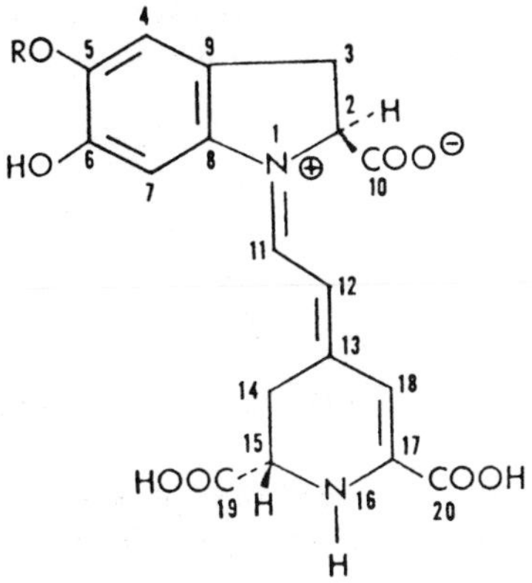

Betanidin, R = H
(XXVII)

Betanin, R = Glucose
(XXVIII)

The anthocyanins and the betalains have different chemical structures and are easily differentiated. Their spectra are different in that the betalains have no absorption peaks in the 270-nm region. Anthocyanins are easily extracted with methanol and very poorly with water. The reverse is true for betalains. In electrophoresis systems with weakly acidic buffers, the anthocyanins go to the cathode and the betalains to the anode. Electrophoresis is actually the method of choice for separating closely related betalains.

The betalains are subject to degradation by thermal processing, as in canning, but usually sufficient pigment is available so that the food (e.g., beets) has an attractive dark red color. The isolated pigment of beets is stable in the pH range 4-6 and this makes it of interest as a potential colorant in foods.

Members of the Phytolacca family (American pokeberry) had a brief claim to fame as adulterants for wine many years ago, when a pokeberry plant in the corner of the vineyard was insurance against a crop of grapes low in pigment content. The addition of pokeberry juice to wine was outlawed in France in 1892. Apart from being a potent colorant, pokeberry juice also contains a purgatory and emetic substance.

VIII. QUINONES AND XANTHONES

The quinones [17] are a large group of yellowish pigments found in the cell sap of flowering plants, fungi, lichens, bacteria, and algae. Over 200 are known, ranging in color from pale yellow to almost black. The largest subgroup is the anthraquinones, of which some members have been used as natural dyestuffs and purgatives for centuries. A typical anthraquinone is emodin (31), which is widely distributed in fungi, lichens, and higher plants. A small subgroup, composed of about 20 pigments, is the napthoquinones (32). Several members of this group are used as dyes, e.g., henna. Juglone, occurring in walnuts, and plumbagin (32) are typical napthoquinones. The anthraquinones usually occur as glycosides but the napthoquinones do not. Another larger subgroup is the benzoquinones, which occur mainly in fungi and some flowering plants. As example is the violet-black compound spinulosin (33). Another subgroup of unique red pigments, the napthacenequinones, confined to the Actinomycetales, is closely related to the tetracycline antibiotics. There are many other subgroups, such as the phenanthraquinones, isoprenoid quinones, and a number with more complex structures.

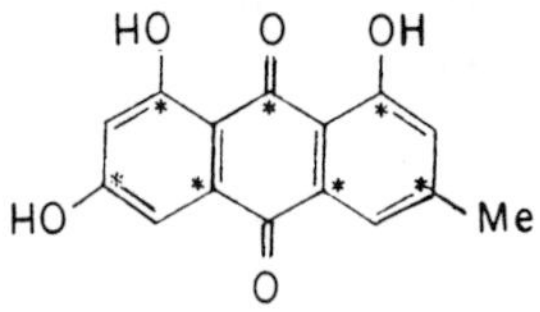

Emodin (XXXI)

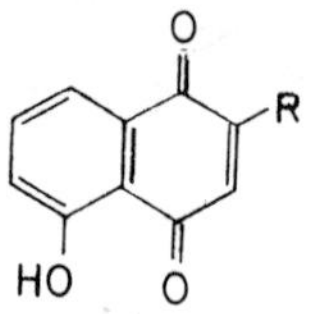

Napthoquinones (XXXII)

Juglone (R = H)
Plumbagin (R = Me)

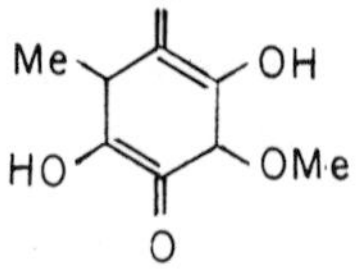

Spinulosin (XXXIII)

The xanthones are a group of 20 yellow pigments which have been confused with the quinones and the flavones. One well-known member is mangiferin (34), which occurs as a glucoside in mangoes. They can be easily distinguished from flavones and quinones by spectral data.

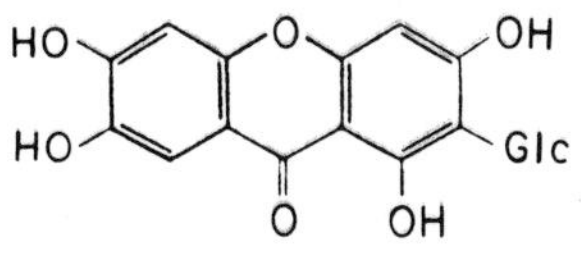

Mangiferin (XXXIV)

IX. CAROTENOIDS

The carotenoids are a group of mainly lipid-soluble compounds responsible for many of the yellow and red colors of plant and animal products. They are very widespread and occur naturally in large quantities. Isler [22] has estimated that over 100,000,000 tons of carotenoids are produced annually by nature. Most of this is in the form of fucoxanthin (42) in various algae and the three main carotenoids of green leaves, lutein (39), violaxanthin (40), and neoxanthin (41). Others, produced in much smaller amounts but occurring very widely, are β-carotene (36), and zeaxanthin (35). Other pigments, such as lycopene (48) in tomatoes, capsanthin (44) in red peppers, and bixin (46) in annatto, predominate in certain plants.

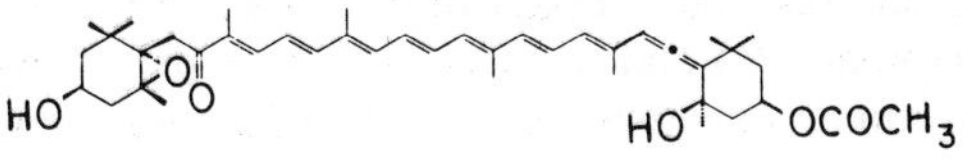

Fucozanthin (XXXXII)

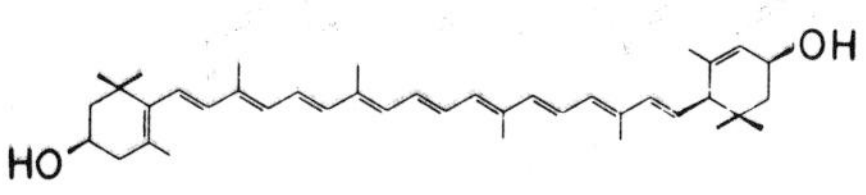

Lutein (XXXIX)

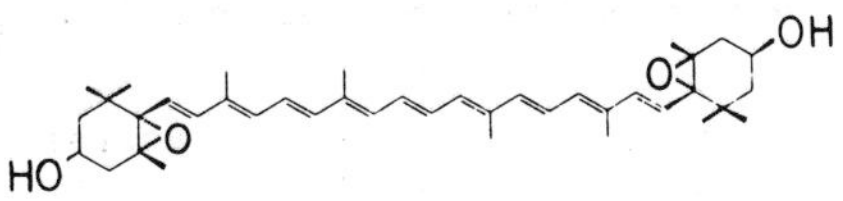

Violaxanthin (XXXX)

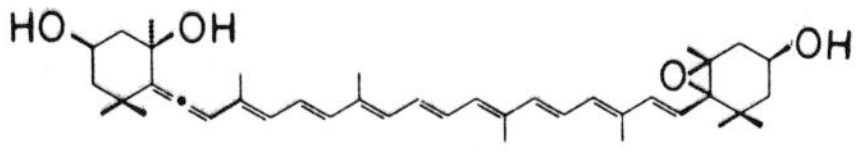

Neoxanthin (XXXXI)

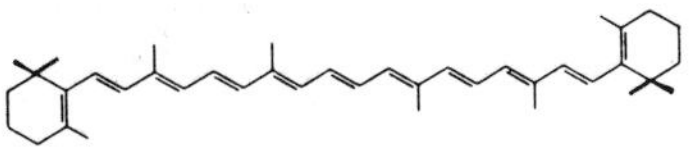

Beta-carotene (XXXVI)

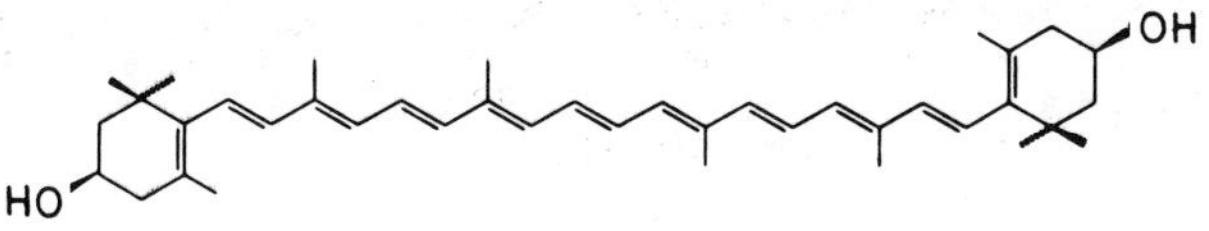

Zeaxanthin (XXXV)

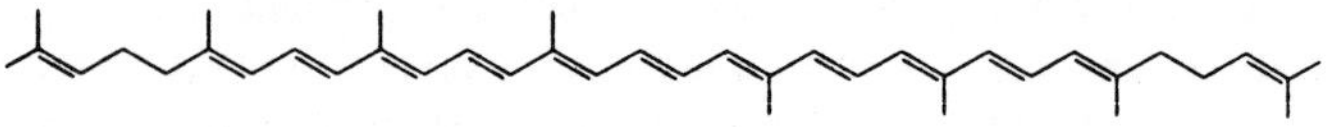

Lycopene (XXXXVIII)

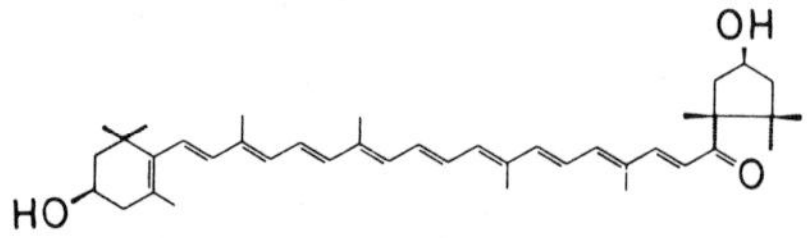

Capsanthin (XXXXIV)

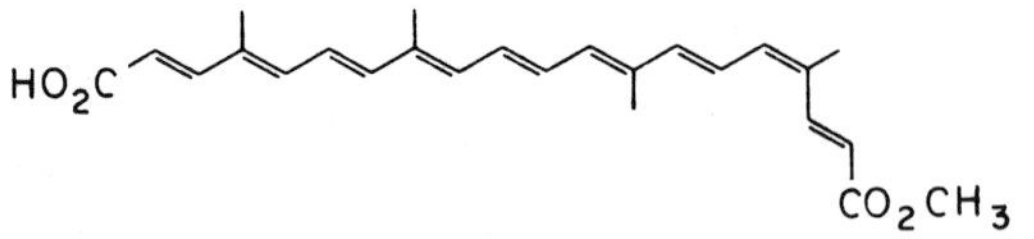

Bixin (XXXXVI)

A. Structure

Carotenoids include a class of hydrocarbons, called carotenes, and their oxygen-ated derivatives, called xanthophylls. They consist of eight isoprenoid units joined in such a manner that the arrangement of isoprenoid units is reversed in the center of the molecule. The basic carbon structure for lycopene (48) shows the symme-trical arrangement around the central pair of carbons. This structure can be cyclyzed to form β-carotene (36) and the 15-15' carbon pair forms the center of the molecule (Fig. 8-12). Other carotenoids have different end groups with the same

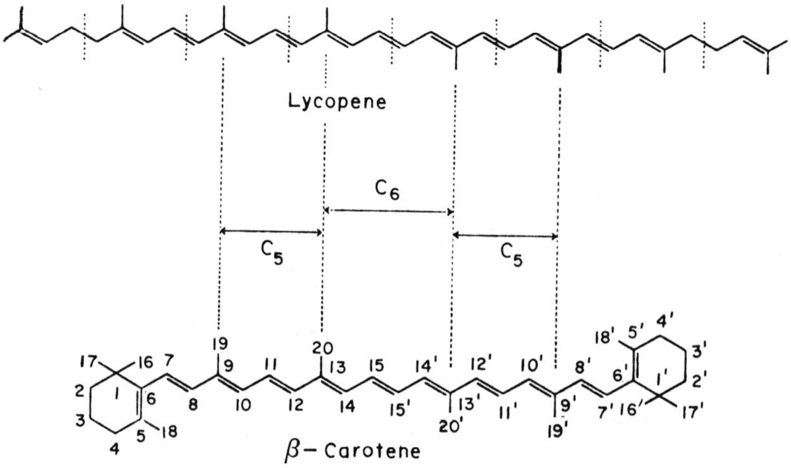

FIG. 8-12. Relationship of lycopene and β-carotene structures showing the symmetry around the 15-15' carbons, and the C_5 (isoprene) repeating units. (From Isler [32]; courtesy of Birkhauser Verlag, Basel.)

central structure. About 60 different end groups are known, comprising about 300 known carotenoids, and new ones are continually being reported. Most of the caro-tenoids reported earlier have a C_{40} central skeleton but recently some have been described which contain more than 40 carbons. They are also named as substituted C_{40} carotenoids. The nomenclature for the carotenoids is too complicated for description here and the latest modification may be found in the report of the IUPAC Commission [1].

Carotenoids can exist in the free state in plant tissue as crystals or amorphous solids, or in solution in lipid media. They also occur as esters or in combination with sugars and proteins. The occurrence of carotenoids as esters of fatty acids has been known for a long time. For example, lutein in autumn leaves is associ-ated with both palmitic and linolenic acids in positions 3 and 3' of lutein. Cap-santhin (44) occurs as the lauric acid ester in paprika. Carotenoid esters have been found in flowers, fruits, and bacteria.

The association of carotenoids with proteins is of more recent investigation, and knowledge has developed primarily from studies of pigments in various inver-tebrates [7]. The association of carotenoids with proteins stabilizes the pigment and also changes the color. For example, the red carotenoid astazanthin (43), when complexed with a protein, forms the blue colorant in lobster shells. Another example is ovoverdin, the green pigment in lobster eggs. Carotenoid-protein complexes are also known in some green leaves, bacteria, fruits, and vegetables.

Astazanthin (XXXXIII)

Carotenoids may also occur in combination with reducing sugars via a glycosidic bond. For many years, crocin, containing two molecules of the sugar gentiobiose united with crocetin (47), was the only pigment of this type known. Crocin is the main pigment in saffron. Lately, a number of carotenoid glycosides have been isolated from bacteria.

Crocetin (XXXXVII)

B. Isolation and Identification

Extraction of carotenoids is normally accomplished by lipid solvents, such as hex-ane or petroleum ether, in the cold and in the absence of strong light. The sol-vents should be treated to remove traces of peroxides in order to minimize the possibility of structural change. Nearly all carotenoids are stable to alkali; there-fore, preliminary saponification with potassium hydroxide in methanol may be used

to facilitate purification. For example, chlorophylls are saponified by this treatment and can be removed by washing with water. Saponification, of course, breaks
fatty acid ester linkages. The carbohydrate or protein complexes with carotenoids
must be extracted with alcohol since they have low solubility in the usual lipid
solvents.

After extraction and preliminary purification by washing, the mixture can be
resolved by chromatography on columns of magnesium oxide and filter aid, alumina, starch, sugar, etc. Thin-layer chromatography on polyamides, silica gel,
cellulose, etc., has been adopted as the method of choice because of speed and good
resolution. Column chromatography is used if larger quantities are desired. If
the pigment mixture is known to be fairly complex, the crude mixture can be fractionated into groups according to their polarity by counter-current liquid-liquid
fractionation. Solvent systems, such as methanol, water, and petroleum ether,
will separate carotenoids into hydrocarbons, monols, diols, epoxide diols, keto-
diols, and polyols. Each group can then be further fractionated by chromatography
into pure pigments.

Identification of carotenoids is based primarily on Rf data, location on a chromatogram, and spectral data in the ultraviolet, visible, and infrared ranges. A
number of specific reactions are available to identify specific chemical groups in
the molecule (e.g., keto groups). Recently, mass spectrometry and nuclear magnetic resources (almost solely proton magnetic resonance) have become very
valuable tools in structure determination. Detailed procedures are available in a
number of books [e.g., 16, 17, 22].

C. Quantitative Analysis

Analyses for total carotenoid content are usually based on extraction of the crude
pigment mixture in a lipid solvent and measurement of optical density at 440 nm.
The pigment content is expressed "as β-carotene" using the absorption coefficients
for β-carotene. If estimates of individual pigments are desired, the pigments must
be extracted and separated, usually by chromatography, and the absorption measured at one of the absorption peaks characteristic of each individual pigment. Absorption coefficients for most known pigments are available in the literature [17].

D. Chemical Reactions

1. PROVITAMIN A

Carotenoids have received a great deal of attention from early researchers because
β-carotene is a precursor of vitamin A, a well-known nutrient in the human diet.
β-Carotene yields two molecules of vitamin A by cleavage at the center of the molecule. Compounds, such as α-carotene (37), which have half of their structure
identical to β-carotene function as precursors for one molecule of vitamin A. Lycopene (48) has no vitamin A activity. The association of vitamin A with retinene
in the visual purple cycle in human vision has been responsible for literally hundreds of papers on carotenoid chemistry and physiology.

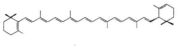

Alpha-carotene (XXXVII)

2. OXIDATION REACTIONS

The main cause of carotenoid degradation in foods is oxidation. The severity of oxidation depends on whether the pigment is in vivo or in vitro and on environmental conditions. In intact living tissue, the stability of the pigments is probably a function of cell permeability and the presence of protective components. For example, lycopene in tomatoes is quite stable but the extracted purified pigment is unstable. Present in many tissues are enzyme systems which degrade carotenoids rapidly. For example, in macerated green leaves, half the carotenoids are lost in 20 min at room temperature. Lipoxidase will interact to degrade carotenoids in a number of foods.

In processed foods, the mechanism of oxidation is complex and depends on many factors. The pigments may autoxidize by reaction with atmospheric oxygen at rates dependent on light, heat, and presence of pro- and antioxidants. The reactions are believed to be caused by free-radical formation with three distinct steps involved. This area has been reviewed by Scott [37]. Carotenoids undergo coupled oxidation in the presence of lipids at rates dependent on the system. Carotenoids are usually more stable in systems with high degrees of unsaturation, possibly because the lipid system itself accepts the free radicals more easily than carotene. Conversely, carotenes are less stable in lipid systems with high degrees of unsaturation, but there are several exceptions to this in the literature. Carotenoids can act as antioxidants or prooxidants, depending on the system.

E. Carotenoids as Food Colors

Carotenoids contained in natural extracts from annatto, saffron, paprika, tomatoes, etc., have been employed as food colorants. Yellow colorants, such as extracts from carrots, palm oil, and butterfat, also have vitamin A activity because of their β-carotene contents. These natural extracts have been supplemented in many cases with synthetic carotenoids.

Three synthesized carotenoids are currently approved by the FDA for addition to human foods. β-Carotene (36) which provides a yellow to orange color is by far the most widely used. β-Apo-8-carotenal (45) provides an orange to red color and canthazanthin (38) provides a red color. Canthazanthin is the most recent carotenoid to be approved and is rapidly gaining in importance particularly since the use of F.D. and C. Red No. 2 has been curtailed. It is possible to reproduce the color produced by Red No. 2 with a mixture of canthazanthin and a small amount of F.D. and C. Violet No. 1.

Beta-apo-8-carotenol (XXXXV)

Canthazanthin (XXXVIII)

Applications of carotenoids as food colorants can be divided into fat-based and water-based categories. The former group includes margarine, butter, oils, etc., and usually requires a 20-30% suspension of a carotenoid in an oil carrier. Stability of carotenoids added in this manner is usually very good. Water-based foods, such as beverages, soups, dairy products, meat products, syrups, or macaroni, require a different carotenoid formulation. It is possible to prepare water-dispersible carotenoids by formation of a colloidal suspension using water-miscible solvents or by emulsification of oily solutions. Synthetic carotenoids are available as oily suspensions, as tiny beadlets coated with gelatin or carbohydrate, or even as microcrystals, depending on the application.

There is no legal limit on the addition of β-carotene to foods, whereas β-apo-8-carotenal and canthazanthin are limited to 15 and 20 mg, respectively, per pound of solid food or pint of liquid food.

X. MISCELLANEOUS NATURAL PIGMENTS

There are a number of groups of compounds the structures of which differ from the usual carotenoid-flavonoid-quinonoid-porphyrin concept of color. The appearance of a colored molecule may be incidental, resulting from a relatively minor structural variation which shifts the absorption of light into the visible area. An example may be taken from the aromatic ketones, in which the simple compounds are colorless and complex derivatives, such as gossypol, are yellow. Gossypol, a toxic substance, has received much attention lately because it is present in cottonseed meal and the meal is a potential source of protein for humans. Many aromatic dienone compounds are found in molds. One cyclic dienone group resembles the flavonoids and one more complex member (dracorubin) is the pigment of "dragons blood," a resin exuded from some palm trees. There is a number of other examples, such as the perinaphthenones, γ-pyrones, sclerotiorins, vulpinic acid pigments, pyrroles, phenazines, phenoxazone, antibiotics, melanins, and compounds similar to riboflavin.

We should not leave the subject of natural pigments without mention of the pale yellow pigment phytochrome, which is so important to overall plant growth. It controls elongation, flowering, germination, induction of dormancy, and production of anthocyanins and carotenoids. Its structure is unknown at this time.

Table 8-4 provides a summary of the various natural pigments and their characteristics.

XI. SYNTHETIC COLORS

In any discussion of food pigments one cannot ignore the synthetic colorants or dyes used so widely in food materials. It is not our purpose to describe all such colorants; however, it is in keeping to discuss the general philosophy of synthetic colorants and their place in food materials.

TABLE 8-4

Summary of Characteristics of Natural Pigments

Pigment groups	Number of compounds	Color	Source	Solubility	Stability
Anthocyanins	120	Orange, red, blue	Plants	Water soluble	pH sensitive, heat labile
Flavonoids	600	Colorless, yellow	Most plants	Water soluble	Fairly heat stable
Leucoanthocyanins	20	Colorless	Plants	Water soluble	Heat stable
Tannins	20	Colorless, yellow	Plants	Water soluble	Heat stable
Betalains	70	Yellow, red	Plants	Water soluble	Heat sensitive
Quinones	200	Yellow to black	Plants, bacteria, algae	Water soluble	Heat stable
Xanthones	20	Yellow	Plants	Water soluble	Heat stable
Carotenoids	300	Colorless, yellow, red	Plants, animals	Lipid soluble	Heat stable
Chlorophylls	25	Green, brown	Plants	Lipid and water soluble	Heat sensitive
Heme pigments	6	Red, brown	Animals	Water soluble	Heat sensitive

There is no question that colorants are to be added to the food supply in the future. With the vast increase in our population and the limited ability of the land to produce food one must look more and more to the area of fabricated or synthetic foods as a possible solution to world food problems.

Since the case for adding colorants is easy to establish, one must then consider what kind of colorants are going to be used. Certainly there is a current trend to carefully reexamine the safety of those synthetic colorants which are now allowed in foods. Certain formerly acceptable colorants have been disallowed and others are under suspicion because of potential health hazards.

Since synthetic colorants and dyes may become illegal as food additives, the food industry may be faced with the problem of what to use in their place. Certainly, the first thing that comes to mind is natural pigments. However, having considered in this chapter some of the frailties, the instabilities, and the problems associated with natural pigments one is confronted with severe problems of just how to cope with the chemical nature of these pigments. A larger problem, however, is to supply natural pigments in the amounts required for coloration of those foods in which their presence is deemed desirable. It is rather hopeless to look at the huge amounts of highly concentrated synthetic colorants which are now being used and even to dream of replacing these with natural pigments. One of the major problems, of course, is that most natural pigments are a vital part of the host material. This means, for example, that the anthocyanins in strawberries cannot be extracted from strawberries and used as a colorant in another food if one expects to sell the strawberries. A different approach is to grow a sufficient amount of a highly pigmented nonfood plant from which the pigment can be extracted economically and used in other food materials. However, this approach also has limitations. Not only would it be difficult to produce enough natural pigments by this means, but it would be very costly. The high cost is based on the assumption that such plants are being produced only for their pigment content. It would, of course, be advantageous to find a plant that is grown for some purpose other than its pigment content. In this instance the pigment would be a recoverable byproduct, the use of which could be economically beneficial. Although this approach is possible, it is still far from reality. Thus, to cease using synthetic colorants totally and to replace them with natural pigments is not feasible at this time.

Another approach which is not so dreamlike is to utilize more fully the inherent optical characteristics of natural pigments and unquestionably safe synthetic colorants, i.e., to take advantage of certain physical phenomena which occur when light strikes an object. At every boundary between two materials of different refractive index, light changes its speed and a small fraction of it is reflected, usually about 4% for most common materials. This may seem like an insignificant amount of reflection, but when we are dealing with many kinds of particulate matter suspended in a medium of different refractive index, reflections occur repeatedly until incident light is thoroughly diffused and total reflectances of up to 80-90% are achieved.

Another phenomena extremely important in the color of an object is internal diffusion. When light penetrates the surface of an object it may be subjected to reflection and refraction if particles are present. One of the requirements for internal diffusion of light, therefore, is the existence of many randomly oriented interfaces between materials of different refractive indices. When this situation occurs, the many encounters caused by refraction of light rays give rise to very high levels of reflection. Also affecting internal diffusion is the particle size of the material within the medium. Scattering, or diffusion, of light in a material increases inversely with the square of the particle diameter, down to a limiting size. Maximum scattering of light occurs when particle diameter reaches approximately 0.1 μm which is about one-fourth the wavelength of light. At this diameter the particles become too small to reflect and refract in the usual manner and reflectance decreases with approximately the cube of particle diameter. The paint industry takes advantage of this relationship by attempting to maintain pigment particle diameter at one-fourth the wavelength of light. The food industry might take note of the paint industry's procedure, particularly when dealing with fabricated foods. For instance, if one were preparing a granulated instant drink it would be desirable to achieve maximum color intensity from the food colors used, whether synthetic or natural, and thus to reduce the expense. It may be possible in making this product to choose dispersable colorant particles with diameters one-fourth the wavelength of light and having a different refractive index than the medium in which they are imbedded. A start in this direction could be made by controlling the particle size and refractive index of "lakes." Lakes for use as food colorants are made by absorbing the pigments on substrates, such as alumina hydrate. This produces an insoluble pigment which can be finely ground in order to achieve dispersability in different media and maximum color intensity.

The preceding discussion is hoped to stimulate thinking concerning new ways of utilizing existing and new food colorants to maximum advantage.

REFERENCES

1. Anonymous, Biochemistry, 10, 4827 (1971).
2. S. Aronoff, The Chlorophylls (L. P. Vernon and G. R. Seeley, eds.), Academic Press, New York, 1966.
3. J. S. Blair, U.S. Patent No. 2,186,003 (1940).
4. J. S. Blair, U.S. Patent No. 2,189,774 (1940).
5. B. W. Baord and Ishan-ul-Haque, Food Technol., 19, 1721 (1965).
6. J. B. S. Braverman, Introduction to the Biochemistry of Foods. Elsevier, New York, 1963.
7. D. F. Cheesman, W. F. Lee, and P. F. Zagalsky, Biol. Rev., 42, 132 (1967).
8. C. O. Chichester, ed., The Chemistry of Plant Pigments. Academic Press, New York, 1972.
9. F. M. Clydesdale and F. J. Francis, Food Technol., 22, 793 (1968).
10. F. M. Clydesdale, Y. D. Lin, and F. J. Francis, J. Food Sci., 37, 45 (1972).
11. J. B. Fox, Jr., J. Agri. Food Chem., 14, 207 (1966).
12. J. B. Fox, Jr., and S. A. Ackerman, J. Food Sci., 33, 364 (1968).
13. J. B. Fox, Jr., W. E. Townsend, S. A. Ackerman, and C. E. Swift, Food Technol., 21, 386 (1967).
14. T. Fuleki and F. J. Francis, J. Food Sci., 33, 72, 78, 266, 471 (1968).
15. T. A. Geissman, The Chemistry of Flavonoid Compounds. Macmillan, New York, 1962.
16. T. W. Goodwin, Carotenoids: Their Comparative Biochemistry. Chemical Publ., New York, 1954.
17. T. W. Goodwin, Chemistry and Biochemistry of Plant Pigments. Academic Press, New York, 1965.
18. S. M. Gupte, H. M. El-Bisi, and F. J. Francis, J. Food Sci., 29 (1963).
19. J. B. Harborne, Comparative Biochemistry of the Flavonoids. Academic Press, New York, 1967.
20. K. A. Harper, Austral. J. Chem., 21, 221 (1968).
21. M. Holden, Biochem. J., 78, 359 (1961).
22. O. Isler, Carotenoids. Birkhauser Verlag, Basel, 1971.
23. I. D. Jones, R. C. White, and E. Gibbs, J. Food Sci., 28, 437 (1963).
24. M. A. Joslyn and G. MacKinney, J. Amer. Chem. Soc., 60, 1132 (1938).
25. L. Jurd, Food Technol., 18, 559 (1964).
26. L. Jurd, J. Food Sci., 29, 16 (1964).
27. F. LaJollo, S. R. Tannenbaum, and T. P. Labuza, J. Food Sci., 36, 850 (1971).
28. R. A. Lawrie, Meat Science. Pergamon Press, New York, 1966.

29. D. H. Lees and F. J. Francis, J. Food Sci., 36, 1056 (1971).

30. Y. D. Lin, F. M. Clydesdale, and F. J. Francis, J. Food Sci., 36, 240 (1971).

31. T. J. Mabry and A. S. Dreiding, Rec. Advan. Phytochem., 1, 145 (1968).

32. T. J. Mabry, K. R. Markham, and M. B. Thomas, The Systematic Identification of Flavonoids. Springer-Verlag, New York, 1970.

33. E. E. Meschter, J. Agri. Food Chem., 1, 574 (1953).

34. C. Y. Peng and P. Markakis, Nature (London), 199, 597 (1963).

35. J. F. Price and B. S. Schweigert, eds., The Science of Meat and Meat Products. 2nd ed., W. H. Freeman, San Francisco, 1971.

36. S. H. Schanderl, C. O. Chichester, and G. L. Marsh, J. Organ. Chem., 27, 3865 (1962).

37. G. Scott, Atmospheric Oxidation and Antioxidants. Elsevier, New York, 1965.

38. A. J. Shrikhande and F. J. Francis, J. Food Sci., 38, 649 (1973).

39. M. S. Starr and F. J. Francis, Food Technol., 22, 1293 (1968).

40. M. S. Starr and F. J. Francis, J. Food Sci., 38, 1043 (1973).

41. C. F. Timberlake and P. Bridle, Chem. Ind. (London), 1489 (1968).

42. C. G. Van Teeling, P. E. Cansfield, and R. A. Gallop, J. Food Sci., 36, 1061 (1971).

43. F. Wagenknecht, F. A. Lee, and F. P. Boyle, Food Res., 17, 343 (1952).

44. G. C. Walker, J. Food Sci., 29, 383 (1964).

45. S. S. Wang, J. F. Haard, and G. R. DiMarco, J. Food Sci., 36, 657 (1971).

Chapter 9

FLAVORS

Rose Marie Pangborn and Gerald F. Russell

Department of Food Science and Technology
University of California
Davis, California

Contents

I. INTRODUCTION

Man has been deeply concerned with the odors and flavors in his environment since ancient times. In 320 BC, for example, the Greek Theophrastus (382-287 BC) assembled a lengthy treatise on odors. Several references to aromas and fragrances were made in the Old and New Testaments of the Bíble. Among the early written classics are Camerarius' study on the nature of smell, published in 1587; Triumphius' discussion of the use and abuse of aromatics in 1695; and Linnaeus' classification of odors in 1756 [64].

The interest of United States food technologists in quantitative measurement of food flavors was evidenced in 1937 when the American Chemical Society sponsored a symposium on Flavor in Foods at Chapel Hill, North Carolina [see Food Research, 2, (1937)]. Crocker's [14] classic little book on food quality, which is still useful today, contains one of the first descriptions of flavor characteristics. The advent of sophisticated analytical techniques, such as gas-liquid chromatography and mass spectrometry, resulted in extensive study of the volatiles in a wide variety of fresh and processed foods, as well as of beverages and other consumer products the odors or flavors of which were important to their acceptance. An interesting and informative experience is in store for the reader who traces involvement of food scientists in flavor chemistry by consulting the following book sequence: Chemistry of Natural Food Flavors [56], Flavor Research and Food Acceptance [49], Proceedings of Flavor Chemistry Symposium [10], Flavor Chemistry [21], The Chemistry and Physiology of Flavors [74], and Flavor Research: Principles and Techniques [80]. In the foregoing texts, the major attention is given to volatiles isolated from specific products, such as bread, wine, meats, fish, dairy products, fruits, and vegetables.

A. Definition of Flavor

The consumer uses the word "flavor" to describe the overall acceptance of a food, embracing all the sensory attributes perceived when the food is placed in the mouth. The food technologist narrows the classification to those characteristics which stimulate the senses of taste and smell, in addition to tactile and thermal sensations. Most sensory analysts limit flavor to the combination of taste (sweet, sour, salty, and bitter stimuli) with odor (volatiles perceived by sniffing or from the mouth via the oropharyngeal pathway). The flavor chemists, in contrast, study chemical compounds which contribute to the characteristic aroma of a food.

Flavor, by definition, is a sensory phenomenon which necessitates human judgement. Therefore, the chemist measures not flavor but the chemical constituents of a product, some of which contribute to the sensation of flavors, while others have little or no sensory significance. As indicated by Hewitt et al. [27], most food flavors have four characteristics in common: (1) they consist of many components, some present in a high proportion but most present in very low proportions in the product; (2) they are minor, usually nonnutritive, constituents of the food, exerting their influence at extremely low concentrations; (3) they are highly specific to the molecular configurations of the respective molecules; and (4) they tend to be labile, thermally unstable compounds.

B. Importance of Flavor to the Consumer

Many times a day we are stimulated by flavors imparted by foods, beverages, and
medicines, as well as by those derived from inedible oral stimulants, such as
toothpaste, mouthwash, chewing gum, and tobacco products. The consumer expects to derive pleasure from his foods, beverages, chewing gum, and tobacco
products; he expects his toothpaste to be inoffensive; and he tolerates any undesirable flavors in his medicine and mouthwash because of the benefits resulting
from their use. Several foods induce pain, e.g., the irritation of the mouth by the
alcohol in distilled spirits and the carbonation in soft drinks; the burning sensations
caused by capsaicin in chili peppers; the pungency of black pepper, ginger, and
curries; and the unique oral and sinus impact of the volatile oils of horseradish.
Nonetheless, millions of people in the world consider small, controlled quantities
of these painful stimulants to be pleasant and highly desirable in their dietaries.

Man derives not only pleasure but satisfaction and security from the flavors of
the foods he consumes. In the modification of existing products, as well as in the
development of new products, it is critical that the flavor be acceptable to the intended consumer, for no matter how safe, how nutritious, how inexpensive, or
how colorful the food may be, if its flavor is undesirable, it is rejected. Even
hungry and nutritionally deprived populations have been known to reject foods that
have flavors strange or offensive to them. The world-wide increase in population
demands the development of new protein sources which can meet at least minimum
flavor acceptability by the people for whom they are intended. In the past the flavor
industry devoted much attention to luxury items which required simple additions of
spices, essential oils, or fruit concentrates. Of more recent concern has been the
need to duplicate natural flavors with synthetic flavorings, due to diminishing supplies of some raw materials in the world market as well as to the constantly rising
cost of natural flavors.

C. Flavor and Nutrition

Man cannot assure adequate nutrition merely by depending upon the palatability of
food or by relying upon appetite. Appetites frequently are trivial in origin, are
fickle and unpredictable, and are influenced more by a person's cultural background
than by physiological needs. Nonetheless, nutritionists should be aware of the
emotional and cultural factors which influence food acceptability, one of the most
important being flavor. Traditionally, nutritionists have been concerned with
measurement of the body's need for proteins, lipids, carbohydrates, minerals, and
vitamins, forgetting that people eat food, not nutrients. Highly flavored items,
such as capsicum peppers, garlic and onions, mustard and pickles, horseradish,
ginger, cloves, and cinnamon, have insignificant nutritive value. However, these
flavors and condiments exert a greater influence on food acceptance than does a
knowledge of nutritional requirements.

During World War II, much to the dismay of the United States Army Quartermaster Corps, the best-fed soldiers in the world often rejected their nutritionally
adequate rations. Nutritionists and dieticians had forgotten that conditions of stress
and physiological and/or social deprivation, such as existed on the battle field and
the mess hall, would cause people to place an unusual importance on the flavor of

their foods. (This latter phenomenon often is exhibited by hospital patients, dormitory residents, and prison inmates.) Consequently, from 1945 to 1962, much pioneering research on consumer acceptance of food flavors, singly and in meal combinations, was conducted by the Quartermaster Food and Container Institute for the Armed Forces in their Chicago laboratories.

D. Importance of Flavor to the Food Processor

The initial acceptance of a food is determined by its appearance, flavor, and texture, in that order. Modern food technologists have developed a large array of tempting products; today the sale of processed foods in the United States exceeds that of fresh foods. Despite the success of commercially prepared foods, processors still are concerned with flavor, from several points of view: (1) prevention of the loss of desirable flavors which may ensue during handling, heat treatment, transport, and storage; (2) avoidance of the development of undesirable flavors, such as oxidative rancidity in fats and oils, light-induced off flavors in milk and beer, and metallic flavors in canned products; (3) development of desirable flavors, as in the roasting of coffee beans, the baking of breads, and the aging and cooking of meats; and (4) fortification of foods with substances which enhance natural flavors and/or mask off flavors. In some cases the volatile flavor substances can be collected from the product during processing and added back; in other cases, specific enzymes can act upon precursors to regenerate lost flavors.

Most present-day flavor research is designed to (1) isolate and identify the volatile components which occur in natural products; (2) measure the volatiles which develop during processing; (3) measure the effect of various unit processes and combinations of processes during handling and subsequent storage; and (4) measure the role of flavor modifiers, enhancers, or potentiators.

E. Approaches to Research on Food Flavor

Why is it so difficult to describe the mouth-watering flavor of a rare beef steak, the full bouquet of a vintage wine, the delicate fragrance of wild berries, or the robust aroma of a good coffee? Primarily because the chemical composition of these materials is so complex, the mechanism by which the human perceives and interprets these stimuli is unknown, and man has such a limited ability to quantify and then verbalize how emotional satisfaction is derived from sensory experiences.

Because of its complexity, flavor has been subdivided into its component parts for analytical laboratory studies, as follows:

1. "Flavor" chemistry: analysis of volatile constituents, primarily by separation of compounds by gas-liquid chromatography (GLC) and subsequent identification by spectroscopic and other methods
2. Sensory analysis: use of human subjects to quantify perceptual experiences, emphasizing one of two approaches:
    a. Quality evaluation: examination of the flavor quality of specific products by experienced judges, e.g., the expert wine tasters, tea tasters, or perfumers

b. Fundamental research: studies dealing primarily with taste and smell, with three major areas of emphasis:
   (1) Physiological: studies of the biological aspects related to sensory perception, e.g., the anatomy and function of the receptors, the influence of pathological conditions, hunger, nutritional status, etc., on receptor function
   (2) Molecular: studies of the physical–chemical properties of molecules and their resultant sensory properties
   (3) Behavioral: studies of psychological factors influencing perception and judgment, e.g., experience, motivation, expectation

II. FLAVORS AND FLAVORINGS IN FOODS

A. Sources of Food Flavors

A flavoring is any chemical compound or natural mixture added to a product to produce all or part of the flavor of the original source. The term "flavor" sometimes is used to denote both the sensation and the substance. In the study of food flavors, chemists extract and concentrate flavoring materials in order to identify individual chemicals which are present and to trace their biogenetic sources. This has led to development of large industries which market natural and synthetic flavorings for food use.

Our understanding of the biosynthetic sources of nonvolatile flavors has followed closely the research developments in the areas of natural product chemistry and biochemistry. For example, many of the organic acids responsible for sour tastes and sugars with a sweet taste are produced by common metabolic pathways in plant and animal systems. Hendrickson [26] reviewed the natural product chemistry of the structure and biosynthesis of complex plant alkaloids, e.g., quinine, which tastes very bitter, and capsaicin and piperine, which produce a physiological "hot" sensation.

Thousands of different compounds have been found in flavor extracts. There is much speculation on the biogenetic precursors of these compounds, since they may lead to development of flavor precursors, but there have been few definitive studies on the mechanisms involved. The fruity and floral character of many products is due primarily to the volatile esters. In one of the few flavor studies where one or two components were shown to impart the principle character of a flavor, esters of fatty acids were identified. Methyl or ethyl trans-2-cis-4-decadienoic acid, which possess the unmistakable odor of Bartlett pears, is produced in high levels near the climacteric point in the developing fruit [34]. It was suggested that the esterification with lower alcohols was a consequence of an enzymic "shutdown" of the process of converting these fatty acids to oils for storage by the plant.

No one class of compounds in plant foods is so ubiquitous as the terpenoids. Flavor chemists have spent a great deal of time identifying terpene structures since volatile terpenes can predominate in the headspace air over a food. The terpenes are found as five-carbon multiples of "isoprene units" that are usually linked together, following an "isoprene rule," to yield terpenes (C_{10}) or sesquiterpenes (C_{15}). The chemists' fascination with the structural isoprene building block is due to its predictive value in establishing the structure of compounds from limited microchemical information. The trace amounts of material isolated frequently precludes traditional determinations of chemical structure.

Flavor chemists have attempted to follow the biosynthetic production of the terpenes since an understanding of these processes may lead to control of flavor in foods. Although the C_5 isoprene units are the backbone of the carbon skeletons, it is now well established that these arise through a C_6 mevalonic acid (the R form in vivo) through decarboxylation, with concomitant loss of the hydroxyl group to give isopentenyl pyrophosphate. Further condensations or polymerizations yield the acyclic progenitors, such as geraniol and farnesyl pyrophosphates. By deuterium labeling, Cornforth et al. [13] found very subtle stereosyntheses that proved enzymic control of these reactions; in fact, they later showed that the enzyme system treated each proton differently on the C-4 methylene and this carbon acted as a center of chirality. The intermediate pyrophosphates may then generate the various cyclic terpene hydrocarbons and alcohols and these in turn may be rearranged, oxidized, or hydrolyzed to yield the individual terpenes.

The production of many flavors depends on a specific treatment. Onions do not release strong odor until flavor precursors are acted upon enzymically. This can be prompted by shearing the onion tissue to allow enzyme and substrate to come into contact. The importance of sulfur compounds in many of the species of Allium (e.g., onion, leeks, garlic, and chives) has been reviewed along with the biogenesis of sulfur compounds [11]. Since that review, many additional volatiles have been elucidated in Allium [8] and at present over 116 compounds have been reported (see also Chapters 6 and 9).

Enzymic and nonenzymic browning reactions can produce many volatile compounds with strong odors [29]. The classical Maillard browning reactions, i.e., reducing sugar-amine interactions, probably generate furfural, hydroxymethyl furfural, and maltol, which occur in dairy products [67] (see also Chapter 3). In their review of the presence of hydrocarbons reported in foods, Johnson et al. [35] concluded that the aromatic hydrocarbons could be natural food volatiles, despite the previous suspicion that these had to be artifacts or contaminants.

The production of desirable meat flavor is dependent on thermal energy causing breakdown products of amino acids and fats. A review of the importance of fatty acids to development of flavors and off flavors in dairy products emphasized the interactions among chemical constituents, their equilibria in solutions and the complexity of chemical reactions that lead to the oxidative and hydrolytic reactions of materials present, and their concentrations in controlling various flavors [42].

The development of volatiles in fresh and cooked vegetables has been reviewed by Johnson et al. [36,37]. The advent of sophisticated instrumentation, such as gas chromatography linked with mass spectrometry (GC-MS), has enabled the flavor chemist to identify hundreds of pyrazines and related products in cooked foods, such as coffee [78] and roasted nut products [41]. The complexity of volatiles in such foods as meats [85] and chicken products [87] continues to generate much research.

B. Extraction of Food Flavorings

There are two main reasons for chemical extraction of a flavor. The first is to prepare a suitable concentrate of volatiles for use in chemical identification studies.

This may require very time-consuming and involved techniques, such as counter-current distribution solvent extractions, elaborate vacuum trapping, spinning band distillations, adsorption–desorption on charcoal or polystyrene adsorbants, or direct GLC entrainment of headspace volatiles. The end product of these methods is designed to yield a very pure and chemically high-quality concentrate for chemical analysis, but frequently tons of food materials may yield only a few milligrams of a high-quality essence. The second reason for obtaining flavor concentrates is for commercial use in food preparations. The concern of the physical chemist and food scientist is to obtain the highest quality concentrates, while maximizing the yield.

Flavorings from such products as herbs and spices can be added to food in the form of concentrates or extracts. These concentrated forms are easier to handle and transport, require less storage space, and are not subject to rodent or micro-bial spoilage. However, an extracted flavor cannot exactly duplicate the original flavor.

1. ESSENTIAL OILS AND OLEORESINS

The major aromas of herbs and spices derive from their essential oils, which are volatile, steam-distillable oils. They differ from fixed oils which are nonvolatile products, such as triglycerides, phopholipids, and waxes. Essential oils are found in the vittae, glands, secretory cells, and spatial tissues of plants. The manner in which they are extracted can have a great effect on the final quality and quantity of essential oil.

Steam distillation is commonly used to obtain essential oils. The main body of plant material is distilled with steam or superheated steam, the distillate is condensed, and most of the oil forms a surface layer which is skimmed and stored as the essential oil. This simple and inexpensive extraction frequently is done in less developed countries, close to the source of the harvested plant. If often yields a product of good quality which requires no further processing. However, the oil may be subjected to further refining or rectifying operations to increase purity. A common practice is to extract the oil with chelating agents to remove trace metals that catalyze oxidation reactions. Disadvantages of this form of extraction are that hydrolysis or polymerization of the oils can occur as they are subjected to the thermal treatment over long periods of time, an example of this being the production of caryophyllene in clove oil from the decomposition of its epoxide. Some desirable higher boiling materials may not be carried over efficiently in the distillation, especially if they are partly soluble in water. Other materials may dissolve in the condensed distillate water and cannot be recovered easily. As a result, the final product may not represent the essential oil as it occurs in the raw material.

Cold pressing can be used to obtain a product consisting mainly of essential oils. This method employs high pressure to force out the essential oils and frequently is used to obtain lemon or orange oils. The resultant oil very closely resembles the original natural product, as no chemical or thermal treatment is used. Some nonvolatile fixed oils may also be extracted in the process.

Flavorings can be obtained by various forms of fat extraction, based on the affinity of the nonpolar essential oils for a nonpolar fat. A hot fat extraction is performed by adding the macerated plant to a hot fat or oil and then extracting the flavoring with a solvent, such as alcohol, after the water has been driven off. Cold-fat extraction (enfleurage) involves repeated exposure of layers of hardened fat to the plant material. Odors are absorbed by the fat and may be extracted later, although occasionally the flavoring may be left in the fat to trap the volatiles until a food is heated to the melting range of the fat. Both of these fat-extraction methods find limited use for food flavorings but are used for perfume fragrances.

Extraction with volatile solvents may yield a superior product. A nonodorous solvent, such as dichloroethane or chloroform, is mixed with the material, the crude slurry is filtered, and the solvent is evaporated, leaving a product rich in essential oil. Usually this method is not thermally destructive to the oil but requires more sophisticated technology than simpler methods, such as steam distillation. If there is an appreciable amount of nonvolatile material in the final concentrate, the product is called an oleoresin, which differs from an essential oil. For example, the steam-distilled essential oil of black pepper is a clear oil with a strong aroma of black pepper, but it is basically tasteless. The oleoresin of black pepper, however, is a dark colored, thick resin which contains nonvolatile material, including piperine which contributes the hot "bite" of the original pepper corn.

Oxygenated substances contribute the main impact character to many essential oils, with less contributions from the hydrocarbons. For this reason, some hydrocarbons have been removed from many concentrated essential oils by such methods as vacuum distillation. A higher "terpeneless" grade of essential oil does not contain the monoterpene hydrocarbon fraction. The "terpeneless and sesquiterpeneless" grade has been distilled and extracted with a polar solvent, such as alcohol, to concentrate the oxygenated compounds. The main advantages of these higher grades of essential oils are their greater flavor concentration and their greater stability to forms of deterioration, such as oxidation and polymerization. The presence of hydrocarbons can be a disadvantage if they are easily oxidized to undesirable byproducts. For example, the presence of limonene in an essential oil may lead to undesirable off flavors if it is easily oxidized by a free-radical mechanism to carvone. Many citrus oils contain over 90% hydrocarbon terpenes and sesquiterpenes and upon exposure to air become oxidized to develop a "turpentine" odor.

2. EXTRACTS

Many natural food flavorings occur in forms that are not well suited to preparation methods that yield high-quality essential oils, but an acceptable flavor concentrate can be obtained as an extract. Extracts are obtained by passing alcohol or an alcohol-water solution through a material to dissolve the main flavor components, e.g., vanilla extract or extracts of raspberry or cherry. Alcohol extractions of this type contain high proportions of oxygenated materials as compared to essential oils, since hydrocarbons present are nonpolar components with low affinity for the polar extraction medium. Many of the substances that are concentrated as extracts have a high water content or the flavor constituents are very labile to other extraction treatments, precluding their conversion into essential oil or oleoresins.

The flavoring components in an extract are diluted by the alcohol present and in some cases do not have a strong flavor. To compensate for lack of potency, a reinforced extract commonly called WONF (with other natural flavors) can be used. A WONF flavoring is an extract with 51% of its flavor from the basic natural product and the remainder derived from any combination of other naturally occuring flavorings. They contain no synthetic chemicals and do not have to be labeled as synthetic or imitation.

Vanillin is a pure chemical which is used as a synthetic or imitation vanilla. "Vanilla" refers to the natural vanilla bean or an extract from the beans. Despite the fact that all vanilla is imported into the United States, it has been shown for many years that there is more "natural" vanilla sold than is imported. This emphasizes the need for developing detection tests to guard against adulteration with synthetic chemicals.

C. Flavor Delivery Systems

1. PLATED FLAVORINGS

If it is desirable for flavors to be blended uniformly through a dry product, the addition of plated flavorings rather than concentrated essential oils may be appropriate. Plated flavorings consist of a neutral carrier, such as sucrose, glucose, or sodium chloride, which is surrounded or plated with a thin layer of flavor concentrate. The appearance is one of a dry powder. In this state, blending characteristics may be superior but the concentrate or oil has more exposed surface area and may be susceptible to rapid oxidation or evaporation.

2. ENCAPSULATED FLAVORINGS

The problem of oxidative deterioration or evaporation of the volatiles may be overcome by the use of encapsulated flavorings. In this form, the essential oil or concentrate is surrounded by an outer coating of a neutral, hardened material. Coating is accomplished by spray drying a slurry of the flavoring with a material, such as acacia gum, which envelops the oil. This powdered product then has the increased blending capabilities of the plated flavorings, while the "sealing" of the flavoring can reduce oxidation. In addition, the product can have increased potency for long periods of time, since evaporative losses are reduced until the protective coating is disrupted by dissolving in water or by mechanical action. These products have widespread usage in dry powder cake mixes, chewing gum, etc.

D. Instrumental and Chemical Analyses of Flavor

Historically, chemical analyses of flavorings have consisted of the determination of structures for principle chemical components and the measurement of chemical parameters useful in quality control. Structure studies centered around classic elementary organic analyses and the chemistry of derivatives, while in quality assurance, such parameters as refractive index, specific gravity, titratable acidity, and colorimetric determinations were measured. Because flavorings are very complex mixtures, little progress was made until modern methods, such as GLC, were developed and refined.

Chemical analysis of a flavoring involves at least three phases - sample preparation, separation and identification, and correlation with the sensory properties.

1. SAMPLE PREPARATION

Usually, a sample requires pretreatment, such as gas or steam distillation, solvent extraction, or adsorption-desorption from charcoal or polystyrene beads, techniques which have been reviewed by Teranishi et al. [80]. After concentration of the sample, only 5 μl or less is injected onto the GLC column. If there is too large a proportion of solvent, volatiles in the concentrate may not be detected and the column can be damaged by overloading. An analysis can be made of the total volatiles present in the sample or of the volatiles in the headspace over the sample. The former requires extraction with a suitable solvent, usually a continuous extraction in a Soxhlet or similar apparatus, yielding a concentrate which is rich in many of the compounds responsible for the odor of the material. However, the proportions of the flavor compounds may differ considerably from that which the human subject sniffs, due to changes in the headspace concentration of individual components arising from differential solubilities in hydrophilic and lipophilic materials in the food sample. In headspace analysis, the air above the food sample is trapped and injected onto the column or entrained at low temperatures at the front of the column. Alternatively, the sample can be freeze concentrated in a U-tube trap by immersion in liquid nitrogen and this concentrate injected onto the column.

2. SEPARATION TECHNIQUES

GLC separation involves partitioning compounds between a moving phase (the carrier gas) and a stationary phase (a nonvolatile liquid phase). One end of the temperature-controlled column is connected to an injector and the other end to a detector. With packed columns, the liquid phase is distributed over the surface of a fine granular support material which provides a large surface area for partitioning. In open tubular capillary columns, a thin film of the liquid phase coats the capillary walls. Upon injection onto the column, the volatile compounds partition themselves between the stationary and mobile phases depending upon their individual affinities for each. If they are all separated, each compound arrives at the detector at its own rate. However, it is usually not possible to obtain complete separation of all components in a complex mixture with only one column.

Because the GLC must be operated at high temperatures, certain problems may arise; e.g., the hot metal surfaces of the injector or the column walls can catalyze changes in individual compounds. In some cases, the resultant chromatogram may bear little resemblance to the actual composition of the volatiles originally injected onto the column. Many troublesome degradations and rearrangements can be avoided by using glass injectors and glass columns. Glass capillaries give excellent separation, as shown in the typical chromatogram in Figure 9-1.

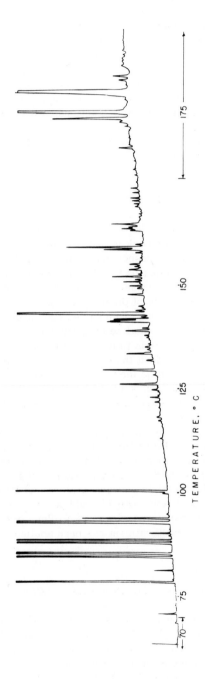

FIG. 9-1. A typical chromatogram of black pepper oil on a 0.25 mm x 65 m open-tubular glass capillary coated with Carbowax 20M. Injection was 1.0 μl of oil with a 50:1 split ratio.

The choice of the liquid phase depends on the particular flavor concentrate, but it is often necessary to use several different columns and liquid phases to resolve components. The type of column used depends on the separation needed. Packed columns usually give poorer resolution but permit the use of larger volumes of injected sample. A greater efficiency can be obtained with wall-coated, 0.01-in. open-tubular capillary columns of stainless steel, but they have a very low capacity and do not allow for trapping of materials eluting from the column for further analyses, such as infrared spectroscopy (IR). Support-coated, open-tubular (SCOT) columns and 0.03-in. open-tubular columns offer intermediate resolution and reasonable sample capacities and allow for trapping of eluting materials. Frequently, the sample is separated into major fractions on packed columns which undergo subsequent separations on capillaries.

Readers unfamiliar with the theory and application of GLC are referred to the review by Giddings and Keller [20].

3. QUANTIFYING THE ANALYSES

As individual components elute from the GLC column, a peak is traced on the chromatogram. The area under the peak is proportional to the amount of material present. Each detector has its own response characteristics to individual compounds, so that response factors must be used in order to quantitate the measurements. The large number of peaks present in complex mixtures makes this task difficult, stimulating the development of other techniques.

Wide differences in total peak areas are obtained even under standardized conditions. One solution has been to normalize the peak areas internally with respect to the total integrated area. Another is to incorporate into the sample internal standards which are carried throughout the entire extraction and injection procedure [70,81]. Internal standards should be inert and not overlap other peaks in the mixture being analyzed. Thus the peaks are normalized with respect to an internal standard and reflect changes which are independent of the amount of sample injected.

Computers have been used to determine relationships between GLC and non-chemical variables. Powers and Keith [69] successfully used stepwise discriminant analyses of GLC peaks to classify coffee blends, utilizing ratioing of normalized peak areas to cross-compare different chromatograms. Biggers et al. [7] applied a peak-ratioing method to differentiate between Arabica and Robusta coffee. Combinations of peak ratios on the "aromagrams" could be used to provide a "quality index" that correlated well with expert tasters, regardless of the degree of coffee roast. A computerized statistical treatment has been applied to brewed tea by Vuataz and Reymond [82].

4. IDENTIFICATION OF COMPONENTS IN FLAVOR EXTRACTS

Recovery of the individual components allows a separate analysis of its sensory properties - a "nasal appraisal." Usually, individual compounds are trapped in capillary tubes, yielding as much as a microliter but frequently less unless repetitive trappings are made and the condensates combined. The identification of compounds is a challenge in microchemical analysis.

Valuable information can be obtained from comparison of retention data from dissimilar columns. However, firm identification cannot be based solely on the fact that a compound has identical retention times or retention indices with a known compound. Retention data are useful in preliminary screening to eliminate certain possibilities and to suggest possible compounds for comparison against the unknown.

The IR or Raman spectrum can be used to identify certain functional groups, providing firm identification if it is an exact match with the spectrum of a compound identified previously. Approximately 100 μg of the sample are needed, although useful information has been obtained with less. This is a nondestructive method, allowing use of the sample for such further tests as ultraviolet (UV) spectroscopy, which is also nondestructive and gives information relative to specific functional groups.

One of the most useful sources of spectral information derives from nuclear magnetic resonance (NMR), despite the fact it is less sensitive than other spectroscopic methods and requires more than 200 μl of sample. This requirement may be lowered somewhat by the use of microcells and/or computer ensemble averaging of spectra, wherein multiple scans of the spectrum are averaged together to increase the signal to noise ratio. The latter increases as the square of the number of scans that are ensemble averaged by the computer.

Much progress has been made by direct coupling and interfacing of the GLC with the mass and infrared spectrometers, allowing for rapid scanning of spectra as they elute from the GLC without the need for intermediate trapping. It is possible to obtain a spectrum every few seconds during the chromatographic separation. By interfacing newer minicomputers to a GC-MS, the massive number of spectra that accumulate during a run of several hours can be stored and retrieved in condensed form for later analyses. In addition, the computer can control the calibration and operation of the mass spectrometer.

New techniques have resulted in a dramatic 10- to 100-fold increase in the sensitivity of IR and NMR spectrometers due to the availability of low-cost computers that can be applied to Fourier transform (FT) spectroscopy. The application of IR interferometry and of NMR pulse methods, followed by Fourier transformation of the resultant "interferogram," permits acquisition of spectral data in considerably less time than do conventional methods. The equipment used in FT-IR spectroscopy is a Michelson interferometer, which generates an interferogram that must be transformed by a digital computer. The technique affords the advantage of obtaining data on all frequencies simultaneously, rather than a slow scan through all frequencies in a monochrometer range. The ability of these FT spectroscopic methods to produce high-quality spectra from microgram and nanogram quantities of flavoring materials undoubtedly will lead to their adoption by chemists concerned with trace compounds.

E. Flavor Potentiators or Modifiers

The term "flavor potentiator" is used to describe substances that enhance desirable flavors or depress undesirable flavors in foods. The potentiators have little or no flavor of their own, but small additions to a food product modify its flavor, usually in a desirably manner. For example, the addition of low levels of L-glutamic acid to meats and soups produces an enhancement which bears no resemblance to the flavor of the glutamic acid.

Two groups of chemical compounds have been used as flavor potentiators: certain L-amino acids, such as L-glutamic acid (MSG), and certain 5'-nucleotides, such as guanosine 5'-monophosphate (5'-GMP), inosine 5'-monophosphate (5'-IMP), and xanthine 5'-monophosphate (5'-XMP). The best known of these is monosodium glutamate (MSG), the action of which was first observed by Japanese workers who were attempting to explain why certain edible seaweeds imparted flavor-enhancing properties to many foods. Pure MSG is odorless but has a distinct taste, which is a mildly pleasant combination of saltiness and sweetness, and some tactile properties, variously described as "mouth satisfaction." Some individuals report that the compound induces considerable salivation. A "meaty" flavor has been erroneously ascribed to MSG, probably due to impurities resulting from protein hydrolysis. Manufacturers of MSG strongly insist that it enhances desirable flavors while minimizing undesirable ones, such as the sharpness of onions, the rawness of vegetables, or bitterness in canned vegetables. Some contend that MSG simply increases saltiness, other investigators believe it adds body and flavor balance to processed foods, while still others say it sensitizes the taste receptors so that the consumer appreciates flavors better.

A condition described as the "Chinese restaurant syndrome," wherein victims suffer from headaches, facial pressure, chest pains, gastric distress, and burning sensations over various body parts, has been found to result from ingestion of large quantities of MSG by people who are hypersensitive to it [73].

The 5'-nucleotides are produced by enzymic degradation of ribonucleic acid or by chemical phosphorylation of inosine that is produced by fermentation. These nucleotides are used as flavor enhancers in soups, gravies, bouillons, canned meats, tomato juice, and other similar products and can be used to replace beef extract. The use of 5'-IMP and 5'-GMP was reported to enhance flavor notes described as meaty, brothy, mouth filling, viscosity, dryness, and astringency, while suppressing sulfide-like flavors. Sourness and sweetness usually were not affected. A review of several experiments involving 5'-nucleotides was published by Kuninaka [44], who described their flavoring action, neurophysiological action, chemical structure, and synergistic action in combination with MSG and two amino acids, tricholomic acid and ibotenic acid.

Maltol, dioctyl sodium sulfosuccinate, and N,N'-di-o-tolyethylene diamine are examples of additional compounds reported to have potentiating action on specific flavors. The relationship between chemical structure and the bitter, bittersweet, sweet, or tasteless isomers of flavanone glycosides obtained from citrus peel has been reported by Horowitz and Gentili [30]. The bitter compounds all contained the disaccharide β-neophesperidose, while the tasteless compounds contained an isomeric disaccharide, β-rutinose. Of particular interest are the neohesperidosyl dihydrochalcones, several of which are many times sweeter than sucrose.

Several compounds have been found to modify perception of sweetness and of sourness. If the leaves of the tropical plant Gymnema sylvestre are chewed, the ability to perceive the sweet tastes of sugars and of artificial sweeteners disappears for several hours. Stocklin [77] has shown that the active principle is a D-glucuronide of a hexahydroxytriterpene. Three other plants seem to modify taste sensations: Eriodictylon californicum, a shrub growing in northern California and known as "yerba santa," also suppresses the sweet taste; the Sudanese plant Bumelia dulcifica is said to change sweetness and bitterness to sourness; and the berry called "miracle fruit" of the Nigerian plant Synsepalum dulcificum changes the sour tastes of acids to sweetness [31]. Kurihara and Beidler [45,46] extracted a glycoprotein as the active principle and described the effect of gymnemic acid on its taste-modifying properties, suggesting some possible mechanisms for its action.

F. Synthetic Sweeteners and Sugar Substitutes

Synthetic sweeteners have two main advantages over the conventional sweetener, sucrose - their considerably lower cost and lower caloric value per unit of sweetness. Undesirable attributes of selected synthetic sweeteners include a bitter aftertaste (e.g., saccharin), a delayed response to perception of the sweetness, and/or unduly prolonged perception of sweetness after the substance is tasted. Since a substitute sweetener must be nontoxic and readily metabolized or excreted by the body, several synthetics have been discontinued when they have been deemed to be unsafe for general consumption, including such products as dulcin (4-ethoxyphenylurea), P-4,000 (5-nitro-2-propoxyanaline), and the cyclamates. At the present time the most widely used artificial sweetener is saccharin (2,3-dihydro-3-oxobenzisosulfonazole), which is about 300 times sweeter than sucrose.

Considerable interest was elicited by the synthesis of L-aspartyl-L-phenylalanine methyl ester by Mazur et al. [50]. This dipeptide ester was reported to be 100-200 times sweeter than sucrose, with taste characteristics very similar to those of sucrose. If this latter compound is approved for food usage, it may prove to be a very important sucrose substitute.

Neohesperidan dihydrochalcone, a sweetener isolated from citrus peels, is synthesized by catalytic hydrogenation of a naturally occurring flavanoid. After hydrogenation of the bitter-tasting neohesperidan, the dihydro compound is about 1,000 times sweeter than sucrose. However, the sweetness sensation reaches its maximum intensity very slowly and persists longer than that of sucrose, which may make it more suited for such products as chewing gum and pharmaceuticals if it is approved for food use by the FDA.

Morris and Cagan [57] isolated and characterized a protein which they named "monellin" from serendipity berries (Dioscoreophyllem cumminsii Diels), a West African fruit. This was the first protein reported to elicit a sweet response in man, with an estimated potency 3,000 times that of sucrose. The sweet sensation persists up to 1 hr.

III. SENSORY PERCEPTION OF FLAVORS

Perception of flavor primarily involves gustation and olfaction, i.e., stimulation of the taste receptors in the mouth and of the olfactory receptors within the nasal passages.

A. The Sense of Taste

Taste is the least complicated of all senses. Technically, taste refers to perception and recognition of the sweet, sour, bitter, and salty qualities of a dissolved substance. The taste sensation is mediated by taste buds, is conducted centrally by the glossopharyngeal and lingual nerves, and is coordinated especially by centers in the posteroventral nuclei of the thalamus. The taste buds are located primarily in the epithelium of the sides of the tongue and the walls of the vallate papillae at the base of the tongue. The taste buds consist of flask-shaped structures of neuro-epithelial sensory cells which terminate peripherally in short, hairlike structures that project into the pore in the overlying epithelium. The gustatory cells located in the taste bud are the actual receptors of the sensation.

1. CHARACTERISTICS OF TASTE BUDS

Taste buds have a limited lifetime, being renewed about every 210 hr, but the response pattern appears to be stable. McCutcheon and Saunders [53], reported that a single fungiform taste papilla in human subjects responded to both sucrose and citric acid with the typical distinctive tastes in a manner that was stable over a month's test.

The total number of taste buds is greatest in newborn infants and gradually diminishes with age. The anterior portion of the tongue is more sensitive to sweet stimuli, the posterior to bitter substances, and the lateral portion to salty and sour stimuli. However, there is considerable overlap. The time between stimulation and perception is shorter for taste than for any other sense - $1.5-4.0 \times 10^{-3}$ sec. There are temporal differences among the tastes also; e.g., the response to a salty substance is much faster than that to a bitter substance. It has been noted that movement of the tongue results in greater gustatory sensitivity, probably by continuously changing the stimulus concentration acting on the taste cells, thus preventing rapid adaptation.

Some physiologists believe that the taste buds operate somewhat like chemical filters that open and close upon stimulation [71]. Beidler [6], however, cites studies with the electron microscope in support of the role of taste cells as transducers and not merely filters. The amount of the taste compound reaching the taste receptors appears to be regulated by metals and metal-binding proteins in the taste buds. Taste sensitivity can be reduced deliberately to the vanishing point by administering thiols and increased by administering heavy metals, such as copper, nickel, and zinc. Thus, it is understandable why we can taste materials which enter the mouth internally from circulating metabolites in our blood stream. For example, intravenous injections of iron or histamine can cause a metallic taste, just as intravenous administration of glucose can elicit oral sensations of sweetness. Drugs used to treat some metallic poisonings, such as penicillamine, which picks up copper, completely eliminate the sense of taste.

2. TASTE THEORIES

The old theory advanced to explain the mechanism of taste perception is known as the "specificity theory." It states that a specific class of stimulus reacts with a specific receptor, the nerve fibers of which travel to a specific portion of the central nervous system (CNS), that portion being different for the various receptor types. The more recent "patterning theory" states that all receptors are alike in that they respond to all taste stimuli, although not equally so. The pattern of neural firing is analyzed by the CNS and identified as indicating the presence of a specific stimulus class.

The complete sequence of events leading from the application of a taste stimulus to the graded potential in the receptor cell and ultimately to the action potentials in the sensory axon is still unknown. The enzyme theory of taste generally has been discounted because it contradicts established neurophysiological evidence. The most acceptable theory at present is Beidler's [5], which indicates that the molecules of the taste stimulus are bound to the outside of the cell membrane by weak physical forces. However, the manner in which the receptor membrane is depolarized by the physical combination of one part of a stimulus molecule and the receptor site is not known.

According to Shallenberger and Acree [75], the sweetness of a sugar varies inversely with the degree to which the hydroxyl groups of the sugar are able to couple intramolecularly by hydrogen bonding. Multiple NO_2 groups and the sulfur atoms in the $-S-S-$ or $C=S$ linkage have been associated with bitter taste, but there is only limited correspondence between bitter taste and molecular structure.

3. TASTE SUBSTANCES

A substance must be water soluble in order to have a taste, even though solubility in water is not directly proportional to taste intensity. Most of the taste substances studied have 20-30 different intensities that can be distinguished by the average person. The number of different taste qualities that can be discriminated has been estimated at 5×10^3, compared with 10^6 for odor qualities.

In general, saltiness is produced by inorganic salts but the only pure salty taste is that of sodium chloride. Other salts tend to have additional tastes, and in some cases the additional taste predominates; e.g., some iodide and bromide salts are bitter, and some inorganic salts of lead and beryllium are sweet. Sweet tastes often are caused by aliphatic hydroxy compounds but sweet-tasting compounds include such diverse molecules as sucrose, dulcin, saccharin, glycine, chloroform, and the abovementioned lead acetate and beryllium chloride. Sourness is caused primarily by proton donors, although this does not entirely account for the sour taste because at the same pH an acid, such as acetic, tastes more sour than an acid such as hydrochloride. Aliphatic carboxylic acids with a long carbon chain are more sour than those with a short chain. Picric acid tastes bitter. Many alkaloids taste bitter - quinine, caffeine, strychnine - but so do nitrogen-free substances, such as lactones, and simple compounds, such as urea and formamide. Bitterness and pharmacological action often are parallel. Although bitterness is associated with unpleasant substances, bitter taste is desirable in such materials as coffee, chocolate, beer, and quinine water.

The so-called water taste is of interest because the chorda tympani nerve, which innervates the anterior two-thirds of the tongue, responds to stimulation by distilled water in the rabbit, cat, dog, and monkey but not in the rat, hamster, sheep, and man. It is possible that animals without the water taste exhibit a baseline neural activity in response to their own saliva. McBurney and Pfaffmann [51] found that the threshold for sodium chloride always just exceeded the sodium concentration of the subject's saliva.

Some substances taste different to different individuals. Thresholds for the taste of phenylthiocarbamide (PTC) fall in a bimodal distribution so that some individuals can be classified as "tasters" and others as "nontasters." The inability to taste PTC is believed to be a simple Mendelian recessive characteristic and is dependent in part on differences in the saliva of tasters and nontasters [18].

The effect of one taste on another has been of considerable interest because foods and other oral stimuli contain a mixture of tastes. In most instances, one taste reduces the perceived intensity of a second taste [60]. In particular, acids and sugars have mutually masking effects, as do salt and sugar (see Figs. 9-2 and 9-3). A noted exception was the observation of a bimodal response to the influence of acid on apparent saltiness. Further studies showed that ethyl alcohol enhanced sweetness and bitterness but reduced saltiness and sourness in water solutions (Fig. 9-4).

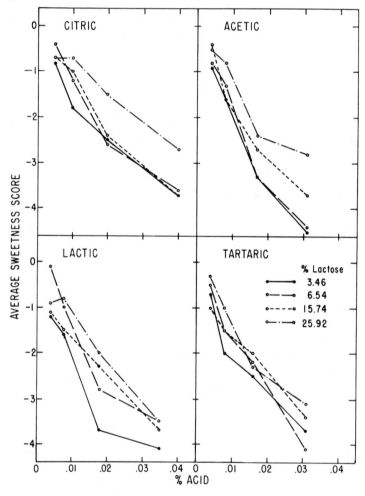

FIG. 9-2. Influence of increasing concentrations of organic acids on perceived sweetness intensity of lactose solutions.

PAIRED PRESENTATION

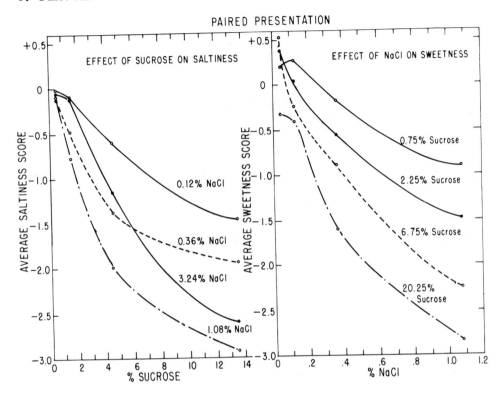

FIG. 9-3. Influence of increasing concentrations of sucrose and of sodium chloride on perceived intensities of saltiness and sweetness, respectively.

For a more detailed review on human taste perception, the summary by Meiselman [54] is recommended.

B. The Sense of Smell

Olfaction was the first distance receptor to evolve in human phylogenesis but it is the least specialized and the most primitive of the senses. Unlike the other distance receptors, localization of odors is inaccurate, unless vision, hearing, or movement of the entire organism is called into play. Furthermore, olfactory adaptation takes place so rapidly that it can progress to a state in which the subject is completely insensitive to an odor.

Odor perception, even more than taste, is subject to numerous nonolfactory influences which are known to occur simultaneously; e.g., the release of flavors from food occurs concomitantly with chewing in a sequential fashion; the thermal receptors are also stimulated when the flavor of coffee or tea is perceived; the appreciation of the fragrance of fruits is often coupled with their attractive color and form; the enjoyment of cigarette smoking is intertwined with manual-visual-oral components.

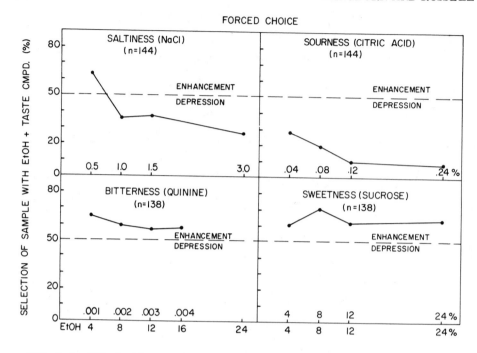

FIG. 9-4. Effect of increasing concentrations of ethyl alcohol on perceived intensities of sweet, sour, salty, and bitter stimuli in solution.

1. OLFACTORY SENSITIVITY

Human olfaction is exceptionally sensitive, as some odorants can be detected in concentrations of 10^{-18} molar and an olfactory receptor can respond to only nine molecules of mercaptan [79]. The critical duration for olfaction in man is about 0.18 sec. It has been estimated that experienced judges can distinguish as many as 10,000 different odor qualities and that for each quality they can distinguish about 20 different levels of intensity. There are marked individual, age, and sex differences in nasal mucous membrane function which can be reflected in odor sensitivity.

Olfactory perception is diminished by some compounds, such as formaldehyde. Thus, many room deodorants operate on the principle of limiting one's ability to smell the odor rather than by removing the odor from the air. Sensitivity to odors and degree of liking for odors differ markedly with age. For example, children under 3 years reportedly react with pleasure to substances which older children and most adults consider offensive. It is unclear whether sensitivity is involved or whether children learn from their parents what odors are pleasant and which are unpleasant, just as they acquire their food habits. Generally, olfactory sensitivity decreases with age. There is an average decrease of primary olfactory fibers of about 1% per year after birth.

2. RECEPTOR FUNCTION AND THEORIES OF OLFACTION

In recent years, much has been learned about the ultrastructure of odor receptors, the electrical properties of the olfactory epithelium, and the role of such compounds as pheromones which control behavior and reproductive processes in many species. However, we do not understand even the most elementary aspects of receptor function. There is general agreement that the initial mechanism of olfactory receptor stimulation depends upon the adsorption of the stimulus molecule to the receptor surface, causing an electrical depolarization of the olfactory cell which initiates nerve impulses in its axonal extension. This adsorption depends upon the molecular structure of the molecule as well as on the character of functional groups, which has been studied extensively by Beets [4], Wright [88], and Davies [15]. Amoore [2] has postulated that there are a specific number of receptor sites in the olfactory mucosa which accommodate compounds with corresponding shapes and sizes, thereby triggering an impulse which is translated into an odor quality. Rather than depending upon the primary odor theory, Davies [15] believes that odorants are adsorbed at the receptor site and that the associated energy leads to puncture of a membrane to effect a nerve impulse. The number of molecules required would vary with the compound. A plot of molecular cross-section of odorants vs the free energy of desorption at a lipid-water interface yielded areas that represented odor classes. Radiation and vibration theories have been advanced, in which the molecules are thought to act indirectly upon receptors. The role of the receptor was analogous to that of an infrared detector in a spectrophotometer, but this theory failed to explain differences in the odors of chiral isomers. Mechanical theories assumed that movement of molecules past the olfactory ephithelium set the olfactory hairs in motion according to the molecular weight of the compound. This theory arose from the observation that odors were perceived only when nasal air was in motion, but it was discredited by microscopic observations that the olfactory cilia were bathed in fluid and that no correlation existed between odors and molecular weight. In general, enzyme theories have been discredited since the number of enzymes and the complexity of an enzyme system is too great to account for the thousands of different odors which can be perceived.

Despite the many attempts to correlate chemical structure with odor quality, results have not been conclusive. Some compounds with completely different functional groups have similar odors, whereas closely related compounds, such as stereoisomers, may have totally distinct odor qualities. For example, the stereoisomers of menthol (menthol, isomenthol, neomenthol, and neosiomenthol) have markedly different odors. Russell and Hills [72] demonstrated that for a series of carvone-related stereoisomers, the chirality of each stereoisomer changed its odor character from spearmint-like to caraway-like. With other compounds, the chirality of the molecule had no effect on the odor quality.

It should be remembered that up until recently these theories have been speculative. They must be tested experimentally and must have validity across the entire olfactory system, encompassing the anatomy and physiology of the receptors, the physical and chemical characteristics of the stimuli, and the behavior of the animal.

C. Tasting versus Sniffing

The chemist should like to have some assurance that sniffing the compounds eluting from a chromatograph or those being perceived from the headspace over a food product are indeed directly related to those which people perceive when a food is placed in the mouth during normal consumption. In the latter situation, the temperature of the oral cavity, amount and composition of saliva, and tactile sensations complicate the sensations perceived but are inoperative during simple sniffing.

Methyl stillingate, a character impact compound isolated from Bartlett pears, was dispersed in distilled water and presented in eight concentrations to trained judges for evaluation by sniffing as well as by mouth [65]. As indicated in Figure 9-5, significantly higher intensity ratings were assigned for odor intensity than for taste intensity at the same concentrations. Subsequent studies using vanillin dispersed in distilled water showed no differences between odor intensity and taste intensity. With acetic acid, however, significantly greater intensities were assigned to solutions evaluated by mouth than by sniffing because of the predominant sour taste which could not be predicted from the odor. Wasserman [84] measured the thresholds for three phenolic components of hickory smoke, guaiacol, 4-methylguaiacol, and 2,6-dimethoxyphenol, and found that all were perceived in lower concentrations when tasted than when shiffed. Furthermore, as shown in Table 9-1, the first two compounds had lower odor thresholds in water than in mineral oil, with the reverse for the third compound.

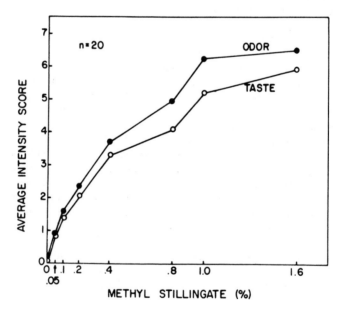

FIG. 9-5. Average intensity scores for solutions of methyl stillingate, a character impact compound isolated from Bartlett pears. Odor intensity was measured by sniffing and taste intensity by oral evaluation [65].

TABLE 9-1

Taste and Odor Thresholds of Three Phenols
Present in Wood Smoke[a]

| | In water | | In oil |
Phenol	Taste (ppm)	Odor (ppm)	Odor (ppm)
Guaiacol	0.013	0.021	0.070
4-Methyl guaiacol	0.065	0.090	0.400
2,6-Dimethoxyphenol	1.65	1.85	0.34

[a]Adapted from Wasserman [84].

Results from such studies as the foregoing emphasize two important factors in odor evaluation: (1) results from sniffing vs flavor by mouth may lead to different conclusions about the flavor of a product and (2) the medium of dispersion can influence the quality and the intensity of odor or flavor perceived.

D. The Interaction of the Senses in Flavor Perception

1. INFLUENCE OF VISUAL CHARACTERISTICS ON FLAVOR

To a large extent, we recognize, discriminate, and select foods with the eye. Through conditioning and association, we expect an item of a certain shape and color to have a specific odor, taste, and texture. Appearance of the product is identified with previously experienced quality and serves as an instant indicator of good or bad, according to the product's intended use. For example, we associate discoloration, fading of color, and shriveling of the surface with less desirable flavors. In contrast, there is little to commend the appearance of such foods as caviar, black olives, dried prunes or figs, truffles, raw oysters, or squid, yet these items are considered to be delicacies by experienced consumers.

In studies on the influence of color on food flavors, judges almost invariably identified the atypically colored samples incorrectly. Hall [25] described an experiment in which sherbets in six flavors were prepared in their natural or commonly associated color, in an inappropriate color, and uncolored. As anticipated, subjects were highly successful in identifying flavors presented in the customary colors, less so with flavors presented in uncolored form, and very unsuccessful with deceptive colors.

According to Pangborn [61], sweetness discrimination was not influenced by red, green, or yellow coloring in unflavored aqueous solutions. In pear nectar, by contrast, there was a pronounced tendency to designate the green colored samples as the least sweet [62]. Perhaps the green samples were associated with underripe fruit. In another experiment, food colorings were added to a dry white table wine to simulate the appearance of reisling, sautern, sherry, rosé, claret,

and burgundy wine types [63]. Judges who seldom or never used wine demonstrated no color-sweetness relationships, but experienced wine judges, despite their
greater sensitivity to constituents of wine, attributed significantly greater sweetness to the rosé-colored wine and the least sweetness to the claret-colored wine.
This is a logical error because wine judges know that rosé wines traditionally have
a higher residual sugar content than do the others.

One object lesson that can be learned from the foregoing studies is that the appearance of a product must be either standardized or masked if judges are to give
a critical analysis of flavor. In sensory tests, it is recommended that the appearance and color of the product be evaluated under a standard source of illumination and quantified in terms of deviation from a reference sample. Then, aliquots of the same samples should be represented to the judges for flavor evaluation
under illumination which effectively equalizes or minimizes the visual differences.
In this manner, flavor does not bias the visual judgments and appearance does not
influence the flavor evaluations.

2. INTERACTION OF TASTE, ODOR, TEXTURE, AND FLAVOR

Once taken into the mouth, foods and beverages make at least a dual and usually a
multiple impression. The tissues of the mouth, throat, and nasal cavity are so
innervated and so interrelated that any or all of four sensory systems operate
simultaneously. The cutaneous sensibilities of the mouth react to texture, tingle,
and astringency, as well as to chemical burning or biting or cooling. Thermal effects are readily perceived and the sense of taste obviously is involved. However,
it is olfaction which furnishes the most elaborate experiences associated with
flavor. A summary of the major functions of the oral caviry, as related to food
intake, is presented in Table 9-2. Pain features very predominently and is the
unifying sensation among all the sensory modalities. When the intensity of the
stimulus, be it visual, auditory, tactile, olfactory, thermal, or gustatory, becomes too strong, the receptor registers pain.

TABLE 9-2

Summary of the Principle Physiological and Sensory Functions
of the Oral Cavity Related to Food Intake

Oral structure	Physiological and/or sensory function
Temporomandibular joint	Hinge movement, biting Lateral movement, chewing Protrusion-withdrawal, chewing
Lips, cheeks	Transfer food and drink into mouth Retain material in mouth Regulate volume in mouth Sensitive to tactile, thermal stimuli[a]
Hard palate	Wrinkled surface provides "traction" to prevent food slippage on tongue

TABLE 9-2 (Continued)

Oral structure	Physiological and/or sensory function
Hard palate (cont.)	Highly sensitive to tactile, thermal stimuli[a]
Tongue	Crushing food; mixing food with saliva Positioning food between teeth Selective mastication Removing food residues from mouth Taste buds Sensitive to tactile, thermal, gustatory stimuli[a]
Teeth and periodontal membrane	Chewing Sensitive to pressure, thermal stimuli[a]
Salivary glands and oral mucosa	Cleanse mouth Lubricate mouth for swallowing and speaking Dilute oral stimuli Secrete amylase and other constituents Excrete constituents, e.g., alcohol, heavy metals Functions in thirst-water balance
Oropharyngeal area	Sensitive to tactile, thermal, odor stimuli[a]

[a]Extremely high intensities of tactile, thermal, gustatory, and olifactory stimuli elicit pain.

It is conceivable that changes in the texture of a food or the viscosity of a beverage can alter the odor and flavor characteristics by changing the rate with which the stimuli reach the gustatory and olfactory receptors. Conversely, various taste and odor compounds could alter the perceived oral viscosity by changing the rheological behavior of the viscous material. Pangborn et al. [66] reported that hydrocolloidal food thickeners depressed the sourness of citric acid and the bitterness of caffeine. Carboxymethylcellulose gums enhanced the intensity of sodium chloride and sodium saccharin but depressed the intensities of sucrose, citric acid, and caffeine. The odor of butyric acid was substantially reduced by addition of the hydrocolloids, whereas the other three odorants tested (acetaldehyde, acetophenone, methyl sulfide) were unaffected. With more complex beverages, Misaghi [55] observed that increasing concentrations of the five gums tested depressed flavor and odor intensities of both tomato juice and orange juice at solution temperatures of 0° and 22°C. Similar conclusions were obtained in subsequent experiments using instant coffee as the medium of dispersion. Thus, it can be concluded that increasing the viscosity of the liquid media studied consistently lowers the perceived intensities of taste, odor, and flavor.

E. Sensory versus GLC Measurements

1. GENERAL CONSIDERATIONS

Headspace vapor analysis, in which the volatiles present above the surface of a foodstuff are analyzed by GLC, is analogous to the mechanics of human sniffing, and therefore may be expected to yield comparable results. That this is not true is demonstrated in Table 9-3. Both GLC and human olfaction vary widely in sensitivity to different molecular species and to different compounds of the same chemical type. The lower limits of GLC flame ionization detection of acetone is 0.03 ppm, yet 500 ppm are needed for smell. Vanillin and methyl salicylate are relatively nonvolatile compounds and yet have low odor detection thresholds.

It is evident, therefore, that the sensitivities of the two measurements can differ widely in magnitude. Human judgments represent integrated responses, whereas the chromatograph is a physical separator. The responses of the GLC generally are linear, whereas the relationship between sensory response magnitude and stimulus magnitude is believed to be a power function. No known instrument or combination of instrumental and chemical techniques can completely duplicate the human olfactory capacity and versatility. The human senses, of course, cannot duplicate instrumental analyses.

Wick [86] has asked three pertinent questions to stimulate thinking on the possible relations between instrumental and sensory measurements: (1) What quantity of the commonly occurring volatile components of foods must be present in a sniff (10-100 ml air) in order to be smelled? (2) What corresponding quantity is necessary for detection by the most sensitive chromatographic measurements? (3) What is the similarity between these quantities? An even more elementary question

TABLE 9-3

Detection of Selected Compounds by Gas Chromatography and Olfaction[a]

Compound	BP (°C)	GLC (ppm)	Smell (ppm)
In aqueous solution			
n-Propanal	61	0.0025	0.17
n-Butanal	76	0.12	0.07
n-Hexanal	131	0.3	0.03
Acetone	56	0.03	500
2-Butanone	80	0.017	50
Dimethyl sulfide	38	0.002	0.012
Methyl mercaptan	8	0.013	0.002
Methyl salicylate	222	–	0.01
In air: (mg/liter)			
2-Heptanone	150	6.5×10^{-4}	8.97×10^{-4}
Vanillin	285	–	1.1×10^{-9}

[a]Adapted from Wick [86].

confronts the sensory analyst: What qualitative and/or quantitative human responses can be of use to the chemist in his approach to flavor?

Human judgment can supplement GLC analyses by (1) identifying the compound(s) if any, which contributes to the characteristic aroma of the product; (2) describing the quality and relative intensities of individual peaks and "families" of peaks; (3) establishing the relative importance of the odor of the complex essence, as well as of isolated fractions, to the total flavor picture (i.e., odor, taste, and other oral sensations); (4) determining what no instrument can approach - affective value, i.e., pleasantness–unpleasantness, palatability, and acceptability.

According to Sjöström and Cairncross [76], natural flavoring materials can be classified into four principal types from a sensory standpoint: (1) the primary component or components which form the nucleus around which the essential characteristics of odor are built and which bear the burden of flavor; (2) the principal supporting components which blend, modify, and support the principal characteristic and possibly provide interesting character notes; (3) components that do not provide interesting character notes and neither add nor detract from the essential ingredients; and (4) components that may be considered undesirable and actually detract from the overall effect of both the primary and secondary components. In the latter class they have included nonactive components which develop undesirable effects on aging.

2. DESCRIPTIVE ANALYSES

One of the first attempts to directly relate sensory with GLC analyses of headspace vapors was reported by McCarthy et al. [52]. A total of 200 chromatographic analyses were conducted on several banana varieties at successive stages of ripening under controlled conditions and were compared with 55 sensory sessions utilizing the "flavor profile" developed by A. D. Little, Inc. The characteristic bananalike flavor was found to be due to the amyl esters of acetic, propionic, and butyric acids, while distinctive fruity and estery notes were attributed to butyl acetate, butyl butyrate, hexyl acetate, and amyl butyrate. Table 9-4 demonstrates the intensities ascribed to flavor qualities for two varieties of bananas at four levels of ripeness. Note both qualitative and quantitative changes in flavor characteristics.

In a comparison of GLC with sensory analysis of anethole, citral, methyl salicylate, and safrole (similar molecular weights and boiling points), Kendall and Neilson [39] concluded that in both an aqueous–ethanol system and a hexadecane system, the sensory panel had much lower detection thresholds for all compounds than the detection levels of the GLC with a flame ionization detector. Odor intensity and quality were influenced by minor, normal contaminants as well as by the major components, both of which could be monitored by GLC. The chromatography of vapor from combinations of compounds did not indicate the presence of any new component to account for the development of new odor characters or, conversely, suppression of an odor. Furthermore, binary, tertiary, and quaternary combinations of compounds produced an unpredictable pattern of change in both odor intensity and quality. Subsequently, Kendall and Neilson [40] found strong sensory evidence that the various odor phenomena resulting from mixing four pure odorants could not be defined by measurable changes in the chromatographic behavior of the components. A significant finding was the considerable influence of subthreshold

TABLE 9-4

Development of Amplitude Levels and Intensity of
Characteristic Flavor Notes during Ripening of Banana Fruit Varieties[a]

	Gros Michel				Valery			
Amplitude	Yellow green) ([b]	Green tips ½	Full yellow 1	Flecked w/brown 1	Yellow green 1	Green tips 1	Full yellow 2	Flecked w/brown 2
Flavor notes								
Sweet	0	½	1½	1½	1	1	2	2
Sour	2½	2	1½	1	2	2	1	1
Banana	) (	½	1	1	1	1½	2	2
Amyl acetate	0	0	1	½	½	½	1	1
Amyl propionate	0	0	0	½	0	) (	1½	1½
Butyl butyrate	0	0	0	0	0	0	) (	½
Amyl butyrate	0	0	0	) (	) (	) (	½	1
Green	2	1½	1	0	1½	1½	1	0
Woody	1	½	) (	0	½	0	0	0

[a]Adapted from McCarthy et al. [52].
[b]Threshold

concentrations of one compound on the odor intensity of a second. This phenomenon has been studied also by Guadagni et al. [22,23], who have observed additive effects in mixtures rather than synergistic, subractive, or independent effects.

Using a combination of difference and descriptive testing, Jennings et al. [32] established the relative intensity of chromatographic fractions from pear essence. Characterization of the fractions indicated which were pleasant or unpleasant and which resembled the odor of pears. Aroma intensities of the esters of 2,4-decadienoic acid correlated well with the magnitude of their absorptions in the ultraviolet spectrum at 263-267 nm [28]. Scaling of odor intensity was used to obtain a mathematical basis upon which to treat statistically the relative effects of sample treatment, judges, and sensory replications. Additionally, judges were trained to utilize descriptive terminology to characterize the qualitative attributes of the recovered essence at varying dilutions.

In a unique study, Ottoson and von Sydow [59] measured electrophysiological responses from the olfactory membrane of a frog to gas chromatographic fractions from a concentrate of black currants. Although there was no direct correlation between the amplitude of the chromatographic peak and that of the electrical response, it was possible to calculate the relative stimulative efficiency of the components in the concentration at which they were present in the original mixture. Subsequently, Drake et al. [16] compared flavor across three distinct systems, gas chromatography, human olfaction, and animal electrophysiology.

3. "NOSING THE EFFLUENT"

Sniffing and characterizing of odorous components eluted from the GLC is done routinely by chemists in many laboratories. Fuller et al. [19] investigated the capability of a professional perfumer, stationed in a glass boothlike structure adjacent to the GLC, to identify odors in the exit helium stream. After the perfumer was familiarized with over 150 pure single aromatics and natural isolates, relative retention times were determined and the perfumer's ability to distinguish and identify the components of complex known mixtures was measured. Results of several tests with various 15-component mixtures showed that the perfumer could correctly identify 10 of the 15 by chemical name. Additionally, such compounds as methyl 2-octynoate were detected at only a few parts per 100,000, which did not record a peak on the GLC. These investigators demonstrated how a human sensor could assist the chemist in the quick identification of peaks, detection of impurities in material of over 99% purity, and judging whether or not a supposedly single peak is completely resolved by sensory examination of both sides.

Guadagni et al. [24] trained 12 judges to sniff the exit port of a GLC and describe the characteristic odor of each fraction that emerged from the column when 20 μl of apple essence were injected into the instrument. Responses from three trials were expressed as percentage identifying the peak as apple or applelike and compared with corresponding evaluation of the peaks collected in 100 ml of distilled water. One finding was that the fraction with the most intense odor was present in the least amount. Differences in peak area increased in a logarithmic fashion as the degree of odor difference between samples increased. Establishing the relationship between degree of odor difference and total peak area difference could be of value in determination of quality-control limits for some products. These investigators concluded that GLC's contribution to quality control depended on: (1) determination of which peaks contributed to the characteristic product aroma; (2) determination of the relative importance or effectiveness of each peak; (3) development of reliable techniques for relating the physical to the sensory response; and (4) establishment of a mathematical relation between the two types of measurement.

Klose et al. [43] developed a method for fractionating cooked chicken aroma at room temperature by passing nitrogen gas laden with the aroma through solid absorbants. Trained judges, stationed at a smelling cup at one end of the apparatus, characterized the unabsorbed effluents in terms of known odors of compounds previously established to be present in the total volatiles.

An excellent summary of problems encountered in the correlation of sensory and instrumental data was presented by von Sydow [83].

Two warnings might be issued relative to stationing human subjects at the hot exit port of the GLC. In a few isolated cases, toxic materials can be eluted and there is an apochryphal account of a chemist smelling burning hair, only to discover it came from his own nostrils!

4. ODOR AND FLAVOR THRESHOLDS

Although knowledge of threshold concentrations gives useful information on the relative stimulating properties of compounds, it should be recognized that thresholds are statistical end points influenced by temperature, relative humidity, stability, and purity of the stimuli; the psychophysical method employed; and judge variability. Since thresholds are so largely dependent on methods, decrease with training, and vary from determination to determination, a range rather than one value is more meaningful.

F. Special Problems in Odor and Flavor Measurement

1. MEDIUM OF DISPERSION

Since the olfactory receptors respond to compounds in the vapors emanating from the sample source, the ideal medium of dispersion should be air. In an ideal system, the odorous material would be delivered to a human subject who could sniff normally and give a response which could be expressed in some common scientific unit. Such factors as temperature, humidity, air pressure, and air velocity should be standardized. Also required are quantitative control of odor concentration, a supply of odor-free air, and the use of odorless and easily cleaned materials of construction. Use of a precision olfactometer where the latter set of conditions are met may not allow testing of mixtures of compounds, as deviations from ideal gas laws may invalidate calculations upon which the concentrations are determined. Therefore, it is common to disperse odorants in distilled water or mineral oil and express the units in terms of the dilution.

Patton [68] compared his flavor threshold data for fatty acids dispersed in water with those of Feron and Govignon [17], who used a neutral edible oil media, as follows:

Fatty acid	Water (ppm)	Oil (ppm)
C_4	6.8	0.6
C_6	5.4	2.5
C_8	5.8	350.0
C_{10}	3.5	200.0

The data agree with observations by Lea and Swoboda [48] for aliphatic aldehydes which yield lower thresholds in water than in oils. Patton suggested that bonding to solvent molecules tends to reduce volatilization of polar components from water in a manner similar to that in which oils "fix" nonpolar odorants. Using direct headspace gas chromatographic analyses, Nawar [58] reported differential results on the influence of dispersion in water and in oil on headspace concentrations of ethanol, heptane, and 2-heptanone. Dilution with water caused an increase in the concentration of selected volatiles in the headspace.

2. EFFECT OF NONVOLATILES ON ODOR

It is well known that nonvolatile solutes can increase the partial pressures of volatile constituents and thereby increase their concentration in the vapor phase.

Jennings [33] observed that additions of NaCl increased the headspace concentration of $1-^{14}C$-ethyl acetate at all temperatures studied. Nawar [58] reported that glucose increased the headspace response of 800 and 8,000 ppm of 2-heptanone in aqueous systems but to a lesser extent than did Na_2SO_4.

Although it is not known whether sugar increases the fugacity of a medium, it is commonly observed that sweetness enhances apparent flavor intensity of both artificially flavored solutions and natural food products. Kendall and Nielson [40] found mainly qualitative changes in the odor of a quaternary mixture of compounds as a result of additions of 10% sucrose, 1% salt, or 0.1% MSG.

G. Taste, Odor, and Acceptance of Flavor Stimuli

Although flavor greatly influences the acceptance of foods and dozens of other consumer products which emit volatile compounds, there need not be any relation between the intensity of the response to flavor and how much it is liked or disliked. Degree of liking for a food flavor may increase up to some optimum point, after which it becomes too intense and even offensive. Large individual differences exist among people in their affective responses to aromas and tastes as a result of their cultural backgrounds, their individual perceptual sensitivities, and their frame of reference during the testing. Consequently, there is no simple relation between the acceptance of a food, beverage, or flavoring and the quality or intensity of its chemical components. Even though the economy of commercial enterprises may depend greatly upon such knowledge, it is difficult to determine beforehand what types of substances are highly acceptable to a given population. For example, independent of the flavor quality of a product, unfamiliarity is a great obstacle to the introduction of any new food or beverage. Even the most adventuresome individual who readily "tries anything once" does not change his long-term consumption patterns very rapidly. A British observer stated, "This even applies to North America where economic growth, a competitive mentality, and the power of advertising greatly favour innovation" [38].

H. Sensory Methodology

1. LABORATORY TESTS

a. Selection and Training of Judges. The sensitivity and reproducibility of the judges influences the final results of a flavor evaluation to a greater extent than any other variable. Unless the judges are selected on the basis of their sensitivity to the variable under study, more variation in the results is often obtained attributable to judges than to the experimental treatments.

The following recommendations have been found to improve the reliability of the judgments [1]:

1. From the available population, select at least twice as many judges as
    needed, making certain that each is interested in participating and can be
    present during the entire test period. At a group meeting explain the

objectives of the study and demonstrate the range of sensory properties to be expected. Posting results during the training period and providing light refreshments stimulate interest and cooperation.

2. To select the most sensitive judges, present two samples varying in a known parameter, which is related to the sensory variable that is to be studied ultimately. For example, if one is selecting judges to evaluate "skunky" flavor in beer, samples varying in amount of time exposed to light could be presented. There appears to be little or no relationship between a judge's general sensitivity to sweet, sour, salty, and bitter taste stimuli and his or her ability to judge flavors.

3. After judges have been selected, allow two or three test periods to acquaint them with the experimental samples. This is most easily done by proceeding with the scheduled testing design, discarding the results from the first two or three sessions, and then presenting these samples toward the end of the study to complete the experimental design.

4. Judges should be treated as individual measuring devices, allowing sufficient replication per treatment per judge. If necessary, eliminate scores of any judge who shows unreasonable inconsistency during a study. Do not substitute judges. Judges are no more interchangeable than are treatments.

5. In analyzing data, test for effect of individual judge variation. If means are reported, give the range and the standard deviation. In all cases, indicate the number of individual determinations constituting each mean.

The investigator and the assisting technician should participate on their own panels. By direct participation, the investigator establishes rapport with the judges and is better able to interpret their responses. However, in most cases, the investigator's judgments should not be included in the final analysis, as he has much more prior knowledge of the treatments than other judges and may introduce unmeasurable bias.

Although differences in ability between smokers and nonsmokers have not been demonstrated conclusively, it is recommended that judges refrain from smoking at least one-half hour before testing to minimize the tobacco flavor in the mouth and the odors they may bring into the test room. Differences in sensitivity between men and women have not been established, except in descriptive analysis, where women may be more articulate due to their daily contact with foods and cooking odors. In general, better results are obtained using judges between the ages of 18 and 40 years of age.

b. Physical Environment. The test room should be quiet and conducive to thought-ful evaluation of the test samples. It is preferable that individual, partitioned booths be used so that judges do not influence one another. The temperature, humidity, and illumination in the test room should be controlled, and extraneous odors and distracting interruptions should be avoided. Distilled water should be provided for oral rinsing. Generally, swallowing is not permitted in order to avoid sensory fatigue and postingestion effects.

c. <u>Preparation and Presentation of Samples</u>. Samples should be properly coded and randomly presented so that judges have no clue to their identity. It is essential to use an appropriate experimental design with sufficient replication, e.g., 40 or more evaluations per treatment. Such factors as quantity, temperature, color, size, and shape should be standardized so that the only variable is the one under direct consideration. The number of samples presented at one session depends on: (1) the product, (2) the intensity of the characteristic being judged, (3) the method of evaluation, (4) the experience of the judge, and (5) time and commodity available. Reliable judgments have been obtained on up to 36 samples of milk, but only eight samples of beer, six of ice cream, and three of tomato catsup per session.

d. <u>Difference Tests</u>. Often a trained panel is used to determine whether differences can be perceived between two samples or among several treatments. One of the most sensitive difference tests is the paired comparison, wherein two samples are presented and the judge is asked to state which of the two has the greater amount of the designated quality, e.g., which is sweeter or which has greater vanilla flavor. The probability of obtaining a correct response due to chance alone is 0.5.

When the experimenter does not know in advance which sensory parameter is to be altered by the treatment, a triangle test can be used, wherein three samples are presented, two of which are identical and one different. The judge is required to indicate the odd sample, without the necessity of describing the difference. The probability of obtaining a correct response due to chance alone is 0.33. Despite its statistical advantage, the triangle test is a more difficult task than the paired comparison, as in actual practice it consists of three paired comparisons, i.e., the first vs the second, the first vs the third, and the second vs the third sample.

A useful variation of the paired comparison can be called "deviation from the reference." A labeled reference sample is presented, followed by a series of 3-12 samples, with the judge requested to indicate the degree to which each coded sample deviates in flavor from the reference. Usually one or more hidden references are included within the series to test the reproducibility of the judges.

e. <u>Quality-Quantity Evaluation</u>. In addition to measurement of differences between treatments, frequently it is desirable to establish intensity of the characteristic or levels of quality. The laboratory panel is much better suited to the former as quality can be a rather nebulous concept, depending on the intended use of the product, the conditions of testing, and the frame of reference of the judge. Trained judges are capable of evaluating intensities of sensory properties independently of degree of liking. With quality judgments, however, individual experience and preferences influence the nature of the quality ascribed.

Ranking of a series of samples in increasing or decreasing order of intensity often is used in screening of experimental samples. To avoid sensory fatigue and loss of attention, a maximum of six samples is recommended. Inclusion of one or more control samples or of standards having a designated quality can improve the precision of ranks. Ranking is rapid, allows testing of multiple samples, is simple to administer, and lends itself to use of fixed scales with control or reference samples. However, the noted disadvantage of ranking is that it disregards the degree of difference between samples. Also, because of the direct relative nature of the rank, the values cannot be compared directly with values from another set of data.

Scoring is the oldest of all sensory testing systems and is most frequently used due to its diversity, simplicity, and ease of statistical analysis. It consists of evaluating, on a preestablished scale, single or multiple factors that influence intensity or quality. To increase precision, the number of points allowed should be at least as many as the differences which trained judges can distinguish. Usually, experienced judges can distinguish 7-12 intensity levels. Since judges have a tendency to avoid the extremes on any scale, it is customary to use scales with 9-15 intervals. One disadvantage of the traditional scoring technique is that the judge is forced to arrange the experimental samples within the finite boundaries of the numerical scale given. To provide judges with an infinite scale, experimenters have used magnitude estimation or ratio scaling, wherein a control is presented followed by the experimental samples. The judge is asked to rate the intensity of the samples in terms of how many times greater it is than the reference. Responses can vary from one to infinity.

Descriptive sensory analysis has been used extensively in the food and flavor industry. The best-known descriptive method is the flavor profile developed by the Arthur D. Little Co., Cambridge, Massachusetts [12]. Unlike difference testing, descriptive analysis concentrates on all sensory properties in relation to each other. Usually, open discussion sessions are held, where samples are judged according to three criteria: (1) a written description of the single components that can be detected by sniffing and by tasting, listed in the order of their appearance; (2) the intensity of each of these components; and (3) the overall judgment or "amplitude." Upon completion of individual examinations, the findings are discussed in open sessions, one person acting as moderator. Standards, consisting of pure chemical compounds, or more complex items are continually consulted in order to verify the descriptive terms. Testing and open discussions are continued until agreement between judges is obtained, after which a composite "profile" is developed. Examples of profile results of banana flavor were shown previously in Table 9-4. The main advantage of this method is that individual components as well as the overall aspects of the product are evaluated critically, making the method a good quality-control tool. In addition, reference to designated standards serves to anchor the descriptions and increase reliability. If carefully used, descriptive analysis has an excellent potential. As traditionally used it suffers from several serious disadvantages: (1) it is a very expensive method of analysis because selecting, training, and conducting panels is extremely time consuming; (2) results cannot be expressed mathematically and therefore cannot be analyzed statistically; and (3) an open-discussion session is employed exclusively wherein judges continually influence each other's opinions. The second disadvantage can be remedied easily by using scoring or magnitude estimation in combination with the descriptive terms. The last disadvantage could be corrected by placing a portable partition on the discussion table, so that open briefings could be held followed by separate, isolated judgments.

2. CONSUMER TESTING

After samples have been screened by laboratory panels, the consumer reaction can
be assessed by consumer groups representing the population that purchases and
consumes the foods. Hedonic scales are frequently used for this purpose.

Hedonics relates to the psychology of pleasant and unpleasant states of con-
sciousness. In hedonic scaling, affective responses, i.e., like and dislike, are
measured on a rating scale. This method frequently is used at the consumer level
since it reflects the attitudes of a group of people toward certain foods under a
given set of conditions. Usually a nine-point structured scale is used, with terms
ranging from "like extremely" through "neither like or dislike," to "dislike extremely." For analysis, the terms are converted to integers. The hedonic scale
is simple and flexible, judges do not need previous experience, and data can be
handled by analysis of variance. Disadvantages include lack of precision, high
variability in ratings from a group of observers, inability to use the method for
quality-control purposes, and limited application unless large populations are used.

For detailed descriptions of sensory procedures and methodologies see texts by
Amerine et al. [1], ASTM [3], and Larmond [47].

3. APPLICATION OF SENSORY TESTS IN THE FLAVOR INDUSTRY

In a series of articles on flavor evaluation, Buchel [9], of Naarden, Inc., pointed
out that often the human nose is more sensitive than instrumental detectors. To
efficiently measure sensory responses to flavors and flavorings, he recommends
the following: (1) "If a sample of flavoring is to be evaluated, we have to ask
ourselves first of all, what kind of performance we expect from this material. If
the flavor is meant to substitute for another ingredient, without any noticeable
effect in the final food product, then a 'difference-similarity' test is required."
(2) "When the flavoring is intended to be an improvement to the product, without
changing the original character of the food, then we want to test for 'preference.'"
(3) "Finally, if a total new flavor concept is to be introduced, it is the 'acceptability' that we are mainly interested in." For difference tests, they begin with four
to six highly trained experts, and if the results are satisfactory they continue with
a semitrained panel of 30 persons. For preference and acceptance, they extend
the testing of selected samples to untrained consumers.

The literature in this chapter has only been reviewed up to January 1, 1972.

REFERENCES

1. M. A. Amerine, R. M. Pangborn, and E. B. Roessler, Principles of Sensory
   Evaluation of Food. Academic Press, New York, 1965.
2. J. E. Amoore, Molecular Basis of Odor. Charles C Thomas, Springfield,
   Ill., 1970.
3. American Society for Testing and Materials, STP 433: Basic Principles of Sen-
   sory Evaluation. STP 434: Manual on Sensory Testing Methods. STP 440:
   Correlation of Subjective-Objective Methods in the Study of Odors and Taste.
   American Society of Testing and Materials, Philadelphia, 1968.

4. M. G. J. Beets, in Molecular Structure and Organoleptic Quality. SCI Mono-graph No. 1, 1957, pp. 54-90.

5. L. M. Beidler, J. Gen. Physiol., 38, 133 (1954).

6. L. M. Beidler, in Second Symposium on Oral Sensation and Perception (J. F. Bosma, ed.), Charles C Thomas, Springfield, Ill., 1970, pp. 100-108.

7. R. E. Biggars, J. J. Hilton, and M. A. Gianturco, J. Chromatog. Sci., 7, 453 (1969).

8. M. Boelens, P. J. de Valois, H. J. Wobben, and A. van der Gen, J. Agri. Food Chem., 19, 984 (1971).

9. J. A. Buchel, in Flavor Thoughts. Naarden, Inc., Baltimore, Md., 1972.

10. Campbell Soup Company, Proceedings, Flavor Chemistry Symposium - 1961. Camden, N.J., 1961.

11. J. F. Carson, in Chemistry and Physiology of Flavor (H. W. Schultz, E. A. Day, and L. M. Libbey, eds.), AVI Publ., Westport, Conn., 1967, pp. 390-405.

12. J. F. Caul, in Advances in Food Research. Academic Press, New York, 1957, pp. 1-40.

13. J. W. Cornforth, R. H. Cornforth, G. Popjak, and L. Yengoyan, J. Biol. Chem., 241, 3970 (1966).

14. E. C. Crocker, Flavor. McGraw-Hill, New York, 1945.

15. J. T. Davies, J. Theoret. Biol., 8, 1 (1965).

16. B. Drake, B. Johansson, and E. von Sydow, Scand. J. Psychol., 10, 89 (1969).

17. R. Feron and M. Govignon, Ann. Fals. Expert. Chim., 54, 308 (1961).

18. R. Fischer and F. Griffin, Arzneim.-Frosch., 14, 673 (1964).

19. G. H. Fuller, R. Steltenkamp, and G. A. Tisserand, in Recent Advances in Odor: Theory, Measurement, and Control (H. E. Whipple, ed.), New York Academy of Science, New York, 1964, pp. 711-724.

20. J. C. Giddings and R. A. Keller, Advances in Chromatography. Vol. 9, Marcel Dekker, New York, 1970.

21. R. F. Gould, Flavor Chemistry, Advances in Chemistry Series 56. American Chemical Society, Washington, D.C., 1966.

22. D. G. Guadagni, R. G. Buttery, and S. Okano, J. Sci. Food Agri., 10, 761 (1963).

23. D. G. Guadagni, R. G. Buttery, S. Okano, and H. K. Burr, Nature (London), 200, 1288 (1963).

24. D. G. Guadagni, S. Okano, R. G. Buttery, and H. K. Burr, Food Technol., 20, 166 (1966).

25. R. L. Hall, in Flavor Research and Food Acceptance (A. D. Little, Inc., ed.), Reinhold, New York, 1958, pp. 224-240.

26. J. B. Hendrickson, The Molecules of Nature. W. A. Benjamin, New York, 1965.

27. E. J. Hewitt, D. A. M. Mackay, and S. Z. Lewin, in Flavor Research and Food Acceptance (A. D. Little, Inc., ed.), Reinhold, New York, 1958, pp. 262-289.

28. D. E. Heinz, R. M. Pangborn, and W. G. Jennings, J. Food Sci., 29, 756 (1964).

29. J. E. Hodge, in Chemistry and Physiology of Flavors (H. W. Schultz, E. A. Day, and L. M. Libbey, eds.), AVI Publ., Westport, Conn., 1967, pp. 465-491.

30. R. M. Horwitz and B. Gentili, J. Agri. Food Chem., 17, 696 (1969).
31. G. E. Inglett, B. Dowling, J. J. Albrecht, and F. A. Hoglan, J. Agri. Food Chem., 13, 284 (1965).
32. W. G. Jennings, S. Leonard, and R. M. Pangborn, Food Technol., 14, 587 (1960).
33. W. G. Jennings, J. Food Sci., 30, 445 (1965).
34. W. G. Jennings, in Chemistry and Physiology of Flavor (H. W. Schutz, E. A. Day, and L. M. Libbey, eds.), AVI Publ., Westport, Conn., 1967, pp. 419-430.
35. A. E. Johnson, H. E. Nursten, and R. A. Self, Chem. Ind., January, 10, (1969).
36. A. E. Johnson, H. E. Nursten, and A. A. Williams, Chem. Ind., May, 556, (1971).
37. A. E. Johnson, H. E. Nursten, and A. A. Williams, Chem. Ind., October, 1212, (1971).
38. H. Kalmus and S. J. Hubbard, The Chemical Senses in Health and Disease. Charles C Thomas, Springfield, Ill. (1960).
39. D. A. Kendall and A. J. Neilson, in Recent Advances in Odor: Theory, Measurement, and Control (H. E. Whipple, ed.), New York Academy of Science, New York, 1964, pp. 567-575.
40. D. A. Kendall and A. J. Neilson, J. Food Sci., 31, 268 (1966).
41. T. E. Kinlin, R. Muralidhara, A. O. Pittet, A. Sanderson, and J. P. Waldradt, J. Agri. Food Chem., 20, 1021 (1972).
42. J. E. Kinsella, Chem. Ind., January, 35, (1969).
43. A. A. Klose, H. H. Palmer, H. Lineweaver, and A. A. Campbell, J. Food Sci., 31, 638 (1966).
44. A. Kuninaka, in Flavor Chemistry, Advances in Chemistry Series 56 (R. F. Gould, ed.), American Chemical Society, Washington, D.C., 1966, pp. 261-274.
45. K. Kurihara and L. M. Beidler, Science, 161, 1241 (1968).
46. K. Kurihara and L. M. Beidler, Nature (London), 222, 1176 (1969).
47. E. Larmond, Methods for Sensory Evaluation of Food. Publ. 1284, Canada Department of Agriculture, Ottawa, 1970.
48. C. H. Lea and P. A. T. Swoboda, Chem. Ind., 1958, 1289 (1958).
49. A. D. Little, Inc., Flavor Research and Food Acceptance. Reinhold, New York, 1958.
50. R. H. Mazur, J. M. Schlatter, and A. H. Goldkemp, J. Amer. Chem. Soc., 91, 2684 (1969).
51. D. H. McBurney and C. Pfaffmann, J. Exp. Psychol., 65, 523 (1963).
52. A. L. McCarthy, J. K. Palmer, C. P. Shaw, and E. E. Anderson, J. Food Sci., 28, 379 (1963).
53. N. B. McCutcheon and J. Saunders, Science, 175, 214 (1972).
54. H. L. Meiselman, in CRC Critical Reviews in Food Technology, (T. E. Furia, ed.), (3) 89-119 (1972).
55. Z. Misaghi, M.S. Thesis, University of California, Davis, 1972.
56. J. H. Mitchell, Jr., N. J. Leinen, E. M. Mrak, and S. D. Bailey, Chemistry of Natural Food Flavors. Quartermaster Food and Container Institute for the Armed Forces, Chicago, Ill., 1957.
57. J. A. Morris and R. A. Cagan, Biochem. Biophys. Acta, 261, 114 (1972).

58. W. W. Nawar, Food Technol., 20, 213 (1966).

59. D. Ottoson and E. von Sydow, Life Sci., 3, 1111 (1964).

60. R. M. Pangborn, Food Res., 25, 245 (1960).

61. R. M. Pangborn, Amer. J. Psychol., 73, 229 (1960).

62. R. M. Pangborn and B. Hansen, Amer. J. Psychol., 76, 315 (1963).

63. R. M. Pangborn, H. W. Berg, and B. Hansen, Amer. J. Psychol., 76, 492 (1963).

64. R. M. Pangborn, Food Technol., 18, 63 (1964).

65. R. M. Pangborn, in Proceedings of the Second International Congress of Food Science and Technology (D. J. Tilgner and A. Borys, eds.), Warsaw, 1968, pp. 303-317.

66. R. M. Pangborn, I. M. Trabue, and A. S. Szczesniak, J. Texture Stud., 4(2), 224 (1973).

67. S. Patton, J. Agri. Food Chem., 6, 132 (1958).

68. S. Patton, J. Food Sci., 29, 679 (1964).

69. J. J. Powers and E. S. Keith, J. Food Sci., 33, 207 (1968).

70. H. M. Richard, G. F. Russell, and W. G. Jennings, J. Chromatog. Sci., 9, 560 (1971).

71. N. Robbins, in Second Symposium on Oral Sensation and Perception (J. F. Bosma, ed.), Charles C Thomas, Springfield, Ill., 1970, pp. 71-79.

72. G. F. Russell and J. I. Hills, Science, 172, 1043 (1971).

73. H. H. Schaumburg, R. Byck, R. Gerstl, and J. H. Mashman, Science, 163, 3869 (1969).

74. H. W. Schultz, E. A. Day, and L. M. Libbey, The Chemistry and Physiology of Flavors. AVI Publ., Westport, Conn., 1967.

75. R. S. Shallenberger and T. E. Acree, in Handbook of Sensory Physiology, Vol. IV, Chemical Senses. Part 2. Taste. Springer-Verlag, Berlin, 1971, pp. 221-277.

76. L. B. Sjöström and S. E. Cairncross, in Flavor Research and Food Acceptance (A. D. Little, Inc., ed.), Reinhold, New York, 1958, pp. 257-261.

77. W. Stocklin, J. Agri. Food Chem., 17, 704 (1969).

78. M. Stoll, M. Winter, F. Guatschi, I. Flament, and B. Willhalm, Helv. Chim. Acta, 50, 628 (1967).

79. M. Stuiver, Ph.D. Thesis, Rijks University, Groningen, The Netherlands, 1958.

80. R. Teranishi, I. Hornstein, P. Issenberg, and E. L. Wick, Flavor Research. Principles and Techniques. Food Sci. Ser. Vol. 1, Marcel Dekker, New York, 1971.

81. R. Tressl and W. G. Jennings, J. Agri. Food Chem., 21, 189 (1972).

82. L. Vuataz and D. Reymond, J. Chromatog. Sci., 9, 168 (1971).

83. E. von Sydow, Food Technol., 25, 40 (1971).

84. A. E. Wasserman, J. Food Sci., 31, 1005 (1966).

85. A. E. Wasserman, J. Agri. Food Chem., 20, 737 (1972).

86. E. L. Wick, Food Technol., 19, 145 (1965).

87. R. A. Wilson and I. Katz, J. Agri. Food Chem., 20, 741 (1972).

88. R. H. Wright, The Science of Smell. Basic Books, New York, 1964.

Chapter 10

OTHER DESIRABLE CONSTITUENTS OF FOOD

R. C. Lindsay

Department of Food Science
University of Wisconsin-Madison
Madison, Wisconsin

Contents

I. INTRODUCTION

Carbohydrates, fats, proteins, water, and minerals comprise the great bulk of
food and are discussed at length in appropriate chapters. The minor constituents
of foods form a varied group of relatively simple chemicals which contribute functional properties and nutritional qualities or which in some cases are only incidentally present. Many of the minor constituents are dealt with in other chapters.
Included are antioxidants (Chapter 4), amino acids (Chapter 5), vitamins and minerals (Chapter 7), pigments (Chapter 8), flavors (Chapter 9), potentially hazardous
substances (Chapter 11), and emulsifiers (Chapter 12). In spite of seemingly extensive coverage devoted to minor food constituents in other chapters, there remains a
substantial number of compounds that do not readily fit into already discussed areas.
It is to this group of constituents, both natural and added, that attention is given
here.

II. ACIDS

A. General Information

Both organic and inorganic acids occur extensively in natural systems, where they
function in a variety of roles ranging from intermediary metabolites to components
of buffer systems. Acids are added for numerous purposes in foods and food
processing where they provide the benefits of many of their natural actions. One of
the most important functions of acids in foods is participation in buffering systems,
and this aspect is discussed in Section IV. The use of acids and acid salts in chemical leavening systems, the role of specific acidic microbial inhibitors (e.g., sorbic acid, benzoic acid) in food preservation, and the function of acids as chelating
agents are also discussed in subsequent sections of this chapter. Acids are important in the setting of pectin gels (Chapter 3), they serve as defoaming agents and
emulsifiers, and they induce coagulation of milk proteins (Chapters 5 and 14) in the
production of cheese and cultured dairy products, such as sour cream. In natural
culturing processes lactic acid (CH_3-CHOH-COOH) produced by streptococci and
lactobacilli causes coagulation by lowering the pH to near the isoelectric point of
casein. Cheeses can be produced by adding rennet and acidulants, such as citric
acid and hydrochloric acids, to cold milk (4°-8°C). Subsequent warming of milk
(to 35°C) produces a uniform gel structure [73,88,101]. Addition of acid to warm

milk results in a protein precipitate rather than a gel. Glucono-δ-lactone also can be used for slow acid production in cultured dairy products [27,76] and in chemical leavening systems because it slowly hydrolyzes in aqueous systems to form gluconic acid [1].

$$CH_2OH-CH-CHOH-CHOH-CHOH-C \overset{O}{\underset{}{\overset{''}{}}} \quad \underset{-H_2O}{\overset{+H_2O}{\rightleftharpoons}} \quad CH_2OH-(CHOH)_4-COOH$$

$$\underset{\text{Glucono-δ-lactone}}{\underline{\hspace{2cm} O \hspace{2cm}}} \qquad\qquad \text{Gluconic acid}$$

$$(10\text{-}1)$$

Dehydration of lactic acid yields lactide, a cyclic dilactone

$$(\underline{OCH(CH_3)COOCH(CH_3)CO}$$

that also can be used as a slow-release acid in aqueous systems.

Acids, such as citric, are added to some moderately acid fruits and vegetables to lower the pH to a value below 4.5. In canned foods this permits sterilization to be achieved under less severe thermal conditions than is necessary for less acid products and has the added advantage of precluding the growth of hazardous microorganisms.

Acids, such as potassium acid tartrate, are employed in the manufacture of fondant and fudge to induce limited hydrolysis or inversion of sucrose (Chapter 3). Inversion can lead to greater sweetness, and the presence of fructose and glucose inhibits excessive growth of sucrose crystals by providing a more complex crystallization syrup.

One of the most important contributions of acids to foods is that of providing a sour or tart taste [43]. Acids also have the ability to modify and intensify the taste perception of other flavoring agents. The hydrogen ion or hydronium ion (H_3O^+) is generally believed to trigger the sour taste response (Chapter 9). Short-chain free fatty acids (C_2-C_{12}) contribute significantly to the aroma of foods. For example, butyric acid at relatively high concentrations contributes strongly to the characteristic flavor of hydrolytic rancidity but in lower concentrations it contributes to the typical flavor of such products as cheese and butter.

A number of organic acids are available for food applications [44]. Some of the more commonly used acids are acetic, CH_3COOH; lactic, $CH_3-CHOH-COOH$; citric, $HOOC-CH_2-COH(COOH)-CH_2-COOH$; malic, $HOOC-CH(OH)-CH_2-COOH$; fumaric, $HOOC-CH=CH-COOH$; succinic, $HOOC-CH_2-CH_2-COOH$; and tartaric, $HOOC-CH(OH)-CH(OH)-COOH$. Phosphoric acid, H_3PO_4, is the only inorganic acid extensively employed as a food acidulant. Phosphoric acid is an important acidulant in flavored carbonated beverages, particularly in colas and root beer. The other mineral acids (e.g., HCl, H_2SO_4) are usually too highly dissociated for food applications, and their use may lead to problems with quality attributes of foods.

B. Chemical Leavening Systems

Chemical leavening systems are composed of compounds that react to release gas in a dough or batter under appropriate conditions of moisture and temperature.

During baking, this gas release along with expansion of entrapped air and moisture vapor imparts a characteristic porous, cellular structure to finished foods. Chemical leavening systems are found in self-rising flours, prepared baking mixes, household and commercial baking powders, and refrigerated dough products.

Carbon dioxide is the only gas generated from currently used chemical leavening systems, and it is derived from a carbonate or bicarbonate salt. The most common leavening salt is sodium bicarbonate ($NaHCO_3$), although ammonium carbonate, $(NH_4)_2CO_3$, and bicarbonate, NH_4HCO_3, are sometimes used in cookies. Both of the ammonium salts decompose at baking temperatures and thus do not require, as does sodium bicarbonate, an added leavening acid for functionality. Potassium bicarbonate ($KHCO_3$) has been employed as a component of leavening systems in sodium-free diets, but its application is limited because of its hygroscopic nature and slight bitter flavor [84].

Sodium bicarbonate is quite soluble in water (619 g per 100 ml) and ionizes completely:

$$NaHCO_3 \longrightarrow Na^+ + HCO_3^- \tag{10-2}$$

$$HCO_3^- + H_2O \longrightarrow H_2CO_3 + OH^- \tag{10-3}$$

$$HCO_3^- \longrightarrow CO_3^{2-} + H^+ \tag{10-4}$$

These reactions, of course, apply only to simple water solutions. In dough systems the ionic distribution becomes much more complex since proteins and other naturally occurring ionic species are available to participate in the reactions. In the presence of hydrogen ions provided mainly by leavening acids, and to some extent by the dough, sodium bicarbonate reacts to release carbon dioxide.

$$R-O^-, H^+ + NaHCO_3 \longrightarrow R-O^-, Na^+ + H_2O + CO_2 \tag{10-5}$$

The proper balance of acid and sodium bicarbonate are essential because excess sodium bicarbonate imparts a soapy taste to bakery products, while an excess of acid leads to tartness and sometimes bitterness. The neutralizing power of leavening acids is not uniform and the relative activity of an acid is given by its neutralizing value. The neutralizing value of an acid is determined by calculating the parts by weight of sodium bicarbonate that neutralize 100 parts by weight of the leavening acid [111]. However, in the presence of natural flour ingredients, the amount of leavening acid required to give neutrality or any other desired pH in a baked product may be quite different from the theoretical amount determined for a simple system. Still, neutralizing values are useful in determining initial formulations for leavening systems. Residual salts from a properly balanced leavening process help stabilize the pH of finished products.

Leavening acids are often not easily recognized as acids in the usual sense, yet they must provide hydrogen ions to release carbon dioxide. The phosphates and potassium acid tartrate are metal salts of partially neutralized acids, while sodium aluminum sulfate reacts with water to yield sulfuric acid:

$$Na_2SO_4 \cdot Al_2(SO_4)_3 + 6\ H_2O \longrightarrow Na_2SO_4 + 2\ Al(OH)_3 + 3\ H_2SO_4 \tag{10-6}$$

As mentioned earlier, glucono-δ-lactone is an intramolecular ester (or lactone) that hydrolyzes slowly in aqueous systems to yield gluconic acid.

Leavening acids generally exhibit limited water solubility at room temperature, but some are less soluble than others. This difference in solubility or availability accounts for the initial rate of carbon dioxide release at room temperature and is the basis for classifying leavening acids according to speed. For example, if the compound is moderately soluble, carbon dioxide is rapidly evolved and the acid is referred to as fast acting. Conversely, if the acid is slightly soluble, it will be a slow-acting leavening acid. Leavening acids usually release a portion of the carbon dioxide prior to baking and the remainder under elevated temperatures of the baking process.

General patterns of carbon dioxide release at 27°C for fast-acting monocalcium phosphate monohydrate [$Ca(HPO_4)_2 \cdot H_2O$] and slow-acting 1-3-8 sodium aluminum phosphate, $NaH_{14}Al_3(PO_4)_8 \cdot 4 H_2O$, are shown in Figure 10-1. Over 60% of the carbon dioxide is released very quickly from the more soluble monocalcium phosphate monohydrate, while only 20% of the potential carbon dioxide is released from the less soluble 1-3-8 sodium aluminum phosphate during a 10-min reaction period. Because of a hydrated alumina coating, the latter mentioned leavening acid reacts to only a small extent until activated by heat. Also shown in Figure 10-1 is the low temperature release pattern of carbon dioxide from coated anhydrous monocalcium phosphate, $Ca(HPO_4)_2$. The crystals of this leavening acid were coated with compounds of slightly soluble alkali metal phosphates. The gradual release of carbon dioxide over the 10-min reaction period corresponds to the time required for water to penetrate the coating. This behavior is very desirable in some products that encounter a delay prior to baking.

The release of the remainder of the carbon dioxide from leavening systems during baking provides the final modifying action on texture. In most leavening systems the rate at which carbon dioxide is released greatly accelerates as the

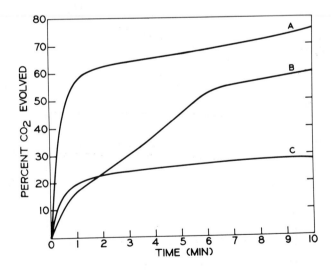

FIG. 10-1. Carbon dioxide production at 27°C from the reaction of $NaHCO_3$ with (a) monocalcium phosphate·H_2O, (b) coated anhydrous monocalcium phosphate, and (c) 1-3-8 sodium aluminum phosphate. (Data from Stahl and Ellinger [111].)

temperature is elevated. The effect of elevated temperatures on the release rate of carbon dioxide from slow-acting sodium acid pyrophosphate ($Na_2H_2P_2O_7$) is presented in Figure 10-2. Even a slight increase in temperature (from 27°C to 30°C) noticeably accelerates gas production. Temperatures near 60°C cause a complete release of carbon dioxide within 1 min. Some leavening acids are less sensitive to high temperatures and do not exhibit vigorous activity until temperatures near the maximum baking temperature are obtained. Calcium phosphate ($CaHPO_4$) is unreactive at room temperature because it forms a slightly alkaline solution at this temperature. However, upon heating above approximately 60°C, hydrogen ions are released, thereby activating the leavening process. This slow action confines its use to products requiring long baking times, such as some types of cakes. Formulations of leavening acids employing one or more acidic components are common, and systems are often tailored for specific dough or batter applications.

Leavening acids currently employed include potassium acid tartrate, sodium aluminum sulfate, glucono-δ-lactone, and ortho- and pyrophosphates. The phosphates include calcium phosphate, sodium aluminum phosphate, and sodium acid pyrophosphate. Some general properties of commonly used leavening acids are given in Table 10-1. It must be remembered that these are only examples and that an extensive technology has developed for modification and control of the phosphate leavening acids [111].

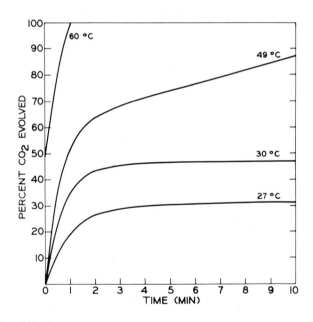

FIG. 10-2. Effect of temperature on the rate of carbon dioxide evolution from the reaction of $NaHCO_3$ and slow-acting sodium acid pyrophosphate. (Reprinted from Ref. [111], p. 201; courtesy of the AVI Publishing Co., Inc.)

TABLE 10-1

Some Properties of Common Leavening Acids[a]

Acid	Formula	Neutralizing value[b]	Relative reaction rate at room temperature[c]
Sodium aluminum sulfate	$Na_2SO_4 \cdot Al_2(SO_4)_3$	100	Slow
Calcium phosphate di-hydrate	$CaHPO_4 \cdot 2\ H_2O$	33	None
Monocalcium phosphate monohydrate	$Ca(HPO_4)_2 \cdot H_2O$	80	Fast
Sodium aluminum phos-phate-1-3-8	$NaH_{14}Al_3(PO_4)_8 \cdot 4\ H_2O$	100	Slow
Sodium acid pyrophosphate (slow type)	$Na_2H_2P_2O_7$	72	Slow
Potassium acid tartrate	$KHC_4H_4O_6$	50	Fast
Glucono-δ-lactone	$C_6H_{10}O_6$	55	Slow

[a]Refer to Stahl and Ellinger [111].
[b]In simple model systems; parts by weight of $NaHCO_3$ that will neutralize 100 parts by weight of the leavening acid.
[c]Rate of CO_2 evolution in the presence of $NaHCO_3$.

Baking "powders" account for a large part of the chemical leaveners used in both the home and in bakeries. These preparations include sodium bicarbonate, suitable leavening acids, and starch and other extenders. Federal standards for baking powder require the formula must yield at least 12% by weight of available carbon dioxide and most contain 26-30% by weight of sodium bicarbonate [84]. Traditional baking powders of the potassium acid tartrate type have been largely replaced by "double-acting" preparations. In addition to $NaHCO_3$ and starch, these baking powders usually contain calcium monophosphate monohydrate, $Ca(HPO_4)_2 \cdot H_2O$, which provides rapid action during the mixing stage, and sodium aluminum sulfate, $Na_2SO_4 \cdot Al_2(SO_4)_3$, which does not react appreciably until the temperature increases during baking.

The increase in convenience foods has stimulated sales of prepared baking mixes and refrigerated dough products. In white and yellow cake mixes, the most widely used leavening acid blend contains anhydrous calcium monophosphate, $Ca(HPO_4)_2$, and sodium aluminum phosphate, $NaH_{14}Al_3(PO_4)_8 \cdot 4\ H_2O$, while chocolate cake mixes usually contain anhydrous calcium monophosphate and sodium acid pyrophosphate ($Na_2H_2P_2O_7$) [111]. Typical blends of acids contain 10-20% fast-acting anhydrous monophosphate and 80-90% of the slower acting sodium aluminum phosphate or sodium acid pyrophosphate compounds. The leavening acids in prepared biscuit mixes usually consist of 30–50% anhydrous calcium monophosphate and 50–70% sodium aluminum phosphate or sodium acid pyrophosphate. The earliest self-rising flours and corn meal mixes contained calcium monophosphate monohydrate, $Ca(HPO_4)_2 \cdot H_2O$, but coated anhydrous calcium monophosphate and sodium aluminum phosphate are in common use today [111].

Refrigerated doughs for biscuit and roll products require limited initial carbon dioxide release during preparation and packaging and considerable gas release during baking. Formulations for biscuits usually contain from 1.0 to 1.5% sodium bicarbonate and from 1.4 to 2.0% slow-acting leavening acids, such as coated calcium monophosphate and sodium acid pyrophosphate based on total dough weight. The pyrophosphates are useful in dough because they can be manufactured with a wide range of reactivities. For example, pyrophosphatase in flour is capable of hydrolyzing sodium acid pyrophosphate (1)

$$
\begin{array}{ccc}
OH & & OH \\
| & & | \\
NaO-P-O-P-ONa \\
\Downarrow & & \Downarrow \\
O & & O
\end{array}
$$

(1)

to orthophosphates, and the reaction of sodium bicarbonate and pyrophosphate yields some trisodium monohydrogen pyrophosphate which also can be hydrolyzed to orthophosphates. This enzymic action leads to gas production that assists in sealing packages of refrigerated dough, but it can also lead to formation of large crystals of orthophosphates that may be mistaken for broken glass by the consumer.

III. BASES

Basic or alkaline substances are used in a variety of applications in foods and food processing. While the majority of applications involve buffering and pH adjustments, other functions include carbon dioxide evolution, enhancement of color and flavor, and chemical peeling. The role of carbonate and bicarbonate salts in carbon dioxide production during baking has been discussed previously.

Alkali treatments are imposed on several food products for the purpose of color and flavor improvement. Ripe olives are treated with solutions of sodium hydroxide (0.25-2.0%) to aid in removal of the bitter principal and to develop a darker color [83]. Pretzels are dipped in a solution of 1.25% sodium hydroxide at 85°-88°C (186°-190°F) prior to baking to alter proteins and starch so that the surface becomes smooth and deep brown during baking [84]. It is believed that the NaOH treatment used to prepare hominy and tortilla dough destroys disulfide bonds which are base labile [121]. Small amounts of sodium bicarbonate are used in the manufacture of peanut brittle candy to enhance sugar-amino browning and to provide, through release of carbon dioxide, a somewhat porous structure. Bases, usually sodium bicarbonate, are also used in cocoa processing for the production of dark (Dutch) chocolate. The elevated pH enhances sugar-amino browning reactions, resulting in a smoother, less acid and bitter chocolate flavor, a darker color, and a slightly improved solubility [69].

Food systems sometimes require adjustment to higher pH values to achieve more stable or more desirable characteristics. For example, alkaline salts, such as disodium phosphate, trisodium phosphate, and sodium citrate, are used in the preparation of processed cheese (3%) to increase the pH (5.7-6.3) and to aid in protein dispersion. The alkaline salts also interact with proteins in cheese to improve their emulsification and water-binding capacities [105].

Popular instant milk-gel puddings are prepared by combining dry mixes containing pregelatinized starch and cold milk and allowing them to stand for a short time at refrigerator temperatures. Alkaline salts, such as tetrasodium pyrophosphate ($Na_4P_2O_7$) and disodium phosphate (Na_2HPO_4), in the presence of calcium ions in milk cause milk proteins to gel in combination with the pregelatinized starch. The optimum pH for acceptable puddings falls between 7.5 and 8.0. Although some of the necessary alkalinity is contributed by alkaline phosphate salts, other alkalizing agents are often added to achieve the desired pH [34].

The addition of phosphates and citrates changes the salt balance in fluid milk products by forming complexes with proteins and ions of calcium and magnesium. The complex mechanism is incompletely understood, but depending on the type and concentration of salt added, the milk protein system can undergo stabilization, gelation, or destabilization [38,90].

Alkaline agents are used to neutralize excess acid in the production of such foods as cultured butter. Prior to churning, the cream is fermented by lactic acid bacteria so that it contains about 0.75% titratable acidity expressed as lactic acid [59]. Alkalis are then added to achieve a titratable acidity of approximately 0.25%. The reduction in acidity improves churning efficiency and retards the development of oxidative off flavors. Several materials, including sodium bicarbonate, $NaHCO_3$; sodium carbonate, Na_2CO_3; magnesium carbonate, $MgCO_3$; magnesium oxide, MgO; calcium hydroxide, $Ca(OH)_2$; and sodium hydroxide, NaOH, are utilized alone or in combination as neutralizers for foods. Solubility, foaming as a result of carbon dioxide release, and strength of the base influence the selection of the alkaline agent. The use of alkaline agents or bases in excessive amounts leads to soapy or "neutralizer" flavors, especially when substantial quantities of free fatty acids are present.

Strong bases are employed for peeling a number of fruits and vegetables. Exposure of the product to hot solutions (60°-82°C) of sodium hydroxide (about 3%) with subsequent mild abrasion effects peel removal with substantial reductions in plant waste water over other conventional peeling techniques. Differential solubilization of cell and tissue constituents (particularly soluble are the pectic substances in the middle lamella) provides the basis for caustic peeling processes [62].

IV. BUFFER SYSTEMS AND SALTS

A. Buffers and pH Control in Foods

Since most foods are complex materials of biological origin, they contain many substances that can participate in pH control and buffering systems. Included are proteins, organic acids, and weak inorganic acid phosphate salts. Lactic acid and phosphate salts along with proteins are important for pH control in animal tissue, while polycarboxylic acids, phosphate salts, and proteins are important in plant tissues. The buffering effects of amino acids and proteins and the influence of pH and salts on their functionalities are discussed in Chapter 5. In plants, buffering systems containing citric acid (lemons, tomatoes, rhubarb), malic acid (apples, tomatoes, lettuce), oxalic acid (rhubarb, lettuce) and tartaric acid (grapes, pineapple) are common and they usually function in conjunction with phosphate salts in maintaining pH control. Milk acts as a complex buffer because of its content of carbon dioxide, proteins, phosphate, citrate, and a number of minor constituents [65].

In situations where the pH must be altered, it is usually desirable to stabilize the pH at the desired level through a buffer system. This is accomplished naturally when lactic acid is produced in cheese and pickle fermentations. Also, in some instances where substantial amounts of acids are used in foods and beverages, it is desirable to reduce the sharpness of acid tastes and obtain smoother product flavors without inducing neutralization flavors. This usually can be accomplished by establishing a buffer system in which the salt of a weak organic acid is dominant. The common ion effect is the basis for obtaining pH control in these systems, and the system develops when the added salt contains an ion which is already present in an existing weak acid. The added salt immediately ionizes, resulting in repressed ionization of the acid with reduced acidity and a more stable pH. The effectiveness of a buffer depends on the concentration of the buffering substances. Since there is a pool of undissociated acid and dissociated salt, buffers resist changes in pH. For example, relatively large additions of a strong acid, such as hydrochloric acid, to an acetic acid-sodium acetate system causes hydrogen ions to react with the acetate-ion pool to form more slightly ionized acetic acid, and the pH remains relatively stable. In a similar manner, an addition of sodium hydroxide yields a reaction of hydroxyl ions with hydrogen ions to form undissociated water molecules.

Titration of buffered systems and resulting titration curves (e.g., pH vs volume of base added) reveal their resistance to pH change. If a weak acid buffer is titrated with a base, there is a gradual but steady increase in the pH as the system approaches neutralization; i.e., the change in pH per milliliter of added base is small. Weak acids are only slightly dissociated at the beginning of the titration. However, the addition of hydroxyl ion shifts the equilibrium to the dissociated species and eventually the buffer is overcome.

In general, for an acid HA in equilibrium with ions H^+ and A^-, Eq. (10-7), the equilibrium is expressed as in Eq. (10-8):

$$HA \rightleftharpoons H^+ + A^- \tag{10-7}$$

$$K_a^1 = \frac{[H^+][A^-]}{[HA]} \tag{10-8}$$

The constant K_a^1 is the apparent dissociation constant and is characteristic of individual acids. The apparent dissociation constant, K_a^1, becomes equal to the hydrogen ion concentration $[H^+]$ when the anion concentration $[A^-]$ becomes equal to the concentration of undissociated acid $[HA]$. This situation gives rise to an inflection point on a titration curve, and the pH corresponding to this point is referred to as the pK_a^1 of the acid. Therefore, for a weak acid, pH is equal to pK_a^1 when the concentrations of the acid and conjugate base are equal, Eq. (10-9).

$$pH = pK_a^1 = -\log_{10} [H^+] \tag{10-9}$$

A convenient method for calculating the approximate pH of a buffer mixture, given the pK_a^1 of the acid, is provided by Eq. (10-12). This equation is arrived at by first solving Eq. (10-8) for $[H^+]$ to yield Eq. (10-10).

$$[H^+] = K_a^1 \frac{[HA]}{[A^-]} = K_a^1 \frac{[acid]}{[salt]} \tag{10-10}$$

Since the salt in solution is almost completely dissociated, it is assumed equal to the concentration of the conjugate base $[A^-]$. The negative logarithms of the terms yield Eq. (10-11). By substituting pH for $-\log [H^+]$ and pK_a^1 for $-\log K_a^1$, Eq. (10-12) is obtained. The pH of a buffer system derived from any weak acid which dissociates to H^+ and A^- can be calculated by using Eq. (10-12).

$$-\log [H^+] = -\log K_a^1 - \log \frac{[acid]}{[salt]} \tag{10-11}$$

$$pH = pK_a^1 + \log \frac{[acid]}{[salt]} = pK_a^1 + \log \frac{[A^-]}{[HA]} \tag{10-12}$$

In calculating the pH values of buffer solutions, it is important to recognize that the apparent dissociation constant K_a^1 differs from K_a, the true dissociation constant. However, for any buffer, the value of K_a^1 remains constant as the pH is varied, provided the total ionic strength of the solution remains unchanged [126]. The sodium salts of gluconic, acetic, citric, and phosphoric acids are commonly used for pH control and tartness modification in the food industry. The citrates are usually preferred over phosphates for tartness modification since they yield smoother sour flavors [43]. When low-sodium products are required, potassium buffer salts may be substituted for sodium salts. In general, calcium salts are not used because of their limited solubilities and incompatibilities with other components in the system. The effective buffering ranges for combinations of common acids and salts are pH 2.1–4.7 for citric acid–sodium citrate, pH 3.6–5.6 for acetic acid–sodium acetate, and pH 2.0–3.0, 5.5–7.5, and 10–12, respectively, for the three ortho- and pyrophosphate anions.

B. Salts in Processed Dairy Foods

Salts are used extensively in processed cheese to promote a uniform, smooth texture. These salts are sometimes considered emulsifying agents in this role. Salts used for cheese processing include mono-, di-, and trisodium phosphate; dipotassium phosphate; sodium hexametaphosphate; sodium acid pyrophosphate; tetrasodium pyrophosphate; sodium aluminum phosphate; sodium citrate; calcium citrate; sodium tartrate; and sodium potassium tartrate. Although the emulsifying mechanism remains obscure, it has been suggested that salt added to processed cheese binds calcium of the p-casein complex, with a consequent rearrangement and exposure of solubilizing groups in the protein. It also has been suggested that the salt emulsifiers provide anions that form bridges between protein molecules and thereby contribute to cheese structure [105].

The addition of certain phosphates, such as trisodium phosphate, to evaporated milk prevents separation of the butterfat and aqueous phases. The amount required varies with the season of the year and the source of milk. Concentrated milk that is sterilized by a high-temperature, short-time method frequently gels upon storage. The addition of polyphosphates, such as sodium hexametaphosphate and sodium tripolyphosphate, prevents gel formation through an unresolved mechanism which involves complexing of calcium and magnesium by phosphates [90].

C. Phosphates and Water Binding in Animal Tissues

The addition of certain phosphates increases the water-holding capacity of raw and cooked meats, and these phosphates are used in the production of sausages, in the curing of ham, and to decrease drip losses in poultry and seafoods. Sodium tripolyphosphate ($Na_5P_3O_{10}$) is the most commonly added phosphate in processed meat, poultry, and seafoods. It is often used in blends with sodium hexametaphosphate [$(NaPO_3)_n$, n = 10–15] to increase tolerance to calcium ions that exist in brines used in meat curing. Ortho- and pyrophosphates often precipitate if used in salt brines containing substantial amounts of calcium.

The mechanism by which alkaline phosphates and polyphosphates enhance meat hydration is not clearly understood despite extensive studies. The action may involve the influence of pH changes (Chapter 5), ionic strength effects, and specific phosphate anion interactions with divalent cations and myofibrillar proteins [51]. Many believe that calcium complexing and a resulting loosening of the tissue structure is one major function of polyphosphates. It is also believed that binding of polyphosphate anions and simultaneous cleavage of crosslinkages between actin and myosin results in increased electrostatic repulsion between peptide chains and a swelling of the system. If exterior water is available, it then can be taken up in an immobilized state within the loosened protein network. Furthermore, because the ionic strength has been increased, the interaction between proteins is perhaps reduced to a point where part of the myofibrillar proteins form a colloidal solution. In comminuted meat products, such as bologna and sausage, the addition of sodium chloride (2.5–4.0%) and polyphosphate (0.35–0.5%) contributes to a more stable emulsion and, after cooking, to a cohesive network of coagulated proteins.

If the phosphate-induced solubilization occurs primarily on the surface of tissues, as is the case with polyphosphate-dipped (6–12% solution with 0.35–0.5% retention) fish fillets, shellfish, and poultry, a layer of coagulated protein is formed during cooking and this aids moisture retention [79].

V. CHELATING AGENTS

Chelating agents or sequestrants play a significant role in food stabilization through reactions with metallic and alkaline earth ions to form complexes that alter the properties and effects of the ions in foods. Many of the chelating agents employed in the food industry are natural substances, such as polycarboxylic acids (citric, malic, tartaric, oxalic, and succinic), polyphosphoric acids (adenosine triphosphate and pyrophosphate), and macromolecules (porphyrins, proteins). Many metals exist in a naturally chelated state. Examples include magnesium in chlorophyll;

copper, zinc, and manganese in various enzymes; iron in proteins, such as ferritin; and iron in the porphyrin ring of hemoglobin. When these ions are released by hydrolytic or other degradative reactions, they are free to participate in reactions that lead to discoloration, oxidative rancidity, turbidity, and flavor changes in foods. Chelating agents are sometimes added to complex these metal ions and thereby stabilize the foods.

Any molecule or ion with an unshared electron pair can coordinate or complex with metal ions. Therefore, compounds containing two or more functional groups, such as -OH, -SH, -COOH, $-PO_3H_2$, C=O, $-NR_2$, -S-, and -O-, in proper geometrical relation to each other can chelate metals in a favorable physical environment. Citric acid and its derivatives, various phosphates, and salts of ethylenediamine tetraacetic acid (EDTA) are the most popular chelating agents used in foods. Usually the ability of a chelating agent (ligand) to form a five- or six-membered ring with a metal is necessary for stable chelation. For example, EDTA forms chelates of high stability with calcium because of an initial coordination with the electron pairs of its nitrogen atoms and with the free electron pairs of the anionic oxygen atoms of two of the four carboxyl groups (Eq. 10-13).

$$Ca^{2+} + \quad \begin{array}{c} ^-OOCCH_2 \quad\quad CH_2COO^- \\ NCH_2CH_2N \\ ^-OOCCH_2 \quad\quad CH_2COO^- \end{array} \rightleftharpoons \begin{array}{c} ^-OOCCH_2 \; CH_2 —— CH_2 \; CH_2COO^- \\ N \quad\quad\quad\quad N \\ H_2C \quad Ca \quad CH_2 \\ | \quad\quad / \backslash \quad\quad | \\ OC \_\_ O \; O \_\_ CO \end{array}$$

EDTA   EDTA-Ca^{2+} complex

$$(10\text{-}13)$$

The spatial configuration of the calcium–EDTA complex is such that it allows additional coordination of the calcium with the free electron pairs of the anionic oxygen atoms of the remaining two carboxyl groups, and this results in an extremely stable complex utilizing all six electron donor groups [12].

In addition to steric and electronic considerations, such factors as pH influence the formation of metal chelates. The nonionized carboxylic acid group is not an efficient donor group but the carboxylate ion functions effectively. Judicious raising of the pH allows dissociation of the carboxyl group and enhances chelating efficiency. In some instances hydroxyl ions compete for metal ions and reduce the effectiveness of chelating agents. Metal ions exist in solution as hydrated complexes (metal·H_2OM^+), and the rate at which these complexes are disrupted influences the rate which they can be complexed with chelating agents. The relative efficiency of chelating agents for different ions can be determined from stability or equilibrium constants (K = [metal·chelating agent]/[metal] [chelating agent]). For example, for calcium the stability constant (expressed as log k) is 10.7 with EDTA, 5.0 with pyrophosphate, and 3.5 with citric acid [41]. As the stability constant (k) increases, more of the metal is complexed, leaving less metal in cation form (i.e., the metal in the complex is more tightly bound).

Chelating agents are not antioxidants in the sense that they arrest oxidation by chain termination or serve as oxygen scavengers. They are, however, valuable antioxidant synergists since they remove metal ions which catalyze oxidation (Chapter 4). When a chelating agent is selected for an antioxidant synergist role, its solubility must be considered. Citric acid and citrate esters (20-200 ppm) in propylene glycol solution are solubilized by fats and oils and thus are effective synergists in all-lipid systems [106]. In contrast, Na_2EDTA and Na_2CA-EDTA dissolve to only a limited extent and are not effective in pure fat systems. The EDTA salts (to 500 ppm), however, are very effective antioxidants in emulsion systems, such as salad dressings, mayonnaise, and margarine, because they can function in the aqueous phase.

Polyphosphates and EDTA are used in canned seafoods to prevent the formation of glassy crystals of struvite or magnesium ammonium phosphate ($MgNH_4PO_4 \cdot 6 H_2O$). Seafoods contain substantial amounts of magnesium ions which sometimes react with ammonium phosphate during storage to give crystals that may be mistaken as glass contamination. Chelating agents complex magnesium and minimize struvite formation [87]. Chelating agents also can be used to complex iron, copper, and zinc in seafoods to prevent reactions, particularly with sulfides, that lead to product discoloration (Chapter 5).

The addition of chelating agents to vegetables prior to blanching can inhibit metal-induced discolorations and can remove calcium from pectic substances in cell walls and thereby promote tenderness.

While citric and phosphoric acids are employed as acidulants in soft drink beverages, they also chelate metals which otherwise may promote oxidation of flavor compounds, such as terpenes, and catalyze discoloration reactions. Chelating agents also stabilize fermented malt beverages by complexing copper. Free copper catalyzes oxidation of polyphenolic compounds which subsequently interact with proteins to form permanent hazes or turbidity [58].

The extremely efficient chelating abilities of some agents, notably EDTA, has caused speculation that excessive usage in foods may lead to the depletion of calcium and other minerals in the body. To deal with this concern, levels and applications are regulated, and calcium is added to food systems through the use of the Na_2Ca salt of EDTA rather than the all sodium (Na, Na_2, Na_3, or Na_4 EDTA) or acid forms.

VI. STABILIZERS AND THICKENERS

Many hydrocolloid materials are widely used in foods for their unique textural, structural, and functional characteristics, e.g., they provide stabilization for emulsions, suspensions, and foams and general thickening properties. Most of these materials, which are sometimes classes as gums, are derived from natural sources, although some are chemically modified to achieve desired characteristics. Many stabilizers and thickeners are polysaccharides, such as gum arabic, guar gum, carboxymethylcellulose, carrageenan, agar, starch, and pectin. The chemistry of these and related carbohydrates is discussed in Chapter 3. Gelatin, a protein derived from collagen, is one of the few noncarbohydrate stabilizers used extensively and it is discussed in Chapters 5 and 12. Since all effective stabilizers and thickeners are hydrophilic and are dispersed in solution as colloids they are often referred to as hydrocolloids. General properties of useful hydrocolloids include significant solubility in water, a capability to increase viscosity, and in some cases an ability to form gels. Some specific functions of hydrocolloids include improvement and stabilization of texture, inhibition of crystallization (sugar, ice), stabilization of emulsions and foams, improvement (reduced stickiness) of icings on baked goods, and encapsulation of flavors [70,123,124]. Hydrocolloids are generally used at concentrations of about 2% or less because many exhibit limited dispersibility, and the desired functionality is provided at these levels. The efficacy of hydrocolloids in many applications is directly dependent on their ability to increase viscosity. For example, this is the mechanisms by which hydrocolloids stabilize oil in water emulsions. They cannot function as true emulsifiers since they lack the necessary combination of strong hydrophilic and lipophilic properties.

VII. POLYHYDRIC ALCOHOLS IN FOODS

Polyhydric alcohols are carbohydrate compounds that contain only hydroxyl groups as functional groups (Chapter 3), and as a result they are generally water-soluble, hygroscopic materials that exhibit moderate viscosities at high concentrations in water. While the number of available polyhydric alcohols is substantial, only a few are of importance in food applications, and these include propylene glycol, $CH_2OH-CHOH-CH_3$; glycerol, $CH_2OH-CHOH-CH_2OH$; and sorbitol and mannitol (both are epimers of $CH_2OH-CHOH-CHOH-CHOH-CHOH-CH_2OH$). With a few exceptions, such as propylene glycol and xylitol, most polyhydric alcohols occur naturally, although they usually are not noted for food functional roles in these situations. For example, free glycerol is known to exist in wine and beer as a result of fermentation, and sorbitol occurs in fruits, such as pears, apples, and prunes. The polyhydroxy structures of these compounds result in water-binding properties that have been exploited in foods. Specific functions of polyhydric alcohols include control of viscosity and texture, bulking, retention of moisture, reduction of water activity, control of crystallization, improvement or retention of softness, improvement of rehydration properties of dehydrated foods, and solubilization of flavor compounds [32,48,50,61].

Sugars and polyhydric alcohols are similar, except that sugars contain aldo or keto groups (free or bound) that adversely affect their chemical stability, especially at high temperatures. Many applications of polyhydric alcohols in foods rely on concurrent contributions of functional properties from sugars, proteins, starches, and gums. Polyhydric alcohols are sweet but less so than sucrose. Short-chain members are slightly bitter at high concentrations. The taste of polyhydric alcohols is generally of limited concern when the amount added is low (2-10%). However, when used at high levels, such as in intermediate moisture foods (glycerol, 25%) and dietary sugar-free candies (sorbitol, 40%), these substances contribute greatly to product taste.

Recently, attention has been given to the development of polymeric forms of polyhydric alcohols for food applications. While ethylene glycol (CH_2OH-CH_2OH) is toxic, polyethylene glycol 6,000 is allowed in some food coating and plasticizing applications. Polyglycerol, $CH_2OH-CHOH-CH_2-(O-CH_2-CHOH-CH_2)_n-O-CH_2-CHOH-CH_2OH$, formed from glycerol through an alkaline-catalyzed polymerization, exhibits useful properties. It can be further modified by esterification with fatty acids to yield materials with lipidlike characteristics [4]. These polyglycerol materials have been approved for food use because the hydrolysis products, glycerol and fatty acids, are metabolized normally.

Intermediate moisture (IM) foods deserve some discussion since polyhydric alcohols make an important contribution to the stability of some of these products. IM foods contain substantial moisture (15-30%) yet are shelf stable to microbiological deterioration without refrigeration. Several familiar foods, including dried fruits, jams, jellies, marshmallows, fruit cake, and jerky, owe their stability to IM characteristics. Some of these items may be rehydrated prior to consumption, but all possess a plastic texture and can be consumed directly. While moist shelf-stable pet foods have found ready acceptance in recent years, new forms of intermediate moisture foods for human consumption have not as yet become popular. Nevertheless, meat, vegetable, fruit, and combination prepared dishes are under development and may eventually become important forms of preserved foods.

Most IM foods possess water activities of 0.70-0.85 and those containing humectants contain moisture contents of about 20 g of water per 100 g of solids (83% H_2O by weight). If IM foods with a water activity of about 0.85 water activity are prepared by desorption, they are still susceptible to attack by molds and yeasts. To overcome this problem, a heat process can be given the ingredients during preparation along with the addition of an antimycotic agent, such as sorbic acid. However, in view of recent findings about adsorptive procedures for preparing IM foods, it should be possible to prepare stable intermediate moisture foods without the need for chemical growth inhibitors [71].

To obtain the desired water activity it is usually necessary to add a humectant which binds water and maintains a soft palatable texture. Relatively few substances, including glycerol, sucrose, glucose, propylene glycol, and sodium chloride, are sufficiently effective in lowering the water activity to be of value in preparing IM foods [8,9,68]. Figure 10-3 illustrates the effectiveness of the polyhydric alcohol, glycerol, on the water activity of a cellulose model system. Note that in a 10% glycerol system a water activity of 0.9 corresponds to a moisture content of only 25 g H_2O per 100 g solids, whereas the same water activity in a 40% glycerol system corresponds to a moisture content of 75 g H_2O per 100 g solids. The principal flavor criticism for glycerol systems is a sweet-bitter sensation. This drawback also exists for sucrose and glucose applications. However, many foods show promise when combinations of glycerol, salt, propylene glycol, and sucrose are employed.

VIII. ANTICAKING AGENTS

Several conditioning agents are used to maintain free-flowing characteristics of granular and powdered forms of foods that are hygroscopic in nature. In general, these materials function by readily absorbing excess moisture, by coating particles to impart a degree of water repellency, and/or by providing an insoluble particulate diluent to the mixture. Calcium silicate ($Ca SiO_3 \cdot X H_2O$) is used to prevent caking in baking powder (to 5%), table salts (to 2%), and in other foods and food ingredients. Finely divided calcium silicate absorbs liquids in amounts up to two and one-half times its weight and still remains free flowing. In addition to absorbing water, calcium silicate also effectively absorbs oils and other nonpolar organic compounds. This characteristic makes it useful in complex powdered mixes and in certain spices which contain free essential oils [112].

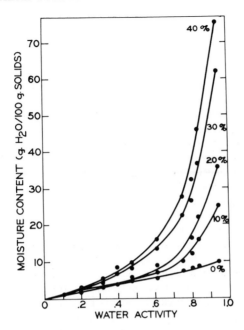

FIG. 10-3. Moisture sorption isotherms of cellulose model systems for various amounts of glycerol at 37°C. (Reprinted from Ref. [72], p. 86; courtesy of The American Oil Chemists Society.)

Food-grade calcium and magnesium salts of long-chain fatty acids are derived from tallow and are used as conditioning agents for dehydrated vegetable products, salt, onion and garlic salt, and a variety of other food ingredients and mixes in powder form. Calcium stearate is often added to powdered foods to prevent agglomeration, to promote free flow during processing, and to insure freedom from caking during the shelf life of the finished product. Calcium stearate is essentially insoluble in water but adheres well to particles and provides a partial water repellent coating for the particles. Commercial stearate powders have a high bulk density (about 20 lb/cu ft) and possess large surface areas that make their use as conditioners (0.5-2.5%) reasonably economical. Calcium stearate is also used as a release lubricant (1%) in the manufacture of pressed tablet-form candy [97].

Other anticaking agents employed in the food industry include sodium silicoaluminate, tricalcium phosphate, magnesium silicate, and magnesium carbonate [21]. These materials are essentially insoluble in water and exhibit variable abilities to absorb moisture. Their use levels are similar to those for other anticaking agents (e.g., about 1% sodium silicoaluminate is used in powdered sugar). Anticaking agents are either metabolized (stearates) or exhibit no toxic actions at levels employed in food [40].

IX. FIRMING AGENTS

Thermal processing or freezing of plant tissues usually causes softening because
the cellular structure is modified. Stability and integrity of these tissues are dependent on maintenance of intact cells and firm molecular bonding between constituents of cell walls. The pectic substances (Chapters 3 and 15) are extensively
involved in structure stabilization through crosslinking of their free carboxyl groups
with polyvalent cations. Although considerable amounts of polyvalent cations are
naturally present, calcium salts (0.1-0.25% as calcium) are frequently added.
This increases firmness through enhanced crosslinking and the formation of relatively insoluble calcium pectinate and pectate. These stabilized structures support the tissue mass, and integrity is maintained even through heat processing.
Fruits, including tomatoes, berries, and apple slices, are commonly firmed by
adding one or more calcium salts prior to canning or freezing. The most commonly used salts include calcium chloride, calcium citrate, calcium sulfate, calcium
lactate, and monocalcium phosphate. Most calcium salts are sparingly soluble
and some contribute a bitter flavor [62].

Acidic alum salts, sodium aluminum sulfate, $NaAl(SO_4)_2 \cdot 12\ H_2O$; potassium
aluminum sulfate; ammonium aluminum sulfate; and aluminum sulfate, $Al_2(SO_4)_3 \cdot$
$18\ H_2O$, are added to cucumber pickle products prepared from fermented, salt-
brined pickles to make the products more crisp and firm [35]. The trivalent
aluminum ion is believed to be involved in the crisping process through the formation of complexes with pectin substances [83]. However, recent investigations
have demonstrated that aluminum sulfate has an opposite softening effect on fresh-
pack or pasteurized pickles and should not be included in these products [35]. The
reasons for the softening are not understood, but the presence of aluminum sulfate
counteracts the firming effects provided by pH adjustment to near 3.8 with acetic
or lactic acids.

The firmness and texture of some vegetables and fruits can be manipulated during processing without the use of direct additives. For example, the enzyme pectin
methylesterase is activated during low-temperature blanching (70-82 °C for 3-
15 min) rather than inactivated as is the case during usual blanching (88-100 °C
for 3 min). The degree of firmness produced following low-temperature blanching
can be controlled by the holding time prior to retorting [83,117,118]. Pectin
methylesterase hydrolyzes esterified methanol (sometimes referred to as methoxyl
groups) from carboxyl groups on pectin to yield pectinic and pectic acids. Pectin
lacks substantial numbers of free carboxyl groups, rendering it water soluble and
free to migrate from the cell wall. In contrast, pectinic acid and pectic acid
possess large numbers of free carboxyl groups and they are relatively insoluble,
especially in the presence of calcium ions. As a result they remain in the cell wall
during processing and produce firm textures [109]. Firming effects through activation of pectin methyl esterase have been observed for snap beans, potatoes,
cauliflower, and sour cherries. Addition of calcium ions in conjunction with enzyme
activation leads to additive firming effects.

X. CLARIFYING AGENTS

In beer, wine, and many fruit juices the formation of hazes or sediments and oxidative deterioration are long-standing problems. Natural phenolic substances are

involved in these phenomena. The chemistry of this important group, including anthocyanins, flavonoids, leucoanthocyanogens and tannins, is discussed in Chapter 8. Proteins and pectin substances participate with polyphenols in the formation of haze-forming colloids. Specific enzymes have been utilized to partially hydrolyze high molecular weight proteins and pectic substances (Chapter 6) and thereby reduce the tendency toward haze formation. However, in some instances excess enzymic activity can adversely affect other properties, such as desirable foam formation in beer.

An important means of manipulating polyphenolic composition to control both its desirable and undesirable effects is to use various clarifying (fining) agents and adsorbants. Preformed haze can be at least partially removed by filter aids, such as diatomaceous earth. Many of the clarifying agents which have been used affect the polyphenolic content more or less incidentally without having significant selectivity for phenolic compounds. Adsorption is usually maximal when solubility of the adsorbate is minimal, and suspended or nearly insoluble materials, such as a tannin-protein complexes, tend to collect at any interface. As the activity of the adsorbent increases, the less soluble substances still tend to be adsorbed preferentially but more soluble compounds are also adsorbed.

Bentonite, a montmorillonite clay, is representative of many similar and moderately effective minerals which have been employed as clarifying agents. Montmorillonite is a complex hydrated aluminum silicate with exchangeable cations, frequently sodium ions. In aqueous suspension bentonite behaves as small platelets of insoluble silicate. The bentonite platelets have a negative charge and a very high surface area of about 750 m^2/g. Bentonite is a rather selective adsorbant for protein, and evidently this adsorption results from an attraction between the positive charges of the protein and the negative charges of the silicate. A particle of bentonite covered with adsorbed protein will adsorb some phenolic tannins on or along with the protein [108]. Bentonite is used as a clarifying or fining agent for wines to prevent protein precipitation. Doses of the order of a few pounds per 1,000 gal usually reduce the protein content of wine from 50-100 mg/liter to a stable level of less than 10 mg/liter. Bentonite rapidly forms a heavy compact sediment and is often employed in conjunction with final filtration to remove precipiated colloids.

The important clarifying agents which have a selective affinity for tannins, leucoanthocyanogens, and other polyphenols include proteins and certain synthetic resins, such as the polyamides and polyvinylpyrrolidone (PVP). Gelatin and isinglass (obtained from the swim bladder of fish) are the proteins most commonly used to clarify beverages. It appears that the most important, although probably not the only, linkage between tannins and proteins are the hydrogen bonds between phenolic hydroxyl groups and amide bonds in proteins. The addition of small amounts of gelatin (1.5-6.0 oz per 100 gal) to apple juice causes aggregation and precipitation of a gelatin-tannin complex which on settling enmeshes and removes other suspended solids. The exact amount of gelatin for each use must be determined at the time of processing. Juices containing low levels of polyphenolics are supplemented with added tannin or tannic acid (0.005-0.01%) to facilitate flocculation of the gelatin [116].

At low concentrations, gelatin and other soluble clarifying agents can act as protective colloids; at higher concentrations they can cause precipitation and at still higher concentrations they can again fail to cause precipitation. Hydrogen bonding between the colloidal clarifying agents and water accounts for their solubilities. Molecules of the clarifying agent and polyphenol can combine in different proportions to either neutralize or enhance the hydration and solubility of a given colloidal particle. The most nearly complete disruption of H bonding between water and either the protein or the polyphenol gives the most complete precipitation. This can be expected to occur when the amount of dissolved clarifying agent roughly equals the weight of the tannin being removed.

The synthetic resins (polyamides and PVP) have found applications especially in the stabilization of wines to prevent browning in white wines [13] and to prevent hazes in beer [26]. These polymers are available in both soluble and insoluble forms, but requirements for little or no residual polymer in beverages have stimulated use of the high molecular weight crosslinked formed that are insoluble. The synthetic resins have been particularly useful in the brewing industry where reversible refrigeration–induced haze (chill haze) and permanent haze (that which is associated with the development of oxidized flavors) are serious problems. These hazes are caused by formation of complexes between native proteins and leucoanthocyanogens from malted barley. Excessive removal of proteins leads to defective foam character, but the selective removal of polyphenols extends the stability of beer. Initial applications have involved polyamides (Nylon 66), but greater efficiency has been achieved through the use of crosslinked polyvinylpyrrolidone (2). Treatment with 3–5 lb of insoluble PVP per 100 barrels of beer provides control of chill haze and improves storage stability [26,86]. PVP is added after fermentation and prior to filtration and it rapidly adsorbs polyphenols. Just as bentonite removes some tannins along with preferentially adsorbed protein, selective tannin adsorbents remove some proteins along with the phenolics.

(2)

In addition to the adsorbants already discussed, activated charcoal and other materials have been employed. Activated charcoal is quite reactive but it adsorbs appreciable amounts of smaller molecules (flavors, pigments) along with the larger compounds that contribute to haze formation. Tannic acid (tannin) is used to precipitate proteins, but its presence can potentially lead to the undesirable effects described previously. Other insoluble proteins (keratin, casein, and zein) and soluble proteins (sodium caseinate, egg albumen, and serum albumin) also have selective adsorptive capacities for polyphenols, but they have not been extensively employed.

XI. FLOUR BLEACHING AGENTS AND BREAD IMPROVERS

Freshly milled wheat flour has a pale yellow tint and yields a sticky dough that does not handle or bake well. When the flour is stored, it slowly becomes white and undergoes an aging or maturing process that improves its baking qualities. It is a usual practice to employ chemical treatments to accelerate these natural processes and to use other additives to enhance yeast leavening activity and to retard onset of staling.

Flour bleaching involves primarily the oxidation of carotenoid pigments. This results in degradation of the conjugated double-bond system of carotenoids to a less conjugated colorless system. The dough-improving action of oxidizing agents is believed to involve the oxidation of sulfhydryl groups in gluten proteins. Oxidizing agents employed may participate in bleaching only, in both bleaching and dough improving, or in dough improving only [52]. One commonly used flour bleaching agent, benzoyl peroxide, $(C_6H_5CO)_2O_2$, exhibits only a bleaching or decolorizing action but does not influence baking properties. Materials that act both as bleaching and improving agents include chlorine gas, Cl_2, chlorine dioxide, ClO_2; nitrosyl chloride, NOCl; and oxides of nitrogen (nitrogen dioxide, NO_2, and nitrogen tetroxide, N_2O_4). These oxidizing agents are gaseous and exert their action immediately upon contact with flour. Oxidizing agents that serve primarily as dough improvers exert their action during the dough stages rather than in the flour. Included in this group are potassium bromate, $KBrO_3$; potassium iodate, KIO_3; calcium iodate, $Ca(IO_3)_2$; and calcium peroxide, CaO_2.

Benzoyl peroxide is usually added to flour (0.025-0.075%) at the mill. It is a powder and is usually added along with carrier and stabilizing agents, such as calcium sulfate, magnesium carbonate, dicalcium phosphate, calcium carbonate, and sodium aluminum phosphate. Benzoyl peroxide is a free-radical initiator (see Chapter 4) and it requires several hours after addition to decompose into available free radicals for initiation of carotenoid oxidation [62].

The gaseous agents for oxidizing flour show variable bleaching efficiencies but effectively improve baking qualities of suitable flours. Treatment with chlorine dioxide slightly improves flour color but gives flour with improved dough handling properties. Chlorine gas, often containing a small amount of nitrosyl chloride, is used extensively as a bleach and improver for soft wheat cake flour. Hydrochloric acid is formed from oxidation reactions of chlorine and the resulting slightly lowered pH values lead to improved cake baking properties. Nitrogen tetroxide (N_2O_4) and other oxides of nitrogen, produced by passing air through an intense electric arc, are only moderately effective bleaching agents but they produce good baking qualities in treated flours [84].

Oxidizing agents that are utilized primarily for dough improvement may be added to flour (10-40 ppm) at the mill. They are, however, often incorporated into a dough conditioner mix containing a number of inorganic salts and then added at the bakery. Potassium bromate, an oxidizing agent used extensively to improve doughs, remains unreactive until yeast fermentation lowers the pH of the dough sufficiently to activate it. As a result it acts rather late in the process and causes increased loaf volume, improved loaf symmetry, and improved crumb and texture characteristics.

Early investigators proposed that the improved baking qualities resulting from treatment with oxidizing agents were attributable to inhibition of proteolytic enzymes present in flour [67]. However, this theory has been replaced by the view that dough improvers oxidize sulfhydryl groups (-SH) in the proteins of gluten to yield an increased number of intermolecular disulfide bonds (-S-S-). This cross-linking allows gluten proteins to form a thin, tenacious network of protein films that comprise the vesicles for leavening. The result is a tougher, drier, more extensible dough that gives rise to improved characteristics in the finished products. Excessive treatments of flour with oxidizing agents must be avoided since they lead to inferior products with gray crumb color, irregular grain, and reduced loaf volume [84].

Inorganic salts incorporated into dough conditioners include ammonium chloride, NH_4Cl; ammonium sulfate, $(NH_4)_2SO_4$; calcium sulfate, $CaSO_4$; ammonium phosphate, $(NH_4)_3PO_4$; and calcium phosphate, $CaHPO_4$. They are added to doughs to facilitate growth of yeast and to aid in control of pH. The principal contribution of ammonium salts is to provide a ready source of nitrogen for yeast growth. The phosphate salts improve dough apparently by buffering the pH at a slightly lower value than normal. This is especially important when water supplies are alkaline.

Other types of materials are also used as dough improvers in the baking industry. Calcium stearyl-2-lactylate $[(C_{17}H_{35}COOC(CH_3)HCOOC(CH_3)HCOO)_2Ca]$ and similar emulsifying agents are used at low levels (to 0.5%) to improve mixing qualities of dough and to promote increased loaf volume [115]. Hydrocolloid gums have been used in the baking industry to improve the water-holding capacity of doughs and to modify the functional properties of doughs and baked products [45]. Carrageenan, carboxymethylcellulose, locust bean gum, and methylcellulose are among the more useful hydrocolloids in baking applications. Methylcellulose and carboxymethylcellulose have been found to retard retrogradation and staling in bread, and they also retard migration of moisture to the product surface during subsequent storage. Carrageenan (0.1%) softens the crumb texture of sweet dough products. Several hydrocolloids (e.g., carboxymethylcellulose at 0.25%) can be incorporated into doughnut mixes to significantly decrease the amount of fat absorbed during frying. This benefit apparently arises because of improvements in the dough and because a more effective hydrated barrier is established on the surface of the doughnuts [70].

XII. ANTIOXIDANTS

Oxidation reactions occur when electrons are removed from an atom or group of atoms, and for each reaction there is a corresponding reduction reaction that involves the addition of electrons to an atom or a group of atoms. Oxidation reactions may or may not involve the addition of oxygen atoms or the removal of hydrogen atoms from the substance being oxidized. Oxidation-reduction reactions are common in biological systems and also are common in foods. While some oxidation reactions are beneficial in foods, others can lead to detrimental effects, including oxidative degradation of vitamins (Chapter 7), pigments (Chapter 8), and lipids (Chapter 4), with loss of nutritional value and development of off flavors. Control of undesirable oxidation reactions in foods is usually achieved by employing processing and packaging techniques that exclude oxygen and by adding appropriate chemical agents.

Prior to the development of specific chemical technology for the control of free-radical mediated lipid oxidation, the term "antioxidant" was applied to all substances that inhibited oxidation reactions regardless of the mechanism. For example, ascorbic acid was considered an antioxidant and was employed to prevent enzymic browning of cut surfaces of fruits and vegetables (Chapter 6). In this application ascorbic acid functions as a reducing agent by transferring hydrogen atoms back to quinones that are formed by enzymic oxidation of phenolic compounds. In closed systems ascorbic acid reacts readily with oxygen (Chapter 7) and thereby serves as an oxygen scavenger [6]. Likewise, sulfurous acid and sulfites are readily oxidized in food systems to sulfonates and sulfate and thereby function as effective antioxidants in such foods as dried fruits [64].

More recently the term "food antioxidants" has been applied to those compounds that interrupt the free-radical chain reaction involved in lipid oxidation (Chapter 4); however, the term should not be used in such a narrow sense. The most commonly employed food antioxidants are phenolic substances. Antioxidants often exhibit variable degrees of efficiency in protecting food systems, and combinations often provide greater overall protection that can be accounted for through the simple additive effects of each [114]. Thus mixed antioxidants sometimes have a synergistic action, the mechanisms for which are still largely unresolved. It has been proposed, however, that ascorbic acid can regenerate phenolic antioxidants by supplying hydrogen atoms to phenoxy radicals that form when the antioxidants yield hydrogen atoms to the lipid oxidation chain reaction [6]. In order to achieve this action in lipids, ascorbic acid must be made less polar so it can dissolve in fats. This is done by esterification to fatty acids to form such compounds as ascorbyl palmitate.

The presence of metallic ions, particularly copper and iron, promotes lipid oxidation through a catalytic action [60]. These prooxidants are frequently inactivated by adding chelating agents, such as citric acid or EDTA. In this role chelating agents are also referred to as synergists since they greatly enhance the action of the phenolic antioxidants. However, they are ineffective as antioxidants when employed alone.

Many naturally occurring substances possess antioxidant capabilities, and the tocopherols are noted examples (Chapter 4). Gossypol, which occurs naturally in cottonseed, is also an antioxidant but it has toxic properties (Chapter 11). Other naturally occurring antioxidants are coniferyl alcohol (found in plants) and guiaconic and guiacic acid (from gum guaiac) [92,112]. All of these are structurally related to butylated hydroxyanisole (BHA), butylated hydroxytoluene (BHT), propyl gallate, and di-t-butylhydroquinone (TBHQ), which are synthetic phenolic antioxidants currently approved for use in foods. Nordihydroguairetic acid, a compound related to some of the constituents of gum guaiac, is an effective antioxidant but its use directly in foods has been suspended because of toxicological effects. All of these phenolic substances serve as oxidation terminators by participating in the reactions through resonance-stabilized free-radical forms [114].

Thiodipropionic acid ($HOOC-CH_2-CH_2-S-CH_2-CH_2-COOH$) and dilauryl thiodipropionate are approved food antioxidants. The thiodipropionates act as secondary antioxidants in that they break down hydroperoxides formed during lipid oxidation to relatively stable end products [36]. While these materials have found extensive application in stabilizing polyolefin resins, the food industry has not readily accepted them.

XIII. NONNUTRITIVE SWEETENERS

Nonnutritive sweeteners encompass a broad group of substances that have been found to evoke a sweet taste or enhance the perception of sweet tastes. Although the list of potentially useful nonnutritive sweeteners is growing, only a few are currently available for food applications. The recent ban on the use of cyclamates in the United States has stimulated a search for alternate low-calorie sweeteners because of the demand for low-calorie foods and beverages in the present society. Most nonnutritive sweeteners bear little resemblance to the characteristic poly-hydric structures of naturally occurring sugars (Chapter 3).

Both the sodium and calcium salts of cyclamic acid were widely employed before these compounds were prohibited because of evidence suggesting they were carcino-genic. The basic structure of cyclamate (3) provides a reason for suspecting the compound to be a potential carcinogen because hydrolysis of the sulfamate ester leads to the formation of cyclohexylamine (4), a known metabolite and carcinogen [75,100]. The primary route of elimination is the urine, and this exposes the bladder to an active carcinogen. The FDA ban occurred because implants of cyclamates in laboratory animals caused bladder cancer [11].

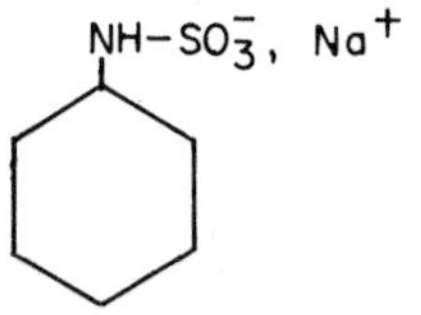

Sodium Cyclamate
(Sodium cycyclohexane sulfamate
(3)

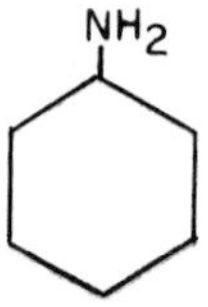

Cyclohexylamine
(4)

The primary nonnutritive sweetener available currently is saccharin (5), and both calcium and sodium salts are used. The level of use for saccharin depends on the intensity of sweetness desired; however, a slightly bitter flavor often re-sults at relatively high concentrations. The commonly accepted rule of thumb is that saccharin is about 300 times as sweet as sucrose in concentrations up to the equivalent of a 10% sucrose solution [104].

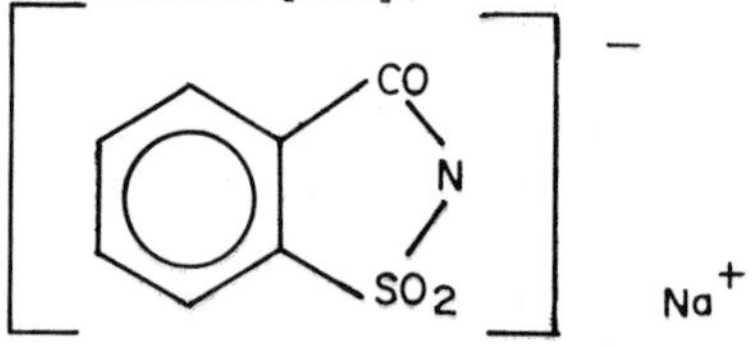

Sodium Saccharin
(Sodium ortho−benzosulfimide)
(5)

Glycyrrhizic acid is a natural, sweet-tasting substance that is found in licorice root and is considered a low-calorie sweetener. The root extract contains both the calcium and sodium salts of glycyrrhizic acid. Glycyrrhizic acid is a plant glyco-side which on hydrolysis yields 2 moles of glucuronic acid and 1 mole of glycry-yhetinic acid (a triterpene related to aleanolic acid) [113]. The sweet taste of glycyrrhizic acid is detectable at one-fiftieth the threshold taste level of sucrose. Glycyrrhizic acid is used primarily in tobacco products and to some extent in foods and beverages. Its slight licorice flavor influences its suitability for some applica-tions [22,78].

Substances structurally related to glycyrrhizic acid have been discovered recently. Stevioside is a naturally occurring sweetener found in the leaves of Stevia rebaudiana Bertoni, and it is 300 times as sweet as sucrose [54]. Somewhat related are the dihydrochalcone sweeteners which are derived from the bitter flavanones of citrus. Intensely sweet substances are produced by hydrogenation of (1) naringin to yield naringin dihydrochalcone, (2) neohesperidin to yield neohesperidin dihydrochalcone, or (3) hesperidin to yield hesperedin dihydrochalcone 4'-O-glucoside [56]. All of these sweet substances are related in that they contain (1→2)-linked disaccharides. The dihydrochalcones are undergoing required feeding trials and are not yet allowed in foods.

Another potentially useful low-calorie sweetener is aspartylphenylalanine methyl ester, which exhibits a relatively intense sweet taste. Use of this sweetener may be limited because it lacks stability in food systems. The amide-linked amino acids and the methyl ester are potentially labile to both chemical hydrolysis and microbiological attack [37,85].

The tropical African fruits, katemfe and serendipity berry, contain very sweet substances that qualify as low-calorie sweeteners. Katemfe contains two substances, thaumatin I and II, which are alkaline proteins each with a molecular weight of about 20,000 daltons. On a molar basis these substances are about 10^5 times as sweet as sucrose. The serendipity berry contains a sweet protein substance, monellin, which has a molecular weight of about 11,500 daltons, and it has characteristics similar to those sweeteners found in katemfe. The potential use of these substances is limited since they are unstable to heat and exhibit a complete loss of sweetness below pH 2 at room temperature [93,119].

Another basic protein, miraculin, has been isolated from miracle fruit (Synsepalum dulcificum). It is tasteless but has the peculiar property of changing sour taste to sweet. This material is a glycoprotein with a molecular weight of 42,000 daltons [120]. Similar to other protein sweeteners, miraculin is heat labile and is inactivated at low pH values. Further, the taste effects of miraculin persist for a long time and this may limit its use.

XIV. ANTIMICROBIAL AGENTS

A. Sulfites and Sulfur Dioxide

Sulfur dioxide long has been used in foods as a general food preservative. Currently, the forms employed include sulfur dioxide gas and the sodium or potassium salts of sulfite, bisulfite, or metabisulfite. In aqueous solution sulfur dioxide [13,14] and sulfite salts form sulfurous acid and ions of bisulfite and sulfite [64].

$$SO_2 + H_2O \rightleftharpoons H_2SO_3 \tag{10-14}$$

$$2 H_2SO_3 \rightleftharpoons H^+, HSO_3^- + 2 H^+, SO_3^{2-} \tag{10-15}$$

The relative proportion of each form depends on the pH of the solution, and at pH 4.5 or lower the HSO_3^- ion and undissociated sulfurous acid predominate [64]. It has been shown that sulfur dioxide is most effective as an antimicrobial agent in acid media, and this effect is believed to result from undissociated sulfurous acid, which is the dominant form below pH 3.0 [10,25]. Sulfurous acid inhibits yeasts, molds, and bacteria, but not always to the same degree. This is particularly true at high pH values where it has been suggested that the HSO_3^- ion is effective against bacteria but not against yeasts [33,102]. The enhanced antimicrobial effect of sulfur dioxide at low pH values may result because undissociated sulfurous acid can more easily penetrate the cell wall. Postulated mechanisms by which sulfurous acid inhibits microorganisms include the reaction of bisulfite with acetaldehyde in the cell, the reduction of essential disulfide linkages in enzymes, and the formation of bisulfite addition compounds which interfere with respiratory reactions involving nicotinamide dinucleotide [17].

Of the known inhibitors of nonenzymic browning in foods (Chapter 3), sulfur dioxide is the most effective and acceptable. The chemical mechanism by which sulfur dioxide inhibits nonenzymic browning is not fully understood, but it probably involves bisulfite interactions with active carbonyl groups. Bisulfite combines reversibly with reducing sugars and aldehydic intermediates and more strongly with α-dicarbonyls and α,β-unsaturated aldehydes [103]. These bisulfite addition products appear to retard the browning process which, when coupled with the bleaching action of sulfur dioxide on melanoidin pigments, results in effective inhibition of nonenzymic browning.

Sulfur dioxide also inhibits certain enzyme-catalyzed reactions, notably enzymic browning. The production of pigments by enzyme-catalyzed oxidation of phenolic compounds can lead to a serious problem during the handling of some fresh fruits and vegetables (Chapter 6). However, the use of sulfite or metabisulfite sprays or of dips with or without added citric acid provides effective control of enzymic browning in prepeeled and presliced potatoes, carrots, and apples [24].

Sulfur dioxide also functions as an antioxidant in a variety of food systems, but it is not usually employed for this purpose. When sulfur dioxide is added to beer, the development of oxidized flavors is inhibited significantly during storage [16]. The red color of fresh meat also can be effectively maintained by the presence of sulfur dioxide. However, this practice is not permitted because of the potential for masking deterioration in abused meat products.

When added to flour, sulfur dioxide effects a reversible cleavage of protein disulfide bonds and this can have desirable effects on the baking properties of bread doughs [103]. Prior to drying certain fruits, gaseous sulfur dioxide is often applied, and this is sometimes done in the presence of buffering agents (i.e., $NaHCO_3$). This treatment prevents browning and bleaches anthocyanin pigments. The resulting properties are desired in such products as those used to make white wine and maraschino cherries [24].

Sulfur dioxide and sulfites are metabolized to sulfate and are excreted in the urine without any obvious pathological results [77]. Levels of sulfur dioxide encountered in dried fruits sometimes approach 2,000 ppm; however, levels above 500 ppm give a noticeable disagreeable flavor [17].

B. Nitrite and Nitrate Salts

The potassium and sodium salts of nitrite and nitrate are commonly used in curing mixtures for meats to develop and fix the color, to inhibit microorganisms, and to develop characteristic flavors. Nitrite, rather than nitrate, is apparently the functional constituent. Nitrites in meat form nitric oxide, which reacts with heme compounds to form nitrosomyoglobin, the pigment responsible for the pink color of cured meats (Chapter 8). Sensory evaluations also indicate that nitrite contributes to cured meat flavor but the details are poorly understood [122]. Furthermore, nitrites (150-200 ppm) inhibit clostridia in canned-comminuted and cured meats [18,19,107]. In this regard, nitrite is more effective at pH 5.0-5.5 than it is at higher pH values. The antimicrobial mechanism of nitrite is unknown, but it has been suggested that nitrite reacts with sulfhydryl groups to create compounds that are not metabolized by microorganisms under anaerobic conditions [15].

Recently, nitrites have been shown to be involved in the formation of low, but possibly toxic, levels of nitrosamines in certain cured meats. The chemistry and health implications of nitrosamines are discussed in Chapter 11. Nitrate salts also occur naturally in many foods, including such vegetables as spinach [3]. The accumulation of high amounts of nitrate in plant tissues grown on heavily fertilized soils is of concern, particularly in infant foods prepared from these tissues. The reduction of nitrate to nitrite in the intestine, with subsequent absorption, could lead to cyanosis due to methemoglobin formation [46]. For these reasons, the use of nitrites and nitrates in foods is being questioned. The antimicrobial capability of nitrite provides some justification for its use in cured meats in which growth of Clostridium botulinum is possible. However, in cured products where botulism does not present a hazard, there appears to be little justification for adding nitrates and nitrites [7].

C. Sorbic Acid

Straight-chain monocarboxylic aliphatic fatty acids exhibit antimycotic activity and α-unsaturated fatty acid analogs are especially effective. Sorbic acid (C-C=C-C=C-COOH) and its sodium and potassium salts are widely used to inhibit mold and yeasts in a wide variety of foods, including cheese, baked products, fruit juices, wine, and pickles. Sorbic acid is particularly effective in preventing mold growth, and it contributes little flavor at the concentrations employed (to 0.3% by weight). The method of application may involve direct incorporation, surface coatings, or incorporation in a wrapping material. The activity of sorbic acid increases as the pH decreases, indicating that the undissociated form is more inhibitory than the dissociated form. In general, sorbic acid is effective up to pH 6.5, which is considerably above the effective pH ranges for propionic and benzoic acids [17].

The antimycotic action of sorbic acid appears to arise because molds are unable to metabolize the α-unsaturated diene system of its aliphatic chain. It has been suggested that the diene structure of sorbic acid interferes with cellular dehydrogenases which normally dehydrogenate fatty acids as the first step in oxidation [89]. This inhibitory effect does not extend to higher animals [28], and all evidence indicates that animals and man metabolize sorbic acid in much the same manner as they do naturally occurring fatty acids [29].

Several microorganisms, including a few molds, have been shown to metabolize sorbic acid, and it has been suggested that this metabolism proceeds through β oxidation, similar to that in mammals [89]. Short-chain (C_2-C_{12}) saturated fatty acids are also moderately inhibitory to many molds, such as Penicillium roqueforti. However, some of these molds are capable of mediating β oxidation of saturated fatty acids to corresponding β-keto acids, especially when the concentration of the acid is only marginally inhibitory [74]. Decarboxylation of the resulting β-keto acid yields the corresponding methyl ketone, Eq. (10-16), which does not exhibit antimicrobial properties.

$$\text{R-C-C-COOH} \xrightarrow{\text{oxid}} \text{R-C-}\overset{\overset{\text{O}}{\|}}{\text{C}}\text{-COOH} \longrightarrow \text{R-}\overset{\overset{\text{O}}{\|}}{\text{C}}\text{-C} + CO_2 \tag{10-16}$$

Fatty acid $\qquad\qquad$ β-Keto acid $\qquad$ Methyl ketone

Some hold that the various fatty acids which have some degree of antimycotic activity cause changes in cell permeability by attaching to the cell surface. In addition, unsaturated fatty acids may undergo oxidation and the resulting free radicals could exert an inhibitory action by attaching to critical sites of cell membranes. These mechanisms, however, are speculative at this time.

A specific mechanism for deactivating the antimicrobial properties or sorbic acid has been demonstrated in molds, especially P. roqueforti [80]. This involves direct decarboxylation of sorbic acid to yield the hydrocarbon 1,3-pentadiene, Eq. (10-17).

$$\text{C-C=C-C=C-COOH} \xrightarrow[\text{P. roqueforti}]{} \text{C-C=C-C=C} + CO_2 \tag{10-17}$$

Sorbic acid $\qquad$ 1,3-Pentadiene

The intense aroma of this compound can cause gasoline- or hydrocarbon-like off flavors when mold growth occurs in the presence of sorbic acid, especially on the surface of cheese treated with sorbate.

D. Propionic Acid

Propionic acid (C-C-COOH) and its sodium and calcium salts exert antimicrobial activity against molds and a few bacteria. It occurs naturally in Swiss cheese (up to 1% by wt) where it is produced by Propionibacterium shermanii [17]. Propionic acid has found extensive use in the bakery field, where it not only inhibits molds effectively but also is active against the ropy bread organism, Bacillus mesentericus [94]. Levels of use generally range up to 0.3% by weight. As with other carboxylic acid antimicrobial agents, the undissociated form of propionic acid is active, and the range of effectiveness extends up to pH 5.0 in most applications [95]. The toxicity of propionic acid to molds and certain bacteria is related to the inability of these organisms to metabolize the three-carbon skeleton [55]. In mammals, propionic acid is metabolized in a manner similar to other fatty acids, and it has not been shown to cause any toxic effects at the levels utilized [47].

E. Acetic Acid

The preservation of foods with acetic acid (CH_3COOH) in the form of vinegar dates to antiquity. In addition to vinegar (4% acetic acid) and acetic acid, also used in food are sodium acetate, CH_3COONa; potassium acetate, CH_3COOK; calcium acetate, $(CH_3-COO)_2Ca$; and sodium deacetate, $CH_3-COONa \cdot CH_3-COOH \cdot 1/2\ H_2O$. The salts are used in bread and other baked goods (0.1–0.4%) to prevent ropiness and the growth of molds and do not interfere with yeast [17]. Vinegar and acetic acid are used in pickled meats and fish products. If fermentable carbohydrates are present, at least 3.6% acid must be present to prevent growth of lactic acid bacilli and yeasts. The acid is also used in foods, such as catsup, mayonnaise, and pickles, primarily for flavor, but these products also benefit from the concurrent antimicrobial action. The antimicrobial activity of acetic acid increases as the pH is decreased, a property analogous to that found for other aliphatic fatty acids.

F. Benzoic Acid

Benzoic acid (C_6H_5COOH) has been widely employed as an antimicrobial agent in foods and occurs naturally in cranberries, prunes, cinnamon, and cloves [17]. The undissociated acid is the form with antimicrobial activity, and benzoic acid exhibits optimum activity in the pH range of 2.5–4.0 and thus is well suited for use in acid foods, such as fruit juices, carbonated beverages, pickles, and sauerkraut. Since the sodium salt of benzoic acid is more soluble in water than the acid form, the former is generally used. Once in the product some of the salt converts to the active acid form. It is most active against yeasts and bacteria and least active against molds [23]. Often benzoic acid is used in combination with sorbic acid or parabens, and levels of use usually range from 0.05 to 0.1% by weight.

Benzoic acid has been found to cause no deleterious effects when used in small amounts [17]. It is readily eliminated from the body primarily after conjugation with glycine (Eq. 10-18) to form hippuric acid (benzoyl glycine). This detoxification step precludes accumulation of benzoic acid in the body.

| Benzoic acid | Glycine | Hippuric acid | (10-18) |

G. p-Hydroxybenzoate Alkyl Esters

The parabens are a group of alkyl esters of p-hydroxybenzoic acid that have been used widely as antimicrobial agents in foods, pharmaceutical products, and cosmetics. The methyl (6), propyl, and heptyl esters are used domestically, and in some other countries the ethyl and butyl esters are used as well [17].

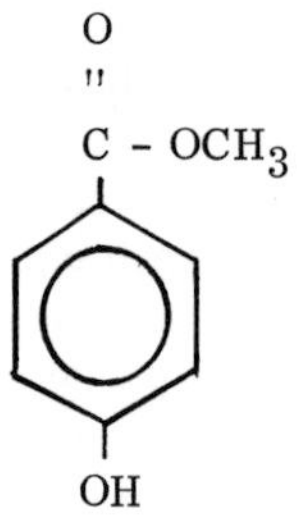

$$
\underset{\displaystyle (6)}{
\begin{array}{c}
O \\
\| \\
C - OCH_3
\end{array}
}
$$

Structure: benzene ring with C(=O)-OCH₃ group at top and OH group at bottom, labeled (6).

Parabens are used as microbial preservatives in baked goods, soft drinks, beer, olives, pickles, jams and jellies, and syrups. They have little effect on flavor, are effective inhibitors of molds and yeasts (0.05–0.1% by wt), and are relatively ineffective against bacteria, especially gram-negative bacteria [98]. The antimicrobial activity of parabens increases with increases in the length of the alkyl chain, but this decreases their water solubility and, as a result, the shorter chain members are used. In contrast to other antimycotic agents the parabens are active at pH 7 and higher, apparently because of their ability to remain undissociated at neutral pH values [1]. The phenolic group provides a weak acid character to the molecule. The ester linkage is stable to hydrolysis even under retort temperatures. The parabens have many properties in common with benzoic acid and they are often used together. Parabens exhibit a low order of toxicity and are excreted in the urine after hydrolysis of the ester group and subsequent metabolic conjugation [66,81].

H. Epoxides

Most antimicrobial agents used in foods exhibit inhibitory rather than lethal effects at the concentrations employed. However, exceptions occur with ethylene (7) and propylene (8) oxides. These epoxide compounds, which do not have natural counterparts, find applications in certain low-moisture foods. In order that they achieve intimate contact with microorganisms the epoxides are applied to the gaseous phase, and after adequate exposure most of the residual unreacted epoxide is removed by flushing and evacuation. The epoxides are reactive cyclic ethers that destroy all forms of microorganism, including spores and even viruses [99], but the mechanism of action of epoxides is not known. In the case of ethylene oxide it has been proposed that alkylation of essential intermediary metabolites with a hydroxyethyl group ($-CH_2-CH_2-OH$) accounts for the lethal results [98]. The site of attack would be any labile hydrogen in the metabolic system. The epoxides also react with water to form corresponding glycols (Eq. 10–19).

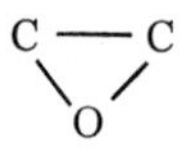

Structures: (7) ethylene oxide — C—C with O bridging below; (8) propylene oxide — C—C—C with O bridging below.

(7) 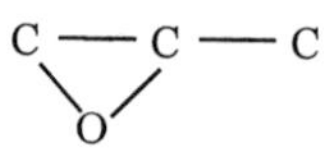   (8)

$$C \underset{O}{\overset{\diagup\diagdown}{-\!\!\!-}} C + H_2O \quad\longrightarrow\quad \underset{OH}{\overset{|}{C}} \underset{OH}{\overset{|}{-\!\!\!-\!\!\!-}} C \qquad\qquad (10\text{-}19)$$

Ethylene oxide   Ethylene glycol

However, the toxicity of the glycols is extremely low and therefore cannot account for any inhibitory effect.

Since the majority of the active epoxide is removed from the treated food and the glycols formed are of low toxicity, these gaseous sterilants may seem likely to be used extensively. Their use, however, is limited to dry items, such as nutmeats and spices. Spices often contain high microbial loads and are destined for incorporation into perishable foods. Thermal sterilization is unsuitable because the flavor compounds are volatile and the product is generally unstable. Thus, treatment with epoxides is a suitable method for reducing the microbial load.

The potential formation of relatively toxic chlorohydrins as a result of reactions between epoxides and inorganic chlorides (Eq. 10-20) is a cause of some concern [2]. However, there are reports that dietary chlorohydrin in low concentrations causes no ill effect [125]. Another consideration in the use of epoxides involves their possible adverse effects on vitamins, including riboflavin, niacin, and pyridoxine [5].

$$C \underset{O}{\overset{\diagup\diagdown}{-\!\!\!-}} C + Cl^-,\ H^+ \quad\longrightarrow\quad \underset{OH}{\overset{|}{C}} \underset{Cl}{\overset{|}{-\!\!\!-\!\!\!-}} C \qquad\qquad (10\text{-}20)$$

Ethylene   Inorganic   Ethylene
oxide   chloride   chlorohydrin

Ethylene oxide is more reactive than propylene oxide and is also more volatile and flammable. For safety purposes, ethylene oxide is often supplied in mixture consisting of 10% ethylene oxide and 90% carbon dioxide. The product to be sterilized is placed in a closed chamber; the chamber is evacuated and then pressurized to 30 lb with the ethylene oxide-carbon dioxide mixture. This pressure is needed to provide a concentration of epoxide sufficient to kill microorganisms in a reasonable time. When propylene oxide is used, sufficient heat must be applied to maintain the epoxide in a gaseous state [17].

I. Antibiotics

Antibiotics include a wide group of antimicrobial agents produced naturally by a variety of microorganisms. They exhibit selective antimicrobial activity and their applications in medicine have contributed significantly to the field of chemotherapy. The successes of antibiotics in controlling pathogenic microorganisms in living animals have led to extensive investigations into their potential applications in food preservation. However, because of the fear that routine use of antibiotics causes resistant organisms to evolve, their application to foods is not currently permitted in the United States. The development of resistant strains of organisms is of particular concern if the antibiotic used in food is also used in a medical application.

Although antibiotics are not used for food preservation in the United States, some other countries allow limited use of a relatively few antibiotics. These include nisin, chlortetracycline, oxytetracycline, and pimaricin [17]. Most actual or proposed applications of antibiotics in foods involve their use as adjuncts to other methods of food preservation. Notably, these include delaying spoilage of perishable foods during refrigeration and reducing the severity of a thermal process. Fresh meats, fish, and poultry are perishable products which may benefit from the action of broad-spectrum antibiotics. In fact, a few years ago the United States' Food and Drug Administration permitted dipping whole poultry carcasses into solutions of chlortetracycline or oxytetracycline. This increased the shelf life of the poultry, and residual antibiotics were safely destroyed by usual cooking methods [91].

Nisin has been explored extensively for applications in food preservation. This polypeptide antibiotic is active against gram-positive organisms and it is not used in medical applications. Nisin is produced by lactic streptococci [82], and in some parts of the world it is used to prevent spoilage of dairy products, such as processed cheese and condensed milk. Nisin is not effective against gram-negative spoilage organisms, and some strains of clostridia are resistant. However, nisin is essentially nontoxic to humans, does not lead to cross-resistance with medical antibiotics, and is degraded harmlessly in the intestinal tract [53].

Pimaricin is an antifungal substance with a macrolide or lactone ring structure attached to a sugar moiety through a glycoside linkage [17]. Its toxicity to humans is low and it is effective against microorganisms in concentrations of 10-100 ppm. It is allowed in only a few countries and its applications have been limited to surface coatings on cheeses.

The biochemical modes of actions for antibiotics are just coming into focus, with research efforts directed toward the molecular level. In addition, there is a continuing search for natural preservatives that are hoped to be suitable for application to foods. However, the necessarily stringent requirements placed on substances for food applications indicate that a difficult task lies ahead.

J. Diethyl Pyrocarbonate

Diethyl pyrocarbonate has been used as an antimicrobial food additive for beverages, such as fruit juices, wine, and beer. The advantage of diethyl pyrocarbonate is that it can be used in a cold-pasteurization process for aqueous solutions, following which it readily hydrolyzes to ethanol and carbon dioxide (Eq. 10-21).

$$H_5C_2O-\overset{\overset{O}{\|}}{C}-O-\overset{\overset{O}{\|}}{C}-OC_2H_5 \overset{H_2O}{\longrightarrow} 2\ C_2H_5OH \quad + \quad 2\ CO_2 \qquad (10\text{-}21)$$

Diethyl pyrocarbonate   Ethanol

Usage levels between 120 and 300 ppm in acid beverages (below pH 4.0) cause complete destruction of yeasts in about 60 min [96]. Other organisms, such as lactic acid bacteria, are more resistant and sterilization is achieved only when the microbial load is low (less than 500 per milliliter) and the pH is below 4.0. The low pH retards the rate of diethyl pyrocarbonate decomposition and intensifies its effectiveness [110].

Concentrated diethyl pyrocarbonate is an irritant. However, since hydrolysis is essentially complete within 24 hr in acid beverages, there is little concern for direct toxicity. Unfortunately, diethyl pyrocarbonate reacts with a variety of compounds to form carbethoxy derivatives and ethyl esters. Diethyl pyrocarbonate reacts readily with ammonia to yield urethane (ethyl carbamate) (Eq. 10-22).

$$H_5C_2\text{-O-}\overset{\overset{\text{O}}{\|}}{C}\text{-O-}\overset{\overset{\text{O}}{\|}}{C}\text{-OC}_2H_5 + 2\ NH_3 \longrightarrow 2\ H_5C_2O\text{-}\overset{\overset{\text{O}}{\|}}{C}\text{-NH}_2 \qquad (10\text{-}22)$$

Diethyl   Ammonia   Urethane
   Pyrocarbonate   (ethyl carbamate)

Urethane is a known carcinogen but, until recently, there had been no reports of urethane formation in foods treated with diethyl pyrocarbonate. Sensitive isotope dilution techniques have revealed that orange juice, beer, and wine previously treated with diethyl pyrocarbonate (250-500 ppm) can contain from 0.17 to 2.6 ppm of urethane [14]. Since ammonia is ubiquitous in plant and animal tissues, it is probable that foods treated with diethyl pyrocarbonate contain some of the carcinogenic urethane. Because of this, diethyl pyrocarbonate is no longer permitted in foods in the United States.

XV. GASES AND PROPELLANTS

Gases, both reactive and inert, play important roles in the food industry. For example, hydrogen is used to hydrogenate unsaturated fats (Chapter 4), chlorine is used to bleach flour (see Section XI) and sanitize equipment, sulfur dioxide is used to inhibit enzymic browning in dried fruits (see Section XIV, A), ethylene gas is used to promote ripening of fruits (Chapter 15), ethylene oxide is used as a sterilant for spices (see Section XIV, H), and air is used to oxidize ripe olives for color development. However, the functions and properties of essentially inert gases used in food are the topics of primary concern in this section.

A. Protection from Oxygen

Some processes for oxygen removal involve the use of inert gases, such as nitrogen or carbon dioxide, to flush a headspace, to strip or sparge a liquid, or to blanket a product during or after processing. Carbon dioxide is not totally without chemical influence because it is soluble in water and can lead to a tangy, carbonated taste in some foods. The ability of carbon dioxide to provide a dense, heavier than air, gaseous blanket over a product makes it attractive in many processing applications. Nitrogen blanketing requires thorough flushing, followed by a slight positive pressure to prevent rapid diffusion of air into the system. A product that is thoroughly evacuated, flushed with nitrogen, and hermetically sealed exhibits increased stability against oxidative deterioration [63].

B. Carbonation

The addition of carbon dioxide (carbonation) to liquid products, such as carbonated soft drinks, beer, some wines, and certain fruit juices, causes them to become effervescent, tangy, slightly tart, and somewhat tactual. The quantity of carbon dioxide used and the method of introduction vary widely with the type of product [63]. For example, beer becomes partially carbonated during the fermentation process but is further carbonated prior to bottling. Beer usually contains three to four volumes of carbon dioxide (one volume of beer at 60°F and 1 atm pressure contains three to four volumes of carbon dioxide gas at the same temperature and pressure). Carbonation is often carried out at lowered temperatures (4°C) and elevated pressures to increase carbon dioxide solubility. The retention of large amounts of carbon dioxide in solutions at atmospheric pressure has been ascribed to surface adsorption by colloids and to chemical binding. It is well established that carbamino compounds are formed in some products by rapid, reversible reactions between carbon dioxide and free amino groups of amino acids and proteins [39]. In addition, formulation of carbonic acid (H_2CO_3) and bicarbonate ions (HCO_3^-) also aids in stabilizing the carbon dioxide system. Spontaneous release of carbon dioxide from beer, i.e., gushing, has been associated with trace metallic impurities and with the presence of oxalate crystals which provide nuclei for nucleation of gas bubbles [57].

C. Propellants

Some fluid food products can be dispersed as liquids, foams, or sprays from pressurized aerosol containers. Since the propellant usually comes into intimate contact with the food, it becomes an incidental food component or ingredient. The principal propellants for pressure dispensing of foods are nitrous oxide, nitrogen, and carbon dioxide [30,49,63]. Foam-type products are frequently dispensed by nitrous oxide and carbon dioxide because these propellants are quite soluble in water and their expansion during dispensing assists in the formation of the foam. Carbon dioxide is also employed for such products as cheese spreads, where tanginess and tartness are acceptable characteristics. Nitrogen, because of its low solubility in water and fats, is used to dispense liquids in which foaming should be avoided (catsup, edible oils, syrups). The use of all of these gases in foods is regulated and the pressure must not exceed 100 psig at 21°C (70°F) or 135 psig at 54°C (130°F). At these conditions, none of the gases liquifies and a large portion of the container is occupied by the propellant. Thus, as the product is dispensed the pressure drops, and this can lead to difficulties with product uniformity and completeness of dispensing. The gaseous propellants are nontoxic, nonflammable, economical, and usually do not cause objectionable color or flavors. However, carbon dioxide, when used alone, imparts an undesirable taste to some foods.

More recently liquified propellants (LP) have been developed and approved for food use. Although LP's have been used extensively in nonedible products, the common LP's are not acceptable in foods because of problems with off flavors, corrosiveness, or toxicity [49]. The LP's approved for foods are octafluorocyclobutane, or Freon C-318 ($CF_2-CF_2-CF_2-CF_2$), and chloropentafluoroethane, or

Freon 115 ($CClF_2$-CF_3) [31]. These propellants exist in the container as a liquid layer situation on top of the food product. An appropriate headspace containing vaporized propellant is also present. Use of an LP enables dispensing to occur at a constant pressure, but the contents first must be shaken to provide an emulsion that foams or sprays upon discharge from the container. Constant pressure dispensing is essential for good performance of spray-type aerosols. These propellants are nontoxic at levels encountered and they do not impart off flavors to foods. They are, however, expensive compared to compressed gas propellants. In addition to applications in spray-type products, LP's are used along with nitrous oxide to dispense whipped cream and foamed toppings [40]. They yield particularly good foams because they are highly soluble in any fat that may be present and they can be effectively emulsified.

XVI. SUMMARY TABLE OF FOOD ADDITIVES

Summarized in Table 10-2 are various kinds of food additives and their functions in food.

TABLE 10-2

Summary Table for Selected Food Additives[a]

Class and general function	Chemical name	Additional or more specific function	Source of discussion in this book
Acidulants (acids)	Acetic acid	Antimicrobial agent	Chapter 10
	Citric acid	Chelating agent	Chapter 4, 10
	Fumaric acid	Chelating agent	Chapter 10
	Glucono-δ-lactone	Leavening agent	Chapter 10
	Hydrochloric acid	–	Chapter 10
	Lactic acid	–	Chapter 10
	Malic acid	Chelating agent	Chapter 10
	Phosphoric acid	–	Chapter 10
	Potassium acid tartrate	Leavening agent	Chapter 10
	Succinic acid	Chelating agent	Chapter 10
	Tartaric acid	Chelating agent	Chapter 10
Alkalies (bases)	Ammonium bicarbonate	CO_2 source	Chapter 10
	Ammonium hydroxide	–	Chapter 10
	Calcium carbonate	–	Chapter 10
	Magnesium carbonate	–	Chapter 10
	Potassium bicarbonate	CO_2 source	Chapter 10
	Potassium hydroxide	–	Chapter 10
	Sodium bicarbonate	CO_2 source	Chapter 10
	Sodium carbonate	–	Chapter 10
	Sodium citrate	Emulsifier salt	Chapter 10
	Trisodium phosphate	Emulsifier salt	Chapter 10

TABLE 10-2 (Continued)

Class and general function	Chemical name	Additional or more specific function	Source of discussion in this book
Anticaking agents	Aluminum phosphate	–	Chapter 10
	Calcium silicate	–	Chapter 10
	Calcium stearate	–	Chapter 10
	Dicalcium phosphate	–	Chapter 10
	Dimagnesium phosphate	–	Chapter 10
	Kaolin	–	–
	Magnesium carbonate	–	–
	Magnesium silicate	–	Chapter 10
	Magnesium stearate	–	Chapter 10
	Sodium silicoaluminate	–	Chapter 10
	Tricalcium phosphate	–	Chapter 10
	Tricalcium silicate	–	Chapter 10
Antimicrobial agents	Acetic acid (and salts)	Bacteria, yeast	Chapter 10
	Benzoic acid (and salts)	Bacteria, yeast	Chapter 10
	Ethylene oxide	General	Chapter 10
	p-Hydroxybenzoate alkyl esters	Mold, yeast	Chapter 10
	Nitrates, nitrites (K, Na salts)	$\underline{C}$. botulinum spores	Chapter 10
	Propionic acid (and salts)	Mold	Chapter 10
	Propylene oxide	General	Chapter 10
	Sorbic acid (and salts)	Mold, yeast	Chapter 10
	Sulfur dioxide and sulfites	General	Chapter 10
Antioxidants	Ascorbic acid (and salts)	Reducing agent	Chapters 4, 7, 10
	Ascorbyl palmitate	Reducing agent	–
	Butylated hydroxyanisole (BHA)	Free-radical terminator	Chapters 4, 10
	Butylated hydroxy toluene (BHA)	Free-radical terminator	Chapters 4, 10
	Ethoxyquin	Free-radical terminator	Chapters 4, 10
	Gum guaiac	Free-radical terminator	Chapters 4, 10
	Propyl gallate	Free-radical terminator	Chapters 4, 10
	Sulfite and metabisulfite salts	Reducing agents	Chapters 4, 10
	Thiodipropionic acid (and esters)	Hydroperoxide decomposer	Chapters 4, 10

TABLE 10-2 (Continued)

Class and general function	Chemical name	Additional or more specific function	Source of discussion in this book
	Thiosulfate salts	Reducing agents	Chapters 4, 10
	α-tocopherol	Free-radical terminator	Chapters 4, 10
Bleaching (oxidizing agents)	Acetone peroxides	Free-radical initiator	Chapter 10
	Benzoyl peroxide	Free-radical initiator	Chapter 10
	Calcium peroxide	Free-radical initiator	Chapter 10
	Hydrogen peroxide	Free-radical initiator	–
Bodying, bulking agents	Glycerine	Bodying, humectant	Chapters 3, 10
	Methylcellulose	Bulking	Chapter 3
	Sodium carboxymethyl-cellulose	Bulking	Chapter 3
	Sorbitol	Bodying, bulking	Chapters 3, 10
	Xanthan (and other gums)	Bodying, bulking	Chapters 3, 10
Buffering salts	Aluminum ammonium sulfate	–	–
	Aluminum sodium sulfate	–	–
	Ammonium phosphate (mono-, dibasic)	–	Chapter 10
	Calcium citrate	–	Chapter 10
	Calcium gluconate	–	Chapter 10
	Calcium phosphate (mono-, tribasic)	–	Chapter 10
	Calcium pyrophosphate	–	Chapter 10
	Potassium acid tartrate	–	Chapter 10
	Potassium citrate	–	Chapter 10
	Potassium phosphate (mono-, dibasic)	–	Chapter 10
	Sodium acetate	–	Chapter 10
	Sodium acid pyrophosphate	–	Chapter 10
	Sodium citrate	–	Chapter 10
	Sodium phosphate (mono-, di-, tribasic)	–	Chapter 10
	Sodium potassium tartrate	–	Chapter 10

TABLE 10-2 (Continued)

Class and general function	Chemical name	Additional or more specific function	Source of discussion in this book
Chelating agents (sequestrants)	Calcium citrate	–	Chapters 4,10
	Calcium disodium EDTA	–	Chapters 4,10
	Calcium gluconate	–	Chapters 4,10
	Calcium phosphate (mono-basic)	–	Chapters 4,10
	Citric acid	–	Chapters 4,10
	Disodium EDTA	–	Chapters 4,10
	Phosphoric acid	–	Chapters 4,10
	Potassium citrate	–	Chapters 4,10
	Potassium phosphate (mono-, dibasic)	–	Chapters 4,10
	Sodium acid pyrophosphate	–	Chapters 4,10
	Sodium citrate	–	Chapters 4,10
	Sodium diacetate	–	Chapters 4,10
	Sodium gluconate	–	Chapters 4,10
	Sodium hexametaphosphate	–	Chapters 4,10
	Sodium phosphate (mono-, di-, tri-)	–	Chapters 4,10
	Sodium potassium tartrate	–	Chapters 4,10
	Sodium tartrate	–	Chapters 4,10
	Sodium thiosulfate	–	Chapters 4,10
	Sodium tripolyphosphate	–	Chapters 4,10
	Sorbitol	–	Chapters 4,10
	Tartaric acid	–	Chapters 4,10
Clarifying agents	Bentonite	Adsorbs proteins	Chapter 10
	Gelatin	Complexes poly-phenols	Chapter 10
	Polyvinylpyrrolidone	Complexes poly-phenols	Chapter 10
	Tannic acid	Complexes proteins	Chapter 10
Color fixatives	Ferrous gluconates	Dark olives	–
	Magnesium chloride	Canned peas	–
	Nitrate, nitrite (po-tassium, sodium)	Cured meat	Chapters 8, 10, 11
Defoaming agents	Aluminum stearate	Yeast processing	–
	Ammonium stearate	Beet sugar proces-sing	–
	Butyl stearate	Beet sugar, yeast	–
	Decanoic acid	Beet sugar, yeast	–

TABLE 10-2 (Continued)

Class and general function	Chemical name	Additional or more specific function	Source of discussion in this book
	Dimethylpolysiloxane	General use	Chapter 12
	Eugenol	Yeast	-
	Lauric acid	Beet sugar, yeast	-
	Mineral oil	Beet sugar, yeast	-
	Oleic acid	General use	-
	Oxystearin	Beet sugar, yeast	-
	Palmitic acid	Beet sugar, yeast	-
	Petroleum waxes	Beet sugar, yeast	-
	Silicon dioxide	General use	-
	Stearic acid	Beet sugar, yeast	-
Emulsifiers and emulsifier salts	Calcium stearoyl-2-lactylate	Dried egg white, bakery	Chapters 10, 12
	Cholic acid	Dried egg white	Chapter 12
	Desoxycholic acid	Dried egg white	Chapter 12
	Dioctyl sodium sulfosuccinate	General	-
	Fatty acids (C_{10}-C_{18})	General	-
	Glycerol mono-, diesters	Shortening, bakery	Chapter 12
	Glycocholic acid	General	Chapter 12
	Lactylic esters of fatty acids	Shortening	Chapter 12
	Lecithin	General	Chapter 12
	Mono- and diglycerides	General	Chapter 12
	Ox bile extract	General	-
	Polyglycerol esters	General	-
	Polyoxyethylene sorbitan esters	General	Chapter 12
	Propylene glycol mono-, diesters	General	Chapter 12
	Potassium phosphate, tribasic	Process cheese	Chapters 10, 12
	Potassium polymetaphosphate	Process cheese	Chapters 10, 12
	Potassium pyrophosphate	Process cheese	Chapters 10, 12
	Sodium aluminum phosphate, basic	Process cheese	Chapters 10, 12
	Sodium citrate	Process cheese	Chapters 10, 12
	Sodium metaphosphate	Process cheese	Chapters 10, 12

TABLE 10-2 (Continued)

Class and general function	Chemical name	Additional or more specific function	Source of discussion in this book
	Sodium phosphate, di-basic	Process cheese	Chapters 10, 12
	Sodium phosphate, monobasic	Process cheese	Chapters 10, 12
	Sodium phosphate, tri-basic	Process cheese	Chapters 10, 12
	Sodium pyrophosphate	Process cheese	Chapters 10, 12
	Sorbitan monooleate	Dietary products	Chapter 12
	Sorbitan monopalmitate	Flavor dispersion	Chapter 12
	Sorbitan monostearate	General	Chapter 12
	Sorbitan tristearate	Confection coatings	Chapter 12
	Stearyl-2-lactylate	Bakery shortening	Chapter 12
	Stearyl monoglyceridyl citrate	Shortenings	Chapter 12
	Taurocholic acid (salts)	Egg whites	Chapter 12
Enzymes	Amylase	Starch conversion	Chapter 6
	Glucose oxidase	Oxygen scavenger	Chapter 6
	Lipase	Dairy flavor developer	Chapter 6
	Papain	Chillproofing beer, meat tenderizer	Chapter 6
	Pepsin	Meat tenderizer	Chapter 6
	Rennin	Cheese production	Chapter 6
Firming agents	Aluminum sulfate(s)	Pickles	Chapter 10
	Calcium carbonate	General	Chapter 10
	Calcium chloride	Canned tomatoes	Chapter 10
	Calcium citrate	Canned potatoes	Chapter 10
	Calcium gluconate	Apple slices	Chapter 10
	Calcium hydroxide	Fruit products	Chapter 10
	Calcium lactate	Apple slices	Chapter 10
	Calcium phosphate, (monobasic)	Tomatoes, canned	Chapter 10
	Calcium sulfate	Canned potatoes, tomatoes	Chapter 10
	Magnesium chloride	Canned peas	Chapter 10
Flavor potentiators	Disodium guanylate	Meats and vegetables	Chapter 9
	Disodium inosinate	Meats and vegetables	Chapter 9
	Maltol	Bakery goods, sweets	Chapter 9
	Monosodium glutamate	Meats and vegetables	Chapter 9
	Sodium chloride	General	–

TABLE 10-2 (Continued)

Class and general function	Chemical name	Additional or more specific function	Source of discussion in this book
Flavoring agents	Essential oils	General	Chapter 9
	Herbs and spices	General	Chapter 9
	Plant extractives	General	Chapter 9
	Synthetic flavor compounds (individual members comprising flavoring agents are too numerous to mention - see refs. [40] and [42] for comprehensive listings)	General	Chapter 9
Food colors	Annatto	Cheese, baked goods	Chapter 8
	Beet powder	Frosting, yogurt	Chapter 8
	Caramel	Confectionary	Chapter 8
	Carotene	Margarine	Chapter 8
	Cochineal	Beverages	–
	F.D. & C. Green No. 3	Mint jelly	Chapter 8
	F.D. & C. Red No. 2 (amaranth)	Cereals, soft drinks	Chapter 8
	F.D. & C. Red No. 3 (erythrosine)	Baked goods	Chapter 8
	Titanium dioxide	White candy	Chapter 8
Gases, propellants	Carbon dioxide	Carbonation	Chapter 10
	Freon C-318	–	Chapter 10
	Freon 115	–	Chapter 10
	Nitrous oxide	–	Chapter 10
	Nitrogen	–	Chapter 10
Humectants	Glycerine	Plasticizing agent	Chapters 3, 10
	Propylene glycol	Plasticizing agent	Chapters 3, 10
	Sorbitol	Crystallization control	Chapters 3, 10
	Mannitol	Crystallization control	Chapters 3, 10
Leavening agents	Ammonium bicarbonate	CO_2 source	Chapter 10
	Ammonium phosphate (dibasic)	–	Chapter 10
	Calcium phosphate	–	Chapter 10
	Glucono-δ-lactone	–	Chapter 10
	Sodium acid pyrophosphate	–	Chapter 10
	Sodium aluminum phosphate	–	Chapter 10
	Sodium aluminum sulfate	–	Chapter 10
	Sodium bicarbonate	CO_2 source	Chapter 10

TABLE 10-2 (Continued)

Class and general function	Chemical name	Additional or more specific function	Source of discussion in this book
Lubricants, coating agents	Acetylated monoglycerides	–	Chapter 10
	Beeswax	–	–
	Castor oil	–	–
	Methyl cellulose	–	Chapter 3
	Mineral oil	–	–
	Petrolatum	–	–
	Stearic acid	–	Chapter 10
Maturing agents, dough conditioners	Acetone peroxides	–	–
	Ammonium chloride	–	Chapter 10
	Ammonium sulfate	–	Chapter 10
	Calcium bromate	–	Chapter 10
	Calcium iodate	–	Chapter 10
	Calcium peroxide	–	Chapter 10
	Calcium phosphate (dibasic)	–	Chapter 10
	Calcium stearoyl-2-lactylate	–	Chapter 10
	Potassium bromate	–	Chapter 10
	Sodium stearoyl-2-lactylate	–	Chapter 10
Nonnutritive sweeteners	Ammonium saccharin	–	Chapters 3, 9, 10
	Calcium saccharin	–	Chapters 3, 9, 10
	Saccharin	–	Chapters 3, 9, 10
	Sodium saccharin	–	Chapters 3, 9, 10
Nutrient, dietary supplements			
Amino acids	Alanine	–	Chapter 5
	Arginine	Essential	Chapter 5
	Aspartic acid	–	Chapter 5
	Cysteine	Essential	Chapter 5
	Cystine	–	Chapter 5
	Glutamic acid	–	Chapter 5
	Histidine	Essential	Chapter 5
	Isoleucine	Essential	Chapter 5
	Leucine	Essential	Chapter 5
	Lysine	Essential	Chapter 5
	Methionine	Essential	Chapter 5

TABLE 10-2 (Continued)

Class and general function	Chemical name	Additional or more specific function	Source of discussion in this book
	Phenylalanine	Essential	Chapter 5
	Proline	–	Chapter 5
	Serine	–	Chapter 5
	Threonine	Essential	Chapter 5
	Valine	Essential	Chapter 5
Minerals	Boric acid	Boron source	Chapter 7
	Calcium carbonate	Breakfast cereals	Chapter 7
	Calcium citrate	Cornmeal	Chapter 7
	Calcium phosphates	Enriched flour	Chapter 7
	Calcium pyrophosphate	Enriched flour	Chapter 7
	Calcium sulfate	Bread	Chapter 7
	Cobalt carbonate	Cobalt source	Chapter 7
	Cobalt chloride	Cobalt source	Chapter 7
	Cobalt sulfate	Cobalt source	Chapter 7
	Cupric chloride	Copper source	Chapter 7
	Cupric gluconate	Copper source	Chapter 7
	Cupric oxide	Copper source	Chapter 7
	Cupric sulfate	Copper source	Chapter 7
	Calcium fluoride	Water fluoridations	Chapter 7
	Ferric phosphate	Iron source	Chapter 7
	Ferric pyrophosphate	Iron source	Chapter 7
	Ferrous gluconate	Iron source	Chapter 7
	Ferrous sulfate	Iron source	Chapter 7
	Iodine	Iodine source	Chapter 7
	Iodide, cuprous	Table salt	Chapter 7
	Iodate, potassium	Iodine source	Chapter 7
	Magnesium oxide	Magnesium source	Chapter 7
	Magnesium phosphates	Magnesium source	Chapter 7
	Magnesium sulfate	Magnesium source	Chapter 7
	Magnesium chloride	Manganese source	Chapter 7
	Manganese citrate	Manganese source	Chapter 7
	Manganese oxide	Manganese source	Chapter 7
	Molybdate, ammonium	Molybderrum source	Chapter 7
	Nickel sulfate	Nickel source	Chapter 7
	Phosphates, calcium	Phosphorous source	Chapter 7
	Phosphates, sodium	Phosphorous source	Chapter 7
	Potassium chloride	NaCl Substitute	Chapter 7
	Zinc chloride	Zinc source	Chapter 7
	Zinc stearate	Zinc source	Chapter 7
Vitamins	p-Aminobenzoic acid	B complex factor	Chapter 7
	Biotin	–	Chapter 7
	Carotene	Provitamin A	Chapter 7

TABLE 10-2 (Continued)

Class and general function	Chemical name	Additional or more specific function	Source of discussion in this book
	Niacin	B complex vitamin	Chapter 7
	Niacinamide	Enriched flour	Chapter 7
	Pantothenate, calcium	B complex vitamin	Chapter 7
	Pyridoxine hydrochloride	B complex vitamin	Chapter 7
	Riboflavin	B complex vitamin	Chapter 7
	Thiamine hydrochloride	Vitamin B_1	Chapter 7
	Tocopherol acetate	Vitamin E_1	Chapter 7
	Vitamin A acetate	–	Chapter 7
	Vitamin B_{12}	–	Chapter 7
	Vitamin D	–	Chapter 7
Miscellaneous	Betaine hydrochloride	Dietary supplement	–
	Choline chloride	Dietary supplement	–
	Folic acid	Nutrient	–
	Inositol	Dietary supplement	–
	Linoleic acid	Essential fatty acid	Chapter 4
	Rutin	Dietary supplement	–
Stabilizers and thickeners	Acacia gum	Foam stabilizer	Chapters 3, 10, 12
	Agar	Ice cream	Chapters 3, 10, 12
	Alginic acid	Ice cream	Chapters 3, 10, 12
	Carrageenan	Chocolate drinks	Chapters 3, 10, 12
	Guar gum	Cheese foods	Chapters 3, 10, 12
	Hydroxypropyl cellulose	General	Chapters 3, 10, 12
	Locust bean gum	Salad dressing	Chapters 3, 10, 12
	Methylcellulose	General	Chapters 3, 10, 12
	Pectin	Jellies	Chapters 3, 10, 12
	Sodium carboxymethyl cellulose	Ice cream	Chapters 3, 10, 12
	Tragacanth gum	Salad dressing	Chapters 3, 10, 12
	Xanthan gum	Salad dressing	Chapters 3, 10, 12
Yeast nutrients	Ammonium chloride	–	Chapter 10
	Ammonium phosphate (dibasic)	–	Chapter 10

TABLE 10-2 (Continued)

Class and general function	Chemical name	Additional or more specific function	Source of discussion in this book
	Ammonium sulfate	–	Chapter 10
	Calcium carbonate	–	Chapter 10
	Calcium phosphate (di-basic)	–	Chapter 10
	Calcium sulfate	–	Chapter 10
	Potassium chloride	–	Chapter 10
	Potassium phosphate (di-basic)	–	Chapter 10

aFor additional information see Refs. [20], [21], [40], and [42].

REFERENCES

1. T. R. Aalto, M. C. Firman, and N. E. Rigler, J. Amer. Pharmacol. Assoc., 42, 449 (1953).
2. A. M. Ambrose, AMA Arch. Ind. Hyg. Occup. Med., 2, 591 (1950).
3. M. R. Aston, The Occurrence of Nitrates and Nitrites in Foods, Literature Survey No. 7. B.F.M.I.R.A., Leatherhead, Surrey, England, April 1970.
4. V. K. Babayan, Food Prod. Devel., 2(2), 58 (1968).
5. H. Bakerman, M. Romine, J. A. Schricker, S. M. Takahashi, and O. Mickelsen, J. Agri. Food Chem., 4, 956 (1956).
6. J. C. Bauerfeind and D. M. Pinkert, in Advances in Food Research (C. O. Chichester, E. M. Mrak, and G. F. Stewart, eds.), Academic Press, New York, 1970, p. 219.
7. D. D. Bills, K. I. Hildrum, R. A. Scanlon, and L. M. Libbey, J. Agri. Food Chem., 21, 876 (1973).
8. D. Bone, Food Technol., 27, 71 (1973).
9. M. C. Brockmann, Food Technol., 24, 60 (1970).
10. B. I. Brown, J. Food Technol., 7, 153 (1972).
11. G. T. Bryan and E. Erturk, Science, 167, 996 (1970).
12. D. H. Bush and J. C. Bailar, J. Amer. Chem. Soc., 75, 4574 (1953).
13. A. Caputi and R. G. Peterson, Amer. J. Enol. Viticult., 16(1), 9 (1965).
14. E. A. Carter, G. D. Drummey, and K. J. Isselbacher, Science, 174, 1248 (1971).
15. A. G. Castellani and C. F. Niven, Jr., Appl. Microbiol., 3, 154 (1955).
16. L. Chapon and E. Urion, Wallerstein Labs Comm., 23, 38 (1960).
17. D. F. Chichester and F. W. Tanner, Jr., in Handbook of Food Additives (T. E. Furia, ed.), 2nd ed., CRC Press, Cleveland, 1972, p. 115.
18. L. N. Christiansen, R. W. Johnston, D. A. Kautter, J. W. Howard, and W. J. Aunan, Appl. Microbiol., 25, 357 (1973).

19. L. N. Christiansen, R. B. Tompkin, A. B. Shaparis, T. U. Kueper, R. W. Johnston, D. A. Kautter, and O. J. Kolari, Appl. Microbiol., 27, 733 (1974).

20. Committee on Food Protection, Food and Nutrition Board, Chemicals Used in Food Processing, NAS-NRC Publ. 1274. National Academy of Sciences, Washington, D.C., 1965.

21. Committee on Food Protection, Food and Nutrition Board, Food Chemicals Codex, NAS-NRC Publ. 1949. 2nd ed., National Academy of Sciences, Washington, D.C., 1972, p. 136.

22. M. K. Cook, Food Eng., 45(5), 145 (1973).

23. W. V. Cruess, Ind. Eng. Chem., 24, 648 (1932).

24. W. V. Cruess, Commercial Fruit and Vegetable Products. 4th ed., McGraw-Hill, New York, 1948, p. 248.

25. W. V. Cruess and J. H. Irish, J. Bacteriol., 23, 163 (1932).

26. R. V. Dahlstrom and M. R. Sfat, Brewer's Dig., 47, 75 (1972).

27. D. D. Deane and E. G. Hammond, J. Dairy Sci., 43, 1421 (1960).

28. H. J. Deuel, Jr., R. Alfin-Slater, C. S. Weil, and H. F. Smyth, Food Res., 19, 1 (1954).

29. H. J. Deuel, Jr., C. F. Calbert, L. Anisfeld, H. McKeehan, and H. D. Blunden, Food Res., 19, 13 (1954).

30. E. I. du Pont de Nemours and Co., General Background on Food Aerosols. Wilmington, Del., June 1960.

31. E. I. du Pont de Nemours and Co., Food Propellent "Freon" 115. Wilmington, Del., August 1965.

32. J. W. Du Ross and W. H. Knightly, Mfg. Confect. J., 43, 26 (1963).

33. E. J. Dyett and D. D. M. Shelly, J. Appl. Bacteriol., 29(3), 439 (1966).

34. R. H. Ellinger, in Handbook of Food Additives (T. E. Furia, ed.), 2nd ed., CRC Press, Cleveland, 1972, p. 617.

35. J. L. Etchells, T. A. Bell, and L. J. Turney, J. Food Sci., 37, 442 (1972).

36. Evans Chemetics, Inc., Thiodipropionate Antioxidants. Darien, Conn., 1966, p. 1.

37. N. R. Farnsworth, Cosmet. Perfum., 88(7), 27 (1973).

38. K. K. Fox, M. K. Harper, V. H. Holsinger, and M. J. Pallansch, J. Dairy Sci., 47, 179 (1964).

39. J. S. Fruton and S. Simmonds, General Biochemistry. 2nd ed., Wiley, New York, 1958, p. 919.

40. T. E. Furia, ed., Handbook of Food Additives. 2nd ed., CRC Press, Cleveland, 1972, p. 783.

41. T. E. Furia, in Handbook of Food Additives (T. E. Furia, ed.), 2nd ed., CRC Press, Cleveland, 1972, p. 271.

42. T. E. Furia and N. Bellanca, eds., Fenaroli's Handbook of Flavor Ingredients. CRC Press, Cleveland, 1971.

43. W. H. Gardner, Food Acidulants. Allied Chemical Corp., New York, 1966.

44. W. H. Gardner, in Handbook of Food Additives (T. E. Furia, ed.), 2nd ed., CRC Press, Cleveland, 1972, p. 225.

45. M. Glicksman, in Advances in Food Research (C. O. Chichester, E. M. Mrak, and G. F. Stewart, eds.), Vol. 11, Academic Press, New York, 1962, p. 109.

46. S. Govindarajan, Food Prod. Devel., 6, 33 (1972).

47. D. Graham, H. Teed, and H. C. Grice, J. Pharmacy and Pharmacol., 6, 534 (1954).

48. W. C. Griffin and M. J. Lynch, in Handbook of Food Additives (T. E. Furia, ed.), 2nd ed., CRC Press, Cleveland, 1972, p. 431.

49. S. Gross, ed., Modern Packaging Encyclopedia. Vol. 44, McGraw-Hill, New York, 1971, p. 258.

50. D. W. Grover, J. Soc. Chem. Ind., 66, 201 (1947).

51. R. Hamm, in Symposium: Phosphates in Food Processing (J. M. deMan and P. Melnychyn, eds.), AVI Publ., Westport, Conn., 1971, p. 65.

52. C. G. Harrel, Ind. Eng. Chem., 44, 75 (1952).

53. B. Heinemann and R. Williams, J. Dairy Sci., 49, 312 (1966).

54. J. E. Hodge and G. E. Inglett, in Symposium-Sweeteners (G. E. Inglett, ed.), AVI Publ., Westport, Conn., 1974, p. 216.

55. C. Hoffman, T. R. Schweitzer, and G. Dalby, Food Res., 4, 539 (1939).

56. R. M. Horowitz, in Comparative Biochemistry of the Flavinoids (J. B. Harborne, ed.), Academic Press, New York, 1967, p. 545.

57. J. S. Hough, D. E. Briggs, and R. Stevens, Malting and Brewing Science. Chapman and Hall, London, 1971, p. 643.

58. J. R. Hudson, J. Inst. Brewing, 64, 157 (1958).

59. O. F. Hunziker, The Butter Industry. 3rd ed., Printing Products Corp., Chicago, 1940, p. 238.

60. K. U. Ingold, in Symposium on Foods: Lipids and Their Oxidation (H. W. Schultz, E. A. Day, and R. O. Sinnhuber, eds.), AVI Publ., Westport, Conn., 1962, p. 93.

61. M. B. Jacobs, Amer. Perfum. Essent. Oil Rev., 47(10), 53 (1945).

62. M. B. Jacobs, The Chemistry and Technology of Food and Food Products. 2nd ed., Interscience, New York, 1951, p. 485.

63. M. A. Joslyn, in Food Processing Operations: Their Management, Machines, Materials, and Methods (M. A. Joslyn and J. L. Heid, eds.), Vol. 3, AVI Publ., Westport, Conn., 1964, p. 335.

64. M. A. Joslyn and J. B. S. Braverman, in Advances in Food Research (E. M. Mrak and G. F. Stewart, eds.), Academic Press, New York, 1954, p. 97.

65. R. Jenness and S. Patton, Principles of Dairy Chemistry. Wiley, New York, 1959, p. 218.

66. P. S. Jones, D. Thigpen, J. L. Morrison, and A. P. Richardson, J. Amer. Pharmaceut. Assoc., 45, 268 (1956).

67. H. Jorgenson, Cereal Chem., 16, 51 (1939).

68. M. Kaplow, Food Technol., 24, 53 (1970).

69. N. W. Kempf, The Technology of Chocolate. The Manufacturing Confectioner Co., Oak Park, Ill., p. 39.

70. R. E. Klose and M. Glicksman, in Handbook of Food Additives (T. E. Furia, ed.), 2nd ed., CRC Press, Cleveland, 1972, p. 295.

71. T. P. Labuza, S. Cassil, and A. J. Sinskey, J. Food Sci., 37, 160 (1972).

72. T. P. Labuza, N. D. Heidelbaugh, M. Silver, and M. Karel, J. Amer. Oil Chem. Soc., 48, 86 (1971).

73. W. A. Larson, N. F. Olson, C. A. Ernstrom, and W. M. Breene, J. Dairy Sci., 50, 1711 (1967).

74. R. C. Lawrence, J. Gen. Microbiol., 44, 393 (1966).

75. M. S. Legator, K. A. Palmer, S. Green, and K. W. Peterson, <u>Science, 165</u>, 1139 (1969).
76. R. C. Lindsay, E. A. Day, and L. A. Sather, <u>J. Dairy Sci.</u>, <u>50</u>, 25 (1967).
77. M. F. Lockett and I. L. Natoff, <u>J. Pharmacy and Pharmacol.</u>, <u>12</u>, 488 (1960).
78. MacAndrews and Forbes Co. Technical Bull., <u>Ammoniated Glycyrrhizin-Natural Sweetener and Flavor Potentiator.</u> Camden, N.J., 1972.
79. J. H. Mahon, K. Schlamb, and E. Brotsky, in <u>Symposium: Phosphates in Food Processing</u> (J. M. de Man and P. Malnychyn, eds.), AVI Publ., Westport, Conn., 1971, p. 158.
80. E. H. Marth, C. M. Capp, L. Hazenzahl, H. W. Jackson, and R. V. Hussong, <u>J. Dairy Sci.</u>, <u>49</u>, 1197 (1966).
81. C. Matthew, J. Davidson, E. Bauer, J. L. Morrison, and A. P. Richardson, <u>J. Amer. Pharmaceut. Assoc.</u>, <u>45</u>, 260 (1956).
82. A. T. R. Mattick and A. Hirsch, <u>Nature</u> (London), <u>154</u>, 551 (1944).
83. S. A. Matz, <u>Food Texture</u>. AVI Publ., Westport, Conn., 1962, p. 241.
84. S. A. Matz, <u>Bakery Technology and Engineering</u>. 2nd ed., AVI Publ., Westport, Conn., 1972, p. 40.
85. R. H. Mazur, in <u>Symposium-Sweeteners</u> (G. E. Inglett, ed.), AVI Publ., Westport, Conn., 1974, p. 159.
86. W. D. McFarlane and P. D. Bayne, in <u>Proceedings of the 10th Congress of the European Brewery Convention</u>. Elsevier, New York, 1961, p. 278.
87. E. P. McFee and J. A. Peters, <u>Food Eng.</u>, <u>25</u>(1), 67 (1953).
88. T. F. McNurlin and C. A. Ernstrom, <u>J. Dairy Sci.</u>, <u>45</u>, 647 (1962).
89. D. Malnick, F. H. Luckmann, and C. M. Gooding, <u>Food Res.</u>, <u>19</u>, 44 (1954).
90. P. Melnychyn and J. M. Wolcott, in <u>Symposium: Phosphates in Food Processing</u> (J. M. de Man and P. Melnychyn, eds.), AVI Publ., Westport, Conn., 1971, p. 49.
91. W. E. Meredith, H. H. Weiser, and A. R. Winter, <u>Appl. Microbiol.</u>, <u>13</u>, 86 (1965).
92. H. S. Mitchell and H. C. Black, <u>Ind. Eng. Chem.</u>, <u>35</u>, 50 (1943).
93. J. A. Morris, <u>Mfg. Confect.</u>, <u>52</u> (7), 38 (1972).
94. D. K. O'Leary and R. D. Kralovec, <u>Cereal Chem.</u>, <u>18</u>, 730 (1941).
95. J. C. Olson, Jr. and H. Macy, <u>J. Dairy Sci.</u>, <u>28</u>, 701 (1945).
96. C. S. Ough and J. L. Ingraham, <u>Amer. J. Enol. Viticult.</u>, <u>12</u>, 149 (1961).
97. S. B. Penick & Co. <u>Food Plus-A-Tives for Better Food Processing</u>. New York, 1973.
98. C. R. Phillips, <u>Amer. J. Hyg.</u>, <u>50</u>, 280 (1949).
99. C. R. Phillips and S. Kaye, <u>Amer. J. Hyg.</u>, <u>50</u>, 270 (1949).
100. J. M. Price, C. C. Biava, B. L. Oser, E. E. Vogen, J. Steinfeld, and H. L. Ley, <u>Science</u>, <u>167</u>, 1131 (1970).
101. E. L. Quarne, W. A. Larson, and N. F. Olson, <u>J. Dairy Sci.</u>, <u>51</u>, 848 (1968).
102. O. Rahn and J. E. Conn, <u>Ind. Eng. Chem.</u>, <u>36</u>, 185 (1944).
103. A. C. Roberts and D. J. McWeeny, <u>J. Food Technol.</u>, <u>7</u>(3), 221 (1972).
104. A. Salant, in <u>Handbook of Food Additives</u> (T. E. Furia, ed.), 2nd ed., CRC Press, Cleveland, 1972, p. 523.

105. L. G. Scharpf, in Symposium: Phosphates in Food Processing (J. M. de Man and P. Melnychyn, eds.), AVI Publ., Westport, Conn., 1971, p. 120.
106. A. W. Schwab, R. M. Cooney, C. D. Evans, and J. C. Cowan, J. Amer. Oil Chem. Soc., 30, 177 (1953).
107. J. G. Sebranek and R. G. Cassens, J. Milk Food Technol., 36, 76 (1973).
108. V. L. Singleton, Tech. Quart. Master Brewers Assoc. Amer., 4, 245 (1967).
109. W. A. Sistrunk and R. F. Cain, Food Technol., 14, 357 (1960).
110. D. F. Splittstoesser and M. Wilkison, Appl. Microbiol., 25, 853 (1973).
111. J. E. Stahl and R. H. Ellinger, in Symposium: Phosphates in Food Processing (J. M. de Man and P. Melnychyn, eds.), AVI Publ., Westport, Conn., 1971, p. 194.
112. P. G. Stecher, ed., The Merck Index. 8th ed., Merck & Co., Rahway, N.J., 1968, p. 195.
113. H. Storm, in abstracts of papers presented at Division of Agriculture and Food Chemistry, 165th Meeting, American Chemical Society, Dallas, Texas, April 1973.
114. B. N. Stuckey, in Handbook of Food Additives (T. E. Furia, ed.), CRC Press, Cleveland, 1972, p. 185.
115. J. B. Thompson and B. D. Buddemeyer, Cereal Chem., 31, 296 (1954).
116. D. K. Tressler and M. A. Joslyn, The Chemistry and Technology of Fruit and Vegetable Juice. AVI Publ., Westport, Conn., 1954, p. 536.
117. J. P. van Buren, Food Eng., 45, 127 (1973).
118. J. P. van Buren, J. C. Moyer, D. E. Wilson, W. B. Robinson, and D. B. Hand, Food Technol., 14, 233 (1960).
119. H. van der Wel, FEBS Letters, 21(1), 88 (1972).
120. H. van der Wel, in Symposium-Sweeteners (G. E. Inglett, ed.), AVI Publ., Westport, Conn., 1974, p. 194.
121. J. S. Wall, in Symposium on Foods: Proteins and Their Reactions (H. W. Schultz and A. F. Anglemeir, eds.), AVI Publ., Westport, Conn., 1964, p. 334.
122. A. E. Wasserman and F. Talley, J. Food Sci., 37, 536 (1972).
123. G. Wellner, Food Eng., 25(8), 94 (1953).
124. S. J. Werbin, Bakers Dig., 24(4), 21 (1953).
125. F. Wesley, F. Rourke, and O. Darbishire, J. Food Sci., 30, 1037 (1965).
126. E. H. White, Chemical Background for the Biological Sciences. 2nd ed., Prentice-Hall, Englewood Cliffs, N.J., 1970, p. 45.

Chapter 11

UNDESIRABLE OR POTENTIALLY UNDESIRABLE CONSTITUENTS OF FOOD

Gerald N. Wogan

Department of Nutrition and Food Science
Massachusetts Institute of Technology
Cambridge, Massachusetts

Contents

I. INTRODUCTION

A very diverse group of nonnutrient chemicals that find their way into foods and food raw materials are of interest by virtue of their undesirable or potentially undesirable properties with respect to food safety. Chemically, these substances represent a wide range of compounds from simple inorganic salts, on the one hand, to large macromolecules, on the other. Their presence in foods represents real or potential health risks of differing character and magnitude to populations consuming them. The spectrum of possible risks extends from the danger of acute poisoning in a few instances to the potential but as yet undefined risk of prolonged exposure to compounds for which there is evidence of mutagenic activity in experimental test systems. Evidence for actual risks to man also ranges in specific circumstances from well-documented cases of human exposure and response to implications derived from purely experimental situations.

Given its multifaceted character, the general problem of toxicants in foods can logically by discussed by organizing available information around the general themes of the chemistry of agents involved, characteristics of biological responses, or sources and routes of exposure. The latter organization, around sources of substances involved, is utilized in this chapter because it is more in keeping with the general organization of the book. Within this framework, the discussion includes a general survey of presently known problem areas, with more detailed presentation only of important examples of individual or classes of related substances in each major area. Available information is briefly summarized dealing with the chemical nature of compounds; their sources and routes of entry into the food supply; their effects in biological systems pertinent to the question of food safety; evidence of human exposure and response; and the nature of control measures to reduce or eliminate hazards if they exist.

II. NATURAL CONSTITUENTS OF FOODS

A. Plant Foodstuffs

Nature has provided plants with the capability of synthesizing a multitude of chemicals that cause toxic reactions when eaten by man or animals. In the course of his evolution, man must have learned by trial and error to avoid those plants that cause acute, easily recognizable poisoning [32] or to develop processing methods that reduce or eliminate the toxicity. Nonetheless many foodstuffs that are still regularly consumed, including some of the major sources of plant protein of nutritional value, contain substances that are toxic if consumed in sufficient quantities. For the most part, their existence has been recognized for a long time, and ordinary levels of intake of them are low enough to avoid apparent signs of toxicity. However, grossly increased intakes are sometimes necessitated, for example, by acute food shortages in developing countries, and mass poisonings have been known to occur under those circumstances. Cognizance must also be taken of the existence of these toxicants in formulation of novel products utilizing plant protein sources.

Table 11-1 presents some essential features of most of the major toxicants in plant foodstuffs but other relevant points dealing with some of these problems should be briefly summarized.

1. PROTEASE INHIBITORS, HEMAGGLUTININS, AND SAPONINS

It is useful for this discussion to consider these three groups of substances together. Although they are not all related chemically or toxicologically, they are often present simultaneously in the same groups of pulses, legumes, and cereals. Indeed, much of what we now know about them has resulted from research stimulated by such early observations as the fact that the nutritive value of soybean meal is improved by heating, or that raw kidney beans cause weight loss and death when fed to rats.

TABLE 11-1

Toxic Constituents of Plant Foodstuffs

Toxins	Chemical nature	Main food sources	Major toxicity symptoms
Protease inhibitors	Proteins (mol wt 8,000– 24,000)	Beans (soy, mung, kidney, navy, lima); chick pea; peas, potato (sweet, white); cereals	Impaired growth and food utilization; pancreatic hypertrophy
Hemagglutin- ins	Proteins (mol wt 36,000– 132,000)	Beans (castor, soy, kidney, black, yellow, jack); len- tils; peas	Impaired growth and food utilization; agglutination of erythrocytes in vitro; mitogenic activity to cell cultures in vitro
Saponins	Glycosides	Soybeans, sugarbeets, peanuts, spinach, asparagus	Hemolysis of erythro- cytes in vitro
Goitrogens	Thioglycosides	Cabbage and related species; turnips; rutabaga; radish; rapeseed; mustard	Hypothyroidism and thy- roid enlargement
Cyanogens	Cyanogenetic glucosides	Peas and beans; pulses; linseed; flax; fruit kernels; cassava	HCN poisoning
Gossypol pigments	Gossypol	Cottonseed	Liver damage; hemor- rhage; edema
Lathyrogens	β-Aminopropi- onitrile and derivatives	Chick pea; vetch	Osteolathyrism (skeletal deformities)
	β-N-Oxalyl-L- α, β-diamino- propionic acid	Chick pea	Neurolathyrism (CNS damage)
Allergens	Proteins?	Practically all foods	Allergic responses in sensitive individuals
Cycasin	Methylazoxy- methanol	Nuts of Cycas genus	Cancer of liver and other organs
Favism	Unknown (gly- cosides?)	Fava beans	Acute hemolytic anemia

The protease inhibitors [31] are proteins that have the property in vitro of inhibiting proteolytic enzymes by binding to the enzyme, apparently in a 1:1 molar ratio. Although a great deal of sophisticated physical biochemistry has been done on the structure and mode of action of these inhibitors, their role in animal nutrition and toxicology remains largely undefined. Their ability to impair protein hydrolysis is possibly related to impaired nutritive value of raw products containing them, but this has not been conclusively proved. When fed to animals in purified form, the chief toxicological response is pancreatic hypertrophy, the significance of which is not clear. Since these inhibitors are inactivated by heating, their destruction may be related to the improved nutritive value of heated soybean meal.

Hemagglutinins [25,26] are also proteins that have in common the ability to cause agglutination of red blood cells in vitro. This effect, which is highly specific for each protein, results from binding to the erythrocyte plasma membrane, and the hemagglutinins have been referred to as "lectins" because of their specificity of binding. Lectins also have the ability to stimulate mitosis in cell cultures and have become useful tools in the study of membrane structure and function.

Although many hemagglutinins are known to exist, only a few have been isolated in pure form. Some purified proteins in this class are lethal when fed or injected into animals, the most toxic being castor bean ricin, which has an LD_{50} of 5 $\mu g/$ kg in rats. By contrast, soybean and kidney bean lectins are less toxic by a factor of 1,000, and those from lentils and peas are nontoxic. The toxicity of all hemagglutinins is destroyed by moist (but not dry) heat.

Saponins [7] are glycosides that occur in a wide variety of plants and are characterized by three properties: bitter taste; foaming in aqueous solutions, and hemolysis of red blood cells. They are highly toxic to fish and other aquatic cold-blooded animals, but their effects in higher animals is variable. Chemically, they occur in two groups according to the nature of the sapogenin moiety conjugated with hexoses, pentoses, or uronic acids. The sapogenins are steroids (C_{27}) or triterpenoids (C_{30}). Interest in this group of substances has been initiated mainly by their hemolytic activity, but this property seems to be unimportant with respect to in vivo toxicity.

2. GOITROGENS

Goitrogens [58] are thioglucoside antithyroid agents that occur in plants of the family Cruciferae, most representatives of importance as foods being in the genus Brassica. These compounds are also responsible for the pungent nature of such plants. All natural thioglucosides, of which about 50 have been identified, occur in association with the enzyme(s) that hydrolyze them to yield glucose and bisulfate when wet, unheated tissue is crushed. Intramolecular arrangements may take place in the aglycone to yield also isothiocyanate, nitrile, or thiocyanate (Fig. 11-1).

Although the role of these antithyroid substances in the etiology of human endemic goiter is apparently minimal, their presence in commodities used as animal feeds is of considerable economic importance.

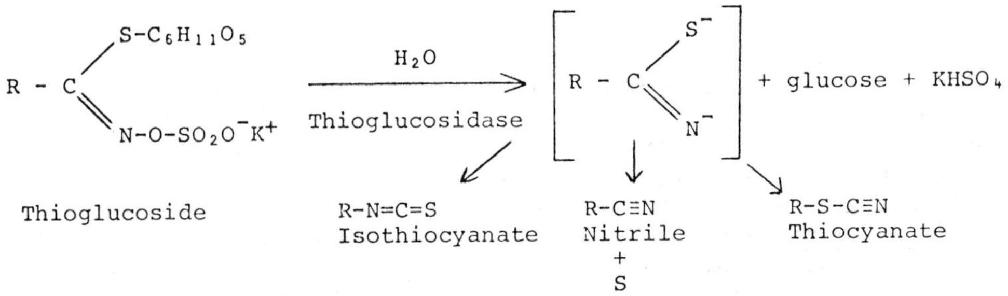

FIG. 11-1. Hydrolysis products of thioglucosides.

3. CYANOGENS

Cyanide in trace amounts is widely distributed in plants and occurs mainly in the form of cyanogenetic glucosides [39]. Three glucosides have been identified in edible plants: amygdalin (benzaldehyde cyanohydrin glucoside); dhurrin (p-hydroxybenz-aldehyde cyanohydrin glucoside); and linamarin (acetone cyanohydrin glucoside). Amygdalin is present in bitter almonds and other fruit kernels; dhurrin, in sorghum and related grasses; and linamarin, in pulses, linseed, and cassava. HCN yields as high as 245 mg per 100 g from cassava and 800 mg per 100 g from immature bamboo shoots have been reported. The lethal dose of HCN for man is in the order of 0.5-3.5 mg/kg body weight, and occasionally sufficient quantities of cyanogen-etic foods are consumed to cause fatal poisoning in humans. The possibility of chronic toxicity resulting from regular consumption of low levels has been sug-gested but not proved.

4. GOSSYPOL

Gossypol (Fig. 11-2) and several closely related pigments occur in pigment glands of cottonseeds at levels of 0.4-1.7% [5]. It is a highly reactive substance and causes a variety of toxic symptoms in domestic and experimental animals. It also causes a reduction of nutritive value of cottonseed flour, a protein source of increasing importance for human feeding. Glandless, gossypol-free cottonseed is now being developed by selective plant breeding.

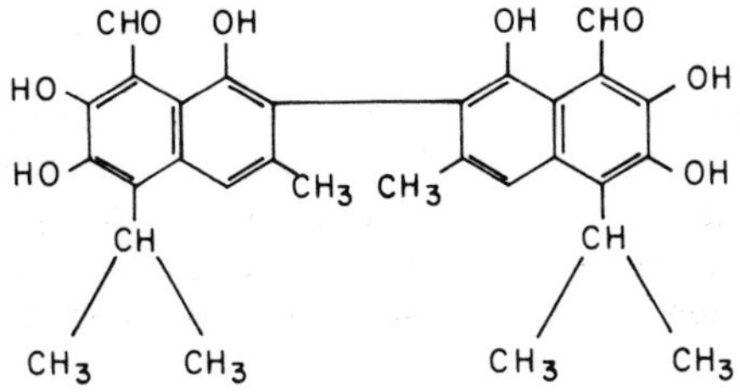

FIG. 11-2. Gossypol.

5. OTHER PLANT TOXICANTS

The other plant toxicants listed in Table 11-1 create problems of different types but tend to be of concern to more restricted populations by virtue of patterns of intake or sensitivity to the toxic agents. Human neurolathyrism [45], a crippling disease that results from degenerative lesions of the spinal cord, is known to occur only in India. Although it is associated with ingestion of certain varieties of Lathyrus sativus, the causative agent is unknown. The toxic amino acids listed in Table 11-1 induce lesions in animals reminiscent in some respects of those in humans and occur naturally in the plant. They are therefore suspected, but not proved, to be involved in causing the disease.

Food allergens [41] are usually normal components of foods, and their undesirable properties are the result of altered reactivity (i.e., allergy) in individuals who respond to such otherwise innocuous substances. The range of food constituents known to cause allergic responses in sensitive individuals is very wide and incorporates virtually all kinds of foods.

Cycasin [65] represents still another kind of problem. This compound, the glucoside of methylazoxymethanol, is a normal component of a number of plants that serve as an emergency source of starch for some populations in the Pacific and Japan. Although it has very potent carcinogenic activity in animals, it appears that traditional methods of processing the starch effectively remove the toxic substance. Its importance to man is therefore uncertain.

Favism [34] is a clinical syndrome in man consisting of acute hemolytic anemia and related symptoms resulting from the ingestion of fava beans (Vicia faba) or inhalation of pollen of the plant. The disease shows a remarkable localization in the insular and littoral regions of the Mediterranean area and has been attributed to an inborn error of metabolism with an ethnic distribution. Susceptible individuals have a deficiency of glucose-6-phosphate dehydrogenase in erythrocytes, which sensitizes them to the active agents in the bean, resulting in acute hemolytic damage.

B. Animal Foodstuffs

Poisonous animals, i.e., those whose tissues are toxic and cause adverse responses when eaten, are restricted almost entirely to marine forms. Their presence among the edible species of marine animals creates a problem that seems certain to become increasingly important as man turns to the oceans for additional sources of animal protein. The problem is especially difficult because present knowledge about the nature of the toxic agents and factors determining their occurrence is so limited that it is impossible to predict with any certainty when and where toxins are present.

More than 1,000 species of marine organisms are known to be poisonous or venomous, and many of these are edible forms or otherwise enter the food chain [22-24]. Toxins causing them to be poisonous vary considerably in their chemistry and toxicology. Some appear to be proteins of large molecular weight, while others are quaternary ammonium compounds of small size; most have not been isolated or purified.

Two main types of poisoning by marine animals are recognized: fish poisoning (that resulting from eating fish containing poisonous tissues); and shellfish poisoning (resulting from ingestion of shellfish that have concentrated toxins from plankton constituting their food supply). These are known, respectively, as icthyotoxism and paralytic shellfish poisoning [43].

1. PARALYTIC SHELLFISH POISONING

This syndrome is caused by eating clams or mussels that have ingested toxic dinoflagellates and effectively concentrate the toxic agents contained in them. Shellfish become toxic when local conditions favor growth (blooms) of the dinoflagellates beyond their normal numbers; such circumstances are often referred to as "red tides." The organisms involved along the American coastlines are usually species of Gonyaulax, although other genera and species are also toxic [46].

The toxic agent has been isolated and purified from cultures of the dinoflagellate and from toxic shellfish. It has an empirical formula of $C_{10}H_{17}N_7O_4 \cdot 2$ HCl but its structure has not yet been elucidated. It is stable to heat and not destroyed by cooking.

The purified toxin has an LD_{50} of 9 μg/kg body weight in mice and the estimated total lethal dose for man is thought to be between 1 and 4 mg. The toxin depresses respiratory and cardiovascular regulatory centers in the brain, and death usually results from respiratory failure. The fatality rate of affected individuals is 1-10% in most outbreaks.

2. ICTHYOTOXISM

About 500 species of marine fishes are known to be poisonous when eaten, and many of these are among edible varieties. Poisoning syndromes resulting from their ingestion are variable in character and are usually designated by the kind of fish involved: ciguatera; tetraodon; scombroid; clupeoid; cyclostome; or elasmobranch. The general character of the problem can be illustrated by selected examples.

Ciguatera poisoning is the most common form of fish poisoning. It can occur following ingestion of a wide variety of commonly used food fishes, such as groupers, sea basses, and snappers. This form of toxicity is associated with the food chain relationship of the fish. The toxic agent apparently arises in a blue-green algae and is then passed directly to herbivorous fish and indirectly to carnivorous species [20]. The toxic agent has been isolated in pure form and has an empirical formula of $C_{35}H_{65}NO_8$. Its LD_{50} in mice is 80 μg/kg body weight, but its precise mode of action is unknown. Death of poisoned individuals appears to be due to cardiovascular collapse.

Clupeoid poisoning sometimes occurs following eating of certain herring, anchovies, tarpons, and bonefishes and is particularly prevalent in the Caribbean. The situation may be related to ciguatera poisoning, but the source and character of the toxin are unknown. The clinical syndrome, however, is well characterized and death is common.

Tetrodon (puffer fish) poisoning is probably the most widely known and studied fish poisoning [42]. Puffer fish are not widely used for food but are consumed under special circumstances in Japan, where fatal poisonings occasionally are reported. Tetrodotoxin is probably the most lethal of all the fish poisons.

The few examples serve to emphasize the importance of additional research into the occurrence and nature of toxins in marine animals. Such information is imperative to determining which marine animals can be safely harvested and which cannot.

III. INTENTIONAL FOOD ADDITIVES

Intentional food additives are chemicals added to foods to accomplish one or more general objectives: improvement of nutritive value; maintenance of freshness; creation of some desirable sensory property; or aid in processing. At present, upwards of 3,000 chemicals are added to foods for these purposes [19]. Their large number and the fact that relatively large quantities of some of them are ingested regularly over a lifetime emphasize the importance of establishment of conditions that assure their safe use.

In most technologically developed countries, use of food additives is regulated through legal mechanisms that not only specify precisely the conditions under which the additive can be used but also require evidence from studies in experimental animals that the compound does not induce adverse responses that are of significance to human health. During the last two decades, the amount and kinds of animal data required by regulatory agencies and other groups charged with the responsibility of safety evaluation has become greater and more sophisticated. Evidence is required from at least two species regarding acute and chronic toxicity; a variety of biochemical indices of toxicity; effects on reproduction; tests for carcinogenic, mutagenic, or teratogenic effects; and information on metabolic fate of the material.

Every newly proposed food additive must undergo this complete toxicological evaluation before a regulation permitting its use is issued. Under these conditions, such additives can be considered to be safe within the limits of the ability of animal testing to detect toxicological hazard. The great majority of food additives fall into this category, although they have not all undergone testing of the same intensive nature.

New evidence has become available, however, that indicates the existence of toxicological problems with certain individual intentional food additives that have not been previously recognized. Since it is not feasible to attempt a detailed discussion of all classes of food additives, two examples of current interest are discussed as illustrative of the kinds of problems that can arise.

A. Nitrites and N-Nitroso Compounds

Sodium nitrite has a long history of use as a preservative and color stabilizer, particularly in meat and fish products. Regulations governing its maximum permitted use levels were based on no-effect levels with respect to acute toxicity in animals. Recently, however, it has been discovered that the use of nitrite may present another kind of hazard through its ability to interact with amines or amides, with the formation of N-nitroso derivatives of considerable toxicological interest.

Nitrosamines can form by the reaction of secondary or tertiary amines with N_2O_3, the active nitrosating reagent in most food products, through the following types of reaction:

$$R_2NH + N_2O_3 \longrightarrow R_2N \cdot NO + HNO_2 \tag{11-1}$$

$$R_3N + N_2O_3 \longrightarrow R_2N \cdot NO + R \tag{11-2}$$

Nitrosation of amines may take place in foods during storage or processing, and nitrosamines may then be ingested as such. Alternatively, it has been shown that nitrosation can also take place in the strongly acid conditions of the human stomach, in which case ingestion of the precursors can lead to a local formation of nitrosamines or nitrosamides.

The kinetics of nitrosamine formation from secondary amines is a third-order reaction with a pH optimum of 3.4, the pK_a of nitrous acid:

$$v = k_n [HNO_2]^2 [amine] \tag{11-3}$$

Detailed investigations of the prevalence of this type of food contamination are currently underway. Although quantitative studies on levels of preformed nitrosamines in foods have been hampered by lack of adequate analytical methodology, limited surveys have indicated that nitrosamines can indeed be detected in certain food products. Meats, fish, and cheese are the principal types of products contaminated, and representative data so far indicate that levels of nitrosamines generally found are in the range of 10-40 ppb. Dimethylnitrosamine is the predominant compound in most instances, but others have also been identified [13,14,47,48, 57,59].

N-Nitroso compounds are of toxicological interest because many of the known representatives of the class have potent carcinogenic activity in animals. Approximately 80% of more than 100 such compounds so far tested are carcinogenic for onr or more tissues of experimental animals [33]. Furthermore, formation of carcinogenic levels of nitrosamines in vivo by the simultaneous feeding of high levels of nitrite and amines to animals has been demonstrated [38,53].

In general, the levels of nitrosamines so far detected in foods have been far below the effective dose in animals. However, these observations have stimulated a reconsideration of the use of nitrite as an additive and also additional research on conditions under which nitrosation can take place in vivo and in foods. The possible role of nitrosamines in the etiology of human cancers with widely different geographical distribution is also under investigation.

B. Carrageenan

"Carrageenan" is a family of naturally occurring hydrocolloids consisting of high molecular weight linear sulfated polysaccharides. They are commercially extracted from several related species of red seaweeds and are widely used by the food and other industries as stabilizers, thickeners, and gelling agents.

Chemically, carrageenans share the common feature of regularly repeating linear structure of alternating $\alpha(1,3)$-linked and $\beta(1,4)$-linked galactose units. The 1,3-linked units occur as monosulfates and the 1,4-linked units as mono- and disulfates, the anhydride and anhydride sulfate. Food-grade carrageenans have average molecular weights of 100,000 or higher, and those less than 10,000 are not used as food additives.

These substances have a long history of use, and applications have been increasing, particularly during the last decade. Estimated average daily intake per capita in the United States currently is about 0.5 mg/kg body weight; infants on formula diets ingest as much as 50-80 mg/kg/day.

The toxicology of carrageenan in animals is influenced by route of administration. It is a strongly inflammatory substance when injected subcutaneously or intraperitoneally. Early feeding studies in rats indicated that it was toxicologically inert when orally ingested, apparently owing to lack of absorption. However, more recent studies have linked oral ingestion of partially hydrolyzed carrageenan to ulcerative colitis and other tissue changes in the gastrointestinal tract of some species of laboratory animals [36,60-62]. Recent feeding studies with natural carrageenan used in food applications show that it is not ulcerogenic in monkeys and rats but has some undesirable effects in guinea pigs [1,4,8,35,55]. It thus appears that native, undegraded carrageenan is not ulcerogenic to most laboratory species, apparently due to its lack of absorption through the intestinal mucosa. The ulcerogenic action in guinea pigs is thought to indicate that herbivorous animals have the ability to absorb the high molecular weight material.

Further investigation of this problem is now in progress, involving especially studies on the metabolic fate of carrageenan, as well as further evaluation of effects of chronic feeding of the substance as it is used in foods.

IV. PRODUCTS OF MICROBIAL GROWTH

A. Mycotoxins

Mold spores are ubiquitously distributed in nature, and the ease with which they germinate and grow on foods and feeds, especially if they become moist, is familiar to everyone. The fact that moldiness generally results in unpleasant flavors or other undesirable changes in products has also been known for a long time. Another feature of mold spoilage was first recognized long ago, but its importance has come to be widely appreciated only within the last two decades. Some molds have the capacity to manufacture, during their growth period, chemical substances that are poisonous or produce toxic symptoms of various kinds when foods or feeds containing them are eaten by man or animals. These chemicals are referred to generically as mycotoxins, and the toxicity syndrome produced by them is called mycotoxicoses.

Contamination of the food supply by mycotoxins gives rise to problems of several kinds. A direct hazard to human health can result when mycotoxin-contaminated foods are eaten by man. It is important to note that mycotoxins remain in the food long after the mold that has produced them has died and can therefore be present in foods that are not visibly moldy. Furthermore, many kinds of mycotoxins, but not all, are relatively stable substances that survive the usual conditions of cooking or processing. Problems of a somewhat different character can be created if livestock feed becomes contaminated by mycotoxins. In addition to the losses generated by toxicity syndromes that may occur in the animals themselves, mycotoxins or metabolic products of them can remain as residues in meat or be passed into milk and eggs and thus eventually be consumed by man.

Historically, mass poisoning of human populations by mycotoxins has been recorded in two circumstances. Ergotism, a toxicosis resulting from eating grains contaminated with Claviceps purpurea occured in epidemic proportions during the Middle Ages. Indeed, more restricted outbreaks have been documented as recently as 1951 in France. Alimentary toxic aleukia (ATA) is a mycotoxicosis caused by eating grain that became moldy as a result of overwintering in the field, as discussed later. Both toxicoses are of acute onset and are clearly associated with consumption of large doses of the toxic substances responsible for the illnesses.

In contrast to the small number of documented mycotoxicoses in humans, there are literally hundreds of reports in the literature of toxicity syndromes in livestock that have been attributed to moldy feeds. In a few such instances, the causative fungi and toxic agents have been identified, but in most cases they remain unknown.

It is important to consider mycotoxins from the perspective of their real or possible significance to human health. In this context, based on present knowledge, the toxins and fungi producing them fall into one or more of the following general categories:

1. Mycotoxins known by direct evidence of exposure and response to have caused some form of toxicity in man;
2. Mycotoxins known to be toxic to animals and that have been identified by chemical assay in human foods or foodstuffs, but without evidence of human exposure or response;
3. Fungi, isolated from human foods or foodstuffs, that produce mycotoxins under laboratory conditions but without evidence of actual occurrence of mycotoxins in foods;
4. Mycotoxins occurring in feeds or forage of domestic animals, causing toxicity syndromes in them, and presenting the possible risk of human exposure through residues in edible tissues or products;
5. Fungi isolated from animal feeds, litter, or various other sources that produce metabolites with toxic properties in experimental bioassays, but without evidence of occurrence in foods or feeds or of poisoning in animals or man.

1. MYCOTOXINS IN HUMAN FOODS AND FOODSTUFFS

Information in Table 11-2 is organized within this framework and deals only with those problems that fall within the first three categories, i.e., where there is direct evidence or reasonable expectation of human exposure. For a detailed review of mycotoxins in these as well as in the remaining categories, the reader is referred to comprehensive reviews of the entire area [11,28,29,63,64].

TABLE 11-2

Mycotoxins and Toxin-producing Fungi from Human Foods
or Foodstuffs

Toxin or syndrome	Fungal sources	Foods mainly affected	Chief pharmacological effects after ingestion	References
		Aspergillus toxins		
Aflatoxins	A. flavus, A. parasiticus	Peanuts, oil seeds; grains; pulses, and others	Toxic to liver; carcinogenic to liver of several animals and possibly man	[12,21,64]
Sterigmatocystin	A. nidulans, A. versicolor	Cereal grains	Toxic and carcinogenic to liver of rats	[12]
Ochratoxins	A. ochraceous	Cereal grains; green coffee	Toxic to kidney of rats	[56]
		Penicillium toxins		
Luteoskyrin	P. islandicum	Rice	Toxic, possibly carcinogenic to liver of rats	[44]
Patulin	P. articae; P. claviformi; others	Apple products	Edema; toxic to kidney of rats	[10]
		Fusarium toxins		
Zearalenone	Gibberella zeae	Corn	Hyperestrogenism in swine and laboratory animals	[37]
Alimentary toxic aleukia (ATA)	F. poae, F. sporotrichioides	Millet and other cereal grains	Panleukocytopenia due to bone marrow damage; mortality up to 60% in human epidemics	[27]
12,13-Epoxytricothecanes	Fusarium spp., Trichoderma spp., Glio-	Corn; other cereal grains	Cardiovascular collapse; increased clotting	[3]

TABLE 11-2 (Continued)

Toxin or syndrome	Fungal sources	Foods mainly affected	Chief pharmacological effects after ingestion	References
	cladium spp., Tricothecium spp.		time; leuko-penia; may have been involved in ATA in man	

It is clear from the evidence summarized in Table 11-2 that mycotoxins present public health hazards of a wide range of types and severity. Aside from ergotism, as mentioned earlier, alimentary toxic aleukia is the only mycotoxicosis for which there is extensive direct evidence of mass human poisoning. That syndrome, for which the exact chemical agents were never identified, occurred in various areas of the USSR during the later years of World War II. Epidemics of the syndrome involving many thousands of persons were associated with the use of millet and other grains that could not be harvested at the usual time and were allowed to over-winter in the field. The grains became heavily molded with the spring thaws but were used because of food shortages, and the toxicosis was the result.

The significance to man of the remaining mycotoxins listed in the table, except for the aflatoxins, must be assessed from inferences drawn from limited data on occurrence and biological activity of the various substances involved. It is not possible to make a meaningful generalization based on presently available evidence.

2. AFLATOXINS

Because research on aflatoxins has stimulated additional studies in the mycotoxin field, and because much is known about them including their significance to man, this group of mycotoxins warrants further brief elaboration. Various aspects of the field have been comprehensively surveyed [21,64].

Aflatoxins are produced by a few strains of Aspergillus flavus or A. parasiticus, the spores of which are widely disseminated, especially in soil. Although toxin-producing fungi usually produce only two or three aflatoxins under a given set of conditions, a total of 14 chemically related toxins or derivatives has been identified. One of these, aflatoxin B_1 (Fig. 11-3), is most frequently found in foods and is also the most potent toxin of the group.

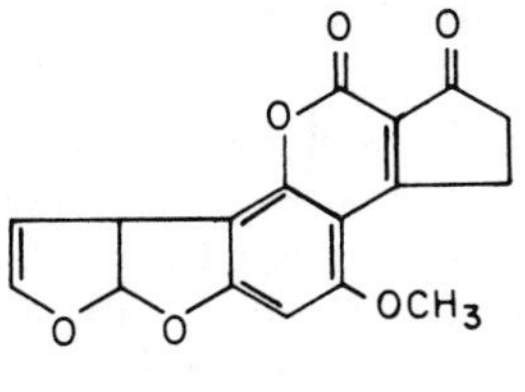

FIG. 11-3. Aflatoxin B_1.

With respect to substrate, requirements for toxin production are relatively non-specific, and the mold can produce the compounds on virtually any food (or indeed on synthetic media) that supports growth. Thus, any food material must be considered liable to aflatoxin contamination if it becomes moldy. However, experience has shown that the frequency and levels of aflatoxin found varies greatly among foods collected in a given region and in different regions.

As regards their toxic and other biological effects, the aflatoxins are very interesting compounds. Acute or subacute poisoning can be produced in animals by feeding aflatoxin-contaminated diets or by dosing with purified preparations of the toxins. Although there are species differences in responsiveness to acute toxicity, no completely refractory species of animal is known. Symptoms of poisoning are produced in most domestic animals by aflatoxin levels in the feed of 10-100 ppm or less. Although cattle tolerate relatively high levels of the toxin, they secrete in milk aflatoxin M_1, a derivative that is also toxic.

Aflatoxin B_1 is among the most potent chemical carcinogens known, and it is this property that has provided an important stimulus for research on these mycotoxins. Carcinogenic activity of various aflatoxins has been demonstrated experimentally in the duck, the rainbow trout, the ferret, the rat, the mouse, and the rhesus monkey. Rainbow trout are an extremely sensitive species, developing cancer when fed diets containing less than 1 ppb aflatoxin B_1, and a high incidence of liver cancer is induced in rats by feeding diets containing more than 15 ppb aflatoxin B_1.

A very important aspect in the history of the aflatoxin problem is the early and continuing emphasis that has been placed on the development of assay methods for detecting and quantitating levels of the toxins in foods. Availability of such methods, coupled with application of appropriate technology, has served to minimize the risk of human exposure to aflatoxins in countries possessing the necessary technological capabilities. It follows that the risk of contamination of food supplies is greater in developing countries with less advanced agricultural and other technologies. It is indeed from those regions that the currently available information on implications of aflatoxins to human health has come.

This information derives from field studies designed on the basis of the following lines of evidence. With respect to both toxic and carcinogenic actions in animals, aflatoxins affect mainly, although not exclusively, the liver. It is reasonable to assume man to respond similarly and liver disease, particularly liver cancer, is the principal illness presumed to be associated with aflatoxin exposure. It has been known for a long time that liver cancer, a relatively uncommon form of cancer in the United States and Europe, occurs at much higher frequency in some populations in other parts of the world, particularly in central and southern Africa and Asia. Several field studies have been conducted to determine whether elevated liver cancer incidence is associated with aflatoxin exposure.

One such study, conducted in Uganda, included collection and analysis for aflatoxins in foods eaten by several tribal groups within the country [2]. Tribal groups with the highest incidence of the disease also ate the most frequently contaminated foods.

A study of similar general design and purpose was conducted in Thailand, but in this case cooked samples of foods as eaten were systematically collected, and actual aflatoxin intake values were calculated [49-52,54]. Again, elevated liver cancer incidence was associated with higher levels of aflatoxin intake. Data of a similar character have recently been obtained in a third study conducted in Kenya.

This epidemiological information cannot be said to establish a cause-effect relationship between liver cancer induction and aflatoxin exposure. Indeed, it is very likely that many factors are involved in the induction of the disease. The above data, however, do strongly suggest that the risk of liver cancer is higher in populations exposed to elevated aflatoxin exposure and therefore provide a strong argument for minimizing exposure.

Practically nothing is known about the acute effects of aflatoxins in humans. However, certain lines of evidence are accumulating that suggest that aflatoxins and/or other mycotoxins may be involved in some types of acute poisoning in children. During the study in Thailand described above, it was possible to study children dying of a form of acute encephalitis with degeneration of the liver and other visceral organs, a malady known as Reye's syndrome. When tissues from children fatally affected by the disease were analyzed, it was found that aflatoxin B_1 was identifiable in liver, brain, and other tissues at far higher amounts and frequency than in tissues of children from the same region dying of other causes. This circumstantial evidence suggests that aflatoxins may have been involved in the disease. Of considerable interest is the fact that a sample of rice eaten by one child immediately before he became ill contained some aflatoxin B_1 and also contained viable fungal spores that proved to be capable of producing not only aflatoxins, but four other toxic materials of unknown character.

One portion of the study in Thailand also included the isolation of fungi from food samples and screening them for their ability to produce toxic materials. Fungi were isolated from the samples and cultured on sterile medium, and extracts of the culture were administered to rats. Using this screening procedure, more than 50 fungi were isolated that proved to be capable of producing toxic materials other than aflatoxins or other known mycotoxins. This kind of result has been reported by several other investigators studying human or animal foods or feeds.

The presence of these toxigenic molds on human foods presents an obvious potential risk to public health. It is unknown to what extent that potential is expressed. However, its existence provides strong motivation for implementing all available techniques for minimizing contamination of foods by mycotoxins.

B. Bacterial Toxins

Just as growth of spoilage molds can introduce toxic chemicals into foods, the growth of certain bacteria can also result in the production of pharmacologically active agents. Botulism, associated with the growth of Clostridium botulinum, is probably the best known form of food poisoning because of the extraordinary potency of the toxin involved and the high fatality rate. Poisoning by the enterotoxins produced by Staphylococcus aureus, although a much less serious illness, occurs far more frequently. These two forms of bacterially induced food poisoning are the most clearly recognizable syndromes in this category, but a variety of less well-defined food-borne bacterial toxins are known to exist [40].

1. BOTULISM

Botulism is the disease resulting from the ingestion of foods contaminated with the preformed toxin produced by Clostridium botulinum, an anaerobic, spore-forming bacillus. Various aspects of conditions for growth and toxin production, as well as isolation and characterization of the toxin, have been comprehensively reviewed [9].

Clostridia with the capacity to produce toxin are ubiquitously distributed, with a natural habitat in the soil, where they are present as spores. Food contamination can readily occur. However, in spite of the wide distribution of various types of botulinum spores in nature, the prevalence of one of another kind of botulinum poisoning in a given locality is apparently attributable mainly to the dietary habits of the local inhabitants.

Six serological types of toxin-producing Clostridium botulinum are known, designated A, B, (Cα, Cβ), D, E, and F. Of these types, only A, B, and E have been frequently associated with botulism in humans. The toxins produced by these organisms are proteins. The precise molecular weight of the active form of the molecule as it exerts its action is unknown. However, crystalline toxin A as isolated from cultures of the bacterium has a molecular weight of 900,000. This molecule can be chromatographically separated into two fractions of molecular weight 128,000 (α), and 500,000 (β), both of which retain toxicity. Therefore the actual size of the toxic subunit is not clear.

The site of action of botulinum toxin has been established as those synapses in the peripheral nervous system which depend upon acetylcholine for transmission of nerve impulses. Death is a consequence of suffocation resulting from paralysis of the diaphragm and other muscles involved in respiration.

The potency of botulinum toxin is well known. In its purified form, 1 μg of the toxin contains about 200,000 minimum lethal doses for a mouse, and it is suspected that not much more than 1 μg of the toxin may be fatal for man. Botulinum toxins are thermolabile, losing their biological activity upon heating for 30 min at 80°C. This has great practical significance, since the toxins are inactivated by heat processing or most ordinary cooking conditions.

Today the most frequent cause of botulism in man is inadequately heated or cured foods prepared in the home. Commercially prepared foods have been remarkably safe, with the exception of small-scale outbreaks over the last decade involving such products as smoked whitefish, canned tuna, canned liver paste, and canned vichysoisse. Much work is now in progress to prevent similar recurrences in the future.

2. ENTEROTOXINS PRODUCED BY STAPHYLOCOCCUS AUREUS

Staphylococcal food poisoning is perhaps the most commonly experienced form of food-borne toxicity. The topic has recently been comprehensively reviewed [6,15] and only the main points relevant to this discussion are presented here.

Symptoms of the poisoning generally appear 2 to 3 hr after eating and consist of salivation followed by nausea, vomiting, abdominal cramps, and diarrhea. Most patients return to normal in 24–48 hr and death is rare. Because so few affected individuals seek medical treatment, the actual incidence of poisoning is unknown but is thought to be very large. Only outbreaks affecting large numbers of individuals usually come to the attention of public health officials.

The cause of the disease is the growth and toxin production by Staphylococcus aureus, a common organism on the skin and external epithelial tissues of man and animal. Only a few of the various subtypes of S. aureus produce enterotoxin, and this capacity is difficult to predict except by direct isolation of toxin from contaminated foods.

At least four immunologically distinct enterotoxins are known to exist, and they are designated types A, B, C, and D. Physicochemical studies of enterotoxins A, B, and C have shown them to be proteins of similar composition, with molecular weights in the range of 30,000-35,000.

The pharmacological mode of action of the toxins is not clearly understood. They are very potent in producing their effects. The emetic dose of enterotoxin B in monkeys has been shown to be 0.9 mg/kg body weight, and it has been estimated that humans respond to as little as 1 μg of enterotoxin A.

Based on serological procedures, it has been found that enterotoxin A is most frequently encountered, followed by D, B, and C in that order. Emetic activity for monkeys is retained in crude culture extracts even after 1 hr of boiling. Purified toxins are somewhat more sensitive to heat inactivation but still must be regarded as comparatively stable from the viewpoint of their toxicological activity.

Three conditions must be met for staphylococcal food poisoning to occur: (1) enterotoxin-producing organisms must be present; (2) the food must support toxin production (baked beans, roast fowl, potato salad, chicken salad, custards, and cream-filled bakery products are common vehicles); and (3) the food must remain at a suitable temperature for sufficient time for toxin production (4 hr or more at ambient temperature).

V. UNINTENTIONAL ADDITIVES

Unintentional food additives comprise chemicals that become part of the food supply inadvertently, through several different routes. For the most part, they are residues resulting from processing or other manipulation involved in food production and distribution or enter foods through purely accidental circumstances [18]. Major categories of more important examples of this type of contaminant are summarized in the following sections.

A. Factors Arising from Processing

1. FUMIGANTS

Ethylene oxide is commonly used as a fumigant to sterilize foods under conditions in which steam heat is impractical. This and other epoxides can produce adverse effects by destroying essential nutrients or by reacting chemically with food components to produce toxic products. Among other products that are of interest toxicologically, ethylene oxide can combine with inorganic chlorides to form the corresponding chlorhydrin. Ethylene chlorhydrin has been found in whole and ground spices fumigated commercially at concentrations up to 1,000 ppm. The chlorhydrins are relatively toxic to animals, but effects of chronic exposure to low levels has not been evaluated and no tolerance limits have been set.

2. SOLVENT EXTRACTION AND THE PRODUCTION OF TOXIC FACTORS

Studies of trichloroethylene-extracted oil-bearing seeds present an excellent example of the kind of problem that arises when there is an interaction between the substance being processed and the solvent, with the production of a highly toxic product, although the chemical used in processing is itself nontoxic.

Extraction of various oil seeds with trichloroethylene was formerly practiced in several countries, until the practice had to be abandoned when it was found that the extracted residue was toxic when fed to animals. Soybean oil meal, for example, when extracted in this fashion, invariably caused aplastic anemia when fed to cattle. Ultimately, it was shown that the toxic factor was S-(dichlorovinyl)-L-cysteine, which was produced by interaction of the solvent with cysteine in the proteins of the soybean meal.

3. PRODUCTS OF LIPID OXIDATION

A large number of changes can be induced in lipids of foods during processing by commercial methods. Important among these from a toxicological point of view are some of the oxidative and polymerization reactions that take place, particularly after prolonged heating. For example, several investigators have shown that fatty acid monomers and dimers differing from their natural counterparts accumulate during abusive deep-fat frying and similar heating conditions. Such heated oils when fed to rats result in depressed growth and food efficiency and also in liver enlargement. The mechanisms responsible for these changes are unknown, but the not uncommon occurrence of these conditions in commercial practice (especially in small facilities for group feeding) makes further investigation of the problem worthwhile.

4. CARCINOGENS IN SMOKED FOODS

The smoking of food for preservation and flavoring is one of the oldest forms of food processing. Despite its long use, surprisingly little is known about the toxicological connotations of the practice. For example, it is well known that products that are exposed directly to wood smoke become contaminated with polycyclic aromatic hydrocarbons, many of which are known to be carcinogenic for animals. It has, in fact, been suggested (but not proved) that the high incidence of stomach cancer in Iceland may be somehow associated with the habitual consumption of heavily smoked meats and meat products. Woodsmoke condensate contains many other classes of compounds (phenolics, acids, carbonyls, and alcohols), most of which have not been adequately investigated for toxicological activity.

B. Accidental Contaminants

1. HEAVY METALS

Heavy metals have been among substances receiving increased attention as widespread environmental contaminants and as accidental food contaminants. They enter the environment mainly as a result of industrial pollution and find their way into the food chain through a number of routes. The two metals of principal concern in this connection are mercury and cadmium [16,17].

Toxicological implications of mercury depend heavily on the chemical form involved. Exposure to organic mercurials, especially methyl mercury, is more dangerous than is exposure to inorganic salts. The central nervous system is the main site of toxic action of both forms, but exposure to methyl mercury is much more ominous, since lesions induced by it are irreversible. Human response data are available from a mass-poisoning episode in the Minimata Bay area of Japan, in which clinical signs of poisoning were evident when intakes of methyl mercury exceeded 4 μg/kg body weight. Taking into account the total dietary sources of mercury, a "tolerable weekly intake" of 300 μg total mercury per person, of which not more than 200 μg should be methyl mercury, has been established.

Practically all of the methyl mercury in the diet comes through contaminated fish; other foods generally contain less than 100 ppb of total (inorganic and organic) mercury. In recent years, marketbasket surveys reveal daily intake of 1-20 μg of total mercury per individual in the United States and Western Europe.

Cadmium is widely distributed in the environment and is readily absorbed when eaten. All available information deals with inorganic salts; no toxicological information is available on organic compounds containing cadmium.

A small proportion of ingested cadmium is stored in the kidneys in the form of a metal-protein complex. Long-term exposure to excessive amounts results in renal tubular damage in animals and man. Other long-term effects include anemia, liver dysfunction, and testicular damage.

Human exposure to cadmium takes place mainly through foods, most of which contain less than 50 ppb of the metal. Representative intakes in various parts of the world are in the range of 40-60 μg per person per day, and a tolerance of 400-500 μg per week has been established.

2. POLYCHLORINATED BIPHENYLS (PCB'S)

The discovery in 1966 of PCB's in fish attracted attention among the scientific community, since it was thought that these chemicals were used only in closed, controlled systems. Subsequent research has revealed that they are in fact widespread environmental contaminants with many possible implications to public health [30].

With respect to PCB's in foods, current information suggests that (1) they rarely appear in fresh fruits and vegetables; (2) they are frequently found in fish, poultry, milk, and eggs; and (3) thay can enter foods through migration from packaging materials. Levels generally encountered are in the range 1–40 ppm, with an average of less than 2 ppm.

The toxicological implication of these residues is not entirely clear. Although these chemicals do not have a high order of acute or chronic toxicity to animals, they accumulate in adipose tissues, and evidence of human poisoning has been reported at very high levels of intake.

3. CHLORINATED NAPHTHALENES

These substances are of interest because they have proved to be the causative agents in a previously unknown disease of cattle known as bovine hyperkeratosis.

This toxic syndrome is of great economic importance since it kills large numbers of cattle in affected herds. The compounds are commonly used in wood preservatives and lubricating oils, and the problem arises when feedstuffs become contaminated with machine oil during processing. Other domestic animal species are also susceptible to poisoning, and the compounds are toxic to man. No evidence exists as to the possible presence of these contaminants in other portions of the food chain.

VI. SUMMARY AND CONCLUSIONS

This brief review has indicated the main features of the nature of real or potential problems created by the entry, through one route or another, of toxic substances into the human food supply. It is important that these problems be evaluated from the perspective of minimization of their possible impact on public health. Each of them offers interesting scientific and intellectual challenges of its own, and effective control measures require somewhat different scientific inputs.

In these terms, our present state of knowledge with regard to specific problem areas is highly variable. Some are well defined, and a large body of scientific information is at hand, as in the cases of certain of the natural constituents of plant foods or intentional additives. (This is not to say, however, that all problems in these areas are solved.) Other important problems, however, are still in their earliest stages of definition and obviously merit considerable further study, as in the instance of nitrosation of food constituents, producing compounds of possibly great public health importance.

In all of these areas, progress toward problem recognition and definition and evolution of control measures can be most effectively made by multidisciplinary research efforts, involving the joint participation of chemists, biologists, microbiologists, toxicologists, and epidemiologists. The need for this kind of approach is manifest in such problems of current interest as the nitrosamines. In this, as in other areas, food chemistry plays a role of pivotal importance.

REFERENCES

1. R. Abraham and L. Goldberg, Abstract No. 19, Society of Toxicology, Eleventh Annual Meeting, March 1972.
2. M. E. Alpert, M. S. R. Hutt, G. N. Wogan, and C. S. Davidson, Cancer, 28, 253 (1971).
3. J. R. Bamburg and F. M. Strong, in Microbial Toxins (S. Kadis, A. Ciegler, and S. J. Ajl, eds.), Vol. 7, Academic Press, New York, 1971, pp. 207-292.
4. K. F. Benitz, R. Abraham, L. Goldberg, and F. Coulston, Abstract No. 18, Society of Toxicology, Eleventh Annual Meeting, March 1972.
5. L. C. Berardi and L. A. Goldblatt, in Toxic Constituents of Plant Foodstuffs (I. E. Liener, ed.), Academic Press, New York, 1969, pp. 211-266.
6. M. S. Bergdoll, in Microbial Toxins (T. C. Montie, S. Kadis, and S. J. Ajl, eds.), Vol. 3, Academic Press, New York, 1970, pp. 265-326.
7. Y. Birk, in Toxic Constituents of Plant Foodstuffs (I. E. Liener, ed.), Academic Press, New York, 1969, pp. 169-210.

8. S. Bonfils, Lancet, ii, 414 (1970).

9. D. A. Boroff and B. R. DasGupta, in Microbial Toxins (S. Kadis, C. Montie, and S. J. Ajl, eds.), Vol. 2A, Academic Press, New York, 1971, pp. 1-68.

10. A. Ciegler, R. W. Detroy, and E. B. Lillehoj, in Microbial Toxins (A. Ciegler, S. Kadis, and S. J. Ajl, eds.), Vol. 6, Academic Press, New York, 1971, pp. 409-434.

11. A. Ciegler, S. Kadis, and S. J. Ajl, eds., Microbial Toxins. Vol. 6, Academic Press, New York, 1971.

12. R. W. Detroy, E. B. Lillehoj, and A. Ciegler, in Microbial Toxins (A. Ciegler, S. Kadis, and S. J. Ajl, eds.), Vol. 6, Academic Press, New York, 1971, pp. 4-178.

13. T. Fazio, J. N. Damico, J. W. Howard, R. H. White, and J. O. Watts, J. Food Agri. Chem., 19, 250 (1971).

14. W. Fiddler, R. C. Doerr, J. R. Ertel, and A. E. Wasserman, J. Assoc. Off. Anal. Chem., 54, 1160 (1971).

15. E. M. Foster and M. S. Bergdoll, in The Safety of Foods (J. C. Ayres, F. R. Blood, C. O. Chichester, H. D. Graham, R. S. McCutcheon, J. J. Powers, B. S. Schweigert, A. D. Stevens, and G. Zweig, eds.), AVI Publ., Westport, Conn., 1968, pp. 159-167.

16. L. Friberg, M. Piscator, and G. Nordberg, Cadmium in the Environment. Chemical Rubber Company Press, Cleveland, 1971.

17. L. Friberg and J. Vostal, Mercury in the Environment. Chemical Rubber Company Press, Cleveland, 1972.

18. L. Friedman and S. I. Shibko, in Toxic Constituents of Plant Foodstuffs (I. E. Liener, ed.), Academic Press, New York, 1969, pp. 349-408.

19. T. E. Furia, Handbook of Food Additives. Chemical Rubber Company Press, Cleveland, 1972.

20. J. H. Gentile, in Microbial Toxins (S. Kadis, A. Ciegler, and S. J. Ajl, eds.), Vol. 7, Academic Press, New York, 1971, pp. 27-66.

21. L. A. Goldblatt, Aflatoxin - Scientific Background, Control, and Implications. Academic Press, New York, 1969.

22. B. W. Halstead, Poisonous and Venomous Marine Animals. Vol. I, United States Government Printing Office, Washington, D.C., 1965.

23. B. W. Halstead, Poisonous and Venomous Marine Animals. Vol. II, United States Government Printing Office, Washington, D.C., 1967.

24. B. W. Halstead, Poisonous and Venomous Marine Animals. Vol. III, United States Government Printing Office, Washington, D.C., 1970.

25. W. G. Jaffé, in The Safety of Foods (J. C. Ayres, F. R. Blood, C. O. Chichester, H. D. Graham, R. S. McCutcheon, J. J. Powers, B. S. Schweigert, A. D. Stevens, and G. Zweig, eds.), AVI Publ., Westport, Conn., 1968, pp. 61-67.

26. W. G. Jaffé, in Toxic Constituents of Plant Foodstuffs (I. E. Liener, ed.), Academic Press, New York, 1969, pp. 69-101.

27. A. Z. Joffe, in Microbial Toxins (S. Kadis, A. Ciegler, and S. J. Ajl, eds.), Vol. 7, Academic Press, New York, 1971, pp. 139-189.

28. S. Kadis, A. Ciegler, and S. J. Ajl, eds., Microbial Toxins. Vol. 7, Academic Press, New York, 1971.

29. S. Kadis, A. Ciegler, and S. J. Ajl, eds., Microbial Toxins. Vol. 8, Academic Press, New York, 1972.

30. D. H. K. Lee and H. L. Falk, Environ. Health Persp., Experimental Issue No. 1, April 1972.

31. I. E. Liener and M. L. Kakade, in Toxic Constituents of Plant Foodstuffs (I. E. Liener, ed.), Academic Press, New York, 1969, pp. 7-68.

32. A. C. Leopold and R. Ardrey, Science, 176, 512 (1972).

33. P. N. Magee and J. M. Barnes, Advan. Cancer Res., 10, 163 (1967).

34. J. Mager, A. Razin, and A. Hershko, in Toxic Constituents of Plant Foodstuffs (I. E. Liener, ed.), Academic Press, New York, 1969, pp. 293-318.

35. M. Maillet, S. Bonfils, and R. E. Lister, Lancet, ii, 415 (1970).

36. R. Marcus and J. Watt, Lancet, ii. 489 (1969).

37. C. J. Mirocha, C. M. Christensen, and G. H. Nelson, in Microbial Toxins (S. Kadis, A. Ciegler, and S. J. Ajl, eds.), Vol. 7, Academic Press, New York, 1971, pp. 107-138.

38. S. S. Mirvish, M. Greenblatt, and V. R. C. Kommineni, J. Natl. Cancer Inst., 48, 1311 (1972).

39. R. C. Montgomery, in Toxic Constituents of Plant Foodstuffs (I. E. Liener, ed.), Academic Press, New York, 1969, pp. 143-157.

40. D. A. A. Mossel, in The Safety of Foods (J. C. Ayres, F. R. Blood, C. O. Chichester, H. D. Graham, R. S. McCutcheon, J. J. Powers, B. S. Schweigert, A. D. Stevens, and G. Zweig, eds.), AVI Publ., Westport, Conn., 1968, pp. 168-182.

41. F. Perlman, in Toxic Constituents of Plant Foodstuffs (I. E. Liener, ed.), Academic Press, New York, 1969, pp. 319-348.

42. F. E. Russell, in Advances in Marine Biology (F. S. Russell, ed.), Vol. 3, Academic Press, London, 1965, pp. 255-384.

43. F. E. Russell, in The Safety of Foods (J. C. Ayres, F. R. Blood, C. O. Chichester, H. D. Graham, R. S. McCutcheon, J. J. Powers, B. S. Schweigert, A. D. Stevens, and G. Zweig, eds.), AVI Publ., Westport, Conn., 1968, pp. 68-81.

44. M. Saito, M. Enomoto, and T. Tatsuno, in Microbial Toxins (A. Ciegler, S. Kadis, and S. J. Ajl, eds.), Vol. 6, Academic Press, New York, 1971, pp. 299-380.

45. P. S. Sarma and G. Padmanaban, in Toxic Constituents of Plant Foodstuffs (I. E. Leiner, ed.), Academic Press, New York, 1969, pp. 267-291.

46. E. J. Schantz, in Microbial Toxins (S. Kadis, A. Ciegler, and S. J. Ajl, eds.), Vol. 7, Academic Press, New York, 1971, pp. 3-26.

47. N. P. Sen, B. Donaldson, J. R. Iyengar, and T. Panalaks, Nature (London), 241, 473 (1973).

48. N. P. Sen, L. A. Schwinghamer, B. A. Donaldson, and W. F. Miles, J. Agri. Food Chem., 20, 1280 (1972).

49. R. C. Shank, N. Bhamarapravati, J. E. Gordon, and G. N. Wogan, Food Cosmet. Toxicol., 10(2), 171 (1972).

50. R. C. Shank, J. B. Gibson, A. Nondasuta, and G. N. Wogan, Food Cosmet. Toxicol., 10(1), 61 (1972).

51. R. C. Shank, J. B. Gibson, and G. N. Wogan, Food Cosmet. Toxicol., 10(1), 51 (1972).

52. R. C. Shank, J. E. Gordon, A. Nondasuta, B. Subhamani, and G. N. Wogan, Food Cosmet. Toxicol., 10(1), 71 (1972).

53. R. C. Shank and P. M. Newberne, Food Cosmet. Toxicol., 10, 887 (1972).

54. R. C. Shank, P. Siddhichai, B. Subhamani, N. Bhamarapravati, J. E. Gordon, and G. N. Wogan, Food Cosmet. Toxicol., 10(2), 181 (1972).

55. M. Sharratt, P. Grasso, F. Carpanini, and S. Gangolli, Gastroenterology, 61, 410 (1971).

56. P. S. Steyn, in Microbial Toxins (A. Ciegler, S. Kadis, and S. J. Ajl, eds.), Vol. 6, Academic Press, New York, 1971, pp. 179-205.

57. G. M. Telling, T. A. Bryce, and J. Althorpe, J. Agri. Food Chem., 19, 937 (1971).

58. C. H. VanEtten, in Toxic Constituents of Plant Foodstuffs (I. E. Liener, ed.), Academic Press, New York, 1969, pp. 103-142.

59. A. E. Wasserman, W. Fiddler, R. C. Doerr, S. F. Osman, and C. J. Dooley, Food Cosmet. Toxicol., 10, 681 (1972).

60. J. Watt and R. Marcus, J. Pharm. Pharmacol., 21, 1875 (1969).

61. J. Watt and R. Marcus, Gastroenterology, 59, 760 (1970).

62. J. Watt and R. Marcus, J. Pharm. Pharmacol., 22, 130 (1970).

63. G. N. Wogan, in Foodborne Infections and Intoxications (H. Riemann, ed.), Academic Press, New York, 1969, pp. 395-451.

64. G. N. Wogan, in Methods in Cancer Research (H. Busch, ed.), Academic Press, New York, 1973, pp. 309-344.

65. M. G. Yang and O. Mickelsen, in Toxic Constituents of Plant Foodstuffs (I. E. Liener, ed.), Academic Press, New York, 1969, pp. 159-167.

Chapter 12

FOOD DISPERSIONS

William D. Powrie and Marvin A. Tung

Department of Food Science
University of British Columbia
Vancouver, British Columbia, Canada

Contents

I. INTRODUCTION

Food systems can be divided into two major categories, namely, intact edible
tissues and food dispersions. Sliced strawberries, diced potatoes, and fish fillets

are examples of intact tissue systems which consist of cells interconnected by adhesive polymers and/or by membranes. Edible plant tissue consists for the most part of parenchyma cells which are roughly spherical in shape and have diameters ranging from 50 to 300 μm. Pectic substances are the major cementing components between these cells. Meat, essentially intact muscle tissue, is made up of parallel-oriented fiberlike cells (called fibers) which are interconnected by connective tissue. By mechanically shearing the tissue cells or by altering the intercellular adhesives and membranes, intact tissue can be converted to complex food dispersions, such as tomato juice, mashed potatoes, and meat emulsions.

A food dispersion is a system consisting of one or more dispersed or discontinuous phases in a continuous phase. A dispersion can be as simple as sugar and protein solutions or as complex as whipped cream, which contains a wide variety of dispersed molecules and particles. The types of dispersed particles in food dispersions include crystals, amorphous solid matter, cell fragments, cells, liquid droplets, and gas bubbles. In most cases, the continuous phase is either water or an edible oil.

Dispersions can be classified on the basis of the size or physical state of particles. Colloidal dispersions contain particles ranging in size from 1 nm to 0.5 μm, and coarse dispersions have particles with dimensions greater than 0.5 μm. A solution (molecular dispersion) is a one-phase system with the molecules having dimensions below 1 nm. In contrast, colloidal and coarse dispersions consist of two or more phases. The transparency, osmotic pressure, diffusion properties, and rheological characteristics of uniphase solutions (e.g., sucrose solution) are much different than those of di- and polyphase dispersions.

Systems with two phases (diphase) can be categorized into eight different combinations of phases (solid, S; liquid, L; gaseous, G) but only five are of importance in food science (Table 12-1). The most common diphase food systems are sols (S/L), emulsions (L/L), and foams (G/L).

TABLE 12-1

Diphase Food Dispersions

Dispersed phase (A)	Continuous phase (B)	A/B	Name of dispersion	Example
Solid (S)	Liquid (L)	S/L	Sol	Skim milk
Liquid (L)	Liquid (L)	L/L	Emulsion	French dressing
Gas (G)	Liquid (L)	G/L	Foam	Meringue
Gas (G)	Solid (S)	G/S	Solid foam	Foam candy
Solid (S)	Gas (G)	S/G	Solid aerosol	Smoke for flavoring food

Many foods consist of two or three dispersed phases in a continuous phase. For example, whipped cream and mayonnaise are tetraphase systems with oil droplets, aggregated protein particles, and gas bubbles as dispersed phases and water as the continuous phase. Tetraphase systems can be symbolized by L-S-G/L, with the letters before the slash indicated dispersed phases and the letter after denoting the continuous phase. Alternatively, the aforementioned tetraphase system can be termed an emulso-sol-foam.

Stability of a food dispersion is dependent on interfacial characteristics, particle size distribution, viscosity of the continuous phase, phase-volume ratio, and density difference between phases. Any alteration in the abovementioned properties can lead to destabilization of the dispersion, whereupon the dispersed particles clump together to form aggregates and, if liquid in nature, they may ultimately coalesce to form a second bulk phase (e.g., an oil layer). Destabilization of colloidal particles in a sol may bring about the formation of an elastic gel which is composed of two intermingled continuous phases. For example, in a fruit jelly, destabilized pectin polymers interconnect to form a three-dimensional continuous phase intermingled with a continuous sugar solution.

II. SURFACE AND INTERFACIAL PHENOMENA

A. Principles

Since surface or interfacial characteristics have a bearing on the formation, physical properties and stability of food dispersions, it is essential to introduce the basic concepts of surface phenomena prior to consideration of specific food dispersions.

Commonly, the boundary between a liquid and a gas is designated as a "surface," whereas with other combinations of phases, the junction is termed an "interface." Molecules at an interface or surface behave differently than like molecules that are in the bulk phase. Since a molecule in the interior (bulk) of a liquid phase is attracted equally in all directions to other molecules in its immediate environment, the attractive forces are balanced (Fig. 12-1). Molecules at a surface or interface are not surrounded completely by other molecules of the same type and the same physical state, however, and thus the net attractive force for each molecule is directed toward the interior of the phase in which the molecule resides. The inward attraction tends to reduce the number of molecules at the surface or interface and as a result the surface or interfacial area is reduced to a minimum. The forces causing a reduction in surface or interfacial area are referred to, respectively, as surface tension and interfacial tension. These tensions, γ, are expressed in dynes per centimeter at constant temperature, pressure, and concentration.

The intermolecular attractions which are responsible for surface and interfacial tensions of liquid involve hydrogen bonding and London dispersion forces. With polar compounds, such as water, both of these forces are important, whereas only London dispersion forces are operative in nonpolar liquids, such as triglycerides.

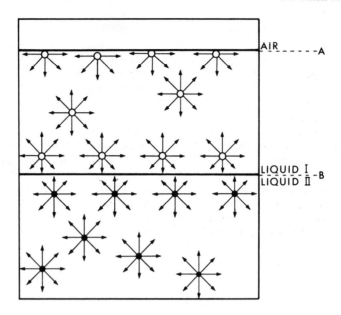

FIG. 12-1. Attractive forces between molecules at the surface, at the interface, and in the interior of the liquid phases.

To increase the area of a surface, work is required to overcome the forces of
attraction so that interior molecules can move to the surface region. The work of
surface expansion is expressed in ergs per square centimeter, which is numeri-
cally the same as surface tension, γ, in dynes per centimeter (1 erg is equal to 1
dyne-cm). Moreover, the work in ergs per square centimeter is equal to the free-
energy change of expansion. The total surface energy, E_S, required to expand a
surface by 1 cm^2 is the sum of the work and heat inputs and is usually expressed as

$$E_s = \gamma - T \frac{d\gamma}{dT} \qquad\qquad (12\text{-}1)$$

where γ is the surface tension and T is absolute temperature in °K. The term
$T(d\gamma/dT)$ represents the amount of heat energy which must be supplied to maintain
the expanding surface at a constant temperature. If the surface of water is at 20°C,
the value of $T(d\gamma/dT)$ is –47.7 ergs/cm^2, γ is 72.8 ergs/cm^2, and thus E_S is
120.5 ergs/cm2.

With an increase in temperature of a liquid phase, the kinetic energy of the
molecules increases and the attractive forces among them decreases. Thus, the
surface tension of a liquid generally decreases with a rise in temperature. As the
temperature is increased, a critical temperature T_C is eventually reached at which
point the surface tension theoretically is zero.

The variation of surface tension with temperature is represented by the Ramsay
and Shields equation:

$$\gamma \left(\frac{M}{\rho}\right)^{2/3} = k(T_c - T - 6) \qquad\qquad (12\text{-}2)$$

where γ is surface tension (dynes/cm),

      M is molecular weight of liquid,

      ρ is density of the liquid,

      M/ρ is molecular volume,

      k is Eötvö's constant (about two for dissociating liquids, such as water, and for triglycerides),

      T_c is the critical temperature of the liquid, and

      $\gamma(M/\rho)^{2/3}$ is the molecular free surface energy.

One of the most common methods for measuring surface and interfacial tensions of a liquid involves the use of a du Noüy tensiometer, which is essentially a torsion balance with a platinum ring suspended from the beam. The force required to move the ring from the surface or interface is measured directly with this apparatus. The applied force F is approximately equal to the downward pull expressed as $4\pi r\gamma$, where r is the radius of the ring and γ is the surface or interfacial tension in dynes per centimeter. However, since a certain volume of liquid is adsorbed to the rising ring, a correction factor f_c, ranging from about 0.75 to 1.45, must be included in Eq. (12-3) to obtain the true tension value:

$$\gamma = \frac{f_c F}{4\pi r} \qquad\qquad (12\text{-}3)$$

B. Surface and Interfacial Tensions of Purified Liquids

Water and edible triglyceride oils, the most important food liquids, have markedly different surface tension values between 0° and 80°C (Table 12-2). With an increase in temperature from 20° to 80°C, the surface tension of water drops about 10 dynes/cm, whereas the surface tensions of cottonseed and coconut oils decrease only 4-5 dynes/cm.

TABLE 12-2

Influence of Temperature on the Surface Tension of
Water and Vegetable Oils[a]

Temperature (°C)	Water	Surface tension (dynes/cm)		
		Cottonseed oil	Coconut oil	Olive oil
0	72.6	–	–	–
20	72.8	35.4	33.4	33.0
30	71.2	–	–	–
50	67.9	–	–	–
80	62.6	31.3	28.4	–
100	58.9	–	–	–
130	–	27.5	24.0	–

[a]From Halpern [12].

The interfacial tension between edible oil and water is of particular importance in the creation and stability of many food emulsions. To facilitate emulsification, the interfacial tension between water and oil should be below 10 dynes/cm. Interfacial tension values for specific triglycerides and vegetable oils are listed in Table 12-3. The values fall between 12.8 and 18.5 dynes/cm for oil-water systems at 25°C.

C. Surface and Interfacial Tensions of Aqueous Solutions

The presence of a solute influences the surface tension of water. The orientation and concentration of the molecules or ions at the surface of a solution govern the extent of change in the surface tension. Two effects of solutes on surface tension are shown in Figure 12-2. With solutions of inorganic salts and compounds with a large number of hydroxyl groups (e.g., sucrose), surface tension increases slightly as the concentration of the solute increases (curve I). The surface tensions of sucrose solutions at concentrations between 10 and 63% are presented in Table 12-4. Curve II is produced when a surface-active compound (surfactant) is present in solution. Following the rapid drop to a minimum, the surface tension rises and then levels out. The minimum is the result of a small amount of impurity in the surfactant. Surface-active agents, which have a balance of both polar (hydrophilic) and nonpolar (hydrophobic) groups, are adsorbed at the surface of a solution. This results in a reduction in surface tension.

TABLE 12-3

Interfacial Tension between Water and Various Oils[a]

Purified oil	Interfacial tension (dynes/cm)	
	25°C	75°C
Triolein	14.6	13.5
1,3-Dioleo-2-palmitin	14.5	12.3
Peanut (screw press)	18.1	–
Peanut (solvent, extracted)	18.5	–
Cottonseed (screw press)	14.9	–
Olive	17.6	–
Coconut	12.8	–

[a]From Benerito et al. [4] and Singleton and Benerito [23].

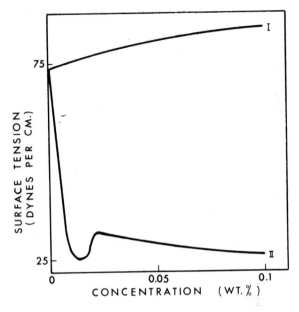

FIG. 12-2. Influence on concentration of compounds (types I and II) on the surface tension of water.

TABLE 12-4

Surface Tension of Sucrose Solution at 21°C

Concentration (g/100 g solution)	Surface tension (dynes/cm)
0	72.7
10	73.4
30	76.2
51	78.7
63	79.6

Added solutes exhibit either positive or negative adsorption. With positive adsorption, the concentration of a solute at the surface is higher than the solute concentration in the bulk and this brings about a type II curve. In contrast, a solution that exhibits negative adsorption has a greater concentration of solute in the bulk fluid than at the surface, and a type I curve results. The surface concentration Γ (moles/cm^2) of a solute can be expressed by Gibbs adsorption equation,

$$\Gamma = -\frac{c}{RT}\frac{\partial\gamma}{\partial c} \qquad\qquad (12\text{-}4)$$

where c is the concentration (moles/liter) of solute, R is the gas constant (8.31 x 10^7 ergs/°K-mole), T is absolute temperature (°K), and γ is surface tension.

To attain a minimum free energy at the surface of a surfactant solution, it is necessary for the surfactant molecules to orient at the surface with their polar groups directed toward the aqueous phase and their hydrocarbon chains directed toward the gaseous (or nonaqueous) phase. As the concentration of surface-active agent is increased, the molecules are adsorbed as a monolayer until the surface region is completely filled. At some higher concentration, additional molecules of surfactant aggregate in the bulk phase to form organized structures, called micelles. Micelles may be spherical or lamellar in shape, and they have an interior consisting of inwardly oriented hydrocarbon chains of surface-active compounds and an exterior of hydrated hydrophilic groups. The lowest surfactant concentration at which the micelles form is known as the "critical micelle concentration" (CMC). The CMC's of many surfactants fall between 0.004 and 0.15 moles/liter. At concentrations greater than the CMC, micelles act as reservoirs of surfactant molecules. When new surfaces are formed, individual molecules move from the micelles to the surface or interface. Light scattering studies indicate that the number of surfactant molecules in micelles range from three to over 100. In solutions of fatty acid salts, micelles contain about 30-50 molecules. Some molecules, such as phospholipids, group together to form complex particles, such as myelin (concentric multilayered) figures rather than single micelles [21].

Proteins, when dissolved in water, reduce surface and interfacial tensions. When protein molecules are present at a surface or interface, they uncoil (surface denaturation), are strongly adsorbed on the surface or interface, and interact with each other to form a viscous film. The surface tensions of freshly prepared protein solutions generally decrease with time since the rate of surface adsorption of these high molecular weight polymers is slow. According to Ghosh and Bull [8], the surface tension of 0.06% egg albumin solution (pH 4.9) at 30°C dropped from about 62 to 48 dynes/cm within a period of 55 min after preparation. As shown in Table 12-5, a variety of milk proteins can reduce the interfacial tension between water and butter oil.

TABLE 12-5

Influence of Milk Proteins on the Interfacial Tension
between Water and Butter Oil at 40°C[a]

Protein	Concentration (%)	Interfacial tension (dynes/cm)
None	–	19.2
Euglobulin	0.2	18
	0.6	18
β-Lactoglobulin	0.2	14
	0.6	14

TABLE 12-5 (Continued)

Protein	Concentration (%)	Interfacial tension (dynes/cm)
α-Lactalbumin	0.2	11
	0.6	11
Interface protein	0.2	11
	0.6	9

[a]From Jackson and Pallansch [14].

Lipids, such as phospholipids, salts of fatty acids, and monoglycerides, have surface-active properties. The surface tensions of phospholipid sols with concentrations between 0.6 and 10% are in the vicinity of 23–27 dynes/cm which are much lower values than those for comparable concentrations of proteins [24]. The influence of monoglyceride concentration on the interfacial tension between water and cottonseed oil is depicted in Figure 12-3.

III. FOOD SOLS

A sol is an S/L dispersion with solid or semisolid particles distributed in a continuous liquid phase. Uniform distribution of the particles in a stable sol is dependent on size, shape, solvation, interfacial forces, concentration, and density of the particles and on viscosity of the continuous phase. Systems consisting of

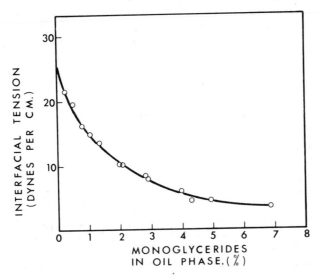

FIG. 12-3. Influence of monoglyceride concentration on the interfacial tension between water and cottonseed oil. (From Kuhrt et al. [17].)

microparticles with diameters between 1 nm and 0.5 μm are called "colloidal sols" and those with macroparticles having diameters above 0.5 μm have been termed "coarse sols" or "suspensions." Rheological, optical, and gas-retaining properties of the two types of sols at a given solids content may be markedly different. Colloidal food sols are made up of long-chain macromolecules and/or micelles consisting of aggregated molecules of proteins, polysaccharides, or lipids. The macroparticles in coarse sols can be crystals, semicrystalline aggregates (i.e., cell-wall fragments), or amorphous flocs. Many food systems exhibit a wide range of particle sizes and thus cannot be categorized on the basis of particle size distribution alone.

Within the colloidal size range, interfacial and inertial forces are significant in governing the properties of sols. Some of these properties are Brownian motion, diffusion through membranes, light scattering, and viscous flow. The nature of the particle-fluid interface is particularly important as a determinant of rheological behavior and stability of sols. In particular, the presence of electrically charged ionic groups and polar groups at the interfaces contribute to particle-particle repulsion and adsorption of stabilizing dipolar water molecules.

Colloidal sols can be further categorized as lyophilic and lyophobic on the basis of the degree of affinity that the dispersed particles have for the aqueous continuous phase. Lyophilic colloids include hydrophilic biopolymers, such as seaweed gums, pectic substances, and proteins, and hydrophilic complex aggregates found in skim milk, egg yolk, and brewed coffee. Sols of the hydrophobic type, e.g., hydrophobic oxides and insoluble salts, are rarely encountered in food systems.

Coarse food sols, such as shortening, peanut butter, applesauce, ketchup, and fondant, possess macroparticles which at moderately high solids concentrations contribute to the plasticity and opacity of the final product. The stability of these sols is governed by the density difference of the phases, viscosity of the continuous phase, particle size, and to a lesser extent interfacial forces. If the density difference is small, then the interfacial force can be important. Other factors being equal, coarse sols are usually much less stable than colloidal sols since particles larger than 4 μm do not exhibit Brownian movement. The higher degree of plasticity of coarse sols can be attributed to extensive particle-particle contact and capillary immobilization of the continuous phase at the surfaces of the macroparticles.

A. Properties of Sols

1. ELECTRICAL DOUBLE LAYER

In a sol possessing a continuous aqueous phase, the particles often have electrically charged surfaces. The ionized groups of proteins, phospholipids, and polysaccharides can be the source of these charges. In the presence of dissolved electrolytes, an electrical double layer may exist around each particle. The double layer consists of (1) approximately a single layer of fixed counterions (Stern layer) adsorbed to the charged surface of each particle and (2) a diffuse layer of counterions distributed in the solution near the interface. Roughly 60–85% of the counterions are located in the Stern layer and these are responsible for a sharp drop in potential across this layer (Fig. 12-4). A Langmuir-type adsorption

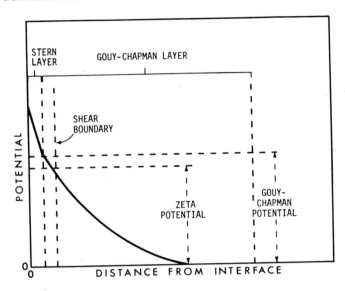

FIG. 12-4. Electrical double layer.

equilibrium is assumed to exist between ions in solution and those in the Stern layer (about 2 Å in thickness), and the adsorption energy includes electrical and van der Waals forces. The diffuse layer (Gouy-Chapman layer) has a thickness of up to several hundred Ångstroms, and the potential gradually falls with increasing distance from the particle surface.

Under the influence of an applied electrical field, the particle along with the Stern layer can move away from the diffuse ion layer at the plane of shear. Zeta potential is the electrical potential across the plane of shear and this potential can be as high as 100 mV.

Stability of a sol with charged particles requires that the forces of repulsion between particles of like charge exceed the forces of attraction. On close approach of two charged particles, the overlapping of double layers interact to increase free energy and to intensify the potential energy of repulsion. The rate of flocculation (reversible particle-particle aggregation) is dependent on the collision frequency of the sol particles, the degree of solvation of particles, and the energy level of the double layer. The addition of salts to a sol can cause flocculation, but the minimum salt concentration required is much higher with hydrophilic sols than with hydrophobic sols. About 3.6 moles/liter of sodium chloride are required to flocculate negatively charged egg albumin. Salts affect hydrophilic sols by reducing the zeta potential on the particles and by withdrawing water from the hydrated surfaces of the particles. Only a small amount of electrolyte is required to lower the zeta potential but a considerable amount is necessary for desolvation of the particles. Solvation alone can inhibit flocculation when the particles have diameters less than 1,000 Å and have solvent layers greater than 20 Å [25].

With a lowering of zeta potential, the viscosity of a hydrophilic sol is reduced. This phenomenon is called the electroviscous effect. If a sol has negatively charged particles, then the ability of cations to lower viscosity occurs in the order: trivalent > divalent > monovalent (equal ionic strength).

Another process by which hydrophilic sols can be destabilized involves the interaction of oppositely charged particles. If a small amount of tannin sol is added to a 1% agar sol, the resulting mixture attains a milky appearance and the particles flocculate in the presence of a small concentration of electrolyte. Presumably the surfaces of the flocs are occupied by a large number of somewhat hydrophobic phenolic groups of the tannin molecules.

The stability of protein sols is decreased when the pH is adjusted so that net charges on the particles are reduced. In normal skim milk (around pH 6.7), caseinate micelles which are negatively charged can be destabilized by lowering the pH to about 4.7 [26]. At this pH (the isoelectric point of casein), the micelles have approximately equal numbers of negatively and positively charged groups and thus they can readily form aggregates.

2. RHEOLOGY OF SOLS

Although hydrophobic sols have viscosities similar to water at the same temperature, the viscosities of hydrophilic sols are much greater than that of water and are increased markedly by a decrease in temperature or an increase in particle concentration. Indeed at particle concentrations greater than 20%, sols may exhibit plasticity.

In order to understand the rheological characteristics of sols and other colloidal systems, knowledge of some basic rheological terms is needed. The viscosity of a fluid is a measure of the resistance to flow or shear and is highly dependent on the surface characteristics of dispersed particles. The unit of viscosity, the poise, is the tangential force required to maintain a velocity of 1 cm/sec between two planes with areas of 1 cm^2 and positioned 1 cm apart. When the shear stress (τ) is proportional to the rate of shear ($\dot{\gamma}$), the fluid is Newtonian and behaves in accord with the following relationship:

$$\tau = \eta\dot{\gamma} \qquad\qquad (12\text{-}5)$$

The formula defines the coefficient of viscosity, η, which is a material parameter. Dilute hydrophobic sols and very dilute hydrophilic sols with viscosities similar to that for water exhibit Newtonian behavior. Most hydrophilic sols, in contrast, do not exhibit a straight-line relationship between shearing stress and rate of shear and are therefore termed non-Newtonian fluids. Non-Newtonian food sols can be divided into "pseudo plastic," "dilatant," and "plastic" (Fig. 12-5). The viscosity of a pseudoplastic fluid decreases with increasing rate of shear, whereas the viscosity of a dilatant fluid increases with increasing shear rate. This is shown by the changing slope of the shear stress-shear rate rheograms (Fig. 12-5), since viscosity is the slope of the line at any point. Thus non-Newtonian viscosity is not constant and the term "apparent viscosity" describes the resistance to flow of these fluids. A Bingham plastic substance has a constant viscosity after a definite stress, known as the yield stress (τ_y) is applied; however nonlinear behavior (non-Bingham plastic flow) is also common.

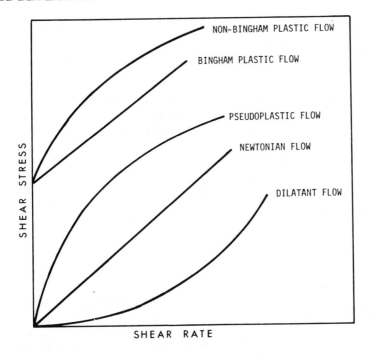

FIG. 12-5. Rheograms of flow behavior of food sols.

Dilute hydrophilic sols, such as milk and gum sols, exhibit pseudo plastic flow; concentrated hydrophilic sols, such as tomato ketchup, applesauce, and fudge, are considered to exhibit non-Bingham plastic flow; and a 35% starch slurry exhibits dilatant properties. The characteristics of these non-Newtonian fluids are dependent on (1) particle size distribution, (2) nature of the particle surfaces, (3) particle shape, and (4) volume of the dispersed phase. Hydrophilic sols consisting of long-chain polymers or fiberlike particles are randomly dispersed and perhaps tangled; thus, they exhibit high viscosities. However, with higher shear rates, the particles tend to orient themselves parallel to the shear field and the viscosity decreases.

Dilatant sols (become more viscous with increasing shear rate) consist of a high concentration of particles which have a tendency to aggregate and form large pockets for entrapment of the continuous phase.

Over a moderate range of shear rate, pseudo plastic and dilatant behavior follows a power law relationship:

$$\tau = m\dot{\gamma}^n \tag{12-6}$$

where m is the consistency coefficient and n is the flow behavior index. Pseudo-plastic fluids are characterized by n < 1, dilatant fluids by n > 1, and Newtonian fluids correspond to n = 1.

As mentioned, a minimum stress (yield stress) must be applied to plastic sols before flow occurs. These systems at rest consist of high concentrations of particles, many of which are aggregated. Thus, a sufficient stress is required to break down the aggregates to bring about flow of the continuous phase. As shear stress is applied at low values, the aggregates deform elastically until the stress exceeds the yield stress and flow occurs. At higher stress values, the flow pattern may be represented by a linear relationship between shear stress and shear rate, as a Bingham plastic, which follows the equation:

$$\tau - \tau_y = \eta_p \dot{\gamma} \qquad\qquad (12\text{-}7)$$

where η_p is the coefficient of plastic viscosity. After the yield value has been exceeded a nonlinear relationship is quite common in food sols, and this non-Bingham plastic flow is accurately described by a power law with yield stress equation:

$$\tau - \tau_y = m\dot{\gamma}^n \qquad\qquad (12\text{-}8)$$

The following factors influence the yield value: (1) concentration of the dispersed phase, (2) presence of flocculating agents, (3) size of dispersed particles, and (4) viscosity of the continuous phase.

If the shear stress of a sol decreases with time during steady shear the material is called: (1) "thixotropic" if the structural breakdown is reversible after a rest time is allowed, or (2) "rheodestructive" if the breakdown is permanent. Time-dependent behavior is caused by the gradual detachment of particles from small aggregates and the nonlinear shear stress decay often is in accord with one of the following models:

$$\tau = A_1 - B_1 \log t \qquad\qquad (12\text{-}9)$$

or

$$\log (\tau - \tau_e) = A_2 - B_2 t \qquad\qquad (12\text{-}10)$$

where t is time, τ_e is a minimum equilibrium shear stress achieved at a given shear rate, and A_1, A_2, B_1, and B_2 are constants for the selected sol. Because of the combined effects of shear rate and time dependence, the rheological description of concentrated sols is quite complex.

The viscosity of sols containing high molecular weight polymers at a given concentration generally increases with increasing chain length in accord with the Staudinger equation:

$$\eta_{sp} = \frac{\eta - \eta_s}{\eta_s} = KMc \qquad\qquad (12\text{-}11)$$

where η_{sp} is specific viscosity of the sol, η is viscosity of the sol, η_s is viscosity of the continuous phase, K is a constant, M is the molecular weight of the polymer, and c is the concentration.

3. OPTICAL PROPERTIES OF SOLS

In food sols, particles may be large enough to reflect and refract incident light so that an opaque appearance occurs. However, if the particles are in the colloidal size range, incident light is scattered and polarized to some extent (Tyndall phenomenon). Highly solvated colloidal particles do not scatter as much light as hydrophobic particles because their refractive indices are very similar to that of the continuous phase.

The light reflection, I_R, of large-particle sols is dependent on the size and concentration of particles and can be expressed as:

$$I_R = K\frac{c}{d} \qquad (12\text{-}12)$$

where K is a constant, c is concentration, and d is the diameter of particles (applicable only to particles that are greater than about 1 μm in diameter).

B. Formation of Sols

The formation of food sols involves either (1) the process of aggregation of molecules to form micro- and macroparticles or (2) a dispersion or peptization process whereby a large mass is subdivided into particles of suitable size and shape.

In the aggregation process, the combining of molecules must be controlled to insure the proper particle size distribution and, in addition, the continuous phase must have specific chemical and physical properties to maintain the proper size distribution. Controlled crystallization, isoelectric precipitation, and thermal coagulation are examples of aggregation processes. To form small crystals, a supersaturated system must be created or a melt (such as oil or water) must be cooled. Supersaturation (S) occurs when the ratio in Eq. (12-13) exceeds a value of 1.0:

$$S = \frac{\text{g solute per 100 g water at temperature T}}{\text{g solute per 100 g water when saturated at temperature T}} \qquad (12\text{-}13)$$

During the cooling of a solution, the system may pass from the stable zone (unsaturated), into the metastable zone (slightly supersaturated), and finally into the labile zone (highly supersaturated), where spontaneous crystallization occurs.

With sucrose solutions, the metastable zone ranges between supersaturation values of 1.0 and 1.3 wherein crystallization can be induced by external seeding with particles, such as added sucrose crystals [18]. Fondant, a sol consisting of sucrose crystals dispersed in a saturated sugar solution, can be produced by cooling a saturated solution of sucrose to a specific level of supersaturation and initiating crystallization by agitation. The size and number of sucrose crystals in the final fondant are governed by the degree of supersaturation, temperature at which crystallization is induced, viscosity of the syrup phase, degree of agitation, and the presence of crystal inhibitors. In the manufacture of shortening, the melted fat is cooled to a suitable temperature to initiate nucleation and crystallization of those triglycerides that have melting points above ambient temperature.

Optimum plasticity can be achieved by the formation of small, stable crystals (β' polymorphic form) at a concentration level of around 20-25% at 20°C [27].

The dispersion process for sol formation involves disintegration or subdivision of masses by (1) addition of peptizing agents, such as salts, acids, bases, or enzymes; (2) heating; (3) removal of flocculating agents; or (4) mechanical disruption, e.g., grinding, comminuting, or colloid milling.

IV. FOOD GELS

A food gel consists of a continuous phase of interconnected particles and/or macromolecules intermingled with a continuous liquid phase such as water. Gels possess various degrees of rigidity, elasticity, and brittleness, depending on the type and concentration of the gelling agent, the salt content, and pH of the aqueous phase, and the temperature. The gelling agents, present at levels of 10% or less, may be polysaccharides, proteins, or colloidal complex particles, such as caseinate micelles. Firm gels can be prepared from a few types of gums, pectins, and gelatin at levels of 1% or lower. Gels prepared with colloidal particles are generally not very rigid even when the solids content is considerably higher than 1%. Some gels can be melted (liquefied) and reset with the addition or removal of thermal energy, and these have been designated as thermoreversible. Gels with covalent bonds between the molecules or complex particles, however, are generally thermoirreversible.

A sol can be transformed into a gel under various conditions, such as (1) temperature change, (2) chemical alteration of the gelling agent, (3) reduction in the number of charged groups by adjustment of pH or addition of salt and (4) addition of a water-competitive compound, such as a sugar. During the sol-gel transformation, a three-dimensional network is formed involving interaction of specific groups on polymer chains or particles to form crosslinkages at the sites of junction zones. The aqueous phase is entrapped in the interstitial areas of this structure. With some gelling agents, the junction zones consist of microcrystallites involving specific chain units arranged in a crystal-like fashion. Bonds in the junction zones are electrostatic, hydrophobic, covalent, and hydrogen bonds. Thermoreversible gels have a preponderance of intermolecular hydrogen bonds, whereas in protein gels a few disulfide linkages per polymer chain may be sufficient to render them thermoirreversible.

During the storage of a gel, the system may shift to a more stable state with changes in junction zones and solvent-solute relationships. This process leads to syneresis, which involves the spontaneous release of water and the contraction of the gel volume. Further information on food gels is given in Chapters 3 and 5 and in Refs. [1,3,7,13,16,20,28].

V. EMULSIONS

A. Introduction

When an immiscible liquid is dispersed as small droplets (dispersed phase) in another immiscible liquid (continuous phase) by mechanical agitation, an emulsion is created. A simple emulsion, as just described, is generally unstable and if it is allowed to stand for a short time, the dispersed droplets either rise and co-alesce to form a floating layer or settle and coalesce to form a sedimented layer, depending on the densities of the two phases. Emulsion stability can be promoted by adding an emulsifying agent to one of the phases prior to emulsion formation [2,11]. An emulsifying agent is a surface-active agent that lowers the interfacial tension and forms a physical barrier around each droplet so as to impede their coalescence (combining of small droplets to form larger droplets).

A food emulsion is basically a two-phase system consisting of a liquid or plastic lipid (such as oils, fats, waxes, or essential oils) and water. Most of the dis-persed droplets in food emulsions have diameters between 0.1 and 10 μm. Oil in water (O/W) emulsions consist of lipid droplets dispersed in water, and water in oil (W/O) emulsions are made up of water droplets dispersed in a continuous oil phase. Food emulsions may possess, in addition to the two liquid phases, solid particles (e.g., coagulated protein clumps) and gas bubbles. The following are examples of food emulsions: butter (W/O), margarine (W/O), mayonnaise (O/W), salad dressing (O/W), milk (O/W), cream (O/W), nondairy creamer (O/W), chip dip (O/W), and ice cream mix (O/W).

B. Identification of Emulsion Type

Several methods have been commonly used to identify the type of food emulsion.

1. CONDUCTIVITY METHOD

When two electrodes are immersed in an emulsion, an electric current can pass readily through an O/W type but very little can be carried through the W/O type (except for emulsions with a dispersed phase volume exceeding 60%). Current flow in the system can be detected with an ammeter or a light bulb.

2. DYE METHOD

This method is based on the ability of a dye to dissolve in the continuous phase. A small amount of powdered dye (either water soluble or oil soluble) is mixed into the emulsion and the emulsion-dye system is examined with a microscope to note any dissolution of the dye. If the dye is water soluble, then an O/W emulsion be-comes colored uniformly. In contrast, if the water-soluble dye exists as small undissolved particles in the continuous phase, then the emulsion is a W/O type. Any of the food coal tar dyes are suitable water-soluble dyes and Sudan III can be employed as the oil-soluble dye.

3. DILUTION METHOD

Dilution of an emulsion with either water or oil can be employed to assess the emulsion type. If a drop of water is mixed with a few drops of emulsion, the original characteristics of the emulsion do not change if the emulsion is an O/W type. Water is not miscible with the continuous phase of a W/O emulsion.

4. FLUORESCENT METHOD

Since oils fluoresce under ultraviolet light, a uniform fluorescent field becomes apparent with a W/O emulsion. With an O/W emulsion, however, the field is non-uniform.

C. Functional Attributes of Food Emulsions

Acceptability of food emulsions is dependent on such attributes as appearance (color, opacity), textural characteristics (viscosity, plasticity, oiliness), and flavor. To be more specific, the following features of food emulsions make them advantageous:

1. Oil-soluble flavoring and coloring matter or vitamins can be incorporated as components in the dispersed oil phase of an O/W emulsion.
2. Opacity of a fluid product can be created by dispersing droplets with diameters ranging from 0.05 to 1.0 μm in the continuous phase.
3. A high degree of plasticity can be achieved by raising the concentration of the dispersed liquid to about 60% or above (e.g., mayonnaise).
4. Oil can be introduced into a system without imparting an oily sensation (e.g., mayonnaise).

D. Physical Properties of Emulsions

1. DROPLET SIZE DISTRIBUTION

With most food emulsions, droplet size distribution is Gaussian. The range of droplet sizes is dependent on type and concentration of the emulsifying agent; the mechanical treatment, such as colloid milling and homogenization; and storage time. Very few droplets in an emulsion are smaller than 0.25 μm in diameter and the largest droplets may have diameters as high as 50 μm. Droplet size distribution can be determined by measuring the diameters of 500-2,000 droplets under a microscope. Other methods of estimating size distribution involve light scattering, centrifugal sedimentation or flotation in a density gradient, or passage of droplets through orifices of known size (e.g., Coulter counter).

2. OPTICAL PROPERTIES

The opacity of an emulsion is governed by droplet size distribution, droplet concentration, and difference between the refractive indices of the two phases. An emulsion is transparent when the refractive indices of the phases are the same or when droplet diameters are 0.05 μm or less. Opacity of an emulsion is enhanced as the average droplet size increases from 0.05 to 1 μm, the latter value yielding approximately maximum opacity. The effect of droplet size on the appearance of an emulsion is shown in Table 12-6.

3. RHEOLOGY OF EMULSIONS

Very dilute emulsions exhibit Newtonian flow with a straight-line relationship between shearing stress (τ) and shear rate ($\dot{\gamma}$). In more concentrated emulsions, the droplets interact with one another to form aggregates and thus the systems possess non-Newtonian behavior. These emulsions may exhibit pseudo plasticity or non-Bingham plasticity. Many factors influence the rheological behavior of food emulsion, including those given in the following sections.

a. Viscosity of the Continuous Phase

The viscosity of the continuous phase is a major factor governing the rheological behavior of an emulsion. Equation (12-14) expresses a direct proportionality between the viscosity of the continuous phase and apparent viscosity of emulsion:

$$\eta = \eta_0 X \tag{12-14}$$

where η is apparent viscosity of the emulsion; η_0 is viscosity of the continuous phase, and X is a factor representing the summation of all other properties influencing the viscosity of the emulsion. In many food emulsions, gums are added to the continuous phase to enhance stability as well as to increase viscosity of the emulsion. Gum acacia can stabilize emulsions by being adsorbed at the oil-water interface to form a hydrated film and by increasing the viscosity of the continuous phase [22].

TABLE 12-6

Effect of Droplet Size on Emulsion Appearance

Particle size	Appearance
Macroglobules	Two phases may be distinguished
Greater than 1 μm	Milky-white emulsion
1 μm to about 0.1 μm	Blue-white emulsion
0.1 μm to 0.05 μm	Gray semitransparent
0.05 μm and smaller	Transparent

aFrom Griffin and Lynch [11].

b. Viscosity of the Dispersed Phase

The viscosity of the dispersed phase is significant only when it behaves like a
liquid. Since small droplets in emulsions generally behave like rigid spheres,
their influence on viscosity is usually slight.

c. Concentration of the Dispersed Phase

The apparent viscosity of an emulsion is usually similar to that of the continuous
phase if this phase constitutes the major portion of the emulsion. However, when
the dispersed phase is increased to a volume greater than that of the continuous
phase, the apparent viscosity of the emulsion increases. In other words, as the
droplets increase in number and occupy a greater total volume, droplet contact
increases and causes a rise in viscosity. Only 74% of the total volume of an emulsion can be occupied by the dispersed phase when the droplets are spherical, uniform in size, and not distorted by pressure. When the dispersed phase exceeds
74% of the emulsion, droplets are distorted and the emulsion has a high degree of
plasticity.

d. Interfacial Film and Emulsifying Agents

When an emulsifying agent is added to one of the phases of an emulsion, a strong
interfacial film of oriented emulsifier molecules is formed around each droplet
during emulsification. The chemical nature and concentration of the emulsifying
agent have definite influences on the apparent viscosity of the emulsion. A high
viscosity generally results from a relatively high concentration of emulsifier, and
this effect is attributable to enhanced adsorption of some types of molecules (proteins) and to entrapment of the continuous phase in micelles formed from excess
emulsifier molecules.

e. Electroviscous Effect

Droplets in an emulsion may have double-layer charges at their interfaces. These
charges generally arise by ionization, adsorption, or frictional contact and they
may have a profound influence on viscosity. When an emulsion is sheared, the
symmetry of the electric double layer around each droplet is distorted and the
interaction between ions in the electrical double layer is affected. This leads to
dissipation of energy and an increase in viscosity.

E. Formation of Emulsions

During formation of an emulsion, the disruption of bulk liquids to produce small
droplets is the prime process and, thereafter, stabilization of the droplets is
paramount.

The most common method for preparing an emulsion is by mechanically dispersing one bulk liquid phase in another. If a portion of one liquid phase is extended in another by mixing, two spherical droplets form when the length of the extended portion exceeds its circumference $(2\pi r)$. The next step in emulsification is the breaking up of large drops into small droplets by shear from a beater blade or from passage of the coarse emulsion through a colloid mill or homogenizer.

To form an emulsion, work is required to create new interfaces. The amount of work required to disperse 1 ml of olive oil as droplets of 5 μm diameter in 10 ml of water is about 274,800 ergs. This value does not include other work inputs, such as that for setting the liquids in motion. An emulsifier added to this olive oil-water system would reduce the interfacial tension from 22.9 to 3 dynes/cm at 20°C, and the amount of work needed to create the new surfaces would be only 36,000 ergs. Obviously, a large amount of work is saved by incorporating an emulsifying agent into the system. Furthermore, emulsifiers enhance formation of small droplets and reduce the rate at which droplets coalesce.

1. HLB SYSTEM FOR EMULSION FORMULATION

Since numerous food emulsifiers are available, a systematic approach to emulsifier selection is needed to insure that the desired emulsion type be formed quickly and economically. The HLB method, developed by Griffin [9,10], has been used successfully for this purpose. The letters HLB represent "hydrophile-lipophile balance," which is the ratio of the weight percentages of hydrophilic and hydrophobic groups in an emulsifier molecule. Emulsifiers with HLB values below nine are lipophilic, those with HLB values from 11 to 20 are hydrophilic, and those with values between eight and 11 are intermediate.

Although HLB values can be determined experimentally, Griffin [10] developed equations for calculating HLB values for some types of nonionic emulsifiers. For most fatty acid esters of polyhydric alcohols, values can be estimated from Eq. (12-15):

$$HLB = 20(1 - \frac{S}{A}) \qquad (12\text{-}15)$$

where S is the saponification number of the ester and A is the acid number of the acid. HLB values of a variety of common emulsifiers are presented in Table 12-7.

Emulsifiers with HLB values in the range of three to six will promote W/O emulsions, whereas O/W emulsions are formed with emulsifiers having HLB values between eight and 18.

The solubility of an emulsifier is related to the HLB value. As shown in Table 12-8, the dispersibility of an emulsifier in water increases as its HLB value increases. Emulsifiers with HLB values greater than 13 form clear solutions in water.

TABLE 12-7

HLB Values for Emulsifiers[a]

Emulsifier	HLB value
Potassium oleate	20.0
Sodium oleate	18.0
Polyoxyethylene sorbitan monooleate	15.0
Polyoxyethylene sorbitan monostearate	14.9
Gum acacia	11.9
Gum tragacanth	11.9
Methylcellulose	10.5
Polyoxyethylene sorbitan tristearate	10.5
Gelatin	9.8
Sorbitan monostearate	4.7
Mono- and diglycerides (about 61–69% total mono)	3.5
Glycerol monostearate	3.4
Propylene glycol monostearate	3.4
Mono- and diglycerides (about 48–52% total mono)	2.8
Oleic acid	1.0

[a]From Becher [2] and Griffin and Lynch [11].

TABLE 12-8

Dispersibility in Water of Emulsifiers with Various HLB Values[a]

Dispersibility	HLB range
No dispersibility	1–4
Poor dispersibility	3–6
Milky dispersion by agitation	6–8
Stable milky dispersion	8–10
Translucent to clear dispersion	10–13
Clear solution	13+

[a]From Becher [2].

To achieve a stable emulsion, a blend of two or more emulsifiers (combinations of lipophilic and hydrophilic compounds) is generally necessary. When blending two emulsifiers (A and B) to achieve an intermediate HLB of X, the percentage of each compound may be estimated from the following formulas:

$$\%A = \frac{100\ (X - HLB_B)}{HLB_A - HLB_B} \qquad\qquad (12\text{-}16)$$

$$\%B = 100 - \%A \qquad\qquad (12\text{-}17)$$

For example, the amounts of polyxoyethylene sorbitan oleate (HLB of 15.0) and sorbitan oleate (HLB of 4.3) required to produce an HLB value of 12 are as follows:

$$\text{Percent polyoxyethylene sorbitan oleate} = (\frac{12.0 - 4.3}{15.0 - 4.3})\ 100 = 72$$

Percent sorbitan oleate = 28

At a given HLB value, emulsion stability can vary depending on the emulsifiers used. Each pair of emulsifiers may result in a different degree of stability. Thus, a series of emulsions, prepared from various emulsifier blends with the same HLB values, should be evaluated to determine the most suitable pair.

The emulsifier HLB value selected depends on the type of emulsion desired (O/W, W/O) and the type of oil. To form O/W emulsions with vegetable oils, an emulsifier system with an HLB values between seven and 12 is essential. However, a W/O emulsion prepared from cottonseed oil requires an emulsifier HLB value of about five.

2. STABILIZING AGENTS

Stabilizing agents for emulsions can be classed as (1) emulsifiers oriented at the oil-water interface, (2) finely divided particles adsorbed at the interface, and (3) water-dispersible hydrocolloids which increase the viscosity of the continuous phase. When these three classes of stabilizing agents are used in combination, optimum emulsion stability can be achieved.

a. Food Emulsifiers

Food emulsifiers are surface-active agents which consist of hydrophilic and hydrophobic moeities. These compounds are categorized as ionic (cationic, anionic, and amphoteric) and nonionic. The major disadvantage of ionic emulsifiers in food emulsions is that they can react with various ions (hydrogen ions, di- and trivalent inorganic ions, or oppositely charged emulsifier ions) to form complexes which may have reduced emulsifying power and low solubility in both liquid phases. In contrast, nonionic emulsifiers are generally soluble in one of the phases and do not react with the abovementioned ions. For this reason, nonionic emulsifiers are used extensively in the food industry.

Some desirable characteristics of food emulsifiers are:

1. Ability to reduce interfacial tension below 10 dynes/cm (preferably 5 dynes/cm)
2. Ability to be rapidly adsorbed at the interface
3. Possession of a proper balance of hydrophilic and hydrophobic groups so that the desired type of emulsion (O/W, W/O) can be stabilized
4. Ability to impart a large electrokinetic potential to dispersed droplets
5. Ability to function effectively at low concentrations
6. Resistance to chemical change
7. Lack of odor, color, and toxicity
8. Economical.

Food emulsifiers are derived from biological materials or are synthesized from purified fatty acids, triglycerides, and hydrophilic compounds. Muscle, egg yolk, and milk can be used in the preparation of emulsions since they contain stabilizing agents.

(1) Salts of Fatty Acids (Ionic). Salts of fatty acids are not generally added to food as emulsifiers, but they may be present in trace amounts in some ingredients of a food emulsion. The HLB values (Table 12-7) for the potassium and sodium oleates are 20.0 and 18.0, respectively, whereas oleic acid has an HLB value of 1.

(2) Sodium Stearoyl-2-lactylate (Ionic). Sodium stearoyl-2-lactylate is a predominantly hydrophilic emulsifier which can be used to create very stable O/W emulsions capable of withstanding at least six freeze-thaw cycles. The commercial product contains several lactylated compounds, but the most common component has the structure:

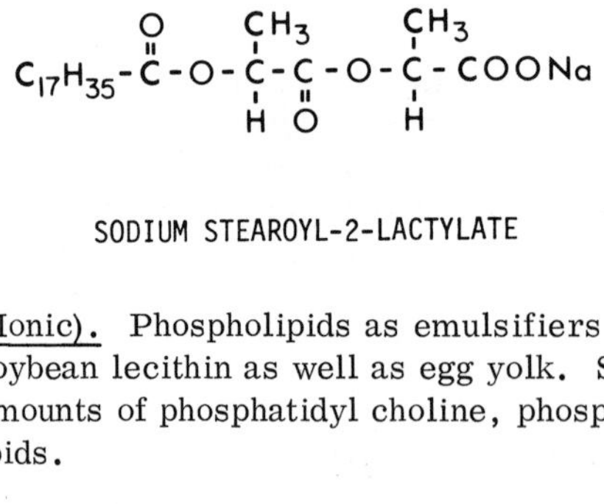

$$C_{17}H_{35}-\overset{O}{\overset{\|}{C}}-O-\overset{CH_3}{\underset{\underset{H}{|}}{\overset{|}{C}}}-\overset{\overset{O}{\|}}{C}-O-\overset{CH_3}{\underset{\underset{H}{|}}{\overset{|}{C}}}-COONa$$

SODIUM STEAROYL-2-LACTYLATE

(3) Phospholipids (Ionic). Phospholipids as emulsifiers are added to emulsions in the form of crude soybean lecithin as well as egg yolk. Soybean lecithin contains approximately equal amounts of phosphatidyl choline, phosphatidyl ethanolamine, and inositol phospholipids.

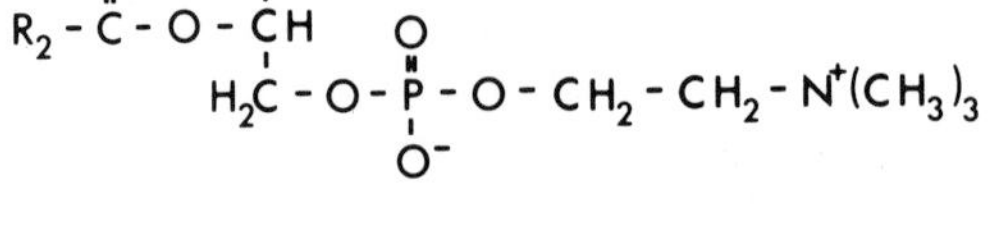

PHOSPHATIDYL CHOLINE

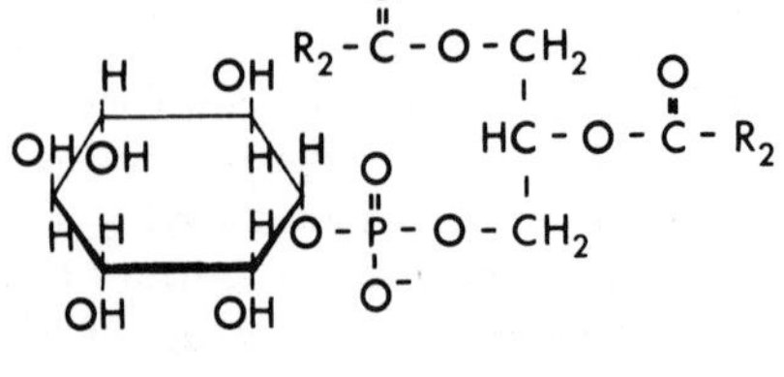

PHOSPHATIDYL INOSITOL

PHOSPHATIDYL ETHANOLAMINE   DIPHOSPHOINOSITIDE

These phospholipids are oil soluble but can be dispersed in water. Crude lecithin is available unbleached (dark brown) or bleached with hydrogen peroxide so that the produce can be used in light colored emulsions. Commercial lecithin is fractionated into alcohol-soluble and -insoluble fractions to provide emulsifiers rich in particular phospholipids. The compositions of these fractions are presented in Table 12-9. The alcohol-soluble fraction is rich in phosphatidyl choline, has an HLB value between 14 and 15, and promotes O/W emulsions. The alcohol-insoluble fraction promotes W/O emulsions. Commercial lecithin is hydroxylated with lactic acid to improve its hydrophilic nature and its ability to stabilize O/W emulsions.

(4) Proteins (Ionic). Proteins are polyionic compounds with surface-active properties and some can assist in the formation and stabilization of O/W emulsions. The amino acid composition and sequence, as well as the secondary, tertiary, and quaternary structure, are major factors which govern their effectiveness. During emulsification, the soluble protein polymers uncoil through cleavage of intramolecular hydrogen bonds and form elastic films on the droplets. Protein fractions from soybeans, rape seed, sunflower seeds, and casein have emulsifying properties.

TABLE 12-9

Composition of Fractionated Soybean Lecithin[a]

| | Wt % of total soybean lecithin | | |
	Unfractionated	Alcohol-soluble fraction	Alcohol-insoluble fraction
Phosphatidyl ethanolamine	32.6	32.5	32.6
Phosphatidyl choline	32.6	65.1	4.6
Phosphatidyl inositol	34.8	2.4	62.8

[a]From Puski and Szuhaj [19].

(5) Glycerol Esters (Nonionic). Glycerol esters, such as mono- and diesters of fatty acids, lactated monoglycerides, and diacetyl tartaric acid monoglycerides, are used widely as emulsifiers.

$$\begin{array}{l} H_2C-OH \\ HC-O-\overset{O}{\overset{\|}{C}}(CH_2)_{16}CH_3 \\ H_2C-OH \end{array}$$

2-MONOSTEARIN

$$\begin{array}{l} \quad\;\; \overset{O}{\overset{\|}{}} \\ H_2C-O-\overset{\|}{C}(CH_2)_{16}CH_3 \\ HC-O-\overset{}{C}(CH_2)_{16}CH_3 \\ H_2C-OH\;\;\overset{}{O} \end{array}$$

1,2-DISTEARIN

Glycerolysis of fats is a common method of preparing mono- and diglycerides. Refined fats are subjected to temperatures between 180° and 250°C in the presence of an alkaline catalyst, such as NaOH or Ca(OH)$_2$. The fatty acids in the resulting partial glycerides are governed by the fatty acid composition of the starting fat. The partial glyceride products consist of about 45% mono-, 44% di-, and 10% tri-glycerides. Normally about 90% of the monoglycerides are in the α form. By molecular distillation, a product containing about 90% monoglyceride can be produced from the above mixture.

By direct esterification of equimolar amounts of fatty acids and glycerol held at around 250°C for 2-3 hr in the presence of a catalyst (such as an acid, a base. or a metal oxide), a mixture of mono- and diglycerides with minor amounts of glycerol and fatty acids can be formed.

The hydrophilic character of monoglycerides can be increased by introducing hydroxy carboxylic acids (lactic, tartaric) into the molecule through an ester linkage. Lactated or lactylated monoglycerides, such as glycerol lactate palmitate, are produced by refluxing fatty acids, glycerol, and lactic acid at about 180°C for 12 hr in the presence of CO$_2$.

(6) Polyglycerol Esters (Nonionic). Since polyglycerol fatty acids have a wide range of HLB values, they have broad potential applications in preparing food emulsions. The hydrophilic nature of these esters is dependent on the number of free hydroxyl groups in the polyglycerol chain. Glycerol can be polymerized to polyglycerol by heating it under vacuum in the presence of either alkaline or acidic catalysts. Polymer chains with 2-30 units of glycerol are formed at 250°-275°C when sodium hydroxide or acetate is used as a catalyst. Ether linkages are present in the linear chains. Esterification of the polyalcohols with fatty acids can occur at 190°-220°C with alkaline catalysts.

(7) Propylene Glycol Fatty Acids (Nonionic). Fatty acid mono- and diesters of propylene glycol can be formed by exposing propylene glycol and desired fatty acids to temperatures of 170°-210°C in the presence of acid or alkaline catalysts. Commercial grades of glycol esters, such as propylene glycol monostearate (PGMS), consist of about 55-63% monoester, with the remainder essentially as diester. These emulsifiers, along with monoglycerides, are effective in emulsifying fat in cakes.

(8) Sorbitan Fatty Acid Esters (Nonionic). Each type of commercial sorbitan ester is a mixture of compounds with varying degrees of anhydrization of sorbitol and esterification.

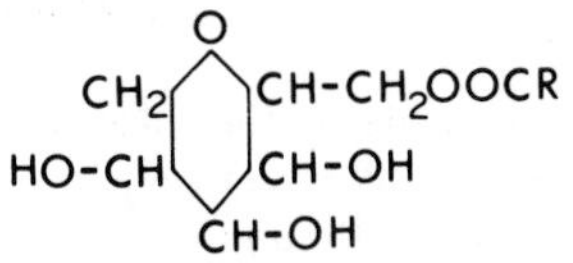

1,5-SORBITAN ESTER

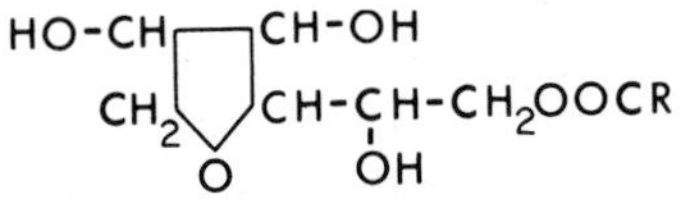

1,4-SORBITAN ESTER

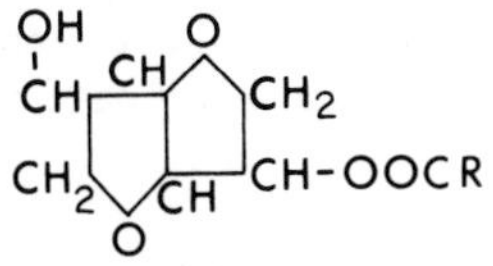

ISOSORBIDE ESTER

These esters are prepared by heating sorbitol with fatty acids at 180°-250°C in the presence of a catalyst, such as NaOH or H_2SO_4. Formation of the internal ether linkages occurs in the sorbitol molecules to form mostly 1,4-sorbitan and isosorbide, which are subsequently esterified. Transesterification of sorbitol with triglycerides of a fat is one method of producing esters with a wide variety of fatty acids. Anhydrohexitol esters can be prepared by first synthesizing the hexitans and then esterifying with fatty acids.

(9) Polyoxyethylene Sorbitan Fatty Acids (Nonionic). To increase the hydrophilic nature of sorbitan fatty acids, polyoxyethylene chains with hydrophilic -0- groups can be added.

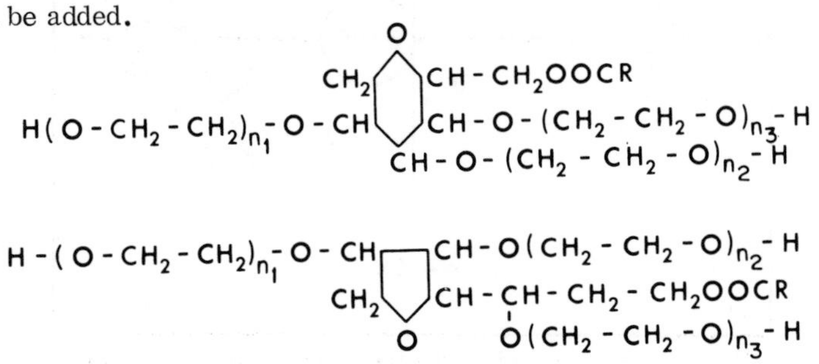

POLYOXYETHYLENE SORBITAN ESTERS

The HLB values of these compounds range from about 10 to 19, depending on the type of fatty acid present. These esters are prepared by reacting ethylene oxide with a sorbitan fatty acid ester in the presence of sodium methylate at about 100°C under pressure. The polyoxyethylene chains interact with hydroxyl groups of the sorbitan through ether linkages.

b.   Finely Divided Solids

Many finely divided solids, which do not ordinarily exhibit surface activity, can function as stabilizing agents for emulsions. Particles of hydroxides of magnesium, aluminum, and calcium, as well as diatomaceous earth, silicates, coagulated proteins, and plant cell fragments (ground spices), adsorb at oil-water interfaces and function to prevent coalescence.

The distribution of solid particles in an emulsion depends on the interfacial tensions in the system, namely the tension between solid and water, γ_{sw}; the tension between water and oil, γ_{wo}; and the tension between solid and oil, γ_{so}. Three situations may exist in the system:

1. If $\gamma_{so} > \gamma_{wo} + \gamma_{sw}$, then the solid is present in the aqueous phase.
2. If $\gamma_{sw} > \gamma_{wo} + \gamma_{so}$, then the solid is present mostly in the oil phase.
3. If $\gamma_{wo} > \gamma_{sw} + \gamma_{so}$, or if none of the three interfacial tensions is greater than the sum of the other two, the solid particles concentrate at the boundary.

Figure 12-6 shows the three possible positions of solid particles at the interface. In the case of (a) in Figure 12-6, the particles are wetted more by the oil than by the water. Thus, a W/O emulsion probably would form. On the other hand, in (c) of Figure 12-6 the particle is wetted more by water than oil and thus an O/W emulsion is more likely to form. Equal wettability of particles by oil and water can bring about the formation of either an O/W or a W/O emulsion.

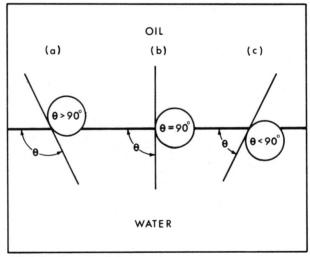

FIG. 12-6.   Distribution of solid particles at an oil-water interface.

In many instances, hydrated small particles can produce either O/W or W/O emulsions and the resulting emulsion type depends on the method of preparation. For example, if olive oil is added to a bentonite slurry, an O/W emulsion forms; but if the bentonite slurry is added to the oil phase, a W/O emulsion forms.

c. Hydrocolloids

Hydrocolloids, such as plant gums and gelatin, act as stabilizers in O/W emulsions by increasing the viscosity of the continuous water phase (auxiliary emulsifiers) and sometimes by forming strong interfacial films around the oil droplets (primary emulsifiers). Plant gums that are used in food emulsions are highly hydrophilic polysaccharides with either anionic or nonionic properties. Anionic gums include pectin, alginate, xanthan, tragacanth, agar, carrageenan, and arabic. Guar, locust bean, carboxymethylcellulose, hydroxypropylcellulose, and methylcellulose gums are nonionic. At a 1% level, guar and xanthan gums increase the viscosity of water to a much greater extent than the other abovementioned gums.

The stability of gums in emulsions is dependent on pH, the presence of electrolytes, and temperature. Some anionic gums can interact with proteins to form insoluble complexes. For example, κ-carrageenan can interact with milk proteins to form a gel-like structure which can help stabilize an emulsion. κ-Carrageenan also can form complexes with egg albumin, acid-extracted soya albumin, and acid-extracted gelatin. Methylcellulose, with 1.3–2.6 methoxy groups per anhydroglucose unit, is soluble in cold water, but above 40°C, its solubility diminishes. Emulsions prepared with carboxymethylcellulose are unstable in the acid pH range, whereas emulsions containing methylcellulose are stable between pH 2 and 10.

Strong films form when either gum arabic or carrageenan is present at the interfaces between oil droplets and the water phase [22]. In emulsions with gum arabic, the thickness of the multilayered films is about 0.1 μm. After repeated washing of the droplets, an elastic monolayer of this gum remains. Gum arabic is used widely for preparing citrus oil emulsions and spray-dried flavoring matter. Neither of these gums reduces interfacial tension very much, and so a considerable amount of work is necessary to prepare emulsions when a gum is the primary emulsifier.

As shown in Table 12-7, the HLB values of some gums and gelatin fall in the range of 8–13.2, indicating that these gums are suitable for preparing O/W emulsions.

F. Stability of Emulsions

During the storage of food emulsions, physical changes in the dispersed droplets may take place, with subsequent reduction of quality attributes. Stability changes in food emulsions can occur through the processes of creaming, flocculation, and coalescence.

The creaming phenomenon involves the flotation or sedimentation of dispersed emulsified droplets, and eventually the system changes into two emulsion layers, one richer and the other poorer in the disperse phase than the original emulsion. The rate of creaming is dependent on the density difference between the dispersed and continuous phases, the droplet size, and the viscosity of the continuous phase. The velocity, V, of droplet separation can be expressed by Stokes equation:

$$V = \frac{2r^2 g(d_1 - d_2)}{9\eta}$$ (12-18)

where r is droplet radius, g is acceleration due to gravity, η is viscosity of the continuous phase, and d_1 and d_2 are densities of the two phases.

Flocculation is the agglomeration of droplets to form loose and irregular clusters. Since flocculation increases effective droplet size, rate of creaming is enhanced. Generally, agglomerated droplets can be redispersed by mixing or shaking since weak interdroplet forces (van der Walls) are responsible for flocculation.

Coalescence, the irreversible union of small droplets to yield larger droplets, can occur after flocculation if the stabilizing interfacial film of emulsifying agent(s) is ruptured. Coalescence is a thermodynamically spontaneous process and ultimately leads to separation of the two phases into two distinct layers. The rate of coalescence is governed by the resistance of the emulsifier interfacial layer to shear and distortion which may arise during agitation or freezing of the emulsion.

Emulsions can be stabilized against creaming, flocculation, and coalescence by introducing a strong interfacial film around each droplet, adding electric charges to the droplet surfaces, and increasing the viscosity of the continuous phase.

1. INTERFACIAL FILMS

The strength, compactness, and elasticity of interfacial films around droplets greatly influence the stability of an emulsion [15]. Emulsifiers having low molecular weights are adsorbed at the interface in the form of closely packed monomolecular films when their concentration is above the critical micelle concentration (CMC). A combination of two emulsifiers, one oil soluble and the other water soluble, is frequently more effective for stabilization than a single emulsifier. These emulsifier molecules interact to form densely packed monolayer complexes, which are strongly adsorbed at the interfaces and lower the interfacial tension to values as low as 0.1 dyne/cm (oil-water interfacial tensions are in range of 13-20 dynes/cm).

Macromolecular emulsifiers, which can stabilize O/W emulsions, form macromolecular films on the oil droplets. Protein molecules can be adsorbed as a monolayer at an interface after they uncoil and orient themselves with hydrocarbon side chains directed toward the oil phase and hydrophilic groups directed toward the water phase. In some food emulsions, droplet films consist of layers of protein complexes. For example, in ice cream, droplet films about 10 nm thick are composed of a layer of subunits of caseinate micelles [5]. The composition of the films become especially complex when multicomponent emulsifying agents, such as egg yolk, are used. The electron micrograph of mayonnaise in Figure 12-7 shows a thick speckled area and a membrane around each droplet. Presumably the speckled region is composed of coalesced low-density lipoproteins and microparticles of granules [6].

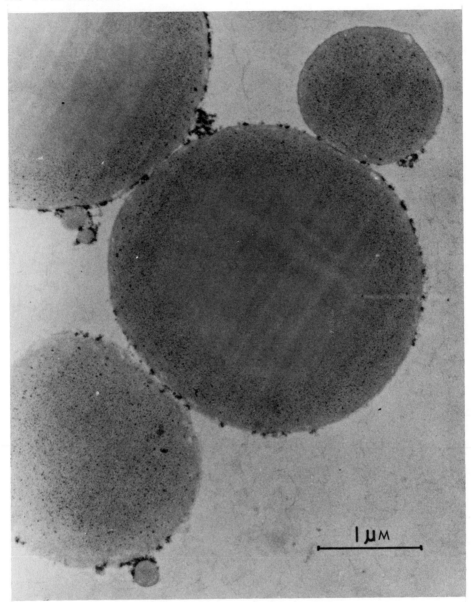

FIG. 12-7. Electron micrograph of mayonnaise [6].

In O/W emulsions, films composed of low molecular weight nonionic and ionic emulsifiers, as well as hydrophilic macromolecules, such as proteins, are surrounded by about one to two layers of strongly bound water molecules. These ice-like layers act as additional physical barriers to coalescence.

Some films exhibit surface elasticity when an external force is exerted on the droplets. In emulsions containing low molecular weight emulsifiers, localized film expansion can lead to an increase in interfacial tension if there is a lag in adsorption of additional emulsifier molecules from the bulk solution. This increase tends to counteract the thinning of the protective film. Elasticity E (dynes/cm) can be expressed by Gibbs equation:

$$E = 2A \frac{d\gamma}{dA} \qquad\qquad (12-19)$$

where A is the area occupied by the emulsifier molecules and γ is interfacial tension. In contrast, food emulsions with macromolecular emulsifiers may have a three-dimensional tangled-polymer gel as an interfacial film, and any force which tends to thin this film may be opposed by a large osmotic force and the elastic nature of the macromolecules. Shear elasticity of protein films has been correlated with stability against coalescence.

As mentioned earlier, if an emulsion contains dispersed droplets which are all of one size and perfectly spherical, the volume of the dispersed phase (ϕ) cannot exceed 74.02%. However, in food emulsions, a range of droplet sizes exists and the droplets may be closely packed and distorted. Thus ϕ values in excess of 74.02% can occur. With thick, elastic films around droplets, ϕ values of such emulsions as mayonnaise can be as high as 85% without significant coalescence over a storage period of 1 year.

2. ELECTRICAL CHARGE

Emulsions can be stabilized against flocculation by electrostatic charges on the surfaces of dispersed droplets. With regard to O/W emulsions, surface charges can originate from ionization of groups on ionic emulsifiers, adsorption of ions from the aqueous phase on nonionic emulsifier layers, or frictional contact between droplet surfaces and the aqueous medium. Charged droplets are surrounded by a diffuse double layer of counterions. A detailed discussion of the double layer is presented in Section III and is applicable to emulsions. Repulsion of the droplets occurs when the diffuse double layers overlap. The repulsive energy is a function of the quantity κH_O, where κ is the reciprocal of the effective radius of the double layer and H_O is the distance between the droplets. In emulsions with protein films, the rate of flocculation increases as the pH of the continuous phase is adjusted closer to the isoelectric point of the protein.

VI. FOAMS

A. Introduction

A foam is a dispersion of gas bubbles in a liquid (or semisolid) phase. Thus, the bubbles are separated from each other by liquid (or semisolid) walls (also called films or lamellae) that are elastic in stable foams. The diameters of foam bubbles range from about 1 μm to several centimeters. Depending on the bubble sizes and wall thicknesses, a foam can be almost as dense as the continuous liquid phase or almost as light as the dispersed gaseous phase. Typical food foams include whipped cream, ice cream, cake, bread, marshmallow, meringue, and the froth on beer.

Typical food foams (1) contain large amounts of entrapped gas (low density), (2) have an extensive surface area between the gaseous and continuous liquid phases, (3) have a higher concentration of solute at surfaces than in the bulk liquid, (4) have walls which are turgid and rigid or semirigid and elastic, and (5) reflect light so they have an opaque appearance. One or more of these properties may be required to provide desirable textural qualities and eye appeal or may be essential for a process operation. For example, low density and a thin-walled, turgid structure are essential for fluffiness, a textural quality which is a summation of touch sensations in the mouth and sound sensations that occur when bubbles burst as the tongue presses the foam against the palate. The tenderness of a foam, such as cake, is dependent on bubble volume as well as the thickness and rheological properties of the lamellae. A process called foam mat drying is based on the fact that water evaporates rapidly from the foam walls which have extensive surfaces per unit volume. Introduction of air into cream during the churning process may cause adsorption of the lipid-protein complexes at the air-liquid surfaces and thereby remove these emulsion-stabilizing substances from the oil-water interface.

B. Formation of a Foam

The formation of a foam is dependent on the presence of a foaming agent in the continuous phase prior to dispersion of gas. Pure liquids and saturated solutions (except surface-active agents) are not capable of forming foams. The foaming agent must be adsorbed at the surface to reduce surface tension and to provide a distinct surface layer which resists coalescence of gas bubbles. Foaming agents may be classified as (1) surface-active lipids, (2) glucosides, (3) cellulose derivatives, and (4) proteins. Selection of the type of foaming agent is determined by the foam properties desired, such as textural characteristics, density, and stability.

Foams can be formed by either dispersion or condensation. In the former method, gas is injected into the foaming solution through orifices or is introduced by beating the solution with rotating blades or ribbons. In the condensation method, gas under pressure is dissolved in the solution that is to be foamed. When the pressure is released, some dissolved gas leaves solution and all of the gas in the system expands to create a foam. Whipped cream from an aerosol container is formed by this method.

In low-density foams, the bubbles are deformed into polyhedral shapes and considerable internal pressure is present. The slight positive gas pressure on the interior wall of a gas bubble provides turgidity which diminishes with a decrease in surface tension. The gas pressure in a bubble can be expressed by Laplace's equation:

$$P = P_a + \frac{4\gamma}{R} \qquad\qquad (12\text{-}20)$$

where P_a is atmospheric pressure, γ is surface tension, and R is the bubble's radius of curvature. From this relationship, it is apparent that small bubbles have large internal pressures.

The stability and density of a foam is influenced by bubble size. Bubble size in foams formed by vertical gas injection through an orifice can be calculated from Eq. (12-21):

$$R^3 = \frac{3r\gamma}{2g\rho}$$

(12-21)

where R is radius of the bubble, r is radius of the orifice, γ is surface tension of the foaming solution, g is acceleration due to gravity, and ρ is density of the foaming solution. It is evident that bubble size is proportional to the radius of the orifice and surface tension, and inversely proportional to density. When gas is introduced into a solution by mechanical agitation, bubble size is dependent essentially on surface tension, as well as on rate and duration of shear.

C. Foam Stability

Persistence of a foam, defined as the length of time that a unit volume of gas can remain in a foam, is related to the resistance of foam walls to bursting stresses. Foams are thermodynamically unstable since the total free energy decreases upon collapse. A major reason for the collapse of a foam is that liquid in the bubble walls diminishes until a portion of the wall reaches a critical thickness of between 50 and 150 Å, whereupon coalescence occurs. Loss of liquid in walls is caused by (1) gravitational force, (2) a suction effect at the periphery of the wall due to the high curvature, (3) evaporation of the solvent, and (4) deformation forces brought about by gas movement (diffusion) from small bubbles to larger ones.

Foam stability can be enhanced by increasing the elasticity of the bubble wall, by increasing the viscosity of the solution and the wall surfaces, or by introducing particulate matter. Elasticity is related to the surface tension change which results in response to deformation of the foam wall. The degree of elasticity can be calculated from the Gibbs equation:

$$E = 2A \frac{d\gamma}{dA}$$

(12-22)

where E, A, and γ are, respectively, elasticity, surface area, and surface tension. For a foam to be stable, the surface tension must change rapidly to oppose any force which distorts the lamellae. If the surface of a lamella contains molecules of an adsorbed foaming agent, any extension of the surface by a force brings about a decrease in the concentration of surface molecules. As a result, the surface tension increases and the external force is counteracted to inhibit further extension. Subsequently, surface molecules of a foaming agent move from a region of low surface tension to the region of high surface tension and drag underlying water molecules with them, and the original wall thickness is restored. Without any adsorbed molecules at the surface, the solution would have an elasticity value of zero. A pure liquid falls into this category and thus does not foam.

If, during deformation of the foam, molecules of foaming agent move too rapidly from the bulk of the solution to the lamella, the surface tension gradient are quickly destroyed and insufficient water is transferred to restore the original thickness of the lamella. Such a situation occurs in solutions containing high concentrations of foaming agents and these solutions exhibit poor foam stability.

The rate of drainage in a foam can be reduced by increasing the viscosity of the liquid in the lamellae and in the surface layer itself. Gums and proteins (such as gelatin) are excellent stabilizing agents which, at low concentrations (around 0.5-2%), increase markedly the viscosity of a solution. Sometimes sugars are used in foams to increase viscosity as well as to act as sweetening agents. A foam can be destabilized by reducing the viscosity of the liquid in the lamellae by increasing temperature or degrading water-binding polymers that may be present.

The viscosity of the surface layers of foams can be increased by adding a polar foam stabilizer to a solution containing a foaming agent. As a consequence, the life of the foam is lengthened considerably. Primary alcohols, glycerol, and glyceryl ethers have been found to be particularly effective in increasing surface viscosity and foam life.

Native proteins at the water-air interface denature (uncoil) and orient themselves with their hydrophobic groups directed toward the air phase and their hydrophilic groups directed toward the water phase. Aggregation of denatured protein molecules forms a "skin" which increases the surface viscosity and stability of the foam. More extensive aggregation of denatured molecules in the bulk region brings about formation of large particles, called coagulum. Protein coagulum has a high water-binding capacity and thus contributes to a decrease in the rate of drainage from the foam. Isoelectric precipitation of proteins can also reduce drainage through extensive entrapment of water in these particles.

Finely divided materials, such as spices and cocoa with sufficient hydrophobic character, can migrate to the foam surfaces, increase surface viscosity, and enhance foam stability. The quantity of particulate matter which can concentrate at the surface depends on the hydrophilic-hydrophobic balance of the particles, particle size, and concentration of the foaming agent.

D. Foam Destruction

During the manufacture of many food products, undesirable foams are formed. In the concentration of fruit juices, maple syrup, coffee extracts, vegetable oils, and corn syrups, or in a fermentation process, excessive foaming may lead to a loss of product and reduced rates of processing. Antifoam agents are sometimes added to food systems at levels of about 10-100 ppm. Water-insoluble dimethyl polysiloxanes (silicone oils) are used almost exclusively as antifoaming agents in the food industry. An effective antifoam agent generally causes immediate collapse of a foam and retards additional foam formation for several hours. Antifoam agents lower the surface tension of the foaming solution and tend to produce an expanded surface film. An antifoam agent in a foam spreads as a monolayer or lens which displaces the stabilizing foam film and the underlying liquid until thinning of the bubble walls is sufficient to cause bursting.

REFERENCES

1. American Chemical Society, Physical Functions of Hydrocolloids. Advances in Chemistry Series, 25, Washington, D.C., 1960.

2. P. Becher, Emulsions, Theory and Practice. 2nd ed., Reinhold, New York, 1965.

3. R. Beeby, R. D. Hill, and N. S. Snow, in Milk Proteins (H. A. McKenzie, ed.), Vol. II, Academic Press, New York, 1971, pp. 421–465.

4. R. R. Benerito, W. S. Singleton, and R. O. Feuge, J. Phys. Chem., 58, 831 (1954).

5. K. G. Berger and G. W. White, J. Food Technol., 6, 285 (1971).

6. C. M. Chang, W. D. Powrie, and O. Fennema, Can. Inst. Food Sci. Technol. J., 5, 134 (1972).

7. D. French, in Symposium on Foods: Carbohydrates and Their Roles (H. W. Schultz, R. F. Cain, and R. W. Wrolstad, eds.), AVI Publ., Westport, Conn., 1969, pp. 26–54.

8. S. Ghosh and H. B. Bull, Biochem. Biophys. Acta, 66, 150 (1963).

9. W. C. Griffin, J. Soc. Cosmet. Chem., 1, 311 (1949).

10. W. C. Griffin, J. Soc. Cosmet. Chem., 5, 249 (1954).

11. W. C. Griffin and M. J. Lynch, in Handbook of Food Additives (T. E. Furia, ed.), 2nd ed., Chemical Rubber Company Press, Cleveland, 1972, pp. 397–429.

12. A. Halpern, J. Phys. Colloid Chem., 53, 895 (1949).

13. W. F. Harrington and P. H. Von Hippel, in Advances in Protein Chemistry (C. B. Anfinson, M. L. Anson, K. Bailey, and J. T. Edsall, eds.), Vol. 16, Academic Press, New York, 1961, pp. 1–138.

14. R. H. Jackson and M. Pallansch, J. Agri. Food Chem., 9, 424 (1961).

15. J. A. Kitchener and P. R. Mussellwhite, in Emulsion Science (P. Sherman, ed.), Academic Press, New York, 1968, pp. 78–130.

16. R. E. Klose and M. Glicksman, in Handbook of Food Additives (T. E. Furia, ed.), 2nd ed., Chemical Rubber Company Press, Cleveland, 1972, pp. 295–359.

17. N. H. Kuhrt, E. A. Welch, and F. J. Kovarik, J. Amer. Oil Chem. Soc., 27, 310 (1950).

18. R. Lees, Factors Affecting Crystallization in Boiled Sweets, Fondants and Other Confectionery. Scientific and Technical Survey No. 42, British Food Manufacturing Industries Research Association, Leatherhead, Surrey, England, 1965.

19. G. Puski and B. Szuhaj, in Soy, The Wonder Bean (P. Melnychyn, ed.), American Association of Cereal Chemists, St. Paul, Minn., 1971.

20. D. A. Rees, in Advances in Carbohydrate Chemistry and Biochemistry (M. L. Wolfrom, S. T. Tipson, and D. Horton, eds.), Vol. 24, Academic Press, New York, 1969, pp. 267–332.

21. N. Robinson, Trans. Faraday Soc., 56, 1260 (1960).

22. E. Shotton and R. F. White, in Rheology of Emulsions (P. Sherman, ed.), MacMillan, New York, 1963, pp. 59–71.

23. W. S. Singleton and R. R. Benerito, J. Amer. Oil Chem. Soc., 32, 23 (1955).

24. R. Vincent, W. D. Powrie, and O. Fennema, J. Food Sci., 31, 643 (1966).

25. M. J. Vold, J. Colloid Sci., 16, 1 (1961).

26. D. F. Waugh, in Milk Proteins (H. A. McKenzie, ed.), Vol. II, Academic Press, New York, 1971, pp. 3–85.

27. T. J. Weiss, Food Oils and Their Uses. AVI Publ., Westport, Conn., 1970.

28. O. B. Wurzburg, in Handbook of Food Additives (T. E. Furia, ed.), 2nd ed. Chemical Rubber Company Press, Cleveland, 1972, pp. 361–395.

GENERAL REFERENCES

A. W. Adamson, Physical Chemistry of Surfaces. Interscience, New York, 1960.

American Chemical Society, Physical Functions of Hydrocolloids. Advances in Chemistry Series, 25, Washington, D.C., 1960.

P. Becher, Emulsions, Theory and Practice. 2nd ed., Reinhold, New York, 1965.

H. Bennett, J. L. Bishop, Jr., and M. F. Wulfinghoff, Practical Emulsions. Vols. I and II, Chemical Publishing Co., New York, 1968.

J. J. Bickerman, Foams. Springer-Verlag, New York, 1973.

British Food Manufacturers Industrial Research Association, Gelation and Gelling Agents. Symposium Proceedings, 13, Leatherhead, Surrey, England, 1972.

M. Glicksman, Gum Technology in the Food Industry. Academic Press, New York, 1969.

W. C. Griffin and M. J. Lynch, in Handbook of Food Additives (T. E. Furia, ed.), 2nd ed., Chemical Rubber Company Press, Cleveland, 1972, pp. 397–429.

J. L. Kavanau, Structure and Function on Biological Membranes. Vol. I, Holden-Day, San Francisco, 1965.

I. A. Macdonald, J. Amer. Oil Chem. Soc., 45, 584A (1968).

L. I. Osipow, Surface Chemistry. Reinhold, New York, 1962.

S. Ross, Chemistry and Physics of Interfaces. American Chemical Society, Washington, D.C., 1965.

P. Sherman, ed., Rheology of Emulsions. MacMillan, New York, 1963.

P. Sherman, ed., Emulsion Science. Academic Press, New York, 1968.

P. Sherman, Industrial Rheology. Academic Press, New York, 1970.

T. J. Weiss, Food Oils and Their Uses. AVI Publ., Westport, Conn., 1970.

O. B. Wurzburg, in Handbook of Food Additives (T. E. Furia, ed.), 2nd ed., Chemical Rubber Company Press, Cleveland, 1972, pp. 361–395.

Chapter 13

CHARACTERISTICS OF MUSCLE TISSUE

Herbert O. Hultin

Department of Food Science and Nutrition
University of Massachusetts
Amherst, Massachusetts

Contents

I. INTRODUCTION

Since earliest times, man has had a desire to satisfy his hunger with animal food. There is evidence that many people in many cultures have lived chiefly on this type of food. It is difficult to explain man's desire for animal products. It may be for evolutionary reasons related to the high performance and good health of men who have been able to obtain sufficient amounts of these products, or it simply may be due to the sensory appeal of these tissues. Whatever the case, these foods have been very important in cultural traditions; e.g., meat was often given to the most prominent individuals in a society. In our day, meals are still often designed around meat or animal products.

Many types of animal tissues have been, and are, used as foods. Of these, muscle tissues, milk, and related products are the most important from an economic and quantitative standpoint. The term "meat" refers to muscle, especially that from mammals, which has undergone certain chemical and biochemical changes following death. However, because of the long-standing importance of meat in the diet, the term has often been used synonymously with food. Many muscle tissues are not generally referred to as meat, e.g., fish muscle. In this chapter, the terms "muscle" and "meat" are used interchangeably but with the forwarning that, generally speaking, muscle is considered to be a more appropriate term for the functional tissue and meat a more appropriate term for the tissue after it has passed through certain changes following death of the animal involved. Furthermore, meat often implies a product which includes some adipose (fat) tissue and bone.

II. NUTRITIVE VALUE

In addition to its esthetic appeal, meat is important because of its high nutritive content. The approximate analysis of lean muscle tissue is given in Table 13-1. This composition is relatively constant for a wide variety of animals. Meat composition varies mostly in lipid content which may be evident as different degrees of

TABLE 13-1

Composition of Lean Muscle Tissue[a]

Species	Composition (%)			
	Water	Protein	Lipid	Ash
Beef	70–73	20–22	4–8	1
Pork	68–70	19–20	9–11	1.4
Chicken	73.7	20–23	4.7	1
Lamb	73	20	5–6	1.6
Cod	81.2	17.6	0.3	1.2
Salmon	64	20–22	13–15	1.3

[a]This information was compiled from Ref. [119].

marbling in some mammalian meats. The tissues of certain fatty fish vary greatly in this component. The total composition of meat varies depending on the amount of fat, bone, and skin which is included in the sample.

As shown in Table 13-1, protein makes up about 20% of the lean portion of meat. Not only is the protein content of muscle tissue very large, but the quality of the protein is also very high, containing a ratio of amino acids very similar to that required for maintenance and growth of human tissue. The amino acid makeup of various muscle proteins has been summarized by Bodwell and McClain [14]. Of the total nitrogen content of muscle, approximately 95% is protein and 5% is smaller peptides and amino acids.

The lipid components of muscle tissue vary more widely than do the amino acids. In addition to species variations, the lipid components of muscle can be markedly influenced by diet. Basically, the lipid composition of meat can be categorized as lipids from the muscle tissue and lipids from adipose tissue. The lipid composition of these two tissues can be quite different. The lean portion contains greater proportions of phospholipids, and these are located in membranes of the cell. Lean muscle contains about 0.5-1% phospholipids. The fatty acids of phospholipids are more unsaturated than those of triglycerides. Consequently, fatty acids in the lean portion of meat have a higher degree of unsaturation than those in adipose tissue. Oxidation of the highly unsaturated fatty acids found in the membrane fractions of muscle may be very important in some of the deteriorative reactions of meat. Pork fat is more unsaturated than beef, while lamb fat is more saturated than beef fat. Within a species, red muscle contains more lipid than white muscle.

In recent years, the relatively high content of saturated fatty acids in muscle tissue has been a source of controversy as to its role in producing certain forms of atherosclerosis. As yet, however, there has been no firm scientific evidence demonstrating that fats from muscle tissue are deleterious to health when eaten in reasonable quantities. The cholesterol content of meat (about 75 mg per 100 g [113]) is well below that which is considered undesirable for humans.

Muscle tissue is an excellent source of some of the vitamins of the B complex, especially thiamine, riboflavin, niacin, B_6, and B_{12}. However, the vitamin B content of muscle varies considerably depending on the species and on the type of muscle within a species. In addition, the levels of the B vitamins are also influenced by breed, age, sex, and general health of the animal. Less work has been performed on the fat-soluble vitamins, but the levels of vitamins A, D, E, and K in meats are generally rather low, although the amount of vitamin E (tocopherols) can be influenced by the diet of the animal. Ascorbic acid is present only at very low levels in meat.

Meat is a good source of iron and phosphorus and a rather poor source of calcium (approximately 10 mg per 100 g of meat). Meat generally contains from 60 to 90 mg of sodium per 100 g and about 300 mg of potassium per 100 g of lean tissue. The minerals and water-soluble B complex vitamins are found in the lean portion of the meat. The content of these substances therefore will vary depending on the amount of fat tissue and bone in a particular cut of meat.

In this chapter, the structural and chemical features of muscle tissue are considered, with emphasis on the changes that occur following death and during storage and processing. These changes will be related to their effects on the texture, color, flavor, and nutritional attributes of the muscle tissue.

III. MUSCLE STRUCTURE

A. Skeletal Muscle

Skeletal muscle is composed of long, narrow, multinucleated cells (fibers) which range from a few to several centimeters in length and from 10 to 100 μm in diameter. The fibers are arranged in a parallel fashion to form bundles, and groups of bundles form a muscle.

Surrounding the whole muscle is a heavy sheath of connective tissue, called the "epimysium" (see Fig. 13-1). From the inner surface of the epimysium, other connective tissue penetrates the interior of the muscle, separating the groups of fibers into bundles. This connective tissue layer is termed the "perimysium," and extending from this are finer sheaths of connective tissue that surround each muscle fiber. These last sheaths are termed "endomysia." The connective tissue sheaths merge at the termini of the muscle with large masses of connective tissue tendons, these serving to anchor the muscle to the skeleton. The long components of the circulatory system are located in the perimysium, whereas the smallest units (capillaries) are within the endomysium.

Figure 13-2 is a diagrammatic view of a muscle fiber. The surface of the muscle fiber is termed the "sarcolemma." It is generally considered that the sarcolemma is composed of three layers: an outer network of collagen fibrils, a middle or amorphous layer, and an inner plasma membrane [68]. Invaginations of the plasma membranes form the transverse (T) system [35,59,117]. The ends of this T system meet in the interior of the cell close to two terminal sacs of the sarcoplasmic reticulum. The sarcoplasmic reticulum is a membranous system located in the cell (fiber) and generally arranged parallel to the main axis of the cell. The meeting of the T system and the sarcoplasmic reticulum (triadic joint)

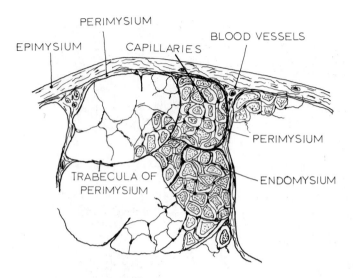

FIG. 13-1. Muscle cross-section, illustrating the arrangement of connective tissue into epimysium, perimysium, and endomysium and the relationship to muscle fibers and fiber bundles. The typical position of blood vessels is also shown. (Reprinted from Ref. [45], p. 653, by courtesy of J. B. Lippincott Co.)

occurs in different intrafiber locations in different muscles. The triadic joint appears to exist most frequently at or around the Z lines (p. 583) in fish and frog muscle and at the junction of the A and I bands (p. 583) in reptiles, birds, and mammals [117].

The T system has the function of extending the plasma membrane into the interior of the muscle and it is this phenomenon which allows the muscle cell to respond as a unit (essentially no lag period in the interior of the cell). Depolarization of the plasma membrane and its intracellular extension (T system) triggers liberation of calcium from terminal sacs of the sarcoplasmic reticulum [21]. This liberation of calcium activates ATPase of the contractile proteins and allows contraction to occur [33]. The calcium functions by relieving magnesium inhibition of muscle ATPase. Relaxation is achieved in part by a reversal of the process and the sequestering of calcium by the sarcoplasmic reticulum [50,88].

Mitochondria serve as prime energy transducers for the muscle cell and these organelles are located throughout the cell. In some cases there is a concentration of mitochondria near the Z line or near the plasma membrane. Nuclei are distributed near the surface of the muscle cell and have an important role in protein synthesis. Although the function of the Golgi apparatus is not completely clear, it is believed to have a secretory role.

Lysosomes are subcellular fractions which contain large quantities of hydrolytic enzymes and serve a digestive role in the cell. It is not clear as yet whether lysosomes exist as part of the muscle cell per se or whether lysosomal enzymes are contributed by phagocytic cells which are present in the circulatory system [5,13, 97]. The proteolytic enzymes of these bodies are termed "cathepsins." Several cathepsins with differing activities have been isolated.

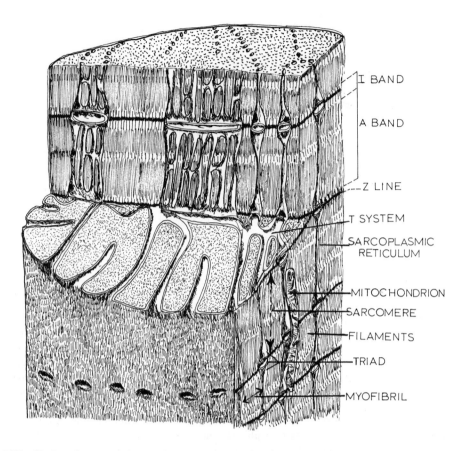

FIG. 13-2. Cutaway of muscle fiber showing the outer membrane and its invaginations (T system), which run horizontally and meet with two terminal sacs of the longitudinal sarcoplasmic reticulum in the triad. Repetitive cross-striations are also indicated. (Adapted from Ref. [102].)

Glycogen particles and lipid droplets also occur in some muscle cells, depending on the state of the muscle.

All of these cellular components, as well as the contractile apparatus which is discussed next, are bathed in the so-called sarcoplasm, a semifluid material which contains soluble components, such as myoglobin, some enzymes, and some metabolic intermediates of the cell.

Each muscle fiber contains many smaller fibrils (myofibrils) which constitute the contractile apparatus. The myofibrils are surrounded by the sarcoplasm and some of the elements discussed above, such as mitochondria, the T system, and the sarcoplasmic reticulum.

The characteristic striated appearance of skeletal muscle is due to a specific repetitive arrangement of proteins in the myofibrils. This arrangement is shown in Figure 13-3. The dark bands of the fibrils are anisotropic or birefringent when

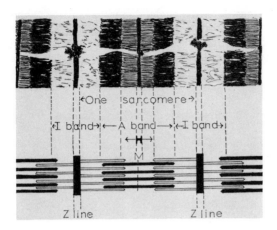

FIG. 13-3. Striated muscle in longitudinal section. The I band consists only
of thin filaments. The A band is darker where it consists of overlapping thick and
thin filaments and lighter in the H zone, where it consists solely of thick filaments.
The M line is caused by a bulge in the center of each thick filament, and the
pseudo-H zone is a bare region on either side of the M line. (Adapted from Ref.
[60].)

viewed in polarized light. The bands which appear lighter are isotropic. Therefore, the darker bands are termed A (for anisotropic) bands, and the lighter bands
are called I (for isotropic) bands. In the center of each of the I bands is a dark
line, called the Z line. In the center part of the A band is a zone which is lighter
than the rest of the A band. This is called the H zone, and frequently at the center
of this H zone there exists a darker M line. The basic contractile unit is termed
the "sarcomere" and is defined as the material located between and including two
adjacent Z lines.

A sarcomere is comprised of thick and thin longitudinal filaments. The A band
is comprised of thick filaments, whereas the I band is composed of thin filaments.
The thin filaments extend outward from the Z lines in both directions, and in parts
of the A band the thin filaments overlap the thick filaments. The lighter zone in
the A band, or H zone, is that area where the thin filaments do not overlap the
thick filaments. The contractile state of the muscle has an important bearing on
the size of these various bands and zones, since during contraction the thin and
thick filaments slide past each other. The length of the A band remains constant,
while the I band and the H zone both shorten during contraction.

Thin filaments are apparently imbedded in or connected to the Z-line material
(or disk), and because of this, the Z line presumably serves as an anchor during
the contractile process. The M line is located in the area of the myosin filaments
where projections on the myosin headpieces are not observed (Section IV.A.1).
The M line probably serves to keep the filaments in the correct geometric position [99].

Striated muscle from other vertebrates as well as invertebrates has essentially
the same structure as that discussed above for mammalian muscle. However,
there may be some differences in the arrangement of the myofibrils, the amount of

sarcoplasm, the relationship of the nuclei and mitochondria to the other components in the muscle cell, the arrangement of the sarcoplasmic reticulum, and the
location of the triadic joint. Furthermore, solubility characteristics of the contractile proteins of striated scallop muscle [89] differ from those of vertebrate
muscle.

B. Smooth or Involuntary Muscle

Smooth muscle fibers do not show the characteristic striations of voluntary or
skeletal muscle. Certain organs containing smooth muscle, such as the gizzards
of birds and intestinal tissue, are used for food.

C. Cardiac (Heart) or Striated Involuntary Muscle

Heart tissue is used as food directly or may be incorporated into sausage products.
The myofibrillar structure of heart muscle is similar to that of striated skeletal
muscles but cardiac fibers contain larger numbers of mitochondria than do skeletal fibers. The fiber arrangement of cardiac muscle is also somewhat less regular
than that observed in skeletal muscle.

IV. PROTEINS OF THE MUSCLE CELL

The proteins of muscle can be roughly categorized into contractile, soluble, and
insoluble elements. The soluble fraction can be extracted from muscle with water
or dilute salt solution and is made up of enzymes, such as those involved in glycolysis, and the muscle pigment, myoglobin. Although there is some question as
to whether all of these proteins are soluble in situ [92], they are nevertheless
easily extractable. The contractile proteins are soluble in salt solutions of high
ionic strength but not in water or dilute salt solutions. The insoluble fraction remains after treatment with salt solutions of high ionic strengths and it consists of
connective tissue proteins, membrane proteins, and usually some unextracted
contractile proteins. These fractions are discussed separately.

A. Contractile Proteins

1. MYOSIN

The protein of the thick filaments is myosin. It is a very elongated protein molecule with a molecular weight of approximately 470,000 daltons. Myosin contains
two identical polypeptide chains, and each has a high degree of α-helical structure.
In addition, the two chains are supercoiled, that is, wound around each other as
illustrated in Figure 13-4. The molecule has a globular head which is responsible
for its enzymic (ATPase) activity and its ability to interact with actin. The globular heads are in two fractions and represent the termini of the two polypeptide
chains making up this molecule. Myosin can be cleaved near the head region by

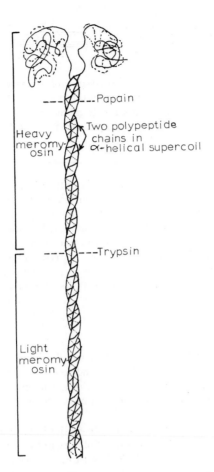

FIG. 13-4. Schematic representation of the myosin molecule, showing its globular head and long tail and the points of enzymic fragmentation. (Adapted from Ref. [79].)

proteolytic enzymes, such as trypsin, producing two fractions of the protein. One of these is called light meromyosin and the other, which contains the globular head structures of the myosin molecule, is called heavy meromyosin. Separated heavy meromyosin retains its ability to interact with actin and its ATPase activity.

Myosin represents approximately 50-60% of the myofibrillar or contractile proteins [48]. Each thick filament contains some 400 molecules of myosin [57]. These molecules polarize when they interact, joining in head to tail fashion in two directions as illustrated in Figure 13-5. It is undoubtedly this polarity which allows contraction to occur. Thick filaments can be reformed from isolated myosin molecules.

FIG. 13-5. Possible arrangement of myosin molecules with globular regions
at either end and the straight-shaft portion in the center. The polarities of the
myosin molecules are reversed on either side of the center, but all molecules on
the same side have the same polarity. (Reprinted from Ref. [58], p. 289, by
courtesy of Academic Press, Inc.)

Myosin can be extracted from muscle with a salt solution (ionic strength about
0.6) of slightly alkaline pH. It can then be purified by repeated cycles of precipitation, followed by resolubilization in salt solution of high concentration. Solutions
commonly used for extraction are 0.3M KCl and 0.15M phosphate at pH 6.5 [41],
or 0.47M KCl, 0.1M phosphate, and 0.01M pyrophosphate at pH 6.5 [51]. If a
short period of time is used for the extraction, a crude myosin, called myosin A,
is produced. If longer periods of extraction (e.g., overnight) are used, then a
crude actomyosin preparation, called myosin B, is obtained.

2. ACTIN

A major protein of the thin filaments is actin, which comprises 15-30% of the myofibrillar protein of muscle [57]. Actin is bound to the structure of the muscle
much more firmly than is myosin. Extraction of actin can be accomplished by prolonged exposure of a muscle powder (obtained by acetone extraction) with an aqueous
solution of ATP [2].
   Actin probably exists in muscle as a double-helical structure of so-called
fibrous actin, or F actin (see Fig. 13-6). Globular actin, or G actin, is the monomeric form of the protein and it is stable in water, where it can also exist as a
dimer. Globular actin binds ATP very firmly and, in the presence of magnesium,
spontaneously polymerizes to form F actin with the concurrent hydrolysis of bound
ATP to give bound ADP and inorganic phosphate. Globular actin also polymerizes
in the presence of neutral salts at a concentration of approximately 0.15M.

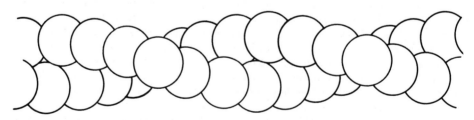

FIG. 13-6. Arrangement of actin in double-helical structure.

3. ACTOMYOSIN

When purified actin and myosin are mixed in vitro, a complex, called actomyosin, is formed. Actomyosin has a high viscosity and also exhibits a large flow birefringence. Although actin by itself has no enzymic activity, it significantly modifies the ATPase activity of myosin in the actomyosin complex. Pure myosin requires Ca^{2+} for its activity and is inhibited by Mg^{2+}. The ATPase activity of actomyosin, however, is stimulated by Mg^{2+} [104]. Sulfhydryl groups are involved in the interaction between myosin and actin [7]. The complex of actomyosin can be dissociated in the presence of ATP and/or ADP and magnesium ions [70]. It is most likely that a similar type of combination between actin and myosin occurs in muscle cells and is probably intimately involved with contraction. The interaction of actin and myosin in the absence of ATP and ADP, and the plasticizing effect of these nucleotides when they are present, is a very important factor influencing the quality of meat.

4. OTHER CONTRACTILE PROTEINS

Tropomyosin B is another protein found in thin filaments [19]. It is a long rodlike molecule which has a molecular weight of about 68,000 daltons [121]. It probably consists of two identical polypeptide chains, again entwined in a double-helical structure similar to that found in the tail region, or light meromyosin region, of myosin. Tropomyosin B consists almost entirely of an α-helix structure and it forms a complex with F actin when the two proteins are mixed [108]. It is thought that tropomyosin B is located in one of the grooves of the double helix of F actin [30].

Another protein found in some specialized muscles is tropomyosin A. This is located principally in the "catch" muscle of bivalves. It apparently functions to lock actin and myosin together so the shell can remain closed without an expenditure of energy.

Troponins A and B bind to tropomyosin B and all of these are often extracted together. Troponin A confers calcium sensitivity to the tropomyosin B-troponin-actomyosin complex, while troponin B inhibits myofibrillar ATPase activity [49]. There is apparently at least one other component associated with the tropomyosin-troponin A and B complex, the role of which has not yet been determined [77]. The complex of tropomyosin and the troponins are collectively designated the "relaxing factor" [105].

Two other proteins which are found in small quantities but which may have an important role in muscle function are α-actinin and β-actinin. These proteins are most likely closely associated with the thin filaments. α-Actinin can cause gelation of F actin, a temperature-dependent phenomenon which is reversed in the presence of tropomyosin B [28,108]. It is believed that α-actin is also involved in the structure of the Z line and it may form an anchor or interlocking component with actin at the Z line [18]. The role of β-actinin is not known with certainty but it may be associated with troponin.

Other as yet unidentified proteins are probably also present as parts of the contractile apparatus.

B. Contraction

Although it is not the purpose of this chapter to delve into the physiology of muscle in the living animal, it is necessary to have some knowledge of the normal functioning and interactions of contractile proteins in the living cell in order to understand postmortem changes.

Muscle is stimulated by an electrical nervous impulse which is responsible for depolarization of the muscle cell membrane. The transverse tubular system of the muscle appears to be an extension of the cell membrane [35,59,117], and its role therefore appears to be to transmit the stimulus (depolarization) to the interior of the muscle cell so that the whole cell can react as a unit. As described in Section III.A, the transverse system joins two other bulbous projections from the sarcoplasmic reticulum near the myofibrils. In some manner, depolarization of the transverse tubular system causes a release of calcium from the terminal sacs of the sarcoplasmic reticulum [21]. The calcium that is released interacts with the troponin-tropomyosin complex, which then has the capacity to interfere with the binding of Mg-ATP at the relaxing site of the myofibril [109]. This relaxing site is, in fact, an inhibitory site which is responsible for preventing myofibrillar ATPase activity. When the inhibition is overcome, ATP is hydrolyzed by the actomyosin complex. This hydrolysis provides energy for the systematic changes which take place in the contractile proteins and lead to the phenomenon of contraction. Thus, the contractile process is regulated by the amount of free calcium ions that are released into the sarcoplasm. Regulation of ATPase activity by calcium is mediated through the relaxing system, which consists of tropomyosin, troponin A (the calcium-sensitizing factor), and troponin B (an inhibitor of the magnesium-stimulated ATPase of myofibrils).

C. Mechanism of Contraction

The exact mechanism by which the energy released during hydrolysis of ATP is converted into the mechanical energy of muscle contraction is not fully understood at the molecular level. Currently, the most popular theory is that of Hanson and Huxley [61], who have proposed that when muscle contracts the thin and thick filaments slide past each other (see Fig. 13-7). In some way, the globular head portion of the myosin molecule interacts with actin and then pulls the actin filaments parallel to the fiber axis. Maximal contraction varies from 20 to 50% of the rest length of the sarcomere. Since interaction of the filaments occurs through cross-bridges, it is generally agreed that tension must be developed and carried by these cross-bridges. There is at this time, however, no generally agreed upon mechanism for the production of force within the sarcomere.

D. Relaxation

Relaxation occurs when calcium ions are removed from the sarcoplasm. This takes place by an active, energy-supported transport or by sequestering of calcium by the sarcoplasmic reticulum. The actomyosin ATPase system is activated when the calcium concentration of the sarcoplasm increases to approximately 0.5-1 μM.

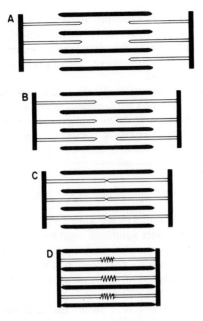

FIG. 13-7. Contraction states of a sarcomere showing thick (dark) filaments and thin (light) filaments attached to the Z lines. If B is taken as the schematic representation of a sarcomere from resting muscle, A represents that from a stretched muscle and C and D those from muscle contracted to different degrees. The jagged lines in the thin filaments in D represent those portions of the thin filaments which overlap each other.

When the calcium ion is reduced to a concentration below this, the myofibrils again lose the capacity to hydrolyze ATP. ATP then functions as a plasticizing agent, causing separation of actin and myosin, and the sarcomeres relax to their rest lengths. The sarcoplasmic reticulum can be fragmented and isolated and this calcium-sequestering activity demonstrated. Separated fragments of the sarcoplasmic reticulum of pig muscle rapidly lose their ability to sequester calcium [40], but this loss has not been observed in comparable components of chicken muscle postmortem [52].

E. Soluble Components of the Muscle Cell

Soluble proteins of the muscle cell are known by various terms, for example, myogen, which is a water extract of muscle, or simply sarcoplasmic extract. In any case, the soluble proteins of the muscle cell constitute a very significant portion of the proteins of the cell, usually from 25 to 30% of the total proteins.

Most of these soluble proteins are enzymes, principally glycolytic enzymes, but other enzymes are present as well, including those of the pentose shunt and such auxiliary enzymes as creatine kinase and AMP deaminase. The oxygen storage component of the muscle cell, myoglobin, is also a water-soluble protein. The high viscosity of the sarcoplasm is probably attributable to the presence of soluble proteins that are present in concentrations as high as 20-30% [103]. In some species, glyceraldehyde-3-phosphate dehydrogenase comprises approximately 10% of this soluble protein [22]. As noted above, these proteins may not be soluble in vivo but they are easily solubilized.

Other soluble constituents of the sarcoplasm include various nitrogen-containing compounds, such as amino acids and nucleotides; some soluble carbohydrates (intermediates in glycolysis); such acids as lactic acid, which is the major end product of glycolysis; a number of enzymic cofactors; and inorganic ions, including inorganic phosphate, potassium, sodium, magnesium, calcium, and iron.

F. Insoluble Components of the Muscle Cell

Some components of the muscle cell are not soluble in either water or dilute salt solutions or in the concentrated salt solutions used to extract some of the contractile proteins. This category includes unextractable contractile proteins, portions of membrane systems, glycogen granules, and fat droplets. Part of the insoluble fraction of meat is composed of these elements but the majority consists of connective tissue proteins.

Most of the lipid material in the cell is associated with the membranes and these materials are typically rich in phospholipids. The phospholipid content of a membrane varies from one membrane to another. There is approximately 90% phospholipid in the lipid fraction of mitochondria [34] and about 50% phospholipid in the lipid fraction of plasma membrane [65]. The total lipid content of the muscle cell is small, being only about 3-4% of the total weight of the cell [39]. It is extremely important, however, since it is involved in the structure of the membranes, and as we shall see later, it is very important in some deteriorative reactions.

The major phospholipids are lecithin (phosphatidyl choline), phosphatidyl ethanolamine, phosphatidyl serine, phosphatidyl inositol, and some of the acidic glycerol phosphatides, e.g., cardiolipin. The amounts of each of these substances vary with the particular subcellular fraction concerned. This is also somewhat true of the kinds of fatty acids that make up the phospholipids. Furthermore, compositional differences of the sort just mentioned also exist among muscles of any given species and among muscles of different species.

The principal neutral lipids in muscle are triglycerides and cholesterol.

Proteins of the membrane fractions are usually very insoluble unless the material is treated with detergents (surface-active agents). These fractions are therefore usually not extractable with most aqueous solvents.

V. MUSCLE TYPES

Differences in pigmentation among muscles are obvious, and muscles are accordingly classified as either white or red. There may be differences even among muscles of the same organism, for example, the white breast muscle of the chicken or turkey and the dark muscles of the leg. Moreover, there is often a graduation of color in an individual muscle, with redness increasing from periphery to axis. In general, white muscles are capable of fast contractions, whereas many red muscles contract much more slowly.

It is also known that a simple classification based on overall appearance of the muscle is not very accurate or useful. This is because most muscles are made up of both red and white fibers, with red muscles containing a preponderance of so-called red fibers and white muscles containing a preponderance of so-called white fibers. Therefore, muscles may differ in the degree of "redness" or "whiteness."

In addition to the difference in color, there are many morphological and biochemical differences between red and white fibers [10,36]. Red fibers tend to be smaller, contain more mitochondria, possess greater concentrations of myoglobin and lipid, and are more generously supplied with blood than are white fibers. However, glycogen and many of the enzymes related to glycolysis tend to be less abundant in red fibers than in white. In addition, red fibers have thicker sarcolemma, a much less extensive and more poorly developed sarcoplasmic reticulum, less sarcoplasm, and a less granular appearance than do white fibers. The Z lines of red muscle fibers also tend to be rougher and thicker than those observed in white muscle fibers. In some cases, it has been shown that there are differences in the isoenzyme contents of the various muscles [101].

Even the classification of fibers as either red or white is arbitrary and incomplete. Histochemically, there is another type of fiber, called the intermediate fiber, which has many properties (e.g., size and level of enzymes) intermediate between those of white and red fibers.

It is generally considered that red and white muscles have different functions in the living animal. Red fibers, because of their well-developed vascular system, copious supply of oxygen, and high content of myoglobin, are ideally suited for oxidative metabolism. This role is further attested to by their low content of glycolytic and related enzymes and by their relatively high content of mitochondria, which function in respiratory utilization of oxygen. It has been suggested, therefore, that red muscles function best for sustained activity [36]. In contrast, white muscles are presumably best suited for vigorous activity for a short period of time.

Our understanding of muscle fiber types is gradually evolving. More recent work has led to the classification of muscle fibers into three categories: fast-twitch red, fast-twitch white, and slow-twitch intermediate. These categories are based on speed of contraction and histochemical assessment of oxidative and glycolytic capacities [9]. A yet more recent paper [100] characterizes muscle types as fast-twitch oxidative glycolytic, fast-twitch glycolytic, and slow-twitch oxidative. These categories are based on a more careful examination of some of the histochemical, morphological, and biochemical properties of muscle.

An understanding of the differences among muscle fibers is important in food science since many of the characteristics of muscle postmortem are a function of muscle fiber type. For example, muscle color and susceptibility to cold shortening (Section VIII.A) are influenced greatly by fiber type. Muscles with a preponderance of white fibers generally are much less susceptible to cold shortening than muscles that have a majority of red fiber types.

VI. CONNECTIVE TISSUE

Connective tissue consists of various fibers, several different cell types, and amorphous ground substances. Connective tissues hold and support the muscle through the component tendons, epimysium, perimysium, and endomysium. The relationship between connective tissue and muscle cells is so intimate that most likely all substances passing in or out of the muscle cell diffuse through some type of connective tissue.

The amorphous ground substance is a nonstructured mixture of carbohydrates, proteins, and lipids. Some of this mixture surrounds each cell as part of the sarcolemma.

Several types of cells are found in the connective tissue. These include fibroblasts, mesenchyme cells, macrophages, lymphoid cells, mast cells, and eosinophilic cells.

The fat cell deserves special attention. Fat cells appear to arise from undifferentiated mesenchyme cells, usually developing around the blood vessels in muscle. As a fat cell develops, it begins to accumulate droplets of liquid. These droplets grow by coalescence and, eventually, in the mature fat cell, only a single large drop of fat exists. The cytoplasm surrounds the fat droplet, and the subcellular organelles are located in this thin cytoplasmic layer. Fat cells are located outside the primary muscle bundles, i.e., in the perimysial spaces or subcutaneously, but not in the endomysial area. Lipid in the latter area is usually associated with membranes or it exists as tiny fat droplets distributed in the muscle fiber itself.

The amount of fat that accumulates in an animal depends on age, the level of nutrition, exercise, and other physiological factors that function in the specific muscle in question. Initially, fat generally tends to accumulate abdominally or under the skin and only later does it accumulate around the muscle. The latter accumulation leads to the so-called marbling of meat. Since this is the last fat to be deposited, a large quantity of feed is necessary to develop marbling. The amount of fat surrounding and within muscles is not constant but can increase or decrease depending on the food intake of the animal and other factors. The amount of fat surrounding the major muscles influences the appearance or "finish" of the meat.

The membranes surrounding fat cells contain small amounts of phospholipids and some cholesterol but by far the largest part of the lipid content of adipose tissue is triglyceride and free fatty acids. This fat can be extracted from the carcass by rendering, which simply involves heating to melt the fat and to rupture the fat cells. This fat can be used as such, e.g., lard, or it can be chemically modified for use in the manufacture of shortenings and margarines. The fat component of meat is very important since some is needed to produce a satisfactory flavor and mouthfeel; however, excessive amounts simply decrease the usable lean portion without improving these quality attributes.

A. Collagen

The major fraction of connective tissue is collagen. This component is important because it contributes significantly to toughness. Also, the partially denatured product of collagen, gelatin, is a useful ingredient in many food products since it serves as the basis for temperature-dependent geltype desserts. Collagen is abundant in tendons, skin, bone, the vascular system of animals, and the connective tissue sheaths surrounding muscle. It has been reported that collagen comprises one-third or more of the total protein of mammals [78]. A portion of collagen is soluble in neutral salt solution, part is soluble in acid, and another fraction is insoluble.

The basic unit of the collagen fiber is tropocollagen, a long cylindrical protein about 2,800 Å long and 14-15 Å in diameter. It consists of three polypeptide chains (two of which are similar) wound around each other in a suprahelical fashion. The two types of chains are designated 1 and 2, and they are approximately the same size. Each chain has a molecular weight of about 100,000 daltons; yielding a total molecular weight of about 300,000 daltons for tropocollagen [14]. In some instances single strands of the peptides which make up tropocollagen are crosslinked with covalent bonds. When two of the peptides are joined in this fashion it is called a β component and when all three are joined, the product is known as a γ component. The solubility of collagen decreases as intermolecular crosslinking increases. The peptides in tropocollagen have substantial helical contents, but these helices differ from the typical α helix because the large content of proline interferes with the α-helical structure. Tropocollagen molecules are linked end to end and adjacently to make up the collagen fibril, as shown in Figure 13-8. There is a periodicity in the cross-striations of collagen at about 640-700 Å. Collagen fibrils are sometimes arranged in parallel fashion to give great strength, as in tendons, or they may be highly branched and disordered, as in skin.

The amino acid composition of collagen is unusual in that glycine represents nearly one-third of the total residues, and this amino acid is distributed uniformly at every third position throughout most of the molecule. This repetitive occurrence of glycine does not include the first 15 or so amino acid residues from the N terminus and the first 10 or so from the C terminus of the molecule [112]. Collagen is also unique in being the only protein that (1) has a large content of hydroxyproline (up to 10%) and (2) contains the amino acid hydroxylysine. It also has a large

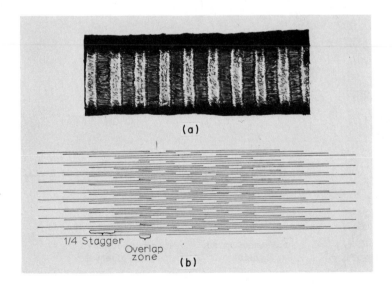

(a)

1/4 Stagger

Overlap zone

(b)

FIG. 13-8. Diagrammatic (a) and schematic (b) representations of the alignment of tropocollagen molecules in the native collagen fibril. (Reprinted from Ref. [6], p. 1001, by courtesy of Dr. A. J. Bailey.)

concentration of proline. Collagen has a poor spectrum of amino acids from a nutritional point of view; e.g., tryptophan is almost totally absent from collagen.

Two important oxidations take place in the polypeptides which comprise collagen. These are the conversion of proline to hydroxyproline and the conversion of lysine to hydroxylysine. This latter compound, as well as lysine, is further oxidized in some of the residues to α-amino adipic Δ-semialdehyde. Oxidation of proline and lysine to their hydroxylated residues is catalyzed by proline hydroxylase and lysine hydroxylase, respectively [44,67]. These enzyme systems utilize molecular oxygen, α-ketoglutarate, ferrous ion, and some reducing system which is probably ascorbate. Ascorbic acid aids in wound healing through its role in synthesis of collagen. The production of the α-amino adipic Δ-semialdehyde is catalyzed by an enzyme called lysyl oxidase [106].

The covalent crosslinks involved in the β and γ components of tropocollagen and the intermolecular crosslinks between tropocollagen molecules form spontaneously by the condensation of aldehyde groups. This may involve an aldol condensation-type reaction (described above) or formation of a Schiff base when the aldehyde reacts with an amino group [111]. Some examples of these reactions are outlined in Figure 13-9. These crosslinks in collagen increase with increasing age [38]. This partially explains why meat from older animals is tougher than that from younger animals, even though there is generally more collagen in the muscle tissue of younger animals.

Collagenase enzymes occur naturally in muscle [71] and they also accompany contaminating microorganisms. These enzymes generally result in only limited breaking of the three collagen chains, and loss of helical structure generally does not occur. The importance of collagenase in the breakdown of collagen in situ is not known but it may have some importance in postmortem tenderization.

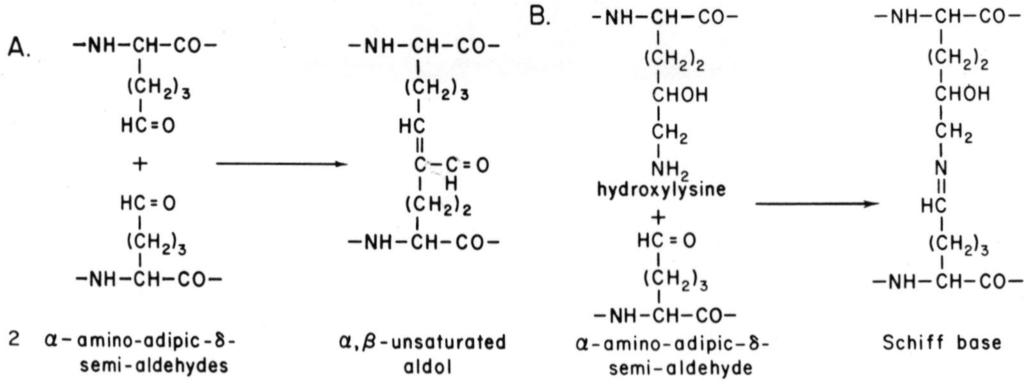

A.

$-NH-CH-CO-$
$\quad\ |$
$\quad (CH_2)_3$
$\quad\ |$
$\quad HC=O$

$\quad +$

$\quad HC=O$
$\quad\ |$
$\quad (CH_2)_3$
$\quad\ |$
$-NH-CH-CO-$

$\longrightarrow$

$-NH-CH-CO-$
$\quad\ |$
$\quad (CH_2)_3$
$\quad\ |$
$\quad HC$
$\quad\ \|$
$\quad C-C=O$
$\quad | \ H$
$\quad (CH_2)_2$
$\quad\ |$
$-NH-CH-CO-$

2 α-amino-adipic-δ-semi-aldehydes

α,β-unsaturated aldol

B.

$-NH-CH-CO-$
$\quad\ |$
$\quad (CH_2)_2$
$\quad\ |$
$\quad CHOH$
$\quad\ |$
$\quad CH_2$
$\quad\ |$
$\quad NH_2$
hydroxylysine

$\quad +$

$\quad HC=O$
$\quad\ |$
$\quad (CH_2)_3$
$\quad\ |$
$-NH-CH-CO-$

α-amino-adipic-δ-semi-aldehyde

$\longrightarrow$

$-NH-CH-CO-$
$\quad\ |$
$\quad (CH_2)_2$
$\quad\ |$
$\quad CHOH$
$\quad\ |$
$\quad CH_2$
$\quad\ |$
$\quad N$
$\quad\ \|$
$\quad HC$
$\quad\ |$
$\quad (CH_2)_3$
$\quad\ |$
$-NH-CH-CO-$

Schiff base

FIG. 13-9. Crosslink formation in collagen by side chain groups. (a) Aldol condensation followed by loss of water. (b) Schiff base formation. Lysine would react in a manner analogous to hydroxylysine.

B. Conversion of Collagen to Gelatin

Collagen fibrils shrink as the temperature is raised to a level characteristic of a given species [42]. When collagen is heated to a temperature above this critical temperature, some intermolecular bonds, some intramolecular bonds (Schiff base and aldol condensation bonds), and a few main-chain peptide bonds are hydrolyzed. This results in conversion of the tristranded collagen structure to a more amorphous form, known as gelatin [116]. These changes constitute denaturation of the collagen molecule but not to the point of a completely unstructured product. If this happens, glue instead of gelatin is produced.

After gelatin is produced and the temperature is lowered to below the critical value, there is a partial renaturation of the collagen molecule, involving what is called the "collagen fold" [116]. Apparently those parts of collagen that are rich in the imino acid residues proline and hydroxyproline regain some of their structure, following which they can apparently interact. When many molecules are involved, a three-dimensional structure is produced which is responsible for the gel that is observed at low temperatures. This collagen fold is absolutely dependent on temperature. Above the melting temperature, the structure degrades and so does the gel. The strength of the gel that is formed is proportional to the square of the concentration of gelatin and directly proportional to molecular weight [116]. Ionic strength and pH seem to have only small influences on gel structure over the range of values encountered in food products.

Processing of collagen into gelatin involves three major steps. There is first the removal of noncollagenous components from the stock (skin and bones), then the conversion of collagen to gelatin by heating in the presence of water, and finally recovery of gelatin in the final form. The molecular properties of gelatin depend on the number of bonds that are broken in the parent collagen molecules. Removal of noncollagenous material may be done with acid or with alkali, and the procedures used influence the properties of the gelatin.

Conversion of collagen to gelatin occurs during normal cooking of meat, and this accounts for the gel-like material that is sometimes evident in meat after heating and cooling. An aspic type of product, for example, results from the conversion of collagen to gelatin. Conversion of collagen molecule to the much less structured gelatin can also play an important role in the tenderness of the meat, especially meat of poor quality. This kind of meat (e.g., pot roast or stew meat) has a high content of collagen and is usually cooked for a long time in water to achieve the desired tenderness, i.e., the desired conversion of collagen to gelatin.

Since collagenase enzymes are apparently present in muscle and collagen cross-linkages are easily broken, one may expect that significant changes in collagen can occur during postmortem aging and that these changes can have a desirable effect on tenderness. Information on this point, however, is inconclusive. Several workers have reported that there is little change in collagen solubility (which is based in part on the number of crosslinkages in the collagen) on aging. Furthermore, it has been reported that collagen content is not affected significantly by postmortem conditions [55]. Other workers [69,90], however, have reported either a significant change in the amount of intramuscular connective tissue, i.e., perimysial and endomysial collagen, or a change in the molecular structure of intramuscular collagen during postmortem holding. Thus, the exact meaning of the results seen to date remains uncertain.

VII. BIOCHEMICAL CHANGES OCCURRING IN MUSCLE POSTMORTEM

A. Biochemical Changes Related to Energy Metabolism

Muscle is a highly specialized tissue, and its functioning represents a classical example of conversion of chemical to mechanical energy in living systems. Muscle requires a large outlay of energy to rapidly operate the contractile apparatus (Section IV.B). This energy is derived immediately from the high-energy compound ATP. Creatine phosphate then rapidly transfers its high-energy phosphate to ADP so that the ATP level may not decrease too much during activity. Resynthesis of ATP from ADP and creatine phosphate is catalyzed by the enzyme creatine kinase. The enzyme adenylate kinase converts two molecules of ADP to one molecule of ATP and one molecule of AMP; this reaction also serves as a source of ATP for the muscle cell.

For long-term activity, the muscle must rely on the oxidation of substrates, usually either carbohydrate or lipid in nature. Lipid metabolism seems to be an especially important source of utilizable energy in muscles which exhibit sustained activity [98], for example, those which support sustained running or sustained flights of migratory birds. Carbohydrates are also an important energy source for muscle. Glycogen is the most important source of carbohydrate energy, but glucose is also utilized. In red muscles and in muscles which are not working extremely hard, it is likely that most of the energy is supplied via the Krebs cycle and the mitochondrial electron transport system (aerobic respiration). This system provides a large quantity of ATP molecules per molecule of substrate utilized and allows for the complete combustion of substrate to carbon dioxide and water.

The mitochondrial system, however, requires oxygen and in some instances, when the muscle is under heavy stress, the oxygen available is not sufficient to maintain mitochondrial function. The anaerobic glycolytic system may then become predominant. This is especially likely in white muscles, which are generally involved in sporatic bursts of activity requiring very large amounts of energy. During anaerobic glycolysis, glycogen is converted by the Emden-Meyerhoff pathway through a series of phosphorylated six-carbon and three-carbon intermediates, until finally pyruvate is produced. Pyruvate is then reduced to lactate. The system requires the cofactor NAD^+ and continually regenerates the NAD^+ that it requires to operate the system. The terminal enzyme of the sequence, lactate dehydrogenase, is principally responsible for regeneration of NAD^+. In anaerobic glycolysis, ATP production is much less efficient than it is in aerobic respiration. For example, anaerobic glycolysis yields only 2 or 3 moles of ATP per mole of glucose, compared to 36 or 37 when aerobic respiration is operative. Also, anaerobic glycolysis results in incomplete oxidation of substrates and accumulation of lactic acid. Lactic acid can penetrate the cell membrane and much of it is removed to the blood, where it goes to the liver and is used to resynthesize glucose. It is then carried back to the muscle, where eventually glycogen is reproduced. The production of lactic acid during contraction may lead to a temporary reduction of pH in the living muscle cell [91]. Obviously, anaerobic glycolysis is favored only under conditions where the mitochondrial system cannot function, i.e., under conditions of limited oxygen. The amount of anaerobic glycolysis that occurs in a given muscle is, therefore, dependent on many factors, including the vascular system, the muscle, the amount of myoglobin, and the number of mitochondria.

We are principally interested in these reactions because many of them proceed after death of the animal and have an important bearing on the food quality of the muscle. Muscle tissue is often referred to as "dead," as opposed to postharvest fruits and vegetables, which are said to be "alive." The distinction is mostly due to differences in the physiology and morphology of muscle tissue as compared to plant tissue. Animal tissues are more highly organized than plant tissues, and life processes of animals rely heavily on a highly developed circulatory system. After death, all circulation ceases, and this rapidly brings about important changes in the muscle tissue. The principal changes are attributable to a lack of oxygen, the development of anaerobic conditions, and the accumulation of certain waste products, especially lactic acid. Plant tissue is less dependent on a highly developed circulatory system than animal tissue, and although certain substances are no longer available to the fruit or vegetable after harvest (see Chapter 15), oxygen can be taken up directly by the plant tissues and waste products can be removed from the cytoplasm by accumulation in the large vacuoles which are present in mature parenchymatous tissue. Thus, although the enzymes of muscle postmortem are still subject to the same control mechanisms as in the live tissue, they are faced with an entirely different environment.

It is believed that cells in general try to maintain a high energy level [20]. The energy level of a cell is expressed as "energy charge" which is defined by Eq. (13-1) [4].

$$\text{Energy charge} = (\text{ATP} + 1/2\text{ADP})/(\text{ATP} + \text{ADP} + \text{AMP}) \qquad (13\text{-}1)$$

The muscle cell postmortem tries to maintain a high energy charge but it has restrictions imposed on it because the circulatory system has been disrupted. In a short time, the mitochondrial system ceases to function in all but surface cells, since internal oxygen is rapidly depleted. Metabolism of some substrates, such as lipids, ceases at this time. ATP is gradually depleted through the action of various ATPases, some being contributed by the contractile proteins but most coming from the membrane systems [12]. Some ATP is temporarily regenerated by the conversion of creatine phosphate to creatine and the transfer of its phosphate to ADP. The adenylate kinase reaction discussed on p. 596 may also function here. After the creatine phosphate has been used up, which occurs fairly rapidly, anaerobic glycolysis continues to regenerate some ATP with the end product lactic acid accumulating. Glycolytic activity may cease because of exhaustion of substrate or, more likely, because of the decrease in pH caused by glycolysis. As glycolytic activity slows down, ATP concentration decreases. Most of the ATP loss usually occurs in 24 hr or less, depending on the species and the circumstances.

Although on a molecular basis, the hydrogen ions generated come from hydrolysis of ATP and not from production of lactate, there is a close correlation between the amount of lactate produced and the pH decline [15]. This relationship occurs because there is an almost linear relationship between the ATP produced by the glycolytic system (and hence the ATP that may be hydrolyzed later) and the amount of lactate produced.

The decrease in pH that accompanies postmortem glycolysis has an important bearing on meat quality. One point of concern is the rate of glycolysis and the concomitant pH decrease. Since there are some 20-odd enzymes involved, glycolysis can conceivably be controlled at many points, depending on the particular subcellular conditions. However, there seems to be certain points in the scheme which are especially important in controlling the rate of glycolysis. In some muscles the phosphorylase step, that is, the conversion of glycogen to glycose 1-phosphate, is the controlling step [94]. This is true, for example, in "slow-glycolyzing" muscles of the pig [64]. However, in "fast-glycolyzing muscles," control is also exerted by phosphofructokinase. In muscle minces in which inorganic phosphate is included, the eventual rate-limiting step is the one controlled by glyceraldehyde-3-phosphate dehydrogenase. This is attributed to hydrolysis of NAD catalyzed by endogenous nucleotide pyrophosphatase [95]. The decrease in concentration of this cofactor limits the activity of the dehydrogenase.

The rate of pH drop also may be affected by the amount of buffering capacity of muscle. Generally, white muscles have relatively large contents of amino acids, carnosine, and anserine, and these probably function as buffering agents in the muscle cell [23].

A second aspect that is important in postmortem muscle is the extent of glycolysis, i.e., how much glycolysis occurs. Under ordinary circumstances, the factor that limits the extent of postmortem glycolysis is pH. When the pH gets low enough, certain critical enzymes, especially phosphofructokinase, are inhibited and glycolysis ceases. The pH where this occurs is generally around 5.1-5.5.

The final pH that is attained is called the "ultimate pH," and this value has an important influence on the textural quality of meat, its water-holding capacity, its resistance to microorganisms, and its color. If an animal prior to slaughter is stressed or exercised vigorously its glycogen content is decreased substantially and a higher ultimate pH is likely to result postmortem. This commonly occurs with fish muscle since fish often struggle vigorously during harvest and prior to death. A similar depletion of substrate can be achieved by the antemortem injection of certain hormones, such as epinephrine [26]. It is possible that other phenomena also have a bearing on ultimate pH, for example, hydrolysis of the cofactor NAD or inactivation of a key enzyme by some handling stress.

Both the rate of pH decline and the ultimate pH are important in controlling the quality of meat. A too rapid drop in pH postmortem has been associated with the pale-soft-exudative (PSE) conditions that are especially common in pork [17,120]. Characteristic attributes are a soft texture, poor water-holding capacity, and a pale color. This is caused by a combination of effects, all of which are caused by denaturation of certain muscle proteins. If a substantial decline in pH occurs before the muscle has been cooled to a sufficiently low temperature (e.g., pH 6.0 and 35°C), denaturation is excessive and PSE symptoms are likely [80].

However, if an animal is vigorously exercised prior to slaughter, its glycogen level may be low, and if so the final meat is dark, firm, and dry. These "dark-cutting" muscles are particularly common in beef. It is possible that high-pH meat may be dark due to maintenance of mitochondrial activity for a longer than normal period of time [3]. Active mitochondria may compete with myoglobin for oxygen at the surface of the meat, thus reducing the amount of oxymyoglobin that is formed.

1. CONSEQUENCES OF ATP DEPLETION

The consequences of ATP depletion in a muscle cell are in part similar to those that presumably occur in any cell where energy sources are depleted. Biosynthetic reactions come to a halt and there is a loss of the cell's ability to maintain its integrity, especially with respect to membrane systems [43]. There is an additional unique phenomenon which occurs with muscle cells. ATP and ADP serve as plasticizers for actin and myosin [70]. When these nucleotides are present, they prevent interaction of these two proteins. When ATP and ADP are depleted postmortem, actin and myosin interact and the muscle passes into a state known as rigor mortis. This means literally the "stiffness of death." The stiffness is due to the tension developed by antagonistic muscles. This tension cannot be relieved because ATP and/or ADP are absent. Individual muscles may not become stiff, but they do become inextensible. When there is sufficient ATP and/or ADP, muscle can be stretched a reasonably length before it breaks. In the state of rigor, however, the muscle ATP has been depleted and it consequently cannot be stretched significantly without breaking [25,53].

The rate of loss of ATP postmortem is closely related to decline in pH and is affected by such factors as species, type of muscle, individual variation among animals, and temperature of the carcass. The ultimate pH of many species is close to pH 5.5, although it may be somewhat higher for some; e.g., 5.9 is common in chicken muscle. The average initial ATP content of many muscles is in the range of 3-5 mg per gram of fresh tissue, and the time at which most of the ATP is degraded can be used as a rough indication of the time of rigor onset. The time postmortem for rigor onset may be as little as 2-4 hr in the chicken [25], 10-24 hr in beef muscle [27,83], and up to 50 hr in whale muscle [82]. The time for rigor onset is greatly dependent on temperature. Beef muscle held at 37°C can go into rigor in as little as 4 hr postmortem.

2. AGING OF MUSCLE

When muscle stands for 2 weeks or more at 0.5°-2°C, it becomes more tender. This tenderization process has been described as "resolution of rigor." There has been much discussion as to exactly what constitutes resolution of rigor and why tenderization occurs. It appears that it is not caused by the breaking of actomyosin bonds, at least not in the way that ATP does this. It has been suggested that resolution results from hydrolysis of some structural proteins in the muscle cell by indigenous cathepic enzymes. In any event, cleavage of some sarcomeres at the Z line has been noted in aged muscle. In one sense, then, the state of rigor is not resolved since actomyosin linkages are not reversed. However, resolution does occur in the sense that the muscle becomes more tender and presumably undergoes some structural changes. It should be noted, however, that details of these structural changes have not been easy to demonstrate. One of the problems may be that small molecular weight fragments have, for the most part, been looked for, whereas the tenderization procedure may involve cleavage of proteins into only one or two large fragments.

B. ATP Breakdown to Hypoxanthine

Another important consequence of the loss of ATP in muscle postmortem is its conversion to hypoxanthine, as shown in Figure 13-10. Certain 5'-mononucleotides are important flavor enhancers in muscle foods [63]. In order for these compounds

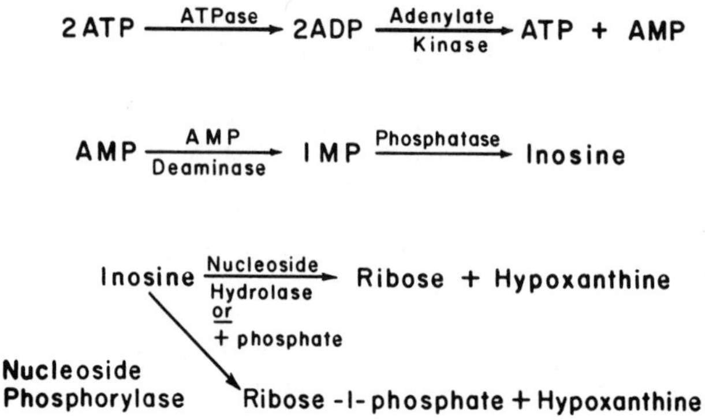

$$2\,ATP \xrightarrow{\text{ATPase}} 2ADP \xrightarrow[\text{Kinase}]{\text{Adenylate}} ATP \;+\; AMP$$

$$AMP \xrightarrow[\text{Deaminase}]{\text{AMP}} IMP \xrightarrow{\text{Phosphatase}} \text{Inosine}$$

$$\text{Inosine} \xrightarrow[\substack{\text{Hydrolase} \\ \text{or} \\ +\text{ phosphate}}]{\text{Nucleoside}} \text{Ribose} \;+\; \text{Hypoxanthine}$$

**Nucleoside
Phosphorylase**   Ribose -I- phosphate + Hypoxanthine

FIG. 13-10. Conversion of ATP to hypoxanthine in postmortem muscle.

to have flavor-enhancing properties, the ribose component must be phosphorylated at position 5' and the purine component must be hydroxylated at position 6. Compounds that fall into this category are IMP (inosinic acid) and GMP (guanylic acid). ATP is first converted to ADP and then to AMP by a disproportionation reaction. AMP is then deaminated to IMP, a flavor enhancer. IMP, however, can degrade to inosine and eventually to hypoxanthine. Hypoxanthine has a bitter flavor and it has been suggested as the cause of off flavors in stored fish [62]. Hypoxanthine also may cause off flavors in unheated irradiated beef since some enzyme activity remains (enzymes are more difficult to destroy by ionizing radiations than are microorganisms). Irradiated beef therefore should be exposed to a heat treatment sufficient to inactivate enzymes so that hypoxanthine production and other detrimental enzyme-catalyzed changes do not occur.

It has also been proposed, especially with fish, that levels of ATP and its breakdown products serve as indicators of the freshness of tissue [107]. IMP, inosine, or hypoxanthine may be determined for this purpose. This approach has so far proved less successful and has been studied less extensively in muscle tissues from warm-blooded animals than in muscle tissues from cold-blooded animals.

The advantage of testing for these breakdown products is that they may serve as a means of detecting early deterioration in meat. These products also may have significance in muscle tissue which is canned, e.g., herring, mackeral, or salmon. Since the enzymic reactions are stopped during processing, analysis of the canned product for these components should indicate the quality of the raw fish that has been used.

C. Loss of Calcium-sequestering Ability

One possible reason for increased ATPase activity postmortem and the tendency for muscle to contract is a loss in the ability of the sarcoplasmic reticulum to sequester calcium [40]. The sarcoplasmic reticulum releases its calcium with aging postmortem. Loss of its ability to control the calcium content of the sarcoplasm is probably due both to a deterioration in the energy generating systems of the muscle and to an increased permeability of the sarcoplasmic reticulum with postmortem age (this permits greater leakage of calcium from the membrane). Increased levels of calcium in the sarcoplasm may cause contractile proteins to more fully display their ATPase potential and may initiate the activity of ATPases in membrane systems. This, in turn, would cause increased activity of the glycolytic system and a more rapid decline in pH. The sarcoplasmic reticulum of postmortem chicken, however, does not lose its ability to sequester calcium [52].

D. Z-Line Disintegration

During the aging of muscle postmortem there is a tendency for the Z line to disintegrate. This is evident both from increased fragmentation of myofibrils during homogenization [110] and from disorganization and eventual disappearance of the Z line [24]. This disruption may result from breakage of links joining thin filaments to the Z line or simply from solubilization of Z-line proteins. There is some indication that magnesium stabilizes the Z line and calcium hastens its disintegration [37]. As mentioned, the latter process may be involved in "resolution of rigor." It has been shown that there is a calcium-activated protease in muscle which participates in Z-line destruction postmortem [122].

VIII. THE EFFECTS OF POSTMORTEM CHANGES ON QUALITY ATTRIBUTES OF MEAT

A. Texture and Water-holding Capacity

One of the important biochemical events in muscle tissue postmortem is the reduction in pH. Both the extent and the rate of pH change are important. If a low enough pH is obtained at an undesirably high temperature, considerable denaturation of contractile and/or sarcoplasmic proteins may occur. If the sarcoplasmic proteins are denatured they may adsorb to contractile proteins, thus modifying the physical properties of the contractile proteins, including their ability to hold water.

If fatty acids are produced during the postmortem phase of meat storage, such as by the actions of lipases or phospholipases, they may interact with contractile proteins and denature them. This has been suggested as an important factor in the deterioration of texture of fish muscle during frozen storage [66].

A major phenomenon which affects the texture of meat is the interaction of actin and myosin after depletion of ATP and ADP. Associated with this interaction is an increase in toughness, and meat is sometimes aged to partially overcome this effect. If meat is cooked and eaten before it passes into rigor, i.e., before actin and myosin interact, it is very tender [84].

Dissolution and disintegration of the Z line is related to increased tenderization of meat during postmortem aging. However, it probably is not the only factor of importance since the Z line is intact in tender prerigor muscle. Furthermore, disintegration of the Z line appears to occur well in advance of substantial tenderization during aging. It appears very probable that both disintegration of the Z line and some rupture of thin and thick filaments are involved in postmortem tenderization.

A particularly important aspect of the development of toughness in meat involves the state of the sarcomere when actomyosin is formed, that is, the extent to which thin and thick filaments overlap. This is controlled by several factors in the early postmortem period. Since critical changes in sarcomere length require the presence of ATP, either as a plasticizing agent so thin and thick filaments can slip past each other or as an energy source for contraction, it is necessary to deal principally with the prerigor period when ATP and ADP are still abundant.

If muscle is excised from the skeleton in a prerigor state, it is susceptible to rapid contraction. The extent of shortening depends on many factors, including the nature of the specific muscle involved, the temperature at which the muscle is held, the elapsed time between death and excision, and the physiological state of the muscle at the time of death (Section X). At high (physiological) temperatures, contraction is great. As the temperature is reduced, contraction of excised prerigor muscles decreases and for some muscles minimum contraction occurs at about 10°-20°C. If these muscles are exposed to still lower temperatures, in the range of 10°-0°C, increased contraction again occurs [80] (Fig. 3-11). This behavior is particularly noticeable and of commercial importance with beef and lamb muscle.

The shortening which occurs at low nonfreezing temperatures is termed "cold shortening." Muscles that are highly susceptible to cold shortening (beef, lamb) should be maintained at temperatures above 10°C until they pass into rigor; otherwise undesirable changes in tenderness occur.

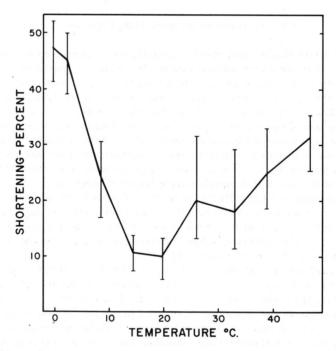

FIG. 3-11. Relation between shortening of beef muscle and storage temperature postmortem. Vertical lines represent standard deviations. (Reprinted from Ref. [80], p. 788, by courtesy of Dr. R. H. Locker.)

Marsh and Leet [86] have shown (Fig. 13-12) that toughness increases as shortening increases, up to a point where the muscle is approximately 60% of its rest length (40% contraction). This length represents the point at which the myosin filaments just reach the Z line, i.e., the I band just disappears. With greater shortening, the muscle loses toughness rapidly. The reason for this tenderization is not completely clear but it may result because thin and thick filaments slide past each other to an extent exceeding that which occurs in vivo, thus leading to severe, irreversible disruption of the sarcomere.

Data relating muscle shortening to water-holding capacity (drip) are shown in Figure 13-13. Drip losses do not become excessive until shortening exceeds about 40% of the original length. This behavior is in accord with the previously stated belief that severe disruption of the muscle fiber occurs when shortening exceeds about 40%.

Muscles on the carcass also can undergo some cold shortening, although skeletal attachments limit the amount. The extent to which this occurs depends on whether the muscle has been severed during slaughter (e.g., sternomandibularis or neck muscle), whether the temperature is conducive to cold shortening, whether a temperature gradient exists along the muscle during prerigor cooling (so some parts contract and other parts stretch), whether the muscle is naturally anchored at both ends or one end only (e.g., longissiums dorsi), the species being handled, and how the carcass is positioned during the prerigor phase. Significant changes in tenderness in a particular muscle can be accomplished by holding the carcass in certain positions [56]. It has been well documented that stretched muscles (governed by the way the carcass is hung) are more tender than unstretched muscles.

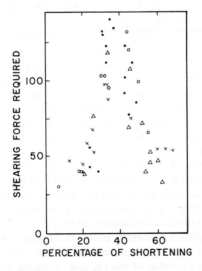

FIG. 13-12. The relationship between shortening and tenderness in heat-denatured beef muscle. Shortening was produced by treatments of varying temperature and time and by freezing-thawing. (Reprinted from Ref. [86], p. 635, by courtesy of Macmillan Journals, Ltd.)

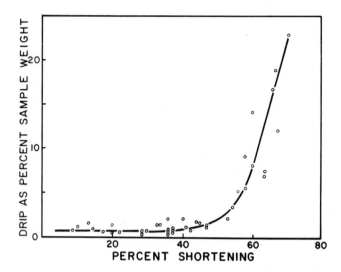

FIG. 13-13. The relation between "drip" exudation (as percent of frozen sample weight) and extent of thaw shortening (as percent of initial excised length). (Reprinted from Ref. [87], p. 456, by courtesy of Institute of Food Technologists.)

Furthermore, a high positive correlation has been established between sarcomere length and degree of tenderness [54]. Excision of a muscle prerigor, of course, removes the physical restraints on contraction and the muscle can undergo tremendous shortening, sometimes up to 60-70% of its rest length [86]. This results in a highly disrupted (tender) muscle and one with very poor water-holding capacity.

A phenomenon related to cold shortening is freeze-thaw contraction or "thaw rigor." If a muscle is frozen prerigor, it often undergoes considerable shortening during rapid thawing. This can be accompanied by a toughening of the muscle (if contraction is less than 40%) and poor water-holding capacity (if contraction exceeds 40%). For this reason, meat which is to be frozen generally should be in rigor or postrigor if optimal quality is desired. However, thaw rigor can be avoided in fish by holding frozen prerigor samples at normal temperatures of frozen storage for about 2 months [16]. Thaw rigor in frozen prerigor lamb, beef, or poultry can be avoided by holding the frozen muscles at -3°C for a time equal to that normally used during chilling [11].

A suggestion has been made by Marsh [85] that the fundamental cause of both cold shortening and freeze-thaw contraction is the inability of the sarcoplasmic reticulum in the muscle to control the calcium concentration in the sarcoplasm. In cold shortening, low nonfreezing temperatures alone apparently impair the ability of the sarcoplasmic reticulum to sequester calcium. In thaw rigor, direct or indirect effects of ice crystals apparently result in almost total destruction of the functionality of the sarcoplasmic reticulum. In either case, the release of calcium would inhibit the relaxing proteins of the muscle, causing uncontrolled contraction of the muscle.

B. Color

Color of muscle is principally affected by pH, which controls the physical state of the myofibrils and hence the reflection of light from muscle [17]. In addition, pH influences the functioning of mitochondria and their ability to compete with myoglobin for oxygen [3], and it also may affect the metmyoglobin-reducing systems in muscle. If these reducing systems are inactivated by an unfavorable pH, one can expect more rapid oxidation of bright red oxymyoglobin to brown metmyoglobin.

Since myoglobin can exist in either a reduced or an oxidized state, its form (and color) is determined by the oxidation-reduction potential of the system. With long-term storage, the reducing substances may be depleted and when this happens myoglobin converts to an oxidized (Fe^{3+}) state (brown metmyoglobin).

During most slaughtering procedures, some hemoglobin from the blood remains in the muscle. Estimates of the amount range from 5 to 40% of the total pigment. With respect to meat color, the principal difference between myoglobin and hemoglobin is that binding of O_2 to hemoglobin is sensitive to pH, whereas with myoglobin it is not. The colors formed from each type of pigment and the reactions required to produce these colors are identical. Meat pigments are discussed further in Chapter 8.

C. Flavor

Little is known concerning the effect of postmortem handling on the development of a normal cooked flavor in meat. However, proteolysis and nucleotide metabolism may produce compounds which contribute significantly to flavor or which react on cooking to produce flavor. Flavor is highly dependent on the particular cut of meat and its chemical composition.

D. Nutritional Quality

The changes that occur in meat portmortem mainly affect color and texture and have little effect on nutritional quality. The only possible exception to this is when muscle loses large amounts of fluid (e.g., during thaw rigor or with PSE pork). Then soluble nutrients may be lost if the exuded fluid is not collected and consumed with the final product. Amino acids and vitamins, especially those of the B complex, are most affected.

IX. ANTEMORTEM FACTORS AFFECTING POSTMORTEM BIOCHEMICAL CHANGES

For any given animal, several antemortem factors are of importance in determining the course of postmortem events. Most of these factors influence the level of muscle glycogen, although mechanical damage can occur by rough handling (bruising) or fighting (bites).

Glycogen is depleted by several stress conditions and, in general, it is desirable to minimize the stress conditions as much as possible. Stress conditions include exercise, fasting, cold temperatures, and fear. Not all animals react in the same way or to the same degree to any one of these stresses. It is very difficult, for example, to deplete cattle of glycogen by exercising, whereas significant lowering of the glycogen content of pig muscles can occur with relatively mild exercise [72]. Within a given species, there may be variations among breeds or even sexes. It is possible literally to frighten some stress-susceptible animals to death.

The ultimate pH of fish is generally much higher than that of warm-blooded animals because the means of catching the fish allows them to struggle for a long time before death, thus reducing their glycogen contents.

Generally, it is desirable to reach a moderately low ultimate pH, since this gives improved resistance to microbial spoilage and, in the case of red meats, provides a more desirable color. As mentioned earlier (Section VII.A), the ultimate pH should be achieved slowly, that is, glycolysis should be slow and complete. Many stress-susceptible animals show a tendency to give a rapid decrease in pH, even though the ultimate pH is no lower or may be even considerably higher than that of non-stress-susceptible animals. This is undesirable since low pH values are attained before the muscle is cooled adequately, resulting in protein denaturation and toughness.

X. EFFECTS OF PROCESSING ON MEAT COMPONENTS

The purpose of many food-processing techniques is to slow down or prevent deleterious changes from occurring in food materials. These deleterious changes are often caused by contaminating microorganisms, by chemical reactions among natural components of the food tissues, or by simple physical occurrences (dehydration). The reactions may be chemically catalyzed or catalyzed by native enzymes of the tissue.

The procedures used to prevent changes in foods caused by microorganisms or chemical-physical reactions are (1) removal of water; (2) removal of other active components, such as oxygen or glucose; (3) use of chemical additives; (4) lowering of temperature; (5) input of energy; and (6) packaging. Most of the unit operations in food processing are based on combinations of two or more of these fundamental procedures. Very often, however, when one desirable objective is achieved other undesirable consequences occur. This is especially true when the principal objective of the processing procedure is to reduce the microbial population. Conditions designed to do this very often lead to extensive chemical and physical changes in the foods. In this section, the effects of various food processing techniques on chemical components and quality attributes of meat are considered.

A. Refrigeration

The most widely used process in meat preservation is refrigeration. This procedure is not only used for meat that is to be sold "fresh" but is very often employed for meat that is to be processed by other procedures.

Refrigeration preserves muscle tissue by retarding growth of microorganisms and by slowing chemical and enzymic reactions. Generally speaking, a temperature as low as possible without freezing is desirable. During postmortem cooling and subsequent refrigerated storage, control of relative humidity is very important.

If considerable moisture is lost from the surface, the weight reduction becomes economically undesirable and the meat pigment, myoglobin, also oxidizes to brown metmyoglobin. However, a small amount of moisture loss from the surface is desirable since this tends to retard growth of microorganisms.

Beef muscle, after cooling postmortem, is sometimes aged at refrigerated temperatures for 1-2 weeks to allow for tenderization. After relatively long-term storage at refrigerator temperatures, growth of microorganisms on the meat may necessitate some surface trimming. Mold growth may impart a musty flavor which is considered desirable by some.

The susceptibility of meat to microbial spoilage depends on the ratio of cut surface to weight. Small cuts spoil more rapidly than large cuts. Ground meat is especially susceptible to spoilage by microorganisms.

The major deleterious effects which occur during cooling of muscle are caused by cold shortening.

One other item of interest is that some enzymes exhibit a decrease in Michaelis constant with a decrease in temperature [31]. This decrease means that at low substrate concentrations, the enzyme retains a higher proportion of its maximal activity. In muscle tissue most substrates, especially those taking part in rate-limiting reactions, would not be present in sufficiently high quantities to saturate the enzymes. Therefore, lowering the temperature does not necessarily slow down enzyme-catalyzed reactions as much as one may expect. An example of a physical phenomenon which may be related to this is the dependence of cold shortening on temperature, where a minimal value of shortening occurs around 15°-20°C [80]. Another example is the rate of loss of ATP which is minimal in chicken muscle at about 20°C [25]. The major point is that decreases in rates of enzyme-catalyzed reactions do not always correlate well with decreases in temperature.

B. Freezing

Freezing is an excellent process for preserving the quality of meat for a long period. It functions by a combination of internal dehydration (ice crystal formation) and lowering of temperature. Although some microorganisms can survive storage at very low temperatures, there generally is no opportunity for growth of microorganisms if recommended storage temperatures are maintained.

As discussed in Section VIII A, one generally should not freeze meat prior to the development of rigor. If this is done, the muscle may contract on thawing, giving increased toughness and exudation of fluid. This thaw exudate (drip), in addition to being unsightly, represents economic and nutritional losses if it is not utilized.

Although freezing rate has some influence on the quality of thawed-cooked meat, it is generally a factor of secondary importance since changes during frozen storage, as conducted commercially, frequently obscure any benefits of rapid freezing (minimal drip) that exist initially. Exceptions to this statement can occur when the time of frozen storage is short, the temperature of frozen storage is below -18°C, or meat with a large surface to mass ratio (e.g., ground meat) is being frozen.

A major problem arising from improper (very slow) freezing and storage procedures is the phenomenon of excessive thaw exudate referred to above. During the initial formation of ice crystals, especially in extracellular spaces, a very high concentration of salt develops in the muscle. This increase in salt concentration, along with the possible concomitant change in pH, may cause extensive denaturation of muscle proteins [81,93]. These proteins then lose a great deal of their capacity to bind water. This loss in water-binding ability of the proteins, along with cellular damage arising from mechanical disruption of the muscle cells by ice crystals, is responsible in large part for the thaw exudate.

Enzymes generally are not inactivated by the freezing process and many continue to function in frozen meat. Enzymes with low activation energies, e.g., lipoxygenase, retain considerable activity, oftentimes more than is expected by extrapolation of Arrhenius plots. Freezing damage to the tissue (enzyme delocalization) and changes in environmental conditions (pH, ionic strength, substrate concentration) or changes in the Michaelis constant may account for this behavior.

There is a redistribution of certain enzymes among subcellular fractions when meat is frozen and thawed. A procedure measuring the redistribution of the mitochondrial isoenzyme of glutamate-oxaloacetate transaminase has been tested to differentiate frozen and thawed beef, pork, and chicken from the unfrozen products [46,47]. However, this procedure may not be suitable for pork since procedures other than freezing and thawing can damage pig muscle mitochondria and cause redistribution of this enzyme [115].

The major enzymes that appear to be involved in the spoilage of meat during long-term frozen storage are those that act on fats. Lipases and phospholipases release free fatty acids from the lipids of the meat. These free fatty acids may then undergo oxidation, with or without the aid of lipoxygenase. This problem is especially important in products with a high degree of unsaturated fatty acids, such as pork and seafoods.

Another problem that may ensue from the release of free fatty acids from triglycerides or phospholipids is related to the fact that free fatty acids are surface-active agents. Thus, they can combine with proteins and denature them. This may be a major cause of the undesirable toughening that codfish muscle undergoes during frozen storage [1]. There is also some indication that the major source of fatty acids in lean fish is phospholipids of the membrane systems and not triglycerides [96].

Dehydration of the surface of the meat during the freezing process or during subsequent frozen storage (freezer burn) is an additional problem that can occur if improper packaging techniques are employed. Freezer burn occurs when the equilibrium vapor pressure above the surface of the meat is greater than that in the air, thus causing ice crystals to sublime. Oxidation of the heme pigment usually occurs in the desiccated tissue.

C. Heating

The amount of thermal energy that is applied to muscle tissue in processing and cooking brings about substantial changes in the tissue. The extent of these changes is dependent on the amount of energy applied and this varies from the mild heat treatments used in preparation for eating or for pasteurization processes to the much more severe treatments used to produce commercially sterile products.

Heating of meat, of course, is frequently done to destroy some or all of the microorganisms present. It does, however, have other functions, one of which is inactivation of enzymes. Whether or not one obtains complete inactivation of enzymes depends on the extent of the heat treatment. Some of the enzymes of muscle will survive short treatments at temperatures of 60° or 70°C [76]. However, most heat treatments result in enzyme inactivation. Myosin and actomyosin are also enzymes, and their activities are destroyed during most heat treatments. Conventional heat treatments also have the general effect of denaturing most of the meat proteins. Textural changes result from this since contractile proteins become somewhat tougher as heating progresses. However, very often this is counteracted, especially in the tougher cuts of meat, by a concomitant conversion of the collagen of connective tissue to gelatin. This is, of course, the reason for cooking tough cuts of meat for a long period of time in the presence of water. Some firming of muscle tissue by heating is considered desirable; however, too much can lead to a tough, dry product even with the best cuts of meat.

Another consequence of denaturation of muscle proteins is a decrease in water-binding capacity. This decrease in water-binding capacity may produce juiciness (free moisture), which is considered desirable. Heat denaturation and surface dehydration that take place on cooking cause a surface layer to form that tends to retard loss of fluid from the meat until it is cut and eaten.

The emulsifying capacities of muscle proteins are also greatly decreased by heating.

During heating, fat is melted, adipose tissue cells are ruptured, and there is a significant redistribution of fat. When the meat is eaten warm, the melted fat serves to increase palatability of the product by giving a desirable mouthfeel, especially at the end of the chewing period when most of the aqueous juices have been lost.

Myoglobin also undergoes denaturation during heating. Denaturation of this protein causes a rapid release of the heme pigment from the globin part of the molecule, and free heme is very sensitive to oxidation [75]. On heating, therefore, red meat will generally turn brown due to the formation of the oxidized pigment, hemin (see Chapter 8).

With severe heating, there will be further changes in the proteins and free amino acids of the meat, with production of some volatile breakdown products. Sulfur-containing compounds are produced, including hydrogen sulfide, mercaptans, sulfides, and disulfides, as well as aldehydes, ketones, alcohols, volatile amines, and others (see Chapter 5). Lipid components may also break down into volatile products, such as aldehydes, ketones, alcohols, acids, or hydrocarbons (see Chapter 4). Some of these volatile compounds, in both the fat and the lean portions of the meat, contribute to the flavor and odor of cooked meat.

Commercial heating generally has moderately detrimental effects on the vitamin content of meat. Thiamine is sensitive to heat, and some of this may be destroyed on cooking or thermal processing. Certain amino acids may interact with glucose and/or ribose of the meat (Maillard reaction) and the nutritional values of these amino acids are lost when this occurs (see Chapter 3). Lysine, arginine, histidine, and methionine seem to be particularly susceptible to degradation via this route. However, the conditions used during commercial sterilization generally have little detrimental effect on the nutritive value of proteins and lipids.

Some muscles cannot withstand the extreme conditions of temperature that are needed for sterilization without undergoing extensive changes in quality. Pork is an example of a meat that does not tolerate high temperatures well. Thus, a moderate heat treatment is usually used for pork preservation, often along with a curing process and subsequent refrigeration of the product.

D. Dehydration

Preservation of muscle tissue by dehydration is an ancient practice, originating at least 3,000 years ago. The quality resulting from the early techniques was, however, extremely poor by our standards, and this technique was used only because of dire necessity.

Drying can be successfully employed for both raw and cooked meat; however, the quality of the final reconstituted product is superior when the meat is cooked prior to dehydration [73]. The reason for this is not clear, but it may be that protein denaturation which occurs during heating in the presence of the original moisture is less severe than that which occurs during the combined process of heating and moisture removal.

The type of dehydration also will have a very significant effect on the quality of the final product. Conventional air drying, which is done at relatively high temperatures, has more detrimental effects on muscle tissue than a process, such as freeze dehydration, which involves a low temperature and sublimation of ice. In addition to the difference in temperature between these two kinds of dehydration, there is also a difference in salt concentration. During air drying there is an increase in salt concentration throughout the tissue [73]. As moisture evaporates, more moisture is drawn to the surface, and salts become more and more concentrated as the moisture is removed. Removal of water causes the muscle tissue to shrink substantially, and the high salt concentration tends to destabilize the proteins, partly because of the increased ionic strength of the aqueous medium and partly because of changes in pH. In freeze dehydration, where water is converted directly from the solid state to the gaseous state, the increase in solute concentration is more evenly distributed, and the product is at a lower temperature than during dehydration by conventional means. Thus, there is less damage from salt effects.

When muscle tissue is air dried, there is a loss in volume which is accompanied by smaller spaces among the groups of muscle fibers. This shrinkage is greater with precooked muscle than with raw [118].

Heat denaturation effects on raw muscle occur in stages [73]. From 0° to 20°C, there is a loss in native structure of protein as measured by water-binding capacity. This is presumably due to denaturation of sarcoplasmic proteins. The next major loss in water-binding capacity occurs over the range 40°-50°C and is most likely due to denaturation of contractile proteins. This denaturation continues up to about 80°C. Collagen changes at relatively high temperatures, being converted to gelatin at around 100°C. The changes in collagen tend to increase water-binding capacity, but the effect is slight and not enough to offset the decrease caused by denaturation of sarcoplasmic and contractile proteins.

During high-temperature drying, melting of fat in the tissues also occurs. Fat in excess of about 35–40% (fresh weight basis) usually cannot be retained by dehydrated tissue [73].

Of all the quality attributes, texture is the one most severely altered by dehydration. The change in texture is determined principally by the extent of denaturation of the muscle proteins, and this in turn is highly dependent on the pH of the meat at the start of dehydration. Even a very good freeze-drying procedure results in some lowering of the water-holding capacity of muscle if the process is carried out near the isoelectric points of the proteins. If one starts at a high ultimate pH, relatively small decreases occurs in the water-binding capacity of muscle during dehydration. Measurements of rehydration, extractability of proteins, and ATPase activity all have been used to measure in a rough way the amount of denatured protein in dehydrated muscle.

Some changes in dehydrated meat also occur during storage. The extent of these changes depends in large part of the conditions of storage (temperature, oxygen level, moisture content), as well as on the processing procedure and on the quality of the initial raw material.

Lipid oxidation is a major factor limiting the shelf life of dehydrated muscle tissue. The highly unsaturated nature of pork lipids and lipids from fatty-type fishes is such that it is impractical to store these products in dehydrated form for extended periods without some other type of protective treatment. In the case of pork, this has meant the addition of antioxidants. Oxidative changes are greater in dehydrated raw muscle tissue than in dehydrated cooked muscle because in raw tissue such enzymes as lipoxygenase may survive the dehydration treatment.

Lipid oxidation results principally in undesirable flavors which can make the meat unacceptable. There also may be some destruction of oxidizable nutrients, such as essential fatty acids, as well as oxidation of heme pigments which leads to discoloration. Lipid oxidation of meat can be minimized by packaging it in a container from which oxygen is excluded and by storing it at a low temperature. Some of the breakdown products of lipid oxidation also can interact with proteins, causing textural changes.

Another major type of deterioration in dehydrated muscle tissue involves nonenzymic browning. Glucose and phosphorylated sugar derivatives and a large number of amino groups from either free amino acids or proteins are present in meat. These can interact by means of the Maillard reaction (discussed in Chapter 3), resulting in dark pigments. When the sugars react with proteins, the physical properties of the proteins can change, resulting in a toughening or hardening of the texture. A small decrease in nutritive value can also occur when essential amino acids, such as lysine, participate in this reaction. Nonenzymic browning also leads to desirable changes in flavor, some of which are typical of cooked meat. Some vitamins, especially thiamine, can also degrade during storage of dehydrated muscle tissue.

E. Curing

The production of cured meat is an ancient process. Curing involves the use of sodium chloride and sodium nitrite and/or sodium nitrate. Sugar may or may not be added along with other ingradients to improve flavor. The addition of sodium chloride inhibits microorganisms. As discussed in Chapter 8, nitrite produces the cured meat pigment, nitric oxide hemochromagen. This effect of nitrite was perhaps discovered accidentally due to impurities in sodium chloride. Many research workers believe that sodium nitrate provides a source of nitrite in the meat by means of bacterial reduction.

During the curing process, whether it be by dry curing, where salt is rubbed onto the surface of the meat, or by use of a curing pickle, where the meat is submerged in a strong salt solution, the high osmotic pressure of the external fluid initially draws water and soluble proteins out of the meat. Later, salt diffuses into the meat and binds to the proteins, causing some of the expelled protein to diffuse back in. The net effect of this process is a swelling of the meat. The salt-protein complex that forms binds water well; thus, the water-binding capacity of proteins generally increases during curing. The final meat contains increased ash due to the absorbed salts.

If meat with a high ultimate pH is used for curing, salt penetration is difficult since the fibers are enlarged [74]. In pork that is pale, soft, and exudative (a low pH is reached too quickly postmortem), the water-binding capacity of the cured product may be low. Even though salt penetration can occur easily, this advantage is apparently offset by the large amount of denatured protein, which has poor water-holding capacity [74]. Freezing of meat prior to the curing process also increases the penetration rate of salt because this process partially disrupts the meat structure.

It has been claimed that nitrite has a significant beneficial effect on the flavor of cured meats. The nature of these flavors is poorly understood. Nitrite also has an inhibitory effect on Clostridium botulinum.

Curing appears to have little effect on either the quality of proteins or the stability of the B vitamins [74].

A major detrimental change that can occur in cured meat during storage is the oxidation of nitric oxide hemochromagen (pink) to brown metmyoglobin [8]. The rate of oxidation increases with increasing oxygen content; therefore, cured meat preferably should be packaged in a container from which oxygen is excluded.

The presence of salt in cured meat enhances oxidation of lipid components, thus considerably reducing the shelf life. Ascorbic acid in the presence of a metal-chelating agent, such as polyphosphate, can effectively forestall this oxidative reaction [74].

Recently, concern has arisen over the potential hazard of using nitrite in cured meats since this compound reacts with amines, especially secondary amines, to form N-nitrosamines which may be carcinogenic [29]. Although N-nitrosamines should not form in meat if the concentration of nitrite does not exceed United States federal regulations, commercial samples of frankfurters have occasionally been found that do contain this compound [32]. In these instances, it has been suggested that improper mixing may have resulted in high local concentrations of nitrite, thereby favoring the formation of nitrosamines.

F.   Other Chemical Additives

Many chemical additives in addition to those used for curing are added to meat products. Most of these chemicals are either antimicrobial or flavoring agents and they may be added intentionally, such as acetic acid (vinegar for pickling meat), or they may be produced by fermentation, such as lactic acid in certain types of dry sausage.

Smoking is often used in conjunction with salting and curing, and it is considered highly desirable because of the flavor that accrues from it. Many of the chemical components of smoke are effective antimicrobial agents if present in sufficient concentration. Wood smoke may have other effects, however, that depend on direct interaction with the meat components. For example, many of the components of smoke are effective antioxidants. In using the same smoking procedure, differences in flavor can be produced in different meat products. Therefore, it is clear that an interaction of smoke with meat components does take place.

G. Preservation by Ionizing Radiation

Although ionizing radiation has not been approved for processing of food products, it does constitute a potentially useful form of preservation. Aside from inactivation of microorganisms, one of the major effects of ionizing radiation on meat is alteration of pigments [114]. If raw or cured meat is exposed to large doses of ionizing radiation, it turns brown. The color of cooked meat is not affected by ionizing radiations in air, but a pink color develops in the absence of oxygen. However, on exposure to air it reverts to its original brown color. The pink color of irradiated cooked meat is attributable to a denatured globin hemochrome pigment.

Sterilizing doses of ionizing radiation result in the breakdown of various lipids and proteins to compounds which have distinct and often undesirable odors [114]. These odors vary with the particular muscle tissue that is treated and range all the way from extremely unpleasant odors, in the case of beef, to rather mild odors, in the cases of pork and chicken. Furthermore, irradiated beef steak is sometimes bitter, and this may result from the conversion of ATP to hypoxanthine. Many of these reactions can be prevented by lowering the temperature at which irradiation takes place. Temperatures of -80°C or below greatly lessen undesirable side effects without seriously decreasing destruction of microorganisms [114]. This occurs because microorganisms are primarily destroyed by direct interaction with the ionizing radiation, whereas most of the undesirable changes in chemical components occur from the indirect effects of free radicals produced during irradiation.

The tenderness of beef may be increased by treatment with ionizing radiations in the megarad range.

Generally, enzymes are not completely inactivated by irradiation treatments sufficient to sterilize the product. Therefore, for long-term storage it is necessary to heat the meat to approximately 70°C, i.e., cook it prior to irradiation and storage.

H. Packaging

The basic reasons for packaging processed muscle tissue have been discussed above. In summary, frozen meat should be packaged to prevent loss of moisture and freezer burn. Dehydrated products must be packaged to prevent the entrance of water and oxygen, so that nonenzymic browning and oxidative reactions do not occur. Cured meat should be packaged to exclude oxygen so that nitric oxide hemochromagen does not oxidize to brown denatured metmyoglobin. Packages for fresh meat must be reasonably impermeable to moisture to prevent weight loss but must be permeable to oxygen so that the fresh red bloom of the oxygenated myoglobin pigment can be maintained.

REFERENCES

1. M. L. Anderson and E. M. Ravesi, J. Fish. Res. Bd. Can., 26, 2727 (1969).
2. H. Arnold and D. Pette, Eur. J. Biochem., 6, 163 (1968).
3. C. R. Ashmore, W. Parker, and L. Doerr, J. Anim. Sci., 34, 46 (1972).
4. D. E. Atkinson and G. M. Walton, J. Biol. Chem., 242, 3239 (1967).
5. M. E. Bailey, in Proceedings of the 24th Annual Reciprocal Meat Conference, National Live Stock and Meat Board, Chicago, 1971, pp. 134-170.
6. A. J. Bailey, J. Sci. Food Agri., 23, 995 (1972).
7. G. Bailin and M. Barany, Biochim. Biophys. Acta, 140, 208 (1967).
8. J. Bard and W. E. Townsend, in The Science of Meat and Meat Products (J. F. Price and B. S. Schweigert, eds.), 2nd ed., Freeman, San Francisco, 1971, pp. 452-470.
9. R. J. Barnard, V. R. Edgerton, T. Furukawa, and J. B. Peter, Amer. J. Physiol., 220, 410 (1971).
10. G. R. Beecher, R. G. Cassens, W. G. Hoekstra, and E. J. Briskey, J. Food Sci., 30, 969 (1965).
11. J. R. Behnke, O. Fennema, and R. G. Cassens, J. Food Sci., 38, 539 (1973).
12. J. R. Bendall, J. Physiol., 114, 71 (1951).
13. J. W. C. Bird, in Proceedings of the 24th Annual Reciprocal Meat Conference, National Live Stock and Meat Board, Chicago, 1971, pp. 67-95.
14. C. E. Bodwell and P. E. McClain, in The Science of Meat and Meat Products (J. F. Price and B. S. Schweigert, eds.), 2nd ed., Freeman, San Francisco, 1971, pp. 78-133.
15. C. E. Bodwell, A. M. Pearson, and M. E. Spooner, J. Food Sci., 30, 766 (1965).
16. F. Bramsnase, in Quality and Stability of Frozen Foods (W. B. Van Arsdale, M. J. Copley, and R. L. Olson, eds.), Wiley-Interscience, New York, 1969, p. 228.
17. E. J. Briskey and R. G. Kauffman, in The Science of Meat and Meat Products (J. F. Price and B. S. Schweigert, eds.), 2nd ed., Freeman, San Francisco, 1971, pp. 367-401.
18. E. J. Briskey, K. Seraydarian, and W. F. H. M. Mommaerts, Biochim. Biophys. Acta, 133, 424 (1967).
19. D. L. D. Caspar, C. Cohen, and W. Longley, J. Mol. Biol., 41, 87 (1969).
20. A. G. Chapman, L. Fall, and D. E. Atkinson, J. Bacteriol., 108, 1072 (1971).
21. L. L. Constantin and R. J. Podolsky, Nature (London), 210, 483 (1966).
22. G. T. Cori, M. W. Selin, and C. F. Cori, J. Biol. Chem., 173, 605 (1948).
23. C. L. Davey, Arch. Biochem. Biophys., 89, 303 (1960).
24. C. L. Davey and M. R. Dickson, J. Food Sci., 35, 56 (1970).
25. D. deFremery and M. F. Pool, Food Res., 25, 73 (1963).
26. D. deFremery and M. F. Pool, J. Food Sci., 28, 173 (1963).
27. J. G. Disney, M. J. Follett, and P. W. Ratcliff, J. Sci. Food Agri., 18, 314 (1967).
28. W. Drabikowski and E. Nowak, Eur. J. Biochem., 5, 209 (1968).
29. H. Druckrey, R. Preussmann, S. Ivankovic, D. Schmäl, J. Afkham, G. Blum, H. D. Memmel, M. Muller, P. Petropoules, and H. Schneider, Z. Krebsforsch., 69, 103 (1967).

30. S. Ebashi, M. Endo, and I. Ohtsuki, Quart. Rev. Biophys., 2, 351 (1969).
31. J. D. Ehmann and H. O. Hultin, J. Food Sci., 38, 1119 (1973).
32. W. Fiddler, E. G. Piotrowski, J. W. Pensabene, R. C. Doerr, and A. E. Wasserman, J. Food Sci., 37, 668 (1972).
33. R. S. Filo, D. F. Bohr, and J. C. Ruegg, Science, 147, 1581 (1965).
34. S. Fleischer and G. Rouser, J. Amer. Oil Chem. Soc., 42, 588 (1965).
35. C. Franzini-Armstrong and K. R. Porter, Nature (London), 202, 355 (1964).
36. J. C. George and A. J. Berger, Avian Myology., Academic Press, New York, 1966, pp. 25-114.
37. D. E. Goll, M. Arakawa, M. H. Stromer, W. A. Busch, and R. M. Robson, in Physiology and Biochemistry of Muscle as a Food (E. J. Briskey, R. G. Cassens and B. B. Marsh, eds.), 2nd ed., University of Wisconsin Press, Madison, 1970, pp. 755-800.
38. D. E. Goll, R. W. Bray, and W. G. Hoekstra, J. Food Sci., 29, 622 (1964).
39. S. Govindarajan, Ph.D. Thesis, University of Massachusetts, Amherst, 1973.
40. M. L. Greaser, R. G. Cassens, W. G. Hoekstra, and E. J. Briskey, J. Food Sci., 34, 633 (1969).
41. F. Guba, in Studies from the Institute of Medical Chemistry, University Szeged (A. Szent-Györgyi, ed.), Vol. 3, S. Karger A.G., Basel, 1943, pp. 40-45.
42. K. H. Gustavson, The Chemistry and Reactivity of Collagen. Academic Press, New York, 1956.
43. N. F. Haard, J. Food Sci., 37, 504 (1972).
44. J. Halme, K. I. Kivirikko, and K. Simons, Biochim. Biophys. Acta, 198, 460 (1970).
45. A. W. Ham, Histology. 6th ed., Lippincott, Philadelphia, 1969.
46. R. Hamm and L. Kormendy, J. Food Sci., 34, 452 (1969).
47. R. Hamm, L. Kormendy, and L. Tetzlaff, Z. Lebensmittel Unters. Forschg., 147, 71 (1971).
48. J. Hanson and H. E. Huxley, Biochim. Biophys. Acta, 23, 250 (1957).
49. D. J. Hartshorne and H. Mueller, Biochem. Biophys. Res. Comm., 31, 647 (1968).
50. W. Hasselbach and M. Makinose, Biochem. Z., 333, 518 (1961).
51. W. Hasselbach and G. Schneider, Biochem. Z., 321, 462 (1951).
52. J. D. Hay, R. W. Currie, F. H. Wolfe, and E. J. Sanders, J. Food Sci., 38, 700 (1973).
53. P. V. J. Hegarty and C. E. Allen, J. Food Sci., 37, 652 (1972).
54. H. K. Herring, R. G. Cassens, and E. J. Briskey, J. Food Sci., 30, 1049 (1965).
55. H. K. Herring, R. G. Cassens, and E. J. Briskey, J. Food Sci., 32, 534 (1967).
56. R. L. Hostetler, B. A. Link, W. A. Landmann, and H. A. Fitzhugh, J. Food Sci., 38, 264 (1973).
57. H. E. Huxley, in The Cell (J. Brachet and A. E. Mirsky, eds.), Vol. IV, Academic Press, New York, 1960, pp. 365-481.
58. H. E. Huxley, J. Mol. Biol., 7, 281 (1963).
59. H. E. Huxley, Nature (London), 202, 1067 (1964).
60. H. E. Huxley, Sci. Amer., 213, 18 (1965). Offprint No. 1026.
61. H. E. Huxley and J. Hanson, Nature (London), 173, 973 (1954).

62. N. R. Jones, Proc. 11th Intl. Congr. Refrig., Munich., 1963, p. 917.

63. N. R. Jones and J. Murray, J. Sci. Food Agri., 15, 684 (1964).

64. L. L. Kastenschmidt, W. G. Hoekstra, and E. J. Briskey, J. Food Sci., 33, 151 (1968).

65. A. M. Kidwai, M. A. Radcliffe, E. Y. Lee, and E. E. Danual, Biochim. Biophys. Acta, 298, 593 (1973).

66. F. J. King, M. L. Anderson, and M. A. Steinberg, J. Food Sci., 27, 363 (1962).

67. K. I. Kivirikke, K. Shudo, S. Sakakibara, and D. J. Prockop, Biochemistry, 11, 122 (1972).

68. T. Kono, F. Kakuma, M. Homma, and S. Fukuda, Biochim. Biophys. Acta, 88, 155 (1964).

69. W. G. Kruggel and R. A. Field, J. Food Sci., 36, 1114 (1971).

70. M. J. Kushmerick and R. E. Davies, Biochim. Biophys. Acta, 153, 279 (1968).

71. E. Laakkonen, J. W. Sherbon, and G. H. Wellington, J. Food Sci., 35, 181 (1970).

72. R. A. Lawrie, Meat Science. Pergamon Press, Oxford, 1966, p. 119.

73. R. A. Lawrie, Meat Science. Pergamon Press, Oxford, 1966, pp. 212-236.

74. R. A. Lawrie, Meat Science. Pergamon Press, Oxford, 1966, pp. 236-251.

75. R. A. Lawrie, Meat Science. Pergamon Press, Oxford, 1966, p. 273.

76. R. A. Lawrie, J. Sci. Food Agri., 19, 233 (1968).

77. L.-W. Lee and S. Watanabe, J. Biol. Chem., 245, 3004 (1970).

78. A. L. Lehninger, Biochemistry. Worth, New York, 1970, p. 115.

79. A. L. Lehninger, Biochemistry. Worth, New York, 1970, p. 589.

80. R. H. Locker and C. J. Hagyard, J. Sci. Food Agri., 14, 787 (1963).

81. R. M. Love, in Cryobiology (H. T. Meryman, ed.), Academic Press, New York, 1966, pp. 317-405.

82. B. B. Marsh, Biochim. Biophys. Acta, 9, 127 (1952).

83. B. B. Marsh, J. Sci. Food Agri., 5, 70 (1954).

84. B. B. Marsh, Rept. Meat Ind. Res. Inst. New Zealand, 1964, p. 16.

85. B. B. Marsh, in The Physiology and Biochemistry of Muscle as a Food (E. J. Briskey, R. G. Cassens, and J. C. Trautman, eds.), 1st ed., University of Wisconsin Press, Madison, 1966, p. 225.

86. B. B. Marsh and N. G. Leet, Nature (London), 211, 635 (1966).

87. B. B. Marsh and N. G. Leet, J. Food Sci., 31, 450 (1966).

88. A. Martonosi and R. Feretos, J. Biol. Chem., 239, 648 (1964).

89. J. J. Matsumoto, W. J. Dyer, J. R. Dingle, and D. G. Ellis, J. Fish. Res. Bd. Can., 24, 873 (1967).

90. P. E. McClain, G. J. Creed, E. R. Wiley, and I. Hornstein, J. Food Sci., 35, 258 (1970).

91. J. V. McLoughlin, J. Food Sci., 35, 717 (1970).

92. R. L. Melnick and H. O. Hultin, J. Cell. Physiol., 81, 139 (1973).

93. H. T. Meryman, in Cryobiology (H. T. Meryman, ed.), Academic Press, New York, 1966, pp. 1-114.

94. R. P. Newbold and C. A. Lee, Biochem. J., 97, 1 (1965).

95. R. P. Newbold and R. K. Scopes, J. Food Sci., 36, 209 (1971).

96. J. Olley and J. A. Lovern, J. Sci. Food Agri., 11, 644 (1960).

97. F. C. Parrish, in Proceedings of the 24th Annual Reciprocal Meat Conference, National Live Stock and Meat Board, Chicago, 1971, pp. 97-133.

98. P. Paul and B. Issekutz, J. Appl. Physiol., 22, 615 (1967).

99. F. A. Pepe, in Progress in Biophysics and Molecular Biology (J. A. V. Butler and D. Noble, eds.), Vol. 22, Pergamon Press, New York, 1971, p. 77-96.

100. J. B. Peter, R. J. Barnard, V. R. Edgerton, C. A. Gillespie, and K. E. Stempel, Biochemistry, 11, 2627 (1972).

101. J. B. Peter, S. Sawaki, R. J. Barnard, V. R. Edgerton, and C. A. Gillespie, Arch. Biochem. Biophys., 144, 304 (1971).

102. K. R. Porter and C. Franzini-Armstrong, Sci. Amer., 212, 72 (1965). Offprint No. 1007.

103. R. N. Sayre and E. J. Briskey, J. Food Sci., 28, 675 (1963).

104. M. C. Schaub and M. Ermini, Biochem. J., 111, 777 (1969).

105. M. C. Schaub, S. V. Perry, and W. Häcker, Biochem. J., 126, 237 (1972).

106. R. C. Siegel, S. R. Pinnell, and G. R. Martin, Biochemistry, 9, 4486 (1970).

107. J. Spinelli, M. Eklund, and D. Miyauchi, J. Food Sci., 29, 710 (1964).

108. J. A. Spudich and S. Watt, J. Biol. Chem., 246, 4866 (1971).

109. J. M. Stewart and H. M. Levy, J. Biol. Chem., 245, 5764 (1970).

110. K. Takahashi, T. Fukazawa, and T. Yasui, J. Food Sci., 32, 409 (1967).

111. M. L. Tanzer, Science, 180, 561 (1973).

112. W. Traub and K. A. Piez, in Advances in Protein Chemistry (C. B. Anfinsen, J. T. Edsall, and F. M. Richards, eds.), Vol. 25, Academic Press, New York, 1971, pp. 243-352.

113. C. Tu, W. D. Powrie, and O. Fennema, J. Food Sci., 32, 30 (1967).

114. W. M. Urbain, in The Science of Meat and Meat Products (J. F. Price and B. S. Schweigert, eds.), 2nd ed., Freeman, San Francisco, 1971, pp. 426-434.

115. P. Vandekerchkhove, D. Demeyer, and H. Henderickx, J. Food Sci., 37, 636 (1972).

116. A. Veis, The Macromolecular Chemistry of Gelatin, Academic Press, New York, 1964.

117. S. M. Walker and G. R. Schrodt, Nature (London), 211, 935 (1966).

118. H. Wang, F. Andrews, E. Rasch, D. M. Doty, and H. R. Kraybill, Food Res., 18, 351 (1953).

119. B. K. Watt and A. L. Merrill, eds., Composition of Foods. Agriculture Handbook No. 8, U.S. Department of Agriculture, Washington, D.C., December 1963.

120. J. Wismer-Pedersen and E. J. Briskey, Nature (London), 189, 318 (1961).

121. E. F. Woods, J. Biol. Chem., 242, 2859 (1967).

122. A. Suzuki, Y. Nonami, and D. E. Goll, Agr. Biol. Chem. 39, 1461 (1975).

Chapter 14

CHARACTERISTICS OF EDIBLE FLUIDS OF ANIMAL ORIGIN: MILK

J. Robert Brunner

Department of Food Science and Human Nutrition
Michigan State University
East Lansing, Michigan

Contents

I. INTRODUCTION

Although man utilizes, in addition to the milk of his own kind, milks of various species of domesticated mammals indigenous to his locale, the western breeds of dairy cattle (<u>Bos</u> <u>taurus</u>) constitute the dominant source of milk for the highly industrialized dairy industry in the United States. Considering the necessarily restricted length of this chapter, therefore, I shall confine my presentation to the salient aspects of the composition and characteristics of normal cows' milk. Certainly, the lack of detail in the treatment of the subject matter will provoke the inquisitive mind. Therefore, the following reference works are recommended for supplemental study: Principles of Dairy Chemistry [19], Fundamentals of Dairy Chemistry [5], and Milk Proteins, Chemistry and Molecular Biology, Vols. I and II [6].

II. COMPOSITION OF COWS' MILK

Milk is the normal secretion of the mammary gland and is defined by the United States Public Health Service (Pub. 229, 1965) as "the lacteal secretion, practically free from colostrum, obtained by the complete milking of one or more healthy cows, which contains not less than 8-1/4% of milk-solids-not-fat and not less than 3-1/4% of milkfat." State and local regulations specify compositional variance from the federal standard ranging from 8.0 to 9.0% MSNF and from 3.0 to 3.8% fat. By definition and for esthetic reasons, colostrum - the secretion immediately following parturition - is excluded.

A. Variations in Gross Composition

The multitude of components comprising milk are commonly categorized simply as milkfat (3-6%), protein (3-4%), lactose (~5.0%), and ash (~0.7%), which collectively represent a total solids content of 11.5-14.5%. Water, of course, representing the continuous phase, accounts for the balance, viz., 85.5-88.5%. Compositional data usually reported for milk reflect average values from many analyses and thus represent an oversimplification. Among the many factors which influence the composition of individual, herd, and composite milks, breed characteristics (Table 14-1) and seasonal effects (Table 14-2) are the most significant. Variations in the composition of composite milk are generally anticipated and compensated for by the processor through the practice of compositional standardization.

TABLE 14-1

Representative Gross Composition of Milk of Cows of Different Breeds[a]

Breed	Water	Fat	Protein	Lactose	Ash	Total solids
Guernsey	85.35	5.05	3.90	4.96	0.74	14.65
Jersey	85.47	5.05	3.78	5.00	0.70	14.53
Ayrshire	86.97	4.03	3.51	4.81	0.68	13.03
Brown Swiss	86.87	3.85	3.48	5.08	0.72	13.13
Holstein[b]	87.72	3.41	3.32	4.87	0.68	12.28

Note: All units are in percentages.
[a]Compiled from data presented by Corbin and Whittier [12].
[b]Represents predominate dairy breed in the United States.

TABLE 14-2

Influence of Season on Gross Composition of Milk[a]

Month	Fat	Protein	Lactose	Ash	Total solids
January	4.31	3.67	4.87	0.72	13.57
February	4.22	3.62	4.89	0.72	13.45
March	4.16	3.56	4.98	0.71	13.41
April	4.10	3.54	5.01	0.71	13.37
May	4.10	3.53	5.04	0.71	13.37
June	3.96	3.45	5.02	0.70	13.13
July	3.95	3.46	5.02	0.70	13.12
August	3.95	3.54	5.00	0.69	13.18
September	4.10	3.62	4.96	0.70	13.38
October	4.24	3.66	4.92	0.71	13.53
November	4.27	3.69	4.88	0.72	13.55
December	4.30	3.65	4.92	0.72	13.59

Note: All units are in percentages.

[a]Compiled from data presented by Corbin and Whittier [12]; representing 2,426 samples from 1,482 individuals of six breeds.

Classical analytical procedures for determining the fat, protein, lactose, and ash contents of milk are outlined in the AOAC handbook [1]. In recent years, high-speed, semiautomatic procedures for making these determinations have been introduced; the most sophisticated of these is the IRMA (infrared milk analyzer), an infrared spectrophotometer adapter to the simultaneous determination of fat, protein, and lactose [14].

B. Components of Cows' Milk

Although the gross composition of cows' milk provides useful information for the herdsman and processor, it does not describe adequately the compositional complexity of milk. Contemporary analytical chemists have at their disposal highly sensitive and discerning instruments and techniques which have made possible a more detailed resolution of milk. The development of spectrophotometric, chromatographic, electrophoretic, and ultracentrifugal procedures has been most useful in this regard. Thus, in the following paragraphs we will consider in essential detail the components constituting the principal classes of materials indigenous to cows' milk.

1. LIPIDS

The principal component of the lipid phase is milkfat, a complex mixture of triglycerides. Other lipid materials, notably phospholipids, sterols, carotenoids,
and the fat-soluble vitamins A, D, E, and K, are present in amounts ranging from
traces to about 1.0% of the total lipid material (Table 14-3). Variations in the distribution of the lipid components, particularly the fatty acid composition of the
triglycerides, reflect breed and management factors, as previously noted. In this
respect, it is noteworthy that the fatty acid composition of the phospholipids is essentially unaffected by factors which contribute markedly to changes in the fatty
acid composition of the triglycerides. It should be noted that milk synthesis begins
in the cow's rumen; hence, factors affecting its function become apparent in the
quantity and composition of the milk produced.

TABLE 14-3

Lipid Composition of Milk[a]

| Lipid class | Approximate concentration | |
	Percentage of total lipid (range of values)	g/liter[b]
Triglycerides	97–98	39.0
Diglycerides	0.25–0.48	0.14
Monoglycerides	0.016–0.038	0.01
Ketoacid glycerides	0.85–1.28	0.4
Aldehydogenic glycerides	0.011–0.015	0.005
Glyceryl ethers	0.011–0.023	0.007
Free fatty acids	0.10–0.44	0.1
Phospholipids	0.2–1.0	0.3
Cerebrosides	0.013–0.066	0.02
Sterols	0.22–0.41	0.1
Squalene	0.007	0.003
Carotenoids	0.0007–0.009	0.002
Fat-soluble vitamins[c]		

[a]Compiled from data presented by Kurtz [25] and by Jenness and Patton [19].
[b]Based on milk of average composition containing 4.0% total milk lipid.
[c]See Table 14-10.

a. Milkfat

An extensive analysis of milkfat revealed the presence of 64 different fatty acid residues, ranging from 4 to 26 carbon atoms (Table 14-4). Twenty-seven of these were present in concentrations of less than 0.1%, collectively accounting for only 1% of the total fatty acid concentration. Typically for the milkfat of ruminants, considerable amounts of short-chain fatty acids, C_4-C_{10}, were found. The concentration of butyric acid reported in this study is atypically low; values on the order of 8-12% are more frequently reported. Saturated acids with even numbers of carbon atoms accounted for 58.57% of the total acids. Fatty acids with odd numbers of carbon atoms (1.99%) and branched carbon chains (1.53%) raised the saturated fatty acid content to 62.09%. Unsaturated fatty acids, 33.27% monounsaturated and 3.82% polyunsaturated, accounted for 37.09% of the total fatty acids.

TABLE 14-4

Fatty Acid Composition of Milkfat[a]

Acid[b]	%	Acid[b]	%
Saturated acids			
4:0	2.79	5:0	0.01
6:0	2.34	7:0	0.02
8:0	1.06	9:0	0.03
10:0	3.04	11:0	0.03
12:0	2.87	13:0	0.06
14:0	8.94	15:0	0.79
16:0	23.8	17:0	0.70
18:0	13.2	19:0	0.27
20:0	0.28	21:0	0.04
22:0	0.11	23:0	0.03
24:0	0.07	25:0	0.01
26:0	0.07	–	–
Branched-chain acids			
14:0 br	0.10	13:0 br	0.04
16:0 br	0.17	15:0 brA[c]	0.24
18:0 br	Trace	15:0 brB[c]	0.38
20:0 br	Trace	17:0 brA[c]	0.35
–	–	17:0 brB[c]	0.25
Monounsaturated acids			
10:1[d]	0.27	15:1	0.07
12:1[e]	0.14	17:1	0.27
14:1[e]	0.76	19:1	0.06
16:1[f]	1.79	21:1	0.02
18:1[f]	29.6	23:1	0.03

TABLE 14-4 (Continued)

Acid[b]	%	Acid[b]	%
20:1	0.22	–	–
22:1	0.03	–	–
24:1	0.01	–	–

Polyunsaturated acids

Dienes		Trienes	
18:2	2.11	18:3	0.50
18:2 c,t; conj[g]	0.63	18:3 conj[g]	0.01
18:2 t,t; conj[g]	0.09	20:3	0.11
20:2	0.05	22:3	0.02
22:2	0.01	–	–

Tetraenes		Pentaenes	
20:4	0.14	20:5	0.04
22:4	0.05	22:5	0.06

[a]Compiled from data presented by Herb et al. [16] from an analysis of solvent-extracted lipids obtained from the cream portion of composite Ayrshire milk.
[b]Figures preceding the colon designate the number of carbon atoms comprising the acid, whereas those following the colon designate the number of unsaturated bonds in the carbon chain.
[c]A and B designate isomers.
[d]Terminal double bond.
[e]Includes cis, trans, and terminal double-bond isomers.
[f]Includes cis and trans isomers.
[g]c,t = cis,trans; t,t = trans,trans; and conj = conjugated.

Obviously, milkfat is unusually complex. With 64 fatty acids present, we can expect a minimum of 1.25×10^5 to 1.30×10^5 different glycerides, depending upon whether we apply the "even" or "random" distribution theory and accept but one form of the positional isomers G (ACB) and G (CAB). It appears that neither the even nor the random distribution theories can be applied exclusively to milkfat. The concensus is that the unsaturated acids are evenly distributed but that the saturated acids follow the rule of random distribution. Interestingly, a high-melting glyceride fraction (M.P. 52-53 °C), crystallized at 22 °C from milkfat dissolved in acetone, represents a relatively distinct group of glycerides, containing predominantly trisaturated glycerides composed principally of C_{14}, C_{16}, and C_{18} acids. In opposition to the crystallization habit of the mixed triglycerides of total milkfat, this high-melting glyceride fraction exhibits distinct polymorphic phase transitions, viz., $\gamma \to \alpha \to \beta^1 \to \beta$, when a rapidly chilled specimen is slowly warmed.

b. Phospholipids

Phospholipids constitute a relatively small but significant portion of the total milk lipids. The principal components are phosphatidyl choline (~30%), phosphatidyl ethanolamine (~30%), phosphatidyl serine (~10%), sphingomyelin (~25%), and, to a lesser extent, phosphatidyl inositol, cerebrosides, and plasmalogens. As previously noted, the fatty acid composition of the phospholipids is rather constant, seemingly unaffected by diet and seasonal variations. No appreciable amounts of acids below C_{10} are present. The dominant saturated acids are C_{16} and C_{18}, whereas the unsaturated acids $C_{18:1}$ and $C_{18:2}$ account for about one-half of the fatty acids of phosphatidyls choline, serine, and ethanolamine. Sphingomyelin is characterized by low concentrations of unsaturated acids; the saturated acids C_{16}, C_{18}, C_{22}, and C_{23} accounting for about 80% of the total acids.

c. Other Lipids

With the possible exception of the phospholipids, keto acid glycerides constitute the most abundant of the minor lipids of milk. Each keto acid associates with two fatty acids in a triglycerides and consists mostly of isomeric ketostearic acids. Small amounts of glyceride-bound δ-hydroxy acids have been reported which presumably contribute to the formation of δ-lactones and the desirable coconut-like flavor of heated milkfat. Small amounts of free fatty acids, monoglycerides, and diglycerides are usually found in milk. Whether these compounds are of endogenous origin or result from the action of lipase on triglycerides is not entirely clear.

Cholesterol and trace amounts of the related sterols, lanosterol and 7-dehydrocholesterol, are present in milk. Cholesteryl esters, containing predominantly both saturated and unsaturated long-chain fatty acids, account for 10-15% of the total cholesterol. Squalene, a precurssor of cholesterol, and a series of carotenoid provitamins A, which impart the yellow color to milkfat, have been reported in trace amounts. Finally, the fat-soluble vitamins A, D, E, and K reside in the lipid phase. The tocopherol (Vitamin E) content of milk is markedly influenced by the quality of the roughage consumed by the cow and serves as an antioxidant for the lipid system.

2. PROTEINS

That milk protein consists of a heterogeneous mixture has been long recognized. Classical methods employed for the separation of these proteins into gross fractions are based on solubility at specific values of pH and in the presence high concentrations of neutral salts. Casein, the principal milk protein, is precipitated by acidification of milk or skim milk to pH 4.6 at 20°C. When enzymically coagulated by rennin, as occurs in the cheese-making process, the modified casein is designated as calcium p-caseinate. The remaining proteins of skim milk are classified as whey proteins and can be resolved into albumin (soluble) and globulin (insoluble) fractions based on their solubility in solutions half-saturated with ammonium sulfate. Rowland [33] extended the chemical fractionation procedure into a scheme capable of distributing the nitrogen content of milk between five fractions:

casein (78.3%), albumin (9.1%), globulin (3.5%), "protease-peptone" (4.1%), and nonprotein nitrogen (5.0%). In addition to the proteins found exclusively in the skim milk portion, there is a small amount of specific protein material associated with the lipid phase which is commonly referred to as fat globule membrane protein.

None of the protein fractions so far mentioned represents homogeneous entities. Beginning in 1934 with Palmer's [30] crystallization of β-lactoglobulin from whey, scientists have endeavored to resolve the complexities of the milk protein system. With the possible exception of blood, no other biological system has been so thoroughly investigated. Much of the progress to this end, including the development of milk protein nomenclature, has been summarized in the four reports of the American Dairy Science Association's Committee on Milk Protein Nomenclature, Classification, and Methodology [9,18,31,38].

The principal milk proteins and some of their pertinent characteristics are listed in Table 14-5.

a. Caseins

Whole casein is defined as a heterogeneous group of associated phosphoproteins precipitated from skim milk at pH 4.6 and 20°C, It consists of three principal components, α_{s1}-casein (~55%), β-casein (~25%), and k-casein (~15%), and several minor components, notably, γ-casein (~5%). The caseins exist as genetically controlled polymorphic species, differing in one or more internally substituted or deleted amino acid residues which can be identified in gel electropherograms (Fig. 14-1).

α_{s1}-Caseins are characterized by their sensitivity to low concentrations of calcium ions (0.4M $CaCl_2$, pH 7.0). k-Caseins are soluble at these conditions, serving to stabilize the α_{s1}-caseins in milk. Also, they represent the specific substrate for the primary action of rennin; insoluble para-k-casein and soluble glycomacropeptide being formed. β-Caseins associate into polymeric species at temperatures above 8.5°C, dissociating into monomer subunits at lower temperatures. γ-Caseins resemble β-caseins in composition and behavior and possibly represent degradation products of the β-caseins or incomplete products of biological synthesis. At pH 7.0, the caseins tend to associate as the temperature is increased, whereas at pH 12 they dissociate into monomeric units.

Amino acid compositions for representative casein components are given in Table 14-6. They are characterized by a relatively low ratio of polar to apolar residues and high concentrations of proline. k-Caseins contain two cysteine residues per mole which seem to exist, at least in isolated specimens, as intermolecular disulfide bonds. Also, k-caseins exist as mixed species, varying in carbohydrate concentration from 0 to ~12%. Essentially all of the carbohydrate moieties are attached to the C-terminal glycomacropeptide portion of the molecule. The phosphate groups in caseins are covalently linked predominantly with serine residues as monoesters (R-O-P). Significantly, most of the phosphorylated residues occur in close proximity, no doubt contributing to the unique properties of the caseins.

TABLE 14-5

Distribution and Properties of the Principal Milk Proteins[a]

Component	Approximate concentration Percentage of total protein (range of values)	g/liter	Polymorphs	P	-SH	-S-S-	Approximate molecular weight	Isoelectric point pH
Caseins	75-85	(25.0)[b]						4.6
α_{s1}-Casein	45-55	13.7	A, B, C, D	8	0	0	23,500	5.0
β-Casein	25-35	6.2	A^1, A^2, A^3, B, C, D	5	0	0	24,000	4.5
k-Casein	8-15	3.7	A, B	1	2	0	19,000[c]	3.7-4.2
γ-Casein	3-7	1.2	A^1, A^2, A^3, B	1	0	0	20,000	5.8
Whey proteins	15-25	(5.2)[b]						
β-Lactoglobulin	7-12	3.0	A, B, C, D	0	1	2	18,000	5.3
α-Lactaalbumin	2-5	0.7	A, B	0	0	4	14,200	5.1
Immunoglobulins[d]	1.5-2.5	0.6	-[e]	0	0	Variable[f]	160,000[g]	5.6-6.0
Serum albumin	0.7-1.3	0.3		0	1	17	69,000	4.7
Minor proteins	2.0-4.0	0.6						

[a]Compiled partially from data presented by Jenness [17], Rose et al. [31], and Swaisgood [36].

[b]Assumed average composition: 2.50% casein, 0.52% whey protein.

[c]Molecular weight of carbohydrate-free species; species containing up to five carbohydrate moieties ($\sim$600 daltons per moiety) exist.

[d]Heterogeneous mixture of glycoproteins.

[e]Primary structure is individually variable.

[f]Four chain molecules, consisting of two light and two heavy chains intermolecularily bound through -S-S- groups. Light and heavy chains contain intramolecular -S-S- loops.

[g]Approximate molecular weight of monomers IgG1 and IgG2; IgM is a pentamer ($\sim$1,000,000) and IgA is a dimer ($\sim$300,000).

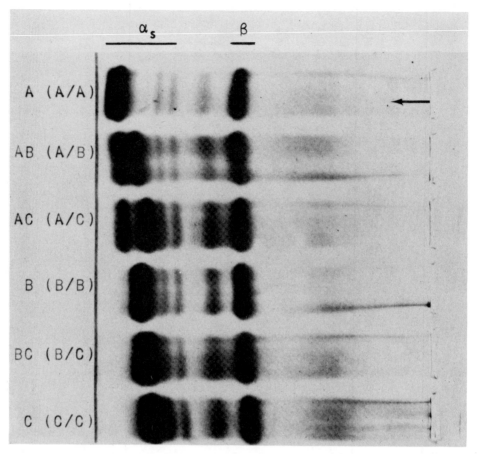

FIG. 14-1. Starch gel (urea) electropherograms of caseins isolated from six individual cows. The heavily stained zones at the front of the patterns represent genetically controlled polymorphic forms of α_{s1}-caseins A, B, and C. The β-casein present in these samples was of a single genetic type. (Adapted from Kiddy et al. [22], by courtesy of the American Dairy Science Association.)

b. Whey proteins

The noncasein proteins of skim milk are designated whey proteins and they consist principally of β-lactoglobulin (~60%), α-lactalbumin, immunoglobulins, serum albumin, and the complex proteose-peptone fraction (see Tables 14-5 and 14-6). With the exception of the proteose-peptone fraction, whey proteins are heat labile and form associated complexes when milk is heated. It should be mentioned here that the composition of whey with regard to its complement of minor proteins and ionic activity reflects the method employed for the removal of casein. Accordingly, whey resulting from acid precipitation of casein is designated acid whey; whereas whey obtained following coagulation of casein with rennin is identified as rennin whey.

(1) β-Lactoglobulin. This protein represents the most thoroughly investigated protein of milk. It exists in several genetic variants, differing in minor but significant ways, which contribute to its environmentally influenced association-dissociation phenomena. At the pH of normal milk (~6.6-6.7) and at 20°C, two monomeric subunits (18,000 daltons) exist in stable equilibrium as a dimer (36,000 daltons). This protein is uniquely characterized in milk as the principal source of sulfhydryl (-SH) groups (one per mole) which can be either active or inactive depending on the spacial configuration of the protein. In this regard, many of the phenomena related to the effect of heat on milk are vested in the activity of the thiol group.

(2) α-Lactalbumin. This is the second most abundant protein found in whey, and it possesses the lowest molecular weight of the major milk proteins (14,200 daltons). Like β-lactoglobulin, it can be readily crystallized from solution and exhibits complex pH-dependent association-dissociation phenomena and conformational changes. The amino acid profile of α-lactalbumin is characterized by its high content of tryptophan. It contains no free sulfhydryl groups, although its cystine content is high (four residues per mole). Interestingly, it is the only milk protein in which the aspartic acid content exceeds that of glutamic acid. Although immunologically different, it contains many of the same amino acid sequences as lysozyme.

Unlike the other major proteins of milk, α-lactalbumin has a definite biological function. It represents the B protein of lactose synthetase, the enzyme system which catalyzes the reaction uridine diphosphate galactose (UDP-gal) + glucose → lactose + UDP. In the absence of α-lactalbumin, component A (galactosyl transferase) of the lactose synthetase system acts to transfer the galactose of UDP-galactose to such compounds as N-acetyl glucosamine but not to glucose.

(3) Immunoglobulins. Whey immunoglobulins are similar to the immunoglobulins of blood, consisting of large glycoprotein molecules which possess antibody activities. They constitute the major protein of colostrum and serve to transmit passive immunity to the newborn calf. The relatively low concentration of immunoglobulin found in normal milk acts in symphony with the lipid phase to produce the "creaming" phenomenon. Immunoglobulins appear to be monomers or polymers of a four-chain, disulfide-crosslinked molecule designated IgG. IgM is a pentamer (~1,000,000 daltons) of IgG; IgA is often a dimer (~380,000 daltons); and IgG is usually a monomer (~160,000 daltons). IgG contains about 2-3% carbohydrate, whereas IgM and IgA contain about 10%. The primary structures of immunoglobulins are specific to their origins, thus, these proteins are uniquely heterogeneous among milk proteins.

(4) Minor Proteins. Whey serum albumin is identical to blood serum albumin and enters milk by a different route than do proteins synthesized in the udder. It is a fairly large molecule (69,000 daltons) and is characterized by a high content of cystine (17 residues per mole) and one free sulfhydryl. Small amounts of lactoferrin, an iron-binding red protein, and serum transferrin, identical to blood serum transferrin, are found in skim milk. Lactoferrin is synthesized in the udder and absorbs iron from serum transferrin.

TABLE 14-6

Amino Acid Composition of the Principal Proteins of Milk[a]

Amino acid residue	Caseins							
	αs_1-B (23,613 daltons)		β-A[1] (24,020 daltons)		k-A (19,037 daltons)		γ-A[1] (20,560 daltons)	
	R/mole[b]	R (wt %)[c]	R/mole	R (wt %)	R/mole	R (wt %)	R/mole	R (wt %)
Aspartic acid	15	7.3	9	4.3	12	7.3	7	3.9
Threonine	5	2.1	9	4.0	15	8.0	8	3.9
Serine	16	6.0	16	5.8	13	6.0	11	4.7
Glutamic acid	39	21.3	39	21.1	27	18.3	32	20.1
Proline	17	7.0	34	13.8	20	10.2	33	15.6
Glycine	9	2.2	5	1.2	2	0.6	4	1.1
Alanine	9	2.7	5	1.5	14	5.2	5	1.7
Cysteine	0	0	0	0	0	0	0	0
1/2 Cystine	0	0	0	0	2	1.1	0	0
Valine	11	4.6	19	7.8	11	5.7	17	8.2
Methionine	5	2.8	6	3.3	2	1.4	6	3.8
Isoleucine	11	5.3	10	4.7	12	7.1	7	3.9
Leucine	17	8.1	22	10.4	8	4.8	19	10.5
Tyrosine	10	7.0	4	2.7	9	7.7	4	3.2
Phenylalanine	8	5.0	9	5.5	4	3.1	9	6.4
Tryptophan	2	1.6	1	0.8	1	1.0	1	1.0
Lysine	14	7.6	11	5.9	9	6.1	10	6.2
Histidine	5	2.9	6	3.4	3	2.2	6	4.0
Arginine	6	4.0	4	2.6	5	4.1	2	1.5

[a]Compiled from data presented by Swaisgood [36], McKenzie [28], and Gordon and
[b]Number of residues per mole of protein derived from primary sequence. Values for
[c]Weight percentage of residues per mole of protein. Values for serum albumin and
per 100 grams of protein. (Residue wt = molecular wt - 1 mole of H_2O.)

Whey proteins					
β-Lg-A (18,000 daltons)		α-La-B (14,176 daltons)		Serum albumin (69,000 daltons)	Immunoglobulins (150,000–1,000,000
R/mole	R (wt %)	R/mole	R (wt %)	R (wt %)	daltons; R (wt %)
16	10.2	21	17.1	9.4	8.1
8	4.5	7	5.0	4.9	8.9
7	3.4	7	4.3	3.5	9.5
25	17.9	13	11.9	14.4	10.7
8	4.3	2	1.4	4.1	8.4
3	1.0	6	2.4	1.4	4.0
14	5.5	3	1.5	5.0	3.8
1	0.6	0	0	5.5	2.7
4	2.3	8	5.8		
10	5.5	6	4.2	5.0	8.1
4	2.9	1	0.9	0.7	0.8
10	6.3	8	6.4	2.2	2.6
22	13.8	13	10.4	10.6	8.3
4	3.6	4	4.6	4.6	6.0
4	3.3	4	4.2	5.9	3.5
2	2.1	4	5.3	0.5	2.4
15	10.7	12	10.9	11.2	6.0
2	1.5	3	2.9	3.3	1.8
3	2.6	1	1.1	5.3	3.7

Whittier [13]. Polymorphic variants selected represent most prevalent forms.
β-Lg-A represent most probable numbers calculated for four independent analyses.
the immunoglobulins were recalculated from data expressed as grams of amino acids

The proteose-peptone fraction represents a poorly defined heterogenous group (~8-10 components) of heat- and acid-stable phosphoglycoproteins, ranging in molecular weight from ~4,000 to ~200,000. These proteins have been grouped and designated as components 3, 5, and 8, according to their relative position in a moving-boundary electrophoretic pattern of whey proteins at pH 8.6. Components 5 and 8 exist in association with micellar casein as well as in the whey, and conceivably they may be minor caseins. Component 3, the most homogenous of the three component groups, is restricted to whey. Proteose-peptones are characterized by low contents of aromatic and sulfur amino acids and the presence of carbohydrate moieties.

A small amount of proteinaceous material exists as components of the fat globule membrane. The intricacies of this interesting lipid-protein complex are considered in more detail subsequently (p. 638). For the present, it suffices to state that the protein system of the membrane complex is poorly defined, consisting of a highly associated group of specific proteins unlike any of the other milk proteins. They have been classified simply as "soluble" or "insoluble" relative to their dispersibility in saline. Recent electrophoretic investigations of the membrane material in polyacrylamide gels containing strong dissociating agents, viz., sodium dodecyl sulfate and mercaptoethanol, revealed numerous zones, most of which have been identified as lipoglycoproteins.

c. Enzymes

Enzymes exist as simple protein molecules or as apoproteins in lipoprotein complexes. The enzymes in milk are distributed throughout the entire system, some bound to the fat globule surface; some associated with the casein micelles; and some existing in free, colloidal suspension (see Table 14-7). Despite the array of enzymes present in milk, only a few are of particular significance to the food scientist.

TABLE 14-7

Enzymes Identified in Milk

Enzyme (trivial name)	Classification[a] number	Distribution[b]
α-Mannosidase	E.C.3.2.1.24	MC
Lipase	E.C.3.1.1.3	MC
Protease	E.C.3.4.4.-	MC
Esterase	E.C.3.1.1.1	S
Lactoperoxidase	E.C.1.11.1.7	S
Lysozyme	E.C.3.2.1.17	S
α-Amylase	E.C.3.2.1.1	S

TABLE 14-7 (Continued)

Enzyme (trivial name)	Classification[a] number	Distribution[b]
β-Amylase	E.C.3.2.1.2	S
Ribonuclease	E.C.2.7.7.16	S
Sulfhydryl oxidase	E.C.1.8.3.-	S
Catalase	E.C.1.11.1.6	FGM, MC, S
Alkaline phosphatase	E.C.3.1.3.1	FGM, S
Acid phosphatase	E.C.3.1.3.2	FGM, S
Aldolase	E.C.4.1.2.7	FGM, S
Xanthine oxidase	E.C.1.2.3.2	FGM
Phosphodiesterase	E.C.3.1.4.1	FGM
NADH-cytochrome c reductase	E.C.1.6.2.1	FGM, ER
Acetylcholinesterase	E.C.3.1.1.7	FGM
Mg^{2+}-activated ATPase	E.C.3.6.1.4	FGM
Glucose-6-phosphatase	E.C.3.1.3.9	FGM
5'-Nucleotidase	E.C.3.1.3.5	FGM, PM[c]
UDP-Galactose hydrolase	-	FGM, PM[c]
UDP-Glucose hydrolase	-	FGM, PM[c]
UDP-Galactosyl transferase	E.C.2.4.1.22	GM, S
Triglyceride synthetase	-	ER

[a]According to Committee on Enzymes of the International Union of Biochemists [2].

[b]Designates location in milk; viz., MC, micellar casein; S, serum (whey); FGM, fat globule membrane; GM, Golgi membrane; PM, plasma membrane; and ER, endoplasmic reticulum.

[c]Serve as marker enzymes for PM and FGM.

(1) Alkaline phosphatase. This enzyme exists in the form of a lipoprotein complex and is distributed between the lipid (FGM) and aqueous phases. Fortuitously, the enzyme is essentially inactivated by normal pasteurization procedures. Thus, its detection in pasteurized dairy products signifies inadequate heat treatment.

(2) Lipase. Although an equivocal issue, available information favors the concept that more than one type of lipase exist in milk: a "membrane lipase" which irreversibly adsorbs to the fat globule membrane when milk is cooled, and a "plasma lipase" which remains in the skim milk phase until activated by some form of mechanical agitation. Apparently the release of membrane material from the fat globules predisposes the fat to lipolytic attack by plasma lipase. Several workers have shown that milk lipase is associated with casein micelles and in particular with the k-casein component. Fortunately, the lipases are inactivated by pasteurization.

(3) Protease. This fairly heat-stable proteolytic enzyme is associated with the casein fraction and may contribute significantly to the physical instability of dairy products given high-temperature, short-time treatments.

(4) Xanthine Oxidase. This enzyme is found in high concentrations in the fat globule membrane. It consists of a high molecular weight protein which firmly binds 2 moles of flavine adenine dinucleotide (FAD), 8 moles of iron, and 2 moles of molybdenum. The enzymic degradation of FAD yields flavin mononucleotide (FMN) and riboflavin. It may well be that xanthine oxidase gives rise to the high riboflavin content of cow's milk.

3. LACTOSE

The principal carbohydrate of milk is lactose (milk sugar), a disaccharide of galactose and glucose. It is formed by the coupled action of N-galactosyl transferase and α-lactalbumin (lactose synthetase) to effect the linking of galactose and glucose; glucose being supplied to the udder by the blood. Lactose is the principal osmotic agent in milk, enabling the transport of water from blood. Apparently, the unique structural properties of this sugar inhibit its transport across membranes in normal udders.

Lactose is about one-fifth as sweet as sucrose and together with the salts of milk is responsible for the characteristic flavor of milk. When crystallized from concentrated whey at temperatures below 93.5°C, lactose assumes the α-hydrate form, containing 1 mole of water. The "tomahawk"-shaped crystals are sparingly soluble and impart a gritty feel when placed in the mouth. This characteristic is responsible for the "sandy" defect frequently encountered in high-solids ice cream. When crystallization takes place at temperatures above 93.5°C, needlelike β-anhydride crystals form which are sweeter and more soluble than crystals of α-hydrate. When a solution of lactose is dried rapidly, a noncrystalline "glass" is produced which is very unstable and hydroscopic.

4. ASH AND SALTS

Milk ash and milk salts are not synonymous terms. Ash is the white residue remaining after the incineration of milk at 600°C, and it consists of the oxides of sodium, potassium, calcium, magnesium, iron, phosphorus, and sulfur, plus some chloride. The sulfur and portions of the phosphorus and iron are derived from proteins. The salts of milk are the phosphates, chlorides and, citrates of potassium, sodium, calcium, and magnesium (Table 14-8). Sodium, potassium, and chlorides are entirely ionized, whereas the phosphates, calcium, magnesium, and citrate exist partly in soluble form and partly as colloidal complexes in a highly labile equilibrium with the casein complex. Approximately two-thirds of the total calcium content of milk is colloidally dispersed and only one-tenth exists in ionic form. The state of equilibrium between ionic calcium and its bound or complexed forms plays a significant role in the physical stability of processed dairy products. Upon acidification, more calcium is ionized and this contributes to destabilization of casein. Upon dialysis, the calcium phosphate complex dissociates, releasing the micellular subunits. High temperatures shift the equilibrium in favor of the complexed form, thus reducing the concentration of the ionic species and increasing stability of the casein system.

TABLE 14-8

Concentration and Distribution of the Principal Salts of Milk[a]

Constituent	Concentration (mg/100 g)	
	Mean	Range of values
Total calcium	117.7	110.9–120.3
Total magnesium	12.1	11.4–13.0
Total citric acid	176.0	166–192
Total phosphorus	95.1	79.8–101.7
Sodium	58	47–77
Potassium	140	133–171
Chloride	104.5	89.8–127.0
Colloidal inorganic Ca	49.7	41.8–54.0
Caseinate Ca	31.4	28.9–33.9
Soluble unionized Ca	25.3	21.9–28.8
Ionized Ca	11.4	10.5–12.8
Colloidal Mg	4.3	7.0–8.5
Soluble Mg	7.8	7.0–8.5
Colloidal citric acid	19	15–22
Soluble citric acid	158	143–175
Colloidal inorganic P	29.3	24.9–31.1
Casein P	21.5	18.7–23.0
Soluble inorganic P	33.6	27.0–38.9
Ester P	10.6	7.7–13.1

[a]Compiled from data of White and Davies [41].

In addition to the major salts, milk contains many trace elements, reflecting to some extent the characteristics of the feed consumed (Table 14-9). A few trace elements, such as molybdenum and iron, are integral constituents of enzymes.

5. VITAMINS

The vitamins found in milk are listed in Table 14-10. As previously indicated, the fat-soluble vitamins are components of the lipid phase, whereas the B vitamins and vitamin C reside in the aqueous phase. Excepting vitamin K, the concentrations of fat-soluble vitamins depend on the amounts consumed in the feed. The concentrations of vitamin K and the water-soluble vitamins are independent of feed since they are synthesized in the cow's rumen or tissues. Aside from their obvious value as micronutrients, many of the vitamins play roles in the flavor stability of milk. Many of the B vitamins exist in various chemical forms as free species or complexed with proteins.

TABLE 14-9

Trace Elements in Milk[a]

Element	Concentration (μg/liter)
Aluminum	460
Arsenic	50
Boron	270
Bromine	200
Chromium	15
Cobalt	0.6
Copper	130
Fluorine	150
Iodine	43
Iron	450
Lead	40
Manganese	22
Molybdenum	73
Silenium	40-1,270
Silicon	1,430
Zinc	3,900

[a]Compiled from data presented by Corbin and Whittier [12]. Values representative of milk from cows on normal ration, viz., nonsupplemented.

TABLE 14-10

Vitamin Content of Fresh Milk[a]

Fat-soluble vitamins		Water-soluble vitamins	
Vitamin	Concentration	Vitamin	Concentration (mg/liter)
Vitamin A	1,070–1,770 (IU/liter)[b]	Thiamine	0.20–0.80
Vitamin D	13.7–33 (IU/liter)[c]	Riboflavin	0.81–2.58
Vitamin E	0.20–1.84 (mg/liter)	Nicotinic acid (niacin)	0.30–2.00
Vitamin K	0–4,000 (D-GU/liter)[d]	Pantotheric acid	2.60–4.90
		Pyroxidine	0.22–1.90
		Biotin	0.012–0.060
		Folic acid	0.0004–0.0062
		Vitamin B_{12}	0.0024–0.0074
		Ascorbic acid	16.5–27.5[e]
		Choline	43–218
		Inositol	60–180
		Orotic acid	47–105

[a]Compiled from data presented by Hartman and Dryden [15].
[b]IU = 0.3 μg of vitamin A alcohol.
[c]IU = 1 mg/liter: market milk is usually fortified to ~420 IU/liter.
[d]Dan - Glavind Unit = 0.04 μg menadione.
[e]Values for commercial milk: 2.4–20.5 mg/liter.

III. STRUCTURE OF MILK

Although the solids content of milk is relatively high, it is a free-flowing liquid of relatively low viscosity (~2.0 poise). This desirable attribute is a ramification of the manner in which its principal components are assembled at the time of secretion. As food scientists, we are not concerned primarily with this fascinating physiological function of the cow. Yet, we would be remiss if we did not acknowledge the excellent work currently being directed to elucidating the secretory process. Briefly summarized, secretion involves intracellular processes in which fat droplets are extruded from the apical end of the secretory cell, enshrouded with plasma membrane and small amounts of closely associated cytoplasmic components, and released into the lumen of the udder. Concomitant with this process is the replenishment of plasma membrane by Golgi vacuolar membrane. Apparently, the proteins synthesized on the endoplasmic reticulum are assembled in Golgi vacuoles. This is also the site where casein components acquire their characteristic micellar structure and lactose is synthesized. When the protein-laden vacuole makes contact with the acinar plasma membrane, it "blends" to form new plasma membrane, discharging its contents into the lumen. Figure 14-2 contains schematic and pictorial representations of these processes.

The typical whitness of milk results from the multireflection of transmitted light by suspended fat globules and casein micelles. Whey, which is devoid of fat globules and casein, is a greenish (attributed to riboflavin), transparent liquid.

A. The Lipid Phase

As already indicated, most of the lipids of milk are dispersed in a stable emulsion of membrane-coated fat droplets, ranging in size from about 2 to 10 μm and in numbers approximating 3×10^9 per cubic centimeter.

1. THE CREAMING PHENOMENON

The rising of fat globules and subsequent formation of a cream layer represents one of the fundamental properties of normal cow's milk. Admittedly, the creaming property is no longer of practical interest to the dairy industry because most milk processed for the fluid market is homogenized, thus eliminating formation of a cream layer. Nevertheless, the mechanism remains an intriguing one to dairy scientists.

The rate of rise of individual fat globules can be estimated from Stokes' law for the rate of settling of spherical particles, viz., $V = r^2 2(d_1 - d_2)g/9\eta$, where r is radius of the globule, d_1 is density of the plasma phase, d_2 is density of the fat phase, g is the gravitational constant, and η is specific viscosity of the plasma phase. Accordingly, 50 hr has been estimated as the time required for the fat globules of milk to rise into a cream layer. This is far in excess of the observed time of 20-30 min, so other factors must be involved. During the creaming process, we observe the formation of clusters of fat globules which increase the effective radius (r) and thus the velocity of rise. Cluster formation is initiated by cooling milk to about 4°C. However, when washed fat globules are suspended in a model system devoid of whey proteins, they fail to cluster, nor do they cluster when added to heated (~170°C for 30 min) skim milk. Thus, the clustering and creaming of the fat phase must be attributed to activity of some components of the whey protein system. Recent investigations have revealed that the macroimmuno-globulins, IgM and possibly IgA, are specifically involved. Upon cooling, IgM, a cryoglobulin, associates into larger complexes and with the fat globule surface, forming clusters which accelerate formation of a cream layer.

2. FAT GLOBULE MEMBRANE

The complex lipid-protein material constituting the fat globule membrane has been studied extensively from both its compositional and its structural aspects. Although analytical data vary somewhat, reflecting procedures used to isolate the membrane material, it is generally agreed that membrane preparations contain

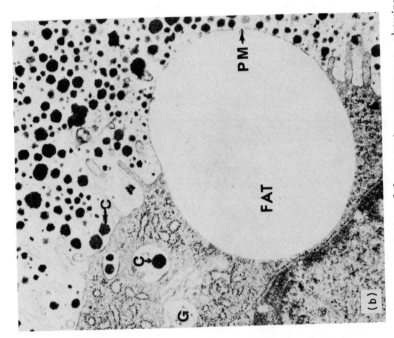

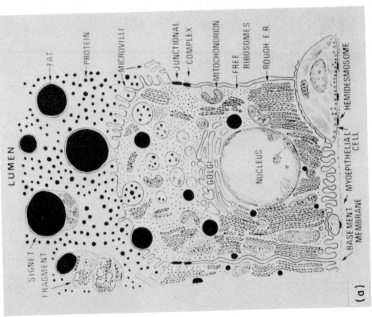

FIG. 14-2. The mechanism of milk secretion. (a) A schematic representation of the secretory processes, showing the secretion of plasma membrane-covered fat globules into the mammary lumen and a concomitant release of proteins from Golgi vacuoles. Note that the vacuolar membrane becomes part of the plasma membrane. (Reprinted from Linzell and Peaker [27], by courtesy of the American Physiological Society.) (b) An electron photomicrograph of a section from a secretory cell, showing the same processes represented in (a) in which G designates an intracellular Golgi vacuole, C designates casein micelles in the interior of a vacuole and in the lumen, and PM identifies the plasma membrane which will eventually cover the protruding fat droplet. (Reprinted from Toben et al. [39], by courtesy of J. B. Lippincott Co.)

neutral lipids, phospholipids, and protein (Table 14-11). Analyses of phospholipids found in specimens of fat globule membrane and cellular membranes are reported in Table 14-12. These data support the concept that the plasma membrane is indeed the source of the fat globule membrane. The concept is further substantiated by the identification of 5'-nucleotidase, a plasma membrane-specific enzyme, in the fat globule membrane. Also, gel electropherograms of plasma membrane and fat globule membrane proteins show essentially similar protein patterns.

TABLE 14-11

Composition of the Lipid Portion of a Fat Globule Membrane Preparation[a]

Component	Percentage of membrane lipids	Percentage of whole membrane
Carotenoids	0.45	0.30
Squalene	0.61	0.40
Cholesterol esters	0.79	0.54
Triglycerides[b]	53.41	36.12
Free fatty acids	6.30	4.26
Cholesterol	5.17	3.50
Diglycerides	8.14	5.49
Monoglycerides	4.66	3.14
Phospholipids	20.35	13.76
Totals	99.88	67.51[c]

[a]From Thompson et al. [37]: isolated from pooled milk source.
[b]Contains large portion of a high-melting glyceride fraction (M.P. 52°-53°C).
[c]Specimen contained 32.5% protein.

TABLE 14-12

Percentage Distribution of Phospholipids in Membranes of Mammary Cell Organelle and the Fat Globule Membrane[a]

Phospholipid	Endoplasmic reticulum	Golgi apparatus	Plasma[b] membrane	Fat globule membrane[b]
Sphinogomyelin	5.7 5.7	12.7	19.6	19.1
Phosphatidyl choline	57.1	46.8	38.9	38.0
Phosphatidyl serine	4.1	6.0	6.4	5.0

TABLE 14-12 (Continued)

Phospholipid	Endoplasmic reticulum	Golgi apparatus	Plasma[b] membrane	Fat globule membrane[b]
Phosphatidyl inositol	5.7	7.1	5.8	8.0
Phosphatidyl ethanolamine	23.6	27.1	24.1	27.4
Lysophosphatidyl choline	1.6	0.4	3.4	1.7
Lysophosphatidyl ethanol-amine	2.1	0.1	0.9	0.6

[a]From data of Keenan and Huang [20].
[b]Note the compositional similarity of plasma membrane and fat globule membrane.

Structural characteristics of the fat globule membrane have been elucidated by electron microscopy. The photomicrographs, shown in Figure 14-3, reveal the presence of a typical tripartite membrane structure in specimens fixed and sectioned by conventional procedures. Numerous relatively large spherical particles, possibly of cytoplasmic origin. are apparent on the underside of the membrane [21]. These structures are dramatically portrayed in the freeze-fractured specimen. Although typical membrane structures are apparent in milk immediately following secretion, their survival intact in the normal milk supply is doubtful. Apparently the influences of mechanical manipulation and other components of the milk system exert a degrading effect on the membrane structure, causing it to reorient into disordered layers up to about 25 nm in thickness.

About 50% of the phospholipids of milk are found in the skim milk portion. It has been assumed that these are components of lipoprotein particles released from the fat globule surface by agitation. Although this may account, in part, for their presence in skim milk, recent evidence suggests that portions of the plasma membrane, viz., microvilli, and other lipoprotein particles not normally associated with the fat globule membrane per se constitute the principal source of plasma phospholipids.

B. The Casein Complex

In normal milk at the temperature of secretion (38 °C), essentially all of the casein components are in the form of colloidally dispersed micelles, ranging in size from about 80 to 300 nm and composed of discrete subunits of about 10-20 nm which are associated through calcium and/or complex calcium phosphate salt bridges (Fig. 14-4). When calcium ions are removed by chelating agents or by exhaustive dialysis, the micelles dissociate into subunits. Upon reintroduction of calcium ions, the subunits recluster into micelles. At temperatures lower than 8.5°C β-casein, γ-casein, and much of the k-casein dissociate from the complex, leaving α_s-

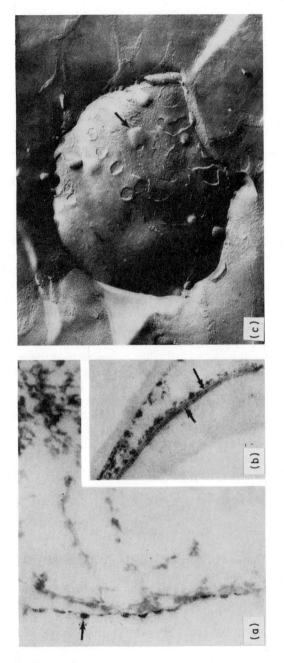

FIG. 14-3. Electron photomicrographs of the fat globule membrane. (a) A thin section of an OsO$_4$-fixed, epoxy-embedded fat globule, showing (arrow) dense areas of cytoplasmic materials in the membrane region. (Courtesy of W. Buchheim [11].) (b) A similar preparation, showing (arrow) a typical tripartite membrane structure. (Courtesy of P. S. Stewart [35].) (c) A freeze-fractured specimen of milk, showing (arrow) the membrane surface of a fat globule. Note the smooth surface and underlying particulates of cytoplasmic material of about 30–80 nm in diameter. (Adapted from Knoop [24], by courtesy of Volkswirtschaftlicher Verlag GmbH.)

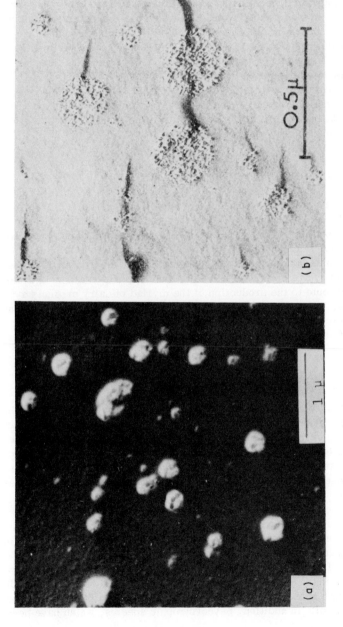

FIG. 14-4. Electron photomicrographs of casein micelles. (a) A specimen fixed with glutaraldehyde and shadowed with platinum. (Data of Brunner [7].) (b) A specimen prepared by the freeze-fracture technique. The micelles prepared by the latter technique appear to be open structured and somewhat larger than the micelles in (a). Also, the micellar subunits are clearly distinguishable and an occasional, an unassociated subunit can be recognized. (Reprinted from Knoop [24], by courtesy of Volkswirtschaftlicher Verlag GmbH.)

caseins as the structural matrix. Upon warming, the dissociated components re-assemble in the complex. Once the micellar structure is disturbed, it is unlikely that it can be reassembled in its original state.

The precise microstructure of the subunits, as well as that of the micelle, is a matter for speculation at the present time. Most of the prevailing theories on structure can be grouped into two general categories: a coat-core model, in which all of the k-casein is located in the coat; or a model in which the k-casein is distributed throughout the subunits of the micelle (see Fig. 14-5). The most convincing argument for the first model rests on the observation that the size of experimentally simulated micelles is influenced by the amount of k-casein present in the system, i.e., the more k-casein, the smaller the micelles. In support of the second model, recent experiments have demonstrated that when polymerized papain (too large a molecule to enter interstitial spaces of the micelle) is allowed to hydrolyze micellar casein, the unhydrolyzed portion contains about the same proportion of α_{s1}-, β-, and k-caseins throughout the course of the reaction.

IV. EFFECTS OF PROCESSING ON PROPERTIES OF MILK

Milk is a perishable raw material which must be stabilized against bacterial spoilage and is converted into consumable products through a multiplicity of processing procedures. Pasteurization and more rigorous heat treatments, such as sterilization, are required for microbiological control in the interest of public health. Other processes, such as homogenization, concentration, dehydration, freezing, renneting, and churning, are employed to modify the composition and indigenous properties of milk enroute to the production of the myriad of dairy products available to the consumer. In most instances the effects of these processes on the milk system are fairly well understood. In the ensuing discussions, only the most characteristic effects are considered.

A. Procedures Related to Milk Production

The production and transportation of milk has yielded to mechanization. Pipeline milking systems, refrigerated bulk tank storage, insulated tank transports, and every other day pickup have replaced the 10-gal can and daily collection of past years. The introduction of these highly efficient procedures has effectively lowered the cost of milk procurement. However, certain practices inherent to the system have engendered new problems. One of these, a rancid flavor defect resulting from lipolysis of milkfat by plasma lipases, occurs in milking systems which subject milk to extensive agitation. Agitation of milk at temperatures of 30°-35°C is critical, resulting in displacement of membrane material from fat globules and adsorption of plasma lipases. The problem is usually eliminated by removing "risers" from the pipeline system and by rapid cooling of the milk.

At normal values of pH 6.6-6.7, milk is quite stable to normal processing procedures. A decrease in pH contributes to the tendency for both fat globules and casein micelles to aggregate. The microbiological quality of milk has an obvious bearing on changes in pH. In addition, psychrotrophic species, which have become

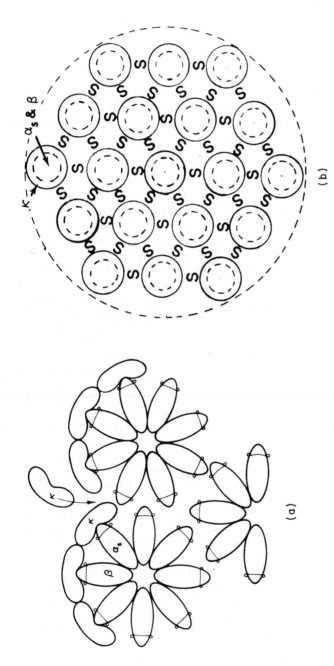

(a)

(b)

FIG. 14-5. Two conceptual models depicting organization of the components of micellar casein. Model A proposes that α_s- and β-caseins associate stoichiometrically in rosette configurations which in turn interassociate to form micellar core with k-casein oriented at the peripheral layer. (Adapted from Waugh and Noble [40], by courtesy of the American Chemical Society.) Model B depicts the micelle as associated subunits of uniform composition, consisting of α_s- and β-casein complexes covered with a layer of k-α_s-casein complex. (Adapted from Morr [29], by courtesy of the American Dairy Science Association.) Both models allow for association of subunits through calcium and colloidal calcium phosphate linkages which are indicated in Model B by S.

increasingly more prevalent in contemporary milk supplies, elaborate destablizing lipolytic and proteolytic enzymes. This problem is generally alleviated by careful attention to sanitary aspects of milk handling.

Upon delivery to the processor, milk is either clarified to remove cell debris and other extraneous matter or separated into cream and skim milk portions. Both processes are accomplished by passing either cold or warm milk through a centrifuge. The effects of agitation and gravitational forces inherent to the process cause some erosion of the fat globule membrane material which then accompanies the skim milk phase. Cold separation at 5°-10°C, although less efficient, is frequently more convenient and less destructive to the membrane. Also, cold-separated cream contains more of the cryoglobulin (IgM) fraction than warm-separated cream and this results in a more viscous product.

B. Heat Treatment

Pasteurization (61.8°C for 30 min, 71.8°C for 15 sec) represents a minimum heat treatment for the destruction of pathogenic organisms (based on destruction of M. tuberculosis). Fortuitously, many of the degrading enzymes, viz., lipolytic lipases, are inactivated by this treatment. Pasteurized products are nonsterile and possess limited shelf life at refrigerator temperatures. Ultrahigh-temperature pasteurization (93.4°C for 3 sec to 149.5°C for 1 sec) in conjunction with aseptic packaging produces a product essentially lacking a "heated" flavor and possessing increased shelf life. In-can sterilization (116.7°C for 12-15 min or 129.6°C for 3-5 min) is employed to achieve complete destruction of bacteria and spores. Processes in excess of normal pasteurization treatments induce significant changes in the chemical and physical characteristics of the milk system.

Cream layer formation proceeds normally in unhomogenized pasteurized milk and only small amounts of heat-labile whey proteins are denatured. At more severe heat treatments, creaming is impaired and greater portions of the whey proteins are denatured (see Fig. 14-6). Milk processed in this manner has a characteristic "cooked" flavor which can be partially alleviated by vacuum treatment. High temperatures favor displacement of fat membrane material, rendering the lipid phase less stable and necessitating homogenization to achieve physical stability.

Heat-induced protein-protein interactions can be extensive and complex. Heat-labile whey proteins interact with themselves as well as with casein micelles. The mechanism of interaction is believed to be that of disulfide interchange, initiated principally through the free sulfhydryl group of β-lactoglobulin. It should be recalled that k-casein contains a disulfide structure which no doubt constitutes the specific reactant in the casein system. In the absence of micellar casein, heat-denatured whey proteins aggregate and precipitate.

Significantly, milk processed at high temperatures does not form a normal curd when treated with rennin; hence such milk cannot be used to produce cheese. Apparently, the enzyme-specific site on k-casein is obscured by the complexed whey proteins, or the whey-protein-casein complex does not form a normal gel structure. This effect of heat on skim milk is not apparent when sulfhydryl-blocking agents are added prior to heating.

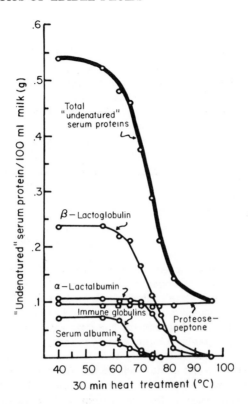

FIG. 14-6. The denaturation of whey (serum) protein components in milk heated for 30 min at temperatures ranging from 40° to 96°C. Quantitative values were estimated from moving-boundary electrophoretic patterns of the undenatured proteins. (Adapted from Larson and Rolleri [26], by courtesy of the American Dairy Science Association.)

At higher protein and salt concentrations, viz., in evaporated milk of commerce, the casein-whey protein complex forms a gel-like structure during the in-can sterilization process. This gel, which is induced by a relatively high activity of calcium ions, is dispersed by agitation and contributes to the desirable viscosity characteristics of the product. If excessive, the aggregation step can result in insoluble particles, a defect known as "graininess." In such instances, it is necessary to shorten the time of sterilization or to implement procedures to reduce the activity of calcium ions. The latter can be achieved either by increasing the heat treatment given the milk prior to concentration and/or by adding a "stabilizing" phosphate salt.

Heat also effects rates of degradative chemical reactions. Aside from the partial destruction of vitamin C and portions of the B vitamins, high-temperature processes induce the so-called "browning" reaction (see Chapter 3) which progresses during storage until the products are no longer acceptable. The principal participants of this reaction are the ϵ-amino groups of the protein lysine and lactose.

C. Homogenization

Homogenization is a standard industrial practice employed to effect stabilization of the lipid phase against gravity separation. Although the effects of homogenization are most apparent in the lipid phase, significant alterations in the protein system also occur. Homogenization is accomplished by warming milk to liquify the fat and then forcing it at high pressure (~2,500 psi) and high velocity (~600–800 fps) through restricted passages. Fat globules are reduced in size from 3–10 μm to <2 μm in diameter, which is commensurate with a four to sixfold increase in surface area (Fig. 14-7). The newly formed fat droplets are no longer coated exclusively with the original membrane material. Instead, they are covered with an adsorbed layer of plasma proteins, including casein micelles, micellar subunits, and reminants of the membrane material (Fig. 14-8). Increased dispersion of the lipid phase and its resurfaced interfacial layer imparts to homogenized milk characteristics unlike those of unhomogenized milk. Homogenized milk is whiter in appearance, bland in flavor, less heat stable, more sensitive to light-induced oxidation, and less sensitive to copper-induced oxidation and it possesses greater foaming capacity and lower curd tension then unhomogenized milk.

The interesting feature of homogenized milk is not the small size of the fat globules but rather the fixed state of their dispersion; i.e., they show no tendency to form clusters. This noncreaming characteristic has been attributed to denaturation of the creaming factor. Apparently, homogenization induced formation of an IgM-k-casein complex. Casein-complexed IgM is incapable of cryoaggregation, so the bridging of fat globules to form clusters is prevented. However, inactivation of the clustering agent does not explain adequately the extraordinary stability of the fat emulsion. It seems reasonable, therefore, to look at the nature of the "new" membrane for additional insight. Because casein is the principal component, factors which are responsible for maintaining the dispersion of micellar casein in the plasma must be operative.

Another of the interesting properties of homogenized milk is its low curd tension. Homogenization at 2,000 psi reduces the curd tension of pasteurized milk from about 55 g to 20 g. This has been attributed to (1) an increased number of fat globules serving as points of weakness in the gel structure and (2) immobilization of casein at the fat-plasma interface, resulting in a reduction of casein in the plasma phase. It is inconceivable that a reduction of approximately 10% in the effective concentration of the plasma casein can produce such a dramatic change in curd tension. Conceivable, then, the interaction between IgM and casein renders a large portion of the casein unavailable to the action of rennin.

Finally, let us consider the effect of homogenization on the flavor of milk. The characteristically bland flavor associated with homogenized milk is a ramification of the casein-surfaced fat globules. Because lipases are associated with the casein fraction, it is imperative that milk be properly pasteurized prior to homogenization to inactivate this enzyme system. If this is not done, a disagreeable rancid flavor develops. Contamination with raw milk should be avoided for the same reason. Furthermore, the increased surface of the fat phase enhances absorption of light and development of light-induced oxidized flavor. Conversely, the opportunity for ionic copper to catalyze the oxidation of milk lipids is retarded. It has been demonstrated that the amount of copper required to produce the copper-induced oxidation defect must be increased about four- to five-fold, which is roughly equivalent to the increased surface of the fat phase.

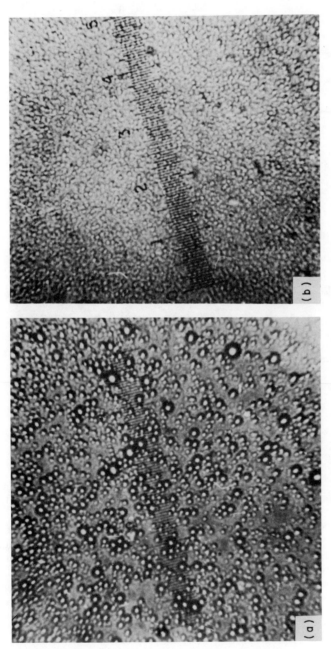

FIG. 14-7. Photomicrographs of unhomogenized (a) and homogenized milk (b). The random sized fat globules (3–10 μm) present in unhomogenized milk are reduced in size by homogenization to globules of uniform size (<2 μm). (Adapted from Brunner [10], by courtesy of the AVI Publishing Co.)

FIG. 14-8. Electron photomicrograph of a freeze-fractured specimen of homogenized cream. A designates the core of a fat globule and C identifies casein
micelles and subunits adsorbed to the fat globule surface. Occasional intact casein
micelles are apparent in the plasma phase. Apparently the subunits comprising
casein micelles are utilized to partially resurface the lipid phase in homogenized
milk products. A single casein micelle is frequently associated with more than one
fat globule. (Reprinted from Knoop [24], by courtesy of Volkswirtschaftlicher
Verlag GmbH.)

D. Dehydration and Freezing

In a sense, dehydration and freezing exert similar stresses on the milk system. Both treatments remove available water, producing a concentrated system of high ionic activity. The fat globule membrane is eroded by both treatments, setting free a portion of the lipid phase. Thus, homogenization is a required preliminary process for products which are to be frozen or dehydrated. Also, protein-protein interactions are more prevalent in concentrated products and may cause product instability.

The solubility of lactose approaches a critical stage in concentrated milk products and may crystallize in the insoluble α-hydrate form. In spray-dried milk products, lactose assumes a "glassy" or amorphous state which is quite hydroscopic. Such products must be protected from moisture to avoid the onset of lactose crystallization and subsequent caking.

E. Churning

The process of churning butter from cream utilizes the denaturation effects of violent agitation to denude the fat globule surface, the membrane material being eliminated in the buttermilk. To be effective, churning must be performed at a temperature conducive to the clumping of fat globules, being adjusted upward or downward a few degrees to compensate for variations in the triglyceride composition and thus the physical state of the fat. The churning of cream is ineffective at temperatures at which all of the fat is either in the liquid or the solid state. Hence, there must be a balance between the two physical states, permitting the blending of liquid and solid fat in a kind of "cementing" action. Churning can be accomplished by either batch or continuous processes, yielding butter of discrete physical characteristics (see Table 14-13) but probably indistinguishable to the consumer. The underlying principle of churning involves destabilization of cream, an oil in water emulsion, to form a product in which fat represents the continuous phase and contains up to 16% of finely dispersed water droplets.

One of the important operations in the butter-making process is the control of fat crystallization and the associated hardness or spreadibility of the butter. For instance, rapid cooling of the cream prior to churning increases crystallization of fat and the hardness of the butter produced. The hardness of butter can be somewhat reduced by "working" prior to printing (forming). Batch-churned butter exhibits two crystalline forms, α and β', in which the β' (stable form) predominates. In continuously churned butter the α form prevails but gradually transforms to the β' form following printing.

F. Rennin Treatment

The process of making cheese involves destabilization of micellar casein to form a casein curd. This is accomplished through the addition either of rennet, obtained from the abomasum of milk-fed calves, or of renninlike enzymes of microbiological or plant origin. The primary action of rennin on casein is specific, cleaving the peptide bond between phenylalanine and methionine in the k-casein

TABLE 14-13

Properties of Conventional Butter and Butter Made by
Continuous Processes[a]

Properties	Conventional butter	Continuous processes		
		Fritz	Alfa	Cherry-Burrell
Microscopic structure	Fat globules and water droplets in free fat			Water droplets in free fat
Dielectric constant[b]	5–8	5–7	6–8	–
Globular fat	2–46%, 3.5–4 μm	12–17%, 3.5–4.2 μm	11–31%, 3.3–4.1 μm	Few globules
Free fat (%)	54–98	83–88	69–89	100
Aqueous phase (diam. of droplets)	<1–>30 μm	<1–>15 μm	<1–<7 μm	<1–30 μm
Gaseous phase (% vol)	~3	~7	<1	N_2 added to 4–5%
Consistency	Tendency to openness	Tendency to crumbliness	Close texture	–

[a]Compiled from King [23].
[b]Dielectric constant of cream at 80°C is ~130; butterfat ~3.

component, thus setting free a glycomacropeptide (~6,000 daltons). The remaining protein, viz., p-k-casein (~12,000 daltons), is no longer soluble and relinquishes its role as the stabilizing agent for micellar casein. The secondary step in the reaction involves formation of an insoluble casein gel (see Fig. 14-9). The tertiary phase involves a general proteolytic action of rennin on all of the protein components. In the cheese-making process, the curd is cut at an appropriate time and allowed to undergo syneresis and firm; the latter occurrences being accelerated by mild heating. The final characteristic of the cheese depends to a large extent on the flora of the starter culture employed and the conditions and time of ripening. It should be remembered that cheese is essentially the casein fraction of milk and may or may not contain milkfat.

V. NUTRITIVE VALUE OF MILK

Milk and milk products account for a significant portion of the total food consumed in the United States, amounting daily to about 1.5 lb (whole milk equivalent) per capita. From the compositional data presented in Section II of this chapter, it is apparent that milk contains a broad distribution of essential nutrients. Based on

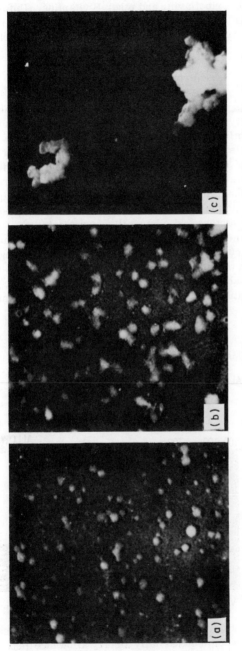

FIG. 14-9. Electron photomicrographs of casein micelles in skim milk showing the effect of the action of remnin on their progressive aggregation into a gel structure: (a) After 1 min; (b) after 4 min; (c) after 8 min. (Adapted from Schmidt [34], by courtesy of Nederlands Instituut voor Zuivelonderzoek (NIZO).)

the recommended dietary allowances established by the National Research Council [4], one quart of vitamin D-fortified milk provides a significant portion of the required nutrients (Fig. 14-10). Milk is an especially rich course of high-quality protein, calcium, phosphorus, riboflavin, and other B vitamins. Unfortified milk is a poor source of vitamin D, vitamin C, and iron. Most of the fluid milk processed for the retail trade is fortified with 400 IU of vitamin D per quart.

A. Protein Quality

Total milk protein represents one of the highest quality proteins available rivaled by meat and surpassed only by egg proteins. In Table 14-14, the amounts of essential amino acids in total milk protein, whey protein, and casein are compared with the FAO [3] recommended standard based on egg protein. The principal but relatively minor deficiency of milk proteins is in the content of the sulfur-bearing residues, viz., cystine, cysteine, and methionine. Milk proteins represent an unusually rich source of lysine. In concentrated products, such as evaporated milk and some types of milk powder, a portion of the lysine is rendered unavailable through interaction with lactose and other milk constituents.

Concomitant with development of the dairy industry has been the gradual replacement of breast milk by cow's milk for infant feeding. Chief among the feeding problems associated with this phenomenon is allergic sensitivity to cow's milk proteins. According to available information, all of the milk proteins, individually and as a group, have been implicated. In particular, much attention has been

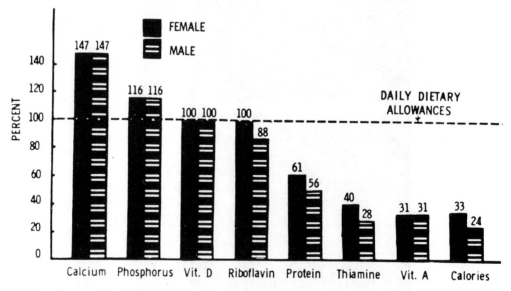

FIG. 14-10. Major nutrients contributed by 1 quart of milk compared to the National Research Council's recommended daily dietary allowance [4]. Milk was fortified with 400 IU of vitamin D. (Reprinted from Rusoff [32], by courtesy of the American Dairy Science Association.)

TABLE 14-14

Essential Amino Acid Patterns of Milk Proteins Compared to the
Essential Amino Acid Pattern of Whole Hen-Egg Protein[a]

Essential amino acid	Whole milk protein[b]	Whey protein[b]	Casein[c]	Whole egg protein[d]
Isoleucine	112	117	119	129
Leucine	199	234	179	172
Lysine	168	191	160	125
Phenylalanine	104 ⎫ 210	82 ⎫ 144	98 ⎫ 221	114 ⎫ 195
Tyrosine[e]	106 ⎭	62 ⎭	123 ⎭	81 ⎭
Methionine	51 ⎫ 60	35 ⎫ 58	55 ⎫ 61	61 ⎫ 107
Cystine[e]	9 ⎭	23 ⎭	6 ⎭	46 ⎭
Threonine	89	103	96	99
Tryptophan	42	57	33	31
Valine	123	98	140	141

[a]A/E ratios, where A is the milligrams of a given essential amino acid and E is the grams of total essential amino acids.

[b]For Holstein milk [8].

[c]Calculated from data of Gordon and Whittier [13], representing a total casein fraction.

[d]FAO (1965) pattern for egg protein [3].

[e]Since methionine and phenylalanine are utilized by the body for synthesis of cystine and tyrosine, respectively, the requirements for these two essential amino acids can be partially met by cystine and tyrosine present in the diet.

focused in β-lactoglobulin which seems to be a potent antigen. Even denaturation of whey proteins by heat is not always effective in altering their antigenicity for sensitized individuals. When this situation is encountered, the best course of action is to remove milk proteins from the diet, substituting proteins from another source, viz., human milk, goat's milk or soy proteins.

B. Lipid Quality

Milk lipids (triglycerides) contain relatively high concentrations of saturated fatty acids and low concentrations of the essential polyunsaturated fatty acids, linoleic and linolenic. A popular contemporary concept equates the consumption of predominantly saturated animal fats with the onset of atherosclerosis. Under such circumstances the levels of plasma cholesterol and β-lipoproteins are high. However, there are many facets to this problem which have not been resolved. Thus, it seems unjust, at this time, to indict milkfat per se as a principal cause for the high incidence of antherosclerosis in our society.

C. Lactose Intolerance

Although it has been difficult to assign a specific nutritional role to lactose, there is some evidence that it plays an important role in absorption of calcium and amino acids across the gut. Within the past few years, numerous reports have appeared concerning lactose intolerance in older children and adults in some non-Caucasian races. This intolerance results in severe dehydrating diarrhea and vomiting and has been attributed to a lack of intestinal lactase in affected individuals. Apparently this deficiency is rare among Caucasians, most of whom have been nurtured by the cow for generations. Interestingly, some workers have observed that lactose intolerance is associated with allergenic reaction to milk proteins; when milk protein is removed from the diet, there has been subsidence of intolerance to lactose. Unfortunately, much of the sensational revelations concerning intolerance to lactose represent extrapolation from experimentally administered doses of lactose. Thus, it seems unwise to recommend elimination of milk, with its myriad of essential nutrients, from the diet.

D. Vitamin Stability

The fat-soluble vitamins of milk are quite stable to heat and other processing treatments. However, significant destruction of vitamins A and E does occur in the presence of oxidized lipids or when products are exposed to light. Vitamin C is the most labile of the water-soluble vitamins. It exists initially in the form of L-ascorbic acid, which is slowly oxidized to biologically active dehydroascorbic acid, which further degrades to biologically inactive diketogluconic acid and other products. This transformation is induced by contaminating copper ions or by exposure to light radiation of less than 500 nm. Riboflavin is also sensitive to light-induced oxidation and participates in photooxidative degradation of other milk constituents, viz., vitamin C, lipids, and proteins. With the exception of thiamin, which is about 50% destroyed during moderately severe heating such products as evaporated milk, the B vitamins are relatively heat stable. The B vitamins of milk exist partially in a free state and partially bound to proteins. Thus, the biological activity of the bound forms may depend on their release upon ingestion.

REFERENCES

1. Association of Official Agricultural Chemists, Official Methods of Analysis (W. Horwitz, ed.; P. Chichilo and H. Reynolds, assoc. eds.), 11th ed., Assoc. Off. Agri. Chem., Washington, D.C., 1970.
2. M. Florkin and E. H. Stotz, eds., Comprehensive Biochemistry. Vol. 13, Elsevier, New York, 1965.

3. Food and Agriculture Organization, Protein Requirements, FAO, UN Nutr. Meeting Rept. Ser. 37, 1965.
4. Food and Nutrition Board, Recommended Dietary Allowances. 7th rev. ed., National Academy of Sciences, National Research Council, Publ. 1694, Washington, D.C., 1969.
5. B. H. Webb and A. H. Johnson, eds., Fundamentals of Dairy Chemistry. AVI Publ., Westport, Conn., 1965.
6. H. A. McKenzie, ed., Milk Proteins, Chemistry and Molecular Biology. Vols. I and II, Academic Press, New York, 1970 and 1971.
7. J. R. Brunner, unpublished data, 1969.
8. J. R. Brunner, unpublished data, 1973.
9. J. R. Brunner, C. A. Ernstrom, R. A. Hollis, B. L. Larson, R. McL. Whitney and C. A. Zittle, J. Dairy Sci., 43, 901 (1960).
10. J. R. Brunner, in Fundamentals of Dairy Chemistry (B. H. Webb and A. H. Johnson, eds.), AVI Publ., Westport, Conn., 1965, pp. 403-505.
11. W. Buchheim, personal communication, 1971.
12. E. A. Corbin and E. O. Whittier, in Fundamentals of Dairy Chemistry (B. H. Webb and A. H. Johnson, eds.), AVI Publ., Westport, Conn., 1965, pp. 1-36.
13. W. G. Gordon and E. O. Whittier, in Fundamentals of Dairy Chemistry (B. H. Webb and A. H. Johnson, eds.), AVI Publ., Westport, Conn., 1965, pp. 54-90.
14. J. D. S. Goulden, J. Dairy Res., 31, 273 (1964).
15. A. M. Hartman and L. P. Dryden, in Fundamentals of Dairy Chemistry (B. H. Webb and A. H. Johnson, eds.), AVI Publ., Westport, Conn., 1965, pp. 261-338.
16. S. F. Herb, P. Magidman, F. E. Luddy, and R. W. Riemenschneider, J. Amer. Oil Chem. Soc., 39, 142 (1962).
17. R. Jenness, in Milk Proteins, Chemistry and Molecular Biology (H. A. McKenzie, ed.), Vol. I, Academic Press, New York, 1970, pp. 17-40.
18. R. Jenness, B. L. Larson, T. L. McMeekin, A. M. Swanson, C. H. Whitnah, and R. McL. Whitney, J. Dairy Sci., 39, 536 (1956).
19. R. Jenness and S. Patton, Principles of Dairy Chemistry. Wiley, New York, 1958.
20. T. W. Keenan and C. M. Huang, J. Dairy Sci., 55, 1586 (1972).
21. T. W. Keenan, D. E. Olson, and H. H. Mollenhauer, J. Dairy Sci., 54, 295 (1971).
22. C. A. Kiddy, J. O. Johnson, and M. P. Thompson, J. Dairy Sci., 47, 147 (1964).
23. N. King, Dairy Ind., 20, 409 (1955).
24. E. Knoop, Milchwissenschaft, 27, 364 (1972).
25. F. E. Kurtz, in Fundamentals of Dairy Chemistry (B. H. Webb and A. H. Johnson, eds.), AVI Publ., Westport, Conn., 1965, pp. 91-169.
26. B. L. Larson and G. D. Rolleri, J. Dairy Sci., 38, 351 (1955).
27. J. L. Linzell and M. Peaker, Physiol. Rev., 51, 564 (1971).
28. H. A. McKenzie, in Milk Proteins, Chemistry and Molecular Biology (H. A. McKenzie, ed.), Vol. II, Academic Press, New York, 1971, pp. 257-330.
29. C. V. Morr, J. Dairy Sci., 50, 1744 (1967).
30. A. H. Palmer, J. Biol. Chem., 104, 359 (1934).

31. D. Rose, J. R. Brunner, E. B. Kalan, B. L. Larson, P. Melnychyn, H. E. Swaisgood, and D. F. Waugh, J. Dairy Sci., 53, 1 (1970).

32. L. L. Rusoff, J. Dairy Sci., 53, 1296 (1970).

33. S. J. Rowland, J. Dairy Res., 30, 42 (1938).

34. D. G. Schmidt, Off. Org. K. Ned. Zuivelbond, 57, 848 (1965); also cited in Dairy Sci., Abstr., 28, 44 (1966).

35. P. S. Stewart, M.S. Thesis, University of Guelph, Guelph, Canada, 1970; See also, P. S. Stewart, and D. M. Irvine, 18th Intl. Dairy Cong. Proc., Melbourne, 1E, 71 (1971).

36. H. E. Swaisgood, Crit. Rev. Food Technol., 4, 375 (1973).

37. M. P. Thompson, J. R. Brunner, C. M. Stine, and K. Lindquist, J. Dairy Sci., 44, 1589 (1961).

38. M. P. Thompson, N. P. Tarassuk, R. Jenness, H. A. Lillevik, U. S. Ashworth, and D. Rose, J. Dairy Sci., 48, 159 (1965).

39. H. Toben, J. B. Josimovich, and H. Salazar, Endocrinology, 90, 1569 (1972).

40. D. F. Waugh and R. W. Noble, J. Amer. Chem. Soc., 87, 2246 (1965).

41. J. C. D. White and D. T. Davies, J. Dairy Res., 25, 236 (1958).

Chapter 15

CHARACTERISTICS OF EDIBLE FLUIDS OF
ANIMAL ORIGIN: EGGS

William D. Powrie

Department of Food Science
University of British Columbia
Vancouver, British Columbia, Canada

Contents

I. INTRODUCTION

Whole eggs, yolk, and albumen (egg white) are excellent sources of nutrients and, in addition, have valuable functional properties. A survey of the nutritional value of eggs has been presented by Cook and Briggs [13]. Shell eggs consist of 8–11% shell, 56–61% albumen, and 27–32% yolk. Liquid whole egg, which has a solids content between 25 and 26.5%, is composed of about 36% yolk and 64% albumen. Commercially prepared liquid yolk contains between 15 and 20% albumen since some albumen adheres to vitelline membranes of the separated intact yolk. According to Standards of Identity of the United States Food and Drug Administration, commercial liquid yolk must contain not less than 43% total egg solids.

Egg products are commonly marketed in the following forms: (1) refrigerated, (2) frozen, or (3) spray dried. In compliance with FDA regulations, all egg products must be pasteurized to destroy viable Salmonella organisms. For refrigerated and frozen egg products, pasteurization is carried out in a heat exchanger prior to cooling or freezing. In the case of spray-dried albumen, the liquid product may be pasteurized prior to drying or the dried product may be stored at a high temperature for Salmonella inactivation. The addition of 10% sucrose or 10% NaCl to commercial frozen yolk is common practice to prevent gelation (viscosity increase). Frozen salted yolks are used for the manufacture of mayonnaise and salad dressing, whereas frozen sugared yolk is preferred for bakery products and ice cream. Frozen plain yolk without added sugar or salt is used in noodles and baby foods. Prior to spray drying, albumen is usually desugared by a glucose oxidase treatment to obviate nonenzymic browning in the dry albumen during storage.

Recent reviews on the chemistry of egg components have been written by Baker [2], Brooks and Taylor [6], Cook [12], Feeney [17], Parkinson [28], Powrie [30], and Shenstone [39].

II. STRUCTURE AND COMPOSITION OF THE SHELL AND SHELL MEMBRANES

A. Egg Shell

The egg shell is composed of (1) a matrix of interwoven protein fibers and (2) interstitial calcite (calcium carbonate) crystals in a proportion of about 1:50. In addition, the surface of the shell is covered by a cuticle, a foamy layer of protein. Figure 15-1 is a diagram of a radial section of the shell [40]. The matrix consists of two regions, the mamillary matrix and the spongy matrix. Microscopic studies have shown that the matrix fibers pass through calcite instead of simply surrounding them. Undoubtedly the matrix has a significant influence on shell strength. The matrices are made up of protein-mucopolysaccharide complexes. The polysaccharides contain chondroitin sulfates A and B, galactosamine, glucosamine, galactose, mannose, fucose, and sialic acid.

According to Romanoff and Romanoff [35] the elemental composition of the egg shell is 98.2% calcium, 0.9% magnesium, and 0.9% phosphorus (present in the shell as phosphate). Brooks and Hale [4] indicated that shell hardness increases with increases in magnesium content.

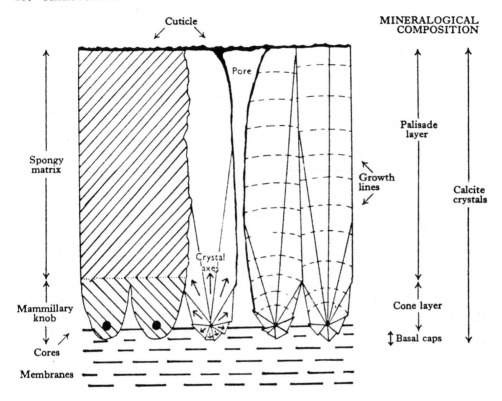

FIG. 15-1. Schematic cross-section of an egg shell.

Numerous funnel-shaped pore canals (7,000-17,000 per egg) are distributed at right angles to the shell surface and form passages between the shell membrane and the cuticle. The pore canals are filled with protein fibers which restrict microbial entry into the egg.

The water-insoluble protein cuticle forms a protective coating (about 10-30 μm thick) on the entire surface of the egg. The cuticle is made up of mucoproteins with hexosamine, galactose, mannose, and fucose as constituents of the polysaccharides.

B. Shell Membranes

Two membranes with thicknesses of 48 μm and 22 μm reside between the inner surface of the shell and the albumen. The membranes are composed of protein-polysaccharide fibers. The outer shell membrane is attached firmly to the shell by numerous cones on the inner shell surface and by fiber associations. The outer membrane has six layers of fibers oriented alternately in different directions, whereas the inner membrane has three layers of fibers which are parallel to the shell and at right angles to each other.

III. COMPOSITION OF ALBUMEN AND YOLK

A. Albumen

Albumen is made up of four distinct layers: outer fluid (thin) albumen, viscous albumen (thick), inner fluid albumen (thin), and a chalaziferous layer. The proportions and moisture contents of the layers are presented in Table 15-1. The wide range in the proportion of layers has been attributed to breed, environmental conditions, size of egg, and rate of egg production [35].

The major constituent of the albumen layers is water, which decreases somewhat in amount from the outer to the inner albumen layers (Table 15-1). The water content of mixed albumen ranges from 87 to 89% and is dependent on the strain and age of the hens [30].

The proximate analysis of albumen is listed in Table 15-2. Protein is the major constituent in albumen solids. The variability of protein content (9.7-10.6%) in albumen can be attributed primarily to age of the bird. The amount of lipid in albumen (about 0.03%) is negligible compared to that of yolk. The carbohydrates in albumen are in combined (with protein) and free forms and can reach a level of about 1%. Approximately 98% of the free carbohydrate (about 0.5%) of the albumen is glucose. The elemental composition of the ash of albumen is presented in Table 15-3, and the total amount does not vary appreciably. The predominant cations are potassium and sodium.

TABLE 15-1

Proportion and Moisture Content of Albumen Layers

Layer	Percent albumen		Percent moisture
	Mean	Range	
Outer thin white	23.2	10-60	88.8
Thick white	57.3	30-80	87.6
Inner thin white	16.8	1-40	86.4
Chalaziferous (including chalazae)	2.7		84.3

TABLE 15-2

Composition of Albumen, Yolk, and Whole Egg

Egg component	Percent solids content	Percent protein	Percent lipid	Percent carbohydrate	Percent ash
Albumen	11.13	9.7-10.6	0.03	0.4-0.9	0.5-0.6
Yolk	52.3-53.5	15.7-16.6	31.8-35.5	0.2-1.0	1.1
Whole egg	25-26.5	12.8-13.4	10.5-11.8	0.3-1.0	0.8-1.0

TABLE 15-3

Elemental Composition of Albumen and Yolk

Element	Percent in albumen	Percent in yolk
Sulfur	0.195	0.016
Potassium	0.145–0.167	0.112–0.360
Sodium	0.161–0.169	0.070–0.093
Phosphorus	0.018	0.543–0.980
Calcium	0.008–0.02	0.121–0.262
Magnesium	0.009	0.032–0.128
Iron	0.0009	0.0053–0.011

B. Yolk

The solids content of yolk is in the vicinity of 50%. Yolk from fresh eggs has a solids content of 52–53% but the yolk solids drop about 2% when eggs are stored at refrigerated temperatures for 1–2 weeks because water migrates into the yolk from the albumen. Proteins and lipids are the major constituents of yolk, with minor amounts of carbohydrates and minerals also present (Table 15-2). The protein content of yolk is about 16%, with limited variability. The amount of lipid varies between about 32 and 36% and this variation can be attributed to the strain of bird rather than to diet. The yolk lipid fraction contains approximately 66% triglyceride, 28% phospholipid, 5% cholesterol, and minor amounts of other lipids. Rhodes and Lea [34] estimated the composition of yolk phospholipids as 73.0% phosphatidyl choline, 15.5% phosphatidyl ethanolamine, 5.8% lysophosphatidyl choline, 2.5% sphingomyelin, 2.1% lysophosphatidyl ethanolamine, 0.9% plasmalogen, and 0.6% inositol phospholipid.

The fatty acid composition of yolk lipid is influenced by the types of fatty acids in the diet of the hen. The total amount of saturated fatty acids, primarily palmitic and stearic, does not change with an alteration of dietary fatty acid composition, but linoleic acid increases with oleic acid decreases when the level of dietary poly-unsaturated fatty acids is elevated.

The fatty acid content of yolk lipid fractions is tabulated in Table 15-4 [31]. Palmitic and stearic acids amount to about 30% of the triglycerides, whereas they amount to about 49% in lecithin and 54% in cephalin.

The amount of carbohydrate (combined and free) in yolk may be as high (1%) as that in albumen. The content of free carbohydrate has been estimated to be 0.2%. Protein-bound carbohydrates are mannose-glucosamine polysaccharides.

As shown in Table 15-3, the major elements in the yolk ash (about 1.1%) are calcium, potassium, and phosphorus.

IV. PROTEINS IN ALBUMEN

Albumen can be considered as a protein system consisting of ovomucin fibers in an aqueous solution of numerous globular proteins. The protein composition of the

TABLE 15-4

Fatty Acid Composition of Lipid Fractions of
Yolk and Dietary Lipid

Fatty acid	Percent of total fatty acids				
	Crude lipid	Triglyceride	Lecithin	Cephalin	Dietary lipid
16:0	23.5	22.5	37.0	21.6	14.0
16:1	3.8	7.3	0.6	trace	2.7
18:0	14.0	7.5	12.4	32.5	2.4
18:1	38.4	44.7	31.4	17.3	29.1
18:2	16.4	15.4	12.0	7.0	44.4
18:3	1.4	1.3	1.0	2.0	3.2
20:4	1.3	0.5	2.7	10.2	0.8
20:5 22:5	0.4	0.2	0.8	3.0	0.8
22:6	0.8	0.6	2.1	6.4	1.3

thin and thick layers of albumen differs only in the ovomucin content (four times greater amount in the thick albumen). Protein fractions can be separated by step-wise addition of ammonium sulfate and by ion-exchange chromatography. Several types of electrophoretic techniques have been used to separate albumen proteins. Seven major peaks, including ovalbumins A_1 and A_2; globulins G_1, G_2, and G_3; ovomucoid; and conalbumin, were obtained with moving-boundary electrophoresis [18]. With polyacrylamide disk-gel electrophoresis, Chang et al. [11] were able to separate albumen protein into 12 bands, whereas 19 protein bands were obtained by several investigators using starch-gel electrophoresis. Variation in the number of bands from albumen of various strains and inbred lines has been attributed to genetic polymorphism. The relative amounts of proteins in albumen, and some of their properties are presented in Table 15-5 [2].

A. Ovalbumin

Ovalbumin, the major protein fraction in albumen, is classed as a phosphoglyco-protein since phosphate and carbohydrate moeities are attached to the polypeptide chain. Purified ovalbumin is made up of three components, A_1, A_2, and A_3, which differ only in phosphorus content. A_1 has two phosphates per molecule, A_2 has one, and A_3 has none. The relative proportion of the A_1, A_2, and A_3 components is about 85:12:3. The ovalbumin molecule contains four sulfhydryl and two disulfide groups.

TABLE 15-5

Proteins in Egg Albumen

Protein	Relative amount in albumen (%)	Isoelectric point	Molecular weight	Characteristics
Ovalbumin	54	4.6	45,000	Phosphoglyco-protein
Conalbumin	13	6.6	80,000	Binds metals, especially iron
Ovomucoid	11	3.9–4.3	28,000	Inhibits trypsin
Lysozyme (G$_1$ globulin)	3.5	10.7	14,600	Lyzes some bacteria
G$_2$ globulin	4.0 ?	5.5	30,000–45,000	–
G$_3$ globulin	4.0 ?	5.8	?	–
Ovomucin	1.5	?	?	Sialoprotein
Flavoprotein	0.8	4.1	35,000	Binds riboflavin
Ovoglycoprotein	0.5 ?	3/9	24,000	Sialoprotein
Ovomacroglobulin	0.5	4.5–4.7	760,000–900,000	?
Ovoinhibitor	0.1	5.2	44,000	Inhibits several proteases
Avidin	0.05	9.5	53,000	Binds biotin

The carbohydrate content of ovalbumin is about 2% D-mannose and 1.2% 2-amino-2-deoxy-D-glucose, or an average of five and three residues, respectively, of these sugars per molecule of protein. The carbohydrate moeity of ovalbumin has a molecular weight between 1,560 and 1,580. During storage of eggs, ovalbumin is converted to S-ovalbumin, a more heat-stable protein, conceivably through sulfhydryl-disulfide interchange.

Ovalbumin in solution is readily denatured and coagulated by exposure to new surfaces but is resistant to thermal denaturation. When albumen at pH 9 was heated to 62°C for 3.5 min, Lineweaver et al. [24] found that only 3-5% of the ovalbumin was altered significantly.

B. Conalbumin

Conalbumin, prepared by fractional precipitation of albumen with ammonium sulfate, consists of two forms in the approximate ratio of 4:1. Conalbumin contain neither phosphorus nor sulfhydryl groups. About 0.8% hexose and 1.4% hexosamine is present in this protein.

Conalbumin is more heat sensitive but less susceptible to surface denaturation than ovalbumin. Cunningham and Lineweaver [16] showed that 1% conalbumin in phosphate-bicarbonate buffer had a minimum heat stability near pH 6, at which value 40% of the conalbumin was altered during heating to 57°C for 10 min. Conalbumin at pH 9 was not altered significantly when the solution was heated under the same conditions. The heat stability of conalbumin in albumen is similar to that for conalbumin in the buffer.

Di- and trivalent metallic ions are bound firmly by conalbumin. Two atoms of Fe^{+3}, Al^{+3}, Cu^{+2}, or Zn^{+2} per molecule of conalbumin form stable complexes at about pH 6. These complexes are red, colorless, yellow, and colorless, respectively. Conalbumin complexed with metallic ions is heat stable. Presumably the iron ion is bound by three phenolic hydroxyl groups as well as by one carbonate ion.

C. Ovomucoid

Ovomucoid is a glycoprotein which exists in three forms, all of which have trypsin-inhibiting abilities. The carbohydrate composition of ovomucoid is 1.0-1.5% D-galactose, 4.3-4.7% D-mannose, 12.5-15.4% 2-amino-2-deoxyglucose, 0.4-4% sialic acid, and 6-9% total hexoses. The carbohydrate is present as three oligosaccharides, each attached to the polypeptide through an asparaginyl residue. The polypeptide, with eight disulfide linkages, possesses about 22% of the fully extended chain as helical structure.

Ovomucoid in acidic media is very resistant to heat denaturation, but in alkaline solutions this protein is altered rapidly at 80°C.

D. Lysozyme

Lysozyme, an enzyme with lytic action on bacterial cell walls, consists of three components which can be separated by cation-exchange chromatography. Its isoelectric point of 10.7 is much higher than that of other albumen proteins and its molecular weight (14,600) is the lowest. Lysozyme consists of 129 amino acid residues and its primary structure has been successfully elucidated. Four disulfide linkages but no free SH groups are present on each polypeptide molecule.

Thermal inactivation of lysozyme is dependent on pH and temperature. Lysozyme is much more heat sensitive in egg albumen than when present alone in a phosphate buffer between pH 7 and 9. When egg albumen is heated for 10 min at 63.5°C, lysozyme is inactivated to a greater degree as the pH is increased above 7.

E. Ovomucin

Ovomucin is a glycoprotein which contributes to the gel-like structure of thick albumen. This protein is not soluble in water but can be solubilized by a dilute salt solution at pH 7 or above. Ovomucin consists of three components which can be separated by moving-boundary electrophoresis. The carbohydrate content of the purified protein is around 30%, with 10-12% as hexosamine, 15% as hexose, and 2.6-8% as sialic acid.

Purified ovomucin in solution is resistant to heat denaturation. Cunningham and Lineweaver [16] found that ovomucin solutions with pH values between 7.1 and 9.4 did not change in optical density during heating for 2 hr at about 90°C.

Ovomucin and lysozyme can form a water-soluble complex through electrostatic interaction. Over the pH range 7.2-10.4, protein interaction decreases as the pH is elevated. Presumably the ovomucin-lysozyme complex contributes to the gel-like structure of thick albumen, but contradictory hypotheses have been presented. Cotterill and Winter [15] have postulated that the thinning of thick albumen during egg storage is caused by a reduction in the amount of naturally occurring ovomucin-lysozyme complex as the pH rises to 9.5.

F. Other Albumen Proteins

Avidin, a biotin-binding protein, is composed of three components, A, B, and C. Ovoglobulins G_2 and G_3 are excellent foaming agents. Ovoinhibitor is capable of inhibiting trypsin and chymotrypsin. Flavoprotein is made up of two types of apo-protein which bind riboflavin tightly.

V. MICROSTRUCTURE OF YOLK PARTICLES

Yolk can be classed as a dispersion containing a variety of particles distributed uniformly in a protein (livetin) solution. The types of particles are (1) yolk spheres, (2) granules, (3) low-density lipoprotein, and (4) myelin figures.

Chang [10] found numerous spheres with diameters of about 20 μm in white yolk but only a few spheres (about 40 μm in diameter) were observed in yellow yolk (about 99% of the total yolk). Bellairs [3] noted three types of sphere surfaces: (1) lamellated capsules (several layers of membrane), (2) unit membranelike structures, and (3) naked surfaces. The majority of spheres have naked surfaces.

Granules are smaller and more numerous than yolk spheres. Although sphere diameters are as large as 1.7 μm, the majority of granules have diameters between about 1.0 and 1.3 μm [10]. Electron micrographs indicate that granules are made up of electron-dense subunits which can be dispersed by diluting yolk with 0.34M NaCl. At higher salt concentrations the native structure of the subunits is destroyed with the formation of small and large globules (300-1,000 Å), myelin figures (560-1,300 Å), and electron-dense fluffy masses which are made up of entangled strands to which electron-dense microparticles are attached. The microparticles, which are roughly circular, have average diameters of about 100 Å.

Round profiles (diameters of 250 Å) were noted in electron micrographs of yolk. These profiles are considered to be low-density lipoproteins which exist as individual particles uniformly distributed throughout the yolk.

VI. PROTEINS AND LIPOPROTEINS IN GRANULES
AND PLASMA

By high-speed centrifugation, yolk can be separated into sedimented granules and a clear supernatant, called plasma. The granules make up about 19-23% of the yolk solids. Granules on a moisture-free basis contain about 34% lipid, 60% protein, and 6% ash. About 37% of the total lipid consists of phospholipids, mainly phosphatidyl choline (82%) and phosphatidyl ethanolamine (15%).

Plasma represents about 78% of liquid yolk and has a moisture content of about 49%. On a dry weight basis, plasma consists of 77-81% lipid, 2% ash, and about 18% protein.

A. Proteins and Lipoproteins in Granules

According to Burley and Cook [8], granules are composed of 70% α- and β-lipovitellins, 16% phosvitin, and 12% low-density lipoprotein. Radmonski and Cook [32,33] showed that lipovitellins and phosvitin had an affinity for each other and suggested that a phosvitin-lipovitellin complex was a basic unit of the granule. The electron-dense subunits in the granule are composed of low-density lipoproteins surrounded by phosvitin strands with lipovitellin attached.

1. PHOSVITIN

Phosvitin, with a molecular weight between 36,000 and 40,000, contains about 10% phosphorus and thereby represents about 80% of the protein phosphorus in yolk. This phosphoprotein can be separated by moving-boundary electrophoresis into three peaks but is homogeneous when analyzed by ultracentrifugation. Little or no cysteine and cystine have been found in phosvitin, but an exceptionally high concentration of serine (31% of the total amino acid residues) is present. Phosphate in the protein is presumably esterified with serine.

Taborsky [41] reported that ferric ions are bound tightly to phosvitin to form a soluble complex. According to Greengard et al. [20], phosvitin is the iron carrier of yolk.

2. LIPOVITELLINS

The high-density lipoprotein fraction, lipovitellin, can be separated into α- and β-lipovitellins by moving-boundary electrophoresis or by chromatography using a column of either hydroxyapatite, Dowex-1, or triethylaminoethyl cellulose. The apparent lipid and protein P contents of these proteins depend on the type of column used in the chromatographic separation (Table 15-6). The lipid in α- and β-lipoprotein includes 40% neutral lipid and 60% phospholipid [27]. The phospholipid fraction of each protein contains 75% phosphatidyl choline, 18% phosphatidyl ethanolamine, and 7% sphingomyelin and lysophospholipids.

At pH values below 7, lipoproteins exist as dimers. With an increase in pH, however, monomers are gradually formed. The molecular weights of α- and β-lipoprotein dimers are in the vicinity of 400,000.

TABLE 15-6

Lipid and Protein Phosphorus Contents of α- and β-
Lipovitellins (LV) Isolated by Column Chromatography

Chromatographic column	Lipid content (%)		Protein P (%)	
	α-LV	β-LV	α-LV	β-LV
Hydroxyapatite (HA)	20	20	1.20	0.45
Dowex 1, then HA	22	22	0.50	0.27
TEAE cellulose	14.6	16.5	0.54	0.28

B. Proteins and Lipoproteins in Plasma

Plasma is composed of a globular protein fraction, called livetin, and a low-density lipoprotein fraction. The livetin and lipoprotein fractions represent about 11 and 66%, respectively, of the total yolk solids.

1. LIVETIN

Three components (α-, β-, and γ-livetins) can be separated by moving-boundary and paper electrophoresis, but with disk gel electrophoresis 16 protein bands can be obtained from the livetin fraction [30]. The chemical composition and molecular weights of α-, β-, and γ-livetins are presented in Table 15-7. Livetins are presumably derived from the blood of the hen. Williams [42] identified α-livetin as serum albumin, β-livetin as α_S-glycoprotein, and γ-livetin as γ-globulin.

TABLE 15-7

Composition of Livetins

	α-Livetin	β-Livetin	γ-Livetin
Nitrogen (%)	14.3	14.3	15.6
Hexose (%)	-	7	2.6
Hexosamine (%)	-	-	1.8
Molecular weight	80,000	45,000	150,000

2. LOW-DENSITY LIPOPROTEIN

The low-density lipoprotein (LDL) fraction of egg yolk has a density of 0.98 and can be isolated by flotation procedures. The purified LDL fraction contains between 84 and 89% lipid, which is made up of 74% neutral lipid and 26% phospholipid consisting of 71-76% phosphatidyl choline, 16-20% phosphatidyl ethanolamine, and 8-9% sphingomyelin and lysophospholipid [27].

With differential flotation techniques, two components, LDL_1 and LDL_2, have been separated from the LDL fraction. The composition of these fractions is presented in Table 15-8. The average molecular weights of LDL_1 and LDL_2 have been estimated to be 10 and 3 million, respectively [26]. Cook and Martin [14] have postulated that a low-density lipoprotein is a sphere with a triglyceride core upon which phospholipids and proteins are layered.

VII. EFFECTS OF STORAGE AND PROCESSING ON PROPERTIES OF EGGS AND EGG PRODUCTS

A. Storage of Eggs

During the storage of shell eggs, the pH of albumen increases at a temperature-dependent rate from about 7.6 to a maximum value of about 9.7 [38]. In one study,

TABLE 15-8

Composition of Low-density Lipoproteins

	LDL_1	LDL_2
Total lipid (%)	89	86
Lipid phosphorus	1.0	1.14
Lipid molar N/P ratio	1.04	1.14
Cholesterol, percent of lipid	3.3	3.4
Free fatty acid, percent of lipid	5	4.5
Phospholipid composition (%)		
Phosphatidyl choline	84	83
Phosphatidyl ethanolamine	13	14
Nonlipid residue (%)	11	14
Nitrogen, percent of nonlipid residue	14.8	13.7
Phosphorus, percent of nonlipid residue	0.15	0.16

the pH of albumen in eggs rose to 9.2 during a 3-day storage period at 3°C. The rise in pH is caused by a loss of carbon dioxide through pores in the shell. The pH is dependent on the equilibria among dissolved CO_2, HCO_3^-, CO_3^{2-}, and proteins. The concentrations of HCO_3^- and CO_3^{2-} ions are governed by the partial pressure of CO_2 in the external environment. The rise in pH of albumen causes a breakdown in the gel structure of the thick white.

Fresh yolk has a pH of about 6 and this changes very little, even over a prolonged storage period. In one study involving storage temperatures of 2°C and 37°C, the yolk pH rose to 6.4 in about 50 and 18 days, respectively [38].

B. Pasteurization of Egg Products

Liquid egg products are pasteurized by heat to inactivate Salmonella, the pathogenic organism which is sometimes present as a result of contamination. Kline et al. [23] showed that pasteurization of albumen in a commercial heat exchanger (for 2-3 min) at about 53°C caused an increase in whipping time but caused little destruction of Salmonella and did not influence angel cake volume significantly. As the temperature is increased above 53°C, damage to the foaming capability of albumen increases. When albumen is heated for 2 min at 58°C or flash heated to 60°C, albumen turbidity and viscosity increase and angel cake volume decreases. Whole egg and yolk, in contrast, can be pasteurized at temperatures between 60° and 63°C without significant changes in physical and functional properties.

Conalbumin is a heat-sensitive protein which is insolubilized rapidly at temperatures of 58°C and above when the albumen pH is in the region of 6-7 [16]. Ovalbumin, ovomucoid, lysozyme, and ovomucin, however, are heat stable in the vicinity of pH 7. Azari and Feeney [1] showed that the iron-conalbumin complex was much more heat stable than metal-free conalbumin. Cunningham and Lineweaver [16] carried out detailed studies on the influence of polyvalent cations on the heat stability of conalbumin in albumen at pH 7 and 60°C. The Fe^{3+}, Cu^{2+}, and Al^{3+} ions were very effective stabilizers at pH 7 but not at pH 9. When albumen (pH 7) containing 10^{-3} moles of aluminum ions was heated for 13 min at 60°C, the volume and texture of angel cakes prepared from the heated albumen were comparable to those in cakes prepared from unheated albumen but the whipping time was increased. This increase in whipping time was attributed to heat denaturation of the ovomucin-lysozyme complex [19]. Apparently, weak lamella are formed from heat-damaged ovomucin-lysozyme and these are easily broken by mechanical action of the whipping beaters.

Chang et al. [11] reported that 2% sodium hexametaphosphate (SHMP) was effective in inhibiting thermal coagulation of conalbumin in albumen at pH values between 7 and 9, with greatest stabilization occurring at about pH 7. The foam performance of the SHMP-treated albumen heated for 3 min at 61.7°C was damaged only slightly.

C. Freezing of Yolk

When yolk is frozen and stored below -6°C, the viscosity of the thawed product is much higher than that of native yolk [29]. This irreversible change in fluidity has been termed "gelation." The functional properties of yolk are altered during the gelation process. Jorden et al. [22] found that the volume of sponge cakes made with gelled yolk was considerably lower than that of cakes prepared with unfrozen yolks.

The rate and extent of yolk gelation is influenced by rate of freezing, temperature and duration of frozen storage, and rate of thawing. Rapid freezing of yolk in liquid nitrogen prevents significant gelation provided the frozen product is thawed rapidly [25]. As the temperature of frozen storage is lowered below -6°C, the rate of gelation increases until -50°C is reached.

Gelation of yolk can be minimized by prefreezing treatments, such as addition of cryoprotective agents or proteolytic enzymes, or by colloid milling. Sugars, such as sucrose, glucose, and galactose, at the 10% level are effective cryoprotective (antigelling) agents which do not significantly alter the viscosity of the unfrozen yolk. However, NaCl at an 8% level also prevents gelation during freezing, although it increases the viscosity of unfrozen yolk. Treatment of native yolk with proteolytic enzymes, such as trypsin and papain, is an additional approach to preventing gelation during the freezing process. Unfortunately, enzyme-treated yolk has a low emulsifying action compared to untreated yolk, thus preventing commercial use of this method. Colloid milling inhibits but does not prevent yolk gelation.

The mechanism of yolk gelation has been explored by several investigators but complete details are still lacking [10,29]. The basic requisites for initiating yolk gelation are the formation of ice crystals and the lowering of the storage temperature below -6°C (the freezing point of yolk is about 0.58°C). The ice content of frozen yolk at -6°C is about 81% of the initial water content. The fivefold increase in the concentration of soluble salts that occurs in yolk during freezing to -6°C may be responsible in part for gelation. Freezing also reduces the average distance between reactants, such as lipoproteins, in the unfrozen phase, and this enhances aggregation. Constituents in both plasma and granules are involved in gelation, for Chang [10] has shown that the gelation rate for plasma is much slower than that for yolk at temperatures of -10° and -15°C.

Studies indicate that low-density lipoproteins aggregate during frozen storage at temperatures below -6°C [29]. According to Chang [10], the optical density (700 nm) of thawed plasma and yolk solutions (samples diluted with 10% NaCl) increased gradually with frozen storage time at either -10° or -14°C. Furthermore, the electrophoretic mobility of low-density lipoproteins decreased when plasma and yolk were stored at -10° or -14°C.

Electron micrographs of frozen-thawed yolk have shown that granules are disrupted and low-density lipoproteins are released. The large lipid masses, which are apparent in micrographs of frozen yolk, probably form by coalescence of low-density lipoproteins.

The gelled nature of thawed yolk may be attributable to water entrapment within aggregates of lipoproteins.

D. Spray-dried Egg Products

During spray drying and subsequent storage of dry whole egg, yolk, and albumen, the following types of chemical and physical changes can occur: a decrease in solubility or dispersibility, undesirable changes in color, a decrease in whipping power, and development of off odors.

Unstored, spray-dried whole egg has a high solubility (95-98% dispersible in 10% KCl) but has about half the foaming power of fresh whole egg in the making of sponge cake [6]. The loss of foaming power was attributed by Brooks and Hawthorne [5] to liberation of free fat. Microscopic studies have shown that large fat droplets are present in whole egg powder, whereas none have been noted in native whole egg. After spray-dried whole egg is stored for only 3 hr, the foaming capability of the reconstituted product is almost completely lost [23]. During storage of spray-dried whole egg for 3-4 months at about 27°C, common changes are development of a brown color and an off flavor and a decrease in dispersibility. The Maillard reaction involving the amino group of cephalin (phosphatidyl ethanolamine) and glucose has been found to be involved in deteriorative changes. Hawthorne and Brooks [21] studied whole eggs and found that removal of naturally occurring glucose by yeast fermentation prior to drying retarded both discoloration and loss of dispersibility. Off-flavor development in stored whole egg powder has been attributed to oxidation of fatty acids in phospholipids.

The addition of sucrose and corn syrup solids to whole yolk before spray drying will retard the Maillard reaction in the dried product during storage and will minimize the loss of foaming power brought about by drying. Flavor stability is improved gradually as the level of sugar solids is increased to 5% for sucrose and 10% for corn syrup solids. At higher levels of sugars (10-15%), the rate of autoxidation of egg lipids increases and an off flavor develops gradually.

When egg yolk is spray dried, the foaming ability of the rehydrated product is lower than that of the native yolk [37]. Further, yolk stored at 13°C develops an off flavor in about 4 months. Schultz et al. [37] presented evidence to support the concept that drying of yolk causes irreversible changes in the structure of low-density lipoproteins which results in foam-inhibiting free lipids. As the concentration of added sucrose is raised to the 15% level, the foaming ability of reconstituted spray-dried yolk increases. Ultracentrifugal studies by Schultz et al. [37] showed that low-density lipoproteins were protected by sucrose during drying.

Functional properties of albumen are not altered appreciably during the spray-drying process [7]. However, during storage of the dried product, brown discoloration develops, albumen solubility decreases, and its ability to produce angel cakes of acceptable volume declines [9]. A decrease of 26% in volume of angel cake was observed when dried albumen was stored for 2 weeks at 104°F. When glucose is removed prior to drying, none of the abovementioned changes occurs during normal storage.

REFERENCES

1. P. R. Azari and R. E. Feeney, J. Biol. Chem., 232, 293 (1958).
2. C. M. A. Baker, in Egg Quality, A Study of the Hen's Egg (T. C. Carter, ed.), Oliver and Boyd, Edinburgh, Scotland, 1968.
3. R. Bellairs, J. Biophys. Biochem. Cytol., 11, 207 (1961).
4. J. Brooks and H. P. Hale, Nature (London), 175, 848 (1955).
5. J. Brooks and J. R. Hawthorne, J. Soc. Chem. Ind., 63, 310 (1944).
6. J. Brooks and D. J. Taylor, Spec. Rept. Food Invest. Bd., DSIR, No. 60g, 1955.

7. S. L. Brown and M. E. Zabik, Food Technol., 21, 87 (1967).
8. K. W. Burley and W. H. Cook, Can. J. Biochem. Physiol., 39, 1295 (1961).
9. A. F. Carlin and J. C. Ayres, Food Technol., 5, 172 (1951).
10. C. M. Chang, Ph.D. Thesis, University of Wisconsin, Madison, 1969.
11. P. K. Chang, W. D. Powrie, and O. Fennema, J. Food Sci., 35, 774 (1970).
12. W. H. Cook, in Egg Quality, A Study of the Hen's Egg (T. C. Carter, ed.), Oliver and Boyd, Edinburgh, Scotland, 1968, pp. 91-109.
13. F. Cook and G. M. Briggs, in Egg Science and Technology (W. J. Stadelman and O. J. Cotterill, eds.), AVI Publ., Westport, Conn., 1973.
14. W. H. Cook and W. G. Martin, Can. J. Biochem. Physiol., 40, 1273 (1962).
15. O. J. Cotterill and A. R. Winter, Poultry Sci., 34, 679 (1955).
16. F. E. Cunningham and H. Lineweaver, Food Technol., 19, 1442 (1965).
17. R. E. Feeney, in Proteins and Their Reactions (H. W. Schultz and A. F. Anglemier, eds.), AVI Publ., Westport, Conn., 1964.
18. R. H. Forsythe and J. F. Foster, Arch. Biochem., 20, 161 (1949).
19. J. A. Garibaldi, J. W. Donovan, J. G. Davis, and S. L. Comino, J. Food Sci., 33, 514 (1968).
20. O. Greengard, A. Sentenac, and N. Mendelsohn, Biochim. Biophys. Acta,

21. J. R. Hawthorne and J. Brooks, J. Soc. Chem. Ind., 63, 232 (1944).
22. R. Jordan, B. N. Luginbill, L. E. Dawson, and C. J. Echterling, Food Res., 17, 177 (1952).
23. L. Kline, T. F. Sugihara, M. L. Bean, and K. Ijichi, Food Technol., 19, 105 (1965).
24. H. Lineweaver, F. E. Cunningham, J. A. Garibaldi, and K. Ijichi, ARS 74-39, U.S. Department of Agriculture, Washington, D.C., 1967.
25. A. Lopez, C. R. Fellers, and W. D. Powrie, J. Milk Food Technol., 17, 334 (1954).
26. W. G. Martin, J. Augustyniak, and W. H. Cook, Biochim. Biophys. Acta, 84, 714 (1964).
27. W. G. Martin, W. G. Tattrie, and W. H. Cook, Can. J. Biochem. Physiol., 41, 657 (1963).
28. T. L. Parkinson, J. Sci. Food Agri., 17, 101 (1966).
29. W. D. Powrie, in Low Temperature Biology of Foodstuffs (J. Hawthorn and E. J. Rolfe, eds.), Pergamon Press, Oxford, 1968, pp. 319-331.
30. W. D. Powrie, in Egg Science and Technology (W. J. Stadelman and O. J. Cotterill, eds.), AVI Publ., Westport, Conn., 1973, pp. 61-90.
31. O. S. Privett, M. L. Bland, and J. A. Schmidt, J. Food Sci., 27, 463 (1962).
32. M. W. Radmonski and W. H. Cook, Can. J. Biochem., 42, 395 (1964).
33. M. W. Radmonski and W. H. Cook, Can. J. Biochem., 42, 1203 (1964).
34. D. N. Rhodes and C. H. Lea, Biochem. J., 54, 526 (1957).
35. A. L. Romanoff and A. Romanoff, The Avian Egg. Wiley, New York, 1949.
36. A. Saari, W. D. Powrie, and O. Fennema, J. Food Sci., 29, 307 (1964).
37. J. R. Schultz, H. E. Snyder, and R. H. Forsythe, J. Food Sci., 33, 507 (1968).
38. P. F. Sharp and C. K. Powell, Ind. Eng. Chem., 23, 196 (1931).
39. F. S. Shenstone, in Egg Quality, A Study of the Hen's Egg (T. C. Carter, ed.), Oliver and Boyd, Edinburgh, Scotland, 1968.

40. K. Simkiss, in Egg Quality, A Study of the Hen's Egg (T. C. Carter, ed.), Oliver and Boyd, Edinburgh, Scotland, 1968.

41. G. Taborsky, Biochemistry, 2, 266 (1963).

42. J. Williams, Biochem. J., 83, 346 (1962).

Chapter 16

CHARACTERISTICS OF EDIBLE PLANT TISSUES

Norman F. Haard

Department of Food Science
Rutgers The State University
New Brunswick, New Jersey

Contents

I. INTRODUCTION

Plant tissues supply all of man's food, either directly or indirectly through animals.
The number of crops which fit into man's dietary picture is probably between 1,000
and 2,000 species. Some 100-200 species are of major importance in world trade
and 15 species provide the bulk of world food crops: rice, wheat, sorghum, and
barley; sugarcane and sugar beets; potato, sweet potato, and cassava; bean, soybean, and peanut; coconut and banana [56]. Many of these crops are associated
with legends and songs which illustrate their fascinating roles in the history of different cultures. It has been said that crop production, the management of useful
plants, is the basis of civilization.

The economic plant groupings which enter man's food chain include the Gramin-
eae (cereals), Leguminosae (legumes), root crops, stem and leaf crops, fruit and
seed "vegetables," and a wide array of plants which are used for extractives and
derivatives (e.g., spices, beverages, oils). Many volumes have been written to
describe the characteristics of these plant tissues, and it is beyond the scope of
this chapter to provide details on a single commodity, no less all of these crops.
The intent of this section is to outline the compositional and physiological similarities and diversities of harvested plant tissues and to point out how these properties
appear to relate to changes in quality during storage and processing. The future
course of this area promises to be soul stirring to the food scientist and all important to mankind.

II. CHEMICAL COMPOSITION

The chemical compositions of specific tissues are related to their food quality indices and their stabilities. Detached plant parts, like all living organisms, contain
a very wide range of different chemical compounds and show considerable variation
in composition. Apart from the obvious interspecies differences, an individual
fruit, vegetable, or cereal grain, being largely composed of living tissues which
are metabolically active, is constantly changing in composition. The rate and extent of such changes can depend on the growing conditions prior to harvest, the
stage of maturity of the harvested tissue, the physiological role of the organ or
leaf, the genetic pool of the specific cells, and the environment in which the harvested commodity is contained. This innate variability of botanical structures must
always be kept in mind when the details of chemical composition are considered.

A. Water

The predominent chemical substance of most plant tissues is water, which generally represents about 70-90% of the fresh weight but may comprise more than 90%
of the fresh weights of tomato, celery, pumpkin, lettuce, etc. Other commodities,
such as cereals (e.g., wheat, barley, rice), pulses (e.g., soybeans, peanuts,
beans), and nuts, contain less than 10-20% water.

In the intact growing plant, the amount of water in the tissue depends on the
amount of water absorbed through the roots and the amount lost by transpiration.
Given an unlimited supply of available moisture, the water content of viable tissue

assumes a characteristic maximum value which is associated with a state of complete turgor of the component cells. At turgor, the internal pressure (up to nine or more atmospheres) developed in the vascular system of the cell by osmotic forces is balanced by the inward pressure of the fully extended cell wall. The maximum water content of a given tissue may vary considerably because of fine structural differences and may be markedly affected by cultural conditions which influence structural differentiation.

Water is not always present in sufficient quantity to maintain full tissue turgor. An inadequate supply of water may lead to wilting of leafy commodities since they are the normal sites for transpiration. The susceptibility of a commodity to water loss is related to the water vapor deficit of the surrounding atmosphere and to the extent to which its external surface is structurally modified to reduce water loss. Apart from the effect of water vapor deficit on wilting and weight loss, one must' recognize that water loss may evoke pronounced physiological changes in certain plant tissues (discussed in Section IV.A.5). The interaction of water with other molecular constituents and its role in cellular metabolism are discussed in Chapters 2 and 16.

B. Carbohydrates

Most of the solid matter of fruits, vegetables, pulses, nuts, and cereals is carbohydrate. The total carbohydrate content can be as low as 2% of the fresh weight in some curcurbitatious fruits or in nuts; over 30% in starchy vegetables, and over 60% in some pulses and cereals. In general, approximately 75% of the dry weight of plant material is made up of carbohydrates. Total carbohydrates are generally regarded as consisting of simple sugars, polysaccharides (such as starch, cellulose, and hemicelluloses), and pectic substances, although substances in this last group are not strictly carbohydrates.

1. CELL-WALL CONSTITUENTS

The principal cell-wall constituents are cellulose, hemicelluloses, and pectins (Table 16-1). Other non-carbohydrate materials, such as peptides, proteins, and lignin, are associated with carbohydrates [63]. Chemically, cellulose is a glucose polymer in which individual glucose units are condensed by β-1,4 linkages (β-1,4-glucan). Cellulose often contains paracrystalline regions in which the molecules are arranged in fibrils, parallel groups of which form bundles (see Chapter 3). It is largely insoluble and indigestible to human beings and, accordingly, it provides the bulk of "unavailable carbohydrate" in human food. The nutritional value of otherwise good protein sources, such as coconut meal, is severely reduced because of interference from these indigestable constituents.

The hemicelluloses are a heterogeneous group of polysaccharides which may contain numerous kinds of hexose and pentose monosaccharide units and, in some instances, residues of glucuronic acid. These ill-defined polymers can be classified according to the types of sugar residues predominating and they are often referred to as xylans, arabinogalactans, glucomannans, etc.

TABLE 16-1

Principal Cell-wall Constituents

Common name	Chemical nature	Linkages and crosslinkages with carbohydrates
Cellulose	$\beta(1\rightarrow4)$-linked glucose	Polymer of up to 12,000 glucose units; shows crystalline regions in which the molecules are arranged in fibrils, parallel groups of which form bundles: interactions with other wall constituents are likely
Hemicellulose xylans	$\beta(1\rightarrow4)$-linked xylose	Polymer of 150-200 units, mostly xylose; with uronic acid residues, one of which is generally acetylated; may contain side chain $\beta(1\rightarrow3)$ links with arabinose
Glucomannans	$\beta(1\rightarrow4)$ randomly linked glucose and mannose	Strongly adsorbed to cellulose microfibrils; may contain $\alpha(1\rightarrow6)$ linkages with galactose
Arabinogalactans	$\beta(1\rightarrow3)$-linked galactose	Arabinose units linked $\beta(1\rightarrow3)$ or $\beta(1\rightarrow6)$ to galactose; also occurs as a constituent of pectic substances
Pectin substances	$\alpha(1\rightarrow4)$-linked galacturonic acid	Contain $\alpha(1\rightarrow6)$-linked rhamnose and lesser quantities of fucose, xylose, and galactose linked $\beta(1\rightarrow4)$ to main and side chains; variable numbers of uronide carboxylate groups are esterified as methyl esters; regarded as filler substances within cell-wall matrix and they influence water distribution
Lignin	Insoluble, high molecular weight polymer of coumaryl, coniferyl, and sinapyl alcohols	Contains 100 or more aromatic units which are high in methoxyl groups; penetrates wall, producing secondary thickening, and acts as a hydrophobic filler; forms covalent links with wall carbohydrates
Cell-wall protein extension	Hydroxyproline-rich protein	Various o-glycosidic, N-glycosidic, ester, and Schiff base links with polysaccharides; hydroxyquinone chelate bridges with lignin

The pectic substances are an equally ill-defined group of cell-wall and intracellular polymers. Pectin is generally regarded as α-1,4-linked galacturonic acid residues which are esterified to varying degrees with methanol. However, purified pectin invariably contains significant quantities of covalently linked nonuronide sugars, such as rhamnose, arabinose, and xylose [5]. The pectins have been extensively studied because of their role in fruit softening [61] and because of their commercial use as a gelation agents [122]. The albedo (whitish spongy layer) of the peel of citrus fruits is an especially rich source of pectin, containing up to 50% pectin on a dry weight basis. Some other waste vegetable tissues are also excellent sources of pectin.

The relative proportions of cellulose, hemicellulose, and pectin vary greatly from tissue to tissue, from species to species, and with maturity of the plant. The bran layers of wheat and other cereals and the vascular tissue of certain commodities, such as asparagus and celery, contain an abundance of these substances [108]. In some soft vegetable tissues, these constituents represent up to 50% of the dry matter of the cell wall. Cellulose is invariably present in plants in excess of about 25% (dry weight basis), whereas the content of hemicelluloses and pectins may be less than 5%.

Since we are discussing cell-wall constituents, it is appropriate to mention a noncarbohydrate, lignin, which is always associated with cell walls. Lignin is a three-dimensional polymer comprised of phenyl propane units, such as syringaldehyde and vanillin, which are linked together in various ways through aliphatic three-carbon side chains. Lignification of cell walls, notably those of xylem and sclerenchymatous tissues, confers considerable rigidity and toughness to the wall [54]. As we shall see, changes of cell-wall constituents are closely related to textural changes in stored and processed commodities.

2. STARCH AND OTHER POLYSACCHARIDES

The principal carbohydrate of plant tissues which is not associated with cell walls is starch, a linear (α-1,4) or branched (α-1,4; 1,6) polymer of D-glucose units (see Chapter 3). Amylose and amylopectin vary in characteristic proportion and size in different species and varieties. Starch is housed in intracellular plastids or granules which have characteristic sizes and shapes. Industrially, starch is obtained either from root plants, such as potatoes, or from cereals, which may contain up to 40% starch on a fresh weight basis [93]. Starch metabolism plays an important role in the changes which occur in many fruits and vegetables during storage and processing. Although starch contributes more calories to the normal human diet than any other single substance, it is absent or negligible in such crops as most ripe fruits, many vegetables, and soybeans.

Polysaccharides other than starch also occur in intracellular regions, but these substances are not common to all plant cells and they are usually present in small amounts. Examples are α-D-1,4-linked glycopyranose of sweet corn; β-glucans of mango fruits, oats, etc.; and fructans, which contain D-fructose as the main unit linked glycosidically 2,1 and 2,6 [55]. Gums and mucilages also are found in plants, but it seems that mechanical injury or microbial infection triggers their formation. These carbohydrates are chemically similar to the hemicelluloses and some, such as carageenan, gum arabic, locust bean gum, and gum tragacanth, are widely used as food additives because they form aqueous colloidal suspensions of high viscosity (see Chapter 3). Similar mucilagenous substances are believed to provide rye dough with its unusual mixing properties.

3. SIMPLE SUGARS

The relative proportions of sucrose and reducing sugars (glucose and fructose) vary with the tissue and with maturity [65]. The sugar contents of fruits and vegetables vary from negligible (e.g., avacado, spinach) to over 20% (fresh weight basis; FWB) in ripe bananas. In general, fruits and vegetables contain more reducing sugars than sucrose but in certain vegetables, e.g., parsnip, carrot, beetroot, onion, sweet corn, and peas, and in some ripe fruits, such as banana, pineapple, peach, and melon, the reverse is true. Sugarcane and sugar beets are, of course, important economic crops because of their high sucrose contents. Other sugars, such as xylose, mannose, arabinose, galactose, maltose, sorbose, octulose, and cellobiose, also may be present in plant tissues, and in specific instances they may constitute a major portion of the total sugars (Table 16-2). The sugar alcohol, sorbitol, has been identified in a number of fruits, including apple, pear, cherry, and plum.

TABLE 16-2

Some Monosaccharide Sugars Found in Plant Tissues[a]

Sugar	Occurrence
Triose	
D-Glyceraldehyde	D-Glyceraldehyde 3-phosphate is an intermediary metabolite
Dihydroxyacetone	Dihydroxyacetone phosphate is an intermediary metabolite
Tetrose	
D-Erythrose	D-Erythrose 4-phosphate is an intermediary metabolite
Aldopentoses	
D-Ribose	Ribose 5'-phosphate is an intermediary metabolite; found in furanose form as component of ribonucluc acid, coenzymes, flavor-enhancing nucleotides
D-Xylose	Widely distributed as a constituent of xylan
L-Arabinose	Occurs as free sugar and in cell-wall polysaccharides and gums
Ketopentoses D-ribulose	D-Ribulose 5-phosphate is an intermediary metabolite
D-xylulose	D-Xylulose 5-phosphate is an intermediary metabolite

TABLE 16-2 (Continued)

Sugar	Occurrence
Aldohexoses	
D-Glucose	Most widely distributed monosaccharide; found free, as phosphate esters, as components of polysaccharides, and in glucosides
D-Galactose	Found free in some berries; frequently found in polysaccharides and glycosides
L-Galactose	Occurs in certain gums and agar
D-Mannose	Occurs widely in gums and mannans
Ketohexose	
D-Fructose	The only ketohexose commonly found in plants; notable free and in the disaccharide (sucrose) form in fruit; phosphate esters are important metabolites
Heptuloses	
D-Sedoheptulose	Occurs free in various succulent tissues; phosphate esters are metabolites
D-Mannoheptulose	Occurs free in avocado
Sugar alcohols	
Glycerol	Important as building block of glyceride lipids
Sorbitol	Occurs free in many fruits and leaves
Myoinositol	Occurs widely in plants both free and in phytic acid (notably cereals); a vitamin for many animals
Sugar acids	
Glyoxylic acid	Important in organic acid metabolism
Glucuronic acid	Widely distributed as glycoside of phenols, alcohols
L-Ascorbic acid	Occurs widely in free form; an essential vitamin for man and other animals

[a]From Ref. [98].

C. Proteins and Other N Compounds

Proteins, although commonly representing less than 1% (FWB) of plant tissues, always play important roles as structural constituents of cellular membranes and as biocatalysts. The significance of fruits and vegetables as dietary sources of protein is generally small compared with that of cereals and pulses. Starchy vegetables contain between 0.5 and 2.0% (FWB). In many developing countries the contribution of starchy vegetables to the total dietary protein is quite high. Nonstarchy vegetables are generally richer in protein than are fruits, but the level in most cases is below 3% (FWB). The protein content of fruits seldom rise above 1.5% (FWB), and most of this amount is accounted for by enzymes and membrane systems. Despite its relatively low protein content of 1.1-2.9% (FWB), the banana undoubtedly is a principal protein source in some tropical areas. Legumes and cereals, with between 2.9 and 8.2% protein (FWB), contain considerable amounts of storage protein. Soybeans sometimes contain over 40% protein on a dry weight basis.

Most information available on protein contents of plant tissues is inaccurate because it is normally obtained by multiplying the nitrogen content by the factor 6.25. The inaccuracy arises because appreciable amounts of nonprotein nitrogen often exist in plant tissues [16]. Approximately two-thirds of potato tuber nitrogen is in the form of free amino acids and up to 70% of the nitrogen in certain varieties of apple is nonprotein. Besides amino acids, plant tissues may contain appreciable quantities of amines, such as asparagine and glutamine, as well as other nitrogenous compounds, notably, purines, pyrimidines, nucleosides, nucleotides, betaines, alkaloids, porphyrins, and nonproteinogenic amino acids (e.g., β-alanine, γ-amino butyric acid) (Table 16-3). Certain plant tissues, e.g., citrus fruits, tomato, strawberry, gooseberry, and blackberry, may contain more than half of their nonprotein nitrogen as amines of aspartic (asparagine) and glutamic (glutamine) acids. In addition, amines having pharmacological properties, e.g., serotonin, tyramine, dopamine, and epinephrine, are also present in some fruit and vegetable tissues [110].

TABLE 16-3

Non-protein Nitrogenous Compounds Found in Plant Tissues

Substance	Structure	Occurrence
γ-Amino butyric acid	$CH_2-CH_2-CH-COOH$ $\qquad\qquad\qquad NH_2$	Grapefruit, lemon, grape, raspberry, avacado, potato
Choline	CH_3 $CH_3-\overset{+}{N}-CH_2CH_2OH$ CH_3	Grapefruit, grape, potato, eggplant; universally distributed as part of lecithin
Glutathione	$\qquad\qquad\qquad SH$ $\qquad\qquad\qquad CH_2$ H $HOOC-C-CH_2-CH_2-C-NH-C-C-N-CH_2-COOH$ $NH_2\qquad\quad O\qquad H\ O\ H$	Citrus fruit, grape, potato
Pipecolic acid		Apple, cherry, peach, grape, raspberry, avacado

TABLE 16-3 (Continued)

Substance	Structure	Occurrence
Asparagine	$\overset{NH_2}{\underset{\overset{\|}{O}}{C}}-CH_2-\overset{H}{\underset{NH_2}{C}}-COOH$	Widely distributed
Solanidine		Potato, toxic alkaloid
Dopamine		Banana fruit
Ornithine	$NH_2-CH_2-CH_2-CH_2-\overset{NH_2}{CH}-COOH$	Cherry, plum, lime, grape, avacado, mango, papaya, rhubarb
S-Methyl L-cysteine sulfoxide	$CH_3-\overset{O}{S}-CH_2-\overset{NH_2}{CH}-COOH$	Onion, cabbage, turnip
Taurine	$NH_2-CH_2-CH_2SO_3H$	Peach, papaya, fig, potato

The compositions, heterogeneities, molecular weights, nutritional qualities, and functional properties of plant storage proteins are discussed in Chapter 5.

D. Lipids and Related Compounds

In plant tissues, lipids, like proteins, may be largely confined to the cytoplasmic membranes or they also may be present as reserve material (Table 16-4). The content of lipid materials in fruits and vegetables is generally between 0.1 and 1% (FWB). Avacado and olive are unusual in having lipid contents of about 20% (FWB). Most of the reserve lipid in whole grain cereals is located in the germ, which con-

TABLE 16-4

Lipid Contents of Some Fruits[a]

Source	Lipid content (% DWB)
Oil-palm trees	74–81
Avacado	35–70
Olive	30–70
Laurel	24–55
Grape	0.2
Banana	0.1
Apple	0.06

[a]From Ref. [11].

TABLE 16-5

Principal Fatty Acids of Reserve Triglycerides[a]

Source	Fatty acids (kind and percent of total fatty acid content of triglycerides in each source)							
	Lauric	Myristic	Palmitic	Stearic	Oleic	Linoleic	Linolenic	Arachidonic
Coconut	45	20	5	3	6	–	–	–
Palm kernel	55	12	6	4	10	–	–	–
Olive	–	–	15	–	75	10	–	–
Peanut	–	–	9	6	51	26	–	–
Cotton-seed	–	–	23	–	32	45	–	–
Corn	–	–	6	2	44	48	–	–
Soybean	–	–	11	2	20	64	3	–
Sunflower	–	–	6	4	31	57	–	–
Wheat	–	3	18	7	16	51	4	2
Rye	–	6	11	4	18	35	7	2

[a]Adapted from Borgstrom [11]. The spectrum of fatty acids in a vegetable oil will influence its functional properties (e.g., solidification temperature, tendency to oxidize, smoke point, flash point, flavor, nutritive value).

TABLE 16-6

Phospholipid Composition of Apple Tissue[a]

| Lipids | Pulp | | | Peel |
	Whole	Mitochondria	Microsomes	
All lipids	(% of total lipids in each source)			
Neutral lipids	24	10	+	85
Glycolipids	Trace	Trace	Trace	5.5
Phospholipids	75	90	+	9.5
Phospholipids	(% of total phospholipids in each source)			
Lyso compounds	1	–	0.3	–
Phosphatidyl inositol	1.6	5	14.7	18.2
Phosphatidyl choline	32.6	45	39.5	33.8
Phosphatidyl glycerol	Trace	7	7.6	9.5
Phosphatidyl serine	6.9	3	12.2	Trace
Phosphatidyl ethanolamine	38.7	35	25.6	18.2
Diphosphatidyl glycerol	3.8	–	0.1	8.7
Phosphatidic acid	16.3	5	–	11.6

[a]Ben Abdelkader et al. [6]. The permeability and stress susceptability of biological membranes may be influenced by the nature and content of phospholipids.

tains up to 15% oil. Nuts are especially rich sources of fat: pecan, 73%; walnut,
64%; and peanut, 45%.

Storage lipids contain triglycerides of variable fatty acid compositions (Table
16-5). Fats obtained from fruit flesh or fruit coatings, such as olive oil and
Chinese vegetable tallow, generally contain large amounts of palmitic, oleic, and
linoleic acids. Coconut oil is an exception, since it contains a high percentage of
saturated fatty acids. In plant tissues that contain no storage fats, lipids are usually present in cellular membranes as phospholipids or glycolipids (Table 16-6).
Seeds, especially soybeans, contain up to 8% phospholipid, most of which is reserve material. Phospholipids are used commercially as emulsifiers. Other compound lipids found in some plant tissues are galactolipids, sulfolipids, and lipoproteins.

Lipid substances are particularly prominent in the protective surfaces of plant
organs. These include waxes (Table 16-7) and the cutin acids (Table 16-8, Fig.
16-1).

It is appropriate, at this point, to mention the groups of lipophillic substances
which contribute to the characteristic flavor of plant tissues. Although present in
trace quantities, they markedly influence flavor. In some instances these are dissolved in terpenoid hydrocarbons to form the so-called essential oils. These oils
may be present in special oil sacs, as in the skins of citrus fruits or the leaves of
peppermint. More commonly, however, these substances are more uniformly

TABLE 16-7

Chemical Compositions of Two Fruit Waxes[a]

Product and wax fractions	Percent of total waxes	Distribution of chain lengths in each fraction						
		C_{12}	C_{14}	C_{16}	C_{18}	C_{20}	C_{22}	C_{23}
Apple								
Paraffins	33							Trace
Alcohols	19					Trace	Trace	Trace
Diols	2.5					Trace	30	–
Saturated fatty acids	14.4	Trace	Trace	62.5	13.9	3	1	Trace
Unsaturated fatty acids	25			0.5	99.5			
Hydroxy acids	6	11.4	8.9	10	11	7.7	5	
Grape								
Paraffins	1.2	Trace	Trace	Trace	Trace	Trace	Trace	5.7
Alcohols, free	51.4					0.1	1.3	1.2
Alcohols, esterified	11.5					0.2	1.7	1.7
Aldehydes	15.4			0.2	0.8	1.7	0.4	0.6
Acids, free	9		0.4	4.6	9.5	12.2	7.8	1.4
Acids, esterified			0.4	5.3	18.1	31.7	18.0	1.5

[a]From Mazliak [77].

distributed in the tissue. The odoriferous substances in fruits are largely oxygenated compounds (esters, alcohols, acids, aldehydes, and ketones), many of which are derivatives of terpenoid hydrocarbons or lower aliphatic acids and alcohols. Some 100 or more of these compounds may contribute to the subtle flavor of aromatic tissues [82]. The quantity and balance of flavor compounds may be very critical to the specific sensory response which they evoke.

The range of volatile constituents present in vegetables and other plant tissues is generally more limited than that of fruits. Individual acids, alcohols, aldehydes, and ketones have been found in certain species but esters are generally lacking.

(% of total weight of fraction)											
C_{24}	C_{25}	C_{26}	C_{27}	C_{28}	C_{29}	C_{30}	C_{31}	C_{32}	C_{33}	C_{34}	C_{35}
Trace	Trace	Trace	2	Trace	96.5	Trace	Trace				
15.8	Trace	35	Trace	28.8	Trace	5.25					
40	–	20	–	10							
1	Trace	2	Trace	4.5	Trace	8					
3.5	17.2	3.8	19.5	2.6	22.1	2.4	14.8	1.1	1.9	–	0.4
14.2	5.7	42.6	5.3	21.3	4.4	3.3		Trace		Trace	
11.6	6.2	44.4	6.6	20.7	2.5	1.2		Trace			
12.4	2.8	41.7	2.5	21.8	1.1	7.5	0.5	2.8			
12.8	2.6	18.0	1.2	10.6	1.0	3.3	2.3	2.0			
9.8	1.4	3.9	0.7	2.3	0.7	1.2	0.3	1.2			

It should be noted that nonlipid substances also contribute to the flavor of plant tissues [102]. Members of the family Cruciferae (cabbage, brussel sprouts, cauliflower, turnip, radish, watercress, etc.) and species of Allium (onion, garlic, etc.) are rich in sulfur–containing compounds, such as glycosides of isothiocyanates and sulfides, and these compounds contribute significantly to flavor (Table 16-9 and Chapters 6 and 9). Bitter tastes may be caused by certain flavonoids (e.g., naringin of grapefruit, the curcurbitaciñs of curcurbitaceous fruits, and oleuropein of olive) and by terpenoids (e.g., limonin of citrus fruits) [39]. Other constituents, mainly sugars and organic acids, also contribute to the overall taste characteristics of plant tissues. Many of these flavor constituents (e.g., in curcurbita-

TABLE 16-8

Identified Cutin Acids in Apple Cuticle[a,b]

Acid	Percent of total cutin acids
Monobasic acid	
Tetradecanois	0.01
Palmitic	0.29
Oleic + linoleic	0.64
Stearic	0.06
Eicosanoic	0.06
Decosanoic	0.10
Methyl tetradecanoic	0.02
Dibasic acid	
Hexadecane-1,16-dioic	0.22
Heptadecadiene-1,17-dioic	
Heptadec-9-ene-1,17-dioic	0.09
Octadeca-9,12-diene-1,18-dioic	0.06
Octadec-9-ene-1,18-dioic	0.28
Octadecane-1,18-dioic	0.04
Monohydroxy monobasic acids	
16-Hydroxyhexadecanoic	8.0
18-Hydroxy-octadeca-9,12-dienoic	13.0
18-Hydroxy-octadec-9-enoic	5.0
Vic-dihydroxy dibasic acids	
8,9-Dihydroxyheptadecane-1,17-dioic	0.18
9,10-Dihydroxyoctadecane-1,18-dioic	0.06
Dihydroxy monobasic acids	
10,16-Dihydroxyhexadecanoic	24.0
Trihydroxy monobasic acids	
9,10,18-Trihydroxyocatadecenoic	3.0
Erythro-9,10,18-trihydroxyoctadecanoic	7.0
Threo-9,10,18-trihydroxyoctadecanoic	17.0

[a]Unidentified acids are not quoted.
[b]From Eglinton and Hunneman [26].

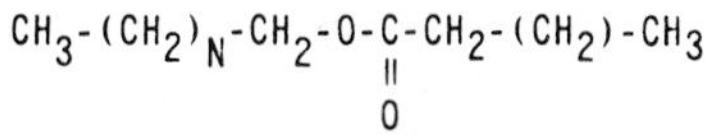

$$CH_3-(CH_2)_N-CH_2-O-\underset{\substack{\| \\ O}}{C}-CH_2-(CH_2)-CH_3$$

WAX ESTER

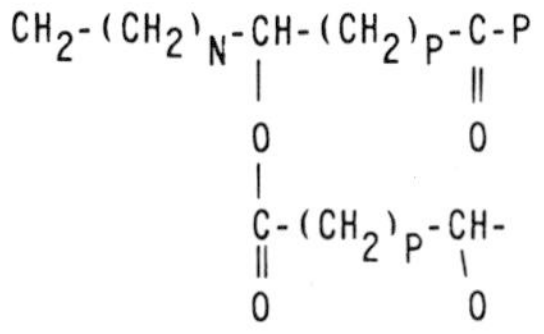

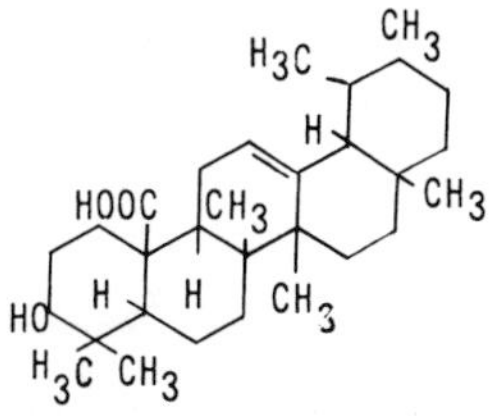

$$CH_2-(CH_2)_N-CH-(CH_2)_P-\underset{\substack{\| \\ O}}{C}-P$$
$$\underset{\substack{| \\ O}}{}$$
$$\underset{\substack{\| \\ O}}{C}-(CH_2)_P-CH-$$

CUTIN ESTOLIDE   URSOLIC ACID (TRITERPENOID)

FIG. 16-1. Examples of lipid substances which accumulate in the outer epidermal membranes of certain vegetative tissues. In its broad and common meaning, the term "natural waxes" refers not only to wax esters (combination of a fatty acid with a long-chain monoalcohol) but also to hydrocarbons (paraffins, olefins), fatty acids (normal, hydroxylated ethylenic), ketones, alcohols (primary, secondary), aldehydes, etc. All of these compounds have high molecular weights, properties of water repellance, melting points between 40° and 100°C, and paracrystallinity at ambient temperature.

TABLE 16-9

Examples of Nonlipid Flavor Constituents and Their Formation

Commodity	Enzyme	Substrate	Products
Crucifera (cabbage, mustard, horse-radish, water-cress)	Thioglucosidases (myrosinase, siningrinase)	Siningrin (black pepper)	Glucose, sulfate, allyisothiocynate
Alliums (onion, garlic)	L-Cystein sulfox-ide lyase	Alliins	Sulfenic acids, pyruvate, ammonia, thiosulf-inates (allicins); thiosulfonates
Tomato	α-Alanine amino-transferase	L-Alanine, 2-oxyoglutarate	Pyruvate, glutamate
Citrus	Geraniol oxido-reductases	Geraniol	Geranial, cit-ronellol, citronellal
Miscellaneous	5'-Phosphodies-terases	Ribonucleic acid	5'-Nucleotides

ceous fruits and <u>Alliums</u>) are not synthesized by the plant until the cells are disrupted and precursor molecules are made available for enzyme-catalyzed reactions
[103]. In this way we find that the environment of the mouth may influence flavor
biogenesis and hence taste perception in different individuals. It also should be
emphasized that cooking of plant tissues generally causes the formation of flavor
compounds not present in the raw material.

E. Organic Acids

A wide range of organic acids are present in plant tissues (Table 16-10). Many of
these acids are present in small quantities and are intermediaries in basic metabolism, notably in the tricarboxylic acid cycle, the glyoxylic acid route, and the
shikimic acid pathway. Other acids, so far not linked with any metabolic pathways
and not known to have any physiological significance, can accumulate in plant tissues in considerable quantity. Consequently, fruits and vegetables are normally
acid and sometimes sour in taste. The acid level ranges from very low (sweet
corn and leguminous seeds) up to about 50 m-equivs of acid per 100 g of certain
fruits (black currant and loganberry) and up to 40 m-equiv per 100 g of spinach.

1. ALIPHATIC PLANT ACIDS

The most widely occurring and abundant acids in edible plant tissues are citric and
malic, each of which can constitute up to 3% (FWB) of a given tissue. Citric acid
constitutes the major acid of citrus fruits, currants, raspberries, loganberries,
strawberries, cranberries, blueberries, pineapples, and pears; whereas malic
acid predominates in apples, most drupe fruits (plums, cherries, apricots, etc.),
curcurbitacous fruits, banana, and rhubarb. Vegetables containing citric as the
principal acid include potato, sweet potato, leguminous seeds, many leafy vegetables, tomato, and beetroot. In curcutbits, lettuce, artichoke, broccoli, cauliflower, okra, onion, celery, carrot, parsnip, turnip, and green beans, malic is
the main acid. Instances where neither malate nor citrate predominate include
grapes, which accumulate tartaric acid, spinach (oxalic), and blackberry (isocitric).

Organic acids are in constant metabolic flux in most vegetables and fruits. For
example, levels of citric and malic acids in many excised leaves are responsive to
light and exhibit diurnal cycles [127]. The overall acidities of many fruits decline
during ripening, although some specific acids actually increase. Organic acids are
generally localized in subcellular vacuoles and these vacuoles sometimes show a
characteristic distribution within the tissue (e.g., citramalic acid is confined to the
peel).

TABLE 16-10

Organic Acids Occurring in Plant Tissues[a]

Fruits	Acids
Apples	Malic, quinic, α-ketoglutaric, oxalacetic, citric, pyruvic, fumaric, lactic, and succinic acids
Apricots	Malic and citric acids
Avocados	Tartaric acid
Bananas	Malic, citric, tartaric, and traces of acetic and formic acids
Blackberries	Isocitric, malic, lactoisocitric, shikimic, quinic, and traces of citric and oxalic acids
Blueberries	Citric, malic, glyceric, citramalic, glycolic, succinic, glucuronic, galacturonic, shikimic, quinic, glutamic, and aspartic acids
Boysenberries	Citric, malic and isocitric acids
Cherries	Malic, citric, tartaric, succinic, quinic, shikimic, glyceric, and glycolic acids
Cranberries	Citric, malic and benzoic acids
Currants	Citric, tartaric, malic, and succinic acids
Elderberries	Citric, malic, shikimic, and quinic acids
Figs	Citric, malic, and acetic acids
Gooseberries	Citric, malic, shikimic, and quinic acids
Grapefruit	Citric, tartaric, malic, and oxalic acids
Grapes	Malic and tartaric (3:2), citric, and oxalic acids
Lemons	Citric, malic, tartaric, and oxalic acids (no isocitric acid)
Limes	Citric, malic, tartaric, and oxalic acids
Orange peel	Malic, citric, and oxalic acids
Oranges	Citric, malic, and oxalic acids
Peaches	Malic and citric acids
Pears	Malic, citric, tartaric, and oxalic acids
Pineapples	Citric and malic acids

TABLE 16-10 (Continued)

Fruits	Acids
Plums	Malic, tartaric, and oxalic acids
Quinces	Malic acid (no citric acid)
Strawberries	Citric, malic, shikimic, succinic, glyceric, glycolic, and aspartic acids
Youngberries	Citric, malic, and isocitric acids

Vegetables	Acid
Beans	Citric, malic, and small amounts of succinic and fumaric acids
Broccoli	Malic, citric (3:2), oxalic, and succinic acids
Carrots	Malic, citric, isocitric, succinic, and fumaric acids
Mushrooms	Lactarimic, cetostearic, fumaric, and allantoic acids
Peas	Malic acid
Potatoes	Malic, citric, oxalic, phosphoric, and pyroglutamic acids
Rhubarb	Malic, citric and oxalic acids
Tomatoes	Citric, malic, oxalic, succinic, glycolic, tartaric, phosphoric, hydrochloric, sulfuric, fumaric, pyrrolidonecarboxylic, and galacturonic acids

[a]Acids which occur in appreciable quantities are underscored. The relative amount of each acid varies widely with the variety, degree of ripeness, and seasonal influences. Complete identification of all the acids present in many of the products is obviously lacking in many instances. From Gardner [36].

2. CARBOCYCLIC PLANT ACIDS

Various aromatic acids are found in edible plant tissues [46], e.g., chlorogenic acid in potatoes and most pome fruits, benzoic acid in cranberries, caffeic acid in coffee beans, digitalin and protocatechuic acids in peas and gall nuts, and p-coumarylquinic acid in apples and pears (Fig. 16-2). The alicyclic acids, quinic and shikimic, are widely distributed in plant tissues. They are precursors of aromatic organic acids (especially chlorogenic) which are important because of their participation in enzymic browning of bruised or otherwise wounded fruits and vegetables and in aftercook blackening in potatoes.

F. Mineral Elements

The mineral level in plant tissues is usually expressed in terms of ash content. The ash content may vary from less than 0.1% (FWB) to as much as 4.4% in

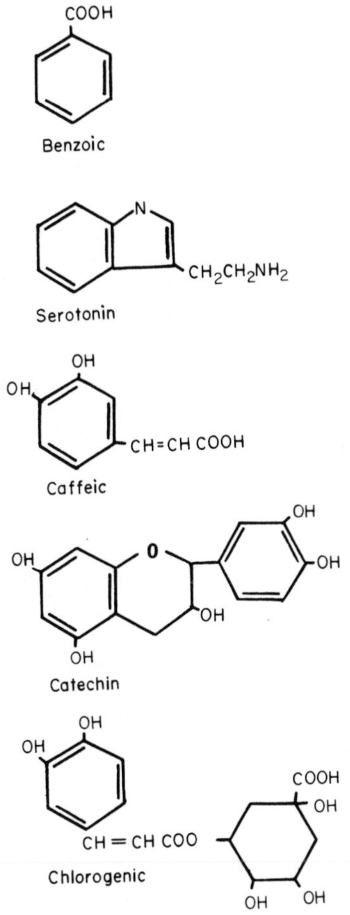

FIG. 16-2.   Examples of carbocyclic acids which occur in plant tissues.

Kohlrabi or 4.9% in whole soybeans [25].   The growing plant, through selective
absorption from the soil, contains in varying proportions the full range of mineral
elements which are present in the medium of cultivation.   Mineral content appears
to be principally influenced by the species or variety.   Little is known of any general relations between cultivation or fertilization practices and mineral constituents
of the plant.

     The distribution of particular mineral elements is known to vary in particular
tissues.   In apple, the contents of calcium, potassium, magnesium, and phosphorous have been observed to increase severalfold acropetally from the outer cortex
to the core [86].   In pea, phosphorous is many times richer in the cotyledons than
in the testa, whereas the difference is reversed for calcium.

     The most abundant mineral elements, the so-called macronutrients, are potas-
sium, calcium, magnesium, iron, phosphorus, sulfur, and nitrogen, together with
certain other elements, such as sodium, aluminum, and silicon, which are often

present at slightly lower concentrations. The micronutrients, copper, manganese, zinc, boron, molybdenum, and chlorine, are also present but in trace amounts. The single most abundant element in fruits and vegetables in potassium, which usually exists at levels between 60 and 600 mg per 100 g of tissue (FWB). However, in parsley, the potassium content sometimes exceeds 1 wt %. Potassium and other minerals occur mainly in salts of organic acids. The pH of fruit tissue is closely related to the potassium-organic acid balance.

Natural variations in the amounts of macronutrients other than potassium are shown in Table 16-11. Some Ca^{2+} is apparently associated with pectic substances and cell-wall materials. Tissues containing abundant amounts of oxalic acid are observed to contain crystals of calcium oxalate. Some minerals are important constituents of enzyme prosthetic groups (e.g., magnesium in chlorophyll; iron in the heme compounds, peroxidase, catalase and cytochromes), some serve as co-factors (e.g., phosphorus in ATP, PO_4^{2-}), and others form part of major cell constituents (e.g., phosphorus in phospholipids, nucleic acids).

The influence of mineral elements on metabolic events in harvested edible plants is undoubtedly profound, although the details of their roles are still largely obscure. Various physiological disorders of stored fruit have been related to mineral content and distribution (Table 16-12). For example, in apples, the calcium concentration was lowest just below the peel and at the nose of fruit where "bitter pit" (local cell necrosis) was most commonly observed. Pears susceptible to cork spot also are frequently deficient in this macronutrient [75]. The content of other minerals, notably, K, P, and Mg, also related to the incidence of storage disorders. There is evidence that calcium delimits localization and activity of peroxidase, an enzyme involved in the accumulation of phenolic pools and in deposition of lignin [96]. Pre- or postharvest application of parts per million levels of pyrophosphate can

TABLE 16-11

Normal Range of Some Macronutrients in Vegetative Tissues[a]

Element	Normal range (mg/100 g FWB)	Especially rich sources
Ca	3–300	Spinach may contain up to 600 mg per 100 g FWB
Mg	2–90	Sweet corn
P	7–230	Seeds and young growing parts
Na	0–124	Celery
Cl	1–180	Celery
S	2–170	High-protein tissues
Fe	0.1–4	Parsley contains up to 8 mg per 100 g FWB

[a]Adapted from Duckworth [25]. When considering the influence of minerals on metabolic control, one must take compartmentalization into account. Many minerals are concentrated in vacuoles or as salt crystals (e.g., calcium oxalate).

TABLE 16-12

Senescence Breakdown Indices in Bulk Samples of Apples
as Influenced by Calcium Content[a]

Ca (mg/100 g FWB)	Breakdown index[b]
3.5	112
3.7	52
4.1	0

[a]Adapted from Perry [87].

[b]Senescence breakdown indices (maximum = 300: none = 0) were determined after 189 days storage at 2.8°C.

dramatically decrease conversion of sugar to starch in harvested sweet corn (Fig. 16-3). There are undoubtedly many yet unknown ways in which minerals delimit biochemical reactions and thereby affect the quality of harvested plant tissues. Finally, minerals can markedly influence the texture (e.g., calcium interaction with demethylated pectins), color (interaction of various ions with pigments and metal cans), flavor, and nutritive value of edible plants during and after processing [30].

G. Enzymes

The importance of enzymes to the quality of edible plant tissues cannot be overemphasized. Apart from determining chemical composition and stress susceptibility before and after harvest, they can cause marked changes in the quality of processed products. All of the quality indices of edible plants are influenced to some degree by the particular enzymes (dependant on species, variety, maturity, etc.) involved in anabolic and catabolic reactions. Senescence of plant tissues is generally associated with the emergence of numerous hydrolytic enzymes (e.g., polygalacturonase, chlorophyllase, proteases, esterases, carbohydrases, DNAase, RNAse) and oxidative enzymes (e.g., peroxidase, catalase, amino acid oxidases, lipoxidase, and phenolases) [119]. It is important to recognize that the mere occurrence of an enzyme in a given tissue does not imply catalytic activity at all times. This concept of "metabolic control" is discussed later.

H. Pigments

The principal pigments of plant tissues, the chlorophylls, carotenoids and flavonoids, are discussed in Chapter 8. The kinds and amounts of pigments in plant tissues depend on species, variety, maturity, growing conditions, etc. [17]. Most of these pigments undergo considerable change during storage and processing. Chlorophylls a and b, which occur to an extent of 0.1% (FWB) in green leaves, are

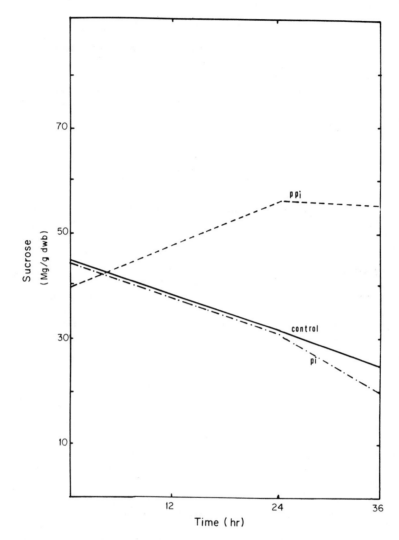

FIG. 16-3. Effect of pyrophosphate (PPi) and phosphate (Pi) treatment on sucrose remaining in sweet corn after harvest [4]. A 5-ml aliquot containing 1 mM PPi or Pi was injected into the central parenchyma tissue of the ear prior to storage at room temperature. The authors also observed that PPi markedly inhibited the enzyme ADP-glucose pyrophosphorylase and hypothesized that PPi affected starch synthesis by blocking ADP-glucose synthesis.

localized in chloroplasts and typically decline with the onset of plant senescence. The yellow, orange, or red carotenoid pigments are associated, in small quantities (0.005-0.008% FWB), with chlorophyll and, in addition, may occur in nongreen tissues as small crystals in the cytoplasm or in membrane-limited chromoplasts.

Carotenoids located in regions other than chloroplasts may, in specific instances, accumulate to an extent of about 0.1% (FWB) and are responsible for the yellow to red color of numerous fruits and vegetables (e.g., carrot, sweet potato, squash, citrus, tomato, watermelon, apricot, and red peppers).

The water-soluble anthocyanin pigments are responsible for the characteristic red, blue, or purple color of various fruits and vegetables (e.g., red cabbage, radish, eggplant, cherry, strawberry). Flavonoid compounds and related substances (not possessing the complete flavonoid structure) can affect texture (lignin and polymerized leucoanthocyanins), enzymic browning (catechins, leucoanthocyanins), and flavor (astringent tannins, bitter substances).

The extent of pigment synthesis and degradation in detached fruits and vegetables is often markedly influenced by conditions of storage. Mention should be made of two growth substances which have general effects on the metabolism of specific pigments. The naturally occurring plant hormone, ethylene, generally initiates catabolism of chlorophylls in mature green plants. Commercial use of ethylene gas to force degreening of lemons and celery has been employed for many years. In contrast, the synthetic molecule, 2-(4-chlorophenylthio)-triethylamine hydrochloride (CPTA), has the general effect of markedly enhancing synthesis of specific carotenoids in most plant tissues [19].

I. Vitamins

Edible plant tissues vary widely in their vitamin contents. Variety, growing conditions, stage of maturity, and postharvest handling, storage, and processing all may influence vitamin content. Vitamins are usually not distributed uniformly in plant tissues. The old addage "it's a sin to eat the potato and throw away the skin" makes reference to the fact that thiamine and ascorbic acid are most abundant in the cortex area. Although wheat is an excellent source of B vitamins, the bran and germ, which contain the bulk of these nutrients, are usually removed during processing. Some examples of edible plant tissues which serve as important sources of specific vitamins are shown in Table 16-13.

The vitamin contents of commodities can be influenced significantly by growing conditions, the stage of maturity at harvest, and postharvest practices [49]. For example, vitamin C is maximal in a fully ripe banana; vine ripened tomatoes have a higher ascorbic acid content than those ripened after harvest; and tomatoes grown in a greenhouse have lower vitamin A levels than those grown in the field. Furthermore, substantial amounts of vitamins can be lost by holding plant tissues in a nonrefrigerated state following harvest. Far too little effort has been made to harvest, store, and process plant tissues under conditions that result in maximum retention of nutrients.

III. STRUCTURE

A. Classification

No attempt will be made here to outline the taxonomy of edible plant tissues. The internationally accepted rules prescribe that each plant be distinguished by two

TABLE 16-13

Edible Plants That Are Important Sources of Vitamins[a]

B-Carotene	Thiamine	Riboflavin	Niacin	Ascorbic acid
Green leaves	Whole grain	Green leaves	Dried yeast	Citrus fruits
Other green vegetables	Wheat germ	Legumes	Peanuts	Tomatoes
Apricots	Dried yeast	Buds (broccoli)		Cabbage
Yellow vegetables	Legumes			Strawberries
Tomato	Nuts			Peas
	Chard			Potato
	Spinach			Peppers

[a]Adapted from Hughes and Bennion [49]. The spectrum and amounts of vitamins in a given commodity may be influenced by preharvest and postharvest handling as well as variety.

primary identifying names, the generic name and the specific name. The author of a plant name is often listed after the specific name, e.g., the Latin name for wheat is <u>Triticum aestivum</u>, L., where the L. stands for Linnaeus, the father of modern taxonomy. Species may be subdivided into subspecies or varieties. More important for our consideration is the classification of edible plants into groups according to their appearance and use. These groupings are not very accurate but are useful for our purpose. Consideration will be given to four categories of edible plant tissues based on their appearance: roots, stems, leaves, and fruits. Foods, of course, are also classified on the basis of their ecomonic use, e.g., fruits, vegetables, nuts, grains, berries, bulbs, or tubers. This type of categorization is based on custom rather than on botanical systematics and accordingly varies in different cultures.

Each tissue is structurally adapted to carry out a particular function. Much of the metabolic activity of the plant is carried out in relatively unspecialized tissue, called parenchyma, which generally makes up the bulk of edible plant tissues. The outer cell layer is called the epidermis and is structurally adapted to protect the organ. Specialized tissues, called collenchyma and sclerenchyma, provide structural support. Water, minerals, and solute molecules are transported through the vascular tissues, xylem and phloem.

The chemical composition of a given tissue often relates to the constituent cell types although, not in obvious ways. For example, many plant tissues contain considerably less solids than fluid milk and yet have rigid structures.

1. ROOTS

The economically important root crops include sugar beets, sweet potatoes and yams, and cassava. The basic anatomical structure of root tissue is illustrated in Figure 16-4a. The surface of roots consist of an epidermal layer, followed inwardly by the cortex, which is made up of a number of layers of thin-walled storage cells [38]. Roots of most plants have more or less extensive areas in which the innermost cortical layer (endodermis) is partially suberized and other areas where it may be completely suberized. The central portion of a root is comprised of the cambium, which contains the xylem and phloem cells (vascular elements) and associated parenchyma. Fleshy roots are formed by secondary growth of the cambia (Fig. 16-4b, c). This secondary growth is to the outside (phloem) and to the inside (xylem) of the cambia [25]. The secondary vascular tissues of such crops consist of small groups of conducting elements scattered throughout a matrix of parenchyma tissue, the latter being responsible for the fleshy consistency. In beet root, an anomalous type of secondary growth occurs. A series of concentric cambia is formed, each individual cambium giving rise to phloem centrifugally and xylem centripetally, producing alternate layers of the two tissues. Multiple cambia are also formed in sweet potato, but in this instance they arise around individual groups of cells in the original secondary xylem and they are not arranged in concentric fashion.

2. STEMS

The "stem crops" are relatively unimportant except where a particular commodity may be a basic food in a local area. Two notable exceptions are the potato, with a world production in excess of 300 million tons per annum, and sugarcane which is grown to the extent of nearly 0.5 million tons annually. Other reasonably important stem crops include asparagus, bamboo shoot, rhubarb, and kohlrabi. Underground stems, (rhyzomes, bulbs) are modified structures and are exemplified by potatoes and onions.

A stem may be defined as an axis which bears leaves and buds and is characterized by the possession of nodes, the points of attachment of the appendages, and internodes, the regions between two successive modes [38]. Topographically, a stem consists of four distinct regions: the cortex, located between the epidermis and vascular system; and the pith, which forms the central core of cells (Fig. 16-5a). Parenchyma cells are the basic cell type of the cortex and pith regions. In the outer cortical regions, there may be zones of collenchyma and schlerenchyma cells which provide mechanical support and flexibility. The secondary tissues exhibit different forms, as illustrated by the dicotyledonous potato (Fig. 16-5b). In potato, the bundles of vascular tissue are characteristically arranged in a single ring and the phloem is normally external to the xylem in each bundle. The potato is somewhat atypical in having small strands of internal phloem. Monocots, such as asparagus, more typically have complete vascular bundles scattered throughout the parenchymatous ground tissue (Fig. 16-5c). In bulbs, such as onion and garlic, the organ consists of a short stem which bears a series of fleshy leaves above and around the stem.

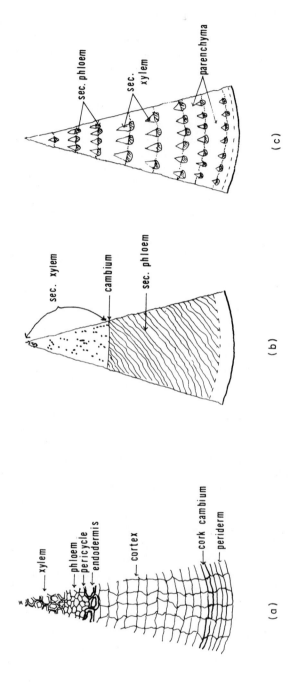

FIG. 16-4. Diagrammatic illustration of anatomical structure of root tissue in cross-section (a). Fleshy roots are formed by secondary growth of meristematic tissue, called cambia. A typical example is carrot (b), where the cambia forms phloem to the outside and xylem to the inside. The conducting elements are scattered throughout a mass of parenchyma tissue. Beet root shows a different kind of secondary growth, in which a series of concentric cambia are formed (c).

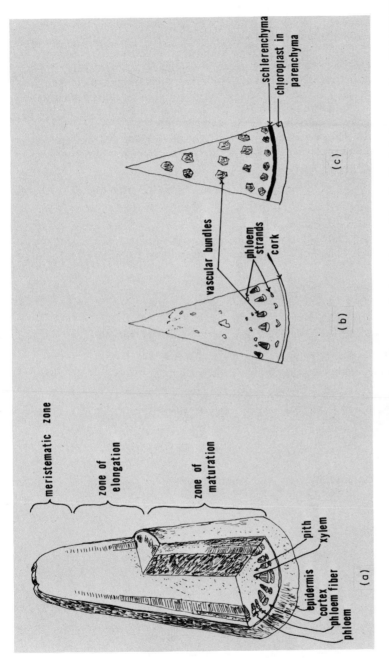

FIG. 16-5. Diagrammatic illustration of anatomical structure of stem tissue (a). In dicotyledonous stem structures, such as potato (b), the vascular bundles are arranged in a single ring, as seen in transverse section. Monocotyledons, represented by asparagus (c), show a characteristic scattering of vascular bundles throughout the parenchymatous ground tissue. A photomicrograph of asparagus is shown in Fig. 16-35a.

3. LEAF CROPS

Examples of leaf vegetables are lettuce, mustard greens, chard, spinach, water-cress, parsley, and cabbage. A leaf is typically a flat and expanded organ, primarily involved with photosynthesis, but deviations in morphology and function may occur [38]. The leaf is composed of tissues which are fundamentally similar to those found in stem and root but their organization is usually different (Fig. 16-6). The epidermis contains a well-developed cuticle in most instances and stomata are characteristically present. Beneath the epidermal layer lie a series of elongated, closely packed palisade cells which are rich in chloroplasts. The irregular loose arrangement of parenchyma cells beneath the palisade results in a spongelike tissue (spongy mesophyll) that provides the air space necessary for gaseous exchange in photosynthesis and transpiration. The vascular system consists of netlike veins in dicots and parallel veins in monocots.

4. FRUITS

Botanically, a fruit is a ripened ovary or the ovary with adjoining parts, i.e., it is the seed-bearing organ. The flesh of fruit may be developed from the floral recep-

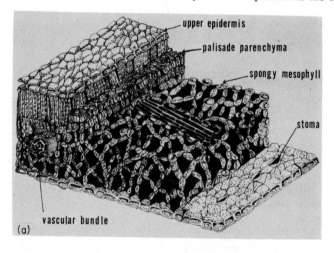

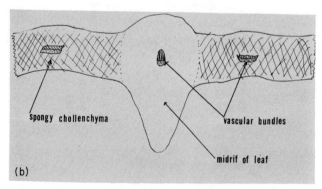

FIG. 16-6. Diagrammatic illustrations of anatomical structures of a typical leaf tissue (a) and a transverse section of lettuce (b), showing distribution of vascular bundles in spongy chollenchyrma.

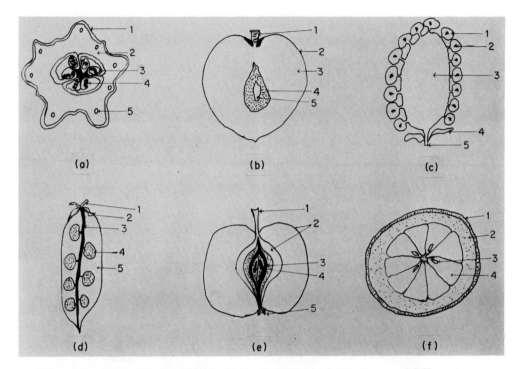

FIG. 16-7. Diagrammatic illustrations of anatomical structures of different types of fruit: (a) pepo (cucumber, squash, pumpkin) in cross-section [(1) rind (receptacular), (2) flesh (ovary wall), (3) placenta, (4) seed, (5) vascular bundle] (b) drupe (cherry, peach, plum) in longitudinal section [(1) pedicel, (2) skin (ovary wall), (3) flesh (ovary wall), (4) pit (stony ovary wall), (5) seed]; (c) aggregate (raspberry, strawberry, blackberry) in longitudinal section [(1) fleshy ovary wall, (2) seed (stony ovary wall plus seed), (3) fleshy receptacle, (4) sepal, (5) pedicel]; (d) legume (pea, soybean, lima bean) in longitudinal section [(1) pedicel, (2) sepel, (3) vascular bundles, (4) seed, (5) pod (ovary wall)]; (e) pome (apple, pear) in longitudinal section [(1) pedicel, (2) skin and flesh (receptacle), (3) leathery carpel (ovary wall), (4) seed, (5) calyx (sepals and stamens)]; (f) hespiridium (citrus) in cross-section [(1) collenchymatous exocarp (the flavedo), (2) parenchymatous mesocarp (the albedo), (3) seed, (4) endocarp of juice sacs formed by breakdown of groups of parenchyma-like cells]; (g) kernel of wheat, longitudinal and cross-sectional views. (Courtesy of The Wheat Flour Institute.)

tacle, from carpellary tissue, or from extrafloral structures, such as bracts [38,56]. Whatever its origin, it is generally largely composed of parenchymatous tissue. The vascular tissues are poorly developed in most instances, although there are exceptions, such as pineapple, where structural tissue is extensive. Fruit types include the berry (tomato, grape), hesperidium (citrus), pepo (cucumber, squash), drupe (cherry, peach), aggregate (strawberry, raspberry), multiple (fig, pineapple), pome (apple, pear), legume (soybean, pea), capsule (okra), caryopsis (corn), and the nut (chestnut). The anatomical features of some of these fruit types are illustrated in Figure 16-7. Legumes, capsules, caryopses, and nuts are not thought of as fruits by the layman. From the popular standpoint, fruits are usually eaten raw as a dessert, and they possess characteristic aromas and flavors due to the presence of various organic esters.

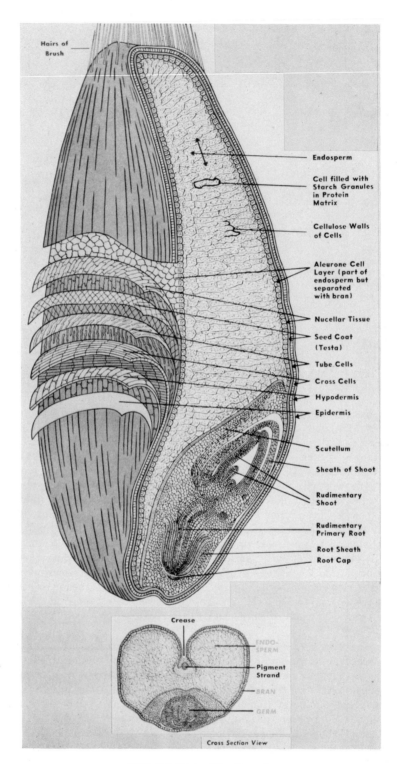

Hairs of Brush

Endosperm

Cell filled with Starch Granules in Protein Matrix

Cellulose Walls of Cells

Aleurone Cell Layer (part of endosperm but separated with bran)

Nucellar Tissue

Seed Coat (Testa)

Tube Cells

Cross Cells

Hypodermis

Epidermis

Scutellum

Sheath of Shoot

Rudimentary Shoot

Rudimentary Primary Root

Root Sheath

Root Cap

Crease

ENDO-SPERM

Pigment Strand

BRAN

GERM

Cross Section View

FIG. 16-7(g). (Continued)

B. Tissue and Cell Structure

Now that we have examined the distribution of tissue in various plant organs, let us look at the cellular and subcellular structures present in these tissues.

1. PARENCHYMA TISSUE

The Greek word "parenchyma" meaning "that which is poured in beside," is descriptive of the soft or succulent tissue which surrounds the hardened or woody tissues. This tissue is the most abundant type present in edible plants and it is composed of undifferentiated cells which develop directly from the meristematic tissues of growing roots or stems. A mature parenchyma cell possesses a thin cell wall and the bulk of the cell volume is occupied by large vacuoles. These cells are generally isodiametric and polyhedral in shape, containing between 11 and 20 faces which are in contact with other cells. Cell size (50-300 μm) and shape is characteristic for a given species. The extent of cellular contact also varies with the commodity. For example, air spaces account for less than 1 vol % of potato parenchyma and as much as 25 vol % of apple parenchyma. Examples of parenchyma tissues are illustrated in Figure 16-8.

Between the walls of adjacent cells is a region, the middle lamella, composed primarily of pectic substances. These substances serve as intercellular "cement" and their nature largely determines the textural properties of the tissue. For example, the different textures of "melting" (e.g., peach) and "nonmelting" (e.g., apple) fruit appear to relate to the ready ability of the cells to slide apart in the former tissue but not in the latter.

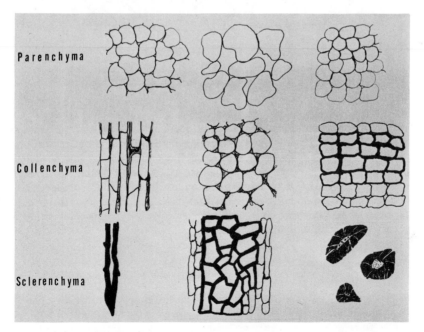

FIG. 16-8. Diagrammatic illustrations of parenchymatous and supporting tissues.

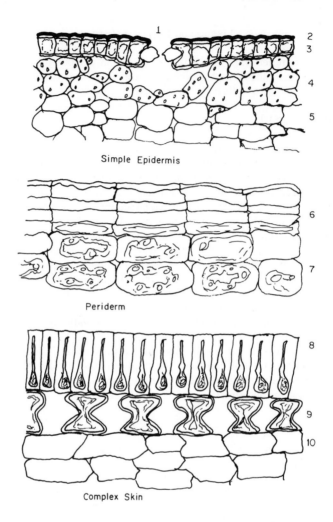

Simple Epidermis

Periderm

Complex Skin

FIG. 16-9. Diagrammatic illustration of protective tissues. (a) Simple epidermis, such as asparagus stem; (b) periderm, such as potato tuber; and (c) complex "skin," such as the testa of a pea. (1) Stoma, (2) cuticle, (3) epidermis, (4) chloroplast containing parenchyma, (5) unspecialized parenchyma, (6) corky tissue, (7) parenchyma cells containing developing starch granules, (8) compact layer of elongated epidermal cells with heavily thickened walls (primarily hemicellulosic in pea), (9) hypodermal layer of hourglass-shaped cells with large intercellular spaces, (10) parechymatous inner layer.

2. PROTECTIVE TISSUES

Protective tissues develop at the surface of plant organs, forming the "peel" or "skins" of the commodity. The outermost layer of cells is called the epidermis. These cells fit together compactly with no air spaces and their outer walls are usually rich in wax and cutin. An extracellular surface layer, called the cuticle, is usually present outside the epidermis (Fig. 16-9). Another feature of the epidermis is the presence of hairlike protrusions, called trichomes.

The surfaces of underground storage organs are usually protected by a thin layer of cork which is formed by a layer of meristematic cells, called the cork cambium or phellogen. The cork cambium generally arises from a layer of cells within the epidermis and is impregnated with the lipophillic substance suberin.

The epidermis of leaves, fruits, and some stems contains small pores, called stomata, each surrounded by guard cells which regulate the passage of gases and water. In cork-covered organs, the stomata are replaced by structures, called lenticels, in which pores are formed by the breaking apart of cork cells.

More elaborate structural modification of epidermal tissue is found in seeds, such as cereals, and in the pericarps of some fruits, such as citrus and banana.

3. SUPPORTING TISSUES

Collenchyma tissue is characterized by elongated cells which have unevenly thickened walls (Fig. 16-8). It is found particularly in petioles, stems, and leaves, occupying the ridges which are often situated on the surface of the organ (e.g., strands of the outer edge of celery petioles). Thickened primary walls are especially rich in pectin and hemicelluloses, giving the walls unusual plasticity. Collenchyma tissue, although relatively soft, resists degradation during cooking and mastication.

Sclerenchyma cells are uniformly thick-walled cells which are normally lignified. Unlike parenchyma and collenchyma cells, mature sclerenchyma is nonliving, normally devoid of cytoplasm, and composed mainly of a cell wall. The two main types of sclerenchyma cells are "fibers" and sclereids (Fig. 16-8). Fibers are elongated (up to 10 cm) and are generally found in closely knit strands, commonly in association with vascular tissue. These fibers are not perturbed by cooking and they give rise to the stringy textures of asparagus and green beans. Sclereids are responsible for the gritty texture of pear and quince fruit and are especially abundant in the shells of nuts and other seeds and in the testas of some seeds.

4. VASCULAR TISSUES

The vascular tissues, xylem and phloem, are complex tissues that are composed of simple and specialized cells. These cells are continuous throughout most plant tissues. The characteristic cell type of the xylem is the vessel element, a tubular-cell (vessel) through which water is transported. The walls of vessels are unevenly thickened in patterns characteristic of the species. The vessels are intermixed with xylem parenchyma cells, fibers, and other cell types.

Phloem tissue consists mainly of a series of specialized cells, called sieve elements, phloem parenchyma cells, and companion cells. Sieve elements are arranged longitudinally, forming long tubes for the transport of aqueous solutions of organic matter. The phloem is normally associated with the xylem in vascular bundles, although it may also occur as isolated strands in regions where it is surrounded by storage tissue. The phloem is a relatively soft tissue which has little influence on the texture of edible foods. Little, if anything, is known of the functionality of phloem in physiological events postharvest.

C. Subcellular Structure

1. NUCLEI

The main components of "typical" plant cells are illustrated in Figure 16-10. The largest plant cell organelle is the nucleus, which appears to have the same struc-

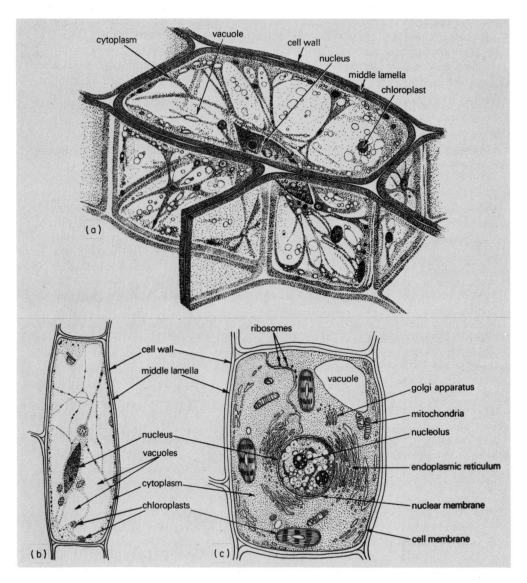

FIG. 16-10. Diagrammatic representation of a mature plant cell. (a) light microscope; (b) light microscope section; (c) electron microscope image. (Reprinted from Ref. [14], courtesy of <u>Scientific American.</u>)

ture and functions as the animal nucleus. Nuclei of higher plants, such as onion, are about 8 μm in diameter and contain about 3,000 pores in the nuclear envelope. Comparatively little work has been done on nuclei in mature plant cells, such as those of interest to food scientists. Future lines of research dealing with biochemical controls in edible plant tissues will undoubtedly involve investigation of this organelle.

2. MITOCHONDRIA

Mitochondria are the sites of respiration and other assorted cellular functions and these activities, particularly electron transfer and oxidative phosphorylation, have been fairly well characterized in mature and senescing plant cells. In meristematic cells, mitochondria contain few cristae and respiration is partly fermentative; during growth and differentiation, the cristae increase along with the contents of enzymes involved in the Kreb's cycle and in the electron-transfer pathway; in mature tissue, respiration may proceed via alternate metabolic pathways, such as the pentose shunt, and mitochondrial enzymes appear to decline somewhat; finally, during senescence, mitochondrial activity declines, cristae dilate, and in some instances the entire membrane structure becomes disorganized [115]. Considerable effort has been expended to determine whether mitochondria remain functional during the early stages of senescence. Mitochondria of ripening fruit appear to remain intact and functional despite the general collapse of cellular compartmentation at this time [97]. Indeed, there is evidence that retention of coupled respiration is essential to the normal course of ontogenic events, such as dormancy and ripening.

Mitochondria also possess nonrespiratory functions, such as ion transport, transhydrogenation, water pumping, oxidation of lipids, and synthesis of a wide assortment of metabolites [44]. Examples of some enzymes found in association with plant mitochondria are provided in Chapter 6. Numerous enzymes involved in flavor biogenesis, such as transaminases in tomato, thioglycosidases in cabbage, and C-S lyase in onions, are located in mitochondria [102,126]. It has been observed that active calcium transport increases concomitantly with climacteric respiration of banana fruit (Table 16-14). Mitochondria may serve to monitor the cellular concentration of this important nutrient (e.g., see Table 16-12). Finally,

TABLE 16-14

Influence of Stage of Fruit Ripeness on Succinate-driven
Accumulation of Calcium Ions by Isolated Banana Mitochondria[a]

Description of fruit extracted	Active calcium accumulation (μmole/mg protein N/15 min)
Full green, preclimacteria	0.488
Yellow flush, climacteric	0.726
Full yellow, postclimacteric	1.625

[a]Haard and Hultin [44].

it should be mentioned that plant mitochondria, like those from animal tissues, contain nonnuclear DNA and are capable of limited protein synthesis [18]. Little has been done to characterize such ancillary functions in mature and senescing plant tissue and this remains an important area for future investigation.

3. PLASTIDS

A feature common to most, if not all, plant cells is the presence of organelles of variable shape and size, called plastids. These bodies often serve as centers for the accumulation of various products of cellular metabolism. Those containing pigments are referred to as chromoplasts, and the most common example is the chloroplast, a chromoplast containing chlorophylls and associated pigments. Chloroplasts, of course, are the seat of photosynthetic activity and are accordingly a starting point of our food chain. These organelles are also a source of cytoplasmic DNA and the protein synthesizing machinery. While it is outside the scope of this chapter to outline the biochemistry of photosynthesis, all students of food science should be familiar with this important process. The enterprising scientist who unravels the mystery of what controls the channeling of the sun's energy into synthesis of proteins rather than carbohydrate will add untold dimensions to the solution of world food problems.

The only other pigments which occur in special chromoplasts are the carotenoids and they tend to occur in a crystalline form. However, needle-shaped crystals of carotenoid pigments can also occur in areas other than plastids. Carrots and tomatoes are good examples of commodities rich in carotenoid chromoplasts.

Colorless plastids, or leukoplasts, can act as sites for the accumulation of storage materials, such as starch. Starch grains have characteristic size, shape, and optical properties depending on the specific tissues [93] and these properties are often a useful means of detecting food adulteration (Fig. 6-11). Starch metabolism is one of the more important events in postharvest commodities. There is some evidence that integrity of the leukoplast wall is related to the availability of the starch pool for metabolism [84]. Electron micrographs of granules attacked by enzymes and modified by acid treatment are shown in Figure 16-12. During heating, such as blanching or cooking, the starch granule is disrupted and the starch becomes hydrated (gelatinized; see Chapter 3).

Small inclusions of protein may also be present in some cells, although these are not generally referred to as plastids. In the peripheral region of the potato tuber, cuboidal protein crystals occur in parenchyma cells. Proteins also occur in aleurone grains in certain seeds and in fruits, such as sweet corn.

4. VACUOLES

Vacuoles are membrane-limited cavities located within the cytoplasm and they contain aqueous inclusions of salts and various organic metabolites. In mature cells the numerous vacuoles evolve into a large void which occupies the majority of the cell. The extensive vacuolar development in plants may relate to the lack of efficient circulatory, filtration, and excretory systems, such as those in animals. It also appears that plant vacuoles are involved in generation of hydrostatic pressure which results in cell turgidity.

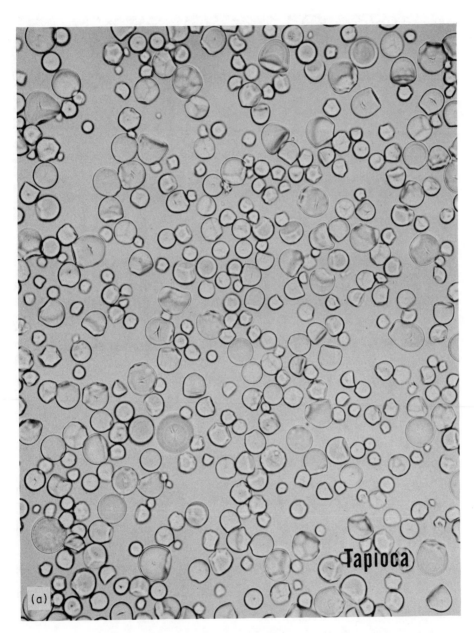

FIG. 16-11. Photomicrographs of starch granules from four sources. Note the characteristic size and shape of each type of starch granule. (Reprinted from Ref. [80a], courtesy of Academic Press.)

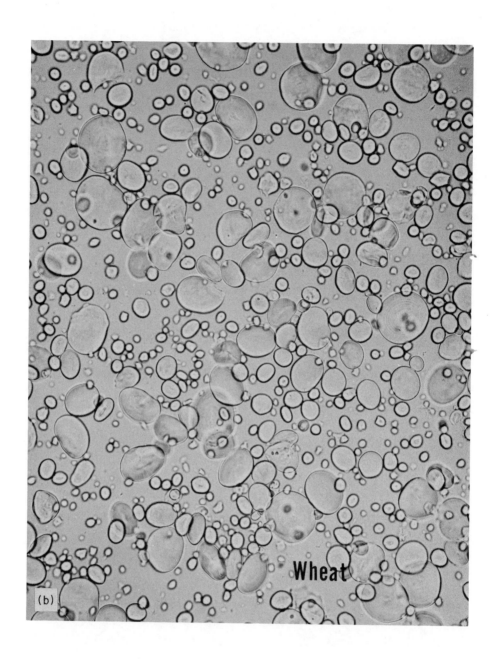

FIG. 16-11. (Continued)

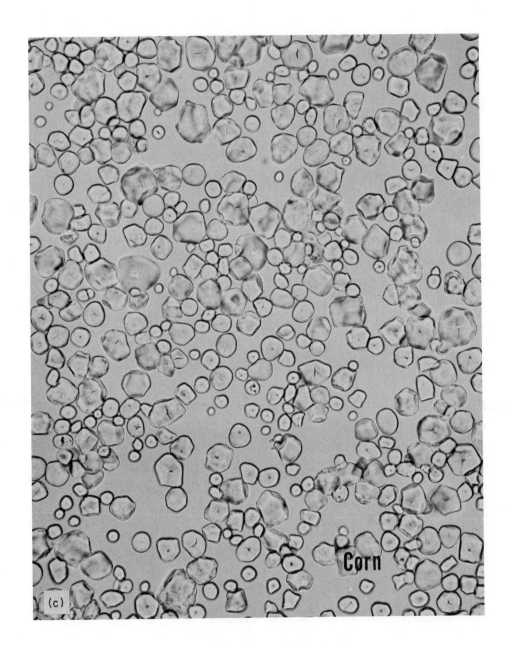

FIG. 16-11. (Continued)

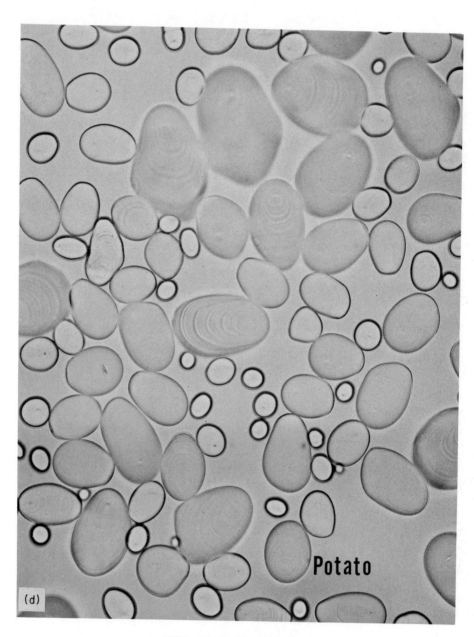

FIG. 16-11 (Continued)

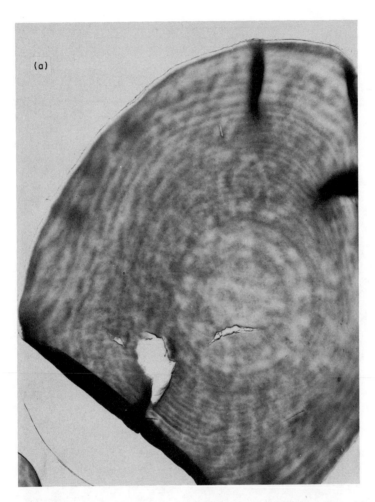

FIG. 16-12. Electron micrographs of "waxy" cornstarch granules: (a) untreated, (b) digested with α-amylase (note partial erosion of granule structure),
(c) acid modified and (d) treated with glucoamylase (note extreme disintegration).
Strains of corn which are practically devoid of amylose are referred to as "waxy"
varieties because of the waxy appearance of the cut grain. (Reprinted from Ref.
[124], courtesy of Academic Press, New York.)

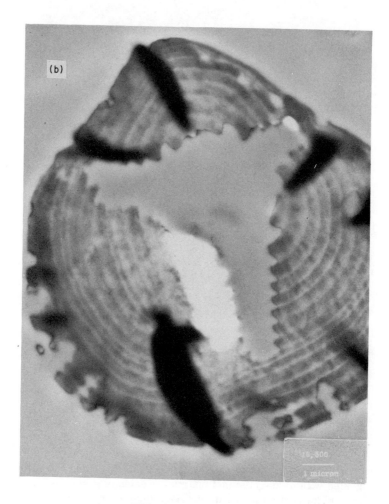

FIG. 16-12. (Continued)

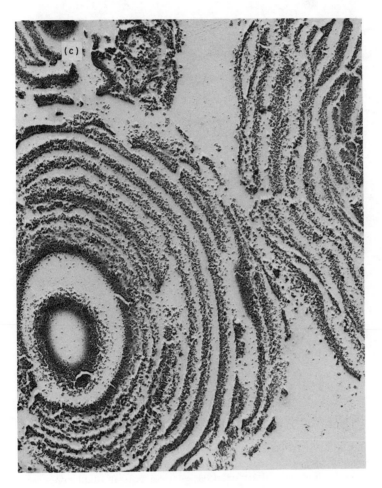

FIG. 16-12. (Continued)

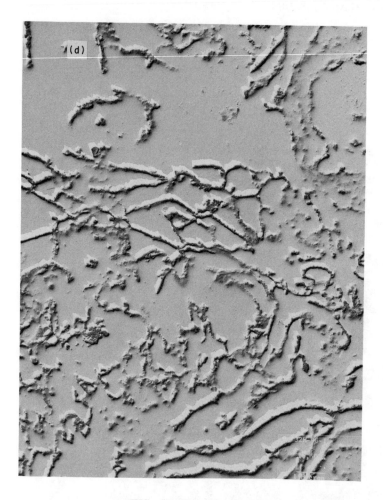

FIG. 16-12. (Continued)

5. SPHEROSOMES AND PEROXISOMES

Particles containing hydrolytic enzymes (e.g., spherosomes or lysosomes) and oxidative enzymes (peroxisomes) also have been identified in certain higher plants [34]. These inclusions are likely candidates for a role in plant senescence and stress susceptibility in edible tissues and are certain to be the objects of future investigation.

IV. PHYSIOLOGY

Innumerable physiological processes take place in edible plant tissue after harvest. On removal from the parent plant, such tissues are deprived of their normal supplies of water, minerals, and also, in some instances, simple organic molecules (e.g., sugars, hormones) which normally are translocated to them from other parts of the plant. With the possible exception of some short-lived photosynthetic activity in green leafy structures, synthesis of organic products from carbon dioxide and water ceases at the point of harvest. However, most tissues remain capable of transforming many of the constituents already present. These physiological processes can be either beneficial or detrimental to the edible quality of a particular commodity. Many of the metabolic shifts which occur in plant tissues and are important to edible quality have yet to be characterized. More important, the metabolic controls on such processes are poorly understood. This area promises to be one of unparalleled importance in food science.

The kind and intensity of physiological activity in detached plants determines, to a large extent, their storage longevities. Some organs, such as seeds, fleshy roots, tubers, and bulbs, are morphologically and physiologically adapted to maintain themselves in a dormant state until environmental conditions are favorable for germination or growth. Metabolic activity, although depressed, is not completely halted in such tissues. The tissues of most fruits and vegetables, in contrast, are physiologically primed for senescence rather than dormancy. Fleshy fruits are unusual in that maturation normally is followed by a ripening process which is associated with the development of optimal eating quality. Unfortunately, ripening is rapidly followed by senescence and a decline in edible value.

A. Comparative Biochemistry

If we represent the set of all chemical reactions occurring in plant tissues as a large circle, we can on the basis of current knowledge imagine a subset consisting of reactions that are basically identical in all plant tissues (Fig. 16-13). This "common core" includes basal events, such as activation of amino acids preparatory to protein synthesis, mitochondrial-linked respiration, and anabolism of certain cell-wall materials. In addition to reactions common to all detached plant parts, we can represent additional subsets of reactions which are common to large groups of organs, such as photosynthesis in green plants or certain aspects of organic acid metabolism. A large number of reactions occurring in one grouping may also be common to other groupings. Finally, there are reactions that are highly specific to individual families, or even subspecies, such as the biogenesis or biodeterioration of volatile flavor substances. Because of what Seymour Hutner called "mammalian chauvinism" and Carl Price referred to as "Escherichia coli chauvinism," we know little about the subsets of biochemical reactions in edible plant tissues compared to our knowledge of rats and E. coli. Here, we discuss two important "core reactions" which are of central importance in detached plant parts - respiration and gene expression - and we review some of the ancillary biochemical events which have an important bearing on the quality of edible food.

B. Core Reactions

1. RESPIRATION

There is a fairly consistent relationship between respiratory rate and storage life of fleshy plant tissues (Table 16-15; Fig. 16-14). Commodities which exhibit rapid

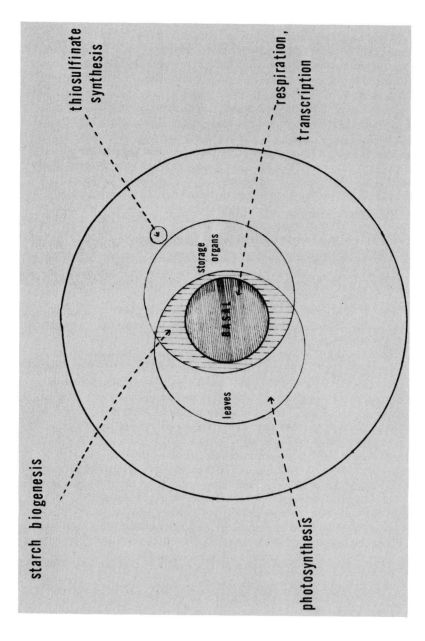

FIG. 16-13. Geometric representation of chemical reactions which occur in the plant kingdom. The outer circle encloses all reactions occurring in plant tissues, while the inner darkened circle represents a subset of reactions basic to all plant cells. The overlapping inner circles, which include basal reactions, represent subsets of reactions common to all members of a given group (leaf and storage organs in this example). Examples of reactions common to specific subsets are shown.

TABLE 16-15

Respiration Rates and Perishability of Fruits and Vegetables[a]

Commodity	Respiration (mg CO_2/kg/hr) 5°C	25°C	Storage life (weeks) at 5°C
Peas	50	475	1
Asparagus	45	260	2-3
Avacado	10	400	2-4
Turnips	6	17	16-20
Apples	3	30	12-32

[a]Adapted from Ref. [113]; data are representative and vary with variety and cultivation practice of a particular commodity. Note that the Q_{10} for respiration may differ with different commodities.

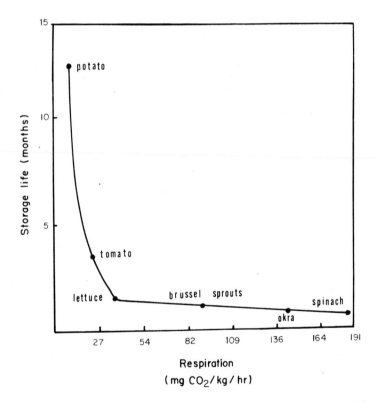

FIG. 16-14. Relation between initial respiration rate and storage life (to unsalable condition) of selected vegetables stored at 15.5°C. (Reprinted from Ref. [101], courtesy of AVI Publ. Co.)

carbon dioxide evolution and oxygen consumption are generally quite perishable, while those with slow respiration may be stored satisfactorily for relatively long periods of time. Moreover, the shelf life of a given commodity can be greatly extended by placing it in an environment which retards respiration (e.g., refrigeration, controlled atmosphere, hypobaric conditions).

We have already mentioned that coupled respiration appears to endure through the early stages of plant senescence [44]. Although respiratory rates of different commodities differ widely, it is not clear why they do so. One simple cannot account for the balance of energy in rapidly respiring vegetables and ripening fruits (Fig. 16-15). The relatively rapid rate of respiration in leguminous seeds and certain vegetables, such as sweet corn and asparagus, appears to relate to starch synthesis and the biogenesis of supporting tissues. In some instances, there also appears to be a close relationship between respiratory rate and depletion of carbohydrates. For example, harvested peas undergo a dramatic loss in sweet taste because of the swift oxidation of sucrose.

The relative importance of different oxidative cycles (Kreb's cycle, glyoxylate shunt; Embden-Meyerhof pathway, pentose phosphate cycle) appears to vary from species to species, from organ to organ, and with the ontogeny of the plant. Glycolysis and Kreb's cycle-mediated oxidation appear to be the principal pathways; although pentose phosphate oxidation can account for approximately one-third of glucose catabolism in some instances [24]. The relative importance of the pentose cycle appears to increase in mature tissues and it is known to be operative in pepper, tomato, cucumber, lime, orange, and banana fruits. It would be interesting to relate the functional advantage of pentose cycle oxidation (e.g., increased reducing power) to biosynthetic events in mature tissues. One indication that biological oxidations undergo shifts during senescence is a change in respiratory quotient (ratio of CO_2 evolved to O_2 absorbed) [109]. The respiratory quotient (RQ) is a useful qualitative guide to changes in metabolic pathways or the emergence of nonrespiratory decarboxylase or oxygenase systems (Table 16-16). The rise in RQ during climacteric respiration of fruit is indicative of increased decarboxylation or decreased carboxylation. It is known that the activity of the malic enzyme increases during ripening of apple and pear fruit.

It is generally believed that the final electron acceptor in fruits and vegetables is mitochondrial cytochrome oxidase because the oxygen action spectra (concentration vs affinity of cytochrome oxidase), unlike that of other enzymes, such as polyphenoloxidases, ascorbic acid oxidase, monoamine oxidase, or indole acetic acid oxidase, is analogous to that of in situ respiration. The affinity of these other oxidases (which are generally present in mature plant tissues) for oxygen may differ considerably in the cellular environment (in situ) and they should accordingly not be discounted as participants in respiratory control.

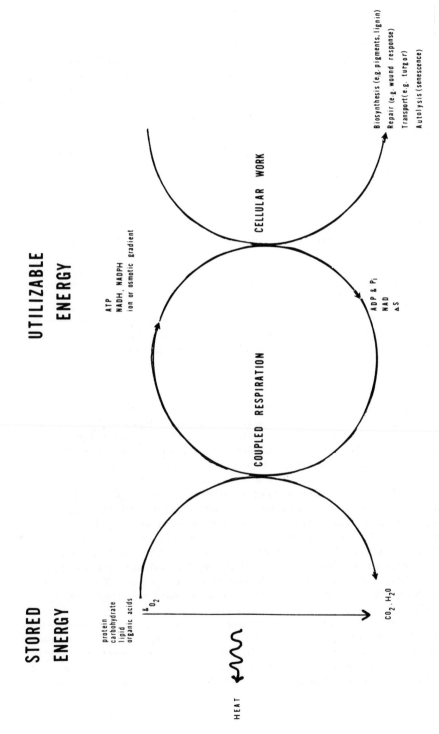

FIG. 16-15. Respiratory oxidation of stored chemical energy to utilizable energy (coupled) and to heat (uncoupled).

TABLE 16-16

Respiratory Quotients of Some Detached Plant Parts[a]

System	Respiratory quotient
Leaves rich in carbohydrates	1.0
Germinating starchy seeds	1.0
Germinating linseed	0.64
Germinating buckwheat seed	0.48
Maturing linseed	1.22
Mature apples in air	1.0
Overripe apples in air	1.3
Apples browning in air containing chloroform vapor	0.25
Apples treated with HCN	2.0
Wheat seedlings in 5-20% O_2	0.95
Wheat seedlings in 3% O_2	3.34

[a]Suggestion: using a set of metabolic charts, rationalize the differences in respiratory quotients on the basis of storage materials being oxidized and metabolic pathways.

a. Respiratory Patterns. Most fleshy fruits show a characteristic rise in respiration more or less coincident with the obvious changes in color, flavor, and texture associated with ripening (Table 16-17). This respiratory rise, called the climacteric [60], has been the subject of considerable study because it marks the onset of senescence. The relative magnitude of the climacteric burst varies considerably in different fruits and many fruits do not appear to exhibit a rise after harvest [8] (Fig. 16-16). This latter group has traditionally been categorized as nonclimacteric, although it may be that such fruits are postclimacteric when harvested [2].

No clear metabolic differences have been demonstrated between climacteric and nonclimacteric fruits, although ripening in fruits categorized as nonclimacteric often proceeds more slowly. The relation of the climacteric rise to ripening indices is not particularly clear. Under a wide range of conditions it has been observed that climacteric respiration is concomitant with ripening. There is, however, evidence that the respiratory rise can be separated from other ripening indices [33].

Detached stem, root, and leaf tissues normally respire at a steady rate or show a gradual decline in respiration rate with the onset of senescence, when environment conditions are invariant (Fig. 16-16). Most stress conditions, such as mechanical damage and exposure to extreme temperatures, may result in a burst of respiratory activity [66], although there is no apparent autonomous climacteric.

TABLE 16-17

Classification of Edible Fruits According to Respiratory Patterns

Climacteric		Nonclimacteric	
Common name	Scientific name	Common name	Scientific name
Apple	Pyrus malus	Cherry	Prunus avium
Apricot	Prunius armeniaca	Cucumber	Cucumis sativus
Avacado	Persea gratissima	Fig	Ficus carica
Banana	Musa saplentum	Grape	Vitus vinifera
Cherimoya	Annona cherimola	Grapefruit	Citrus paradisi
Feijoa	Feifoa sellowiana	Lemon	Citrus limon
Mango	Mangifera indica	Melon	Cucumis melo
Papaya	Carica papaya	Orange	Citris sinensis
Passion fruit	Passiflora edulis	Pineapple	Ananas comosus
Papaw	Asimina triloba	Strawberry	Frugaria vesc americana
Peach	Prunus persica		
Pear	Pyrus communis		
Plum	Prunus americana		
Sapote	Casimiroa adulis		
Tomato	Lycopersicum esculentum		

The relationship of respiration to wounding and other stress conditions is discussed in Section V.A.1.

b. Respiratory Control. Temperature and the concentration of carbon dioxide and oxygen in the environment are the principal factors which can be manipulated to curtail biological oxidations and accompanying reactions. The temperature range over which detached edible plant tissues can function normally is quite variable (Table 16-18). The upper limit for most fleshy commodities lies between 30° and 35°C but wide variations in tolerance to low temperatures are found [124]. Physiological disorders resulting from storing commodities at temperature extremes are discussed in Section V.A.2. Within the "physiological" temperature range for a species, the rate of respiration usually increases as the temperature is raised, and the extent of the change in respiration rate is expressed in terms of a Q_{10} value. For most fruit and vegetable species Q_{10} values vary from 7 to less than 1, although values between 1 and 2 are most common (Fig. 16-17).

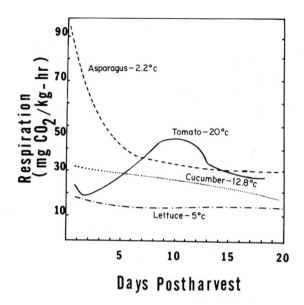

FIG. 16-16. Respiratory patterns of a stem (asparagus), a leafy vegetable (lettuce), a nonclimacteric fruit (cucumber), and a climacteric fruit (tomato). The magnitude of the climacteric rise varies with different fruits but is always coincident with ripening. (Reprinted from Ref. [101], courtesy of AVI Publishing Company.)

TABLE 16-18

Chilling Injury of Commodities Stored below Critical
Nonfreezing Temperatures[a]

Commodity	Minimum storage temperature (°C)	Character of injury
Apples	3	Internal browning, soft rot, scald, etc.
Bananas	13	Dull color, flavor, failure to ripen
Cranberries	2	Rubbery texture, red flesh
Olives	7	Internal browning
Oranges	3	Pitting, brown stain
Potatoes	4	Accumulation of reducing sugars
Tomatoes	9	Water soaking and soft rot

[a]Adapted from Ref. [113]. The critical chilling temperature will often vary with the variety and cultivation practices.

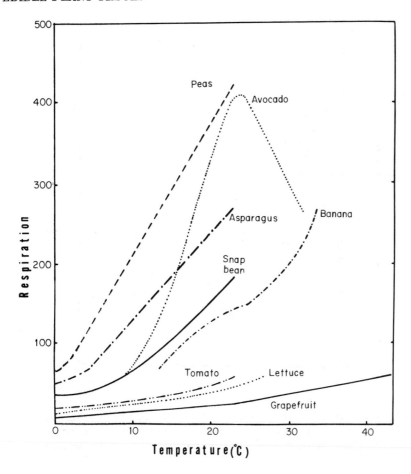

FIG. 16-17. Respiration rate as a function of storage temperature for various commodities. (Reprinted from Ref. [25], courtesy of Pergamon Press.)

Lowering temperature delays the time of onset as well as the magnitude of the respiratory burst in climacteric fruit [97]. The respiration of potato tubers has been fairly well studied with respect to storage temperature [85]. Transfer of tubers from cold storage (e.g., 4°C) to warmer temperatures (e.g., 20°C) results on an initial burst in respiratory activity followed by equilibration to an intermediate level of activity (Fig. 16-18).

In general, either a reduction in oxygen tension (below 21%) or an increase in carbon dioxide concentration (above 0.3%) will slow respiration and associated deteriorative reactions. Diminution of oxygen or enrichment of carbon dioxide beyond limits which are characteristic for a species results in injury (Table 16-19). Injuries resulting from excessive carbon dioxide or insufficient oxygen are manifest in several ways, notably localized necrosis (e.g., core breakdown, pitting).

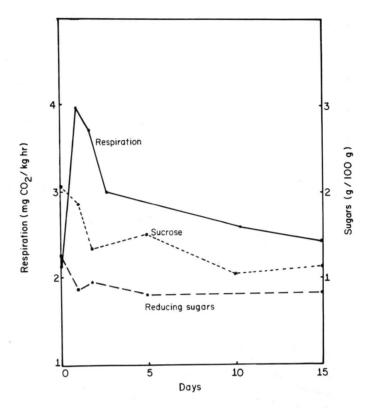

FIG. 16-18. Changes in the amounts of reducing and nonreducing sugars and the rate of respiration when potatoes previously stored at 10°C are moved to 21°C. (Reprinted from Ref. [85], courtesy of The Institute of Food Technologists.)

TABLE 16-19

Susceptibility of Fruits and Vegetables to Extremes in CO_2 and O_2 Concentrations[a]

Commodity	Minimum O_2 tolerance (%)	Maximum CO_2 tolerance (%)
Apple	3	2–5
Asparagus	5	10
Cauliflower	–	8
Cherries	3	7
Lettuce	1	4
Strawberries	1	45

[a]From Ref. [113] and unpublished data. These values will vary with variety, cultivation practices, and storage temperature.

2. PROTEIN SYNTHESIS

There are many indications that protein synthesis is an event of fundamental importance during plant senescence [10,13,51]. Increased levels of specific enzymes have been noted in detached and deteriorating plant tissues [59]. For example, aldolase, carboxylase, chlorophyllase, phosphorylase, phosphatase, invertase, pectic enzymes, lipase, ribonuclease, peroxidase, phenolase, transaminase, o-methyltransferase, catalase, and indoleacetic acid oxidase are among those enzymes known to emerge in ripening fruit. In most instances, it is not yet clear whether the emergence of such enzymes is the direct consequence of gene direction. It has been generally observed that plant senescence is accompanied by increased RNA synthesis and increased incorporation of amino acids into proteins. Indeed, there appears to be an absolute requirement for continued protein synthesis in ripening fruit [13]. For example, cycloheximide, an inhibitor of protein synthesis, inhibits degreening, softening, and ripening in ethylene-treated banana fruit (Fig. 16-19).

The previously mentioned occurrence of cytoplasmic DNA leads one to suspect that enzymes, such as chlorophyllase (degreening) and transaminase (flavor biogenesis), are respectively synthesized via chloroplast and mitochondrial DNA.

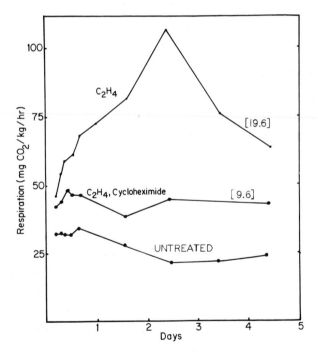

FIG. 16-19. Effect of cycloheximide (2 μg/ml) on the respiration rate and sugar content of banana slices vented continuously with 10-15 ppm ethylene. Numerals in brackets are the percent soluble solids at the completion of the experiment. (Reprinted from Ref. [13], courtesy of Pergamon Press.)

The recent findings that gene-directed events are an integral part of plant senescence have tremendous importance since these findings open new avenues of approach to commodity preservation. Manipulation of gene expression through chemical and physical treatments may well supplant conventional methods of fresh commodity preservation, i.e., refrigeration and storage in modified atmospheres. Recently, mutant cultivars of fruit have been developed. These fruit remain mature, without ripening for indefinite periods of time.

3. MANIPULATION OF CORE REACTIONS BY CONTROLLING ENZYME ACTIVITIES

We have much to learn of the many enzymes which mediate physiological events in postharvest cells. However, the real trick and the key to future progress lies in our understanding of enzyme control. The mere presence of an enzyme does not alone indicate its functionality in association with a given physiological event. We have already mentioned that subtle differences in microconstituents, such as inorganic ions, can profoundly influence the direction of metabolism by modifying the activity of a particular enzyme. Some modes of enzyme control and examples of their specific implications in postharvest systems are outlined in Table 16-20. Special mention should be made of the plant hormones which appear to be important regulators of senescence and stress response in postharvest commodities [41]. Of the five known categories of plant hormones (four are shown in Fig. 16-20), ethylene gas has received most of the attention until recent years. The propensity of this gas to "trigger" ripening of fruit [21] and generally promote senescence in plant tissues has led to the descriptive name "ripening hormone" (Fig. 16-21). Recent evidence clearly points to the involvement of other hormones in fruit ripening. The juvenile hormones (auxins [118], cytokinins [116], and gibberellins [100]) clearly repress ripening, while there is some evidence that abscisins promote the onset of senescence phenomena, such as ripening [76]. As with other physiological events, such as seed germination, it appears that plant hormones act in concert to control senescence-linked events.

TABLE 16-20

Modes of Enzyme Control

Control mechanism	Example
Protein antienzyme	Invertase inhibitor in potato tuber [92]
Isozyme variants	Cytoplasmic and mitochondrial malic dehydrogenase [59b]
Compartmentalization	Organic acid metabolism in potato tuber [83]
Cooperativity	Indole-3-acetic acid oxidase in ripening pear [32]
Allotopy	Peroxidase in developing pear fruit [96]
Biosynthesis	Malic enzyme in ripening pear fruit [33]

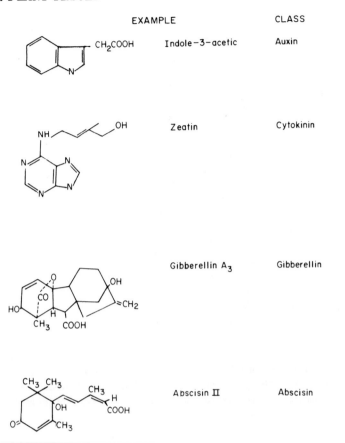

FIG. 16-20. Some plant hormones and their structures.

The mechanism of hormone action, notably that of ethylene in ripening fruit, has received considerable study. Some suggested loci of hormone action are outlined in Figure 16-22. Today, we have no precise biochemical description of how hormones elicit their physiological effects. To establish a definite corollary one must relate the control site to other possible loci of action. For example, if a given hormone appears to trigger DNA transcription in situ, one must ask whether this is an indirect consequence of promoting feedback inhibition and stimulating accumulation of a particular end product.

C. Ancillary Physiological Events

Aside from the core reactions we must consider those subsets of reactions which are unique to species or groups of tissue and which affect the edible quality of the commodity. We have already mentioned the dynamic nature of chemical constituents of edible plant tissues. Here we briefly consider some enzymes which influence texture, flavor, and color of these systems. Other than for a few reactions,

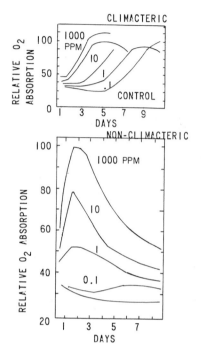

FIG. 16-21. Influence of ethylene on the respiratory rates of climacteric and nonclimacteric fruits. Note that increased ethylene concentration results in the early onset of climacteric respiration in climacteric fruits and in an increased respiratory burst in the nonclimacteric fruit.

especially pectin catabolism in fruit and starch metabolism in potato, relatively little information is available concerning enzyme systems which affect the quality of fresh commodities.

1. CHANGES IN CELL-WALL CONSTITUENTS

Quantitatively the most important biochemical changes taking place in harvested vegetative tissues involve carbohydrates. Fruit ripening and the softening of vegetative tissues is usually accompanied by catabolism of cell-wall polysaccharides [54]. Pectin-degrading enzymes have been studied extensively in ripening fruit. The two major groups of pectin enzymes found in mature plant tissues are esterases and polygalacturonases. While polygalacturonase activity has been demonstrated in relatively few fruits (tomato, pear, pineapple, avadaco [48]), pectinesterase is commonly encountered and is often observed to increase during ripening [117]. The amounts and types of pectic enzymes in fruits have an important bearing on the clarity or cloud stability of fruit juices and other derived beverages [57]. In orange and tomato juices where a stable colloidal suspension is desired, the presence of pectinesterases and polygalacturonases is undesirable. In contrast,

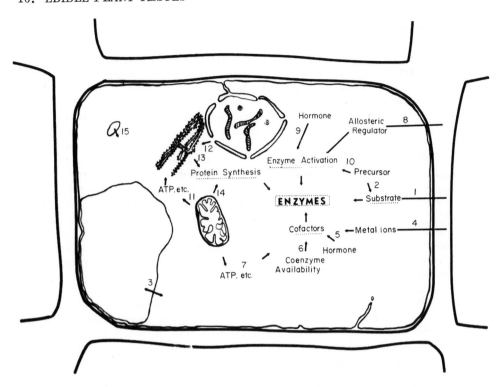

FIG. 16-22. Conceivable loci of hormone action at the cell level, and impact on enzyme catalysis: (1) transport or release of substrate, (2) conversion of substrate precursor, (3) transport of solute from intracellular compartments, (4) transport or release of metal ions, (5) hormone functioning directly as cofactor, (6) transport or release of cofactor, (7) biosynthesis of cofactor, (8) availability or release of allosteric effector, (9) hormone functioning directly as enzyme effector, (10) conversion of precursor to active enzyme, (11) provision of utilizable energy for protein synthesis, (12) transcription, (13) translation, (14) cytoplasmic coded protein synthesis, and (15) release of autolytic enzymes from lysosome. (Reprinted from Ref. [41], courtesy of Chemical Rubber Company.)

the presence of pectin enzymes is beneficial in such products as lime, apple, and grape juices, where a clear beverage is considered desirable.

Other cell-wall-degrading enzymes, such as cellulase and hemicellulases, are presumably active in edible plant tissues, although their contributions to changes in texture are not clear. While cellulase activity increases in ripening tomato fruit, it does not appear to markedly influence concomitant softening [47]. Cell-wall polysaccharides are known to be the major source of sugars generated in such postharvest products as citrus and in some fruits which contain negligible starch. The toughening of vegetative tissues, such as asparagus and the pods of many leguminous species, which occurs shortly after harvest appears related to synthesis of cell-wall materials.

2. STARCH-SUGAR TRANSFORMATIONS

The synthesis of starch or its degradation to simple sugars is an important reaction in postharvest commodities. In potatoes, sugars are undesirable since they can cause (1) poor texture after baking or boiling, or (2) an undesirable sweet taste and excessive browning after frying. The conversion of starch to sucrose and reducing sugars is promoted when most tuber species are stored in nonfreezing temperatures below 40°-45°C. It is not known why exposure of potatoes to a low temperature stimulates starch catabolism, nor is it entirely clear which enzymes are involved. A number of conceivable loci of control are illustrated in Figure 16-23. Amylases, which are important in starch catabolism in germinating tubers, do not appear to be very active in the dormant potato [37]. It has been suggested that phosphorylase is instrumental in causing sugar accumulation at low nonfreezing temperatures. Some have found that phosphorylase exhibits increased activity in tubers during storage at low temperatures [52], whereas others have reported that the enzyme exhibits no significant change in activity or proportion of isoenzymes during cold storage [53]. This is a moot point since there are a multitude of other modes by which phosphorylase may be turned on in response to cold stress (Table 16-20).

Such modes of control may only be manifest in situ. The activity of invertase in potatoes increases during storage at low nonfreezing temperatures [91]. This enzyme appears to be controlled by a proteinaceous inhibitor which is metabolized at a low temperature. According to this scheme, sucrose, or perhaps sucrose phosphate, functions to limit starch hydrolysis via feedback control on phosphorylase or by promotion of starch synthesis via ADP glucose-starch glucosyltransferase. Although phosphorylase catalyzes the synthesis of α-1,4-glycosidic linkages in vitro, many workers believe that in vivo it is involved primarily in starch breakdown [123]. One must also consider that low temperatures may disrupt or modify membranes surrounding starch granules, and this may serve to delimit enzyme contact with glucan [84]. There is also a host of other means by which the low-temperature response can be explained, but none is as appealing as that involving enzyme-catalyzed steps of the glycolytic scheme.

Hydrolysis of starch to simple sugars is among the more prominent changes occurring in most ripening fruits. Again, it is not known which enzymes are involved, although in ripening mangoes, increases in the activities of amylase and invertase parallel decreases in starch from 6% to a trace. In ripening fruits, low temperatures generally retard starch hydrolysis. Does this indicate that different modes of metabolic control are operative in potatoes and fruit?

In some commodities, notably seeds (peas, corn, beans) and underground storage organs (sweet potato, potato, carrot) synthesis of starch, rather than degradation, may predominate after harvest [4]. Starch synthesis is generally optimal at temperatures above ambient. Diminution of sugars in vegetables is closely associated with loss of desirable quality. The principal enzymes in starch synthesis appear to be those in photosynthetic tissues, namely fructose transglycosidase, adenosine diphosphate glucose:starch glucosyltransferase, UDPG pyrophosphorylase, and ADPG-pyrophosphorylase. However, the details of this scheme have not been determined for commodities of interest to the food scientist. Decreases in sugars may also result from their oxidation via mitochondrial-linked reactions [85].

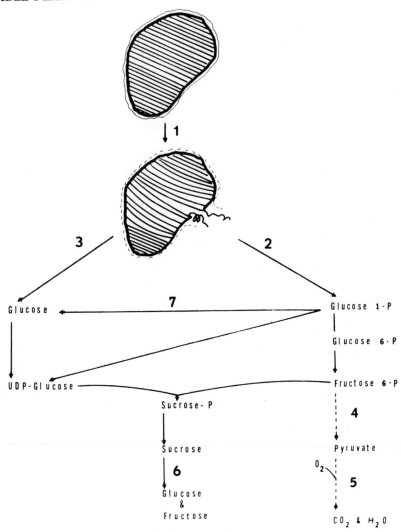

FIG. 16-23. Some possible control loci of starch catabolism in plant tissues:
(1) disruption of the plastid membrane by low temperature or enzymes; unpacking
of the "crystalline" starch granule by "hydrogen bondase" or some other initiating
enzyme; hormonal modification of the plastid membrane. (2) Hydrolysis of glucan
to glucose 1-phosphate via phosphorylase biosynthesis, or activation of unique isoenzyme species; modulation by cylic AMP or hormones. (3) Hydrolysis of glucan
to dextrins, maltose, and glucose via amylases (biosynthesis or activation of α-
amylase, β-amylase, maltase, glycoamlyase, etc.). (4) Feedback control on phosphorylase (e.g., glucose 1-phosphate accumulation) via glycolytic enzymes (e.g.,
phosphofructokinase). (5) Feedback control on phosphorylase, glycolytic enzymes,
etc., via respiration control (e.g., energy charge). (6) Feedback control on phosphorylase, by sucrose via invertase or invertase inhibitor. (7) Activation or biosynthesis of glucose-1-phosphatase. Cofactors and minor reactants for indicated
reactions are not included.

3. METABOLISM OF ORGANIC ACIDS

We have already mentioned that organic acids are constantly changing in ripening fruit and tend to diminish during final senescence of most plant tissues. Much of this loss is undoubtedly attributable to their oxidation in respiratory metabolism. The respiratory quotient is approximately 1.0 when sugars are substrates, increases to 1.33 when malate or citrate are substrates, and further increases to 1.6 when tartrate is the substrate [111]. Some suggested pathways associating respiratory metabolism with organic acid synthesis are shown in Figure 16-24. Enzymes involved in organic acid metabolism include the malic enzyme, phosphoenolpyruvate carboxylase, pyruvate kinase, and pyruvate decarboxylase. There is evidence that the activity of malic enzyme increases in climacteric pears and apples (de novo synthesis demonstrated in pears) and that the activity of pyruvate decarboxylase increases with climacteric respiration in apples, pears, and bananas.

The metabolism of aromatic organic acids via the shikimic acid pathway (Fig. 16-25) is important because of its relationship to protein metabolism (aromatic amino acids), accumulation of substrate for enzymic browning (e.g., chlorogenic acid), and lignin deposition (phenyl propane residues) [95]. It also should be mentioned that acetate participates in the synthesis of phenolic compounds, lipids, and volatile flavor compounds. Apart from their general impact on flavor, texture, and color, certain organic acids appear to modify the metabolism of plant hormones and are thereby implicated in the control of senescence. For example, the finding that chlorogenic acid modifies the activity of indole-3-acetic acid oxidase may well relate to the increased concentration of this acid in the green blotchy areas of defective tomatoes [121] and in pear fruits which fail to ripen [95]. That is, ripening, which is dependent on auxin metabolism, may alternately be controlled by substances (such as chlorogenic acid) which are effectors of indole-3-acetic acid oxidase activity.

D. Lipid Metabolism

Although the lipid components of most plant tissues used as food are present at relatively low levels, their metabolism appears to be an important element of senescence. Oxidative enzymes, such as lipoxygenase, and hydrolytic enzymes, such as phospholipases, have received the most attention [128]. The aging of various plant tissues is associated with a decline in polyunsaturated fatty acids [35]. It is tempting to speculate that autolysis of membrane lipids is related to cellular decompartmentalization and leakage which occurs during this stage of development. In addition to their role in ontogenic development, lipolytic enzymes are involved in the development of off flavors in processed foods. For example, many plant tissues must be blanched to inactivate lipoxygenases prior to freezing; otherwise offflavors develop during frozen storage [88].

The lipids of tissues which accumulate fat deposits (e.g., palm, olive, avacado) have a composition markedly different from those which are part of the functional cell framework. Little is known concerning the metabolic control of triglyceride accumulation in these tissues during development, nor is it clear whether the enzyme systems that participate in synthesis of reserve lipids are the same as those which synthesize membrane lipids.

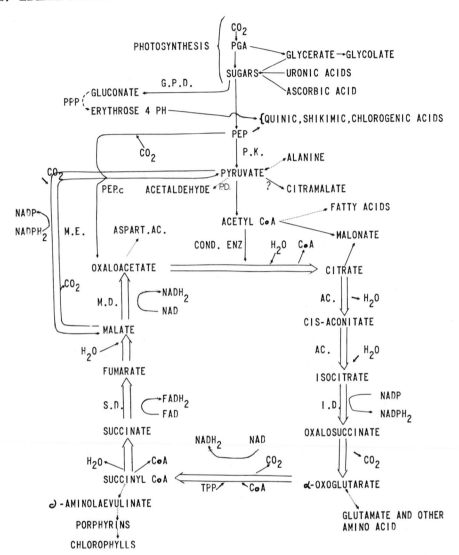

FIG. 16-24. Krebs cycle (⇄) with some other modes of organic acid synthesis (→) or synthesis of other important constituents (•••→). Abbreviations: AC, aconitase; Cond. en2., condensing enzyme; GPD, glucose-6-phosphate dehydrogenase; ID, isocitric dehydrogenase; MD, malate dehydrogenase; ME, malic enzyme; PEPc, phosphoenal pyruvate carboxyllase and carboxykinase; PGA, phosphoglyceric acid; PD, pyruvate decarboxylase; PK, pyruvate kinase; PPP, pentose phosphate pathway; SD, succinic dehydrogenase; TPP, thiamine pyrophosphate. (Reprinted from Ref. [111], courtesy of Academic Press.)

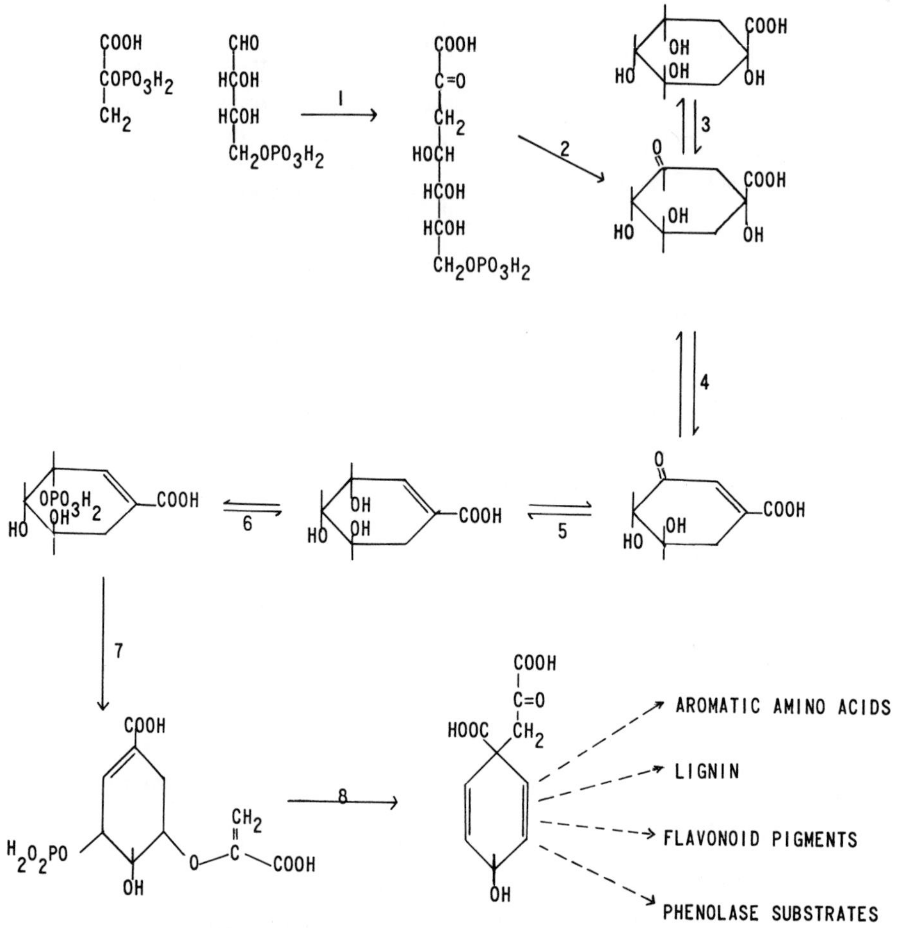

FIG. 16-25. Biosynthesis of some important cell constituents via the shikimic acid pathway. (1) Phosphoenolpyruvate + D-erythrose 4-phosphate to 3-deoxy-D-arabinoheptulosonic acid 7-phosphate; (2) to 5-dehydroquinic acid; (3) to quinic acid; (4) to 5-dehydroshikimic acid; (5) to shikimic acid; (6) to 5-phosphoshikimic acid; (7) to 3-(enolpyruvate ether) of phosphoshikimic acid; (8) to prephenic acid. Although this scheme is based on studies with microorganisms, there is ample evidence that this pathway operates in higher plants.

E. Pigment Metabolism

1. CAROTENOIDS

The biosynthesis of carotenoids and related terpenoids is an important event in many edible plant tissues. Biosynthesis of these compounds occurs through the universal system for isoprene compounds and it involves the formation of mevalonic acid from acetyl CoA [17]. Carotenoid formation in detached plant parts may be influenced by storage conditions. In certain instances these reactions are stimulated by oxygen, inhibited by light and high temperatures, and affected by the hormones ethylene and abscisic acid [59]. The most common catalytic agents for carotenoid destruction appear to be the lipoxygenases (indirectly via lipid oxidation) and the peroxidases (which appear to promote β-carotene degradation directly).

2. FLAVONOIDS AND RELATED PIGMENTS

The biosynthesis of these aromatic pigments takes place in a number of stages. The pathway for synthesis of the basic $C_6:C_3$ structure which comprises the A phenyl ring is known (Fig. 16-25), although less is known of reactions involved in the formation of specific pigments. Anthocyanin synthesis is stimulated by light and is often affected by temperature [106]. The purple pigment, betain, of red cabbage is synthesized and accumulates when cabbage is placed in storage below 10°C [14]. The use of N-dimethylaminosuccinamic acid (B-9) sprays has been observed to induce early formation of anthocyanins in cherry [22].

The catabolism of anthocyanin pigments is not very well understood. Various anthocyanins can be oxidized by products of the polyphenoloxidase reaction on hydroxycinnamic acid derivatives and flavones. Decolorization of anthocyanins can be catalyzed by decolorizing enzyme systems (some of which are glycosidases) found to exist in leaf and fruit tissues [114]. These enzymes presumably contribute to the loss in the bright colors characteristic of many fruits and vegetables postharvest.

The metabolism of other aromatic pigments is not well understood. The astringent tannins (dimers of flavones, etc.) are condensed during ripening of many fruits, resulting in loss of their capacity to complex with saliva proteins and loss of their astringent properties [40]. We should also mention that aromatic compounds have been long suspected of playing a role in disease resistance of plants. Phenolics, oxidized by either the plant tissue or a parasite, may be potent antifungal agents and are potent inhibitors of pectic enzymes [3]. Active pectic enzymes are commonly necessary for pathogens to successfully invade plant tissue. It also has been suggested that oxidized phenols modify specific biochemical events in plants, e.g., auxin catabolism and coupled respiration.

3. CHLOROPHYLL

One of the more obvious changes that occurs in senescing plant tissues containing chlorophyll is the loss of a characteristic green color. Peel and sometimes pulp degreening is associated with the ripening of most fruit, and "yellowing" is a characteristic of most leaf and stem tissues consumed as vegetables. Chlorophyll degradation is accompanied by synthesis of other pigments in a number of detached plant tissues. Chlorophyll metabolism is markedly influenced by environmental parameters, such as light, temperature, and humidity, and the effects of these factors are specific for the tissue. For example, light accelerates degradation of chlorophyll in ripening tomatoes and promotes formation of the pigment in cold-stored potato tubers. Chlorophyllase emergence is associated with the buildup of endogenous ethylene, and chlorophyll degradation can be promoted by application of parts per million levels of this hormone [68]. It is a common commercial practice to utilize this principle for degreening citrus fruit and other commodities, such as celery. Chlorophyllase is a hydrolytic enzyme which converts chlorophylls a and b to their respective chlorophyllides (see Chapter 8). Present evidence actually suggests that chlorophyllase does not catalyze the initial step of chlorophyll degradation in senescing plant tissues [120]. The initial steps of chlorophyll degradation require molecular oxygen, and removal of the phytol chain occurs in later steps. In most instances it has been observed that chlorophyllase activity parallels synthesis rather than degradation. Most studies have shown that chlorophyllase declines during chlorophyll degradation, although there are some exceptions [68]. It is conceivable that chlorophyll degradation is catalyzed more effectively by oxidative enzymes, such as lipoxygenase, than by chlorophyllases. Lipoxygenase has been observed to consistently emerge during plant senescence and it is known to contribute to loss of chlorophyll in frozen vegetables.

F. Aroma Compounds – Biogenesis and Degradation

We have mentioned a variety of reactions which influence the flavor of fruits and vegetables. These include the metabolic reactions associated with phenolic substances, carbohydrates, and organic acids. Development of compounds responsible for the more subtle notes of flavor are catalyzed by a wide variety of enzymes. Some examples of enzymes related to flavor biogenesis are illustrated in Table 16-9. In some instances, such as with species of Allium and Curcurbites, the compounds responsible for aroma are not synthesized until the cells are disrupted [104]. Here we have a situation where enzyme-catalyzed formation of flavor substances occurs in the mouth during decompartmentation of cells. The concept of flavor precursors which are converted to flavor compounds on exposure to appropriate enzymes has been known for some time. Indeed, a commercial process exists whereby flavor potentiating enzymes are added back to processed foods just prior to consumption to regenerate the fresh flavor which was lost as a consequence of heating or dehydration [62]. This method takes advantage of the fact that precursor molecules may be stable to heat or dehydration, whereas the flavor enzymes are labile.

Less is known of enzymes responsible for catabolism of esters, aldehydes, ketones, etc., during aging of plant tissues, although these products are generally short lived. In Bartlett pears, the rapid diminution of 2,4-decadienoic acid esters is associated with increased esterase activity. Oxidative enzymes are known to generate compounds responsible for off flavor in improperly processes vegetables and fruits. These compounds are often chemically similar to those which provide desirable flavor.

V. REACTIONS TO STRESS

Now that we have been introduced to the basic character of plant tissues we can begin to examine some of the problems which confront the food scientist. Here we consider the stress response of plant tissues in which the treatment is (1) unintentional and leads to undesirable physiological change and (2) intentional and leads to relatively long-term stability of the tissue in its protected state.

A. Physiological Responses to Injury

Throughout its life cycle, the intact plant must respond to challenges from the environment. A plant's reactions to stress are normally in the direction of protection, e.g., prevention of water loss, adaptation to temperature extremes, or the development of physical and chemical barriers to pathogens. When injury is such that the tissue cannot adapt to the situation, the response may be one of gene-directed death of particular cells or groups of cells. The responses of a given tissue to various environmental challenges is important because these responses indicate the range of commercial conditions that can be successfully imposed on the living tissue.

1. WOUNDING

Mechanical wounding generally causes a temporary, localized burst of respiration and cell division. New specialized protective tissues may form which prevent desiccation and resist invasion by microorganisms. In fleshy storage organs the wounded cells commence synthesis of messenger RNA [64], resulting in an increased polysome content and protein synthesis (Fig. 16-26). In sweet potatoes, attack by pathogens or mechanical injury results in production of phenolic acids (chlorogenic, isochlorogenic, caffeic). Synthesis of these compounds is mediated

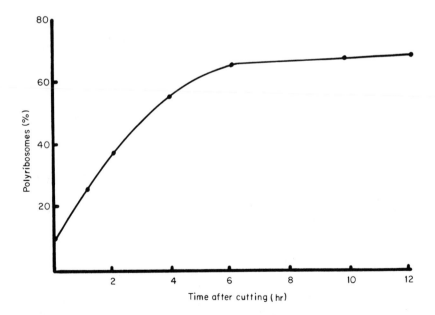

FIG. 16-26. The polyribosome content of carrot disks following cutting. Accompanying the increase in polyribosomes there are increases in both the rate of amino acid incorporation into proteins and the protein content of the tissue. (Reprinted from Ref. [61], courtesy of The U.S. National Academy of Sciences.)

by the enzymes phenylalanine ammonia-lysase and tyrosine ammonia-lyase [112], which deaminate the respective amino acids to cinnamic and p-coumaric acid (Fig. 16-27). These enzymes are absent in healthy tissue and their rapid formation in cut or infected tissues is dependent on protein synthesis. Induction of peroxidase isozymes is also closely associated with wound response, although it is not clear what role the enzymes play (Fig. 16-28) [70]. The degree to which different varieties respond to fungal infection suggests that the production of peroxidase is a prime factor in disease resistance. In some instances, the tissue is able to respond to wounding and pathogen invasion by producing fungitoxic substances, called phytoalexins (Fig. 16-29). It is not clear how such compounds are formed or why they have antimicrobial properties. There is considerable evidence that activation of genes controlling enzymes associated with injury response is controlled by the hormones cytokinin, auxin, and ethylene. Recent reports indicating that phytoalexins may occur in commercial foods are important because these compounds have been implicated in various disorders of human health, including emphysema and liver toxicity [12].

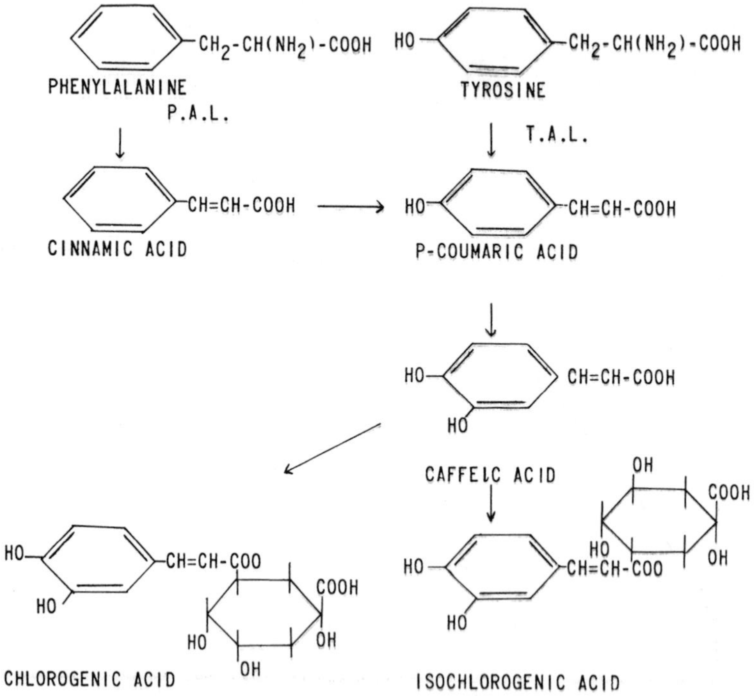

FIG. 16-27. Synthetic pathways of phenolic acids which develop in certain plant tissues (e.g., sweet potato roots) in response to mechanical injury of infection. PAL, phenylalanine ammonia lyase; TAL, tyrosine ammonia lyase.

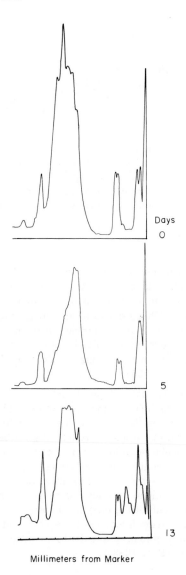

Days

0

5

13

Millimeters from Marker

FIG. 16-28. Densitometric tracings of peroxidase isozymes separated by polyacrylamide gel electrophoresis. The indicated changes occurred as a result of chilling stress in preclimacteric banana fruit. Bacterial and fungal attack of plant tissues can also cause a change in isoperoxidase distribution. Disease resistance and stress response appear to be closely related to specific shifts in the distribution of isoperoxidases.

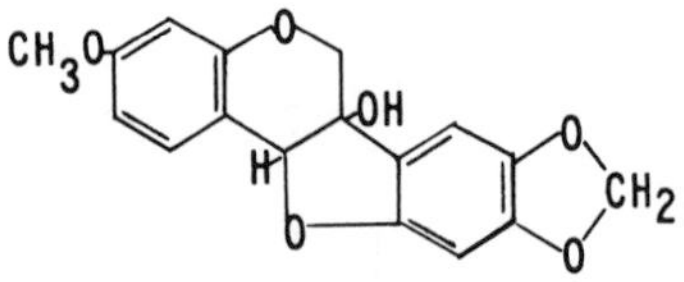

FIG. 16-29. Structure of the phytoalexin pisatin. This compound is synthesized by the host tissue (endocarp of detached pea pods) on exposure to various
pathogenic or nonpathogenic fungi. Exposing a tissue to a nonpathogenic microbe
before exposure to a pathogenic microbe results in increased disease resistance.
Pathogens not affected by a specific phytoalexin have the ability to degrade the
compound.

Browning which occurs on cut or bruised surfaces of many plant tissues results
when polyphenoloxidase (phenolase) catalyzes oxidative conversion of phenolic
substances such as chlorogenic acid, to brown end products, known as melanoidins
([27]; see also Chapter 6). These enzymic browning reactions are considered
desirable in certain instances, such as during tea fermentation, and undesirable in
others, such as during processing of fruit slices or juices. The propensity of a
given tissue to brown may vary with its enzyme content and sometimes with its
content of phenolic substances [95].

Numerous methods have been developed to inhibit enzymic browning because of
its undesirable effects on fresh fruits and vegetables. These methods include exclusion of oxygen by immersing the product in water; inhibition of the reaction by
NaCl, antioxidants (ascorbate), acids (to reduce the pH below 3.0 with, for example, citric, malic, or phosphoric acid); or treatment with sulfur dioxide or sulfites.
The latter chemicals, at concentrations as low as 1 ppm, have been observed to
inhibit the phenolase enzyme system. Apparently, SO_2 may directly inhibit the
enzyme or may act on the quinone product and reduce it back to the original phenols.
An interesting method for controlling enzymic browning in tissue slices is to induce or add the enzyme m-O-methyltransferase [29]. Methylation of the o-
dihydroxy structure results in loss of substrate specificity and accordingly decreased enzymic browning (Fig. 16-30).

2. EXPOSURE TO ADVERSE TEMPERATURES

A group of disorders known as low-temperature or chilling injuries sometimes
occurs at temperatures somewhat above the freezing point of tissues. Some plant
tissues, such as pear fruit and lettuce, do not normally suffer from low chilling
temperatures but for many tissues there is a critical temperature below which
chilling injury occurs (Table 16-18). The extent of low-temperature injury is time-

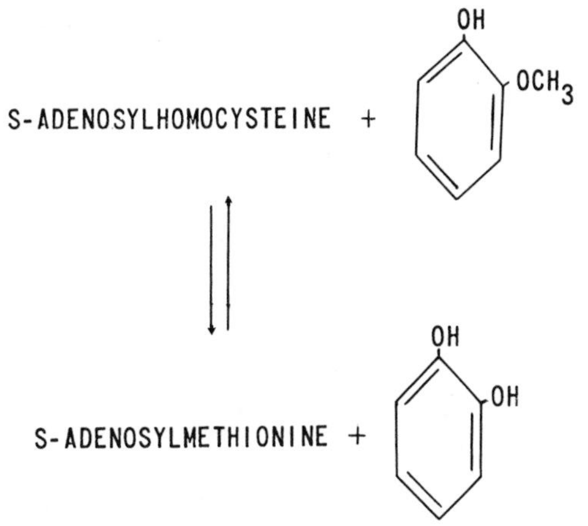

FIG. 16-30. Control of enzymic browning by conversion of the o-dihydroxy substrate to the methylated product.

temperature dependent. Long exposure of commodities to temperatures just below their critical values gives an effect comparable to that exhibited following short-term exposure to lower temperatures. Visible effects of chilling injury range from necrosis of local cellular regions to complete decomposition of the tissue.

It is not clear what specific biochemical events are responsible for chilling injury, although it is generally believed that the various metabolic reactions in a given tissue are affected differently during exposure to low nonfreezing temperatures. This apparently results in underproduction of certain essentials and overproduction of other substances to a point where they become toxic. For example, accumulations of ethanol, acetaldehyde, and oxaloacetic acid are associated with low-temperature breakdown of certain fruits [80].

Other lines of evidence suggest that chilling injury is related to the fragility of biological membranes [72]. The amounts of unsaturated fatty acids in membrane phospholipids are notably higher in species insensitive to chilling (Table 16-21). Apparently, a temperature-induced change in the activation energy of membrane-bound enzymes is associated with phase changes in the lipid components of membranes (Fig. 16-31). Phase changes which occur in membrane lipids at chilling temperatures have been related to perturbation of mitochondrial respiration. Furthermore, mitochondria from chilling-resistant tissues show the capacity to swell to a greater extent than those from sensitive species. These effects are presumably related to the plasticity of the membrane, which in turn is a function of the degree of unsaturation in the phospholipids. Still other lines of evidence

TABLE 16-21

Degree of Fatty Acid Saturation in Plant Phospholipids as
Related to Chilling Injury

Fatty acids[a] unsaturated/saturated	Number of species	
	Sensitive	Resistant
2.0	5	1
2.0-2.5	6	5
2.6-3.0	2	5
3.0	0	3

[a]Mole % basis.

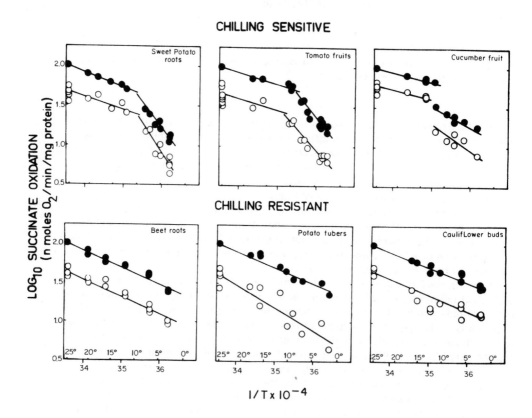

FIG. 16-31. Phase changes in the membrane lipids of mitochondria from chilling-sensitive plants. (Reprinted from Ref. [71], courtesy of American Association of Plant Physiologists.)

suggest that chilling-insensitive cells can adapt to unfavorable temperatures by peroxidase-catalyzed oxidation of sulfhydryl groups in membrane proteins [79]. Development of cold hardiness is often associated with emergence of specific iso-zymes of peroxidase [45].

Exposure of plant tissues to abnormally high temperatures may also produce characteristic injuries in specific commodities. Storage of many varieties of fruit above 30°C results in failure to ripen normally, and this condition may result from a breakdown of the ethylene-synthesizing machinery [9].

3. CARBON DIOXIDE INJURY

Many commodities are sensitive to increases in atmospheric carbon dioxide that can occur during storage without proper ventilation (CO_2 is generated from respir-ation) or during storage involving controlled but improper levels of carbon dioxide. The tolerance of different tissues to carbon dioxide is quite variable (Table 16-19). Some fruits, notably sweet cherries, plums, and peaches, are not very susceptible to carbon dioxide injury and can be stored at CO_2 concentrations up to at least 20% (v/v in atmosphere). The sensitivity of a given tissue to carbon dioxide can be in-fluenced by other storage parameters. The mechanisms of CO_2 injury and re-sistance to injury are not clear. Toxic levels of succinic acid were observed to accumulate in CO_2-injured apples (brown hearted [50]), and the disorder in pears has been related to alterations in the structure and function of organelle membranes (FIG. 16-32).

4. OXYGEN DEPRIVATION

Diminution of atmospheric oxygen below critical levels can also result in injury of certain commodities. In most cases, plant tissues can tolerate oxygen concen-trations as low as 5% (v/v in atmosphere) and in some unusual examples (e.g., radish) a tissue may be stored without adversity in an environment completely devoid of oxygen. Tissue necrosis resulting from oxygen deprivation is probably a consequence of metabolic shifts to anaerobic respiration, allowing ethyl alcohol and other toxic end products of glycolysis to accumulate.

5. WATER VAPOR DEFICIT

It is generally recommended that fresh fruits and vegetables be stored at relative humidities sufficient to minimize moisture loss and maintenance of cell turgor while not so high as to favor microbial growth. The tendency for commodities to lose moisture at a given relative humidity is related to the nature and amounts of specialized cells at the tissue surfaces.

Relative humidity can markedly influence physiological processes of stored plant tissues. For example, the ripening of preclimacteric fruit is influenced by atmospheric moisture. When stored at 25% relative humidity instead of the recommended 80-85% relative humidity, banana fruits fail to ripen and do not undergo a climacteric respiration rise [43], whereas green tomatoes and pears

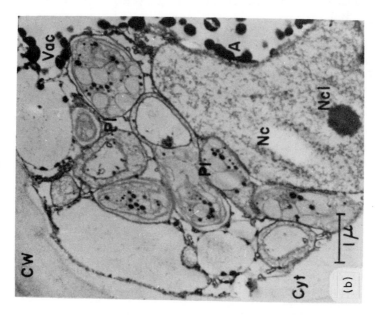

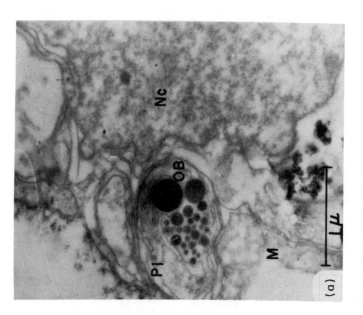

FIG. 16-32. Effect of carbon dioxide on the structure of pears. (a) Air controls: ultrastructure of plastids (Pl) showing the laminar arrangement, the position of osmophilic bodies (OB), the structural continuity with a mitochondrion (M), and the nucleus (Nc). (b) In 10% CO_2: note change of plastid from laminar form to oval vasculated form. Cell wall, CW; cytoplasm, Cyt; vasuole, vac; aggregates of polyphenols, A.

[42] stored at 25% relative humidity exhibit a bimodal climacteric and intensification of ripening indices (Fig. 16-33). These effects may be caused by alteration of gaseous exchange at the fruit peel. It is not clear why these fruits differ in their responses to water vapor deficit.

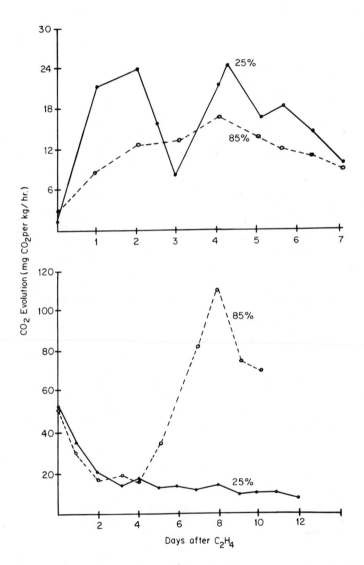

FIG. 16-33. Respiratory patterns of banana (-lower-) and pear (-upper-) fruits as influenced by percent relative humidity in the atmosphere [42,43].

Atmospheric moisture levels also influence the severity of chilling injury in certain fruits. Core breakdown and soft scald of apples is minimized by storage at a low relative humidity, and low-temperature breakdown of citrus fruits is lessened when fruits are wrapped in wax paper to minimize moisture loss [74]. There is mounting evidence that the plant hormone abscisic acid is associated with the susceptibility of plant tissues to water deficits [67]. The unique property of this hormone to counterbalance the effects of juvenile hormones (auxins, gibberellins, cytokinins) may relate to the influence of water vapor deficit on physiological processes. The general area relating plant hormones to stress response is deserving of further study.

6. IONIZING RADIATION

Low doses of ionizing radiation have been successfully applied experimentally to prolong the storage life of fresh fruits and vegetables [90]. The inhibition of sprouting in potatoes, onions, and carrots as well as the destruction of insect pests in stored grains may be accomplished with 10-25 krad doses. Control of mold growth requires in excess of 100 krads and destruction of pathogenic bacteria necessitates a dose of 500-1,000 krads. Here we wish to briefly concern ourselves with the impact of this stress on physiological processes in plant tissue.

Usually, the quality of fruits and vegetables is adversely affected by doses of ionizing radiation in excess of 200 krads. The physiological changes induced by irradiation may bring about the death of cells long after treatment. Commodities show characteristic symptoms of irradiation damage. For example, apples exposed to 1,000 krads exhibit a ring of necrotic tissue, not unlike core flush, adjacent to the core. Moreover, citrus fruit and bananas have been shown to exhibit peel lesions at doses as low as 25 krad. Local tissue necrosis appears to relate to the emergence of peroxidase and catalase in citrus fruit, and the pulp softening observed in irradiated plant tissues is associated with activation of pectic enzymes.

Results of low-dose irradiation studies on pear fruit provide an interesting story [99]. Exposure of preclimacteric fruit to a 0.25 Mrad dose delays ripening, while a 1.5 Mrad dose inhibits ripening irreversibly. In both instances mitochondrial respiration is uncoupled; however, in the instance where ripening is only delayed, the cell system is able to restore coupling, presumably through de novo synthesis of mitochondria, and the fruit eventually ripens normally (Table 16-22).

TABLE 16-22

Mitochondrial Recovery of Respiratory Control in Vivo as Revealed by
Split Doses and as Affected by Climacteric State of the
Pear Fruit when Exposed to Ionizing Radiation[a]

Radiation dose	Respiratory control (RCR-1)	
	Preclimacteric	Climacteric
0 krad	3.2	2.8
500 krad	2.1	1.8

TABLE 16-22 (Continued)

Radiation dose	Respiratory control (RCR-1)	
	Preclimacteric	Climacteric
1,000 krad	0.3	0.1
500 krad, 24 hr, 500 krad	2.4	0.4
500 krad, 24 hr, 500 krad, 24 hr, 500 krad	2.3	0.1

[a]Data from Romani [99]. The organelles were isolated and assayed for respiratory control immediately after the final dose. In the absence of respiratory control the respiration rate in state 3 (absence of ADP) and state 4 (presence of ADP) are equal. A respiratory control of 3.2 is indicative of efficient coupling of electron transfer to ATP synthesis, while lower values indicate an uncoupling or decrease in the efficiency of oxidative phosphorylation.

7. AIR POLLUTANTS

Brief mention should be made of the influence of air pollutants on physiological processes in plant tissues. Postharvest commodities show different susceptibilities to air pollutants, and this form of stress has become of increasing concern in urban areas. Automobile emissions, especially ethylene, can accelerate tissue necrosis at parts per million levels. The volatile components of photochemical smog [O_3, PANS (peroxyacyl nitrates), and NO_2] are known to create undesirable injury symptoms in a wide array of fruits and vegetables.

B. Stresses Incurred During Processing

The basic purpose of food processing is to curtail the activity of microorganisms and enzymes which may otherwise adversely affect the edible quality of food, and to do so with minimal damage to native qualities. The most common techniques for long-term preservation of plant tissues are dehydration, thermal processing, freezing, and fermentation. Because of the severity of the first three processes, the product itself usually undergoes rather extensive changes and the effects of these processes therefore are considered here.

1. THERMAL PROCESSING AND COOKING

Blanching and thermal sterilization are the most common types of heat processes used for plant tissues. Blanching is a mild heat treatment involving exposure of plant tissues to water or steam for a few minutes at about 100 °C and 1 atm pressure. Prior to freezing, dehydration, or irradiation, blanching is done primarily to inactive enzymes, whereas prior to heat sterilization blanching is done for several reasons, the most important being to remove air from the tissue. During moderately severe thermal processes, such as sterilization or cooking, damage to the edible quality and nutritive value of plant tissue may result from (1) leakage of solutes into the surrounding medium, (2) mechanical loss of solids, (3) volatilization, (4) oxidation, and (5) hydrolysis and other degradative reactions. The design of a thermal process will depend on the objectives desired. For example, slow or moderate heating allows activation of enzymes which can affect color, texture, flavor, and nutritive value. This occurrence can be either desirable or undesirable, depending on the product.

a. Texture Changes. The cellular architecture of plant tissues is slightly disrupted during heating, with a resulting increase in permeability of the cells. Consequently, turgor pressure is lost or diminished and normally crisp tissues bend to become flacid. Extracellular and vascular air is also lost during heating and this results in a change in texture. Cellulose destruction is apparently slight under most circumstances. Changes in pectic substances may also occur during heating. Slightly alkaline conditions cause extensive cleavage of the polygalacturonate chain by a transelimination reaction. Slow heating and brief heat shock (e.g., blanching) may activate pectinmethylesterase resulting in partial demethylation of pectic substances. Calcium, either naturally occurring or added, can then form ionic bridges between adjacent molecules of pectin by means of the newly freed carboxyl groups, and this results in increased intercellular cohesion and firmness.

Decomposition of insoluble pectin substances by exposure to high temperature may result in undesirably soft textures. Hydrolysis of pectic substances is time-temperature dependent and is also influenced by product pH and the storage conditions after heating. It has been shown that partial conversion of protopectin to pectin occurs during heat processing of both clingstone and freestone peaches [89]. Since fresh, ripe clingstone peaches have extensive amounts of protopectin in the cell walls, partial hydrolysis during heating does not markedly affect the final texture of the canned product. In contrast, freestone peaches undergo considerable diminution of cell-wall materials during normal ripening; thus, the added loss of insoluble pectin during heating results in a canned product with a mushy texture.

There are a number of tricks available to the processor that enable him to minimize excessive softening of plant tissues during thermal processing. These include the use of less mature produce, the addition of acids (e.g., citric acid to pimentoes), the addition of calcium salts, and the use of low processing temperatures (e.g., 80°-85°C for apricots).

Schlerenchymatic tissues retain their rigid structure even after prolonged heating. This is presumeably due to the intractable nature of the lignocellulose associated with the cell walls of these tissues.

Fruits heated in sucrose syrups tend to be firmer than those heated in the absence of this solute. If a substantial concentration of sugar exists in the syrup, water is withdrawn from the fruit [107]. The effect of water removal is to bring cell-wall polysaccharides closer together, permitting greater interaction by means of hydrogen bonding and van der Waals forces. This results in increased cell rigidity.

Gelatinization of starch also may have a profound effect on the texture of tissues, notably potatoes. The method of heating (e.g., boiling, steaming, baking, frying) a tissue will influence its water content and accordingly the degree of gelatinization and its texture (e.g., soggy, mealy). Starch gelatinization is discussed in detail in Chapter 3.

b. Flavor Changes. Flavor may be affected in various ways by thermal processing. Volatile compounds may escape or be destroyed. Members of the cabbage and onion families lose considerable amounts of volatile flavor compounds both by evaporation and decomposition. In many heat-processed vegetables (cabbage, corn), formation of hydrogen sulfide and other volatile sulfur compounds gives rise to a characteristic cooked flavor [105]. In plain tin cans, sulfides may interact with the tin coating of cans, giving rise to black stannous sulfide.

Characteristic cooked flavors also can develop when aldehydes, ketones, esters, and acids in plant tissues undergo oxidative and hydrolytic transformations during heating. In plain tin cans, the reduction of aldehydes and ketones to primary and secondary alcohols appears to occur at the tin-acid interface. Off flavors in some canned fruits and vegetables are attributable to the formation of ammonium pyrorolidonecarboxylate from the cyclization of glutamine [73] (Fig. 16-34).

Failure to completely inactivate enzymes may result in flavor changes during processing and subsequent storage. In some instances, enzymes are fairly heat resistant (e.g., peroxidase), and in others the enzyme is located in an area where it is physically protected. An example of the latter is a β-glucosidase of plum kernels [20]. Peroxidase, which can be responsible for off flavors in thermal-processed vegetables, is capable of regenerating activity after high-temperature, short0time processing [81]. Enzyme regeneration is discussed in Chapter 6.

c. Color Changes. Plant pigments undergo numerous transformations during thermal processing and these changes are discussed in Chapter 8. In addition to changes in the major natural pigments, other changes in coloration can occur during heating. For example, the interaction of leucoanthocyanins (colorless) with metal ions can result in pink discoloration of many fruits [26]. Furthermore, if precautions are not taken to prevent phenolase activity during the initial stages of heating, the product may develop a brown color. Finally, nonenzymic or Maillard-type browning may contribute to the development of dark pigments when conditions are favorable for these reactions (heat, relatively high pH).

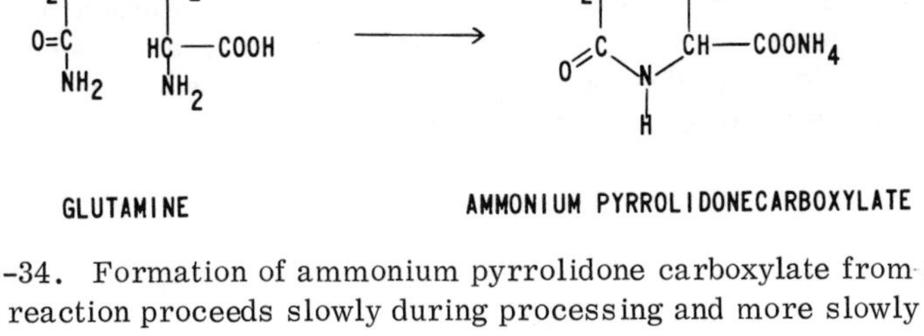

GLUTAMINE   AMMONIUM PYRROLIDONECARBOXYLATE

FIG. 16-34. Formation of ammonium pyrrolidone carboxylate from glutamic acid. The reaction proceeds slowly during processing and more slowly during storage.

d. Vitamin Losses. Losses of vitamins during heating of plant tissues range from
slight to substantial, depending on the vitamin and the conditions. Substantial
amounts of water-soluble vitamins can be lost by leaching. Chemical degradation
can also occur; e.g., ascorbic acid and thiamine become increasingly heat labile
as the pH is raised to near neutral or above. Relative stabilities of the various
vitamins and their modes of degradation are discussed in Chapter 7.

2. FREEZING

Lowering the temperature well below the freezing point of a product provides an
environment where microbial growth is stopped and reaction rates are generally
retarded. A properly conducted freezing process results in only minor changes in
the flavor, color, and nutritive value of plant tissues; however, texture of delicate
tissues can be greatly damaged. Plant tissues are generally blanched prior to
freezing to inactivate enzymes which otherwise would catalyze reactions leading to
undesirable changes in all quality attributes [28].

a. Texture Changes. Damage to texture is the most important change occurring
in plant tissues during freezing, frozen storage, and thawing [15]. Texture softening is primarily attributed to the collapse of individual cells (Fig. 16-35, a and
b). The disruption of cell structure appears to be physical since ultrarapid freezing (small ice crystals) results in a thawed product with textural and water-holding
properties superior to that achieved by slow freezing (large crystals). Furthermore, there is no apparent chemical change in cell-wall constituents during
freezing.

b. Color Changes. Chemical degradation of pigments in frozen plant tissues is
not important unless degradative enzymes are not sufficiently inactivated by blanching or other means. Accordingly, it is important that enzymes, such as lipoxygenase, anthocyanase, and polyphenoloxidases, be inactivated when they are originally present in a particular tissue. There are some reports of postthawing discolorations, such as development of a blue color in strawberries [58]. This type
of disorder probably results from formation of metal-pigment complexes in cells
disrupted by the freezing process.

c. Flavor Changes. Significant changes in the flavor and aroma of properly frozen
plant tissues are usually evident only after prolonged storage. Enzymic or nonenzymic oxidative reactions may be responsible since these reactions can proceed
slowly at normal temperatures of commercial storage. There has been considerable study of the role of residual peroxidase and lipoxygenase activities as the
causes of off flavors in stored frozen vegetables [88].

d. Vitamin Changes. There appears to be little change in the vitamin content of
plant tissue as a result of the freezing alone. On thawing, some portion of the
water-soluble vitamins may be lost in the thaw exudate and in the cooking medium
for vegetables. Vitamins, notably ascorbic acid, may undergo extensive decline
during long-term storage in the frozen state via enzymic or metal ion-catalyzed
reactions, particularly if oxygen is not properly excluded.

3. DEHYDRATION

As with freezing, the principle of dehydration is to create in the tissue a water
activity sufficiently low to preclude growth of microorganisms and to greatly retard chemical reactions. The extents of physical, chemical, and biochemical
changes in the tissue are very much dependent on the mode of dehydration employed
and the nature of the product. Hence, a given fruit processed by sun drying,
vacuum drying, osmotic dehydration, or freeze drying can exhibit wide differences
in physical and chemical properties [78].

a. Texture Changes.. The texture of dried tissue is greatly dependent on the method
of moisture removal, but in most instances texture is severely damaged. Freeze-
dried vegetables may possess texture characteristics similar to that achieved by
simple freezing (reasonably good), whereas a comparable sample which has been
air dried often bears little resemblance to the fresh tissue. If dehydration involves high temperatures, an impervious layer may develop on the outer surface
of the commodity (case hardening) and this may cause a rubbery or otherwise intractable texture. Various chemical changes, such as protein denaturation and
condensation reactions, are undoubtedly involved, although they are not well
understood.

b. Color Changes. The principal color change of dried plant tissues, especially
fruits, is browning, and this may be of either enzymic (if improperly blanched) or
nonenzymic origin. If browning is undesirable, it is necessary to inhibit the reactions involved. Sulfur dioxide is applied principally to prevent nonenzymic
browning, although it is also effective against enzymic browning. Chlorophyll is
frequently converted to the undesirable pheophytin form if hot air is used during
dehydration. Carotenoids appear to be stable in many dehydrated products provided blanching has effectively inactivated oxidative enzymes. Anthocyanins are
generally unstable during conventional dehydration and they assume a greyish color
if sulfuring is not employed. The nature of these pigment changes are not well
understood, although from the previous discussion both enzymic and nonenzymic
reactions can be expected to be involved. Further details on this subject are presented in Chapter 8.

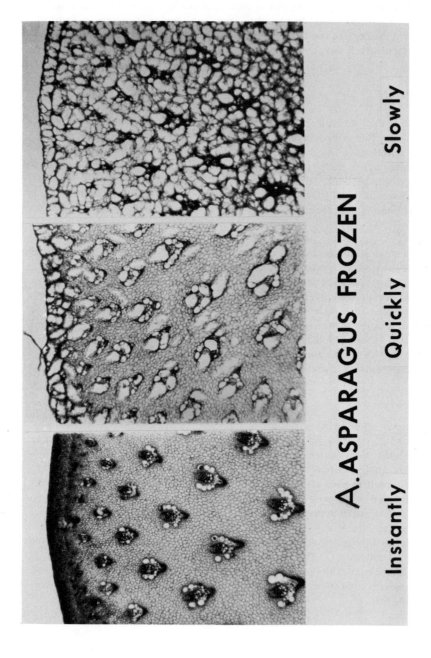

A. ASPARAGUS FROZEN

Instantly   Quickly   Slowly

FIG. 16-35. Influence of freezing rate (instantly, frozen in less than 1 min; quickly, frozen in about 5 min; slowly, frozen in 20 min or more) on the fine structure of asparagus (a) and green beans (b). (Part (b) reprinted from Ref. [15], courtesy of Society of Chemical Industry, London.)

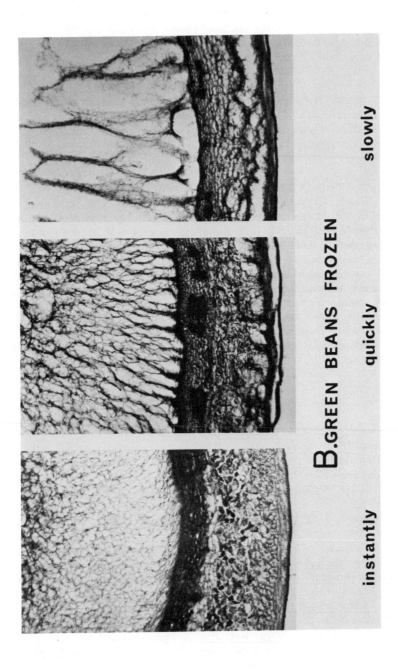

FIG. 16-35 (Continued)

c. Flavor Changes. As can be expected, there is considerable loss of native volatile flavor compounds during conventional dehydration, and new flavor substances may be generated as a result of the Maillard reaction and other chemical reactions. For example, during dehydration of prunes, crotonaldehyde is formed from acetaldehyde and contributes to the dehydrated flavor.

d. Vitamin Changes. Dehydrated vegetative tissues may undergo considerable loss in vitamins, especially ascorbic acid and vitamin A, if precautions are not taken to prevent oxidation. Treatment with sulfur dioxide lessens destruction of vitamin C but accelerates destruction of thiamine.

VI. FUTURE AVENUES OF RESEARCH AND DEVELOPMENT

A wide spectrum of fundamental and applied lines of research confront food scientists. As utilizable agricultural lands diminish, the problems of food availability are certain to grow and botanical sources of protein are certain to supplant animal sources. The time is ripe for the food scientist to tackle problems of photosynthesis and the mechanism of transducing the sun's energy into storage proteins. We need to better understand the ancillary metabolic modes which affect food quality, and much remains to be learned of the nature of physiological and processing stresses on plant tissues. One can readily envision the use of plant tissue cultures to selectively produce flavors, nutrients, pigments, and other food additives. Technological advances in food productivity and preservation most certainly hinge on this information.

REFERENCES

1. F. A. Abeles, Ann. Rev. Plant Physiol., 23, 259 (1972).
2. Y. Aharoni, Plant Physiol., 43, 99 (1968).
3. P. J. Allen, in Plant Pathology (J. Horsfall and A. Demond, eds.), Vol. 1, Academic Press, New York, 1959, p. 435.
4. J. Amir, R. D. Wright, and J. H. Cherry, J. Agri. Food Chem., 19, 954 (1971).
5. G. O. Aspinall, J. W. T. Craig, and J. L. Whyte, Carbohydrate Research. Elsevier, Amsterdam, 1969, p. 442.
6. A. Ben Abdelkadar, A. M. Catesson, P. Mazliak, A. Thibaudin, and A. Tremolieres, Bull. Soc. Physiol. Veg., 14, 323 (1968).
7. J. Biale, in Handbuch der Pflanzen physiologie (W. Ruhland, ed.), Springer Verlag, Berlin, 1960, p. 536.
8. J. Biale, Advan. Food Res., 10, 293 (1960).
9. J. B. Biale and R. E. Young, Endeavor, 21, 164 (1962).
10. J. Bonner, Prog. Chem. Org. Nat. Prod., 16, 138 (1958).
11. G. Borgstrom, Principles of Food Science II. Food Microbiology and Biochemistry. Macmillan, London, 1968, p. 12.

12. M. Boyd and B. Wilson, J. Agri. Biol. Chem., 20, 428 (1972).
13. C. J. Brady, P. B. H. O'Connell, J. K. Palmer, and R. M. Smillie, Phytochemistry, 9, 1037 (1970).
14. J. B. S. Braverman, Introduction to the Biochemistry of Foods, Elservier, New York, 1963, p. 223.
15. M. S. Brown, J. Sci. Food Agri., 18, 77 (1967).
16. L. F. Burroughs, in Biochemistry of Fruits and Their Products (A. C. Hulme, ed.), Vol. 1, Academic Press, New York, 1970, p. 119.
17. C. O. Chichester, ed., The Chemistry of Plant Pigments. Academic Press, New York, 1972.
18. G. O. Clark-Walker and A. W. Linnane, J. Cell. Biol., 34, 1 (1967).
19. C. W. Coggins, H. Henning, and Y. Yokoyama, Science, 168, 1589 (1970).
20. J. Conchic, A. L. Gelman, and G. A. Levy. Biochem. J., 103, 609 (1967).
21. W. Crocker, A. E. Hitchcock, and P. W. Zimmerman, Plant Res., 7, 231 (1935).
22. E. D. Dekazos, J. Food Sci., 35, 242 (1970).
23. D. R. Dilley, in Biochemistry of Fruits and Their Products (A. C. Hulme, ed.), Vol. 1, Academic Press, New York, 1970, p. 179.
24. W. P. Doyle and C. H. Wang, Can. J. Bot., 36, 483 (1958).
25. R. B. Duckworth, Fruits and Vegetables. Pergamon Press, New York, 1966, p. 28.
26. G. Englington and D. H. Hunneman, Phytochemistry, 7, 313 (1968).
27. N. A. M. Eskin, H. M. Henderson, and R. J. Townsend, Biochemistry of Foods. Academic Press, New York, 1971, Chapter 3.
28. B. J. Finkle, in Biochemistry of Fruits and Their Products (A. C. Hulme, ed.), Vol. 2, Academic Press, New York, 1971, Chapter 19.
29. B. J. Finkle and R. F. Nelson, Nature (London), 197, 902 (1963).
30. G. G. Freeman and M. Mossadejhi, J. Sci. Food Agri., 23, 387 (1972).
31. C. Frenkel, Ph.D. Thesis, Washington State University, Pullman, Washington, 1967.
32. C. Frenkel and N. F. Haard, Plant Physiol., 52, 380 (1973).
33. C. Frenkel, I. Klein, and D. R. Dilley, Plant Physiol., 43, 1146 (1968).
34. P. G. Gahan, in Plant Cell Organelles (J. B. Pridham, ed.), Academic Press, New York, 1968, Chapter 13.
35. T. Galliard, Phytochemistry, 7, 1915 (1968).
36. W. H. Gardner, Food Acidulants, Allied Chem. Corp., New York, 1966.
37. S. J. Gerbrandy and J. D. Verleur, Phytochemistry, 10, 261 (1971).
38. P. Gray, ed., The Encyclopedia of the Biological Sciences. Van Nostrand Reinhold, New York, 1970.
39. F. P. Griffiths and B. J. Lime, Food Technol., 13, 430 (1959).
40. J. L. Goldstein and T. Swain, Phytochemistry, 2, 371 (1963).
41. N. F. Haard, CRC Crit. Rev. Food Technol., 2, 305 (1971).
42. N. F. Haard, Biol. Plan., 13, 141 (1971).
43. N. F. Haard and H. O. Hultin, Phytochemistry, 8, 2149 (1969).
44. N. F. Haard and H. O. Hultin, J. Food Sci., 35, 751 (1970).
45. N. F. Haard and D. Timbie, J. Food Sci., 38, 642 (1973).
46. T. Harborne, ed., Biochemistry of Phenolic Compounds. Academic Press, New York, 1964.

47. G. E. Hobson, J. Food Sci., 33, 588 (1968).

48. G. E. Hobson, Nature (London), 195, 804 (1971).

49. O. Hughes and M. Bennion, Introductory Foods. Macmillan, London, 1970, Chapters 3 and 4.

50. A. C. Hulme, Nature (London), 178, 218 (1956).

51. A. C. Hulme, M. J. C. Rhodes, T. Gaillard, and L. S. C. Wooltorton, Plant Physiol., 43, 1154 (1968).

52. R. B. Hyde and J. W. Morrison, Amer. Potato J., 41, 163 (1964).

53. J. Ioannou, G. Chism, and N. F. Haard, J. Food Sci., 38, 1022 (1973).

54. F. A. Isherwood, in Recent Advances in Food Science, Vol. 3, Biochemistry and Biophysics (J. M. Leitch and D. N. Rhodes, eds.), Butterworth, 1963, p. 300.

55. F. A. Isherwood, in The Biochemistry of Fruit and Their Products. (A. C. Hulme, ed.), Vol. 1, Academic Press, New York, 1970, p. 33.

56. J. Janick, R. W. Schery, F. W. Woods, and V. M. Ruttan, in Plant Science. W. A. Freeman, San Francisco, 1969, Chapter 3.

57. M. A. Josyln, in Fruit and Vegetable Juice Processing Technology (D. K. Tressler and M. A. Joslyn, eds.), AVI Publ., Westport, Conn., 1961.

58. S. Jurd and S. Asen, Phytochemistry, 5, 1263 (1966).

59. A. K. Khudairi, Amer. Sci., 60, 696 (1972).

60. F. Kidd and C. West, Rep. Food Invest. Bd. 1921, p. 14, 1921.

61. S. Kon, J. Food Sci., 33, 437 (1968).

62. K. S. Koningsbacher, E. J. Hewitt, and R. L. Evans, Food Technol., 13, 128 (1959).

63. D. T. A. Lamport, Ann. Rev. Plant Physiol., 21, 235 (1970).

64. C. J. Leaver and J. L. Key, Proc. Natl. Acad. Sci. U.S., 57, 133 (1967).

65. C. Y. Lee, R. S. Shallenberger, and M. T. Vittum, N.Y. Food Life Sci. Bull., 1, 1 (1970).

66. J. Levitt, Responses of Plants to Environmental Stresses. Academic Press, New York, 1972.

67. C. H. A. Little and D. C. Eidt, Nature (London), 220, 498 (1968).

68. N. E. Looney and M. E. Patterson, Nature (London), 214, 1245 (1967).

69. M. Lovrekovich and M. Stahman, Phytopathology, 58, 193 (1968).

70. B. S. Luh, S. J. Leonard, and D. S. Patel, Food Technol., 14, 53 (1960).

71. J. M. Lyons and J. K. Raison, Plant Physiol., 45, 386 (1970).

72. J. M. Lyons, T. A. Wheaton, and H. K. Pratt, Plant Physiol., 39, 262 (1964).

73. A. A. Mahdi, A. C. Rice, and K. G. Weckel, J. Agri. Food Chem., 9, 143 (1961).

74. D. Martin, T. L. Lewis, and J. Cerny, Austral. J. Agri. Res., 18, 271 (1967).

75. J. L. Mason and M. F. Welsh, Hort. Sci., 5, 447 (1970).

76. S. Mayak and A. H. Halevy, Plant Physiol., 50, 341 (1972).

77. P. Mazliak, in Biochemistry of Fruits and Their Products (A. C. Hulme, ed.), Vol. 1, Academic Press, New York, 1970, p. 209.

78. D. M. McBean, M. A. Joslyn, and F. S. Bury, in Biochemistry of Fruits and Their Products (A. C. Hulme, ed.), Vol. 2, Academic Press, New York, 1971, Chapter 18.

79. B. H. McGown, T. C. Hall, and G. E. Beck, Plant Physiol., 44, 210 (1969).
80. T. Murata, Physiol. Plantarum, 22, 401 (1969).
80a. W. C. Mussolman and J. A. Wagoner, Cereal Chemistry, 45, 162 (1968).
81. E. A. Nebesky, W. B. Esselen, A. M. Kaplan, and C. A. Fellers, Food Res., 15, 114 (1950).
82. H. E. Nursten, in Biochemistry of Fruits and Their Products (A. C. Hulme, ed.), Vol. 1, Academic Press, New York, 1970, p. 239.
83. A. Oaks and R. G. S. Bidwell, Ann. Rev. Plant Physiol., 21, 43 (1970).
84. I. Ohod, I. Friedberg, Z. Neeman, and M. Schramm, Plant Physiol., 47, 465 (1971).
85. L. Paez and H. O. Hultin, J. Food Sci., 35, 46 (1972).
86. M. A. Perring and B. G. Wilkinson, J. Sci. Food Agri., 16, 438 (1965).
87. M. A. Perry, J. Sci. Food Agri., 19, 186 (1968).
88. A. Pinsky, S. Grossman, and M. Trop, J. Food Sci., 36, 571 (1971).
89. H. L. Postlmayr, B. S. Luh, and S. J. Leonard, Food Technol., 10, 618 (1956).
90. Preservation of Fruits and Vegetables by Radiation. Proceedings of a panel of joint FAO/IAEA, International Atomic Energy Agency, Vienna, 1968.
91. R. Pressey, Arch. Biochem. Biophys., 113, 667 (1966).
92. R. Pressey, J. Food Sci., 37, 521 (1972).
93. J. A. Radley, Starch and its Derivatives. Chapman and Hall, London, 1968.
94. J. K. Raison, J. M. Lyons, and W. W. Thomson, Arch. Biochem. Biophys., 142, 83 (1971).
95. A. S. Ranadive and N. F. Haard, J. Sci. Food Agri., 22, 86 (1971).
96. A. S. Ranadive and N. F. Haard, J. Food Sci., 37, 381 (1972).
97. M. J. C. Rhodes, in Biochemistry of Fruits and Their Products (A. C. Hulme, ed.), Vol. 1, Academic Press, New York, 1972, p. 529.
98. T. Robinson, The Organic Constituents of Higher Plants. Burgess Publ., Minneapolis, 1963, Chapter 2.
99. R. J. Romani and R. Yu, Arch. Biochem. Biophys., 127, 283 (1968).
100. L. Russo, H. C. Dostal, and K. C. Leopold, Bioscience, 18, 109 (1968).
101. A. L. Ryall and W. J. Lipton, Handling, Transportation and Storage of Fruits and Vegetables. Vol. 1, AVI Publ., Westport, Conn., 1972, p. 9.
102. S. Schwimmer, Arch. Biochem. Biophys., 130, 312 (1969).
103. S. Schwimmer, J. Food Sci., 37, 530 (1972).
104. S. Schwimmer, J. Food Sci., 37, 530 (1972).
105. J. I. Simpson and E. G. Halliday, Food Res., 7, 300 (1942).
106. R. M. Smock, Proc. Amer. Soc. Hort. Sci., 88, 80 (1966).
107. C. Sterling, Food Technol., 13, 629 (1959).
108. C. Sterling, in Recent Advances in Food Science, Vol. 3, Biochemistry and Biophysics (J. M. Leitch and D. N. Rhodes, eds.), Butterworth, London, 1963, p. 259.
109. M. Thomas, Plant Physiology. 4th ed., J. and A. Churchill, London, 1956, p. 308.
110. S. Undenfriend, Arch. Biochem. Biophys., 85, 487 (1959).
111. R. Ulrich, in Biochemistry of Fruits and Their Products (A. C. Hulme, ed.), Vol. 1, Academic Press, New York, 1970, p. 89.
112. I. Uritani, T. Asahi, T. Menamekawa, H. Hyoda, K. O. Shima, and M. Kejima, in Dynamic Role of Molecular Constituents in Plant-Parasite Interactions (C. Mirocha and I. Uritani, eds.), American Phytopathology Society, Minneapolis, 1967, p. 342.

113. USDA Handbook No. 66, U.S. Government Printing Office, Washington, D.C., 1968.

114. J. P. Van Buren, D. M. Scheiner, and A. C. Wagenknect, Nature (London), 185, 165 (1960).

115. J. L. Van Lancker, in Metabolic Conjugation and Metabolic Hydrolysis (W. H. Fishman, ed.), Vol. 1, Academic Press, New York, 1970, p. 355.

116. J. Van Overbeek, U.S. Patent 3,013,885 (1961).

117. K. Vas, M. Nedbalek, H. Scheffer, and G. Kovacs-Proszt, Kruchtsaft-Ind., 12, 164.

118. M. Vendrell, Austral. J. Biol. Sci., 22, 601 (1969).

119. J. E. Varner, Ann. Rev. Plant Physiol., 12, 45 (1961).

120. G. C. Walker, J. Food Sci., 29, 383 (1964).

121. J. R. L. Walker, J. Sci. Food Agri., 13, 363 (1962).

122. R. H. Waters and M. P. Hood, Food Technol., 18, 130 (1964).

123. W. J. Whelan, Nature (London), 190, 954 (1961).

124. B. G. Wilkinson, in Biochemistry of Fruits and Their Products (A. C. Hulme, ed.), Vol. 1, Academic Press, New York, 1970, p. 537.

125. L. S. C. Wooltorton, J. D. Jones, and A. C. Hulme, Nature (London), 207, 999 (1965).

126. M. H. Yu, L. E. Olson and D. K. Salunkhe, Phytochemistry, 7, 561 (1968).

127. M. Zuker, Ann. Rev. Plant Physiol., 23, 133 (1972).

Chapter 17

INTEGRATION OF CHEMICAL AND BIOLOGICAL CHANGES IN FOODS AND THEIR INFLUENCE ON QUALITY

Steven R. Tannenbaum

Department of Nutrition and Food Science
Massachusetts Institute of Technology
Cambridge, Massachusetts

Contents

I. INTRODUCTION

Since foods are derived from materials of biological origin, they invariably contain the entire complex milieu of chemical substances required to sustain life. Each of these classes of chemicals (proteins, carbohydrates, lipids, etc.) has been the subject of one or more chapters in this volume, and each chapter has in turn been a condensation of a much larger body of literature. Therefore, the goal of the food scientist, to understand and control the assorted phenomena described in this volume for each and every class of food product, may appear at first to be naive and unreachable. In the encyclopedic sense this latter statement is probably correct. Even a large computer, which had stored in its memory every paper and chapter on food that had ever been written, would be incapable of describing all of the significant chemical reactions which occurred during the thermal processing of a pea, much less that of a more complex product, such as vegetable soup.

Fortunately, the decisions one makes in the course of optimizing the conditions of processing or storage of a food can be arrived at in a more efficient manner. The key word in the previous sentence is "optimizing." We accept the philosophy that certain chemical changes are inevitable if we wish to ensure the safety of the food at the time of its consumption; however, we concurrently seek to minimize those changes which reduce the quality of the product. Thus, it is desirable to establish an analytical approach to the chemistry of food preservation - one in which facts derived from the study of apple spoilage can at least partially enhance our understanding of the spoilage of other products.

II. ANALYTICAL APPROACH

There are four necessary components to this approach: (1) determining those properties that are important characteristics of safe, high-quality foods, (2) determining those chemical and biochemical reactions that have important influences on loss of quality and/or wholesomeness of foods, (3) integrating the first two points so that one understands how the key chemical and biochemical reactions influence quality and safety, and (4) applying this understanding to the various situations encountered during storage and processing of food.

A. Quality and Safety Attributes

It is essential to reiterate that safety is the first requisite of any food. In the broad sense this is taken to mean that a food is free of any harmful chemical or microbial contamination at the time of its consumption. Often this concept for practical reasons is used in its operational sense. In the canning industry, commercial sterility as applied to low-acid foods is taken to mean the absence of viable spores of <u>Clostridium</u> <u>botulinum</u>. This in turn may be translated into a specific set of heating conditions for a specific product in a specific package. Given this information one can then approach optimization of retention of other quality attributes through techniques which have been discussed in Chapter 7. Similarly, in such a product as peanut butter, operational safety may be taken as the absence of aflatoxins, carcinogenic substances produced by certain species of molds (Chapter 11). Steps taken to prevent growth of the mold in question may or may not interfere with the retention of some other quality attribute; nevertheless the conditions for safety must be satisfied.

A simple list of some quality attributes of food and some undesirable changes they can undergo is given in Table 17-1. The major attributes are texture, flavor, color, and nutritive value. The changes that can occur, with the exception of those involving nutritive value, are readily evident to the consumer. That is, they are macroscopic changes arising from the entire gestalt of microscopic of chemical changes which take place in the product during processing or storage. The major subheadings of Table 17-1 are linked later in this chapter to specific chemical reactions.

TABLE 17-1

Classification of Undesirable Changes That Can Occur in Food

Attribute	Undesirable change
Texture	a. Loss of solubility b. Loss of water-holding capacity c. Toughening d. Softening
Flavor	Development of: e. Rancidity (hydrolytic or oxidative) f. Cooked or caramel flavors g. Other off flavors
Color	h. Darkening i. Bleaching j. Development of other off colors
Nutritive value	Loss or degradation of: k. Vitamins l. Minerals m. Proteins n. Lipids

B. Chemical and Biochemical Reactions

There are many reactions which can lead to the deterioration of food quality or impairment of food safety. Some of the more important classes of these reactions are listed in Table 17-2. Each reaction class can involve different reactants or substrates depending on the specific food and the particular conditions for processing or storage. They are treated as reaction classes because the general nature of the substrates or reactants are similar for all foods. Thus, nonenzymic browning involves reactions of carbonyl compounds which can arise from such diverse prior reactions as oxidation of ascorbic acid or hydrolysis of starch. Lipid oxidation may involve primarily triglycerides in one food and phospholipids in another, but in both, the autoxidation of unsaturated fatty acids is the prime event.

It is unnecessary to review each reaction in Table 17-2 since each, as indicated, has been treated in some depth elsewhere in this volume.

C. Effect of Reactions on the Quality and Safety of Food

The reactions listed in Table 17-2 can lead to deterioration of the quality attributes described in Table 17-1, and sometimes to impairment of food safety. Integration of the information contained in both tables can lead to an understanding of the causes of food deterioration. Deterioration of food usually consists of a series

TABLE 17-2

Chemical and Biochemical Reactions That Can Lead to
Deterioration of Food Quality or Impairment of Safety

Class of reaction	Chapters
Nonenzymic browning	3, 7, 14, 15
Enzymic browning	6, 16
Lipid hydrolysis	4, 6
Lipid oxidation	4, 7, 11
Protein denaturation	5, 6, 13
Protein crosslinking	5, 13
Oligo- and polysaccharide hydrolysis	3, 6, 13, 14
Protein hydrolysis	5, 6, 13
Polysaccharide synthesis	3, 6, 13, 14
Degradation of specific natural pigments	8, 13, 14, 16
Glycolytic changes	3, 6, 13, 14, 16
Nitrosation of amines	10, 11, 13

of events, each with a set of consequences, and these in turn ultimately manifest themselves as one or more of the macroscopic changes listed in Table 17-1. Examples of sequences of this type are shown in Table 17-3. Note particularly that a given quality attribute can be altered as a result of several different primary events. If Table 17-3 could be enlarged to include most of the information in this volume, and if this information were assembled with the primary events arranged horizontally at the bottom of a page, the intermediate consequences at the center of the page, and the quality manifestations at the top, the assembled data would approximate the shape of a triangle.

Note that the sequences in Table 17-3 can be applied in two directions. Operating from left to right one can predict possible macroscopic events by considering a particular chemical reaction or physical event and its perturbation of other constituents in the system. Alternatively, one can determine the probable cause(s) of an observed quality change by considering all primary events that are possibly involved and then isolating, by approximate chemical tests, the key primary event. The interested reader might attempt to conceive, from his or her own experience, additions to Table 17-3. The utility of constructing such sequences is that they encourage one to approach problems of food deterioration in an analytical manner.

Figure 17-1 is a summary of the reactions and interactions of the major constituents of food. The major cellular pools of carbohydrates, lipids, proteins, and their intermediary metabolites are shown on the left-hand side of the diagram. The exact nature of these pools is dependent upon the physiological state of the

TABLE 17-3

Cause and Effect in the Deterioration of Food

Primary event	Consequence	Manifestation (see Table 17-1)
Hydrolysis of lipids	Free fatty acids react with protein	Texture: a, b, c Flavor: e, g Nutrit. val.: m
Hydrolysis of polysaccharides	Sugars react with proteins	Texture: a, b, c Flavor: f Color: h Nutrit. val.: k, m
Oxidation of lipids	Oxidation products react with many other constituents	Texture: a, b, c Flavor: e Color: h and/or i Nutri. val.: k, m, n
Bruising of fruit	Cells broken, enzymes released, oxygen accessible	Texture: d Flavor: g Color: h Nutrit. val.: k
Heating of green vegetables	Cell walls and membranes lose integrity, acids released, enzymes released	Texture: d Flavor: g Color: j Nutrit. val.: k, l
Heating of muscle tissue	Proteins denature and aggregate, enzymes inactivated	Texture: b and c or d Flavor: f Color: j Nutrit. val.: k

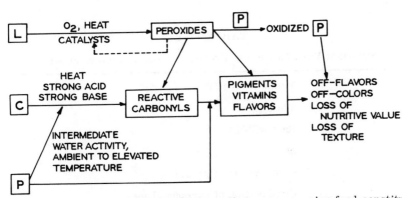

FIG. 17-1. Summary of chemical interactions among major food constituents. L, Lipid pool (triglycerides, fatty acids, phospholipids); C, carbohydrate pool (polysaccharides, sugars, organic acids, etc.); P, protein pool (proteins, peptides, amino acids, and other N-containing substances).

tissue at the time of processing or storage. Each class of compound can undergo its own characteristic type of deterioration. Of great interest is the common role that carbonyl compounds play in the deterioration process. They arise from lipid oxidation and carbohydrate degradation and lead to destruction of nutritional value, to off colors, and to off flavors.

D. Analysis of Situations Encountered During Storage and Processing of Food

Having before us a description of the attributes of high-quality, safe foods, the significant chemical reactions involved in deterioration of food, and the relation of the two, we can now begin to consider how to apply this information to situations encountered during the storage and processing of food.

The variables that are important during the storage and processing of food are listed in Table 17-4. Temperature is perhaps the most important of these variables because of its broad influence on all types of chemical reactions. The effect of temperature on an individual reaction can be expressed by the Arrhenius equation, $k = Ae^{-\Delta E/RT}$. Data conforming to the Arrhenius equation yield a straight line when $\log k$ is plotted versus $1/T$. The Arrhenius plots in Figure 17-2 represent reactions important in food deterioration. It is evident that food reactions generally conform to the Arrhenius relationship over a certain intermediate temperature range but that deviations from this relationship can occur at high or low temperatures [14]. Thus, it is important to remember that the Arrhenius relationship for food systems can be used only over a range of temperatures that has been experimentally tested. Deviations from the Arrhenius relationship can occur because of the following events, most of which are induced by either high or low temperatures: (1) enzyme activity may be lost, (2) the reaction pathway may change or it may be influenced by a competing reaction(s), (3) the physical state of the system may change, or (4) one or more of the reactants may become depleted.

A variety of processes, including refrigeration, canning, and freezing, depend primarily on the effects of temperature to lessen the rate at which foods deteriorate.

TABLE 17-4

Important Variables in the Processing and Storage of Foods

Temperature (T)
Time (t)
Rate (dT/dt)
pH
Composition of product
Composition of gaseous phase
Water activity (a_W)

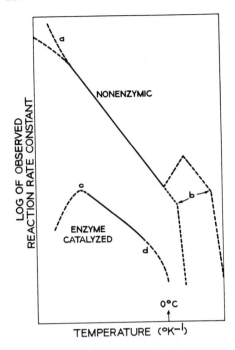

FIG. 17-2. Conformity of important deteriorative reactions in food to the Arrhenius relationship. (a) Above a certain value of T there may be deviations from linearity due to a change in the path of the reaction. (b) As the temperature is lowered below the freezing point of the system, the ice phase (essentially pure) enlarges and the fluid phase, which contains all of the solutes, diminishes. This concentration of solutes in the unfrozen phase can decrease reaction rates (supplement the effect of decreasing temperature) or increase reaction rates (oppose the effect of declining temperature), depending on the nature of the system (see Chapter 2). (c) For an enzymic reaction there is a temperature range in which denaturation of the enzyme competes with formation of reaction product. (d) In the vicinity of the freezing point of water, subtle changes, e.g., the dissociation of an enzyme complex, can lead to a sharp drop in reaction rate.

The second variable in Table 17-4 is time, and this should be considered together with the rate at which temperature changes with time. During storage of a food product, one frequently wants to know the time the food can be expected to remain above a certain level of quality. Therefore, one is interested in time with respect to the integral of chemical and/or microbiological changes which occur during a specified storage period, and in the way these changes combine to determine a specified storage life for the product.

During processing, attention should be given primarily to the time variable as it appears in the rate expression, usually the rate of temperature change in a process, since this determines the relative rates of competing chemical reactions and the rate at which microorganisms are destroyed.

Time also can have an important influence on the relative importance of concurrent reactions. For example, if a given food can deteriorate by both lipid oxidation and nonenzymic browning, and if the products of the browning reaction are antioxidants, it is important to know whether the time scales for the two reactions overlap sufficiently to cause a significant interaction.

Another variable, pH, influences the rates of many chemical and enzymic reactions. Extreme pH values are usually required for severe inhibition of microbial growth or enzymic processes, and these conditions can result in acceleration of acid- or base-catalyzed reactions. In contrast, relatively small pH changes can cause profound changes in the quality of some foods, e.g., muscle (Chapter 13).

The composition of the product is important since this determines the reactants available for chemical transformation. Particularly important in this regard is the relationship that exists between the quality of the raw material and the quality of the finished product. For example: (1) the manner in which fruits and vegetables are handled postharvest can influence sugar content and this, in turn, influences the degree of browning obtained during dehydration or deep-fat frying (Chapter 16). (2) The manner in which animal tissues are handled postmortem influences the extent of microbial contamination and growth, and the extents and rates of proteolysis, glycolysis and ATP degradation, and these in turn can influence storage life, water-holding capacity, toughness, flavor, and color. (3) The blending of raw materials may cause unexpected interactions, e.g., the rate of oxidation can be accelerated or inhibited depending on the amount of salt present.

In fabricated foods, the composition can be controlled by adding approved chemicals, such as acidulants, chelating agents or antioxidants, or by removing undesirable reactants, e.g., removal of glucose from dehydrated egg albumen.

The composition of the gaseous phase is important mainly with respect to the availability of oxygen as a reactant. In situations where it is desirable to limit oxygen it is unfortunately almost impossible to achieve complete exclusion. The consequences of a small amount of residual oxygen sometimes become apparent during subsequent behavior of the product. For example, the early formation of a small amount of dehydroascorbic acid can lead to browning during storage.

One of the more important variables controlling reaction rates in foods is water activity (a_w). Numerous investigators have shown a_w to be an important factor in enzyme reactions [1], lipid oxidation [11,15], nonenzymic browning [7,11], sucrose hydrolysis [16], chlorophyll degradation [12], anthocyanin degradation [8], and in many other reactions. Some of these relationships were shown earlier in Chapter 2 (Fig. 2-10). The role that water plays in chemical deterioration of foods is complicated by the fact that it usually performs more than a single function. For example:

1. Water may be a reactant in the system, as in such hydrolytic reactions as sucrose hydrolysis or lipolysis.
2. Water is usually the primary solvent in the system and as such influences the diffusion of reactants and reaction products. In this sense water or the lack of it has an important bearing on reactions rates in dehydrated or frozen foods.
3. Water may influence the catalytic properties of metals by shielding them or by forming inactive metal hydroxides. The removal of water may expose new surfaces and allow interactions between lipids and proteins, or proteins

and proteins, and these interactions do not normally occur in the presence of water.

4. Water may be the product of a reaction, as in nonenzymic browning, and thus be almost autocatalytic at very low water activities.

As can be seen from Figure 2-10 (Chapter 2), most reactions tend to decrease in rate below an a_w corresponding to the range for intermediate moisture foods (0.75-0.85), and this is primarily due to the reduced solvent capacity of the decreased water phase. Oxidation of lipids and associated secondary effects, such as carotenoid decoloration, are exceptions to this rule, i.e., these reactions accelerate at the lower end of the a_w scale. In these instances, water, because of its scarcity, is apparently unable to serve as an antioxidant; i.e., it cannot interact significantly with catalysts, lipid hydroperoxides, and free radicals [9,10]. Some reactions, such as nonenzymic browning, reach a peak reaction rate at an intermediate a_w. This behavior is characteristic of multiple-reactant systems where the rate is strongly influenced by dilution.

III. THE ANALYTICAL APPROACH AS APPLIED TO SPOILAGE OF A SPECIFIC FOOD COMMODITY

In order to better understand the analytical approach just presented, it is useful to examine the spoilage characteristics of an individual food under different conditions of processing and storage. The example chosen is fish, since it is processed in a number of different ways and information is available on its modes of deterioration. For further details, the reader is referred to Chapter 13 and additional references [2-6,13,17,18].

A. Icing or Refrigeration

A summary of the causes of fish deterioration is given in Table 17-5. Icing is an important method of preservation, since almost all fish must be held under refrigeration while awaiting further processing or while being transported to the market. An exception is fish meal which, however, is not intended for human consumption. The storage life of iced fish is greatly influenced by storage temperature, and it is highly desirable that fish be held as near as possible to, but not below, their freezing points. Iced fish deteriorates primarily as a result of the growth of microorganisms; e.g., the production of trimethylamine from trimethlamine N-oxide is caused by microorganisms. However, the endogenous enzyme systems in the fish flesh as well as the enzymes which originate in the digestive system of fish are also factors in deterioration.

Important biochemical transformations involved in the deterioration of fish include autolysis of proteins, degradation of glycogen, and the subsequent process of glycolysis and breakdown of ATP. This latter reaction is of importance with respect to the formation of flavor compounds (inosine) and the precursors of nonenzymic browning (ribose). Furthermore, the rate of and extent to which glycolysis occurs influences the toughness and water-holding capacity of the muscle. Oxidation of highly unsaturated fish lipids also is possible, but this usually occurs only

TABLE 17-5

Causes of Fish Deterioration During Processing and Storage

Cause of deterioration	Treatment			
	Icing or refrigeration	Freezing	Canning	Dehydration
Microbial growth	x			
Various enzyme-catalyzed reactions (autolysis, etc.)	x			
Lipid hydrolysis		x		
Lipid oxidation	x	x		x
Various off flavors			x	x
Browning, nonenzymic			x	x
"Rusting"		x		
Pigment changes				x
Softening			x	
Toughening		x		x
Freezer burn		x		

if an extensive amount of biochemical degradation has taken place. Thus the conditions maintained during the early stages of refrigerated storage predetermine the composition of the system at the time of further processing and influence the particular reactions which lead to further deterioration.

B. Freezing

Fish can be frozen in the round (dressed but whole) or after filleting. In either case it is desirable to coat (glaze) the surface of the flesh with a layer of ice. This retards the entrance of oxygen and avoids dessication of the flesh. Dessication can lead to a defect known as freezer burn. Freezer burn is accelerated by fluctuation of storage temperature since this encourages sublimation of ice from the tissue. The exposed surfaces absorb oxygen readily, with concommitant oxidation of the highly unsaturated lipids.

The occurrence of "rusting" on the surfaces of some species of fish is thought to result from a browning reaction between amines (from bacterial metabolism) and carbonyls (from lipid oxidation). Rusting can be prevented by a surface glaze of ice.

Hydrolysis of lipids, primarily phospholipids, occurs readily down to temperatures of -18°C, releasing free fatty acids which can oxidize or interact with proteins. A characteristic change in fish during frozen storage is toughening brought about by protein changes, particularly aggregation of actomyosin. These protein changes are retarded by neutral lipids and accelerated by fatty acids, at least in model systems. Both lean and fatty species are subject to this type of deterioration.

C. Canning

Only a few species of fish are canned since the flesh must be capable of resisting the severe thermal process without undue disintegration. During canning, changes occur in flavor, color, and texture. Many species cannot be canned because nonenzymic browning reactions are excessive. The degradation of ATP to ribose is thought to be very important in this respect.

D. Dehydration

The prime deteriorative reactions which occur during dehydration are those which have already been mentioned. Oxidation of lipids is a major problem leading to further changes in proteins, bleaching of carotenoid pigments, and nonenzymic browning (resulting from carbonyls that are generated by a breakdown of hydroperoxides). Browning also occurs as a result of carbonyl-amine condensations involving ribose and glucose. Stability of dehydrated fish is strongly influenced by those factors which determine the amount and type of lipid in the fish, i.e., sex, age, season of catch, and type of food.

In many instances, dehydration is accompanied by the same types of deteriorative processes that occur during freezing. This is not surprising since both processes involve a reduction of water in the tissue, either by physical removal or by internal crystallization, and this results in concentration of reactants in the remaining water and disruption of membranes and other cell structures. Thus, new surfaces are exposed to oxygen, and aggregation and disaggregation take place among proteins, lipids, and other constituents of the system.

In all instances the initial quality strongly influences subsequent performance in processing and storage. This is true not only for fish but for all foods. The final quality of the product is the most perfect indicator we have of the sum of chemical and biochemical changes which have occurred between the garden or the sea and our table.

REFERENCES

1. L. W. Acker, J. Food Technol., 23, 1257 (1969).
2. C. H. Castell, B. A. Moor, P. M. Jamgard, and W. E. Neal, J. Fish. Res. Bd. Can., 23, 1385 (1966).
3. J. J. Connell, in Low Temperature Biology of Foodstuffs (J. Hawthorne and E. J. Rolfe, eds.), Pergamon Press, New York, 1968, p. 333.

4. J. J. Connell, in Proteins and Their Reactions (H. W. Schultz and A. F. Anglemier, eds.), AVI Publ., Westport, Conn., 1964.

5. W. J. Dyer, Cyrobiology, 3, 297 (1967).

6. W. J. Dyer, in Low Temperature Biology of Foodstuffs (J. Hawthorne and E. J. Rolfe, eds.), Pergamon Press, New York, 1968, p.

7. K. Eichner and M. Karel, J. Agri. Food Chem., 20, 218 (1972).

8. J. A. Erlandson and R. E. Wrolstad, J. Food Sci., 37, 592 (1971).

9. M. Karel, CRC Crit. Rev. Food Technol., 4, 329 (1973).

10. T. P. Labuza, CRC Crit. Rev. Food Technol., 2, 355 (1971).

11. T. P. Labuza, S. R. Tannenbaum, and M. Karel, Food Technol., 24, 543 (1970).

12. F. Lajollo, S. R. Tannenbaum, and T. P. Labuza, J. Food Sci., 36, 850 (1971).

13. F. Martinez and T. P. Labuza, J. Food Sci., 33, 241 (1968).

14. D. J. McWeeney, J. Food Technol., 3, 15 (1968).

15. D. G. Quast and M. Karel, J. Food Sci., 37, 584 (1972).

16. T. Schobell, S. R. Tannenbaum, and T. P. Labuza, J. Food Sci., 34, 324 (1969).

17. H. L. A. Tarr, J. Food Sci., 31, 846 (1966).

18. H. L. A. Tarr and R. E. A. Gadd, J. Fish. Res. Bd. Can., 22, 755 (1965).

SUBJECT INDEX

A

Acetic acid, antimicrobial properties, 492, 493
Acids, functions in food, 466, 477, 499; see also specific acids
Activation energy
  spore inactivation, 356, 357
  vitamin destruction, 356, 357, 368
Adulteration, see "Food adulteration"
Aging meat, 331, 599, 601
Amino acids
  characteristics, 207-213
  chemical reactions, 222-227
  dissociation constant, 209-211
  isoelectric points, 210, 211
  most prevalent, 212
  optical isomers, 213
  structures, 207-209
  titration curves, 210-212
  ultraviolet absorption spectra, 213
Analysis with enzymes, 314
Anthocyanins, see also "Pigments" and "Colors"
  complexes, 408, 409
  derivatives as colorants, 409
  description, 402
  enzymic degradation, 408
  identification, 404
  mentioned, 66
  molar extinction coefficient, 404
  pH effects, 405-407
  quantitative analysis, 404-406
  reaction with ascorbic acid, 407, 408
  reaction with peroxide, 408
  reaction with sulfites, 407
  separation, 403, 404
  stability, 405
  structures, 402

Antibiotics, 495, 496
Anticaking agents, 480, 481, 500
Antioxidants
  general discussion, 486, 487
  kinds, 500, 501
  mechanisms, 182, 183
  sulfites, 490
  synergism, 184, 185
  types, 183-185
Arrhenius equation, 296, 299
Ascorbic acid
  analysis, 360, 361
  degradation, 361-366
  involvement in nonenzymic browning, 363, 364
  nomenclature, 70, 71
  properties, 360, 361
  structure, 360

B

Bases, functions in food, 472, 473, 499
Benzoic acid, 493
Betalains, 413-415
Biotin, 374
Blair process, 392
Blanching, plant tissues, 753
Bleaching agents, flour, 485, 501
Bound water, see "Water, bound"
Browning reactions
  Amadori compounds, 83, 84
  caramelization, 81, 82
  carbonyl-amine, 85, 355
  defined, 72
  enzymes involved, 80
  enzymic, 325-329, 694, 738, 746
  flavors, 87, 91, 92, 432